How to Use This Book

This book starts at the beginning, taking people who know nothing about COBOL and stepping them through 21 lessons and on to programming proficien~

Within this book, you'll find hands-on tutorials, timely ⁻¹
stand technical information to help you get your footing
by writing simple programs, and progress to complex, use
apply to your day-to-day situations. This book also address
and offers useful solutions to apply.

Who Should Read This Book

Whether you are a complete novice to programming or a programmer ready to take the plunge into COBOL, this book is for you. The book walks you day by day through the process of learning COBOL. In addition, if you're feeling really ambitious, you can plunge into the six Bonus Day chapters at the end of the book, which give you even more information about programming with COBOL. You can go chapter by chapter through the lessons, or just choose those lessons that most interest you. Either way, this book is the perfect companion for anyone ready to learn programming in COBOL.

Conventions

This book uses several different typefaces to help you differentiate between COBOL code and regular text. COBOL code appears in the book in a `special` typeface. Placeholders within the code—words to represent the type of infomation you need to enter in the code—appear in a `special italic` typeface.

 In addition, when new terms are introduced in the text, a New Term icon appears to the left of the text to indicate that term is being defined.

 The type icon denotes a new program for you to enter into your editor.

 The output icon highlights the results of compiling and executing the program.

 Analysis of the programs reveals insights and information about several key lines of the listing.

Throughout this book, the emphasis has been on providing useful information in a way that is fast, easy, and fun.

Teach
Yourself
COBOL
in 21 days,
Second Edition

Teach Yourself
COBOL
in 21 days, Second Edition

Mo Budlong

SAMS
PUBLISHING

201 West 103rd Street
Indianapolis, Indiana 46290

I want to dedicate this book to the army of programmers and computer professionals who are already sweating or will shortly be sweating with the rest of us over the year 2000 problem.

Copyright © 1997 by Sams Publishing
SECOND EDITION

International Standard Book Number: 0-672-31137-2

Library of Congress Catalog Card Number: 97-67492

2000 99 98 97   4 3 2 1

Interpretation of the printing code: the rightmost double-digit number is the year of the book's printing; the rightmost single-digit, the number of the book's printing. For example, a printing code of 97-1 shows that the first printing of the book occurred in 1997.

Composed in AGaramond and MCPdigital by Macmillan Computer Publishing

Printed in the United States of America

Trademarks

President   Richard K. Swadley

Publisher and Director of Acquisitions   Jordan Gold

Director of Product Development   Dean Miller

Executive Editor   Chris Denny

Managing Editor   Brice P. Gosnell

Indexing Manager   Johnna L. VanHoose

Director of Marketing   Kelli S. Spencer

Product Marketing Manager   Wendy Gilbride

Marketing Coordinator   Linda B. Beckwith

Acquisitions Editor
Chris Denny

Development Editor
Rich Alvey

Production Editor
Ryan Rader

Copy Editors
Drew Cupp
Gayle Johnson

Indexer
Bruce Clingaman

Technical Reviewer
Lee Ann Phillips

Editorial Coordinators
Mandie Rowell
Katie Wise

Technical Edit Coordinator
Lynette Quinn

Editorial Assistants
Carol Ackerman
Andi Richter
Rhonda Tinch-Mize
Karen Williams

Cover Designer
Tim Amrhein

Cover Illustrator
Eric Lindley

Book Designer
Gary Adair

Copy Writer
David Reichwein

Production Team Supervisors
Brad Chinn
Andrew Stone

Production
Rick Bond
Betsy Deeter
Michael Dietsch
Lana Dominguez

Overview

Contents

Acknowledgments

In this second edition of *Teach Yourself COBOL in 21 Days*, I have had a chance to correct errors from the first edition, expand on areas that needed elaboration, and write about many of the new and exciting things that are happening in the COBOL world. But most important to me, I have been able to act on the feedback that I have had from readers of the first edition. All of it was good, and all of it was helpful. There are way too many of you to thank. There were lots of little suggestions and a couple of major ones, and they all have been incorporated. I want to thank you all.

This is my third project for Sams and Macmillan, and I want to thank Chris Denny for noticing that the first edition was climbing the sales charts and for realizing that it was time for a new edition.

I want to thank Heather Mlodinow, an accomplished COBOL programmer who reviewed the technical end of the first edition, and Lee Ann Phillips who reviewed the second edition. Lee Ann was a tough editor, but she was usually right, and I am particularly indebted to her for additional material on dates and calendars. Greg Adams, president of International Digital Scientific, Inc., also reviewed the dates chapters and provided helpful suggestions. All the Sams and Macmillan editors and crew have been terrific. Ryan Rader, Rich Alvey, Drew Cupp, Heather Butler, Mary Ann Abramson, Fran Hatton, and Gayle Johnson all gave excellent advice and encouragement.

Mostly, I want to thank my wife Helen, who was not only my first line editor, but the first guinea pig to take the course. In fact, all three of the trial students—Helen, Victoria St. James, and Colleen Lerian—were patient and capable and made it very easy to adjust the book to get it right for a newcomer to COBOL. The book is much better because of their efforts.

In order to do this job properly, I needed to get my hands on a great deal of software and hardware, and I want to thank Micro Focus Inc. for providing Micro Focus Personal COBOL and Micro Focus Professional COBOL, as well as a lot of encouragement.

Acucobol Inc. graciously made its ACUCOBOL-85 package available.

A huge team is involved in taking a manuscript from the author's pen (or word processor) to final print. A lot of help, advice, and changes are contributed by this team. But ultimately the book is the author's work, and therefore I want to stress that I have made every effort to provide useful and accurate information, but any errors you find are mine alone.

About the Author

Mo Budlong has been a programmer and hardware engineer for 25 years. He has written several computer books, including *COBOL Dates and the Year 2000*, *Moving from COBOL to C*, *COBOL Cookbooks Volumes 1, 2*, and *3*, and the *C100 Manual*. He currently writes regular columns for UNIX magazines in the U.S. and England, including the monthly "UNIX 101" column for *SunWorld Online*, a Web-based magazine. As a software consultant, he programs in multiple languages, including C/C++, Visual Basic, SQL, and numerous Assembly languages, and he has several software packages currently on the market.

Tell Us What You Think!

As a reader, you are the most important critic and commentator of our books. We value your opinion and want to know what we're doing right, what we could do better, what areas you'd like to see us publish in, and any other words of wisdom you're willing to pass our way. You can help us make strong books that meet your needs and give you the computer guidance you require.

Do you have access to the World Wide Web? Then check out our site at http://www.mcp.com.

 NOTE

> If you have a technical question about this book, call the technical support line at 317-581-3833 or send e-mail to support@mcp.com.

As the team leader of the group that created this book, I welcome your comments. You can fax, e-mail, or write me directly to let me know what you did or didn't like about this book—as well as what we can do to make our books stronger. Here's the information:

Fax: 317-581-4669

E-mail: programming_mgr@sams.mcp.com

Mail: Christopher Denny
            Comments Department
            Sams Publishing
            201 W. 103rd Street
            Indianapolis, IN 46290

Introduction

COBOL is a language that was developed specifically for business programming. It actually can be used for a wide range of programs and programming problems, but it is most popular for handling traditional business activities. COBOL excels in accounting systems and related activities such as inventory control, retail sales tracking, contact management, commissions, payroll—the list is almost endless.

It is the most widespread commercial programming language in use today. It is English-like and easy to read. This makes it very popular with nonprogrammers. Financial officers frequently can read a section of a COBOL program and understand what it is doing with figures, without having to rely on programmers to interpret the program for them.

There is no doubt that COBOL is the most successful programming language ever. With an estimated 80 million lines of COBOL code in use just in the United States, it remains a key language of choice for business applications.

Four years ago, the popular computer media were chanting a funeral dirge for COBOL. Today, the tune has changed remarkably. Nearly every major software and information systems magazine has carried recent articles about the year 2000 problem and the need for COBOL programmers to handle the problem.

Major software companies are backing this resurgence with research and development dollars. A wide range of new COBOL-based products has been announced by Micro Focus Inc., Acucobol Inc., Computer Associates International Inc., Fujitsu Inc., and many more.

Programming work is available in COBOL for entry-level, intermediate, and advanced programmers. This cannot be said of other languages, which usually require high intermediate-to-expert experience before you can market that skill.

An additional factor has spurred the demand for COBOL programmers—the approach of the year 2000. Over the years, thousands of programs have been written using only a 4 digit date. When the computer has to calculate into and beyond the year 2000, all kinds of problems arise. Millions of lines of code have to be corrected before the year 2000, and there are just not enough COBOL programmers available. The situation is not limited to COBOL programs, but because COBOL has been the language of preference for business applications for so long, there are vastly more COBOL programs in existence. The magnitude of the year 2000 crisis has caused experienced software experts to predict dire consequences. It is estimated that the cost of fixing the problem will run into the billions of dollars. The demand for COBOL programmers increases almost weekly, as more and more companies realize the scope of the year 2000 problem and begin to allocate resources for its solution.

Although planning, supervision, and management of a year 2000 project requires highly skilled, experienced technicians, there is lots of work that entry-level programmers can do. In fact, a *ComputerWorld* article on the need for training COBOL programmers quotes Sheldon Glasser, a veteran consultant, as recommending that entry-level personnel be used for maintenance work to free up more highly skilled programmers for the more difficult year 2000 work. *Teach Yourself COBOL in 21 Days* has been revised to include more information on dates and the year 2000 problem.

Other magazines such as *Information Technology Training Association* and *Unisphere* have stressed the importance of getting novices trained and productive fast. With fewer than 1,000 days until the year 2000, there's no time to waste on academic or theoretical exercises. I wanted to create a way for students to be able to quickly and easily learn the language, and the feedback in calls and letters as well as media response has been encouraging in this regard. This book is being used in college and other courses across the country as well as in businesses and as a home study course.

Although the enormous demand for programmers to fix year 2000 problems probably will not continue far into the new millennium, undoubtedly the demand for COBOL programmers will continue. Many companies are putting off other maintenance and development that is not crucial in favor of completing their year 2000 projects. Given the amount of money that is being invested in updating and correcting existing COBOL code and the date problems in it, no one will want to throw away that investment in the near future—which means COBOL is here to stay for another round.

Additionally, recent developments in COBOL include a graphical user interface that works for COBOL programs running on PCs and UNIX-based systems. This has created a trend in downsizing—taking existing COBOL programs from mainframes and minicomputers and moving them to PCs as COBOL applications.

COBOL is also a good general-purpose language and can be used for creating simple or very complex programs. It has been standardized since 1968, and learning it on any computer enables you to use it on other computers.

COBOL has invaded UNIX, an area that was dominated by the C language. A friend of mine recently called who was desperately looking for COBOL programmers. He is a systems administrator for a large network of UNIX computers at a major oil company. He has been a C purist for years, but the company has decided to buy a business package in COBOL, and he needed help immediately. COBOL obviously has a long and healthy life ahead of it.

About This Book

Teach Yourself COBOL in 21 Days went through many versions before it was right for the job. Several adventurous volunteers agreed to learn COBOL from scratch by doing each lesson as I completed it, and I installed revisions based on their feedback. For the second edition, each day's text incorporated suggestions from the first edition users and then underwent multiple revisions to ensure that it could be easily understood and that the correct gradient approach was used. Concepts are introduced slowly and repeated many times. The first edition included four Bonus Day lessons. This new edition has been extended to include two additional Bonus Day lessons, with emphasis on the year 2000 problem.

In many cases, it is difficult to illustrate a programming point by using a full program. The point being highlighted gets lost against the background of all the other things going on in the program.

The answer to this is to write short programs just to show how something works. The problem with this approach is that some examples are silly or trivial programs. One of my more determined volunteers frequently showed up at my desk looking perplexed and asking, "I understand what the program is doing, but why would anyone ever want a program like this?"

The answer always is, "No one would; the example is only to illustrate how that part of the language works." I have revised each chapter and added specific comments indicating which examples aren't "real" programs. If I've missed any of these, and you see a program that seems to do something silly, irrelevant, or useless, be tolerant. Review the program as an example of how the language works and not as a program that you might use for some purpose.

Lots of code is used. COBOL experience comes from writing, reading, and understanding lots of code. Sometimes one point is illustrated by repeating a whole program with only that one point changed.

Programming Style

It is impossible to write a book about a programming language without spilling over into programming style. I have tried to balance teaching you good programming habits and teaching you the language.

It also is one of the realities of COBOL that a great deal of COBOL programming consists of maintaining existing programs written by other people. Some of these existing programs are just plain awful. You have to know a little about the "dark side" of programming to be able to deal with these. Techniques are described that you should never use, but you do need to know what is going on in a program when you see it.

Which is the best programming style is debated almost as hotly as which is the best programming language. You probably will run into some criticism of the programming styles used in this book. Don't get tangled up by it; you always can improve your style.

Who Should Use This Book?

Teach Yourself COBOL in 21 Days, Second Edition is aimed at beginners. It also is suitable for anyone who needs a refresher in COBOL, and for entry-level programmers who want to take their next step in COBOL. This book also can be used by experienced programmers who do not know COBOL.

What I Expect from You

You are expected to have some familiarity with the computer that you will use with this book. I would not expect people who have no experience with computers to be interested in learning COBOL as their first step with computers.

This is not an academic book. I expect that a person wanting to learn COBOL programming will actually do the exercises, write the code, compile it, and run it. You will not learn to program by just reading about it. You have to learn to use the tools by practicing their use. Therefore, you must either own a COBOL compiler or have access to one in order to get the most out of your study.

You should have good English and computer dictionaries available in order to look up words you do not fully understand. It is impossible to understand what you are studying if you do not know the meaning of the words used.

Two things are important if you are new or relatively new to programming. Don't skip anything. The course is organized to be a gradual accumulation of skills. Skipping a section will cause problems in later sections. Also, be sure to do all the exercises. Frequently, the explanations and examples in a chapter are based on an assumption that you completed the exercises at the end of a preceding chapter.

The other important point is to use good study habits. Study with a schedule and with a definite intention to get through some portion of the course. You must also read and understand questions and exercises before you begin doing them.

Working with Your Computer

You must know how to do four things in order to work with this book. These are covered in the first chapters of the book, and you must master these skills. You will be using them again and again as you progress through the book. If you skimp on any of them, you will hit a wall somewhere in this course. You must learn how to do the following:

☐ Edit a text file. An editor is somewhat similar to a word processor but does not have all the formatting features. The editor is used to write the programs in the book.

☐ Compile. A compiler converts the file that you have just edited into something that will run on your computer as a program.

☐ Link. This might not be necessary on your system, but you must find out whether it is needed, and you must learn how to do it. Linking takes the executable program created by the compiler and links it with any programs that your computer needs in order to be able to operate.

☐ Run. You must know how to execute a program when it is ready to run.

These four steps are covered in some detail in the manual for your compiler, and in Appendix C, "Editing, Compiling, and Linking." If you aren't familiar with these by the time you finish Day 1, "Your First COBOL Program," you will be in trouble for the rest of the course.

Target Compiler and Computers

Teach Yourself COBOL in 21 Days, Second Edition was written in such a way that it can be used with most computers and most versions of COBOL. There is a great deal of difference in the way different computers behave and the way versions of COBOL interact with the user.

The programs are written to work with Micro Focus COBOL, Micro Focus Personal COBOL, LPI COBOL, ACUCOBOL on UNIX or MS-DOS computers, and VAX COBOL on VAX VMS computers. The programs also should work with IBM COBOL for the AIX computer, RM COBOL, Realia COBOL, and Microsoft COBOL. There probably are many others.

All the volunteers worked with Micro Focus Personal COBOL, and the book tends to favor that compiler because it is a full compiler at a reasonable price. This makes it a good tool for self-teaching.

You *must* have a COBOL compiler in your computer system in order to be able to master the basic COBOL programming skills. If you do not have a compiler, an order form for one is included at the back of the book.

Supporting Material

Teach Yourself COBOL in 21 Days, Second Edition includes several appendixes designed to supplement points touched on in the text:

☐ Appendix A, "Answers," contains the answers to all the quiz questions and exercises posed at the end of each chapter.

☐ Appendix B, "ASCII," contains the ASCII character chart.

☐ Appendix C, "Editing, Compiling, and Linking," describes how to edit, compile, link, and run using various computers and versions of COBOL.

☐ Appendix D, "Handling Compiler Errors," covers some of the trickier compiler errors produced by COBOL compilers and how to track them down.

☐ Appendix E, "Summary of COBOL Syntax," is a brief listing of the syntax of the COBOL language used in this book.

☐ Appendix F, "Transaction Processing," describes methods of updating groups of files simultaneously to prevent data corruption.

☐ Appendix G, "Glossary," includes definitions of unusual terms used in the book.

The Companion Disk

A low-cost companion disk is available from the author, Mo Budlong, for $15.00 through King Computer Services, Inc., PO Box 728, Tujunga, CA 91043-0728. (See the King Computer Services order form at the back of the book.) This disk offer is made by the author and not by Sams Publishing. The disk will save you a lot of typing. It contains all the programs in the book, including sample programs for the exercises. If you choose to order the disk, it will be sent to you quickly so that you can begin work as soon as possible.

Teach Yourself COBOL in 21 Days, Second Edition will enable you to take the bold step into the world of COBOL programming. It is an exciting world. Happy programming!

At a Glance

As you begin your first week of learning to become a COBOL programmer, you will start to see why COBOL is one of the most commonly used programming languages, despite being one of the oldest. Aside from familiarity with an editor and the structure of the language, you'll find that the most important tool is experience. Experience is gained only by doing things. Learning by doing is regarded by many as the most effective form of learning. This book is designed to encourage you to perform many real-world tasks at a pace designed for the beginner.

This book is set up around a series of concepts that build on each other. Each day ends with a workshop containing a quiz and exercises that focus on specific concepts. Appendix A lists possible answers for the quiz questions and programs for the exercises. Don't be discouraged if your programs don't look exactly like those found in Appendix A. More than one answer is always possible. Because learning by doing is so effective, take advantage of the quizzes and exercises. They let you know whether you're on course or whether you need to return to a day and review a certain concept.

Where You're Going

The first week covers the fundamentals of the COBOL programming language. Don't underestimate the power of this material! COBOL is much like English, so you don't need to focus on cryptic symbols and meanings. Instead, you can focus on the lessons and underlying principles.

On Day 1, "Your First COBOL Program," you'll write your first program and immediately focus on why COBOL is so easy to learn. Day 2, "Using Variables and Constants," helps you focus on how to use variables to store and manipulate information in your program. Day 3, "A First Look at Structured COBOL," focuses on the overall structure of the COBOL program and lays the groundwork for many important concepts. Day 4, "Decision Making," and Day 5, "Using PERFORM, GO TO, and IF to Control Programs," focus on the mechanisms used to control which statements are executed, when they should execute, and how many times they should execute. Day 6, "Using Data and COBOL Operators," contributes significantly to your understanding of how to manipulate information stored within variables and reinforces the information covered on Day 1. Day 7, "Basics of Design," teaches you how to break down a task, identify processing loops, and work your way through the steps of program design.

Day 1

Your First COBOL Program

Let's start with some basics. You might find that some of this revisits material you know, particularly if you already are a programmer. COBOL sets somewhat rigid requirements for the layout, contents, and order of a program. You must be familiar with these in order to program in COBOL.

Today's lesson covers the following topics:

- [ ] What is a computer?
- [ ] What is a program?
- [ ] What is a programming language?
- [ ] What is COBOL?
- [ ] The "Hello World" program.
- [ ] The parts of a COBOL program.
- [ ] The elements of code layout.

☐ Commenting a COBOL program.

☐ What is a shell program?

Today, you'll write your first program and learn the basic parts of a COBOL program.

What Is a Computer?

A computer is a machine that can add, subtract, multiply, divide, and perform other mathematical and logical functions on numbers. A computer recognizes some numbers as numbers, and it also can recognize words by translating the words into numbers. At one time, you could talk to a computer only in numbers, but modern computers can accept words on-screen, translate them into command numbers, and then execute them.

The heart of a computer is the machine that does the addition, subtraction, multiplication, and division, and also moves data from one location to another. This is called the *central processing unit* (CPU), because it processes the data. In personal computing, the computer itself frequently is named after the CPU. A computer that uses a CPU called the 80286 is sometimes called a 286. Machines that use the 80386 usually are sold as 386 machines, and those that use the 80486 CPU are called 486 machines. The arrival of 80586 chips heralded a name change. These are called Pentiums. Will 80686 chips be called Hexiums?

To be useful, the computer also must have a way to be given the numbers to process (the *input*) and a method of presenting results to the user (the *output*). The input to a computer usually is entered with a keyboard. Other input devices include bar code readers, optical character readers (OCR), scanners, and mice. The output from a computer usually is displayed on a monitor (or screen) or printed on paper or can be written out to a file on a disk.

To perform large calculations, the computer needs some place to store temporary or intermediate results. This temporary storage for the computer frequently is called *main memory*, *primary memory*, or *primary storage* and usually is stored inside the main box of the computer. Think of the memory storage area inside the computer as a giant scratch pad for programs. Early personal computers had as little as 4 kilobytes (4KB) of memory. (A *kilobyte* is a bit more than 1,000 bytes; a byte can store one character of data, such as A, X, or @.) The personal computer boom brought the price of memory down to the point that computers now commonly sell with a starting memory of 4 or 8 megabytes (8MB) and can be upgraded to 32MB or more. (A *megabyte* is about a million bytes.)

To save results so that they can be reused, the computer needs some place to store information on a permanent or long-term basis. The problem with main memory is that it needs to have power all the time. When a computer is switched off, the contents of main memory are lost. The computer needs something that will retain information even when power is switched off. This is the task of secondary storage. Secondary storage is permanent and continues to function even after power is gone. Secondary storage comes most commonly in the form of diskettes (or floppies), hard disks, and tapes. Data is recorded on diskettes, hard drives, and tapes in a manner similar to the way that music is stored on a music tape cassette. A CD-ROM (compact disc–read-only memory) is another type of secondary storage. It is most commonly used as a permanent storage device and contains data that cannot be modified; such as the text of encyclopedias and dictionaries, or a complete listing of businesses in a country. There are more expensive devices available that can write to a CD-ROM that can be used for the initial storage of the dictionary, encyclopedia, or whatever.

The central processing unit requires that any program to be run and any data to be processed must be in main memory. Whenever you run a program, it is loaded from the secondary storage device (disk) into main or primary memory before it is executed. Whenever you work on data, such as editing a file, the file is first loaded into main memory from the disk drive (secondary storage). The editing is done directly in main memory and then must be saved back to disk. The central processing unit can neither execute a program directly from disk nor manipulate data directly on the disk.

Figures 1.1 through 1.4 illustrate the relationship between the CPU, main memory, and disk storage.

In Figure 1.1, the user has typed a command or clicked a button to start a word processing program. The CPU locates the program on the disk, loads it into main memory, and then begins executing the instructions in the word processing program.

Figure 1.1.

When the user starts a word processing program, the CPU loads the program from a hard disk into memory.

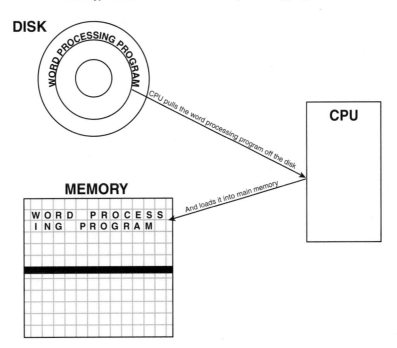

User types a command to start a word processing program

In Figure 1.2, the word processing program is running and the user types a command or clicks a button to load a document for editing. The CPU locates the document on the disk and loads it, ready to be edited, into main memory.

Figure 1.2.

When the user asks for a document to be edited, the CPU loads the document from a hard disk into memory.

Word processing program opens a document

User requests a document to be opened for editing.

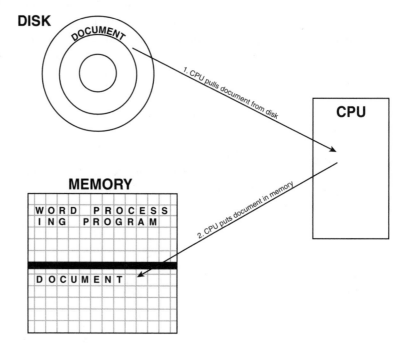

In Figure 1.3, the word processing program is running and the user types a letter "A" to be added to the document. The CPU collects the letter typed at the keyboard and places it in the document in memory.

In Figure 1.4, the user has requested that the document be saved. The CPU collects all the memory containing the document and writes it to the hard disk.

The CPU, input, output, main memory, and secondary storage all work together to form a computer.

Figure 1.3.
When the user types the letter "A," the CPU collects the character from the keyboard and inserts it into main memory.

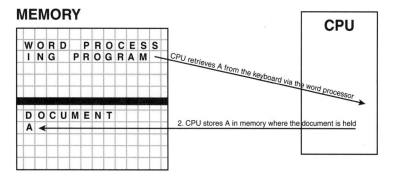

Figure 1.4.
When the user asks for the document to be saved, it is pulled from memory and written back to the hard disk.

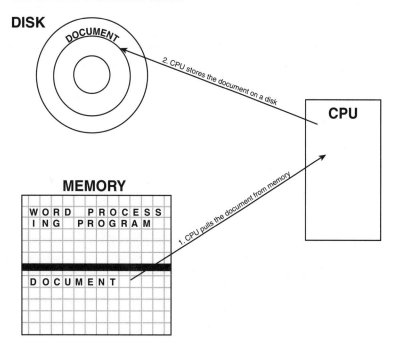

What Is a Program?

A computer is an incredibly stupid device. It doesn't do anything unless and until it is told to do so.

When a computer is first switched on, the CPU starts looking through main memory for an instruction. You can think of it as being in a perpetual state of readiness.

The computer is designed so that a small portion of main memory is permanent; it retains its contents even when the power is switched off. This permanent memory is placed at the location where the CPU begins searching for its first instruction after powering up. Consequently, it finds this permanent instruction immediately. This permanent area of memory contains a sequence of instructions that the computer executes on power-up. The instructions look something like this:

- ☐ Test the monitor.
- ☐ Test the keyboard.
- ☐ Test all of the main memory and display the results on the monitor.
- ☐ Test any other devices that need to be tested, including disk drives.
- ☐ Load the *operating system* program from secondary storage (the disk) into main memory. The operating system is a master program that controls a computer's basic functions and allows other programs to access the computer's resources, such as the disk drives, printer, keyboard, and screen. (In practice, this step is a little more complicated, but the principle is correct.) For an MS-DOS–compatible computer, the operating system is MS-DOS (Microsoft Disk Operating System).
- ☐ Jump to the first, previously loaded instruction at the beginning of the MS-DOS operating system.

From this point on, the CPU is executing instructions within the MS-DOS operating system.

If you could read the first few instructions of the MS-DOS operating system in English, they might look something like what you see in Table 1.1.

Table 1.1. The first few instructions of the MS-DOS operating system as they might appear in English.

Instruction Number	Instruction	Comment
001	Display the prompt	Put the > prompt on the screen.
002	Wait for a keypress	
003	Was a key pressed?	

Instruction Number	Instruction	Comment
004	`If not, GO TO 002`	If no key was pressed, go back and try again.
005	`Get the key value`	
006	`Save the key value`	Store the value in main memory.
007	`Display the key value`	
008	`Was the value (ENTER)?`	Determine whether the Enter key was pressed, signaling the end of command input.
009	`If not, GO TO 002`	The user is still typing, so keep getting keypresses.
010	`GO TO do the command`	The user pressed Enter, so jump to the instruction that will try to execute the command. This part of the program is not shown.

The set of instructions is written in English to represent the steps of a program. The program is executed so quickly that you see no visible delay between typing the key and seeing it appear on-screen, even though the action of saving the key value occurs between the keystroke and the display.

What Is a Programming Language?

The CPU expects instructions to arrive as numeric codes. These numeric codes are not easily read by human beings. A *programming language* is a set of English-like instructions that includes a set of rules (syntax) for putting the instructions together to create commands.

A translator changes the English-like commands into numeric codes that the computer can understand. The most common type of translator is a compiler. The *compiler* is a program that reads the English-like commands in a file and then creates another file containing computer-readable numeric codes or commands.

In the previous example, the CPU cannot understand the English-like instruction WAS A KEY PRESSED?, but a programming language might accept this as a valid command and translate it into codes that the CPU can recognize.

The term *program* is used loosely to refer to the actual application that is executed by the CPU, as well as the file of English-like commands originally written by the programmer before it was translated into the program that the CPU executes.

In strict terms, the English-like commands in a file are called *source code*, and the translated numeric codes placed in the output file are a runable program called *executable code*. The computer cannot directly execute source code as if it were a program. However, even experienced programmers will say, "I wrote a program to calculate the month-end balance." What they really mean is, "I wrote a source code file containing English-like commands that, when compiled, will produce an executable program file that, when run, will calculate the month-end balance." It is definitely easier to say, "I wrote a program."

What Is COBOL?

COBOL is a programming language especially aimed at solving business problems. You will see as you work through this book that COBOL solves a lot more than just business problems and can be used as a solution to many data processing problems.

New Term   *COBOL* is an acronym for Common Business Oriented Language.

Note

COBOL was developed by the Conference on Data Systems Languages (CODASYL), convened in 1959 by the Department of Defense. COBOL compilers became available in 1960, but they were not standardized. The American National Standards Institute (ANSI) standardized a version of COBOL in 1968. The language was revised and updated by ANSI in 1974 and again in 1985. These standards sometimes are called COBOL or COBOL-68, COBOL-74, or COBOL-85. Most compilers are now COBOL-85 standard, but there still are a few COBOL-74 versions out there. This book is written against the COBOL-85 standard, but you will have no trouble using a COBOL-74 compiler for any of the examples.

Because the year 2000 problem might be one of the reasons that you are studying this book, it is worth noting that legacy code could be written in any of the earlier COBOL standards. If you are taking this course to bring yourself up to speed for an update effort, you will need to learn the quirks and differences of the particular COBOL version that you will be working on. This book covers the core of COBOL-85 and will give you about 95% of any version of COBOL that you might work with. Throughout the book there are tips on differences that you might find in other versions of COBOL.

The future of COBOL is fairly bright. A new COBOL standard is being drafted even as I write this. This standard is intended to take

COBOL into the future and certainly well beyond the year 2000. The amount of money that is being invested in correcting date problems in existing COBOL code is a sure indicator that no one is planning to dispose of COBOL in the near future.

Approximately 90% of all COBOL code runs in a character-based environment, which means that most COBOL screens are 80 columns wide by 24 or 25 characters high and do not contain graphics. Although there are versions of COBOL on the market that act in a Windows-like environment, this book is not intended to be a course in COBOL for Windows. This means that throughout the book, you will be running or executing your programs on an MS-DOS computer or in an MS-DOS window that has been opened on a Windows computer. The MS-DOS window is an 80 × 24 character window and represents the kind of display that you might see when coding COBOL on a mainframe or minicomputer.

The "Hello World" Program

The "Hello world" program has become almost trite. Writing a program that prints "Hello world" on-screen usually is the first program you learn in any language. Listing 1.1 is a basic COBOL program that will display "Hello world". The format of a COBOL program is covered in the following sections.

TYPE   **Listing 1.1. "Hello world" in COBOL.**

```
000100 IDENTIFICATION DIVISION.
000200 PROGRAM-ID. HELLO.
000300 ENVIRONMENT DIVISION.
000400 DATA DIVISION.
000500 PROCEDURE DIVISION.
000600
000700 PROGRAM-BEGIN.
000800     DISPLAY "Hello world".
000900
001000 PROGRAM-DONE.
001100     STOP RUN.
```

ANALYSIS A COBOL program always contains four divisions. These four divisions always have the same names:

- ☐ IDENTIFICATION DIVISION
- ☐ ENVIRONMENT DIVISION
- ☐ DATA DIVISION
- ☐ PROCEDURE DIVISION

In Listing 1.1, lines 000100 and 000200 are the IDENTIFICATION DIVISION. This division is used to identify basic information about the program. In this example, the IDENTIFICATION DIVISION contains only the PROGRAM-ID, HELLO.

Line 000300 is the ENVIRONMENT DIVISION, which is used to identify the environment in which the program is running. Remember that COBOL is intended to run on many different types of machines, and this section is used to handle the differences between various computers. In this case, the program has no specialized machine requirements, so the ENVIRONMENT DIVISION is empty.

Line 000400 is the DATA DIVISION, which will contain any data that the program operates on. This program has no data, so the DATA DIVISION is empty.

Lines 000500 through 001100 are the PROCEDURE DIVISION. This is the meat of the program—the part that does the work intended by the programmer. The PROCEDURE DIVISION contains two paragraphs at line 000700 (PROGRAM-BEGIN) and line 001000 (PROGRAM-DONE). The term *paragraph* has a special definition in COBOL that will be covered a bit later in today's lesson. All the actual work in this program is done by line 000800.

If you have not yet installed your software, review Appendix C, "Editing, Compiling, and Linking," and the installation instructions in your software documentation; then complete the installation procedure. Make sure that you end up with a C> prompt under MS-DOS, and create your working directories as described in Appendix C. Change to your working directory before you begin editing hello.cbl.

It is extremely important that you type (edit), compile, and, if necessary, link this program to produce a running program. If you can't get this program to run, the remainder of this book will be an exercise in theory with no practical application. If you are using some other editor and COBOL combination, consult your local documentation or someone who is experienced with the system. Don't pass over this exercise without getting it to run. It is the simplest program to edit, compile, link, and run.

Before you start typing, you should note a couple of things. The first six character positions of each line are used for line numbering. The seventh character position is always blank. The commands at lines 000800 and 001100 begin at position 12. Everything else starts at position 8.

The editor that comes with Micro Focus Personal COBOL actually skips positions 1 through 7 and leaves the cursor positioned at column 8. If you are using this editor, use the left arrow key to move to column 1 to type the line numbers and the lines. Columns 1 through 7 are traditionally used for line numbering in COBOL. Most larger systems will use line numbers. The practice of skipping or not requiring line numbers is common with PC COBOL compilers and very modern compilers, but at the moment it is the exception rather than the rule. This book uses line numbers in keeping with the practice of most larger systems, and to provide a convenient way to refer to lines of code when a program is being analyzed in the text.

It's preferable to use spaces instead of the Tab key while editing, and you should break the habit of using the Tab key. Many personal computer–based COBOL compilers can handle tab characters, but the language was not designed originally to allow tabs in the source code file, and their presence can cause trouble on larger machines.

If you are using Micro Focus Personal COBOL, start your editor by typing the following line and pressing Enter:

```
pcobol hello.cbl
```

The extension .cbl is the default extension for many MS-DOS based COBOL compilers. On the VAX minicomputer manufactured by Digital Equipment Corporation, the default extension is .COB, and you would use a command such as:

```
EDIT HELLO.COB
```

Do	Don't

DO type each line exactly as it appears in Listing 1.1. Review your work carefully.

DON'T make typing errors. Some of the typing errors that can cause serious problems when you are compiling include misspelling the name of a DIVISION (for example, INDENTIFICATION DIVISION), adding an unnecessary hyphen (for example, DATA-DIVISION), or omitting any of the periods. Note that everything ends with a period (.); in fact, line 000200 has two periods in it.

NEW TERM   Checking source code created with an editor for typographical and other errors before compiling it is referred to as *desk-checking*.

NEW TERM   COBOL compilers are prone to produce cascading errors. A *cascading error* is one or more errors (sometimes hundreds) generated by the compiler when the problem really is one simple error earlier in the program. Code containing a missing period can produce a stream of apparent errors on some compilers that can be traced back in the program to that single error. The missing period itself might not even be mentioned as an error by the compiler, but it causes later problems that do show up.

When you have completed your check, close and save the file. Under Micro Focus Personal COBOL, hold down the Alt key while pressing F4, and then release both keys and press Enter.

Now you are ready to compile your program. Under Micro Focus Personal COBOL, press F2 until check is displayed on the status line (the fifth line from the bottom of the screen) and press Enter.

NEW TERM Under Micro Focus Personal COBOL, the process of compiling is called *checking*. The Micro Focus Personal COBOL compiler actually is called the *checker*.

The program should compile with no errors or warnings. If there are errors or warnings, re-edit your source code file, hello.cbl, desk-check it (compare it to the example in the book), and locate the error. The compiler might tell you the line number at which the error occurred, and you can go straight to that line.

COBOL compilers are dependent on correct punctuation, so bad punctuation can sometimes confuse the compiler. If the compiler says you have an error on a particular line, but you can't seem to find it, look one or two lines earlier to check whether you left out a period or started a line in an incorrect column. You also might want to check Appendix D, "Handling Compiler Errors," to help you track down errors.

After the program compiles cleanly, you are ready to run it. Exit from the COBOL development environment, if you are in one. For Micro Focus Personal COBOL, press Esc. The bottom row of the screen will display the message "Exit from Personal COBOL." Press the Y key to exit.

To run the program, type cls and press Enter to clear the screen. Then type the following and press Enter:

pcobrun hello

The program runs and displays your "Hello World" text, along with some Micro Focus copyright information, as shown in the output that follows.

OUTPUT
```
Personal COBOL version 2.0 from Micro Focus
PCOBRUN V2.0.02  Copyright (C) 1983-1993 Micro Focus Ltd.
Hello world

C:>
```

Congratulations, you've completed your first program. If you are not excited about this, try exclaiming "Wow! My first COBOL program!" a couple of times.

The output display is approximately what you should see on your screen under Microfocus Personal COBOL. Other versions of COBOL will produce different display arrangements and may or may not include copyright notices. The key point is that the message Hello world will be displayed on-screen.

If you did not get the expected results, do not despair. Go back to the beginning of this section and review all the work. Particularly review Appendix C and the installation instructions in your software documentation, and run the tests to make sure that your editor is installed correctly. Check all the spelling in the program and run it through the compiler (checker) again until there are no error messages.

The Parts of a COBOL Program

Recall that a COBOL program is made up of four mandatory divisions. They always appear in the program in the order shown in Listing 1.2.

TYPE **Listing 1.2. COBOL's four divisions.**

```
000100 IDENTIFICATION DIVISION.
000200 ENVIRONMENT DIVISION.
000300 DATA DIVISION.
000400 PROCEDURE DIVISION.
```

The IDENTIFICATION DIVISION marks the beginning of a COBOL program. The name of the program, which you assign, will be entered as a statement in the IDENTIFICATION DIVISION (more on this in a moment).

The ENVIRONMENT DIVISION contains statements or commands to describe the physical environment in which the program is running. The main use of the ENVIRONMENT DIVISION is to describe the physical structure of files that will be used in the program. You won't be working with files in these early lessons, so for now this DIVISION will be little used.

The DATA DIVISION contains statements describing the data used by the program. The DATA DIVISION and the PROCEDURE DIVISION are the most important divisions in a COBOL program; they do 95 percent of the work. You will start working in the DATA DIVISION in Day 2, "Using Variables and Constants."

The PROCEDURE DIVISION contains the COBOL statements that the program will execute after the program starts running. The PROCEDURE DIVISION is the real workhorse of a COBOL program. Without a PROCEDURE DIVISION, you wouldn't have a program, because all the other divisions are used to create the environment and data that are used by the PROCEDURE DIVISION to actually do something.

You already have seen `hello.cbl` (in Listing 1.1). It contains no data, no environment, and only one significant statement, which is in the PROCEDURE DIVISION. However, without the DISPLAY "Hello" command, the program would do nothing at all.

Each DIVISION in a COBOL program is broken down into smaller units, like an outline. Briefly, a DIVISION can contain SECTIONs, a SECTION can contain paragraphs, and paragraphs can contain sentences. For the moment, you can ignore SECTIONs, which are introduced in Day 2. Think of a COBOL program as DIVISIONs containing paragraphs containing sentences.

The requirements for the contents of each different DIVISION can vary, but most compilers require that only two things be present in a COBOL program—other than the four divisions—in order to compile it:

- PROGRAM-ID
- STOP RUN

The PROGRAM-ID is a paragraph that must appear in the IDENTIFICATION DIVISION and is used to give the program a name.

There must also be one paragraph in the PROCEDURE DIVISION that contains the STOP RUN statement.

Listing 1.3 is an example of the smallest possible COBOL program that will compile and run on any COBOL compiler. It contains the PROGRAM-ID paragraph and only one paragraph in the PROCEDURE DIVISION.

The paragraph PROGRAM-DONE contains only one sentence, STOP RUN. This sentence causes the program to stop running when the sentence is executed. Most versions of COBOL require this explicit command as a way of identifying the point in the program where the program terminates.

TYPE **Listing 1.3. `minimum.cbl`, the irreducible minimum COBOL program.**

```
000100 IDENTIFICATION DIVISION.
000200 PROGRAM-ID. MINIMUM.
000300 ENVIRONMENT DIVISION.
000400 DATA DIVISION.
000500 PROCEDURE DIVISION.
000600
000700 PROGRAM-DONE.
000800     STOP RUN.
```

OUTPUT *Nothing!*

ANALYSIS Clearly, `minimum.cbl` does even less than `hello.cbl`. In fact, `minimum.cbl` does nothing except stop running as soon as it starts. Its only function is to illustrate the minimum syntax that the COBOL compiler will accept.

Of all the errors that you can make in typing a COBOL program, an incorrect DIVISION name is one of the hardest errors to locate. In one compiler that I tested, misspelling the name of the IDENTIFICATION DIVISION as INDENTIFICATION DIVISION caused the compiler to report that the PROCEDURE DIVISION was missing. This is a difficult error to spot because the real problem was three divisions away, and everything about the PROCEDURE DIVISION was fine. It is important that the DIVISIONs be typed correctly.

Listing 1.4 is more useful than `minimum.cbl`. You will recognize some similarities to `hello.cbl`, but I have divided a couple of the lines to illustrate a few more things about COBOL.

TYPE | **Listing 1.4. Three levels of COBOL grammar.**

```
000100 IDENTIFICATION DIVISION.
000200 PROGRAM-ID. SENTNCES.
000300 ENVIRONMENT DIVISION.
000400 DATA DIVISION.
000500 PROCEDURE DIVISION.
000600
000700 PROGRAM-BEGIN.
000800     DISPLAY "This program contains four DIVISIONS,".
000900     DISPLAY "three PARAGRAPHS".
001000     DISPLAY "and four SENTENCES".
001100 PROGRAM-DONE.
001200     STOP RUN.
```

OUTPUT
```
C>pcobrun comment
Personal COBOL version 2.0 from Micro Focus
PCOBRUN V2.0.02  Copyright (C) 1983-1993 Micro Focus Ltd.
This program contains four DIVISIONS,
three PARAGRAPHS
and four SENTENCES
```

ANALYSIS Strictly speaking, the PROGRAM-ID, SENTNCES, is a sentence, but it has such a specialized role in a COBOL program (identifying the program) that it is not usually considered to be a sentence. The program is named `sentnces.cbl` (with the word `sentnces` deliberately shortened) because some operating systems (especially MS-DOS) limit filenames to eight characters plus an extension, and many compilers limit program names to eight characters.

DO match the filename and program name; for example, sentnces.cbl is the file name and SENTNCES is the PROGRAM-ID.

DON'T add confusion by using a PROGRAM-ID that is different from the filename.

I will stick with the use of eight or fewer characters for the names of programs and files throughout the text.

The sentnces.cbl program contains all four DIVISIONs, three paragraphs (PROGRAM-ID, PROGRAM-BEGIN, and PROGRAM-DONE), and four sentences (the three DISPLAY statements in PROGRAM-BEGIN and STOP RUN at line 001200).

The paragraph name, PROGRAM-ID, is a required paragraph name and must be typed exactly as PROGRAM-ID. The paragraph names PROGRAM-BEGIN and PROGRAM-DONE are names I assigned when I wrote the program. Any of the paragraphs in the PROCEDURE DIVISION are given names you assign. The two paragraphs could have been named DISPLAY-THE-INFORMATION and PROGRAM-ENDS-HERE.

All the special words in COBOL (such as PROGRAM-ID, DATA, DIVISION, STOP, and RUN), as well as the paragraph names and program name (such as SENTNCES, PROGRAM-BEGIN, and PROGRAM-DONE), are created using the uppercase letters of the alphabet A through Z, the digits 0 through 9, and the hyphen (-). The designers of COBOL chose to allow a hyphen as a way of improving the readability of COBOL words. PROGRAM-BEGIN is easier to read than PROGRAMBEGIN.

The designers of COBOL also allowed for blank lines, such as line 000600 in Listing 1.4. Blank lines mean nothing in COBOL and can be used to spread things out to make them more readable.

You should type, compile (and, if necessary, link), and run Listing 1.4. See Appendix C for details. You might need to review this appendix a couple of times before you are completely comfortable with each of the steps involved in editing, compiling, and running.

Listing 1.4 illustrates the line-by-line organization of a COBOL program. There also is a left-to-right organization that determines what can be placed in certain columns.

A COBOL source code file has five areas, extending from left to right across the page. The first six characters or columns of a line are called the *sequence number area*. This area is not processed by the compiler, or if it is processed, it provides you only with warnings that numbers are out of sequence (if they are).

Character position 7 is called the *indicator area*. This seventh position is usually blank. If an asterisk is placed in this column, everything else on that line is ignored by the compiler. This is used as a method to include comments in your source code file.

The four character positions 8 through 11 are called *Area A*. DIVISIONs and paragraphs (and SECTIONs) must start in Area A. It is good coding practice to start DIVISIONs, SECTIONs, and paragraph names at column 8 rather than some random place in Area A.

Character positions 12 through 72 are called *Area B*. Sentences must start and end within Area B. It is good coding practice to start sentences at column 12 rather than some random place in Area B.

COBOL was designed as an 80-column language, but there is no formal definition of character positions 73 through 80. This is called the *identification area* (which has nothing to do with the IDENTIFICATION DIVISION).

The identification area is left to the designer of the COBOL compiler to use as needed. COBOL editors on large computers usually allow you to define an eight-character modification code that is inserted into the identification area whenever a line is changed or a new line is added. If you add lines to an existing program or change existing lines, it could be useful to know which lines were changed. Modification codes can be used to track down where a particular change was made. Modification codes are especially useful in companies where many programmers can work on many files. It helps keep track of changes, when they occurred, and who made them.

Some special COBOL editors place a modification code automatically in positions 73 through 80. This method of marking lines as modified usually depends on a special editor set up for COBOL that inserts these codes automatically. You probably will never see modification codes using COBOL on a PC.

Listing 1.5 is comment.cbl, which really is sentnces.cbl with a comment included and some lines that have been tagged with modification codes. I have deliberately left some of the sequence numbers out, or put them in incorrect order. The compiler will compile this without an error, but it might generate a warning that lines are out of order or sequence numbers are not consecutive. The compiler doesn't really care what is in the first six positions, but it might provide some warning information. Because of the width limits in a book, the example modification codes in Listing 1.5 do not actually start in column 73 as they must in a real COBOL example.

TYPE **Listing 1.5. The areas of a COBOL program.**

Sequence number area	Indicator area	Area A	Area B	Identification area

```
000100 IDENTIFICATION DIVISION.
000200 PROGRAM-ID. COMMENT.
000300 ENVIRONMENT DIVISION.
       DATA DIVISION.                              MB072197
000500 PROCEDURE DIVISION.
000600
000700* This is a comment.                         MB072197
000800* This paragraph displays information about the program.  MB072197
000900 PROGRAM-BEGIN.
003700     DISPLAY "This program contains four DIVISIONS,".  MB072197
003800     DISPLAY "three PARAGRAPHS".              MB072197
001000     DISPLAY "and four SENTENCES".
001100 PROGRAM-DONE.
001200     STOP RUN.
```

Note that the output is the same as sentnces.cbl:

OUTPUT
```
C>pcobrun comment
Personal COBOL version 2.0 from Micro Focus
PCOBRUN V2.0.02  Copyright (C) 1983-1993 Micro Focus Ltd.
This program contains four DIVISIONS,
three PARAGRAPHS
and four SENTENCES

C>
```

ANALYSIS As a historical note, the very first COBOL programs were written using punch cards. Each card carried one line of code that had been carefully entered using a keypunch machine (a kind of typewriter that punches holes in cards). The stack of punched cards was carried to the computer and fed into it using a card reader. An "out of sequence" warning was used to let you know that you probably had dropped the punch card deck and hadn't put them back together in the correct sequence. Compiler error messages also referred to line numbers, and locating an error was difficult without line numbers on the cards. PC COBOL compilers rarely give warnings about sequence.

Lines 000700 and 000800 contain an asterisk in column 7, the indicator area. Everything beyond the asterisk is ignored and can be used as a comment, as in the example.

DIVISIONs and paragraphs start in Area A but can extend into Area B.

Sentences begin and end in Area B. In Listing 1.5, sentences appear at lines 003700, 003800, 001000, and 001200.

What Is a Shell Program?

Because COBOL has a certain minimum amount of code that is required for all programs, it is a good practice to maintain a COBOL program that contains the minimum requirements.

 A COBOL program that contains the minimum requirements usually is called a *shell program*, a *skeleton program*, or a *boilerplate program.*

If you copy this shell program to a new file before you start editing the new program, you can save yourself extra typing. Listing 1.6, cobsh101.cbl, is your first version of the COBOL shell program. As you progress through the days, you'll gradually add more and more pieces to the shell; eventually, you'll have a complete shell to use in all projects.

TYPE **Listing 1.6. Your first version of a COBOL shell.**

```
000100 IDENTIFICATION DIVISION.
000200 PROGRAM-ID. COBSHL01.
000300 ENVIRONMENT DIVISION.
000400 DATA DIVISION.
000500 PROCEDURE DIVISION.
000600 PROGRAM-BEGIN.
000700
000800 PROGRAM-DONE.
000900     STOP RUN.
```

Type Listing 1.6 and compile it to ensure that everything in it is correct. You will use this shell, and versions of it, many times before you are through with these lessons.

As you will see in the next few days, PC-based COBOL compilers are much less stringent about following the rules described in today's lesson. However, COBOL is intended to be a portable language that allows code to be moved to other computers. Another computer probably will be using another COBOL compiler that might require compliance to all the strict rules of COBOL. When you start breaking the rules, you limit your code to a compiler that can handle the loose syntax, and this might make it extremely difficult to move your code to another machine or compiler.

Summary

Today's lesson introduced you to some computer and programming basics, including the following:

☐ A computer processes numbers and is made up of a central processing unit, input devices, output devices, main memory, and secondary storage.

☐ A computer can't do anything without a program.

☐ A program is a series of instructions that the central processing unit executes to process data, usually using some input data and providing some sort of output.

☐ A programming language is a method of writing a source code file in an English-like language that a human being can understand.

☐ A compiler translates the source code file into instructions that the central processing unit can understand and execute.

☐ A COBOL program contains four DIVISIONs: the IDENTIFICATION DIVISION, the ENVIRONMENT DIVISION, the DATA DIVISION, and the PROCEDURE DIVISION.

☐ A DIVISION can be broken down into paragraphs. Some divisions have required paragraphs, such as the PROGRAM-ID paragraph in the IDENTIFICATION DIVISION.

☐ The names of the paragraphs in the PROCEDURE DIVISION are assigned by the programmer.

☐ The work of a COBOL program is done in sentences that contain the commands of a program and appear within a paragraph.

☐ A COBOL program is written in 80-column format. The columns are divided into the following areas:

    ☐ Columns 1 through 6 are the sequence area and can be used by the programmer for line numbering. Line numbering is optional.

    ☐ Column 7 is the indicator area. An asterisk (*) in column 7 causes everything to the right of the asterisk to be treated as a comment.

    ☐ Columns 8 through 11 are Area A, and columns 12 through 72 are Area B. DIVISION names, SECTION names, and paragraph names must begin in Area A, but they can extend into Area B. Sentences begin and end in Area B.

    ☐ Columns 73 through 80 are undefined and are not processed by the COBOL compiler, but some COBOL editors use these columns to tag lines with modification codes.

Today, you also learned how to type, compile, and run several simple COBOL programs.

Q&A

Q Why is so much of COBOL in uppercase?

A COBOL was developed in the days when computer terminals and keypunch machines used only uppercase letters. The entire language was defined in terms of this all-uppercase state of affairs. You can display uppercase and lowercase messages, such as Hello world, because terminals now have uppercase and lowercase capability. However, the actual elements of COBOL—the DIVISIONs, the paragraph names such as PROGRAM-BEGIN, and the verbs such as DISPLAY—originally were designed in uppercase only.

Q What does a blank line in a program do?

A Nothing. The compiler skips blank lines. You can put blank lines anywhere you want in the program to improve readability.

Q Does COBOL use line numbers?

A Yes, but they are optional. Most compilers ignore them or can be set to ignore them. Some compilers on larger computers will process the line numbers and provide a warning if the line numbers are out of sequence, but this is not an error.

Q Can I put anything in a comment?

A Yes. As long as the asterisk appears at column 7, everything after the asterisk is ignored and has no effect on the compiler. You can write English sentences or gobbledygook, although the usual practice is to provide some information that describes what the program is doing, or why it is doing it.

You can do this on as many lines as necessary to complete the comment.

Q Will my comments appear in the program when it runs?

A No. Comments appear only in the source code file, and they will not be included in the compiled program. Comments are intended to document the source code. The computer can read only the compiled code, and the comments wouldn't mean anything to the computer, so they are not included in the resulting program.

Q Why do paragraph names have hyphens in them?

A Paragraph names in COBOL are limited to 30 characters and may only contain uppercase letters (A through Z), digits (0 through 9), and the hyphen (-). The hyphen is used to improve the readability of paragraphs and the names of data (which is covered in Day 2). Some modern compilers allow paragraph names, division names, and other elements of COBOL to be typed in lowercase.

Workshop

Quiz

1. What is the output of the following program?

```
000100 IDENTIFICATION DIVISION.
000200 PROGRAM-ID. BYEBYE.
000300 ENVIRONMENT DIVISION.
000400 DATA DIVISION.
000500 PROCEDURE DIVISION.
000600
000700 PROGRAM-BEGIN.
000800     DISPLAY "Bye bye birdie".
000900 PROGRAM-DONE.
001000     STOP RUN.
```

2. How many DIVISIONs are in the following program, byebye.cbl?

```
000100 IDENTIFICATION DIVISION.
000200 PROGRAM-ID. BYEBYE.
000300 ENVIRONMENT DIVISION.
000400 DATA DIVISION.
000500 PROCEDURE DIVISION.
000600
000700 PROGRAM-BEGIN.
000800     DISPLAY "Bye bye birdie".
000900 PROGRAM-DONE.
001000     STOP RUN.
```

3. How many paragraphs?

4. How many sentences?

5. What is wrong with the following, bad01.cbl?

```
000100 IDENTIFICATION DIVISION.
000200 PROGRAM-ID. BAD01.
000300 ENVIRONMENT DIVISION.
000400
000500 PROCEDURE DIVISION.
000600
000700 PROGRAM-BEGIN.
000800     DISPLAY "I'm bad!".
000900 PROGRAM-DONE.
001000     STOP RUN.
```

6. What is wrong with the following, bad02.cbl?

```
000100 IDENTIFICATION DIVISION.
000200 PROGRAM-ID. BAD02.
000300 ENVIRONMENT DIVISION.
000400 DATA DIVISION.
000500 PROCEDURE DIVISION.
000600
000700 PROGRAM-BEGIN.
000800 DISPLAY "I'm bad!".
000900 PROGRAM-DONE.
001000     STOP RUN.
```

Hint: Where are sentences supposed to begin?

Note: Some compilers might not give an error on compiling BAD02, but might only provide a warning.

7. What is wrong with the following, bad03.cbl?

```
000100 IDENTIFICATION DIVISION.
000200 PROGRAM-ID. BAD03.
000300 ENVIRONMENT DIVISION.
000400 DATA DIVISION.
000500 PROCEDURE DIVISION.
000600     This program displays a message.
000700 PROGRAM-BEGIN.
000800     DISPLAY "I'm really bad!".
000900 PROGRAM-DONE.
001000     STOP RUN.
```

Exercises

1. Modify the `hello.cbl` program to display `I am a COBOL programmer.`

   Hint: Copy the `hello.cbl` program to `iam.cbl`:

   ```
   copy hello.cbl iam.cbl
   ```

   Then use your editor or pcobol to change the `PROGRAM-ID` and `DISPLAY` statements.

2. Use the computer to compile each of the bad examples (`bad01.cbl`, `bad02.cbl`, and `bad03.cbl`) to get a feel for the types of error messages that your compiler produces.

   COBOL-85 compilers are much more relaxed than earlier standards. The `ENVIRONMENT`, `DATA`, and `PROCEDURE DIVISION`s are optional under ANSI 85, although what a program would do without a `PROCEDURE DIVISION` is a bit of a mystery. The results of compiling these programs are interesting.

   Both Micro Focus Personal COBOL and ACUCOBOL found nothing wrong with `bad01.cbl`. Apparently, if a program contains no data, it doesn't need to have a `DATA DIVISION`.

   Micro Focus Personal COBOL handled `bad02.cbl` without a hiccup.

   ACUCOBOL produced a warning that a sentence was starting in Area A.

   Both Micro Focus Personal COBOL and ACUCOBOL generated errors on `bad03.cbl` and would not compile it.

3. Modify `bad01.cbl` so that it compiles without errors or warnings.

4. Modify `bad02.cbl` so that it compiles without errors or warnings.

5. Modify `bad03.cbl` so that it compiles without errors or warnings.

Day 2

Using Variables and Constants

The DATA DIVISION is a critical subject to understand in COBOL. Today's lesson covers the basics, but you will be returning to the DATA DIVISION again and again throughout this book.

Today, you learn about the following topics:

- ☐ What is a constant?
- ☐ What is a variable?
- ☐ Defining numeric variables in COBOL.
- ☐ Naming variables in COBOL.
- ☐ More on using DISPLAY.
- ☐ Defining and using variables.
- ☐ Defining pictures.
- ☐ Using the MOVE verb.
- ☐ Formatting output.
- ☐ Tips on layout and punctuation.
- ☐ Continuation characters.

What Is a Constant?

The data in COBOL programs falls into two broad categories: constants and variables.

NEW TERM   A *constant* is a value that cannot be modified while the program is running.

You already have used constants in the hello.cbl program and examples in Day 1, "Your First COBOL Program." In Listing 1.1, the string "Hello world" is a constant.

In hello.cbl, there is no way to modify the display of "Hello world" without editing the program and recompiling it, as shown in Listing 2.1. This effectively creates a new program.

TYPE   **Listing 2.1. Modifying a constant by editing and recompiling.**

```
000100 IDENTIFICATION DIVISION.
000200 PROGRAM-ID. HELLO.
000300 ENVIRONMENT DIVISION.
000400 DATA DIVISION.
000500 PROCEDURE DIVISION.
000600
000700 PROGRAM-BEGIN.
000800     DISPLAY "I said, Hello world".
000900
001000 PROGRAM-DONE.
001100     STOP RUN.
```

If you want to display both messages, you have to use code similar to what you see in Listing 2.2; however, this merely uses two different constants in one program.

TYPE   **Listing 2.2. Adding another constant.**

```
000100 IDENTIFICATION DIVISION.
000200 PROGRAM-ID. HELOHELO.
000300 ENVIRONMENT DIVISION.
000400 DATA DIVISION.
000500 PROCEDURE DIVISION.
000600
000700 PROGRAM-BEGIN.
000800     DISPLAY "Hello world".
000900     DISPLAY "I said, Hello world".
001000 PROGRAM-DONE.
001100     STOP RUN.
```

Numeric constants can be used in a similar way. Listing 2.3 includes examples of numeric constants (55 and 12.607). Note the difference between character constants, such as "Hello world", and numeric constants, such as 12.607. Character constants are enclosed in quotation marks. Numeric constants are not.

NEW TERM   Character constants also are called *string constants*.

TYPE   **Listing 2.3. String and numeric constants.**

```
000100 IDENTIFICATION DIVISION.
000200 PROGRAM-ID. CONST.
000300 ENVIRONMENT DIVISION.
000400 DATA DIVISION.
000500 PROCEDURE DIVISION.
000600
000700 PROGRAM-BEGIN.
000800     DISPLAY "Hello world".
000900     DISPLAY 55.
001000     DISPLAY 12.607.
001100 PROGRAM-DONE.
001200     STOP RUN.
```

Character constants can contain spaces, such as the space between the words in "Hello world". Without the double quotation marks at each end, the compiler would have trouble recognizing all of the character constant; it would not know where the constant ended. The following is a classic example of this problem:

DISPLAY THIS IS THE DISPLAY.

DISPLAY is a COBOL verb. In this example, the first occurrence of the word DISPLAY is the COBOL verb for displaying information. The compiler could become confused as to whether the second occurrence of the word DISPLAY is part of the message to be displayed or is another DISPLAY verb. To keep the compiler from having a nervous breakdown, the programmer is required to write the following:

DISPLAY "THIS IS THE DISPLAY".

Every popular programming language includes a requirement that character constants be enclosed in some sort of quotation marks or other signaling characters to indicate the exact beginning and end of the character constant. COBOL uses double quotation marks at the beginning and end of the characters.

Numeric constants such as the following do not contain *white space*, and it is much easier for the compiler to recognize them as numbers:

DISPLAY 12.607.

Most popular languages do not require any special characters to signal a numeric constant.

White space is a general term to cover any blank characters. A space is white space, as is a tab, though you won't use tabs in COBOL programs. They are called white space because they print as white spaces on white paper when sent to a printer.

What Is a Variable?

Computers are capable of dealing with a large amount of data, and the data should be able to change while the computer is running. So, how do you change data? You use something called a variable.

 A *variable* is a value that can be changed while the program is running.

When a variable is created in a program, an area of memory is set aside to hold values. In most programming languages, including COBOL, a variable is given a name. The name can be used in the program to refer to the value.

The value stored in memory can be modified while the program is running by using the variable name. You'll see some examples of using variables later in today's lesson; but you first must understand how to define a variable.

Defining Numeric Variables in COBOL

The following is an example of a COBOL numeric variable. Variable names use the same characters as paragraph names: A through Z, 0 through 9, and the hyphen (-). This is described more fully in the section "Naming Variables in COBOL," later in today's lesson.

```
001400 01  THE-NUMBER              PICTURE IS 9999.
```

A COBOL variable definition contains at least three parts:

☐ The level number
☐ The name
☐ The PICTURE

In the syntax, the level number is 01. For now, every variable you will be using will have a level number of 01. The level number 01 must be in Area A, columns 8 through 11. In the previous code fragment, the 01 starts in column 8.

The second part of the variable definition is the name of the variable and, in this case, is THE-NUMBER. This is the data name used to identify the variable. The data name is assigned by the programmer. The variable will be referred to by its data name, THE-NUMBER, anywhere in the program that the variable must be set or modified. The name of the variable must start in Area B, columns 12 through 72. In this example, THE-NUMBER starts in column 12.

The PICTURE defines two things about a variable: the size of the variable (the number of bytes used in memory for the value) and the type of data that can be stored in the variable. In this example, the picture 9999 indicates that four numeric characters can be stored in the variable named THE-NUMBER. Similarly, a variable with a PICTURE IS 99 could hold two numeric characters. The PICTURE IS clause and the actual picture 9999 must start somewhere in Area B, columns 12 through 72.

The PICTURE IS clause in the definition of a variable is the COBOL syntax for introducing the size of a variable and the type of data that a variable holds.

The 9999 in the picture does not indicate that the variable contains the value 9999. It indicates that the variable can be used for numeric values in the range 0 through 9,999. The 9999 picture indicates that four numeric digits can be stored in this variable. The picture 9999 will hold any of the values from 0 through 9,999. The values 17 and 6,489 will both fit in THE-NUMBER, but the value 65,413 is too large.

Look at Listing 2.4, add01.cbl, for the general format of the program now that it contains variables. Three variables are created in this program: FIRST-NUMBER, SECOND-NUMBER, and THE-RESULT. Each variable has the level number 01. The first two have pictures of 99 and will hold values ranging from 0 through 99. The third variable, THE-RESULT, has a picture of 999 and will hold a value of 0 through 999. Once again, the PICTURE IS clause does not set the value of the variable; it sets only the largest and smallest values that a variable can hold and the fact that the variable will hold numeric data.

TYPE   **Listing 2.4. Using variables.**

```
000100 IDENTIFICATION DIVISION.
000200 PROGRAM-ID. ADD01.
000300 ENVIRONMENT DIVISION.
000400 DATA DIVISION.
000500
000600 WORKING-STORAGE SECTION.
000700
000800 01  FIRST-NUMBER      PICTURE IS 99.
000900 01  SECOND-NUMBER     PICTURE IS 99.
001000 01  THE-RESULT        PICTURE IS 999.
001100
001200 PROCEDURE DIVISION.
001300
001400 PROGRAM-BEGIN.
001500
001600     DISPLAY "Enter the first number.".
001700
001800     ACCEPT FIRST-NUMBER.
001900
002000     DISPLAY "Enter the second number.".
002100
```

continues

Listing 2.4. continued

```
002200        ACCEPT SECOND-NUMBER.
002300
002400        COMPUTE THE-RESULT = FIRST-NUMBER + SECOND-NUMBER.
002500
002600        DISPLAY "The result is:".
002700        DISPLAY THE-RESULT.
002800
002900 PROGRAM-DONE.
003000        STOP RUN.
003100
```

Load and compile or type in with your editor and compile Listing 2.4, add01.CBL. When you run the program, you will be asked to enter the first number, as shown in the following output. Note that the final blank line 003100 in the listing has no effect on the program. You can leave it out if you wish.

```
C>pcobrun add01

Enter the first number.
```

First, type **97** and then press Enter. You will be asked for a second number, in a screen looking something like this:

```
C>pcobrun add01


Enter the first number.
97
Enter the second number.
```

Now type **33** and press Enter. The two numbers are added together and displayed:

```
C>pcobrun add01

Enter the first number.
97
Enter the second number.
33
The result is:
130

C>
```

ANALYSIS Take a look at the DATA DIVISION. Here is your first example of a section, the WORKING-STORAGE SECTION. A SECTION in COBOL is created by typing a name, similar to a paragraph name, followed by one or more spaces, followed by the word SECTION and a period. SECTIONs in COBOL can be required or optional, depending on which DIVISION they are in. WORKING-STORAGE SECTION is a reserved name and a required section in the DATA DIVISION if your program uses any variables—and most programs do.

Do	Don't

DO precede the word SECTION with at least one space (WORKING-STORAGE SECTION).

DON'T precede SECTION with an extra hyphen (WORKING-STORAGE-SECTION).

Each of the variables is defined with a 01, a variable name, and a PICTURE. The PICTURE IS clauses are lined up on the right. There is no reason for this other than tidiness. As long as the PICTURE clause starts and ends in Area B, there are no other restrictions on alignment or position.

Now look at Listing 2.4 again, but this time from the perspective of a running program. In the DATA DIVISION, space is created for two variables with pictures of 99 and one variable with a picture of 999.

In the PROCEDURE DIVISION, a message is displayed for the user at line 001600, asking the user to enter the first variable. At line 001800, this value is accepted from the keyboard, using the ACCEPT verb. ACCEPT is a verb that causes the program to wait for input from the keyboard. Digits can be typed until the user presses Enter. When the user presses Enter, the value of the digits entered is moved to the variable named immediately after the ACCEPT verb.

When the program is running and encounters the sentence

```
ACCEPT FIRST-NUMBER
```

the computer stops and waits for the user to type. Whatever value is typed is stored in the two bytes of FIRST-NUMBER.

At line 002000, the user is asked for another number. This is accepted at line 002200 using the ACCEPT verb and stored in SECOND-NUMBER.

At line 002400, the COBOL COMPUTE verb is used to add the two values together. In the following statement, the values that have been stored at FIRST-NUMBER and SECOND-NUMBER are retrieved and added together, using + to perform the addition:

```
COMPUTE THE-RESULT = FIRST-NUMBER + SECOND-NUMBER.
```

The result of this addition is stored at THE-RESULT.

Finally, in lines 002600 and 002700, the result of the addition is displayed.

In this example, two of the variables—FIRST-NUMBER and SECOND-NUMBER—have been modified or "varied" by the user entering values at the keyboard. The third variable, THE-RESULT, was modified by the program. The program uses the COMPUTE statement to calculate a new value and store it in THE-RESULT. This is what variables are all about: the ability to vary their values while the program is running.

Some versions of COBOL (ACUCOBOL, for example) are picky about accepting data from the keyboard. If a field is defined with a PICTURE IS 99, you must enter two digits in response to an ACCEPT. To enter the number 3, you must enter 03. To enter 7 into a PICTURE 99999 field, you must enter 00007. ACUCOBOL includes an option to change this behavior, and I am informed that, as of their version 3.0 compiler, the ACCEPT verb behaves in a more relaxed manner, allowing numeric entry without the preceding zeroes. Other versions of COBOL, such as Micro Focus Personal COBOL, use this more relaxed approach to ACCEPT. If you want to enter a 3 into a PICTURE 999, just enter a 3 and press Enter. The COBOL language will correctly store 003 in the PICTURE 999.

For the time being, enter all the digits to avoid any problems. If a program complains of non-numeric data in a numeric field, you probably have not entered enough leading zeroes.

Type the program from Listing 2.4 into your computer and compile it. Run it several times, entering different values each time. You will see that the three variables truly are variable, because their values are determined while the program is running. You do not have to edit and recompile the program each time that you want to get a new result.

Take one more look at Listing 2.4, add01.cbl, for a quick review. Line numbers appear in columns 1 through 6, the sequence area. Comments start in the indicator area, and they start with an asterisk in that column. DIVISIONs, SECTIONs, paragraphs, and the 01 level number of a variable start in columns 8, Area A. Everything else starts and ends in Area B, usually at column 12.

Naming Variables in COBOL

COBOL variable names are similar to paragraph and section names because they can use any of the uppercase alphabet characters, the digits 0 through 9, and the hyphen (but not as a starting character). COBOL variable and paragraph names are limited to 30 characters. Table 2.1 provides some examples of valid and invalid variable names.

Table 2.1. Valid and invalid variable names.

Valid Name	Invalid Name	Explanation of Invalid Name
TOTAL-DOLLARS	TOTAL-$	Uses an invalid $ in the name
SUM-OF-COLUMNS	sum-of-columns	Uses lowercase letters
7-BY-5	7_BY_5	Uses the invalid _ character in the name
MINUS-RESULT	-RESULT	Starts with a hyphen
BOEING-707-SEATS	BOEING-707-MAXIMUM-SEATING-CAPACITY	Exceeds 30 characters

2

Some modern compilers have disposed of the uppercase requirement and will accept variable names such as sum-of-columns and 7-by-5, but it is a good practice to use uppercase because it makes your code more portable between COBOL compilers.

More on Using DISPLAY

The DISPLAY verb can be used to display more than one value at a time, like so:

```
DISPLAY "The result is " THE-RESULT.
```

It is used this way in Listing 2.5, add02.cbl. The only change in this program is that lines 002600 and 002700 have been combined into a single DISPLAY line, and the colon (:) in the message has been replaced with a space.

TYPE   **Listing 2.5. Combining values in one DISPLAY statement.**

```
000100 IDENTIFICATION DIVISION.
000200 PROGRAM-ID. ADD02.
000300 ENVIRONMENT DIVISION.
000400 DATA DIVISION.
000500
000600 WORKING-STORAGE SECTION.
000700
000800 01  FIRST-NUMBER        PICTURE IS 99.
000900 01  SECOND-NUMBER       PICTURE IS 99.
001000 01  THE-RESULT          PICTURE IS 999.
001100
001200 PROCEDURE DIVISION.
001300
001400 PROGRAM-BEGIN.
001500
001600     DISPLAY "Enter the first number.".
001700
001800     ACCEPT FIRST-NUMBER.
001900
002000     DISPLAY "Enter the second number.".
002100
002200     ACCEPT SECOND-NUMBER.
002300
002400     COMPUTE THE-RESULT = FIRST-NUMBER + SECOND-NUMBER.
002500
002600     DISPLAY "The result is " THE-RESULT.
002700
002800
002900 PROGRAM-DONE.
003000     STOP RUN.
003100
```

This is the output from a sample session with `add02.cbl`. The result line is combined into one line of display:

```
C>pcobrun add02

Enter the first number.
16
Enter the second number.
93
The result is 109

C>
```

Defining and Using Variables

When you define a variable in the WORKING-STORAGE SECTION of the DATA DIVISION, you are providing information for the compiler about the size of the variable and the type of data that can be stored in it.

A numeric variable is used to store numbers. The picture character used to represent a digit in a numeric variable is a 9, as in this example:

```
01   THE-NUMBER          PICTURE IS 99.
```

This description defines a variable named THE-NUMBER that can be used to hold a numeric variable that is two digits long; in other words, any value in the range of 0 through 99.

New Term Variables that can hold character data are called alphanumeric variables.

Alphanumeric data contains one or more printable characters. Some examples of alphanumeric values are Hello, ??506^%$A, and 123-B707. An alphanumeric variable is defined in the same way as a numeric variable, except that the picture character used to represent one alphanumeric character is an X. The following syntax example defines an alphanumeric variable that can hold a word or message of no more than 10 characters:

```
001200 01 THE-MESSAGE     PICTURE IS XXXXXXXXXX.
```

An alphanumeric variable can also be used to hold numbers (such as storing 123 in a PICTURE IS XXX variable), but you will not be able to use the values as numbers. For example, you could display the PICTURE IS XXX variable containing 123, but you couldn't use the COMPUTE verb to add 1 to it.

In Listing 2.6, a modified version of `hello.cbl` named `hello02.cbl` illustrates the use of alphanumeric variables.

Listing 2.6. Using an alphanumeric variable.

```
000100 IDENTIFICATION DIVISION.
000200 PROGRAM-ID. HELLO02.
000300 ENVIRONMENT DIVISION.
000400 DATA DIVISION.
000500
000600 WORKING-STORAGE SECTION.
000700
000800 01  THE-NAME      PICTURE IS XXXXXXXXXX.
000900
001000 PROCEDURE DIVISION.
001100
001200 PROGRAM-BEGIN.
001300
001400     DISPLAY "Enter someone's name.".
001500
001600     ACCEPT THE-NAME.
001700
001800     DISPLAY "Hello " THE-NAME.
001900
002000 PROGRAM-DONE.
002100     STOP RUN.
```

The following is an example of the output from `hello02.cbl`, using `Erica` as the name entered at the keyboard:

OUTPUT
```
C>pcobrun hello02


Enter someone's name.
Erica
Hello Erica

C>
```

ANALYSIS At line `001400`, the user is asked to enter a name. At line `001600`, the ACCEPT verb will cause the computer to accept input from the keyboard until the user presses Enter. Whatever is typed (up to 10 characters) will be stored in THE-NAME. THE-NAME then is displayed in a hello message.

Defining Pictures

So far, you've defined small variables, but you also can define longer ones in COBOL. Numeric variables can be as large as 18 digits:

```
01  THE-NUMBER    PICTURE IS 999999999999999999.
```

Numeric variables are limited to 18 digits, but the length of alphanumeric variables is limited by the version of COBOL that you have. LPI COBOL has a limit of 32,767 characters. ACUCOBOL has a limit of 65,520 characters. The Professional Micro Focus COBOL compiler (big brother to Micro Focus Personal COBOL) has a limit of a whopping 256 million characters.

Defining long variables could become a tedious task if every X and 9 had to be spelled out explicitly; and typing in long strings of X or 9 could result in errors. In addition, having to type PICTURE IS for every variable can get tiring in large programs. Fortunately, COBOL allows some abbreviations that make the task less cumbersome.

The word IS in PICTURE IS is optional, and the word PICTURE can be abbreviated as PIC. This abbreviation is used so commonly that it is rare to see a program containing PICTURE IS:

```
01   THE-MESSAGE     PIC XXXXXX.
```

The second abbreviation is even more useful. The picture itself can be abbreviated by typing one picture character followed by the number of repetitions of that character in parentheses. Thus, PIC XXXXXX becomes PIC X(6), and PIC 99999 becomes PIC 9(5). The 18-digit number shown earlier becomes the following:

```
01   THE-NUMBER      PIC 9(18).
```

This works even when the repetition is one, so it is possible to describe PIC X as PIC X(1). When you are reading a listing, it sometimes is easier to determine the size of a variable quickly by scanning the values in parentheses. Some programmers make it a practice always to include the size in parentheses.

If you want to use the abbreviations to cut down on keystrokes, abbreviate anything exceeding a length of four. PIC XXXX and PIC X(4) require the same number of keystrokes, so for the sake of typing speed, it doesn't matter which you use. PIC X is faster to type than PIC X(1), but PIC X(5) is faster to type than PIC XXXXX.

You might find the use of parentheses is dictated by the style manual of the company that is using the program. If it is for your own use, pick the one that is more comfortable for you.

Introducing the MOVE Verb

The MOVE verb in COBOL is a general-purpose verb, used to store a value in a variable. The general syntax for MOVE is the following:

```
MOVE value TO variable.
```

In this syntax, `variable` must be a variable defined in the DATA DIVISION, and `value` can be another variable or a constant.

Here are some examples:

```
MOVE 12 TO THE-NUMBER.
MOVE ONE-NUMBER TO ANOTHER-NUMBER.
MOVE "XYZ" TO THE-MESSAGE.
```

MOVE is used to set a variable to a specific value. For example, if you're going to use the variable THE-COUNTER as a counter and you need the count to start at 1, you might use the following as one method of setting up the variable with a starting value:

```
MOVE 1 TO THE-COUNTER.
```

MOVE in COBOL does not move memory physically from one place to another. It copies values from the source variable and stores them in the target variable. Table 2.2 describes the effect of some different MOVE examples that move constants and variables into variables. All variables are assumed to be defined in the WORKING-STORAGE SECTION.

Table 2.2. Examples of the MOVE verb.

Command	Effect
MOVE 19 TO THE-NUMBER	Stores 19 in the variable THE-NUMBER, or sets THE-NUMBER to a value of 19
MOVE "Hello" TO THE-MESSAGE	Stores Hello in the variable THE-MESSAGE, or sets THE-MESSAGE to contain Hello
MOVE A-NUMBER TO THE-NUMBER	Locates the variable named A-NUMBER, gets the value stored there, and copies it or moves it to the variable named THE-NUMBER
MOVE THE-OLD-NAME TO THE-NEW-NAME	Locates the variable named THE-OLD-NAME, gets the value stored there, and copies it or moves it to the variable named THE-NEW-NAME

Listing 2.7 is a program designed solely to provide examples of the MOVE verb. It combines PICTURE abbreviations, multiple DISPLAY statements, and MOVE statements to display two messages, with message numbers, on the screen. This will give you a further idea of the uses and effects of MOVE.

Listing 2.7. Using MOVE.

```
000100 IDENTIFICATION DIVISION.
000200 PROGRAM-ID. HELLO03.
000300 ENVIRONMENT DIVISION.
000400 DATA DIVISION.
000500
000600 WORKING-STORAGE SECTION.
000700
000800 01  THE-MESSAGE      PIC X(20).
000900 01  THE-NAME         PIC X(10).
001000 01  THE-NUMBER       PIC 99.
001100
001200 PROCEDURE DIVISION.
001300
001400 PROGRAM-BEGIN.
001500
001600     DISPLAY "Enter someone's name.".
001700
001800     ACCEPT THE-NAME.
001900
002000     MOVE "Hello" TO THE-MESSAGE.
002100
002200     MOVE 1 TO THE-NUMBER.
002300
002400     DISPLAY "Message "
002500             THE-NUMBER
002600             ": "
002700             THE-MESSAGE
002800             THE-NAME.
002900
003000     MOVE "Say Goodnight," TO THE-MESSAGE.
003100
003200     MOVE 2 TO THE-NUMBER.
003300
003400     DISPLAY "Message "
003500             THE-NUMBER
003600             ": "
003700             THE-MESSAGE
003800             THE-NAME.
003900
004000
004100 PROGRAM-DONE.
004200     STOP RUN.
004300
```

OUTPUT   C>pcobrun hello03

```
Enter someone's name.
Gracie
Message 01: Hello               Gracie
Message 02: Say Goodnight,      Gracie

C>
```

ANALYSIS Lines 000800, 000900, and 001000 contain abbreviated PICTURES. THE-MESSAGE is a 20-character alphanumeric field, and THE-NAME is a 10-character alphanumeric field. The user is asked to enter a name, and this is accepted from the keyboard into THE-NAME at line 001800.

In lines 002000 and 002200, MOVE is used to move values to THE-MESSAGE and the THE-NUMBER. Lines 002400 through 002800 contain one long DISPLAY statement. Notice that this long statement ends with only one period, on line 002800. COBOL sentences can spread over more than one line as in this example, as long as they remain within Area B, which is columns 12 through 72. This DISPLAY creates one line of display information containing the values Message, THE-NUMBER, :, THE-MESSAGE, and THE-NAME, one after the other on a single line:

```
Message 01: Hello            Charlie
```

Similar logic is repeated at lines 003000 through 003800, and a second line is displayed. See if you can guess how the output will appear before taking a look.

Note that the output from hello03.cbl is shown for an input name of Gracie. Listing 2.7 is a good program for practice. First type, edit, and compile hello03.cbl, and try it a couple of times. Then copy the program to hello04.cbl and edit it. Try different constants and display orders for the DISPLAY statements. Here are a couple of alternatives for the first DISPLAY statement:

```
DISPLAY "Line "
THE-NUMBER
"> "
THE-MESSAGE
THE-NAME.


DISPLAY THE-MESSAGE
THE-NAME
" was Number "
THE-NUMBER.
```

The following are sample output lines from these two formats:

```
Line 01> Hello            Charlie
Hello            Charlie was Number 01
```

One of the features of the MOVE verb is that it will pad a variable with spaces to the end if the value that is being moved into an alphanumeric field is too short to fill the field. This is convenient; it's almost always what you want. In the line MOVE "Hello" TO THE-MESSAGE, the first five characters of THE-MESSAGE are filled with Hello, and the remaining character positions are filled with spaces. (In Bonus Day 2, "Miscellaneous COBOL Syntax," you learn how to move a field while dropping the trailing space used for padding.)

MOVE pads numeric variables by filling them with zeroes to the left. Notice that a numeric value with a PIC 99 containing a value of 1 will display as 01 in Listing 2.7. This is because of the padding action of the MOVE verb.

Values that are too long are truncated. If THE-MESSAGE is defined as a PIC X(7), the line

```
MOVE "Hello world" to THE-MESSAGE
```

results in THE-MESSAGE containing Hello w and the rest of the value falling off the end.

Moving a value that is too large to a numeric variable results in a similar truncation, but on the left side. If THE-NUMBER is defined as a PIC 9999, the following line results in THE-NUMBER containing 1784:

```
MOVE 61784 TO THE-NUMBER
```

There isn't room for all five digits, so only the four digits on the right are picked up on the move.

Formatting Output

Listing 2.8 is another example of some of the principles you have learned. It displays three lines of a nursery rhyme involving some work that Jack had to do. The ADD verb (which is new in this listing) increments the value of THE-NUMBER as each line is displayed. In the DISPLAY statements, a space is used to separate the line number from the statement. Remember that the asterisk in column 7 is used to place a comment in the code.

Type   Listing 2.8. Using the ADD verb.

```
000100 IDENTIFICATION DIVISION.
000200 PROGRAM-ID. JACK01.
000300 ENVIRONMENT DIVISION.
000400 DATA DIVISION.
000500
000600 WORKING-STORAGE SECTION.
000700
000800 01   THE-MESSAGE        PIC X(50).
000900 01   THE-NUMBER         PIC 9(2).
001000
001100 PROCEDURE DIVISION.
001200 PROGRAM-BEGIN.
001300
001400* Set up and display line 1
001500     MOVE 1 TO THE-NUMBER.
001600     MOVE "Jack be nimble," TO THE-MESSAGE.
001700     DISPLAY THE-NUMBER " " THE-MESSAGE.
001800
001900* Set up and Display line 2
002000     ADD 1 TO THE-NUMBER.
```

```
002100     MOVE "Jack be quick," TO THE-MESSAGE.
002200     DISPLAY THE-NUMBER " " THE-MESSAGE.
002300
002400* Set up and display line 3
002500     ADD 1 TO THE-NUMBER.
002600     MOVE "Jack jump over the candlestick." TO THE-MESSAGE.
002700     DISPLAY THE-NUMBER " " THE-MESSAGE.
002800
002900 PROGRAM-DONE.
003000     STOP RUN.
003100
```

OUTPUT

```
01 Jack be nimble,
02 Jack be quick,
03 Jack jump over the candlestick.


C>
C>
```

ANALYSIS   It is possible to use a variable as though it were a constant. In Listing 2.9, an additional variable, A-SPACE, is created. This variable is set to a value at the start of the program and then used in each message. The output of jack02.cbl should be identical to that of jack02.cbl.

NEW TERM   Setting a variable to a starting value is called *initializing*.

TYPE   ## Listing 2.9. Another method of formatting.

```
000100 IDENTIFICATION DIVISION.
000200 PROGRAM-ID. JACK02.
000300 ENVIRONMENT DIVISION.
000400 DATA DIVISION.
000500
000600 WORKING-STORAGE SECTION.
000700
000800 01  THE-MESSAGE     PIC X(50).
000900 01  THE-NUMBER      PIC 9(2).
001000 01  A-SPACE         PIC X.
001100
001200 PROCEDURE DIVISION.
001300 PROGRAM-BEGIN.
001400
001500* Initialize the space variable
001600     MOVE " " TO A-SPACE.
001700
001800* Set up and display line 1
001900     MOVE 1 TO THE-NUMBER.
002000     MOVE "Jack be nimble," TO THE-MESSAGE.
002100     DISPLAY THE-NUMBER A-SPACE THE-MESSAGE.
002200
```

continues

Listing 2.9. continued

```
002300* Set up and Display line 2
002400     ADD 1 TO THE-NUMBER.
002500     MOVE "Jack be quick," TO THE-MESSAGE.
002600     DISPLAY THE-NUMBER A-SPACE THE-MESSAGE.
002700
002800* Set up and display line 3
002900     ADD 1 TO THE-NUMBER.
003000     MOVE "Jack jump over the candlestick." TO THE-MESSAGE.
003100     DISPLAY THE-NUMBER A-SPACE THE-MESSAGE.
003200
003300 PROGRAM-DONE.
003400     STOP RUN.
003500
```

Layout and Punctuation

As the programs you are working on get larger, it is a good idea to start paying attention to layout and other features of COBOL that can help make your code more readable.

Commas can be used in COBOL to separate items in a list:

```
DISPLAY THE-NUMBER, " ", THE-MESSAGE.
```

There are arguments for and against the use of commas. As far as the COBOL compiler is concerned, commas are optional; the compiler ignores them completely. The only use, therefore, is to improve readability. In a list of variables, the commas help to separate the elements when you are reading the code.

Serious problems result from mistyping a period for a comma. If the screen does not provide a clear display or the printer is printing the source code with a feeble ribbon, it is possible to mistake a comma for a period. A period is not optional and is a critical piece of COBOL syntax used to end sentences. The confusion of a comma for a period has caused some serious problems in programs, and it might be better to leave commas out unless there is a compelling reason to use them.

A sentence does not have to begin and end on one line. As long as it stays out of Area A (columns 8 through 11), a sentence can spread over multiple lines. Listing 2.7, hello03.cbl, uses this technique to clearly separate each value that is being displayed. Listing 2.10 is a version of jack02.cbl that spreads the DISPLAY sentence out in order to clarify what is being displayed. This will compile and run identically to jack02.cbl, but it is a little easier to read.

TYPE   **Listing 2.10. Spreading out a sentence.**

```
000100 IDENTIFICATION DIVISION.
000200 PROGRAM-ID. JACK03.
000300 ENVIRONMENT DIVISION.
000400 DATA DIVISION.
000500
000600 WORKING-STORAGE SECTION.
000700
000800 01  THE-MESSAGE        PIC X(50).
000900 01  THE-NUMBER         PIC 9(2).
001000 01  A-SPACE            PIC X.
001100
001200 PROCEDURE DIVISION.
001300 PROGRAM-BEGIN.
001400
001500* Initialize the space variable
001600     MOVE " " TO A-SPACE.
001700
001800* Set up and display line 1
001900     MOVE 1 TO THE-NUMBER.
002000     MOVE "Jack be nimble," TO THE-MESSAGE.
002100     DISPLAY
002200         THE-NUMBER
002300         A-SPACE
002400         THE-MESSAGE.
002500
002600* Set up and Display line 2
002700     ADD 1 TO THE-NUMBER.
002800     MOVE "Jack be quick," TO THE-MESSAGE.
002900     DISPLAY
003000         THE-NUMBER
003100         A-SPACE
003200         THE-MESSAGE.
003300
003400* Set up and display line 3
003500     ADD 1 TO THE-NUMBER.
003600     MOVE "Jack jump over the candlestick." TO THE-MESSAGE.
003700     DISPLAY
003800         THE-NUMBER
003900         A-SPACE
004000         THE-MESSAGE.
004100
004200 PROGRAM-DONE.
004300     STOP RUN.
004400
```

Remember that, when you are reading COBOL programs, a sentence continues until a period is encountered, no matter how many lines it takes.

Continuation Characters

When an alphanumeric value is too long to fit on a single line, it can be continued on the next line by using a continuation character. In Listing 2.11, the columns have been included. The message must be continued to the end of Area B (column 72) and ends without a closing quote. The next line begins with a hyphen (-) in column 7 to indicate that the previous quoted string is being continued. The rest of the message starts with a quote and continues as long as is necessary to complete the message. Lines can be continued over more than one line if necessary.

Listing 2.11. The continuation character.

```
         1         2         3         4         5         6         7         8
12345678901234567890123456789012345678901234567890123456789012345678901234567890
000500 01  LONG-MESSAGE    PIC X(80) VALUE "This is an incredibly long m
000600-    "essage that will take more than one line to define".
```

Summary

Today, you learned the basics about COBOL's DATA DIVISION, including the following:

☐ The WORKING-STORAGE SECTION of the DATA DIVISION is used to create space for the variables of a program.

☐ Variables in WORKING-STORAGE are given names. The names are assigned by the programmer.

☐ Variables can be named using the uppercase characters A through Z, the digits 0 through 9, and the hyphen (-). The hyphen cannot be the first character of a variable name.

☐ Variables are divided into two broad classes: alphanumeric and numeric.

☐ Alphanumeric variables can hold printable characters: A through Z, a through z, 0 through 9, spaces, symbols, and punctuation characters.

☐ Numeric variables can hold numbers.

☐ Alphanumeric values must be enclosed in double quotation marks when being moved to variables.

☐ Numeric values being moved to numeric variables do not require quotation marks.

☐ The MOVE verb moves an alphanumeric value to an alphanumeric variable and pads the variable with spaces on the right if the value is too short to fill the variable.

2

- The MOVE verb moves a numeric value to a numeric variable and pads the value on the left with zeroes if the value is too small to fill the variable.
- The DISPLAY verb can display more than one value or variable at a time.
- A COBOL sentence can contain commas for punctuation. They do not affect the behavior of the final program, but they can be included to improve readability.
- A COBOL sentence ends with a period. It can spread over several lines of the source code file, as long as it stays within Area B, columns 12 through 72.
- A continuation character can be used to continue a literal on one or more subsequent lines.

Q&A

Q Are there other limits on variable names?

A For now, you should ensure that each variable name is different. You have up to 30 characters to use for a variable name, so you should have no trouble coming up with different names.

Q When should you use a variable, and when should you use a constant?

A Most of the work in programming is done with variables. You can use a constant inside the PROCEDURE DIVISION when it will never need to be changed.

Even when a constant will never change, it sometimes is clearer to use a variable, because it explains what is happening. In the following example, the first line indicates that the sales amount is being multiplied by the constant .10 (10 percent), but gives no information on why. The value .10 is a constant because it cannot be changed without first editing the program and recompiling it. The second version indicates that some logic is being executed to calculate a sales commission:

```
MULTIPLY SALES-AMOUNT BY .10.
MULTIPLY SALES-AMOUNT BY COMMISSION-RATE.
```

Workshop

Quiz

1. How many bytes of memory are used by the following variable?

   ```
   01  CUSTOMER-NAME          PIC X(30).
   ```

2. What type of data can be stored in CUSTOMER-NAME?

3. If you move a value to CUSTOMER-NAME, such as

   MOVE "ABC Company" TO CUSTOMER-NAME.

   only the first 11 characters of the variable are filled with the value. What is placed in the remaining 19 character positions?

4. What is the largest number that can be moved using MOVE to the following variable?

   01   UNITS-SOLD   PIC 9(4).

5. What is the smallest value that can be moved using MOVE to UNITS-SOLD?

6. If 12 is moved to UNITS-SOLD, as in

   MOVE 12 to UNITS-SOLD.

   what values are stored in the four numeric positions of UNITS-SOLD?

Exercises

1. Modify add02.cbl from Listing 2.5 to display a message that tells the user what the program will do.

   Hint: Add a message at line 001500.

2. Pick a poem or phrase of your own choosing that has four or more lines (but no more than 10 lines) and display it on the screen with line numbers.

3. Repeat this poem but have the line numbers start at 05 and increment by 5.

   Hint: You can start by moving 5 to THE-NUMBER, and then increment the value by using ADD 5 TO THE-NUMBER for each line that is being printed.

Day 3

A First Look at Structured COBOL

COBOL is a structured language. You already have seen some of the rules for layout, but structure goes deeper than just physical layout. Structuring applies to the DATA and the PROCEDURE DIVISIONs of a COBOL program. Today, you learn the structure of the PROCEDURE DIVISION and explore the following topics:

- [ ] A new COBOL shell.
- [ ] Program flow.
- [ ] Paragraph names.
- [ ] What is STOP RUN?
- [ ] What is the PERFORM verb?
- [ ] When to use PERFORM.
- [ ] SECTIONs in the PROCEDURE DIVISION.

A New COBOL Shell

From now on, all programs will have some sort of data in them, so it is a good idea to modify cobshl01.cbl, created in Day 1, "Your First COBOL Program." Listing 3.1, cobshl02.cbl, now includes WORKING-STORAGE.

TYPE **Listing 3.1. A new COBOL shell including data.**

```
000100 IDENTIFICATION DIVISION.
000200 PROGRAM-ID. COBSHL02.
000300 ENVIRONMENT DIVISION.
000400 DATA DIVISION.
000500 WORKING-STORAGE SECTION.
000600
000700 PROCEDURE DIVISION.
000800 PROGRAM-BEGIN.
000900
001000 PROGRAM-DONE.
001100     STOP RUN.
```

Program Flow

The normal course of execution of a COBOL program is from the first statement in the PROCEDURE DIVISION to the last. Let's look at Listing 3.2, add01.cbl, line by line.

TYPE **Listing 3.2. Top-to-bottom execution.**

```
000100 IDENTIFICATION DIVISION.
000200 PROGRAM-ID. ADD03.
000300 ENVIRONMENT DIVISION.
000400 DATA DIVISION.
000500
000600 WORKING-STORAGE SECTION.
000700
000800 01  FIRST-NUMBER      PICTURE IS 99.
000900 01  SECOND-NUMBER     PICTURE IS 99.
001000 01  THE-RESULT        PICTURE IS 999.
001100
001200 PROCEDURE DIVISION.
001300
001400 PROGRAM-BEGIN.
001500     DISPLAY "This program will add 2 numbers.".
001600     DISPLAY "Enter the first number.".
001700
001800     ACCEPT FIRST-NUMBER.
001900
```

3

```
002000      DISPLAY "Enter the second number.".
002100
002200      ACCEPT SECOND-NUMBER.
002300
002400      COMPUTE THE-RESULT = FIRST-NUMBER + SECOND-NUMBER.
002500
002600      DISPLAY "The result is " THE-RESULT.
002700
002800
002900 PROGRAM-DONE.
003000      STOP RUN.
003100
```

ANALYSIS   The program starts executing at line 001300 in the PROCEDURE DIVISION. Blank lines are skipped, so nothing happens on that line. Line 001400 is a paragraph name. Paragraphs in COBOL are used as bookmarks. The program doesn't do anything for line 001400 except to note internally that it has started a paragraph named PROGRAM-BEGIN.

At line 001500, the program displays a message on-screen. At line 001600, another is displayed. Line 001700 is blank, so it is skipped. At line 001800, the program stops, waits for keyboard input, and places the results in the variable FIRST-NUMBER.

This type of step-by-step action occurs until line 002900, when the program notes that it has begun executing a paragraph named PROGRAM-DONE. At line 003000, the statement STOP RUN is executed, and this halts the execution of the program.

Paragraph Names

Because paragraph names are used only as bookmarks, it is possible to insert more paragraph names into this program. Remember that you can assign your own paragraph names. The rules for naming paragraphs are similar to the rules for naming variables:

☐ A paragraph name can contain 30 characters. In fact, a paragraph name can be longer than 30 characters, but the compiler will warn you that it will use only the first 30 characters of the name. The remaining characters can be included in the name but the compiler will ignore them.

☐ The characters can be A through Z, 0 through 9, and the hyphen (-). Some compilers also allow the lowercase characters a through z.

☐ The paragraph name must not start with the hyphen.

☐ Paragraph names must start in Area A, columns 8 through 11, and must end with a period.

DO use uppercase paragraph names if you want your code to be portable.

DON'T use lowercase paragraph names. Even the simplest COBOL programs have a tendency to survive and grow. One day, you might find yourself porting the program to a new computer, and you will curse yourself for having used lowercase.

Listing 3.3 is sprinkled with some extra paragraph names. If you compare Listing 3.2 and Listing 3.3, you will see that the sentences are identical. Because a paragraph name does not cause any command to be executed, these two programs behave identically. Enter them both into the computer and compile them. Run them one after the other and you will see no difference.

TYPE | **Listing 3.3. Adding extra paragraph names.**

```
000100 IDENTIFICATION DIVISION.
000200 PROGRAM-ID. ADD04.
000300 ENVIRONMENT DIVISION.
000400 DATA DIVISION.
000500
000600 WORKING-STORAGE SECTION.
000700
000800 01  FIRST-NUMBER      PIC 99.
000900 01  SECOND-NUMBER     PIC 99.
001000 01  THE-RESULT        PIC 999.
001100
001200 PROCEDURE DIVISION.
001300
001400 PROGRAM-BEGIN.
001500
001600     DISPLAY "This program will add 2 numbers.".
001700
001800 GET-FIRST-NUMBER.
001900
002000     DISPLAY "Enter the first number.".
002100
002200     ACCEPT FIRST-NUMBER.
002300
002400 GET-SECOND-NUMBER.
002500
002600     DISPLAY "Enter the second number.".
002700
002800     ACCEPT SECOND-NUMBER.
002900
003000 COMPUTE-AND-DISPLAY.
003100     COMPUTE THE-RESULT = FIRST-NUMBER + SECOND-NUMBER.
003200
003300     DISPLAY "The result is " THE-RESULT.
003400
003500
```

```
003600 PROGRAM-DONE.
003700     STOP RUN.
003800
```

ANALYSIS   Listing 3.4 includes an empty paragraph at line 001400. At lines 001500, 001800,
002400, and 003000, the paragraph names have been changed to STEP-01, STEP-02,
and so on. If you inspect the code, you will notice that, because of the placement of the
paragraph names, the paragraph PROGRAM-BEGIN contains no statements. Some compilers
allow this, and others complain of an empty paragraph with either a warning or an error.
Personal COBOL and ACUCOBOL both allow it. If you want to test your compiler, you
can type this and compile it.

TYPE   **Listing 3.4. An empty paragraph.**

```
000100 IDENTIFICATION DIVISION.
000200 PROGRAM-ID. ADD05.
000300 ENVIRONMENT DIVISION.
000400 DATA DIVISION.
000500
000600 WORKING-STORAGE SECTION.
000700
000800 01  FIRST-NUMBER      PIC 99.
000900 01  SECOND-NUMBER     PIC 99.
001000 01  THE-RESULT        PIC 999.
001100
001200 PROCEDURE DIVISION.
001300
001400 PROGRAM-BEGIN.
001500 STEP-01.
001600     DISPLAY "This program will add 2 numbers.".
001700
001800 STEP-02.
001900
002000     DISPLAY "Enter the first number.".
002100
002200     ACCEPT FIRST-NUMBER.
002300
002400 STEP-03.
002500
002600     DISPLAY "Enter the second number.".
002700
002800     ACCEPT SECOND-NUMBER.
002900
003000 STEP-04.
003100     COMPUTE THE-RESULT = FIRST-NUMBER + SECOND-NUMBER.
003200
003300     DISPLAY "The result is " THE-RESULT.
003400
003500
003600 PROGRAM-DONE.
003700     STOP RUN.
003800
```

3

What Is STOP RUN?

In any programming language, certain words have special meanings in the language. In COBOL, DISPLAY "Hello" causes the word Hello to be displayed on-screen. DISPLAY has a special meaning in COBOL. It means "put the next thing on the screen."

NEW TERM *Reserved words* are reserved in the language to have a special meaning, and the programmer cannot use these words for some other purpose.

The words DATA and DIVISION appearing together mean that the section of the program where data is defined is beginning. DATA, DIVISION, and DISPLAY are reserved words. Therefore, if you create a program that displays something, it would be incorrect to name the program DISPLAY as in the following:

PROGRAM-ID. DISPLAY.

The compiler probably would complain of an invalid program name, because DISPLAY is reserved for a special meaning in COBOL. You already have learned several reserved words: COMPUTE, ACCEPT, ADD, PROCEDURE, DIVISION, and others. You learn about most of them as you move through this book.

Do	**Don't**
DO name programs, variables, and paragraphs with descriptive names that make their use obvious. **DON'T** name programs, variables, or paragraphs with reserved words.	

You also have seen that WORKING-STORAGE is a reserved word for the name of the SECTION in the DATA DIVISION that contains the data. The compiler will complain if you try to name a variable WORKING-STORAGE. That combination of words is reserved for use by COBOL.

STOP RUN has appeared in every program so far. STOP RUN is a sentence in COBOL, just as DISPLAY "Hello" is. STOP and RUN are both reserved words, and the sentence STOP RUN does exactly what it says; it stops the execution of the program.

Some COBOL implementations do not require a STOP RUN; for example, Personal COBOL does not. Most compilers will compile a program that does not include a STOP RUN, and the problem, if there is one, occurs while the program is running. A program will come to the end and appear to start over again, or it will come to the end and crash with some sort of ABORT message. If you want to check out your COBOL compiler, take any of the examples already covered and remove the PROGRAM-DONE paragraph and the STOP RUN sentence. Compile the program and then try to run it. See what happens when the program reaches the end.

3

STOP RUN can occur anywhere in the program, and it will stop execution. In all the examples so far, the STOP RUN is placed in its own separate paragraph to make it stand out as the end of the program, but Listing 3.2 could have been written without the PROGRAM-DONE paragraph name, as long as it included STOP RUN. It would have worked as well. In Listing 3.5, the STOP RUN at line 002400 causes the program to terminate at that spot.

TYPE | **Listing 3.5. A forced STOP RUN.**

```
000100 IDENTIFICATION DIVISION.
000200 PROGRAM-ID. ADD06.
000300 ENVIRONMENT DIVISION.
000400 DATA DIVISION.
000500
000600 WORKING-STORAGE SECTION.
000700
000800 01  FIRST-NUMBER      PIC 99.
000900 01  SECOND-NUMBER     PIC 99.
001000 01  THE-RESULT        PIC 999.
001100
001200 PROCEDURE DIVISION.
001300
001400 PROGRAM-BEGIN.
001500     DISPLAY "This program will add 2 numbers.".
001600
001700
001800     DISPLAY "Enter the first number.".
001900
002000     ACCEPT FIRST-NUMBER.
002100
002200     DISPLAY "Fooled you.".
002300
002400     STOP RUN.
002500
002600     DISPLAY "Enter the second number.".
002700
002800     ACCEPT SECOND-NUMBER.
002900
003000     COMPUTE THE-RESULT = FIRST-NUMBER + SECOND-NUMBER.
003100
003200     DISPLAY "The result is " THE-RESULT.
003300
003400
003500 PROGRAM-DONE.
003600     STOP RUN.
003700
```

Obviously, the PROGRAM-DONE paragraph at line 003500 is misleading in this example because the program stops before this point.

What Is the PERFORM Verb?

A program that executes from beginning to end and then stops might be useful for something, but it wouldn't do much more than the examples already covered. Suppose you had one action that you performed several times in a program. In top-to-bottom execution, you would have to code that same logic over and over.

The PERFORM verb avoids this problem of coding repetitive actions. In order to illustrate the effect of a PERFORM, Listing 3.6 uses another version of the "Hello world" program. A PERFORM is a kind of "jump" with a "bounce back."

TYPE   **Listing 3.6. Using PERFORM.**

```
000100 IDENTIFICATION DIVISION.
000200 PROGRAM-ID. HELLO04.
000300
000400* This program illustrates the use of a PERFORM
000500
000600 ENVIRONMENT DIVISION.
000700 DATA DIVISION.
000800 PROCEDURE DIVISION.
000900
001000 PROGRAM-BEGIN.
001100     DISPLAY "Today's message is:".
001200     PERFORM SAY-HELLO.
001300
001400 PROGRAM-DONE.
001500     STOP RUN.
001600
001700 SAY-HELLO.
001800     DISPLAY "Hello world".
001900
```

OUTPUT

```
Today's message is:
Hello world


C>
C>
```

ANALYSIS   At line 001200, PERFORM SAY-HELLO indicates the following:

1. Locate the paragraph named SAY-HELLO.

2. Jump to that paragraph and start executing there.

3. When that paragraph ends, return to the end of this sentence (PERFORM SAY-HELLO).

A paragraph ends in two ways. Either another paragraph begins or the end of the source code file is reached. In Listing 3.6, the paragraph PROGRAM-BEGIN ends at line 001400 when PROGRAM-DONE begins. The paragraph PROGRAM-DONE ends at line 001700 when SAY-HELLO begins, and SAY-HELLO ends just after line 001900 at the end of the source code file.

Ignoring blank lines (because they will not execute), the sequence of execution in Listing 3.6 is the following:

Line 001000. Internally note that the paragraph PROGRAM-BEGIN has started.

Line 001100. DISPLAY "Today's message is:" on-screen.

Line 001200. Locate the paragraph SAY-HELLO at line 001700. Jump to line 001700, the beginning of SAY-HELLO.

Line 001700. Internally note that the paragraph SAY-HELLO has started.

Line 001800. DISPLAY "Hello world" on-screen.

End of file. COBOL recognizes that it has hit the end of the SAY-HELLO paragraph, but it also knows that it is in the middle of a PERFORM requested at line 001200. Whenever a paragraph ends because of an end-of-file or because a new paragraph starts, COBOL checks whether it is in the middle of a PERFORM. If it is, it returns to the line that requested the PERFORM. In this example, the SAY-HELLO paragraph ends, and execution resumes at the end of line 001200. There are no further instructions on that line, so execution continues at line 001400.

Line 001400. Internally note that the paragraph PROGRAM-DONE has started.

Line 001500. Stop execution of the program.

The top-to-bottom course of a COBOL program continues unless it is interrupted by a PERFORM. The paragraph being performed is also executed top to bottom. When the PERFORM is complete, the program returns to the point just after the PERFORM was requested, and it continues from there to the bottom.

It is important to recognize this "keep-on-trucking" flow of a COBOL program, because it is critical to place your PERFORMed paragraphs below the STOP RUN statement. Listing 3.7 has the SAY-HELLO paragraph placed differently.

TYPE   **Listing 3.7. An incorrectly placed paragraph.**

```
000100 IDENTIFICATION DIVISION.
000200 PROGRAM-ID. HELLO05.
000300
000400* This program illustrates the incorrect placement of a
000500* Paragraph that is the target of a perform
000600
```

continues

Listing 3.7. continued

```
000700 ENVIRONMENT DIVISION.
000800 DATA DIVISION.
000900 PROCEDURE DIVISION.
001000
001100 PROGRAM-BEGIN.
001200     DISPLAY "Today's message is:".
001300     PERFORM SAY-HELLO.
001400
001500 SAY-HELLO.
001600     DISPLAY "Hello world".
001700
001800 PROGRAM-DONE.
001900     STOP RUN.
002000
```

If you followed the steps describing the flow of hello05.cbl, it should come as no surprise that the program displays Hello world twice:

```
Today's message is:
Hello world
Hello world
```

```
C>
C>
```

ANALYSIS Ignoring blank lines, the sequence of execution in Listing 3.7 is as follows:

Line 001100. Internally note that the paragraph PROGRAM-BEGIN has started.

Line 001200. DISPLAY "Today's message is:" on-screen.

Line 001300. Jump to line 001500, the beginning of SAY-HELLO.

Line 001500. Internally note that the paragraph SAY-HELLO has started.

Line 001600. DISPLAY "Hello world" on-screen.

Line 001800. COBOL recognizes that it has hit the end of the SAY-HELLO paragraph, but it also knows that it is in the middle of a PERFORM requested at line 001300. The SAY-HELLO paragraph ends, and execution resumes at the end of line 001300. There are no further instructions on that line, so execution continues at line 001500.

Line 001500. Internally note that the paragraph SAY-HELLO has started.

Line 001600. DISPLAY "Hello world" on-screen.

Line 001800. COBOL recognizes that it has hit the end of the SAY-HELLO paragraph, but in this case it is not in the middle of a PERFORM.

Line 001800. Internally note that the paragraph PROGRAM-DONE has started.

Line 001900. Stop execution of the program.

3

When to Use PERFORM

A PERFORM has several uses in COBOL. First, it is used to section off a repetitive action that is performed in several places or several times in a program to prevent writing the same code over and over.(I hinted at this use when I introduced PERFORM earlier in today's lesson.) This creates two advantages: It not only cuts down on the amount of typing, but it cuts down on the number of potential errors. Less typing means fewer opportunities to copy it incorrectly.

Imagine typing the following retail profit formula five or six times in different places in a program, and you begin to see the sense of putting this in a paragraph called COMPUTE-RETAIL-PROFIT and using the PERFORM verb every time you want it done:

```
COMPUTE MARGIN-PERCENT =
    ( (GOODS-PRICE - GOODS-COST) /
            GOODS-PRICE ) * 100 .
```

The second use of PERFORM might not be so obvious, because the programs used so far in this book have been relatively small. A PERFORM serves to break up a program into smaller, more manageable pieces. If you're changing the sales commission from 10 percent to 11 percent, it's much easier to search through a long program looking for a paragraph named CALCULATE-COMMISSION than to plow through a long list of code not broken into paragraphs. It is very common for programs to perform more than one major task. A payroll system might have a program in it used both to calculate pay totals and to print checks after the hours for each employee are entered into the computer.

A program that carries out these actions might have one area of the program to deal with the calculations, while further down in the program another area of code deals with the printing activity. Above these two areas is the main logic of the program that performs both pieces of the program:

```
MAIN-LOGIC.
    PERFORM CALC-PAYROLL-TOTALS.
    PERFORM PRINT-PAYROLL-CHECKS.
```

The third reason to use a PERFORM is that the program is easier to read and understand if the paragraphs are named sensibly. In the following code fragment, it is fairly easy to figure out what the paragraph PAY-THE-SALESPERSON is doing, even though the whole paragraph is made up of PERFORMs:

```
PAY-THE-SALESPERSON
    PERFORM GET-SALES-TOTAL.
    PERFORM CALCULATE-COMMISSION.
    PERFORM PRINT-THE-CHECK.
```

A fourth reason to use PERFORM would be to conserve memory. Look back at the retail profit formula and imagine that piece of code repeated five or six times in a single program. Each time the formula appears in the program it takes up several bytes of memory. Coding it once in a single paragraph and performing that paragraph five or six times uses far less memory.

Let's take a closer look at the first reason for a PERFORM, which is to handle repetitive code. Listing 3.8, "The Lady from Eiger," is similar to jack03.cbl, used in Day 2, "Using Variables and Constants." At line 001800, THE-NUMBER is initialized to 0, and then (instead of moving 1 to THE-NUMBER at line 002300) 1 is added to THE-NUMBER.

TYPE **Listing 3.8. Repetitive actions.**

```
000100 IDENTIFICATION DIVISION.
000200 PROGRAM-ID. EIGER03.
000300 ENVIRONMENT DIVISION.
000400 DATA DIVISION.
000500
000600 WORKING-STORAGE SECTION.
000700
000800 01  THE-MESSAGE      PIC X(50).
000900 01  THE-NUMBER       PIC 9(2).
001000 01  A-SPACE          PIC X.
001100
001200 PROCEDURE DIVISION.
001300 PROGRAM-BEGIN.
001400
001500* Initialize the space variable
001600     MOVE " " TO A-SPACE.
001700* Start THE-NUMBER at 0
001800     MOVE 0 TO THE-NUMBER.
001900
002000* Set up and display line 1
002100     MOVE "There once was a lady from Eiger,"
002200         TO THE-MESSAGE.
002300     ADD 1 TO THE-NUMBER.
002400     DISPLAY
002500         THE-NUMBER
002600         A-SPACE
002700         THE-MESSAGE.
002800
002900* Set up and Display line 2
003000     MOVE "Who smiled and rode forth on a tiger."
003100         TO THE-MESSAGE.
003200     ADD 1 TO THE-NUMBER.
003300     DISPLAY
003400         THE-NUMBER
003500         A-SPACE
003600         THE-MESSAGE.
003700
003800* Set up and display line 3
003900     MOVE "They returned from the ride" TO THE-MESSAGE.
004000     ADD 1 TO THE-NUMBER.
004100     DISPLAY
004200         THE-NUMBER
004300         A-SPACE
004400         THE-MESSAGE.
004500
```

3

```
004600* Set up and display line 4
004700     MOVE "With the lady inside," TO THE-MESSAGE.
004800     ADD 1 TO THE-NUMBER.
004900     DISPLAY
005000         THE-NUMBER
005100         A-SPACE
005200         THE-MESSAGE.
005300
005400* Set up and display line 5
005500     MOVE "And the smile on the face of the tiger."
005600         TO THE-MESSAGE.
005700     ADD 1 TO THE-NUMBER.
005800     DISPLAY
005900         THE-NUMBER
006000         A-SPACE
006100         THE-MESSAGE.
006200
006300
006400 PROGRAM-DONE.
006500     STOP RUN.
006600
```

OUTPUT

```
01 There once was a lady from Eiger,
02 Who smiled and rode forth on a tiger.
03 They returned from the ride
04 With the lady inside,
05 And the smile on the face of the tiger.


C>
C>
```

ANALYSIS   If you inspect lines 002300 through 002700 and lines 003200 through 003600, you'll find that the actions are identical. These appear again in lines 004000 through 004400. In fact, these two sentences are repeated five times in the program, appearing again in lines 004800 through 005200 and 005700 through 006100.

The DISPLAY command (lines 002400 through 002700, 003300 through 003600, and so on) is rather long because it is a DISPLAY of three variables. The odds of typing incorrectly are reasonably high. A typographical error wouldn't be so bad (because the compiler would complain if something were spelled incorrectly), but suppose that in one of the five instances you left out A-SPACE in the list of variables to display. It wouldn't be a disaster. It would show up the first time you ran the program; one of the lines would look odd, and you would be able to track it down quickly. Unfortunately, not all errors of this sort are so easy to spot. If this were a series of calculations, you might be able to spot an error in the final result, but you wouldn't know where it had originated.

There are two repetitive actions in Listing 3.8:

```
ADD 1 TO THE-NUMBER
```

and

```
DISPLAY THE-NUMBER A-SPACE THE-MESSAGE.
```

It is simple to extract these two lines and create a paragraph that performs both of these actions:

```
ADD-NUMBER-AND-DISPLAY.

ADD 1 TO THE-NUMBER
DISPLAY THE-NUMBER A-SPACE THE-MESSAGE.
```

Listing 3.9 is an example of using this paragraph, with PERFORMs inserted at the appropriate points.

TYPE   **Listing 3.9. Using a PERFORMed paragraph.**

```
000100 IDENTIFICATION DIVISION.
000200 PROGRAM-ID. EIGER04.
000300 ENVIRONMENT DIVISION.
000400 DATA DIVISION.
000500
000600 WORKING-STORAGE SECTION.
000700
000800 01   THE-MESSAGE      PIC X(50).
000900 01   THE-NUMBER       PIC 9(2).
001000 01   A-SPACE          PIC X.
001100
001200 PROCEDURE DIVISION.
001300 PROGRAM-BEGIN.
001400
001500* Initialize the space variable
001600     MOVE " " TO A-SPACE.
001700* Start THE-NUMBER at 0
001800     MOVE 0 TO THE-NUMBER.
001900
002000* Set up and display line 1
002100     MOVE "There once was a lady from Eiger,"
002200          TO THE-MESSAGE.
002300     PERFORM ADD-NUMBER-AND-DISPLAY.
002400
002500* Set up and Display line 2
002600     MOVE "Who smiled and rode forth on a tiger."
002700          TO THE-MESSAGE.
002800     PERFORM ADD-NUMBER-AND-DISPLAY.
002900
003000* Set up and display line 3
003100     MOVE "They returned from the ride" TO THE-MESSAGE.
003200     PERFORM ADD-NUMBER-AND-DISPLAY.
003300
```

3

```
003400* Set up and display line 4
003500     MOVE "With the lady inside," TO THE-MESSAGE.
003600     PERFORM ADD-NUMBER-AND-DISPLAY.
003700
003800* Set up and display line 5
003900     MOVE "And the smile on the face of the tiger."
004000          TO THE-MESSAGE.
004100     PERFORM ADD-NUMBER-AND-DISPLAY.
004200
004300 PROGRAM-DONE.
004400     STOP RUN.
004500
004600 ADD-NUMBER-AND-DISPLAY.
004700     ADD 1 TO THE-NUMBER.
004800     DISPLAY
004900          THE-NUMBER
005000          A-SPACE
005100          THE-MESSAGE.
005200
```

Code eiger04.cbl, compile it, and run it. Work out the flow of each PERFORM and how the program returns to the main stream of the logic. Here is the output of eiger04.cbl:

OUTPUT

```
01 There once was a lady from Eiger,
02 Who smiled and rode forth on a tiger.
03 They returned from the ride
04 With the lady inside,
05 And the smile on the face of the tiger.


C>
C>
```

ANALYSIS At line 002300, the computer locates ADD-NUMBER-AND-DISPLAY at line 004600 and jumps to that line. This paragraph is PERFORMed, and when complete, execution resumes at the end of line 002300. Execution continues on line 002600. Then at line 002800, another jump is made to line 004600, and the program returns to the end of line 002800. This process continues until all five PERFORM requests have been executed and ADD-NUMBER-AND-DISPLAY has been performed five times.

It is possible to request a PERFORM when you already are within a PERFORM, by nesting them together. If a paragraph that is being PERFORMed itself requests a PERFORM of another paragraph, COBOL keeps track of the layers of PERFORMed paragraphs and returns to the correct level.

In general, when a PERFORMed paragraph ends, the program returns to the line that requested the PERFORM, at a position in the line just after the PERFORM was requested. In Listing 3.10, the ADD-NUMBER-AND-DISPLAY paragraph at line 005100 has been broken down into two sentences that each PERFORM smaller paragraphs. These PERFORM sentences refer to paragraphs at lines 005800 and 006100—ADD-THE-NUMBER and DISPLAY-THE-MESSAGE. Each of these paragraphs does only one thing. In practice, you rarely would create a paragraph to execute a single statement, but this example serves to illustrate nested PERFORMs.

Type **Listing 3.10. Nested PERFORMs.**

```
000100 IDENTIFICATION DIVISION.
000200 PROGRAM-ID. EIGER05.
000300
000400* This program illustrates nested PERFORMS
000500 ENVIRONMENT DIVISION.
000600 DATA DIVISION.
000700
000800 WORKING-STORAGE SECTION.
000900
001000 01   THE-MESSAGE       PIC X(50).
001100 01   THE-NUMBER        PIC 9(2).
001200 01   A-SPACE           PIC X.
001300
001400 PROCEDURE DIVISION.
001500 PROGRAM-BEGIN.
001600
001700* Initialize the space variable
001800      MOVE " " TO A-SPACE.
001900* Start THE-NUMBER at 0
002000      MOVE 0 TO THE-NUMBER.
002100
002200* Set up and display line 1
002300      MOVE "There once was a lady from Eiger,"
002400          TO THE-MESSAGE.
002500      PERFORM ADD-NUMBER-AND-DISPLAY.
002600
002700* Set up and Display line 2
002800      MOVE "Who smiled and rode forth on a tiger."
002900          TO THE-MESSAGE.
003000      PERFORM ADD-NUMBER-AND-DISPLAY.
003100
003200* Set up and display line 3
003300      MOVE "They returned from the ride" TO THE-MESSAGE.
003400      PERFORM ADD-NUMBER-AND-DISPLAY.
003500
003600* Set up and display line 4
003700      MOVE "With the lady inside," TO THE-MESSAGE.
003800      PERFORM ADD-NUMBER-AND-DISPLAY.
003900
004000* Set up and display line 5
004100      MOVE "And the smile on the face of the tiger."
004200          TO THE-MESSAGE.
004300      PERFORM ADD-NUMBER-AND-DISPLAY.
004400
004500 PROGRAM-DONE.
004600      STOP RUN.
004700
004800* This paragraph is PERFORMED 5 times from within
004900* PROGRAM-BEGIN. This paragraph in turn PERFORMS
005000* Two other paragraphs
005100 ADD-NUMBER-AND-DISPLAY.
005200      PERFORM ADD-THE-NUMBER.
005300      PERFORM DISPLAY-THE-MESSAGE.
005400
005500* These two paragraphs will each be performed 5 times as
005600* they are each performed every time ADD-NUMBER-AND-DISPLAY
```

3

```
005700* is performed.
005800 ADD-THE-NUMBER.
005900     ADD 1 TO THE-NUMBER.
006000
006100 DISPLAY-THE-MESSAGE.
006200     DISPLAY
006300         THE-NUMBER
006400         A-SPACE
006500         THE-MESSAGE.
006600
```

ANALYSIS   The flow of the program at line 005100 is executed every time PERFORM ADD-NUMBER-AND-DISPLAY is requested:

Line 005100. Internally note that the paragraph ADD-NUMBER-AND-DISPLAY has started.

Line 005200. Locate the paragraph called ADD-THE-NUMBER and jump to it at line 005800.

Line 005800. Internally note that the paragraph ADD-THE-NUMBER has started.

Line 005900. ADD 1 TO THE-NUMBER.

Line 006100. COBOL notes that ADD-THE-NUMBER has ended and returns to line 005200, where there are no further instructions.

Line 005300. Locate the paragraph named DISPLAY-THE-MESSAGE and jump to it at line 006100.

Line 006100. Internally note that the paragraph DISPLAY-THE-MESSAGE has started.

Lines 006200 through 006500. These lines are executed as one long sentence, displaying all the variables.

End of file (the last line of the source code). COBOL notes the end of DISPLAY-THE-MESSAGE and knows it is in the middle of a PERFORM. It returns to line 005300, where there are no further instructions.

Line 005800. (Remember that blank lines and comment lines have no effect on the program, so the next active line is 005800.) COBOL notes that ADD-THE-NUMBER starts here; therefore, the current paragraph, ADD-NUMBER-AND-DISPLAY, must have ended. Execution returns to whatever line originally requested the PERFORM of ADD-NUMBER-AND-DISPLAY.

Do	Don't

DO locate repetitive actions in your programs, and create separate paragraphs containing those actions. Then PERFORM the paragraph wherever those actions are needed.

DON'T keep typing the same code over and over in one program.

It is common for PERFORMs to be nested in COBOL programs. In fact, Listing 3.11 shows how an experienced programmer actually might organize "The Lady from Eiger." The callouts down the right side show you the sequence of execution.

TYPE **Listing 3.11. A structured program.**

```
000100 IDENTIFICATION DIVISION.
000200 PROGRAM-ID. EIGER06.
000300
000400* This program illustrates nested PERFORMS in a
000500* structured program.
000600 ENVIRONMENT DIVISION.
000700 DATA DIVISION.
000800
000900 WORKING-STORAGE SECTION.
001000
001100 01  THE-MESSAGE      PIC X(50).
001200 01  THE-NUMBER       PIC 9(2).
001300 01  A-SPACE          PIC X.
001400
001500 PROCEDURE DIVISION.
001600
001700* LEVEL 1 ROUTINES
001800 PROGRAM-BEGIN. ──────────────────────────────────────1
001900
002000     PERFORM PROGRAM-INITIALIZATION.──────────────────2
002100     PERFORM MAIN-LOGIC.──────────────────────────────6
002200
002300 PROGRAM-DONE.────────────────────────────────────────33
002400     STOP RUN.────────────────────────────────────────34
002500
002600*LEVEL 2 ROUTINES ────────────────────────────────────3
002700 PROGRAM-INITIALIZATION.
002800* Initialize the space variable
002900     MOVE " " TO A-SPACE. ────────────────────────────4
003000* Start THE-NUMBER at 0
003100     MOVE 0 TO THE-NUMBER.────────────────────────────5
003200
003300 MAIN-LOGIC. ─────────────────────────────────────────7
003400* Set up and display line 1
003500     MOVE "There once was a lady from Eiger,"──────┐
003600         TO THE-MESSAGE. ─────────────────────────┘───8
003700     PERFORM ADD-NUMBER-AND-DISPLAY. ─────────────────9
003800
003900* Set up and Display line 2
004000     MOVE "Who smiled and rode forth on a tiger."──┐
004100         TO THE-MESSAGE. ─────────────────────────┘──13
004200     PERFORM ADD-NUMBER-AND-DISPLAY.────────────────14
004300
004400* Set up and display line 3
004500     MOVE "They returned from the ride" TO THE-MESSAGE.──18
004600     PERFORM ADD-NUMBER-AND-DISPLAY. ────────────────19
004700
004800* Set up and display line 4
```

```
004900        MOVE "With the lady inside," TO THE-MESSAGE.————————23
005000        PERFORM ADD-NUMBER-AND-DISPLAY.————————————————————24
005100
005200* Set up and display line 5
005300        MOVE "And the smile on the face of the tiger."————┐
005400            TO THE-MESSAGE.————————————————————————————————┴—28
005500        PERFORM ADD-NUMBER-AND-DISPLAY.————————————————————29
005600
005700* LEVEL 3 ROUTINES
005800* This paragraph is PERFORMED 5 times from within
005900* MAIN-LOGIC.
006000
006100 ADD-NUMBER-AND-DISPLAY.—————————————————————10,15,20,25,30
006200        ADD 1 TO THE-NUMBER.—————————————————11,16,21,26,31
006300        DISPLAY ————————————————————┐
006400            THE-NUMBER               │
006500            A-SPACE                  ├————————12,17,22,27,32
006600            THE-MESSAGE.—————————————┘
006700
```

3

ANALYSIS   The "main" stream of the program runs from line 001800 to line 002400 and is quite short. All the work of the program is accomplished by requesting PERFORMs of other paragraphs. Some of these in turn request other PERFORMs. You should look over this listing and compare it carefully to Listing 3.9. You will see that the effect of the two programs is identical, and both of them use paragraphs to isolate repetitive logic. The version in eiger06.cbl additionally uses paragraphs to break out and document which parts of the code are for initializing (or setting up variables) before the main logic and which parts are the main logic of the code.

Summary

Today, you learned about the structure of the PROCEDURE DIVISION, including the following basics:

- ☐ COBOL programs execute from top to bottom unless that flow is interrupted by a PERFORM.

- ☐ The statements in a PERFORMed paragraph are executed from top to bottom.

- ☐ When a PERFORMed paragraph is completed, flow resumes at the jumping-off point (the point where the PERFORM was requested) and continues down through the statements.

- ☐ COBOL paragraph names can contain up to 30 significant characters. The characters can be A through Z, 0 through 9, and the hyphen (-). Some compilers allow the lowercase characters a through z. The paragraph name must not start with the hyphen. Additionally, paragraph names must start in Area A, columns 8 through 11, and must end with a period.

☐ PERFORMed paragraphs must be placed after the STOP RUN statement.

☐ PERFORM is used to eliminate repetitive coding and break a program into more manageable pieces. It also can be used to document the program if done correctly.

☐ PERFORMs can be nested so that a PERFORMed paragraph can itself request a PERFORM of another paragraph.

☐ COBOL programs frequently are arranged so that a small amount of code is written between the start of the program and STOP RUN. This code usually consists of PERFORM requests on paragraphs that are written after the STOP RUN.

Q&A

Q Are there other limits on COBOL paragraph names?

A Paragraphs (and variables) each should have a unique name. There actually is a way around this limit, but its explanation is beyond the scope of this book. With 30 characters for a paragraph name, you should have no problem coming up with different names for each paragraph.

There is another limit that you should place on yourself for practical purposes. Paragraph names should be descriptive of what is done in the paragraph.

Q How many paragraphs can be included in the PROCEDURE DIVISION?

A This is limited only by the COBOL compiler that you are using. The number always is large enough to support large and fairly complex programs because COBOL is a language designed to handle such problems.

Q How many PERFORMs can be included in a program?

A There is no limit on PERFORMs other than the limits imposed by your compiler on the overall size of programs. See the next question.

Q If one paragraph can PERFORM another paragraph, which in turn can PERFORM another paragraph, how many levels of this nesting (PERFORMs within PERFORMs) are possible?

A This again depends entirely on your COBOL compiler. The number usually is large. Levels of 250 are not uncommon. You would have to write something very complex to nest PERFORMs 250 levels deep.

Q Can a paragraph PERFORM itself as in the following example?

```
DO-SOMETHING.
      PERFORM DO-SOMETHING.
```

A No. This is allowed in some languages, but not in COBOL.

Workshop

Quiz

1. If the code in a paragraph is designed to locate overdue customers, which of the following would be the best name for the paragraph?

   a. LOCATE-CUSTOMERS.

   b. FIND-SOME-STUFF.

   c. LOCATE-OVERDUE-CUSTOMERS.

2. Number the lines of msg01.cbl to show the sequence in which the lines would be executed:

```
000100 IDENTIFICATION DIVISION.
000200 PROGRAM-ID. MSG01.
000300
000400 ENVIRONMENT DIVISION.
000500 DATA DIVISION.
000600
000700 WORKING-STORAGE SECTION.
000800
000900 PROCEDURE DIVISION.
001000
001100 PROGRAM-BEGIN.
001200
001300     PERFORM MAIN-LOGIC.
001400
001500 PROGRAM-DONE.
001600     STOP RUN.
001700
001800 MAIN-LOGIC.
001900     PERFORM DISPLAY-MSG-1.
002000     PERFORM DISPLAY-MSG-2.
002100
002200 DISPLAY-MSG-1.
002300     DISPLAY "This is message 1.".
002400
002500 DISPLAY-MSG-2.
002600     DISPLAY "This is message 2.".
002700
```

Exercises

1. What would be the effect of omitting the PROGRAM-DONE paragraph and STOP RUN sentence from hello04.cbl in Listing 3.6? Copy hello04.cbl to hello06.cbl and edit it to remove lines 001400 and 001500. Compile and run the program. What does the display look like? The display effect should be the same as the output of Listing 3.7, hello05.cbl.

2. Trace the flow of hello06.cbl step by step and work out what is happening. What must appear before any paragraphs that are PERFORMed?

3. Work out where to place a STOP RUN in hello06.cbl to prevent the situation in Exercise 2.

4. Study the following listing, add07.cbl:

```
000100 IDENTIFICATION DIVISION.
000200 PROGRAM-ID. ADD07.
000300 ENVIRONMENT DIVISION.
000400 DATA DIVISION.
000500
000600 WORKING-STORAGE SECTION.
000700
000800 01   FIRST-NUMBER      PIC 99.
000900 01   SECOND-NUMBER     PIC 99.
001000 01   THE-RESULT        PIC 999.
001100
001200 PROCEDURE DIVISION.
001300
001400 PROGRAM-BEGIN.
001500
001600     PERFORM ADVISE-THE-USER.
001700     PERFORM GET-FIRST-NUMBER.
001800     PERFORM GET-SECOND-NUMBER.
001900     PERFORM COMPUTE-AND-DISPLAY.
002000
002100 PROGRAM-DONE.
002200     STOP RUN.
002300
002400 ADVISE-THE-USER.
002500     DISPLAY "This program will add 2 numbers.".
002600
002700 GET-FIRST-NUMBER.
002800
002900     DISPLAY "Enter the first number.".
003000     ACCEPT FIRST-NUMBER.
003100
003200 GET-SECOND-NUMBER.
003300
003400     DISPLAY "Enter the second number.".
003500     ACCEPT SECOND-NUMBER.
003600
003700 COMPUTE-AND-DISPLAY.
003800
003900     COMPUTE THE-RESULT = FIRST-NUMBER + SECOND-NUMBER.
004000     DISPLAY "The result is " THE-RESULT.
004100
```

Copy this to add08.cbl and modify the program so that it adds three numbers instead of two.

Hint: You can add three numbers just by continuing the COMPUTE statement:

```
004600      COMPUTE THE-RESULT = FIRST-NUMBER +
004700                           SECOND-NUMBER +
004800                           THIRD-NUMBER.
```

5. Using add02.cbl (Listing 2.6 from Day 2), redesign the program to use a logic flow similar to eiger06.cbl, with the main stream of the program being a series of PERFORMs.

Hint: Listing 3.3 provides some clues about the natural paragraphs in the program.

3

Day **4**

Decision Making

A program must be able to make decisions about data and to execute different sections of code based on those decisions. Controlling the flow of programs by testing conditions with the IF statement lies at the heart of every program.

This lesson deals almost exclusively with the IF statement and the many options available with it—information critical to understanding programming in COBOL. Today, you learn about the following topics:

- [ ] What is IF?
- [ ] Using IF to control multiple statements.
- [ ] What can you test with an IF?
- [ ] Testing multiple conditions.
- [ ] Using IF-ELSE.

IF

The primary method of changing the flow of a program is by making decisions using the IF verb. The following example demonstrates the IF verb:

```
IF condition
    PERFORM DO-SOMETHING.
```

When COBOL sees an IF, it makes a decision about the condition, and then either requests a PERFORM of DO-SOMETHING or skips that line of the program.

The example in Listing 4.1 uses an IF to decide which message to display. In GET-THE-ANSWER, at line 002300, this program prompts the user to enter Y or N (Yes or No) and accepts a single character from the keyboard and places it in the variable YES-OR-NO. This is not a particularly good program because if the user enters a lowercase y or n, the program does nothing at all. The problem of handling the lowercase entry is addressed later in this chapter. The general problem of handling lowercase versus uppercase data entry is covered in Day 15, "Data Integrity." For now, just press the Caps Lock key on the left of your keyboard to force all data entry into uppercase.

TYPE **Listing 4.1. Testing values using IF.**

```
000100 IDENTIFICATION DIVISION.
000200 PROGRAM-ID. YESNO01.
000300*--------------------------------------------------
000400* This program asks for a Y or N answer, and then
000500* displays whether the user chose yes or no.
000600*--------------------------------------------------
000700 ENVIRONMENT DIVISION.
000800 DATA DIVISION.
000900 WORKING-STORAGE SECTION.
001000
001100 01  YES-OR-NO      PIC X.
001200
001300 PROCEDURE DIVISION.
001400 PROGRAM-BEGIN.
001500
001600     PERFORM GET-THE-ANSWER.
001700
001800     PERFORM DISPLAY-THE-ANSWER.
001900
002000 PROGRAM-DONE.
002100     STOP RUN.
002200
002300 GET-THE-ANSWER.
002400
002500     DISPLAY "Is the answer Yes or No? (Y/N)".
002600     ACCEPT YES-OR-NO.
002700
002800 DISPLAY-THE-ANSWER.
002900     IF YES-OR-NO IS EQUAL "Y"
```

4

```
003000          DISPLAY "You answered Yes.".
003100
003200     IF YES-OR-NO IS EQUAL "N"
003300          DISPLAY "You answered No.".
003400
```

This is the output of yesno01.cbl if you enter a Y:

OUTPUT
```
Is the answer Yes or No? (Y/N)
Y
You answered Yes.


C>
C>
```

ANALYSIS Edit, compile, and run this program; then try it, entering a few different answers. You will notice that it displays a message only if the entry is an uppercase Y or N. When you are comparing alphanumeric variables, the values are case-dependent, so y is not the same as Y, and n is not the same as N.

Do	Don't

DO test for both uppercase and lowercase versions of an alphanumeric field, if either uppercase or lowercase values are valid.

DON'T ignore case differences in a variable if they are important in a program.

In DISPLAY-THE-ANSWER, at lines 002800 through 003300, one of two possible messages is displayed, based on whether the user entered a Y or an N.

At line 002900, the condition being tested is YES-OR-NO IS EQUAL "Y". IS EQUAL are COBOL reserved words used for testing whether two values are equal. The IF sentences in DISPLAY-THE-ANSWER at lines 002900 and 003200 are each two lines long; there is no period until the end of the second line.

When the criteria of a tested condition are met, the condition is considered to be true. When the criteria of a tested condition are not met, the condition is considered to be false. The DISPLAY statement at line 003000 is executed only when the condition being tested by the IF at line 002900 (YES-OR-NO IS EQUAL "Y") is true. When the IF at line 002900 is not true (any character but Y is entered), line 003000 is skipped. The DISPLAY statement at line 003300 is executed only when the condition being tested by the IF at line 003200 (YES-OR-NO IS EQUAL "N") is true. When the IF at line 003200 is not true (any character but N is entered), line 003300 is skipped. When a condition tested by an IF statement is not true, any statements controlled by the IF are not executed.

Depending on the user's input, there are three possible output results from this program:

☐ If YES-OR-NO contains an N when DISPLAY-THE-ANSWER is performed, the IF test at line 002900 is not true, and line 003000 is not executed. However, the IF test at line 003200 is true, and line 003300 is executed.

☐ If YES-OR-NO contains a Y when DISPLAY-THE-ANSWER is performed, the IF test at line 002900 is true, and line 003000 is executed. However, the IF test at line 003200 is false, and line 003300 is not executed.

☐ If YES-OR-NO does not contain a Y or an N when DISPLAY-THE-ANSWER is performed, the IF test at line 002900 is false, and line 003000 is not executed. The IF test at line 003200 also is false, and line 003300 is not executed. In this case, neither message is displayed.

Listing 4.2 adds the extra step of editing the user's answer to adjust for a lowercase y or n.

TYPE **Listing 4.2. Editing the answer.**

```
000100 IDENTIFICATION DIVISION.
000200 PROGRAM-ID. YESNO02.
000300*-------------------------------------------------
000400* This program asks for a Y or N answer, and then
000500* displays whether the user chose yes or no.
000600* The edit logic allows for entry of Y, y, N, or n.
000700*-------------------------------------------------
000800 ENVIRONMENT DIVISION.
000900 DATA DIVISION.
001000 WORKING-STORAGE SECTION.
001100
001200 01  YES-OR-NO      PIC X.
001300
001400 PROCEDURE DIVISION.
001500 PROGRAM-BEGIN.
001600
001700     PERFORM GET-THE-ANSWER.
001800
001900     PERFORM EDIT-THE-ANSWER.
002000
002100     PERFORM DISPLAY-THE-ANSWER.
002200
002300 PROGRAM-DONE.
002400     STOP RUN.
002500
002600 GET-THE-ANSWER.
002700
```

4

```
002800        DISPLAY "Is the answer Yes or No? (Y/N)".
002900        ACCEPT YES-OR-NO.
003000
003100 EDIT-THE-ANSWER.
003200
003300        IF YES-OR-NO IS EQUAL "y"
003400            MOVE "Y" TO YES-OR-NO.
003500
003600        IF YES-OR-NO IS EQUAL "n"
003700            MOVE "N" TO YES-OR-NO.
003800
003900 DISPLAY-THE-ANSWER.
004000        IF YES-OR-NO IS EQUAL "Y"
004100            DISPLAY "You answered Yes.".
004200
004300        IF YES-OR-NO IS EQUAL "N"
004400            DISPLAY "You answered No.".
004500
```

ANALYSIS   In EDIT-THE-ANSWER at line 003300, the program checks to see whether the user entered a y. If true, at line 003400 the program forces this to become a Y. In the same paragraph at lines 003600 and 003700, an n will be changed to an N.

The tests in DISPLAY-THE-ANSWER work correctly now, because the answer has been forced to uppercase Y or N by the EDIT-THE-ANSWER paragraph.

If you edit, compile, and run yesno02.cbl, you will find that uppercase and lowercase versions of y and n are now all valid entries. The program still displays no message if anything else is entered. (I will address this problem later in this chapter, in the section entitled IF-ELSE.)

Using IF to Control Multiple Statements

Listing 4.3 executes multiple statements under the control of the IF tests at lines 004000 and 004400. In each sequence, a PERFORM is requested to display an additional message before the main message is displayed. More than one statement can be executed when an IF tests true:

```
IF condition
    PERFORM DO-SOMETHING
    PERFORM DO-SOMETHING-ELSE.
```

An IF controls all statements under it until the sentence ends. When an IF tests true, all statements up to the next period are executed. When an IF tests false, all statements up to the next period are skipped.

TYPE **Listing 4.3. Controlling multiple statements with IF.**

```
000100 IDENTIFICATION DIVISION.
000200 PROGRAM-ID. YESNO03.
000300*-------------------------------------------------
000400* This program asks for a Y or N answer, and then
000500* displays whether the user chose yes or no.
000600* The edit logic allows for entry of Y, y, N, or n.
000700*-------------------------------------------------
000800 ENVIRONMENT DIVISION.
000900 DATA DIVISION.
001000 WORKING-STORAGE SECTION.
001100
001200 01  YES-OR-NO      PIC X.
001300
001400 PROCEDURE DIVISION.
001500 PROGRAM-BEGIN.
001600
001700     PERFORM GET-THE-ANSWER.
001800
001900     PERFORM EDIT-THE-ANSWER.
002000
002100     PERFORM DISPLAY-THE-ANSWER.
002200
002300 PROGRAM-DONE.
002400     STOP RUN.
002500
002600 GET-THE-ANSWER.
002700
002800     DISPLAY "Is the answer Yes or No? (Y/N)".
002900     ACCEPT YES-OR-NO.
003000
003100 EDIT-THE-ANSWER.
003200
003300     IF YES-OR-NO IS EQUAL "y"
003400         MOVE "Y" TO YES-OR-NO.
003500
003600     IF YES-OR-NO IS EQUAL "n"
003700         MOVE "N" TO YES-OR-NO.
003800
003900 DISPLAY-THE-ANSWER.
004000     IF YES-OR-NO IS EQUAL "Y"
004100         PERFORM IT-IS-VALID
004200         DISPLAY "You answered Yes.".
004300
004400     IF YES-OR-NO IS EQUAL "N"
004500         PERFORM IT-IS-VALID
004600         DISPLAY "You answered No.".
004700
004800 IT-IS-VALID.
004900     DISPLAY "Your answer is valid and".
005000
```

OUTPUT
```
Is the answer Yes or No? (Y/N)
y
Your answer is valid and
You answered Yes.


C>
C>
```

ANALYSIS When the IF at line 004400 tests true, lines 004100 and 004200 are executed, one after the other. Line 004100 is a PERFORM request that causes a message to be displayed at line 004900. A similar action happens when the IF at line 004000 tests true and lines 004500 and 004600 are executed.

What Can You Test with IF?

The condition in an IF verb is a test of one value against another for equality or inequality.

NEW TERM The symbols used to compare two values are called *comparison operators*. The short and long versions of these comparisons are all comparison operators. IS NOT EQUAL, NOT =, =, IS EQUAL, NOT <, >, GREATER THAN, and NOT GREATER THAN are all examples of comparison operators. Tables 4.1 and 4.2 list all of the comparison operators.

Table 4.1 lists the comparisons that can be made and describes their effects.

4

Table 4.1. COBOL comparison operators.

Comparison Operator	Description
IF x IS EQUAL y	True if x equals y
IF x IS LESS THAN y	True if x is less than y
IF x IS GREATER THAN y	True if x is greater than y
IF x IS NOT EQUAL y	True if x does not equal y
IF x IS NOT LESS THAN y	True if x is not less than y (or is equal to or greater than y)
IF x IS NOT GREATER THAN y	True if x is not greater than y (or is equal to or less than y)

The word IS in a comparison is optional, and EQUAL, GREATER THAN, and LESS THAN can be shortened to =, >, and <, respectively. Table 4.2 compares the possible versions of comparisons.

Table 4.2. More COBOL comparison operators.

Optional Operator	Shortest Version
IF x EQUAL y	IF x = y
IF x LESS THAN y	IF x < y
IF x GREATER THAN y	IF x > y
IF x NOT EQUAL y	IF x NOT = y
IF x NOT LESS THAN y	IF x NOT < y
IF x NOT GREATER THAN y	IF x NOT > y

Listing 4.4 repeats yesno03.cbl, using the shortened comparisons.

TYPE   **Listing 4.4.** yesno03.cbl **with shorter comparisons.**

```
000100 IDENTIFICATION DIVISION.
000200 PROGRAM-ID. YESNO04.
000300*-------------------------------------------------
000400* This program asks for a Y or N answer, and then
000500* displays whether the user chose yes or no.
000600* The edit logic allows for entry of Y, y, N, or n.
000700*-------------------------------------------------
000800 ENVIRONMENT DIVISION.
000900 DATA DIVISION.
001000 WORKING-STORAGE SECTION.
001100
001200 01  YES-OR-NO      PIC X.
001300
001400 PROCEDURE DIVISION.
001500 PROGRAM-BEGIN.
001600
001700     PERFORM GET-THE-ANSWER.
001800
001900     PERFORM EDIT-THE-ANSWER.
002000
002100     PERFORM DISPLAY-THE-ANSWER.
002200
002300 PROGRAM-DONE.
002400     STOP RUN.
002500
002600 GET-THE-ANSWER.
002700
002800     DISPLAY "Is the answer Yes or No? (Y/N)".
002900     ACCEPT YES-OR-NO.
003000
003100 EDIT-THE-ANSWER.
003200
003300     IF YES-OR-NO = "y"
003400         MOVE "Y" TO YES-OR-NO.
003500
```

4

```
003600      IF YES-OR-NO = "n"
003700          MOVE "N" TO YES-OR-NO.
003800
003900 DISPLAY-THE-ANSWER.
004000      IF YES-OR-NO = "Y"
004100          PERFORM IT-IS-VALID
004200          DISPLAY "You answered Yes.".
004300
004400      IF YES-OR-NO = "N"
004500          PERFORM IT-IS-VALID
004600          DISPLAY "You answered No.".
004700
004800 IT-IS-VALID.
004900      DISPLAY "Your answer is valid and".
005000
```

For numeric values, all these tests make sense. Less than and greater than are both conditions that easily can be established when you are testing two numbers. But what are you testing when you compare two alphanumeric variables?

When a condition test is performed on alphanumeric variables, the tests usually compare the characters in the two alphanumeric values on the left and right sides of the comparison operator, in ASCII order. (See Appendix B, "ASCII.")

 The sequence in which the characters appear in the ASCII chart is known as the *ASCII collating sequence. Collate* means to assemble in some sort of order—in this case, ASCII order.

ASCII is not the only collating sequence. IBM mainframes use a collating sequence called EBCDIC. In the ASCII collating sequence, numbers appear before uppercase letters, and uppercase letters appear before lowercase letters. In the EBCDIC collating sequence, lowercase letters appear before uppercase letters and numbers appear last. Punctuation characters vary quite a bit in the EBCDIC and ASCII collating sequences. Collating sequences also vary for different spoken languages. Castillian Spanish treats the letter combinations ch and ll as single letters so that llanero sorts after luna and chico sorts after corazon. The examples in this book are based on the English ASCII collating sequence.

In ASCII order, A is less than B, AB is less than ABC, and the uppercase letters are less than the lowercase letters; so, ABC is less than abc. When an alphanumeric variable contains the digits 0 through 9, the digits are less than the characters, so 1BC is less than ABC. Spaces are the lowest of all, so three spaces are less than 00A. Refer to Appendix B for the complete set and sequence of ASCII characters.

Listing 4.5 will accept two words from a user and then display them in ASCII order. You can use this program any time you want to find out the actual ASCII order for two values. The testing is done in the paragraph DISPLAY-THE-WORDS, which starts at line 004100. The actual tests, at lines 004500 and 004900, use a greater than (>) and a not greater than (NOT >) comparison to decide which word to display first.

TYPE   **Listing 4.5. Displaying two words in ASCII order.**

```
000100 IDENTIFICATION DIVISION.
000200 PROGRAM-ID. WRDSRT01.
000300*----------------------------------------------
000400* Accepts 2 words from the user and then displays
000500* them in ASCII order.
000600*----------------------------------------------
000700 ENVIRONMENT DIVISION.
000800 DATA DIVISION.
000900 WORKING-STORAGE SECTION.
001000
001100 01  WORD-1              PIC X(50).
001200 01  WORD-2              PIC X(50).
001300
001400 PROCEDURE DIVISION.
001500 PROGRAM-BEGIN.
001600
001700     PERFORM INITIALIZE-PROGRAM.
001800     PERFORM ENTER-THE-WORDS.
001900     PERFORM DISPLAY-THE-WORDS.
002000
002100 PROGRAM-DONE.
002200     STOP RUN.
002300
002400* Level 2 Routines
002500
002600 INITIALIZE-PROGRAM.
002700     MOVE " " TO WORD-1.
002800     MOVE " " TO WORD-2.
002900
003000 ENTER-THE-WORDS.
003100     DISPLAY "This program will accept 2 words,".
003200     DISPLAY "and then display them".
003300     DISPLAY "in ASCII order.".
003400
003500     DISPLAY "Please enter the first word.".
003600     ACCEPT WORD-1.
003700
003800     DISPLAY "Please enter the second word.".
003900     ACCEPT WORD-2.
004000
004100 DISPLAY-THE-WORDS.
004200
004300     DISPLAY "The words in ASCII order are:".
004400
004500     IF WORD-1 > WORD-2
004600         DISPLAY WORD-2
004700         DISPLAY WORD-1.
004800
004900     IF WORD-1 NOT > WORD-2
005000         DISPLAY WORD-1
005100         DISPLAY WORD-2.
005200
```

4

Here is the sample output of `wrdsrt01.cbl` when the words entered are `beta` and `alpha`:

OUTPUT

```
This program will accept 2 words,
and then display them
in ASCII order.
Please enter the first word.
beta
Please enter the second word.
alpha
The words in ASCII order are:
alpha
beta


C>
```

ANALYSIS Multiple statements are executed within the IF tests at lines `004500` and `004900`. There are two DISPLAY statements under each of the IF tests. If WORD-1 is greater than WORD-2, or if WORD-1 occurs after WORD-2 in the ASCII sorting sequence, WORD-2 is displayed first.

You should edit, compile, and run `wrdsrt01.cbl`; then try it with various pairs of "words," such as ABC and abc, (space)ABC and ABC, or ABCD and ABC, to see how these are arranged in ASCII order.

Please note that many people, including experienced programmers, assume that the opposite of GREATER THAN is LESS THAN. However, testing for only these two conditions misses the case where the two entered words are identical. The complement of GREATER THAN is LESS THAN OR EQUAL which is correctly stated as NOT GREATER THAN.

You also can try a version of `wrdsrt01.cbl` that reverses the test in DISPLAY-THE-WORDS, as in Listing 4.6, which is just a listing of the DISPLAY-THE-WORDS paragraph. Try coding this one as `wrdsrt02.cbl` and satisfy yourself that the results are identical. Note that the test and display order are reversed.

TYPE ## Listing 4.6. Reversing the test and display.

```
004100 DISPLAY-THE-WORDS.
004200
004300     DISPLAY "The words sorted in ASCII order are:".
004400     IF WORD-1 < WORD-2
004500         DISPLAY WORD-1
004600         DISPLAY WORD-2.
004700     IF WORD-1 NOT < WORD-2
004800         DISPLAY WORD-2
004900         DISPLAY WORD-1.
```

You should also try a version of wrdsrt01.cbl that tests incorrectly in DISPLAY-THE-WORDS, as in Listing 4.7. This version tests for LESS THAN and GREATER THAN. Try coding this one as badsrt.cbl and satisfy yourself that the results are identical unless you enter the exact string for WORD-1 and WORD-2, such as ABC and ABC. Note that the test fails to display anything for this condition.

TYPE **Listing 4.7. An incorrect version of the test.**

```
004100 DISPLAY-THE-WORDS.
004200
004300     DISPLAY "The words sorted in ASCII order are:".
004400     IF WORD-1 < WORD-2
004500         DISPLAY WORD-1
004600         DISPLAY WORD-2.
004700     IF WORD-1 > WORD-2
004800         DISPLAY WORD-2
004900         DISPLAY WORD-1.
```

The indentation chosen for the IF is completely arbitrary. As long as the IF starts in and stays within Area B, the arrangement is up to you. Listing 4.8 and Listing 4.9 are equally valid, but in Listing 4.9 it is difficult to tell what is going on, and Listing 4.8 looks a bit sloppy.

Do   **Don't**

DO indent IF conditions carefully. An IF controls all statements up to the period at the end of the sentence.

DON'T use sloppy indenting on an IF. Correct indentation gives a good visual clue of which parts of the program are controlled by the IF.

TYPE **Listing 4.8. Sloppy indenting of an IF.**

```
004100 DISPLAY-THE-WORDS.
004200
004300     DISPLAY "The words sorted in ASCII order are:".
004400     IF WORD-1 < WORD-2
004500       DISPLAY WORD-1
004600             DISPLAY WORD-2.
004700     IF WORD-1 NOT < WORD-2
004800             DISPLAY WORD-2
004900         DISPLAY WORD-1.
```

TYPE **Listing 4.9. Failing to indent an IF.**

```
004100 DISPLAY-THE-WORDS.
004200
004300      DISPLAY "The words sorted in ASCII order are:".
004400      IF WORD-1 < WORD-2
004500      DISPLAY WORD-1
004600      DISPLAY WORD-2.
004700      IF WORD-1 NOT < WORD-2
004800      DISPLAY WORD-2
004900      DISPLAY WORD-1.
```

Testing Multiple Conditions

An IF test also can be used to test more than one condition. Conditions can be combined by using AND, OR, or combinations of both. Listing 4.10 is a short menu program. A menu program is designed to display a series of options on the screen and let the user pick one option to execute. In this menu program, the user has a choice of displaying one of three possible messages.

TYPE **Listing 4.10. Combining tests using OR.**

```
000100 IDENTIFICATION DIVISION.
000200 PROGRAM-ID. MENU01.
000300*-------------------------------------------------
000400* THIS PROGRAM DISPLAYS A THREE CHOICE MENU OF
000500* MESSAGES THAT CAN BE DISPLAYED.
000600* THE USER ENTERS THE CHOICE, 1, 2 OR 3, AND
000700* THE APPROPRIATE MESSAGE IS DISPLAYED.
000800* AN ERROR MESSAGE IS DISPLAYED IF AN INVALID
000900* CHOICE IS MADE.
001000*-------------------------------------------------
001100 ENVIRONMENT DIVISION.
001200 DATA DIVISION.
001300 WORKING-STORAGE SECTION.
001400
001500 01  MENU-PICK       PIC 9.
001600
001700 PROCEDURE DIVISION.
001800 PROGRAM-BEGIN.
001900
002000      PERFORM GET-THE-MENU-PICK.
002100
002200      PERFORM DO-THE-MENU-PICK.
002300
002400 PROGRAM-DONE.
002500      STOP RUN.
002600
```

continues

Listing 4.10. continued

```
002700* LEVEL 2 ROUTINES
002800 GET-THE-MENU-PICK.
002900
003000     PERFORM DISPLAY-THE-MENU.
003100     PERFORM GET-THE-PICK.
003200
003300 DO-THE-MENU-PICK.
003400     IF MENU-PICK < 1 OR
003500        MENU-PICK > 3
003600         DISPLAY "Invalid selection".
003700
003800     IF MENU-PICK = 1
003900         DISPLAY "One for the money.".
004000
004100     IF MENU-PICK = 2
004200         DISPLAY "Two for the show.".
004300
004400     IF MENU-PICK = 3
004500         DISPLAY "Three to get ready.".
004600
004700* LEVEL 3 ROUTINES
004800 DISPLAY-THE-MENU.
004900     DISPLAY "Please enter the number of the message".
005000     DISPLAY "that you wish to display.".
005100* Display a blank line
005200     DISPLAY " ".
005300     DISPLAY "1.  First Message".
005400     DISPLAY "2.  Second Message".
005500     DISPLAY "3.  Third Message".
005600* Display a blank line
005700     DISPLAY " ".
005800     DISPLAY "Your selection (1-3)?".
005900
006000 GET-THE-PICK.
006100     ACCEPT MENU-PICK.
006200
```

Here are sample output results from menu01.cbl for a valid and an invalid response:

```
Please enter the number of the message
that you wish to display.

1.  First Message
2.  Second Message
3.  Third Message

Your selection (1-3)?
2
Two for the show.


C>
C>
```

```
      Please enter the number of the message
      that you wish to display.

      1.   First Message
      2.   Second Message
      3.   Third Message

      Your selection (1-3)?
      5
      Invalid selection


      C>
      C>
```

ANALYSIS The valid menu selections are 1, 2, and 3. The test that the value entered is in a range at lines 003400 through 003500, ending with a display of an invalid entry message at line 003600. If the entered MENU-PICK is less than 1 or greater than 3, it is invalid. Note that the OR on line 003400 combines the two tests within one IF. An OR test is true if either of the tests is true.

Read the comments in the program, because they explain some of the options used to improve the look of the displayed menu. The levels in the comments relate to the level of PERFORM. Routines in level 2 are being performed from the top level of the program, PROGRAM-BEGIN. Routines in level 3 are performed from within routines at level 2.

An AND test is true only if both conditions being tested are true. Listing 4.11 asks the user to enter a number between 10 and 100, excluding 10 and 100. Therefore, the valid range of entries for this program is 011 through 099. Remember that ACUCOBOL will require that you enter the leading zero.

TYPE   ### Listing 4.11. Combining tests with AND.

```
000100 IDENTIFICATION DIVISION.
000200 PROGRAM-ID. RANGE01.
000300*-------------------------------------------------
000400* ASKS USER FOR A NUMBER BETWEEN 10 AND 100
000500* EXCLUSIVE AND PRINTS A MESSAGE IF THE ENTRY
000600* IS IN RANGE.
000700*-------------------------------------------------
000800 ENVIRONMENT DIVISION.
000900 DATA DIVISION.
001000 WORKING-STORAGE SECTION.
001100
001200 01   THE-NUMBER            PIC 999.
001300
001400 PROCEDURE DIVISION.
001500 PROGRAM-BEGIN.
001600
001700      PERFORM GET-THE-NUMBER.
001800
```

continues

Listing 4.11. continued

```
001900     PERFORM CHECK-THE-NUMBER.
002000
002100 PROGRAM-DONE.
002200     STOP RUN.
002300
002400 GET-THE-NUMBER.
002500     DISPLAY "Enter a number greater than 10".
002600     DISPLAY "and less than 100. (011-099)".
002700     ACCEPT THE-NUMBER.
002800
002900 CHECK-THE-NUMBER.
003000     IF THE-NUMBER > 10 AND
003100        THE-NUMBER < 100
003200         DISPLAY "The number is in range.".
003300
```

 At lines 003000 and 003100, THE-NUMBER must be greater than 10 and less than 100 to be valid.

IF-ELSE

When an IF test fails, none of the statements controlled by the IF test are executed. The program continues to the next sentence and skips all the logic. In Listing 4.5 (wrdsrt0103.cbl), at lines 004500 through 005100, two IF tests are done to check the correct order for displaying WORD-1 and WORD-2. In these two comparisons, the second IF test is the exact opposite of the first IF test:

```
WORD-1 > WORD-2
WORD-1 NOT > WORD-2.
```

If you refer to Listing 4.7, you will recall that I had you deliberately create an error in the two tests by testing LESS THAN followed by GREATER THAN. It is entirely possible to make this exact error by accident. Rather than worrying about testing the complementary condition, you can use the ELSE clause of an IF to do it for you. If you are testing a condition and you want to do one set of commands if the condition or conditions are true and another set if they are false, it is easier to use ELSE than to try to word an IF with the opposite condition.

An ELSE has the following form:

```
IF condition
    statement
    statement
ELSE
    statement
    statement.
```

The following is an example of an ELSE statement:

```
IF A < B
    PERFORM ACTION-A
    PERFORM ACTION-B
ELSE
    PERFORM ACTION-C
    PERFORM ACTION-D.
```

ELSE can be used in an IF test to specify what to do when the IF condition does not test as true. An ELSE also can execute multiple statements. In an IF-ELSE statement, when the IF condition is true, all statements up to the ELSE are executed. Otherwise, all statements from the ELSE to the closing period are executed. The period is placed at the end of the last statement in the ELSE.

Listing 4.12 is a slightly improved version of wrdsrt01.cbl. The two IF tests have been replaced by an IF-ELSE. You should be able to copy wrdsrt01.cbl to wrdsrt03.cbl and make the two changes needed easily. Remove the period at the end of line 004700, and change the second IF test to an ELSE.

TYPE **Listing 4.12. Using IF-ELSE.**

```
000100 IDENTIFICATION DIVISION.
000200 PROGRAM-ID. WRDSRT03.
000300*------------------------------------------------
000400* Accepts 2 words from the user and then displays
000500* them in ASCII order.
000600*------------------------------------------------
000700 ENVIRONMENT DIVISION.
000800 DATA DIVISION.
000900 WORKING-STORAGE SECTION.
001000
001100 01  WORD-1              PIC X(50).
001200 01  WORD-2              PIC X(50).
001300
001400 PROCEDURE DIVISION.
001500 PROGRAM-BEGIN.
001600
001700     PERFORM INITIALIZE-PROGRAM.
001800     PERFORM ENTER-THE-WORDS.
001900     PERFORM DISPLAY-THE-WORDS.
002000
002100 PROGRAM-DONE.
002200     STOP RUN.
002300
002400* Level 2 Routines
002500
002600 INITIALIZE-PROGRAM.
002700     MOVE " " TO WORD-1.
002800     MOVE " " TO WORD-2.
002900
```

continues

Listing 4.12. continued

```
003000 ENTER-THE-WORDS.
003100     DISPLAY "This program will accept 2 words,".
003200     DISPLAY "and then display them".
003300     DISPLAY "in ASCII order.".
003400
003500     DISPLAY "Please enter the first word.".
003600     ACCEPT WORD-1.
003700
003800     DISPLAY "Please enter the second word.".
003900     ACCEPT WORD-2.
004000
004100 DISPLAY-THE-WORDS.
004200
004300     DISPLAY "The words in ASCII order are:".
004400
004500     IF WORD-1 > WORD-2
004600         DISPLAY WORD-2
004700         DISPLAY WORD-1
004800     ELSE
004900         DISPLAY WORD-1
005000         DISPLAY WORD-2.
005100
```

The IF-ELSE construction is useful when you are working with combined tests.

Look at Listing 4.11 again and try to work out the opposite test to the test at lines 003000 and 003100. It should be something like the lines in Listing 4.13.

TYPE   Listing 4.13. The original test and its opposite.

```
003000     IF THE-NUMBER > 10 AND
003100         THE-NUMBER < 100
003200         DISPLAY "The number is in range.".
003300
003400     IF THE-NUMBER NOT > 10 OR
003500         THE-NUMBER NOT < 100
000000         DISPLAY "The number is not in range.".
```

Listing 4.14 handles the problem by using ELSE, and it is simpler to code and easier to understand.

TYPE   Listing 4.14. Using ELSE.

```
000100 IDENTIFICATION DIVISION.
000200 PROGRAM-ID. RANGE02.
000300*-------------------------------------------------
000400* ASKS USER FOR A NUMBER BETWEEN 10 AND 100
000500* EXCLUSIVE AND PRINTS A MESSAGE IF THE ENTRY
```

```
000600* IS IN RANGE.
000700*------------------------------------------------
000800 ENVIRONMENT DIVISION.
000900 DATA DIVISION.
001000 WORKING-STORAGE SECTION.
001100
001200 01  THE-NUMBER            PIC 999.
001300
001400 PROCEDURE DIVISION.
001500 PROGRAM-BEGIN.
001600
001700     PERFORM GET-THE-NUMBER.
001800
001900     PERFORM CHECK-THE-NUMBER.
002000
002100 PROGRAM-DONE.
002200     STOP RUN.
002300
002400 GET-THE-NUMBER.
002500     DISPLAY "Enter a number greater than 10".
002600     DISPLAY "and less than 100. (011-099)".
002700     ACCEPT THE-NUMBER.
002800
002900 CHECK-THE-NUMBER.
003000     IF THE-NUMBER > 10 AND
003100        THE-NUMBER < 100
003200        DISPLAY "The number is in range."
003300     ELSE
003400        DISPLAY "The number is out of range.".
003500
```

Listing 4.15 is another version of the yes/no problem. In this listing, the answer is tested for Y or N, and a separate paragraph is performed if the answer is valid. Otherwise (ELSE), an invalid entry message is displayed. The code in the paragraph DISPLAY-YES-OR-NO can be written differently. See whether you can figure out what to change, and then look at the analysis after the listing.

TYPE **Listing 4.15. Using IF-ELSE.**

```
000100 IDENTIFICATION DIVISION.
000200 PROGRAM-ID. YESNO05.
000300*------------------------------------------------
000400* This program asks for a Y or N answer, and then
000500* displays whether the user chose yes or no
000600* or an invalid entry.
000700* The edit logic allows for entry of Y, y, N, or n.
000800*------------------------------------------------
000900 ENVIRONMENT DIVISION.
001000 DATA DIVISION.
001100 WORKING-STORAGE SECTION.
001200
001300 01  YES-OR-NO      PIC X.
```

continues

Listing 4.15. continued

```
001400
001500 PROCEDURE DIVISION.
001600 PROGRAM-BEGIN.
001700
001800     PERFORM GET-THE-ANSWER.
001900
002000     PERFORM EDIT-THE-ANSWER.
002100
002200     PERFORM DISPLAY-THE-ANSWER.
002300
002400 PROGRAM-DONE.
002500     STOP RUN.
002600
002700 GET-THE-ANSWER.
002800
002900     DISPLAY "Is the answer Yes or No? (Y/N)".
003000     ACCEPT YES-OR-NO.
003100
003200 EDIT-THE-ANSWER.
003300
003400     IF YES-OR-NO = "y"
003500         MOVE "Y" TO YES-OR-NO.
003600
003700     IF YES-OR-NO = "n"
003800         MOVE "N" TO YES-OR-NO.
003900
004000 DISPLAY-THE-ANSWER.
004100
004200     IF YES-OR-NO = "Y" OR
004300         YES-OR-NO = "N"
004400             PERFORM DISPLAY-YES-OR-NO
004500     ELSE
004600         DISPLAY "Your entry was invalid.".
004700
004800 DISPLAY-YES-OR-NO.
004900
005000     IF YES-OR-NO = "Y"
005100         DISPLAY "You answered Yes.".
005200
005300     IF YES-OR-NO = "N"
005400         DISPLAY "You answered No.".
005500
```

ANALYSIS   The paragraph DISPLAY-YES-OR-NO is performed only if YES-OR-NO is Y or N, so this paragraph could be simplified by using an ELSE:

```
DISPLAY-YES-OR-NO.

    IF YES-OR-NO = "Y"
        DISPLAY "You answered Yes."
    ELSE
        DISPLAY "You answered No.".
```

Do	Don't

DO type IF and IF-ELSE constructions carefully. An IF controls all statements up to the next ELSE, or to the period at the end of the sentence if there is no ELSE. An ELSE controls all statements up to the period at the end of the sentence.

DON'T use sloppy indenting on IF and IF-ELSE verbs. Correct indentation gives a good visual clue of which parts of the program are controlled by the IF and which are controlled by the ELSE.

A final note in IF-ELSE indentation is that COBOL unfortunately uses the period as a sentence terminator. The period is almost invisible and can even get lost in a listing printed with a poor ribbon. This is another reason that source code should be kept as standardized as possible. Proper IF-ELSE indentations are one way of keeping your code easy to read.

Summary

Today's lesson explored controlling the flow of programs by testing conditions with the IF statement. You learned these basics:

- [ ] The primary method of changing the flow of a program is to use an IF or an IF-ELSE to make a decision, based on the values of variables.
- [ ] Multiple statements can be executed within an IF.
- [ ] The conditional operators used with an IF test are as follows:

Conditional operator	Alternative operator
IS EQUAL	=
IS GREATER THAN	>
IS LESS THAN	<
IS NOT EQUAL	NOT =
IS NOT GREATER THAN	NOT >
IS NOT LESS THAN	NOT <

- [ ] When numeric values are compared, they are compared as numbers.
- [ ] When alphanumeric values are compared, they are compared based on the ASCII collating sequence.
- [ ] Multiple conditions can be tested in an IF by using AND and OR to connect two or more comparisons.

☐ An ELSE can be used to control statements to be executed when the IF test evaluates as false.

☐ Multiple statements can be executed within an ELSE.

☐ The statements controlled by an IF are executed if the condition being tested by an IF is true.

☐ The statements controlled by an ELSE are executed if the condition being tested by the corresponding IF is false.

Q&A

Q Can a numeric variable be tested against an alphanumeric variable?

A Some compilers let you get away with this, but it is a very bad habit. If THE-MESSAGE is a PIC X containing the character "2", and THE-NUMBER is a PIC 9 containing 2, the statement

```
IF THE-MESSAGE = THE-NUMBER
```

could produce the following different results:

☐ The compiler might refuse to compile it and return an error that you cannot compare—unlike data types.

☐ It might compile, run, and test correctly.

☐ It might compile, but the program might crash while running when the test is performed.

☐ It might compile and run, but return random results that test true sometimes and test false other times.

Because only one of these possibilities is what you want, it isn't worth trying to work with a particular compiler's idiosyncrasies. It is also makes it hard to figure out what the program is doing when unlike data types are compared.

Workshop

Quiz

1. In the following paragraph DECIDE-WHAT-TO-DO, which lines are executed when THE-NUMBER equals 7?

```
005200 DECIDE-WHAT-TO-DO.
005300     IF THE-NUMBER = 7 OR
005400         THE-NUMBER < 4
005500         PERFORM ACTION-1
005600         PERFORM ACTION-2
005700     ELSE
005800         PERFORM ACTION-3.
005900
```

2. Which lines are executed when THE-NUMBER equals 6?

3. Which lines are executed when THE-NUMBER equals 2?

4. Which lines are executed when THE-NUMBER equals 4?

Exercises

1. Modify Listing 4.2 to allow Maybe as a third possible answer.

2. Modify Listing 4.4 to allow Maybe as a third possible answer.

   Hint: You can test more than two conditions using AND or OR, as in the following example:

```
004400       IF YES-OR-NO = "Y" OR
004500          YES-OR-NO = "N" OR
004600          YES-OR-NO = "M"
004700          PERFORM DISPLAY-YES-NO-OR-MAYBE
```

Day **5**

Using PERFORM, GO TO, and IF to Control Programs

In COBOL, the flow of a program is controlled almost entirely by IF-ELSE statements, the PERFORM verb, and GO TO, which is a new verb you will look at today. There are some additional versions of the PERFORM verb and the IF-ELSE statement, allowing even more control, and these are covered as well. Today, you learn about the following topics:

- ☐ Using GO TO to control a program.
- ☐ Using PERFORM repetitively.
- ☐ What is a processing loop?
- ☐ Using PERFORM to control a processing loop.

Using GO TO to Control a Program

You can force the program to jump to the beginning of any paragraph with a GO TO. Here is an example:

```
GO TO paragraph-name.
```

A GO TO is like a PERFORM in that the program jumps to a new paragraph. However, when that paragraph is completed, the PERFORM returns to the line at which the PERFORM was requested, but the GO TO does not. When a GO TO reaches the end of the paragraph to which it has jumped, it moves into the next paragraph.

GO TO is written as two words, but it is used as one. The words always appear together. Listing 5.1 uses GO TO to bail out of a program.

TYPE   **Listing 5.1. Using GO TO.**

```
000100 IDENTIFICATION DIVISION.
000200 PROGRAM-ID. QUIT01.
000300 ENVIRONMENT DIVISION.
000400 DATA DIVISION.
000500 WORKING-STORAGE SECTION.
000600
000700 01  YES-OR-NO      PIC X.
000800
000900 PROCEDURE DIVISION.
001000 PROGRAM-BEGIN.
001100
001200     PERFORM SHALL-WE-CONTINUE.
001300     IF YES-OR-NO = "N"
001400         GO TO PROGRAM-DONE.
001500
001600     PERFORM MAIN-LOGIC.
001700
001800 PROGRAM-DONE.
001900     STOP RUN.
002000
002100 SHALL-WE-CONTINUE.
002200     DISPLAY "Continue (Y/N)?".
002300     ACCEPT YES-OR-NO.
002400     IF YES-OR-NO = "n"
002500         MOVE "N" TO YES-OR-NO.
002600
002700 MAIN-LOGIC.
002800     DISPLAY "This is the main logic.".
002900
```

ANALYSIS   At line 001200, a PERFORM is requested of SHALL-WE-CONTINUE. In this paragraph, at lines 002100 and 002200, the user is asked whether he wants to continue. When the user enters a response, a possible "n" is converted to "N" and the logic at line 001300 checks whether the user entered N, and, if so, the program flow at line 001400 jumps straight to PROGRAM-DONE. PROGRAM-DONE contains the now familiar STOP RUN, and execution of the program is terminated.

The alternative is that the user enters something other than N (or n), and line 001300 is skipped. The next executed line is 001600, where the program requests a PERFORM of MAIN-LOGIC. (In this example, the content of MAIN-LOGIC isn't important.)

GO TO is the only four-letter verb in COBOL. (That's a joke.) The use of GO TO in programs is a hotly debated issue, and academics will tell you, "You never use a GO TO," or "One more GO TO out of you, and I'm going to wash your mouth out with soap!" One professor of computer science was so incensed by GO TO that he designed a whole new programming language with no GO TO in it.

If you plan to work with COBOL in the real world, rather than behind closed university doors, you must know what a GO TO does and how to work with and around it. Any working program that you have to modify will be littered with GO TO verbs, and you ignore them at your own peril. Just remember that mentioning a GO TO around some people will make their faces red and cause steam to come out of their ears.

You shouldn't use GO TO in programs that you write, but you will have to deal with GO TO in programs that you modify. Listing 5.2 is an example of a GO TO that would be considered a minor sin by some people. The program, mult01.cbl, displays multiplication tables (such as the ones you had to memorize in school) based on which table the user selects to display.

Listing 5.2. Using GO TO to execute a paragraph several times.

TYPE

```
000100 IDENTIFICATION DIVISION.
000200 PROGRAM-ID. MULT01.
000300*------------------------------------------------
000400* This program asks the user for a number for a
000500* multiplication table,
000600* and then displays a table for that number times
000700* the values 1 through 12.
000800*------------------------------------------------
000900 ENVIRONMENT DIVISION.
001000 DATA DIVISION.
001100 WORKING-STORAGE SECTION.
001200
001300 01   THE-NUMBER        PIC 99.
001400 01   THE-MULTIPLIER    PIC 999.
001500 01   THE-PRODUCT       PIC 9999.
001600
001700 PROCEDURE DIVISION.
001800* LEVEL 1 ROUTINES
001900 PROGRAM-BEGIN.
002000     PERFORM PROGRAM-INITIALIZATION.
```

continues

Listing 5.2. continued

```
002100     PERFORM GET-TABLE-NUMBER.
002200     PERFORM DISPLAY-THE-TABLE.
002300
002400 PROGRAM-DONE.
002500     STOP RUN.
002600
002700* LEVEL 2 ROUTINES
002800 PROGRAM-INITIALIZATION.
002900     MOVE 0 TO THE-MULTIPLIER.
003000
003100 GET-TABLE-NUMBER.
003200     DISPLAY
003300     "Which multiplication table (01-99)?".
003400     ACCEPT THE-NUMBER.
003500
003600 DISPLAY-THE-TABLE.
003700     DISPLAY "The " THE-NUMBER 's table is:".
003800     PERFORM CALCULATE-AND-DISPLAY.
003900
004000* LEVEL 3 ROUTINES.
004100 CALCULATE-AND-DISPLAY.
004200     ADD 1 TO THE-MULTIPLIER.
004300     COMPUTE THE-PRODUCT = THE-NUMBER * THE-MULTIPLIER.
004400     DISPLAY
004500         THE-NUMBER " * " THE-MULTIPLIER " = " THE-PRODUCT.
004600     IF THE-MULTIPLIER < 12
004700         GO TO CALCULATE-AND-DISPLAY.
004800
```

This is the output of mult01.cbl for the 7's table (which I had a great deal of trouble memorizing in school):

OUTPUT

```
Which multiplication table (01-99)?
07
The 07's table is:
07 * 001 = 0007
07 * 002 = 0014
07 * 003 = 0021
07 * 004 = 0028
07 * 005 = 0035
07 * 006 = 0042
07 * 007 = 0049
07 * 008 = 0056
07 * 009 = 0063
07 * 010 = 0070
07 * 011 = 0077
07 * 012 = 0084


C>
C>
```

5

ANALYSIS In PROGRAM-INITIALIZATION, the variable THE-MULTIPLIER is set to 0. In GET-TABLE-NUMBER, the user is asked to select the multiplication table and is prompted for a number between 01 and 99. Remember that some versions of COBOL require that you enter a number with a leading zero, here—03, for example, if you want 3.

These two paragraphs, when performed, set things up for the main activity of the program, which is to display a table of the entered number times 1, times 2, times 3, and so on to 12.

Now look at the paragraph CALCULATE-AND-DISPLAY. THE-MULTIPLIER is initialized to 0 by PROGRAM-INITIALIZATION, so the action of this paragraph is to add 1 to THE-MULTIPLIER, calculate THE-PRODUCT by multiplying THE-MULTIPLIER by THE-NUMBER, and then display this information.

In the COBOL COMPUTE statement, the asterisk (*) is the multiplication symbol.

The DISPLAY statement is organized to display the results as follows:

```
03 * 01 = 0003
03 * 02 = 0006
```

The basic repetitive task of the program to is add 1 to THE-MULTIPLIER, calculate the new product, and display the result. It is necessary to do this 12 times. At line 004600, an IF tests whether THE-MULTIPLIER is less than 12. As long as it is, the program will jump back to the beginning of CALCULATE-AND-DISPLAY. Each time, the program adds 1 to THE-MULTIPLIER and calculates and displays the new product. When THE-MULTIPLIER reaches 12, the IF condition is no longer true. The GO TO CALCULATE-AND-DISPLAY at line 004700 is not executed and the CALCULATE-AND-DISPLAY paragraph ends. The program returns to the end of line 003800 looking for more commands. There are none. No further commands are in DISPLAY-THE-TABLE, so that paragraph ends and the program returns to line 002200, where there also are no further commands. The program proceeds to lines 002400 and 002500 and ends.

It is certainly legitimate to use a GO TO at the bottom of a paragraph to jump back to the top of the paragraph in order to execute the paragraph again under some condition, although some would dispute even that use.

After you've worked with modifying real code, you will find out why GO TO should be discouraged. It is very confusing to be following a paragraph of logic, and find a GO TO to another paragraph somewhere else in the program. Because a GO TO does not bounce back, you have no way of knowing whether the rest of the current paragraph is ever executed or the programmer just skipped everything else for some reason.

One danger of GO TO verbs is the likelihood that the programmer skipped some code for no reason at all (other than carelessness), instead of having some reason to skip the code.

Understand GO TO, because you will find it in various programs. You can avoid GO TO

5

completely, as you will see a little later in today's lesson. So, if you ever work in a shop that has banned the use of GO TO, you can work your way around the stricture.

Using PERFORM Repetitively

Now that you have been warned about the evils of GO TO, how could you write the previous program without one? The PERFORM verb is available for that purpose—in a variety of flavors. One of them allows you to perform a paragraph several times:

```
PERFORM A-PARAGRAPH 10 TIMES.
```

Listing 5.3, mult02.cbl, uses this version of the PERFORM verb to present the same multiplication tables based on the user's selection. Edit, compile, and run this program. It will accept factors up to 99.

TYPE **Listing 5.3. Using PERFORM multiple TIMES.**

```
000100 IDENTIFICATION DIVISION.
000200 PROGRAM-ID. MULT02.
000300*----------------------------------------------------
000400* This program asks the user for a number for a
000500* multiplication table,
000600* and then displays a table for that number times
000700* the values 1 through 12.
000800*----------------------------------------------------
000900 ENVIRONMENT DIVISION.
001000 DATA DIVISION.
001100 WORKING-STORAGE SECTION.
001200
001300 01   THE-NUMBER        PIC 99.
001400 01   THE-MULTIPLIER    PIC 999.
001500 01   THE-PRODUCT       PIC 9999.
001600
001700 PROCEDURE DIVISION.
001800* LEVEL 1 ROUTINES
001900 PROGRAM-BEGIN.
002000     PERFORM PROGRAM-INITIALIZATION.
002100     PERFORM GET-TABLE-NUMBER.
002200     PERFORM DISPLAY-THE-TABLE.
002300
002400 PROGRAM-DONE.
002500     STOP RUN.
002600
002700* LEVEL 2 ROUTINES
002800 PROGRAM-INITIALIZATION.
002900     MOVE 0 TO THE-MULTIPLIER.
003000
003100 GET-TABLE-NUMBER.
003200     DISPLAY
003300     "Which multiplication table (01-99)?".
```

```
003400      ACCEPT THE-NUMBER.
003500
003600 DISPLAY-THE-TABLE.
003700      DISPLAY "The " THE-NUMBER "'s table is:".
003800      PERFORM CALCULATE-AND-DISPLAY 12 TIMES.
003900
004000* LEVEL 3 ROUTINES.
004100 CALCULATE-AND-DISPLAY.
004200      ADD 1 TO THE-MULTIPLIER.
004300      COMPUTE THE-PRODUCT = THE-NUMBER * THE-MULTIPLIER.
004400      DISPLAY
004500         THE-NUMBER " * " THE-MULTIPLIER " = " THE-PRODUCT.
```

ANALYSIS The program is identical to `mult01.cbl` except that the IF and GO TO at lines 004600 and 004700 are removed, and the PERFORM at line 003800 has been replaced with `PERFORM CALCULATE-AND-DISPLAY 12 TIMES`.

Again, the basic repetitive task of the program is to add 1, calculate, and display the result. It is necessary to do this 12 times, and this job is taken care of at line 003800.

When the PERFORM verb is used to perform something a number of times, the COBOL compiler takes care of setting things so that a PERFORM is requested over and over until the number of times is exhausted. When the program is running, it actually jumps down to line 004100 and then back to line 003800 12 times.

The PERFORM...TIMES verb is flexible, and the number of times to perform something can be a variable itself. Here is an example:

```
PERFORM A-PARAGRAPH HOW-MANY TIMES.
```

Listing 5.4 takes the multiplication table program one step further by allowing the user to specify the number of entries to be displayed.

TYPE ## Listing 5.4. Varying the number of entries.

```
000100 IDENTIFICATION DIVISION.
000200 PROGRAM-ID. MULT03.
000300*----------------------------------------------------
000400* This program asks the user for a number for a
000500* multiplication table, and a table size
000600* and then displays a table for that number times
000700* the values 1 through HOW-MANY.
000800*
000900*
001000*----------------------------------------------------
001100 ENVIRONMENT DIVISION.
001200 DATA DIVISION.
001300 WORKING-STORAGE SECTION.
001400
001500 01  THE-NUMBER        PIC 99.
```

continues

Listing 5.4. continued

```
001600 01  THE-MULTIPLIER      PIC 999.
001700 01  THE-PRODUCT         PIC 9999.
001800 01  HOW-MANY            PIC 99.
001900
002000
002100
002200
002300 PROCEDURE DIVISION.
002400* LEVEL 1 ROUTINES
002500 PROGRAM-BEGIN.
002600     PERFORM PROGRAM-INITIALIZATION.
002700     PERFORM GET-TABLE-DATA.
002800     PERFORM DISPLAY-THE-TABLE.
002900
003000 PROGRAM-DONE.
003100     STOP RUN.
003200
003300* LEVEL 2 ROUTINES
003400 PROGRAM-INITIALIZATION.
003500     MOVE 0 TO THE-MULTIPLIER.
003600
003700
003800 GET-TABLE-DATA.
003900     DISPLAY
004000     "Which multiplication table(01-99)?".
004100     ACCEPT THE-NUMBER.
004200
004300     DISPLAY "How many entries would you like (01-99)?".
004400     ACCEPT HOW-MANY.
004500
004600 DISPLAY-THE-TABLE.
004700     DISPLAY "The " THE-NUMBER "'s table is:".
004800     PERFORM CALCULATE-AND-DISPLAY HOW-MANY TIMES.
004900
005000* LEVEL 3 ROUTINES.
005100 CALCULATE-AND-DISPLAY.
005200     ADD 1 TO THE-MULTIPLIER.
005300     COMPUTE THE-PRODUCT = THE-NUMBER * THE-MULTIPLIER.
005400     DISPLAY
005500         THE-NUMBER " * " THE-MULTIPLIER " = " THE-PRODUCT.
005600
```

The following is the output from mult03.cbl for 15 entries of the 15's table:

```
Which multiplication table(01-99)?
15
How many entries would you like (01-99)?
15
The 15's table is:
15 * 001 = 0015
15 * 002 = 0030
15 * 003 = 0045
15 * 004 = 0060
```

```
15 * 005 = 0075
15 * 006 = 0090
15 * 007 = 0105
15 * 008 = 0120
15 * 009 = 0135
15 * 010 = 0150
15 * 011 = 0165
15 * 012 = 0180
15 * 013 = 0195
15 * 014 = 0210
15 * 015 = 0225


C>
C>
```

ANALYSIS   In Listing 5.4, mult03.cbl, the GET-TABLE-NUMBER paragraph has been changed to GET-TABLE-DATA and additionally asks the user for the number of entries to be displayed. This value is stored in the variable HOW-MANY. Instead of performing CALCULATE-AND-DISPLAY 12 TIMES, the program performs it HOW-MANY TIMES.

If you edit, compile, and run this program, you can display the 15's table with 24 or 25 entries. If you enter more than 25 for the number of entries, the first entries in the table will scroll off the top of the screen.

Certain terminals known as block mode terminals do not display all lines. Instead they display one line, wait for you to press Enter, then display the next line, and so on. If this happens to you, consult with your system administrator for verification that you are using block mode terminals. If this is the case, you should consider acquiring the Micro Focus Personal COBOL Compiler to continue these lessons.

The program mult03.cbl contains a few extra blank lines because you will be modifying it shortly. Spend some time going over Listing 5.4 to make sure that you really understand what is happening in the program. Run it several times with different values (with the program in front of you) and work out where you are in the code at each point in the running program.

In mult03.cbl, the flaw, as mentioned before, is that early entries in the table scroll off the screen if more than 20 entries are requested.

You have all the tools you need to correct this problem; it is just a matter of using them. To tidy up the display in the next example, the program halts the display after every 15 lines.

The traditional way of doing this would be to display 15 lines, display Press ENTER to continue . . ., and wait for the user to press the Enter key.

Remember that using the ACCEPT verb causes the computer to wait for input from the keyboard until the user presses Enter. In this case, you want the user to press Enter, but you don't care about any values entered. The simple solution is to ACCEPT a dummy variable.

Edit, compile, and run Listing 5.5, trying numbers of entries greater than 15. The display will pause after 15 lines and wait for you to press Enter; then it will continue the display.

TYPE **Listing 5.5. Pausing after 15 lines.**

```
000100 IDENTIFICATION DIVISION.
000200 PROGRAM-ID. MULT04.
000300*------------------------------------------------
000400* This program asks the user for a number for a
000500* multiplication table, and a table size
000600* and then displays a table for that number
000700* times the values 1 through HOW-MANY.
000800*
000900* The display is paused after each 15 lines.
001000*------------------------------------------------
001100 ENVIRONMENT DIVISION.
001200 DATA DIVISION.
001300 WORKING-STORAGE SECTION.
001400
001500 01   THE-NUMBER        PIC 99.
001600 01   THE-MULTIPLIER    PIC 999.
001700 01   THE-PRODUCT       PIC 9999.
001800 01   HOW-MANY          PIC 99.
001900 01   SCREEN-LINES      PIC 99.
002000
002100 01   A-DUMMY           PIC X.
002200
002300 PROCEDURE DIVISION.
002400* LEVEL 1 ROUTINES
002500 PROGRAM-BEGIN.
002600      PERFORM PROGRAM-INITIALIZATION.
002700      PERFORM GET-TABLE-DATA.
002800      PERFORM DISPLAY-THE-TABLE.
002900
003000 PROGRAM-DONE.
003100      STOP RUN.
003200
003300* LEVEL 2 ROUTINES
003400 PROGRAM-INITIALIZATION.
003500      MOVE 0 TO THE-MULTIPLIER.
003600      MOVE 0 TO SCREEN-LINES.
003700
003800 GET-TABLE-DATA.
003900      DISPLAY
004000      "Which multiplication table (01-99)?".
004100      ACCEPT THE-NUMBER.
004200
004300      DISPLAY "How many entries would you like (01-99)?".
004400      ACCEPT HOW-MANY.
004500
004600 DISPLAY-THE-TABLE.
004700      DISPLAY "The " THE-NUMBER "'s table is:".
```

5

```
004800      PERFORM CALCULATE-AND-DISPLAY HOW-MANY TIMES.
004900
005000* LEVEL 3 ROUTINES.
005100 CALCULATE-AND-DISPLAY.
005200      ADD 1 TO THE-MULTIPLIER.
005300      COMPUTE THE-PRODUCT = THE-NUMBER * THE-MULTIPLIER.
005400      DISPLAY
005500          THE-NUMBER " * " THE-MULTIPLIER " = " THE-PRODUCT.
005600
005700      ADD 1 TO SCREEN-LINES.
005800      IF SCREEN-LINES = 15
005900          DISPLAY "Press ENTER to continue . . ."
006000          ACCEPT A-DUMMY
006100          MOVE 0 TO SCREEN-LINES.
006200
```

Three screens of output occur when mult04.cbl is used to display 31 entries of the 14's table. Here is the first screen:

OUTPUT

```
Which multiplication table (01-99)?
14
How many entries would you like (01-99)?
31
The 14's table is:
14 * 001 = 0014
14 * 002 = 0028
14 * 003 = 0042
14 * 004 = 0056
14 * 005 = 0070
14 * 006 = 0084
14 * 007 = 0098
14 * 008 = 0112
14 * 009 = 0126
14 * 010 = 0140
14 * 011 = 0154
14 * 012 = 0168
14 * 013 = 0182
14 * 014 = 0196
14 * 015 = 0210
Press ENTER to continue . . .
```

After you press Enter, the current display scrolls upward, making room for 15 more lines of tables and another Press ENTER message. The tail end of the first 15 lines still appears at the top of the screen. Here is the output after you press Enter:

OUTPUT

```
14 * 010 = 0140
14 * 011 = 0154
14 * 012 = 0168
14 * 013 = 0182
14 * 014 = 0196
14 * 015 = 0210
Press ENTER to continue . . .
```

5

```
14 * 016 = 0224
14 * 017 = 0238
14 * 018 = 0252
14 * 019 = 0266
14 * 020 = 0280
14 * 021 = 0294
14 * 022 = 0308
14 * 023 = 0322
14 * 024 = 0336
14 * 025 = 0350
14 * 026 = 0364
14 * 027 = 0378
14 * 028 = 0392
14 * 029 = 0406
14 * 030 = 0420
Press ENTER to continue . . .
```

After you press Enter a second time, one more line of information is displayed at the bottom of the screen, leaving the remains of the first two displays of 15 lines at the top:

OUTPUT

```
14 * 015 = 0210
Press ENTER to continue . . .

14 * 016 = 0224
14 * 017 = 0238
14 * 018 = 0252
14 * 019 = 0266
14 * 020 = 0280
14 * 021 = 0294
14 * 022 = 0308
14 * 023 = 0322
14 * 024 = 0336
14 * 025 = 0350
14 * 026 = 0364
14 * 027 = 0378
14 * 028 = 0392
14 * 029 = 0406
14 * 030 = 0420
Press ENTER to continue . . .

14 * 031 = 0434


C>
C>
```

ANALYSIS Listing 5.5 adds two additional variables: SCREEN-LINES to count the number of lines that have been displayed on the screen, and A-DUMMY, which is a dummy variable to be used with ACCEPT. The SCREEN-LINES variable is set to an initial value of 0 in PROGRAM-INITIALIZATION.

All the other changes are in the CALCULATE-AND-DISPLAY paragraph at line 005100. The first part of the paragraph is identical to Listing 5.4, mult03.cbl, up to line 005600. Note that the

5

line numbers have stayed the same for Listing 5.4 and 5.5 because of the extra blank lines in Listing 5.4. The blanks are there to keep the line numbers the same, but this is not a standard programming practice.

At line 005700, 1 is added to the variable. At line 005800, a test is made to determine whether SCREEN-LINES has reached 15 (that is, 15 lines have been displayed). When 15 lines have been displayed, the logic at lines 005900 through 006100 is executed. At line 005900, a message is displayed. At line 006000, A-DUMMY is accepted. Remember that you don't care what value is placed in A-DUMMY; you just want some method of waiting for the user to press Enter. At line 006100, the SCREEN-LINES variable is reset to 0.

If SCREEN-LINES were not reset to 0, it would continue counting up from 15 to 16, 17, and so on. It never again would equal 15, and the IF at line 005800 would never test true. The result would be that the screen would stop after the first 15 entries were displayed, but it wouldn't stop after the next 15.

Listing 5.5 has a minor bug (a logic error) in it. To see the result of the bug, do the following: Run mult04.cbl and enter any multiplication table that you want. For the number of entries, enter an even multiple of 15, such as 15, 30, or 45. After the program has displayed the number of entries, it asks you to press Enter to continue. When you press Enter, nothing else is displayed and the program ends. The Press ENTER message implies to the user that there is more to see when, in fact, there is not. Try following the logic and work out why this happens. You will deal with this bug later in today's lesson, but first you have a few more things to learn about the PERFORM verb.

What Is a Processing Loop?

A computer is designed to do things over and over, but if it does the same thing endlessly, the computer is limited to a single job. In practice, a processing loop is brought to an end by some condition. The condition is set up to be tested at the beginning of each pass through the processing loop or at the last step in the loop. The condition is used to determine whether the processing loop should end or continue. The processing loop is the logic that is performed over and over.

NEW TERM   You have just written a couple programs containing examples of a processing loop. A *processing loop* is one or more paragraphs that are executed over and over. Processing loops (which are almost always controlled by some condition and should be called *controlled processing loops*) are sometimes simply called *loops*.

NEW TERM   The condition that controls the processing loop usually is called the *processing loop control*, or simply the *loop control*.

Sometimes it is difficult to separate completely the processing loop from the control of the loop, and the two areas are referred to jointly as a loop or a processing loop. You should train yourself to spot the processing loop and the control of the processing loop.

Listing 5.6 is a portion of `mult02.cbl` from Listing 5.3.

TYPE | **Listing 5.6. A controlled processing loop.**

```
003800      PERFORM CALCULATE-AND-DISPLAY 12 TIMES.
003900
004000
004100 CALCULATE-AND-DISPLAY.
004200      ADD 1 TO THE-MULTIPLIER.
004300      COMPUTE THE-PRODUCT = THE-NUMBER * THE-MULTIPLIER.
004400      DISPLAY
004500          THE-NUMBER " * " THE-MULTIPLIER " = " THE-PRODUCT.
```

ANALYSIS The processing loop portion is the CALCULATE-AND-DISPLAY paragraph at lines 004100 through 004500. This paragraph is performed over and over.

The control for the processing loop is the PERFORM 12 TIMES statement at line 003800. The condition that controls or ends the loop occurs when the paragraph has been performed 12 times.

Listing 5.7 shows a portion of Listing 5.2, `mult01.cbl`.

TYPE | **Listing 5.7. Another control loop.**

```
003800      PERFORM CALCULATE-AND-DISPLAY.
003900
004000
004100 CALCULATE-AND-DISPLAY.
004200      ADD 1 TO THE-MULTIPLIER.
004300      COMPUTE THE-PRODUCT = THE-NUMBER * THE-MULTIPLIER.
004400      DISPLAY
004500          THE-NUMBER " * " THE-MULTIPLIER " = " THE-PRODUCT.
004600      IF THE-MULTIPLIER < 12
004700          GO TO CALCULATE-AND-DISPLAY.
```

ANALYSIS In this example, the processing loop is also the CALCULATE-AND-DISPLAY paragraph. The control for the loop is at lines 004600 and 004700. The loop ends when THE-MULTIPLIER is no longer less than 12.

A controlled processing loop is one of the key elements of every working program. Remember that one of the main functions of a computer is to perform repetitive tasks. Unless you want the computer to perform the same task forever, you must use some condition to stop the repetition. This is where the control loop comes in.

The control loop is such a key part of any computer program that every programming language includes some specialized verb or statement that can be used to create a controlled processing loop. COBOL is no exception.

Using PERFORM to Control a Processing Loop

The PERFORM verb has some other formats that allow control over a loop. The first of these formats, as you have seen, is using the PERFORM verb with a number of TIMES. The next is PERFORM UNTIL. Use this syntax:

```
PERFORM a paragraph
    UNTIL a condition.
```

The following is an example:

```
PERFORM CALCULATE-AND-DISPLAY
    UNTIL THE-MULTIPLIER > 12.
```

The PERFORM UNTIL sentence is a repetitive request to perform a paragraph, with a built-in IF test in the UNTIL. The PERFORM verb is requested over and over until the condition tests true.

Listing 5.8 illustrates a PERFORM UNTIL.

TYPE **Listing 5.8. Using PERFORM UNTIL.**

```
003800      PERFORM CALCULATE-AND-DISPLAY
003900          UNTIL THE-MULTIPLIER > 12.
004000
004100 CALCULATE-AND-DISPLAY.
004200      ADD 1 TO THE-MULTIPLIER.
004300      COMPUTE THE-PRODUCT = THE-NUMBER * THE-MULTIPLIER.
004400      DISPLAY
004500          THE-NUMBER " * " THE-MULTIPLIER " = " THE-PRODUCT.
```

ANALYSIS At lines 003800 and 003900, the paragraph CALCULATE-AND-DISPLAY is performed repetitively. This repetition stops when THE-MULTIPLIER is greater than 12 (as specified in line 003900). PERFORM UNTIL is one long sentence with the period at the end of line 003900. There is a bug in this example that we will be fixing before the end of the chapter.

A PERFORM UNTIL sentence tests the condition before the perform is executed. COBOL does not allow you to go to a line number, but if it did, a PERFORM UNTIL sentence could be thought of as executing the following logic, which is not proper COBOL code:

```
003800      IF THE-MULTIPLIER > 12 GO TO line 004100.
003900          PERFORM CALCULATE-AND-DISPLAY
004000              GO TO line 003800.
004100* PROGRAM continues here
```

Previous examples started by setting THE-MULTIPLIER to 0. The CALCULATE-AND-DISPLAY paragraph always began by adding 1 to the multiplier, as in Listing 5.8.

If you follow the path of the logic in Listing 5.8, starting at the top of CALCULATE-AND-DISPLAY when THE-MULTIPLIER equals 11, you'll notice an error in the logic (a bug). The paragraph adds 1 to THE-MULTIPLIER, making it 12, and displays the results for 12. The program then returns to line 003900, falls through to line 004000, where it jumps back up to line 003800, and checks the condition again. THE-MULTIPLIER equals 12 (so it is not greater than 12), however, and the paragraph CALCULATE-AND-DISPLAY is performed one more time. The first action in CALCULATE-AND-DISPLAY is to add 1 to THE-MULTIPLIER, so the results will be displayed when THE-MULTIPLIER equals 13.

The quickest fix for this is to change the test at line 003900 to test for greater than 11, but it looks a little confusing when you are reading the code. It takes a moment to realize that the loop executes 12 times, because you have to look back through the code to establish that THE-MULTIPLIER originally was set to 0:

```
003800        PERFORM CALCULATE-AND-DISPLAY
003900            UNTIL THE-MULTIPLIER > 11.
```

A solution that works just as well is illustrated in Listing 5.9. This has the advantage of keeping all the key pieces of the loop together in one section of the code.

TYPE **Listing 5.9. Structured loop control.**

```
003700        MOVE 1 TO THE-MULTIPLIER.
003800        PERFORM CALCULATE-AND-DISPLAY
003900            UNTIL THE-MULTIPLIER > 12.
004000
004100 CALCULATE-AND-DISPLAY.
004200        COMPUTE THE-PRODUCT = THE-NUMBER * THE-MULTIPLIER.
004300        DISPLAY
004400            THE-NUMBER " * " THE-MULTIPLIER " = " THE-PRODUCT.
004500        ADD 1 TO THE-MULTIPLIER.
```

ANALYSIS The variable THE-MULTIPLIER first is set to a value of 1. The paragraph CALCULATE-AND-DISPLAY is performed until THE-MULTIPLIER is greater than 12. Because THE-MULTIPLIER starts with an initially correct value of 1, the ADD 1 TO THE-MULTIPLIER logic is moved to the end of CALCULATE-AND-DISPLAY.

It is much quicker to figure out that the loop is performed with THE-MULTIPLIER ranging in value from 1 through 12.

Listing 5.9 also illustrates a very common method of constructing and controlling a processing loop. These are the three steps of this construction:

1. Set up a variable with the value that it must have when the loop is entered for the first time. This variable is called the loop control variable. In this case, THE-MULTIPLIER must start off with a value of 1 at line 003700.

2. Request a PERFORM of the loop until the variable is out of range—in this case, PERFORM CALCULATE-AND-DISPLAY (at line 003800) UNTIL THE-MULTIPLIER > 12 (at line 003900).

3. In the loop, do whatever processing is called for. At the end of the loop or after each pass through the loop, increment the loop control variable. In this case, the loop control variable is increased by 1 at line 004500.

Look again at Listing 5.9 for these three steps. Based on the first step, the value in THE-MULTIPLIER must be set to 1. This is the first value that THE-MULTIPLIER must have on entry to the loop (CALCULATE-AND-DISPLAY). This is taken care of at line 003700.

In the second step, CALCULATE-AND-DISPLAY is performed until the MULTIPLIER is greater than 12, at lines 003800 and 003900.

In the final step, the variable that controls the loop, THE-MULTIPLIER, is modified as the last step in the loop. The ADD 1 logic is moved and now occurs at the end of CALCULATE-AND-DISPLAY at line 004500. The requested paragraph is performed over and over until the condition tests true.

Using PERFORM VARYING UNTIL

The three steps of process loop control are so common in programs that the PERFORM verb has been extended even further, to allow the first and last steps to be incorporated directly into the PERFORM verb:

```
PERFORM a paragraph
VARYING a variable
FROM a value BY a value
UNTIL a condition.
```

The following is an example:

```
PERFORM CALCULATE-AND-DISPLAY
VARYING THE-MULTIPLIER
FROM 1 BY 1
UNTIL THE-MULTIPLIER > 12.
```

This is an extension of PERFORM UNTIL.

Compare the partial programs in Listings 5.10 and 5.11. They produce the same results using different versions of the PERFORM verb. (I've inserted the blank line in Listing 5.10 in the middle of the PERFORM UNTIL logic to keep the line numbers the same in the two listings. Remember that the blank line means nothing; even if it appears in the middle of a sentence, it is ignored.)

TYPE **Listing 5.10. Using PERFORM UNTIL in a loop.**

```
003700        MOVE 1 TO THE-MULTIPLIER.
003800        PERFORM CALCULATE-AND-DISPLAY
003900
004000            UNTIL THE-MULTIPLIER > 12.
004100
004200 CALCULATE-AND-DISPLAY.
004300        COMPUTE THE-PRODUCT = THE-NUMBER * THE-MULTIPLIER.
004400        DISPLAY
004500            THE-NUMBER " * " THE-MULTIPLIER " = " THE-PRODUCT.
004600        ADD 1 TO THE-MULTIPLIER.
```

TYPE **Listing 5.11. Using PERFORM VARYING UNTIL.**

```
003700
003800        PERFORM CALCULATE-AND-DISPLAY
003900          VARYING THE-MULTIPLIER FROM 1 BY 1
004000            UNTIL THE-MULTIPLIER > 12.
004100
004200 CALCULATE-AND-DISPLAY.
004300        COMPUTE THE-PRODUCT = THE-NUMBER * THE-MULTIPLIER.
004400        DISPLAY
004500            THE-NUMBER " * " THE-MULTIPLIER " = " THE-PRODUCT.
004600
```

ANALYSIS In Listing 5.10, initializing THE-MULTIPLIER at line 003700 and adding 1 to THE-MULTIPLIER at line 004600 have been replaced by a single line at 003900 in Listing 5.11.

A PERFORM VARYING UNTIL can be broken down into the following steps (again assuming that COBOL allows you to go to a line number, which it doesn't):

```
003700        MOVE 1 TO THE-MULTIPLIER.
003800        IF THE-MULTIPLIER > 12 GO TO line 004200.
003900        PERFORM CALCULATE-AND-DISPLAY.
004000        ADD 1 TO THE-MULTIPLIER.
004100        GO TO line 003800.
004200* Program continues here
```

Listing 5.12 shows the multiplication tables program again, using PERFORM VARYING UNTIL to control the processing loop.

TYPE   **Listing 5.12. Using** PERFORM VARYING UNTIL.

```
000100 IDENTIFICATION DIVISION.
000200 PROGRAM-ID. MULT05.
000300*--------------------------------------------------
000400* This program asks the user for a number for a
000500* multiplication table, and a table size and then
000600* displays a table for that number times the values
000700* 1 through HOW-MANY using PERFORM VARYING UNTIL.
000800*--------------------------------------------------
000900 ENVIRONMENT DIVISION.
001000 DATA DIVISION.
001100 WORKING-STORAGE SECTION.
001200
001300 01  THE-NUMBER      PIC 99.
001400 01  THE-MULTIPLIER  PIC 999.
001500 01  THE-PRODUCT     PIC 9999.
001600 01  HOW-MANY        PIC 99.
001700
001800 PROCEDURE DIVISION.
001900* LEVEL 1 ROUTINES
002000 PROGRAM-BEGIN.
002100     PERFORM PROGRAM-INITIALIZATION.
002200     PERFORM GET-TABLE-DATA.
002300     PERFORM DISPLAY-THE-TABLE.
002400
002500 PROGRAM-DONE.
002600     STOP RUN.
002700
002800* LEVEL 2 ROUTINES
002900 PROGRAM-INITIALIZATION.
003000*    MOVE 0 TO THE-MULTIPLIER.
003100* is no longer needed
003200
003300 GET-TABLE-DATA.
003400     DISPLAY
003500     "Which multiplication table(01-99)?".
003600     ACCEPT THE-NUMBER.
003700
003800     DISPLAY "How many entries would you like (01-99)?".
003900     ACCEPT HOW-MANY.
004000
004100 DISPLAY-THE-TABLE.
004200     DISPLAY "The " THE-NUMBER "'s table is:".
004300     PERFORM CALCULATE-AND-DISPLAY
004400         VARYING THE-MULTIPLIER
004500             FROM 1 BY 1
004600             UNTIL THE-MULTIPLIER > HOW-MANY.
004700
004800* LEVEL 3 ROUTINES.
004900 CALCULATE-AND-DISPLAY.
005000
005100     COMPUTE THE-PRODUCT = THE-NUMBER * THE-MULTIPLIER.
005200     DISPLAY
005300         THE-NUMBER " * " THE-MULTIPLIER " = " THE-PRODUCT.
005400
```

5

Solving the Press ENTER Problem

Remember the bug in Listing 5.5, mult04.cbl? It displays a Press ENTER message, even when there is nothing else to display. Now we're going to solve this problem; you'll find the solution in mult05.cbl. The processing loop from mult05.cbl is shown in Listing 5.13.

TYPE   **Listing 5.13. The processing loop from mult05.cbl.**

```
004900 CALCULATE-AND-DISPLAY.
005000
005100     COMPUTE THE-PRODUCT = THE-NUMBER * THE-MULTIPLIER.
005200     DISPLAY
005300         THE-NUMBER " * " THE-MULTIPLIER " = " THE-PRODUCT.
005400
```

The two important points in any processing loop are the top of the loop and the bottom of the loop. These might seem obvious at first glance, but you must understand two things about these points. If the processing loop is constructed correctly, you know at the top of the loop that the rest of the loop is going to be executed. At the bottom of the loop, you know that the loop has been executed. Now you can try to use these two points in the loop to solve the Press ENTER problem.

There really are two problems. One is to count the number of lines that have been displayed, which is fairly simple to do. The other is to display a Press ENTER message (and wait for the user) when only 15 lines have been displayed and there is more data to display.

The obvious place to count the lines is at the end of the loop where it is obvious that one line has been displayed (the loop has been executed). Listing 5.14 adds the instruction to count the lines at line 5400.

TYPE   **Listing 5.14. Counting the lines.**

```
004900 CALCULATE-AND-DISPLAY.
005000
005100     COMPUTE THE-PRODUCT = THE-NUMBER * THE-MULTIPLIER.
005200     DISPLAY
005300         THE-NUMBER " * " THE-MULTIPLIER " = " THE-PRODUCT.
005400     ADD 1 TO SCREEN-LINES.
```

The second problem (displaying a Press ENTER message at the correct point) seems to fit at the top of the loop. There you know that a line is about to be displayed. If you make the program stop the user at this point and the user presses Enter, you can be certain that at least one more line will be displayed. Listing 5.15 is a complete listing, using a test for SCREEN-LINES at the top of the loop and adding to SCREEN-LINES at the bottom of the loop. Code, compile, and run this listing; try any number of entries, including multiples of 15. You will see that the minor bug in mult04.cbl has been eliminated.

TYPE **Listing 5.15. Eliminating the Press ENTER bug.**

```
000100 IDENTIFICATION DIVISION.
000200 PROGRAM-ID. MULT06.
000300*--------------------------------------------------------
000400* This program asks the user for a number for a
000500* multiplication table, and a table size
000600* and then displays a table for that number
000700* times the values 1 through HOW-MANY.
000800*
000900* The display is paused after each 15 lines.
001000*--------------------------------------------------------
001100 ENVIRONMENT DIVISION.
001200 DATA DIVISION.
001300 WORKING-STORAGE SECTION.
001400
001500 01  THE-NUMBER        PIC 99.
001600 01  THE-MULTIPLIER     PIC 999.
001700 01  THE-PRODUCT        PIC 9999.
001800 01  HOW-MANY           PIC 99.
001900 01  SCREEN-LINES       PIC 99.
002000
002100 01  A-DUMMY            PIC X.
002200
002300 PROCEDURE DIVISION.
002400* LEVEL 1 ROUTINES
002500 PROGRAM-BEGIN.
002600     PERFORM PROGRAM-INITIALIZATION.
002700     PERFORM GET-TABLE-DATA.
002800     PERFORM DISPLAY-THE-TABLE.
002900
003000 PROGRAM-DONE.
003100     STOP RUN.
003200
003300* LEVEL 2 ROUTINES
003400 PROGRAM-INITIALIZATION.
003500
003600     MOVE 0 TO SCREEN-LINES.
003700
003800 GET-TABLE-DATA.
003900     DISPLAY
004000     "Which multiplication table(01-99)?".
004100     ACCEPT THE-NUMBER.
004200
004300     DISPLAY "How many entries would you like (01-99)?".
004400     ACCEPT HOW-MANY.
004500
004600 DISPLAY-THE-TABLE.
004700     DISPLAY "The " THE-NUMBER "'s table is:".
004800     PERFORM CALCULATE-AND-DISPLAY
004900         VARYING THE-MULTIPLIER
005000             FROM 1 BY 1
005100             UNTIL THE-MULTIPLIER > HOW-MANY.
005200
005300* LEVEL 3 ROUTINES.
005400 CALCULATE-AND-DISPLAY.
```

continues

5

Listing 5.15. continued

```
005500
005600        IF SCREEN-LINES = 15
005700            DISPLAY "Press ENTER to continue . . ."
005800            ACCEPT A-DUMMY
005900            MOVE 0 TO SCREEN-LINES.
006000
006100        COMPUTE THE-PRODUCT = THE-NUMBER * THE-MULTIPLIER.
006200        DISPLAY
006300            THE-NUMBER " * " THE-MULTIPLIER " = " THE-PRODUCT.
006400
006500        ADD 1 TO SCREEN-LINES.
006600
```

You now have seen several ways of avoiding a GO TO. You can use PERFORM to control a processing loop in different ways, and it should be possible to set up the control in such a way that GO TO can be avoided.

Do	Don't

DO understand GO TO so that you know what it is doing when you see it in a program.

DON'T use a GO TO in a program that you write.

DO use PERFORM, PERFORM UNTIL, PERFORM VARYING, and PERFORM nn TIMES to control loops. If a problem seems to require GO TO to solve it, it can be solved better using one of the versions of PERFORM.

Summary

Today, you learned how to use PERFORM, GO TO, and IF to control programs. The following are the basic truths about those three statements:

☐ A GO TO verb can be used to make the program jump to the beginning of another paragraph or back to the beginning of the current paragraph.

☐ Using a GO TO verb to jump out of one paragraph to the start of another paragraph is bad programming practice. Don't do it.

☐ The PERFORM verb can be used to perform a paragraph a number of times. The number of times can be a constant, as in this example:

```
PERFORM DO-SOMETHING 10 TIMES
```

The number of times can also be a variable, as in this example:

```
PERFORM DO-SOMETHING THE-NUMBER TIMES
```

☐ A processing loop is one paragraph (or more) performed over and over in a program.

☐ A processing loop must be controlled by some condition that will cause the loop to stop, or the loop will go on forever.

☐ Controlled processing loops in COBOL can be executed by using the following three variations of the PERFORM verb:

```
PERFORM a paragraph number TIMES.

PERFORM a paragraph
     UNTIL condition.

PERFORM a paragraph
     VARYING a variable
          FROM starting value BY increment value
          UNTIL condition.
```

☐ The key steps in setting up a loop are as follows:

1. Initialize a value for the first pass through the loop.

2. Perform the processing loop until a condition is met.

3. Increment the control variable at the end of the loop or after each pass through the loop.

☐ The top of the loop can be used to insert code that will be executed only if the loop will be executed.

☐ The bottom of the loop can be used to insert code that will be executed each time the loop is completed.

Q&A

Q Can I perform something zero times?

A Yes, you should be able to. I have tested several COBOL compilers, and they all allow this—in effect not performing at all. If the user enters 00 for HOW-MANY in mult02.cbl, the result is the following:

```
Which multiplication table(01-99)?
15
How many entries would you like (01-99)?
00
The 15's table is:


C>
C>
```

Q Why is THE-MULTIPLIER defined as a PIC 999 in all the sample programs when a PIC 99 should be large enough for a value from 1 to 99?

A The answer lies in the extremes. In most of the examples, CALCULATE-AND-DISPLAY is performed until THE-MULTIPLIER is greater than HOW-MANY. This test is performed in various ways in the examples but is essentially the same test.

If the user enters 99 for HOW-MANY, an interesting problem shows up when THE-MULTIPLIER is defined as a PIC 99. On each pass through CALCULATE-AND-DISPLAY, 1 is added to THE-MULTIPLIER. What happens when THE-MULTIPLIER equals 99 and you add 1 to it? THE-MULTIPLIER should go to 100, but a PIC 99 is too small to hold that value. The 100 is truncated on the left to 00, and THE-MULTIPLIER can never reach a value where it is greater than HOW-MANY if HOW-MANY equals 99. Adding the extra digit to the picture of THE-MULTIPLIER allows it to go to 100 as a value.

Whenever you write a program, it is practically mandatory that you test it at the extremes of the data. If the user is allowed to enter 00 through 99, what happens if the user enters 99? What happens if the user enters 0?

Workshop

Quiz

1. How many times will DISPLAY-HELLO be performed in the following example?

```
003600      PERFORM DISPLAY-HELLO 10 TIMES.
003700
003800 DISPLAY-HELLO.
003900      DISPLAY "hello".
004000
```

2. If THE-COUNT is defined as a numeric variable, how many times will DISPLAY-HELLO be performed in the following example?

```
003600      PERFORM DISPLAY-HELLO
003700          VARYING THE-COUNT FROM 1 BY 1
003800          UNTIL THE-COUNT > 5.
003900
004000 DISPLAY-HELLO.
004100      DISPLAY "hello".
004200
```

3. In each of the previous examples, which lines contain the processing loop and which lines contain the control for the processing loop?

Exercise

Code two different ways to perform a paragraph named A-PARAGRAPH eight times.

Day **6**

Using Data and COBOL Operators

One truth about COBOL is that you will never learn everything about the data used by a program and the DATA DIVISION. Each day's lesson gives you enough of a grasp of the DATA DIVISION that you can work comfortably with data. Today, you dive back into the DATA DIVISION and learn about the following topics:

- ☐ Initializing variables
- ☐ SPACES and ZEROES
- ☐ Experimenting with truncated variables
- ☐ Multiple moves
- ☐ Decimal data
- ☐ Positive and negative numbers
- ☐ Displaying decimals and signs
- ☐ Suppressing leading zeroes
- ☐ Adding commas
- ☐ COBOL numeric operators

Initializing Variables

When you define a variable in WORKING-STORAGE, you also can assign it an initial value. This is a convenient method of setting variables to start with a known value.

Variables are initialized with a VALUE IS clause, as shown in lines 000900 and 001000 of Listing 6.1. Note that the period closing the variable definition is at the end of the initializer, so the sequence is the level number, the variable name, PICTURE IS (or PIC), the picture, VALUE IS, the initializer, and finally the period.

TYPE **Listing 6.1. Initializing a variable in WORKING-STORAGE.**

```
000100 IDENTIFICATION DIVISION.
000200 PROGRAM-ID. JACK04.
000300 ENVIRONMENT DIVISION.
000400 DATA DIVISION.
000500
000600 WORKING-STORAGE SECTION.
000700
000800 01  THE-MESSAGE      PIC X(50).
000900 01  THE-NUMBER       PIC 9(2) VALUE IS 1.
001000 01  A-SPACE          PIC X    VALUE IS " ".
001100
001200 PROCEDURE DIVISION.
001300 PROGRAM-BEGIN.
001400
001500* Set up and display line 1
001600     MOVE "Jack be nimble," TO THE-MESSAGE.
001700     DISPLAY
001800         THE-NUMBER
001900         A-SPACE
002000         THE-MESSAGE.
002100
002200* Set up and Display line 2
002300     ADD 1 TO THE-NUMBER.
002400     MOVE "Jack be quick," TO THE-MESSAGE.
002500     DISPLAY
002600         THE-NUMBER
002700         A-SPACE
002800         THE-MESSAGE.
002900
003000* Set up and display line 3
003100     ADD 1 TO THE-NUMBER.
003200     MOVE "Jack jump over the candlestick." TO THE-MESSAGE.
003300     DISPLAY
003400         THE-NUMBER
003500         A-SPACE
003600         THE-MESSAGE.
003700
003800 PROGRAM-DONE.
003900     STOP RUN.
004000
004100
```

The word IS in a value clause is optional; the initialization could be written as the following:

```
01   THE-NUMBER           PIC 9(2) VALUE 1.
```

Compare Listing 6.1 to Listing 2.10 in Day 2, "Using Variables and Constants." Notice that using the initializers in WORKING-STORAGE has eliminated the need for two of the MOVE statements, at lines 001600 and 001900, in the PROCEDURE DIVISION.

If you want a variable to have a default value that will be used in the program, you must initialize it in WORKING-STORAGE. A variable that is not initialized has an undefined value until something is moved to it.

NEW TERM   An *undefined value* is one that can contain any value.

For numeric variables, this can become a problem. If you attempt to use the DISPLAY (ADD 1) statement with a numeric variable that contains an undefined value, you probably will produce an error. This does not cause a compiler error, but usually causes an error while the program is running. The program usually aborts with a message such as this:

```
ATTEMPT TO PERFORM ARITHMETIC WITH NON-NUMERIC DATA
```

or

```
VARIABLE THE-NUMBER DOES NOT CONTAIN NUMERIC DATA
```

Initializing a variable in WORKING-STORAGE has the same effect as a MOVE to the variable. If the initializing value is shorter than the PICTURE of an alphanumeric field, the field is padded on the right with spaces. If the initializing value is too small for a numeric variable, the variable is padded on the left with zeroes.

Listing 6.2, jack05.cbl, takes initialization one step further by initializing all the variables ready to print the first line of the poem.

TYPE   **Listing 6.2. Short initializers.**

```
000100 IDENTIFICATION DIVISION.
000200 PROGRAM-ID. JACK05.
000300 ENVIRONMENT DIVISION.
000400 DATA DIVISION.
000500
000600 WORKING-STORAGE SECTION.
000700
000800 01   THE-MESSAGE      PIC X(50)
000900      VALUE "Jack be nimble,".
001000
001100 01   THE-NUMBER       PIC 9(2) VALUE IS 1.
001200 01   A-SPACE          PIC X    VALUE IS " ".
001300
```

6

continues

Listing 6.2. continued

```
001400 PROCEDURE DIVISION.
001500 PROGRAM-BEGIN.
001600
001700* Line 1 is set up, so just display it
001800     DISPLAY
001900         THE-NUMBER
002000         A-SPACE
002100         THE-MESSAGE.
002200
002300* Set up and Display line 2
002400     ADD 1 TO THE-NUMBER.
002500     MOVE "Jack be quick," TO THE-MESSAGE.
002600     DISPLAY
002700         THE-NUMBER
002800         A-SPACE
002900         THE-MESSAGE.
003000
003100* Set up and display line 3
003200     ADD 1 TO THE-NUMBER.
003300     MOVE "Jack jump over the candlestick." TO THE-MESSAGE.
003400     DISPLAY
003500         THE-NUMBER
003600         A-SPACE
003700         THE-MESSAGE.
003800
003900 PROGRAM-DONE.
004000     STOP RUN.
004100
```

The output from all three versions of JACK is identical.

OUTPUT

```
C>

01 Jack be nimble,
02 Jack be quick,
03 Jack jump over the candlestick.

C>
```

ANALYSIS The definition for the variable, THE-MESSAGE, is at lines 000800 and 000900. The definition is broken up into two lines. The 01 level starts in Area A, but only the level number of the variable is required to start in Area A. The remainder of the definition (the variable name, picture, and value) falls within Area B (columns 12 through 72).

The initializer for THE-MESSAGE—in this case, "Jack be nimble"—is clearly too short for the PICTURE, and the remainder of THE-MESSAGE is filled with spaces by the compiler when it encounters the VALUE clause. Similarly, THE-NUMBER is initialized with a 1, and the compiler fills the variable space with 01 when it encounters the VALUE IS clause.

6

Note that initializing a variable with a VALUE in WORKING-STORAGE is the same as using MOVE to give it a value. Thereafter, you can use MOVE to assign values to the variable later in the program. THE-MESSAGE, initialized at lines 000800 and 000900, is modified by a MOVE at line 002500 and again later at line 003300.

SPACES **and** ZEROES

Variables that are not initialized contain undefined values until a MOVE moves something to them. It is a good practice to initialize variables in WORKING-STORAGE. The usual practice is to initialize numeric variables to zero and alphanumeric variables to spaces. COBOL has provided reserved words for this, primarily to make clearer what is happening.

Both of the following initializations do the job. Remember that an initializer works like a MOVE, padding the remainder of the variable with spaces or zeroes. Therefore, moving a single space to an alphanumeric variable is the same as filling it with spaces, as you see here:

```
01   THE-MESSAGE      PIC X(50) VALUE " ".
01   THE-NUMBER       PIC 9(4)  VALUE 0.
```

Instead of a quoted space (which isn't clear), or a 0 (zero) that can be confused with the letter O, COBOL has reserved the words SPACE, SPACES, ZERO, ZEROS, and ZEROES to represent these values. This initialization is clearer:

```
01   THE-MESSAGE      PIC X(50) VALUE SPACES.
01   THE-NUMBER       PIC 9(4)  VALUE ZEROES.
```

SPACE and SPACES both mean "fill with spaces." ZERO, ZEROS, and ZEROES all mean "fill with zeroes." The singular and plural versions produce the identical effect. SPACE is the same as SPACES, and ZERO is the same as ZEROS and ZEROES.

SPACES and ZEROES also can be used in MOVE commands, like this:

```
MOVE SPACES TO THE-MESSAGE.
MOVE ZERO TO THE-NUMBER.
```

Do	Don't

DO initialize variables in the DATA DIVISION when they are defined, or in the PROCEDURE DIVISION before they are used.

DON'T perform any arithmetic functions on an uninitialized numeric variable.

6

Truncated Values

A *truncated value* occurs when a value that is too large for a numeric variable is moved to the numeric variable, or when a value that is too long for an alphanumeric variable is moved to the alphanumeric variable.

The compiler conveniently fills variables with blanks or zeroes when short or small values are moved to them, or when short or small values are used to initialize them. What happens when a value that is too large or too long is moved to a variable or is used to initialize a variable?

The short answer is that you lose some data. What you lose depends on the type of variable that is the target of the MOVE. An alphanumeric variable truncates the right end of the value until the value fits in the variable. A numeric variable truncates the left end of the value until the value fits. (There is an exception to this for decimal values, which you will learn about in "Decimal Data," later in this chapter.)

Listing 6.3 illustrates the effect of truncation on variables. It moves a message to successively smaller alphanumeric variables, and a numeric value to successively smaller numeric variables. All the resulting values are displayed.

TYPE   **Listing 6.3. Truncating variables.**

```
000100 IDENTIFICATION DIVISION.
000200 PROGRAM-ID. TRUNC01.
000300 ENVIRONMENT DIVISION.
000400 DATA DIVISION.
000500 WORKING-STORAGE SECTION.
000600
000700 01  6-BYTES      PIC X(6).
000800 01  5-BYTES      PIC X(5).
000900 01  4-BYTES      PIC X(4).
001000 01  3-BYTES      PIC X(3).
001100 01  2-BYTES      PIC X(2).
001200 01  1-BYTE       PIC X(1).
001300
001400 01  5-DIGITS     PIC 9(5).
001500 01  4-DIGITS     PIC 9(4).
001600 01  3-DIGITS     PIC 9(3).
001700 01  2-DIGITS     PIC 9(2).
001800 01  1-DIGIT      PIC 9(1).
001900
002000 PROCEDURE DIVISION.
002100 PROGRAM-BEGIN.
002200
002300     MOVE "Hello" TO 6-BYTES.
002400     MOVE "Hello" TO 5-BYTES.
002500     MOVE "Hello" TO 4-BYTES.
002600     MOVE "Hello" TO 3-BYTES.
002700     MOVE "Hello" TO 2-BYTES.
002800     MOVE "Hello" TO 1-BYTE.
002900
```

```
003000        MOVE 2397 TO 5-DIGITS.
003100        MOVE 2397 TO 4-DIGITS.
003200        MOVE 2397 TO 3-DIGITS.
003300        MOVE 2397 TO 2-DIGITS.
003400        MOVE 2397 TO 1-DIGIT.
003500
003600        DISPLAY 6-BYTES.
003700        DISPLAY 5-BYTES.
003800        DISPLAY 4-BYTES.
003900        DISPLAY 3-BYTES.
004000        DISPLAY 2-BYTES.
004100        DISPLAY 1-BYTE.
004200
004300        DISPLAY 5-DIGITS.
004400        DISPLAY 4-DIGITS.
004500        DISPLAY 3-DIGITS.
004600        DISPLAY 2-DIGITS.
004700        DISPLAY 1-DIGIT.
004800
004900
005000 PROGRAM-DONE.
005100        STOP RUN.
005200
```

The output of trunc01.cbl shows characters being lopped off the right side of Hello and digits being lopped off the left side of 2397:

```
Hello
Hello
Hell
Hel
He
H
02397
2397
397
97
7


C>
C>
```

You might find when you compile trunc01.cbl that the compiler will return warnings about truncation. Many compilers will provide warnings on the numeric moves to 3-DIGITS, 2-DIGITS, and 1-DIGIT. This usually is something like the following:

```
HIGH ORDER DIGIT TRUNCATION MAY OCCUR IN MOVE AT LINE 003200
```

A few compilers give warnings on the alphanumeric truncation in the moves to 4-BYTES, 3-BYTES, 2-BYTES, and 1-BYTE:

```
VALUE MAY BE TRUNCATED IN MOVE AT LINE 002500
```

6

It is more common to warn about numeric truncation because it usually has more serious effects on the outcome of a program. Numeric values in a program are usually used somewhere in a calculation, and a truncation can produce errors that are not easily visible.

Listing 6.4, trunc02.cbl, demonstrates the truncation of values by initializing the variables with values that are too large or too long. You might find that trunc02.cbl will not even compile with your compiler. Truncation in initializers in WORKING-STORAGE is treated more severely than a truncation in a MOVE statement, and this listing might produce one or more errors and fail to compile. This program will not compile with the Microfocus Personal COBOL compiler and generates the error "VALUE literal too large. Literal truncated." for lines 000900 through 001200. It also generates the error "VALUE too long for data item or has too many decimal positions." for lines 001600 through 001800. The ACUCOBOL compiler provides the more general error "VALUE size error" for the same lines.

TYPE **Listing 6.4. Truncation in initializers.**

```
000100 IDENTIFICATION DIVISION.
000200 PROGRAM-ID. TRUNC02.
000300 ENVIRONMENT DIVISION.
000400 DATA DIVISION.
000500 WORKING-STORAGE SECTION.
000600
000700 01  6-BYTES      PIC X(6) VALUE "Hello".
000800 01  5-BYTES      PIC X(5) VALUE "Hello".
000900 01  4-BYTES      PIC X(4) VALUE "Hello".
001000 01  3-BYTES      PIC X(3) VALUE "Hello".
001100 01  2-BYTES      PIC X(2) VALUE "Hello".
001200 01  1-BYTE       PIC X(1) VALUE "Hello".
001300
001400 01  5-DIGITS     PIC 9(5) VALUE 2397.
001500 01  4-DIGITS     PIC 9(4) VALUE 2397.
001600 01  3-DIGITS     PIC 9(3) VALUE 2397.
001700 01  2-DIGITS     PIC 9(2) VALUE 2397.
001800 01  1-DIGIT      PIC 9(1) VALUE 2397.
001900
002000 PROCEDURE DIVISION.
002100 PROGRAM-BEGIN.
002200
002300
002400     DISPLAY 6-BYTES.
002500     DISPLAY 5-BYTES.
002600     DISPLAY 4-BYTES.
002700     DISPLAY 3-BYTES.
002800     DISPLAY 2-BYTES.
002900     DISPLAY 1-BYTE.
003000
003100     DISPLAY 5-DIGITS.
003200     DISPLAY 4-DIGITS.
003300     DISPLAY 3-DIGITS.
003400     DISPLAY 2-DIGITS.
003500     DISPLAY 1-DIGIT.
```

```
003600
003700
003800 PROGRAM-DONE.
003900     STOP RUN.
004000
```

If `trunc02.cbl` does compile, its output is the same as the output of `trunc01.cbl`.

Multiple MOVE Statements

A MOVE verb can be used to move the same value to multiple targets. Here is the syntax:

```
MOVE source TO destination destination destination . . . .
```

Listing 6.5, `trunc03.cbl`, uses multiple moves to achieve the same result as `trunc01.cbl`. (Listing 6.5 only illustrates the convenience of using a multiple MOVE. It isn't a useful program.)

TYPE **Listing 6.5. Using multiple MOVE statements.**

```
000100 IDENTIFICATION DIVISION.
000200 PROGRAM-ID. TRUNC03.
000300 ENVIRONMENT DIVISION.
000400 DATA DIVISION.
000500 WORKING-STORAGE SECTION.
000600
000700 01  6-BYTES     PIC X(6).
000800 01  5-BYTES     PIC X(5).
000900 01  4-BYTES     PIC X(4).
001000 01  3-BYTES     PIC X(3).
001100 01  2-BYTES     PIC X(2).
001200 01  1-BYTE      PIC X(1).
001300
001400 01  5-DIGITS    PIC 9(5).
001500 01  4-DIGITS    PIC 9(4).
001600 01  3-DIGITS    PIC 9(3).
001700 01  2-DIGITS    PIC 9(2).
001800 01  1-DIGIT     PIC 9(1).
001900
002000 PROCEDURE DIVISION.
002100 PROGRAM-BEGIN.
002200
002300     MOVE "Hello" TO 6-BYTES 5-BYTES
002400                     4-BYTES 3-BYTES
002500                     2-BYTES 1-BYTE.
002600
002700     MOVE 2397 TO 5-DIGITS
002800                  4-DIGITS
002900                  3-DIGITS
```

continues

Listing 6.5. continued

```
003000                    2-DIGITS
003100                    1-DIGIT.
003200
003300    DISPLAY 6-BYTES.
003400    DISPLAY 5-BYTES.
003500    DISPLAY 4-BYTES.
003600    DISPLAY 3-BYTES.
003700    DISPLAY 2-BYTES.
003800    DISPLAY 1-BYTE.
003900
004000    DISPLAY 5-DIGITS.
004100    DISPLAY 4-DIGITS.
004200    DISPLAY 3-DIGITS.
004300    DISPLAY 2-DIGITS.
004400    DISPLAY 1-DIGIT.
004500
004600
004700 PROGRAM-DONE.
004800    STOP RUN.
004900
```

Decimal Data

So far, all the numbers you've worked with have been positive whole numbers (integers), but COBOL is a business language, which should be able to deal with decimal numbers, dollars and cents, and percentages.

In order to put a decimal point in a number, you must put a decimal point in the PICTURE of a variable. The character in a numeric PICTURE that represents a decimal point is an uppercase V.

The following variable holds values ranging from 000.00 to 999.99.

```
01   THE-VALUE        PIC 999V99.
```

Any constant values that you move to a decimal variable or use to initialize a decimal variable are written in conventional format, as in these examples:

```
01   THE-VALUE        PIC 999V99 VALUE 19.24.
01   THE-VALUE        PIC 999V99 VALUE ZERO.
MOVE 26.15 TO THE-VALUE.
```

If you attempt to move a value containing too many decimals, the number is truncated on the right, and some of the decimal information will be lost. In this example, THE-VALUE ends up containing 467.23:

```
MOVE 467.237 TO THE-VALUE.
```

Truncation still takes place from the high end as well. In this example, THE-VALUE ends up containing 923.46 because the number is truncated on both the left and the right:

```
MOVE 6923.468 TO THE-VALUE.
```

WARNING

I have stressed truncation in numbers because of the effect it can have on calculations. It is important to plan the size of numeric variables so that they are large enough to hold the largest possible values that may occur during the program.

Positive and Negative Numbers

COBOL numbers can also contain a positive or negative sign. The PICTURE character for a sign is an initial S. The S must be the first character in the picture.

The following variable holds values ranging from -999.99 to +999.99.

```
01   THE-VALUE        PIC S999V99.
```

The following variable holds values ranging from -9999 to +9999.

```
01   THE-VALUE        PIC S9999.
```

The abbreviations used in a picture still can be used in a numeric picture containing a sign or a decimal. For example, the following two variable definitions will produce the same size and type of variable.

```
01   THE-VALUE        PIC S999999V9999.
```

```
01   THE-VALUE        PIC S9(6)V9(4).
```

It looks like some sort of strange code, but it is simple to decipher if you remember that any number in parentheses in a PICTURE is a signal to repeat the preceding character the number of times in parentheses. So 9(6) expands to 999999 and 9(4) expands to 9999.

Displaying Decimals and Signs

In COBOL, numbers that will be displayed are treated differently from numbers that are used for calculations. COBOL was designed to do a lot of number calculating (addition, subtraction, multiplication, and division). Numbers that contain an S for a sign (positive or negative) or a V for a decimal are stored in memory in a special format that speeds up calculations. However, this format does not display correctly.

6

The designers of COBOL recognized the need to include in the design of the language a way to display numeric values. After all, the output of a program isn't much good if a user can't understand it.

The idea behind the design is that all calculations are performed with numeric variables (variables whose pictures contain only numbers, an S for a sign, and a V for a decimal). After the calculations are complete, the resulting value is moved to a display variable, and the display variable is put on-screen through a DISPLAY statement.

A numeric variable stipulated by a DISPLAY statement uses different PICTURE characters for the sign and the decimal.

The PICTURE character for a sign in a numeric variable that will be used for a DISPLAY is the minus sign (-). The PICTURE character for a decimal in a numeric variable that will be used for DISPLAY is the decimal point or period.

The following variable holds the values -999.99 through 999.99 for display purposes:

```
01    DISPLAY-VALUE      PIC -999.99.
```

The display sign (-) displays only when the value is negative. If DISPLAY-VALUE contains -46.17, it displays as the following:

```
-046.17
```

However, the number 55.03 displays as follows:

```
055.03
```

A program performing calculation and display might contain WORKING-STORAGE and code as in Listing 6.6. In practice, a sales commission usually would not be negative (unless the salesperson generated a pile of refunds), but the example does show the difference between the PICTURE of a signed value used for calculation at line 000800 and the PICTURE of a signed value used for display at line 001300.

Type **Listing 6.6. Using numeric and display variables.**

```
000700 WORKING-STORAGE SECTION.
000800 01    SALES-TOTAL           PIC S9(5)V99   VALUE 44707.66.
000900 01    COMMISSION-PERCENT    PIC 99         VALUE 11.
001000 01    PERCENT-AS-DECIMAL    PIC V99.
001100 01    THE-COMMISSION        PIC S9(5)V99   VALUE ZERO.
001200
001300 01    DISPLAY-COMMISSION    PIC -9(5).99.
......
002500* Divide commission by 100 to convert to decimal
002600    COMPUTE PERCENT-AS-DECIMAL =
002700       COMMISSION-PERCENT / 100.
002800
```

```
002900     COMPUTE THE-COMMISSION =
003000        PERCENT-AS-DECIMAL * SALES-TOTAL.
003100
003200     MOVE THE-COMMISSION TO DISPLAY-COMMISSION.
003300
003400     DISPLAY "The Commission is "
003500        DISPLAY-COMMISSION.
```

The - also can be placed at the end of the picture rather than at the beginning. It is fairly common in business programs to see display values specified as follows:

```
01    THE-DISPLAY-VALUE              PIC 999999.99-.
```

Suppressing Leading Zeroes

You can suppress leading zeroes to improve the display of a number. In the previous example, if -55.17 is moved to THE-DISPLAY-VALUE and then displayed, it appears on the screen as the following:

```
000055.17-
```

In a display variable, you can suppress the display of leading zeroes, using Z to replace 9 in the picture of the variable. Here is an example:

```
01    THE-DISPLAY-VALUE              PIC ZZZZZ9.99-.
```

When entered like this, a value of -54.27 moved to THE-DISPLAY-VALUE displays as the following:

```
54.27-
```

Leading zeroes are suppressed by the Z in the PICTURE statement.

Using a PICTURE of ZZZZZ9.99- enables the value 0 to display as this:

```
0.00
```

If you suppress all zeroes with a PICTURE of ZZZZZZ.ZZ-, a value of 0 displays as a blank because all zeroes are suppressed.

Commas can be inserted in the picture to provide commas in the final display, like this:

```
01    DISPLAY-COMMISSION        PIC ZZ,ZZ9.99-.
```

A value of 12345.67 moved to DISPLAY-COMMISSION displays as the following:

```
12,345.67
```

NEW TERM   The minus sign (–), decimal point (.), comma (,) and the character Z are called *editing characters.* A numeric variable that contains an editing character is called an *edited numeric variable.* Edited numeric variables should be used only to display values and should not be used in calculations. There are other editing characters, but these are the main ones.

WARNING

> Editing characters should never be mixed with S or V in a PICTURE.
> PIC S99.99 and PIC -ZZV99 are illegal PICTUREs, and your compiler will generate an error if you try to create a PICTURE that mixes the two types.

Before you leap into writing a program that uses decimal or signed data, you need to know how to enter signed and decimal data using ACCEPT. Numeric data that is entered into a computer probably will be entered by the user with editing characters, such as a plus sign or a minus sign, a decimal point, and commas.

If you ACCEPT values into a numeric field, such as a PIC 9(6)V99, characters such as signs and commas entered by the user will be invalid. In order to allow the user to enter digits and editing characters, it is necessary to use ACCEPT to accept values into an edited numeric variable.

The easiest way to create a PICTURE for a field into which this type of numeric data will be accepted is to make it as large as possible by including all possible editing characters. If you want to allow the user to enter a number as large as 999,999.99 with a sign, the picture for the field should be PIC -ZZZ,ZZZ.ZZ. This PICTURE allows the user to enter all possible editing characters including commas, a sign, and a decimal point. You also could use the following:

```
01   ENTRY-FIELD               PIC ZZZ,ZZZ.ZZ-.
```

When a display variable is used as a data entry field with ACCEPT, the PICTURE of the variable does not control what the user can enter. For example, it doesn't matter whether the minus sign (-) is placed at the beginning or the end of the PICTURE statement. The user still can enter a minus in a leading or trailing position. When an ACCEPT of ENTRY-FIELD is used in a program, the ACCEPT verb uses the size of the PICTURE, 11 characters (eight characters, a comma, a minus sign, and a decimal point), to determine how many characters the user is allowed to enter and assumes that the user will be entering digits, and possibly a sign, commas and/or a decimal point as the input.

After the user enters data and presses Enter, the ACCEPT verb looks at the 11 (or fewer) characters and tries to sort out the digits, minus signs, commas, or decimal points. It turns the result into a number that can be moved to a true numeric variable.

Unfortunately, the following three different versions of ACCEPT can be used for numeric entry:

```
ACCEPT ENTRY-FIELD.

ACCEPT ENTRY-FIELD WITH CONVERSION.

ACCEPT ENTRY-FIELD CONVERT.
```

Micro Focus Personal COBOL uses the first version. ACUCOBOL uses the second and third versions; VAX COBOL use the second; and LPI COBOL uses the third. You have to consult your COBOL manual to check which one your version uses.

NOTE

> The listings in today's lesson use ACCEPT ENTRY-FIELD because this code was compiled and tested using a Micro Focus compiler. The other versions are commented out in the code. You can change the one you use to fit your compiler.

Code, compile, and run Listing 6.7, entering various values to get an idea how the formatting works. You might want to try editing the program to add additional formats or to try out longer fields.

TYPE **Listing 6.7. Edited formats.**

```
000100 IDENTIFICATION DIVISION.
000200 PROGRAM-ID. NUMS01.
000300*----------------------------------------------
000400* Illustrates how decimal data is displayed
000500* when edited.
000600*----------------------------------------------
000700 ENVIRONMENT DIVISION.
000800 DATA DIVISION.
000900 WORKING-STORAGE SECTION.
001000
001100 01   ENTRY-FIELD    PIC -ZZZ,ZZZ.ZZ.
001200 01   THE-VALUE      PIC S999999V99.
001300
001400 01   EDITED-DISPLAY-1     PIC -999999.99.
001500 01   EDITED-DISPLAY-2     PIC ZZZZZ9.99-.
001600 01   EDITED-DISPLAY-3     PIC ZZZZZZ.ZZ-.
001700 01   EDITED-DISPLAY-4     PIC ZZZ,ZZZ.ZZ-.
001800
001900 PROCEDURE DIVISION.
002000 PROGRAM-BEGIN.
002100
002200     DISPLAY "PLEASE ENTER A VALUE".
002300     ACCEPT ENTRY-FIELD.
002400*or  ACCEPT ENTRY-FIELD CONVERT.
```

6

continues

Listing 6.7. continued

```
002500*or  ACCEPT ENTRY-FIELD WITH CONVERSION.
002600     MOVE ENTRY-FIELD TO THE-VALUE.
002700
002800     MOVE THE-VALUE TO EDITED-DISPLAY-1
002900                      EDITED-DISPLAY-2
003000                      EDITED-DISPLAY-3
003100                      EDITED-DISPLAY-4.
003200
003300     DISPLAY ENTRY-FIELD     "|"
003400             EDITED-DISPLAY-1 "|"
003500             EDITED-DISPLAY-2 "|"
003600             EDITED-DISPLAY-3 "|"
003700             EDITED-DISPLAY-4 "|".
003800
003900     IF THE-VALUE NOT = ZERO
004000        GO TO PROGRAM-BEGIN.
004100
004200 PROGRAM-DONE.
004300     STOP RUN.
004400
```

The output of nums01.cbl shows the results of various numeric entry values. The user input is shown in boldface type. Entry stops when you enter zero.

OUTPUT
```
PLEASE ENTER A VALUE
-1
-       1.00|-000001.00|    1.00-|      1.00-|        1.00-|
PLEASE ENTER A VALUE
234,56
23,456.00| 023456.00| 23456.00 | 23456.00 | 23,456.00 |
PLEASE ENTER A VALUE
10606-
- 10,606.00|-010606.00| 10606.00-| 10606.00-| 10,606.00-|
PLEASE ENTER A VALUE
123.45
123.45| 000123.45|    123.45 |    123.45 |    123.45 |
PLEASE ENTER A VALUE
1234.5
1,234.50| 001234.50|   1234.50 |   1234.50 |  1,234.50 |
PLEASE ENTER A VALUE
-1678.98
-  1,678.98|-001678.98|   1678.98-|   1678.98-|  1,678.98-|
PLEASE ENTER A VALUE
```

ANALYSIS The code in Listing 6.7 allows data entry to be accepted into a display variable field at line 002300 and then moves it to a calculation field. From there, it is moved to several different edited numeric fields. The original entry and the different versions of the edited numeric fields are displayed.

COBOL Numeric Operations

You already have worked with several COBOL numeric operators; now it is time to round them up in one section.

The COBOL COMPUTE verb is a general-purpose verb that can be used to calculate results. Arithmetic expressions in the COMPUTE verb use the arithmetic operators: + (addition), - (subtraction), * (multiplication), and / (division). You can use parentheses to affect the order in which operations are performed.

When parentheses appear in an expression, the value within the innermost parentheses is evaluated first. Assuming that THE-VALUE contains 100 and THE-PERCENT contains .25, these are the steps for evaluating the sample compute statement:

1. COMPUTE THE-RESULT = ((THE-VALUE * THE-PERCENT) + 14) / 6
2. COMPUTE THE-RESULT = ((25) + 14) /6
3. COMPUTE THE-RESULT = (39) / 6
4. COMPUTE THE-RESULT = 6.5

The COMPUTE verb has two optional clauses: ROUNDED and ON SIZE ERROR. ROUNDED rounds the result up or down as necessary, based on the results of the calculation. The ON SIZE ERROR logic is performed if the result is larger than the variable that is used to store the result.

The statement that follows ON SIZE ERROR also is executed if a COMPUTE statement attempts to do something impossible, such as divide by zero. Dividing by zero causes a lot of problems for a computer. It is an error that can occur in a COMPUTE statement that uses division (/), or one that uses the DIVIDE verb (which is covered later in today's lesson).

In the following syntax, clauses in brackets ([ ]) are optional. In a COMPUTE statement, the result is stored in the variable on the left of the equals (=) sign, like this:

```
COMPUTE numeric variable
    [ROUNDED] =
    arithmetic expression
    [ ON SIZE ERROR
      do something else ]
```

In the following examples, the first COMPUTE statement uses all of the options.

```
COMPUTE THE-RESULT
    ROUNDED =
    (BASE-VALUE * 10) +
    (A-VALUE / 50)
    ON SIZE ERROR
    DISPLAY "Warning Size error."

COMPUTE THE-RESULT = 12 * 15.

COMPUTE THE-RESULT
    ROUNDED =
    (BASE-VALUE * 10) / 1.5.
```

6

A divide-by-zero error might occur in a program that calculated the sales dollars generated per day per salesperson by dividing a salesperson's monthly total sales revenue by the number of days worked that month. If one of the sales staff were off all month because of a serious illness, but some income came in that month from a previous month's sale, trying to compute the dollars per day would cause a divide-by-zero error.

```
COMPUTE DOLLARS-PER-DAY = MONTH-DOLLARS / DAYS-WORKED.
```

A program containing this COMPUTE statement would crash if DAYS-WORKED equals 0. An ON SIZE ERROR traps this condition and displays an error, so that the program can continue:

```
002600      COMPUTE DOLLARS-PER-DAY =
002700        MONTH-DOLLARS / DAYS-WORKED
002800          ON SIZE ERROR
002900            DISPLAY "Division by zero error".
```

The ADD verb is available in two versions. Both versions have options similar to the COMPUTE verb. In the first, a value (which can be a constant or a variable) is added to second value (which must be a variable). The result is stored in the variable, like this:

```
ADD value TO variable
    [ROUNDED]
    [ ON SIZE ERROR
    do something ]
```

In each of the following examples, the result of the addition is stored in THE-VALUE:

```
ADD 1.17 TO THE-VALUE.
```

```
ADD A-VALUE TO THE-VALUE
    ROUNDED.
```

```
ADD 1.17 TO THE-VALUE
    ROUNDED
    ON SIZE ERROR
    DISPLAY "Add - overflow"
```

In the second version, two values are added together and the reserved word GIVING is used to indicate a variable into which the result is stored. The values can be constants or variables.

```
ADD value TO value
    GIVING variable [ROUNDED]
    [ ON SIZE ERROR
    do something ]
```

In each example, the result of the addition is stored in THE-SUM, as shown here:

```
ADD 17.5 TO THE-VALUE
    GIVING THE-SUM ROUNDED
    ON SIZE ERROR
    DISPLAY "Add - overflow"
```

```
ADD 17.5 TO 22.7
    GIVING THE-SUM
```

```
ADD A-VALUE TO THE-VALUE
    GIVING THE-SUM
    ON SIZE ERROR
    DISPLAY "Add - overflow"
```

Subtraction is handled by the SUBTRACT verb, and it comes in the following two versions that are similar to ADD. The second version of SUBTRACT also uses GIVING.

```
SUBTRACT value
    FROM variable [ROUNDED]
    [ ON SIZE ERROR
    do something ]

SUBTRACT value FROM value
    GIVING variable [ROUNDED]
    [ ON SIZE ERROR
    do something ]
```

The following are examples of subtraction with the SUBTRACT verb:

```
SUBTRACT  1.17
    FROM THE-VALUE ROUNDED
    ON SIZE ERROR
    DISPLAY "Subtract - overflow

SUBTRACT 17.5 FROM THE-VALUE
    GIVING THE-DIFFERENCE ROUNDED
    ON SIZE ERROR
    DISPLAY "Subtract-overflow"
```

Multiplication is handled by the MULTIPLY verb, and the following syntax for both versions of MULTIPLY is similar to ADD and SUBTRACT:

```
MULTIPLY value
    BY variable [ROUNDED]
    [ ON SIZE ERROR
    do something ]

MULTIPLY value BY value
    GIVING variable [ROUNDED]
    [ ON SIZE ERROR
    do something ]
```

The result is stored in the second value (for example, THE-VALUE) for the first version, and the second version uses GIVING to name a variable—in this case, THE-PRODUCT—to store the result:

```
MULTIPLY 1.17
    BY THE-VALUE ROUNDED
    ON SIZE ERROR
    DISPLAY "Multiply-overflow"

MULTIPLY 17.5 BY THE-VALUE
    GIVING THE-PRODUCT ROUNDED
    ON SIZE ERROR
    DISPLAY "Multiply-overflow"
```

6

Division with the DIVIDE verb comes in several versions, which follow. It has versions with
and without the GIVING clause, and it also includes the capability of storing the remainder of
a division in a separate variable. There also are versions that allow you to divide BY or divide
INTO.

```
DIVIDE value
    INTO variable [ROUNDED]
    [ ON SIZE ERROR
    do something ]

DIVIDE value INTO value
    GIVING variable [ROUNDED]
    [ ON SIZE ERROR
    do something ]

DIVIDE value INTO value
    GIVING variable [ROUNDED]
    REMAINDER variable
    [ ON SIZE ERROR
    do something ]

DIVIDE value BY value
    GIVING variable [ROUNDED]
    [ ON SIZE ERROR
    do something ]

DIVIDE value BY value
    GIVING variable [ROUNDED]
    REMAINDER variable
    [ ON SIZE ERROR
    do something ]
```

The following are examples of division with the DIVIDE verb:

```
DIVIDE 56.2
    INTO THE-VALUE ROUNDED
    ON SIZE ERROR
    DISPLAY "Divide-error"

DIVIDE 56.2 INTO THE-VALUE
    GIVING THE-QUOTIENT ROUNDED
    ON SIZE ERROR
    DISPLAY "Divide-error"

DIVIDE 15 INTO THE-VALUE
    GIVING THE-QUOTIENT ROUNDED
    REMAINDER THE RE-REMAINDER
    ON SIZE ERRROR
    DISPLAY "Divide-error"

DIVIDE 56.2 BY THE-VALUE
    GIVING THE-QUOTINT ROUNDED
    ON SIZE ERROR
    DISPLAY "Divide-error"

DIVIDE 15 BY 7
    GIVING THE-QUOTIENT ROUNDED
    REMAINDER THE-REMAINDER
    ON SIZE ERROR
    DISPLAY "Divide-error"
```

Summary

Today, you learned more about COBOL's DATA DIVISION, including the following basics:

- ☐ When a variable is declared in WORKING-STORAGE, it also can be given an initial value with a VALUE or VALUE IS clause.

- ☐ A variable that is not initialized in WORKING-STORAGE contains undefined values and must be initialized if it is expected to have a default value.

- ☐ Initializing a variable in WORKING-STORAGE has the same effect as a MOVE to the variable. If the initializing value is too small for an alphanumeric field, the field is padded on the right with spaces. If the initializing value is too small for a numeric variable, the variable is padded on the left with zeroes.

- ☐ SPACE and SPACES are reserved COBOL words that mean "fill with spaces." ZERO, ZEROS, and ZEROES are reserved COBOL words that mean "fill with zeroes."

- ☐ If a value is too large or too long when moved to a target variable, you will lose some data. An alphanumeric variable truncates characters from the right of the value until the value will fit in the variable. A numeric variable truncates digits from the left of the value until the value will fit. The compiler might warn you or return errors when initializing with or moving values that are too large or too long.

- ☐ A MOVE verb can be used to move the same value to multiple targets.

- ☐ The decimal in a numeric PICTURE is a V, and the sign in a numeric picture is a leading S. The following variable will hold values ranging from -99.9 through 99.9.

  ```
  01   THE-VALUE      PIC S99V9.
  ```

- ☐ Variables whose pictures contain only the characters 9, S, and V are numeric variables and can be used in calculations.

- ☐ Variables whose pictures contain Z, -, ., and , are edited numeric variables intended to be used for displaying or printing variables. You have seen the effect of some of these editing characters on the display of a number.

- ☐ How to use the COMPUTE, ADD, SUBTRACT, MULTIPLY and DIVIDE verbs.

Q&A

Q If I can use ZEROES and SPACES to initialize a variable, can I also move ZEROES and SPACES to a variable?

A Yes. Both of the following statements behave as you would expect them to by moving spaces or zeroes to variables:

```
MOVE SPACES TO THE-MESSAGE.

MOVE ZEROES TO THE-NUMBER.
```

6

Q **Does truncation happen in signed (positive and negative) numbers?**

A Yes. If you move -2371.16 to a `PIC S999V99`, the result is stored as -371.16. If you move a number with a negative sign to a picture that does not have a sign, the sign is truncated. If you move -456.78 to a `PIC 999V99`, the result is stored as 456.78.

Workshop

Quiz

1. What is the value in `BIG-NUMBER` after the `MOVE`?

   ```
   01  BIG-NUMBER        PIC 9(5).

       MOVE 4976 TO BIG-NUMBER
   ```

2. What is the value in `SMALL-NUMBER` after the `MOVE`?

   ```
   01  SMALL-NUMBER      PIC 9(2).

       MOVE 4976 TO SMALL-NUMBER.
   ```

   Hint: Numbers are truncated from the left.

3. After the following move, `THE-VALUE` contains `000.00`. Why?

   ```
   01  THE-VALUE         PIC 999V99.

       MOVE 1000.001 TO THE-VALUE.
   ```

Exercises

1. If you haven't done so, compile `trunc01.cbl` and make a note of any warnings provided by your compiler. If your compiler has a manual that lists the meanings of warnings, look them up in the manual and become familiar with them.

2. Compile `trunc02.cbl` and look up any errors generated by the compiler.

6

Day **7**

Basics of Design

You now have enough tools to begin designing your own programs. A simple approach to design will make your efforts worthwhile. Today, you learn about the following topics:

- [ ] Why write a program?
- [ ] Defining the job.
- [ ] Breaking down the task.
- [ ] Identifying the processing loops.
- [ ] What is pseudocode and how do you use it?
- [ ] Identifying the main processing loop.
- [ ] The steps to program design.
- [ ] A compound interest program.

Why Write a Program?

A program's primary goal is to take a repetitive task that would be mind-numbingly dull for a person to perform, and reduce it to a set of rote steps performed over and over by the machine.

A task is suitable for a program if the task involves doing one thing over and over. For example, going through the list of all books loaned out by a library, checking the return dates, determining which books are overdue, and printing an overdue notice to send to the offending cardholder is an ideal task for a computer program. This task is repetitive because it processes each book with the same steps:

1. Look up the loan date.
2. Check whether it is overdue.
3. If it is overdue, print a notice.

A task also is suitable for a program if it does only one thing once, but the program is run several times. For example, a program would be helpful to design and print signs for a retail store. Someone will design a sign and print it each time there is a sale. Unless you are keen on that individual artistic look, a sign-printing program will do this task repeatedly with a uniform quality of result.

If you are planning to move and need to put up a sign offering a garage sale, this is probably an unsuitable candidate for a program, unless you hold a garage sale every weekend and need to print signs that often.

In the early lessons of this book, several programs were presented that were not true candidates for programs. The "Hello world" program and the programs to display poems really didn't qualify as necessary programs, but they were coded simply to introduce you to the language.

The multiplication tables programs were good candidates. They executed an action repeatedly by multiplying two numbers, displaying the result, and moving on to the next number.

Some repetitive tasks make lousy programs because of the limitations of computers. Although you might make yourself a cup of coffee the same way each morning, it really wouldn't work as a program. Very few computers have a coffee maker as a standard output device.

If the job involves processing data, it is a good bet that a program will help expedite the task. (This is not always true. How about the repetitive task of going through all the people you know and selecting 50 people to invite to a party? Unless the computer knows who is on your A list, it will not be able to do this job even though it is repetitive and is data processing.)

Defining the Job

When you have decided that a job is suitable for a computer, you need to come up with a job description for the program. This doesn't have to be detailed, but it does have to be precise. Some job descriptions of computer programs that have been discussed or have appeared in previous lessons include the following:

☐ Review all books out on loan and send overdue notices to the holders of all overdue books.

☐ Accept a sign text from the user, format a sign under user control, and print one or more copies of it.

☐ Display a multiplication table for any value from 1 to 99, displaying any number of entries from 1 to 99.

☐ Display multiplication tables for any value from 1 to 99, displaying any number of entries from 1 to 99.

Notice the difference between the last two. This is an example of precision without detail. The job descriptions are of two similar but slightly different programs.

Breaking Down the Task

When you have a job description, you can start breaking the job into smaller jobs. This is the point at which you need to have some knowledge of what the programming language is capable of doing.

Let's try breaking down the fourth job description in the previous list, because you're familiar with a version of this program. This will be a version of the multiplication tables that lets the user enter more than one table and display it.

The job description is to display multiplication tables for any value from 1 to 99, displaying any number of entries from 1 to 99.

Without worrying about the order of things, start by breaking the job description into component tasks, with a brief description of what the computer will have to do to execute this part of the task.

Original Job Description	Computer Task
Display multiplication tables	Display multiplication tables over and over.
For any value from 1 to 99	Ask the user for the table to display (1–99).
Display any number of entries from 1 to 99	1. Ask the user for the number of entries (1–99). 2. Display each entry from 1 through the number specified by the user.

The smaller tasks themselves might have to be broken down again. This process might have to be performed over and over until the tasks are small enough to be described in terms the computer can process.

7

Identifying the Processing Loops

Processing loops begin to stand out when the job is broken into smaller tasks. Recall from Day 5, "Using PERFORM, GO TO, and IF to Control Programs," that a processing loop is any task that is done over and over based on the detailed task descriptions.

You should be able to identify two loops now. The first displays a selected table repeatedly. The second displays an entry repeatedly until the number of entries specified by the user is reached.

After you have identified a loop, it is helpful to think of the loop as doing one thing over and over instead of doing all the things once. Table 7.1 illustrates the difference between the normal way of thinking about doing things repeatedly, and the computer-oriented way of thinking about processing loops.

Table 7.1. Normal thinking versus computer thinking.

Normal Thinking	Computer Thinking
Display several tables.	Display one table over and over, changing some value each time.
Display all the entries.	Display one entry over and over, changing some value each time.

NEW TERM   *Pseudocode* is a convenient way to write code without having to labor over the syntax of every line. It also allows you to leave gaps when you don't know the answer yet. Good pseudocode should be written in something that approximates the target language. There are no real rules for pseudocode, except that it should be helpful when designing a program.

Now that you have the program job, tasks, and processing loops identified, the next step is to start putting it together with pseudocode. The first task is identifying the whole program. What does it do? The program displays a bunch of tables. In computer "loopthink" it displays one table over and over, with something changed during each display. Listing 7.1 is a pseudocode statement for this.

Note that the first example of pseudocode violates two COBOL syntax rules. All words are not in uppercase, and the sentence does not end with a period. This is typical of pseudocode. It is like COBOL but does not have to honor all syntax rules.

TYPE   **Listing 7.1. The first pseudocode.**

```
THE-PROGRAM
    DISPLAY-ONE-TABLE over and over
```

"Over and over" is good enough for the programmer, but a computer program needs to be more precise so that the computer knows when to stop. This translates into an UNTIL condition. For the moment, I will leave things open-ended and change the pseudocode to that of Listing 7.2.

TYPE **Listing 7.2. The main action of the program in pseudocode.**

```
THE-PROGRAM
    DISPLAY-ONE-TABLE
        UNTIL something???
```

The next step is to look at DISPLAY-ONE-TABLE. What actions do you have to do to display one table? Basically, there are only two actions, which are to get the table and display it. Listing 7.3 expands the pseudocode with these steps.

TYPE **Listing 7.3. Expanding the code.**

```
THE-PROGRAM
    DISPLAY-ONE-TABLE
        UNTIL something???

DISPLAY-ONE-TABLE
    GET-WHICH-TABLE
    DISPLAY-THE-TABLE
```

GET-WHICH-TABLE resolves into simple COBOL commands to display a message and accept an answer. Now, what do you have to do to display the table? There are also two steps to this. First, get the number of entries. Next, display one entry until that number of entries is exhausted. Listing 7.4 includes the actions for GET-WHICH-TABLE and DISPLAY-THE-TABLE.

TYPE **Listing 7.4. Expanding on DISPLAY-THE-TABLE.**

```
THE-PROGRAM
    DISPLAY-ONE-TABLE
        UNTIL something???

DISPLAY-ONE-TABLE
    GET-WHICH-TABLE
    DISPLAY-THE-TABLE

GET-WHICH-TABLE
    DISPLAY "Which table? (01-99)"
    ACCEPT THE-TABLE
```

continues

Listing 7.4. continued

```
DISPLAY-THE-TABLE
    GET-HOW-MANY-ENTRIES
    DISPLAY-ONE-ENTRY
        UNTIL all entries are displayed
```

Now you can apply your knowledge of COBOL to the problem. The entries to be displayed range from 1 to the number entered by the user. This seems a good place to use a VARYING option. Listing 7.5 expands on this in DISPLAY-THE-TABLE and also tackles the problem of getting the number of entries.

TYPE **Listing 7.5. The program takes shape.**

```
THE-PROGRAM
    DISPLAY-ONE-TABLE
        UNTIL something???

DISPLAY-ONE-TABLE
    GET-WHICH-TABLE
    DISPLAY-THE-TABLE

GET-WHICH-TABLE
    DISPLAY "Which table? (01-99)"
    ACCEPT THE-TABLE

DISPLAY-THE-TABLE
    GET-HOW-MANY-ENTRIES
    DISPLAY-ONE-ENTRY
      VARYING THE-ENTRY FROM 1 BY 1
        UNTIL THE-ENTRY > HOW-MANY-ENTRIES

GET-HOW-MANY-ENTRIES
    DISPLAY "How many entries (01-99)?"
    ACCEPT HOW-MANY-ENTRIES
```

The last piece of the program is the task of displaying one entry. Listing 7.6 puts the final piece of the pseudocode together.

TYPE **Listing 7.6. The core of the program in pseudocode.**

```
THE-PROGRAM
    DISPLAY-ONE-TABLE
        UNTIL something???

DISPLAY-ONE-TABLE
    GET-WHICH-TABLE
    DISPLAY-THE-TABLE
```

```
GET-WHICH-TABLE
    DISPLAY "Which table? (01-99)"
    ACCEPT THE-TABLE

DISPLAY-THE-TABLE
    GET-HOW-MANY-ENTRIES
    DISPLAY-ONE-ENTRY
      VARYING THE-ENTRY FROM 1 BY 1
        UNTIL THE-ENTRY > HOW-MANY-ENTRIES

GET-HOW-MANY-ENTRIES
    DISPLAY "How many entries (01-99)?"
    ACCEPT HOW-MANY-ENTRIES

DISPLAY-ONE-ENTRY
    COMPUTE THE-PRODUCT = THE-TABLE * THE-ENTRY
    DISPLAY THE-TABLE " * "
            THE-ENTRY " = "
            THE-PRODUCT
```

You don't want the program to turn into a runaway train, so you still have an UNTIL to resolve in THE-PROGRAM. This is where the user wants the process to stop. You could establish this by asking users whether they want to continue or to see another table.

When should the user be asked? After each table is displayed. Remember the two key parts of a processing loop are the top and the bottom. The question could be asked at the bottom of DISPLAY-ONE-TABLE. Listing 7.7 covers the sections that have been added in DISPLAY-ONE-TABLE and the new section GO-AGAIN. In GO-AGAIN, I made a design choice about the user's answer. I could have checked for y, Y, n, or N and provided an invalid entry message for anything else, but this felt like overkill for such a simple program. Instead, I chose to test only for y and convert it to Y. Then, anything other than Y is changed to N, forcing any entry other than Y or y to be treated as no.

TYPE   **Listing 7.7. The pseudocode is almost complete.**

```
THE-PROGRAM
    DISPLAY-ONE-TABLE
        UNTIL YES-NO = "N"

DISPLAY-ONE-TABLE
    GET-WHICH-TABLE
    DISPLAY-THE-TABLE
    GO-AGAIN

GET-WHICH-TABLE
    DISPLAY "Which table? (01-99)"
    ACCEPT THE-TABLE
```

continues

Listing 7.7. continued

```
DISPLAY-THE-TABLE
    GET-HOW-MANY-ENTRIES
    DISPLAY-ONE-ENTRY
        VARYING THE-ENTRY FROM 1 BY 1
            UNTIL THE-ENTRY > HOW-MANY-ENTRIES

GO-AGAIN
    DISPLAY "Go Again (Y/N)?"
    ACCEPT YES-NO
    IF YES-NO = "y"
        MOVE "Y" TO YES-NO
    IF YES-NO NOT = "Y"
        MOVE "N" TO YES-NO

GET-HOW-MANY-ENTRIES
    DISPLAY "How many entries (01-99)?"
    ACCEPT HOW-MANY-ENTRIES

DISPLAY-ONE-ENTRY
    COMPUTE THE-PRODUCT = THE-TABLE * THE-ENTRY
    DISPLAY THE-TABLE " * "
            THE-ENTRY " = "
            THE-PRODUCT
```

Now comes the tidying up. First, look at the loops. There is a potential problem in the control of the first loop in THE-PROGRAM. Recall the following loop steps:

1. Initialize for the first pass through the loop.

2. Do the loop.

3. Modify the variable that controls the loop as the last step of the loop, or after each pass through the loop.

There is no loop step 1 for DISPLAY-ONE-TABLE. This can be fixed by forcing YES-NO to an initial value of "Y". This ensures that DISPLAY-ONE-TABLE is executed when the loop is entered for the first time.

```
THE-PROGRAM
    MOVE "Y" TO YES-NO
    DISPLAY-ONE-TABLE
        UNTIL YES-NO = "N"
```

The second area to clean up has been dealt with once before—the problem of displaying 15 lines at a time. You can use the top of the DISPLAY-ONE-ENTRY loop for a Press ENTER message, and use the bottom of the loop to add 1 to SCREEN-LINES.

Because this program will display more than one table, it is necessary to start SCREEN-LINES at zero before each table is displayed. Listing 7.8 is the final version of the pseudocode.

TYPE | Listing 7.8. The final pseudocode.

```
THE-PROGRAM
    MOVE "Y" TO YES-NO
    DISPLAY-ONE-TABLE
        UNTIL YES-NO = "N"

DISPLAY-ONE-TABLE
    GET-WHICH-TABLE
    DISPLAY-THE-TABLE
    GO-AGAIN

GET-WHICH-TABLE
    DISPLAY "Which table? (01-99)"
    ACCEPT THE-TABLE

DISPLAY-THE-TABLE
    GET-HOW-MANY-ENTRIES
    MOVE 0 TO SCREEN-LINES
    DISPLAY-ONE-ENTRY
      VARYING THE-ENTRY FROM 1 BY 1
        UNTIL THE-ENTRY > HOW-MANY-ENTRIES

GO-AGAIN
    DISPLAY "Go Again (Y/N)?"
    ACCEPT YES-NO
    IF YES-NO = "y"
        MOVE "Y" TO YES-NO
    IF YES-NO NOT = "Y"
        MOVE "N" TO YES-NO

GET-HOW-MANY-ENTRIES
    DISPLAY "How many entries (01-99)?"
    ACCEPT HOW-MANY-ENTRIES

DISPLAY-ONE-ENTRY
    IF SCREEN-LINES = 15
        PRESS-ENTER
    COMPUTE THE-PRODUCT = THE-TABLE * THE-ENTRY
    DISPLAY THE-TABLE " * "
            THE-ENTRY " = "
            THE-PRODUCT
    ADD 1 TO SCREEN-LINES

PRESS-ENTER
    DISPLAY "Press ENTER to continue"
    ACCEPT A-DUMMY
```

What's left? I deliberately chose a pseudocode that translated readily into COBOL code. Remember that pseudocode is supposed to help with the design. In fact, the pseudocode is now very close to a COBOL program.

Basically, you need to clean up the punctuation by adding some periods, add some PERFORM statements, create variables in WORKING-STORAGE, compile, and test. The result is shown in Listing 7.9. The pseudocode is almost identical to the PROCEDURE DIVISION.

7

TYPE **Listing 7.9. The final program.**

```
000100 IDENTIFICATION DIVISION.
000200 PROGRAM-ID. MULT07.
000300*--------------------------------------------------
000400* This program asks the user for a number for a
000500* multiplication table, and a table size
000600* and then displays a table for that number
000700* times the values 1 through HOW-MANY.
000800*
000900* The display is paused after each 15 lines.
001000*--------------------------------------------------
001100 ENVIRONMENT DIVISION.
001200 DATA DIVISION.
001300 WORKING-STORAGE SECTION.
001400
001500 01  THE-TABLE          PIC 99.
001600 01  THE-ENTRY          PIC 999.
001700 01  THE-PRODUCT        PIC 9999.
001800 01  HOW-MANY-ENTRIES   PIC 99.
001900 01  SCREEN-LINES       PIC 99.
002000
002100 01  A-DUMMY            PIC X.
002200
002300 01  YES-NO             PIC X.
002400
002500 PROCEDURE DIVISION.
002600
002700 PROGRAM-BEGIN.
002800     MOVE "Y" TO YES-NO.
002900     PERFORM DISPLAY-ONE-TABLE
003000         UNTIL YES-NO = "N".
003100
003200 PROGRAM-DONE.
003300     STOP RUN.
003400
003500 DISPLAY-ONE-TABLE.
003600     PERFORM GET-WHICH-TABLE.
003700     PERFORM DISPLAY-THE-TABLE.
003800     PERFORM GO-AGAIN.
003900
004000 GET-WHICH-TABLE.
004100     DISPLAY
004200      "Which multiplication table(01-99)?".
004300     ACCEPT THE-TABLE.
004400
004500 DISPLAY-THE-TABLE.
004600     PERFORM GET-HOW-MANY-ENTRIES.
004700
004800     MOVE 0 TO SCREEN-LINES.
004900
005000     PERFORM DISPLAY-ONE-ENTRY
005100         VARYING THE-ENTRY
005200             FROM 1 BY 1
005300             UNTIL THE-ENTRY > HOW-MANY-ENTRIES.
005400
```

```
005500 GO-AGAIN.
005600     DISPLAY "Go Again (Y/N)?".
005700     ACCEPT YES-NO.
005800     IF YES-NO = "y"
005900         MOVE "Y" TO YES-NO.
006000     IF YES-NO NOT = "Y"
006100         MOVE "N" TO YES-NO.
006200
006300 GET-HOW-MANY-ENTRIES.
006400     DISPLAY
006500       "How many entries would you like (01-99)?".
006600     ACCEPT HOW-MANY-ENTRIES.
006700
006800 DISPLAY-ONE-ENTRY.
006900
007000     IF SCREEN-LINES = 15
007100         PERFORM PRESS-ENTER.
007200     COMPUTE THE-PRODUCT = THE-TABLE * THE-ENTRY.
007300     DISPLAY
007400         THE-TABLE " * " THE-ENTRY " = " THE-PRODUCT.
007500
007600     ADD 1 TO SCREEN-LINES.
007700
007800 PRESS-ENTER.
007900     DISPLAY "Press ENTER to continue . . .".
008000     ACCEPT A-DUMMY.
008100     MOVE 0 TO SCREEN-LINES.
008200
```

Identifying the Main Processing Loop

Although a processing loop is supposed to be a section of the program that is performed over and over, it does not have to be. The main processing loop, the main action that the program does, is not always performed repeatedly. You saw in earlier versions of the multiplication tables program in Day 5 that the main processing loop need not be performed over and over. Yet the program is still a valid computer program.

If the main processing loop doesn't have to be a true loop, how do you identify it? One way is to pretend that whatever the program is going to do, it will be doing it over and over. If the original job description had been to display only one multiplication table, you could add "do it over and over" while you are designing it.

When you have used this trick in thinking to identify the main activity (and thereby the main processing loop) of the program, the design can be completed, and the program can be converted easily to a single loop version.

An interesting feature of processing loops is that they work for one occurrence in the loop just as well as they do for all occurrences. Listing 7.10, mult08.cbl, is identical to mult07.cbl, but certain lines have been commented out. Commenting out code is a common practice. Instead

7

of deleting the whole line, simply place an asterisk in column 7. This causes the line to be treated as a comment, and it is therefore ignored by the compiler. It has the same effect as deleting the line, but it leaves the code there. This practice is used when something is being changed and you need to refer to the original.

TYPE **Listing 7.10. Converting** `mult07.cbl` **to perform a single loop.**

```
000100 IDENTIFICATION DIVISION.
000200 PROGRAM-ID. MULT08.
000300*-----------------------------------------------
000400* This program asks the user for a number for a
000500* multiplication table, and a table size
000600* and then displays a table for that number
000700* times the values 1 through HOW-MANY.
000800*
000900* The display is paused after each 15 lines.
001000*-----------------------------------------------
001100 ENVIRONMENT DIVISION.
001200 DATA DIVISION.
001300 WORKING-STORAGE SECTION.
001400
001500 01  THE-TABLE         PIC 99.
001600 01  THE-ENTRY         PIC 999.
001700 01  THE-PRODUCT       PIC 9999.
001800 01  HOW-MANY-ENTRIES  PIC 99.
001900 01  SCREEN-LINES      PIC 99.
002000
002100 01  A-DUMMY           PIC X.
002200
002300*01  YES-NO            PIC X VALUE "Y".
002400
002500 PROCEDURE DIVISION.
002600
002700 PROGRAM-BEGIN.
002800*     MOVE "Y" TO YES-NO.
002900      PERFORM DISPLAY-ONE-TABLE.
003000*         UNTIL YES-NO = "N".
003100
003200 PROGRAM-DONE.
003300      STOP RUN.
003400
003500 DISPLAY-ONE-TABLE.
003600      PERFORM GET-WHICH-TABLE.
003700      PERFORM DISPLAY-THE-TABLE.
003800*     PERFORM GO-AGAIN.
003900
004000 GET-WHICH-TABLE.
004100      DISPLAY
004200      "Which multiplication table(01-99)?".
004300      ACCEPT THE-TABLE.
004400
004500 DISPLAY-THE-TABLE.
004600      PERFORM GET-HOW-MANY-ENTRIES.
004700
```

```
004800      MOVE 0 TO SCREEN-LINES.
004900
005000      PERFORM DISPLAY-ONE-ENTRY
005100          VARYING THE-ENTRY
005200              FROM 1 BY 1
005300              UNTIL THE-ENTRY > HOW-MANY-ENTRIES.
005400
005500*GO-AGAIN.
005600*      DISPLAY "Go Again (Y/N)?".
005700*      ACCEPT YES-NO.
005800*      IF YES-NO = "y"
005900*          MOVE "Y" TO YES-NO.
006000*      IF YES-NO NOT = "Y"
006100*          MOVE "N" TO YES-NO.
006200
006300 GET-HOW-MANY-ENTRIES.
006400      DISPLAY
006500        "How many entries would you like (01-99)?".
006600      ACCEPT HOW-MANY-ENTRIES.
006700
006800 DISPLAY-ONE-ENTRY.
006900
007000      IF SCREEN-LINES = 15
007100          PERFORM PRESS-ENTER.
007200      COMPUTE THE-PRODUCT = THE-TABLE * THE-ENTRY.
007300      DISPLAY
007400          THE-TABLE " * " THE-ENTRY " = " THE-PRODUCT.
007500
007600      ADD 1 TO SCREEN-LINES.
007700
007800 PRESS-ENTER.
007900      DISPLAY "Press ENTER to continue . . .".
008000      ACCEPT A-DUMMY.
008100      MOVE 0 TO SCREEN-LINES.
008200
```

ANALYSIS   Listing 7.10 has been modified to remove all the code pertaining to asking the user to continue and to going again if the user answers yes.

Lines 002300, 002800, 003000, 003800, and 005500 through 006100 have been commented out. The resulting program is a slightly different version of the original multiplication tables program that displays only one table. The mult07.cbl program has been stripped back to a single pass by a few well-placed asterisks, and you have completed an efficient design.

Processing loops are not always obvious. The original versions of the multiplication program, mult01.cbl through mult06.cbl, in Day 5, made only one pass through the main processing loop.

If you are designing a program that performs only one pass of some process, you can imitate the process shown in Listing 7.10, mult08.cbl. Pretend that you are making multiple passes, complete the design, and then cut back to one pass through the loop. This is just a trick to help you think of the main action of a program as a processing loop, even if it is executed only once.

7

A Summary of Design Steps

Before you tackle another design problem, a review of the design steps that you have learned is in order. The following list includes both design and development:

1. Create a job description. This is a precise, but not necessarily detailed, description of what the program will do.

2. Break the job description into tasks. This step adds detail to the precision. The tasks might need to be further broken down until the task descriptions approximate what a computer can do.

3. Identify the processing loops.

4. Identify the main processing loop if it has not become apparent during step 3.

5. Write the program in pseudocode.

6. Convert the pseudocode into actual code.

7. Edit and compile the program.

8. Test the program.

9. Fix any bugs by rewriting the areas of the program that aren't working correctly.

10. Repeat steps 8 and 9 until the program works correctly.

It is not unusual for steps 1 through 5 to take longer than steps 6 through 10, especially if you do a thorough job of design.

A Compound Interest Program

In this example you work through the design of a completely new program that calculates the value of an initial investment after compound interest has accumulated over a period of time.

To calculate compound interest, you need to know the principal, the interest rate over a given period, and the number of periods over which the interest will be compounded. Starting with the steps again, you first create a job description for the program, which is as follows:

Calculate the values of investments based on user input of principals, interest rates, and number of periods.

This can be broken into the following tasks without regard to their order:

1. Calculate the value of an investment over and over.

2. Display the value.

3. Get user input of the principal.

4. Get user input of the interest.

5. Get user input of the number of periods.

The easiest way to calculate compound interest is to calculate the new value of the investment over one period. Then make the new value the investment, and calculate another new value on one period using the new investment value. (See Table 7.2.) This is repeated until all periods are exhausted. Assuming an interest rate of 10 percent over four periods, the value of the investment is calculated in the four steps shown in Table 7.2.

Table 7.2. Calculating compound interest.

Period	1	2	3	4
Principal	1000.00	1100.00	1210.00	1331.00
Rate (10%)	×.10	×.10	×.10	×.10
Interest	=100.00	=110.00	=121.00	=133.10
Plus the original principal	+1000.00	+1100.00	+1210.00	+1331.00
Equals	=1100.00	=1210.00	=1331.00	=1464.10

At the end of each step, the resulting value is moved to the top of the next period and the steps are repeated.

There are more efficient formulas for compound interest, but this one illustrates that even when you don't know the "most proper" formula, you can use a computer to tough it out for you. This helps to add a sixth task to the list.

6. Calculate the new value of an investment for one period over and over.

From these tasks, it is possible to recognize two processing loops at tasks 1 and 6. The loop at task 1 is the main loop for the program.

From your existing experience with pseudocode, put together a quick outline of the program. In Listing 7.11, I've used more formal pseudocode, which approximates COBOL even more closely. Now that you have some experience with DISPLAY and ACCEPT, it's not necessary to spell all this out in pseudocode. Remember that pseudocode is supposed to help during a design, not be extra work to do. The pseudocode is clear enough to indicate that you will display some sort of message and get some user input.

TYPE   **Listing 7.11. Pseudocode for compound interest.**

```
THE-PROGRAM
    MOVE "Y" TO YES-NO
    PERFORM GET-AND-DISPLAY-RESULT
       UNTIL YES-NO = "N".
```

continues

Listing 7.11. continued

```
GET-AND-DISPLAY-RESULT.
    PERFORM GET-THE-PRINCIPAL
    PERFORM GET-THE-INTEREST
    PERFORM GET-THE-PERIODS.
    PERFORM CALCULATE-THE-RESULT.
    PERFORM DISPLAY-THE-RESULT.
    PERFORM GO-AGAIN.

GET-THE-PRINCIPAL.
    ( between 0.01 and 999999.99 )

GET-THE-INTEREST.
    ( between 00.1 and 99.9%)

GET-THE-PERIODS.
    ( between 001 and 999 )

CALCULATE-THE-RESULT.
    PERFORM CALCULATE-ONE-PERIOD
        VARYING THE-PERIOD FROM 1 BY 1
          UNTIL THE-PERIOD > NO-OF-PERIODS.

CALCULATE-ONE-PERIOD.
    COMPUTE EARNED-INTEREST ROUNDED =
        THE-PRINCIPAL * INTEREST-AS-DECIMAL.
    COMPUTE THE-NEW-VALUE =
            THE-PRINCIPAL + EARNED-INTEREST.
    MOVE THE-NEW-VALUE TO THE-PRINCIPAL.

GO-AGAIN
    ( YES OR NO)

DISPLAY-THE-RESULT
    (VALUE = THE-PRINCIPAL)
```

Listing 7.12 is the code that comes from the pseudocode. The paragraphs to get the principal, the interest, and the number of periods have been designed to validate the input data, display an invalid entry message if necessary, and go to the top of the paragraph if an entry error has occurred. Study this listing, code it, compile it, and try it out.

NOTE Remember that the ACCEPT data-name statements have to be adjusted to your computer to ACCEPT data-name CONVERT or just ACCEPT data-name WITH CONVERSION.

TYPE **Listing 7.12. Compound interest.**

```
000100 IDENTIFICATION DIVISION.
000200 PROGRAM-ID. CMPINT01.
000300*------------------------------------------------
000400* Calculates compound interest
000500*------------------------------------------------
000600 ENVIRONMENT DIVISION.
000700 DATA DIVISION.
000800 WORKING-STORAGE SECTION.
000900
001000 01   YES-NO                       PIC X.
001100 01   THE-INTEREST                 PIC 99V9.
001200 01   INTEREST-AS-DECIMAL          PIC V999.
001300 01   THE-PRINCIPAL                PIC 9(9)V99.
001400 01   THE-NEW-VALUE                PIC 9(9)V99.
001500 01   EARNED-INTEREST              PIC 9(9)V99.
001600 01   THE-PERIOD                   PIC 9999.
001700 01   NO-OF-PERIODS                PIC 999.
001800
001900 01   ENTRY-FIELD                  PIC Z(9).ZZ.
002000 01   DISPLAY-VALUE                PIC ZZZ,ZZZ,ZZ9.99.
002100
002200 PROCEDURE DIVISION.
002300 PROGRAM-BEGIN.
002400
002500     MOVE "Y" TO YES-NO.
002600     PERFORM GET-AND-DISPLAY-RESULT
002700         UNTIL YES-NO = "N".
002800
002900 PROGRAM-DONE.
003000     STOP RUN.
003100
003200 GET-AND-DISPLAY-RESULT.
003300     PERFORM GET-THE-PRINCIPAL.
003400     PERFORM GET-THE-INTEREST.
003500     PERFORM GET-THE-PERIODS.
003600     PERFORM CALCULATE-THE-RESULT.
003700     PERFORM DISPLAY-THE-RESULT.
003800     PERFORM GO-AGAIN.
003900
004000 GET-THE-PRINCIPAL.
004100     DISPLAY "Principal (.01 TO 999999.99)?".
004200     ACCEPT ENTRY-FIELD
004300     MOVE ENTRY-FIELD TO THE-PRINCIPAL.
004400     IF THE-PRINCIPAL < .01 OR
004500         THE-PRINCIPAL > 999999.99
004600         DISPLAY "INVALID ENTRY"
004700         GO TO GET-THE-PRINCIPAL.
004800
004900 GET-THE-INTEREST.
005000     DISPLAY "Interest (.1% TO 99.9%)?".
005100     ACCEPT ENTRY-FIELD.
005200     MOVE ENTRY-FIELD TO THE-INTEREST.
005300     IF THE-INTEREST < .1 OR
```

7

continues

Listing 7.12. continued

```
005400        THE-INTEREST > 99.9
005500         DISPLAY "INVALID ENTRY"
005600         GO TO GET-THE-INTEREST
005700    ELSE
005800        COMPUTE INTEREST-AS-DECIMAL =
005900            THE-INTEREST / 100.
006000
006100 GET-THE-PERIODS.
006200    DISPLAY "Number of periods (1 TO 999)?".
006300    ACCEPT ENTRY-FIELD.
006400    MOVE ENTRY-FIELD TO NO-OF-PERIODS.
006500    IF NO-OF-PERIODS < 1 OR
006600        NO-OF-PERIODS > 999
006700         DISPLAY "INVALID ENTRY"
006800         GO TO GET-THE-PERIODS.
006900
007000 CALCULATE-THE-RESULT.
007100    PERFORM CALCULATE-ONE-PERIOD
007200        VARYING THE-PERIOD FROM 1 BY 1
007300            UNTIL THE-PERIOD > NO-OF-PERIODS.
007400
007500 CALCULATE-ONE-PERIOD.
007600    COMPUTE EARNED-INTEREST ROUNDED =
007700        THE-PRINCIPAL * INTEREST-AS-DECIMAL.
007800    COMPUTE THE-NEW-VALUE =
007900            THE-PRINCIPAL + EARNED-INTEREST.
008000    MOVE THE-NEW-VALUE TO THE-PRINCIPAL.
008100
008200 GO-AGAIN.
008300    DISPLAY "GO AGAIN?".
008400    ACCEPT YES-NO.
008500    IF YES-NO = "y"
008600        MOVE "Y" TO YES-NO.
008700    IF YES-NO NOT = "Y"
008800        MOVE "N" TO YES-NO.
008900
009000 DISPLAY-THE-RESULT.
009100    MOVE THE-NEW-VALUE TO DISPLAY-VALUE.
009200    DISPLAY "RESULTING VALUE IS " DISPLAY-VALUE.
009300
```

Here is the output of `cmpint01.cbl` for $1,000.00 invested at 1.1 percent per month, and compounded for 48 months:

```
Principal (.01 TO 999999.99)?
1000
Interest (.1% TO 99.9%)?
1.1
Number of periods (1 TO 999)?
48
RESULTING VALUE IS        1,690.65
GO AGAIN?
```

Before anyone complains about using GO TO in Listing 7.12, I have included Listing 7.13, cmpint02.cbl, which avoids the GO TO logic by using an ENTRY-OK flag. Study the differences in cmpint01.cbl and cmpint02.cbl. The second listing illustrates that you can avoid using a GO TO even when a GO TO seems like a logical choice.

TYPE **Listing 7.13. Avoiding GO TO.**

```
000100 IDENTIFICATION DIVISION.
000200 PROGRAM-ID. CMPINT02.
000300*-------------------------------------------------
000400* Calculates compound interest
000500*-------------------------------------------------
000600 ENVIRONMENT DIVISION.
000700 DATA DIVISION.
000800 WORKING-STORAGE SECTION.
000900
001000 01   YES-NO                      PIC X.
001100 01   ENTRY-OK                    PIC X.
001200 01   THE-INTEREST                PIC 99V9.
001300 01   INTEREST-AS-DECIMAL         PIC V999.
001400 01   THE-PRINCIPAL               PIC 9(9)V99.
001500 01   THE-NEW-VALUE               PIC 9(9)V99.
001600 01   EARNED-INTEREST             PIC 9(9)V99.
001700 01   THE-PERIOD                  PIC 9999.
001800 01   NO-OF-PERIODS               PIC 999.
001900
002000 01   ENTRY-FIELD                 PIC Z(9).ZZ.
002100 01   DISPLAY-VALUE               PIC ZZZ,ZZZ,ZZ9.99.
002200
002300 PROCEDURE DIVISION.
002400 PROGRAM-BEGIN.
002500
002600      MOVE "Y" TO YES-NO.
002700      PERFORM GET-AND-DISPLAY-RESULT
002800          UNTIL YES-NO = "N".
002900
003000 PROGRAM-DONE.
003100      STOP RUN.
003200
003300 GET-AND-DISPLAY-RESULT.
003400      PERFORM GET-THE-PRINCIPAL.
003500      PERFORM GET-THE-INTEREST.
003600      PERFORM GET-THE-PERIODS.
003700      PERFORM CALCULATE-THE-RESULT.
003800      PERFORM DISPLAY-THE-RESULT.
003900      PERFORM GO-AGAIN.
004000
004100 GET-THE-PRINCIPAL.
004200      MOVE "N" TO ENTRY-OK.
004300      PERFORM ENTER-THE-PRINCIPAL
004400          UNTIL ENTRY-OK = "Y".
004500
```

7

continues

Listing 7.13. continued

```
004600 ENTER-THE-PRINCIPAL.
004700     DISPLAY "Principal (.01 TO 999999.99)?".
004800     ACCEPT ENTRY-FIELD.
004900     MOVE ENTRY-FIELD TO THE-PRINCIPAL.
005000     IF THE-PRINCIPAL < .01 OR
005100         THE-PRINCIPAL > 999999.99
005200         DISPLAY "INVALID ENTRY"
005300     ELSE
005400         MOVE "Y" TO ENTRY-OK.
005500
005600 GET-THE-INTEREST.
005700     MOVE "N" TO ENTRY-OK.
005800     PERFORM ENTER-THE-INTEREST
005900         UNTIL ENTRY-OK = "Y".
006000
006100 ENTER-THE-INTEREST.
006200     DISPLAY "Interest (.1% TO 99.9%)?".
006300     ACCEPT ENTRY-FIELD.
006400     MOVE ENTRY-FIELD TO THE-INTEREST.
006500     IF THE-INTEREST < .1 OR
006600         THE-INTEREST > 99.9
006700         DISPLAY "INVALID ENTRY"
006800     ELSE
006900         MOVE "Y" TO ENTRY-OK
007000         COMPUTE INTEREST-AS-DECIMAL =
007100                 THE-INTEREST / 100.
007200
007300 GET-THE-PERIODS.
007400     MOVE "N" TO ENTRY-OK.
007500     PERFORM ENTER-THE-PERIODS
007600         UNTIL ENTRY-OK = "Y".
007700
007800 ENTER-THE-PERIODS.
007900     DISPLAY "Number of periods (1 TO 999)?".
008000     ACCEPT ENTRY-FIELD.
008100     MOVE ENTRY-FIELD TO NO-OF-PERIODS.
008200     IF NO-OF-PERIODS < 1 OR
008300         NO-OF-PERIODS > 999
008400         DISPLAY "INVALID ENTRY"
008500     ELSE
008600         MOVE "Y" TO ENTRY-OK.
008700
008800 CALCULATE-THE-RESULT.
008900     PERFORM CALCULATE-ONE-PERIOD
009000         VARYING THE-PERIOD FROM 1 BY 1
009100             UNTIL THE-PERIOD > NO-OF-PERIODS.
009200
009300 CALCULATE-ONE-PERIOD.
009400     COMPUTE EARNED-INTEREST ROUNDED =
009500         THE-PRINCIPAL * INTEREST-AS-DECIMAL.
009600     COMPUTE THE-NEW-VALUE =
009700             THE-PRINCIPAL + EARNED-INTEREST.
009800     MOVE THE-NEW-VALUE TO THE-PRINCIPAL.
009900
```

```
010000 GO-AGAIN.
010100     DISPLAY "GO AGAIN?".
010200     ACCEPT YES-NO.
010300     IF YES-NO = "y"
010400         MOVE "Y" TO YES-NO.
010500     IF YES-NO NOT = "Y"
010600         MOVE "N" TO YES-NO.
010700
010800 DISPLAY-THE-RESULT.
010900     MOVE THE-NEW-VALUE TO DISPLAY-VALUE.
011000     DISPLAY "RESULTING VALUE IS " DISPLAY-VALUE.
011100
```

ANALYSIS In Listing 7.13, the data entry is treated as a processing loop that is performed until the data that is entered is correct.

For example, at line 004200, the ENTRY-OK flag is set to "N" (not okay) before the loop ENTER-THE-PRINCIPAL is performed. Then ENTER-THE-PRINCIPAL is performed UNTIL ENTRY-OK = "Y" (the data entry is okay). This forces ENTER-THE-PRINCIPAL to be performed at least once. Because the code ENTER-THE-PRINCIPAL is used, the user is prompted for an entry, the entry is accepted, and the entry is checked.

If the entry is okay, the ENTRY-OK flag is set to "Y". This ends the PERFORM UNTIL at lines 004300 and 004400.

If the entry is not okay, an INVALID ENTRY message is displayed, but the ENTRY-OK flag is not changed. On exit, the PERFORM UNTIL at lines 004300 and 004400 finds that the ENTRY-OK flag is not yet "Y" and ENTER-THE-PRINCIPAL is performed one more time. This continues until the user gets it right and the ENTRY-OK flag is set to "Y".

Summary

Today, you learned the basics of program design. The following are the key steps of design and development:

1. Create a job description for the program.
2. Break the job description into tasks until the tasks approximate what the computer will do.
3. Identify the processing loops.
4. Identify the main processing loop if it has not become apparent during step 3.
5. Write the program in pseudocode.
6. Convert the pseudocode into actual code.
7. Edit and compile the program.
8. Test the program.

9. Fix any bugs by rewriting the areas of the program that aren't working correctly.

10. Repeat steps 8 and 9 until the program works correctly.

Pseudocode is any convenient English-like method of describing what a program does. Pseudocode helps with the design of a program and easily converts into the code for the program.

You can avoid GO TO using the PERFORM verb and its variations.

Q&A

Q Do I have to do all of the design steps before I start coding?

A When you are learning, it is good practice to do all steps. This helps you clarify what the program eventually is supposed to do. Even so, you will notice that in the second example, I left out some of the steps of the pseudocode.

You will reach a point when you can "think" in sections of code. For example, you probably already have a rough idea of what the code would look like to ask the user whether to go again. You will be able to shortcut some of the design steps because you will actually be doing them in your head without having to write them all out on paper.

Workshop

Quiz

1. What is the first step in designing the program for the following job description?

   Ask the user for sales amounts and sales tax rates, and use these values to calculate the sales tax on the amount.

2. What are the six design steps?

Exercises

1. Perform all the design steps up to and including the coding of the job described in Quiz question 1. The steps for this are given in the back of the book. If you hit a snag on any step, go ahead and look at the answer for that step. Designing is a skill that comes only with a vast amount of experience. Occasionally, I have seen competent programmers freeze or produce a bad design when they have been asked to design certain programs, and I still have plenty to learn about design. There is no shame in getting help for this exercise.

   Hint: You will be able to use quite a bit of the logic from cmpint02.cbl (shown in Listing 7.13) as the basic model for the program.

2. Complete the following last four steps of the development on the design you did in Exercise 1.

   7. Edit and compile the program.

   8. Test the program.

   9. Fix any bugs by rewriting the areas of the program that aren't working correctly.

  10. Repeat steps 8 and 9 until the program works correctly.

3. Modify the program that you created in Exercise 2 so that it asks for the sales tax percentage only once as the first step of the program, and then asks for sales amounts repeatedly, calculating the sales tax for each entry.

Hint: Use the answer to Exercise 2 from Appendix A, "Answers." You should be able to make this change by moving only one line of code up to become the first line of code in PROGRAM-BEGIN.

7

In Review

After the first week of teaching yourself COBOL, you should be familiar with the basic structure of a COBOL program. Because COBOL is much like the English language in structure and readability, you probably can follow programs containing unfamiliar material—something you might not be able to do when learning other programming languages. By now you should be able to easily recognize and build the four DIVISIONs, design your overall program structure, make decisions using the IF statement, designate the flow of your program using PERFORM and GO TO, and use the various operators to manipulate data stored within your program.

As you continue, focus on what is being accomplished and how it fits within the concepts you've learned so far. The lessons are designed to build on each other and reduce the need to turn back and rehash previous days, but don't feel bad if you need to do so. Although the design of COBOL is simple, this book moves at a rapid pace in order to ensure that you have all the necessary information to quickly become a competent COBOL programmer.

WEEK

2

At a Glance

You've made it through the first week. You can now define the information your program should store and manipulate, and you know how to act on this information. You can be proud of what you've accomplished so far.

8

9

10

11

12

13

14

Where You're Going

The second week focuses on reading information into your program and out to your users. COBOL excels in this area, so don't underestimate the value of these chapters and their quizzes and exercises. After all, the value of any software lies in how easily others can use it. Day 8, "Structured Data," will help you take the information your program uses and organize it into a structured format. You can then more easily model the real-world problems that you face daily. Day 9, "File I/O," and Day 10, "Printing," emphasize the need to effectively and efficiently read information into and out of files and print formatted information on your printer. Day 11, "Indexed File I/O," and Day 12, "More on Indexed Files," provide important information that no COBOL programmer should be without. Day 13, "Deleting Records and Other Indexed File Operations," adds to your growing understanding of indexed files by teaching you to delete unwanted information—a skill as important as collecting necessary information. You'll close the second week with still another day of indexed files on Day 14, "A Review of Indexed Files."

After you finish this week, you should rank yourself as a strong intermediate user. You'll be two-thirds of the way through your 21-day journey.

Day **8**

Structured Data

You can use the DATA DIVISION to organize your data and variables and improve the performance of your program. You also can use it to reduce the amount of code that you have to write.

Today, you learn about the following topics:

- ☐ What is a data structure?
- ☐ How to use a data structure.
- ☐ FILLER and how to use it.
- ☐ Calculating the length of data structures.
- ☐ What is structured data in memory?
- ☐ Nested structure variables.
- ☐ Misusing structures.
- ☐ What is level 77?
- ☐ What is level 88?

What Is a Data Structure?

You might want to create a COBOL program that combines variables to improve the way they display.

 A *data structure*, or *record*, in COBOL is a method of combining several variables into one larger variable.

The program `jack02.cbl` in Day 2, "Using Variables and Constants," used variables to display a poem with line numbers. Variables are defined and displayed as shown in Listing 8.1.

TYPE   **Listing 8.1. An extract from `jack02.cbl`.**

```
000700
000800 01   THE-MESSAGE        PIC X(50).
000900 01   THE-NUMBER         PIC 9(2).
001000 01   A-SPACE           PIC X.
001100
......
001700
001800* Set up and display line 1
001900     MOVE 1 TO THE-NUMBER.
002000     MOVE "Jack be nimble," TO THE-MESSAGE.
002100     DISPLAY THE-NUMBER A-SPACE THE-MESSAGE
002200
```

These three variables can be combined into one record (data structure) and used as a group for the DISPLAY statement. The grouping is done by defining the data as shown in Listing 8.2.

TYPE   **Listing 8.2. A structure or record.**

```
000700
000800 01   THE-WHOLE-MESSAGE.
000900     05   THE-NUMBER      PIC 9(2)   VALUE ZEROES.
001000     05   A-SPACE        PIC X(1)   VALUE SPACE.
001100     05   THE-MESSAGE    PIC X(50) VALUE SPACES.
001200
```

 In Listing 8.2, THE-WHOLE-MESSAGE is a *structure variable* or simply a *structure*. It is occasionally referred to as a *compound variable* or *compound data*.

In a structure variable, the highest-level variable (the one that includes all the individual variables) has the level number 01. The 01 level must appear in Area A (columns 8 through 12). The structure variable name appears in Area B (columns 12 through 72), and it does not have a PICTURE. The variables that fall within the structure begin with numbers higher than 01, and start in Area B (columns 12 through 72).

You can use the individual variables within a structure in the program as though they still were level 01 variables. In addition, you can use the structure variable as a variable. For example, if all the variables within a structure variable can be displayed, the structure variable itself can be displayed as a variable (see Listing 8.3).

TYPE **Listing 8.3. Using a structure.**

```
000700
000800 01   THE-WHOLE-MESSAGE.
000900      05   THE-NUMBER        PIC 9(2)   VALUE ZEROES.
001000      05   A-SPACE          PIC X(1)   VALUE SPACE.
001100      05   THE-MESSAGE      PIC X(50)  VALUE SPACES.
......
001700
001800* Set up and display line 1
001900      MOVE 1 TO THE-NUMBER.
002000      MOVE "Jack be nimble," TO THE-MESSAGE.
002100      DISPLAY THE-WHOLE-MESSAGE.
002200
```

ANALYSIS The individual variables of the structure have higher level numbers than the structure variable. In the following code fragment, the elementary variables have the level number 05. This level number could have been 02, but it is a common practice to skip some numbers between levels.

Figure 8.1 illustrates the positioning of the parts of a structure variable within Area A and Area B.

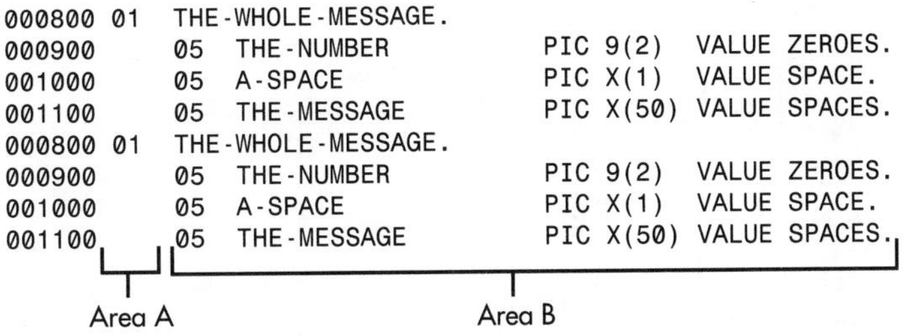

Figure 8.1.
The layout of a structure in Area A and Area B.

```
000800 01   THE-WHOLE-MESSAGE.
000900      05   THE-NUMBER        PIC 9(2)   VALUE ZEROES.
001000      05   A-SPACE          PIC X(1)   VALUE SPACE.
001100      05   THE-MESSAGE      PIC X(50)  VALUE SPACES.
000800 01   THE-WHOLE-MESSAGE.
000900      05   THE-NUMBER        PIC 9(2)   VALUE ZEROES.
001000      05   A-SPACE          PIC X(1)   VALUE SPACE.
001100      05   THE-MESSAGE      PIC X(50)  VALUE SPACES.
```

Area A   Area B

How to Use a Data Structure

One of the primary uses of a structure is to format information for display or printing. One quick way of seeing how structures work is to use one to format output data.

Listing 8.4, cmpint03.cbl, is similar to the compound interest programs in Day 7, "Basics of Design," but it uses a structured variable (a structure) to produce a formatted output.

TYPE   **Listing 8.4. Using a structure to format data.**

```
000100 IDENTIFICATION DIVISION.
000200 PROGRAM-ID. CMPINT03.
000300*-----------------------------------------------
000400* Calculates compound interest
000500*-----------------------------------------------
000600 ENVIRONMENT DIVISION.
000700 DATA DIVISION.
000800 WORKING-STORAGE SECTION.
000900
001000 01  YES-NO                    PIC X.
001100 01  ENTRY-OK                  PIC X.
001200 01  THE-INTEREST              PIC 99V9.
001300 01  INTEREST-AS-DECIMAL       PIC V999.
001400 01  THE-PRINCIPAL             PIC 9(9)V99.
001500 01  WORKING-PRINCIPAL         PIC 9(9)V99.
001600 01  THE-NEW-VALUE             PIC 9(9)V99.
001700 01  EARNED-INTEREST           PIC 9(9)V99.
001800 01  THE-PERIOD                PIC 9999.
001900 01  NO-OF-PERIODS             PIC 999.
002000
002100 01  ENTRY-FIELD               PIC ZZZ,ZZZ,ZZZ.ZZ.
002200
002300 01  THE-WHOLE-MESSAGE.
002400     05  DISPLAY-PRINCIPAL     PIC ZZZ,ZZZ,ZZ9.99.
002500     05  MESSAGE-PART-01       PIC X(4) VALUE " at ".
002600     05  DISPLAY-INTEREST      PIC Z9.9.
002700     05  MESSAGE-PART-02       PIC X(6) VALUE "% for ".
002800     05  DISPLAY-PERIODS       PIC ZZ9.
002900     05  MESSAGE-PART-03       PIC X(16)
003000         VALUE " periods yields ".
003100     05  DISPLAY-VALUE         PIC ZZZ,ZZZ,ZZ9.99.
003200
003300 PROCEDURE DIVISION.
003400 PROGRAM-BEGIN.
003500
003600     MOVE "Y" TO YES-NO.
003700     PERFORM GET-AND-DISPLAY-RESULT
003800         UNTIL YES-NO = "N".
003900
004000 PROGRAM-DONE.
004100     STOP RUN.
004200
004300 GET-AND-DISPLAY-RESULT.
004400     PERFORM GET-THE-PRINCIPAL.
004500     PERFORM GET-THE-INTEREST.
004600     PERFORM GET-THE-PERIODS.
004700     PERFORM CALCULATE-THE-RESULT.
004800     PERFORM DISPLAY-THE-RESULT.
004900     PERFORM GO-AGAIN.
005000
005100 GET-THE-PRINCIPAL.
005200     MOVE "N" TO ENTRY-OK.
005300     PERFORM ENTER-THE-PRINCIPAL
005400         UNTIL ENTRY-OK = "Y".
005500
```

```
005600 ENTER-THE-PRINCIPAL.
005700     DISPLAY "Principal (.01 TO 999999.99)?".
005800     ACCEPT ENTRY-FIELD WITH CONVERSION.
005900     MOVE ENTRY-FIELD TO THE-PRINCIPAL.
006000     IF THE-PRINCIPAL < .01 OR
006100        THE-PRINCIPAL > 999999.99
006200          DISPLAY "INVALID ENTRY"
006300     ELSE
006400          MOVE "Y" TO ENTRY-OK.
006500
006600 GET-THE-INTEREST.
006700     MOVE "N" TO ENTRY-OK.
006800     PERFORM ENTER-THE-INTEREST
006900          UNTIL ENTRY-OK = "Y".
007000
007100 ENTER-THE-INTEREST.
007200     DISPLAY "Interest (.1% TO 99.9%)?".
007300     ACCEPT ENTRY-FIELD WITH CONVERSION.
007400     MOVE ENTRY-FIELD TO THE-INTEREST.
007500     IF THE-INTEREST < .1 OR
007600        THE-INTEREST > 99.9
007700          DISPLAY "INVALID ENTRY"
007800     ELSE
007900          MOVE "Y" TO ENTRY-OK
008000          COMPUTE INTEREST-AS-DECIMAL =
008100                  THE-INTEREST / 100.
008200
008300 GET-THE-PERIODS.
008400     MOVE "N" TO ENTRY-OK.
008500     PERFORM ENTER-THE-PERIODS
008600          UNTIL ENTRY-OK = "Y".
008700
008800 ENTER-THE-PERIODS.
008900     DISPLAY "Number of periods (1 TO 999)?".
009000     ACCEPT ENTRY-FIELD WITH CONVERSION.
009100     MOVE ENTRY-FIELD TO NO-OF-PERIODS.
009200     IF NO-OF-PERIODS < 1 OR
009300        NO-OF-PERIODS > 999
009400          DISPLAY "INVALID ENTRY"
009500     ELSE
009600          MOVE "Y" TO ENTRY-OK.
009700
009800 CALCULATE-THE-RESULT.
009900     MOVE THE-PRINCIPAL TO WORKING-PRINCIPAL.
010000     PERFORM CALCULATE-ONE-PERIOD
010100          VARYING THE-PERIOD FROM 1 BY 1
010200          UNTIL THE-PERIOD > NO-OF-PERIODS.
010300
010400 CALCULATE-ONE-PERIOD.
010500     COMPUTE EARNED-INTEREST ROUNDED =
010600          WORKING-PRINCIPAL * INTEREST-AS-DECIMAL.
010700     COMPUTE THE-NEW-VALUE =
010800              WORKING-PRINCIPAL + EARNED-INTEREST.
010900     MOVE THE-NEW-VALUE TO WORKING-PRINCIPAL.
011000
```

continues

Listing 8.4. continued

```
011100 GO-AGAIN.
011200     DISPLAY "GO AGAIN?".
011300     ACCEPT YES-NO.
011400     IF YES-NO = "y"
011500         MOVE "Y" TO YES-NO.
011600     IF YES-NO NOT = "Y"
011700         MOVE "N" TO YES-NO.
011800
011900 DISPLAY-THE-RESULT.
012000     MOVE THE-PRINCIPAL TO DISPLAY-PRINCIPAL.
012100     MOVE THE-INTEREST   TO DISPLAY-INTEREST.
012200     MOVE NO-OF-PERIODS TO DISPLAY-PERIODS.
012300     MOVE THE-NEW-VALUE TO DISPLAY-VALUE.
012400     DISPLAY THE-WHOLE-MESSAGE.
012500
```

OUTPUT
```
Principal (.01 TO 999999.99)?
14000
Interest (.1% TO 99.9%)?
12.7
Number of periods (1 TO 999)?
14
14,000.00 at 12.7% for  14 periods yields      74,655.69
GO AGAIN?
```

ANALYSIS The structure is defined at lines 002300 to 003100. In DISPLAY-THE-RESULT, at lines 0011900 to 0012400, values are moved to each of the individual elements of the structure, and the whole structure is displayed, rather than the separate parts.

The structure THE-WHOLE-MESSAGE is considered to be one long variable containing subparts. By using it for the DISPLAY, you cut down on the amount of code you have to write to display the same formatted data one piece at a time.

FILLER and How to Use It

Listing 8.5 is the message data structure extracted from cmpint03.cbl. All parts of the message appear as variables with level 05 numbers within THE-WHOLE-MESSAGE. Even parts of the message that do not vary, such as MESSAGE-PART-01, MESSAGE-PART-02, and MESSAGE-PART-03, have been given data names.

 TYPE **Listing 8.5. The structure definition.**

```
002300 01  THE-WHOLE-MESSAGE.
002400     05  DISPLAY-PRINCIPAL          PIC ZZZ,ZZZ,ZZ9.99.
002500     05  MESSAGE-PART-01            PIC X(4) VALUE " at ".
002600     05  DISPLAY-INTEREST           PIC Z9.9.
002700     05  MESSAGE-PART-02            PIC X(6) VALUE "% for ".
```

```
002800        05  DISPLAY-PERIODS          PIC ZZ9.
002900        05  MESSAGE-PART-03          PIC X(16)
003000            VALUE " periods yields ".
003100        05  DISPLAY-VALUE            PIC ZZZ,ZZZ,ZZ9.99.
003200
```

ANALYSIS   Three of the variables within THE-WHOLE-MESSAGE are never used in the main
program. They are MESSAGE-PART-01, MESSAGE-PART-02, and MESSAGE-PART-03 at
lines 002500, 002700, and 002900, respectively. They are used to format part of the display and
are assigned values in the definition, but nothing is ever moved to these values in the program.

MESSAGE-PART-01, MESSAGE-PART-02, and MESSAGE-PART-03 really do not need to exist as
variables with data names because they are never used in the PROCEDURE DIVISION. They exist
only to fill out THE-WHOLE-MESSAGE.

In COBOL, this type of value in a structure variable can be defined as a filler by using the
COBOL reserved word FILLER. Listing 8.6 uses FILLER in the definition of the same structure
variable.

TYPE   **Listing 8.6. How to use FILLER.**

```
002300 01  THE-WHOLE-MESSAGE.
002400        05  DISPLAY-PRINCIPAL        PIC ZZZ,ZZZ,ZZ9.99.
002500        05  FILLER                   PIC X(4) VALUE " at ".
002600        05  DISPLAY-INTEREST         PIC Z9.9.
002700        05  FILLER                   PIC X(6) VALUE "% for ".
002800        05  DISPLAY-PERIODS          PIC ZZ9.
002900        05  FILLER                   PIC X(16)
003000            VALUE " periods yields ".
003100        05  DISPLAY-VALUE            PIC ZZZ,ZZZ,ZZ9.99.
003200
```

A FILLER cannot be treated as a variable. It is used to reserve space in a structure variable. You
can assign a PICTURE and a VALUE to a FILLER when it is defined, but you cannot use MOVE with
FILLER.

Calculating the Length of Data Structures

A data structure is actually a series of individual variables, laid end to end in memory. The
length of a simple data structure, such as this one used to create a displayable message, is the
sum of all the lengths of the individual parts.

Table 8.1 shows how to calculate the length of THE-WHOLE-MESSAGE by adding the lengths of
the parts. THE-WHOLE-MESSAGE is 61 bytes (characters) long.

Table 8.1. Calculating a structure length.

Variable			Length
05	DISPLAY-PRINCIPAL	PIC ZZZ,ZZZ,ZZ9.99.	14
05	FILLER	PIC X(4) VALUE " at ".	4
05	DISPLAY-INTEREST	PIC Z9.9.	4
05	FILLER	PIC X(6) VALUE "% for ".	6
05	DISPLAY-PERIODS	PIC ZZ9.	3
05	FILLER	PIC X(16) VALUE " periods yields ".	16
05	DISPLAY-VALUE	PIC ZZZ,ZZZ,ZZ9.99.	14
01	THE-WHOLE-MESSAGE		61

What Is Structured Data in Memory?

A structure variable is treated as an alphanumeric variable. It has an implied PICTURE of X(*nn*), where *nn* is equal to the length of the structure variable. THE-WHOLE-MESSAGE has an implicit PICTURE of X(61).

You can move a value to a structure variable, but the move will affect the entire length of the variable. A structure variable and the variables that are the elements of a structure occupy the same memory area. When a variable is created by the compiler, it sets aside a number of bytes in memory that can be used to hold data.

Listing 8.7 shows a sample structure variable used to display an employee number and an hourly rate earned.

Type   **Listing 8.7. A sample structure.**

```
000900 01  EMPLOYEE-DATA.
001000     05  FILLER             PIC X(4)
001100         VALUE "Emp ".
001200     05  EMP-NUMBER         PIC 9999.
001300     05  FILLER             PIC X(7)
001400         VALUE " earns ".
001500     05  EMP-HOURLY         PIC Z9.99.
```

The output of this structure, if you move 234 to EMP-NUMBER and 13.50 to EMP-HOURLY and then DISPLAY EMPLOYEE-DATA, is the following:

Output   `Emp 0234 earns 13.50`

Figure 8.2 represents how the bytes in this structure are filled in with these values (234 in EMP-NUMBER and 13.50 in EMP-HOURLY). The top row numbers the bytes from 1 to 20, which is the length of the entire structure. The second row contains the actual values in memory, where position 1 contains 'E', position 2 contains 'm', and so on.

Rows 3 and 4 are the variable names and the picture for each variable.

Figure 8.2.

The memory layout of a structure.

Position	1	2	3	4	5	6	7	8	9	10	11	12	13	14	15	16	17	18	19	20
Value	E	m	p		0	2	3	4		e	a	r	n	s		1	3	.	5	0
Variable picture	FILLER PIC X (4)				EMP-NUMBER PIC 9 (4)				FILLER PIC X (6)							EMP-HOURLY PIC Z9.99				
Structure	EMPLOYEE-DATA (*implied PIC X (20)*)																			

ANALYSIS   The two fillers, as well as EMP-NUMBER and EMP-HOURLY, occupy some bytes that are in the same space in memory as the structure variable EMPLOYEE-DATA.

When you use a command in COBOL to modify a variable in memory, the command looks at variables in memory as individual units. If you move a value to EMP-NUMBER, or use ADD 1 TO EMP-NUMBER, COBOL acts on EMP-NUMBER as if it were a single variable and ignores the fact that EMP-NUMBER is part of the structure EMPLOYEE-DATA.

Regarding a variable as an individual unit also applies to the complete structure. If you move a message to EMPLOYEE-DATA, the command treats EMPLOYEE-DATA as if it were a PIC X(20) (the implied picture) and ignores the fact that EMPLOYEE-DATA has smaller variables within it.

If the following command is executed in a COBOL program containing this same EMPLOYEE-DATA structure, EMPLOYEE-DATA is treated as if it were a single variable and the elements within EMPLOYEE-DATA are ignored (as shown in Figure 8.3):

```
004600     MOVE "No more employees." TO EMPLOYEE-DATA.
004700     DISPLAY EMPLOYEE-DATA.
```

Figure 8.3.

EMPLOYEE-DATA *after moving a value to it.*

Position	1	2	3	4	5	6	7	8	9	10	11	12	13	14	15	16	17	18	19	20
Value	N	o		M	o	r	e		e	m	p	l	o	y	e	e	s	.		
Structure	EMPLOYEE-DATA (*implied PIC X (20)*)																			

The variables in EMPLOYEE-DATA do not disappear, but the MOVE affects all 20 bytes of memory, and the individual variables might no longer contain data that is correct for that variable type. Figure 8.4 adds back the variables in EMPLOYEE-DATA. EMP-NUMBER now contains ore, which certainly is not valid numeric data. This isn't a problem as long as you don't use a command on EMP-NUMBER, such as ADD 1 TO EMP-NUMBER. I'll return to this issue in a moment.

Figure 8.4.

EMPLOYEE-DATA *with the variables added.*

Position	1	2	3	4	5	6	7	8	9	10	11	12	13	14	15	16	17	18	19	20
Value	N	o		M	o	r	e		e	m	p	l	o	y	e	e	s	.		
Variable picture	FILLER PIC X (4)				EMP-NUMBER PIC 9 (4)				FILLER PIC X (6)							EMP-HOURLY PIC Z9.99				
Structure	EMPLOYEE-DATA *(implied PIC X (20))*																			

This use of a structure variable is fairly common in display and print programs that might use a structure to format and display information line by line, and then at the end of the program might move a message to the entire structure and display it. It is not necessarily good programming practice, but you will encounter this use of structure variables in many programs.

Nested Structure Variables

Any structure can contain another structure. In Listing 8.8, THE-MESSAGE is a structure that, in turn, contains two alphanumeric variables—JACKS-NAME and JACKS-TASK. In addition, it uses a VALUE to initialize JACKS-NAME to reduce the size of the message that must be moved for each line of the display. Indenting JACKS-NAME and JACKS-TASK is a matter of style. The indention makes it clear that these variables are subordinate to THE-MESSAGE.

TYPE **Listing 8.8. Structures within structures.**

```
000100 IDENTIFICATION DIVISION.
000200 PROGRAM-ID. JACK06.
000300 ENVIRONMENT DIVISION.
000400 DATA DIVISION.
000500
000600 WORKING-STORAGE SECTION.
000700
000800 01   THE-WHOLE-MESSAGE.
000900     05   THE-NUMBER        PIC 9(2) VALUE 1.
001000     05   A-SPACE           PIC X    VALUE SPACE.
001100     05   THE-MESSAGE.
001200         10   JACKS-NAME    PIC X(5) VALUE "Jack".
001300         10   JACKS-TASK    PIC X(45).
001400
001500 PROCEDURE DIVISION.
001600 PROGRAM-BEGIN.
001700
001800* Set up and display line 1
001900     MOVE "be nimble," TO JACKS-TASK.
002000     DISPLAY THE-WHOLE-MESSAGE.
002100
002200* Set up and Display line 2
002300     MOVE "be quick," TO JACKS-TASK.
002400     ADD 1 TO THE-NUMBER.
002500     DISPLAY THE-WHOLE-MESSAGE.
002600
```

8

```
002700* Set up and display line 3
002800     MOVE "jump over the candlestick." TO JACKS-TASK.
002900     ADD 1 TO THE-NUMBER.
003000     DISPLAY THE-WHOLE-MESSAGE.
003100
003200* Display a closing message
003300     MOVE "That's all folks" TO THE-WHOLE-MESSAGE.
003400     DISPLAY THE-WHOLE-MESSAGE.
003500
003600 PROGRAM-DONE.
003700     STOP RUN.
003800
```

The following is the output of jack06.cbl.

OUTPUT

```
01 Jack be nimble,
02 Jack be quick,
03 Jack jump over the candlestick.
That's all folks


C>
C>
```

ANALYSIS The last action of the program, at line 003300, is to move a value to THE-WHOLE-MESSAGE and then display it at line 003400. This wipes out the previous contents of THE-WHOLE-MESSAGE and overwrites the whole variable structure as though it were a single alphanumeric variable. This effect can be seen in the output of jack06.cbl.

To calculate the length of a structure variable containing one or more other structure variables, apply what you already know about structure variables. Work out the length of the internal structure variables and add them to the length of the level 01 structure. Table 8.2 calculates the size of the structure by turning the structure upside down and calculating a subtotal for THE-MESSAGE and adding that result to the lengths of the other variables in THE-WHOLE-MESSAGE.

Table 8.2. Calculating the length of a complex structure.

Variable			Length
10	JACKS-TASK	PIC X(45).	45
10	JACKS-NAME	PIC X(5) VALUE "Jack".	+ 5
05	THE-MESSAGE.		= 50 (*subtotal*)
05	A-SPACE	PIC X VALUE SPACE.	+ 1
05	THE-NUMBER	PIC 9(2) VALUE 1.	+ 2
01	THE-WHOLE-MESSAGE.		= 53 (*grand total*)

The maximum level number for a variable within a structure is 49. In practice, it is unusual to find a variable structure that uses all 49 levels. You'll rarely go beyond 25 even when you increment by 5.

The last steps of jack06.cbl are to move "That's all folks" to THE-WHOLE-MESSAGE and then display it. This raises an interesting problem. By moving "That's all folks" to THE-WHOLE-MESSAGE, you move values into the areas occupied by THE-NUMBER, A-SPACE, and THE-MESSAGE. For A-SPACE and THE-MESSAGE, this is no problem because they are alphanumeric variables. THE-NUMBER, however, is a numeric variable that occupies the first two bytes of THE-WHOLE-MESSAGE. After the MOVE, it contains the value "Th", the first two characters of "That's all folks", and the value moved to THE-MESSAGE. This is certainly not numeric data.

If you attempt to perform some sort of calculation with THE-NUMBER, your program usually fails with an error because THE-NUMBER contains invalid data. Some versions of COBOL let you display the variable using DISPLAY THE-NUMBER and it actually displays as "Th". Very few versions of COBOL let you perform anything that resembles a mathematical operation with the variable. Listing 8.9 is a deliberate effort to cause the program to crash by attempting to use ADD 1 TO THE-NUMBER when it contains "Th".

TYPE **Listing 8.9. Forcing a numeric error.**

```
000100 IDENTIFICATION DIVISION.
000200 PROGRAM-ID. JACK07.
000300 ENVIRONMENT DIVISION.
000400 DATA DIVISION.
000500
000600 WORKING-STORAGE SECTION.
000700
000800 01   THE-WHOLE-MESSAGE.
000900      05   THE-NUMBER      PIC 9(2) VALUE 1.
001000      05   A-SPACE         PIC X    VALUE SPACE.
001100      05   THE-MESSAGE.
001200           10   JACKS-NAME  PIC X(5) VALUE "Jack".
001300           10   JACKS-TASK  PIC X(45).
001400
001500 PROCEDURE DIVISION.
001600 PROGRAM-BEGIN.
001700
001800* Set up and display line 1
001900     MOVE "be nimble," TO JACKS-TASK.
002000     DISPLAY THE-WHOLE-MESSAGE.
002100
002200* Set up and Display line 2
002300     MOVE "be quick," TO JACKS-TASK.
002400     ADD 1 TO THE-NUMBER.
002500     DISPLAY THE-WHOLE-MESSAGE.
002600
002700* Set up and display line 3
002800     MOVE "jump over the candlestick." TO JACKS-TASK.
```

```
002900      ADD 1 TO THE-NUMBER.
003000      DISPLAY THE-WHOLE-MESSAGE.
003100
003200* Display a closing message
003300      MOVE "That's all folks" TO THE-WHOLE-MESSAGE.
003400      DISPLAY THE-WHOLE-MESSAGE.
003500
003600* A deliberate attempt to blow up the program
003700      DISPLAY THE-NUMBER.
003800      ADD 1 TO THE-NUMBER.
003900      DISPLAY THE-NUMBER.
004000
004100 PROGRAM-DONE.
004200      STOP RUN.
004300
```

The following output and error message produced by Micro Focus Personal COBOL indicates that an error occurred while trying to ADD 1 TO THE-NUMBER. Note that the first DISPLAY at line 003700 of the program worked and displayed "Th".

OUTPUT
```
C>pcobrun jack07
Personal COBOL version 2.0 from Micro Focus
PCOBRUN V2.0.02  Copyright (C) 1983-1993 Micro Focus Ltd.
01 Jack be nimble,
02 Jack be quick,
03 Jack jump over the candlestick.
That's all folks
Th
JACK07 Segment RT : Error 163 at COBOL PC 009A
Description : Illegal Character in Numeric Field

C>

C>
```

The following output for the same program was compiled and run using ACUCOBOL. This produces no error. The program displays "Th" and then adds 1 to THE-NUMBER and displays it again as "Tg". This obviously nutty result is caused by the fact that THE-NUMBER doesn't contain valid data. If you encounter errors such as non-numeric data in a numeric field, or illegal characters in a numeric field, there are two possible causes that you could investigate. The variable might never have been correctly initialized or the program might have used a MOVE statement to fill a structure variable with information that is invalid for one or more numeric variables that are a part of the structure variable. You would never code a program to take advantage of quirky behavior such as "Th" becoming "Tg" in the preceding example. No one would be able to understand what your program was really trying to do because it relies on possibly unpredictable behavior by some brand of compiler and the behavior might disappear when a new version of the compiler was released by the manufacturer.

```
OUTPUT    01 Jack be nimble,
          02 Jack be quick,
          03 Jack jump over the candlestick.
          That's all folks
          Th
          Tg


          C>
          C>
```

If you have moved a value to the structure and need to use THE-NUMBER again as a numeric value, you must reset the value in THE-NUMBER by moving a number to it, like this:

```
MOVE 1 TO THE-NUMBER.
```

Moving a number to reset the value is the only action you should attempt on a numeric variable that contains invalid data.

Do	Don't

DO move values to numeric variables that have undefined or invalid contents before using numeric variables in calculations.

DON'T perform calculations with numeric variables that have undefined values or that have been modified because they are elements of a structure and some value has been moved to the structure.

Misusing Structures

It is common to find programs that define data structures in WORKING-STORAGE that never are used as structures. Variables of one type might be clumped together into a data structure as a form of documentation. Perhaps this is an effort to be tidy.

Grouping variables together under a structure variable because they are similar or to keep things tidy isn't a good practice. It is better to use comments in WORKING-STORAGE to separate groups of variables used for different purposes. The existence of a structure variable implies that it is used somewhere in the program as a variable. It can be misleading to see a structure in WORKING-STORAGE that is not really a structure but is a grab bag of variables. (See Listing 8.10.) Only THE-WHOLE-MESSAGE is actually used as a structure in the program. Be aware of this when you are trying to understand a program that you are reading. The following example is one you are familiar with, and you will recognize immediately what is going on; recognition is harder in an unfamiliar program.

TYPE   ## Listing 8.10. Clumping variables together.

```
000100 IDENTIFICATION DIVISION.
000200 PROGRAM-ID. CMPINT04.
000300*-------------------------------------------------
000400* Calculates compound interest
000500*-------------------------------------------------
000600 ENVIRONMENT DIVISION.
000700 DATA DIVISION.
000800 WORKING-STORAGE SECTION.
000900
001000 01   SOME-FLAGS.
001100      05   YES-NO                   PIC X.
001200      05   ENTRY-OK                 PIC X.
001300
001400 01   CALCULATION-FIELDS.
001500      05   THE-INTEREST             PIC 99V9.
001600      05   INTEREST-AS-DECIMAL      PIC V999.
001700      05   THE-PRINCIPAL            PIC 9(9)V99.
001800      05   WORKING-PRINCIPAL        PIC 9(9)V99.
001900      05   THE-NEW-VALUE            PIC 9(9)V99.
002000      05   EARNED-INTEREST          PIC 9(9)V99.
002100      05   THE-PERIOD               PIC 9999.
002200      05   NO-OF-PERIODS            PIC 999.
002300
002400 01   ENTRY-FIELD                   PIC ZZZ,ZZZ,ZZZ.ZZ.
002500
002600 01   THE-WHOLE-MESSAGE.
002700      05   DISPLAY-PRINCIPAL        PIC ZZZ,ZZZ,ZZ9.99.
002800      05   MESSAGE-PART-01          PIC X(4) VALUE " at ".
002900      05   DISPLAY-INTEREST         PIC Z9.9.
003000      05   MESSAGE-PART-02          PIC X(6) VALUE "% for ".
003100      05   DISPLAY-PERIODS          PIC ZZ9.
003200      05   MESSAGE-PART-03          PIC X(16)
003300           VALUE " periods yields ".
003400      05   DISPLAY-VALUE            PIC ZZZ,ZZZ,ZZ9.99.
003500
003600 PROCEDURE DIVISION.
003700 PROGRAM-BEGIN.
003800
003900      MOVE "Y" TO YES-NO.
004000      PERFORM GET-AND-DISPLAY-RESULT
004100           UNTIL YES-NO = "N".
004200
004300 PROGRAM-DONE.
004400      STOP RUN.
004500
004600 GET-AND-DISPLAY-RESULT.
004700      PERFORM GET-THE-PRINCIPAL.
004800      PERFORM GET-THE-INTEREST.
004900      PERFORM GET-THE-PERIODS.
005000      PERFORM CALCULATE-THE-RESULT.
005100      PERFORM DISPLAY-THE-RESULT.
005200      PERFORM GO-AGAIN.
005300
```

continues

Listing 8.10. continued

```
005400 GET-THE-PRINCIPAL.
005500     MOVE "N" TO ENTRY-OK.
005600     PERFORM ENTER-THE-PRINCIPAL
005700         UNTIL ENTRY-OK = "Y".
005800
005900 ENTER-THE-PRINCIPAL.
006000     DISPLAY "Principal (.01 TO 999999.99)?".
006100     ACCEPT ENTRY-FIELD WITH CONVERSION.
006200     MOVE ENTRY-FIELD TO THE-PRINCIPAL.
006300     IF THE-PRINCIPAL < .01 OR
006400         THE-PRINCIPAL > 999999.99
006500             DISPLAY "INVALID ENTRY"
006600     ELSE
006700         MOVE "Y" TO ENTRY-OK.
006800
006900 GET-THE-INTEREST.
007000     MOVE "N" TO ENTRY-OK.
007100     PERFORM ENTER-THE-INTEREST
007200         UNTIL ENTRY-OK = "Y".
007300
007400 ENTER-THE-INTEREST.
007500     DISPLAY "Interest (.1% TO 99.9%)?".
007600     ACCEPT ENTRY-FIELD WITH CONVERSION.
007700     MOVE ENTRY-FIELD TO THE-INTEREST.
007800     IF THE-INTEREST < .1 OR
007900         THE-INTEREST > 99.9
008000             DISPLAY "INVALID ENTRY"
008100     ELSE
008200         MOVE "Y" TO ENTRY-OK
008300         COMPUTE INTEREST-AS-DECIMAL =
008400                 THE-INTEREST / 100.
008500
008600 GET-THE-PERIODS.
008700     MOVE "N" TO ENTRY-OK.
008800     PERFORM ENTER-THE-PERIODS
008900         UNTIL ENTRY-OK = "Y".
009000
009100 ENTER-THE-PERIODS.
009200     DISPLAY "Number of periods (1 TO 999)?".
009300     ACCEPT ENTRY-FIELD WITH CONVERSION.
009400     MOVE ENTRY-FIELD TO NO-OF-PERIODS.
009500     IF NO-OF-PERIODS < 1 OR
009600         NO-OF-PERIODS > 999
009700             DISPLAY "INVALID ENTRY"
009800     ELSE
009900         MOVE "Y" TO ENTRY-OK.
010000
010100 CALCULATE-THE-RESULT.
010200     MOVE THE-PRINCIPAL TO WORKING-PRINCIPAL.
010300     PERFORM CALCULATE-ONE-PERIOD
010400         VARYING THE-PERIOD FROM 1 BY 1
010500             UNTIL THE-PERIOD > NO-OF-PERIODS.
010600
```

8

```
010700 CALCULATE-ONE-PERIOD.
010800     COMPUTE EARNED-INTEREST ROUNDED =
010900         WORKING-PRINCIPAL * INTEREST-AS-DECIMAL.
011000     COMPUTE THE-NEW-VALUE =
011100             WORKING-PRINCIPAL + EARNED-INTEREST.
011200     MOVE THE-NEW-VALUE TO WORKING-PRINCIPAL.
011300
011400 GO-AGAIN.
011500     DISPLAY "GO AGAIN?".
011600     ACCEPT YES-NO.
011700     IF YES-NO = "y"
011800         MOVE "Y" TO YES-NO.
011900     IF YES-NO NOT = "Y"
012000         MOVE "N" TO YES-NO.
012100
012200 DISPLAY-THE-RESULT.
012300     MOVE THE-PRINCIPAL TO DISPLAY-PRINCIPAL.
012400     MOVE THE-INTEREST  TO DISPLAY-INTEREST.
012500     MOVE NO-OF-PERIODS TO DISPLAY-PERIODS.
012600     MOVE THE-NEW-VALUE TO DISPLAY-VALUE.
012700     DISPLAY THE-WHOLE-MESSAGE.
012800
```

There are some instances when grouping variables together might be useful. Some compilers make a more efficient use of memory if numeric variables are grouped together under a structure variable. Unfortunately, this is not true of all compilers.

What Is Level 77?

When you see data in a structure in a program, you assume that the structure is used somewhere in the program as a structure, and you can be confused if it is not.

A variable that is not a structure can be given a level number of 77 instead of 01:

```
002600 77  YES-NO                          PIC X.
```

A level 77 variable uses the same syntax as a level 01 variable and must also begin in Area A, but a level 77 may not be used for a structure variable.

A level number of 77 indicates to the compiler that the variable named after the 77 is a simple elementary variable and not a structure. This change sometimes speeds up the compiler, and it might improve the memory use of a program. You don't have to worry about using level 77, but you will see it in some programs and you should know what it means when you see it.

Listing 8.11 shows an alternative way of defining the variables in cmpint04.cbl.

Type | **Listing 8.11. Using level 77.**

```
000800 WORKING-STORAGE SECTION.
000900
001000
001100 77  YES-NO                      PIC X.
001200 77  ENTRY-OK                    PIC X.
001300
001400
001500 77  THE-INTEREST                PIC 99V9.
001600 77  INTEREST-AS-DECIMAL         PIC V999.
001700 77  THE-PRINCIPAL               PIC 9(9)V99.
001800 77  WORKING-PRINCIPAL           PIC 9(9)V99.
001900 77  THE-NEW-VALUE               PIC 9(9)V99.
002000 77  EARNED-INTEREST             PIC 9(9)V99.
002100 77  THE-PERIOD                  PIC 9999.
002200 77  NO-OF-PERIODS               PIC 999.
002300
002400 77  ENTRY-FIELD                 PIC ZZZ,ZZZ,ZZZ.ZZ.
002500
002600 01  THE-WHOLE-MESSAGE.
002700     05  DISPLAY-PRINCIPAL       PIC ZZZ,ZZZ,ZZ9.99.
002800     05  MESSAGE-PART-01         PIC X(4) VALUE " at ".
002900     05  DISPLAY-INTEREST        PIC Z9.9.
003000     05  MESSAGE-PART-02         PIC X(6) VALUE "% for ".
003100     05  DISPLAY-PERIODS         PIC ZZ9.
003200     05  MESSAGE-PART-03         PIC X(16)
003300         VALUE " periods yields ".
003400     05  DISPLAY-VALUE           PIC ZZZ,ZZZ,ZZ9.99.
003500
```

What Is Level 88?

Level 88 is a special level number used to improve the readability of COBOL programs and to improve IF tests.

A level 88 looks like a level under another variable, but it's not. It does not have a PICTURE, but it does have a value. A level 88 is always associated with another variable and is a condition name for that variable. Here is an example:

```
002500
002600 01  YES-NO                      PIC X.
002700     88  ANSWER-IS-YES           VALUE "Y".
002800
```

Both of the following conditions test whether YES-NO is equal to "Y":

```
003700     IF YES-NO = "Y"
```

```
003700     IF ANSWER-IS-YES
```

The condition name at line 002700 is another way of saying YES-NO = "Y" and can be used in IF and UNTIL conditions. A level 88 condition name can be used for an alphanumeric or numeric variable.

Listing 8.12, menu02.cbl, is a menu program that displays a message based on a menu pick of 1, 2, or 3, and exits on a 0.

TYPE   **Listing 8.12. Using a level 88 condition name.**

```
000100 IDENTIFICATION DIVISION.
000200 PROGRAM-ID. MENU02.
000300*-----------------------------------------------
000400* THIS PROGRAM DISPLAYS A THREE CHOICE MENU OF
000500* MESSAGES THAT CAN BE DISPLAYED.
000600* THE USER ENTERS THE CHOICE, 1, 2 OR 3, AND
000700* THE APPROPRIATE MESSAGE IS DISPLAYED.
000800* AN ERROR MESSAGE IS DISPLAYED IF AN INVALID
000900* CHOICE IS MADE.
001000*-----------------------------------------------
001100 ENVIRONMENT DIVISION.
001200 DATA DIVISION.
001300 WORKING-STORAGE SECTION.
001400
001500 01  MENU-PICK         PIC 9.
001600     88  PICK-IS-EXIT  VALUE 0.
001700
001800 PROCEDURE DIVISION.
001900 PROGRAM-BEGIN.
002000
002100     MOVE 1 TO MENU-PICK.
002200     PERFORM GET-AND-DO-PICK
002300         UNTIL PICK-IS-EXIT.
002400
002500     DISPLAY "Thank you. Exiting".
002600
002700 PROGRAM-DONE.
002800     STOP RUN.
002900
003000 GET-AND-DO-PICK.
003100     PERFORM GET-THE-MENU-PICK.
003200
003300     PERFORM DO-THE-MENU-PICK.
003400
003500 GET-THE-MENU-PICK.
003600
003700     PERFORM DISPLAY-THE-MENU.
003800     PERFORM GET-THE-PICK.
003900
004000 DO-THE-MENU-PICK.
004100     IF MENU-PICK > 3
004200         DISPLAY "Invalid selection".
004300
```

continues

Listing 8.12. continued

```
004400      IF MENU-PICK = 1
004500          DISPLAY "One for the money.".
004600
004700      IF MENU-PICK = 2
004800          DISPLAY "Two for the show.".
004900
005000      IF MENU-PICK = 3
005100          DISPLAY "Three to get ready.".
005200
005400 DISPLAY-THE-MENU.
000000* Includes the display of some blank lines to
000000* improve the appearance
005500      DISPLAY "Please enter the number of the message".
005600      DISPLAY "that you wish to display.".
005800      DISPLAY " ".
005900      DISPLAY "1.  First Message".
006000      DISPLAY "2.  Second Message".
006100      DISPLAY "3.  Third Message".
006300      DISPLAY " ".
006400      DISPLAY "0.  EXIT".
006500      DISPLAY " ".
006600      DISPLAY "Your selection (1-3)?".
006700
006800 GET-THE-PICK.
006900      ACCEPT MENU-PICK.
```

Line 001600 defines a condition name of PICK-IS-EXIT when MENU-PICK = 0. At line 002100, MENU-PICK is set to 1 so that it does not have a value of 0. If you start MENU-PICK with a value of 0, GET-AND-DO-PICK never will be performed. Instead, GET-AND-DO-PICK is performed until the PICK-IS-EXIT. The UNTIL condition at line 002300 is exactly equivalent to the following:

```
002300          UNTIL MENU-PICK = 0.
```

You also can set up a level 88 condition to test more than one condition. Here's a situation that could use an 88 to sort out a knotty IF test. In Listing 8.12, menu02.cbl, the menu selections are conveniently arranged to be valid if they are 0 through 3. The test for a valid selection at line 004100 is fairly simple because anything above 3 is invalid:

```
004000
004100      IF MENU-PICK > 3
004200          DISPLAY "Invalid selection".
004300
```

If you change your design so that 9 is used to exit, the test for a valid pick becomes complicated. Listing 8.13 and Listing 8.14 show two ways of performing this test. They are both awkward and a little confusing to read.

TYPE **Listing 8.13. A complex IF.**

```
004100      IF MENU-PICK < 1 OR
004200         ( MENU-PICK < 9 AND MENU-PICK > 3)
004300            DISPLAY "Invalid selection".
004400
```

TYPE **Listing 8.14. Another complex IF.**

```
004100      IF MENU-PICK NOT = 1 AND
004200         MENU-PICK NOT = 2 AND
004300         MENU-PICK NOT = 3 AND
004400         MENU-PICK NOT = 9
004500            DISPLAY "Invalid selection".
004600
```

You can set up a level 88 to test for more than one value. The values can be a list of individual values as in Listing 8.15 (commas are optional), a range of values as in Listing 8.16, or a combination of list and range values as in Listing 8.17. Each listing includes comments showing the equivalent tests that must be used when not using an 88.

TYPE **Listing 8.15. Level 88 with a list of values.**

```
002500
002600 01   MENU-PICK            PIC 9.
002700      88  PICK-IS-VALID     VALUES 1, 2, 3, 9.
002800*          MENU-PICK = 1 OR
002900*          MENU-PICK = 2 OR
003000*          MENU-PICK = 3 OR
003100*          MENU-PICK = 9
003200
```

TYPE **Listing 8.16. Level 88 with a range of values.**

```
002500
002600 01   MENU-PICK            PIC 9.
002700      88  PICK-IS-VALID     VALUES 0 THROUGH 3.
002800*          MENU-PICK = 0 OR
002900*          MENU-PICK = 1 OR
003000*          MENU-PICK = 2 OR
003100*          MENU-PICK = 3
003200
```

TYPE **Listing 8.17. Level 88 with range and list values.**

```
002500
002600 01  MENU-PICK                PIC 9.
002700     88  PICK-IS-VALID         VALUES 8, 9, 0 THROUGH 3
002800*         MENU-PICK = 8 OR
002900*         MENU-PICK = 9 OR
003000*         MENU-PICK = 0 OR
003100*         MENU-PICK = 1 OR
003200*         MENU-PICK = 2 OR
003300*         MENU-PICK = 3
003400
```

A variable also can have more than one level 88 condition name associated with it, as shown in Listing 8.18.

TYPE **Listing 8.18. More than one level 88.**

```
002500
002600 01  MENU-PICK                PIC 9.
002700     88  PICK-IS-VALID         VALUES 8, 9, 0 THROUGH 3
002800     88  PICK-IS-EXIT          VALUE 9.
002900
```

Listing 8.19 uses a level 88 to create a condition of PICK-IS-VALID when MENU-PICK equals 1, 2, 3, or 9. Then, another level 88 is used to set up a condition name of PICK-IS-EXIT when MENU-PICK equals 9.

TYPE **Listing 8.19. More level 88.**

```
000100 IDENTIFICATION DIVISION.
000200 PROGRAM-ID. MENU03.
000300*-------------------------------------------------
000400* THIS PROGRAM DISPLAYS A THREE CHOICE MENU OF
000500* MESSAGES THAT CAN BE DISPLAYED.
000600* THE USER ENTERS THE CHOICE, 1, 2 OR 3, AND
000700* THE APPROPRIATE MESSAGE IS DISPLAYED.
000800* AN ERROR MESSAGE IS DISPLAYED IF AN INVALID
000900* CHOICE IS MADE.
001000*-------------------------------------------------
001100 ENVIRONMENT DIVISION.
001200 DATA DIVISION.
001300 WORKING-STORAGE SECTION.
001400
001500 01  MENU-PICK         PIC 9.
001600     88  PICK-IS-EXIT   VALUE 9.
001700     88  PICK-IS-VALID  VALUES 1 THRU 3, 9.
001800
```

```
001900 PROCEDURE DIVISION.
002000 PROGRAM-BEGIN.
002100
002200     MOVE 1 TO MENU-PICK.
002300     PERFORM GET-AND-DO-PICK
002400         UNTIL PICK-IS-EXIT.
002500*            MENU-PICK = 9
002600
002700     DISPLAY "Thank you. Exiting".
002800
002900 PROGRAM-DONE.
003000     STOP RUN.
003100
003200 GET-AND-DO-PICK.
003300     PERFORM GET-THE-MENU-PICK.
003400
003500     PERFORM DO-THE-MENU-PICK.
003600
003700 GET-THE-MENU-PICK.
003800
003900     PERFORM DISPLAY-THE-MENU.
004000     PERFORM GET-THE-PICK.
004100
004200 DO-THE-MENU-PICK.
004300*        NOT ( MENU-PICK = 1 OR 2 OR 3 OR 9 )
004400     IF NOT PICK-IS-VALID
004500         DISPLAY "Invalid selection".
004600
004700     IF MENU-PICK = 1
004800         DISPLAY "One for the money.".
004900
005000     IF MENU-PICK = 2
005100         DISPLAY "Two for the show.".
005200
005300     IF MENU-PICK = 3
005400         DISPLAY "Three to get ready.".
005500
005600* LEVEL 3 ROUTINES
005700 DISPLAY-THE-MENU.
005800     DISPLAY "Please enter the number of the message".
005900     DISPLAY "that you wish to display.".
006000* Display a blank line
006100     DISPLAY " ".
006200     DISPLAY "1.  First Message".
006300     DISPLAY "2.  Second Message".
006400     DISPLAY "3.  Third Message".
006500* Display a blank line
006600     DISPLAY " ".
006700     DISPLAY "9.  EXIT".
006800     DISPLAY " ".
006900     DISPLAY "Your selection (1-3)?".
007000
007100 GET-THE-PICK.
007200     ACCEPT MENU-PICK.
007300
```

The conditions are set up at lines 001600 and 001700. The condition name PICK-IS-VALID is set up when MENU-PICK equals 1, 2, 3, or 9. At lines 002300 and 002400, GET-AND-DO-PICK is performed UNTIL PICK-IS-EXIT (MENU-PICK = 9).

At lines 004300 and 004400, NOT is used to test for an invalid menu pick IF NOT PICK-IS-VALID (if MENU-PICK is not one of the values in the condition name list). You can see how much tidier, and easier to understand, the logic is at line 004400.

Summary

Today, you used the DATA DIVISION to organize your data and variables, improve the performance of your program, and reduce the amount of code that you have to write. You also learned the following basics:

- COBOL variables can be combined into a composite variable called a structure. The variables within a structure variable still can be used as if they are not part of a structure variable.

- Structure variables frequently are used to format data for display purposes. If the individual variables within a structure can be displayed, the structure variable itself can be displayed.

- Parts of a structure variable that are used to hold constant information and are not used in the PROCEDURE DIVISION can be named FILLER.

- The length of a data structure can be calculated by adding the lengths of the individual variables.

- The implicit picture of a structure is PIC X with a length equal to the length of the structure.

- A structure variable can, in turn, contain another structure variable.

- You can give a variable that is not a structure the level number 77.

- You can use a level 88 to set up condition names that can be used to simplify IF and UNTIL tests.

Q&A

Q What happens if I move to a FILLER?

A You can't. The compiler does not recognize FILLER as a variable name; it is used only to reserve space in a structure variable. If you include a command such as MOVE 1 TO FILLER in a program, it will not compile and produces an error. You can move values to a structure variable that contains a FILLER. The MOVE will affect the structure variable and all of the variables within the structure, but you cannot directly move values to a FILLER.

Q **Why do I need to know the lengths of structures?**

A You don't yet, but you will need to know how to calculate this when you start creating printed reports (in Day 10, "Printing").

Workshop

Quiz

1. What is the length of THE-WHOLE-MESSAGE in the following example?

```
000800 01   THE-WHOLE-MESSAGE.
000900      05   THE-NUMBER       PIC 9(2) VALUE 1.
001000      05   A-SPACE          PIC X    VALUE SPACE.
001100      05   THE-MESSAGE.
001200           10   JACKS-NAME  PIC X(5) VALUE "Jack".
001300           10   JACKS-TASK  PIC X(45).
001400
```

2. What is the implied PICTURE of THE-WHOLE-MESSAGE in question 1?

3. What is a data structure?

4. If you move a value to a structure variable, what happens to the values in the individual variables within the structure?

5. In the following code, what is another way of performing the test at line 004600?

```
001800 01   YES-NO             PIC X.
001900      88   ANSWER-IS-YES   VALUE "Y".

004600      IF YES-NO = "Y"
004700         PERFORM DO-SOMETHING.
```

6. In the following code, what is another way of performing the test at lines 004600 and 004700?

```
001800 01   YES-NO             PIC X.
001900      88   ANSWER-IS-VALID   VALUES "Y","N".

004600      IF YES-NO = "Y" OR
004700         YES-NO = "N"
004800         PERFORM DO-SOMETHING.
```

7. Devise a level 88 condition name for YES-NO that would simplify the tests at lines 004600 through 004900 in the following code:

```
001800 01   YES-NO             PIC X.


004600      IF YES-NO = "Y" OR
004700         YES-NO = "y" OR
004800         YES-NO = "N" OR
004900         YES-NO = "n"
005000         PERFORM DO-SOMETHING.
```

Exercises

1. Copy mult07.cbl from Day 7, "Basics of Design," to mult09.cbl, and modify the program to use a data structure to display the results of the multiplication table.

2. Design a structure similar to CUST-DATA that would hold a 5-digit CUST-NUMBER, a 30-character CUST-NAME, a 50-character CUST-ADDRESS, and a 5-digit CUST-ZIP-CODE:

```
001100 01   CUST-DATA.
001200      05   CUST-NUMBER          PIC 9(3).
001300      05   CUST-NAME            PIC X(10).
```

3. Code the CUST-DATA structure with all the fields initialized correctly to zeroes or spaces using VALUE clauses.

8

Day 9

File I/O

Welcome to the big time! Saving data to and retrieving data from a disk depends on you being able to handle files. The primary activity of COBOL programs is storage, retrieval, sorting, and reporting on files of information. Today, you learn about the following topics:

- [ ] What is a file?
- [ ] What is a record?
- [ ] What is a field?
- [ ] Defining a file in COBOL.
- [ ] The logical description of a COBOL file.
- [ ] The physical description of a COBOL file.
- [ ] Opening and closing a file.
- [ ] Adding records to a file.
- [ ] Reading records from a file.
- [ ] The file processing loop.

What Is a File?

Imagine a small company that keeps two card file boxes. One box contains a card for each vendor who supplies raw material to the company. The other contains a card for each customer who has purchased from the company. Close both boxes, label one Vendors and the other Customers, and bring a stranger in to look at the boxes.

The stranger would see two labeled 3×5 inch boxes that take up space on the desk. The stranger might assume that the boxes contain data on customers and vendors, but the boxes could contain half a tuna fish sandwich and the boss's lucky golf ball.

On a computer disk, a file is similar to a card file box. It has a label (the filename on the disk) and takes up space on the disk. The computer has no idea what kind of data is in a file; the file is just a chunk of disk space set aside for data and given a name. The file could be a word processing document file named `james.doc` containing a letter written to James, or it could be an Excel spreadsheet named `bal.xls` containing account balances. These are sometimes called *physical files*.

Back in our hypothetical office, the stranger might open the boxes to check their contents, and he would see that the physical card file box contains a collection of data.

NEW TERM   In a COBOL program, a *file* is a collection of related units of information within a data category. A file might contain all the information (related units of information) about customers (a data category) for a company. This usually is called a *data file* or a *logical file*.

For the file to exist, there must be a physical file on the disk. When the bytes in this file are arranged logically so that a COBOL program can access the information, it becomes a data file to a COBOL program.

What Is a Record?

In terms of the Customer card file analogy, each card contains the information about a single customer, and the card file box itself is the physical file.

NEW TERM   Within a data file, the information about one unit is called a *record*. If a data file contains the information pertaining to all customers, for example, the information about one customer is a record.

Figure 9.1 shows the relationship of a card file of phone numbers to a file record and fields. Each card contains a last name, a first name, and a phone number.

Figure 9.1.

A card file as a file, records, and fields.

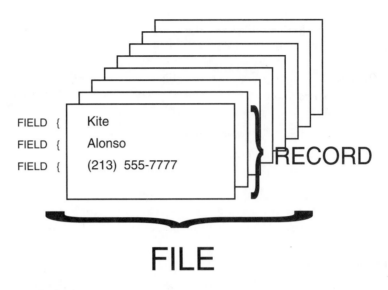

FIELD {   Kite

FIELD {   Alonso

FIELD {   (213) 555-7777

RECORD

FILE

9

What Is a Field?

In the customer file, the customer name is one field and the customer phone number is another field. In the card file analogy, you might place the customer's name on the first line of the card and the phone number on the second line. The first line, then, is the name field and the second line is the phone number field.

NEW TERM A *field* or *data field* is one piece of data contained in a record.

COBOL data files are organized as one or more records containing the same fields in each record. For example, a record for a personal phone book might contain fields for a last name, a first name, and a phone number. These fields would exist in each individual record.

If you displayed the phone file, it might look like the one in Figure 9.2.

Figure 9.2.

The contents of a phone file.

```
Smith        Michael Valentine    818-555-1212
Trent        Jack and Diane       555-9292
Kite         Alonso               (213)555-7777
Mae          Maggie               506 555 1234
Karenina     Ana                  (415) 555-3333
```

In fact, this collection of data is arranged in fields, similar to the card file system, but the layout is slightly different (as shown in Figure 9.3).

Figure 9.3.

File, record, and fields in a data file.

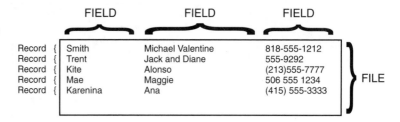

If you could lay a column ruler down over the records as they are displayed, you would see the starting and ending position of each of the fields (as shown in Figure 9.4).

Figure 9.4.

A column ruler against the records.

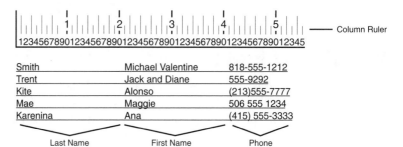

A record layout for the phone record would include a data name and the starting and ending positions in the record for each field (as shown in Figure 9.5).

Figure 9.5.

A customer record layout.

LAST NAME	FIRST NAME	PHONE
1 20	21 40	41 55

An alternative method of creating a record specification is to list the field name, starting position, length, and data type for each field, as shown in Table 9.1. If you are familiar with databases such as dBASE IV, Oracle, Informix, or Access, you will recognize that this type of layout is similar to defining a database file.

Table 9.1. Alternate record layout for a phone record.

Field	Starting Position	Length	Type of Data
LAST NAME	1	20	Alphanumeric
FIRST NAME	21	20	Alphanumeric
PHONE	41	15	Alphanumeric

Defining a File in COBOL

In a COBOL program, the description of a data record is entered as a structure variable. Listing 9.1 shows a COBOL description for the PHONE-RECORD.

TYPE **Listing 9.1. The PHONE-RECORD structure.**

```
002500
002600    01  PHONE-RECORD.
002700        05  PHONE-LAST-NAME      PIC X(20).
002800        05  PHONE-FIRST-NAME     PIC X(20).
002900        05  PHONE-NUMBER         PIC X(15).
003000
```

ANALYSIS When dealing with files, all the variables associated with a file, including the variables in the record, start with an identical prefix. In Listing 9.1, I chose PHONE- as the prefix, although PH- or PHNBK- could have been used as well. The prefix should not be too long because it will appear at the beginning of all variables. PHONE-BOOK- would have been okay, but it is a little long. The prefix convention is a good one, but it is not a requirement of the COBOL language.

In COBOL, a file is defined in two parts: the logical file, which includes the record layout, and the physical file, which includes the name of the file on the disk and how the file will be organized.

The Logical Description of a COBOL File

A logical file is easy to define after you define the record. A logical file is defined in the DATA DIVISION, in a new section called the FILE SECTION. Listing 9.2 shows an example of a logical file definition, which is correctly placed in the FILE SECTION of the DATA DIVISION. FILE SECTION is a reserved name for the section of the DATA DIVISION used to define logical files used in a program.

TYPE **Listing 9.2. A logical COBOL file.**

```
002000
002100 DATA DIVISION.
002200 FILE SECTION.
002300
002400 FD  PHONE-FILE
002500        LABEL RECORDS ARE STANDARD.
002600    01  PHONE-RECORD.
002700        05  PHONE-LAST-NAME      PIC X(20).
002800        05  PHONE-FIRST-NAME     PIC X(20).
002900        05  PHONE-NUMBER         PIC X(15).
```

continues

Listing 9.2. continued

```
003000
003100 WORKING-STORAGE SECTION.
003100
```

ANALYSIS At line 002200, the FILE SECTION appears before the WORKING-STORAGE section in the DATA DIVISION. Because it is a section name, it starts in Area A (columns 8 through 11).

NEW TERM A logical file definition is called a *file descriptor,* or *FD.*

The file descriptor starts at line 002400 and is given the special level number FD. This appears in Area A, followed by a variable name for the logical file in Area B (columns 12 through 72). In this case, the variable name is PHONE-FILE.

The variable name used for a file does not truly name a variable; it really is a file identifier. You cannot move anything to PHONE-FILE, and if you tried to, the compiler probably would generate an error. You do need to open and close a file in order to be able to read data from it and write data to it, and the filename identifier is used with the OPEN and CLOSE commands to open and close the file. (See the section "Opening and Closing a File," later in this chapter.)

A file descriptor frequently is called an FD because it uses the letters FD as a level number. The FD for the PHONE-FILE continues on line 002500 with the statement LABEL RECORDS ARE STANDARD and ends with a period on that line.

The LABEL RECORDS ARE STANDARD clause is a holdover from the days of processing files on tape. Before disk drives became inexpensive, most large data files were written to and read from tape drives. There were two ways to store a file on a tape: labeled and unlabeled. The FD indicated which type of labeling was used on the tape.

All files are labeled so they have a name on the disk. Any file to be processed on a disk drive should include LABEL RECORDS ARE STANDARD. Some recent COBOL compilers have recognized that much more processing these days is done on disk, and the LABEL RECORDS clause is optional. You should include the clause to keep your COBOL compatible across different machines and COBOL compilers.

After the FD, filename, and LABEL clause, the variable structure that describes the record begins at line 002600. The variable structure that describes a record is often simply called a record and is a level 01 variable structure with the individual variables defined under it.

The Physical Description of a COBOL File

The physical description of the file fits in the ENVIRONMENT DIVISION.

 The *physical description* of a COBOL file is a set of statements designed to identify the physical name of the file on the disk drive, and how the file is organized.

The ENVIRONMENT DIVISION is reserved to provide information on the physical computer on which COBOL is running. Different types of computers have different ways of naming files on a disk, so it makes sense that this information is placed in the ENVIRONMENT DIVISION. A physical file description is placed in the FILE-CONTROL paragraph in the INPUT-OUTPUT SECTION of the ENVIRONMENT DIVISION.

The INPUT-OUTPUT SECTION is a reserved name for the section of the ENVIRONMENT DIVISION that is used to define physical files used in a program and to define which areas of memory will be used by the files while they are being processed.

The FILE-CONTROL paragraph is a reserved name for a paragraph in the INPUT-OUTPUT SECTION of the ENVIRONMENT DIVISION, and it is used to define all the physical files used in a program.

Listing 9.3 shows an example of a physical file description. The INPUT-OUTPUT SECTION at line 000500 begins in Area A. The FILE-CONTROL paragraph at line 000600 also begins in Area A.

TYPE **Listing 9.3. The physical PHONE-FILE.**

```
000400 ENVIRONMENT DIVISION.
000500 INPUT-OUTPUT SECTION.
000600 FILE-CONTROL.
000700     SELECT PHONE-FILE
000800         ASSIGN TO "phone.dat"
000900         ORGANIZATION IS SEQUENTIAL.
001000
001100 DATA DIVISION.
```

ANALYSIS The SELECT statement that defines the physical file begins at line 000700. The SELECT clause uses the logical filename (PHONE-FILE) and associates it with a physical filename on the disk by using the ASSIGN TO "phone.dat" at line 000800.

The last line of the SELECT clause at line 000900 specifies that the file organization is SEQUENTIAL. SEQUENTIAL organization indicates that records in the file are processed in sequence. When a record is written to the file, it always is appended to the end of the file. When a file is opened and read, the first read retrieves the first record and each subsequent read retrieves each next record.

If you think of this in terms of the card file of names and phone numbers, it means that every new card file is added at the back end of the card file box, and you must find a card by reading from the first card in the box to the last.

NOTE

> The SELECT clause in Listing 9.3 is suitable for MS-DOS machines. On some machines, it might be necessary to omit the extension and use ASSIGN TO "phone" or force the filename to uppercase and use ASSIGN TO "PHONE".

Opening and Closing a File

Before you can do anything to the contents of a file, you must open the file. When you open a file, you have to specify an OPEN mode. A mode indicates the type of processing that you intend to do on the file. The following syntax is used:

OPEN mode file-name

These are examples of the four OPEN modes, and Table 9.2 describes what happens to the file in each one:

OPEN OUTPUT PHONE-FILE

OPEN EXTEND PHONE-FILE

OPEN INPUT PHONE-FILE

OPEN I-O PHONE-FILE

Table 9.2. Effects of OPEN modes.

Open Mode	Effect
OUTPUT	If the file does not exist, it is created and records can be added to the file. If the file does exist, the old file is destroyed, a new one is created, and any new records can be added to it.
EXTEND	If the file does not exist, it is created and records can be added to the file. If the file does exist, it is opened and records can be appended to the end of it.
INPUT	If the file exists, it is opened and records can be read from the file. If the file does not exist, the OPEN fails and an error occurs.
I-O	If the file exists, it is opened for reading and writing. If the file does not exist, the open fails and an error occurs.

Notice that files opened for INPUT or I-O can cause an error if the file does not physically exist on the disk.

Some versions of COBOL allow you to add the reserved word OPTIONAL to a SELECT clause to prevent these errors. (See Listing 9.4.) The word OPTIONAL indicates that if the file is opened in INPUT or I-O mode, the file is created automatically if it does not exist. If your version of COBOL supports OPTIONAL, use it. Micro Focus Personal COBOL, ACUCOBOL, LPI COBOL, and VAX COBOL all support it.

TYPE **Listing 9.4.** SELECT OPTIONAL.

```
000300
000400 ENVIRONMENT DIVISION.
000500 INPUT-OUTPUT SECTION.
000600 FILE-CONTROL.
000700     SELECT OPTIONAL PHONE-FILE
000800         ASSIGN TO "phone.dat"
000900         ORGANIZATION IS SEQUENTIAL.
001000
001100 DATA DIVISION.
```

Closing a file is a lot less complicated; you simply use the reserved word CLOSE. It doesn't matter what the original open mode was. Here is an example:

```
CLOSE filename
```

For the last listing, you would use the following:

```
CLOSE PHONE-FILE
```

Adding Records to a File

Adding a record to a file involves writing a record. The following syntax is simple:

```
WRITE file-record
```

To continue the phone number file example, use the following:

```
WRITE PHONE-RECORD
```

In Listing 9.5, phnadd01.cbl, all the elements of the program should be recognizable to you. The user is repeatedly asked for a last name, a first name, and a phone number. Study phnadd01.cbl; then code it, compile it, and run it to create your own phone file. All your entries are written to the file one after the other. In this listing, you open a new file and only add records to it. Therefore, opening in EXTEND mode is suitable.

TYPE   **Listing 9.5. Creating a file and adding records.**

```
000100 IDENTIFICATION DIVISION.
000200 PROGRAM-ID. PHNADD01.
000300*------------------------------------------------
000400* This program creates a new data file if necessary
000500* and adds records to the file from user entered
000600* data.
000700*------------------------------------------------
000800 ENVIRONMENT DIVISION.
000900 INPUT-OUTPUT SECTION.
001000 FILE-CONTROL.
001100     SELECT OPTIONAL PHONE-FILE
001200*or   SELECT PHONE-FILE
001300         ASSIGN TO "phone.dat"
001400*or       ASSIGN TO "phone"
001500         ORGANIZATION IS SEQUENTIAL.
001600
001700 DATA DIVISION.
001800 FILE SECTION.
001900 FD  PHONE-FILE
002000     LABEL RECORDS ARE STANDARD.
002100 01  PHONE-RECORD.
002200     05  PHONE-LAST-NAME    PIC X(20).
002300     05  PHONE-FIRST-NAME   PIC X(20).
002400     05  PHONE-NUMBER       PIC X(15).
002500
002600 WORKING-STORAGE SECTION.
002700
002800* Variables for SCREEN ENTRY
002900 01  PROMPT-1              PIC X(9) VALUE "Last Name".
003000 01  PROMPT-2              PIC X(10) VALUE "First Name".
003100 01  PROMPT-3              PIC X(6) VALUE "Number".
003200
003300 01  YES-NO               PIC X.
003400 01  ENTRY-OK             PIC X.
003500
003600 PROCEDURE DIVISION.
003700 MAIN-LOGIC SECTION.
003800 PROGRAM-BEGIN.
003900
004000     PERFORM OPENING-PROCEDURE.
004100     MOVE "Y" TO YES-NO.
004200     PERFORM ADD-RECORDS
004300         UNTIL YES-NO = "N".
004400     PERFORM CLOSING-PROCEDURE.
004500
004600 PROGRAM-DONE.
004700     STOP RUN.
004800
004900* OPENING AND CLOSING
005000
005100 OPENING-PROCEDURE.
005200     OPEN EXTEND PHONE-FILE.
005300
```

9

```
005400 CLOSING-PROCEDURE.
005500     CLOSE PHONE-FILE.
005600
005700 ADD-RECORDS.
005800     MOVE "N" TO ENTRY-OK.
005900     PERFORM GET-FIELDS
006000         UNTIL ENTRY-OK = "Y".
006100     PERFORM ADD-THIS-RECORD.
006200     PERFORM GO-AGAIN.
006300
006400 GET-FIELDS.
006500     MOVE SPACE TO PHONE-RECORD.
006600     DISPLAY PROMPT-1 " ? ".
006700     ACCEPT PHONE-LAST-NAME.
006800     DISPLAY PROMPT-2 " ? ".
006900     ACCEPT PHONE-FIRST-NAME.
007000     DISPLAY PROMPT-3 " ? ".
007100     ACCEPT PHONE-NUMBER.
007200     PERFORM VALIDATE-FIELDS.
007300
007400 VALIDATE-FIELDS.
007500     MOVE "Y" TO ENTRY-OK.
007600     IF PHONE-LAST-NAME = SPACE
007700         DISPLAY "LAST NAME MUST BE ENTERED"
007800         MOVE "N" TO ENTRY-OK.
007900
008000 ADD-THIS-RECORD.
008100     WRITE PHONE-RECORD.
008200
008300 GO-AGAIN.
008400     DISPLAY "GO AGAIN?".
008500     ACCEPT YES-NO.
008600     IF YES-NO = "y"
008700         MOVE "Y" TO YES-NO.
008800     IF YES-NO NOT = "Y"
008900         MOVE "N" TO YES-NO.
009000
```

The following shows the output of `phnadd01.cbl` after two entries:

OUTPUT
```
Last Name   ?
KARENINA
First Name ?
ANA
Number      ?
 (818) 555-4567
GO AGAIN?
Y
Last Name   ?
PENCIL
First Name ?
ARTHUR
Number      ?
 (515) 555-1234
GO AGAIN?
```

ANALYSIS   The listing includes some of the options for the SELECT statement at lines 001200 and 001400. The prompts used to ask the user for input are defined at lines 002900 through 003100.

At line 004000, OPENING-PROCEDURE is performed as the first step of the program. At line 004400, CLOSING-PROCEDURE is performed as the last step of the program. These two paragraphs at lines 005100 and 005400 open and close the file. It is a fairly common arrangement for the first step of a program to open all the files required by the program and for the last step of the program to close all open files.

The ADD-RECORDS loop, at lines 005700 through 006200, asks the user for all the fields UNTIL ENTRY-OK = "Y", and then writes the record to the file.

At line 006400, the GET-FIELDS paragraph initializes the PHONE-RECORD to spaces and then asks the user for each of the three fields. The entries are validated (checked for correct entry) in VALIDATE-FIELDS. The only validation is to check that the last name is entered.

Reading Records from a File

In order to open a file and read it successfully, the physical and logical file definition in the program (FD and SELECT) must match the FD and SELECT used to create the file, at least as far as record length. If they don't match, unpredictable results will occur. Physical files, logical files, and how they are described in COBOL programs are covered in more detail in Day 17, "Alternate Keys."

Do	Don't

DO ensure that if more than one program accesses the same file, both programs use the same SELECT, and an FD of the same length to describe the file.

DON'T try to open a file with a SELECT or FD that is different from the SELECT or FD used to create the file. There are special cases where you can do this, but they are used in data conversions.

DON'T change the record layout of a file by adding fields that change the length of the record without also re-creating the data file.

A file to be opened for reading should be opened in INPUT mode with the following syntax:

```
READ filename NEXT RECORD.
```

Here is an example:

```
READ PHONE-FILE NEXT RECORD.
```

Because the SELECT clause for the file says that it is organized as a SEQUENTIAL file, every READ on the file is a request to retrieve the next record. Each READ reads the next record in the file. There actually are two types of read for a file: READ and READ NEXT. Because a SEQUENTIAL file is organized to be accessed one record after another, a READ and READ NEXT have the same effect on a SEQUENTIAL file. There are other types of file organization that you will begin to explore in Day 11, "Indexed File I/O." For these other file organizations, READ and READ NEXT do not have the same effect.

Because the intention in a READ on a SEQUENTIAL file is to get the next record, it is a good idea to add NEXT to the READ statement, as shown in the following syntax, because it makes the intention clear:

```
READ filename [NEXT RECORD]
```

The following is an example:

```
READ PHONE-FILE
```

```
READ PHONE-FILE NEXT RECORD
```

NOTE

For a SEQUENTIAL file, READ and READ NEXT RECORD are identical.

You need to know one other thing about READ NEXT. How do you know when all the records in a file have been read? If you don't find out, your program will keep attempting to read the next record when nothing is left in the file to read. The READ NEXT statement can include a clause that is executed if the file has reached the end. The following is the syntax for handling an AT END condition:

```
READ filename [NEXT RECORD]
    AT END
    do something
```

For your phone number file, the following will work:

```
READ PHONE-FILE NEXT RECORD
    AT END
    MOVE "Y" TO END-OF-FILE
```

Listing 9.6, phnlst01.cbl, lists all the records in your data file. Before you start looking over the code, take a look at the output of phnlst01.cbl.

TYPE   **Listing 9.6. Displaying the phone file.**

```
000100 IDENTIFICATION DIVISION.
000200 PROGRAM-ID. PHNLST01.
```

continues

Listing 9.6. continued

```
000300*--------------------------------------------------
000400* This program displays the contents of the
000500* phone file.
000600*--------------------------------------------------
000700 ENVIRONMENT DIVISION.
000800 INPUT-OUTPUT SECTION.
000900 FILE-CONTROL.
001000     SELECT OPTIONAL PHONE-FILE
001100*or  SELECT PHONE-FILE
001200         ASSIGN TO "phone.dat"
001300*or      ASSIGN TO "phone"
001400         ORGANIZATION IS SEQUENTIAL.
001500
001600 DATA DIVISION.
001700 FILE SECTION.
001800 FD   PHONE-FILE
001900     LABEL RECORDS ARE STANDARD.
002000 01   PHONE-RECORD.
002100     05   PHONE-LAST-NAME      PIC X(20).
002200     05   PHONE-FIRST-NAME     PIC X(20).
002300     05   PHONE-NUMBER         PIC X(15).
002400
002500 WORKING-STORAGE SECTION.
002600
002700* Structure for SCREEN DISPLAY
002800 01   FIELDS-TO-DISPLAY.
002900     05   PROMPT-1             PIC X(10) VALUE "Last Name:".
003000     05   DISPLAY-LAST-NAME    PIC X(20).
003100     05   PROMPT-2             PIC X(6) VALUE "First:".
003200     05   DISPLAY-FIRST-NAME   PIC X(20).
003300     05   PROMPT-3             PIC X(3) VALUE "NO:".
003400     05   DISPLAY-NUMBER       PIC X(15).
003500
003600 01   END-OF-FILE             PIC X.
003700
003800 01   SCREEN-LINES           PIC 99.
003900 01   A-DUMMY                PIC X.
004000
004100 PROCEDURE DIVISION.
004200 MAIN-LOGIC SECTION.
004300 PROGRAM-BEGIN.
004400
004500     PERFORM OPENING-PROCEDURE.
004600     MOVE ZEROES TO SCREEN-LINES.
004700     MOVE "N" TO END-OF-FILE.
004800     PERFORM READ-NEXT-RECORD.
004900     PERFORM DISPLAY-RECORDS
005000         UNTIL END-OF-FILE = "Y".
005100     PERFORM CLOSING-PROCEDURE.
005200
005300 PROGRAM-DONE.
005400     STOP RUN.
005500
```

9

```
005600 OPENING-PROCEDURE.
005700     OPEN INPUT PHONE-FILE.
005800
005900 CLOSING-PROCEDURE.
006000     CLOSE PHONE-FILE.
006100
006200 DISPLAY-RECORDS.
006300     PERFORM DISPLAY-FIELDS.
006400     PERFORM READ-NEXT-RECORD.
006500
006600 DISPLAY-FIELDS.
006700     IF SCREEN-LINES = 15
006800        PERFORM PRESS-ENTER.
006900     MOVE PHONE-LAST-NAME TO DISPLAY-LAST-NAME.
007000     MOVE PHONE-FIRST-NAME TO DISPLAY-FIRST-NAME.
007100     MOVE PHONE-NUMBER TO DISPLAY-NUMBER.
007200     DISPLAY FIELDS-TO-DISPLAY.
007300
007400     ADD 1 TO SCREEN-LINES.
007500
007600 READ-NEXT-RECORD.
007700     READ PHONE-FILE NEXT RECORD
007800        AT END
007900        MOVE "Y" TO END-OF-FILE.
008000
008100 PRESS-ENTER.
008200     DISPLAY "Press ENTER to continue . . ".
008300     ACCEPT A-DUMMY.
008400     MOVE ZEROES TO SCREEN-LINES.
008500
```

9

OUTPUT

```
C>pcobrun phnlst01
Personal COBOL version 2.0 from Micro Focus
PCOBRUN V2.0.02  Copyright (C) 1983-1993 Micro Focus Ltd.
    Last Name:KARENINA        First:ANITA       NO:(818) 555-4567
    Last Name:PENCIL          First:ARTHUR      NO:(515) 555-1234
    Last Name:BUDLONG         First:MO          NO:(818) 555-4444
    Last Name:ATREIDES        First:JESSICA     NO:606-555-7777
    Last Name:CORTEZ          First:HERNAN      NO:555-4567
    Last Name:WAYNE           First:BOB         NO:555-4332
    Last Name:ADALE           First:ALLEN       NO:415-555-6666
    Last Name:NOTTINGHAM      First:MARY        NO:415-555-6789
    Last Name:TUCK            First:FRANCINE    NO:213-555-2345
    Last Name:SCARLET         First:BILL        NO:202-555-6789
    Last Name:PLUM            First:PETRA       NO:202-555-5678
    Last Name:RED             First:ERIC        NO:424-555-3456
    Last Name:ANGEL           First:DESTINY     NO:616-555-2345
    Last Name:BACH            First:JOHN        NO:555-6789
    Last Name:BAGGINS         First:BILBO       NO:555-9876
    Press ENTER to continue . .
```

ANALYSIS   The OPEN at line 005700 is in INPUT mode. After the open, an END-OF-FILE is set up and the first record is read at lines 004700 and 004800. The READ-NEXT-RECORD paragraph at line 007600 uses the AT END clause of a READ NEXT to set the END-OF-FILE flag to "Y" when the records in the file are exhausted.

The DISPLAY-RECORDS paragraph at line 006200 displays the fields and then performs the READ-NEXT-RECORD paragraph. The READ-NEXT-RECORD paragraph sets the END-OF-FILE flag, so DISPLAY-RECORDS UNTIL END-OF-FILE ="Y" works correctly to control the loop.

The DISPLAY-FIELDS paragraph at line 006600 includes stopping for the user to press Enter after every 15 lines of display.

COBOL programs frequently process a file from one end to the other. This is such a common processing problem that it's worth looking at the techniques used in this example to control the processing loop.

Listing 9.7 shows the READ NEXT logic from phnlst01.cbl. In any program that reads a file from one end to the other, it is important that the paragraph or command used to read the next record sets a flag when the file reaches the end. This flag is used elsewhere in the program to determine that the processing loop reading through the file must stop.

TYPE   **Listing 9.7. READ-NEXT logic from phnlst01.cbl.**

```
007600 READ-NEXT-RECORD.
007700      READ PHONE-FILE NEXT RECORD
007800         AT END
007900           MOVE "Y" TO END-OF-FILE.
008000
```

Do   **Don't**

DO ensure that whenever a file is read sequentially using READ NEXT, some flag is set to indicate the end of a file.

DON'T ignore the possible end-of-file condition by leaving out a test for it in the main logic of the program.

The File Processing Loop

The phnlst01.cbl program includes a piece of coding that is important to understand when you are writing processing loops that involve reading through a file. Listing 9.8 repeats the two key parts of the program, but you might also want to refer to Listing 9.6.

Listing 9.8. The control of the processing loop from

TYPE `phnlst01.cbl.`

```
004700        MOVE "N" TO END-OF-FILE.
004800        PERFORM READ-NEXT-RECORD.
004900        PERFORM DISPLAY-RECORDS
005000            UNTIL END-OF-FILE = "Y".
......
......* The processing loop
006200 DISPLAY-RECORDS.
006300        PERFORM DISPLAY-FIELDS.
006400        PERFORM READ-NEXT-RECORD.
006500
......
......
007600 READ-NEXT-RECORD.
007700        READ PHONE-FILE NEXT RECORD
007800            AT END
007900            MOVE "Y" TO END-OF-FILE.
008000
```

ANALYSIS At lines `004700` and `004800`, the first record in the file is read before the processing loop starts. At lines `004900` and `005000`, the processing loop is performed until the end of the file. At line `006400`, the next record is read at the end of the processing loop.

The style of processing loop for handling a file illustrated by these three pieces of code is very effective and easy to code. You can think of it as three key pieces to use when processing a file from one end to the other:

1. Set a flag that keeps track of whether the file is at the end to reflect a "not at end" condition and read the first record.

2. Perform the processing loop until the file is at end.

3. Read the next record at the bottom of the processing loop.

Compare these three pieces of a file processing loop to the three parts of controlling any processing loop from Day 5, "Using PERFORM, GO TO, and IF to Control Programs," as shown in Table 9.3. You will see that a file processing loop is just a specialized version of a processing loop. The control variable is the "at end" flag for the file.

Table 9.3. Comparing a processing loop to a file processing loop.

Processing Loop Action	File Processing Loop Action
1. Initialize a value for the first pass through the loop.	1. Set an "at end" flag to reflect a "not at end" condition and read the first record.

continues

Table 9.3. continued

Processing Loop Action	File Processing Loop Action
2. Perform the processing loop until a condition is met.	2. Perform the processing loop until the file ends.
3. Increment or modify the control variable at the end of the loop or after each pass through the loop.	3. Read the next record at the end of the processing loop.

In fact, this comparison makes it possible to improve the description of the three parts of a processing loop, as in Table 9.4.

Table 9.4. An improved statement of processing loop design.

Processing Loop Action	Comments
1. Attempt to set up all variables and conditions needed for the first pass through the loop.	This includes setting up one or more loop control variables, and can include reading a record from a file.
2. Perform the processing loop until one or more conditions are met.	
3. At the end of the loop, attempt to set up all conditions for the next pass through the loop.	This includes modifying the loop control variables, and can include reading the next record.

The general description of a processing loop now covers earlier control loops that you have studied as well as the somewhat specialized control loop used to process a file one record at a time.

Summary

Saving data to and retrieving data from a disk depends on being able to handle files. Today, you learned the following basics:

☐ A physical file is a named area of a disk containing some sort of data.

☐ A logical file in COBOL is a physical file that is organized into fields and records.

☐ Accessing a file in COBOL requires both a logical and a physical definition of the file.

☐ The physical definition of the file is created with a SELECT statement in the I-O CONTROL paragraph of the INPUT-OUTPUT SECTION of the ENVIRONMENT DIVISION.

☐ The logical definition of a file is created with an FD in the FILE SECTION of the DATA DIVISION and includes the record layout.

☐ A file can be opened in four modes: EXTEND, OUTPUT, I-O, and INPUT. EXTEND creates a new file, or opens an existing one, and allows records to be added to the end of the file. OUTPUT creates a new file—or destroys an existing file and creates a new version of it—and allows records to be added to the file. INPUT opens an existing file for reading only and returns an error if the file does not exist. I-O mode opens a file for reading and writing and causes an error if the file does not exist.

☐ The errors caused by INPUT mode and I-O mode when you attempt to open a file that does not exist can be changed by including the OPTIONAL clause in the SELECT statement for the file, if your compiler allows it.

☐ Use CLOSE with a filename to close an open file, regardless of the open mode.

☐ Use WRITE with a file-record to write a record to a file.

☐ Read the next record in a file by using READ filename NEXT RECORD. The READ NEXT command includes syntax to allow you to set a flag when the file has reached the end or last record.

☐ These are the three parts to processing a file sequentially and organizing the logic:

1. Set a flag to reflect a "not-at-end" condition and read the first record.
2. Perform the processing loop until the file is at end.
3. Read the next record at the bottom of the processing loop.

Q&A

Q Can I print the contents of phone.dat?

A Yes. Day 10, "Printing," covers printing data files. Printing is one of the most common instances of processing a file by reading all the way through it one record at a time.

Q Is writing to a file the same as adding to a file?

A Yes. The WRITE command adds a new record to a file.

Q Why is the filename in PHNADD01.CBL (phone.dat) in lowercase?

A The physical filename you assign depends on the requirements of the computer on which the program will be compiled. Under MS-DOS, filenames always are converted to uppercase no matter what you use for the name. Using ASSIGN TO "phone.dat" or ASSIGN TO "PHONE.DAT" creates a file named PHONE.DAT. Other computers have other requirements. In UNIX, case is not converted, and phone.dat and PHONE.DAT are two different names for two different files. The examples given in phnadd01.cbl, phnlst01.cbl, and other programs in this chapter use lowercase because it is common to several different computers.

Workshop

Quiz

If you add a field to the PHONE-RECORD to include the extension and recompile the program, will the original file phone.dat process correctly using the new program?

Exercises

1. Copy `phnadd01.cbl` to `phnadd02.cbl`. Add a field to PHONE-RECORD to include a phone extension, and add all the logic needed to ask the user for this new field and store it in the file. Remember that your original data file, `phone.dat`, will not be processed correctly by this new file definition, and you will have to delete or rename the existing `phone.dat` file before you run `phnadd02.cbl`.

   Hint: The new record layout is the following:

   ```
   002100 01   PHONE-RECORD.
   002200      05   PHONE-LAST-NAME      PIC X(20).
   002300      05   PHONE-FIRST-NAME     PIC X(20).
   002400      05   PHONE-NUMBER         PIC X(15).
   002500      05   PHONE-EXTENSION      PIC X(5).
   ```

2. Copy `phnlst01.cbl` to `phnlst02.cbl` and modify it to display the additional extension field.

   Hint: You will find that the result will not display correctly on an 80-column screen, and you will need to shorten the prompts so that everything can be squeezed into 80 columns. If you use prompts as suggested in the following, everything will fit:

   ```
   002900 01   DISPLAY-FIELDS.
   003000      05   PROMPT-1             PIC X(4) VALUE "Lst:".
   003100      05   DISPLAY-LAST-NAME    PIC X(20).
   003200      05   PROMPT-2             PIC X(4) VALUE "1st:".
   003300      05   DISPLAY-FIRST-NAME   PIC X(20).
   003400      05   PROMPT-3             PIC X(3) VALUE "NO:".
   003500      05   DISPLAY-NUMBER       PIC X(15).
   003600      05   PROMPT-4             PIC X(4) VALUE "Xtn:".
   003700      05   DISPLAY-EXTENSION    PIC X(5).
   003800
   ```

   ```
   Smith          Michael Valentine    818-555-1212
   Trent          Jack and Diane       555-9292
   Kite           Alonso               (213)555-7777
   Mae            Maggie               506 555 1234
   Karenina       Ana                  (415) 555-3333
   ```

Day 10

Printing

Reporting on the data in files by using the printing features of COBOL is one of the main activities of COBOL programs. The reports are what end users see most often, and they are the area where users have the most requests for changes. You'll probably spend more time coding (and modifying) report programs than any other type of program. Acquiring good basics of printing reports on files will serve you throughout your COBOL career.

In today's lesson, you learn about the following topics:

- [ ] Printing basics
- [ ] Controlling the printer
- [ ] A simple printing program
- [ ] A simple report program
- [ ] Creating test data
- [ ] Laying out a report

Printing Basics

You already have learned most of the steps for printing, because in COBOL you send data to the printer by writing data to a file. In COBOL, the printer is defined as a file, and it is opened, closed, and written to as though it were a file.

Like any file, the printer file requires both a logical and a physical definition. Listings 10.1 and 10.2 compare the differences between a SELECT statement for a file and the SELECT statement for a print file.

TYPE **Listing 10.1. A SELECT statement for a file.**

```
000400 ENVIRONMENT DIVISION.
000500 INPUT-OUTPUT SECTION.
000600 FILE-CONTROL.
000700     SELECT PHONE-FILE
000800         ASSIGN TO "phone.dat"
000900         ORGANIZATION IS SEQUENTIAL.
001000
001100 DATA DIVISION.
```

TYPE **Listing 10.2. A SELECT statement for a print file.**

```
000400 ENVIRONMENT DIVISION.
000500 INPUT-OUTPUT SECTION.
000600 FILE-CONTROL.
000700     SELECT PHONE-FILE
000800         ASSIGN TO PRINTER
000900         ORGANIZATION IS LINE SEQUENTIAL.
001000
001100 DATA DIVISION.
```

The difference between the listings is the ASSIGN clause at line 00800. A normal disk file is assigned to a filename on the disk. A printer file is assigned to the COBOL reserved word PRINTER.

At line 000900, the ORGANIZATION for the printer file is changed to LINE SEQUENTIAL.

A line sequential file is similar to a sequential file, but it usually has carriage return and line feed characters added to the end of each record. These are added automatically every time a record is written. This format is suitable for printing or displaying. The format also is suitable for a file that is to be edited using a text editor. In fact, the source code files that you are editing whenever you write a program are line sequential files. In this case, the printer file is organized as a line sequential file because a carriage return and line feed are "added" at the end of each line and are sent to the printer to cause the print head to return to the left margin (carriage return) and drop down one line (line feed).

ORGANIZATION IS LINE SEQUENTIAL is commonly used in many versions of COBOL for the organization of the printer file, but it is not the only organization. I have also seen ORGANIZATION IS SEQUENTIAL and ORGANIZATION IS PRINTER.

The ASSIGN statement you use varies slightly for different versions of COBOL, usually based on the device name used on your system for the printer. Table 10.1 compares some different versions of COBOL.

Table 10.1. Versions of the ASSIGN clause.

COBOL Version	How to ASSIGN to PRINTER
Micro Focus COBOL or Personal COBOL	ASSIGN TO PRINTER
LPI COBOL	ASSIGN TO PRINT
	or
	ASSIGN TO PRINTER
ACUCOBOL version 2.0	ASSIGN TO PRINTER
VS COBOL	ASSIGN TO "PRINTER"
VAX COBOL	ASSIGN TO SYS$PRINT?

NEW TERM Because the printer is a device that is treated like a file in COBOL programs, a file used for printing is sometimes called a *printer file* or a *printer device file*.

On MS-DOS computers, writing a record "into" a printer file actually sends the record directly to the printer attached to your computer. When you write from the printer file, you send characters directly to the printer.

NEW TERM On larger computers with many users and one or more printers, writing to the printer file actually writes to a temporary file on the disk. When the printer file is closed, the temporary file is passed on to another program that handles the scheduling of the printers. The scheduling program usually is called a *spooler* or a *print queue manager*. This program sends the temporary file to the printer.

The second difference between data files and print files is shown in Listings 10.3 and 10.4. A data file uses LABEL RECORDS ARE STANDARD, and a print file uses LABEL RECORDS ARE OMITTED. A printer is a device and does not require labeling (filenames).

Listing 10.3. The file definition for a data file.

```
002000 DATA DIVISION.
002100 FILE SECTION.
002200 FD  PHONE-FILE
002300     LABEL RECORDS ARE STANDARD.
002400 01  PHONE-RECORD.
002500     05  PHONE-LAST-NAME      PIC X(20).
002600     05  PHONE-FIRST-NAME     PIC X(20).
002700     05  PHONE-NUMBER         PIC X(15).
002800     05  PHONE-EXTENSION      PIC X(5).
002900
```

Listing 10.4. The file definition for a printer file.

```
003000 FD  PRINTER-FILE
003100     LABEL RECORDS ARE OMITTED.
003200 01  PRINTER-RECORD          PIC X(80).
003300
```

Controlling the Printer

In addition to printing a string of characters on paper, a COBOL program has to tell the printer when to advance one line down the page. It also might have to tell the printer when to advance to the next page.

When a WRITE command is used on a printer file, the command can include instructions to force the printer to advance one or more lines. The syntax for this is the following:

```
WRITE a-record BEFORE ADVANCING a-number.
```

The BEFORE ADVANCING phrase causes one or more carriage return and line feed characters to be sent to the printer after the line is printed.

 A *carriage return* is a command sent to a printer that causes the print head to return to the left margin of the paper.

 A *line feed* is a command sent to a printer that causes the print head to move down one line.

The carriage return and line feed combination is used to move the print head to the left edge of the paper (carriage return) and down one line (line feed).

The advancing phrase also can be used to force the printer to eject the last page and prepare to start a new one. The *advancing* command in the following example sends a form feed to the printer after printing a line:

```
WRITE a-record BEFORE ADVANCING PAGE.
```

 A *form feed* is a command sent to a printer that causes the printer to eject the last sheet of paper and prepare to start printing at the top of a new sheet.

You also might advance the paper before printing a line. Table 10.2 compares the effects of various versions of BEFORE ADVANCING and AFTER ADVANCING.

Table 10.2. Controlling the printer with WRITE.

Code	Effect
WRITE PRINTER-RECORD BEFORE ADVANCING 1.	Sends the characters in PRINTER-RECORD to the printer, then advances the printer one line
WRITE PRINTER-RECORD AFTER ADVANCING 1.	Advances the printer one line, then sends the characters in PRINTER-RECORD to the printer
WRITE PRINTER-RECORD BEFORE ADVANCING 5.	Sends the characters in PRINTER-RECORD to the printer, then advances the printer five lines
WRITE PRINTER-RECORD AFTER ADVANCING 3.	Advances the printer three lines, then sends the characters in PRINTER-RECORD to the printer
WRITE PRINTER-RECORD BEFORE ADVANCING PAGE.	Sends the characters in PRINTER-RECORD to the printer, then advances the printer to the next page
WRITE PRINTER-RECORD AFTER ADVANCING PAGE.	Advances the printer to the next page, then sends the characters in PRINTER-RECORD to the printer

NEW TERM The BEFORE ADVANCING and AFTER ADVANCING clauses of the WRITE verb are called *carriage control clauses* or *carriage control information*. They control the positioning of the print head before or after a line is printed.

Most earlier COBOL programs use AFTER ADVANCING for carriage control. In fact, if you omit carriage control information when writing to a print file, each WRITE is treated as if you had included AFTER ADVANCING 1.

10

Most of the examples in this book use BEFORE ADVANCING. BEFORE ADVANCING has advantages for modern printers, particularly laser printers that expect to receive a form feed as the last command. This form feed causes the laser printer to print all of the last data received and eject the last page of the report.

It is a good practice to use either BEFORE or AFTER consistently in all of your code. You will see in more complex printing programs that it's easier to tell which line you are on when BEFORE or AFTER is used consistently in a program.

A Simple Printing Program

The simplest way to illustrate printing is to modify phnadd02.cbl from Appendix A, "Answers," for Day 9, "File I/O," so that it echoes each record to the printer as you add it. Listing 10.5 shows phnadd03.cbl, a modified version of phnadd02.cbl. Make sure that you have a printer attached to your computer, that the printer is on, and that the printer is ready to receive characters to print. Usually the printer will have a READY light that is on. If you run the program when the printer is not ready, it might lock up your computer.

TYPE **Listing 10.5. Echoing to the printer.**

```
000100 IDENTIFICATION DIVISION.
000200 PROGRAM-ID. PHNADD03.
000300*--------------------------------------------------
000400* This program creates a new data file if necessary
000500* and adds records to the file from user entered
000600* data. The records are written to the data file
000700* and echoed to the printer.
000800*--------------------------------------------------
000900 ENVIRONMENT DIVISION.
001000 INPUT-OUTPUT SECTION.
001100 FILE-CONTROL.
001200     SELECT PHONE-FILE
001300         ASSIGN TO "phone.dat"
001400         ORGANIZATION IS SEQUENTIAL.
001500
001600     SELECT PRINTER-FILE
001700         ASSIGN TO PRINTER
001800         ORGANIZATION IS LINE SEQUENTIAL.
001900
002000 DATA DIVISION.
002100 FILE SECTION.
002200 FD  PHONE-FILE
002300     LABEL RECORDS ARE STANDARD.
002400 01  PHONE-RECORD.
002500     05  PHONE-LAST-NAME    PIC X(20).
002600     05  PHONE-FIRST-NAME   PIC X(20).
002700     05  PHONE-NUMBER       PIC X(15).
002800     05  PHONE-EXTENSION    PIC X(5).
002900
```

```
003000 FD  PRINTER-FILE
003100     LABEL RECORDS ARE OMITTED.
003200 01  PRINTER-RECORD          PIC X(80).
003300
003400 WORKING-STORAGE SECTION.
003500
003600* Variables for SCREEN ENTRY
003700 01  PROMPT-1              PIC X(9)  VALUE "Last Name".
003800 01  PROMPT-2              PIC X(10) VALUE "First Name".
003900 01  PROMPT-3              PIC X(6)  VALUE "Number".
004000 01  PROMPT-4              PIC X(9)  VALUE "Extension".
004100
004200 01  YES-NO               PIC X.
004300 01  ENTRY-OK             PIC X.
004400
004500 PROCEDURE DIVISION.
004600 MAIN-LOGIC SECTION.
004700 PROGRAM-BEGIN.
004800
004900     PERFORM OPENING-PROCEDURE.
005000     MOVE "Y" TO YES-NO.
005100     PERFORM ADD-RECORDS
005200         UNTIL YES-NO = "N".
005300     PERFORM CLOSING-PROCEDURE.
005400
005500 PROGRAM-DONE.
005600     STOP RUN.
005700
005800* OPENING AND CLOSING
005900
006000 OPENING-PROCEDURE.
006100     OPEN EXTEND PHONE-FILE.
006200     OPEN OUTPUT PRINTER-FILE.
006300
006400 CLOSING-PROCEDURE.
006500     CLOSE PHONE-FILE.
006600     MOVE SPACE TO PRINTER-RECORD.
006700     WRITE PRINTER-RECORD BEFORE ADVANCING PAGE.
006800     CLOSE PRINTER-FILE.
006900
007000 ADD-RECORDS.
007100     MOVE "N" TO ENTRY-OK.
007200     PERFORM GET-FIELDS
007300         UNTIL ENTRY-OK = "Y".
007400     PERFORM ADD-THIS-RECORD.
007500     PERFORM GO-AGAIN.
007600
007700 GET-FIELDS.
007800     MOVE SPACE TO PHONE-RECORD.
007900     DISPLAY PROMPT-1 " ? ".
008000     ACCEPT PHONE-LAST-NAME.
008100     DISPLAY PROMPT-2 " ? ".
008200     ACCEPT PHONE-FIRST-NAME.
008300     DISPLAY PROMPT-3 " ? ".
008400     ACCEPT PHONE-NUMBER.
008500     DISPLAY PROMPT-4 " ? ".
008600     ACCEPT PHONE-EXTENSION.
```

10

continues

Listing 10.5. continued

```
008700      PERFORM VALIDATE-FIELDS.
008800
008900 VALIDATE-FIELDS.
009000      MOVE "Y" TO ENTRY-OK.
009100      IF PHONE-LAST-NAME = SPACE
009200          DISPLAY "LAST NAME MUST BE ENTERED"
009300          MOVE "N" TO ENTRY-OK.
009400
009500 ADD-THIS-RECORD.
009600      MOVE PHONE-RECORD TO PRINTER-RECORD.
009700      WRITE PHONE-RECORD.
009800      WRITE PRINTER-RECORD BEFORE ADVANCING 1.
009900
010000 GO-AGAIN.
010100      DISPLAY "GO AGAIN?".
010200      ACCEPT YES-NO.
010300      IF YES-NO = "y"
010400          MOVE "Y" TO YES-NO.
010500      IF YES-NO NOT = "Y"
010600          MOVE "N" TO YES-NO.
010700
```

The following is the on-screen output of `phnadd03.cbl`:

OUTPUT
```
Last Name ?
MARTINSON
First Name ?
RICKY
Number ?
555-1234
Extension ?
405
GO AGAIN?
Y
Last Name ?
JONES
First Name ?
JOHN
Number ?
555-4321
Extension ?
1122
GO AGAIN?
N


C>
C>
```

10

This is the printed output of phnadd03.cbl:

OUTPUT
```
MARTINSON        RICKY             555-1234      405
JONES            JOHN              555-4321      1122
```

ANALYSIS The SELECT and FD for the PRINTER-FILE are at lines 001600 through 001800 and lines 002900 through 003100. No record for the PRINTER-FILE is created as a variable because there is no need for fields within the PRINTER-RECORD, as you will learn later.

The OPENING-PROCEDURE is modified to open the PRINTER-FILE. Printer files can be opened only in OUTPUT mode, as shown at line 006100.

Before you look at the closing procedure, check lines 009600 and 009800 in ADD-THIS-RECORD. PRINTER-RECORD is filled in by moving the PHONE-RECORD to it at line 009600. Then the PRINTER-RECORD is written at line 009800.

The closing procedure at line 006400 seems odd. Just before the printer file is closed, a record of spaces is written, followed by a form feed (BEFORE ADVANCING PAGE). This forces the last page out of the printer. It doesn't hurt to do this on a standard dot-matrix printer, and it's necessary for laser printers. As I mentioned before, laser printers expect a form feed as the last command.

The only information put in the PRINTER-RECORD is either a complete copy of the PHONE-RECORD at line 009600 or SPACE at line 006400, so there is no need for the PRINTER-RECORD to be created as a structure.

A Simple Report Program

The example printing program is a variation of phnadd02.cbl from Appendix A. It echoes records as they are added to the file. Most COBOL printing programs (sometimes called report programs) are designed to read the contents of an existing file and print the information.

Printing programs, which are also called report programs, are similar to display programs such as phnlst01.cbl (see Appendix A).

You can derive the first version of a printing program that prints all records in a file, phnprt01.cbl, almost directly from phnlst02.cbl. You might want to compare the report program in Listing 10.6 to phnprt01.cbl.

TYPE **Listing 10.6. A report program.**

```
000100 IDENTIFICATION DIVISION.
000200 PROGRAM-ID. PHNPRT01.
000300*-------------------------------------------------
000400* This program prints the contents of the
000500* phone file.
```

continues

Listing 10.6. continued

```
000600*-------------------------------------------------
000700 ENVIRONMENT DIVISION.
000800 INPUT-OUTPUT SECTION.
000900 FILE-CONTROL.
001000      SELECT OPTIONAL PHONE-FILE
001100*or   SELECT PHONE-FILE
001200           ASSIGN TO "phone.dat"
001300*or        ASSIGN TO "phone"
001400           ORGANIZATION IS SEQUENTIAL.
001500
001600      SELECT PRINTER-FILE
001700           ASSIGN TO PRINTER
001800           ORGANIZATION IS LINE SEQUENTIAL.
001900
002000 DATA DIVISION.
002100 FILE SECTION.
002200 FD   PHONE-FILE
002300      LABEL RECORDS ARE STANDARD.
002400 01   PHONE-RECORD.
002500      05   PHONE-LAST-NAME      PIC X(20).
002600      05   PHONE-FIRST-NAME     PIC X(20).
002700      05   PHONE-NUMBER         PIC X(15).
002800      05   PHONE-EXTENSION      PIC X(5).
002900
003000 FD   PRINTER-FILE
003100      LABEL RECORDS ARE OMITTED.
003200 01   PRINTER-RECORD            PIC X(80).
003300
003400 WORKING-STORAGE SECTION.
003500
003600* Structure for PRINTING
003700 01   FIELDS-TO-PRINT.
003800      05   PROMPT-1             PIC X(4) VALUE "Lst:".
003900      05   PRINT-LAST-NAME      PIC X(20).
004000      05   PROMPT-2             PIC X(4) VALUE "1st:".
004100      05   PRINT-FIRST-NAME     PIC X(20).
004200      05   PROMPT-3             PIC X(3) VALUE "NO:".
004300      05   PRINT-NUMBER         PIC X(15).
004400      05   PROMPT-4             PIC X(4) VALUE "Xtn:".
004500      05   PRINT-EXTENSION      PIC X(5).
004600
004700 01   END-OF-FILE        PIC X.
004800
004900 01   PRINT-LINES        PIC 99.
005000
005100 PROCEDURE DIVISION.
005200 MAIN-LOGIC SECTION.
005300 PROGRAM-BEGIN.
005400
005500      PERFORM OPENING-PROCEDURE.
005600      MOVE ZEROES TO PRINT-LINES.
005700      MOVE "N" TO END-OF-FILE.
005800      PERFORM READ-NEXT-RECORD.
```

10

```
005900      PERFORM PRINT-RECORDS
006000           UNTIL END-OF-FILE = "Y".
006100      PERFORM CLOSING-PROCEDURE.
006200
006300 PROGRAM-DONE.
006400     STOP RUN.
006500
006600 OPENING-PROCEDURE.
006700     OPEN INPUT PHONE-FILE.
006800     OPEN OUTPUT PRINTER-FILE.
006900
007000 CLOSING-PROCEDURE.
007100     CLOSE PHONE-FILE.
007200     MOVE SPACE TO PRINTER-RECORD.
007300     WRITE PRINTER-RECORD BEFORE ADVANCING PAGE.
007400     CLOSE PRINTER-FILE.
007500
007600 PRINT-RECORDS.
007700     PERFORM PRINT-FIELDS.
007800     PERFORM READ-NEXT-RECORD.
007900
008000 PRINT-FIELDS.
008100     IF PRINT-LINES = 55
008200         PERFORM NEW-PAGE.
008300     MOVE PHONE-LAST-NAME TO PRINT-LAST-NAME.
008400     MOVE PHONE-FIRST-NAME TO PRINT-FIRST-NAME.
008500     MOVE PHONE-NUMBER TO PRINT-NUMBER.
008600     MOVE PHONE-EXTENSION TO PRINT-EXTENSION.
008700     MOVE FIELDS-TO-PRINT TO PRINTER-RECORD.
008800     WRITE PRINTER-RECORD BEFORE ADVANCING 1.
008900
009000     ADD 1 TO PRINT-LINES.
009100
009200 READ-NEXT-RECORD.
009300     READ PHONE-FILE NEXT RECORD
009400         AT END
009500         MOVE "Y" TO END-OF-FILE.
009600
009700 NEW-PAGE.
009800     MOVE SPACE TO PRINTER-RECORD.
009900     WRITE PRINTER-RECORD BEFORE ADVANCING PAGE.
010000     MOVE ZEROES TO PRINT-LINES.
010100
```

10

The printer output of phnprt01.cbl looks something like the following:

```
Lst:MARTINSON      1st:RICKY        NO:555-1234      Xtn:405
Lst:JONES          1st:JOHN         NO:555-4321      Xtn:1122
Lst:Smith          1st:Michael      NO:(213) 555-7075 Xtn:476
Lst:Fitzhugh       1st:Adrianne     NO:(202) 555-7017 Xtn:23
```

ANALYSIS   A printer file has been added in FILE-CONTROL and in the FILE SECTION of the DATA
DIVISION. The OPENING-PROCEDURE and CLOSING-PROCEDURE paragraphs include an
appropriate OPEN and CLOSE for the PRINTER-FILE, including a closing form feed to eject the
last page. The DISPLAY-FIELDS paragraph in phnlst02.cbl has been changed to a PRINT-
FIELDS paragraph, which loads the fields and prints them.

One interesting area of change is at lines 008100 and 008200. Here is the original phnlst02.cbl
(ignoring line numbering differences):

```
007000      IF SCREEN-LINES = 15
007100         PERFORM PRESS-ENTER.
```

This is the phnprt01.cbl program:

```
008100      IF PRINT-LINES = 55
008200         PERFORM NEW-PAGE.
```

The SCREEN-LINES variable has been changed to a PRINT-LINES variable, and the size of a print
page has been set to 55. A print page usually has 66 (sometimes 68) lines on which you can
print data. Laser printers might have fewer lines. If you print from the top to the bottom of
the page, the output might appear cluttered, so it is common to allow a margin. I have chosen
55 lines as the breakpoint.

In the original phnlst02.cbl, the user is asked to press Enter to continue, as in the following:

```
008500 PRESS-ENTER.
008600      DISPLAY "Press ENTER to continue . . ".
008700      ACCEPT A-DUMMY.
008800      MOVE ZEROES TO SCREEN-LINES.
```

In a printing program, this pause between screens is changed into a page break (form feed):

```
009700 NEW-PAGE.
009800      MOVE SPACE TO PRINTER-RECORD.
009900      WRITE PRINTER-RECORD BEFORE ADVANCING PAGE.
010000      MOVE ZEROES TO PRINT-LINES.
```

Code and compile phnprt01.cbl. If you have not done so yet, code and compile phnadd02.cbl
from Appendix A. Delete the old data file, phone.dat, and use phnadd02.cbl to create a new
file. Then add several phone numbers to the phone.dat file, and run phnprt01.cbl to print
these entries. If you have more than 55 entries, phnprt01.cbl inserts a page break after
printing 55 entries and starts a new page for the remaining entries.

If you don't feel like entering this many phone numbers, you can use the information in the
next section to learn how to build test data to test your printing program.

Creating Test Data

Creating test data is one way of setting up proper conditions to test COBOL programs. The main thing to keep in mind is that you want the test data to provide fields that will test all the necessary conditions in your program. For phnprt01.cbl, you need to test these conditions:

☐ Does the program print all the records in a file?

☐ Does the program print all the data in each field?

☐ Does the program stop correctly at the end of the file?

☐ Does the program insert a page break correctly?

The test data doesn't have to make sense, as long as it tests those conditions.

The program phnbld01.cbl in Listing 10.7 creates a number of dummy records, based on a quantity entered by the user.

TYPE Listing 10.7. Creating test data for phnprt01.cbl.

```
000100 IDENTIFICATION DIVISION.
000200 PROGRAM-ID. PHNBLD01.
000300*------------------------------------------------
000400* This program creates a new data file and fills
000500* it with test data.
000600* The test records are written to the data file
000700* and echoed to the printer.
000800*------------------------------------------------
000900 ENVIRONMENT DIVISION.
001000 INPUT-OUTPUT SECTION.
001100 FILE-CONTROL.
001200     SELECT PHONE-FILE
001300         ASSIGN TO "phone.dat"
001400         ORGANIZATION IS SEQUENTIAL.
001500
001600     SELECT PRINTER-FILE
001700         ASSIGN TO PRINTER
001800         ORGANIZATION IS LINE SEQUENTIAL.
001900
002000 DATA DIVISION.
002100 FILE SECTION.
002200 FD  PHONE-FILE
002300     LABEL RECORDS ARE STANDARD.
002400 01  PHONE-RECORD.
002500     05  PHONE-LAST-NAME      PIC X(20).
002600     05  PHONE-FIRST-NAME     PIC X(20).
002700     05  PHONE-NUMBER         PIC X(15).
002800     05  PHONE-EXTENSION      PIC X(5).
002900
003000 FD  PRINTER-FILE
003100     LABEL RECORDS ARE OMITTED.
```

continues

Listing 10.7. continued

```
003200 01  PRINTER-RECORD           PIC X(80).
003300
003400 WORKING-STORAGE SECTION.
003500
003600 01  HOW-MANY                 PIC 999.
003700 01  ENTRY-FIELD              PIC ZZZ.
003800
003900 01  PRINT-LINES              PIC 99 VALUE ZEROES.
004000 01  FORMATTED-NUMBER.
004100     05  FILLER               PIC X(6) VALUE "(404) ".
004200     05  FILLER               PIC X(4) VALUE "555-".
004300     05  PHONE-COUNTER        PIC 9(4) VALUE ZERO.
004400
004500 PROCEDURE DIVISION.
004600 MAIN-LOGIC SECTION.
004700 PROGRAM-BEGIN.
004800
004900     PERFORM OPENING-PROCEDURE.
005000     PERFORM GET-HOW-MANY.
005100     MOVE ZEROES TO PRINT-LINES.
005200     PERFORM ADD-RECORDS
005300         VARYING PHONE-COUNTER
005400         FROM 1 BY 1 UNTIL
005500             PHONE-COUNTER > HOW-MANY.
005600     PERFORM CLOSING-PROCEDURE.
005700
005800 PROGRAM-DONE.
005900     STOP RUN.
006000
006100* OPENING AND CLOSING
006200
006300 OPENING-PROCEDURE.
006400     OPEN OUTPUT PHONE-FILE.
006500     OPEN OUTPUT PRINTER-FILE.
006600
006700 CLOSING-PROCEDURE.
006800     CLOSE PHONE-FILE.
006900     MOVE SPACE TO PRINTER-RECORD.
007000     WRITE PRINTER-RECORD BEFORE ADVANCING PAGE.
007100     CLOSE PRINTER-FILE.
007200
007300 GET-HOW-MANY.
007400     DISPLAY "How many test entries (1-999)".
007500     ACCEPT ENTRY-FIELD.
007600*or  ACCEPT ENTRY-FIELD WITH CONVERSION.
007700     MOVE ENTRY-FIELD TO HOW-MANY.
007800
007900 ADD-RECORDS.
008000     PERFORM FORMAT-THE-RECORD.
008100     PERFORM ADD-THIS-RECORD.
008200
008300 FORMAT-THE-RECORD.
008400     MOVE "Joshua-----------X" TO PHONE-FIRST-NAME.
008500     MOVE "Johnson----------X" TO PHONE-LAST-NAME.
008600     MOVE "12345" TO PHONE-EXTENSION.
```

```
008700       MOVE FORMATTED-NUMBER TO PHONE-NUMBER.
008800
008900 ADD-THIS-RECORD.
009000       WRITE PHONE-RECORD.
009100       PERFORM PRINT-THIS-RECORD.
009200
009300 PRINT-THIS-RECORD.
009400       IF PRINT-LINES NOT < 55
009500           PERFORM NEW-PAGE.
009600       MOVE PHONE-RECORD TO PRINTER-RECORD.
009700       WRITE PRINTER-RECORD BEFORE ADVANCING 1.
009800       ADD 1 TO PRINT-LINES.
009900
010000 NEW-PAGE.
010100       MOVE SPACE TO PRINTER-RECORD.
010200       WRITE PRINTER-RECORD BEFORE ADVANCING PAGE.
010300       MOVE ZEROES TO PRINT-LINES.
010400
```

10

The following output of phnbld01.cbl prints when you request 77 entries:

```
Johnson-----------XJoshua-----------X(404) 555-0001 12345
Johnson-----------XJoshua-----------X(404) 555-0002 12345
Johnson-----------XJoshua-----------X(404) 555-0003 12345
Johnson-----------XJoshua-----------X(404) 555-0004 12345
Johnson-----------XJoshua-----------X(404) 555-0005 12345
Johnson-----------XJoshua-----------X(404) 555-0006 12345
Johnson-----------XJoshua-----------X(404) 555-0007 12345
Johnson-----------XJoshua-----------X(404) 555-0008 12345
Johnson-----------XJoshua-----------X(404) 555-0009 12345
Johnson-----------XJoshua-----------X(404) 555-0010 12345
Johnson-----------XJoshua-----------X(404) 555-0011 12345
Johnson-----------XJoshua-----------X(404) 555-0012 12345
Johnson-----------XJoshua-----------X(404) 555-0013 12345
Johnson-----------XJoshua-----------X(404) 555-0014 12345
Johnson-----------XJoshua-----------X(404) 555-0015 12345
Johnson-----------XJoshua-----------X(404) 555-0016 12345
Johnson-----------XJoshua-----------X(404) 555-0017 12345
Johnson-----------XJoshua-----------X(404) 555-0018 12345
Johnson-----------XJoshua-----------X(404) 555-0019 12345
Johnson-----------XJoshua-----------X(404) 555-0020 12345
Johnson-----------XJoshua-----------X(404) 555-0021 12345
Johnson-----------XJoshua-----------X(404) 555-0022 12345
Johnson-----------XJoshua-----------X(404) 555-0023 12345
Johnson-----------XJoshua-----------X(404) 555-0024 12345
Johnson-----------XJoshua-----------X(404) 555-0025 12345
Johnson-----------XJoshua-----------X(404) 555-0026 12345
Johnson-----------XJoshua-----------X(404) 555-0027 12345
Johnson-----------XJoshua-----------X(404) 555-0028 12345
Johnson-----------XJoshua-----------X(404) 555-0029 12345
Johnson-----------XJoshua-----------X(404) 555-0030 12345
Johnson-----------XJoshua-----------X(404) 555-0031 12345
Johnson-----------XJoshua-----------X(404) 555-0032 12345
Johnson-----------XJoshua-----------X(404) 555-0033 12345
Johnson-----------XJoshua-----------X(404) 555-0034 12345
```

```
Johnson-----------XJoshua-----------X(404) 555-0035 12345
Johnson-----------XJoshua-----------X(404) 555-0036 12345
Johnson-----------XJoshua-----------X(404) 555-0037 12345
Johnson-----------XJoshua-----------X(404) 555-0038 12345
Johnson-----------XJoshua-----------X(404) 555-0039 12345
Johnson-----------XJoshua-----------X(404) 555-0040 12345
Johnson-----------XJoshua-----------X(404) 555-0041 12345
Johnson-----------XJoshua-----------X(404) 555-0042 12345
Johnson-----------XJoshua-----------X(404) 555-0043 12345
Johnson-----------XJoshua-----------X(404) 555-0044 12345
Johnson-----------XJoshua-----------X(404) 555-0045 12345
Johnson-----------XJoshua-----------X(404) 555-0046 12345
Johnson-----------XJoshua-----------X(404) 555-0047 12345
Johnson-----------XJoshua-----------X(404) 555-0048 12345
Johnson-----------XJoshua-----------X(404) 555-0049 12345
Johnson-----------XJoshua-----------X(404) 555-0050 12345
Johnson-----------XJoshua-----------X(404) 555-0051 12345
Johnson-----------XJoshua-----------X(404) 555-0052 12345
Johnson-----------XJoshua-----------X(404) 555-0053 12345
Johnson-----------XJoshua-----------X(404) 555-0054 12345
Johnson-----------XJoshua-----------X(404) 555-0055 12345
```

(New page starts here.)

```
Johnson-----------XJoshua-----------X(404) 555-0056 12345
Johnson-----------XJoshua-----------X(404) 555-0057 12345
Johnson-----------XJoshua-----------X(404) 555-0058 12345
Johnson-----------XJoshua-----------X(404) 555-0059 12345
Johnson-----------XJoshua-----------X(404) 555-0060 12345
Johnson-----------XJoshua-----------X(404) 555-0061 12345
Johnson-----------XJoshua-----------X(404) 555-0062 12345
Johnson-----------XJoshua-----------X(404) 555-0063 12345
Johnson-----------XJoshua-----------X(404) 555-0064 12345
Johnson-----------XJoshua-----------X(404) 555-0065 12345
Johnson-----------XJoshua-----------X(404) 555-0066 12345
Johnson-----------XJoshua-----------X(404) 555-0067 12345
Johnson-----------XJoshua-----------X(404) 555-0068 12345
Johnson-----------XJoshua-----------X(404) 555-0069 12345
Johnson-----------XJoshua-----------X(404) 555-0070 12345
Johnson-----------XJoshua-----------X(404) 555-0071 12345
Johnson-----------XJoshua-----------X(404) 555-0072 12345
Johnson-----------XJoshua-----------X(404) 555-0073 12345
Johnson-----------XJoshua-----------X(404) 555-0074 12345
Johnson-----------XJoshua-----------X(404) 555-0075 12345
Johnson-----------XJoshua-----------X(404) 555-0076 12345
Johnson-----------XJoshua-----------X(404) 555-0077 12345
```

ANALYSIS Each record is identical except for the last four digits of the phone number field. The PHONE-FIRST-NAME field is filled in with Joshua-----------X to test the full 20 characters of the printed field. Similarly, the PHONE-LAST-NAME field is filled in with Johnson-----------X to test the printing of that field, and the PHONE-EXTENSION is filled in with 12345.

10

The trick of creating a different phone number is taken care of by the structure at lines 004000 through 004400. This sets up a structure containing (404) and 555-, followed by a PHONE-COUNTER. At line 005000, a routine is performed to ask the user how many test records to create. At lines 005200 through 005500, the routine to add records to the file is performed while varying the PHONE-COUNTER from 1 through HOW-MANY entries.

At lines 08300 through 008700, the record is filled in. When the record is added in the routine at 008900, it also is printed, ensuring that you have an accurate record of what exactly was placed in the file.

Edit, compile, and run phnbld01.cbl to create a test file large enough to test the printing capabilities of phnprt01.cbl. Then run phnprt01.cbl to see an output report with a page break in it.

By examining the output, you verify that phnprt01.cbl passes all these test criteria:

☐ The program prints all the records in a file.

☐ The program prints all the data in each field.

☐ The program stops correctly at the end of the file.

☐ The program inserts a page break correctly.

The following output of phnprt01.cbl using 77 entries was created by phnbld01.cbl:

```
Lst:Johnson-----------X1st:Joshua-----------XNO:(404) 555-0001 Xtn:12345
Lst:Johnson-----------X1st:Joshua-----------XNO:(404) 555-0002 Xtn:12345
Lst:Johnson-----------X1st:Joshua-----------XNO:(404) 555-0003 Xtn:12345
Lst:Johnson-----------X1st:Joshua-----------XNO:(404) 555-0004 Xtn:12345
Lst:Johnson-----------X1st:Joshua-----------XNO:(404) 555-0005 Xtn:12345
Lst:Johnson-----------X1st:Joshua-----------XNO:(404) 555-0006 Xtn:12345
Lst:Johnson-----------X1st:Joshua-----------XNO:(404) 555-0007 Xtn:12345
Lst:Johnson-----------X1st:Joshua-----------XNO:(404) 555-0008 Xtn:12345
Lst:Johnson-----------X1st:Joshua-----------XNO:(404) 555-0009 Xtn:12345
Lst:Johnson-----------X1st:Joshua-----------XNO:(404) 555-0010 Xtn:12345
Lst:Johnson-----------X1st:Joshua-----------XNO:(404) 555-0011 Xtn:12345
Lst:Johnson-----------X1st:Joshua-----------XNO:(404) 555-0012 Xtn:12345
Lst:Johnson-----------X1st:Joshua-----------XNO:(404) 555-0013 Xtn:12345
Lst:Johnson-----------X1st:Joshua-----------XNO:(404) 555-0014 Xtn:12345
Lst:Johnson-----------X1st:Joshua-----------XNO:(404) 555-0015 Xtn:12345
Lst:Johnson-----------X1st:Joshua-----------XNO:(404) 555-0016 Xtn:12345
Lst:Johnson-----------X1st:Joshua-----------XNO:(404) 555-0017 Xtn:12345
Lst:Johnson-----------X1st:Joshua-----------XNO:(404) 555-0018 Xtn:12345
Lst:Johnson-----------X1st:Joshua-----------XNO:(404) 555-0019 Xtn:12345
Lst:Johnson-----------X1st:Joshua-----------XNO:(404) 555-0020 Xtn:12345
Lst:Johnson-----------X1st:Joshua-----------XNO:(404) 555-0021 Xtn:12345
Lst:Johnson-----------X1st:Joshua-----------XNO:(404) 555-0022 Xtn:12345
Lst:Johnson-----------X1st:Joshua-----------XNO:(404) 555-0023 Xtn:12345
Lst:Johnson-----------X1st:Joshua-----------XNO:(404) 555-0024 Xtn:12345
Lst:Johnson-----------X1st:Joshua-----------XNO:(404) 555-0025 Xtn:12345
Lst:Johnson-----------X1st:Joshua-----------XNO:(404) 555-0026 Xtn:12345
Lst:Johnson-----------X1st:Joshua-----------XNO:(404) 555-0027 Xtn:12345
Lst:Johnson-----------X1st:Joshua-----------XNO:(404) 555-0028 Xtn:12345
```

10

```
Lst:Johnson-----------X1st:Joshua-----------XNO:(404) 555-0029 Xtn:12345
Lst:Johnson-----------X1st:Joshua-----------XNO:(404) 555-0030 Xtn:12345
Lst:Johnson-----------X1st:Joshua-----------XNO:(404) 555-0031 Xtn:12345
Lst:Johnson-----------X1st:Joshua-----------XNO:(404) 555-0032 Xtn:12345
Lst:Johnson-----------X1st:Joshua-----------XNO:(404) 555-0033 Xtn:12345
Lst:Johnson-----------X1st:Joshua-----------XNO:(404) 555-0034 Xtn:12345
Lst:Johnson-----------X1st:Joshua-----------XNO:(404) 555-0035 Xtn:12345
Lst:Johnson-----------X1st:Joshua-----------XNO:(404) 555-0036 Xtn:12345
Lst:Johnson-----------X1st:Joshua-----------XNO:(404) 555-0037 Xtn:12345
Lst:Johnson-----------X1st:Joshua-----------XNO:(404) 555-0038 Xtn:12345
Lst:Johnson-----------X1st:Joshua-----------XNO:(404) 555-0039 Xtn:12345
Lst:Johnson-----------X1st:Joshua-----------XNO:(404) 555-0040 Xtn:12345
Lst:Johnson-----------X1st:Joshua-----------XNO:(404) 555-0041 Xtn:12345
Lst:Johnson-----------X1st:Joshua-----------XNO:(404) 555-0042 Xtn:12345
Lst:Johnson-----------X1st:Joshua-----------XNO:(404) 555-0043 Xtn:12345
Lst:Johnson-----------X1st:Joshua-----------XNO:(404) 555-0044 Xtn:12345
Lst:Johnson-----------X1st:Joshua-----------XNO:(404) 555-0045 Xtn:12345
Lst:Johnson-----------X1st:Joshua-----------XNO:(404) 555-0046 Xtn:12345
Lst:Johnson-----------X1st:Joshua-----------XNO:(404) 555-0047 Xtn:12345
Lst:Johnson-----------X1st:Joshua-----------XNO:(404) 555-0048 Xtn:12345
Lst:Johnson-----------X1st:Joshua-----------XNO:(404) 555-0049 Xtn:12345
Lst:Johnson-----------X1st:Joshua-----------XNO:(404) 555-0050 Xtn:12345
Lst:Johnson-----------X1st:Joshua-----------XNO:(404) 555-0051 Xtn:12345
Lst:Johnson-----------X1st:Joshua-----------XNO:(404) 555-0052 Xtn:12345
Lst:Johnson-----------X1st:Joshua-----------XNO:(404) 555-0053 Xtn:12345
Lst:Johnson-----------X1st:Joshua-----------XNO:(404) 555-0054 Xtn:12345
Lst:Johnson-----------X1st:Joshua-----------XNO:(404) 555-0055 Xtn:12345
```

(New page starts here.)

```
Lst:Johnson-----------X1st:Joshua-----------XNO:(404) 555-0056 Xtn:12345
Lst:Johnson-----------X1st:Joshua-----------XNO:(404) 555-0057 Xtn:12345
Lst:Johnson-----------X1st:Joshua-----------XNO:(404) 555-0058 Xtn:12345
Lst:Johnson-----------X1st:Joshua-----------XNO:(404) 555-0059 Xtn:12345
Lst:Johnson-----------X1st:Joshua-----------XNO:(404) 555-0060 Xtn:12345
Lst:Johnson-----------X1st:Joshua-----------XNO:(404) 555-0061 Xtn:12345
Lst:Johnson-----------X1st:Joshua-----------XNO:(404) 555-0062 Xtn:12345
Lst:Johnson-----------X1st:Joshua-----------XNO:(404) 555-0063 Xtn:12345
Lst:Johnson-----------X1st:Joshua-----------XNO:(404) 555-0064 Xtn:12345
Lst:Johnson-----------X1st:Joshua-----------XNO:(404) 555-0065 Xtn:12345
Lst:Johnson-----------X1st:Joshua-----------XNO:(404) 555-0066 Xtn:12345
Lst:Johnson-----------X1st:Joshua-----------XNO:(404) 555-0067 Xtn:12345
Lst:Johnson-----------X1st:Joshua-----------XNO:(404) 555-0068 Xtn:12345
Lst:Johnson-----------X1st:Joshua-----------XNO:(404) 555-0069 Xtn:12345
Lst:Johnson-----------X1st:Joshua-----------XNO:(404) 555-0070 Xtn:12345
Lst:Johnson-----------X1st:Joshua-----------XNO:(404) 555-0071 Xtn:12345
Lst:Johnson-----------X1st:Joshua-----------XNO:(404) 555-0072 Xtn:12345
Lst:Johnson-----------X1st:Joshua-----------XNO:(404) 555-0073 Xtn:12345
Lst:Johnson-----------X1st:Joshua-----------XNO:(404) 555-0074 Xtn:12345
Lst:Johnson-----------X1st:Joshua-----------XNO:(404) 555-0075 Xtn:12345
Lst:Johnson-----------X1st:Joshua-----------XNO:(404) 555-0076 Xtn:12345
Lst:Johnson-----------X1st:Joshua-----------XNO:(404) 555-0077 Xtn:12345
```

Examination of the output does reveal a problem. The fields are all jammed end-to-end, with no space between the end of one field and the beginning of the prompt for the next field.

Laying Out a Report

Usually, a COBOL report program looks more like the example lines in Figure 10.1.

COBOL report layouts usually are worked out on a printer spacing sheet. A blank printer spacing sheet is shown in Figure 10.2. The printer spacing sheet uses 80 columns (or 132 for wide-carriage printers) to represent printing positions. You can buy these at a stationery shop or simply adapt graph paper to do the same job.

Figure 10.1.

The layout of a COBOL report program.

PHONE BOOK REPORT			Page: 1
Last Name	First Name	Number	Ext.
Johnson------------x	Joshua------------x	(404) 555-0001	12345
Johnson------------x	Joshua------------x	(404) 555-0002	12345
Johnson------------x	Joshua------------x	(404) 555-0003	12345
Johnson------------x	Joshua------------x	(404) 555-0004	12345
Johnson------------x	Joshua------------x	(404) 555-0005	12345
Johnson------------x	Joshua------------x	(404) 555-0006	12345

PHONE BOOK REPORT			Page: 2
Last Name	First Name	Number	Ext.
Johnson------------x	Joshua------------x	(404) 555-0052	12345
Johnson------------x	Joshua------------x	(404) 555-0053	12345
Johnson------------x	Joshua------------x	(404) 555-0054	12345
Johnson------------x	Joshua------------x	(404) 555-0055	12345
Johnson------------x	Joshua------------x	(404) 555-0056	12345
Johnson------------x	Joshua------------x	(404) 555-0057	12345
Johnson------------x	Joshua------------x	(404) 555-0058	12345

The spacing sheet for this sample report program is shown in Figure 10.3. The layout is done by hand and helps to calculate the spacing of the output data in a report. When you have determined the spacing, you can work out what the data should look like in the program.

Figure 10.2.
A printer spacing sheet.

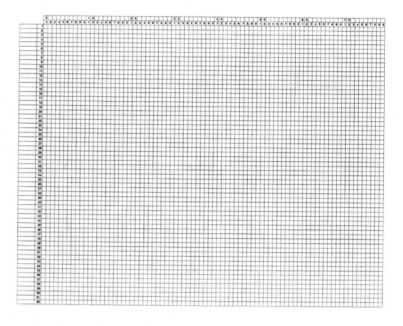

Figure 10.3.
A COBOL printer layout sheet.

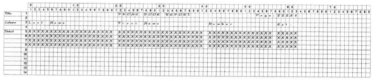

The main part of the report is detail lines holding enough space for each field, with a space between each field, as shown in Listing 10.8.

TYPE **Listing 10.8. The structure for the report detail.**

```
005400
005500 01 DETAIL-LINE.
005600    05  PRINT-LAST-NAME      PIC X(20).
005700    05  FILLER               PIC X(1) VALUE SPACE.
005800    05  PRINT-FIRST-NAME     PIC X(20).
005900    05  FILLER               PIC X(1) VALUE SPACE.
006000    05  PRINT-NUMBER         PIC X(15).
006100    05  FILLER               PIC X(1) VALUE SPACE.
006200    05  PRINT-EXTENSION      PIC X(5).
006300
```

The top line of the report is a title line; the structure shown in Listing 10.9 holds the title for the report and an incrementing page number.

TYPE | **Listing 10.9. The structure for the title.**

```
003700 01   TITLE-LINE.
003800      05  FILLER              PIC X(21) VALUE SPACE.
003900      05  FILLER              PIC X(17) VALUE
004000      "PHONE BOOK REPORT".
004100      05  FILLER              PIC X(15) VALUE SPACE.
004200      05  FILLER              PIC X(5) VALUE "Page:".
004300      05  PRINT-PAGE-NUMBER   PIC ZZZZ9.
004400
```

The second line at the top of each page of the report is for column headings; the structure shown in Listing 10.10 is used to print the columns. The column headings do not change, so all the values in COLUMN-HEADINGS are defined as FILLER.

TYPE | **Listing 10.10. The column headings.**

```
004600 01   COLUMN-HEADINGS.
004700      05  FILLER              PIC X(9)  VALUE "Last Name".
004800      05  FILLER              PIC X(12) VALUE SPACE.
004900      05  FILLER              PIC X(10) VALUE "First Name".
005000      05  FILLER              PIC X(11) VALUE SPACE.
005100      05  FILLER              PIC X(6)  VALUE "Number".
005200      05  FILLER              PIC X(10) VALUE SPACE.
005300      05  FILLER              PIC X(4)  VALUE "Ext.".
```

With the data structure defined, you now can consider the program. Printing the information differs only slightly from phnprt01.cbl. The difference is that the logic to start another page must include ending the last page by inserting a form feed, incrementing the page number, and then printing the title line and the column heading line.

Starting a new page is really two separate problems, because first you must end the old page and then start the new one. The new page logic has to be broken into two pieces because you need to be able to start a new page at the beginning of the report (print the title and column headings) without ending an old page (insert a form feed).

Listing 10.11 is the program that results from this modification to the layout and logic, and it also includes some new features.

TYPE | **Listing 10.11. The final report program.**

```
000100 IDENTIFICATION DIVISION.
000200 PROGRAM-ID. PHNPRT02.
000300*-------------------------------------------------
000400* This program prints the contents of the
000500* phone file.
```

continues

Listing 10.11. continued

```
000600*--------------------------------------------------
000700 ENVIRONMENT DIVISION.
000800 INPUT-OUTPUT SECTION.
000900 FILE-CONTROL.
001000     SELECT OPTIONAL PHONE-FILE
001100*or  SELECT PHONE-FILE
001200         ASSIGN TO "phone.dat"
001300*or      ASSIGN TO "phone"
001400         ORGANIZATION IS SEQUENTIAL.
001500
001600     SELECT PRINTER-FILE
001700         ASSIGN TO PRINTER
001800         ORGANIZATION IS LINE SEQUENTIAL.
001900
002000 DATA DIVISION.
002100 FILE SECTION.
002200 FD  PHONE-FILE
002300     LABEL RECORDS ARE STANDARD.
002400 01  PHONE-RECORD.
002500     05  PHONE-LAST-NAME     PIC X(20).
002600     05  PHONE-FIRST-NAME    PIC X(20).
002700     05  PHONE-NUMBER        PIC X(15).
002800     05  PHONE-EXTENSION     PIC X(5).
002900
003000 FD  PRINTER-FILE
003100     LABEL RECORDS ARE OMITTED.
003200 01  PRINTER-RECORD          PIC X(80).
003300
003400 WORKING-STORAGE SECTION.
003500
003600* Structure for printing a title line
003700 01  TITLE-LINE.
003800     05  FILLER              PIC X(21) VALUE SPACE.
003900     05  FILLER              PIC X(17) VALUE
004000     "PHONE BOOK REPORT".
004100     05  FILLER              PIC X(15) VALUE SPACE.
004200     05  FILLER              PIC X(5) VALUE "Page:".
004300     05  PRINT-PAGE-NUMBER   PIC ZZZZ9.
004400
004500* Structure for printing a column heading
004600 01  COLUMN-HEADINGS.
004700     05  FILLER              PIC X(9)  VALUE "Last Name".
004800     05  FILLER              PIC X(12) VALUE SPACE.
004900     05  FILLER              PIC X(10) VALUE "First Name".
005000     05  FILLER              PIC X(11) VALUE SPACE.
005100     05  FILLER              PIC X(6)  VALUE "Number".
005200     05  FILLER              PIC X(10) VALUE SPACE.
005300     05  FILLER              PIC X(4)  VALUE "Ext.".
005400
005500 01 DETAIL-LINE.
005600     05  PRINT-LAST-NAME     PIC X(20).
005700     05  FILLER              PIC X(1) VALUE SPACE.
005800     05  PRINT-FIRST-NAME    PIC X(20).
005900     05  FILLER              PIC X(1) VALUE SPACE.
006000     05  PRINT-NUMBER        PIC X(15).
```

```
006100     05   FILLER                PIC X(1) VALUE SPACE.
006200     05   PRINT-EXTENSION       PIC X(5).
006300
006400 01  END-OF-FILE               PIC X.
006500
006600 01  PRINT-LINES               PIC 99.
006700 01  PAGE-NUMBER               PIC 9(5).
006800
006900 PROCEDURE DIVISION.
007000 MAIN-LOGIC SECTION.
007100 PROGRAM-BEGIN.
007200
007300     PERFORM OPENING-PROCEDURE.
007400     MOVE ZEROES TO PRINT-LINES
007500                    PAGE-NUMBER.
007600     PERFORM START-NEW-PAGE.
007700     MOVE "N" TO END-OF-FILE.
007800     PERFORM READ-NEXT-RECORD.
007900     IF END-OF-FILE = "Y"
008000         MOVE "No records found" TO PRINTER-RECORD
008100         WRITE PRINTER-RECORD BEFORE ADVANCING 1.
008200     PERFORM PRINT-RECORDS
008300         UNTIL END-OF-FILE = "Y".
008400     PERFORM CLOSING-PROCEDURE.
008500
008600 PROGRAM-DONE.
008700     STOP RUN.
008800
008900 OPENING-PROCEDURE.
009000     OPEN INPUT PHONE-FILE.
009100     OPEN OUTPUT PRINTER-FILE.
009200
009300 CLOSING-PROCEDURE.
009400     CLOSE PHONE-FILE.
009500     PERFORM END-LAST-PAGE.
009600     CLOSE PRINTER-FILE.
009700
009800 PRINT-RECORDS.
009900     PERFORM PRINT-FIELDS.
010000     PERFORM READ-NEXT-RECORD.
010100
010200 PRINT-FIELDS.
010300     IF PRINT-LINES NOT < 55
010400         PERFORM NEXT-PAGE.
010500     MOVE PHONE-LAST-NAME TO PRINT-LAST-NAME.
010600     MOVE PHONE-FIRST-NAME TO PRINT-FIRST-NAME.
010700     MOVE PHONE-NUMBER TO PRINT-NUMBER.
010800     MOVE PHONE-EXTENSION TO PRINT-EXTENSION.
010900     MOVE DETAIL-LINE TO PRINTER-RECORD.
011000     WRITE PRINTER-RECORD BEFORE ADVANCING 1.
011100
011200     ADD 1 TO PRINT-LINES.
011300
011400 READ-NEXT-RECORD.
011500     READ PHONE-FILE NEXT RECORD
011600         AT END
011700         MOVE "Y" TO END-OF-FILE.
```

continues

Listing 10.11. continued

```
011800
011900 NEXT-PAGE.
012000     PERFORM END-LAST-PAGE.
012100     PERFORM START-NEW-PAGE.
012200
012300 START-NEW-PAGE.
012400     ADD 1 TO PAGE-NUMBER.
012500     MOVE PAGE-NUMBER TO PRINT-PAGE-NUMBER.
012600     MOVE TITLE-LINE TO PRINTER-RECORD.
012700     WRITE PRINTER-RECORD BEFORE ADVANCING 2.
012800     MOVE COLUMN-HEADINGS TO PRINTER-RECORD.
012900     WRITE PRINTER-RECORD BEFORE ADVANCING 2.
013000     MOVE 4 TO PRINT-LINES.
013100
013200 END-LAST-PAGE.
013300     MOVE SPACE TO PRINTER-RECORD.
013400     WRITE PRINTER-RECORD BEFORE ADVANCING PAGE.
013500     MOVE ZEROES TO PRINT-LINES.
013600
```

The following is output from phnprt02.cbl when run against a test data file containing 77 entries created with phnbld01.cbl:

OUTPUT

```
                         PHONE BOOK REPORT              Page:    1

Last Name                First Name               Number        Ext.
Johnson-----------X Joshua-----------X (404) 555-0001   12345
Johnson-----------X Joshua-----------X (404) 555-0002   12345
Johnson-----------X Joshua-----------X (404) 555-0003   12345
Johnson-----------X Joshua-----------X (404) 555-0004   12345
Johnson-----------X Joshua-----------X (404) 555-0005   12345
Johnson-----------X Joshua-----------X (404) 555-0006   12345
Johnson-----------X Joshua-----------X (404) 555-0007   12345
Johnson-----------X Joshua-----------X (404) 555-0008   12345
Johnson-----------X Joshua-----------X (404) 555-0009   12345
Johnson-----------X Joshua-----------X (404) 555-0010   12345
Johnson-----------X Joshua-----------X (404) 555-0011   12345
Johnson-----------X Joshua-----------X (404) 555-0012   12345
Johnson-----------X Joshua-----------X (404) 555-0013   12345
Johnson-----------X Joshua-----------X (404) 555-0014   12345
Johnson-----------X Joshua-----------X (404) 555-0015   12345
Johnson-----------X Joshua-----------X (404) 555-0016   12345
Johnson-----------X Joshua-----------X (404) 555-0017   12345
Johnson-----------X Joshua-----------X (404) 555-0018   12345
Johnson-----------X Joshua-----------X (404) 555-0019   12345
Johnson-----------X Joshua-----------X (404) 555-0020   12345
Johnson-----------X Joshua-----------X (404) 555-0021   12345
Johnson-----------X Joshua-----------X (404) 555-0022   12345
Johnson-----------X Joshua-----------X (404) 555-0023   12345
Johnson-----------X Joshua-----------X (404) 555-0024   12345
Johnson-----------X Joshua-----------X (404) 555-0025   12345
Johnson-----------X Joshua-----------X (404) 555-0026   12345
Johnson-----------X Joshua-----------X (404) 555-0027   12345
```

```
Johnson-----------X Joshua-----------X (404) 555-0028  12345
Johnson-----------X Joshua-----------X (404) 555-0029  12345
Johnson-----------X Joshua-----------X (404) 555-0030  12345
Johnson-----------X Joshua-----------X (404) 555-0031  12345
Johnson-----------X Joshua-----------X (404) 555-0032  12345
Johnson-----------X Joshua-----------X (404) 555-0033  12345
Johnson-----------X Joshua-----------X (404) 555-0034  12345
Johnson-----------X Joshua-----------X (404) 555-0035  12345
Johnson-----------X Joshua-----------X (404) 555-0036  12345
Johnson-----------X Joshua-----------X (404) 555-0037  12345
Johnson-----------X Joshua-----------X (404) 555-0038  12345
Johnson-----------X Joshua-----------X (404) 555-0039  12345
Johnson-----------X Joshua-----------X (404) 555-0040  12345
Johnson-----------X Joshua-----------X (404) 555-0041  12345
Johnson-----------X Joshua-----------X (404) 555-0042  12345
Johnson-----------X Joshua-----------X (404) 555-0043  12345
Johnson-----------X Joshua-----------X (404) 555-0044  12345
Johnson-----------X Joshua-----------X (404) 555-0045  12345
Johnson-----------X Joshua-----------X (404) 555-0046  12345
Johnson-----------X Joshua-----------X (404) 555-0047  12345
Johnson-----------X Joshua-----------X (404) 555-0048  12345
Johnson-----------X Joshua-----------X (404) 555-0049  12345
Johnson-----------X Joshua-----------X (404) 555-0050  12345
Johnson-----------X Joshua-----------X (404) 555-0051  12345
```

(New page starts here.)

```
                    PHONE BOOK REPORT              Page:    2

Last Name             First Name           Number          Ext.

Johnson-----------X Joshua-----------X (404) 555-0052  12345
Johnson-----------X Joshua-----------X (404) 555-0053  12345
Johnson-----------X Joshua-----------X (404) 555-0054  12345
Johnson-----------X Joshua-----------X (404) 555-0055  12345
Johnson-----------X Joshua-----------X (404) 555-0056  12345
Johnson-----------X Joshua-----------X (404) 555-0057  12345
Johnson-----------X Joshua-----------X (404) 555-0058  12345
Johnson-----------X Joshua-----------X (404) 555-0059  12345
Johnson-----------X Joshua-----------X (404) 555-0060  12345
Johnson-----------X Joshua-----------X (404) 555-0061  12345
Johnson-----------X Joshua-----------X (404) 555-0062  12345
Johnson-----------X Joshua-----------X (404) 555-0063  12345
Johnson-----------X Joshua-----------X (404) 555-0064  12345
Johnson-----------X Joshua-----------X (404) 555-0065  12345
Johnson-----------X Joshua-----------X (404) 555-0066  12345
Johnson-----------X Joshua-----------X (404) 555-0067  12345
Johnson-----------X Joshua-----------X (404) 555-0068  12345
Johnson-----------X Joshua-----------X (404) 555-0069  12345
Johnson-----------X Joshua-----------X (404) 555-0070  12345
Johnson-----------X Joshua-----------X (404) 555-0071  12345
Johnson-----------X Joshua-----------X (404) 555-0072  12345
Johnson-----------X Joshua-----------X (404) 555-0073  12345
Johnson-----------X Joshua-----------X (404) 555-0074  12345
Johnson-----------X Joshua-----------X (404) 555-0075  12345
Johnson-----------X Joshua-----------X (404) 555-0076  12345
Johnson-----------X Joshua-----------X (404) 555-0077  12345
```

10

The logic called NEW-PAGE in phnprt01.cbl has been changed to NEXT-PAGE. NEXT-PAGE at line 011900 has been broken into two separate actions: END-LAST-PAGE and START-NEW-PAGE.

END-LAST-PAGE at lines 013200 through 013500 performs the familiar task of forcing a form feed.

The START-NEW-PAGE logic at lines 012300 through 013000 takes care of starting the top of a new page. It adds 1 to the page number, moves the new page number to PRINT-PAGE-NUMBER in the TITLE-LINE, writes TITLE-LINE, and advances two lines. The COLUMN-HEADINGS are written, also followed by two lines, and the PRINT-LINES variable is set to 4 to indicate the number of lines used on the page so far.

The main logic of the program, at lines 007300 through 008400, opens the files, initializes the PRINT-LINES and PAGE-NUMBER variables, starts a new page ready for printing, and reads the first record in the file.

Before the main loop is entered, the logic tests for an immediate end-of-file at line 007900. It is a good practice to have some handling for an empty file, and this program prints a "No records found" message. Without this message, all you see on the report is a title and columns. The message makes it clear that the data file contained no records.

Trace out the logic for this program until you feel comfortable with it, and then code, compile, and run it against the test file created with phnbld01.cbl.

Summary

Reporting on the data in files is one of the main activities of COBOL programs. Today, you learned the following basics about coding, modifying, and printing reports:

- ☐ COBOL treats the printer as if it were a file, using open, close, and write.
- ☐ When you write to a printer file, you might be writing directly to the physical printer or to a temporary disk file that is processed by a print queue manager or spooler.
- ☐ You can control the line advancing and page advancing of a printer by using the BEFORE ADVANCING clause in a WRITE command.
- ☐ COBOL report programs usually are laid out using a printer spacing sheet that represents the columns on a printed page. It helps to work out how space is needed for filler in a report.
- ☐ You can break pages by ending the last page and starting the new page as two separate actions.

10

Q&A

Q Can I use `phnbld01.cbl` to create some test data, and then manually add additional data to the file?

A Yes. Run `phnbld01.cbl` to create the initial data; then run `phnadd02.cbl` from the answers in Appendix A for Day 9, and you will be able to add data to the end of the file. If you then run `phnprt02.cbl`, a report will be printed containing the test data, followed by the entries that you created yourself.

Workshop

Quiz

In Listing 10.11, what would be the effect of changing line 007600 to read as follows?

```
007600      PERFORM NEXT-PAGE.
```

Exercises

1. Copy `phnprt02.cbl` to `phnprt03.cbl` and modify it so that two spaces appear between each column of data.

2. Using graph paper or anything similar to a printer spacing chart, design a report layout for a customer file containing the following record definition:

```
001100 01  CUSTOMER-RECORD.
001200     05   CUSTOMER-NUMBER    PIC 9(4).
001300     05   CUSTOMER-NAME      PIC X(20).
001400     05   CUSTOMER-PHONE     PIC X(15).
001500     05   CUSTOMER-BALANCE   PIC S9(5)V99.
```

Hint: The printed picture for the CUSTOMER-NUMBER would be ZZZ9, and for the CUSTOMER-BALANCE it would be ZZ,ZZ9.99-.

Day 11

Indexed File I/O

The real power of COBOL data processing lies in indexed files. They are the central repository of data for virtually every COBOL system in use. Today, you learn about the following topics:

- [ ] What is an indexed file?
- [ ] Indexed files in COBOL.
- [ ] Adding records to an indexed file.
- [ ] Handling file errors.
- [ ] Retrieving records in key order.
- [ ] Formatting long records for display.

What Is an Indexed File?

From Day 9, "File I/O," and Day 10, "Printing," you learned that sequential files allow you to add records to the end of the file and you learned how to do that. You also learned that sequential files only allow you to process the file one record at a time, from beginning to end, and you learned some techniques to execute that style of file processing. This method is acceptable for small files, but businesses can process files containing thousands of customers and hundreds of thousands of parts. Imagine how many records the customer file of a large bank or the inventory file of a car parts store might have.

An indexed file can store the same information as a sequential file, but a separate index is created that keeps the records sorted in alphabetical or numerical order. When you create an indexed file, you specify which fields to use for the indexing. When you write records to an indexed file, the index in the file is kept sorted in order by the index. You can use these index fields to retrieve records rapidly in a sequence that is different from the actual order of the records in the file.

Listing 11.1 shows a customer record. This is a fairly straightforward record layout except that the phone number has been broken down into area code, prefix, and number.

TYPE   **Listing 11.1. A customer record.**

```
001100 01   CUSTOMER-RECORD.
001200      05   CUSTOMER-NAME          PIC X(20).
001300      05   CUSTOMER-ADDRESS-1     PIC X(20).
001400      05   CUSTOMER-ADDRESS-2     PIC X(20).
001500      05   CUSTOMER-ZIP           PIC 9(5).
001600      05   CUSTOMER-PHONE.
001700           10   CUSTOMER-AREA-CODE    PIC 9(3).
001800           10   CUSTOMER-PREFIX       PIC 9(3).
001900           10   CUSTOMER-PHONE-NO     PIC 9(4).
```

If you display the records in the order in which they were added to the file, the file might look like the example shown in Figure 11.1.

Figure 11.1.

Sample records for the customer file.

Name	Address 1	Address 2	ZIP	Phone		
				Area Code	Pre-fix	Num-ber
Johnson and Sons	1212 Main Street	Stanton, NJ	80815	217	555	4381
ABC Company	1234 Park Street	Overton, IL	60655	202	555	2341
Amphora Inc.	1414 15th Street	South Beach, CA	90945	213	555	9187
Xeno Phobe Inc	1112 M St.	Washington, DC	08074	202	555	4345
Brothers Karamazof	6067 South Highway	Indianapolis, IN	10016	404	555	5056
Acme Iron	4048 Upton St.	Pittsburgh, PA	02006	276	555	1212
Alpha Omega	9099 Icon Ave.	North Port, LA	40448	919	555	3030
Malio Bros.	2065 Highland Ave.	South Beach, CA	90945	213	555	7776

A field can be named as an index; as each record is added to the file, information also is stored in the index area of the file to indicate the correct order of records for that index.

For example, suppose you use the name field as an index and you want to see the records sorted by name. The records would appear as shown in Figure 11.2.

Figure 11.2.

Records sorted on the name field.

Name	Address 1	Address 2	ZIP	Phone Area Code	Pre-fix	Num-ber
ABC Company	1234 Park Street	Overton, IL	60655	202	555	2341
Acme Iron	4048 Upton Street	Pittsburgh, PA	02006	276	555	1212
Alpha Omega	9099 Icon Ave.	North Port, LA	40448	919	555	3030
Amphora Inc.	1414 15th St.	South Beach, CA	90945	213	555	9187
Brothers Karamazof	6067 South Highway	Indianapolis, IN	10016	404	555	5056
Johnson and Sons	1212 Main Street	Stanton, NJ	80815	217	555	4381
Malio Bros.	2065 Highland Ave.	South Beach, CA	90945	213	555	7776
Xeno Phobe Inc	1112 M St.	Washington, DC	08074	202	555	4345

If you also specify the zip code and area code as indexes, you then could sort the records by zip code (as shown in Figure 11.3) or by area code (as shown in Figure 11.4).

Figure 11.3.

Records sorted on the zip code field.

Name	Address 1	Address 2	ZIP	Phone Area Code	Pre-fix	Num-ber
Acme Iron	4048 Upton St.	Pittsburgh, PA	02006	276	555	1212
Xeno Phobe Inc	1112 M St.	Washington, DC	08074	202	555	4345
Brothers Karamazof	6067 South Highway	Indianapolis, IN	10016	404	555	5056
Alpha Omega	9099 Icon Ave.	North Port, LA	40448	919	555	3030
ABC Company	1234 Park Street	Overton, IL	60655	202	555	2341
Johnson and Sons	1212 Main Street	Stanton, NJ	80815	217	555	4381
Amphora Inc.	1414 15th St.	South Beach, CA	90945	213	555	9187
Malio Bros.	2065 Highland Ave.	South Beach, CA	90945	213	555	7776

Figure 11.4.

Records sorted on the area code field.

Name	Address 1	Address 2	ZIP	Phone Area Code	Pre-fix	Num-ber
ABC Company	1234 Park Street	Overton, IL	60655	202	555	2341
Xeno Phobe Inc	1112 M St.	Washington, DC	08074	202	555	4345
Amphora Inc.	1414 15th St.	South Beach, CA	90945	213	555	9187
Malio Bros.	2065 Highland Ave.	South Beach, CA	90945	213	555	7776
Johnson and Sons	1212 Main Street	Stanton, NJ	80815	217	555	4381
Acme Iron	4048 Upton St.	Pittsburgh, PA	02006	276	555	1212
Brothers Karamazof	6067 South Highway	Indianapolis, IN	10016	404	555	5056
Alpha Omega	9099 Icon Ave.	North Port, LA	40448	919	555	3030

In these examples, the indexed fields are fields in which duplicates might occur, and in fact do occur. Amphora Inc. and Malio Bros. both have the same zip code and area code. In a large customer base, it also is possible that customer names would be duplicated.

The index allows you to retrieve records in sorted order, but if your record contains a field that is unique from record to record, you might use that index to retrieve an individual record, rather than just retrieving records in sorted order.

In business programming, it is common to add a customer number to the customer record that is used as an index containing unique values (as shown in Listing 11.2).

TYPE **Listing 11.2. Adding a customer number.**

```
001100 01   CUSTOMER-RECORD.
001200      05   CUSTOMER-NUMBER        PIC 9(4).
001300      05   CUSTOMER-NAME          PIC X(20).
001400      05   CUSTOMER-ADDRESS-1     PIC X(20).
001500      05   CUSTOMER-ADDRESS-2     PIC X(20).
001600      05   CUSTOMER-ZIP           PIC 9(5).
001700      05   CUSTOMER-PHONE.
001800           10   CUSTOMER-AREA-CODE    PIC 9(3).
001900           10   CUSTOMER-PREFIX       PIC 9(3).
002000           10   CUSTOMER-PHONE-NO     PIC 9(4).
```

In Figure 11.5, records appear in the order of the unique index, but you also can request a read on a file to return a single record whose customer number is equal to a specific value.

Figure 11.5.

Records with a unique index.

Number	Name	Address 1	Address 2	ZIP	Phone		
					Area Code	Prefix	Number
1001	Johnson and Sons	1212 Main Street	Stanton, NJ	80815	217	555	4381
1002	ABC Company	1234 Park Street	Overton, IL	60655	202	555	2341
1003	Amphora Inc.	1414 15th Street	South Beach, CA	90945	213	555	9187
1004	Xeno Phobe Inc.	1112 M St.	Washington, DC	08074	202	555	4345
1005	Brothers Karamazof	6067 South Highway	Indianapolis, IN	10016	404	555	5056
1006	Acme Iron	4048 Upton St.	Pittsburgh, PA	02006	276	555	1212
1007	Alpha Omega	9099 Icon Ave.	North Port, LA	40448	919	555	3030
1008	Malio Bros.	2065 Highland Ave.	South Beach, CA	90945	213	555	7776

Indexed Files in COBOL

If you have ever wondered why you are given an account number, customer number, or card number by the companies you deal with, the answer lies in the need to create a unique value that can be used to identify your individual record in a computer file.

NEW TERM In a COBOL indexed file, one field must be designed so that it will contain a unique value for each record. This field is set up as the primary index for the file. This primary index is called the *primary key* or sometimes simply the *key*.

Most companies and agencies opt for a numbering system to resolve the problem of creating a unique (and unchanging) field to identify an individual record. This is a workable compromise, although in some cases it creates an artificial piece of data (such as a customer number) associated with a record.

You establish a key (an index) in a file in the physical definition of the file (the SELECT statement). Listing 11.3 is a full FD statement for the customer file we've been working on in this chapter. From the file descriptor and record layout, there is no way to tell that the file is indexed or what the key is. All this information is taken care of in the SELECT statement.

TYPE **Listing 11.3. FD for a keyed file.**

```
000900 FD   CUSTOMER-FILE
001000      LABEL RECORDS ARE STANDARD.
001100 01   CUSTOMER-RECORD.
001200      05  CUSTOMER-NUMBER          PIC 9(4).
001300      05  CUSTOMER-NAME            PIC X(20).
001400      05  CUSTOMER-ADDRESS-1       PIC X(20).
001500      05  CUSTOMER-ADDRESS-2       PIC X(20).
001600      05  CUSTOMER-ZIP             PIC 9(5).
001700      05  CUSTOMER-PHONE.
001800          10  CUSTOMER-AREA-CODE   PIC 9(3).
001900          10  CUSTOMER-PREFIX      PIC 9(3).
002000          10  CUSTOMER-PHONE-NO    PIC 9(4).
```

Listing 11.4 is a SELECT statement for the customer file as it would appear if the file were being treated as a sequential file.

TYPE **Listing 11.4. A SELECT statement for a sequential file.**

```
000300      SELECT CUSTOMER-FILE
000400          ASSIGN TO "customer.dat"
000500          ORGANIZATION IS SEQUENTIAL.
```

Compare this to the SELECT statement for the customer file as an indexed file, as shown in Listing 11.5.

TYPE **Listing 11.5. A SELECT statement for a keyed file.**

```
000300      SELECT CUSTOMER-FILE
000400          ASSIGN TO "customer.dat"
000500          ORGANIZATION IS INDEXED
000600          RECORD KEY IS CUSTOMER-NUMBER
000700          ACCESS MODE IS DYNAMIC.
```

ANALYSIS At line 000500, the organization of the file is specified as INDEXED. After you have specified INDEXED for a file organization, you must name a field that appears in the file record as the key (primary index) to the file. At line 000600, this field is identified with the clause RECORD KEY IS CUSTOMER-NUMBER.

Line 000700 specifies the access mode DYNAMIC. You don't need to be too concerned about access modes—you almost always will use DYNAMIC—but a brief explanation is in order. The following are the three ways of accessing an indexed file:

☐ SEQUENTIAL

☐ RANDOM

☐ DYNAMIC

SEQUENTIAL access is the default and indicates that records will be accessed one after the other in the order of the primary key. RANDOM access indicates that the file will be accessed one record at a time, and for each access, an exact value for the primary key will be specified. DYNAMIC access combines SEQUENTIAL and RANDOM, indicating that records can be accessed randomly, one at time, or one after the other in sequence. You usually will use DYNAMIC because most programs need to access records both ways.

The OPEN and CLOSE for an indexed file are identical to the OPEN and CLOSE that you already have seen for a sequential file. Listing 11.6 opens a vendor file in output mode and then closes it.

TYPE **Listing 11.6. Creating an empty vendor file.**

```
000100 IDENTIFICATION DIVISION.
000200 PROGRAM-ID. VNDBLD01.
000300*------------------------------------------------
000400* Create an Empty Vendor File.
000500*------------------------------------------------
000600 ENVIRONMENT DIVISION.
000700 INPUT-OUTPUT SECTION.
000800 FILE-CONTROL.
000900
001000     SELECT VENDOR-FILE
001100         ASSIGN TO "vendor"
001200         ORGANIZATION IS INDEXED
001300         RECORD KEY IS VENDOR-NUMBER
001400         ACCESS MODE IS DYNAMIC.
001500
001600 DATA DIVISION.
001700 FILE SECTION.
001800
001900 FD  VENDOR-FILE
002000     LABEL RECORDS ARE STANDARD.
002100 01  VENDOR-RECORD.
002200     05  VENDOR-NUMBER             PIC 9(5).
002300     05  VENDOR-NAME               PIC X(30).
002400     05  VENDOR-ADDRESS-1          PIC X(30).
002500     05  VENDOR-ADDRESS-2          PIC X(30).
002600     05  VENDOR-CITY               PIC X(20).
002700     05  VENDOR-STATE              PIC X(2).
002800     05  VENDOR-ZIP                PIC X(10).
002900     05  VENDOR-CONTACT            PIC X(30).
003000     05  VENDOR-PHONE              PIC X(15).
003100
003200 WORKING-STORAGE SECTION.
```

```
003300
003400 PROCEDURE DIVISION.
003500 PROGRAM-BEGIN.
003600     OPEN OUTPUT VENDOR-FILE.
003700     CLOSE VENDOR-FILE.
003800
003900 PROGRAM-DONE.
004000     STOP RUN.
004100
```

ANALYSIS The SELECT statement has some differences that you need to study. The ASSIGN TO clause, at line 001100, assigns the physical filename as "vendor" with no extension. The extension is omitted deliberately. Different versions of COBOL create indexed files in different ways:

☐ Under ACUCOBOL, a new file is created using the assigned name exactly as given. After data is placed in the file, this file includes all the data as well as the index information. The new version 4 of ACUCOBOL, which is in beta test as of this writing, will use a two-file approach similar to those described for LPI COBOL and Microfocus COBOL.

☐ Under LPI COBOL, ASSIGN TO "vendor" creates two files. One, named vendor.dat, contains the data, and the other, named vendor.idx, contains the index information.

☐ Under Micro Focus COBOL, ASSIGN TO "vendor" creates two files. One, named vendor, contains the data, and the other, named vendor.idx, contains the index information.

For systems that create two files, such as LPI COBOL, Micro Focus COBOL, and the upcoming version 4.0 of ACUCOBOL, you don't need to worry about the two files within your COBOL program. When you open the file, the COBOL version takes care of gathering together the data portion of the file and the index portion of the file and opening them for you as though they were one file.

Because these different conventions exist (and there are others), it is best to give indexed files a physical name that contains no extension and let the version of COBOL take care of adding whatever extensions it needs for internal housekeeping.

The vendor record itself at lines 002100 through 003000 lays out a record for a file containing vendor names and addresses, which will be used in an accounts payable system that you develop over this and the following chapters. The vendor contact field can be used to place the name of a contact.

NEW TERM A *vendor* is someone who sells you goods or services and to whom you end up paying money for those goods or services.

You use this file definition to create a bills tracking and payment system gradually.

 An *accounts payable system* tracks the bills you have, their due dates, and what you've paid, and it gives you information on future cash requirements needed to pay bills as they come due.

Although this program doesn't appear to do anything useful, it does have a purpose. In Day 9, you learned that it is possible to create a new file where one did not exist previously by using the OPTIONAL clause in a SELECT statement:

```
SELECT OPTIONAL PHONE-FILE
```

It also is possible to create a file by opening the file in EXTEND mode. This applies to SEQUENTIAL files, but OPTIONAL and EXTEND modes, are sometimes unavailable for indexed files.

Because COBOL syntax varies in the use of OPTIONAL in the SELECT clause, and because OPEN EXTEND is sometimes unavailable for indexed files, a program such as vndbld01.cbl is one way of ensuring that the vendor file is created. It is not uncommon in COBOL systems to have a set of programs, such as vndbld01.cbl, that are used only once to create a new set of empty files when the system is first installed.

Code, compile, and run this program; then perform a directory display of files named vendor to see which files were actually created in response to this command.

Under MS-DOS, enter the following:

```
DIR VENDOR*
```

You might see one of the following three displays, depending on your version of COBOL (or possibly another naming convention):

Files Listed Under LPI COBOL	*Files Listed Under MF COBOL*	*Files Listed Under ACUCOBOL*
VENDOR.DAT	VENDOR	VENDOR
VENDOR.IDX	VENDOR.IDX	

Adding Records to an Indexed File

Adding records to an indexed file is mechanically identical to adding records to a sequential file; you fill each of the fields of the record with a value and then write the record. Listing 11.7, vndnew01.cbl, is a rudimentary program that accepts input for all fields and writes (adds) one record to the file.

Listing 11.7. Adding indexed records.

```
000100 IDENTIFICATION DIVISION.
000200 PROGRAM-ID. VNDNEW01.
000300*------------------------------------------------
000400* Add a record to an indexed Vendor File.
000500*------------------------------------------------
000600 ENVIRONMENT DIVISION.
000700 INPUT-OUTPUT SECTION.
000800 FILE-CONTROL.
000900
001000     SELECT VENDOR-FILE
001100         ASSIGN TO "vendor"
001200         ORGANIZATION IS INDEXED
001300         RECORD KEY IS VENDOR-NUMBER
001400         ACCESS MODE IS DYNAMIC.
001500
001600 DATA DIVISION.
001700 FILE SECTION.
001800
001900 FD  VENDOR-FILE
002000     LABEL RECORDS ARE STANDARD.
002100 01  VENDOR-RECORD.
002200     05  VENDOR-NUMBER             PIC 9(5).
002300     05  VENDOR-NAME               PIC X(30).
002400     05  VENDOR-ADDRESS-1          PIC X(30).
002500     05  VENDOR-ADDRESS-2          PIC X(30).
002600     05  VENDOR-CITY               PIC X(20).
002700     05  VENDOR-STATE              PIC X(2).
002800     05  VENDOR-ZIP                PIC X(10).
002900     05  VENDOR-CONTACT            PIC X(30).
003000     05  VENDOR-PHONE              PIC X(15).
003100
003200 WORKING-STORAGE SECTION.
003300
003400 PROCEDURE DIVISION.
003500 PROGRAM-BEGIN.
003600     OPEN I-O VENDOR-FILE.
003700     PERFORM MAIN-PROCESS.
003800     CLOSE VENDOR-FILE.
003900
004000 PROGRAM-DONE.
004100     STOP RUN.
004200
004300 MAIN-PROCESS.
004400     PERFORM INIT-VENDOR-RECORD.
004500     PERFORM ENTER-VENDOR-FIELDS.
004600     WRITE VENDOR-RECORD.
004700
004800 INIT-VENDOR-RECORD.
004900     MOVE SPACE TO VENDOR-RECORD.
005000     MOVE ZEROES TO VENDOR-NUMBER.
```

continues

Listing 11.7. continued

```
005100
005200 ENTER-VENDOR-FIELDS.
005300     PERFORM ENTER-VENDOR-NUMBER.
005400     PERFORM ENTER-VENDOR-NAME.
005500     PERFORM ENTER-VENDOR-ADDRESS-1.
005600     PERFORM ENTER-VENDOR-ADDRESS-2.
005700     PERFORM ENTER-VENDOR-CITY.
005800     PERFORM ENTER-VENDOR-STATE.
005900     PERFORM ENTER-VENDOR-ZIP.
006000     PERFORM ENTER-VENDOR-CONTACT.
006100     PERFORM ENTER-VENDOR-PHONE.
006200
006300 ENTER-VENDOR-NUMBER.
006400     DISPLAY "ENTER VENDOR NUMBER (00001-99999)".
006500     ACCEPT VENDOR-NUMBER.
006600
006700 ENTER-VENDOR-NAME.
006800     DISPLAY "ENTER VENDOR NAME".
006900     ACCEPT VENDOR-NAME.
007000
007100 ENTER-VENDOR-ADDRESS-1.
007200     DISPLAY "ENTER VENDOR ADDRESS-1".
007300     ACCEPT VENDOR-ADDRESS-1.
007400
007500 ENTER-VENDOR-ADDRESS-2.
007600     DISPLAY "ENTER VENDOR ADDRESS-2".
007700     ACCEPT VENDOR-ADDRESS-2.
007800
007900 ENTER-VENDOR-CITY.
008000     DISPLAY "ENTER VENDOR CITY".
008100     ACCEPT VENDOR-CITY.
008200
008300 ENTER-VENDOR-STATE.
008400     DISPLAY "ENTER VENDOR STATE".
008500     ACCEPT VENDOR-STATE.
008600
008700 ENTER-VENDOR-ZIP.
008800     DISPLAY "ENTER VENDOR ZIP".
008900     ACCEPT VENDOR-ZIP.
009000
009100 ENTER-VENDOR-CONTACT.
009200     DISPLAY "ENTER VENDOR CONTACT".
009300     ACCEPT VENDOR-CONTACT.
009400
009500 ENTER-VENDOR-PHONE.
009600     DISPLAY "ENTER VENDOR PHONE".
009700     ACCEPT VENDOR-PHONE.
009800
```

The following is the output for vndnew01.cbl after entering vendor number 00002, with user entries highlighted:

OUTPUT

```
ENTER VENDOR NUMBER (ALL 5 DIGITS) 00001-99999
00002
ENTER VENDOR NAME
ABC PRINTING
ENTER VENDOR ADDRESS-1
1624 FOOTHILL BLVD
ENTER VENDOR ADDRESS-2
SUITE 34
ENTER VENDOR CITY
LOS ANGELES
ENTER VENDOR STATE
CA
ENTER VENDOR ZIP
91042
ENTER VENDOR ATTENTION
CHARLES JOHANSSEN
ENTER VENDOR PHONE
(818) 555-4321


C>
C>
```

ANALYSIS
The MAIN-PROCESS at lines 004300 through 004600 initializes a vendor record, enters all the vendor fields, and then writes the record. You should have no trouble following the logic.

Code, compile, and run this program three times, each time adding a record for vendor numbers 00001, 00002, and 00003 to the file. You can enter anything you want for the other fields, but the VENDOR-NUMBER must be different for each entry. Before you go any further or experiment with this program or file, study the next section, which covers a problem with indexed files that you might bump into while trying to add these records.

Don't worry if you add some fields incorrectly. You tackle changing records in Day 12, "More on Indexed Files," and you will be able to correct any errors you make.

Handling File Errors

After you have entered vendors 00001, 00002, and 00003, run the program again and try to enter another vendor. Give this vendor one of the numbers that already has been used in the file.

The primary key must contain a value that is unique in each record, so attempting to add a record with a primary key value that already exists in the file will cause some sort of error. Most versions of COBOL end the program abruptly when a file error occurs, as in the following sample output for ACUCOBOL. This output error message is caused by attempting to add a record with a duplicate primary key value of 00002.

```
OUTPUT    ENTER VENDOR NUMBER (ALL 5 DIGITS) 00001-99999
          00002
          ENTER VENDOR NAME
          ABC PRINTING
          ENTER VENDOR ADDRESS-1
          1624 FOOTHILL BLVD
          ENTER VENDOR ADDRESS-2
          SUITE 34
          ENTER VENDOR CITY
          LOS ANGELES
          ENTER VENDOR STATE
          CA
          ENTER VENDOR ZIP
          91042
          ENTER VENDOR ATTENTION
          CHARLES JOHANSSEN
          ENTER VENDOR PHONE
          (818) 555-4321

          File error 22 on vendor
          COBOL error at 000027 in vndnew01

          C>
          C>
```

No error message occurs under Micro Focus Personal COBOL, but the record is not written to the file.

To give you a better idea of file errors, Listing 11.8, vnderr01.cbl, uses READ NEXT to create a different type of file error deliberately. (The program isn't particularly well designed; I'm only trying to illustrate an error condition.)

TYPE **Listing 11.8. Creating an error at the end of the file.**

```
000100 IDENTIFICATION DIVISION.
000200 PROGRAM-ID. VNDERR01.
000300*----------------------------------------------------
000400* Forces an error by reading past the end of a file.
000500*----------------------------------------------------
000600 ENVIRONMENT DIVISION.
000700 INPUT-OUTPUT SECTION.
000800 FILE-CONTROL.
000900
001000     SELECT VENDOR-FILE
001100         ASSIGN TO "vendor"
001200         ORGANIZATION IS INDEXED
001300         RECORD KEY IS VENDOR-NUMBER
001400         ACCESS MODE IS DYNAMIC.
001500
001600 DATA DIVISION.
001700 FILE SECTION.
001800
001900 FD  VENDOR-FILE
```

```
002000      LABEL RECORDS ARE STANDARD.
002100 01   VENDOR-RECORD.
002200      05   VENDOR-NUMBER              PIC 9(5).
002300      05   VENDOR-NAME                PIC X(30).
002400      05   VENDOR-ADDRESS-1           PIC X(30).
002500      05   VENDOR-ADDRESS-2           PIC X(30).
002600      05   VENDOR-CITY                PIC X(20).
002700      05   VENDOR-STATE               PIC X(2).
002800      05   VENDOR-ZIP                 PIC X(10).
002900      05   VENDOR-CONTACT             PIC X(30).
003000      05   VENDOR-PHONE               PIC X(15).
003100
003200
003300 WORKING-STORAGE SECTION.
003400
003500 77  FILE-AT-END         PIC X.
003600
003700 PROCEDURE DIVISION.
003800 PROGRAM-BEGIN.
003900      PERFORM OPENING-PROCEDURE.
004000      PERFORM MAIN-PROCESS.
004100      PERFORM CLOSING-PROCEDURE.
004200
004300 PROGRAM-DONE.
004400      STOP RUN.
004500
004600 OPENING-PROCEDURE.
004700      OPEN I-O VENDOR-FILE.
004800
004900 CLOSING-PROCEDURE.
005000      CLOSE VENDOR-FILE.
005100
005200 MAIN-PROCESS.
005300
005400      MOVE "N" TO FILE-AT-END.
005500      PERFORM READ-NEXT-RECORD.
005600      PERFORM READ-AND-DISPLAY
005700           UNTIL FILE-AT-END = "Y".
005800
005900 READ-AND-DISPLAY.
006000      DISPLAY VENDOR-NUMBER.
006100      PERFORM READ-NEXT-RECORD.
006200
006300 READ-NEXT-RECORD.
006400      READ VENDOR-FILE NEXT RECORD.
006500*          AT END MOVE "Y" TO FILE-AT-END.
006600
```

The output for two different versions of COBOL follows. Assume that the vendor file contains records with the key values 00001, 00002, and 00003. The following output shows an at-end error in Micro Focus Personal COBOL. The last vendor number is displayed twice before the actual error occurs:

OUTPUT

```
C>pcobrun vnderr01
Personal COBOL version 2.0 from Micro Focus
PCOBRUN V2.0.02  Copyright (C) 1983-1993 Micro Focus Ltd.
00001
00002
00003
00003
Error accessing file : vendor
VNDERR01 Segment RT : Error 146 at COBOL PC 00AB
Description : No current record defined for sequential read

C>

C>
```

The following output shows an at-end error in ACUCOBOL. The error occurs at the exact end of the file:

OUTPUT

```
00001
00002
00003

File error 10 on vendor
COBOL error at 000048 in VNDERR01

C>
C>
```

ANALYSIS At lines 005900 and 006000, the program reads through the vendor file, displaying the vendor number for each record as it is read.

At line 006500, the statement that should have trapped the AT END condition has been commented out, so the FILE-AT-END flag is never set to "Y" and the program just keeps trying to read records even though it has reached the end of the file.

The program automatically aborts with an error message after the end of file is reached.

After you've entered three records using vndnew01.cbl, code, compile, and run vnderr01.cbl to see the effects of the end-of-file condition for your particular version of COBOL.

Now copy vnderr01.cbl to vnderr02.cbl and rewrite vnderr02.cbl so that the final lines read as in Listing 11.9. Remove the period at the end of line 006400, and remove the asterisk on line 006500.

TYPE   **Listing 11.9. Fixing** vnderr02.cbl.

```
006300 READ-NEXT-RECORD.
006400     READ VENDOR-FILE NEXT RECORD
006500         AT END MOVE "Y" TO FILE-AT-END.
```

The following is the output of the repaired vnderr01.cbl:

```
00001
00002
00003
```

The usual behavior of a COBOL program performing input and output to a file is to abort if a file error is encountered. You can change this usual behavior if you provide some explicit step or steps to be taken in the event of a file error. In the case of a READ NEXT command, the explicit steps to take in the event of an error are given with the AT END clause.

The AT END clause in the READ NEXT statement actually does two things. First, it overrides the normal COBOL behavior of aborting on a file error. This is done out of sight and is built in as part of the behavior of the AT END clause. The second thing is explicitly stated by the commands that follow AT END. In this case, "Y" is moved to END-OF-FILE.

NEW TERM   The AT END clause is called a file error condition clause.

The WRITE command for an indexed file includes a file error condition clause that can be used to trap duplicate key errors. This clause is INVALID KEY and has the following syntax:

```
WRITE file-record
    INVALID KEY
        do something
```

Here is an example of a file error condition clause:

```
WRITE VENDOR-RECORD
    INVALID KEY
        MOVE "Y" TO DUPLICATE-FLAG
```

Do   Don't

DO stay aware of file error conditions, and program so that you trap these conditions and handle them correctly.

DON'T ever use a file error condition as the natural way to stop a program. It would be a poor design to print records until the program crashed. Yes, all the records would be printed, but the resulting error message would confuse the end user, and it is very sloppy style.

Now that you know how to handle duplicate key errors, look at Listing 11.10. It shows an improved version of a program to add records to the vendor file. It allows records to be added one after the other by asking for each field.

TYPE **Listing 11.10. Improving additions to the vendor file.**

```
000100 IDENTIFICATION DIVISION.
000200 PROGRAM-ID. VNDNEW02.
000300*-----------------------------------------------
000400* Add a record to an indexed Vendor File.
000500*-----------------------------------------------
000600 ENVIRONMENT DIVISION.
000700 INPUT-OUTPUT SECTION.
000800 FILE-CONTROL.
000900
001000     SELECT VENDOR-FILE
001100         ASSIGN TO "vendor"
001200         ORGANIZATION IS INDEXED
001300         RECORD KEY IS VENDOR-NUMBER
001400         ACCESS MODE IS DYNAMIC.
001500
001600 DATA DIVISION.
001700 FILE SECTION.
001800
001900 FD  VENDOR-FILE
002000     LABEL RECORDS ARE STANDARD.
002100 01  VENDOR-RECORD.
002200     05  VENDOR-NUMBER              PIC 9(5).
002300     05  VENDOR-NAME                PIC X(30).
002400     05  VENDOR-ADDRESS-1           PIC X(30).
002500     05  VENDOR-ADDRESS-2           PIC X(30).
002600     05  VENDOR-CITY                PIC X(20).
002700     05  VENDOR-STATE               PIC X(2).
002800     05  VENDOR-ZIP                 PIC X(10).
002900     05  VENDOR-CONTACT             PIC X(30).
003000     05  VENDOR-PHONE               PIC X(15).
003100
003200 WORKING-STORAGE SECTION.
003300
003400 01  VENDOR-NUMBER-FIELD           PIC Z(5).
003500
003600 PROCEDURE DIVISION.
003700 PROGRAM-BEGIN.
003800     OPEN I-O VENDOR-FILE.
003900     PERFORM GET-NEW-VENDOR-NUMBER.
004000     PERFORM ADD-RECORDS
004100         UNTIL VENDOR-NUMBER = ZEROES.
004200     CLOSE VENDOR-FILE.
004300
004400 PROGRAM-DONE.
004500     STOP RUN.
004600
004700 GET-NEW-VENDOR-NUMBER.
004800     PERFORM INIT-VENDOR-RECORD.
004900     PERFORM ENTER-VENDOR-NUMBER.
005000
005100 INIT-VENDOR-RECORD.
005200     MOVE SPACE TO VENDOR-RECORD.
005300     MOVE ZEROES TO VENDOR-NUMBER.
005400
```

11

```
005500 ENTER-VENDOR-NUMBER.
005600     DISPLAY "ENTER VENDOR NUMBER (1-99999)".
005700     DISPLAY "ENTER 0 TO STOP ENTRY".
005800     ACCEPT VENDOR-NUMBER-FIELD.
005900*OR  ACCEPT VENDOR-NUMBER-FIELD WITH CONVERSION.
006000
006100     MOVE VENDOR-NUMBER-FIELD TO VENDOR-NUMBER.
006200*OR  MOVE WITH CONVERSION VENDOR-NUMBER-FIELD
006300*        TO VENDOR-NUMBER.
006400
006500 ADD-RECORDS.
006600     PERFORM ENTER-REMAINING-FIELDS.
006700     PERFORM WRITE-VENDOR-RECORD.
006800     PERFORM GET-NEW-VENDOR-NUMBER.
006900
007000 WRITE-VENDOR-RECORD.
007100     WRITE VENDOR-RECORD
007200         INVALID KEY
007300         DISPLAY "RECORD ALREADY ON FILE".
007400
007500 ENTER-REMAINING-FIELDS.
007600     PERFORM ENTER-VENDOR-NAME.
007700     PERFORM ENTER-VENDOR-ADDRESS-1.
007800     PERFORM ENTER-VENDOR-ADDRESS-2.
007900     PERFORM ENTER-VENDOR-CITY.
008000     PERFORM ENTER-VENDOR-STATE.
008100     PERFORM ENTER-VENDOR-ZIP.
008200     PERFORM ENTER-VENDOR-CONTACT.
008300     PERFORM ENTER-VENDOR-PHONE.
008400
008500 ENTER-VENDOR-NAME.
008600     DISPLAY "ENTER VENDOR NAME".
008700     ACCEPT VENDOR-NAME.
008800
008900 ENTER-VENDOR-ADDRESS-1.
009000     DISPLAY "ENTER VENDOR ADDRESS-1".
009100     ACCEPT VENDOR-ADDRESS-1.
009200
009300 ENTER-VENDOR-ADDRESS-2.
009400     DISPLAY "ENTER VENDOR ADDRESS-2".
009500     ACCEPT VENDOR-ADDRESS-2.
009600
009700 ENTER-VENDOR-CITY.
009800     DISPLAY "ENTER VENDOR CITY".
009900     ACCEPT VENDOR-CITY.
010000
010100 ENTER-VENDOR-STATE.
010200     DISPLAY "ENTER VENDOR STATE".
010300     ACCEPT VENDOR-STATE.
010400
010500 ENTER-VENDOR-ZIP.
010600     DISPLAY "ENTER VENDOR ZIP".
010700     ACCEPT VENDOR-ZIP.
010800
```

continues

Listing 11.10. continued

```
010900 ENTER-VENDOR-CONTACT.
011000     DISPLAY "ENTER VENDOR CONTACT".
011100     ACCEPT VENDOR-CONTACT.
011200
011300 ENTER-VENDOR-PHONE.
011400     DISPLAY "ENTER VENDOR PHONE".
011500     ACCEPT VENDOR-PHONE.
011600
```

The following is the output of vndnew02.cbl when a duplicate key value is entered:

```
ENTER VENDOR NUMBER (1-99999)
ENTER 0 TO STOP ENTRY
1
ENTER VENDOR NAME
JOE DOAKS
ENTER VENDOR ADDRESS-1
1212 FOURTH ST.
ENTER VENDOR ADDRESS-2

ENTER VENDOR CITY
LOS ANGELES
ENTER VENDOR STATE
CA
ENTER VENDOR ZIP
94321
ENTER VENDOR CONTACT
JOSEPH DOAKS
ENTER VENDOR PHONE
(213) 555-6543
RECORD ALREADY ON FILE
ENTER VENDOR NUMBER (1-99999)
ENTER 0 TO STOP ENTRY
```

ANALYSIS The user first is asked for the VENDOR-NUMBER field; if the user enters a vendor number of 00000, this signals the end of data entry. This approach was used instead of asking the user for all the fields and then asking whether the user wants to go again. It works perfectly well, because you usually wouldn't want to put a vendor with the number 00000 in the file.

The data entry for the VENDOR-NUMBER is handled by accepting data into an edited numeric field, VENDOR-NUMBER-FIELD, and then moving the result to VENDOR-NUMBER. This saves the user from having to enter all five digits. This field is defined at line 003400, and the data entry is taken care of at lines 005500 through 006300 in the ENTER-VENDOR-NUMBER routine.

The program uses the VENDOR-NUMBER as the flag to stop the program. In this case, the VENDOR-NUMBER is not only a piece of data for the file; it is the variable that controls the main processing loop of the program. At line 003900, the user is asked to enter a new vendor number—GET-NEW-VENDOR-NUMBER. The user can enter 0 at this point, causing the program to stop

11

immediately. If the user does not, the main processing loop, ADD-RECORDS, is performed at lines 004000 and 004100 until VENDOR-NUMBER = ZEROES.

The main processing loop, ADD-RECORDS (at lines 006500 through 006800) enters the remaining fields, writes the vendor record, and asks the user for another vendor number to add by performing GET-NEW-VENDOR-NUMBER. This sets up the loop control variable before going into the loop (line 003900) and then changes the loop control variable at the bottom of the loop (line 006800).

At line 005300, the VENDOR-NUMBER is initialized to a zero value. Then ADD-RECORDS is performed until the user enters a value of zeroes for a vendor number.

At lines 004700 through 004900, the GET-NEW-VENDOR-NUMBER paragraph takes care of initializing the vendor record—assuming that a new record will be added to the file—and then actually getting the user input of the vendor number.

The writing of the record in WRITE-VENDOR-RECORD at line 007000 uses INVALID KEY to trap the file error condition and displays "RECORD ALREADY ON FILE" at line 007300.

Retrieving Records in Key Order

Use vndnew02.cbl to add some additional records to the vendor file. In particular, add them out of order. Add a vendor number 00022; then add vendor number 00006. You do not have to enter all the missing numbers between the vendor number values. An indexed file is quite comfortable with gaps in it, and a file could contain only vendor number 00001 and vendor number 08706 without causing any bad effects.

After you have entered some records out of order, you need to be able to display them. Listing 11.11 is a simple program. It is intended only to illustrate that regardless of the order you use to put records into the file, when you start retrieving them, they are returned from the file in primary key order.

TYPE **Listing 11.11. Showing the records.**

```
000100 IDENTIFICATION DIVISION.
000200 PROGRAM-ID. VNDREC01.
000300*------------------------------------------------
000400* Display vendor number and
000500* name in order.
000600*------------------------------------------------
000700 ENVIRONMENT DIVISION.
000800 INPUT-OUTPUT SECTION.
000900 FILE-CONTROL.
001000
```

continues

Listing 11.11. continued

```
001100      SELECT VENDOR-FILE
001200          ASSIGN TO "vendor"
001300          ORGANIZATION IS INDEXED
001400          RECORD KEY IS VENDOR-NUMBER
001500          ACCESS MODE IS DYNAMIC.
001600
001700 DATA DIVISION.
001800 FILE SECTION.
001900
002000 FD   VENDOR-FILE
002100      LABEL RECORDS ARE STANDARD.
002200 01   VENDOR-RECORD.
002300      05   VENDOR-NUMBER              PIC 9(5).
002400      05   VENDOR-NAME                PIC X(30).
002500      05   VENDOR-ADDRESS-1           PIC X(30).
002600      05   VENDOR-ADDRESS-2           PIC X(30).
002700      05   VENDOR-CITY                PIC X(20).
002800      05   VENDOR-STATE               PIC X(2).
002900      05   VENDOR-ZIP                 PIC X(10).
003000      05   VENDOR-CONTACT             PIC X(30).
003100      05   VENDOR-PHONE               PIC X(15).
003200
003300 WORKING-STORAGE SECTION.
003400
003500 77  FILE-AT-END          PIC X.
003600
003700 PROCEDURE DIVISION.
003800 PROGRAM-BEGIN.
003900
004000      PERFORM OPENING-PROCEDURE.
004100
004200      MOVE "N" TO FILE-AT-END.
004300      PERFORM READ-NEXT-RECORD.
004400      IF FILE-AT-END = "Y"
004500          DISPLAY "NO RECORDS FOUND"
004600      ELSE
004700          PERFORM DISPLAY-VENDOR-FIELDS
004800              UNTIL FILE-AT-END = "Y".
004900
005000      PERFORM CLOSING-PROCEDURE.
005100
005200
005300 PROGRAM-DONE.
005400      STOP RUN.
005500
005600 OPENING-PROCEDURE.
005700      OPEN I-O VENDOR-FILE.
005800
005900 CLOSING-PROCEDURE.
006000      CLOSE VENDOR-FILE.
006100
006200 DISPLAY-VENDOR-FIELDS.
006300      DISPLAY "NO: " VENDOR-NUMBER
006400              " NAME: " VENDOR-NAME.
```

11

```
006500
006600     PERFORM READ-NEXT-RECORD.
006700
006800 READ-NEXT-RECORD.
006900     READ VENDOR-FILE NEXT RECORD
007000         AT END MOVE "Y" TO FILE-AT-END.
007100
```

OUTPUT
```
NO: 00001 NAME: AERIAL SIGNS
NO: 00002 NAME: ABC PRINTING
NO: 00003 NAME: CHARLES SMITH AND SONS
NO: 00014 NAME: RANIER GRAPHICS
NO: 01176 NAME: ABERCROMBIE AND OTHERS
NO: 01440 NAME: ZINZINDORFF INC.


C>
C>
```

ANALYSIS This program opens the vendor file and displays the vendor number and vendor name for all the records.

Formatting Long Records for Display

The vendor record is too long to display on an 80-column screen. The next display program treats the screen as though it were a scrolling printer, so you have to resort to a printer spacing chart to work out the display. Some 80-column displays cause an extra line feed if a character is printed in position 80, so you'll work with only 79 columns.

Figure 11.6 shows the pattern for the layout.

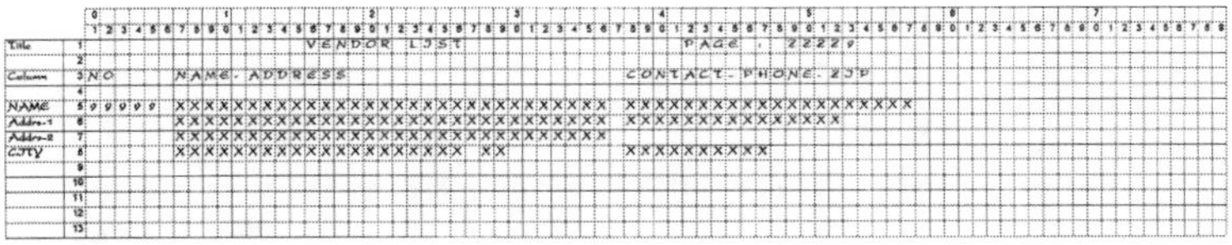

Figure 11.6.

Spacing chart for the display.

Listing 11.12, vnddsp01.cbl, is a program to display the vendor records. Code, compile, and run vnddsp01.cbl. You will see that as the records are displayed, they are displayed in ascending VENDOR-NUMBER order, regardless of the order in which they originally were entered.

TYPE **Listing 11.12. Displaying the vendor records.**

```
000100 IDENTIFICATION DIVISION.
000200 PROGRAM-ID. VNDDSP01.
000300*------------------------------------------------
```

continues

Listing 11.12. continued

```
000400* Display records in the Vendor File.
000500*-------------------------------------------------
000600 ENVIRONMENT DIVISION.
000700 INPUT-OUTPUT SECTION.
000800 FILE-CONTROL.
000900
001000     SELECT VENDOR-FILE
001100         ASSIGN TO "vendor"
001200         ORGANIZATION IS INDEXED
001300         RECORD KEY IS VENDOR-NUMBER
001400         ACCESS MODE IS DYNAMIC.
001500
001600 DATA DIVISION.
001700 FILE SECTION.
001800
001900 FD  VENDOR-FILE
002000     LABEL RECORDS ARE STANDARD.
002100 01  VENDOR-RECORD.
002200     05  VENDOR-NUMBER                PIC 9(5).
002300     05  VENDOR-NAME                  PIC X(30).
002400     05  VENDOR-ADDRESS-1             PIC X(30).
002500     05  VENDOR-ADDRESS-2             PIC X(30).
002600     05  VENDOR-CITY                  PIC X(20).
002700     05  VENDOR-STATE                 PIC X(2).
002800     05  VENDOR-ZIP                   PIC X(10).
002900     05  VENDOR-CONTACT               PIC X(30).
003000     05  VENDOR-PHONE                 PIC X(15).
003100
003200
003300
003400
003500 WORKING-STORAGE SECTION.
003600
003700
003800
003900 01  DETAIL-LINE.
004000     05  DISPLAY-NUMBER     PIC 9(5).
004100     05  FILLER            PIC X      VALUE SPACE.
004200     05  DISPLAY-NAME      PIC X(30).
004300     05  FILLER            PIC X      VALUE SPACE.
004400     05  DISPLAY-CONTACT   PIC X(30).
004500
004600 01  CITY-STATE-DETAIL.
004700     05  DISPLAY-CITY      PIC X(20).
004800     05  FILLER            PIC X VALUE SPACE.
004900     05  DISPLAY-STATE     PIC X(2).
005000
005100 01  COLUMN-LINE.
005200     05  FILLER        PIC X(2)  VALUE "NO".
005300     05  FILLER        PIC X(4)  VALUE SPACE.
005400     05  FILLER        PIC X(12) VALUE "NAME-ADDRESS".
005500     05  FILLER        PIC X(19) VALUE SPACE.
005600     05  FILLER        PIC X(17) VALUE "CONTACT-PHONE-ZIP".
005700
```

```
005800 01   TITLE-LINE.
005900      05   FILLER              PIC X(15) VALUE SPACE.
006000      05   FILLER              PIC X(11)
006100           VALUE "VENDOR LIST".
006200      05   FILLER              PIC X(15) VALUE SPACE.
006300      05   FILLER              PIC X(5) VALUE "PAGE:".
006400      05   FILLER              PIC X(1) VALUE SPACE.
006500      05   DISPLAY-PAGE-NUMBER PIC ZZZZ9.
006600
006700 77   FILE-AT-END             PIC X.
006800 77   A-DUMMY                 PIC X.
006900 77   LINE-COUNT              PIC 999 VALUE ZERO.
007000 77   PAGE-NUMBER             PIC 99999 VALUE ZERO.
007100 77   MAXIMUM-LINES           PIC 999 VALUE 15.
007200
007300 77   DISPLAY-RECORD          PIC X(79).
007400
007500 PROCEDURE DIVISION.
007600 PROGRAM-BEGIN.
007700
007800      PERFORM OPENING-PROCEDURE.
007900      MOVE ZEROES TO LINE-COUNT
008000                     PAGE-NUMBER.
008100
008200      PERFORM START-NEW-PAGE.
008300
008400      MOVE "N" TO FILE-AT-END.
008500      PERFORM READ-NEXT-RECORD.
008600      IF FILE-AT-END = "Y"
008700          MOVE "NO RECORDS FOUND" TO DISPLAY-RECORD
008800          PERFORM WRITE-DISPLAY-RECORD
008900      ELSE
009000          PERFORM DISPLAY-VENDOR-FIELDS
009100              UNTIL FILE-AT-END = "Y".
009200
009300      PERFORM CLOSING-PROCEDURE.
009400
009500
009600 PROGRAM-DONE.
009700      STOP RUN.
009800
009900 OPENING-PROCEDURE.
010000      OPEN I-O VENDOR-FILE.
010100
010200 CLOSING-PROCEDURE.
010300      CLOSE VENDOR-FILE.
010400
010500 DISPLAY-VENDOR-FIELDS.
010600      IF LINE-COUNT > MAXIMUM-LINES
010700          PERFORM START-NEXT-PAGE.
010800      PERFORM DISPLAY-THE-RECORD.
010900      PERFORM READ-NEXT-RECORD.
011000
011100 DISPLAY-THE-RECORD.
011200      PERFORM DISPLAY-LINE-1.
```

continues

Listing 11.12. continued

```
011300      PERFORM DISPLAY-LINE-2.
011400      PERFORM DISPLAY-LINE-3.
011500      PERFORM DISPLAY-LINE-4.
011600      PERFORM LINE-FEED.
011700
011800 DISPLAY-LINE-1.
011900      MOVE SPACE TO DETAIL-LINE.
012000      MOVE VENDOR-NUMBER TO DISPLAY-NUMBER.
012100      MOVE VENDOR-NAME TO DISPLAY-NAME.
012200      MOVE VENDOR-CONTACT TO DISPLAY-CONTACT.
012300      MOVE DETAIL-LINE TO DISPLAY-RECORD.
012400      PERFORM WRITE-DISPLAY-RECORD.
012500
012600 DISPLAY-LINE-2.
012700      MOVE SPACE TO DETAIL-LINE.
012800      MOVE VENDOR-ADDRESS-1 TO DISPLAY-NAME.
012900      MOVE VENDOR-PHONE TO DISPLAY-CONTACT.
013000      MOVE DETAIL-LINE TO DISPLAY-RECORD.
013100      PERFORM WRITE-DISPLAY-RECORD.
013200
013300 DISPLAY-LINE-3.
013400      MOVE SPACE TO DETAIL-LINE.
013500      MOVE VENDOR-ADDRESS-2 TO DISPLAY-NAME.
013600      IF VENDOR-ADDRESS-2 NOT = SPACE
013700          MOVE DETAIL-LINE TO DISPLAY-RECORD
013800          PERFORM WRITE-DISPLAY-RECORD.
013900
014000 DISPLAY-LINE-4.
014100      MOVE SPACE TO DETAIL-LINE.
014200      MOVE VENDOR-CITY TO DISPLAY-CITY.
014300      MOVE VENDOR-STATE TO DISPLAY-STATE.
014400      MOVE CITY-STATE-DETAIL TO DISPLAY-NAME.
014500      MOVE VENDOR-ZIP TO DISPLAY-CONTACT.
014600      MOVE DETAIL-LINE TO DISPLAY-RECORD.
014700      PERFORM WRITE-DISPLAY-RECORD.
014800
014900 READ-NEXT-RECORD.
015000      READ VENDOR-FILE NEXT RECORD
015100          AT END MOVE "Y" TO FILE-AT-END.
015200
015300 WRITE-DISPLAY-RECORD.
015400      DISPLAY DISPLAY-RECORD.
015500      ADD 1 TO LINE-COUNT.
015600
015700 LINE-FEED.
015800      MOVE SPACE TO DISPLAY-RECORD.
015900      PERFORM WRITE-DISPLAY-RECORD.
016000
016100 START-NEXT-PAGE.
016200
016300      PERFORM END-LAST-PAGE.
016400      PERFORM START-NEW-PAGE.
016500
016600 START-NEW-PAGE.
```

11

```
016700        ADD 1 TO PAGE-NUMBER.
016800        MOVE PAGE-NUMBER TO DISPLAY-PAGE-NUMBER.
016900        MOVE TITLE-LINE TO DISPLAY-RECORD.
017000        PERFORM WRITE-DISPLAY-RECORD.
017100        PERFORM LINE-FEED.
017200        MOVE COLUMN-LINE TO DISPLAY-RECORD.
017300        PERFORM WRITE-DISPLAY-RECORD.
017400        PERFORM LINE-FEED.
017500
017600 END-LAST-PAGE.
017700        PERFORM PRESS-ENTER.
017800        MOVE ZERO TO LINE-COUNT.
017900
018000 PRESS-ENTER.
018100        DISPLAY "PRESS ENTER TO CONTINUE. . .".
018200        ACCEPT A-DUMMY.
018300
```

```
                      VENDOR LIST              PAGE:     1

      NO    NAME-ADDRESS                  CONTACT-PHONE-ZIP

      00001 CECILLE JOHNSON AND CO.       CHARLES SMITH
            1212 MAIN ST                  (213) 555-1234
            LOS ANGELES          CA       91042

      00002 ABC PRINTING                  LINDA JOHANSSEN
            1624 FOOTHILL BLVD            (818) 555-4321
            SUITE 34
            LOS ANGELES          CA       91042

      00003 CHARLES SMITH AND SONS        CHARLES SMITH
            1453 SOUTH STREET             (213) 555-4432
            LOS ANGELES          CA       92345

      PRESS ENTER TO CONTINUE. . .
```

NOTE A few level-77 data items are thrown into WORKING-STORAGE so that you will get accustomed to seeing them in programs. You could use 01 for these.

ANALYSIS The organization of the program is similar to a report program. A DETAIL-LINE, COLUMN-LINE, and TITLE-LINE are defined at lines 003900, 005100, and 005800, respectively.

A programmer might use DETAIL-LINE for multiple purposes. Even though it is defined to contain DISPLAY-NUMBER, DISPLAY-NAME, and DISPLAY-CONTACT, the DISPLAY-NAME field will be used to display VENDOR-NAME, but it also will be used to display VENDOR-ADDRESS-1, VENDOR-ADDRESS-2, VENDOR-CITY, and VENDOR-STATE. The DISPLAY-CONTACT field will be used to display VENDOR-PHONE and VENDOR-ZIP, as well as VENDOR-CONTACT.

A 79-byte DISPLAY-RECORD at line 007300 is used throughout the program. Information to be displayed is moved to this field and then displayed by performing WRITE-DISPLAY-RECORD, a routine at line 015300 that displays the DISPLAY-RECORD and adds 1 to the LINE-COUNT. By forcing all displays to be performed using this same paragraph, it's possible to track accurately how many lines are displayed.

The main processing loop at line 010500 is DISPLAY-VENDOR-FIELDS. This checks to see whether a new page is needed, displays the record, and reads the next record.

DISPLAY-THE-RECORD at line 011100 has the task of displaying four separate lines in order to display all the fields of a single record. This is followed by a line feed. Displaying lines 1 and 2 at lines 011800 and 012600 is fairly straightforward.

In DISPLAY-LINE-3 at line 013300, I realized that not all vendors have two lines of address information, and that VENDOR-ADDRESS-2 could be blank. You can see examples of this in lines 7 and 17 of the output for Listing 11.12. Nothing else is formatted for this display line, so I decided to test the field and print the line only if it is not blank, rather than waste space on the screen. This test is at line 013600.

Displaying the fourth line of information presented an unusual problem. Up to this point, all the information to be displayed could fit very neatly within the single DETAIL-LINE defined at line 003900. Name, address 1, and address 2 all fit into the 30-character DISPLAY-NAME at line 004200. Contact and phone both fit into the 30-character DISPLAY-CONTACT at line 004400. The city, state, and zip code information didn't fit quite as neatly.

I could have added another detail line, as shown in Listing 11.13.

TYPE **Listing 11.13. A second detail line for vnddsp01.cbl.**

```
004500 01  2ND-DETAIL-LINE.
004600     05  FILLER           PIC X(6) VALUE SPACE.
004700     05  DISPLAY-CITY     PIC X(20).
004800     05  FILLER           PIC X VALUE SPACE.
004900     05  DISPLAY-STATE    PIC XX.
005000     05  FILLER           PIC X(8) VALUE SPACE.
005100     05  DISPLAY-ZIP      PIC X(10).
```

Using the 2ND-DETAIL-LINE, DISPLAY-LINE-4 changes to look like Listing 11.14.

TYPE **Listing 11.14. Using 2ND-DETAIL-LINE.**

```
014000 DISPLAY-LINE-4.
014100     MOVE SPACE TO 2ND-DETAIL-LINE.
014200     MOVE VENDOR-CITY TO DISPLAY-CITY.
014300     MOVE VENDOR-STATE TO DISPLAY-STATE.
```

```
014400
014500          MOVE VENDOR-ZIP TO DISPLAY-ZIP.
014600          MOVE 2ND-DETAIL-LINE TO DISPLAY-RECORD.
014700          PERFORM WRITE-DISPLAY-RECORD.
```

ANALYSIS There was no need for a full second detail line, because VENDOR-ZIP still would fit within DISPLAY-CONTACT. A small formatting field, CITY-STATE-DETAIL at lines 004600 through 004900, was created to be used to format the 20 characters of city and two characters of state. At lines 014200 and 014300, values are moved into DISPLAY-CITY and DISPLAY-STATE, which are both with the structure variable CITY-STATE-DETAIL. At line 014400, this entire structure, now containing the values I have moved to it, is moved to DISPLAY-NAME.

Summary

COBOL data processing relies on indexed files. They are the central repository of data for virtually every COBOL system in use. Today, you learned the following basics about indexed files:

☐ An indexed file in COBOL is a file structure that allows you to create a file and add records to it so that you can retrieve them in one of two ways. The records can be retrieved by a unique value in the file, or they can be retrieved in a sorted order that is determined at the time the records are written.

☐ A record in an indexed file must contain at least one field that is unique to that record. That field is used as the primary index or primary key of the file.

☐ The primary key is frequently a number; that number then can be used as the unique identifier of a particular record.

☐ The logical description of an indexed file (the FD) is not different from any other file. The logical description defines the record and fields in the record.

☐ A file is identified as an indexed file by using ORGANIZATION IS INDEXED in the SELECT statement and by naming the field that is to be used as the primary key for the file. The SELECT statement also should include ACCESS MODE IS DYNAMIC.

☐ In many larger systems, programmers write a simple program so that you can open an indexed file in output mode to create an empty file as part of the initial setting up of the system.

☐ Adding records to an indexed file is identical mechanically to adding records to a sequential file. You fill each of the fields of the record with a value and then write the record.

☐ If you attempt to add a record to a file with a value in the primary key that is identical to a record already in the file, it will cause a file error condition.

11

☐ File error conditions, such as reading past the end of a file or attempting to write a record with a duplicate key value, usually cause a COBOL program to abort. Using AT END in a READ NEXT command and INVALID KEY in a WRITE command overrides the abort condition and allows the program to continue.

☐ The natural order of records in an indexed file is in primary key order, and when the records are retrieved sequentially, they are retrieved in primary key order.

Q&A

Q Does a primary key have to be numeric?

A No. An alphanumeric field can be used as a primary key.

Q If it doesn't have to be numeric, what order does it use?

A It usually uses the collating sequence of the machine on which the program was compiled. For minicomputers and PCs, this is ASCII sequence, shown in Appendix B, "ASCII." Basically, numbers appear before alphabetic characters, and uppercase alphabet characters appear before lowercase ones.

Workshop

Quiz

1. A salesperson's contact file is organized with records using the FD in the following code:

```
000900 FD  CONTACT-FILE
001000     LABEL RECORDS ARE STANDARD.
001100 01  CONTACT-RECORD.
001200     05  CONTACT-BIRTH-DATE    PIC 9(6).
001300     05  CONTACT-NAME          PIC X(20).
001400     05  CONTACT-ADDRESS-1     PIC X(20).
001500     05  CONTACT-ADDRESS-2     PIC X(20).
001600     05  CONTACT-ZIP           PIC 9(5).
001700     05  CONTACT-PHONE.
001800         10  CONTACT-AREA-CODE  PIC 9(3).
001900         10  CONTACT-PREFIX     PIC 9(3).
002000         10  CONTACT-PHONE-NO   PIC 9(4).
```

The contact file also is organized as an indexed file using a SELECT statement, as in the following code:

```
000300     SELECT CONTACT-FILE
000400         ASSIGN TO "contact"
000500         ORGANIZATION IS INDEXED
000600         RECORD KEY IS CONTACT-BIRTH-DATE
000700         ACCESS MODE IS DYNAMIC.
```

If the file is expected to have hundreds of entries, what is wrong with `CONTACT-BIRTH-DATE` as a primary key?

2. Of the existing fields in the `CONTACT-RECORD`, which one has a better chance than `CONTACT-BIRTH-DATE` of being unique?

Exercises

1. Design a better way of defining the contact file so that you can create a unique key within the record.

2. Another way of handling the city, state, and zip code lines in `vnddsp01.cbl` is to use a `DETAIL-LINE`, as shown in the following code:

```
003900 01  DETAIL-LINE.
004000     05  DISPLAY-NUMBER     PIC 9(5).
004100     05  FILLER            PIC X      VALUE SPACE.
004200     05  DISPLAY-NAME.
004300         10  DISPLAY-CITY   PIC X(20).
004400         10  FILLER        PIC X(1) VALUE SPACE.
004500         10  DISPLAY-STATE  PIC X(2).
004600         10  FILLER        PIC X(7) VALUE SPACE.
004700     05  FILLER            PIC X      VALUE SPACE.
004800     05  DISPLAY-CONTACT    PIC X(30).
```

Also, you should change `DISPLAY-LINE-4` by removing the code at line `014400`, as in the following code:

```
014000 DISPLAY-LINE-4.
014100     MOVE SPACE TO DETAIL-LINE.
014200     MOVE VENDOR-CITY TO DISPLAY-CITY.
014300     MOVE VENDOR-STATE TO DISPLAY-STATE.
014400
014500     MOVE VENDOR-ZIP TO DISPLAY-CONTACT.
014600     MOVE DETAIL-LINE TO DISPLAY-RECORD.
014700     PERFORM WRITE-DISPLAY-RECORD.
```

Can you explain why?

3. Print out copies of `phnprt02.cbl` from Day 10, "Printing," and `vnddsp01.cbl`. Mark out sections of the two programs that behave in similar ways. Although one prints to a printer and the other displays on-screen, the basic logical design of the two programs is similar. You can print these most simply in MS-DOS by entering the following:

```
PRINT phnprt02.cbl
PRINT vnddsp01.cbl
```

If you are using another type of computer, consult your manual.

11

Day 12

More on Indexed Files

Indexed files make it easy to change or delete the contents of a file while maintaining the order of records in the file. Today, you learn about the following topics:

☐ Using COPY files

☐ Programming with COPY files

☐ Using a listing file

☐ Changing records in an indexed file

Using COPY Files

A COPY file is a convenient way of cutting down on the amount of typing you do and reducing the possibility for errors in a program. How do you use them? In Day 11, "Indexed File I/O," you created six programs that accessed the vendor file: vndbld01.cbl, vnderr01.cbl, vnderr02.cbl, vndnew01.cbl, vndnew02.cbl, and vnddsp02.cbl. Regardless of whatever else was going on in the programs, all of them had identical SELECT statements and file descriptors for the vendor file.

You have yet to write programs to change, delete, and print records; these also need to describe the vendor file. This brings the total number of programs to at least nine, and there are probably more. It seems wasteful (and increases the possibility of errors) to have to retype the SELECT and FD every time they are used. Is there a solution? The COPY statement to the rescue!

Any part of a COBOL program can be written in a separate file. In the main file, you can include the separate program file by using a COPY statement. When the main program is compiled, the compiler includes the text in the COPY file, as though you had typed the text into the main file.

```
001200      COPY "FDVENDOR.CBL".
```

The COPY statement starts in Area B (columns 12 through 72) and is followed immediately by the name of the file to COPY and a period. For most MS-DOS COBOL compilers, enclose the filename in double quotation marks and then end the statement with a period. If you are working on another machine, check your manual.

The COPY statement can include comments, and it is organized like a standard COBOL source file with a sequence area, indicator area, Area A, and Area B.

Listings 12.1 and 12.2 are each complete edited files containing the SELECT statement and FD for the vendor file. Listing 12.3 is vndbld02.cbl, a revised version of vndbld01.cbl. It uses COPY statements to include slvnd01.cbl and fdvnd01.cbl. Both of these listings are used in Listing 12.3 to create a vendor file. You should create them now.

TYPE   **Listing 12.1.** slvnd01.cbl.

```
000100*--------------------------------
000200* SLVND01.CBL
000300*--------------------------------
000400      SELECT VENDOR-FILE
000500          ASSIGN TO "vendor"
000600          ORGANIZATION IS INDEXED
000700          RECORD KEY IS VENDOR-NUMBER
000800          ACCESS MODE IS DYNAMIC.
000900
```

TYPE   **Listing 12.2.** fdvnd01.cbl.

```
000100*--------------------------------
000200* FDVND01.CBL
000300*--------------------------------
000400 FD  VENDOR-FILE
000500      LABEL RECORDS ARE STANDARD.
000600 01  VENDOR-RECORD.
000700      05  VENDOR-NUMBER         PIC 9(5).
000800      05  VENDOR-NAME           PIC X(30).
```

```
000900     05   VENDOR-ADDRESS-1          PIC X(30).
001000     05   VENDOR-ADDRESS-2          PIC X(30).
001100     05   VENDOR-CITY               PIC X(20).
001200     05   VENDOR-STATE              PIC X(2).
001300     05   VENDOR-ZIP                PIC X(10).
001400     05   VENDOR-CONTACT            PIC X(30).
001500     05   VENDOR-PHONE              PIC X(15).
001600
```

Listing 12.3 is an example of a Vendor file creation program. If you run it, it will delete any existing vendor file. You might want to copy your current vendor file to backup directory before running this program. After you have tested that a vendor file is created, you can restore your originals.

TYPE   **Listing 12.3. Using COPY files.**

```
000100 IDENTIFICATION DIVISION.
000200 PROGRAM-ID. VNDBLD02.
000300*--------------------------------------------------
000400* Create an Empty Vendor File.
000500*--------------------------------------------------
000600 ENVIRONMENT DIVISION.
000700 INPUT-OUTPUT SECTION.
000800 FILE-CONTROL.
000900
001000     COPY "SLVND01.CBL".
001100
001200 DATA DIVISION.
001300 FILE SECTION.
001400
001500     COPY "FDVND01.CBL".
001600
001700 WORKING-STORAGE SECTION.
001800
001900 PROCEDURE DIVISION.
002000 PROGRAM-BEGIN.
002100     OPEN OUTPUT VENDOR-FILE.
002200     CLOSE VENDOR-FILE.
002300
002400 PROGRAM-DONE.
002500     STOP RUN.
002600
```

ANALYSIS   The result of compiling vndbld02.cbl using the two COPY files is a program that is identical in function to the original vndbld01.cbl.

NEW TERM   The COPY command is not a programming command. It is a command to the compiler to tell it to pull the pieces of different files together into one file and then compile the resulting file. A command that controls the compiler's behavior is called a *compiler directive*, and the COPY command is sometimes called the COPY *directive*.

12

The COPY directive makes it possible to code the SELECT and FD for a file only once, and then to include it in all programs that access that file.

Programming with COPY Files

If all programs use the COPY directive for files, how do you know the names of variables in a file description? Most systems have many files. An accounts payable system has a vendor file, a bills-due file and possibly a historical bills-paid file, and a check file used for check reconciliation. It also has some sort of control file that is used to store the next check number to be used and the next vendor number to be used. These are enough for a small accounts payable system.

The primary way of keeping track of all these is to print the FD for each of the files in the system and keep them in a loose-leaf binder. Each member of the programming staff might have one of these binders, or binders can be placed centrally so that everyone has access to them.

The FD should include helpful comments that can be used by the programmer, and the comments do not necessarily need to relate only to the programming side of the computer system.

Listings 12.4, 12.5, and 12.6 are sample file descriptors that could be printed. The printed copy of the FD could be kept on hand when coding a program as an aid to help with program design. If the FD is adequately commented, there usually is no need to include a printout of the COPY file for the SELECT statement. You should code these files and keep them on hand as you will be using them in this and subsequent chapters.

TYPE   **Listing 12.4.** fdvnd02.cbl.

```
000100*-------------------------------
000200* FDVND02.CBL
000300* Primary Key - VENDOR-NUMBER
000400* VENDOR-ADDRESS-2 not always used
000500*    so may be SPACES
000600* VENDOR-PHONE is usually the
000700*    number for VENDOR-CONTACT
000800* All fields should be entered in
000900*    UPPER case.
001000*-------------------------------
001100 FD  VENDOR-FILE
001200     LABEL RECORDS ARE STANDARD.
001300 01  VENDOR-RECORD.
001400     05   VENDOR-NUMBER          PIC 9(5).
001500     05   VENDOR-NAME            PIC X(30).
001600     05   VENDOR-ADDRESS-1       PIC X(30).
001700     05   VENDOR-ADDRESS-2       PIC X(30).
001800     05   VENDOR-CITY            PIC X(20).
001900     05   VENDOR-STATE           PIC X(2).
```

12

```
002000        05  VENDOR-ZIP              PIC X(10).
002100        05  VENDOR-CONTACT          PIC X(30).
002200        05  VENDOR-PHONE            PIC X(15).
002300
```

TYPE **Listing 12.5.** fdchk01.cbl.

```
000100*- - - - - - - - - - - - - - - - - - - - - - - - - - - - - -
000200* FDCHK01.CBL
000300* Primary Key - CHECK-KEY
000400*   if you use more than 1 check
000500*   account to pay bills, using
000600*   check numbers only may
000700*   cause duplicates.
000800* CHECK-INVOICE is the vendor's
000900*   invoice that this check paid
001000*   and can be blank.
001100* CHECK-CLEARED = "Y" once the
001200*   the check is reported cashed
001300*   on a bank statement. Setting
001400*   this flag is done in the
001500*   check clearance program
001600*   chkclr.cbl.
001700* CHECK-REFERENCE for any notes
001800*   about the check.
001900* CHECK-VENDOR can be zero for a
002000*   general check to someone who
002100*   is not a regular vendor, but
002200*   CHECK-REFERENCE should be
002300*   filled in with payee.
002400*- - - - - - - - - - - - - - - - - - - - - - - - - - - - - -
002500 FD  CHECK-FILE
002600     LABEL RECORDS ARE STANDARD.
002700 01  CHECK-RECORD.
002800     05  CHECK-KEY.
002900         10  CHECK-ACCOUNT          PIC 9(10).
003000         10  CHECK-NUMBER           PIC 9(6).
003100     05  CHECK-AMOUNT               PIC S9(6)V99.
003200     05  CHECK-INVOICE              PIC X(15).
003300     05  CHECK-VENDOR               PIC 9(5).
003400     05  CHECK-REFERENCE            PIC X(30).
003500     05  CHECK-CLEARED              PIC X.
003600
```

TYPE **Listing 12.6.** fdbill01.cbl.

```
000100*- - - - - - - - - - - - - - - - - - - - - - - - - - - - - -
000200* FDBILL01.CBL
000300* Primary Key - BILL-NUMBER
```

12

continues

Listing 12.6. continued

```
000400* BILL-DATE, BILL-DUE and BILL-PAID
000500*   are all dates in CCYYMMDD format.
000600*-------------------------------
000700 FD  BILL-FILE
000800     LABEL RECORDS ARE STANDARD.
000900 01  CHECK-RECORD.
001000     05  BILL-NUMBER          PIC 9(6).
001100     05  BILL-DATE            PIC 9(8).
001200     05  BILL-DUE             PIC 9(8).
001300     05  BILL-AMOUNT          PIC S9(6)V99.
001400     05  BILL-INVOICE         PIC X(15).
001500     05  BILL-VENDOR          PIC 9(5).
001600     05  BILL-NOTES           PIC X(30).
001700     05  BILL-PAID            PIC 9(8).
001800
```

Using a Listing File

If pieces of the program are in other files, how do you ever get to see the whole program?

 A *listing file*, *source listing*, or simply a *listing* is a report produced by the compiler on the program that it has just compiled. This can be sent directly to the printer, or it can be created as a separate file that can be displayed or sent to the printer.

A listing file contains the code of the original file being compiled and all COPY files included in their correct places in the file. The listing file usually will include additional information about how the compile went, whether any warnings or errors were given by the compiler, and sometimes information on how variables are used in the program. It sometimes includes a list of all paragraph names in the program and what lines perform these paragraphs.

The method of producing a listing file varies enormously from compiler to compiler. Check your COBOL manual index under *listing*, and you should find instructions for producing a listing file.

In Micro Focus Personal COBOL, you specify whether you want a listing file created and what information that you want in your listing file just before compiling (checking) the program. The program vndnew03.cbl copies slvnd01.cbl and fdvnd02.cbl. In Figure 12.1, the Micro Focus Personal COBOL compiler is set up and ready to compile and produce a listing to the printer. To set this up, press F2 until check is ready to run, press F4 until the list option is displayed as Print, and then press F7 until XRef+Ref is selected. See the highlighted entries.

Listing files are notorious for being poorly documented. I have never found in any manual or other reference material a clear explanation of a listing file produced by a COBOL compiler. Listing files also differ from compiler to compiler. You usually have to carefully analyze a listing file to learn how to extract the information you need from it and to ignore the rest.

Figure 12.1.

Micro Focus Personal COBOL ready to generate a listing at the printer.

```
┌VNDNEW03.CBL─────────────────────────────────────────────────────────────────┐
│ 000100 IDENTIFICATION DIVISION.                                              │
│ 000200 PROGRAM-ID. VNDNEW03.                                                 │
│ 000300*----------------------------------------------                        │
│ 000400* Add a record to an indexed Vendor File.                             │
│ 000500*----------------------------------------------                        │
│ 000600 ENVIRONMENT DIVISION.                                                 │
│ 000700 INPUT-OUTPUT SECTION.                                                 │
│ 000800 FILE-CONTROL.                                                         │
│ 000900                                                                        │
│ 001000     COPY "SLVND01.CBL".                                               │
│ 001100                                                                        │
│ 001200 DATA DIVISION.                                                        │
│ 001300 FILE SECTION.                                                         │
│ 001400                                                                        │
│ 001500     COPY "FDVND02.CBL".                                               │
│ 001600                                                                        │
│ 001700 WORKING-STORAGE SECTION.                                             │
│ 001800                                                                        │
│ 001900 01  VENDOR-NUMBER-FIELD            PIC Z(5).                          │
└──────────────────────────────────────────────────────────────────────────────┘
 Edit-VNDNEW03──────101-lines──────Line-1──────Col-8──── ─   -Ins-Caps-  -Scroll
 F1=help F2=COBOL F3=insert-line F4=delete-line F5=repeat-line F6=restore-line
 F7=retype-char F8=restore-char F9=word-left F10=word-right      Alt Ctrl Escape
```

Listing 12.7 shows the listing file generated by Micro Focus Personal COBOL for vndnew03.cbl. The vndnew03.cbl program is a minor revision on vndnew02.cbl that includes COPY files to illustrate the parts of a listing file.

TYPE | **Listing 12.7. A listing file.**

```
* Micro Focus Personal COBOL v2.0.02 L2.0 revision 002 02-Jan-94 03:58 Page   1
*                               VNDNEW03.CBL
* Options: WB ERRQ EDITOR(MF) LIST() XREF REF ANIM ENSUITE(2) CONFIRM
1 IDENTIFICATION DIVISION.                                          0
2 PROGRAM-ID. VNDNEW03.                                           230
3*------------------------------------------------
4* Add a record to an indexed Vendor File.
5*------------------------------------------------
6 ENVIRONMENT DIVISION.                                           230
7 INPUT-OUTPUT SECTION.                                           230
8 FILE-CONTROL.                                                   230
9                                                                 230
*   10     COPY "SLVND01.CBL".                                        230
11*-------------------------------
12* SLVND01.CBL
13*-------------------------------
14     SELECT VENDOR-FILE                                         230
15        ASSIGN TO "vendor"                                      230
16        ORGANIZATION IS INDEXED                                 230
```

continues

12

Listing 12.7. continued

```
17         RECORD KEY IS VENDOR-NUMBER                        230
18         ACCESS MODE IS DYNAMIC.                            2C3
19                                                            2C3
20                                                            2C3
21 DATA DIVISION.                                             2C3
22 FILE SECTION.                                              2C3
23                                                            2C3
*   24     COPY "FDVND02.CBL".                                    2C3
25*------------------------------
26* FDVND01.CBL
27* Primary Key - VENDOR-NUMBER
28* VENDOR-ADDRESS-2 not always used
29*    so may be SPACES
30* VENDOR-PHONE is usually the
31*    number for VENDOR-CONTACT
32* All fields should be entered in
33*    UPPER case.
34*------------------------------
35 FD   VENDOR-FILE                                           2C3
36      LABEL RECORDS ARE STANDARD.                           2C3
37 01   VENDOR-RECORD.                                        2C8
38      05   VENDOR-NUMBER        PIC 9(5).                   2C8
39      05   VENDOR-NAME          PIC X(30).                  2CD
40      05   VENDOR-ADDRESS-1     PIC X(30).                  2EB
41      05   VENDOR-ADDRESS-2     PIC X(30).                  309
42      05   VENDOR-CITY          PIC X(20).                  327
43      05   VENDOR-STATE         PIC X(2).                   33B
44      05   VENDOR-ZIP           PIC X(10).                  33D
45      05   VENDOR-CONTACT       PIC X(30).                  347
46      05   VENDOR-PHONE         PIC X(15).                  365
47                                                            374
48                                                            374
49 WORKING-STORAGE SECTION.                                   378
50                                                            378
51 01   VENDOR-NUMBER-FIELD             PIC Z(5).             378
52                                                            378
53 PROCEDURE DIVISION.                                        0
54 PROGRAM-BEGIN.                                             39
55      OPEN I-O VENDOR-FILE.                                 3A
56      PERFORM GET-NEW-VENDOR-NUMBER.                        56
57      PERFORM ADD-RECORDS                                   59
* Micro Focus Personal COBOL v2.0.02 L2.0 revision 002 02-Jan-94 03:58 Page   2
*                               VNDNEW03.CBL
58          UNTIL VENDOR-NUMBER = ZEROES.                     67
59      CLOSE VENDOR-FILE.                                    67
60                                                            7D
61 PROGRAM-DONE.                                              7D
62      STOP RUN.                                             7E
63                                                            7F
64 GET-NEW-VENDOR-NUMBER.                                     7F
65      PERFORM INIT-VENDOR-RECORD.                           80
66      PERFORM ENTER-VENDOR-NUMBER.                          83
67                                                            86
68 INIT-VENDOR-RECORD.                                        86
```

12

```
69      MOVE SPACE TO VENDOR-RECORD.                               87
70      MOVE ZEROES TO VENDOR-NUMBER.                              8E
71                                                                 94
72 ENTER-VENDOR-NUMBER.                                            94
73      DISPLAY "ENTER VENDOR NUMBER (1-99999)".                   95
74      DISPLAY "ENTER 0 TO STOP ENTRY".                           B5
75      ACCEPT VENDOR-NUMBER-FIELD.                                CD
76*OR   ACCEPT VENDOR-NUMBER-FIELD WITH CONVERSION.
77                                                                 D5
78      MOVE VENDOR-NUMBER-FIELD TO VENDOR-NUMBER.                 D5
79*OR   MOVE WITH CONVERSION VENDOR-NUMBER-FIELD
80*        TO VENDOR-NUMBER.
81                                                                 DC
82 ADD-RECORDS.                                                    DC
83      PERFORM ENTER-REMAINING-FIELDS.                            DD
84      PERFORM WRITE-VENDOR-RECORD.                               E0
85      PERFORM GET-NEW-VENDOR-NUMBER.                             E3
86                                                                 E6
87 WRITE-VENDOR-RECORD.                                            E6
88      WRITE VENDOR-RECORD                                        E7
89          INVALID KEY                                            E7
90              DISPLAY "RECORD ALREADY ON FILE".                  107
91                                                                 122
92 ENTER-REMAINING-FIELDS.                                         122
93      PERFORM ENTER-VENDOR-NAME.                                 123
94      PERFORM ENTER-VENDOR-ADDRESS-1.                            126
95      PERFORM ENTER-VENDOR-ADDRESS-2.                            129
96      PERFORM ENTER-VENDOR-CITY.                                 12C
97      PERFORM ENTER-VENDOR-STATE.                                12F
98      PERFORM ENTER-VENDOR-ZIP.                                  132
99      PERFORM ENTER-VENDOR-CONTACT.                              135
100     PERFORM ENTER-VENDOR-PHONE.                                138
101                                                                13B
102 ENTER-VENDOR-NAME.                                             13B
103      DISPLAY "ENTER VENDOR NAME".                              13C
104      ACCEPT VENDOR-NAME.                                       150
105                                                                155
106 ENTER-VENDOR-ADDRESS-1.                                        155
107      DISPLAY "ENTER VENDOR ADDRESS-1".                         156
108      ACCEPT VENDOR-ADDRESS-1.                                  16F
109                                                                174
110 ENTER-VENDOR-ADDRESS-2.                                        174
111      DISPLAY "ENTER VENDOR ADDRESS-2".                         175
112      ACCEPT VENDOR-ADDRESS-2.                                  18E
113                                                                193
114 ENTER-VENDOR-CITY.                                             193
115      DISPLAY "ENTER VENDOR CITY".                              194
* Micro Focus Personal COBOL v2.0.02 L2.0 revision 002 02-Jan-94 03:58 Page   3
*                         VNDNEW03.CBL
116      ACCEPT VENDOR-CITY.                                       1A8
117                                                                1AD
118 ENTER-VENDOR-STATE.                                            1AD
119      DISPLAY "ENTER VENDOR STATE".                             1AE
120      ACCEPT VENDOR-STATE.                                      1C3
121                                                                1C8
```

12

continues

Listing 12.7. continued

```
122 ENTER-VENDOR-ZIP.                                              1C8
123     DISPLAY "ENTER VENDOR ZIP".                                1C9
124     ACCEPT VENDOR-ZIP.                                         1DC
125                                                                1E1
126 ENTER-VENDOR-CONTACT.                                          1E1
127     DISPLAY "ENTER VENDOR CONTACT".                            1E2
128     ACCEPT VENDOR-CONTACT.                                     1F9
129                                                                1FE
130 ENTER-VENDOR-PHONE.                                            1FE
131     DISPLAY "ENTER VENDOR PHONE".                              1FF
132     ACCEPT VENDOR-PHONE.                                       214
133                                                                219
* Micro Focus Personal COBOL v2.0.02 L2.0 revision 002
*
* Total Messages:     0
* Data:        1012    Code:        563    Dictionary:       1515
* Micro Focus Personal COBOL v2.0.02 L2.0 revision 002 02-Jan-94 03:58 Page  4
*                              VNDNEW03.CBL (XREF)            FILES
* VENDOR-FILE                    Indexed
*       14#      35      55      59                           (X     4)
*
*
*               1 files
* Micro Focus Personal COBOL v2.0.02 L2.0 revision 002 02-Jan-94 03:58 Page  5
*                              VNDNEW03.CBL (XREF)            DATA
* VENDOR-ADDRESS-1               Alphanumeric
*       40#     108*                                          (X     2)
*
* VENDOR-ADDRESS-2               Alphanumeric
*       41#     112*                                          (X     2)
*
* VENDOR-CITY                    Alphanumeric
*       42#     116*                                          (X     2)
*
* VENDOR-CONTACT                 Alphanumeric
*       45#     128*                                          (X     2)
*
* VENDOR-NAME                    Alphanumeric
*       39#     104*                                          (X     2)
*
* VENDOR-NUMBER                  Numeric DISPLAY
*       17      38#     58?     70*     78*                   (X     5)
*
* VENDOR-NUMBER-FIELD            Numeric edited
*       51#      75*     78                                   (X     3)
*
* VENDOR-PHONE                   Alphanumeric
*       46#     132*                                          (X     2)
*
* VENDOR-RECORD                  Group length       172
*       37#      69*     88                                   (X     3)
*
* VENDOR-STATE                   Alphanumeric
*       43#     120*                                          (X     2)
```

```
*
* VENDOR-ZIP                      Alphanumeric
*        44#     124*                                          (X    2)
*
* VNDNEW03                        Program name
*         2#                                                   (X    1)
*
*
*              12 data-names
* Micro Focus Personal COBOL v2.0.02 L2.0 revision 002 02-Jan-94 03:58 Page   6
*                                VNDNEW03.CBL (XREF)              PROCS
* ADD-RECORDS                     Paragraph
*        57      82#                                           (X    2)
*
* ENTER-REMAINING-FIELDS          Paragraph
*        83      92#                                           (X    2)
*
* ENTER-VENDOR-ADDRESS-1          Paragraph
*        94     106#                                           (X    2)
*
* ENTER-VENDOR-ADDRESS-2          Paragraph
*        95     110#                                           (X    2)
*
* ENTER-VENDOR-CITY               Paragraph
*        96     114#                                           (X    2)
*
* ENTER-VENDOR-CONTACT            Paragraph
*        99     126#                                           (X    2)
*
* ENTER-VENDOR-NAME               Paragraph
*        93     102#                                           (X    2)
*
* ENTER-VENDOR-NUMBER             Paragraph
*        66      72#                                           (X    2)
*
* ENTER-VENDOR-PHONE              Paragraph
*       100     130#                                           (X    2)
*
* ENTER-VENDOR-STATE              Paragraph
*        97     118#                                           (X    2)
*
* ENTER-VENDOR-ZIP                Paragraph
*        98     122#                                           (X    2)
*
* GET-NEW-VENDOR-NUMBER           Paragraph
*        56      64#      85                                   (X    3)
*
* INIT-VENDOR-RECORD              Paragraph
*        65      68#                                           (X    2)
*
* PROGRAM-BEGIN                   Paragraph
*        54#                                                   (X    1)
*
* PROGRAM-DONE                    Paragraph
*        61#                                                   (X    1)
```

continues

Listing 12.7. continued

```
*
* WRITE-VENDOR-RECORD              Paragraph
*         84        87#                                        (X     2)
*
*
*                16 procedure-names
* End of cross reference listing
```

 ANALYSIS The first thing you need to notice is that all COBOL line numbers have been stripped away and replaced with simple sequence numbers down the left side of the page. Every line not part of the original source code file (vndnew03.cbl) starts with an asterisk.

The COPY files have been included in full at lines 10 through 18 and lines 24 through 46. The numbers down the right side of the page represent addresses in memory where data or code is stored. The first few lines describe the options that were set on the compiler when this listing was created. You essentially can ignore these.

At the end of the listing, after line 128, some statistics about the program are printed, giving the sizes of the data and code created.

I requested a cross-reference (Xref+Ref), which begins on page 4 of the listing. The first page of the cross-reference lists the files used in the program and every line number on which the file is referenced. To the right of this is the number of times the file is referenced. Compare the line numbers listed under VENDOR-FILE (14, 35, 55, and 59) with the actual lines in the listing and you will see that VENDOR-FILE does indeed appear on those lines.

The next page of the cross-reference, page 5 of the listing, is a cross-reference of DATA, the variables used in the program, and the line numbers on which they are used.

Page 6 is a cross-reference of PROCS (paragraph names) in the PROCEDURE DIVISION used in the program. The PROCS listing is very useful in large programs, because every paragraph except PROGRAM-BEGIN and PROGRAM-DONE should appear at least twice in the cross-reference: once when the paragraph is defined, and at least once when it is performed. This part of the listing can be used to spot paragraphs that are never used.

You can use cross-reference listings when you are working on a program away from a computer and also when you are trying to fight your way through a complicated listing.

If a program includes some variable with an ambiguous name such as the OK-TO-DO-IT-FLAG, you have no way of guessing how this flag is really used. A cross-reference listing lets you zero in on every place that the flag is used, and it might help to isolate its purpose.

Changing Records in an Indexed File

Now that you know how to use COPY files, you can get back to the business at hand—indexed files.

In order to change a record in an indexed file, two conditions must be met: the record must exist in the file before it can be changed, and the primary key field of a record cannot be changed in a file.

To change a record in an indexed file, you first must locate the record. To locate a record in an indexed file, use MOVE to move a value to the field that is the primary key to the file and use READ to read the file record. If a record exists with that key value, it is read from the disk. If a record does not exist with that key value, a file error condition occurs that you must trap. The trap for a READ is also INVALID KEY. Use the following syntax:

```
READ file-name RECORD
    INVALID KEY
     do something
```

Here is an example:

```
PERFORM ENTER-VENDOR-NUMBER.
READ VENDOR-FILE RECORD
    INVALID KEY
      MOVE "N" TO RECORD-FOUND.
```

Changing a record involves moving new values to the fields of a record and using the REWRITE verb to rewrite the record. You cannot change the value in the primary key field. You must read the record successfully in the first place before you can execute a REWRITE. A REWRITE also uses INVALID KEY to trap any file error. This is the syntax:

```
REWRITE file-record
    INVALID KEY
     do something
```

The following is an example:

```
REWRITE VENDOR-RECORD
    INVALID KEY
    DISPLAY "ERROR ON REWRITE"
```

On some larger systems where files are shared with many users, there sometimes is an additional requirement that you must be able to lock the record before you perform the REWRITE. This prevents two users from modifying the same record at the same time.

The syntax for a lock varies for different versions of COBOL, but it usually is READ WITH LOCK or READ WITH HOLD. You do not need to use WITH HOLD or WITH LOCK unless the program complains about being unable to rewrite a record.

12

Record-locking is a fairly complex subject and beyond the scope of this book, but one of these two should be enough syntax to get your programs to work correctly:

```
READ file-name RECORD
    WITH LOCK
    INVALID KEY
      do something
```

```
READ file-name RECORD
    WITH HOLD
    INVALID KEY
      do something
```

Here are two examples:

```
READ VENDOR-FILE RECORD
    WITH LOCK
    INVALID KEY
      MOVE "N" TO RECORD-FOUND
```

```
READ VENDOR-FILE RECORD
    WITH HOLD
    INVALID KEY
      MOVE "N" TO RECORD-FOUND
```

A program that allows changes to an indexed file can be broken into two simple tasks:

☐ Get the user to identify a record to change, and ensure that the record is on file.

☐ Get the user to enter the changes to the fields of the record (other than the primary key field) and rewrite the record.

Listing 12.8, vndchg01.cbl, asks the user to supply the vendor number for the record to be changed. It then displays the values in the record fields and asks the user which one to change. The record must exist in the file before it can be changed, and the primary key field of the record cannot be changed.

TYPE Listing 12.8. Changing vendor records.

```
000100 IDENTIFICATION DIVISION.
000200 PROGRAM-ID. VNDCHG01.
000300*-------------------------------
000400* Change records in Vendor File.
000500*-------------------------------
000600 ENVIRONMENT DIVISION.
000700 INPUT-OUTPUT SECTION.
000800 FILE-CONTROL.
000900
001000     COPY "SLVND01.CBL".
001100
001200 DATA DIVISION.
001300 FILE SECTION.
001400
001500     COPY "FDVND02.CBL".
```

```
001600
001700 WORKING-STORAGE SECTION.
001800
001900 77  WHICH-FIELD          PIC 9.
002000 77  RECORD-FOUND         PIC X.
002100
002200 77  VENDOR-NUMBER-FIELD PIC Z(5).
002300
002400 PROCEDURE DIVISION.
002500 PROGRAM-BEGIN.
002600     OPEN I-O VENDOR-FILE.
002700     PERFORM GET-VENDOR-RECORD.
002800     PERFORM CHANGE-RECORDS
002900         UNTIL VENDOR-NUMBER = ZEROES.
003000     CLOSE VENDOR-FILE.
003100
003200 PROGRAM-DONE.
003300     STOP RUN.
003400
003500*-------------------------------
003600* TO GET A VENDOR RECORD, ASK FOR
003700* VENDOR NUMBER, AND THEN TRY TO
003800* READ THE RECORD.
003900*-------------------------------
004000 GET-VENDOR-RECORD.
004100     PERFORM INIT-VENDOR-RECORD.
004200     PERFORM ENTER-VENDOR-NUMBER.
004300     MOVE "N" TO RECORD-FOUND.
004400     PERFORM FIND-VENDOR-RECORD
004500         UNTIL RECORD-FOUND = "Y" OR
004600               VENDOR-NUMBER = ZEROES.
004700
004800 INIT-VENDOR-RECORD.
004900     MOVE SPACE TO VENDOR-RECORD.
005000     MOVE ZEROES TO VENDOR-NUMBER.
005100
005200 ENTER-VENDOR-NUMBER.
005300     DISPLAY " ".
005400     DISPLAY "ENTER VENDOR NUMBER OF THE VENDOR" .
005500     DISPLAY "TO CHANGE (1-99999)".
005600     DISPLAY "ENTER 0 TO STOP ENTRY".
005700     ACCEPT VENDOR-NUMBER-FIELD.
005800*OR  ACCEPT VENDOR-NUMBER-FIELD WITH CONVERSION.
005900
006000     MOVE VENDOR-NUMBER-FIELD TO VENDOR-NUMBER.
006100
006200 FIND-VENDOR-RECORD.
006300     PERFORM READ-VENDOR-RECORD.
006400     IF RECORD-FOUND = "N"
006500         DISPLAY "RECORD NOT FOUND"
006600         PERFORM ENTER-VENDOR-NUMBER.
006700
006800 READ-VENDOR-RECORD.
006900     MOVE "Y" TO RECORD-FOUND.
```

continues

Listing 12.8. continued

```
007000      READ VENDOR-FILE RECORD
007100        INVALID KEY
007200           MOVE "N" TO RECORD-FOUND.
007300
007400*or  READ VENDOR-FILE RECORD WITH LOCK
007500*       INVALID KEY
007600*          MOVE "N" TO RECORD-FOUND.
007700
007800*or  READ VENDOR-FILE RECORD WITH HOLD
007900*       INVALID KEY
008000*          MOVE "N" TO RECORD-FOUND.
008100
008200 CHANGE-RECORDS.
008300      PERFORM GET-FIELD-TO-CHANGE.
008400      PERFORM CHANGE-ONE-FIELD
008500          UNTIL WHICH-FIELD = ZERO.
008600      PERFORM GET-VENDOR-RECORD.
008700
008800*--------------------------------
008900* DISPLAY ALL FIELDS, ASK THE USER
009000* WHICH TO CHANGE.
009100*--------------------------------
009200 GET-FIELD-TO-CHANGE.
009300      PERFORM DISPLAY-ALL-FIELDS.
009400      PERFORM ASK-WHICH-FIELD.
009500
009600*--------------------------------
009700* DISPLAY ALL FIELDS WITH BLANK
009800* LINES ABOVE AND BELOW.
009900*--------------------------------
010000 DISPLAY-ALL-FIELDS.
010100      DISPLAY " ".
010200      PERFORM DISPLAY-VENDOR-NUMBER.
010300      PERFORM DISPLAY-VENDOR-NAME.
010400      PERFORM DISPLAY-VENDOR-ADDRESS-1.
010500      PERFORM DISPLAY-VENDOR-ADDRESS-2.
010600      PERFORM DISPLAY-VENDOR-CITY.
010700      PERFORM DISPLAY-VENDOR-STATE.
010800      PERFORM DISPLAY-VENDOR-ZIP.
010900      PERFORM DISPLAY-VENDOR-CONTACT.
011000      PERFORM DISPLAY-VENDOR-PHONE.
011100      DISPLAY " ".
011200
011300 DISPLAY-VENDOR-NUMBER.
011400      DISPLAY "   VENDOR NUMBER: " VENDOR-NUMBER.
011500
011600 DISPLAY-VENDOR-NAME.
011700      DISPLAY "1. VENDOR NAME: " VENDOR-NAME.
011800
011900 DISPLAY-VENDOR-ADDRESS-1.
012000      DISPLAY "2. VENDOR ADDRESS-1: " VENDOR-ADDRESS-1.
012100
012200 DISPLAY-VENDOR-ADDRESS-2.
012300      DISPLAY "3. VENDOR ADDRESS-2: " VENDOR-ADDRESS-2.
```

12

```
012400
012500 DISPLAY-VENDOR-CITY.
012600     DISPLAY "4. VENDOR CITY: " VENDOR-CITY.
012700
012800 DISPLAY-VENDOR-STATE.
012900     DISPLAY "5. VENDOR STATE: " VENDOR-STATE.
013000
013100 DISPLAY-VENDOR-ZIP.
013200     DISPLAY "6. VENDOR ZIP: " VENDOR-ZIP.
013300
013400 DISPLAY-VENDOR-CONTACT.
013500     DISPLAY "7. VENDOR CONTACT: " VENDOR-CONTACT.
013600
013700 DISPLAY-VENDOR-PHONE.
013800     DISPLAY "8. VENDOR PHONE: " VENDOR-PHONE.
013900
014000 ASK-WHICH-FIELD.
014100     DISPLAY "ENTER THE NUMBER OF THE FIELD".
014200     DISPLAY "TO CHANGE (1-8) OR 0 TO EXIT".
014300     ACCEPT WHICH-FIELD.
014400     IF WHICH-FIELD > 8
014500         DISPLAY "INVALID ENTRY".
014600
014700*--------------------------------
014800* GET DATA ENTRY FOR THE NEW FIELD.
014900* THEN ASK FOR THE NEXT FIELD
015000* TO CHANGE.
015100* CONTINUE UNTIL USER ENTERS 0.
015200*--------------------------------
015300 CHANGE-ONE-FIELD.
015400     PERFORM CHANGE-THIS-FIELD.
015500     PERFORM GET-FIELD-TO-CHANGE.
015600
015700*--------------------------------
015800* ACCEPT DATA ENTRY FOR THE FIELD
015900* SPECIFIED, AND THEN REWRITE THE
016000* RECORD.
016100*--------------------------------
016200 CHANGE-THIS-FIELD.
016300     IF WHICH-FIELD = 1
016400         PERFORM ENTER-VENDOR-NAME.
016500     IF WHICH-FIELD = 2
016600         PERFORM ENTER-VENDOR-ADDRESS-1.
016700     IF WHICH-FIELD = 3
016800         PERFORM ENTER-VENDOR-ADDRESS-2.
016900     IF WHICH-FIELD = 4
017000         PERFORM ENTER-VENDOR-CITY.
017100     IF WHICH-FIELD = 5
017200         PERFORM ENTER-VENDOR-STATE.
017300     IF WHICH-FIELD = 6
017400         PERFORM ENTER-VENDOR-ZIP.
017500     IF WHICH-FIELD = 7
017600         PERFORM ENTER-VENDOR-CONTACT.
017700     IF WHICH-FIELD = 8
017800         PERFORM ENTER-VENDOR-PHONE.
```

12

continues

Listing 12.8. continued

```
017900
018000     PERFORM REWRITE-VENDOR-RECORD.
018100
018200 ENTER-VENDOR-NAME.
018300     DISPLAY "ENTER VENDOR NAME".
018400     ACCEPT VENDOR-NAME.
018500
018600 ENTER-VENDOR-ADDRESS-1.
018700     DISPLAY "ENTER VENDOR ADDRESS-1".
018800     ACCEPT VENDOR-ADDRESS-1.
018900
019000 ENTER-VENDOR-ADDRESS-2.
019100     DISPLAY "ENTER VENDOR ADDRESS-2".
019200     ACCEPT VENDOR-ADDRESS-2.
019300
019400 ENTER-VENDOR-CITY.
019500     DISPLAY "ENTER VENDOR CITY".
019600     ACCEPT VENDOR-CITY.
019700
019800 ENTER-VENDOR-STATE.
019900     DISPLAY "ENTER VENDOR STATE".
020000     ACCEPT VENDOR-STATE.
020100
020200 ENTER-VENDOR-ZIP.
020300     DISPLAY "ENTER VENDOR ZIP".
020400     ACCEPT VENDOR-ZIP.
020500
020600 ENTER-VENDOR-CONTACT.
020700     DISPLAY "ENTER VENDOR CONTACT".
020800     ACCEPT VENDOR-CONTACT.
020900
021000 ENTER-VENDOR-PHONE.
021100     DISPLAY "ENTER VENDOR PHONE".
021200     ACCEPT VENDOR-PHONE.
021300
021400 REWRITE-VENDOR-RECORD.
021500     REWRITE VENDOR-RECORD
021600         INVALID KEY
021700         DISPLAY "ERROR REWRITING VENDOR RECORD".
021800
```

An example of the output from vndchg01.cbl follows. User entries are in bold type.

```
ENTER VENDOR NUMBER OF THE VENDOR
TO CHANGE (1-99999)
ENTER 0 TO STOP ENTRY
00003
VENDOR NUMBER: 00003
1. VENDOR NAME: CHARLES SMITH AND SONS
2. VENDOR ADDRESS-1: 1212 NORTH STREET
3. VENDOR ADDRESS-2:
4. VENDOR CITY: LOS ANGELES
```

```
5. VENDOR STATE: CA
6. VENDOR ZIP: 90064
7. VENDOR CONTACT: CHARLES SMITH
8. VENDOR PHONE: (213) 555-4432
ENTER THE NUMBER OF THE FIELD
TO CHANGE (1-8) OR 0 TO EXIT
2
ENTER VENDOR ADDRESS-1
1435 SOUTH STREET
VENDOR NUMBER: 00003
1. VENDOR NAME: CHARLES SMITH AND SONS
2. VENDOR ADDRESS-1: 1435 SOUTH STREET
3. VENDOR ADDRESS-2:
4. VENDOR CITY: LOS ANGELES
5. VENDOR STATE: CA
6. VENDOR ZIP: 90064
7. VENDOR CONTACT: CHARLES SMITH
8. VENDOR PHONE: (213) 555-4432
ENTER THE NUMBER OF THE FIELD
TO CHANGE (1-8) OR 0 TO EXIT
7
ENTER VENDOR CONTACT
MARTHA HARRISON
VENDOR NUMBER: 00003
1. VENDOR NAME: CHARLES SMITH AND SONS
2. VENDOR ADDRESS-1: 1435 SOUTH STREET
3. VENDOR ADDRESS-2:
4. VENDOR CITY: LOS ANGELES
5. VENDOR STATE: CA
6. VENDOR ZIP: 90064
7. VENDOR CONTACT: MARTHA HARRISON
8. VENDOR PHONE: (213) 555-4432
ENTER THE NUMBER OF THE FIELD
TO CHANGE (1-8) OR 0 TO EXIT
0
ENTER VENDOR NUMBER OF THE VENDOR
TO CHANGE (1-99999)
ENTER 0 TO STOP ENTRY
0
C>
C>
```

ANALYSIS   The control of the main processing loop is at lines 002700 through 002900. This logic starts at 002700 by performing GET-VENDOR-RECORD. Then CHANGE-RECORDS is performed until VENDOR-NUMBER = ZEROES.

The CHANGE-RECORDS processing loop ends by performing GET-VENDOR-RECORD. Figure 12.2 illustrates the relationship between the main processing loop and the loop control logic.

The loop body of CHANGE-RECORDS is itself just another set of loop controls for a lower-level loop at CHANGE-ONE-FIELD, as shown in Figure 12.3.

The GET-VENDOR-RECORD and FIND-VENDOR-RECORD routines at lines 004000 and 006200 are an interesting pair of paragraphs. At lines 004400 through 004600, a perform is requested until two conditions are met. FIND-VENDOR-RECORD is a processing loop that has no body. All the work is done by changing the loop control variables at line 006300. The perform of READ-VENDOR-RECORD changes the RECORD-FOUND variable, and at line 006600, the perform of ENTER-VENDOR-NUMBER changes the VENDOR-NUMBER variable. This is shown in Figure 12.4.

Figure 12.2.

The main processing loop and the loop control.

```
002700        PERFORM GET-VENDOR-RECORD.
002800        PERFORM CHANGE-RECORDS
002900            UNTIL VENDOR-NUMBER = ZEROES.
                                                        LOOP
008200 CHANGE-RECORDS.                                  CONTROL
008300        PERFORM GET-FIELD-TO-CHANGE.
008400        PERFORM CHANGE-ONE-FIELD          LOOP
008500            UNTIL WHICH-FIELD = ZERO.
008600        PERFORM GET-VENDOR-RECORD.
```

Figure 12.3.

A loop within a loop.

```
008200 CHANGE-RECORDS.
008300        PERFORM GET-FIELD-TO-CHANGE.
008400        PERFORM CHANGE-ONE-FIELD
008500            UNTIL WHICH-FIELD = ZERO.
008600        PERFORM GET-VENDOR-RECORD.                LOOP
                                                        CONTROL
015300 CHANGE-ONE-FIELD.
015400        PERFORM CHANGE-THIS-FIELD.        LOOP
015500        PERFORM GET-FIELD-TO-CHANGE.
```

Figure 12.4.

A processing loop with no loop body.

```
004000 GET-VENDOR-RECORD.
004100        PERFORM INIT-VENDOR-RECORD.
004200        PERFORM ENTER-VENDOR-NUMBER.
004300        MOVE "N" TO RECORD-FOUND.
004400        PERFORM FIND-VENDOR-RECORD
004500            UNTIL RECORD-FOUND = "Y" OR
004600                  VENDOR-NUMBER = ZEROES.         LOOP
                                                        CONTROL
006200 FIND-VENDOR-RECORD.
006300        PERFORM READ-VENDOR-RECORD.
006400        IF RECORD-FOUND = "N"
006500            DISPLAY "RECORD NOT FOUND"
006600            PERFORM ENTER-VENDOR-NUMBER.
```

If you haven't already coded Listing 12.1, slvnd01.cbl, and Listing 12.4, fdvnd02.cbl, do so now because you need them for vndchg01.cbl.

This program is the longest one you've coded so far. You might find it easier to understand if you code it, compile it, and print out the program (by entering PRINT vndchg01.cbl for MS-DOS). Then run the program while reading the printed code, and follow where you are in the logic at each point of the program.

12

Summary

Indexed files make it easy to change or delete the contents of a file while maintaining the order of records in the file. Today, you learned these basics about indexed files:

- [ ] You can copy another file into your main source file at compile time by using the COPY directive.

- [ ] It is useful to create all the physical (SELECT) and logical (FD) descriptions of files in a system as separate COPY files. This makes it unnecessary to code the same file description over and over, and helps prevent typing errors.

- [ ] The file descriptors used in creating a COBOL system should be printed and kept in a loose-leaf binder for reference by programmers.

- [ ] A listing file, which prints the entire program including COPY files, can be generated by the compiler.

- [ ] The listing file can include a cross-reference that can be helpful in trying to analyze large programs.

- [ ] A record can be rewritten by moving new values to the record fields and using the REWRITE command. The field containing the primary key cannot be changed. The REWRITE command uses INVALID KEY to trap file error conditions.

- [ ] A record must have been read successfully before a REWRITE command will work.

- [ ] Some systems require that a record must have been read WITH LOCK or WITH HOLD successfully before a REWRITE command will work.

- [ ] The basic layout of a program that allows a user to change records in an indexed file is the following:

  1. Identify the record to be changed.
  2. Read (or hold) the record.
  3. Get the user to enter the changes.
  4. Use the REWRITE command to record the changes.

Q&A

Q If I change a COPY file containing an FD or SELECT statement, does it change the data file?

A No, it changes only the definition of the data file in your program.

12

Q If I do change the definition of a file—by adding an additional field, for example—and the file is described in a COPY file, what do I have to do to make it work correctly with my data files?

A If you have to change a file by adding additional fields or increasing the width of the field, you must convert the data file so that it matches the new definition in the COBOL programs that access the file. After you've done this, all programs that use the COPY file definition of the data file must be recompiled so that the programs now include the new definition of the file. Many systems have utility programs to assist in data file conversions.

Workshop

Quiz

The following code fragment is supposed to read a record in a file. If the record is found, new values are moved in and the record is rewritten. If the record is not found, the same values are used to create a brand-new record by loading the record and writing it. At least, that is what it is supposed to do. Why does it not work that way?

```
003200 ADD-OR-UPDATE.
003300     MOVE "Y" TO RECORD-FOUND-FLAG.
003400     MOVE NEW-NUMBER TO VENDOR-NUMBER.
003500     READ VENDOR-RECORD
003600         INVALID KEY
003700         MOVE "N" TO RECORD-FOUND-FLAG.
003800     IF RECORD-FOUND-FLAG = "N"
003900         PERFORM CHANGE-THIS-RECORD
004000     ELSE
004100         PERFORM ADD-THIS-RECORD.
004200
004300 CHANGE-THIS-RECORD.
004400     PERFORM LOAD-RECORD-VALUES.
004500     REWRITE VENDOR-RECORD
004600         INVALID KEY
004700         DISPLAY "ERROR CHANGING THE RECORD".
004800
004900 ADD-THIS-RECORD.
005000     PERFORM LOAD-RECORD-VALUES.
005100     WRITE VENDOR-RECORD
005200         INVALID KEY
005300         DISPLAY "ERROR ADDING THE RECORD".
005400
005500 LOAD-RECORD-VALUES.
005600     MOVE NEW-NAME TO VENDOR-NAME.
005700     MOVE NEW-ADDRESS-1 TO VENDOR-ADDRESS-1.
005800     MOVE NEW-ADDRESS-2 TO VENDOR-ADDRESS-2.
```

```
005900          MOVE NEW-CITY TO VENDOR-CITY.
006000          MOVE NEW-STATE TO VENDOR-STATE.
006100          MOVE NEW-ZIP TO VENDOR-ZIP.
006200          MOVE NEW-CONTACT TO VENDOR-CONTACT.
006300          MOVE NEW-PHONE TO VENDOR-PHONE.
006400
```

Exercises

1. Describe the bug in the quiz question in English.

2. Rewrite the code in the quiz question to correct the error.

12

Day 13

Deleting Records and Other Indexed File Operations

Master a few more types of access to an indexed file and you have the basics of keeping indexed files updated. Today, you learn about the following topics:

- ☐ A new COBOL program shell
- ☐ Deleting records in an indexed file
- ☐ Displaying records in an indexed file
- ☐ A better way of adding files
- ☐ Printing records in an indexed file

A New COBOL Shell

All the programs that you have worked with have used files. It is time for a new COBOL shell program that makes room for physical and logical file descriptions. You can use this shell or template as the basic starting point for any programs that use files, and it saves a lot of coding. Just copy it to the new COBOL program name and start editing.

Code Listing 13.1 and keep it handy. You'll use this shell for several more days.

TYPE **Listing 13.1. A shell with space for files and comments.**

```
000100 IDENTIFICATION DIVISION.
000200 PROGRAM-ID. COBSHL03.
000300*------------------------------------------------
000400* Comments go here.
000500*------------------------------------------------
000600 ENVIRONMENT DIVISION.
000700 INPUT-OUTPUT SECTION.
000800 FILE-CONTROL.
000900
001000 DATA DIVISION.
001100 FILE SECTION.
001200
001300 WORKING-STORAGE SECTION.
001400
001500 PROCEDURE DIVISION.
001600 PROGRAM-BEGIN.
001700
001800 PROGRAM-DONE.
001900      STOP RUN.
002000
```

Deleting Records in an Indexed File

As time passes, you will need to delete records from a file. You might delete vendors with whom you no longer do business. A bills file might retire records for paid bills from the active file by deleting the records from the main file and writing them to a history file.

The command to delete a record is DELETE *file-name*, and it uses INVALID KEY to trap file-error conditions. Here is the syntax:

```
DELETE file-name RECORD
INVALID KEY
do something
```

The following is an example of DELETE file-name:

13

```
DELETE VENDOR-FILE RECORD
INVALID KEY
DISPLAY "ERROR DURING DELETE"
```

You must read a record successfully before you can delete it. As with REWRITE, some large systems require that the record is read WITH LOCK or WITH HOLD before the DELETE command will succeed.

Listing 13.2 is similar in organization to vndchg01.cbl. The problem with deleting a record is similar to the problem with changing a record. Get the user to identify the record and then read it and delete it.

TYPE **Listing 13.2. Deleting vendor records.**

```
000100 IDENTIFICATION DIVISION.
000200 PROGRAM-ID. VNDDEL01.
000300*------------------------------
000400* Delete records in Vendor File.
000500*------------------------------
000600 ENVIRONMENT DIVISION.
000700 INPUT-OUTPUT SECTION.
000800 FILE-CONTROL.
000900
001000     COPY "SLVND01.CBL".
001100
001200 DATA DIVISION.
001300 FILE SECTION.
001400
001500     COPY "FDVND02.CBL".
001600
001700 WORKING-STORAGE SECTION.
001800
001900 77  OK-TO-DELETE        PIC X.
002000 77  RECORD-FOUND        PIC X.
002100
002200 77  VENDOR-NUMBER-FIELD PIC Z(5).
002300
002400 PROCEDURE DIVISION.
002500 PROGRAM-BEGIN.
002600     OPEN I-O VENDOR-FILE.
002700     PERFORM GET-VENDOR-RECORD.
002800     PERFORM DELETE-RECORDS
002900         UNTIL VENDOR-NUMBER = ZEROES.
003000     CLOSE VENDOR-FILE.
003100
003200 PROGRAM-DONE.
003300     STOP RUN.
003400
003500*------------------------------
003600* TO GET A VENDOR RECORD, ASK FOR
003700* VENDOR NUMBER, AND THEN TRY TO
```

13

continues

Listing 13.2. continued

```
003800* READ THE RECORD.
003900*------------------------------
004000 GET-VENDOR-RECORD.
004100     PERFORM INIT-VENDOR-RECORD.
004200     PERFORM ENTER-VENDOR-NUMBER.
004300     MOVE "N" TO RECORD-FOUND.
004400     PERFORM FIND-VENDOR-RECORD
004500          UNTIL RECORD-FOUND = "Y" OR
004600               VENDOR-NUMBER = ZEROES.
004700
004800 INIT-VENDOR-RECORD.
004900     MOVE SPACE TO VENDOR-RECORD.
005000     MOVE ZEROES TO VENDOR-NUMBER.
005100
005200 ENTER-VENDOR-NUMBER.
005300     DISPLAY " ".
005400     DISPLAY "ENTER VENDOR NUMBER OF THE VENDOR" .
005500     DISPLAY "TO DELETE (1-99999)".
005600     DISPLAY "ENTER 0 TO STOP ENTRY".
005700     ACCEPT VENDOR-NUMBER-FIELD.
005800*OR  ACCEPT VENDOR-NUMBER-FIELD WITH CONVERSION.
005900
006000     MOVE VENDOR-NUMBER-FIELD TO VENDOR-NUMBER.
006100
006200 FIND-VENDOR-RECORD.
006300     PERFORM READ-VENDOR-RECORD.
006400     IF RECORD-FOUND = "N"
006500         DISPLAY "RECORD NOT FOUND"
006600         PERFORM ENTER-VENDOR-NUMBER.
006700
006800 READ-VENDOR-RECORD.
006900     MOVE "Y" TO RECORD-FOUND.
007000     READ VENDOR-FILE RECORD
007100       INVALID KEY
007200         MOVE "N" TO RECORD-FOUND.
007300
007400*or  READ VENDOR-FILE RECORD WITH LOCK
007500*      INVALID KEY
007600*        MOVE "N" TO RECORD-FOUND.
007700
007800*or  READ VENDOR-FILE RECORD WITH HOLD
007900*      INVALID KEY
008000*        MOVE "N" TO RECORD-FOUND.
008100
008200 DELETE-RECORDS.
008300     PERFORM DISPLAY-ALL-FIELDS.
008400     MOVE "X" TO OK-TO-DELETE.
008500
008600     PERFORM ASK-TO-DELETE
008700        UNTIL OK-TO-DELETE = "Y" OR "N".
008800
008900     IF OK-TO-DELETE = "Y"
009000         PERFORM DELETE-VENDOR-RECORD.
009100
```

13

```
009200      PERFORM GET-VENDOR-RECORD.
009300
009400*------------------------------
009500* DISPLAY ALL FIELDS WITH BLANK
009600* LINES ABOVE AND BELOW.
009700*------------------------------
009800 DISPLAY-ALL-FIELDS.
009900      DISPLAY " ".
010000      PERFORM DISPLAY-VENDOR-NUMBER.
010100      PERFORM DISPLAY-VENDOR-NAME.
010200      PERFORM DISPLAY-VENDOR-ADDRESS-1.
010300      PERFORM DISPLAY-VENDOR-ADDRESS-2.
010400      PERFORM DISPLAY-VENDOR-CITY.
010500      PERFORM DISPLAY-VENDOR-STATE.
010600      PERFORM DISPLAY-VENDOR-ZIP.
010700      PERFORM DISPLAY-VENDOR-CONTACT.
010800      PERFORM DISPLAY-VENDOR-PHONE.
010900      DISPLAY " ".
011000
011100 DISPLAY-VENDOR-NUMBER.
011200      DISPLAY "   VENDOR NUMBER: " VENDOR-NUMBER.
011300
011400 DISPLAY-VENDOR-NAME.
011500      DISPLAY "1. VENDOR NAME: " VENDOR-NAME.
011600
011700 DISPLAY-VENDOR-ADDRESS-1.
011800      DISPLAY "2. VENDOR ADDRESS-1: " VENDOR-ADDRESS-1.
011900
012000 DISPLAY-VENDOR-ADDRESS-2.
012100      DISPLAY "3. VENDOR ADDRESS-2: " VENDOR-ADDRESS-2.
012200
012300 DISPLAY-VENDOR-CITY.
012400      DISPLAY "4. VENDOR CITY: " VENDOR-CITY.
012500
012600 DISPLAY-VENDOR-STATE.
012700      DISPLAY "5. VENDOR STATE: " VENDOR-STATE.
012800
012900 DISPLAY-VENDOR-ZIP.
013000      DISPLAY "6. VENDOR ZIP: " VENDOR-ZIP.
013100
013200 DISPLAY-VENDOR-CONTACT.
013300      DISPLAY "7. VENDOR CONTACT: " VENDOR-CONTACT.
013400
013500 DISPLAY-VENDOR-PHONE.
013600      DISPLAY "8. VENDOR PHONE: " VENDOR-PHONE.
013700
013800 ASK-TO-DELETE.
013900      DISPLAY "DELETE THIS RECORD (Y/N)?".
014000      ACCEPT OK-TO-DELETE.
014100      IF OK-TO-DELETE= "y"
014200          MOVE "Y" TO OK-TO-DELETE.
014300      IF OK-TO-DELETE= "n"
014400          MOVE "N" TO OK-TO-DELETE.
014500      IF OK-TO-DELETE NOT = "Y" AND
```

13

continues

Listing 13.2. continued

```
014600        OK-TO-DELETE NOT = "N"
014700          DISPLAY "YOU MUST ENTER YES OR NO".
014800
014900 DELETE-VENDOR-RECORD.
015000    DELETE VENDOR-FILE RECORD
015100        INVALID KEY
015200        DISPLAY "ERROR DELETING VENDOR RECORD".
015300
```

OUTPUT

```
ENTER VENDOR NUMBER OF THE VENDOR
TO DELETE (1-99999)
ENTER 0 TO STOP ENTRY
1
VENDOR NUMBER: 00001
1. VENDOR NAME: JOHNSON AND SON
2. VENDOR ADDRESS-1: 1212 MAIN ST
3. VENDOR ADDRESS-2: # 455
4. VENDOR CITY: LOS ANGELES
5. VENDOR STATE: CA
6. VENDOR ZIP: 91042
7. VENDOR CONTACT: LINDA MARTIN
8. VENDOR PHONE: (213) 555-1234
DELETE THIS RECORD (Y/N)?
N
ENTER VENDOR NUMBER OF THE VENDOR
TO DELETE (1-99999)
ENTER 0 TO STOP ENTRY
1
VENDOR NUMBER: 00001
1. VENDOR NAME: JOHNSON AND SON
2. VENDOR ADDRESS-1: 1212 MAIN ST
3. VENDOR ADDRESS-2: # 455
4. VENDOR CITY: LOS ANGELES
5. VENDOR STATE: CA
6. VENDOR ZIP: 91042
7. VENDOR CONTACT: LINDA MARTIN
8. VENDOR PHONE: (213) 555-1234
DELETE THIS RECORD (Y/N)?
Y
ENTER VENDOR NUMBER OF THE VENDOR
TO DELETE (1-99999)
ENTER 0 TO STOP ENTRY
1
RECORD NOT FOUND
ENTER VENDOR NUMBER OF THE VENDOR
TO DELETE (1-99999)
ENTER 0 TO STOP ENTRY
```

ANALYSIS The primary difference between `vnddel01.cbl` and `vndchg01.cbl` is in DELETE-RECORDS at line 008200. At this point in `vndchg01.cbl`, the user is asked which field to change and data entry is accepted for the changed field. In `vnddel01.cbl`, instead

13

of asking the user for a field, the program asks the user whether this record should be deleted and then deletes the record if the user answers yes.

This gives the user a chance to see the record to make sure that it is the one to be deleted, rather than just deleting it.

One piece of coding you have not seen before appears at line 008700 as a test: UNTIL OK-TO-DELETE = "Y" OR "N". This is equivalent to OK-TO-DELETE = "Y" OR OK-TO-DELETE ="N".

Do	**Don't**
DO give the user a chance to back out, in case the wrong record was chosen for deletion. **DON'T** code programs that let the user find out too late that an irrevocable decision has been made.	

Code, compile, and test this program carefully. It is important in a deletion program to ensure that the record is deleted only when the user answers yes. It can be disconcerting, to say the least, to have records disappear for no apparent reason.

Do	**Don't**
DO test deletion programs carefully, and ensure that they delete records only when the user explicitly gives permission for a delete. **DON'T** let programs carry out unexpected deletions that destroy the integrity of the data in a file.	

To test this program, run it and specify a vendor number. When the record is displayed, enter N for no to the OK TO DELETE question. Then request that record number again. If the record has been deleted accidentally, you will receive a RECORD NOT FOUND message.

Enter a vendor number and specify Y for yes to the OK TO DELETE question. Then request that record number again. This time you should receive the RECORD NOT FOUND message.

The output of vnddel01.cbl illustrates this series of tests.

Displaying Records in an Indexed File

The inquiry program, vndinq01.cbl (shown in Listing 13.3), is almost identical to vnddel01.cbl. The step of asking the user whether to delete the record is dropped completely out of the logic, and the user is prompted for another vendor number.

13

NEW TERM Displaying a single record in an indexed file usually is called an *inquiry*. The user asks for the data on a specific vendor, and the information is displayed on the screen for reference. The program does not allow any changes and is used only for lookup actions.

TYPE **Listing 13.3. Looking up records in a file.**

```
000100 IDENTIFICATION DIVISION.
000200 PROGRAM-ID. VNDINQ01.
000300*-------------------------------
000400* Look Up records in Vendor File.
000500*-------------------------------
000600 ENVIRONMENT DIVISION.
000700 INPUT-OUTPUT SECTION.
000800 FILE-CONTROL.
000900
001000     COPY "SLVND01.CBL".
001100
001200 DATA DIVISION.
001300 FILE SECTION.
001400
001500     COPY "FDVND02.CBL".
001600
001700 WORKING-STORAGE SECTION.
001800
001900 77  RECORD-FOUND        PIC X.
002000
002100 77  VENDOR-NUMBER-FIELD PIC Z(5).
002200
002300 PROCEDURE DIVISION.
002400 PROGRAM-BEGIN.
002500     OPEN I-O VENDOR-FILE.
002600     PERFORM GET-VENDOR-RECORD.
002700     PERFORM INQUIRE-RECORDS
002800         UNTIL VENDOR-NUMBER = ZEROES.
002900     CLOSE VENDOR-FILE.
003000
003100 PROGRAM-DONE.
003200     STOP RUN.
003300
003400*-------------------------------
003500* TO GET A VENDOR RECORD, ASK FOR
003600* VENDOR NUMBER, AND THEN TRY TO
003700* READ THE RECORD.
003800*-------------------------------
003900 GET-VENDOR-RECORD.
004000     PERFORM INIT-VENDOR-RECORD.
004100     PERFORM ENTER-VENDOR-NUMBER.
004200     MOVE "N" TO RECORD-FOUND.
004300     PERFORM FIND-VENDOR-RECORD
004400         UNTIL RECORD-FOUND = "Y" OR
004500               VENDOR-NUMBER = ZEROES.
004600
004700 INIT-VENDOR-RECORD.
```

13

```
004800     MOVE SPACE TO VENDOR-RECORD.
004900     MOVE ZEROES TO VENDOR-NUMBER.
005000
005100 ENTER-VENDOR-NUMBER.
005200     DISPLAY " ".
005300     DISPLAY "ENTER VENDOR NUMBER OF THE VENDOR" .
005400     DISPLAY "TO DISPLAY (1-99999)".
005500     DISPLAY "ENTER 0 TO STOP ENTRY".
005600     ACCEPT VENDOR-NUMBER-FIELD.
005700*OR  ACCEPT VENDOR-NUMBER-FIELD WITH CONVERSION.
005800
005900     MOVE VENDOR-NUMBER-FIELD TO VENDOR-NUMBER.
006000
006100 FIND-VENDOR-RECORD.
006200     PERFORM READ-VENDOR-RECORD.
006300     IF RECORD-FOUND = "N"
006400         DISPLAY "RECORD NOT FOUND"
006500         PERFORM ENTER-VENDOR-NUMBER.
006600
006700 READ-VENDOR-RECORD.
006800     MOVE "Y" TO RECORD-FOUND.
006900     READ VENDOR-FILE RECORD
007000       INVALID KEY
007100         MOVE "N" TO RECORD-FOUND.
007200
007300*or  READ VENDOR-FILE RECORD WITH LOCK
007400*      INVALID KEY
007500*        MOVE "N" TO RECORD-FOUND.
007600
007700*or  READ VENDOR-FILE RECORD WITH HOLD
007800*      INVALID KEY
007900*        MOVE "N" TO RECORD-FOUND.
008000
008100 INQUIRE-RECORDS.
008200     PERFORM DISPLAY-ALL-FIELDS.
008300
008400     PERFORM GET-VENDOR-RECORD.
008500
008600*--------------------------------
008700* DISPLAY ALL FIELDS WITH BLANK
008800* LINES ABOVE AND BELOW.
008900*--------------------------------
009000 DISPLAY-ALL-FIELDS.
009100     DISPLAY " ".
009200     PERFORM DISPLAY-VENDOR-NUMBER.
009300     PERFORM DISPLAY-VENDOR-NAME.
009400     PERFORM DISPLAY-VENDOR-ADDRESS-1.
009500     PERFORM DISPLAY-VENDOR-ADDRESS-2.
009600     PERFORM DISPLAY-VENDOR-CITY.
009700     PERFORM DISPLAY-VENDOR-STATE.
009800     PERFORM DISPLAY-VENDOR-ZIP.
009900     PERFORM DISPLAY-VENDOR-CONTACT.
010000     PERFORM DISPLAY-VENDOR-PHONE.
010100     DISPLAY " ".
010200
```

13

continues

Listing 13.3. continued

```
010300 DISPLAY-VENDOR-NUMBER.
010400     DISPLAY "   VENDOR NUMBER: " VENDOR-NUMBER.
010500
010600 DISPLAY-VENDOR-NAME.
010700     DISPLAY "1. VENDOR NAME: " VENDOR-NAME.
010800
010900 DISPLAY-VENDOR-ADDRESS-1.
011000     DISPLAY "2. VENDOR ADDRESS-1: " VENDOR-ADDRESS-1.
011100
011200 DISPLAY-VENDOR-ADDRESS-2.
011300     DISPLAY "3. VENDOR ADDRESS-2: " VENDOR-ADDRESS-2.
011400
011500 DISPLAY-VENDOR-CITY.
011600     DISPLAY "4. VENDOR CITY: " VENDOR-CITY.
011700
011800 DISPLAY-VENDOR-STATE.
011900     DISPLAY "5. VENDOR STATE: " VENDOR-STATE.
012000
012100 DISPLAY-VENDOR-ZIP.
012200     DISPLAY "6. VENDOR ZIP: " VENDOR-ZIP.
012300
012400 DISPLAY-VENDOR-CONTACT.
012500     DISPLAY "7. VENDOR CONTACT: " VENDOR-CONTACT.
012600
012700 DISPLAY-VENDOR-PHONE.
012800     DISPLAY "8. VENDOR PHONE: " VENDOR-PHONE.
012900
```

The output of vndinq01.cbl follows. I asked for a display of vendor number 00001, but I had deleted it in the previous example while testing vnddel01.cbl. The result was a RECORD NOT FOUND message. Then I requested a display of vendor 00002.

OUTPUT

```
ENTER VENDOR NUMBER OF THE VENDOR
TO DISPLAY (1-99999)
ENTER 0 TO STOP ENTRY
1
RECORD NOT FOUND
ENTER VENDOR NUMBER OF THE VENDOR
TO DISPLAY (1-99999)
ENTER 00000 TO STOP ENTRY
2
VENDOR NUMBER: 00002
1. VENDOR NAME: ABC PRINTING
2. VENDOR ADDRESS-1: 1624 FOOTHILL BLVD
3. VENDOR ADDRESS-2: SUITE 34
4. VENDOR CITY: LOS ANGELES
5. VENDOR STATE: CA
6. VENDOR ZIP: 91042
7. VENDOR CONTACT: CHARLES JOHANSSEN
8. VENDOR PHONE: (818) 555-4321
ENTER VENDOR NUMBER OF THE VENDOR
```

13

```
        TO DISPLAY (1-99999)
        ENTER 0 TO STOP ENTRY
        0
        C>
        C>
```

Notice that the delete program, vnddel01.cbl, is very much like the change program, vndchg01.cbl, only shorter. The inquiry program, vndinq01.cbl, is very much like the delete program but is shorter still.

This is a common relationship. The change program displays all fields and allows changes to individual fields, the delete program displays all fields and allows the whole record to be deleted, and the inquiry program displays all fields and allows no changes.

NEW TERM The four types of programs covered in Day 11, "Indexed File I/O," Day 12, "More on Indexed Files," and today usually are called *maintenance programs*. Programs that allow records to be added, changed, deleted, and looked up in an indexed (or other) file make it possible to maintain the file.

NEW TERM The process of adding, changing, deleting or looking up a record in a data file by entering the data at a terminal is called *transaction processing*. It is also sometimes called *online processing* or *real-time processing*.

A Better Way of Adding Records

When you wrote the first versions of vndnew01.cbl through vndnew03.cbl, you hadn't yet used the READ command to look up a record.

One of the failings of vndnew01, vndnew02, and vndnew03 is that these programs ask the user to enter all the fields for the vendor before letting the user know that a record with that vendor number exists. When a record with that number exists, the user has to select a new number and start entering all over again.

It would be much better to check as soon as possible and let the user correct the VENDOR-NUMBER before going on. Listing 13.4, vndadd01.cbl, uses this approach. The program name now is more in keeping with the four types of maintenance programs: add, change, delete, and inquire (or look up).

TYPE **Listing 13.4. A better way of adding records by checking sooner if the vendor is on file.**

```
000100 IDENTIFICATION DIVISION.
000200 PROGRAM-ID. VNDADD01.
000300*------------------------------------------------
000400* Add a record to an indexed Vendor File.
```

continues

Listing 13.4. continued

```
000500*--------------------------------------------------
000600 ENVIRONMENT DIVISION.
000700 INPUT-OUTPUT SECTION.
000800 FILE-CONTROL.
000900
001000     COPY "SLVND01.CBL".
001100
001200 DATA DIVISION.
001300 FILE SECTION.
001400
001500     COPY "FDVND02.CBL".
001600
001700 WORKING-STORAGE SECTION.
001800
001900 77  RECORD-FOUND                      PIC X.
002000 77  VENDOR-NUMBER-FIELD               PIC Z(5).
002100
002200 PROCEDURE DIVISION.
002300 PROGRAM-BEGIN.
002400     OPEN I-O VENDOR-FILE.
002500     PERFORM GET-NEW-VENDOR-NUMBER.
002600     PERFORM ADD-RECORDS
002700         UNTIL VENDOR-NUMBER = ZEROES.
002800     CLOSE VENDOR-FILE.
002900
003000 PROGRAM-DONE.
003100     STOP RUN.
003200
003300 GET-NEW-VENDOR-NUMBER.
003400     PERFORM INIT-VENDOR-RECORD.
003500     PERFORM ENTER-VENDOR-NUMBER.
003600     MOVE "Y" TO RECORD-FOUND.
003700     PERFORM FIND-NEW-VENDOR-RECORD
003800         UNTIL RECORD-FOUND = "N" OR
003900              VENDOR-NUMBER = ZEROES.
004000
004100 INIT-VENDOR-RECORD.
004200     MOVE SPACE TO VENDOR-RECORD.
004300     MOVE ZEROES TO VENDOR-NUMBER.
004400
004500 ENTER-VENDOR-NUMBER.
004600     DISPLAY " ".
004700     DISPLAY "ENTER VENDOR NUMBER OF THE VENDOR" .
004800     DISPLAY "TO ADD (1-99999)".
004900     DISPLAY "ENTER 0 TO STOP ENTRY".
005000     ACCEPT VENDOR-NUMBER-FIELD.
005100*OR  ACCEPT VENDOR-NUMBER-FIELD WITH CONVERSION.
005200
005300     MOVE VENDOR-NUMBER-FIELD TO VENDOR-NUMBER.
005400
005500 FIND-NEW-VENDOR-RECORD.
005600     PERFORM READ-VENDOR-RECORD.
005700     IF RECORD-FOUND = "Y"
005800         DISPLAY "RECORD ALREADY ON FILE"
```

```
005900          PERFORM ENTER-VENDOR-NUMBER.
006000
006100 READ-VENDOR-RECORD.
006200      MOVE "Y" TO RECORD-FOUND.
006300      READ VENDOR-FILE RECORD
006400        INVALID KEY
006500            MOVE "N" TO RECORD-FOUND.
006600
006700
006800 ADD-RECORDS.
006900      PERFORM ENTER-REMAINING-FIELDS.
007000      PERFORM WRITE-VENDOR-RECORD.
007100      PERFORM GET-NEW-VENDOR-NUMBER.
007200
007300 WRITE-VENDOR-RECORD.
007400      WRITE VENDOR-RECORD
007500          INVALID KEY
007600          DISPLAY "RECORD ALREADY ON FILE".
007700
007800 ENTER-REMAINING-FIELDS.
007900      PERFORM ENTER-VENDOR-NAME.
008000      PERFORM ENTER-VENDOR-ADDRESS-1.
008100      PERFORM ENTER-VENDOR-ADDRESS-2.
008200      PERFORM ENTER-VENDOR-CITY.
008300      PERFORM ENTER-VENDOR-STATE.
008400      PERFORM ENTER-VENDOR-ZIP.
008500      PERFORM ENTER-VENDOR-CONTACT.
008600      PERFORM ENTER-VENDOR-PHONE.
008700
008800 ENTER-VENDOR-NAME.
008900      DISPLAY "ENTER VENDOR NAME".
009000      ACCEPT VENDOR-NAME.
009100
009200 ENTER-VENDOR-ADDRESS-1.
009300      DISPLAY "ENTER VENDOR ADDRESS-1".
009400      ACCEPT VENDOR-ADDRESS-1.
009500
009600 ENTER-VENDOR-ADDRESS-2.
009700      DISPLAY "ENTER VENDOR ADDRESS-2".
009800      ACCEPT VENDOR-ADDRESS-2.
009900
010000 ENTER-VENDOR-CITY.
010100      DISPLAY "ENTER VENDOR CITY".
010200      ACCEPT VENDOR-CITY.
010300
010400 ENTER-VENDOR-STATE.
010500      DISPLAY "ENTER VENDOR STATE".
010600      ACCEPT VENDOR-STATE.
010700
010800 ENTER-VENDOR-ZIP.
010900      DISPLAY "ENTER VENDOR ZIP".
011000      ACCEPT VENDOR-ZIP.
011100
011200 ENTER-VENDOR-CONTACT.
011300      DISPLAY "ENTER VENDOR CONTACT".
```

13

continues

Listing 13.4. continued

```
011400      ACCEPT VENDOR-CONTACT.
011500
011600 ENTER-VENDOR-PHONE.
011700      DISPLAY "ENTER VENDOR PHONE".
011800      ACCEPT VENDOR-PHONE.
011900
```

The following is the output:

```
ENTER VENDOR NUMBER OF THE
VENDOR TO ADD (1-99999)
ENTER 0 TO STOP ENTRY
00002
RECORD ALREADY ON FILE
ENTER VENDOR NUMBER OF THE
VENDOR TO ADD (1-99999)
ENTER 0 TO STOP ENTRY
```

ANALYSIS At line 003300, the GET-NEW-VENDOR-NUMBER routine has been modified to include testing for an existing record. The FIND-NEW-VENDOR-RECORD logic at lines 005500 through 005900 is the reverse of the FIND-VENDOR-RECORD logic used in vndchg01.cbl, vnddel01.cbl, and vndinq01.cbl, and it produces an error message when a record is found, rather than when a record is not found. Compare GET-NEW-VENDOR-NUMBER and GET-NEW-VENDOR-RECORD in vndadd01.cbl with GET-VENDOR-RECORD and FIND-VENDOR-RECORD in vnddel01.cbl or vndinq01.cbl.

Code, compile, and run vndadd01.cbl; then enter a vendor number that is already on file. You are warned about the record-on-file condition immediately.

Printing Records in an Indexed File

The complete set of programs for a data file includes add, change, delete, inquire (or look up), possibly a display program such as vnddsp01.cbl, and a printing program that allows you to report on the contents of the file.

You have already written the printing program, but you might not know it yet. The display program, vnddsp01.cbl, was designed as a program to print records to the screen, as if the screen were a scrolling printer.

Perform a little minor surgery on vnddsp01.cbl and you have the printing program vndrpt01.cbl, shown in Listing 13.5.

TYPE **Listing 13.5. A report program for the vendor file.**

```
000100 IDENTIFICATION DIVISION.
000200 PROGRAM-ID. VNDRPT01.
000300*--------------------------------
000400* Report on the Vendor File.
000500*--------------------------------
000600 ENVIRONMENT DIVISION.
000700 INPUT-OUTPUT SECTION.
000800 FILE-CONTROL.
000900
001000     COPY "SLVND01.CBL".
001100
001200     SELECT PRINTER-FILE
001300         ASSIGN TO PRINTER
001400         ORGANIZATION IS LINE SEQUENTIAL.
001500
001600 DATA DIVISION.
001700 FILE SECTION.
001800
001900     COPY "FDVND02.CBL".
002000
002100 FD  PRINTER-FILE
002200     LABEL RECORDS ARE OMITTED.
002300 01  PRINTER-RECORD          PIC X(80).
002400
002500 WORKING-STORAGE SECTION.
002600
002700 01  DETAIL-LINE.
002800     05  PRINT-NUMBER    PIC 9(5).
002900     05  FILLER          PIC X     VALUE SPACE.
003000     05  PRINT-NAME      PIC X(30).
003100     05  FILLER          PIC X     VALUE SPACE.
003200     05  PRINT-CONTACT   PIC X(30).
003300
003400 01  CITY-STATE-DETAIL.
003500     05  PRINT-CITY      PIC X(20).
003600     05  FILLER          PIC X VALUE SPACE.
003700     05  PRINT-STATE     PIC X(2).
003800
003900 01  COLUMN-LINE.
004000     05  FILLER          PIC X(2)  VALUE "NO".
004100     05  FILLER          PIC X(4)  VALUE SPACE.
004200     05  FILLER          PIC X(12) VALUE "NAME-ADDRESS".
004300     05  FILLER          PIC X(19) VALUE SPACE.
004400     05  FILLER          PIC X(17) VALUE "CONTACT-PHONE-ZIP".
004500
004600 01  TITLE-LINE.
004700     05  FILLER          PIC X(25) VALUE SPACE.
004800     05  FILLER          PIC X(11)
004900         VALUE "VENDOR LIST".
005000     05  FILLER          PIC X(15) VALUE SPACE.
005100     05  FILLER          PIC X(5) VALUE "PAGE:".
```

continues

Listing 13.5. continued

```
005200      05  FILLER             PIC X(1) VALUE SPACE.
005300      05  PRINT-PAGE-NUMBER PIC ZZZZ9.
005400
005500 77  FILE-AT-END          PIC X.
005600 77  LINE-COUNT           PIC 999 VALUE ZERO.
005700 77  PAGE-NUMBER          PIC 99999 VALUE ZERO.
005800 77  MAXIMUM-LINES        PIC 999 VALUE 55.
005900
006000 PROCEDURE DIVISION.
006100 PROGRAM-BEGIN.
006200
006300      PERFORM OPENING-PROCEDURE.
006400      MOVE ZEROES TO LINE-COUNT
006500                     PAGE-NUMBER.
006600
006700      PERFORM START-NEW-PAGE.
006800
006900      MOVE "N" TO FILE-AT-END.
007000      PERFORM READ-NEXT-RECORD.
007100      IF FILE-AT-END = "Y"
007200          MOVE "NO RECORDS FOUND" TO PRINTER-RECORD
007300          PERFORM WRITE-TO-PRINTER
007400      ELSE
007500          PERFORM PRINT-VENDOR-FIELDS
007600              UNTIL FILE-AT-END = "Y".
007700
007800      PERFORM CLOSING-PROCEDURE.
007900
008000 PROGRAM-DONE.
008100      STOP RUN.
008200
008300 OPENING-PROCEDURE.
008400      OPEN I-O VENDOR-FILE.
008500      OPEN OUTPUT PRINTER-FILE.
008600
008700 CLOSING-PROCEDURE.
008800      CLOSE VENDOR-FILE.
008900      PERFORM END-LAST-PAGE.
009000      CLOSE PRINTER-FILE.
009100
009200 PRINT-VENDOR-FIELDS.
009300      IF LINE-COUNT > MAXIMUM-LINES
009400          PERFORM START-NEXT-PAGE.
009500      PERFORM PRINT-THE-RECORD.
009600      PERFORM READ-NEXT-RECORD.
009700
009800 PRINT-THE-RECORD.
009900      PERFORM PRINT-LINE-1.
010000      PERFORM PRINT-LINE-2.
010100      PERFORM PRINT-LINE-3.
010200      PERFORM PRINT-LINE-4.
010300      PERFORM LINE-FEED.
010400
010500 PRINT-LINE-1.
```

13

```
010600        MOVE SPACE TO DETAIL-LINE.
010700        MOVE VENDOR-NUMBER TO PRINT-NUMBER.
010800        MOVE VENDOR-NAME TO PRINT-NAME.
010900        MOVE VENDOR-CONTACT TO PRINT-CONTACT.
011000        MOVE DETAIL-LINE TO PRINTER-RECORD.
011100        PERFORM WRITE-TO-PRINTER.
011200
011300 PRINT-LINE-2.
011400        MOVE SPACE TO DETAIL-LINE.
011500        MOVE VENDOR-ADDRESS-1 TO PRINT-NAME.
011600        MOVE VENDOR-PHONE TO PRINT-CONTACT.
011700        MOVE DETAIL-LINE TO PRINTER-RECORD.
011800        PERFORM WRITE-TO-PRINTER.
011900
012000 PRINT-LINE-3.
012100        MOVE SPACE TO DETAIL-LINE.
012200        MOVE VENDOR-ADDRESS-2 TO PRINT-NAME.
012300        IF VENDOR-ADDRESS-2 NOT = SPACE
012400            MOVE DETAIL-LINE TO PRINTER-RECORD
012500            PERFORM WRITE-TO-PRINTER.
012600
012700 PRINT-LINE-4.
012800        MOVE SPACE TO DETAIL-LINE.
012900        MOVE VENDOR-CITY TO PRINT-CITY.
013000        MOVE VENDOR-STATE TO PRINT-STATE.
013100        MOVE CITY-STATE-DETAIL TO PRINT-NAME.
013200        MOVE VENDOR-ZIP TO PRINT-CONTACT.
013300        MOVE DETAIL-LINE TO PRINTER-RECORD.
013400        PERFORM WRITE-TO-PRINTER.
013500
013600 READ-NEXT-RECORD.
013700        READ VENDOR-FILE NEXT RECORD
013800            AT END MOVE "Y" TO FILE-AT-END.
013900
014000 WRITE-TO-PRINTER.
014100        WRITE PRINTER-RECORD BEFORE ADVANCING 1.
014200        ADD 1 TO LINE-COUNT.
014300
014400 LINE-FEED.
014500        MOVE SPACE TO PRINTER-RECORD.
014600        PERFORM WRITE-TO-PRINTER.
014700
014800 START-NEXT-PAGE.
014900
015000        PERFORM END-LAST-PAGE.
015100        PERFORM START-NEW-PAGE.
015200
015300 START-NEW-PAGE.
015400        ADD 1 TO PAGE-NUMBER.
015500        MOVE PAGE-NUMBER TO PRINT-PAGE-NUMBER.
015600        MOVE TITLE-LINE TO PRINTER-RECORD.
015700        PERFORM WRITE-TO-PRINTER.
015800        PERFORM LINE-FEED.
015900        MOVE COLUMN-LINE TO PRINTER-RECORD.
016000        PERFORM WRITE-TO-PRINTER.
```

continues

Listing 13.5. continued

```
016100      PERFORM LINE-FEED.
016200
016300 END-LAST-PAGE.
016400      PERFORM FORM-FEED.
016500      MOVE ZERO TO LINE-COUNT.
016600
016700 FORM-FEED.
016800      MOVE SPACE TO PRINTER-RECORD.
016900      WRITE PRINTER-RECORD BEFORE ADVANCING PAGE.
017000
```

This output illustrates a sample page of the report created by `vndrpt01.cbl`:

```
VENDOR LIST                  PAGE:     1
NO    NAME-ADDRESS                      CONTACT-PHONE-ZIP
00001 AERIAL SIGNS                      HENRIETTA MARKSON
BURBANK AIRPORT               (818) 555-6066
HANGAR 405
BURBANK              CA       90046
00002 ABC PRINTING                      CHARLES JOHANSSEN
1624 FOOTHILL BLVD            (818) 555-4321
SUITE 34
LOS ANGELES          CA       91042
00003 CHARLES SMITH AND SONS            MARTHA HARRISON
1435 SOUTH STREET            (213) 555-4432
LOS ANGELES          CA       90064
00014 RANIER GRAPHICS                   JULIA SIMPSON
4433 WASHINGTOn ST           (213) 555-6789
LOS ANGELES          CA       90032
01176 ABERCROMBIE AND OTHERS
1234 45TH ST.                (213) 555-6543
SUITE 17
LOS ANGELES          CA       92345
```

ANALYSIS You can create this program by copying `vnddsp01.cbl` and then modifying it. Compare this new program to `vnddsp01.cbl`:

☐ At lines `001200` to `001400` and `002100` to `002300`, the physical and logical descriptions, respectively, are added for the printer file.

☐ The routine `WRITE-DISPLAY-RECORD` is changed to `WRITE-TO-PRINTER` at line `014000`. This routine writes a printer record instead of displaying a `DISPLAY-RECORD`.

☐ At line `016300`, the `END-LAST-PAGE` routine is changed so that it performs a form feed, and the `PRESS-ENTER` routine is replaced with `FORM-FEED` at line `016700`.

13

☐ At line 005800, the MAXIMUM-LINES value is set to 55 instead of 15, and the opening and closing procedures (lines 008300 through 009000) open and close the printer file, as well as performing a final form feed before closing the printer file.

Code, compile, and run this program to get a printed report of the information in your vendor file.

Summary

The basics of keeping indexed files updated include deleting, displaying, adding, and printing records. Today, you learned the following:

☐ Records are deleted by using the DELETE command. The DELETE command uses INVALID KEY to trap file-error conditions.

☐ You must have successfully read a record before you can delete it. Some larger systems might require a READ WITH LOCK or a READ WITH HOLD.

☐ Programs that allow you to add, change, look up, or delete records in a file usually are called maintenance programs.

☐ Change, inquire (look up), and delete programs are usually similar in logic layout.

Q&A

Q **In Listing 13.4, vndadd01.cbl, at lines 007300 through 007700, the WRITE-VENDOR-RECORD paragraph includes a RECORD ALREADY ON FILE message if an attempt is made to write a record that fails. Before this write occurs, the program already has read the record and established that it is not there in READ-VENDOR-RECORD at lines 006100 through 006500. Why does this extra check exist?**

A It is good practice when writing COBOL programs to assume that other users will be accessing the same files. Most COBOL programs run on large multi-user systems. In the vndadd01.cbl program, it is possible for a user to enter a vendor number, establish that the record is not on file, start adding the new fields to the file, and then go on a coffee break before pressing Enter on the final field, causing the new record to be written. If someone adds a record with that primary key in the meantime, the user is in for a surprise upon returning. Rather than let the program crash at this point, an effort is made to trap the file-error condition with a message.

13

Workshop

Quiz

1. Which modes in maintenance programs are usually similar?

    a. Add and change.

    b. Add and delete.

    c. Change, inquire (look up), and delete.

    d. Change, inquire (look up), and print.

2. Describe the similarities between change, inquire, and delete modes.

Exercise

Copy vnddsp01.cbl to vnddsp02.cbl; then modify it so that it uses COPY `"SLVND01.CBL"` and COPY `"FDVND02.CBL"`.

Day 14

A Review of Indexed Files

You have studied indexed files rather intensively for the last three days, and it's important that you review these concepts before you tackle anything new. Today, you take a look at a single program that combines all the maintenance modes—Add, Change, Inquire (Look Up) and Delete—in one program. You also learn more about the following topics:

- ☐ Defining an indexed file
- ☐ Opening and closing indexed files
- ☐ Reading through a file
- ☐ Adding records to indexed files
- ☐ Looking up records in indexed files
- ☐ Changing records in indexed files
- ☐ Deleting records in indexed files
- ☐ Combined maintenance

Defining an Indexed File

An indexed file is defined both logically and physically. The logical description is an FD in the
FILE SECTION of the DATA DIVISION, as shown in Listing 14.1.

TYPE   **Listing 14.1. A logical file description.**

```
001600 DATA DIVISION.
001700 FILE SECTION.
001800
001900 FD   VENDOR-FILE
002000      LABEL RECORDS ARE STANDARD.
002100 01   VENDOR-RECORD.
002200      05   VENDOR-NUMBER                  PIC 9(5).
002300      05   VENDOR-NAME                    PIC X(30).
002400      05   VENDOR-ADDRESS-1               PIC X(30).
002500      05   VENDOR-ADDRESS-2               PIC X(30).
002600      05   VENDOR-CITY                    PIC X(20).
002700      05   VENDOR-STATE                   PIC X(2).
002800      05   VENDOR-ZIP                     PIC X(10).
002900      05   VENDOR-CONTACT                 PIC X(30).
003000      05   VENDOR-PHONE                   PIC X(15).
```

ANALYSIS   The physical description is the SELECT statement in the FILE-CONTROL paragraph of
the INPUT-OUTPUT SECTION of the ENVIRONMENT DIVISION, as shown in Listing 14.2.
At lines 001000 and 001100, the logical VENDOR-FILE is associated with a physical file named
"VENDOR" on the computer hard disk or other storage device. This file will have the physical
name "VENDOR", "VENDOR.DAT", or something similar, on the disk or tape. At line 001200, the
file organization is specified to be indexed. At line 001300, a field in the logical description
of the file (in Listing 14.1) is named as the primary index or primary key to the file. The access
mode is made dynamic at line 001400.

TYPE   **Listing 14.2. Physical description of an indexed file.**

```
000600 ENVIRONMENT DIVISION.
000700 INPUT-OUTPUT SECTION.
000800 FILE-CONTROL.
000900
001000     SELECT VENDOR-FILE
001100         ASSIGN TO "VENDOR"
001200         ORGANIZATION IS INDEXED
001300         RECORD KEY IS VENDOR-NUMBER
001400         ACCESS MODE IS DYNAMIC.
001500
```

Remember that any part of a COBOL program can be written in a separate file and included in the main file by using a COPY statement in the main file. Although you can do this with any part of a program, it is common to do it with the SELECT and FD of a file. By using a COPY statement in any program that uses that file, you can ensure that each program has defined the file in the same way. An example is shown in Listing 14.3.

TYPE **Listing 14.3. Using COPY files.**

```
000600 ENVIRONMENT DIVISION.
000700 INPUT-OUTPUT SECTION.
000800 FILE-CONTROL.
000900
001000     COPY "SLVND01.CBL".
001100
001200 DATA DIVISION.
001300 FILE SECTION.
001400
001500     COPY "FDVND01.CBL".
001600
```

Opening and Closing Indexed Files

You open an indexed file by specifying the open mode and the filename. Output mode creates a new file; I/O mode allows reading and writing access to an existing file. You close a file by naming the file after a CLOSE command. Listings 14.4 and 14.5 show examples of opening and closing files.

TYPE **Listing 14.4. Opening output and closing it.**

```
003500 PROGRAM-BEGIN.
003600     OPEN OUTPUT VENDOR-FILE.
003700     CLOSE VENDOR-FILE.
```

TYPE **Listing 14.5. Opening I/O and closing it.**

```
003400 PROCEDURE DIVISION.
003500 PROGRAM-BEGIN.
003600     OPEN I-O VENDOR-FILE.
003700     PERFORM MAIN-PROCESS.
003800     CLOSE VENDOR-FILE.
```

14

Reading Through a File

When an indexed file is opened in I/O or input mode, the file is usually set up so that a READ NEXT on the file retrieves the record with the lowest primary key value. In Listing 14.6, the READ NEXT action either reads the record with the primary key of the lowest value, or it produces an error if no records are in the file.

TYPE

Listing 14.6. Reading the record with the lowest primary key.

```
003600     OPEN I-O VENDOR-FILE.
003700     READ VENDOR-FILE NEXT RECORD.
```

A READ NEXT should use the AT END condition to trap a file error condition at the end of the file, as shown in Listing 14.7.

TYPE   ### Listing 14.7. Trapping AT END.

```
003600 READ-NEXT-VENDOR-RECORD.
003700     READ VENDOR-FILE NEXT RECORD
003800        AT END MOVE "Y" TO END-OF-FILE.
```

Adding Records to Indexed Files

Records are added to the file by loading the values in the record and using a WRITE command followed by the name of the record. The INVALID KEY condition should be used to trap write errors (as shown in Listing 14.8). These can be caused by trying to write a record with a primary key value that is the same as a record already in the file. Each record in an indexed file must have a unique primary key.

TYPE   ### Listing 14.8. Writing a new record.

```
005100 WRITE-VENDOR-RECORD.
005200     WRITE VENDOR-RECORD
005300        INVALID KEY
005400        DISPLAY "RECORD ALREADY ON FILE".
```

14

Looking Up Records in Indexed Files

A record can be read from an indexed file by moving a value to the field that is the primary key of the file and using READ (as shown in Listing 14.9). The INVALID KEY condition should be used to trap file error conditions that happen when a record does not exist that matches the value requested in the primary key field.

TYPE **Listing 14.9. Using READ to retrieve vendor record.**

```
019800      PERFORM ENTER-VENDOR-NUMBER.
019900      MOVE "Y" TO RECORD-FOUND.
020000      READ VENDOR-FILE RECORD
020100        INVALID KEY
020200          MOVE "N" TO RECORD-FOUND.
020300
```

Changing Records in Indexed Files

You can change a record in an indexed file by reading the original record, loading the new values into the fields of the record, and then using a REWRITE command followed by the name of the record (as shown in Listing 14.10). The primary key of the record cannot be changed using this method, but any other field in the record can be changed.

TYPE **Listing 14.10. Using REWRITE to change a record.**

```
019200      PERFORM ENTER-VENDOR-NUMBER.
019300      PERFORM READ-VENDOR-RECORD.
019400      IF RECORD-FOUND = "Y"
019500        PERFORM LOAD-NEW-VENDOR-DATA
019600        PERFORM REWRITE-VENDOR-RECORD.
019700
019800  READ-VENDOR-RECORD.
019900      MOVE "Y" TO RECORD-FOUND.
020000      READ VENDOR-FILE RECORD
020100        INVALID KEY
020200          MOVE "N" TO RECORD-FOUND.
020300
020400  REWRITE-VENDOR-RECORD.
020500      REWRITE VENDOR-RECORD
020600          INVALID KEY
020700          DISPLAY "ERROR REWRITING VENDOR RECORD".
```

14

Deleting Records in Indexed Files

You can delete a record from an indexed file by reading the original record and then using the DELETE command, followed by the name of the file (as shown in Listing 14.11).

TYPE **Listing 14.11. Using DELETE to remove a record.**

```
019300        PERFORM ENTER-VENDOR-NUMBER.
019400        PERFORM READ-VENDOR-RECORD.
019500        IF RECORD-FOUND = "Y"
019600            PERFORM DELETE-VENDOR-RECORD.
019700
019800 READ-VENDOR-RECORD.
019900     MOVE "Y" TO RECORD-FOUND.
020000     READ VENDOR-FILE RECORD
020100        INVALID KEY
020200            MOVE "N" TO RECORD-FOUND.
020300
020400 DELETE-VENDOR-RECORD.
020500     DELETE VENDOR-FILE RECORD
020600         INVALID KEY
020700         DISPLAY "ERROR DELETING VENDOR RECORD".
```

It is confusing that some file operations are performed using the filename and some are performed using the record name. Two examples of these statements appear at lines 020000 and 020500 in Listing 14.10. Just remember that WRITE and REWRITE use the record name; all other file operations, including those you have not yet learned, use the filename.

Some COBOL programmers try to remember this with the rule "Read a file, write a record." This rule is a little short on detail because it doesn't mention OPEN, CLOSE, DELETE, and REWRITE. It is better to remember, "Write and rewrite a record, do everything else to a file."

Combined Maintenance

All of the four maintenance programs share common elements, and it is possible to combine the four modes into one program and take advantage of this common code.

Whether or not you do this is a matter for system design consideration. In some systems, all users have access to Inquire (Look Up) mode, several might have access to Add or Change mode, and possibly only a few have access to Delete mode. Security is much easier to control when the four modes are separate. Less coding is involved when the four modes are combined. Listing 14.12 combines all four programs into one maintenance program, with a menu for selecting the mode to be used while running the program.

14

TYPE   **Listing 14.12. All modes in one program.**

```
000100 IDENTIFICATION DIVISION.
000200 PROGRAM-ID. VNDMNT01.
000300*--------------------------------
000400* Add, Change, Inquire, and Delete
000500* for the Vendor File.
000600*--------------------------------
000700 ENVIRONMENT DIVISION.
000800 INPUT-OUTPUT SECTION.
000900 FILE-CONTROL.
001000
001100     COPY "SLVND01.CBL".
001200
001300 DATA DIVISION.
001400 FILE SECTION.
001500
001600     COPY "FDVND02.CBL".
001700
001800 WORKING-STORAGE SECTION.
001900
002000 77  MENU-PICK                PIC 9.
002100     88  MENU-PICK-IS-VALID    VALUES 0 THRU 4.
002200
002300 77  THE-MODE                 PIC X(7).
002400 77  WHICH-FIELD              PIC 9.
002500 77  OK-TO-DELETE             PIC X.
002600 77  RECORD-FOUND             PIC X.
002700 77  VENDOR-NUMBER-FIELD      PIC Z(5).
002800
002900 PROCEDURE DIVISION.
003000 PROGRAM-BEGIN.
003100     PERFORM OPENING-PROCEDURE.
003200     PERFORM MAIN-PROCESS.
003300     PERFORM CLOSING-PROCEDURE.
003400
003500 PROGRAM-DONE.
003600     STOP RUN.
003700
003800 OPENING-PROCEDURE.
003900     OPEN I-O VENDOR-FILE.
004000
004100 CLOSING-PROCEDURE.
004200     CLOSE VENDOR-FILE.
004300
004400
004500 MAIN-PROCESS.
004600     PERFORM GET-MENU-PICK.
004700     PERFORM MAINTAIN-THE-FILE
004800         UNTIL MENU-PICK = 0.
004900
005000*--------------------------------
005100* MENU
005200*--------------------------------
005300 GET-MENU-PICK.
005400     PERFORM DISPLAY-THE-MENU.
```

continues

14

Listing 14.12. continued

```
005500        PERFORM GET-THE-PICK.
005600        PERFORM MENU-RETRY
005700            UNTIL MENU-PICK-IS-VALID.
005800
005900 DISPLAY-THE-MENU.
006000        PERFORM CLEAR-SCREEN.
006100        DISPLAY "    PLEASE SELECT:".
006200        DISPLAY " ".
006300        DISPLAY "            1.  ADD RECORDS".
006400        DISPLAY "            2.  CHANGE A RECORD".
006500        DISPLAY "            3.  LOOK UP A RECORD".
006600        DISPLAY "            4.  DELETE A RECORD".
006700        DISPLAY " ".
006800        DISPLAY "            0.  EXIT".
006900        PERFORM SCROLL-LINE 8 TIMES.
007000
007100 GET-THE-PICK.
007200        DISPLAY "YOUR CHOICE (0-4)?".
007300        ACCEPT MENU-PICK.
007400 MENU-RETRY.
007500        DISPLAY "INVALID SELECTION - PLEASE RE-TRY.".
007600        PERFORM GET-THE-PICK.
007700 CLEAR-SCREEN.
007800        PERFORM SCROLL-LINE 25 TIMES.
007900
008000 SCROLL-LINE.
008100        DISPLAY " ".
008200
008300 MAINTAIN-THE-FILE.
008400        PERFORM DO-THE-PICK.
008500        PERFORM GET-MENU-PICK.
008600
008700 DO-THE-PICK.
008800        IF MENU-PICK = 1
008900            PERFORM ADD-MODE
009000        ELSE
009100        IF MENU-PICK = 2
009200            PERFORM CHANGE-MODE
009300        ELSE
009400        IF MENU-PICK = 3
009500            PERFORM INQUIRE-MODE
009600        ELSE
009700        IF MENU-PICK = 4
009800            PERFORM DELETE-MODE.
009900
010000*--------------------------------
010100* ADD
010200*--------------------------------
010300 ADD-MODE.
010400        MOVE "ADD" TO THE-MODE.
010500        PERFORM GET-NEW-VENDOR-NUMBER.
010600        PERFORM ADD-RECORDS
010700            UNTIL VENDOR-NUMBER = ZEROES.
010800
```

14

```
010900 GET-NEW-VENDOR-NUMBER.
011000     PERFORM INIT-VENDOR-RECORD.
011100     PERFORM ENTER-VENDOR-NUMBER.
011200     MOVE "Y" TO RECORD-FOUND.
011300     PERFORM FIND-NEW-VENDOR-RECORD
011400         UNTIL RECORD-FOUND = "N" OR
011500             VENDOR-NUMBER = ZEROES.
011600
011700 FIND-NEW-VENDOR-RECORD.
011800     PERFORM READ-VENDOR-RECORD.
011900     IF RECORD-FOUND = "Y"
012000         DISPLAY "RECORD ALREADY ON FILE"
012100         PERFORM ENTER-VENDOR-NUMBER.
012200
012300 ADD-RECORDS.
012400     PERFORM ENTER-REMAINING-FIELDS.
012500     PERFORM WRITE-VENDOR-RECORD.
012600     PERFORM GET-NEW-VENDOR-NUMBER.
012700
012800 ENTER-REMAINING-FIELDS.
012900     PERFORM ENTER-VENDOR-NAME.
013000     PERFORM ENTER-VENDOR-ADDRESS-1.
013100     PERFORM ENTER-VENDOR-ADDRESS-2.
013200     PERFORM ENTER-VENDOR-CITY.
013300     PERFORM ENTER-VENDOR-STATE.
013400     PERFORM ENTER-VENDOR-ZIP.
013500     PERFORM ENTER-VENDOR-CONTACT.
013600     PERFORM ENTER-VENDOR-PHONE.
013700
013800*-------------------------------
013900* CHANGE
014000*-------------------------------
014100 CHANGE-MODE.
014200     MOVE "CHANGE" TO THE-MODE.
014300     PERFORM GET-VENDOR-RECORD.
014400     PERFORM CHANGE-RECORDS
014500         UNTIL VENDOR-NUMBER = ZEROES.
014600
014700 CHANGE-RECORDS.
014800     PERFORM GET-FIELD-TO-CHANGE.
014900     PERFORM CHANGE-ONE-FIELD
015000         UNTIL WHICH-FIELD = ZERO.
015100     PERFORM GET-VENDOR-RECORD.
015200
015300 GET-FIELD-TO-CHANGE.
015400     PERFORM DISPLAY-ALL-FIELDS.
015500     PERFORM ASK-WHICH-FIELD.
015600
015700 ASK-WHICH-FIELD.
015800     DISPLAY "ENTER THE NUMBER OF THE FIELD".
015900     DISPLAY "TO CHANGE (1-8) OR 0 TO EXIT".
016000     ACCEPT WHICH-FIELD.
016100     IF WHICH-FIELD > 8
016200         DISPLAY "INVALID ENTRY".
016300
016400 CHANGE-ONE-FIELD.
016500     PERFORM CHANGE-THIS-FIELD.
```

14

continues

Listing 14.12. continued

```
016600      PERFORM GET-FIELD-TO-CHANGE.
016700
016800 CHANGE-THIS-FIELD.
016900      IF WHICH-FIELD = 1
017000          PERFORM ENTER-VENDOR-NAME.
017100      IF WHICH-FIELD = 2
017200          PERFORM ENTER-VENDOR-ADDRESS-1.
017300      IF WHICH-FIELD = 3
017400          PERFORM ENTER-VENDOR-ADDRESS-2.
017500      IF WHICH-FIELD = 4
017600          PERFORM ENTER-VENDOR-CITY.
017700      IF WHICH-FIELD = 5
017800          PERFORM ENTER-VENDOR-STATE.
017900      IF WHICH-FIELD = 6
018000          PERFORM ENTER-VENDOR-ZIP.
018100      IF WHICH-FIELD = 7
018200          PERFORM ENTER-VENDOR-CONTACT.
018300      IF WHICH-FIELD = 8
018400          PERFORM ENTER-VENDOR-PHONE.
018500
018600      PERFORM REWRITE-VENDOR-RECORD.
018700
018800*------------------------------
018900* INQUIRE
019000*------------------------------
019100 INQUIRE-MODE.
019200      MOVE "DISPLAY" TO THE-MODE.
019300      PERFORM GET-VENDOR-RECORD.
019400      PERFORM INQUIRE-RECORDS
019500          UNTIL VENDOR-NUMBER = ZEROES.
019600
019700 INQUIRE-RECORDS.
019800      PERFORM DISPLAY-ALL-FIELDS.
019900      PERFORM GET-VENDOR-RECORD.
020000
020100*------------------------------
020200* DELETE
020300*------------------------------
020400 DELETE-MODE.
020500      MOVE "DELETE" TO THE-MODE.
020600      PERFORM GET-VENDOR-RECORD.
020700      PERFORM DELETE-RECORDS
020800          UNTIL VENDOR-NUMBER = ZEROES.
020900
021000 DELETE-RECORDS.
021100      PERFORM DISPLAY-ALL-FIELDS.
021200      MOVE "X" TO OK-TO-DELETE.
021300
021400      PERFORM ASK-TO-DELETE
021500          UNTIL OK-TO-DELETE = "Y" OR "N".
021600
021700      IF OK-TO-DELETE = "Y"
021800          PERFORM DELETE-VENDOR-RECORD.
021900
```

```
022000      PERFORM GET-VENDOR-RECORD.
022100
022200 ASK-TO-DELETE.
022300      DISPLAY "DELETE THIS RECORD (Y/N)?".
022400      ACCEPT OK-TO-DELETE.
022500      IF OK-TO-DELETE = "y"
022600          MOVE "Y" TO OK-TO-DELETE.
022700      IF OK-TO-DELETE = "n"
022800          MOVE "N" TO OK-TO-DELETE.
022900      IF OK-TO-DELETE NOT = "Y" AND
023000          OK-TO-DELETE NOT = "N"
023100          DISPLAY "YOU MUST ENTER YES OR NO".
023200
023300*-------------------------------
023400* Routines shared by all modes
023500*-------------------------------
023600 INIT-VENDOR-RECORD.
023700      MOVE SPACE TO VENDOR-RECORD.
023800      MOVE ZEROES TO VENDOR-NUMBER.
023900
024000 ENTER-VENDOR-NUMBER.
024100      DISPLAY " ".
024200      DISPLAY "ENTER VENDOR NUMBER OF THE VENDOR" .
024300      DISPLAY "TO " THE-MODE " (1-99999)".
024400      DISPLAY "ENTER 0 TO STOP ENTRY".
024500      ACCEPT VENDOR-NUMBER-FIELD.
024600*OR   ACCEPT VENDOR-NUMBER-FIELD WITH CONVERSION.
024700
024800      MOVE VENDOR-NUMBER-FIELD TO VENDOR-NUMBER.
024900
025000 GET-VENDOR-RECORD.
025100      PERFORM INIT-VENDOR-RECORD.
025200      PERFORM ENTER-VENDOR-NUMBER.
025300      MOVE "N" TO RECORD-FOUND.
025400      PERFORM FIND-VENDOR-RECORD
025500          UNTIL RECORD-FOUND = "Y" OR
025600                VENDOR-NUMBER = ZEROES.
025700
025800*-------------------------------
025900* Routines shared Add and Change
026000*-------------------------------
026100 FIND-VENDOR-RECORD.
026200      PERFORM READ-VENDOR-RECORD.
026300      IF RECORD-FOUND = "N"
026400          DISPLAY "RECORD NOT FOUND"
026500          PERFORM ENTER-VENDOR-NUMBER.
026600
026700 ENTER-VENDOR-NAME.
026800      DISPLAY "ENTER VENDOR NAME".
026900      ACCEPT VENDOR-NAME.
027000
027100 ENTER-VENDOR-ADDRESS-1.
027200      DISPLAY "ENTER VENDOR ADDRESS-1".
027300      ACCEPT VENDOR-ADDRESS-1.
027400
027500 ENTER-VENDOR-ADDRESS-2.
027600      DISPLAY "ENTER VENDOR ADDRESS-2".
```

14

continues

Listing 14.12. continued

```
027700      ACCEPT VENDOR-ADDRESS-2.
027800
027900 ENTER-VENDOR-CITY.
028000      DISPLAY "ENTER VENDOR CITY".
028100      ACCEPT VENDOR-CITY.
028200
028300 ENTER-VENDOR-STATE.
028400      DISPLAY "ENTER VENDOR STATE".
028500      ACCEPT VENDOR-STATE.
028600
028700 ENTER-VENDOR-ZIP.
028800      DISPLAY "ENTER VENDOR ZIP".
028900      ACCEPT VENDOR-ZIP.
029000
029100 ENTER-VENDOR-CONTACT.
029200      DISPLAY "ENTER VENDOR CONTACT".
029300      ACCEPT VENDOR-CONTACT.
029400
029500 ENTER-VENDOR-PHONE.
029600      DISPLAY "ENTER VENDOR PHONE".
029700      ACCEPT VENDOR-PHONE.
029800
029900*-------------------------------
030000* Routines shared by Change,
030100* Inquire and Delete
030200*-------------------------------
030300 DISPLAY-ALL-FIELDS.
030400      DISPLAY " ".
030500      PERFORM DISPLAY-VENDOR-NUMBER.
030600      PERFORM DISPLAY-VENDOR-NAME.
030700      PERFORM DISPLAY-VENDOR-ADDRESS-1.
030800      PERFORM DISPLAY-VENDOR-ADDRESS-2.
030900      PERFORM DISPLAY-VENDOR-CITY.
031000      PERFORM DISPLAY-VENDOR-STATE.
031100      PERFORM DISPLAY-VENDOR-ZIP.
031200      PERFORM DISPLAY-VENDOR-CONTACT.
031300      PERFORM DISPLAY-VENDOR-PHONE.
031400      DISPLAY " ".
031500
031600 DISPLAY-VENDOR-NUMBER.
031700      DISPLAY "   VENDOR NUMBER: " VENDOR-NUMBER.
031800
031900 DISPLAY-VENDOR-NAME.
032000      DISPLAY "1. VENDOR NAME: " VENDOR-NAME.
032100
032200 DISPLAY-VENDOR-ADDRESS-1.
032300      DISPLAY "2. VENDOR ADDRESS-1: " VENDOR-ADDRESS-1.
032400
032500 DISPLAY-VENDOR-ADDRESS-2.
032600      DISPLAY "3. VENDOR ADDRESS-2: " VENDOR-ADDRESS-2.
032700
032800 DISPLAY-VENDOR-CITY.
032900      DISPLAY "4. VENDOR CITY: " VENDOR-CITY.
033000
```

14

```
033100 DISPLAY-VENDOR-STATE.
033200     DISPLAY "5. VENDOR STATE: " VENDOR-STATE.
033300
033400 DISPLAY-VENDOR-ZIP.
033500     DISPLAY "6. VENDOR ZIP: " VENDOR-ZIP.
033600
033700 DISPLAY-VENDOR-CONTACT.
033800     DISPLAY "7. VENDOR CONTACT: " VENDOR-CONTACT.
033900
034000 DISPLAY-VENDOR-PHONE.
034100     DISPLAY "8. VENDOR PHONE: " VENDOR-PHONE.
034200
034300*------------------------------
034400* File I-O Routines
034500*------------------------------
034600 READ-VENDOR-RECORD.
034700     MOVE "Y" TO RECORD-FOUND.
034800     READ VENDOR-FILE RECORD
034900       INVALID KEY
035000         MOVE "N" TO RECORD-FOUND.
035100
035200*or  READ VENDOR-FILE RECORD WITH LOCK
035300*       INVALID KEY
035400*         MOVE "N" TO RECORD-FOUND.
035500
035600*or  READ VENDOR-FILE RECORD WITH HOLD
035700*       INVALID KEY
035800*         MOVE "N" TO RECORD-FOUND.
035900
036000 WRITE-VENDOR-RECORD.
036100     WRITE VENDOR-RECORD
036200         INVALID KEY
036300         DISPLAY "RECORD ALREADY ON FILE".
036400
036500 REWRITE-VENDOR-RECORD.
036600     REWRITE VENDOR-RECORD
036700         INVALID KEY
036800         DISPLAY "ERROR REWRITING VENDOR RECORD".
036900
037000 DELETE-VENDOR-RECORD.
037100     DELETE VENDOR-FILE RECORD
037200         INVALID KEY
037300         DISPLAY "ERROR DELETING VENDOR RECORD".
037400
```

The following menu output of vndmnt01.cbl asks the user to select an entry mode:

OUTPUT

```
PLEASE SELECT:
1.  ADD RECORDS
2.  CHANGE A RECORD
3.  LOOK UP A RECORD
4.  DELETE A RECORD
0.  EXIT
YOUR CHOICE (0-4)?
```

ANALYSIS The sections of the program have been moved around to separate the routines that are exclusive to the menu, or to Add, Change, Inquire, and Delete modes.

Other sections have been created to combine the routines that are shared by different modes. Each of these groups of code is commented. Two deliberate errors are in this collection. Two paragraphs are grouped under comments where they don't really belong. This is for the exercises at the end of the chapter. If you happen to spot them, you've got a jump on the exercise.

Even though this program is nearly 400 lines long, it is possible to break it into sections and understand these sections one piece at a time. A couple of changes have been made in Add mode, but overall, the combined program is the same as the code used in the separate programs.

One trick was used in ENTER-VENDOR-NUMBER at line 024000. In the original add, change, delete, and inquire programs, the prompt for the user to enter the vendor number is one of the following:

```
ENTER VENDOR NUMBER OF THE VENDOR
TO ADD (1-99999)
ENTER 0 TO STOP ENTRY

ENTER VENDOR NUMBER OF THE VENDOR
TO CHANGE (1-99999)
ENTER 0 TO STOP ENTRY

ENTER VENDOR NUMBER OF THE VENDOR
TO DISPLAY (1-99999)
ENTER 0 TO STOP ENTRY

ENTER VENDOR NUMBER OF THE VENDOR
TO DELETE (1-99999)
ENTER 0 TO STOP ENTRY
```

These prompts are identical except for the bold keyword.

In vndmnt01.cbl, the display logic has been changed to the code shown in Listing 14.13.

Listing 14.13. A new approach to the vendor number prompt.

TYPE

```
024200      DISPLAY "ENTER VENDOR NUMBER OF THE VENDOR" .
024300      DISPLAY "TO " THE-MODE " (1-99999)".
024400      DISPLAY "ENTER 0 TO STOP ENTRY".
```

ANALYSIS THE-MODE is filled in at the beginning of each mode at lines 010400, 014200, 019200, and 020500 with "ADD", "CHANGE", "DISPLAY", or "DELETE".

The GET-MENU-PICK logic starting at line 005300 displays the menu, asks the user for an entry, and then starts a processing loop if the user has entered an invalid entry. The processing loop consists of displaying an invalid entry message and then asking for another entry. Figure 14.1 illustrates this relationship.

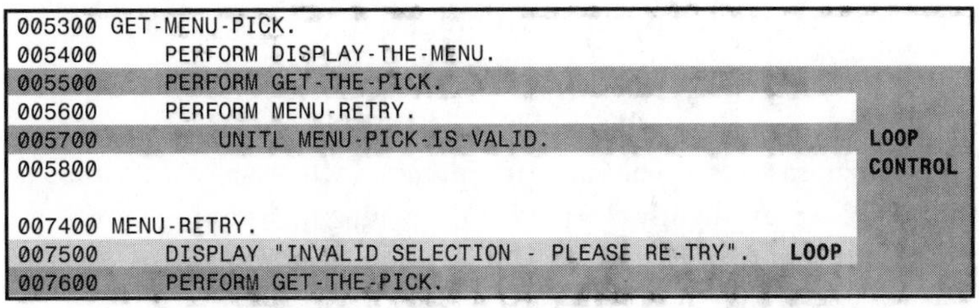

Figure 14.1.

The menu pick loop.

```
005300 GET-MENU-PICK.
005400     PERFORM DISPLAY-THE-MENU.
005500     PERFORM GET-THE-PICK.
005600     PERFORM MENU-RETRY.
005700         UNITL MENU-PICK-IS-VALID.              LOOP
005800                                                CONTROL

007400 MENU-RETRY.
007500     DISPLAY "INVALID SELECTION - PLEASE RE-TRY".  LOOP
007600     PERFORM GET-THE-PICK.
```

One other new coding technique is used in DO-THE-PICK at line 008700. This is the use of a series of IF ELSE combinations linked one to the other as shown in Listing 14.14 (extracted from vndmnt01.cbl).

TYPE **Listing 14.14. Multiple IF ELSE statements.**

```
008700 DO-THE-PICK.
008800     IF MENU-PICK = 1
008900         PERFORM ADD-MODE
009000     ELSE
009100     IF MENU-PICK = 2
009200         PERFORM CHANGE-MODE
009300     ELSE
009400     IF MENU-PICK = 3
009500         PERFORM INQUIRE-MODE
009600     ELSE
009700     IF MENU-PICK = 4
009800         PERFORM DELETE-MODE.
```

This is a series of IF ELSE tests nested inside one another and would be more properly represented with something similar to the code shown in Listing 14.15.

TYPE **Listing 14.15. Indented IF ELSE statements.**

```
008700 DO-THE-PICK.
008800     IF MENU-PICK = 1
008900         PERFORM ADD-RECORDS
009000     ELSE
009100         IF MENU-PICK = 2
009200             PERFORM CHANGE-RECORDS
009300         ELSE
009400             IF MENU-PICK = 3
009500                 PERFORM LOOK-UP-RECORDS
009600             ELSE
009700                 IF MENU-PICK = 4
009800                     PERFORM DELETE-RECORDS.
```

14

ANALYSIS   The first IF tests for a MENU-PICK of 1. If the user picks 1, line 008900 is executed. If 1 is not picked, the code below the ELSE at line 009000 is executed. This section of code starts immediately with another IF test at line 009100. If the MENU-PICK is 2, line 009200 is executed; otherwise, everything below the ELSE at line 009300 is executed. Again, this section of code starts with an IF at line 009400.

This particular method of testing for one of several possible values is very common in programs—especially in menu programs. It usually is written as shown in Listing 14.14, because it is slightly clearer that the paragraph is testing for one possible condition and then performing something based on that one condition. The full analysis of this program is left to you at the end of this chapter as an exercise.

Further information on IF ELSE is in order here. When an IF appears within an IF, it might not be obvious how this works. The inner IF is tested only if the outer IF is true. IF and IF ELSE commands can be nested inside one another. Use this construction to create nested IF statements:

```
IF condition
    do something
    IF condition
        do something
```

In the construction above, the first IF condition is tested. If it is false, none of the remaining statements is performed. If it is true, all statements are performed, including the test at the second IF. Use the following construction for a nested IF-ELSE.

```
    IF condition
    do something
    IF condition
        do something
    ELSE
        do something
ELSE
    do something
```

The first IF is tested. If it is false, the logic under the final ELSE is performed. If the first IF condition tests true, then everything between the IF and the final ELSE is performed, including an inner IF ELSE test.

The following are examples of nested IF statements:

```
IF VENDOR-NUMBER NOT = ZEROES
    PERFORM READ-VENDOR-RECORD
    IF RECORD-FOUND = "N"
        DISPLAY "RECORD NOT FOUND".

IF VENDOR-NUMBER NOT = ZEROES
    PERFORM READ-VENDOR-RECORD
    IF RECORD-FOUND = "N"
        DISPLAY "RECORD NOT FOUND"
    ELSE
        DISPLAY "RECORD WAS FOUND"
ELSE
    DISPLAY "YOU ENTERED ZEROES"
```

The indentation is a matter of style and is used only to indicate which IF matches which ELSE and to make it easier to read.

Figures 14.2 and 14.3 show the relationships caused by nesting IF and IF ELSE commands.

Figure 14.2.
Nested IF *commands.*

```
IF VENDOR-NUMBER NOT = ZEROES              OUTER IF
    PERFORM READ-VENDOR-RECORD
    IF RECORD-FOUND = "N"            INNER IF
        DISPLAY "RECORD NOT FOUND".
```

Figure 14.3.
Nested IF ELSE
commands.

```
IF VENDOR-NUMBER NOT = ZEROES
    PERFORM READ-VENDOR-RECORD                  OUTER
    IF RECORD-FOUND = "N"                        IF ELSE
        DISPLAY "RECORD NOT FOUND"      INNER
    ELSE                                IF ELSE
        DISPLAY "RECORD WAS FOUND"
ELSE
    DISPLAY "YOU ENTERED ZEROES"
```

Do	Don't

DO break up complex IF ELSE logic into smaller paragraphs, or rewrite that area of the program to simplify the problem.

DON'T nest IF commands more than two or three levels. Nesting an IF within another IF can lead to some confusion in the program, and if you find that you need to nest three levels of IF, you might want to rethink the way you are writing the paragraph. You can nest IF ELSE logic in such a way that it is difficult to understand what a program is doing. For an exception to this general rule, see the Q&A section in the Workshop at the end of this chapter.

Code, compile, and run this program; then add, change, delete, and look up records in the vendor file using this one program.

Summary

Today, you reviewed how to define an indexed file in a COBOL program, and the syntax of each type of file operation: OPEN, CLOSE, READ, READ NEXT, WRITE, REWRITE, and DELETE. You also learned the following basics:

☐ An open, input, or I/O on an indexed file usually sets the file up so that a READ NEXT will retrieve the record with the lowest primary key value.

14

☐ WRITE and REWRITE commands use the record name. All other file operations use the filename.

☐ When a variable has more than two possible values and different actions are executed based on those possible values, an IF ELSE IF ELSE IF ELSE series of tests can be used to execute the series of actions.

Q&A

Q The IF ELSE example in Listing 14.15 is nested more than three levels deep. Wasn't such nesting of IF ELSE advised against?

A Yes. Usually you avoid using IF within an IF that is more than two or three levels deep. However, nesting of IF ELSE when you are executing one of several possible options based on the value of a variable is a special case. It is a common practice, especially for menu-type activities, as shown in the example in Listing 14.12, vndmnt01.cbl. The use of this style of IF ELSE is common in programs that perform this type of multiple-choice action because it remains easy to understand (although it is usually written as in the example in Listing 14.14).

Workshop

Quiz

1. If you have created a program containing a CUSTOMER-FILE, and the record for the file is named CUSTOMER-RECORD, what would be the correct command for reading a record in the file?

   a. `READ CUSTOMER-RECORD`
      `INVALID KEY MOVE "N" TO RECORD-FOUND.`

   b. `READ CUSTOMER-FILE RECORD`
      `INVALID KEY MOVE "N" TO RECORD-FOUND.`

2. For the same file, what is the correct command for writing a new record to the file?

   a. `WRITE CUSTOMER-RECORD`
      `INVALID KEY`
      `DISPLAY "RECORD ALREADY ON FILE".`

   b. `READ CUSTOMER-FILE RECORD`
      `INVALID KEY`
      `DISPLAY "RECORD ALREADY ON FILE".`

14

Exercises

1. One of the most useful analysis tools is a plain highlighter or red pen. Print out vndmnt01.cbl four times. Label the first print-out Add Mode. Trace through the program and highlight each paragraph and variable that is used in Add mode. Label the second print-out Change Mode, and highlight all variables and paragraphs used in change mode. Repeat this for Inquire mode, and then again for Delete mode. When these steps are complete, answer the following questions.

   a. Two of the paragraphs are placed incorrectly. They appear in groups of routines that have comments indicating in which modes the routines are used, but the routines actually are not used in the modes indicated. Which routines are they?

   b. Where should these routines be placed correctly?

   c. Which modes use the READ-VENDOR-RECORD routine?

   d. Which modes use the WRITE-VENDOR-RECORD routine?

   e. Which modes use the REWRITE-VENDOR-RECORD routine?

   f. Which modes use the DELETE-VENDOR-RECORD routine?

2. Print a fifth copy of the program, label it Menu, and highlight all the paragraphs and variables used in the menu routines. Obviously, the entire program is run from the menu, so you could say that all routines are part of the menu. Mark only routines up to DO-THE-PICK.

14

In Review

Nearly the entire second week focused on the concept of reading information from files and writing information to files. This is an inherent strength of the COBOL language. Day 8 laid the groundwork in "Structured Data," the key to organizing your program so that it can properly interact with files. Most of your COBOL programs in the real world will focus on obtaining information (either from the person using the program or from a file), manipulating that information, and storing the information either on disk or in printed form. Each of Week 2's programs is designed to focus on specific file functions.

Take a look at everything you've accomplished in two weeks. You've covered many concepts—some easier than others. You'll find the third week much easier, because it focuses on enhancing concepts you've already learned. Remember to focus on how new concepts dovetail with principles you've already learned. Hang in there; you're almost finished!

8

9

10

11

12

13

14

WEEK 3

15

16

17

18

19

20

21

At a Glance

The third (and somewhat final) week gives you the knowledge you need to finish your 21-day journey. You'll also have everything you need—except the experience—to be a power COBOL programmer. Although it might be tempting right now to take what you've learned and run out to apply it, you should finish this third week to ensure that you're ready for anything you might encounter.

Where You're Going

Day 15, "Data Integrity," focuses on the process of keeping intact (and trustworthy) the information your program manages. Day 16, "Using Look Up and Arrays," instills one of the simplest methods of data validation. Day 17, "Alternate Keys," provides advanced coverage of information provided on Day 11, "Indexed File I/O." Day 18, "Calling Other Programs," covers a topic everyone needs to know in the real world—how to use your program to interact with other programs by calling them. Day 19, "Complex Data Entry Problems," and Day 20, "More Complex Data Entry," shed light on a real-world problem: preparing your program for the way users expect to enter data. Day 19 also gives you your first look at the year 2000 problem and some of the techniques used to handle it. Day 21, "Selecting, Sorting, and Reporting," finishes the week by combining the concepts of selecting relevant information, sorting it into the proper order, and preparing a report.

After finishing this week, you will have completed your 21-day journey. Several bonus days have been included to ensure that you're ready to tackle the world.

Day **15**

Data Integrity

As computer systems become larger and larger, the amount of data stored on the computers increases. It is important that this data be as correct as it can be. In today's lesson, you create a file containing state codes, enter data into it using various levels of validation, and learn about the following topics:

- [ ] What is data integrity?
- [ ] What is valid data?
- [ ] How to decide whether to validate data.
- [ ] When to validate data.
- [ ] Required entry validation.
- [ ] Standard field entry.
- [ ] Change mode for simple files.
- [ ] Printing a code file.
- [ ] Converting to uppercase.

What Is Data Integrity?

You probably have heard the phrase, "Garbage in, garbage out." Recall from Day 1, "Your First COBOL Program," that a computer is a stupid machine. It will do only what you tell it to do and cannot make sensible decisions. If you put a silly program into the computer (garbage in), it will execute the silliness without question (garbage out). If you put invalid data into the data files, a program will return that invalid data to you every time you ask for it.

Creating data integrity is the process of ensuring that every field in every record of every file in a system contains only valid data. It is most efficient to do this when the data first is added to a file in the maintenance program.

What Is Valid Data?

Valid data can be broken down into two categories:

☐ Program-level data

☐ Application-level data

Program-level data must be valid to match the criteria of the specified computer or programming language. A numeric variable must contain numeric data, even if it is only zeroes. A record in an indexed file must contain a unique value for the primary key. Invalid data at the program level usually causes a program to fail or crash, and therefore it is fairly easy to spot.

Application-level data must be valid to enable the user to use the system correctly. For example, a program that is used to maintain a file of phone numbers that are critical to a business requires extra care to ensure that phone numbers are entered correctly. How much validation is enough depends on the application.

Listing 15.1 shows the now-familiar logical description of the vendor file.

TYPE **Listing 15.1. Vendor file FD.**

```
000100*-------------------------------
000200* FDVND02.CBL
000300* Primary Key - VENDOR-NUMBER
000400* VENDOR-ADDRESS-2 not always used
000500*    so may be SPACES
000600* VENDOR-PHONE is usually the
000700*    number for VENDOR-CONTACT
000800* All fields should be entered in
000900*    UPPER case.
001000*-------------------------------
001100 FD  VENDOR-FILE
001200     LABEL RECORDS ARE STANDARD.
```

15

```
001300 01   VENDOR-RECORD.
001400      05    VENDOR-NUMBER          PIC 9(5).
001500      05    VENDOR-NAME            PIC X(30).
001600      05    VENDOR-ADDRESS-1       PIC X(30).
001700      05    VENDOR-ADDRESS-2       PIC X(30).
001800      05    VENDOR-CITY            PIC X(20).
001900      05    VENDOR-STATE           PIC X(2).
002000      05    VENDOR-ZIP             PIC X(10).
002100      05    VENDOR-CONTACT         PIC X(30).
002200      05    VENDOR-PHONE           PIC X(15).
002300
```

ANALYSIS   The FD contains some notes at lines 000400 through 000900 about valid data, but this could extend further. If the bill paying system prints envelopes for mailing checks to creditors, the system should be designed so that every record in the vendor file has a valid address that can be printed on the envelopes. If the company that uses this bill-paying system operates in such a way that it is common to call creditors on the phone, the system design requires that VENDOR-CONTACT and VENDOR-PHONE be filled in.

The design of any system probably requires that the VENDOR-NAME always must be filled in. The add and change maintenance portions of the program should be set up to complain to the user if an attempt is made to add a vendor but leave the name blank.

It would be ideal if application-level data validation could check not only that the VENDOR-NAME is entered, but also that the VENDOR-NAME is correct. This is impractical because there is no way the computer could contain a list of all known possible vendors to check against the name. In a case such as VENDOR-NAME, a program usually is designed to enforce that something is entered into this field. Of course, the user could enter XYZ or type ABC Corporashun, and the computer would have no way of recognizing the error.

VENDOR-STATE could be validated by content. The 51 state abbreviations— 50 states plus DC—could be put in another file, and when the user entered the state abbreviation, it could be looked up in the state code file. This style of validation is precise and prevents an error in the VENDOR-STATE field.

Other validations fall somewhere between these two. It might be possible to break down the VENDOR-PHONE and check that it contains the correct number of digits. It might even be possible to look up the area code in an area code file, but it is impractical for the computer to verify that the phone number is correct for that vendor, unless the entire phone directory already exists in the computer for a lookup.

A lot of validation of computer data is done by human inspection of the data. Phone numbers, addresses, and names are some examples, but where the data can be validated by the computer, it should be. The more important the data, the more effort should go into the validation.

Deciding Whether to Validate Data

All data to be put into a computer file should be validated, but only some of the validation can be done by the computer. The rest must be left to a person who will read the report on a file and specify what corrections to make.

Data should be validated by the computer if the validation is easy to perform, if the data is critical, or if the volume of data is large. Easy validations usually can be coded into the program quickly. They should not be overlooked. The fact that they are easy to do doesn't mean they are unimportant.

Suppose that in a bill-paying system, a design decision is made that vendor numbers will start at 10,000. In the program, this validation becomes the following:

```
001100      IF VENDOR-NUMBER < 10000
001200          DISPLAY
001300            "VENDOR NUMBER MUST NOT BE LESS THAN 10000".
```

Critical data can become trickier to validate. A mailing-list company that advertises that it has the most accurate mailing lists might go to the trouble of creating a zip-code file with all the zip codes in the United States and the state for each zip code. When a data-entry operator enters a state and zip code in the main file, the zip code might be looked up in the zip-code file and the state for that zip code would be compared to the state that the operator entered. An error message would be provided if the state and zip code did not match.

Large amounts of data are important to validate because it becomes harder for a human to read all the information and check it. The same mailing-list company might go so far as to include a spelling check on the address fields that would warn the operator that there might be a spelling error in the address, and then ask the operator to double-check it.

Do	Don't

DO use the computer to validate data, and write validation routines into your program wherever and whenever possible.

DON'T neglect to validate critical data in your program.

When to Validate Data

Every maintenance program (a program that enables you to add, change, and delete records) for a file—especially add and change modes—must include the full validation for each field that requires validation.

TIP

Always validate data before it is written to the file.

15

If you are working with a file that contains invalid data, you should track down the program or programs that are putting invalid data in the file and correct the programs. Then correct the data in the file, either by changing the records in change mode or by writing a program that tests all the fields for valid data and reports on the faulty records. The faulty records then can be corrected, possibly with a separate program to do the correction.

You make a serious mistake the first time you see a record or field containing invalid data if you then try to modify a report or any other program to "work around" the invalid data. You have left the error in the data file. The fix in your program has to be made to all other programs that access the file, and the program causing the error in the first place will continue to generate errors.

Do	Don't
DO track down programs that are putting invalid data into files and correct them. **DON'T** attempt to work around bad data. **DO** correct bad data in a data file.	

Required Entry Validation

Required entry validation is the simplest type of validation. It is used to ensure that a user fills in a field that must be filled in. For this example, you are creating a new file of state codes. Listings 15.2 and 15.3 are the logical and physical descriptions of a state code file that contains the two-character codes for state abbreviations and the names of the states.

TYPE **Listing 15.2. The FD for the state code file.**

```
000100*------------------------------
000200* FDSTATE.CBL
000300* Primary Key - STATE-CODE
000400* NAME is required
000500* NAME and CODE should be upper case
000600*------------------------------
000700 FD   STATE-FILE
000800      LABEL RECORDS ARE STANDARD.
000900 01   STATE-RECORD.
001000      05  STATE-CODE            PIC X(2).
001100      05  STATE-NAME            PIC X(20).
001200
```

TYPE | **Listing 15.3. The SELECT statement for the state code file.**

```
000100*--------------------------------
000200* SLSTATE.CBL
000300*--------------------------------
000400     SELECT STATE-FILE
000500         ASSIGN TO "STATE"
000600         ORGANIZATION IS INDEXED
000700         RECORD KEY IS STATE-CODE
000800         ACCESS MODE IS DYNAMIC.
000900
```

Listing 15.4 is similar to vndbld01.cbl. It simply opens output for a new state file. Code the SELECT and FD for the state (shown in Listings 15.2 and 15.3), and then code, compile, and run Listing 15.4, stcbld01.cbl.

TYPE | **Listing 15.4. Creating a new state code file.**

```
000100 IDENTIFICATION DIVISION.
000200 PROGRAM-ID. STCBLD01.
000300*------------------------------------------------
000400* Create an Empty State Code File.
000500*------------------------------------------------
000600 ENVIRONMENT DIVISION.
000700 INPUT-OUTPUT SECTION.
000800 FILE-CONTROL.
000900
001000     COPY "SLSTATE.CBL".
001100
001200 DATA DIVISION.
001300 FILE SECTION.
001400
001500     COPY "FDSTATE.CBL".
001600
001700 WORKING-STORAGE SECTION.
001800
001900 PROCEDURE DIVISION.
002000 PROGRAM-BEGIN.
002100     OPEN OUTPUT STATE-FILE.
002200     CLOSE STATE-FILE.
002300
002400 PROGRAM-DONE.
002500     STOP RUN.
```

Listing 15.5, stcmnt01.cbl, is a simple maintenance program that incorporates add, change, inquire, and delete modes in one program, and it is similar to vndmnt01.cbl.

15

TYPE | **Listing 15.5. Validating field entry.**

```
000100 IDENTIFICATION DIVISION.
000200 PROGRAM-ID. STCMNT01.
000300*-------------------------------
000400* Add, Change, Inquire and Delete
000500* for the State Code.
000600*-------------------------------
000700 ENVIRONMENT DIVISION.
000800 INPUT-OUTPUT SECTION.
000900 FILE-CONTROL.
001000
001100     COPY "SLSTATE.CBL".
001200
001300 DATA DIVISION.
001400 FILE SECTION.
001500
001600     COPY "FDSTATE.CBL".
001700
001800 WORKING-STORAGE SECTION.
001900
002000 77  MENU-PICK               PIC 9.
002100     88  MENU-PICK-IS-VALID   VALUES 0 THRU 4.
002200
002300 77  THE-MODE                PIC X(7).
002400 77  OK-TO-DELETE            PIC X.
002500 77  RECORD-FOUND            PIC X.
002600 77  WHICH-FIELD             PIC 9.
002700
002800
002900
003000
003100
003200
003300 PROCEDURE DIVISION.
003400 PROGRAM-BEGIN.
003500     PERFORM OPENING-PROCEDURE.
003600     PERFORM MAIN-PROCESS.
003700     PERFORM CLOSING-PROCEDURE.
003800
003900 PROGRAM-DONE.
004000     STOP RUN.
004100
004200 OPENING-PROCEDURE.
004300     OPEN I-O STATE-FILE.
004400
004500 CLOSING-PROCEDURE.
004600     CLOSE STATE-FILE.
004700
004800
004900 MAIN-PROCESS.
005000     PERFORM GET-MENU-PICK.
005100     PERFORM MAINTAIN-THE-FILE
005200         UNTIL MENU-PICK = 0.
005300
```

continues

Listing 15.5. continued

```
005400*--------------------------------
005500* MENU
005600*--------------------------------
005700 GET-MENU-PICK.
005800     PERFORM DISPLAY-THE-MENU.
005900     PERFORM ACCEPT-MENU-PICK.
006000     PERFORM RE-ACCEPT-MENU-PICK
006100         UNTIL MENU-PICK-IS-VALID.
006200
006300 DISPLAY-THE-MENU.
006400     PERFORM CLEAR-SCREEN.
006500     DISPLAY "    PLEASE SELECT:".
006600     DISPLAY " ".
006700     DISPLAY "         1.  ADD RECORDS".
006800     DISPLAY "         2.  CHANGE A RECORD".
006900     DISPLAY "         3.  LOOK UP A RECORD".
007000     DISPLAY "         4.  DELETE A RECORD".
007100     DISPLAY " ".
007200     DISPLAY "         0.  EXIT".
007300     PERFORM SCROLL-LINE 8 TIMES.
007400
007500 ACCEPT-MENU-PICK.
007600     DISPLAY "YOUR CHOICE (0-4)?".
007700     ACCEPT MENU-PICK.
007800
007900 RE-ACCEPT-MENU-PICK.
008000     DISPLAY "INVALID SELECTION - PLEASE RE-TRY.".
008100     PERFORM ACCEPT-MENU-PICK.
008200
008300 CLEAR-SCREEN.
008400     PERFORM SCROLL-LINE 25 TIMES.
008500
008600 SCROLL-LINE.
008700     DISPLAY " ".
008800
008900 MAINTAIN-THE-FILE.
009000     PERFORM DO-THE-PICK.
009100     PERFORM GET-MENU-PICK.
009200
009300 DO-THE-PICK.
009400     IF MENU-PICK = 1
009500         PERFORM ADD-MODE
009600     ELSE
009700     IF MENU-PICK = 2
009800         PERFORM CHANGE-MODE
009900     ELSE
010000     IF MENU-PICK = 3
010100         PERFORM INQUIRE-MODE
010200     ELSE
010300     IF MENU-PICK = 4
010400         PERFORM DELETE-MODE.
010500
010600*--------------------------------
010700* ADD
```

```
010800*--------------------------------
010900 ADD-MODE.
011000     MOVE "ADD" TO THE-MODE.
011100     PERFORM GET-NEW-STATE-CODE.
011200     PERFORM ADD-RECORDS
011300         UNTIL STATE-CODE = "ZZ".
011400
011500 GET-NEW-STATE-CODE.
011600     PERFORM INIT-STATE-RECORD.
011700     PERFORM ENTER-STATE-CODE.
011800     MOVE "Y" TO RECORD-FOUND.
011900     PERFORM FIND-NEW-STATE-RECORD
012000         UNTIL RECORD-FOUND = "N" OR
012100               STATE-CODE = "ZZ".
012200
012300 FIND-NEW-STATE-RECORD.
012400     PERFORM READ-STATE-RECORD.
012500     IF RECORD-FOUND = "Y"
012600         DISPLAY "RECORD ALREADY ON FILE"
012700         PERFORM ENTER-STATE-CODE.
012800
012900 ADD-RECORDS.
013000     PERFORM ENTER-REMAINING-FIELDS.
013100     PERFORM WRITE-STATE-RECORD.
013200     PERFORM GET-NEW-STATE-CODE.
013300
013400 ENTER-REMAINING-FIELDS.
013500     PERFORM ENTER-STATE-NAME.
013600
013700*--------------------------------
013800* CHANGE
013900*--------------------------------
014000 CHANGE-MODE.
014100     MOVE "CHANGE" TO THE-MODE.
014200     PERFORM GET-STATE-RECORD.
014300     PERFORM CHANGE-RECORDS
014400         UNTIL STATE-CODE = "ZZ".
014500
014600 CHANGE-RECORDS.
014700     PERFORM GET-FIELD-TO-CHANGE.
014800     PERFORM CHANGE-ONE-FIELD
014900         UNTIL WHICH-FIELD = ZERO.
015000
015100
015200     PERFORM GET-STATE-RECORD.
015300
015400 GET-FIELD-TO-CHANGE.
015500     PERFORM DISPLAY-ALL-FIELDS.
015600     PERFORM ASK-WHICH-FIELD.
015700
015800 ASK-WHICH-FIELD.
015900     PERFORM ACCEPT-WHICH-FIELD.
016000     PERFORM RE-ACCEPT-WHICH-FIELD
016100         UNTIL WHICH-FIELD NOT > 1.
016200
016300
```

continues

Listing 15.5. continued

```
016400 ACCEPT-WHICH-FIELD.
016500     DISPLAY "ENTER THE NUMBER OF THE FIELD".
016600     DISPLAY "TO CHANGE (1) OR 0 TO EXIT".
016700     ACCEPT WHICH-FIELD.
016800
016900 RE-ACCEPT-WHICH-FIELD.
017000     DISPLAY "INVALID ENTRY".
017100     PERFORM ACCEPT-WHICH-FIELD.
017200
017300 CHANGE-ONE-FIELD.
017400     PERFORM CHANGE-THIS-FIELD.
017500     PERFORM GET-FIELD-TO-CHANGE.
017600
017700 CHANGE-THIS-FIELD.
017800     IF WHICH-FIELD = 1
017900         PERFORM ENTER-STATE-NAME.
018000
018100     PERFORM REWRITE-STATE-RECORD.
018200
018300*------------------------------
018400* INQUIRE
018500*------------------------------
018600 INQUIRE-MODE.
018700     MOVE "DISPLAY" TO THE-MODE.
018800     PERFORM GET-STATE-RECORD.
018900     PERFORM INQUIRE-RECORDS
019000         UNTIL STATE-CODE = "ZZ".
019100
019200 INQUIRE-RECORDS.
019300     PERFORM DISPLAY-ALL-FIELDS.
019400     PERFORM GET-STATE-RECORD.
019500
019600*------------------------------
019700* DELETE
019800*------------------------------
019900 DELETE-MODE.
020000     MOVE "DELETE" TO THE-MODE.
020100     PERFORM GET-STATE-RECORD.
020200     PERFORM DELETE-RECORDS
020300         UNTIL STATE-CODE = "ZZ".
020400
020500 DELETE-RECORDS.
020600     PERFORM DISPLAY-ALL-FIELDS.
020700
020800     PERFORM ASK-OK-TO-DELETE
020900     IF OK-TO-DELETE = "Y"
021000         PERFORM DELETE-STATE-RECORD.
021100
021200     PERFORM GET-STATE-RECORD.
021300
021400 ASK-OK-TO-DELETE.
021500     PERFORM ACCEPT-OK-TO-DELETE.
021600     PERFORM RE-ACCEPT-OK-TO-DELETE
021700         UNTIL OK-TO-DELETE = "Y" OR "N".
```

```
021800
021900 ACCEPT-OK-TO-DELETE.
022000     DISPLAY "DELETE THIS RECORD (Y/N)?".
022100     ACCEPT OK-TO-DELETE.
022200     IF OK-TO-DELETE = "y"
022300         MOVE "Y" TO OK-TO-DELETE.
022400     IF OK-TO-DELETE = "n"
022500         MOVE "N" TO OK-TO-DELETE.
022600
022700 RE-ACCEPT-OK-TO-DELETE.
022800     DISPLAY "YOU MUST ENTER YES OR NO".
022900     PERFORM ACCEPT-OK-TO-DELETE.
023000
023100*------------------------------
023200* Routines shared by all modes
023300*------------------------------
023400 INIT-STATE-RECORD.
023500     MOVE SPACE TO STATE-RECORD.
023600
023700 ENTER-STATE-CODE.
023800     PERFORM ACCEPT-STATE-CODE.
023900     PERFORM RE-ACCEPT-STATE-CODE
024000         UNTIL STATE-CODE NOT = SPACE.
024100
024200 ACCEPT-STATE-CODE.
024300     DISPLAY " ".
024400     DISPLAY "ENTER STATE CODE OF THE STATE" .
024500     DISPLAY "TO " THE-MODE
024600                 "(2 UPPER CASE CHARACTERS)".
024700     DISPLAY "ENTER ZZ TO STOP ENTRY".
024800     ACCEPT STATE-CODE.
024900
025000
025100
025200
025300
025400 RE-ACCEPT-STATE-CODE.
025500     DISPLAY "STATE CODE MUST BE ENTERED".
025600     PERFORM ACCEPT-STATE-CODE.
025700
025800 GET-STATE-RECORD.
025900     PERFORM INIT-STATE-RECORD.
026000     PERFORM ENTER-STATE-CODE.
026100     MOVE "N" TO RECORD-FOUND.
026200     PERFORM FIND-STATE-RECORD
026300         UNTIL RECORD-FOUND = "Y" OR
026400                 STATE-CODE = "ZZ".
026500
026600*------------------------------
026700* Routines shared Add and Change
026800*------------------------------
026900 FIND-STATE-RECORD.
027000     PERFORM READ-STATE-RECORD.
027100     IF RECORD-FOUND = "N"
027200         DISPLAY "RECORD NOT FOUND"
```

continues

Listing 15.5. continued

```
027300          PERFORM ENTER-STATE-CODE.
027400
027500 ENTER-STATE-NAME.
027600     PERFORM ACCEPT-STATE-NAME.
027700     PERFORM RE-ACCEPT-STATE-NAME
027800          UNTIL STATE-NAME NOT = SPACES.
027900
028000 ACCEPT-STATE-NAME.
028100     DISPLAY "ENTER STATE NAME".
028200     ACCEPT STATE-NAME.
028300
028400
028500
028600
028700
028800 RE-ACCEPT-STATE-NAME.
028900     DISPLAY "STATE NAME MUST BE ENTERED".
029000     PERFORM ACCEPT-STATE-NAME.
029100
029200*--------------------------------
029300* Routines shared by Change,
029400* Inquire and Delete
029500*--------------------------------
029600 DISPLAY-ALL-FIELDS.
029700   · DISPLAY " ".
029800     PERFORM DISPLAY-STATE-CODE.
029900     PERFORM DISPLAY-STATE-NAME.
030000     DISPLAY " ".
030100
030200 DISPLAY-STATE-CODE.
030300     DISPLAY "   STATE CODE: " STATE-CODE.
030400
030500 DISPLAY-STATE-NAME.
030600     DISPLAY "1. STATE NAME: " STATE-NAME.
030700
030800*--------------------------------
030900* File I-O Routines
031000*--------------------------------
031100 READ-STATE-RECORD.
031200     MOVE "Y" TO RECORD-FOUND.
031300     READ STATE-FILE RECORD
031400        INVALID KEY
031500           MOVE "N" TO RECORD-FOUND.
031600
031700*or  READ STATE-FILE RECORD WITH LOCK
031800*        INVALID KEY
031900*           MOVE "N" TO RECORD-FOUND.
032000
032100*or  READ STATE-FILE RECORD WITH HOLD
032200*        INVALID KEY
032300*           MOVE "N" TO RECORD-FOUND.
032400
032500 WRITE-STATE-RECORD.
032600     WRITE STATE-RECORD
```

15

```
032700              INVALID KEY
032800              DISPLAY "RECORD ALREADY ON FILE".
032900
033000 REWRITE-STATE-RECORD.
033100     REWRITE STATE-RECORD
033200              INVALID KEY
033300              DISPLAY "ERROR REWRITING STATE RECORD".
033400
033500 DELETE-STATE-RECORD.
033600     DELETE STATE-FILE RECORD
033700              INVALID KEY
033800              DISPLAY "ERROR DELETING STATE RECORD".
033900
```

The following output examples of stcmnt01.cbl include the start-up menu, an example of
entering a blank state code, a correct state code, and a state code and state name in lowercase:

```
PLEASE SELECT:
1.   ADD RECORDS
2.   CHANGE A RECORD
3.   LOOK UP A RECORD
4.   DELETE A RECORD
0.   EXIT
YOUR CHOICE (0-4)?
```

OUTPUT
```
ENTER STATE CODE OF THE STATE
TO ADD      (2 UPPER CASE CHARACTERS)
ENTER ZZ TO STOP ENTRY
```

(User pressed Enter here with no entry.)

```
STATE CODE MUST BE ENTERED
ENTER STATE CODE OF THE STATE
TO ADD      (2 UPPER CASE CHARACTERS)
ENTER ZZ TO STOP ENTRY
LA
ENTER STATE NAME
LOUISIANA
ENTER STATE CODE OF THE STATE
TO ADD      (2 UPPER CASE CHARACTERS)
ENTER ZZ TO STOP ENTRY
```

ANALYSIS   stcmnt01.cbl differs from vndmnt01.cbl in one main area: validation. In vndmnt01.cbl,
the user can enter any values, and even enter no values. At lines 023700 through
025700, the ENTER-STATE-CODE routine has been broken into two separate routines: ACCEPT-
STATE-CODE to enter the data, and RE-ACCEPT-STATE-CODE designed to force the user to enter
something. At lines 023900 and 024000, RE-ACCEPT-STATE-CODE is performed until STATE-CODE
NOT = SPACES. The reaccept logic is executed only if the user has entered spaces, which are
invalid for this field. The RE-ACCEPT-STATE-CODE routine at line 025400 displays an error
message and then performs the original routine to get the data—ACCEPT-STATE-CODE. The
RE-ACCEPT-STATE-CODE loop will continue until the user's entry is valid. The identical logic
is used at lines 027500 through 029100 for the state name.

The STATE-CODE is an alphanumeric field, so instead of entering zero to end data entry, the user is asked to enter "ZZ" to end the entry. "ZZ" is not a valid state code, so it can be used.

Standard Field Entry

The style of entry and validation of fields used in stcmnt01.cbl can be reduced to a simple formula. This formula is best expressed in the pseudocode shown in Listing 15.6. Note that I have chosen to include periods in this example of pseudocode. Again, the style to use in pseudocode is your choice unless your company has a standard specification on pseudocode style.

TYPE Listing 15.6. The pseudocode for standard field entry.

```
enter-the-data.
    PERFORM accept-the-data.
    PERFORM re-accept-the-data.
      UNTIL the-data is valid.
accept-the-data.
    DISPLAY a-prompt.
    ACCEPT the-data.
re-accept-the-data.
    DISPLAY error-message.
    PERFORM accept-the-data.
```

Figure 15.1 compares the ENTER-STATE-NAME routine to the pseudocode for a standard field-entry routine.

Figure 15.1.

ENTER-STATE-NAME *as a standard field-entry routine.*

```
ENTER-STATE-NAME.
    PERFORM ACCEPT-STATE-NAME.
    PERFORM RE-ACCEPT-STATE-NAME
      UNTIL STATE-NAME NOT = SPACES.
ACCEPT-STATE-NAME.
    DISPLAY "ENTER STATE NAME".
    ACCEPT STATE-NAME.
RE-ACCEPT-STATE-NAME.
    DISPLAY "STATE NAME MUST BE ENTERED".
    PERFORM ACCEPT-STATE-NAME.
```

```
enter-the-data.
    PERFORM accept-the-data.
    PERFORM re-accept-the-data.
      UNTIL the-data is valid.
accept-the-data.
    DISPLAY a-prompt.
    ACCEPT the-data.
re-accept-the-data.
    DISPLAY error-message.
    PERFORM accept-the-data.
```

Figure 15.2 compares the ENTER-STATE-CODE routine to the pseudocode for a standard field-entry routine. In ACCEPT-STATE-CODE, the logic that corresponds to DISPLAY a-prompt extends over several lines.

This method of data entry does not have to be limited to fields for the file; it can be used for any field that the user must enter or any question that the user is asked. Figure 15.3 shows that ASK-WHICH-FIELD from stcmnt01.cbl also is based on the standard field-entry pattern.

15

Figure 15.2.

ENTER-STATE-CODE *as a standard field-entry routine.*

```
ENTER-STATE-CODE.
    PERFORM ACCEPT-STATE-CODE.
    PERFORM RE-ACCEPT-STATE-CODE
        UNTIL STATE-CODE NOT = SPACE.
ACCEPT-STATE-CODE.
    DISPLAY " ".
    DISPLAY "ENTER STATE CODE OF THE STATE" .
    DISPLAY "TO " THE-MODE
                  "(2 UPPER CASE CHARACTERS)".
    DISPLAY "ENTER ZZ TO STOP ENTRY".
    ACCEPT STATE-CODE.
RE-ACCEPT-STATE-CODE.
    DISPLAY "STATE CODE MUST BE ENTERED".
    PERFORM ACCEPT-STATE-CODE.
```

```
enter-the-data.
    PERFORM accept-the-data.
    PERFORM re-accept-the-data.
        UNTIL the-data is valid.
accept-the-data.
    DISPLAY a-prompt




    ACCEPT the data
re-accept the data
    DISPLAY error-message
    PERFORM accept-the-data
```

Figure 15.3.

ASK-WHICH-FIELD *as a standard field-entry routine.*

```
ASK-WHICH-FIELD.
    PERFORM ACCEPT-WHICH-FIELD.
    PERFORM RE-ACCEPT-WHICH-FIELD
        UNTIL WHICH-FIELD NOT > 1.
ACCEPT-WHICH-FIELD.
    DISPLAY " ".
    DISPLAY "ENTER THE NUMBER OF THE FIELD".
    DISPLAY "TO CHANGE (1) OR 0 TO EXIT".
    ACCEPT WHICH-FIELD.
RE-ACCEPT-WHICH-FIELD.
    DISPLAY "INVALID ENTRY".
    PERFORM ACCEPT-WHICH-FIELD.
```

```
enter-the-data.
    PERFORM accept-the-data.
    PERFORM re-accept-the-data.
        UNTIL the-data is valid.
accept-the-data.
    DISPLAY a-prompt.


    ACCEPT the-data.
re-accept-the-data.
    DISPLAY error-message.
    PERFORM accept-the-data.
```

Listing 15.6, the pseudocode for a standard field-entry routine, is missing one critical step that is included in Listing 15.7.

TYPE **Listing 15.7. A standard field-entry routine including** `edit-check-the-data.`

```
enter-the-data.
    PERFORM accept-the-data.
    PERFORM re-accept-the-data.
      UNTIL the-data is valid.
accept-the-data.
    DISPLAY a-prompt.
    ACCEPT the-data.
    edit-check-the-data.
re-accept-the-data.
    DISPLAY error-message.
    PERFORM accept-the-data.
```

ANALYSIS Within `accept-the-data`, a line has been added to `edit-check-the-data`. This line actually represents two separate actions:

☐ Editing the data includes any forced changes that must be made to data, such as converting y to Y or n to N, as is done with a yes-or-no entry field.

☐ Checking the data includes any additional actions to validate the data, such as checking that the entry is Y or N, as is done with a yes-or-no entry field.

Editing and checking are combined into the single line edit-check-the-data because of the ways in which editing and checking can occur in a program. Some data is edited but not validated (required)—for example, a field that is not required (no validation) but that must be edited (changed) to convert it to uppercase. Some data is validated but not edited—for example, a required phone number field where the data is required but is not changed by the program. Some data, such as WHICH-FIELD, is neither edited nor validated.

Some data receives a bit of both editing and validation. A date field might be entered by the user as "1/7/97", and this format is hard to validate. The first step might be to edit the data by converting it to a standard format such as "19970107". This standard format can be validated as a date; then the field might be edited again and converted to "01/07/97". Because there is no ironclad rule such as "first you edit and then you check," edit-check-the-data is combined into a single line.

ASK-OK-TO-DELETE in Figure 15.4 also is a standard field-entry routine, but this is an example of a routine that uses the edit-check-the-data section of the pseudocode to edit the data, by converting y and n to their uppercase versions.

The GET-MENU-PICK routine shown in Figure 15.5 is a standard field-entry routine with a slight variation. The prompt for the menu field actually is the whole menu followed by "YOUR CHOICE (0-4)?". This is a long and unnecessary prompt to repeat every time the user makes a mistake, so only "YOUR CHOICE (0-4)?" is repeated. This is done by making part of the prompt a separate paragraph, DISPLAY-THE-MENU, and then displaying it once at the beginning of GET-MENU-PICK.

Figure 15.4.

ASK-OK-TO-DELETE *as a standard field-entry routine.*

```
ASK-OK-TO-DELETE.                              enter-the-data.
    PERFORM ACCEPT-OK-TO-DELETE.                   PERFORM accept-the-data.
    PERFORM RE-ACCEPT-OK-TO-DELETE                 PERFORM re-accept-the-data.
        UNTIL OK-TO-DELETE = "Y" OR "N".               UNTIL the-data is valid.
ACCEPT-OK-TO-DELETE.                            accept-the-data
    DISPLAY "DELETE THIS RECORD (Y/N)?".           DISPLAY a-prompt
    ACCEPT OK-TO-DELETE.                            ACCEPT the-data
    IF OK-TO-DELETE= "y"                            edit-check-the-data
        MOVE "Y" TO OK-TO-DELETE.
    IF OK-TO-DELETE= "n"
        MOVE "N" TO OK-TO-DELETE.
RE-ACCEPT-OK-TO-DELETE.                         re-accept-the-data.
    DISPLAY "YOU MUST ENTER YES OR NO".            DISPLAY error-message.
    PERFORM ACCEPT-OK-TO-DELETE.                   PERFORM accept-the-data.
```

You can use this standard field-entry routine as a formula for entering and testing or editing any field.

It is important to understand that the standard field-entry routine in Listing 15.7 and other versions of it elsewhere are just a design. It is not a language requirement, and each COBOL site will have different requirements on how to formulate the steps of a standard field-entry routine.

Figure 15.5.

GET-MENU-PICK *as a standard field-entry routine with a slight variation to handle the large prompt for the field.*

```
GET-MENU-PICK.
    PERFORM DISPLAY-THE-MENU.
    PERFORM ACCEPT-MENU-PICK.
    PERFORM RE-ACCEPT-MENU-PICK
    UNTIL MENU-PICK-IS-VALID.
DISPLAY-THE-MENU.
    PERFORM CLEAR-SCREEN.
    DISPLAY "    PLEASE SELECT:".
    DISPLAY " ".
    DISPLAY "        1.  ADD RECORDS".
    DISPLAY "        2.  CHANGE A RECORD".
    DISPLAY "        3.  LOOK UP A RECORD".
    DISPLAY "        4.  DELETE A RECORD".
    DISPLAY " ".
    DISPLAY "        0.  EXIT".
    PERFORM SCROLL-LINE 8 TIMES.
ACCEPT-MENU-PICK.
    DISPLAY "YOUR CHOICE (0-4)?".
    ACCEPT MENU-PICK.

RE-ACCEPT-MENU-PICK.
    DISPLAY "INVALID SELECTION - PLEASE RE-TRY.".
    PERFORM ACCEPT-MENU-PICK.
```

```
enter-the-data.

    PERFORM accept-the-data.
    PERFORM re-accept-the-data.
        UNTIL the-data is valid.




accept-the-data.
    DISPLAY a-prompt.
    ACCEPT the-data.
    edit-check-the-data.
re-accept-the-data.
    DISPLAY error-message.
    PERFORM accept-the-data.
```

Change Mode for Simple Files

One oddity develops from stcmnt01.cbl, shown in the following output example of changing the record for CA (California):

Output

```
PLEASE SELECT:
1.   ADD RECORDS
2.   CHANGE A RECORD
3.   LOOK UP A RECORD
4.   DELETE A RECORD
0.   EXIT
YOUR CHOICE (0-4)?
2
ENTER STATE CODE OF THE STATE
TO CHANGE (2 UPPER CASE CHARACTERS)
ENTER ZZ TO STOP ENTRY
CA
STATE CODE: CA
1. STATE NAME: CALIFORNIA
ENTER THE NUMBER OF THE FIELD
TO CHANGE (1) OR 0 TO EXIT
1
ENTER STATE NAME
CALIFORNIA
STATE CODE: CA
1. STATE NAME: CALIFORNIA
ENTER THE NUMBER OF THE FIELD
TO CHANGE (1) OR 0 TO EXIT
```

Analysis

Although there is only one modifiable field in the state code record, the user is asked to enter the number of the field to change. In vndmnt01.cbl, the user had the option of up to eight different fields to change. In stcmnt01.cbl, the STATE-CODE is the primary key that cannot be changed, so the user is left with only one field, STATE-NAME, that can be changed.

You can avoid this problem in the data entry by using the changes shown in Listing 15.8, a fragment from stcmnt02.cbl.

TYPE **Listing 15.8. Skip asking the user which field.**

```
014600 CHANGE-RECORDS.
014700     PERFORM GET-FIELD-TO-CHANGE.
014800*    PERFORM CHANGE-ONE-FIELD
014900*         UNTIL WHICH-FIELD = ZERO.
015000     PERFORM CHANGE-ONE-FIELD.
015100
015200     PERFORM GET-STATE-RECORD.
015300
015400 GET-FIELD-TO-CHANGE.
015500     PERFORM DISPLAY-ALL-FIELDS.
015600     PERFORM ASK-WHICH-FIELD.
015700
015800 ASK-WHICH-FIELD.
015900*    PERFORM ACCEPT-WHICH-FIELD.
016000*    PERFORM RE-ACCEPT-WHICH-FIELD
016100*         UNTIL WHICH-FIELD NOT > 1.
016200     MOVE 1 TO WHICH-FIELD.
016300
016400*ACCEPT-WHICH-FIELD.
016500*    DISPLAY "ENTER THE NUMBER OF THE FIELD".
016600*    DISPLAY "TO CHANGE (1) OR 0 TO EXIT".
016700*    ACCEPT WHICH-FIELD.
016800*
016900*RE-ACCEPT-WHICH-FIELD.
017000*    DISPLAY "INVALID ENTRY".
017100*    PERFORM ACCEPT-WHICH-FIELD.
017200
017300 CHANGE-ONE-FIELD.
017400     PERFORM CHANGE-THIS-FIELD.
017500*    PERFORM GET-FIELD-TO-CHANGE.
017600
017700 CHANGE-THIS-FIELD.
017800     IF WHICH-FIELD = 1
017900         PERFORM ENTER-STATE-NAME.
018000
018100     PERFORM REWRITE-STATE-RECORD.
018200
```

The modified output of stcmnt02.cbl skips asking the user for the field to enter and immediately asks for the new state name. In this example, the user re-enters the state name because of an error in the original data entry (CALIFORNIA is misspelled as CALIFORNIB).

15

```
PLEASE SELECT:
1.   ADD RECORDS
2.   CHANGE A RECORD
3.   LOOK UP A RECORD
4.   DELETE A RECORD
0.   EXIT
YOUR CHOICE (0-4)?
2
ENTER STATE CODE OF THE STATE
TO CHANGE (2 UPPER CASE CHARACTERS)
ENTER ZZ TO STOP ENTRY
CA
STATE CODE: CA
1. STATE NAME: CALIFORNIB
ENTER STATE NAME
CALIFORNIA
ENTER STATE CODE OF THE STATE
TO CHANGE (2 UPPER CASE CHARACTERS)
ENTER ZZ TO STOP ENTRY
```

ANALYSIS   This is a modification to stcmnt01.cbl that changes the program so that CHANGE-ONE-FIELD is executed only once, and ASK-WHICH-FIELD is no longer entered by the user but is set to 1 by the computer. The original code is left in but commented out, and the new code appears at lines 015000 and 016200.

Copy stcmnt01.cbl to stcmnt02.cbl and make the changes to this area of the program; then compile and run the program.

Printing a Code File

Printing the state code is fairly simple. Figure 15.6 shows the layout chart for a simple state code report.

Figure 15.6.

Layout for the state codes report.

Listing 15.9, stcrpt01.cbl, is a simple report program based on the layout in Figure 15.6.

TYPE **Listing 15.9. Report on the state codes file.**

```
000100 IDENTIFICATION DIVISION.
000200 PROGRAM-ID. STCRPT01.
000300*------------------------------
000400* Report on the STATE File.
000500*------------------------------
000600 ENVIRONMENT DIVISION.
000700 INPUT-OUTPUT SECTION.
000800 FILE-CONTROL.
000900
001000     COPY "SLSTATE.CBL".
001100
001200     SELECT PRINTER-FILE
001300         ASSIGN TO PRINTER
001400         ORGANIZATION IS LINE SEQUENTIAL.
001500
001600 DATA DIVISION.
001700 FILE SECTION.
001800
001900     COPY "FDSTATE.CBL".
002000
002100 FD  PRINTER-FILE
002200     LABEL RECORDS ARE OMITTED.
002300 01  PRINTER-RECORD              PIC X(80).
002400
002500 WORKING-STORAGE SECTION.
002600
002700 01  DETAIL-LINE.
002800     05  PRINT-CODE       PIC XX.
002900     05  FILLER           PIC XXXX      VALUE SPACE.
003000     05  PRINT-NAME       PIC X(20).
003100
003200 01  COLUMN-LINE.
003300     05  FILLER        PIC X(4)  VALUE "CODE".
003400     05  FILLER        PIC X(2) VALUE SPACE.
003500     05  FILLER        PIC X(4) VALUE "NAME".
003600
003700 01  TITLE-LINE.
003800     05  FILLER            PIC X(25) VALUE SPACE.
003900     05  FILLER            PIC X(11)
004000         VALUE "STATE CODES".
004100     05  FILLER            PIC X(15) VALUE SPACE.
004200     05  FILLER            PIC X(5) VALUE "PAGE:".
004300     05  FILLER            PIC X(1) VALUE SPACE.
004400     05  PRINT-PAGE-NUMBER PIC ZZZZ9.
004500
004600 77  FILE-AT-END       PIC X.
004700 77  LINE-COUNT        PIC 999 VALUE ZERO.
004800 77  PAGE-NUMBER       PIC 99999 VALUE ZERO.
004900 77  MAXIMUM-LINES     PIC 999 VALUE 55.
005000
005100 PROCEDURE DIVISION.
005200 PROGRAM-BEGIN.
005300
005400     PERFORM OPENING-PROCEDURE.
```

15

15

```
005500        MOVE ZEROES TO LINE-COUNT
005600                         PAGE-NUMBER.
005700
005800        PERFORM START-NEW-PAGE.
005900
006000        MOVE "N" TO FILE-AT-END.
006100        PERFORM READ-NEXT-RECORD.
006200        IF FILE-AT-END = "Y"
006300            MOVE "NO RECORDS FOUND" TO PRINTER-RECORD
006400            PERFORM WRITE-TO-PRINTER
006500        ELSE
006600            PERFORM PRINT-STATE-FIELDS
006700                UNTIL FILE-AT-END = "Y".
006800
006900        PERFORM CLOSING-PROCEDURE.
007000
007100 PROGRAM-DONE.
007200        STOP RUN.
007300
007400 OPENING-PROCEDURE.
007500        OPEN I-O STATE-FILE.
007600        OPEN OUTPUT PRINTER-FILE.
007700
007800 CLOSING-PROCEDURE.
007900        CLOSE STATE-FILE.
008000        PERFORM END-LAST-PAGE.
008100        CLOSE PRINTER-FILE.
008200
008300 PRINT-STATE-FIELDS.
008400        IF LINE-COUNT > MAXIMUM-LINES
008500            PERFORM START-NEXT-PAGE.
008600        PERFORM PRINT-THE-RECORD.
008700        PERFORM READ-NEXT-RECORD.
008800
008900 PRINT-THE-RECORD.
009000        MOVE SPACE TO DETAIL-LINE.
009100        MOVE STATE-CODE TO PRINT-CODE.
009200        MOVE STATE-NAME TO PRINT-NAME.
009300        MOVE DETAIL-LINE TO PRINTER-RECORD.
009400        PERFORM WRITE-TO-PRINTER.
009500
009600 READ-NEXT-RECORD.
009700        READ STATE-FILE NEXT RECORD
009800            AT END MOVE "Y" TO FILE-AT-END.
009900
010000 WRITE-TO-PRINTER.
010100        WRITE PRINTER-RECORD BEFORE ADVANCING 1.
010200        ADD 1 TO LINE-COUNT.
010300
010400 LINE-FEED.
010500        MOVE SPACE TO PRINTER-RECORD.
010600        PERFORM WRITE-TO-PRINTER.
010700
010800 START-NEXT-PAGE.
```

continues

Listing 15.9. continued

```
010900
011000      PERFORM END-LAST-PAGE.
011100      PERFORM START-NEW-PAGE.
011200
011300 START-NEW-PAGE.
011400      ADD 1 TO PAGE-NUMBER.
011500      MOVE PAGE-NUMBER TO PRINT-PAGE-NUMBER.
011600      MOVE TITLE-LINE TO PRINTER-RECORD.
011700      PERFORM WRITE-TO-PRINTER.
011800      PERFORM LINE-FEED.
011900      MOVE COLUMN-LINE TO PRINTER-RECORD.
012000      PERFORM WRITE-TO-PRINTER.
012100      PERFORM LINE-FEED.
012200
012300 END-LAST-PAGE.
012400      PERFORM FORM-FEED.
012500      MOVE ZERO TO LINE-COUNT.
012600
012700 FORM-FEED.
012800      MOVE SPACE TO PRINTER-RECORD.
012900      WRITE PRINTER-RECORD BEFORE ADVANCING PAGE.
```

The example of the output from `stcrpt01.cbl` follows the organization designed in the printer layout chart:

```
STATE CODES              PAGE:     1
CODE  NAME
AZ    ARIZONA
CA    CALIFORNIA
FL    FLORIDA
LA    LOUISIANA
NM    NEW MEXICO
WA    WASHINGTON
WI    WISCONSIN
```

Converting to Uppercase

You still haven't done enough to validate the data in the state code file. Listing 15.2, the FD for the state code file, contained comments indicating that the STATE-CODE and STATE-NAME should both be entered in uppercase. When I described running `stcmnt01.cbl`, I said that you should enter the values in uppercase, but just ordering you to do it isn't good enough to ensure that the information really is entered in uppercase and stored in the file in uppercase.

It is possible to validate a field and check each character in the field to ensure that they are all uppercase, but it does involve quite a bit of coding. Instead, it is easier to force everything to become uppercase.

15

Listing 15.10, `upper01.cbl`, is a short program to demonstrate how to convert data to uppercase.

TYPE **Listing 15.10. Converting data to uppercase.**

```
000100 IDENTIFICATION DIVISION.
000200 PROGRAM-ID. UPPER01.
000300*------------------------------------------------
000400* Converts input to upper case.
000500*------------------------------------------------
000600 ENVIRONMENT DIVISION.
000700 INPUT-OUTPUT SECTION.
000800 FILE-CONTROL.
000900
001000 DATA DIVISION.
001100 FILE SECTION.
001200
001300 WORKING-STORAGE SECTION.
001400
001500 77  UPPER-ALPHA           PIC X(26) VALUE
001600     "ABCDEFGHIJKLMNOPQRSTUVWXYZ".
001700 77  LOWER-ALPHA           PIC X(26) VALUE
001800     "abcdefghijklmnopqrstuvwxyz".
001900
002000 77  TEST-FIELD            PIC X(30) VALUE SPACE.
002100 PROCEDURE DIVISION.
002200 PROGRAM-BEGIN.
002300     PERFORM ENTER-TEST-FIELD.
002400     PERFORM CONVERT-AND-ENTER
002500         UNTIL TEST-FIELD = SPACE.
002600
002700 PROGRAM-DONE.
002800     STOP RUN.
002900
003000 ENTER-TEST-FIELD.
003100     DISPLAY "Enter upper or lower case data".
003200     DISPLAY "Leave blank to end".
003300     ACCEPT TEST-FIELD.
003400 CONVERT-AND-ENTER.
003500     PERFORM CONVERT-TEST-FIELD.
003600     PERFORM ENTER-TEST-FIELD.
003700
003800 CONVERT-TEST-FIELD.
003900     INSPECT TEST-FIELD CONVERTING
004000         LOWER-ALPHA TO UPPER-ALPHA.
004100     DISPLAY TEST-FIELD.
```

ANALYSIS This program accepts a 30-character field from the user, converts it to uppercase, and redisplays the converted field below the original. This process continues until the user enters a blank field.

This example uses a new COBOL command—INSPECT CONVERTING. At lines 003900 and 004000, each character in TEST-FIELD is compared to the list of 26 characters in LOWER-ALPHA. If any character is found to match, the character in TEST-FIELD is converted to the corresponding character in UPPER-ALPHA.

The INSPECT CONVERTING command treats all the variables as lists of individual characters. In Listing 15.10, TEST-FIELD is treated as a list of 30 characters to be converted, LOWER-ALPHA is treated as a list of 26 characters to search for in TEST-FIELD, and UPPER-ALPHA is a list of 26 characters to be used as replacements when a match occurs. Both LOWER-ALPHA and UPPER-ALPHA must be the same length.

In this example, INSPECT CONVERTING is used to convert lowercase letters to uppercase letters, but it could be used for any conversion. It happens that UPPER-ALPHA contains the uppercase equivalents of LOWER-ALPHA, but the INSPECT CONVERTING command doesn't care about the content of UPPER-ALPHA. It could contain any 26 characters, numbers, and punctuation marks.

The INSPECT CONVERTING command will perform a character-by-character translation of a field. The syntax is the following:

```
INSPECT    alphanumeric variable
CONVERTING compare value
TO         replace value.
```

Here is an example:

```
CONVERT-TO-UPPER.
INSPECT DATA-FIELD
CONVERTING LOWER-ALPHA
TO         UPPER-ALPHA
```

Listing 15.11, stcmnt03.cbl, includes the earlier changes put into stcmnt02.cbl and adds uppercase conversion in the validation routines at lines 025000 through 025200 and 028400 through 028600.

TYPE   **Listing 15.11. Validating by converting to uppercase.**

```
000100 IDENTIFICATION DIVISION.
000200 PROGRAM-ID. STCMNT03.
000300*--------------------------------
000400* Add, Change, Inquire and Deletes
000500* for the State Code.
000600*--------------------------------
000700 ENVIRONMENT DIVISION.
000800 INPUT-OUTPUT SECTION.
000900 FILE-CONTROL.
001000
001100     COPY "SLSTATE.CBL".
001200
```

15

```
001300 DATA DIVISION.
001400 FILE SECTION.
001500
001600      COPY "FDSTATE.CBL".
001700
001800 WORKING-STORAGE SECTION.
001900
002000 77  MENU-PICK                      PIC 9.
002100     88  MENU-PICK-IS-VALID          VALUES 0 THRU 4.
002200
002300 77  THE-MODE                       PIC X(7).
002400 77  OK-TO-DELETE                   PIC X.
002500 77  RECORD-FOUND                   PIC X.
002600 77  WHICH-FIELD                    PIC 9.
002700
002800 77  UPPER-ALPHA                    PIC X(26) VALUE
002900      "ABCDEFGHIJKLMNOPQRSTUVWXYZ".
003000 77  LOWER-ALPHA                    PIC X(26) VALUE
003100      "abcdefghijklmnopqrstuvwxyz".
003200
003300 PROCEDURE DIVISION.
003400 PROGRAM-BEGIN.
003500      PERFORM OPENING-PROCEDURE.
003600      PERFORM MAIN-PROCESS.
003700      PERFORM CLOSING-PROCEDURE.
003800
003900 PROGRAM-DONE.
004000      STOP RUN.
004100
004200 OPENING-PROCEDURE.
004300      OPEN I-O STATE-FILE.
004400
004500 CLOSING-PROCEDURE.
004600      CLOSE STATE-FILE.
004700
004800
004900 MAIN-PROCESS.
005000      PERFORM GET-MENU-PICK.
005100      PERFORM MAINTAIN-THE-FILE
005200          UNTIL MENU-PICK = 0.
005300
005400*-------------------------------
005500* MENU
005600*-------------------------------
005700 GET-MENU-PICK.
005800      PERFORM DISPLAY-THE-MENU.
005900      PERFORM ACCEPT-MENU-PICK.
006000      PERFORM RE-ACCEPT-MENU-PICK
006100          UNTIL MENU-PICK-IS-VALID.
006200
006300 DISPLAY-THE-MENU.
006400      PERFORM CLEAR-SCREEN.
006500      DISPLAY "    PLEASE SELECT:".
006600      DISPLAY " ".
```

continues

Listing 15.11. continued

```
006700        DISPLAY "          1.   ADD RECORDS".
006800        DISPLAY "          2.   CHANGE A RECORD".
006900        DISPLAY "          3.   LOOK UP A RECORD".
007000        DISPLAY "          4.   DELETE A RECORD".
007100        DISPLAY " ".
007200        DISPLAY "          0.   EXIT".
007300        PERFORM SCROLL-LINE 8 TIMES.
007400
007500 ACCEPT-MENU-PICK.
007600        DISPLAY "YOUR CHOICE (0-4)?".
007700        ACCEPT MENU-PICK.
007800
007900 RE-ACCEPT-MENU-PICK.
008000        DISPLAY "INVALID SELECTION - PLEASE RE-TRY.".
008100        PERFORM ACCEPT-MENU-PICK.
008200
008300 CLEAR-SCREEN.
008400        PERFORM SCROLL-LINE 25 TIMES.
008500
008600 SCROLL-LINE.
008700        DISPLAY " ".
008800
008900 MAINTAIN-THE-FILE.
009000        PERFORM DO-THE-PICK.
009100        PERFORM GET-MENU-PICK.
009200
009300 DO-THE-PICK.
009400        IF MENU-PICK = 1
009500            PERFORM ADD-MODE
009600        ELSE
009700        IF MENU-PICK = 2
009800            PERFORM CHANGE-MODE
009900        ELSE
010000        IF MENU-PICK = 3
010100            PERFORM INQUIRE-MODE
010200        ELSE
010300        IF MENU-PICK = 4
010400            PERFORM DELETE-MODE.
010500
010600*--------------------------------
010700* ADD
010800*--------------------------------
010900 ADD-MODE.
011000        MOVE "ADD" TO THE-MODE.
011100        PERFORM GET-NEW-STATE-CODE.
011200        PERFORM ADD-RECORDS
011300            UNTIL STATE-CODE = "ZZ".
011400
011500 GET-NEW-STATE-CODE.
011600        PERFORM INIT-STATE-RECORD.
011700        PERFORM ENTER-STATE-CODE.
011800        MOVE "Y" TO RECORD-FOUND.
011900        PERFORM FIND-NEW-STATE-RECORD
012000            UNTIL RECORD-FOUND = "N" OR
```

15

15

```
012100                   STATE-CODE = "ZZ".
012200
012300 FIND-NEW-STATE-RECORD.
012400      PERFORM READ-STATE-RECORD.
012500      IF RECORD-FOUND = "Y"
012600          DISPLAY "RECORD ALREADY ON FILE"
012700          PERFORM ENTER-STATE-CODE.
012800
012900 ADD-RECORDS.
013000      PERFORM ENTER-REMAINING-FIELDS.
013100      PERFORM WRITE-STATE-RECORD.
013200      PERFORM GET-NEW-STATE-CODE.
013300
013400 ENTER-REMAINING-FIELDS.
013500      PERFORM ENTER-STATE-NAME.
013600
013700*-------------------------------
013800* CHANGE
013900*-------------------------------
014000 CHANGE-MODE.
014100      MOVE "CHANGE" TO THE-MODE.
014200      PERFORM GET-STATE-RECORD.
014300      PERFORM CHANGE-RECORDS
014400          UNTIL STATE-CODE = "ZZ".
014500
014600 CHANGE-RECORDS.
014700      PERFORM GET-FIELD-TO-CHANGE.
014800*     PERFORM CHANGE-ONE-FIELD
014900*         UNTIL WHICH-FIELD = ZERO.
015000      PERFORM CHANGE-ONE-FIELD.
015100
015200      PERFORM GET-STATE-RECORD.
015300
015400 GET-FIELD-TO-CHANGE.
015500      PERFORM DISPLAY-ALL-FIELDS.
015600      PERFORM ASK-WHICH-FIELD.
015700
015800 ASK-WHICH-FIELD.
015900*     PERFORM ACCEPT-WHICH-FIELD.
016000*     PERFORM RE-ACCEPT-WHICH-FIELD
016100*         UNTIL WHICH-FIELD NOT > 1.
016200      MOVE 1 TO WHICH-FIELD.
016300
016400*ACCEPT-WHICH-FIELD.
016500*     DISPLAY "ENTER THE NUMBER OF THE FIELD".
016600*     DISPLAY "TO CHANGE (1) OR 0 TO EXIT".
016700*     ACCEPT WHICH-FIELD.
016800*
016900*RE-ACCEPT-WHICH-FIELD.
017000*     DISPLAY "INVALID ENTRY".
017100*     PERFORM ACCEPT-WHICH-FIELD.
017200
017300 CHANGE-ONE-FIELD.
017400      PERFORM CHANGE-THIS-FIELD.
017500*     PERFORM GET-FIELD-TO-CHANGE.
017600
```

continues

Listing 15.11. continued

```
017700 CHANGE-THIS-FIELD.
017800     IF WHICH-FIELD = 1
017900         PERFORM ENTER-STATE-NAME.
018000
018100     PERFORM REWRITE-STATE-RECORD.
018200
018300*-------------------------------
018400* INQUIRE
018500*-------------------------------
018600 INQUIRE-MODE.
018700     MOVE "DISPLAY" TO THE-MODE.
018800     PERFORM GET-STATE-RECORD.
018900     PERFORM INQUIRE-RECORDS
019000         UNTIL STATE-CODE = "ZZ".
019100
019200 INQUIRE-RECORDS.
019300     PERFORM DISPLAY-ALL-FIELDS.
019400     PERFORM GET-STATE-RECORD.
019500
019600*-------------------------------
019700* DELETE
019800*-------------------------------
019900 DELETE-MODE.
020000     MOVE "DELETE" TO THE-MODE.
020100     PERFORM GET-STATE-RECORD.
020200     PERFORM DELETE-RECORDS
020300         UNTIL STATE-CODE = "ZZ".
020400
020500 DELETE-RECORDS.
020600     PERFORM DISPLAY-ALL-FIELDS.
020700
020800     PERFORM ASK-OK-TO-DELETE.
020900     IF OK-TO-DELETE = "Y"
021000         PERFORM DELETE-STATE-RECORD.
021100
021200     PERFORM GET-STATE-RECORD.
021300
021400 ASK-OK-TO-DELETE.
021500     PERFORM ACCEPT-OK-TO-DELETE.
021600     PERFORM RE-ACCEPT-OK-TO-DELETE
021700         UNTIL OK-TO-DELETE = "Y" OR "N".
021800
021900 ACCEPT-OK-TO-DELETE.
022000     DISPLAY "DELETE THIS RECORD (Y/N)?".
022100     ACCEPT OK-TO-DELETE.
022200
022300     INSPECT OK-TO-DELETE
022400       CONVERTING LOWER-ALPHA
022500       TO           UPPER-ALPHA.
022600
022700 RE-ACCEPT-OK-TO-DELETE.
022800     DISPLAY "YOU MUST ENTER YES OR NO".
022900     PERFORM ACCEPT-OK-TO-DELETE.
023000
```

15

```
023100*- - - - - - - - - - - - - - - - - - - - - - - - - - - - - - -
023200* Routines shared by all modes
023300*- - - - - - - - - - - - - - - - - - - - - - - - - - - - - - -
023400 INIT-STATE-RECORD.
023500     MOVE SPACE TO STATE-RECORD.
023600
023700 ENTER-STATE-CODE.
023800     PERFORM ACCEPT-STATE-CODE.
023900     PERFORM RE-ACCEPT-STATE-CODE
024000         UNTIL STATE-CODE NOT = SPACE.
024100
024200 ACCEPT-STATE-CODE.
024300     DISPLAY " ".
024400     DISPLAY "ENTER STATE CODE OF THE STATE" .
024500     DISPLAY "TO " THE-MODE
024600             "(2 UPPER CASE CHARACTERS)".
024700     DISPLAY "ENTER ZZ TO STOP ENTRY".
024800     ACCEPT STATE-CODE.
024900
025000     INSPECT STATE-CODE
025100       CONVERTING LOWER-ALPHA
025200       TO          UPPER-ALPHA.
025300
025400 RE-ACCEPT-STATE-CODE.
025500     DISPLAY "STATE CODE MUST BE ENTERED".
025600     PERFORM ACCEPT-STATE-CODE.
025700
025800 GET-STATE-RECORD.
025900     PERFORM INIT-STATE-RECORD.
026000     PERFORM ENTER-STATE-CODE.
026100     MOVE "N" TO RECORD-FOUND.
026200     PERFORM FIND-STATE-RECORD
026300         UNTIL RECORD-FOUND = "Y" OR
026400               STATE-CODE = "ZZ".
026500
026600*- - - - - - - - - - - - - - - - - - - - - - - - - - - - - - -
026700* Routines shared Add and Change
026800*- - - - - - - - - - - - - - - - - - - - - - - - - - - - - - -
026900 FIND-STATE-RECORD.
027000     PERFORM READ-STATE-RECORD.
027100     IF RECORD-FOUND = "N"
027200         DISPLAY "RECORD NOT FOUND"
027300         PERFORM ENTER-STATE-CODE.
027400
027500 ENTER-STATE-NAME.
027600     PERFORM ACCEPT-STATE-NAME.
027700     PERFORM RE-ACCEPT-STATE-NAME
027800         UNTIL STATE-NAME NOT = SPACES.
027900
028000 ACCEPT-STATE-NAME.
028100     DISPLAY "ENTER STATE NAME".
028200     ACCEPT STATE-NAME.
028300
028400     INSPECT STATE-NAME
```

continues

Listing 15.11. continued

```
028500        CONVERTING LOWER-ALPHA
028600        TO            UPPER-ALPHA.
028700
028800 RE-ACCEPT-STATE-NAME.
028900     DISPLAY "STATE NAME MUST BE ENTERED".
029000     PERFORM ACCEPT-STATE-NAME.
029100
029200*--------------------------------
029300* Routines shared by Change,
029400* Inquire and Delete
029500*--------------------------------
029600 DISPLAY-ALL-FIELDS.
029700     DISPLAY " ".
029800     PERFORM DISPLAY-STATE-CODE.
029900     PERFORM DISPLAY-STATE-NAME.
030000     DISPLAY " ".
030100
030200 DISPLAY-STATE-CODE.
030300     DISPLAY "   STATE CODE: " STATE-CODE.
030400
030500 DISPLAY-STATE-NAME.
030600     DISPLAY "1. STATE NAME: " STATE-NAME.
030700
030800*--------------------------------
030900* File I-O Routines
031000*--------------------------------
031100 READ-STATE-RECORD.
031200     MOVE "Y" TO RECORD-FOUND.
031300     READ STATE-FILE RECORD
031400        INVALID KEY
031500           MOVE "N" TO RECORD-FOUND.
031600
031700*or  READ STATE-FILE RECORD WITH LOCK
031800*       INVALID KEY
031900*          MOVE "N" TO RECORD-FOUND.
032000
032100*or  READ STATE-FILE RECORD WITH HOLD
032200*       INVALID KEY
032300*          MOVE "N" TO RECORD-FOUND.
032400
032500 WRITE-STATE-RECORD.
032600     WRITE STATE-RECORD
032700        INVALID KEY
032800        DISPLAY "RECORD ALREADY ON FILE".
032900
033000 REWRITE-STATE-RECORD.
033100     REWRITE STATE-RECORD
033200        INVALID KEY
033300        DISPLAY "ERROR REWRITING STATE RECORD".
033400
033500 DELETE-STATE-RECORD.
033600     DELETE STATE-FILE RECORD
033700        INVALID KEY
033800        DISPLAY "ERROR DELETING STATE RECORD".
033900
```

The output of `stcmnt03.cbl` shows an example of adding `fl florida` in lowercase, but finding that it is stored in uppercase:

```
PLEASE SELECT:
1.  ADD RECORDS
2.  CHANGE A RECORD
3.  LOOK UP A RECORD
4.  DELETE A RECORD
0.  EXIT
YOUR CHOICE (0-4)?
1
ENTER STATE CODE OF THE STATE
TO ADD    (2 UPPER CASE CHARACTERS)
ENTER ZZ TO STOP ENTRY
fl
ENTER STATE NAME
florida
ENTER STATE CODE OF THE STATE
TO ADD    (2 UPPER CASE CHARACTERS)
ENTER ZZ TO STOP ENTRY
zz
```

OUTPUT
```
PLEASE SELECT:
1.  ADD RECORDS
2.  CHANGE A RECORD
3.  LOOK UP A RECORD
4.  DELETE A RECORD
0.  EXIT
YOUR CHOICE (0-4)?
3
ENTER STATE CODE OF THE STATE
TO DISPLAY(2 UPPER CASE CHARACTERS)
ENTER ZZ TO STOP ENTRY
fl
STATE CODE: FL
1. STATE NAME: FLORIDA
ENTER STATE CODE OF THE STATE
TO DISPLAY(2 UPPER CASE CHARACTERS)
ENTER ZZ TO STOP ENTRY
```

ANALYSIS The uppercase conversion is added to the program at lines `002800` through `003100`, `025000` though `025200`, and `028400` through `028600`.

This program also took advantage of the availability of uppercase conversion in the ACCEPT-OK-TO-DELETE routine at line `021900`. The tests are replaced with an INSPECT CONVERTING at lines `022300` through `022500`.

Code, compile, and run `stcmnt03.cbl`, and deliberately enter some lowercase values. Then look up the record and you will see that they have been stored in uppercase.

The addition of the conversion to uppercase for the STATE-CODE and the STATE-NAME now takes advantage of the edit-check-the-data section of the pseudocode for a standard field-entry routine. Figures 15.7 and 15.8 compare the new routines to the standard field-entry routine.

Figure 15.7.

ENTER-STATE-CODE
with uppercase editing.

```
ENTER-STATE-CODE.
PERFORM ACCEPT-STATE-CODE.
    PERFORM RE-ACCEPT-STATE-CODE
        UNTIL STATE-CODE NOT = SPACES.
ACCEPT-STATE-CODE.
    DISPLAY " ".
    DISPLAY "ENTER STATE CODE OF THE STATE" .
    DISPLAY "TO " THE-MODE.
                "(2 UPPER CASE CHARACTERS)".
    DISPLAY "ENTER ZZ TO STOP ENTRY".
    ACCEPT STATE-CODE.
    INSPECT STATE-CODE
      CONVERTING LOWER-ALPHA
        TO          UPPER-ALPHA.
RE-ACCEPT-STATE-CODE.
    DISPLAY "STATE CODE MUST BE ENTERED".
    PERFORM ACCEPT-STATE-CODE.
```

```
enter-the-data.
PERFORM accept-the-data.
    PERFORM re-accept-the-data.
    UNTIL the-data is valid.
accept-the-data.

    DISPLAY a-prompt.



    ACCEPT the-data.
    edit-check-the-data.


re-accept-the-data.
    DISPLAY error-message.
    PERFORM accept-the-data.
```

Figure 15.8.

ENTER-STATE-NAME
with uppercase editing.

```
ENTER-STATE-NAME.
    PERFORM ACCEPT-STATE-NAME.
    PERFORM RE-ACCEPT-STATE-NAME
        UNTIL STATE-NAME NOT = SPACES.
ACCEPT-STATE-NAME.
    DISPLAY "ENTER STATE NAME".
    ACCEPT STATE-NAME.
    INSPECT STATE-NAME
    CONVERTING LOWER-ALPHA
      TO         UPPER-ALPHA.
RE-ACCEPT-STATE-NAME.
    DISPLAY "STATE NAME MUST BE ENTERED".
    PERFORM ACCEPT-STATE-NAME.
```

```
enter-the-data.
    PERFORM accept-the-data.
    PERFORM re-accept-the-data.
    UNTIL the-data is valid
accept-the-data.
    DISPLAY a-prompt.
    ACCEPT the-data.
    edit-check-the-data.


re-accept-the-data.
    DISPLAY error-message.
    PERFORM accept-the-data.
```

There are other ways to convert values to uppercase or lowercase, and these are covered in Bonus Day 5, "Intrinsic Functions and the Year 2000."

Summary

As computer systems become larger and larger, the amount of data stored on the computers increases. In today's lesson, you created a file containing state codes, and you entered data into it using various levels of validation. You also learned the following basics:

☐ Data validation is important in any computer system. The program depends on the correct type of data being in various fields, and the user depends on correct content being in various fields.

☐ Data should be validated whenever the validation is easy to perform, the data is critical, or the volume of data is large.

☐ Always validate data before it is written to the file.

☐ Every maintenance program for a file—especially add and change modes—must include the full validation for each field that requires validation.

☐ Do not try to work around invalid data in a file. Find the cause of the incorrect data and fix it; then correct the incorrect data.

15

15

☐ The simplest form of data validation is requiring that a field be entered and not left blank.

☐ Data can be forced to uppercase by using the INSPECT CONVERTING command.

☐ A standard field-entry routine can be described as the following:

```
enter-the-data.
    PERFORM accept-the-data.
    PERFORM re-accept-the-data.
      UNTIL the-data is valid.
accept-the-data.
    DISPLAY a-prompt.
    ACCEPT the-data.
    edit-check-the-data.
re-accept-the-data.
    DISPLAY error-message.
    PERFORM accept-the-data.
```

Q&A

Q Is data validation part of the COBOL language?

A No. COBOL provides commands that make it possible to validate data, but the actual validation is part of the design of the program. You can write a program that enables you to put any old junk into a file and COBOL will not complain about it, although the users most certainly will.

Workshop

Quiz

1. When should data be validated?

    ☐ Before it is put in the data file.

    ☐ After it has been put in the data file.

    ☐ Any time it is used.

    ☐ After it has been used for a while.

2. What COBOL command can be used to convert a field to uppercase?

3. If the following listing converts DATA-FIELD to uppercase, how would you convert DATA-FIELD to lowercase?

```
010300        INSPECT DATA FIELD
010400            CONVERTING LOWER-ALPHA
010500            TO        UPPER-ALPHA.
```

Exercises

1. Design a standard data entry routine to accept entry for a field called VENDOR-NAME. Assume that appropriate UPPER-ALPHA and LOWER-ALPHA conversion fields exist in WORKING-STORAGE. The field must be entered by the user, and it must be converted to uppercase after the entry is completed. Do this using pencil and paper.

   Hint: You could use ENTER-STATE-NAME as a basis for the routine.

2. Next to the design you have written, write down the parts of the standard field-entry routine.

Day **16**

Using Look Up and Arrays

One of the main methods of validating entered data is to look up the information in another file that contains correct information. In today's lesson, you learn about the following topics:

- ☐ Using look up for validation.
- ☐ Locating invalid data in files.
- ☐ Fixing invalid data in files.
- ☐ What is a table?
- ☐ Looking up data in tables.
- ☐ Using a table in a program.

Using Look Up for Validation

Today, you learn how to use the state code file created in Day 15, "Data Integrity," to check the VENDOR-STATE for correctness when the user is entering data into the vendor file. Listing 16.1 shows a new FD for the vendor file.

TYPE **Listing 16.1. A new FD for the vendor file, indicating which fields are required.**

```
000100*--------------------------------
000200* FDVND03.CBL
000300* Primary Key - VENDOR-NUMBER
000400*
000500* NAME, ADDRESS-1, CITY, STATE,
000600*   and PHONE are required fields.
000700*
000800* VENDOR-STATE must be looked up
000900*   and must exist in the STATE-FILE
001000*   to be valid.
001100* VENDOR-ADDRESS-2 not always used
001200*   so may be SPACES
001300* VENDOR-PHONE is usually the
001400*   number for VENDOR-CONTACT
001500* All fields should be entered in
001600*   UPPER case.
001700*--------------------------------
001800 FD  VENDOR-FILE
001900     LABEL RECORDS ARE STANDARD.
002000 01  VENDOR-RECORD.
002100     05  VENDOR-NUMBER        PIC 9(5).
002200     05  VENDOR-NAME          PIC X(30).
002300     05  VENDOR-ADDRESS-1     PIC X(30).
002400     05  VENDOR-ADDRESS-2     PIC X(30).
002500     05  VENDOR-CITY          PIC X(20).
002600     05  VENDOR-STATE         PIC X(2).
002700     05  VENDOR-ZIP           PIC X(10).
002800     05  VENDOR-CONTACT       PIC X(30).
002900     05  VENDOR-PHONE         PIC X(15).
003000
```

ANALYSIS There is no change in the file layout, but there is a change in the comments indicating which fields are required. The comments indicate that all fields should be uppercase, and all fields are required except for VENDOR-ADDRESS-2 and VENDOR-CONTACT. The VENDOR-STATE also must be looked up in the state codes file.

The original version of vndmnt01.cbl does not include these validations, so today you add those validations, including looking up the state code.

16

You already are familiar with the uppercase and required validations. Listing 16.2 shows an example of the validation logic for the VENDOR-ADDRESS-1 field using the standard field-entry routine developed on Day 15.

TYPE   **Listing 16.2. Entering VENDOR-ADDRESS-1.**

```
030100 ENTER-VENDOR-ADDRESS-1.
030200     PERFORM ACCEPT-VENDOR-ADDRESS-1.
030300     PERFORM RE-ACCEPT-VENDOR-ADDRESS-1
030400         UNTIL VENDOR-ADDRESS-1 NOT = SPACE.
030500
030600 ACCEPT-VENDOR-ADDRESS-1.
030700     DISPLAY "ENTER VENDOR ADDRESS-1".
030800     ACCEPT VENDOR-ADDRESS-1.
030900     INSPECT VENDOR-ADDRESS-1
031000         CONVERTING LOWER-ALPHA
031100         TO          UPPER-ALPHA.
031200
031300 RE-ACCEPT-VENDOR-ADDRESS-1.
031400     DISPLAY "VENDOR ADDRESS-1 MUST BE ENTERED".
031500     PERFORM ACCEPT-VENDOR-ADDRESS-1.
031600
```

VENDOR-ADDRESS-2 is not a required field, so the entry routine is much simpler, as shown in Listing 16.3.

TYPE   **Listing 16.3. Entering VENDOR-ADDRESS-2.**

```
031700 ENTER-VENDOR-ADDRESS-2.
031800     DISPLAY "ENTER VENDOR ADDRESS-2".
031900     ACCEPT VENDOR-ADDRESS-2.
032000     INSPECT VENDOR-ADDRESS-2
032100         CONVERTING LOWER-ALPHA
032200         TO          UPPER-ALPHA.
```

This type of logic can be repeated for all fields in the vendor file. VENDOR-ZIP and VENDOR-PHONE can be validated the same way. Postal codes might contain letters when they are outside the United States, such as the Canadian Postal Code system. Phone numbers rarely contain letters, but using this approach enables you to enter gimmick phone numbers that contain letters.

This works fine until you get to VENDOR-STATE. This field is a required entry field that must be uppercase but also must be tested against the state codes file to ensure that it already exists in that file.

Listing 16.4, vndmnt02.cbl, includes the validations discussed so far. The analysis concentrates particularly on the changes made for handling the VENDOR-STATE.

TYPE   **Listing 16.4. Looking up data in another file to validate it.**

```
000100 IDENTIFICATION DIVISION.
000200 PROGRAM-ID. VNDMNT02.
000300*--------------------------------
000400* Add, Change, Inquire and Delete
000500* for the Vendor File.
000600*--------------------------------
000700 ENVIRONMENT DIVISION.
000800 INPUT-OUTPUT SECTION.
000900 FILE-CONTROL.
001000
001100     COPY "SLVND01.CBL".
001200
001300     COPY "SLSTATE.CBL".
001400
001500 DATA DIVISION.
001600 FILE SECTION.
001700
001800     COPY "FDVND03.CBL".
001900
002000     COPY "FDSTATE.CBL".
002100
002200 WORKING-STORAGE SECTION.
002300
002400 77  MENU-PICK                PIC 9.
002500     88  MENU-PICK-IS-VALID    VALUES 0 THRU 4.
002600
002700 77  THE-MODE                 PIC X(7).
002800 77  WHICH-FIELD              PIC 9.
002900 77  OK-TO-DELETE             PIC X.
003000 77  VENDOR-RECORD-FOUND      PIC X.
003100 77  STATE-RECORD-FOUND       PIC X.
003200
003300
003400 77  VENDOR-NUMBER-FIELD      PIC Z(5).
003500
003600 77  ERROR-MESSAGE            PIC X(79) VALUE SPACE.
003700
003800 77  UPPER-ALPHA              PIC X(26) VALUE
003900     "ABCDEFGHIJKLMNOPQRSTUVWXYZ".
004000 77  LOWER-ALPHA              PIC X(26) VALUE
004100     "abcdefghijklmnopqrstuvwxyz".
004200
004300 PROCEDURE DIVISION.
004400 PROGRAM-BEGIN.
004500     PERFORM OPENING-PROCEDURE.
004600     PERFORM MAIN-PROCESS.
004700     PERFORM CLOSING-PROCEDURE.
004800
004900 PROGRAM-DONE.
```

16

```
005000     STOP RUN.
005100
005200 OPENING-PROCEDURE.
005300     OPEN I-O VENDOR-FILE.
005400     OPEN I-O STATE-FILE.
005500
005600 CLOSING-PROCEDURE.
005700     CLOSE VENDOR-FILE.
005800     CLOSE STATE-FILE.
005900
006000 MAIN-PROCESS.
006100     PERFORM GET-MENU-PICK.
006200     PERFORM MAINTAIN-THE-FILE
006300         UNTIL MENU-PICK = 0.
006400
006500*------------------------------
006600* MENU
006700*------------------------------
006800 GET-MENU-PICK.
006900     PERFORM DISPLAY-THE-MENU.
007000     PERFORM ACCEPT-MENU-PICK.
007100     PERFORM RE-ACCEPT-MENU-PICK
007200         UNTIL MENU-PICK-IS-VALID.
007300
007400 DISPLAY-THE-MENU.
007500     PERFORM CLEAR-SCREEN.
007600     DISPLAY "    PLEASE SELECT:".
007700     DISPLAY " ".
007800     DISPLAY "         1.  ADD RECORDS".
007900     DISPLAY "         2.  CHANGE A RECORD".
008000     DISPLAY "         3.  LOOK UP A RECORD".
008100     DISPLAY "         4.  DELETE A RECORD".
008200     DISPLAY " ".
008300     DISPLAY "         0.  EXIT".
008400     PERFORM SCROLL-LINE 8 TIMES.
008500
008600 ACCEPT-MENU-PICK.
008700     DISPLAY "YOUR CHOICE (0-4)?".
008800     ACCEPT MENU-PICK.
008900
009000 RE-ACCEPT-MENU-PICK.
009100     DISPLAY "INVALID SELECTION - PLEASE RE-TRY.".
009200     PERFORM ACCEPT-MENU-PICK.
009300
009400 CLEAR-SCREEN.
009500     PERFORM SCROLL-LINE 25 TIMES.
009600
009700 SCROLL-LINE.
009800     DISPLAY " ".
009900
010000 MAINTAIN-THE-FILE.
010100     PERFORM DO-THE-PICK.
010200     PERFORM GET-MENU-PICK.
010300
010400 DO-THE-PICK.
010500     IF MENU-PICK = 1
```

continues

16

Listing 16.4. continued

```
010600          PERFORM ADD-MODE
010700      ELSE
010800      IF MENU-PICK = 2
010900          PERFORM CHANGE-MODE
011000      ELSE
011100      IF MENU-PICK = 3
011200          PERFORM INQUIRE-MODE
011300      ELSE
011400      IF MENU-PICK = 4
011500          PERFORM DELETE-MODE.
011600
011700*--------------------------------
011800* ADD
011900*--------------------------------
012000 ADD-MODE.
012100      MOVE "ADD" TO THE-MODE.
012200      PERFORM GET-NEW-RECORD-KEY.
012300      PERFORM ADD-RECORDS
012400          UNTIL VENDOR-NUMBER = ZEROES.
012500
012600 GET-NEW-RECORD-KEY.
012700      PERFORM ACCEPT-NEW-RECORD-KEY.
012800      PERFORM RE-ACCEPT-NEW-RECORD-KEY
012900          UNTIL VENDOR-RECORD-FOUND = "N" OR
013000              VENDOR-NUMBER = ZEROES.
013100
013200 ACCEPT-NEW-RECORD-KEY.
013300      PERFORM INIT-VENDOR-RECORD.
013400      PERFORM ENTER-VENDOR-NUMBER.
013500      IF VENDOR-NUMBER NOT = ZEROES
013600          PERFORM READ-VENDOR-RECORD.
013700
013800 RE-ACCEPT-NEW-RECORD-KEY.
013900      DISPLAY "RECORD ALREADY ON FILE"
014000      PERFORM ACCEPT-NEW-RECORD-KEY.
014100
014200 ADD-RECORDS.
014300      PERFORM ENTER-REMAINING-FIELDS.
014400      PERFORM WRITE-VENDOR-RECORD.
014500      PERFORM GET-NEW-RECORD-KEY.
014600
014700 ENTER-REMAINING-FIELDS.
014800      PERFORM ENTER-VENDOR-NAME.
014900      PERFORM ENTER-VENDOR-ADDRESS-1.
015000      PERFORM ENTER-VENDOR-ADDRESS-2.
015100      PERFORM ENTER-VENDOR-CITY.
015200      PERFORM ENTER-VENDOR-STATE.
015300      PERFORM ENTER-VENDOR-ZIP.
015400      PERFORM ENTER-VENDOR-CONTACT.
015500      PERFORM ENTER-VENDOR-PHONE.
015600
015700*--------------------------------
015800* CHANGE
015900*--------------------------------
```

```
016000 CHANGE-MODE.
016100      MOVE "CHANGE" TO THE-MODE.
016200      PERFORM GET-EXISTING-RECORD.
016300      PERFORM CHANGE-RECORDS
016400          UNTIL VENDOR-NUMBER = ZEROES.
016500
016600 CHANGE-RECORDS.
016700      PERFORM GET-FIELD-TO-CHANGE.
016800      PERFORM CHANGE-ONE-FIELD
016900          UNTIL WHICH-FIELD = ZERO.
017000      PERFORM GET-EXISTING-RECORD.
017100
017200 GET-FIELD-TO-CHANGE.
017300      PERFORM DISPLAY-ALL-FIELDS.
017400      PERFORM ASK-WHICH-FIELD.
017500
017600 ASK-WHICH-FIELD.
017700      PERFORM ACCEPT-WHICH-FIELD.
017800      PERFORM RE-ACCEPT-WHICH-FIELD
017900          UNTIL WHICH-FIELD < 9.
018000
018100 ACCEPT-WHICH-FIELD.
018200      DISPLAY "ENTER THE NUMBER OF THE FIELD".
018300      DISPLAY "TO CHANGE (1-8) OR 0 TO EXIT".
018400      ACCEPT WHICH-FIELD.
018500
018600 RE-ACCEPT-WHICH-FIELD.
018700      DISPLAY "INVALID ENTRY".
018800      PERFORM ACCEPT-WHICH-FIELD.
018900
019000 CHANGE-ONE-FIELD.
019100      PERFORM CHANGE-THIS-FIELD.
019200      PERFORM GET-FIELD-TO-CHANGE.
019300
019400 CHANGE-THIS-FIELD.
019500      IF WHICH-FIELD = 1
019600          PERFORM ENTER-VENDOR-NAME.
019700      IF WHICH-FIELD = 2
019800          PERFORM ENTER-VENDOR-ADDRESS-1.
019900      IF WHICH-FIELD = 3
020000          PERFORM ENTER-VENDOR-ADDRESS-2.
020100      IF WHICH-FIELD = 4
020200          PERFORM ENTER-VENDOR-CITY.
020300      IF WHICH-FIELD = 5
020400          PERFORM ENTER-VENDOR-STATE.
020500      IF WHICH-FIELD = 6
020600          PERFORM ENTER-VENDOR-ZIP.
020700      IF WHICH-FIELD = 7
020800          PERFORM ENTER-VENDOR-CONTACT.
020900      IF WHICH-FIELD = 8
021000          PERFORM ENTER-VENDOR-PHONE.
021100
021200      PERFORM REWRITE-VENDOR-RECORD.
021300
021400*------------------------------
021500* INQUIRE
```

continues

Listing 16.4. continued

```
021600*--------------------------------
021700 INQUIRE-MODE.
021800      MOVE "DISPLAY" TO THE-MODE.
021900      PERFORM GET-EXISTING-RECORD.
022000      PERFORM INQUIRE-RECORDS
022100           UNTIL VENDOR-NUMBER = ZEROES.
022200
022300 INQUIRE-RECORDS.
022400      PERFORM DISPLAY-ALL-FIELDS.
022500      PERFORM GET-EXISTING-RECORD.
022600
022700*--------------------------------
022800* DELETE
022900*--------------------------------
023000 DELETE-MODE.
023100      MOVE "DELETE" TO THE-MODE.
023200      PERFORM GET-EXISTING-RECORD.
023300      PERFORM DELETE-RECORDS
023400           UNTIL VENDOR-NUMBER = ZEROES.
023500
023600 DELETE-RECORDS.
023700      PERFORM DISPLAY-ALL-FIELDS.
023800
023900      PERFORM ASK-OK-TO-DELETE.
024000
024100      IF OK-TO-DELETE = "Y"
024200           PERFORM DELETE-VENDOR-RECORD.
024300
024400      PERFORM GET-EXISTING-RECORD.
024500
024600 ASK-OK-TO-DELETE.
024700      PERFORM ACCEPT-OK-TO-DELETE.
024800
024900      PERFORM RE-ACCEPT-OK-TO-DELETE
025000           UNTIL OK-TO-DELETE = "Y" OR "N".
025100
025200 ACCEPT-OK-TO-DELETE.
025300      DISPLAY "DELETE THIS RECORD (Y/N)?".
025400      ACCEPT OK-TO-DELETE.
025500      INSPECT OK-TO-DELETE
025600        CONVERTING LOWER-ALPHA TO UPPER-ALPHA.
025700
025800 RE-ACCEPT-OK-TO-DELETE.
025900      DISPLAY "YOU MUST ENTER YES OR NO".
026000      PERFORM ACCEPT-OK-TO-DELETE.
026100
026200*--------------------------------
026300* Routines shared by all modes
026400*--------------------------------
026500 INIT-VENDOR-RECORD.
026600      MOVE SPACE TO VENDOR-RECORD.
026700      MOVE ZEROES TO VENDOR-NUMBER.
026800
026900 ENTER-VENDOR-NUMBER.
```

16

```
027000     DISPLAY " ".
027100     DISPLAY "ENTER VENDOR NUMBER OF THE VENDOR" .
027200     DISPLAY "TO " THE-MODE " (1-99999)".
027300     DISPLAY "ENTER 0 TO STOP ENTRY".
027400     ACCEPT VENDOR-NUMBER-FIELD.
027500*OR  ACCEPT VENDOR-NUMBER-FIELD WITH CONVERSION.
027600
027700     MOVE VENDOR-NUMBER-FIELD TO VENDOR-NUMBER.
027800
027900*-------------------------------
028000* Routines shared Add and Change
028100*-------------------------------
028200 ENTER-VENDOR-NAME.
028300     PERFORM ACCEPT-VENDOR-NAME.
028400     PERFORM RE-ACCEPT-VENDOR-NAME
028500         UNTIL VENDOR-NAME NOT = SPACE.
028600
028700 ACCEPT-VENDOR-NAME.
028800     DISPLAY "ENTER VENDOR NAME".
028900     ACCEPT VENDOR-NAME.
029000     INSPECT VENDOR-NAME
029100         CONVERTING LOWER-ALPHA
029200         TO          UPPER-ALPHA.
029300
029400 RE-ACCEPT-VENDOR-NAME.
029500     DISPLAY "VENDOR NAME MUST BE ENTERED".
029600     PERFORM ACCEPT-VENDOR-NAME.
029700
029800 ENTER-VENDOR-ADDRESS-1.
029900     PERFORM ACCEPT-VENDOR-ADDRESS-1.
030000     PERFORM RE-ACCEPT-VENDOR-ADDRESS-1
030100         UNTIL VENDOR-ADDRESS-1 NOT = SPACE.
030200
030300 ACCEPT-VENDOR-ADDRESS-1.
030400     DISPLAY "ENTER VENDOR ADDRESS-1".
030500     ACCEPT VENDOR-ADDRESS-1.
030600     INSPECT VENDOR-ADDRESS-1
030700         CONVERTING LOWER-ALPHA
030800         TO          UPPER-ALPHA.
030900
031000 RE-ACCEPT-VENDOR-ADDRESS-1.
031100     DISPLAY "VENDOR ADDRESS-1 MUST BE ENTERED".
031200     PERFORM ACCEPT-VENDOR-ADDRESS-1.
031300
031400 ENTER-VENDOR-ADDRESS-2.
031500     DISPLAY "ENTER VENDOR ADDRESS-2".
031600     ACCEPT VENDOR-ADDRESS-2.
031700     INSPECT VENDOR-ADDRESS-2
031800         CONVERTING LOWER-ALPHA
031900         TO          UPPER-ALPHA.
032000
032100 ENTER-VENDOR-CITY.
032200     PERFORM ACCEPT-VENDOR-CITY.
032300     PERFORM RE-ACCEPT-VENDOR-CITY
032400         UNTIL VENDOR-CITY NOT = SPACE.
032500
```

continues

Listing 16.4. continued

```
032600 ACCEPT-VENDOR-CITY.
032700     DISPLAY "ENTER VENDOR CITY".
032800     ACCEPT VENDOR-CITY.
032900     INSPECT VENDOR-CITY
033000        CONVERTING LOWER-ALPHA
033100        TO          UPPER-ALPHA.
033200
033300 RE-ACCEPT-VENDOR-CITY.
033400     DISPLAY "VENDOR CITY MUST BE ENTERED".
033500     PERFORM ACCEPT-VENDOR-CITY.
033600
033700 ENTER-VENDOR-STATE.
033800     PERFORM ACCEPT-VENDOR-STATE.
033900     PERFORM RE-ACCEPT-VENDOR-STATE
034000        UNTIL VENDOR-STATE NOT = SPACES AND
034100              STATE-RECORD-FOUND = "Y".
034200
034300 ACCEPT-VENDOR-STATE.
034400     DISPLAY "ENTER VENDOR STATE".
034500     ACCEPT VENDOR-STATE.
034600     PERFORM EDIT-CHECK-VENDOR-STATE.
034700
034800 RE-ACCEPT-VENDOR-STATE.
034900     DISPLAY ERROR-MESSAGE.
035000     PERFORM ACCEPT-VENDOR-STATE.
035100
035200 EDIT-CHECK-VENDOR-STATE.
035300     PERFORM EDIT-VENDOR-STATE.
035400     PERFORM CHECK-VENDOR-STATE.
035500
035600 EDIT-VENDOR-STATE.
035700     INSPECT VENDOR-STATE
035800        CONVERTING LOWER-ALPHA
035900        TO          UPPER-ALPHA.
036000
036100 CHECK-VENDOR-STATE.
036200     PERFORM VENDOR-STATE-REQUIRED.
036300     IF VENDOR-STATE NOT = SPACES
036400        PERFORM VENDOR-STATE-ON-FILE.
036500
036600 VENDOR-STATE-REQUIRED.
036700     IF VENDOR-STATE = SPACE
036800        MOVE "VENDOR STATE MUST BE ENTERED"
036900           TO ERROR-MESSAGE.
037000
037100 VENDOR-STATE-ON-FILE.
037200     MOVE VENDOR-STATE TO STATE-CODE.
037300     PERFORM READ-STATE-RECORD.
037400     IF STATE-RECORD-FOUND = "N"
037500        MOVE "STATE CODE NOT FOUND IN CODES FILE"
037600           TO ERROR-MESSAGE.
037700
037800 ENTER-VENDOR-ZIP.
037900     PERFORM ACCEPT-VENDOR-ZIP.
```

16

```
038000     PERFORM RE-ACCEPT-VENDOR-ZIP
038100         UNTIL VENDOR-ZIP NOT = SPACE.
038200
038300 ACCEPT-VENDOR-ZIP.
038400     DISPLAY "ENTER VENDOR ZIP".
038500     ACCEPT VENDOR-ZIP.
038600     INSPECT VENDOR-ZIP
038700         CONVERTING LOWER-ALPHA
038800         TO          UPPER-ALPHA.
038900
039000 RE-ACCEPT-VENDOR-ZIP.
039100     DISPLAY "VENDOR ZIP MUST BE ENTERED".
039200     PERFORM ACCEPT-VENDOR-ZIP.
039300
039400 ENTER-VENDOR-CONTACT.
039500     DISPLAY "ENTER VENDOR CONTACT".
039600     ACCEPT VENDOR-CONTACT.
039700     INSPECT VENDOR-CONTACT
039800         CONVERTING LOWER-ALPHA
039900         TO          UPPER-ALPHA.
040000
040100 ENTER-VENDOR-PHONE.
040200     PERFORM ACCEPT-VENDOR-PHONE.
040300     PERFORM RE-ACCEPT-VENDOR-PHONE
040400         UNTIL VENDOR-PHONE NOT = SPACE.
040500
040600 ACCEPT-VENDOR-PHONE.
040700     DISPLAY "ENTER VENDOR PHONE".
040800     ACCEPT VENDOR-PHONE.
040900     INSPECT VENDOR-PHONE
041000         CONVERTING LOWER-ALPHA
041100         TO          UPPER-ALPHA.
041200
041300 RE-ACCEPT-VENDOR-PHONE.
041400     DISPLAY "VENDOR PHONE MUST BE ENTERED".
041500     PERFORM ACCEPT-VENDOR-PHONE.
041600
041700*-------------------------------
041800* Routines shared by Change,
041900* Inquire and Delete
042000*-------------------------------
042100 GET-EXISTING-RECORD.
042200     PERFORM ACCEPT-EXISTING-KEY.
042300     PERFORM RE-ACCEPT-EXISTING-KEY
042400         UNTIL VENDOR-RECORD-FOUND = "Y" OR
042500             VENDOR-NUMBER = ZEROES.
042600
042700 ACCEPT-EXISTING-KEY.
042800     PERFORM INIT-VENDOR-RECORD.
042900     PERFORM ENTER-VENDOR-NUMBER.
043000     IF VENDOR-NUMBER NOT = ZEROES
043100         PERFORM READ-VENDOR-RECORD.
043200
043300 RE-ACCEPT-EXISTING-KEY.
043400     DISPLAY "RECORD NOT FOUND"
043500     PERFORM ACCEPT-EXISTING-KEY.
```

continues

Listing 16.4. continued

```
043600
043700 DISPLAY-ALL-FIELDS.
043800     DISPLAY " ".
043900     PERFORM DISPLAY-VENDOR-NUMBER.
044000     PERFORM DISPLAY-VENDOR-NAME.
044100     PERFORM DISPLAY-VENDOR-ADDRESS-1.
044200     PERFORM DISPLAY-VENDOR-ADDRESS-2.
044300     PERFORM DISPLAY-VENDOR-CITY.
044400     PERFORM DISPLAY-VENDOR-STATE.
044500     PERFORM DISPLAY-VENDOR-ZIP.
044600     PERFORM DISPLAY-VENDOR-CONTACT.
044700     PERFORM DISPLAY-VENDOR-PHONE.
044800     DISPLAY " ".
044900
045000 DISPLAY-VENDOR-NUMBER.
045100     DISPLAY "   VENDOR NUMBER: " VENDOR-NUMBER.
045200
045300 DISPLAY-VENDOR-NAME.
045400     DISPLAY "1. VENDOR NAME: " VENDOR-NAME.
045500
045600 DISPLAY-VENDOR-ADDRESS-1.
045700     DISPLAY "2. VENDOR ADDRESS-1: " VENDOR-ADDRESS-1.
045800
045900 DISPLAY-VENDOR-ADDRESS-2.
046000     DISPLAY "3. VENDOR ADDRESS-2: " VENDOR-ADDRESS-2.
046100
046200 DISPLAY-VENDOR-CITY.
046300     DISPLAY "4. VENDOR CITY: " VENDOR-CITY.
046400
046500 DISPLAY-VENDOR-STATE.
046600     PERFORM VENDOR-STATE-ON-FILE.
046700     IF STATE-RECORD-FOUND = "N"
046800         MOVE "**Not found**" TO STATE-NAME.
046900     DISPLAY "5. VENDOR STATE: "
047000             VENDOR-STATE " "
047100             STATE-NAME.
047200
047300 DISPLAY-VENDOR-ZIP.
047400     DISPLAY "6. VENDOR ZIP: " VENDOR-ZIP.
047500
047600 DISPLAY-VENDOR-CONTACT.
047700     DISPLAY "7. VENDOR CONTACT: " VENDOR-CONTACT.
047800
047900 DISPLAY-VENDOR-PHONE.
048000     DISPLAY "8. VENDOR PHONE: " VENDOR-PHONE.
048100
048200*-------------------------------
048300* File I-O Routines
048400*-------------------------------
048500 READ-VENDOR-RECORD.
048600     MOVE "Y" TO VENDOR-RECORD-FOUND.
048700     READ VENDOR-FILE RECORD
048800        INVALID KEY
048900            MOVE "N" TO VENDOR-RECORD-FOUND.
```

```
049000
049100*or   READ VENDOR-FILE RECORD WITH LOCK
049200*        INVALID KEY
049300*          MOVE "N" TO VENDOR-RECORD-FOUND.
049400
049500*or   READ VENDOR-FILE RECORD WITH HOLD
049600*        INVALID KEY
049700*          MOVE "N" TO VENDOR-RECORD-FOUND.
049800
049900 WRITE-VENDOR-RECORD.
050000     WRITE VENDOR-RECORD
050100        INVALID KEY
050200          DISPLAY "RECORD ALREADY ON FILE".
050300
050400 REWRITE-VENDOR-RECORD.
050500     REWRITE VENDOR-RECORD
050600        INVALID KEY
050700          DISPLAY "ERROR REWRITING VENDOR RECORD".
050800
050900 DELETE-VENDOR-RECORD.
051000     DELETE VENDOR-FILE RECORD
051100        INVALID KEY
051200          DISPLAY "ERROR DELETING VENDOR RECORD".
051300
051400 READ-STATE-RECORD.
051500     MOVE "Y" TO STATE-RECORD-FOUND.
051600     READ STATE-FILE RECORD
051700        INVALID KEY
051800          MOVE "N" TO STATE-RECORD-FOUND.
051900
```

The new vndmnt02.cbl limits you to valid state codes, but the original vndmnt01.cbl did not. If you entered an invalid state code using vndmnt01.cbl, vndmnt02.cbl would pick this up and display it.

The sample output illustrates the messages received when a user displays a record containing an invalid state code, attempts to change it to spaces, and then attempts to change it to an invalid state:

OUTPUT

```
ENTER VENDOR NUMBER OF THE VENDOR
TO CHANGE  (1-99999)
ENTER 0 TO STOP ENTRY
1
VENDOR NUMBER: 00001
1. VENDOR NAME: AERIAL SIGNS
2. VENDOR ADDRESS-1: BURBANK AIRPORT
3. VENDOR ADDRESS-2: HANGAR 305
4. VENDOR CITY: BURBANK
5. VENDOR STATE: WX **Not Found**
6. VENDOR ZIP: 90016
7. VENDOR CONTACT: HENRIETTA MARKSON
8. VENDOR PHONE: (818) 555-6066
ENTER THE NUMBER OF THE FIELD
```

```
TO CHANGE (1-8) OR 0 TO EXIT
5
ENTER VENDOR STATE
```

(User pressed Enter here with no entry.1)

```
VENDOR-STATE-MUST BE ENTERED
ENTER VENDOR STATE
ww
STATE CODE NOT FOUND IN CODES FILE
ENTER VENDOR STATE
ca
VENDOR NUMBER: 00001
1. VENDOR NAME: AERIAL SIGNS
2. VENDOR ADDRESS-1: BURBANK AIRPORT
3. VENDOR ADDRESS-2: HANGAR 305
4. VENDOR CITY: BURBANK
5. VENDOR STATE: CA CALIFORNIA
6. VENDOR ZIP: 90016
7. VENDOR CONTACT: HENRIETTA MARKSON
8. VENDOR PHONE: (818) 555-6066
ENTER THE NUMBER OF THE FIELD
TO CHANGE (1-8) OR 0 TO EXIT
```

ANALYSIS In order to look up anything in the state code file, you have to include the file in the program, and the file will have to be opened in the program. Lines 001300 and 002000 include the SELECT and FD for the STATE-FILE. At lines 005400 and 005800, the state file is opened and closed as part of OPENING-PROCEDURE and CLOSING-PROCEDURE.

The STATE-FILE has to be read, so you need a RECORD-FOUND flag for the STATE-FILE. The flag with this name already is used for reading the VENDOR-FILE, so to avoid confusion, the RECORD-FOUND variable is replaced with a VENDOR-RECORD-FOUND and a STATE-RECORD-FOUND at lines 003000 and 003100, respectively. The VENDOR-FILE uses the VENDOR-RECORD-FOUND flag during reads, and the STATE-FILE uses the STATE-RECORD-FOUND flag during reads.

The READ-STATE-RECORD routine appears at lines 051400 through 051800, and the modified READ-VENDOR-RECORD routine appears at lines 048500 through 048900.

The entry and validation of VENDOR-STATE appears at lines 033700 through 037600. The VENDOR-STATE field requires multiple validations because two conditions must be true for the field to be correct. The field must not be spaces, and a record for that state must be found in the state code file.

The ENTER-VENDOR-STATE paragraph at line 034000 has been coded to test for both of these things. In the ACCEPT-VENDOR-STATE paragraph, the editing and checking (validating) of VENDOR-STATE has been broken into a separate paragraph performed at line 034600. The EDIT-CHECK-VENDOR-STATE paragraph at line 035200 is in turn broken into separate routines to edit VENDOR-STATE and check (validate) VENDOR-STATE. In EDIT-VENDOR-STATE at line 035600, the field is converted to uppercase.

The checking (validating) of VENDOR-STATE in CHECK-VENDOR-STATE at line 036100 is broken into two separate paragraphs. At line 036200, the VENDOR-STATE-REQUIRED paragraph is performed. This routine, at line 036600, checks that the field has been entered and sets up an error message for the user if it has not. If the validation of VENDOR-STATE-REQUIRED is passed, at line 036400, the VENDOR-STATE-ON-FILE routine is performed to check that the entered state code appears in the state file.

The VENDOR-STATE-ON-FILE paragraph at line 037100 is fairly straightforward. It moves the VENDOR-STATE to the STATE-CODE and then reads the state code file. If the record is not found, another error message is set up.

The RE-ACCEPT-VENDOR-STATE paragraph at line 034800 could have displayed "INVALID ENTRY" as a catchall error message, but it is helpful to the user to have a more detailed error message. An ERROR-MESSAGE variable is defined at line 003600, filled in at line 036800 or 037500 (depending on the type of error), and then displayed at line 034900. This gives the user a better idea of the problem with the data.

Of course, this assumes that the STATE-FILE contains all the valid states that might be used in vendor addresses, and that these were entered correctly in the first place.

The VENDOR-STATE-ON-FILE routine also can be used to improve the information that is displayed on the screen for the user. At line 046500, the DISPLAY-VENDOR-STATE routine has been modified to display the name of the state, as well as the two-character abbreviation.

At line 046600, VENDOR-STATE-ON-FILE is performed. If the record is not found, the literal "**Not found**" is moved to STATE-NAME. If a record was found, STATE-NAME includes the state name from STATE-FILE. If not found, it includes the message "**Not found**". At lines 046900 through 047100, "5. VENDOR STATE: ", VENDOR-STATE, and STATE-NAME are displayed.

Another new piece of coding worth looking at starts at line 012600 with the GET-NEW-RECORD-KEY paragraph. This logic replaces the GET-NEW-VENDOR logic in vndmnt01.cbl. It is designed to work as a standard field-entry routine, as shown in Figure 16.1.

Figure 16.1.

GET-NEW-RECORD-KEY
as a standard field-entry routine.

```
GET-NEW-RECORD-KEY.                          enter-the-data.
PERFORM ACCEPT-NEW-RECORD-KEY.                PERFORM accept-the-data.
PERFORM RE-ACCEPT-NEW-RECORD-KEY             PERFORM re-accept-the-data.
UNTIL VENDOR-RECORD-FOUND = "N" OR           UNTIL the-data is valid.
VENDOR-NUMBER = ZEROES.
ACCEPT-NEW-RECORD-KEY.                        accept-the-data.
PERFORM INIT-VENDOR-RECORD.                   DISPLAY a-prompt.
PERFORM ENTER-VENDOR-NUMBER.                  ACCEPT the-data.
IF VENDOR-NUMBER NOT = ZEROES                 edit-check-the-data.
PERFORM READ-VENDOR-RECORD.
RE-ACCEPT-NEW-RECORD-KEY.                     re-accept-the-data.
DISPLAY "RECORD ALREADY ON FILE"             DISPLAY error-message.
PERFORM ACCEPT-NEW-RECORD-KEY.               PERFORM accept-the-data.
```

A similar arrangement begins at line `042100` in the `GET-EXISTING-RECORD` routine, which is compared to the standard field-entry routine in Figure 16.2.

Figure 16.2.

`GET-EXISTING-RECORD` *as a standard field-entry routine.*

```
GET-EXISTING-RECORD.                          enter-the-data.
PERFORM ACCEPT-EXISTING-KEY.                  PERFORM accept-the-data.
PERFORM RE-ACCEPT-EXISTING-KEY                PERFORM re-accept-the-data.
UNTIL VENDOR-RECORD-FOUND = "Y" OR            UNTIL the-data is valid.
VENDOR-NUMBER = ZEROES.
ACCEPT-EXISTING-KEY.                          accept-the-data.
PERFORM INIT-VENDOR-RECORD.                   DISPLAY a-prompt.
PERFORM ENTER-VENDOR-NUMBER.                  ACCEPT the-data.
IF VENDOR-NUMBER NOT = ZEROES                 edit-check-the-data.
PERFORM READ-VENDOR-RECORD.
RE-ACCEPT-EXISTING-KEY.                       re-accept-the-data.
DISPLAY "RECORD NOT FOUND"                    DISPLAY error-message.
PERFORM ACCEPT-EXISTING-KEY.                  PERFORM accept-the-data.
```

Locating Invalid Data in Files

The new version of `vndmnt02.cbl` forces uppercase entry, but `vndmnt01.cbl` did not. It is possible for your data file to contain values that are in lowercase if you used `vndmnt01.cbl` to add records.

If you have entered everything in uppercase, take the time to run `vndmnt01.cbl` once again, and add a record with lowercase fields in it. You also might want to enter one record that contains an invalid `VENDOR-STATE`—one that does not appear in the state code file.

In Figure 16.3, the state name has been added to the report immediately after the state code, and part of the report has been moved to the right to make room for the extra 20 characters of state name. A report such as this can be used to identify vendor records that contain fields in lowercase and vendor records that contain invalid state codes.

Figure 16.3.

Spacing chart for `vndrpt02.cbl`.

In Listing 16.5, the state code is looked up using logic similar to that used in `vndmnt02.cbl`.

TYPE **Listing 16.5. Adding the state name to the report.**

```
000100 IDENTIFICATION DIVISION.
000200 PROGRAM-ID. VNDRPT02.
000300*--------------------------------
000400* Report on the Vendor File.
000500*--------------------------------
```

16

```
000600 ENVIRONMENT DIVISION.
000700 INPUT-OUTPUT SECTION.
000800 FILE-CONTROL.
000900
001000     COPY "SLVND01.CBL".
001100
001200     COPY "SLSTATE.CBL".
001300
001400     SELECT PRINTER-FILE
001500         ASSIGN TO PRINTER
001600         ORGANIZATION IS LINE SEQUENTIAL.
001700
001800 DATA DIVISION.
001900 FILE SECTION.
002000
002100     COPY "FDVND02.CBL".
002200
002300     COPY "FDSTATE.CBL".
002400
002500 FD  PRINTER-FILE
002600     LABEL RECORDS ARE OMITTED.
002700 01  PRINTER-RECORD            PIC X(80).
002800
002900 WORKING-STORAGE SECTION.
003000
003100 01  DETAIL-LINE.
003200     05  PRINT-NUMBER     PIC 9(5).
003300     05  FILLER          PIC X      VALUE SPACE.
003400     05  PRINT-NAME       PIC X(30).
003500     05  FILLER          PIC X(15) VALUE SPACE.
003600     05  PRINT-CONTACT    PIC X(30).
003700
003800 01  CITY-STATE-LINE.
003900     05  FILLER           PIC X(6) VALUE SPACE.
004000     05  PRINT-CITY       PIC X(20).
004100     05  FILLER           PIC X VALUE SPACE.
004200     05  PRINT-STATE      PIC X(2).
004300     05  FILLER           PIC X VALUE SPACE.
004400     05  PRINT-STATE-NAME PIC X(20).
004500     05  FILLER           PIC X(1) VALUE SPACE.
004600     05  PRINT-ZIP        PIC X(10).
004700
004800 01  COLUMN-LINE.
004900     05  FILLER          PIC X(2)  VALUE "NO".
005000     05  FILLER          PIC X(4) VALUE SPACE.
005100     05  FILLER          PIC X(12) VALUE "NAME-ADDRESS".
005200     05  FILLER          PIC X(33) VALUE SPACE.
005300     05  FILLER          PIC X(17) VALUE "CONTACT-PHONE-ZIP".
005400
005500 01  TITLE-LINE.
005600     05  FILLER              PIC X(25) VALUE SPACE.
005700     05  FILLER              PIC X(11)
005800         VALUE "VENDOR LIST".
005900     05  FILLER              PIC X(19) VALUE SPACE.
006000     05  FILLER              PIC X(5) VALUE "PAGE:".
006100     05  FILLER              PIC X(1) VALUE SPACE.
```

continues

Listing 16.5. continued

```
006200      05  PRINT-PAGE-NUMBER PIC ZZZZ9.
006300
006400 77  FILE-AT-END           PIC X.
006500 77  STATE-RECORD-FOUND    PIC X VALUE "N".
006600 77  LINE-COUNT            PIC 999 VALUE ZERO.
006700 77  PAGE-NUMBER           PIC 99999 VALUE ZERO.
006800 77  MAXIMUM-LINES         PIC 999 VALUE 55.
006900
007000 PROCEDURE DIVISION.
007100 PROGRAM-BEGIN.
007200
007300      PERFORM OPENING-PROCEDURE.
007400      MOVE ZEROES TO LINE-COUNT
007500                     PAGE-NUMBER.
007600
007700      PERFORM START-NEW-PAGE.
007800
007900      MOVE "N" TO FILE-AT-END.
008000      PERFORM READ-NEXT-RECORD.
008100      IF FILE-AT-END = "Y"
008200          MOVE "NO RECORDS FOUND" TO PRINTER-RECORD
008300          PERFORM WRITE-TO-PRINTER
008400      ELSE
008500          PERFORM PRINT-VENDOR-FIELDS
008600              UNTIL FILE-AT-END = "Y".
008700
008800      PERFORM CLOSING-PROCEDURE.
008900
009000 PROGRAM-DONE.
009100      STOP RUN.
009200
009300 OPENING-PROCEDURE.
009400      OPEN I-O VENDOR-FILE.
009500      OPEN I-O STATE-FILE.
009600      OPEN OUTPUT PRINTER-FILE.
009700
009800 CLOSING-PROCEDURE.
009900      CLOSE VENDOR-FILE.
010000      CLOSE STATE-FILE.
010100      PERFORM END-LAST-PAGE.
010200      CLOSE PRINTER-FILE.
010300
010400 PRINT-VENDOR-FIELDS.
010500      IF LINE-COUNT > MAXIMUM-LINES
010600          PERFORM START-NEXT-PAGE.
010700      PERFORM PRINT-THE-RECORD.
010800      PERFORM READ-NEXT-RECORD.
010900
011000 PRINT-THE-RECORD.
011100      PERFORM PRINT-LINE-1.
011200      PERFORM PRINT-LINE-2.
011300      PERFORM PRINT-LINE-3.
011400      PERFORM PRINT-LINE-4.
011500      PERFORM LINE-FEED.
011600
```

16

```
011700 PRINT-LINE-1.
011800     MOVE SPACE TO DETAIL-LINE.
011900     MOVE VENDOR-NUMBER TO PRINT-NUMBER.
012000     MOVE VENDOR-NAME TO PRINT-NAME.
012100     MOVE VENDOR-CONTACT TO PRINT-CONTACT.
012200     MOVE DETAIL-LINE TO PRINTER-RECORD.
012300     PERFORM WRITE-TO-PRINTER.
012400
012500 PRINT-LINE-2.
012600     MOVE SPACE TO DETAIL-LINE.
012700     MOVE VENDOR-ADDRESS-1 TO PRINT-NAME.
012800     MOVE VENDOR-PHONE TO PRINT-CONTACT.
012900     MOVE DETAIL-LINE TO PRINTER-RECORD.
013000     PERFORM WRITE-TO-PRINTER.
013100
013200 PRINT-LINE-3.
013300     MOVE SPACE TO DETAIL-LINE.
013400     MOVE VENDOR-ADDRESS-2 TO PRINT-NAME.
013500     IF VENDOR-ADDRESS-2 NOT = SPACE
013600         MOVE DETAIL-LINE TO PRINTER-RECORD
013700         PERFORM WRITE-TO-PRINTER.
013800
013900 PRINT-LINE-4.
014000     MOVE SPACE TO CITY-STATE-LINE.
014100     MOVE VENDOR-CITY TO PRINT-CITY.
014200     MOVE VENDOR-STATE TO PRINT-STATE.
014300
014400     MOVE VENDOR-STATE TO STATE-CODE.
014500     PERFORM READ-STATE-RECORD.
014600     IF STATE-RECORD-FOUND = "N"
014700         MOVE "***Not Found***" TO STATE-NAME.
014800     MOVE STATE-NAME TO PRINT-STATE-NAME.
014900
015000     MOVE VENDOR-ZIP TO PRINT-ZIP.
015100     MOVE CITY-STATE-LINE TO PRINTER-RECORD.
015200     PERFORM WRITE-TO-PRINTER.
015300
015400 READ-NEXT-RECORD.
015500     READ VENDOR-FILE NEXT RECORD
015600         AT END MOVE "Y" TO FILE-AT-END.
015700
015800 WRITE-TO-PRINTER.
015900     WRITE PRINTER-RECORD BEFORE ADVANCING 1.
016000     ADD 1 TO LINE-COUNT.
016100
016200 LINE-FEED.
016300     MOVE SPACE TO PRINTER-RECORD.
016400     PERFORM WRITE-TO-PRINTER.
016500
016600 START-NEXT-PAGE.
016700     PERFORM END-LAST-PAGE.
016800     PERFORM START-NEW-PAGE.
016900
017000 START-NEW-PAGE.
017100     ADD 1 TO PAGE-NUMBER.
017200     MOVE PAGE-NUMBER TO PRINT-PAGE-NUMBER.
```

continues

Listing 16.5. continued

```
017300        MOVE TITLE-LINE TO PRINTER-RECORD.
017400        PERFORM WRITE-TO-PRINTER.
017500        PERFORM LINE-FEED.
017600        MOVE COLUMN-LINE TO PRINTER-RECORD.
017700        PERFORM WRITE-TO-PRINTER.
017800        PERFORM LINE-FEED.
017900
018000 END-LAST-PAGE.
018100        PERFORM FORM-FEED.
018200        MOVE ZERO TO LINE-COUNT.
018300
018400 FORM-FEED.
018500        MOVE SPACE TO PRINTER-RECORD.
018600        WRITE PRINTER-RECORD BEFORE ADVANCING PAGE.
018700
018800 READ-STATE-RECORD.
018900        MOVE "Y" TO STATE-RECORD-FOUND.
019000        READ STATE-FILE RECORD
019100            INVALID KEY
019200            MOVE "N" TO STATE-RECORD-FOUND.
019300
```

An example of the output from `vndrpt02.cbl` shows one record containing an invalid state code and a few records containing lowercase values. These are records that must be fixed so that the information in the file is valid:

```
                         VENDOR LIST                    PAGE:    1
          NO    NAME-ADDRESS                  CONTACT-PHONE-ZIP
          00001 AERIAL SIGNS                  HENRIETTA MARKSON
          BURBANK AIRPORT               (818) 555-6066
          HANGAR 305
          BURBANK          WX ***Not Found***   90016
          00002 ABC PRINTING                   CHARLES JOHANSSEN
          1624 Foothill Blvd            (818) 555-4321
          SUITE 34
          LOS ANGELES      CA CALIFORNIA        91042
          00003 CHARLES SMITH AND SONS          Martha Harrison
          1435 SOUTH STREET             (213) 555-4432
          LOS ANGELES      CA CALIFORNIA        90064
          00005 ALIAS SMITH AND JONES           ROBIN COUSINS
          1216 Main Street              415 555-9203
          PALO ALTO        CA CALIFORNIA        90061
          00014 RANIER GRAPHICS                 JULIA SIMPSON
          4433 WASHINGTON ST            (213) 555-6789
          LOS ANGELES      CA CALIFORNIA        90032
          00022 ARTFUL DODGER
          123 UNDERWOOD LANE            202 555-1234
          MARKHAM          WA WASHINGTON        40466
          01176 ABERCROMBIE AND OTHERS
          1234 45TH ST.                 (213) 555-6543
          SUITE 17
          LOS ANGELES      CA CALIFORNIA        92345
          01440 ZINZINDORFF INC.
          1604 7TH ST                   (213) 555-7234
          LOS ANGELES      CA CALIFORNIA        90404
```

16

A SELECT and FD are added for the STATE-FILE. A routine to read the state record, READ-STATE-RECORD, is included at line 018800, and a STATE-RECORD-FOUND variable used in that routine is defined in WORKING-STORAGE at line 006500.

The details for print line 4 containing the city, state code, state, and zip code no longer fit within DETAIL-LINE. Therefore, an additional line, CITY-STATE-LINE, is defined at line 003800 and is used in PRINT-LINE-4, which begins at line 013900.

The logic that uses the state file begins at line 014400 by moving the VENDOR-STATE to STATE-CODE and then reading the record. If the record is not found, the STATE-NAME is filled in with "***Not Found***". The value in STATE-NAME (either the state name or the value "***Not Found***") is moved to PRINT-STATE-NAME. This is part of CITY-STATE-LINE, which also is filled in with the zip code, and then finally printed at line 015200.

Fixing Invalid Data in Files

On Day 15, you learned that if you are working with a file that contains invalid data, you should track down the program or programs that are putting invalid data in the file and correct the programs. Then correct the data in the file. vndmnt02.cbl fixes the problem in vndmnt01.cbl, but now it is necessary to correct the data.

In order to correct the data, you need to convert the data in the vendor file to uppercase. Once again, you use LOWER-ALPHA and UPPER-ALPHA to do this. You already used them in three or four programs. Listing 16.6, wscase01.cbl, is a COPY file that can be used in any program that has to perform case conversion. It saves having to retype LOWER-ALPHA and UPPER-ALPHA each time they are used and includes comments on how to use them. Remember that the COPY file is included by the compiler, as if you had typed it all.

TYPE **Listing 16.6.** wscase01.cbl, **a** COPY **file for case conversion.**

```
000100*-------------------------------
000200* Can be used for case conversion
000300* Ex:
000400*    INSPECT data-field
000500*       CONVERTING LOWER-ALPHA
000600*       TO         UPPER-ALPHA.
000700*-------------------------------
000800
000900 77  UPPER-ALPHA       PIC X(26) VALUE
001000     "ABCDEFGHIJKLMNOPQRSTUVWXYZ".
001100 77  LOWER-ALPHA       PIC X(26) VALUE
001200     "abcdefghijklmnopqrstuvwxyz".
001300
001400
```

Listing 16.7 is a program to convert all the fields in the vendor file to uppercase.

TYPE **Listing 16.7. Fixing the vendor file.**

```
000100 IDENTIFICATION DIVISION.
000200 PROGRAM-ID. VNDFIX01.
000300*-------------------------------
000400* Repairs any lowercase errors in
000500* the vendor file by converting the
000600* the whole record to uppercase.
000700*-------------------------------
000800 ENVIRONMENT DIVISION.
000900 INPUT-OUTPUT SECTION.
001000 FILE-CONTROL.
001100
001200     COPY "SLVND01.CBL".
001300
001400 DATA DIVISION.
001500 FILE SECTION.
001600
001700     COPY "FDVND03.CBL".
001800
001900 WORKING-STORAGE SECTION.
002000
002100 77  VENDOR-AT-END          PIC X VALUE "N".
002200
002300     COPY "WSCASE01.CBL".
002400
002500 PROCEDURE DIVISION.
002600 PROGRAM-BEGIN.
002700     PERFORM OPENING-PROCEDURE.
002800     PERFORM MAIN-PROCESS.
002900     PERFORM CLOSING-PROCEDURE.
003000
003100 PROGRAM-DONE.
003200     STOP RUN.
003300
003400 OPENING-PROCEDURE.
003500     OPEN I-O VENDOR-FILE.
003600
003700 CLOSING-PROCEDURE.
003800     CLOSE VENDOR-FILE.
003900
004000 MAIN-PROCESS.
004100     PERFORM READ-NEXT-VENDOR-RECORD.
004200     PERFORM FIX-VENDOR-RECORDS
004300            UNTIL VENDOR-AT-END = "Y".
004400
004500 FIX-VENDOR-RECORDS.
004600     INSPECT VENDOR-RECORD
004700        CONVERTING LOWER-ALPHA
004800        TO          UPPER-ALPHA.
004900     PERFORM REWRITE-VENDOR-RECORD.
005000
```

16

```
005100      PERFORM READ-NEXT-VENDOR-RECORD.
005200
005300 READ-NEXT-VENDOR-RECORD.
005400      MOVE "N" TO VENDOR-AT-END.
005500      READ VENDOR-FILE NEXT RECORD
005600           AT END MOVE "Y" TO VENDOR-AT-END.
005700
005800*or   READ VENDOR-FILE NEXT RECORD WITH LOCK
005900*          AT END MOVE "Y" TO VENDOR-AT-END.
006000
006100*or   READ VENDOR-FILE NEXT RECORD WITH HOLD
006200*          AT END MOVE "Y" TO VENDOR-AT-END.
006300
006400 REWRITE-VENDOR-RECORD.
006500      REWRITE VENDOR-RECORD
006600           INVALID KEY
006700           DISPLAY "ERROR REWRITING VENDOR RECORD".
006800
```

16

The output of vndrpt02.cbl after vndfix01.cbl has been run verifies that all fields have been converted to uppercase:

OUTPUT

```
                              VENDOR LIST                    PAGE:    1
NO    NAME-ADDRESS                              CONTACT-PHONE-ZIP
00001 AERIAL SIGNS                              HENRIETTA MARKSON
BURBANK AIRPORT                                 (818) 555-6066
HANGAR 305
BURBANK            WX ***Not Found***           90016
00002 ABC PRINTING                              CHARLES JOHANSSEN
1624 FOOTHILL BLVD                              (818) 555-4321
SUITE 34
LOS ANGELES        CA CALIFORNIA                91042
00003 CHARLES SMITH AND SONS                    MARTHA HARRISON
1435 SOUTH STREET                               (213) 555-4432
LOS ANGELES        CA CALIFORNIA                90064
00005 ALIAS SMITH AND JONES                     ROBIN COUSINS
1216 MAIN STREET                                415 555-9203
PALO ALTO          CA CALIFORNIA                90061
00014 RANIER GRAPHICS                           JULIA SIMPSON
4433 WASHINGTON ST                              (213) 555-6789
LOS ANGELES        CA CALIFORNIA                90032
00022 ARTFUL DODGER
123 UNDERWOOD LANE                              202 555-1234
MARKHAM            WA WASHINGTON                 40466
01176 ABERCROMBIE AND OTHERS
1234 45TH ST.                                   (213) 555-6543
SUITE 17
LOS ANGELES        CA CALIFORNIA                92345
01440 ZINZINDORFF INC.
1604 7TH ST                                     (213) 555-7234
LOS ANGELES        CA CALIFORNIA                90404
```

The final error in vendor number `00001` is an invalid state code. This should be corrected manually. Determine the correct code and enter it manually using `vndmnt02.cbl`. The final corrected output of `vndrpt02.cbl` shows a clean file with all data corrected:

OUTPUT

```
                              VENDOR LIST                      PAGE:     1
NO    NAME-ADDRESS                           CONTACT-PHONE-ZIP
00001 AERIAL SIGNS                           HENRIETTA MARKSON
BURBANK AIRPORT                       (818) 555-6066
HANGAR 305
BURBANK             CA CALIFORNIA    90016
00002 ABC PRINTING                           CHARLES JOHANSSEN
1624 FOOTHILL BLVD                    (818) 555-4321
SUITE 34
LOS ANGELES         CA CALIFORNIA    91042
00003 CHARLES SMITH AND SONS                 MARTHA HARRISON
1435 SOUTH STREET                     (213) 555-4432
LOS ANGELES         CA CALIFORNIA    90064
00005 ALIAS SMITH AND JONES                  ROBIN COUSINS
1216 MAIN STREET                      415 555-9203
PALO ALTO           CA CALIFORNIA    90061
00014 RANIER GRAPHICS                        JULIA SIMPSON
4433 WASHINGTON ST                    (213) 555-6789
LOS ANGELES         CA CALIFORNIA    90032
00022 ARTFUL DODGER
123 UNDERWOOD LANE                    202 555-1234
MARKHAM             WA WASHINGTON     40466
01176 ABERCROMBIE AND OTHERS
1234 45TH ST.                         (213) 555-6543
SUITE 17
LOS ANGELES         CA CALIFORNIA    92345
01440 ZINZINDORFF INC.
1604 7TH ST                           (213) 555-7234
LOS ANGELES         CA CALIFORNIA    90404
```

ANALYSIS

This program performs a simple task. It reads each vendor record, converts the whole record to uppercase, and then rewrites the record.

At line `002300`, the COPY file for case conversions, `wscase01.cbl`, is included. The MAIN-PROCESS at line `004000` uses the standard file processing loop of reading the first record and then processing the record until the file ends. The main processing loop is FIX-VENDOR-RECORDS at line `004500`. This applies the case conversion to the entire vendor record and then rewrites the record. At the end of the loop at line `005100`, the next record is read.

On large systems that require a lock or a hold before a record can be changed, READ NEXT also comes with a LOCK or HOLD version. These versions appear commented out at lines `005800` through `006200` in case you need to use them.

Code, compile, and run `vndfix01.cbl` to correct the vendor file. Use `vndrpt02.cbl` to verify that the case conversions have occurred.

What Is a Table?

The `vndrpt02.cbl` program performs file I/O (Input/Output) operations on two different files: the vendor file and the state code file. File I/O operations take time. Disk drives are very slow compared to main memory.

For a small vendor file, this is not particularly a problem. If the vendor file contains 80,000 records, however, the program will have to perform 160,000 file I/O operations—one for each vendor record and one for each state code associated with each vendor record.

Whenever you can avoid performing file operations you should do so, but it is unavoidable that files will be accessed by a computer program. Otherwise, a program would have no way of storing and retrieving information. Although the `vndrpt02.cbl` program has to read through the vendor file to extract all of the information for the report, it is possible to avoid having to read the state code file so many times.

The state code file is small enough (probably 50 records minimum) that it could all be loaded into memory once, and then the state codes could be looked up in memory. It would take 50 file I/O operations to load the state code file into memory and 80,000 file I/O operations to read the vendor file. No additional file I/O operations are needed to look up the state codes in memory. This total of 80,050 operations is close to half of the original 160,000 and represents a substantial increase in the speed of the program.

In order to do this, you use a table or an array to load a file into memory.

 A *table* or an *array* is an area of memory that has been set aside and organized in such a way that it can hold multiple occurrences of the same type of information.

Returning to the file card analogy, using a table in a program is equivalent to pulling the cards out of a card file box and laying them out on the desk, as shown in Figure 16.4. This analogy doesn't hold up completely, because you can't actually pull records out of a file and arrange them in memory, but you can read each record in a file and arrange the data from each record in memory.

Figure 16.4.

Turning a file into a table.

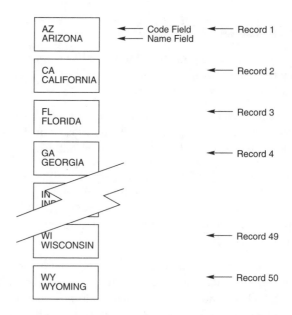

Listing 16.8 is the record for the state code file. What you need is a place in memory to hold 50 occurrences of the data in the STATE-RECORD.

TYPE **Listing 16.8. FD for the state code file.**

```
000100*--------------------------------
000200* FDSTATE.CBL
000300* Primary Key - STATE-CODE
000400* NAME is required
000500* NAME and CODE should be uppercase
000600*--------------------------------
000700 FD  STATE-FILE
000800     LABEL RECORDS ARE STANDARD.
000900 01  STATE-RECORD.
001000     05  STATE-CODE            PIC X(2).
001100     05  STATE-NAME            PIC X(20).
001200
```

Listing 16.9 can be set up in working storage and contains fields that are the same size as the state code and state name fields of the state code file. You load this into memory by reading the state record and then moving STATE-CODE to TABLE-STATE-CODE and STATE-NAME to TABLE-STATE-NAME.

16

TYPE **Listing 16.9. A duplicate of the state code record.**

```
007000 01   TABLE-STATE-RECORD.
007100      05   TABLE-STATE-CODE         PIC XX.
007200      05   TABLE-STATE-NAME         PIC X(20).
```

Listing 16.9 allows for only one occurrence of the state information—and you need 50 occurrences. This is handled by adding an OCCURS clause after the TABLE-STATE-RECORD, as shown in Listing 16.10. This creates space in memory for 50 occurrences of TABLE-STATE-RECORD. The TABLE-STATE-RECORD is 22 bytes long, so this reserves 1,100 bytes (50×22).

TYPE **Listing 16.10. Make it happen 50 times.**

```
007000 01   TABLE-STATE-RECORD OCCURS 50 TIMES.
007100      05   TABLE-STATE-CODE         PIC XX.
007200      05   TABLE-STATE-NAME         PIC X(20).
```

ANALYSIS Adding the OCCURS 50 TIMES works as if you had typed lines 007000 through 007200 in Listing 16.9 50 times. This creates 50 occurrences of TABLE-STATE-RECORD. It also creates multiple occurrences of all the subordinate variables, so 50 occurrences of TABLE-STATE-CODE and TABLE-STATE-NAME are also within the 50 occurrences of TABLE-STATE-RECORD.

If you move something to or from a table variable TABLE-STATE-RECORD (or TABLE-STATE-CODE or TABLE-STATE-NAME), you must add some additional information to identify to or from which occurrence you are moving. You single out a specific variable in a table by adding a number in parentheses after the variable name. This number is called an index or a subscript. This is not the same index as the index to a file, but it is a number that identifies which occurrence of the variable is being referenced. Several examples of this are given in Listing 16.11.

TYPE **Listing 16.11. Examples of using table (array) variables.**

```
018000      MOVE SPACE TO TABLE-STATE-RECORD(5).
018100      MOVE STATE-CODE TO TABLE-STATE-CODE(1).
018200      MOVE STATE-NAME TO TABLE-STATE-NAME(15).
018300      DISPLAY TABLE-STATE-NAME(23).
018400      MOVE TABLE-STATE-CODE(43) TO PRINT-CODE.
```

The examples in Listing 16.11 are not from a real program and don't do anything; they are only examples of the syntax for accessing a table variable with an index or subscript. The index itself can be a variable, as in lines 018500 and 018600 of Listing 16.12.

TYPE **Listing 16.12. A variable used as an index.**

```
018500        MOVE 53 TO STATE-INDEX.
018600        DISPLAY TABLE-STATE-CODE(STATE-INDEX).
```

NEW TERM When you define a table (array), you also can (and usually should) define a variable that specifically is intended to be used as the index for that table. This is called an *index variable*. Listing 16.13 shows an example of the syntax for a table in which STATE-INDEX is the index variable for the TABLE-STATE-RECORD.

Several special commands can be used on tables if the table is given an index. An index variable is given a special status in COBOL programs. It requires no picture or definition other than what is shown in Listing 16.13 at line 007100, but it cannot be used for anything other than as an index to variables in the table.

TYPE **Listing 16.13. Providing an index.**

```
007000 01  TABLE-STATE-RECORD OCCURS 50 TIMES
007100         INDEXED BY STATE-INDEX.
007200     05  TABLE-STATE-CODE        PIC XX.
007300     05  TABLE-STATE-NAME        PIC X(20).
```

Although an index variable such as STATE-INDEX is used as a number that indicates the occurrence of a variable, you can't treat it like a numeric variable. You can't use the COBOL math verbs on it, so you cannot ADD, SUBTRACT, MULTIPLY, or DIVIDE with it.

In order to manipulate an index variable, you must use the SET command. Here is the syntax:

```
SET index variable TO value

SET index variable UP
    BY value

SET index variable DOWN
    BY value
```

The following are examples:

```
SET STATE-INDEX TO 1

SET STATE-INDEX TO A-VALUE

SET STATE-INDEX UP BY 1

SET STATE-INDEX UP
    BY NEXT-AMOUNT

SET STATE-INDEX DOWN BY 1

SET STATE-INDEX DOWN
    BY LAST-AMOUNT
```

16

You can use an index variable in a PERFORM VARYING command. Use this syntax:

```
PERFORM paragraph
    VARYING index variable
    FROM value BY value
        UNTIL condition.
```

The following is an example:

```
PERFORM CLEAR-TABLE
    VARYING STATE-INDEX
    FROM 1 BY 1
        UNTIL STATE-INDEX > 50.
```

Listing 16.14 is sttbrp01.cbl (state code table report). It is based on stcrpt01.cbl, but it prints a report in the state code file by first loading a table of all the state codes and then printing the codes from the table. (In practice, you usually wouldn't use this approach because it doesn't save any time, but I want you to gain some familiarity with table basics before going on to the next topic.)

TYPE   **Listing 16.14. Filling a table from a file.**

```
000100 IDENTIFICATION DIVISION.
000200 PROGRAM-ID. STTBRP01.
000300*--------------------------------
000400* Report on the STATE File.
000500*--------------------------------
000600 ENVIRONMENT DIVISION.
000700 INPUT-OUTPUT SECTION.
000800 FILE-CONTROL.
000900
001000     COPY "SLSTATE.CBL".
001100
001200     SELECT PRINTER-FILE
001300         ASSIGN TO PRINTER
001400         ORGANIZATION IS LINE SEQUENTIAL.
001500
001600 DATA DIVISION.
001700 FILE SECTION.
001800
001900     COPY "FDSTATE.CBL".
002000
002100 FD  PRINTER-FILE
002200     LABEL RECORDS ARE OMITTED.
002300 01  PRINTER-RECORD          PIC X(80).
002400
002500 WORKING-STORAGE SECTION.
002600
002700 01  DETAIL-LINE.
002800     05  PRINT-CODE      PIC XX.
002900     05  FILLER          PIC XXXX     VALUE SPACE.
003000     05  PRINT-NAME      PIC X(20).
003100
```

continues

Listing 16.14. continued

```
003200 01   COLUMN-LINE.
003300      05  FILLER           PIC X(4)  VALUE "CODE".
003400      05  FILLER           PIC X(2) VALUE SPACE.
003500      05  FILLER           PIC X(4) VALUE "NAME".
003600
003700 01   TITLE-LINE.
003800      05  FILLER               PIC X(25) VALUE SPACE.
003900      05  FILLER               PIC X(11)
004000          VALUE "STATE CODES".
004100      05  FILLER               PIC X(15) VALUE SPACE.
004200      05  FILLER               PIC X(5) VALUE "PAGE:".
004300      05  FILLER               PIC X(1) VALUE SPACE.
004400      05  PRINT-PAGE-NUMBER   PIC ZZZZ9.
004500
004600 77  FILE-AT-END            PIC X.
004700 77  LINE-COUNT            PIC 999 VALUE ZERO.
004800 77  PAGE-NUMBER          PIC 99999 VALUE ZERO.
004900 77  MAXIMUM-LINES        PIC 999 VALUE 55.
005000
005100 01   TABLE-STATE-RECORD OCCURS 50 TIMES
005200          INDEXED BY STATE-INDEX.
005300      05  TABLE-STATE-CODE        PIC XX.
005400      05  TABLE-STATE-NAME        PIC X(20).
005500
005600 PROCEDURE DIVISION.
005700 PROGRAM-BEGIN.
005800
005900      PERFORM OPENING-PROCEDURE.
006000      MOVE ZEROES TO LINE-COUNT
006100                     PAGE-NUMBER.
006200
006300      PERFORM START-NEW-PAGE.
006400
006500      SET STATE-INDEX TO 1.
006600      PERFORM PRINT-STATE-FIELDS
006700          UNTIL STATE-INDEX > 50 OR
006800              TABLE-STATE-RECORD(STATE-INDEX) = SPACE.
006900
007000      PERFORM CLOSING-PROCEDURE.
007100
007200 PROGRAM-DONE.
007300      STOP RUN.
007400
007500 OPENING-PROCEDURE.
007600
007700      OPEN I-O STATE-FILE.
007800      PERFORM LOAD-STATE-TABLE.
007900      CLOSE STATE-FILE.
008000
008100      OPEN OUTPUT PRINTER-FILE.
008200
008300 LOAD-STATE-TABLE.
008400      PERFORM CLEAR-TABLE.
008500      SET STATE-INDEX TO 1.
```

16

```
008600      PERFORM READ-NEXT-RECORD.
008700      PERFORM LOAD-ONE-STATE-RECORD
008800          UNTIL FILE-AT-END = "Y" OR
008900               STATE-INDEX > 50.
009000
009100 CLEAR-TABLE.
009200      PERFORM CLEAR-ONE-TABLE-ROW
009300          VARYING STATE-INDEX FROM 1 BY 1
009400            UNTIL STATE-INDEX > 50.
009500
009600 CLEAR-ONE-TABLE-ROW.
009700      MOVE SPACE TO TABLE-STATE-RECORD(STATE-INDEX).
009800
009900 LOAD-ONE-STATE-RECORD.
010000      MOVE STATE-CODE TO TABLE-STATE-CODE(STATE-INDEX).
010100      MOVE STATE-NAME TO TABLE-STATE-NAME(STATE-INDEX).
010200
010300      PERFORM READ-NEXT-RECORD.
010400
010500      IF FILE-AT-END NOT = "Y"
010600          SET STATE-INDEX UP BY 1
010700          IF STATE-INDEX > 50
010800              DISPLAY "TABLE FULL".
010900
011000 CLOSING-PROCEDURE.
011100      PERFORM END-LAST-PAGE.
011200      CLOSE PRINTER-FILE.
011300
011400 PRINT-STATE-FIELDS.
011500      IF LINE-COUNT > MAXIMUM-LINES
011600          PERFORM START-NEXT-PAGE.
011700      PERFORM PRINT-THE-RECORD.
011800      SET STATE-INDEX UP BY 1.
011900
012000 PRINT-THE-RECORD.
012100      MOVE SPACE TO DETAIL-LINE.
012200      MOVE TABLE-STATE-CODE(STATE-INDEX) TO PRINT-CODE.
012300      MOVE TABLE-STATE-NAME(STATE-INDEX) TO PRINT-NAME.
012400      MOVE DETAIL-LINE TO PRINTER-RECORD.
012500      PERFORM WRITE-TO-PRINTER.
012600
012700 READ-NEXT-RECORD.
012800      READ STATE-FILE NEXT RECORD
012900          AT END MOVE "Y" TO FILE-AT-END.
013000
013100 WRITE-TO-PRINTER.
013200      WRITE PRINTER-RECORD BEFORE ADVANCING 1.
013300      ADD 1 TO LINE-COUNT.
013400
013500 LINE-FEED.
013600      MOVE SPACE TO PRINTER-RECORD.
013700      PERFORM WRITE-TO-PRINTER.
013800
013900 START-NEXT-PAGE.
014000
014100      PERFORM END-LAST-PAGE.
```

16

continues

Listing 16.14. continued

```
014200        PERFORM START-NEW-PAGE.
014300
014400 START-NEW-PAGE.
014500        ADD 1 TO PAGE-NUMBER.
014600        MOVE PAGE-NUMBER TO PRINT-PAGE-NUMBER.
014700        MOVE TITLE-LINE TO PRINTER-RECORD.
014800        PERFORM WRITE-TO-PRINTER.
014900        PERFORM LINE-FEED.
015000        MOVE COLUMN-LINE TO PRINTER-RECORD.
015100        PERFORM WRITE-TO-PRINTER.
015200        PERFORM LINE-FEED.
015300
015400 END-LAST-PAGE.
015500        PERFORM FORM-FEED.
015600        MOVE ZERO TO LINE-COUNT.
015700
015800 FORM-FEED.
015900        MOVE SPACE TO PRINTER-RECORD.
016000        WRITE PRINTER-RECORD BEFORE ADVANCING PAGE.
016100
```

The output report of `sttbrp01.cbl` should be identical to the output report created by `stcrpt01.cbl`:

OUTPUT

```
                                      STATE CODES              PAGE:      1
CODE   NAME
AK     ARKANSAS
AL     ALASKA
AZ     ARIZONA
CA     CALIFORNIA
FL     FLORIDA
LA     LOUISIANA
NC     NORTH CAROLINA
NH     NEW HAMPSHIRE
NM     NEW MEXICO
NY     NEW YORK
SC     SOUTH CAROLINA
WA     WASHINGTON
WI     WISCONSIN
```

ANALYSIS The table is defined at line 005100 in WORKING-STORAGE.

The state code file is opened, loaded into the table, and closed—all within the OPENING-PROCEDURE, which starts at line 007500.

The LOAD-STATE-TABLE paragraph at line 008300 starts by clearing the table, using the CLEAR-TABLE routine at lines 009100 through 009800. This is a simple routine that moves spaces to each occurrence of TABLE-STATE-RECORD by varying the STATE-INDEX from 1 through 50.

16

Back at LOAD-STATE-TABLE, at lines 008500 through 008900, the STATE-INDEX is set to 1, the first record in the STATE-FILE is read, and then the table is loaded one record at a time by performing LOAD-ONE-STATE-RECORD until the state file reaches an end or the STATE-INDEX exceeds 50.

LOAD-ONE-STATE-RECORD at line 009900 loads the table elements from the fields in the record and then, at the bottom of the loop (line 010300), reads the next record. If the read is successful, the STATE-INDEX is set up by 1, and if the STATE-INDEX has exceeded 50, an error message is displayed.

This error check is important. If by some accident the state file contained more than 50 records, the records would not load correctly into memory. If the index variable is set to 51, and only 50 elements are in the table, moving a value to TABLE-STATE-CODE(STATE-INDEX) or TABLE-STATE-NAME(STATE-INDEX) has completely unpredictable results. Under some conditions, the program will abort with a warning that an attempt was made to move a value outside the boundaries of the table. Under other conditions, the move succeeds and the values will corrupt some other memory in the program.

If the state file does exceed 50 entries and they are legitimate, you must edit the program so that the table is larger by changing the OCCURS count at line 005100. You will also need to change the value 50 where it occurs in lines 006700, 008900, 009400, and 010700.

The main program loop is set up at line 006500 by setting the STATE-INDEX to 1, and then the main loop is performed until STATE-INDEX > 50 or TABLE-STATE-RECORD(STATE-INDEX) = SPACES. A STATE-TABLE-RECORD might be SPACES if the file did not contain a full 50 records, so printing is stopped as if the whole array had been printed.

The main loop is at line 011400, which is PRINT-STATE-FIELDS. At the end of the loop at line 011800, the loop control variable STATE-INDEX is set UP BY 1.

The printing portion of the program at begins at line 012000. PRINT-THE-RECORD fills in the print line by moving TABLE-STATE-CODE(STATE-INDEX) to PRINT-CODE and TABLE-STATE-NAME(STATE-INDEX) to PRINT-NAME.

You should be able to create sttbrp01.cbl fairly easily by copying stcrpt01.cbl and making modifications to it to match Listing 16.14.

Code, compile, and run sttbrp01.cbl and then rerun stcrpt01.cbl. The output from both programs should be identical. Remember that you usually would not use this style of table operation for a report of this nature. The next example is a much better use of tables.

Looking Up Data in Tables

The real power of tables (arrays) is that they can be searched very quickly for values, and COBOL provides a special command to do it. If a table has been defined with an index variable, the SEARCH command can be used to search the table for a specific piece of information.

The SEARCH command starts from the current value of the index variable, so it is important to remember to set the index to 1 before the search begins.

The search syntax includes an AT END clause that is optional. The COBOL program knows the size of the table, and it knows whether the index has reached the limit of the table. If this occurs, the command following AT END is executed. Otherwise, the SEARCH command starts from the current index variable value and performs the test described by the WHEN condition. If the condition is true, the command associated with the WHEN is executed and the search is ended. The following is the syntax:

```
SEARCH table name
  [AT END
    do something ]
  WHEN condition
    do something.
```

Here is an example:

```
SET STATE-INDEX TO 1.
SEARCH TABLE-STATE-RECORD
  AT END
    PERFORM SEARCH-FAILED
  WHEN
    VENDOR-STATE =
      TABLE-STATE-CODE(STATE-INDEX)
    PERFORM SEARCH-SUCCEEDED
```

Using a Table in a Program

Listing 16.15, vndrpt03.cbl, is a modified version of vndrpt02.cbl, and it uses a table for the state codes.

TYPE   **Listing 16.15. Using a table for a report.**

```
000100 IDENTIFICATION DIVISION.
000200 PROGRAM-ID. VNDRPT03.
000300*-------------------------------
000400* Report on the Vendor File.
000500*-------------------------------
000600 ENVIRONMENT DIVISION.
000700 INPUT-OUTPUT SECTION.
```

16

```
000800 FILE-CONTROL.
000900
001000     COPY "SLVND01.CBL".
001100
001200     COPY "SLSTATE.CBL".
001300
001400     SELECT PRINTER-FILE
001500        ASSIGN TO PRINTER
001600        ORGANIZATION IS LINE SEQUENTIAL.
001700
001800 DATA DIVISION.
001900 FILE SECTION.
002000
002100     COPY "FDVND02.CBL".
002200
002300     COPY "FDSTATE.CBL".
002400
002500 FD  PRINTER-FILE
002600     LABEL RECORDS ARE OMITTED.
002700 01  PRINTER-RECORD           PIC X(80).
002800
002900 WORKING-STORAGE SECTION.
003000
003100 01  DETAIL-LINE.
003200     05  PRINT-NUMBER    PIC 9(5).
003300     05  FILLER          PIC X     VALUE SPACE.
003400     05  PRINT-NAME      PIC X(30).
003500     05  FILLER          PIC X(15) VALUE SPACE.
003600     05  PRINT-CONTACT   PIC X(30).
003700
003800 01  CITY-STATE-LINE.
003900     05  FILLER          PIC X(6) VALUE SPACE.
004000     05  PRINT-CITY      PIC X(20).
004100     05  FILLER          PIC X VALUE SPACE.
004200     05  PRINT-STATE     PIC X(2).
004300     05  FILLER          PIC X VALUE SPACE.
004400     05  PRINT-STATE-NAME PIC X(20).
004500     05  FILLER          PIC X(1) VALUE SPACE.
004600     05  PRINT-ZIP       PIC X(10).
004700
004800 01  COLUMN-LINE.
004900     05  FILLER          PIC X(2)  VALUE "NO".
005000     05  FILLER          PIC X(4) VALUE SPACE.
005100     05  FILLER          PIC X(12) VALUE "NAME-ADDRESS".
005200     05  FILLER          PIC X(33) VALUE SPACE.
005300     05  FILLER          PIC X(17) VALUE "CONTACT-PHONE-ZIP".
005400
005500 01  TITLE-LINE.
005600     05  FILLER              PIC X(25) VALUE SPACE.
005700     05  FILLER              PIC X(11)
005800         VALUE "VENDOR LIST".
005900     05  FILLER              PIC X(19) VALUE SPACE.
006000     05  FILLER              PIC X(5) VALUE "PAGE:".
006100     05  FILLER              PIC X(1) VALUE SPACE.
006200     05  PRINT-PAGE-NUMBER PIC ZZZZ9.
006300
```

16

continues

Listing 16.15. continued

```
006400 77  FILE-AT-END              PIC X.
006500 77  STATE-FILE-AT-END        PIC X VALUE "N".
006600 77  LINE-COUNT               PIC 999 VALUE ZERO.
006700 77  PAGE-NUMBER              PIC 99999 VALUE ZERO.
006800 77  MAXIMUM-LINES            PIC 999 VALUE 55.
006900
007000 01  TABLE-STATE-RECORD OCCURS 50 TIMES
007100     INDEXED BY STATE-INDEX.
007200     05  TABLE-STATE-CODE         PIC XX.
007300     05  TABLE-STATE-NAME         PIC X(20).
007400
007500 PROCEDURE DIVISION.
007600 PROGRAM-BEGIN.
007700
007800     PERFORM OPENING-PROCEDURE.
007900     MOVE ZEROES TO LINE-COUNT
008000                    PAGE-NUMBER.
008100
008200     PERFORM START-NEW-PAGE.
008300
008400     MOVE "N" TO FILE-AT-END.
008500     PERFORM READ-NEXT-RECORD.
008600     IF FILE-AT-END = "Y"
008700         MOVE "NO RECORDS FOUND" TO PRINTER-RECORD
008800         PERFORM WRITE-TO-PRINTER
008900     ELSE
009000         PERFORM PRINT-VENDOR-FIELDS
009100             UNTIL FILE-AT-END = "Y".
009200
009300     PERFORM CLOSING-PROCEDURE.
009400
009500 PROGRAM-DONE.
009600     STOP RUN.
009700
009800 OPENING-PROCEDURE.
009900     OPEN I-O VENDOR-FILE.
010000
010100     OPEN I-O STATE-FILE.
010200     PERFORM LOAD-STATE-TABLE.
010300     CLOSE STATE-FILE.
010400
010500     OPEN OUTPUT PRINTER-FILE.
010600
010700 LOAD-STATE-TABLE.
010800     PERFORM CLEAR-TABLE.
010900     SET STATE-INDEX TO 1.
011000     PERFORM READ-NEXT-STATE-RECORD.
011100     PERFORM LOAD-ONE-STATE-RECORD
011200         UNTIL STATE-FILE-AT-END = "Y" OR
011300             STATE-INDEX > 50.
011400
011500 CLEAR-TABLE.
011600     PERFORM CLEAR-ONE-TABLE-ROW
011700         VARYING STATE-INDEX FROM 1 BY 1
```

16

```
011800          UNTIL STATE-INDEX > 50.
011900
012000 CLEAR-ONE-TABLE-ROW.
012100     MOVE SPACE TO TABLE-STATE-RECORD(STATE-INDEX).
012200
012300 LOAD-ONE-STATE-RECORD.
012400     MOVE STATE-CODE TO TABLE-STATE-CODE(STATE-INDEX).
012500     MOVE STATE-NAME TO TABLE-STATE-NAME(STATE-INDEX).
012600
012700     PERFORM READ-NEXT-STATE-RECORD.
012800
012900     IF STATE-FILE-AT-END NOT = "Y"
013000         SET STATE-INDEX UP BY 1
013100         IF STATE-INDEX > 50
013200             DISPLAY "TABLE FULL".
013300
013400 CLOSING-PROCEDURE.
013500     CLOSE VENDOR-FILE.
013600     PERFORM END-LAST-PAGE.
013700     CLOSE PRINTER-FILE.
013800
013900 PRINT-VENDOR-FIELDS.
014000     IF LINE-COUNT > MAXIMUM-LINES
014100         PERFORM START-NEXT-PAGE.
014200     PERFORM PRINT-THE-RECORD.
014300     PERFORM READ-NEXT-RECORD.
014400
014500 PRINT-THE-RECORD.
014600     PERFORM PRINT-LINE-1.
014700     PERFORM PRINT-LINE-2.
014800     PERFORM PRINT-LINE-3.
014900     PERFORM PRINT-LINE-4.
015000     PERFORM LINE-FEED.
015100
015200 PRINT-LINE-1.
015300     MOVE SPACE TO DETAIL-LINE.
015400     MOVE VENDOR-NUMBER TO PRINT-NUMBER.
015500     MOVE VENDOR-NAME TO PRINT-NAME.
015600     MOVE VENDOR-CONTACT TO PRINT-CONTACT.
015700     MOVE DETAIL-LINE TO PRINTER-RECORD.
015800     PERFORM WRITE-TO-PRINTER.
015900
016000 PRINT-LINE-2.
016100     MOVE SPACE TO DETAIL-LINE.
016200     MOVE VENDOR-ADDRESS-1 TO PRINT-NAME.
016300     MOVE VENDOR-PHONE TO PRINT-CONTACT.
016400     MOVE DETAIL-LINE TO PRINTER-RECORD.
016500     PERFORM WRITE-TO-PRINTER.
016600
016700 PRINT-LINE-3.
016800     MOVE SPACE TO DETAIL-LINE.
016900     MOVE VENDOR-ADDRESS-2 TO PRINT-NAME.
017000     IF VENDOR-ADDRESS-2 NOT = SPACE
017100         MOVE DETAIL-LINE TO PRINTER-RECORD
017200         PERFORM WRITE-TO-PRINTER.
017300
```

16

continues

Listing 16.15. continued

```
017400 PRINT-LINE-4.
017500     MOVE SPACE TO CITY-STATE-LINE.
017600     MOVE VENDOR-CITY TO PRINT-CITY.
017700     MOVE VENDOR-STATE TO PRINT-STATE.
017800
017900     PERFORM LOOK-UP-STATE-CODE.
018000
018100     MOVE VENDOR-ZIP TO PRINT-ZIP.
018200     MOVE CITY-STATE-LINE TO PRINTER-RECORD.
018300     PERFORM WRITE-TO-PRINTER.
018400
018500 LOOK-UP-STATE-CODE.
018600     SET STATE-INDEX TO 1.
018700     SEARCH TABLE-STATE-RECORD
018800         AT END
018900           MOVE "***Not Found***" TO PRINT-STATE-NAME
019000           WHEN VENDOR-STATE = TABLE-STATE-CODE(STATE-INDEX)
019100           MOVE TABLE-STATE-NAME(STATE-INDEX)
019200              TO PRINT-STATE-NAME.
019300
019400     IF STATE-NAME = SPACE
019500         MOVE "*State is Blank*" TO PRINT-STATE-NAME.
019600
019700 READ-NEXT-RECORD.
019800     READ VENDOR-FILE NEXT RECORD
019900         AT END MOVE "Y" TO FILE-AT-END.
020000
020100 WRITE-TO-PRINTER.
020200     WRITE PRINTER-RECORD BEFORE ADVANCING 1.
020300     ADD 1 TO LINE-COUNT.
020400
020500 LINE-FEED.
020600     MOVE SPACE TO PRINTER-RECORD.
020700     PERFORM WRITE-TO-PRINTER.
020800
020900 START-NEXT-PAGE.
021000     PERFORM END-LAST-PAGE.
021100     PERFORM START-NEW-PAGE.
021200
021300 START-NEW-PAGE.
021400     ADD 1 TO PAGE-NUMBER.
021500     MOVE PAGE-NUMBER TO PRINT-PAGE-NUMBER.
021600     MOVE TITLE-LINE TO PRINTER-RECORD.
021700     PERFORM WRITE-TO-PRINTER.
021800     PERFORM LINE-FEED.
021900     MOVE COLUMN-LINE TO PRINTER-RECORD.
022000     PERFORM WRITE-TO-PRINTER.
022100     PERFORM LINE-FEED.
022200
022300 END-LAST-PAGE.
022400     PERFORM FORM-FEED.
022500     MOVE ZERO TO LINE-COUNT.
022600
022700 FORM-FEED.
```

16

```
022800       MOVE SPACE TO PRINTER-RECORD.
022900       WRITE PRINTER-RECORD BEFORE ADVANCING PAGE.
023000
023100 READ-NEXT-STATE-RECORD.
023200       MOVE "N" TO STATE-FILE-AT-END.
023300       READ STATE-FILE NEXT RECORD
023400           AT END
023500               MOVE "Y" TO STATE-FILE-AT-END.
023600
```

ANALYSIS   The definition of the TABLE-STATE-RECORD occurs at lines 007000 through 007300.

At lines 009800 through 010500, the opening procedure has been modified to open the STATE-FILE, load it into a table, and then close the file. The STATE-FILE itself is no longer needed in the program because all the information has been pulled into memory.

The LOAD-STATE-TABLE paragraph, at line 010700, starts by clearing the table using the CLEAR-TABLE routine at lines 011500 through 012100. This is a simple routine that moves spaces to each occurrence of TABLE-STATE-RECORD by varying the STATE-INDEX from 1 through 50.

Back at LOAD-STATE-TABLE, at lines 010900 through 011300, the STATE-INDEX is set to 1, the first record in the STATE-FILE is read, and then the table is loaded one record at a time by performing LOAD-ONE-STATE-RECORD until the state file reaches an end or the STATE-INDEX exceeds 50.

LOAD-ONE-STATE-RECORD at line 012300 loads the table elements from the fields in the record and then, at the bottom of the loop (line 012700), reads the next record. If the read is successful, the STATE-INDEX is set up by 1, and if the STATE-INDEX has exceeded 50, an error message is displayed.

If the state file does exceed 50 entries and they are legitimate, it is necessary to edit the program so that the table is larger by changing the OCCURS count at line 007000. You will also need to change the value 50 at lines 011300, 011330, 011800, and 013100.

The logic for using the table begins in PRINT-LINE-4 at line 017400, where LOOK-UP-STATE-CODE is performed in order to locate the state name.

LOOK-UP-STATE-CODE at line 018500 starts by setting the state index to 1, and then the search is performed at lines 018700 through 019200. The search attempts to match the VENDOR-STATE to the TABLE-STATE-CODE(STATE-INDEX) and, if successful, the TABLE-STATE-NAME(STATE-INDEX) is moved to PRINT-STATE-NAME.

If the match fails, the AT END logic at lines 018800 and 018900 takes over, and a "***Not Found***" message is moved to PRINT-STATE-NAME.

At line `019400`, one final test is made to check whether the `PRINT-STATE-NAME` field is still blank. This is a case of being extra safe. If the state file does not contain all 50 states, some of the table entries will contain spaces. If a vendor record contains a `VENDOR-STATE` that is spaces (which is invalid), the search will find a match, because somewhere in the table after the actual entries, `VENDOR-STATE = TABLE-STATE-CODE(STATE-INDEX)` will be true because both variables contain spaces. This is caused by invalid data in the vendor file, so an extra message is displayed.

Code, compile, and run `vndrpt03.cbl`. The output should be identical to `vndrpt02.cbl`. You probably won't notice a speed difference unless you have many records in your vendor file, but you will know how to use tables.

The code in vndrpt03.cbl can be improved even more, by creating an additional variable containing `NUMBER-OF-STATES` as in the following:

```
01   NUMBER-OF-STATES         PIC 99 VALUE 50.
```

When 50 is used in the code, use the variable instead, as in the following two examples.

```
011200          UNTIL STATE-FILE-AT-END = "Y" OR
011300              STATE-INDEX > NUMBER-OF-STATES.

013100          IF STATE-INDEX > NUMBER-OF-STATES
013200              DISPLAY "TABLE FULL".
```

The advantage of this is that if the number of states is increased by adding DC, VI for Virgin Islands, PR for Puerto Rico and so on, it is possible to modify the program to accommodate the larger table by changing only two lines of code.

```
007000 01   TABLE-STATE-RECORD OCCURS 50 TIMES
007100          INDEXED BY STATE-INDEX.
```

becomes

```
007000 01   TABLE-STATE-RECORD OCCURS 60 TIMES
007100          INDEXED BY STATE-INDEX.
```

and

```
01   NUMBER-OF-STATES         PIC 99 VALUE 50.
```

becomes

```
01   NUMBER-OF-STATES         PIC 99 VALUE 60.
```

Summary

One of the main methods of validating entered data is to look up the information in another file that contains correct information. Today, you learned the following basics:

☐ Using code files is an effective way to validate input information.

☐ The user-entered field is validated by moving it to the key of a code file and reading the code file. If the record is not found, it is assumed that the user entered the information incorrectly.

☐ Code files can be loaded into tables and searched. For long reports, this can speed up the process.

☐ You create a table by using the OCCURS clause and, optionally, an INDEXED BY clause.

☐ Using INDEXED BY makes it easier to do searches on tables.

☐ Index variables are manipulated by using the SET command.

Q&A

Q **In Listing 16.15, vndrpt03.cbl, the loading of TABLE-STATE-CODE and TABLE-STATE-NAME is done by moving the individual fields from STATE-RECORD, as in the following:**

```
012400       MOVE STATE-CODE TO TABLE-STATE-CODE(STATE-INDEX).
012500       MOVE STATE-NAME TO TABLE-STATE-NAME(STATE-INDEX).
```

Is it possible to move STATE-RECORD to TABLE-STATE-RECORD(STATE-INDEX)?

A Yes. STATE-RECORD and STATE-TABLE-RECORD(STATE-INDEX) are both alphanumeric variables, and you always can move one to the other:

```
012400       MOVE STATE-RECORD TO TABLE-STATE-RECORD(STATE-INDEX).
```

The real question is, will this work the same way?

TABLE-STATE-RECORD and STATE-RECORD are identical in length and type, and the subordinate variables are identical in length and type, so moving the whole STATE-RECORD to TABLE-STATE-RECORD will have the same effect.

The state file record listing, which is

```
000900 01   STATE-RECORD.
001000      05   STATE-CODE              PIC X(2).
001100      05   STATE-NAME              PIC X(20).
```

and the table listing, which is

```
007000 01   TABLE-STATE-RECORD OCCURS 50 TIMES
007100           INDEXED BY STATE-INDEX.
007200      05   TABLE-STATE-CODE        PIC XX.
007300      05   TABLE-STATE-NAME        PIC X(20).
```

can be compared byte for byte, ignoring the OCCURS clause, and therefore they are equivalent. However, it is a better practice to move the individual fields.

Q Do I need to use tables?

A No, but they are there to improve the efficiency of programs. Many programs do not use tables, but you should know how to use them so that you have an idea of how to improve report speed.

Q Why do you use a table in a report program, but not in a maintenance program?

A You can use a table in a maintenance program, but tables are used primarily to increase speed. Users type very slowly compared to the speed with which a report program looks up records, so you usually don't find the need for a table in a maintenance program.

Workshop

Quiz

1. What would be the correct command to increase an index variable named VENDOR-INDEX by 1?

2. Using the table created in Listing 16.15, what is the value in STATE-INDEX after the following commands are executed?

```
018300      MOVE 14 TO STATE-INDEX.
018400      MOVE "XX" TO TABLE-STATE-CODE(STATE-INDEX).
```

3. What is the value in TABLE-STATE-CODE(STATE-INDEX) after the commands in quiz question 2 are executed?

Exercises

1. Design a table that will hold 100 vendor records. Include an index variable.

   Hint: See the following listing for the vendor record:

```
002000 01  VENDOR-RECORD.
002100     05  VENDOR-NUMBER           PIC 9(5).
002200     05  VENDOR-NAME             PIC X(30).
002300     05  VENDOR-ADDRESS-1        PIC X(30).
002400     05  VENDOR-ADDRESS-2        PIC X(30).
002500     05  VENDOR-CITY             PIC X(20).
002600     05  VENDOR-STATE            PIC X(2).
002700     05  VENDOR-ZIP              PIC X(10).
002800     05  VENDOR-CONTACT          PIC X(30).
002900     05  VENDOR-PHONE            PIC X(15).
```

2. Work out the size of the table created in exercise 1.

Day 17

Alternate Keys

On Day 11, "Indexed File I/O," you learned that it is possible to set up more than one key in a file, in order to retrieve records in a different order than they were entered. You saw examples of how to retrieve in alphabetical and numerical order, and today's lesson teaches you the specifics of completing this task. You also learn about the following topics:

- ☐ What is an alternate key?
- ☐ Creating a file with alternate indexes.
- ☐ What is in a data file?
- ☐ Creating new files from old files.
- ☐ Maintaining a file with alternate keys.
- ☐ What is a key path?
- ☐ Accessing a file on key paths.
- ☐ Looking up records by alternate key.
- ☐ Helping the user with alternate keys.

What Is an Alternate Key?

Although an indexed file must have a unique primary key, it is possible to put other keys in the file. These keys do not have to be unique and can be arranged to return records in a different order than the primary key. Alternate keys are useful for retrieving records in alphabetical order by name, in zip code order, or any of a variety of other sort orders. A sales file could include an alternate key on the customer territory to group information in territory order. An employee file could contain an alternate key on the employment date to provide a sort on seniority of the employee.

Today, you use one of these alternate keys to provide a method of accessing the vendor file in alphabetical vendor name order.

NEW TERM   An *alternate index* or *alternate key* is an additional index in an indexed file that defines an alternative path along which records can be retrieved. The term *path* is used because when you use an alternate index to read records one after the other in a file, the records are read in a different sequence than they would be read using a standard READ NEXT.

An indexed file containing alternate indexes still must have a primary key, but it usually is called an *alternate indexed file* to indicate the existence of the extra keys.

An alternate indexed file is defined in the same way as an indexed file, but some additional information appears in the SELECT statement for the file.

Listing 17.1 is a COPY file containing an FD for an alternate indexed file. Note that it is no different from earlier versions of the FD for the vendor file, except that it includes a comment that VENDOR-NAME is an alternate key with duplicates. The comment does not create an alternate key, and is only there for reference.

TYPE   **Listing 17.1. The FD for an alternate indexed file.**

```
000100*--------------------------------
000200* FDVND04.CBL
000300* Primary Key - VENDOR-NUMBER
000400* Alternate - NAME with duplicates
000500
000600* NAME, ADDRESS-1, CITY, STATE,
000700*   and PHONE are required fields.
000800*
000900* VENDOR-STATE must be looked up
001000*   and must exist in the STATE-FILE
001100*   to be valid.
001200* VENDOR-ADDRESS-2 not always used
001300*   so may be SPACES
001400* VENDOR-PHONE is usually the
001500*   number for VENDOR-CONTACT
```

17

```
001600* All fields should be entered in
001700*    UPPER case.
001800*-------------------------------
001900 FD   VENDOR-FILE
002000      LABEL RECORDS ARE STANDARD.
002100 01   VENDOR-RECORD.
002200      05   VENDOR-NUMBER          PIC 9(5).
002300      05   VENDOR-NAME            PIC X(30).
002400      05   VENDOR-ADDRESS-1       PIC X(30).
002500      05   VENDOR-ADDRESS-2       PIC X(30).
002600      05   VENDOR-CITY            PIC X(20).
002700      05   VENDOR-STATE           PIC X(2).
002800      05   VENDOR-ZIP             PIC X(10).
002900      05   VENDOR-CONTACT         PIC X(30).
003000      05   VENDOR-PHONE           PIC X(15).
003100
```

Listing 17.2 is a COPY file containing a SELECT statement for an alternate indexed file, and this is where the alternate key is actually defined.

TYPE   **Listing 17.2. The SELECT for an alternate indexed file.**

```
000100*-------------------------------
000200* SLVND02.CBL
000300*-------------------------------
000400      SELECT VENDOR-FILE
000500          ASSIGN TO "vendor"
000600          ORGANIZATION IS INDEXED
000700          RECORD KEY IS VENDOR-NUMBER
000800          ALTERNATE KEY
000900              IS VENDOR-NAME WITH DUPLICATES
001000          ACCESS MODE IS DYNAMIC.
001100
```

ANALYSIS   At lines 000800 and 000900, the alternate key is identified as VENDOR-NAME. The WITH DUPLICATES clause on line 000900 indicates that more than one record can exist with the same value in this field. Allowing duplicates in an alternate key field for names is a standard practice because names can be duplicated. If the WITH DUPLICATES clause is omitted, VENDOR-NAME tends to act like a second primary key on the file, and it forces each value in the key to be unique.

If an alternate indexed file is defined with an alternate key in which duplicates are not allowed, attempting to write a record with a key that already is on file has the same effect as attempting to write a file with a duplicate primary key. An INVALID KEY file error condition occurs because a record with that key value already is on file.

Creating a File with Alternate Indexes

Adding the definition in a SELECT statement does not by itself make an alternate indexed file. The file must have been created (opened in output mode) by a program containing that definition for the file.

After the file is created, you can treat it like any other indexed file. Records written to it will be stored correctly with the alternate index values.

Opening a file in output mode destroys the original file if one exists. This presents a problem. You already have created a vendor file without an alternate index and put several records in it. Now you need a new file with the alternate key included. It is possible to convert the original file without losing the data by using the records in the original file and writing them to the new file that has been created.

The method used for this is a program that opens the original file for reading, opens the new file for output, and then copies records from the old file to the new file.

What Is in a Data File?

Recall that when using a COBOL program to open a file, I said that the file must be opened with the same file definition that was used to create it. Now that you are more familiar with COBOL, I am going to change that statement.

In order to sort this out, you need to delve into the inner workings of an indexed file. STATE-FILE is used in this example because the records are shorter and easier to display, but the principle is the same for the vendor file.

What's in a data file? Regardless of whether the file is indexed, the primary content of a data file is data. Figure 17.1 represents the state code file containing five records. The figure also includes a ruler for the 22 bytes in each record.

Figure 17.1.

Five records in a state codes file.

```
ARARKANSAS
CACALIFORNIA
FLFLORIDA
GAGEORGIA
NHNEW HAMPSHIRE
```

```
|   |   1   |   2   |   |  ◄──── RULER
1234567890123456789012
```

The file contains five records of 22 bytes each. The first two bytes of each record is the two-character code for that state. The remaining 20 bytes contain the state name followed by spaces to the end of the record.

An indexed file contains the data records that have been stored in the file, but it also contains additional information. This additional data is information about the file organization, record length, primary key position and length, and any alternate keys. This information is used internally by the COBOL file system but never shows up as data when reading a file through a COBOL program.

Exactly where this information is stored in the file isn't important as long as you know that it is stored there. Figure 17.2 shows this data to indicate that it is in the file, but not as a data record.

Figure 17.2.

Five records in an indexed state codes file.

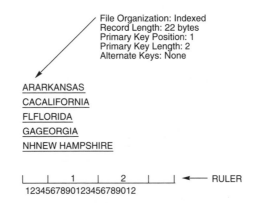

```
File Organization: Indexed
Record Length: 22 bytes
Primary Key Position: 1
Primary Key Length: 2
Alternate Keys: None
```

```
ARARKANSAS
CACALIFORNIA
FLFLORIDA
GAGEORGIA
NHNEW HAMPSHIRE
```

```
|   |   | 1 |   | 2 |   |   | ◄──── RULER
1234567890123456789012
```

With this in mind, it is possible to clarify my earlier statement about opening a file. A file must be opened with a file definition that matches the file organization, record length, and key structure of the actual file. Usually, this is the file definition that was used to create it, but it does not have to be if it matches the file organization, record length, and key structure of that file definition.

Note that the COBOL name for the file (STATE-FILE) and the fields in the record (STATE-CODE, STATE-NAME, and so on) are not actually stored in the data file. They are stored in the COBOL program.

Listings 17.3 and 17.4 are the original SELECT and FD for the state code file.

TYPE Listing 17.3. The original SELECT for the state code file.

```
000100*- - - - - - - - - - - - - - - - - - - - - - - - - - - - -
000200* SLSTATE.CBL
000300*- - - - - - - - - - - - - - - - - - - - - - - - - - - - -
000400    SELECT STATE-FILE
000500        ASSIGN TO "STATE"
000600        ORGANIZATION IS INDEXED
000700        RECORD KEY IS STATE-CODE
000800        ACCESS MODE IS DYNAMIC.
000900
```

TYPE **Listing 17.4. The original FD for the state code file.**

```
000100*---------------------------------
000200* FDSTATE.CBL
000300* Primary Key - STATE-CODE
000400* NAME is required
000500* NAME and CODE should be upper case
000600*---------------------------------
000700 FD  STATE-FILE
000800     LABEL RECORDS ARE STANDARD.
000900 01  STATE-RECORD.
001000     05  STATE-CODE            PIC X(2).
001100     05  STATE-NAME            PIC X(20).
001200
```

Listings 17.5 and 17.6 are another SELECT and FD that also could be used to access the same state code file. Although the data names have been changed, the file organization, record length, and key structure are the same in both definitions.

TYPE **Listing 17.5. A SELECT that will work for the state code file.**

```
000400     SELECT ST-FILE
000500         ASSIGN TO "STATE"
000600         ORGANIZATION IS INDEXED
000700         RECORD KEY IS ST-CODE
000800         ACCESS MODE IS DYNAMIC.
000900
```

TYPE **Listing 17.6. An FD that will work for the state code file.**

```
000700 FD  ST-FILE
000800     LABEL RECORDS ARE STANDARD.
000900 01  ST-RECORD.
001000     05  ST-CODE              PIC X(2).
001100     05  ST-NAME              PIC X(20).
001200
```

If you used Listings 17.5 and 17.6 in a program, you would use the data names from these listings to access the file. When you open the file, you would OPEN I-O ST-FILE. To write the record, you would use WRITE ST-RECORD, but the file would still be accessed correctly.

Listings 17.7 and 17.8 are an extreme (and possibly silly) example of changing things around. The record originally was defined as two fields. What was STATE-CODE is now named THE-KEY, and the 20-character field that was called STATE-NAME is broken up arbitrarily into three smaller fields. Even with the changes, the file organization, record length, and key structure

17

remain the same. This pair of file definitions could be used to open and process the state code file. Of course, using FIRST-5-OF-NAME for anything represents only the first five characters of the original STATE-NAME. 2ND-5-OF-NAME or LAST-10-OF-NAME represents other portions of the original STATE-NAME. It is useless to do something like this, but this extreme example illustrates the point very well.

TYPE | **Listing 17.7. Another SELECT statement that would work.**

```
000400      SELECT THE-FILE
000500          ASSIGN TO "STATE"
000600          ORGANIZATION IS INDEXED
000700          RECORD KEY IS THE-KEY
000800          ACCESS MODE IS DYNAMIC.
000900
```

TYPE | **Listing 17.8. An extreme example of changing the FD.**

```
000700 FD  THE-FILE
000800     LABEL RECORDS ARE STANDARD.
000900 01  THE-RECORD.
001000     05  THE-KEY              PIC X(2).
001100     05  FIRST-5-OF-NAME      PIC X(5).
001200     05  2ND-5-OF-NAME        PIC X(5).
001300     05  LAST-10-OF-NAME      PIC X(10).
```

There are times when a redefinition of the fields in a record can be useful. Suppose that one program that uses the STATE-FILE calculates shipping charges based on whether the shipping address is within the continental United States. The program currently has logic such as that shown in Listing 17.9. It is not a good practice to hard-code special conditions like this, but you will find it in programs that you are asked to modify all the time.

TYPE | **Listing 17.9. The wrong way to test for shipping charges.**

```
021000* Add extra shipping for Alaska and Hawaii
021100     IF STATE-CODE = "HI" OR STATE-CODE = "AK"
021200         PERFORM CHARGE-EXTRA-SHIPPING
021300     ELSE
021400         PERFORM CHARGE-REGULAR-SHIPPING.
```

This code keeps working until the business expands and you need to include state codes for U.S. territories and Canadian provinces. There are just too many of these to hard-code into the program.

17

By inspecting the STATE-FILE you find that none of the states uses the full 20 characters of STATE-NAME, and in every record, the 20th character of the STATE-NAME is a space.

A new FD could be defined that separates out the 20th character to use it as a continental flag as in Listing 17.10.

TYPE   **Listing 17.10. Adding a continental flag to the STATE-FILE.**

```
000100*-------------------------------
000200* FDSTATC.CBL
000300* Primary Key - STATE-CODE
000400* NAME is required
000500* NAME and CODE should be upper case
000600*-------------------------------
000700 FD   STATE-FILE
000800      LABEL RECORDS ARE STANDARD.
000900 01   STATE-RECORD.
001000      05   STATE-CODE          PIC X(2).
001100      05   STATE-NAME          PIC X(19).
001200      05   STATE-CONTINENTAL   PIC X(1).
```

After setting the flag correctly to Y or N for each state, you could test the flag to determine shipping charges as in Listing 17.11.

TYPE   **Listing 17.11. The right way to test for shipping charges.**

```
021000* Add extra shipping for non-continental US
021100      IF STATE-CONTINENTAL = "N"
021200          PERFORM CHARGE-EXTRA-SHIPPING
021300      ELSE
021400          PERFORM CHARGE-REGULAR-SHIPPING.
```

This method of allocating unused characters in existing fields for new fields is a very common practice.

File and data conversions such as adding STATE-CONTINENTAL, and the following conversion of the VENDOR-FILE are very typical tasks that might be assigned to a junior programmer. Being able to do conversions is one way you will be able to perform useful (and paid) work.

Creating New Files from Old Files

You have several things to deal with before you can create a new vendor file out of the existing one. The data names in a program must not be identical, so it is necessary to create a temporary SELECT and FD that can be used to open the original file, but use different data names.

Another problem has to do with the way files are stored on a disk. Two files cannot have the same physical name on a disk. The new file will be called "vendor", so for the purpose of conversion, the old file is renamed "ovendor".

Under MS-DOS, enter the following:

```
DIR vendor*
```

If you are using Micro Focus Personal COBOL, two files are named vendor: VENDOR and VENDOR.IDX. Under ACUCOBOL, one file is named VENDOR. Under other COBOL compilers, two files might be named VENDOR.DAT and VENDOR.IDX. If your system uses two files, both of them must be renamed.

Enter one or more of these commands, depending on the filenames:

```
RENAME VENDOR OVENDOR
RENAME VENDOR.IDX OVENDOR.IDX
RENAME VENDOR.DAT OVENDOR.DAT
```

Listing 17.12, fdovnd01.cbl, is a COPY file of an FD that is created by copying fdvnd03.cbl to fdovnd01.cbl and then changing each data name that starts with VENDOR- so that it starts with OLD-VENDOR-.

Listing 17.13, slvnd01.cbl, is a COPY file of a SELECT statement that is created in a similar way, by copying slvnd01.cbl to slovnd01.cbl and then changing each data name that starts with VENDOR- so that it starts with OLD-VENDOR-.

Create these two files and modify each of them to match Listings 17.12 and 17.13.

TYPE **Listing 17.12. The FD for the original vendor file.**

```
000100*-------------------------------
000200* FDOVND01.CBL
000300* Primary Key - OLD-VENDOR-NUMBER
000400* Original before alt path added
000500* NAME, ADDRESS-1, CITY, STATE,
000600*   and PHONE are required fields.
000700*
000800* OLD-VENDOR-STATE must be looked up
000900*   and must exist in the STATE-FILE
001000*   to be valid.
001100* OLD-VENDOR-ADDRESS-2 not always used
001200*   so may be SPACES
001300* OLD-VENDOR-PHONE is usually the
001400*   number for OLD-VENDOR-CONTACT
001500* All fields should be entered in
001600*   UPPER case.
001700*-------------------------------
001800 FD  OLD-VENDOR-FILE
001900     LABEL RECORDS ARE STANDARD.
002000 01  OLD-VENDOR-RECORD.
```

continues

Listing 17.12. continued

```
002100      05   OLD-VENDOR-NUMBER          PIC 9(5).
002200      05   OLD-VENDOR-NAME            PIC X(30).
002300      05   OLD-VENDOR-ADDRESS-1       PIC X(30).
002400      05   OLD-VENDOR-ADDRESS-2       PIC X(30).
002500      05   OLD-VENDOR-CITY            PIC X(20).
002600      05   OLD-VENDOR-STATE           PIC X(2).
002700      05   OLD-VENDOR-ZIP             PIC X(10).
002800      05   OLD-VENDOR-CONTACT         PIC X(30).
002900      05   OLD-VENDOR-PHONE           PIC X(15).
003000
```

For the SELECT statement, be sure to change line 000500 to read ASSIGN TO "ovendor".

TYPE Listing 17.13. The SELECT for the original vendor file.

```
000100*--------------------------------
000200* SLOVND01.CBL
000300*--------------------------------
000400      SELECT OLD-VENDOR-FILE
000500          ASSIGN TO "ovendor"
000600          ORGANIZATION IS INDEXED
000700          RECORD KEY IS OLD-VENDOR-NUMBER
000800          ACCESS MODE IS DYNAMIC.
```

After these new file definitions are created, it is possible to write a program that converts the old file to the new by reading each record in the old file and writing it to the new file (shown in Listing 17.14).

TYPE Listing 17.14. Creating the new alternate indexed file.

```
000100 IDENTIFICATION DIVISION.
000200 PROGRAM-ID. NEWVND01.
000300*-------------------------------------------------
000400* Create new Vendor File with Alt key from old.
000500*-------------------------------------------------
000600 ENVIRONMENT DIVISION.
000700 INPUT-OUTPUT SECTION.
000800 FILE-CONTROL.
000900
001000      COPY "SLOVND01.CBL".
001100
001200      COPY "SLVND02.CBL".
001300 DATA DIVISION.
001400 FILE SECTION.
001500
```

```
001600        COPY "FDOVND01.CBL".
001700
001800        COPY "FDVND04.CBL".
001900
002000 WORKING-STORAGE SECTION.
002100
002200 77  OLD-VENDOR-FILE-AT-END    PIC X VALUE "N".
002300
002400 PROCEDURE DIVISION.
002500 PROGRAM-BEGIN.
002600        PERFORM OPENING-PROCEDURE.
002700        PERFORM MAIN-PROCESS.
002800        PERFORM CLOSING-PROCEDURE.
002900
003000 PROGRAM-DONE.
003100        STOP RUN.
003200
003300 OPENING-PROCEDURE.
003400        OPEN OUTPUT VENDOR-FILE.
003500        OPEN I-O OLD-VENDOR-FILE.
003600
003700 CLOSING-PROCEDURE.
003800        CLOSE VENDOR-FILE.
003900        CLOSE OLD-VENDOR-FILE.
004000
004100 MAIN-PROCESS.
004200        PERFORM READ-NEXT-OLD-VENDOR-RECORD.
004300        PERFORM PROCESS-ONE-RECORD
004400            UNTIL OLD-VENDOR-FILE-AT-END = "Y".
004500
004600 READ-NEXT-OLD-VENDOR-RECORD.
004700        MOVE "N" TO OLD-VENDOR-FILE-AT-END.
004800        READ OLD-VENDOR-FILE NEXT RECORD
004900            AT END
005000            MOVE "Y" TO OLD-VENDOR-FILE-AT-END.
005100
005200 PROCESS-ONE-RECORD.
005300        MOVE OLD-VENDOR-RECORD TO VENDOR-RECORD.
005400        PERFORM WRITE-VENDOR-RECORD.
005500
005600        PERFORM READ-NEXT-OLD-VENDOR-RECORD.
005700
005800 WRITE-VENDOR-RECORD.
005900        WRITE VENDOR-RECORD
006000            INVALID KEY
006100            DISPLAY "ERROR WRITING VENDOR RECORD".
006200
006300
```

ANALYSIS   Listing 17.14 is a fairly straightforward program. In the OPENING-PROCEDURE at line
003300, it opens the VENDOR-FILE in output mode. This creates the new vendor file
with the alternate index. It then opens OLD-VENDOR-FILE (ovendor) in I/O mode.

The loop control in MAIN-PROCESS at line 004100 follows the procedure of reading the first old vendor record and then performing the processing loop (PROCESS-ONE-RECORD) until OLD-VENDOR-FILE-AT-END = "Y".

The processing loop, PROCESS-ONE-RECORD at line 005200, moves the OLD-VENDOR-RECORD to VENDOR-RECORD, writes the new record, and then at the end of the loop at line 005600, reads the next old vendor record.

Code and compile this program. Be sure that you have renamed the vendor file to "ovendor" before you run it. The new file named "vendor" will contain an alternate index. You won't notice any difference in the file yet, although the file might be larger on the disk.

Maintaining a File with Alternate Keys

You have to modify the maintenance program for the vendor file, vndmnt02.cbl, to allow for the new key in the file. The maintenance for a file with alternate keys can be identical to the maintenance for a standard indexed file. To modify vndmnt02.cbl so that it will maintain the new vendor file, copy it to vndmnt03.cbl. Then make the changes at lines 001100 and 001800 of Listing 17.15, a fragment of vndmnd03.cbl, to include the new SELECT and FD for the vendor file.

TYPE **Listing 17.15. Maintaining a file with alternate keys.**

```
000100 IDENTIFICATION DIVISION.
000200 PROGRAM-ID. VNDMNT03.
000300*-------------------------------
000400* Add, Change, Inquire and Delete
000500* for the Vendor File.
000600*-------------------------------
000700 ENVIRONMENT DIVISION.
000800 INPUT-OUTPUT SECTION.
000900 FILE-CONTROL.
001000
001100     COPY "SLVND02.CBL".
001200
001300     COPY "SLSTATE.CBL".
001400
001500 DATA DIVISION.
001600 FILE SECTION.
001700
001800     COPY "FDVND04.CBL".
001900
002000     COPY "FDSTATE.CBL".
002100
```

Make the changes and compile the program so that you have a maintenance program for the new vendor file.

What Is a Key Path?

Listing 17.16 illustrates a customer record with a primary key of CUSTOMER-NUMBER. This is a fairly straightforward record layout, except that the phone number has been broken down additionally into area code, prefix, and number.

TYPE **Listing 17.16. A customer record.**

```
001000 01   CUSTOMER-RECORD.
001100      05   CUSTOMER-NUMBER        PIC 9(5).
001200      05   CUSTOMER-NAME          PIC X(20).
001300      05   CUSTOMER-ADDRESS-1     PIC X(20).
001400      05   CUSTOMER-ADDRESS-2     PIC X(20).
001500      05   CUSTOMER-ZIP           PIC 9(5).
001600      05   CUSTOMER-PHONE.
001700          10   CUSTOMER-AREA-CODE  PIC 9(3).
001800          10   CUSTOMER-PREFIX     PIC 9(3).
001900          10   CUSTOMER-PHONE-NO   PIC 9(4).
```

A field can be named as an alternate index so that, as each record is added to the file, information also is stored in the alternate index area of the file to indicate the correct order of records for that alternate index.

If you displayed the records in a customer file in primary key order, the file might look somewhat haphazard. This would be reading and displaying the file along the primary key path.

If you request that the name field be used as an index, and that records be presented to you in the order of the name index, they arrive in the order shown in Figure 17.3, along the CUSTOMER-NAME key path.

Figure 17.3.

Records sorted on the name field.

Number	Name	Address 1	Address 2	ZIP	Phone Area Code	Pre fix	Num- ber
00002	ABC Company	1234 Park Street	Overton, IL	60655	202	555	2341
00143	Acme Iron	4048 Upton St.	Pittsburgh, PA	02006	276	555	1212
00144	Alpha Omega	9099 Icon Ave.	North Port, LA	40448	919	555	3030
00140	Amphora Inc.	1414 15th Street	South Beach, CA	90945	213	555	9187
00142	Brothers Karamazof	6067 South Highway	Indianapolis, IN	10016	404	555	5056
00001	Johnson and Sons	1212 Main Street	Stanton, NJ	80815	217	555	4381
00156	Malio Bros.	2065 Highland Ave.	South Beach, CA	90945	213	555	7776
00141	Xeno Phobe Inc.	1112 M St.	Washington, DC	08074	202	555	4345

If you also request that the zip code and area code be used as an index for the records, you can have the records arrive in zip code order (as in Figure 17.4) along the CUSTOMER-ZIP key path, or in area-code order (as in Figure 17.5) along the CUSTOMER-AREA-CODE key path.

Figure 17.4.

Records sorted on the zip code field.

Number	Name	Address 1	Address 2	ZIP	Area Code	Pre-fix	Num-ber
00143	Acme Iron	4048 Upton St.	Pittsburgh, PA	02006	276	555	1212
00141	Xeno Phobe Inc.	1112 M St.	Washington, DC	08074	202	555	4345
00142	Brothers Karamazof	6067 South Highway	Indianapolis, IN	10016	404	555	5056
00144	Alpha Omega	9099 Icon Ave.	North Port, LA	40448	919	555	3030
00002	ABC Company	1234 Park Street	Overton, IL	60655	202	555	2341
00001	Johnson and Sons	1212 Main Street	Stanton, NJ	80815	217	555	4381
00140	Amphora Inc.	1414 15th Street	South Beach, CA	90945	213	555	9187
00156	Malio Bros.	2065 Highland Ave.	South Beach, CA	90945	213	555	7776

Figure 17.5.

Records sorted on the area code field.

Number	Name	Address 1	Address 2	ZIP	Area Code	Pre-fix	Num-ber
00141	Xeno Phobe Inc.	1112 M St.	Washington, DC	08074	202	555	4345
00002	ABC Company	1234 Park Street	Overton, IL	60655	202	555	2341
00140	Amphora Inc.	1414 15th Street	South Beach, CA	90945	213	555	9187
00156	Malio Bros.	2065 Highland Ave.	South Beach, CA	90945	213	555	7776
00001	Johnson and Sons.	1212 Main Street.	Stanton, NJ	80815	217	555	4381
00143	Acme Iron	4048 Upton St.	Pittsburgh, PA	02006	276	555	1212
00142	Brothers Karamazof	6067 South Highway	Indianapolis, IN	10016	404	555	5056
00144	Alpha Omega	9099 Icon Ave.	North Port, LA	40448	919	555	3030

In all the examples, the alternate indexed fields were fields in which duplicates might, and in fact do, occur. Amphora Inc. and Malio Bros. both have the same zip code and area code. In a large customer base, it is possible that customer names would be duplicated.

NEW TERM   The *key path* is the natural sorted order of records as they are read from the file using a particular key.

Listing 17.17 shows an example of the syntax that is used to define a file such as the customer file with multiple keys.

TYPE   **Listing 17.17. The SELECT with multiple alternate keys.**

```
000400      SELECT CUSTOMER-FILE
000500          ASSIGN TO "CUSTOMER"
000600          ORGANIZATION IS INDEXED
000700          RECORD KEY IS CUSTOMER-NUMBER
000800          ALTERNATE KEY IS CUSTOMER-NAME WITH DUPLICATES
000900          ALTERNATE KEY IS CUSTOMER-ZIP WITH DUPLICATES
001000          ALTERNATE KEY IS CUSTOMER-AREA-CODE WITH DUPLICATES
001100          ACCESS MODE IS DYNAMIC.
001200
```

17

Accessing a File on Key Paths

When an alternate indexed file is opened, the key path is set to the primary key. If you READ NEXT through the file, the records will be returned in the order of the primary key. COBOL includes a command that enables you to change the key path—the START command.

The first step to using a START command is to move a value to the field that will be the new key. In the case of the vendor file, the alternate key is the VENDOR-NAME. To set the file up to be able to read all records in VENDOR-NAME order, move the lowest possible value to the VENDOR-NAME (MOVE SPACES TO VENDOR-NAME). After the key is set up, you are ready for the second step. Start the file using the START command.

Listing 17.18 is an example of starting on a new key. What you want to do is start the file at the first record that contains a VENDOR-NAME that is greater than or equal to the spaces that are now in VENDOR-NAME. It seems that you should be able to say START GREATER THAN OR EQUAL. You can under the new COBOL-85 standard, but before that option was added you were limited to a little more awkward syntax. It uses the complement of greater than or equal to which is NOT LESS THAN. In this example, NOT < (NOT LESS THAN) is used to start at the first record whose VENDOR-NAME is equal to or greater than spaces.

TYPE | **Listing 17.18. Starting on the first record of a new key.**

```
020000     MOVE SPACE TO VENDOR-NAME.
020100     START VENDOR-FILE
020200        KEY NOT < VENDOR-NAME
020300          INVALID KEY
020400            MOVE "Y" TO FILE-AT-END.
```

You can do some interesting positioning tricks using the START command. In Listing 17.19, the key is initialized to an A followed by all Zs, and the start is GREATER THAN the key value. This causes the start to position the file at the first record with a VENDOR-NAME greater than "AZZZZZZZZZZZZZZZZZZZZZZZZZZZZZZZ", which probably would be the first vendor name that started with B.

TYPE | **Listing 17.19. Starting partly through the key path.**

```
020000     MOVE "AZZZZZZZZZZZZZZZZZZZZZZZZZZZZZZZ" TO VENDOR-NAME.
020100     START VENDOR-FILE
020200        KEY > VENDOR-NAME
020300          INVALID KEY
020400            MOVE "Y" TO FILE-AT-END.
```

17

The START command originally supported three conditions for determining the starting position, EQUALS, GREATER THAN, and NOT LESS THAN. The COBOL-85 standard added GREATER THAN OR EQUAL TO (>=). Some vendors have extended these to include positioning for LESS THAN, NOT GREATER THAN, and LESS THAN OR EQUAL TO. Here is the syntax for the standard three and the COBOL-85 option:

```
START file name
 KEY NOT < key name
  [ INVALID KEY
    do something ]

START file name
 KEY > key name
  [ INVALID KEY
    do something ]

START file name
 KEY EQUALS key name
  [ INVALID KEY
    do something ]

START file name
 KEY GREATER THAN OR EQUAL TO key name
  [ INVALID KEY
    do something ]
```

The following are examples:

```
MOVE SPACE TO VENDOR-NAME.
START VENDOR-FILE
 KEY NOT < VENDOR-NAME
  INVALID KEY
  MOVE "Y" TO FILE-AT-END.

MOVE "AZZZZZZZZZZZZZZZZZZZ"
    TO VENDOR-NAME.
START VENDOR-FILE
 KEY > VENDOR-NAME
  INVALID KEY
  MOVE "Y" TO FILE-AT-END.

MOVE "JONES AND SONS"
    TO VENDOR-NAME.
START VENDOR-FILE
 KEY EQUALS VENDOR-NAME
  INVALID KEY
  MOVE "N" TO RECORD-FOUND.

START VENDOR-FILE
 KEY GREATER THAN OR EQUAL TO VENDOR-NAME
  INVALID KEY
  MOVE "Y" TO FILE-AT-END.
```

You will usually use START NOT < or the newer START >= (GREATER THAN OR EQUAL TO), which are the most common types of START used in programs. When the START is completed successfully, the key path is changed and any subsequent READ NEXT proceeds to the next record along that path automatically.

The START has two effects: It changes the key path, and it positions the file someplace on that key path. It most commonly is used to position at the beginning of a key path.

A START does not read or acquire a record; it only positions the file ready for a READ or READ NEXT. If you use START NOT LESS THAN (NOT <) or START GREATER THAN (>), the start does not actually read a record. It positions the file so that a READ NEXT will read the record that matches the START condition. You see an example of this in Listing 17.20, the vendor-by-name report.

TYPE | **Listing 17.20. Printing in vendor name order.**

```
000100 IDENTIFICATION DIVISION.
000200 PROGRAM-ID. VNBYNM01.
000300*------------------------------
000400* Report on the Vendor File in
000500* alphabetical name order.
000600*------------------------------
000700 ENVIRONMENT DIVISION.
000800 INPUT-OUTPUT SECTION.
000900 FILE-CONTROL.
001000
001100     COPY "SLVND02.CBL".
001200
001300     COPY "SLSTATE.CBL".
001400
001500     SELECT PRINTER-FILE
001600         ASSIGN TO PRINTER
001700         ORGANIZATION IS LINE SEQUENTIAL.
001800
001900 DATA DIVISION.
002000 FILE SECTION.
002100
002200     COPY "FDVND04.CBL".
002300
002400     COPY "FDSTATE.CBL".
002500
002600 FD  PRINTER-FILE
002700     LABEL RECORDS ARE OMITTED.
002800 01  PRINTER-RECORD          PIC X(80).
002900
003000 WORKING-STORAGE SECTION.
003100
003200 01  DETAIL-LINE.
003300     05  PRINT-NUMBER     PIC 9(5).
003400     05  FILLER           PIC X      VALUE SPACE.
003500     05  PRINT-NAME       PIC X(30).
003600     05  FILLER           PIC X(15) VALUE SPACE.
003700     05  PRINT-CONTACT    PIC X(30).
003800
003900 01  CITY-STATE-LINE.
004000     05  FILLER           PIC X(6) VALUE SPACE.
004100     05  PRINT-CITY       PIC X(20).
004200     05  FILLER           PIC X VALUE SPACE.
```

17

continues

Listing 17.20. continued

```
004300      05  PRINT-STATE        PIC X(2).
004400      05  FILLER             PIC X VALUE SPACE.
004500      05  PRINT-STATE-NAME   PIC X(20).
004600      05  FILLER             PIC X(1) VALUE SPACE.
004700      05  PRINT-ZIP          PIC X(10).
004800
004900 01  COLUMN-LINE.
005000      05  FILLER          PIC X(2)  VALUE "NO".
005100      05  FILLER          PIC X(4) VALUE SPACE.
005200      05  FILLER          PIC X(12) VALUE "NAME-ADDRESS".
005300      05  FILLER          PIC X(33) VALUE SPACE.
005400      05  FILLER          PIC X(17) VALUE "CONTACT-PHONE-ZIP".
005500
005600 01  TITLE-LINE.
005700      05  FILLER             PIC X(20) VALUE SPACE.
005800      05  FILLER             PIC X(24)
005900          VALUE "VENDOR ALPHABETICAL LIST".
006000      05  FILLER             PIC X(11) VALUE SPACE.
006100      05  FILLER             PIC X(5) VALUE "PAGE:".
006200      05  FILLER             PIC X(1) VALUE SPACE.
006300      05  PRINT-PAGE-NUMBER PIC ZZZZ9.
006400
006500 77  FILE-AT-END          PIC X.
006600 77  STATE-FILE-AT-END    PIC X VALUE "N".
006700 77  LINE-COUNT           PIC 999 VALUE ZERO.
006800 77  PAGE-NUMBER          PIC 99999 VALUE ZERO.
006900 77  MAXIMUM-LINES        PIC 999 VALUE 55.
007000
007100 01  TABLE-STATE-RECORD OCCURS 50 TIMES
007200      INDEXED BY STATE-INDEX.
007300      05  TABLE-STATE-CODE     PIC XX.
007400      05  TABLE-STATE-NAME     PIC X(20).
007500 01  NUMBER-OF-STATES         PIC 99 VALUE 50.
007600 PROCEDURE DIVISION.
007700 PROGRAM-BEGIN.
007800
007900      PERFORM OPENING-PROCEDURE.
008000      MOVE ZEROES TO LINE-COUNT
008100                     PAGE-NUMBER.
008200
008300      PERFORM START-NEW-PAGE.
008400
008500      MOVE "N" TO FILE-AT-END.
008600      PERFORM READ-FIRST-RECORD.
008700      IF FILE-AT-END = "Y"
008800          MOVE "NO RECORDS FOUND" TO PRINTER-RECORD
008900          PERFORM WRITE-TO-PRINTER
009000      ELSE
009100          PERFORM PRINT-VENDOR-FIELDS
009200              UNTIL FILE-AT-END = "Y".
009300
009400      PERFORM CLOSING-PROCEDURE.
009500
009600 PROGRAM-DONE.
```

17

```
009700     STOP RUN.
009800
009900 OPENING-PROCEDURE.
010000     OPEN I-O VENDOR-FILE.
010100
010200     OPEN I-O STATE-FILE.
010300     PERFORM LOAD-STATE-TABLE.
010400     CLOSE STATE-FILE.
010500
010600     OPEN OUTPUT PRINTER-FILE.
010700
010800 LOAD-STATE-TABLE.
010900     PERFORM CLEAR-TABLE.
011000     SET STATE-INDEX TO 1.
011100     PERFORM READ-NEXT-STATE-RECORD.
011200     PERFORM LOAD-ONE-STATE-RECORD
011300         UNTIL STATE-FILE-AT-END = "Y" OR
011400             STATE-INDEX > NUMBER-OF-STATES.
011500
011600 CLEAR-TABLE.
011700     PERFORM CLEAR-ONE-TABLE-ROW
011800         VARYING STATE-INDEX FROM 1 BY 1
011900           UNTIL STATE-INDEX > NUMBER-OF-STATES.
012000
012100 CLEAR-ONE-TABLE-ROW.
012200     MOVE SPACE TO TABLE-STATE-RECORD(STATE-INDEX).
012300
012400 LOAD-ONE-STATE-RECORD.
012500     MOVE STATE-CODE TO TABLE-STATE-CODE(STATE-INDEX).
012600     MOVE STATE-NAME TO TABLE-STATE-NAME(STATE-INDEX).
012700
012800     PERFORM READ-NEXT-STATE-RECORD.
012900
013000     IF STATE-FILE-AT-END NOT = "Y"
013100         SET STATE-INDEX UP BY 1
013200         IF STATE-INDEX > NUMBER-OF-STATES
013300             DISPLAY "TABLE FULL".
013400
013500 CLOSING-PROCEDURE.
013600     CLOSE VENDOR-FILE.
013700     PERFORM END-LAST-PAGE.
013800     CLOSE PRINTER-FILE.
013900
014000 PRINT-VENDOR-FIELDS.
014100     IF LINE-COUNT > MAXIMUM-LINES
014200         PERFORM START-NEXT-PAGE.
014300     PERFORM PRINT-THE-RECORD.
014400     PERFORM READ-NEXT-RECORD.
014500
014600 PRINT-THE-RECORD.
014700     PERFORM PRINT-LINE-1.
014800     PERFORM PRINT-LINE-2.
014900     PERFORM PRINT-LINE-3.
015000     PERFORM PRINT-LINE-4.
015100     PERFORM LINE-FEED.
015200
015300 PRINT-LINE-1.
```

continues

Listing 17.20. continued

```
015400        MOVE SPACE TO DETAIL-LINE.
015500        MOVE VENDOR-NUMBER TO PRINT-NUMBER.
015600        MOVE VENDOR-NAME TO PRINT-NAME.
015700        MOVE VENDOR-CONTACT TO PRINT-CONTACT.
015800        MOVE DETAIL-LINE TO PRINTER-RECORD.
015900        PERFORM WRITE-TO-PRINTER.
016000
016100 PRINT-LINE-2.
016200        MOVE SPACE TO DETAIL-LINE.
016300        MOVE VENDOR-ADDRESS-1 TO PRINT-NAME.
016400        MOVE VENDOR-PHONE TO PRINT-CONTACT.
016500        MOVE DETAIL-LINE TO PRINTER-RECORD.
016600        PERFORM WRITE-TO-PRINTER.
016700
016800 PRINT-LINE-3.
016900        MOVE SPACE TO DETAIL-LINE.
017000        MOVE VENDOR-ADDRESS-2 TO PRINT-NAME.
017100        IF VENDOR-ADDRESS-2 NOT = SPACE
017200            MOVE DETAIL-LINE TO PRINTER-RECORD
017300            PERFORM WRITE-TO-PRINTER.
017400
017500 PRINT-LINE-4.
017600        MOVE SPACE TO CITY-STATE-LINE.
017700        MOVE VENDOR-CITY TO PRINT-CITY.
017800        MOVE VENDOR-STATE TO PRINT-STATE.
017900
018000        PERFORM LOOK-UP-STATE-CODE.
018100
018200        MOVE VENDOR-ZIP TO PRINT-ZIP.
018300        MOVE CITY-STATE-LINE TO PRINTER-RECORD.
018400        PERFORM WRITE-TO-PRINTER.
018500
018600 LOOK-UP-STATE-CODE.
018700        SET STATE-INDEX TO 1.
018800        SEARCH TABLE-STATE-RECORD
018900            AT END
019000              MOVE "***Not Found***" TO PRINT-STATE-NAME
019100            WHEN VENDOR-STATE = TABLE-STATE-CODE(STATE-INDEX)
019200              MOVE TABLE-STATE-NAME(STATE-INDEX)
019300                TO PRINT-STATE-NAME.
019400
019500        IF STATE-NAME = SPACE
019600            MOVE "*State is Blank*" TO PRINT-STATE-NAME.
019700
019800 READ-FIRST-RECORD.
019900        MOVE "N" TO FILE-AT-END.
020000        MOVE SPACE TO VENDOR-NAME.
020100        START VENDOR-FILE
020200            KEY NOT < VENDOR-NAME
020300            INVALID KEY MOVE "Y" TO FILE-AT-END.
020400
020500        IF FILE-AT-END NOT = "Y"
020600            PERFORM READ-NEXT-RECORD.
020700
```

```
020800 READ-NEXT-RECORD.
020900     READ VENDOR-FILE NEXT RECORD
021000         AT END MOVE "Y" TO FILE-AT-END.
021100
021200 WRITE-TO-PRINTER.
021300     WRITE PRINTER-RECORD BEFORE ADVANCING 1.
021400     ADD 1 TO LINE-COUNT.
021500
021600 LINE-FEED.
021700     MOVE SPACE TO PRINTER-RECORD.
021800     PERFORM WRITE-TO-PRINTER.
021900
022000 START-NEXT-PAGE.
022100     PERFORM END-LAST-PAGE.
022200     PERFORM START-NEW-PAGE.
022300
022400 START-NEW-PAGE.
022500     ADD 1 TO PAGE-NUMBER.
022600     MOVE PAGE-NUMBER TO PRINT-PAGE-NUMBER.
022700     MOVE TITLE-LINE TO PRINTER-RECORD.
022800     PERFORM WRITE-TO-PRINTER.
022900     PERFORM LINE-FEED.
023000     MOVE COLUMN-LINE TO PRINTER-RECORD.
023100     PERFORM WRITE-TO-PRINTER.
023200     PERFORM LINE-FEED.
023300
023400 END-LAST-PAGE.
023500     PERFORM FORM-FEED.
023600     MOVE ZERO TO LINE-COUNT.
023700
023800 FORM-FEED.
023900     MOVE SPACE TO PRINTER-RECORD.
024000     WRITE PRINTER-RECORD BEFORE ADVANCING PAGE.
024100
024200 READ-NEXT-STATE-RECORD.
024300     MOVE "N" TO STATE-FILE-AT-END.
024400     READ STATE-FILE NEXT RECORD
024500         AT END
024600             MOVE "Y" TO STATE-FILE-AT-END.
024700
```

The output of `vnbynm01.cbl` prints the same information as `vndrpt03.cbl`, but the records are in alphabetical order by name:

```
                         VENDOR ALPHABETICAL LIST          PAGE:    1
NO    NAME-ADDRESS                             CONTACT-PHONE-ZIP
00002 ABC PRINTING                             CHARLES JOHANSSEN
      1624 FOOTHILL BLVD                 (818) 555-4321
      SUITE 34
      LOS ANGELES          CA CALIFORNIA  91042
01176 ABERCROMBIE AND OTHERS
      1234 45TH ST.                      (213) 555-6543
      SUITE 17
      LOS ANGELES          CA CALIFORNIA  92345
```

```
00001 AERIAL SIGNS                              HENRIETTA MARKSON
BURBANK AIRPORT                           (818) 555-6066
HANGAR 305
BURBANK              CA CALIFORNIA         90016
00005 ALIAS SMITH AND JONES                      ROBIN COUSINS
1216 MAIN STREET                         415 555-9203
PALO ALTO            CA CALIFORNIA         90061
00022 ARTFUL DODGER
123 UNDERWOOD LANE                       202 555-1234
MARKHAM              WA WASHINGTON         40466
00003 CHARLES SMITH AND SONS                    MARTHA HARRISON
1435 SOUTH STREET                        (213) 555-4432
LOS ANGELES          CA CALIFORNIA         90064
00014 RANIER GRAPHICS                            JULIA SIMPSON
4433 WASHINGTO ST                        (213) 555-6789
LOS ANGELES          CA CALIFORNIA         90032
01440 ZINZINDORFF INC.
1604 7TH ST                              (213) 555-7234
LOS ANGELES          CA CALIFORNIA         90404
```

 The program is almost identical to vndrpt03.cbl. There are changes in TITLE-LINE (lines 005600 to 006300), and the program uses the new SELECT and FD for the vendor file (lines 001100 and 002200).

The main change begins at line 008600, which performs READ-FIRST-RECORD. READ-FIRST-RECORD begins at line 019800. It sets up the FILE-AT-END flag and moves spaces to the VENDOR-NAME, which will be used as the key to the file.

The START at lines 020100 through 020300 attempts to position the file so that the next READ NEXT will read a record whose VENDOR-NAME is equal to or greater than spaces.

The record has not actually been read, so at line 020600, a READ-NEXT-RECORD is requested.

One thing to note is the use of the INVALID KEY in START at line 020300. A START NOT LESS THAN positions the file so that the next READ NEXT will read a record whose value matches the start condition. If a START NOT LESS THAN fails with a file error condition (INVALID KEY), there is no next record matching the START condition. The only way there can be no next record in a file is if you are at the end of the file. If the START NOT LESS THAN fails, the INVALID KEY file error condition is used to set the FILE-AT-END flag to "Y".

How is it possible to be at the end of the file if you are starting with the lowest possible value for the VENDOR-NAME—all spaces? If a record cannot be located that contains a VENDOR-NAME equal to or greater than spaces, the data file is empty and contains no records. Using the INVALID KEY and FILE-AT-END logic, even when there seems to be no need for it, prevents file errors even if you attempt to report on a new file that contains no records.

It is important to note that aside from START, which switches the key path, the rest of the program remains basically unchanged. When the START is completed successfully, the key path is changed and READ NEXT proceeds to the next and subsequent records along that path automatically.

17

Figure 17.6 is a printer spacing chart for a new vendor report program, vnbynm01.cbl (vendor by name), that prints the same vendor information as vndrpt03.cbl, but in alphabetical name order.

Figure 17.6.

The spacing chart for vnbynm01.cbl.

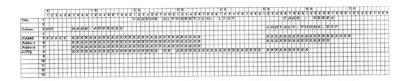

Looking Up Records by Alternate Key

You also can use alternate keys to help a user look up a record. Listing 17.21, vninnm01.cbl, is a vendor inquiry by name.

TYPE   **Listing 17.21. Looking up records by alternate key.**

```
000100 IDENTIFICATION DIVISION.
000200 PROGRAM-ID. VNINNM01.
000300*-------------------------------
000400* Inquire for the Vendor File
000500* using vendor name.
000600*-------------------------------
000700 ENVIRONMENT DIVISION.
000800 INPUT-OUTPUT SECTION.
000900 FILE-CONTROL.
001000
001100     COPY "SLVND02.CBL".
001200
001300     COPY "SLSTATE.CBL".
001400
001500 DATA DIVISION.
001600 FILE SECTION.
001700
001800     COPY "FDVND04.CBL".
001900
002000     COPY "FDSTATE.CBL".
002100
002200 WORKING-STORAGE SECTION.
002300
002400 77  VENDOR-FILE-AT-END        PIC X.
002500 77  STATE-RECORD-FOUND        PIC X.
002600
002700
002800 77  VENDOR-NAME-FIELD         PIC X(30).
002900
003000     COPY "WSCASE01.CBL".
003100
003200 PROCEDURE DIVISION.
003300 PROGRAM-BEGIN.
```

continues

Listing 17.21. continued

```
003400      PERFORM OPENING-PROCEDURE.
003500      PERFORM MAIN-PROCESS.
003600      PERFORM CLOSING-PROCEDURE.
003700
003800 PROGRAM-DONE.
003900      STOP RUN.
004000
004100 OPENING-PROCEDURE.
004200      OPEN I-O VENDOR-FILE.
004300      OPEN I-O STATE-FILE.
004400
004500 CLOSING-PROCEDURE.
004600      CLOSE VENDOR-FILE.
004700      CLOSE STATE-FILE.
004800
004900 MAIN-PROCESS.
005000      PERFORM INQUIRE-BY-NAME.
005100*-------------------------------
005200* INQUIRE
005300*-------------------------------
005400 INQUIRE-BY-NAME.
005500      PERFORM GET-EXISTING-RECORD.
005600      PERFORM INQUIRE-RECORDS
005700          UNTIL VENDOR-NAME = SPACES.
005800
005900 INQUIRE-RECORDS.
006000      PERFORM DISPLAY-ALL-FIELDS.
006100      PERFORM GET-EXISTING-RECORD.
006200
006300*-------------------------------
006400* Locate a record logic
006500*-------------------------------
006600 GET-EXISTING-RECORD.
006700      PERFORM ACCEPT-EXISTING-KEY.
006800      PERFORM RE-ACCEPT-EXISTING-KEY
006900          UNTIL VENDOR-FILE-AT-END NOT = "Y".
007000
007100 ACCEPT-EXISTING-KEY.
007200      PERFORM INIT-FOR-KEY-ENTRY.
007300      PERFORM ENTER-VENDOR-NAME.
007400      IF VENDOR-NAME NOT = SPACES
007500          PERFORM READ-FIRST-VENDOR-RECORD.
007600
007700 RE-ACCEPT-EXISTING-KEY.
007800      DISPLAY "RECORD NOT FOUND"
007900      PERFORM ACCEPT-EXISTING-KEY.
008000
008100*-------------------------------
008200* Field Entry logic
008300*-------------------------------
008400 ENTER-VENDOR-NAME.
008500      PERFORM ACCEPT-VENDOR-NAME.
008600
008700 ACCEPT-VENDOR-NAME.
```

```
008800      DISPLAY "ENTER VENDOR NAME".
008900      ACCEPT VENDOR-NAME.
009000      INSPECT VENDOR-NAME
009100          CONVERTING LOWER-ALPHA
009200          TO          UPPER-ALPHA.
009300
009400*------------------------------
009500* Display logic
009600*------------------------------
009700 DISPLAY-ALL-FIELDS.
009800      DISPLAY " ".
009900      PERFORM DISPLAY-VENDOR-NUMBER.
010000      PERFORM DISPLAY-VENDOR-NAME.
010100      PERFORM DISPLAY-VENDOR-ADDRESS-1.
010200      PERFORM DISPLAY-VENDOR-ADDRESS-2.
010300      PERFORM DISPLAY-VENDOR-CITY.
010400      PERFORM DISPLAY-VENDOR-STATE.
010500      PERFORM DISPLAY-VENDOR-ZIP.
010600      PERFORM DISPLAY-VENDOR-CONTACT.
010700      PERFORM DISPLAY-VENDOR-PHONE.
010800      DISPLAY " ".
010900
011000 DISPLAY-VENDOR-NUMBER.
011100      DISPLAY "   VENDOR NUMBER: " VENDOR-NUMBER.
011200
011300 DISPLAY-VENDOR-NAME.
011400      DISPLAY "1. VENDOR NAME: " VENDOR-NAME.
011500
011600 DISPLAY-VENDOR-ADDRESS-1.
011700      DISPLAY "2. VENDOR ADDRESS-1: " VENDOR-ADDRESS-1.
011800
011900 DISPLAY-VENDOR-ADDRESS-2.
012000      DISPLAY "3. VENDOR ADDRESS-2: " VENDOR-ADDRESS-2.
012100
012200 DISPLAY-VENDOR-CITY.
012300      DISPLAY "4. VENDOR CITY: " VENDOR-CITY.
012400
012500 DISPLAY-VENDOR-STATE.
012600      MOVE VENDOR-STATE TO STATE-CODE.
012700      PERFORM READ-STATE-RECORD.
012800      IF STATE-RECORD-FOUND = "N"
012900          MOVE "**Not found**" TO STATE-NAME.
013000      DISPLAY "5. VENDOR STATE: "
013100          VENDOR-STATE " "
013200          STATE-NAME.
013300
013400 DISPLAY-VENDOR-ZIP.
013500      DISPLAY "6. VENDOR ZIP: " VENDOR-ZIP.
013600
013700 DISPLAY-VENDOR-CONTACT.
013800      DISPLAY "7. VENDOR CONTACT: " VENDOR-CONTACT.
013900
014000 DISPLAY-VENDOR-PHONE.
014100      DISPLAY "8. VENDOR PHONE: " VENDOR-PHONE.
014200
014300*------------------------------
014400* File Related Routines
```

17

continues

Listing 17.21. continued

```
014500*-------------------------------
014600 INIT-FOR-KEY-ENTRY.
014700     MOVE SPACE TO VENDOR-RECORD.
014800     MOVE ZEROES TO VENDOR-NUMBER.
014900     MOVE "N" TO VENDOR-FILE-AT-END.
015000
015100 READ-FIRST-VENDOR-RECORD.
015200     MOVE "N" TO VENDOR-FILE-AT-END.
015300     START VENDOR-FILE
015400        KEY NOT < VENDOR-NAME
015500          INVALID KEY
015600            MOVE "Y" TO VENDOR-FILE-AT-END.
015700
015800     IF VENDOR-FILE-AT-END NOT = "Y"
015900        PERFORM READ-NEXT-VENDOR-RECORD.
016000
016100 READ-NEXT-VENDOR-RECORD.
016200     READ VENDOR-FILE NEXT RECORD
016300        AT END
016400            MOVE "Y" TO VENDOR-FILE-AT-END.
016500
016600 READ-STATE-RECORD.
016700     MOVE "Y" TO STATE-RECORD-FOUND.
016800     READ STATE-FILE RECORD
016900        INVALID KEY
017000            MOVE "N" TO STATE-RECORD-FOUND.
017100
```

The output of vninnm01.cbl illustrates looking up vendors by name rather than by number. For the third entry (user entries are bold), the user enters "b" and all entries are converted to uppercase. No vendor names start with "B" in the file, so the program selects the first record that has a key equal to or greater than "B", which is CHARLES SMITH AND SONS:

Output

```
ENTER VENDOR NAME
abc
VENDOR NUMBER: 00002
1. VENDOR NAME: ABC PRINTING
2. VENDOR ADDRESS-1: 1624 FOOTHILL BLVD
3. VENDOR ADDRESS-2: SUITE 34
4. VENDOR CITY: LOS ANGELES
5. VENDOR STATE: CA CALIFORNIA
6. VENDOR ZIP: 91042
7. VENDOR CONTACT: CHARLES JOHANSSEN
8. VENDOR PHONE: (818) 555-4321
ENTER VENDOR NAME
aber
VENDOR NUMBER: 01176
1. VENDOR NAME: ABERCROMBIE AND OTHERS
2. VENDOR ADDRESS-1: 1234 45TH ST.
3. VENDOR ADDRESS-2: SUITE 17
4. VENDOR CITY: LOS ANGELES
5. VENDOR STATE: CA CALIFORNIA
6. VENDOR ZIP: 92345
```

```
7. VENDOR CONTACT:
8. VENDOR PHONE: (213) 555-6543
ENTER VENDOR NAME
b
VENDOR NUMBER: 00003
1. VENDOR NAME: CHARLES SMITH AND SONS
2. VENDOR ADDRESS-1: 1435 SOUTH STREET
3. VENDOR ADDRESS-2:
4. VENDOR CITY: LOS ANGELES
5. VENDOR STATE: CA CALIFORNIA
6. VENDOR ZIP: 90064
7. VENDOR CONTACT: MARTHA HARRISON
8. VENDOR PHONE: (213) 555-4432
ENTER VENDOR NAME
```

ANALYSIS This program follows the pattern of vndinq01.cbl and the inquire logic of vndmnt03.cbl, but instead of asking the user for the vendor number, it asks the user for the vendor name.

The user is allowed to enter a partial value—"ABER" for ABERCROMBIE, for example—and the program attempts to locate a record that contains a name that is close to that value.

For each name entered by the user, the program attempts to START the file using that value, and if the start is successful, the next record in the file is read. It is possible for a user to enter a name that is beyond the end of the file, such as "ZZZZZZ", so a VENDOR-FILE-AT-END flag is used to trap entries that do not allow a record to be found in the file.

In this version of inquire, the user enters a vendor name of spaces to signal end of entry; anything else is converted to uppercase and then used by the program. At lines 008400 and 008700, ENTER-VENDOR-NAME ACCEPT-VENDOR-NAME takes care of this simple field-entry routine.

The loop control and loop start at line 005400 in 005400 INQUIRE-BY-NAME. This routine starts by getting a valid record (GET-EXISTING-RECORD) and then performing the main loop, INQUIRE-RECORDS, until the user enters a vendor name of spaces (VENDOR-NAME = SPACES).

The main loop itself at 005900 displays all fields; then at the bottom of the loop, line 006100 asks the user for another vendor name to look for by once again performing GET-EXISTING-RECORD.

The GET-EXISTING-RECORD routine at line 006600 is structured as a standard field-entry routine that performs an ACCEPT-EXISTING-KEY and then a RE-ACCEPT-EXISTING-KEY until VENDOR-FILE-AT-END NOT = "Y". This logic is used to force the user to enter a vendor name that is not at the end of the file.

At line 007100, ACCEPT-EXISTING-KEY initializes the vendor record and then gets the user entry of the name to look up. If the name is not spaces, an attempt is made to READ-FIRST-VENDOR-RECORD, which will START the file using the entered vendor name and then try to read the next record in the file. If this causes VENDOR-FILE-AT-END = "Y", then back at line 006800, the program will RE-ACCEPT-EXISTING-KEY until VENDOR-FILE-AT-END NOT = "Y".

The RE-ACCEPT-EXISTING-KEY routine at line 007700 displays an error message and then tries again to ACCEPT-EXISTING-KEY.

The READ-FIRST-VENDOR-RECORD routine at line 015100 is identical to that used in Listing 17.20, vnbynbm01.cbl, and it sets the VENDOR-FILE-AT-END flag if a record cannot be found.

The remainder of the program is used to display the fields in the record, and you are familiar with this type of logic. Code, compile, and run vninnm01.cbl, and use it to look up records in your vendor file.

Helping the User with Alternate Keys

A flaw in vninnm01.cbl makes it awkward for the user. In the following output example, the user wants to look up ABERCROMBIE AND OTHERS and enters "ab". In the sample file, two vendors start with "AB", and ABC PRINTING appears before ABERCROMBIE AND OTHERS in the file in alternate key order. The user's entry retrieves ABC PRINTING, and the user must enter "aber" to zero in on the record that is wanted:

OUTPUT

```
ENTER VENDOR NAME
ab
VENDOR NUMBER: 00002
1. VENDOR NAME: ABC PRINTING
2. VENDOR ADDRESS-1: 1624 FOOTHILL BLVD
3. VENDOR ADDRESS-2: SUITE 34
4. VENDOR CITY: LOS ANGELES
5. VENDOR STATE: CA CALIFORNIA
6. VENDOR ZIP: 91042
7. VENDOR CONTACT: CHARLES JOHANSSEN
8. VENDOR PHONE: (818) 555-4321
ENTER VENDOR NAME
aber
VENDOR NUMBER: 01176
1. VENDOR NAME: ABERCROMBIE AND OTHERS
2. VENDOR ADDRESS-1: 1234 45TH ST.
3. VENDOR ADDRESS-2: SUITE 17
4. VENDOR CITY: LOS ANGELES
5. VENDOR STATE: CA CALIFORNIA
6. VENDOR ZIP: 92345
7. VENDOR CONTACT:
8. VENDOR PHONE: (213) 555-6543
ENTER VENDOR NAME
```

This can become a headache in a large file with many names that are close to one another, and it can be impossible to deal with if two vendors have the same name. In the following sample output, the vendor file contains two firms named ABC PRINTING—one in Los Angeles and one in Pomona:

17

```
VENDOR NUMBER: 00002
1. VENDOR NAME: ABC PRINTING
2. VENDOR ADDRESS-1: 1624 FOOTHILL BLVD
3. VENDOR ADDRESS-2: SUITE 34
4. VENDOR CITY: LOS ANGELES
5. VENDOR STATE: CA CALIFORNIA
6. VENDOR ZIP: 91042
7. VENDOR CONTACT: CHARLES JOHANSSEN
8. VENDOR PHONE: (818) 555-4321
VENDOR NUMBER: 00067
1. VENDOR NAME: ABC PRINTING
2. VENDOR ADDRESS-1: 1606 SOUTH 7TH
3. VENDOR ADDRESS-2:
4. VENDOR CITY: POMONA
5. VENDOR STATE: CA CALIFORNIA
6. VENDOR ZIP: 90404
7. VENDOR CONTACT: HARRIET NELSON
8. VENDOR PHONE: (815) 555-2020
```

The user needs the phone number for the vendor in Pomona but does not know the vendor number. This is a good time to use inquiry by vendor name. However, the next output sample indicates that, in spite of repeated attempts to enter more and more of the company name, vninnm01.cbl always returns the first vendor.

This problem has to do with the way records are stored by alternate key. If an alternate key allows duplicates, and two or more records actually do have the same key value, which one is first? Usually, it is the one that was added to the file first. Sometimes it is the record with the lowest primary index key value. No matter which record is considered to be "first" in the file, vninnm01.cbl will not let you go to the next record:

```
ENTER VENDOR NAME
abc
VENDOR NUMBER: 00002
1. VENDOR NAME: ABC PRINTING
2. VENDOR ADDRESS-1: 1624 FOOTHILL BLVD
3. VENDOR ADDRESS-2: SUITE 34
4. VENDOR CITY: LOS ANGELES
5. VENDOR STATE: CA CALIFORNIA
6. VENDOR ZIP: 91042
7. VENDOR CONTACT: CHARLES JOHANSSEN
8. VENDOR PHONE: (818) 555-4321
ENTER VENDOR NAME
abc print
VENDOR NUMBER: 00002
1. VENDOR NAME: ABC PRINTING
2. VENDOR ADDRESS-1: 1624 FOOTHILL BLVD
3. VENDOR ADDRESS-2: SUITE 34
4. VENDOR CITY: LOS ANGELES
5. VENDOR STATE: CA CALIFORNIA
6. VENDOR ZIP: 91042
7. VENDOR CONTACT: CHARLES JOHANSSEN
8. VENDOR PHONE: (818) 555-4321
```

17

```
ENTER VENDOR NAME
abc printing
VENDOR NUMBER: 00002
1. VENDOR NAME: ABC PRINTING
2. VENDOR ADDRESS-1: 1624 FOOTHILL BLVD
3. VENDOR ADDRESS-2: SUITE 34
4. VENDOR CITY: LOS ANGELES
5. VENDOR STATE: CA CALIFORNIA
6. VENDOR ZIP: 91042
7. VENDOR CONTACT: CHARLES JOHANSSEN
8. VENDOR PHONE: (818) 555-4321
ENTER VENDOR NAME
```

Listing 17.22 is vninnm02.cbl, and it solves the problem.

TYPE   **Listing 17.22. A better alternate key look up.**

```
000100 IDENTIFICATION DIVISION.
000200 PROGRAM-ID. VNINNM02.
000300*-------------------------------
000400* Inquire for the Vendor File
000500* using vendor name.
000600*-------------------------------
000700 ENVIRONMENT DIVISION.
000800 INPUT-OUTPUT SECTION.
000900 FILE-CONTROL.
001000
001100     COPY "SLVND02.CBL".
001200
001300     COPY "SLSTATE.CBL".
001400
001500 DATA DIVISION.
001600 FILE SECTION.
001700
001800     COPY "FDVND04.CBL".
001900
002000     COPY "FDSTATE.CBL".
002100
002200 WORKING-STORAGE SECTION.
002300
002400 77  VENDOR-FILE-AT-END        PIC X.
002500 77  STATE-RECORD-FOUND        PIC X.
002600
002700 77  SEE-NEXT-RECORD          PIC X.
002800
002900 77  VENDOR-NAME-FIELD         PIC X(30).
003000
003100     COPY "WSCASE01.CBL".
003200
003300 PROCEDURE DIVISION.
003400 PROGRAM-BEGIN.
003500     PERFORM OPENING-PROCEDURE.
003600     PERFORM MAIN-PROCESS.
003700     PERFORM CLOSING-PROCEDURE.
003800
```

```
003900 PROGRAM-DONE.
004000     STOP RUN.
004100
004200 OPENING-PROCEDURE.
004300     OPEN I-O VENDOR-FILE.
004400     OPEN I-O STATE-FILE.
004500
004600 CLOSING-PROCEDURE.
004700     CLOSE VENDOR-FILE.
004800     CLOSE STATE-FILE.
004900
005000 MAIN-PROCESS.
005100     PERFORM INQUIRE-BY-NAME.
005200*------------------------------
005300* INQUIRE
005400*------------------------------
005500 INQUIRE-BY-NAME.
005600     PERFORM GET-EXISTING-RECORD.
005700     PERFORM INQUIRE-RECORDS
005800         UNTIL VENDOR-NAME = SPACES.
005900
006000 INQUIRE-RECORDS.
006100     PERFORM SHOW-THIS-RECORD.
006200     PERFORM SHOW-NEXT-RECORD
006300         UNTIL SEE-NEXT-RECORD = "N" OR
006400             VENDOR-FILE-AT-END = "Y".
006500
006600     PERFORM GET-EXISTING-RECORD.
006700
006800
006900*------------------------------
007000* Show records one by one
007100*------------------------------
007200 SHOW-THIS-RECORD.
007300     PERFORM DISPLAY-ALL-FIELDS.
007400     PERFORM GET-SEE-NEXT-RECORD.
007500
007600 SHOW-NEXT-RECORD.
007700     PERFORM READ-NEXT-VENDOR-RECORD.
007800     IF VENDOR-FILE-AT-END NOT = "Y"
007900         PERFORM SHOW-THIS-RECORD.
008000
008100*------------------------------
008200* Get valid record logic
008300*------------------------------
008400 GET-EXISTING-RECORD.
008500     PERFORM ACCEPT-EXISTING-KEY.
008600     PERFORM RE-ACCEPT-EXISTING-KEY
008700         UNTIL VENDOR-FILE-AT-END NOT = "Y".
008800
008900 ACCEPT-EXISTING-KEY.
009000     PERFORM INIT-FOR-KEY-ENTRY.
009100     PERFORM ENTER-VENDOR-NAME.
009200     IF VENDOR-NAME NOT = SPACES
009300         PERFORM READ-FIRST-VENDOR-RECORD.
009400
009500 RE-ACCEPT-EXISTING-KEY.
```

continues

Listing 17.22. continued

```
009600     DISPLAY "RECORD NOT FOUND"
009700     PERFORM ACCEPT-EXISTING-KEY.
009800
009900*--------------------------------
010000* Field Entry logic
010100*--------------------------------
010200 ENTER-VENDOR-NAME.
010300     PERFORM ACCEPT-VENDOR-NAME.
010400
010500 ACCEPT-VENDOR-NAME.
010600     DISPLAY "ENTER VENDOR NAME".
010700     ACCEPT VENDOR-NAME.
010800     INSPECT VENDOR-NAME
010900         CONVERTING LOWER-ALPHA
011000         TO          UPPER-ALPHA.
011100
011200 GET-SEE-NEXT-RECORD.
011300     PERFORM ACCEPT-SEE-NEXT-RECORD.
011400     PERFORM RE-ACCEPT-SEE-NEXT-RECORD
011500         UNTIL SEE-NEXT-RECORD = "Y" OR "N".
011600
011700 ACCEPT-SEE-NEXT-RECORD.
011800     DISPLAY "DISPLAY NEXT RECORD (Y/N)?".
011900     ACCEPT SEE-NEXT-RECORD.
012000
012100     IF SEE-NEXT-RECORD = SPACE
012200         MOVE "Y" TO SEE-NEXT-RECORD.
012300
012400     INSPECT SEE-NEXT-RECORD
012500       CONVERTING LOWER-ALPHA
012600         TO          UPPER-ALPHA.
012700
012800 RE-ACCEPT-SEE-NEXT-RECORD.
012900     DISPLAY "MUST ENTER YES OR NO".
013000     PERFORM ACCEPT-SEE-NEXT-RECORD.
013100
013200*--------------------------------
013300* Display logic
013400*--------------------------------
013500 DISPLAY-ALL-FIELDS.
013600     DISPLAY " ".
013700     PERFORM DISPLAY-VENDOR-NUMBER.
013800     PERFORM DISPLAY-VENDOR-NAME.
013900     PERFORM DISPLAY-VENDOR-ADDRESS-1.
014000     PERFORM DISPLAY-VENDOR-ADDRESS-2.
014100     PERFORM DISPLAY-VENDOR-CITY.
014200     PERFORM DISPLAY-VENDOR-STATE.
014300     PERFORM DISPLAY-VENDOR-ZIP.
014400     PERFORM DISPLAY-VENDOR-CONTACT.
014500     PERFORM DISPLAY-VENDOR-PHONE.
014600     DISPLAY " ".
014700
014800 DISPLAY-VENDOR-NUMBER.
014900     DISPLAY "   VENDOR NUMBER: " VENDOR-NUMBER.
```

17

```
015000
015100 DISPLAY-VENDOR-NAME.
015200      DISPLAY "1. VENDOR NAME: " VENDOR-NAME.
015300
015400 DISPLAY-VENDOR-ADDRESS-1.
015500      DISPLAY "2. VENDOR ADDRESS-1: " VENDOR-ADDRESS-1.
015600
015700 DISPLAY-VENDOR-ADDRESS-2.
015800      DISPLAY "3. VENDOR ADDRESS-2: " VENDOR-ADDRESS-2.
015900
016000 DISPLAY-VENDOR-CITY.
016100      DISPLAY "4. VENDOR CITY: " VENDOR-CITY.
016200
016300 DISPLAY-VENDOR-STATE.
016400      MOVE VENDOR-STATE TO STATE-CODE.
016500      PERFORM READ-STATE-RECORD.
016600      IF STATE-RECORD-FOUND = "N"
016700         MOVE "**Not found**" TO STATE-NAME.
016800      DISPLAY "5. VENDOR STATE: "
016900            VENDOR-STATE " "
017000            STATE-NAME.
017100
017200 DISPLAY-VENDOR-ZIP.
017300      DISPLAY "6. VENDOR ZIP: " VENDOR-ZIP.
017400
017500 DISPLAY-VENDOR-CONTACT.
017600      DISPLAY "7. VENDOR CONTACT: " VENDOR-CONTACT.
017700
017800 DISPLAY-VENDOR-PHONE.
017900      DISPLAY "8. VENDOR PHONE: " VENDOR-PHONE.
018000
018100*--------------------------------
018200* File Related Routines
018300*--------------------------------
018400 INIT-FOR-KEY-ENTRY.
018500      MOVE SPACE TO VENDOR-RECORD.
018600      MOVE ZEROES TO VENDOR-NUMBER.
018700      MOVE "N" TO VENDOR-FILE-AT-END.
018800
018900 READ-FIRST-VENDOR-RECORD.
019000      MOVE "N" TO VENDOR-FILE-AT-END.
019100      START VENDOR-FILE
019200        KEY NOT < VENDOR-NAME
019300          INVALID KEY
019400            MOVE "Y" TO VENDOR-FILE-AT-END.
019500
019600      IF VENDOR-FILE-AT-END NOT = "Y"
019700         PERFORM READ-NEXT-VENDOR-RECORD.
019800
019900 READ-NEXT-VENDOR-RECORD.
020000      READ VENDOR-FILE NEXT RECORD
020100        AT END
020200            MOVE "Y" TO VENDOR-FILE-AT-END.
020300
020400 READ-STATE-RECORD.
020500      MOVE "Y" TO STATE-RECORD-FOUND.
```

continues

Listing 17.22. continued

```
020600      READ STATE-FILE RECORD
020700         INVALID KEY
020800            MOVE "N" TO STATE-RECORD-FOUND.
020900
```

The output from vninnm02.cbl enables the user to step through the file record by record or to skip around, starting with different names:

```
ENTER VENDOR NAME
abc
VENDOR NUMBER: 00002
1. VENDOR NAME: ABC PRINTING
2. VENDOR ADDRESS-1: 1624 FOOTHILL BLVD
3. VENDOR ADDRESS-2: SUITE 34
4. VENDOR CITY: LOS ANGELES
5. VENDOR STATE: CA CALIFORNIA
6. VENDOR ZIP: 91042
7. VENDOR CONTACT: CHARLES JOHANSSEN
8. VENDOR PHONE: (818) 555-4321
DISPLAY NEXT RECORD (Y/N)?
```

(User presses Enter here.)

```
VENDOR NUMBER: 00067
1. VENDOR NAME: ABC PRINTING
2. VENDOR ADDRESS-1: 1606 SOUTH 7TH
3. VENDOR ADDRESS-2:
4. VENDOR CITY: POMONA
5. VENDOR STATE: CA CALIFORNIA
6. VENDOR ZIP: 90404
7. VENDOR CONTACT: HARRIET NELSON
8. VENDOR PHONE: (815) 555-2020
DISPLAY NEXT RECORD (Y/N)?
```

(User presses Enter here.)

```
VENDOR NUMBER: 01176
1. VENDOR NAME: ABERCROMBIE AND OTHERS
2. VENDOR ADDRESS-1: 1234 45TH ST.
3. VENDOR ADDRESS-2: SUITE 17
4. VENDOR CITY: LOS ANGELES
5. VENDOR STATE: CA CALIFORNIA
6. VENDOR ZIP: 92345
7. VENDOR CONTACT:
8. VENDOR PHONE: (213) 555-6543
DISPLAY NEXT RECORD (Y/N)?
n
ENTER VENDOR NAME
z
VENDOR NUMBER: 01440
1. VENDOR NAME: ZINZINDORFF INC.
2. VENDOR ADDRESS-1: 1604 7TH ST
3. VENDOR ADDRESS-2:
```

```
4. VENDOR CITY: LOS ANGELES
5. VENDOR STATE: CA CALIFORNIA
6. VENDOR ZIP: 90404
7. VENDOR CONTACT:
8. VENDOR PHONE: (213) 555-7234
DISPLAY NEXT RECORD (Y/N)?
```

ANALYSIS This program is similar to vninnm01.cbl, but it enables the user to choose the option of looking at the next record after the selected record is displayed.

The differences in the two programs start at line 006000, INQUIRE-RECORDS, in vninnm02.cbl. Rather than displaying all fields and then asking the user for another vendor name, the loop is changed to SHOW-THIS-RECORD and then SHOW-NEXT-RECORD until SEE-NEXT-RECORD = "N" or VENDOR-FILE-AT-END = "Y". The SEE-NEXT-RECORD variable is a yes/no field entered by the user to indicate whether to display the next record. It is defined at line 002700.

At line 007200, the SHOW-THIS-RECORD routine displays all fields and then asks the user whether the next record is wanted. This answer is returned to INQUIRE-RECORDS at line 006200, and if the user has indicated Y by entering the value or simply pressing Enter, the SHOW-NEXT-RECORD routine is performed as a loop.

The SHOW-NEXT-RECORD routine at line 007600 tries to read the next record in the vendor file. If it is successful, it performs SHOW-THIS-RECORD, which displays all fields, and once again asks the user whether the next record is wanted. This loop continues until the user answers N or the read-next takes him or her to the end of the file.

The GET-SEE-NEXT-RECORD routine at line 011200 is a standard field-entry routine. In this case, the user can enter a space, but it is converted to "Y" at lines 012100 and 012200. This gives the user the convenience of pressing Enter to see the next record rather than having to enter a "Y" explicitly. If the user enters something, it must be "Y" or "N" (or the lowercase versions).

The GET-SEE-NEXT-RECORD loop continues until the end of the file is reached, whereupon the user once again is asked for a vendor name.

Code, compile, and run vninnm02.cbl. If you want to, use vndmnt03.cbl to add a vendor with the same name as an existing vendor in the file. You can use vninnm02.cbl to view this record.

Summary

Although an indexed file must have a unique primary key, it is possible to put other keys in the file. These do not need to be unique and can be arranged to return records in a different order than the primary key. Today, you learned these basics:

- ☐ Use an alternate key to return records in a different order than the primary key.
- ☐ Define an alternate key in the SELECT statement by using the ALTERNATE KEY IS clause; you can include an optional WITH DUPLICATES clause.

☐ To create an alternate index in a file, the file must have been created (opened in output mode) by a program containing a file definition that included an alternate key for the file.

☐ After you create the file, you can treat it like any other indexed file. Records written to it will be stored correctly with the alternate index values.

☐ A file must be opened with a file definition that matches the file organization, record length, and key structure of the actual file. Usually, this is the file definition that was used to create it, but it does not have to be, as long as it matches the file organization, record length, and key structure of the file definition that was used to create it.

☐ When an alternate indexed file first is opened, the active path is the primary key path. To switch to an alternate key path, use the START command.

☐ After the START is completed successfully, the key path is changed, and READ NEXT proceeds to the next and subsequent records along that path.

☐ Alternate keys enable you to include routines that make it easier for a user to look up records.

☐ Because alternate keys with duplicates allow records containing duplicate keys, a look up program must be included so that the user can step through the file record by record.

Q&A

Q How many alternate keys can be in a file?

A This varies based on your version of COBOL. Most versions of COBOL allow at least 16 alternate keys, which is plenty for most problems. I have seen some versions of COBOL that allow 63 and even 119 alternate keys.

Workshop

Quiz

1. If a vendor file contained records with the vendor names

   ABC PRINTING

   AZAZEL AND SONS

   CHARLES RUMFORD INC.

   OMEGA MANUFACTURING

   ZYDEC DESIGNS

   which record would be read after the logic in the following listing?

```
018900          MOVE "LINCOLN" TO VENDOR-NAME.
019000          START VENDOR-FILE
019100             KEY NOT < VENDOR-NAME
019200              INVALID KEY
019300                 MOVE "Y" TO VENDOR-FILE-AT-END.
019400
019500          IF VENDOR-FILE-AT-END NOT = "Y"
019600             PERFORM READ-NEXT-VENDOR-RECORD.
019700
019800 READ-NEXT-VENDOR-RECORD.
019900          READ VENDOR-FILE NEXT RECORD
020000             AT END
020100                 MOVE "Y" TO VENDOR-FILE-AT-END.
```

2. What are the keys in the following listing?

   Hint: Don't forget the primary key.

```
000400          SELECT PART-FILE
000500              ASSIGN TO "PARTS"
000600              ORGANIZATION IS INDEXED
000700              RECORD KEY IS PART-NUMBER
000800              ALTERNATE KEY IS PART-VENDOR WITH DUPLICATES
000900              ALTERNATE KEY IS PART-DEPARTMENT WITH DUPLICATES
001000              ALTERNATE KEY IS PART-VENDOR-NUMBER
001100              ACCESS MODE IS DYNAMIC.
001200
```

3. In the listing in question 2, which keys allow duplicates? Which do not?

Exercise

Assuming a customer file with a record layout, as shown in the following listing, create a SELECT statement that defines the CUSTOMER-NUMBER as the primary key, the CUSTOMER-NAME as an alternate key with duplicates, and the CUSTOMER-ZIP as an alternate key with duplicates. The physical name of the file on the disk will be "CUST".

```
000000 FD  CUSTOMER-FILE
000000     LABEL RECORDS ARE STANDARD.
001000 01  CUSTOMER-RECORD.
001100     05  CUSTOMER-NUMBER       PIC 9(5).
001200     05  CUSTOMER-NAME         PIC X(20).
001300     05  CUSTOMER-ADDRESS-1    PIC X(20).
001400     05  CUSTOMER-ADDRESS-2    PIC X(20).
001500     05  CUSTOMER-ZIP          PIC 9(5).
001600     05  CUSTOMER-PHONE.
001700         10  CUSTOMER-AREA-CODE  PIC 9(3).
001800         10  CUSTOMER-PREFIX     PIC 9(3).
001900         10  CUSTOMER-PHONE-NO   PIC 9(4).
```

Day **18**

Calling Other Programs

In practice, a system is composed of many programs that work in concert. So far, you have worked with state codes, file maintenance and report programs, and vendor maintenance and report programs. To get these programs to work together for the user, you need to provide a menu with all these programs available as choices, and then provide the capability of executing these programs based on the user's choice.

Today, you learn about the following topics:

☐ Executing one program from within another

☐ Handling STOP RUN

☐ Calling another program

☐ Creating large menus using calls

☐ Menu programs

Executing One Program from Within Another

It is possible for one COBOL program to execute another program. The syntax for this is simple:

```
CALL "program name"
```

Here is an example:

```
CALL "VNDRPT03"
```

If a CALL is executed within a COBOL program, the calling program is suspended and the called program is executed. When the called program is finished, control is returned to the calling program and execution continues at the next line.

A CALL always is executed by calling the program using only the six- or eight-character program name without an extension. (Some systems allow only six-character filenames.)

A CALL works like a PERFORM, treating another program as if it were one large paragraph. The calling program still is loaded into memory and running, but it is waiting for the called program to complete before it resumes execution.

Handling STOP RUN

Although the syntax for calling another program is simple, there is a complication introduced by our old friend STOP RUN. STOP RUN stops all COBOL programs that you currently are running. If a STOP RUN is executed in a called program, it stops both the called program and the calling program, and control does not return to the calling program. This has not been a problem so far because you have been executing only a single COBOL program.

Listings 18.1 and 18.2 are fragments from a hypothetical vendor menu program and vndrpt03.cbl.

TYPE   **Listing 18.1. Calling vndrpt03.cbl.**

```
020300 CALL-VENDOR-REPORT.
020400     DISPLAY "REPORT IN PROGRESS".
020500     CALL "VNDRPT03".
020600     DISPLAY "REPORT FINISHED".
```

TYPE **Listing 18.2. The top logic in `vndrpt03.cbl`.**

```
007400
007500 PROCEDURE DIVISION.
007600 PROGRAM-BEGIN.
007700
007800     PERFORM OPENING-PROCEDURE.
007900     MOVE ZEROES TO LINE-COUNT
008000                    PAGE-NUMBER.
008100
008200     PERFORM START-NEW-PAGE.
008300
008400     MOVE "N" TO FILE-AT-END.
008500     PERFORM READ-NEXT-RECORD.
008600     IF FILE-AT-END = "Y"
008700        MOVE "NO RECORDS FOUND" TO PRINTER-RECORD
008800        PERFORM WRITE-TO-PRINTER
008900     ELSE
009000        PERFORM PRINT-VENDOR-FIELDS
009100            UNTIL FILE-AT-END = "Y".
009200
009300     PERFORM CLOSING-PROCEDURE.
009400
009500 PROGRAM-DONE.
009600     STOP RUN.
```

18

ANALYSIS At line `020400` in Listing 18.1, a message that the report is underway is displayed for the user, and at line `020500`, the report program is called. This transfers control to line `007500` in Listing 18.2 as if a PERFORM had been requested. At line `009500`, the program is complete and the PROGRAM-DONE paragraph begins and immediately executes a STOP RUN at line `009600`. You want control to return to line `020600` in Listing 18.1, but the STOP RUN brings everything to a halt.

There is another command that can be used to end a program: EXIT PROGRAM. This command checks whether the current program is a called program and, if it is, it returns to the calling program as though the end of a PERFORM had been reached. In most versions of COBOL, EXIT PROGRAM must appear in a paragraph by itself.

EXIT PROGRAM should be used to end a called program, and STOP RUN should be used to end a calling program.

When you write a program, you don't always know whether it will be a called or calling program; you can hedge your bets by including both commands in the program, as shown in Listing 18.3. At the end of each program, just before the paragraph containing STOP RUN, insert a paragraph containing EXIT PROGRAM.

Do   **Don't**

DO be sure to spell EXIT PROGRAM correctly and end it with a period.

DON'T put a hyphen in the command (EXIT-PROGRAM) because the COBOL compilers will mistake this for a paragraph name and will not execute the EXIT PROGRAM command.

TYPE
Listing 18.3. Using EXIT PROGRAM **and** STOP RUN **in the same program.**

```
007500 PROCEDURE DIVISION.
007600 PROGRAM-BEGIN.
007700
007800     PERFORM OPENING-PROCEDURE.
007900     MOVE ZEROES TO LINE-COUNT
008000                       PAGE-NUMBER.
008100
008200     PERFORM START-NEW-PAGE.
008300
008400     MOVE "N" TO FILE-AT-END.
008500     PERFORM READ-NEXT-RECORD.
008600     IF FILE-AT-END = "Y"
008700        MOVE "NO RECORDS FOUND" TO PRINTER-RECORD
008800        PERFORM WRITE-TO-PRINTER
008900     ELSE
009000        PERFORM PRINT-VENDOR-FIELDS
009100           UNTIL FILE-AT-END = "Y".
009200
009300     PERFORM CLOSING-PROCEDURE.
009400
009500 PROGRAM-EXIT.
009600     EXIT PROGRAM.
009700
009800 PROGRAM-DONE.
009900     STOP RUN.
```

ANALYSIS   In Listing 18.3, after the main logic of the program is completed, the program executes the logic in the PROGRAM-EXIT paragraph at line 009500. This performs an EXIT PROGRAM at line 009600. The COBOL program checks to see whether it is a called program. If it is, it returns to the calling program immediately, and the paragraph at line 009800 containing STOP RUN is never executed.

If the program is not a called program, EXIT PROGRAM is ignored and the program continues to lines 009700 and 009800, where the STOP RUN is executed and the program halts.

18

This approach to exiting and stopping is so workable you can include it in your standard COBOL shell. It works for a called or calling program and you don't need to worry about how a program will be used. Listing 18.4 includes this logic, as well as dummy paragraphs, with the basic structure of a program. This is the last general COBOL shell and contains all the parts that you need for the work in the remainder of this book. In a real world work environment, a COBOL shell program will probably have a lot more information in it.

TYPE **Listing 18.4. A final COBOL shell.**

```
000100 IDENTIFICATION DIVISION.
000200 PROGRAM-ID. COBSHL04.
000300*-------------------------------
000400*
000500*-------------------------------
000600 ENVIRONMENT DIVISION.
000700 INPUT-OUTPUT SECTION.
000800 FILE-CONTROL.
000900
001000 DATA DIVISION.
001100 FILE SECTION.
001200
001300 WORKING-STORAGE SECTION.
001400
001500 PROCEDURE DIVISION.
001600 PROGRAM-BEGIN.
001700     PERFORM OPENING-PROCEDURE.
001800     PERFORM MAIN-PROCESS.
001900     PERFORM CLOSING-PROCEDURE.
002000
002100 PROGRAM-EXIT.
002200     EXIT PROGRAM.
002300
002400 PROGRAM-DONE.
002500     STOP RUN.
002600
002700 OPENING-PROCEDURE.
002800
002900 CLOSING-PROCEDURE.
003000
003100 MAIN-PROCESS.
003200
```

NOTE   You have a lot of programs that do not use the EXIT PROGRAM logic; in the subsequent examples, these will be corrected. When this is the only change in the program, only a fragment of the complete listing will be provided.

Calling Another Program

One final note on calling a program—it is important that your source code filename and program ID match. If the program filename is `stcrpt02.cbl`, the `PROGRAM-ID` inside the COBOL program must be `STCRPT02`. Some versions of COBOL, such as ACUCOBOL and Micro Focus Personal COBOL, don't care about this match, but many do. It's also good practice to ensure that these match.

Do	Don't

DO force the source code filename and `PROGRAM-ID` to match.

DON'T forget to double-check these, especially when you are creating programs by copying one file to another and then modifying the new file.

Listing 18.5 shows the corrections you need to make to `stcrpt01.cbl` for the next section of this book. Copy `stcrpt01.cbl` to `stcrpt02.cbl` and add the exit program logic shown at line `007100`. Then recompile the program. Be sure to change the `PROGRAM-ID` to `STCRPT02`.

TYPE **Listing 18.5.** `stcrpt02.cbl` **includes program exit logic.**

```
005100 PROCEDURE DIVISION.
005200 PROGRAM-BEGIN.
005300
005400     PERFORM OPENING-PROCEDURE.
005500     MOVE ZEROES TO LINE-COUNT
005600                    PAGE-NUMBER.
005700
005800     PERFORM START-NEW-PAGE.
005900
006000     MOVE "N" TO FILE-AT-END.
006100     PERFORM READ-NEXT-RECORD.
006200     IF FILE-AT-END = "Y"
006300         MOVE "NO RECORDS FOUND" TO PRINTER-RECORD
006400         PERFORM WRITE-TO-PRINTER
006500     ELSE
006600         PERFORM PRINT-STATE-FIELDS
006700             UNTIL FILE-AT-END = "Y".
006800
006900     PERFORM CLOSING-PROCEDURE.
007000
007100 PROGRAM-EXIT.
007200     EXIT PROGRAM.
007300
007400 PROGRAM-DONE.
007500     STOP RUN.
007600
```

18

Listing 18.6 is stcmnt04.cbl, a modified version of state code maintenance, stcmnt03.cbl.

TYPE **Listing 18.6. State code file maintenance including printing.**

```
000100 IDENTIFICATION DIVISION.
000200 PROGRAM-ID. STCMNT04.
000300*--------------------------------
000400* Add, Change, Inquire and Delete
000500* for the State Code.
000600* Calls the State Codes Report.
000700*--------------------------------
000800 ENVIRONMENT DIVISION.
000900 INPUT-OUTPUT SECTION.
001000 FILE-CONTROL.
001100
001200     COPY "SLSTATE.CBL".
001300
001400 DATA DIVISION.
001500 FILE SECTION.
001600
001700     COPY "FDSTATE.CBL".
001800
001900 WORKING-STORAGE SECTION.
002000
002100 77  MENU-PICK                 PIC 9.
002200     88  MENU-PICK-IS-VALID    VALUES 0 THRU 5.
002300
002400 77  THE-MODE                  PIC X(7).
002500 77  OK-TO-DELETE              PIC X.
002600 77  RECORD-FOUND              PIC X.
002700 77  WHICH-FIELD               PIC 9.
002800
002900     COPY "WSCASE01.CBL".
003000
003100 PROCEDURE DIVISION.
003200 PROGRAM-BEGIN.
003300     PERFORM OPENING-PROCEDURE.
003400     PERFORM MAIN-PROCESS.
003500     PERFORM CLOSING-PROCEDURE.
003600
003700 PROGRAM-EXIT.
003800     EXIT PROGRAM.
003900
004000 PROGRAM-DONE.
004100     STOP RUN.
004200
004300 OPENING-PROCEDURE.
004400     OPEN I-O STATE-FILE.
004500
004600 CLOSING-PROCEDURE.
004700     CLOSE STATE-FILE.
004800
004900
```

continues

Listing 18.6. continued

```
005000 MAIN-PROCESS.
005100     PERFORM GET-MENU-PICK.
005200     PERFORM MAINTAIN-THE-FILE
005300         UNTIL MENU-PICK = 0.
005400
005500*-------------------------------
005600* MENU
005700*-------------------------------
005800 GET-MENU-PICK.
005900     PERFORM DISPLAY-THE-MENU.
006000     PERFORM ACCEPT-MENU-PICK.
006100     PERFORM RE-ACCEPT-MENU-PICK
006200         UNTIL MENU-PICK-IS-VALID.
006300
006400 DISPLAY-THE-MENU.
006500     PERFORM CLEAR-SCREEN.
006600     DISPLAY "    PLEASE SELECT:".
006700     DISPLAY " ".
006800     DISPLAY "        1.  ADD RECORDS".
006900     DISPLAY "        2.  CHANGE A RECORD".
007000     DISPLAY "        3.  LOOK UP A RECORD".
007100     DISPLAY "        4.  DELETE A RECORD".
007200     DISPLAY "        5.  PRINT RECORDS".
007300     DISPLAY " ".
007400     DISPLAY "        0.  EXIT".
007500     PERFORM SCROLL-LINE 8 TIMES.
007600
007700 ACCEPT-MENU-PICK.
007800     DISPLAY "YOUR CHOICE (0-5)?".
007900     ACCEPT MENU-PICK.
008000
008100 RE-ACCEPT-MENU-PICK.
008200     DISPLAY "INVALID SELECTION - PLEASE RE-TRY.".
008300     PERFORM ACCEPT-MENU-PICK.
008400
008500 CLEAR-SCREEN.
008600     PERFORM SCROLL-LINE 25 TIMES.
008700
008800 SCROLL-LINE.
008900     DISPLAY " ".
009000
009100 MAINTAIN-THE-FILE.
009200     PERFORM DO-THE-PICK.
009300     PERFORM GET-MENU-PICK.
009400
009500 DO-THE-PICK.
009600     IF MENU-PICK = 1
009700         PERFORM ADD-MODE
009800     ELSE
009900     IF MENU-PICK = 2
010000         PERFORM CHANGE-MODE
010100     ELSE
010200     IF MENU-PICK = 3
010300         PERFORM INQUIRE-MODE
```

18

```
010400        ELSE
010500        IF MENU-PICK = 4
010600            PERFORM DELETE-MODE
010700        ELSE
010800        IF MENU-PICK = 5
010900            PERFORM PRINT-THE-RECORDS.
011000
011100*-------------------------------
011200* ADD
011300*-------------------------------
011400 ADD-MODE.
011500        MOVE "ADD" TO THE-MODE.
011600        PERFORM GET-NEW-STATE-CODE.
011700        PERFORM ADD-RECORDS
011800            UNTIL STATE-CODE = "ZZ".
011900
012000 GET-NEW-STATE-CODE.
012100        PERFORM INIT-STATE-RECORD.
012200        PERFORM ENTER-STATE-CODE.
012300        MOVE "Y" TO RECORD-FOUND.
012400        PERFORM FIND-NEW-STATE-RECORD
012500            UNTIL RECORD-FOUND = "N" OR
012600                  STATE-CODE = "ZZ".
012700
012800 FIND-NEW-STATE-RECORD.
012900        PERFORM READ-STATE-RECORD.
013000        IF RECORD-FOUND = "Y"
013100            DISPLAY "RECORD ALREADY ON FILE"
013200            PERFORM ENTER-STATE-CODE.
013300
013400 ADD-RECORDS.
013500        PERFORM ENTER-REMAINING-FIELDS.
013600        PERFORM WRITE-STATE-RECORD.
013700        PERFORM GET-NEW-STATE-CODE.
013800
013900 ENTER-REMAINING-FIELDS.
014000        PERFORM ENTER-STATE-NAME.
014100
014200*-------------------------------
014300* CHANGE
014400*-------------------------------
014500 CHANGE-MODE.
014600        MOVE "CHANGE" TO THE-MODE.
014700        PERFORM GET-STATE-RECORD.
014800        PERFORM CHANGE-RECORDS
014900            UNTIL STATE-CODE = "ZZ".
015000
015100 CHANGE-RECORDS.
015200        PERFORM GET-FIELD-TO-CHANGE.
015300*       PERFORM CHANGE-ONE-FIELD
015400*           UNTIL WHICH-FIELD = ZERO.
015500        PERFORM CHANGE-ONE-FIELD.
015600
015700        PERFORM GET-STATE-RECORD.
015800
```

continues

Listing 18.6. continued

```
015900 GET-FIELD-TO-CHANGE.
016000     PERFORM DISPLAY-ALL-FIELDS.
016100     PERFORM ASK-WHICH-FIELD.
016200
016300 ASK-WHICH-FIELD.
016400*    PERFORM ACCEPT-WHICH-FIELD.
016500*    PERFORM RE-ACCEPT-WHICH-FIELD
016600*        UNTIL WHICH-FIELD NOT > 1.
016700     MOVE 1 TO WHICH-FIELD.
016800
016900*ACCEPT-WHICH-FIELD.
017000*    DISPLAY "ENTER THE NUMBER OF THE FIELD".
017100*    DISPLAY "TO CHANGE (1) OR 0 TO EXIT".
017200*    ACCEPT WHICH-FIELD.
017300*
017400*RE-ACCEPT-WHICH-FIELD.
017500*    DISPLAY "INVALID ENTRY".
017600*    PERFORM ACCEPT-WHICH-FIELD.
017700
017800 CHANGE-ONE-FIELD.
017900     PERFORM CHANGE-THIS-FIELD.
018000*    PERFORM GET-FIELD-TO-CHANGE.
018100
018200 CHANGE-THIS-FIELD.
018300     IF WHICH-FIELD = 1
018400         PERFORM ENTER-STATE-NAME.
018500
018600     PERFORM REWRITE-STATE-RECORD.
018700
018800*-------------------------------
018900* INQUIRE
019000*-------------------------------
019100 INQUIRE-MODE.
019200     MOVE "DISPLAY" TO THE-MODE.
019300     PERFORM GET-STATE-RECORD.
019400     PERFORM INQUIRE-RECORDS
019500         UNTIL STATE-CODE = "ZZ".
019600
019700 INQUIRE-RECORDS.
019800     PERFORM DISPLAY-ALL-FIELDS.
019900     PERFORM GET-STATE-RECORD.
020000
020100*-------------------------------
020200* DELETE
020300*-------------------------------
020400 DELETE-MODE.
020500     MOVE "DELETE" TO THE-MODE.
020600     PERFORM GET-STATE-RECORD.
020700     PERFORM DELETE-RECORDS
020800         UNTIL STATE-CODE = "ZZ".
020900
021000 DELETE-RECORDS.
021100     PERFORM DISPLAY-ALL-FIELDS.
021200
```

18

```
021300      PERFORM ASK-OK-TO-DELETE
021400      IF OK-TO-DELETE = "Y"
021500          PERFORM DELETE-STATE-RECORD.
021600
021700      PERFORM GET-STATE-RECORD.
021800
021900 ASK-OK-TO-DELETE.
022000      PERFORM ACCEPT-OK-TO-DELETE.
022100      PERFORM RE-ACCEPT-OK-TO-DELETE
022200          UNTIL OK-TO-DELETE = "Y" OR "N".
022300
022400 ACCEPT-OK-TO-DELETE.
022500      DISPLAY "DELETE THIS RECORD (Y/N)?".
022600      ACCEPT OK-TO-DELETE.
022700
022800      INSPECT OK-TO-DELETE
022900        CONVERTING LOWER-ALPHA
023000        TO          UPPER-ALPHA.
023100
023200 RE-ACCEPT-OK-TO-DELETE.
023300      DISPLAY "YOU MUST ENTER YES OR NO".
023400      PERFORM ACCEPT-OK-TO-DELETE.
023500
023600*--------------------------------
023700* PRINT
023800*--------------------------------
023900 PRINT-THE-RECORDS.
024000      CLOSE STATE-FILE.
024100      DISPLAY "REPORT IN PROGRESS".
024200      CALL "STCRPT02".
024300      OPEN I-O STATE-FILE.
024400
024500*--------------------------------
024600* Routines shared by all modes
024700*--------------------------------
024800 INIT-STATE-RECORD.
024900      MOVE SPACE TO STATE-RECORD.
025000
025100 ENTER-STATE-CODE.
025200      PERFORM ACCEPT-STATE-CODE.
025300      PERFORM RE-ACCEPT-STATE-CODE
025400          UNTIL STATE-CODE NOT = SPACE.
025500
025600 ACCEPT-STATE-CODE.
025700      DISPLAY " ".
025800      DISPLAY "ENTER STATE CODE OF THE STATE" .
025900      DISPLAY "TO " THE-MODE
026000              "(2 UPPER CASE CHARACTERS)".
026100      DISPLAY "ENTER ZZ TO STOP ENTRY".
026200      ACCEPT STATE-CODE.
026300
026400      INSPECT STATE-CODE
026500        CONVERTING LOWER-ALPHA
026600        TO          UPPER-ALPHA.
026700
```

18

continues

Listing 18.6. continued

```
026800 RE-ACCEPT-STATE-CODE.
026900     DISPLAY "STATE CODE MUST BE ENTERED".
027000     PERFORM ACCEPT-STATE-CODE.
027100
027200 GET-STATE-RECORD.
027300     PERFORM INIT-STATE-RECORD.
027400     PERFORM ENTER-STATE-CODE.
027500     MOVE "N" TO RECORD-FOUND.
027600     PERFORM FIND-STATE-RECORD
027700         UNTIL RECORD-FOUND = "Y" OR
027800             STATE-CODE = "ZZ".
027900
028000*------------------------------
028100* Routines shared Add and Change
028200*------------------------------
028300 FIND-STATE-RECORD.
028400     PERFORM READ-STATE-RECORD.
028500     IF RECORD-FOUND = "N"
028600         DISPLAY "RECORD NOT FOUND"
028700         PERFORM ENTER-STATE-CODE.
028800
028900 ENTER-STATE-NAME.
029000     PERFORM ACCEPT-STATE-NAME.
029100     PERFORM RE-ACCEPT-STATE-NAME
029200         UNTIL STATE-NAME NOT = SPACES.
029300
029400 ACCEPT-STATE-NAME.
029500     DISPLAY "ENTER STATE NAME".
029600     ACCEPT STATE-NAME.
029700
029800     INSPECT STATE-NAME
029900       CONVERTING LOWER-ALPHA
030000         TO          UPPER-ALPHA.
030100
030200 RE-ACCEPT-STATE-NAME.
030300     DISPLAY "STATE NAME MUST BE ENTERED".
030400     PERFORM ACCEPT-STATE-NAME.
030500
030600*------------------------------
030700* Routines shared by Change,
030800* Inquire and Delete
030900*------------------------------
031000 DISPLAY-ALL-FIELDS.
031100     DISPLAY " ".
031200     PERFORM DISPLAY-STATE-CODE.
031300     PERFORM DISPLAY-STATE-NAME.
031400     DISPLAY " ".
031500
031600 DISPLAY-STATE-CODE.
031700     DISPLAY "   STATE CODE: " STATE-CODE.
031800
031900 DISPLAY-STATE-NAME.
032000     DISPLAY "1. STATE NAME: " STATE-NAME.
032100
```

```
032200*-------------------------------
032300* File I-O Routines
032400*-------------------------------
032500 READ-STATE-RECORD.
032600     MOVE "Y" TO RECORD-FOUND.
032700     READ STATE-FILE RECORD
032800         INVALID KEY
032900             MOVE "N" TO RECORD-FOUND.
033000
033100*or  READ STATE-FILE RECORD WITH LOCK
033200*        INVALID KEY
033300*            MOVE "N" TO RECORD-FOUND.
033400
033500*or  READ STATE-FILE RECORD WITH HOLD
033600*        INVALID KEY
033700*            MOVE "N" TO RECORD-FOUND.
033800
033900 WRITE-STATE-RECORD.
034000     WRITE STATE-RECORD
034100         INVALID KEY
034200         DISPLAY "RECORD ALREADY ON FILE".
034300
034400 REWRITE-STATE-RECORD.
034500     REWRITE STATE-RECORD
034600         INVALID KEY
034700         DISPLAY "ERROR REWRITING STATE RECORD".
034800
034900 DELETE-STATE-RECORD.
035000     DELETE STATE-FILE RECORD
035100         INVALID KEY
035200         DISPLAY "ERROR DELETING STATE RECORD".
035300
```

The output of stcmnt04.cbl includes a menu option for printing the file and a progress message while stcrpt02.cbl is running:

```
PLEASE SELECT:

    1.   ADD RECORDS
    2.   CHANGE A RECORD
    3.   LOOK UP A RECORD
    4.   DELETE A RECORD
    5.   PRINT RECORDS

    0.   EXIT




YOUR CHOICE (0-5)?
5
REPORT IN PROGRESS
```

ANALYSIS Listing 18.6 adds a menu pick that enables you to print the file. The changes to the menu are at lines 002200, 007200, and 007800.

The DO-THE-PICK routine at line 009500 has had a selection added at lines 010800 and 010900 to perform PRINT-THE-RECORDS if MENU-PICK = 5. The PRINT-THE-RECORDS routine at line 023900 closes the state file, displays a message for the user, calls stcrpt02, and then opens the state file.

Closing and reopening the state file is a good practice. Some COBOL versions allow you to open a file more than once, but many do not. The state file already is open in stcmnt04.cbl and will be opened again in stcrpt02.cbl. If you close the state code file before calling STCRPT02, you can avoid any possible conflict.

Note that stcmnt04.cbl also has been changed at lines 003700 and 003800 to include the exit program logic.

If you are using Micro Focus Personal COBOL or ACUCOBOL, you can create this program by editing and compiling. Other versions of COBOL might require an additional step. If you have been using a version of COBOL that requires a link step, you need to link this program to stcrpt02.

For example, under VAX VMS enter the following:

```
LINK /EXE=STCMNT04 STCMNT04.OBJ STCRPT02.OBJ
```

This creates a program named STCMNT04.EXE by linking the two programs together. Consult your manual for how to link with other versions of COBOL.

After you have created this program, run it and select 5 to print the file; you should get a copy of the report produced by stcrpt02.cbl.

Creating Large Menus Using Calls

For the vendor file, you have several programs that could be added to the vendor maintenance menu. Copy vnbynm01.cbl to vnbynm02.cbl. Change the PROGRAM-ID and then make the changes in Listing 18.7 to include exit program logic. Compile the program so that it is ready to run.

TYPE ## Listing 18.7. The changes for vnbynm02.cbl.

```
007600 PROCEDURE DIVISION.
007700 PROGRAM-BEGIN.
007800
007900     PERFORM OPENING-PROCEDURE.
008000     MOVE ZEROES TO LINE-COUNT
008100                    PAGE-NUMBER.
008200
```

```
008300      PERFORM START-NEW-PAGE.
008400
008500      MOVE "N" TO FILE-AT-END.
008600      PERFORM READ-FIRST-RECORD.
008700      IF FILE-AT-END = "Y"
008800          MOVE "NO RECORDS FOUND" TO PRINTER-RECORD
008900          PERFORM WRITE-TO-PRINTER
009000      ELSE
009100          PERFORM PRINT-VENDOR-FIELDS
009200              UNTIL FILE-AT-END = "Y".
009300
009400      PERFORM CLOSING-PROCEDURE.
009500
009600 PROGRAM-EXIT.
009700      EXIT PROGRAM.
009800
009900 PROGRAM-DONE.
010000      STOP RUN.
010100
```

Listing 18.8 is created by copying vninnm02.cbl to vninnm03.cbl and making the needed changes. Be sure to change the PROGRAM-ID.

TYPE **Listing 18.8. Changes for vninnm03.cbl.**

```
003400 PROGRAM-BEGIN.
003500      PERFORM OPENING-PROCEDURE.
003600      PERFORM MAIN-PROCESS.
003700      PERFORM CLOSING-PROCEDURE.
003800
003900 PROGRAM-EXIT.
004000      EXIT PROGRAM.
004100
004200 PROGRAM-DONE.
004300      STOP RUN.
```

To modify vndrpt03.cbl, copy it to vndrpt04.cbl and make the changes shown in Listings 18.9 and 18.10. The vendor report program needs to be changed to use the new SELECT and FD for the vendor file. Be sure to change the PROGRAM-ID. Compile the program so that it is ready to run.

TYPE **Listing 18.9. Fixing the SELECT and FD in vndrpt04.cbl.**

```
000100 IDENTIFICATION DIVISION.
000200 PROGRAM-ID. VNDRPT04.
000300*--------------------------------
000400* Report on the Vendor File.
000500*--------------------------------
```

continues

Listing 18.9. continued

```
000600 ENVIRONMENT DIVISION.
000700 INPUT-OUTPUT SECTION.
000800 FILE-CONTROL.
000900
001000     COPY "SLVND02.CBL".
001100
001200     COPY "SLSTATE.CBL".
001300
001400     SELECT PRINTER-FILE
001500         ASSIGN TO PRINTER
001600         ORGANIZATION IS LINE SEQUENTIAL.
001700
001800 DATA DIVISION.
001900 FILE SECTION.
002000
002100     COPY "FDVND04.CBL".
002200
002300     COPY "FDSTATE.CBL".
002400
```

TYPE **Listing 18.10. Adding the program exit logic in** `vndrpt04.cbl`**.**

```
007500 PROCEDURE DIVISION.
007600 PROGRAM-BEGIN.
007700
007800     PERFORM OPENING-PROCEDURE.
007900     MOVE ZEROES TO LINE-COUNT
008000                    PAGE-NUMBER.
008100
008200     PERFORM START-NEW-PAGE.
008300
008400     MOVE "N" TO FILE-AT-END.
008500     PERFORM READ-NEXT-RECORD.
008600     IF FILE-AT-END = "Y"
008700         MOVE "NO RECORDS FOUND" TO PRINTER-RECORD
008800         PERFORM WRITE-TO-PRINTER
008900     ELSE
009000         PERFORM PRINT-VENDOR-FIELDS
009100             UNTIL FILE-AT-END = "Y".
009200
009300     PERFORM CLOSING-PROCEDURE.
009400
009500 PROGRAM-EXIT.
009600     EXIT PROGRAM.
009700
009800 PROGRAM-DONE.
009900     STOP RUN.
010000
```

18

These new programs can be called now by another program, and you can create a vendor maintenance program that gives the user any of these options.

Listing 18.11, vndmnt04.cbl, adds three more menu selections to the vendor maintenance menu. Menu pick 5 allows a look up by name and calls VNINNM03, menu pick 6 prints the vendor report and calls VNDRPT04, and menu pick 7 prints the vendor report by name and calls VNDBYNM02.

TYPE **Listing 18.11. Vendor maintenance with several options.**

```
000100 IDENTIFICATION DIVISION.
000200 PROGRAM-ID. VNDMNT04.
000300*-------------------------------
000400* Add, Change, Inquire and Delete
000500* for the Vendor File.
000600* Menu includes inquire by name,
000700* the vendor report, and the vendor
000800* report in name order.
000900*-------------------------------
001000 ENVIRONMENT DIVISION.
001100 INPUT-OUTPUT SECTION.
001200 FILE-CONTROL.
001300
001400     COPY "SLVND02.CBL".
001500
001600     COPY "SLSTATE.CBL".
001700
001800 DATA DIVISION.
001900 FILE SECTION.
002000
002100     COPY "FDVND04.CBL".
002200
002300     COPY "FDSTATE.CBL".
002400
002500 WORKING-STORAGE SECTION.
002600
002700 77  MENU-PICK                  PIC 9.
002800     88  MENU-PICK-IS-VALID      VALUES 0 THRU 7.
002900
003000 77  THE-MODE                   PIC X(7).
003100 77  WHICH-FIELD                PIC 9.
003200 77  OK-TO-DELETE               PIC X.
003300 77  VENDOR-RECORD-FOUND        PIC X.
003400 77  STATE-RECORD-FOUND         PIC X.
003500
003600
003700 77  VENDOR-NUMBER-FIELD        PIC Z(5).
003800
003900 77  ERROR-MESSAGE              PIC X(79) VALUE SPACE.
004000
```

continues

18

Listing 18.11. continued

```
004100      COPY "WSCASE01.CBL".
004200
004300 PROCEDURE DIVISION.
004400 PROGRAM-BEGIN.
004500      PERFORM OPENING-PROCEDURE.
004600      PERFORM MAIN-PROCESS.
004700      PERFORM CLOSING-PROCEDURE.
004800
004900 PROGRAM-EXIT.
005000      EXIT PROGRAM.
005100
005200 PROGRAM-DONE.
005300      STOP RUN.
005400
005500 OPENING-PROCEDURE.
005600      OPEN I-O VENDOR-FILE.
005700      OPEN I-O STATE-FILE.
005800
005900 CLOSING-PROCEDURE.
006000      CLOSE VENDOR-FILE.
006100      CLOSE STATE-FILE.
006200
006300 MAIN-PROCESS.
006400      PERFORM GET-MENU-PICK.
006500      PERFORM MAINTAIN-THE-FILE
006600          UNTIL MENU-PICK = 0.
006700
006800*-------------------------------
006900* MENU
007000*-------------------------------
007100 GET-MENU-PICK.
007200      PERFORM DISPLAY-THE-MENU.
007300      PERFORM ACCEPT-MENU-PICK.
007400      PERFORM RE-ACCEPT-MENU-PICK
007500          UNTIL MENU-PICK-IS-VALID.
007600
007700 DISPLAY-THE-MENU.
007800      PERFORM CLEAR-SCREEN.
007900      DISPLAY "    PLEASE SELECT:".
008000      DISPLAY " ".
008100      DISPLAY "        1.  ADD RECORDS".
008200      DISPLAY "        2.  CHANGE A RECORD".
008300      DISPLAY "        3.  LOOK UP A RECORD".
008400      DISPLAY "        4.  DELETE A RECORD".
008500      DISPLAY "        5.  LOOK UP BY NAME".
008600      DISPLAY "        6.  PRINT RECORDS".
008700      DISPLAY "        7.  PRINT IN NAME ORDER".
008800      DISPLAY " ".
008900      DISPLAY "        0.  EXIT".
009000      PERFORM SCROLL-LINE 8 TIMES.
009100
009200 ACCEPT-MENU-PICK.
009300      DISPLAY "YOUR CHOICE (0-7)?".
009400      ACCEPT MENU-PICK.
```

18

```
009500
009600 RE-ACCEPT-MENU-PICK.
009700     DISPLAY "INVALID SELECTION - PLEASE RE-TRY.".
009800     PERFORM ACCEPT-MENU-PICK.
009900
010000 CLEAR-SCREEN.
010100     PERFORM SCROLL-LINE 25 TIMES.
010200
010300 SCROLL-LINE.
010400     DISPLAY " ".
010500
010600 MAINTAIN-THE-FILE.
010700     PERFORM DO-THE-PICK.
010800     PERFORM GET-MENU-PICK.
010900
011000 DO-THE-PICK.
011100     IF MENU-PICK = 1
011200         PERFORM ADD-MODE
011300     ELSE
011400     IF MENU-PICK = 2
011500         PERFORM CHANGE-MODE
011600     ELSE
011700     IF MENU-PICK = 3
011800         PERFORM INQUIRE-MODE
011900     ELSE
012000     IF MENU-PICK = 4
012100         PERFORM DELETE-MODE
012200     ELSE
012300     IF MENU-PICK = 5
012400         PERFORM INQUIRE-BY-NAME
012500     ELSE
012600     IF MENU-PICK = 6
012700         PERFORM PRINT-VENDOR-REPORT
012800     ELSE
012900     IF MENU-PICK = 7
013000         PERFORM PRINT-BY-NAME.
013100
013200*--------------------------------
013300* ADD
013400*--------------------------------
013500 ADD-MODE.
013600     MOVE "ADD" TO THE-MODE.
013700     PERFORM GET-NEW-RECORD-KEY.
013800     PERFORM ADD-RECORDS
013900         UNTIL VENDOR-NUMBER = ZEROES.
014000
014100 GET-NEW-RECORD-KEY.
014200     PERFORM ACCEPT-NEW-RECORD-KEY.
014300     PERFORM RE-ACCEPT-NEW-RECORD-KEY
014400         UNTIL VENDOR-RECORD-FOUND = "N" OR
014500             VENDOR-NUMBER = ZEROES.
014600
014700 ACCEPT-NEW-RECORD-KEY.
014800     PERFORM INIT-VENDOR-RECORD.
```

continues

Listing 18.11. continued

```
014900      PERFORM ENTER-VENDOR-NUMBER.
015000      IF VENDOR-NUMBER NOT = ZEROES
015100          PERFORM READ-VENDOR-RECORD.
015200
015300 RE-ACCEPT-NEW-RECORD-KEY.
015400    DISPLAY "RECORD ALREADY ON FILE"
015500    PERFORM ACCEPT-NEW-RECORD-KEY.
015600
015700 ADD-RECORDS.
015800    PERFORM ENTER-REMAINING-FIELDS.
015900    PERFORM WRITE-VENDOR-RECORD.
016000    PERFORM GET-NEW-RECORD-KEY.
016100
016200 ENTER-REMAINING-FIELDS.
016300    PERFORM ENTER-VENDOR-NAME.
016400    PERFORM ENTER-VENDOR-ADDRESS-1.
016500    PERFORM ENTER-VENDOR-ADDRESS-2.
016600    PERFORM ENTER-VENDOR-CITY.
016700    PERFORM ENTER-VENDOR-STATE.
016800    PERFORM ENTER-VENDOR-ZIP.
016900    PERFORM ENTER-VENDOR-CONTACT.
017000    PERFORM ENTER-VENDOR-PHONE.
017100
017200*-------------------------------
017300* CHANGE
017400*-------------------------------
017500 CHANGE-MODE.
017600    MOVE "CHANGE" TO THE-MODE.
017700    PERFORM GET-EXISTING-RECORD.
017800    PERFORM CHANGE-RECORDS
017900        UNTIL VENDOR-NUMBER = ZEROES.
018000
018100 CHANGE-RECORDS.
018200    PERFORM GET-FIELD-TO-CHANGE.
018300    PERFORM CHANGE-ONE-FIELD
018400        UNTIL WHICH-FIELD = ZERO.
018500    PERFORM GET-EXISTING-RECORD.
018600
018700 GET-FIELD-TO-CHANGE.
018800    PERFORM DISPLAY-ALL-FIELDS.
018900    PERFORM ASK-WHICH-FIELD.
019000
019100 ASK-WHICH-FIELD.
019200    PERFORM ACCEPT-WHICH-FIELD.
019300    PERFORM RE-ACCEPT-WHICH-FIELD
019400        UNTIL WHICH-FIELD < 9.
019500
019600 ACCEPT-WHICH-FIELD.
019700    DISPLAY "ENTER THE NUMBER OF THE FIELD".
019800    DISPLAY "TO CHANGE (1-8) OR 0 TO EXIT".
019900    ACCEPT WHICH-FIELD.
020000
020100 RE-ACCEPT-WHICH-FIELD.
020200    DISPLAY "INVALID ENTRY".
```

```
020300      PERFORM ACCEPT-WHICH-FIELD.
020400
020500 CHANGE-ONE-FIELD.
020600      PERFORM CHANGE-THIS-FIELD.
020700      PERFORM GET-FIELD-TO-CHANGE.
020800
020900 CHANGE-THIS-FIELD.
021000      IF WHICH-FIELD = 1
021100          PERFORM ENTER-VENDOR-NAME.
021200      IF WHICH-FIELD = 2
021300          PERFORM ENTER-VENDOR-ADDRESS-1.
021400      IF WHICH-FIELD = 3
021500          PERFORM ENTER-VENDOR-ADDRESS-2.
021600      IF WHICH-FIELD = 4
021700          PERFORM ENTER-VENDOR-CITY.
021800      IF WHICH-FIELD = 5
021900          PERFORM ENTER-VENDOR-STATE.
022000      IF WHICH-FIELD = 6
022100          PERFORM ENTER-VENDOR-ZIP.
022200      IF WHICH-FIELD = 7
022300          PERFORM ENTER-VENDOR-CONTACT.
022400      IF WHICH-FIELD = 8
022500          PERFORM ENTER-VENDOR-PHONE.
022600
022700      PERFORM REWRITE-VENDOR-RECORD.
022800
022900*-------------------------------
023000* INQUIRE
023100*-------------------------------
023200 INQUIRE-MODE.
023300      MOVE "DISPLAY" TO THE-MODE.
023400      PERFORM GET-EXISTING-RECORD.
023500      PERFORM INQUIRE-RECORDS
023600          UNTIL VENDOR-NUMBER = ZEROES.
023700
023800 INQUIRE-RECORDS.
023900      PERFORM DISPLAY-ALL-FIELDS.
024000      PERFORM GET-EXISTING-RECORD.
024100
024200*-------------------------------
024300* DELETE
024400*-------------------------------
024500 DELETE-MODE.
024600      MOVE "DELETE" TO THE-MODE.
024700      PERFORM GET-EXISTING-RECORD.
024800      PERFORM DELETE-RECORDS
024900          UNTIL VENDOR-NUMBER = ZEROES.
025000
025100 DELETE-RECORDS.
025200      PERFORM DISPLAY-ALL-FIELDS.
025300
025400      PERFORM ASK-OK-TO-DELETE.
025500
025600      IF OK-TO-DELETE = "Y"
025700          PERFORM DELETE-VENDOR-RECORD.
025800
```

18

continues

Listing 18.11. continued

```
025900      PERFORM GET-EXISTING-RECORD.
026000
026100 ASK-OK-TO-DELETE.
026200      PERFORM ACCEPT-OK-TO-DELETE.
026300
026400      PERFORM RE-ACCEPT-OK-TO-DELETE
026500         UNTIL OK-TO-DELETE = "Y" OR "N".
026600
026700 ACCEPT-OK-TO-DELETE.
026800      DISPLAY "DELETE THIS RECORD (Y/N)?".
026900      ACCEPT OK-TO-DELETE.
027000      INSPECT OK-TO-DELETE
027100        CONVERTING LOWER-ALPHA TO UPPER-ALPHA.
027200
027300 RE-ACCEPT-OK-TO-DELETE.
027400      DISPLAY "YOU MUST ENTER YES OR NO".
027500      PERFORM ACCEPT-OK-TO-DELETE.
027600
027700*--------------------------------
027800* Routines shared by all modes
027900*--------------------------------
028000 INIT-VENDOR-RECORD.
028100      MOVE SPACE TO VENDOR-RECORD.
028200      MOVE ZEROES TO VENDOR-NUMBER.
028300
028400 ENTER-VENDOR-NUMBER.
028500      DISPLAY " ".
028600      DISPLAY "ENTER VENDOR NUMBER OF THE VENDOR" .
028700      DISPLAY "TO " THE-MODE " (1-99999)".
028800      DISPLAY "ENTER 0 TO STOP ENTRY".
028900      ACCEPT VENDOR-NUMBER-FIELD.
029000*OR  ACCEPT VENDOR-NUMBER-FIELD WITH CONVERSION.
029100
029200      MOVE VENDOR-NUMBER-FIELD TO VENDOR-NUMBER.
029300
029400*--------------------------------
029500* INQUIRE BY NAME
029600*--------------------------------
029700 INQUIRE-BY-NAME.
029800      PERFORM CLOSING-PROCEDURE.
029900      CALL "VNINNM03".
030000      PERFORM OPENING-PROCEDURE.
030100
030200*--------------------------------
030300* PRINT
030400*--------------------------------
030500 PRINT-VENDOR-REPORT.
030600      PERFORM CLOSING-PROCEDURE.
030700      DISPLAY "VENDOR REPORT IN PROGRESS".
030800      CALL "VNDRPT04".
030900      PERFORM OPENING-PROCEDURE.
031000
031100*--------------------------------
031200* PRINT BY NAME
```

```
031300*--------------------------------
031400 PRINT-BY-NAME.
031500     PERFORM CLOSING-PROCEDURE.
031600     DISPLAY " REPORT BY NAME IN PROGRESS".
031700     CALL "VNBYNM02".
031800     PERFORM OPENING-PROCEDURE.
031900
032000*--------------------------------
032100* Routines shared Add and Change
032200*--------------------------------
032300 ENTER-VENDOR-NAME.
032400     PERFORM ACCEPT-VENDOR-NAME.
032500     PERFORM RE-ACCEPT-VENDOR-NAME
032600         UNTIL VENDOR-NAME NOT = SPACE.
032700
032800 ACCEPT-VENDOR-NAME.
032900     DISPLAY "ENTER VENDOR NAME".
033000     ACCEPT VENDOR-NAME.
033100     INSPECT VENDOR-NAME
033200         CONVERTING LOWER-ALPHA
033300         TO         UPPER-ALPHA.
033400
033500 RE-ACCEPT-VENDOR-NAME.
033600     DISPLAY "VENDOR NAME MUST BE ENTERED".
033700     PERFORM ACCEPT-VENDOR-NAME.
033800
033900 ENTER-VENDOR-ADDRESS-1.
034000     PERFORM ACCEPT-VENDOR-ADDRESS-1.
034100     PERFORM RE-ACCEPT-VENDOR-ADDRESS-1
034200         UNTIL VENDOR-ADDRESS-1 NOT = SPACE.
034300
034400 ACCEPT-VENDOR-ADDRESS-1.
034500     DISPLAY "ENTER VENDOR ADDRESS-1".
034600     ACCEPT VENDOR-ADDRESS-1.
034700     INSPECT VENDOR-ADDRESS-1
034800         CONVERTING LOWER-ALPHA
034900         TO         UPPER-ALPHA.
035000
035100 RE-ACCEPT-VENDOR-ADDRESS-1.
035200     DISPLAY "VENDOR ADDRESS-1 MUST BE ENTERED".
035300     PERFORM ACCEPT-VENDOR-ADDRESS-1.
035400
035500 ENTER-VENDOR-ADDRESS-2.
035600     DISPLAY "ENTER VENDOR ADDRESS-2".
035700     ACCEPT VENDOR-ADDRESS-2.
035800     INSPECT VENDOR-ADDRESS-2
035900         CONVERTING LOWER-ALPHA
036000         TO         UPPER-ALPHA.
036100
036200 ENTER-VENDOR-CITY.
036300     PERFORM ACCEPT-VENDOR-CITY.
036400     PERFORM RE-ACCEPT-VENDOR-CITY
036500         UNTIL VENDOR-CITY NOT = SPACE.
036600
036700 ACCEPT-VENDOR-CITY.
```

18

continues

Listing 18.11. continued

```
036800     DISPLAY "ENTER VENDOR CITY".
036900     ACCEPT VENDOR-CITY.
037000     INSPECT VENDOR-CITY
037100          CONVERTING LOWER-ALPHA
037200          TO              UPPER-ALPHA.
037300
037400 RE-ACCEPT-VENDOR-CITY.
037500     DISPLAY "VENDOR CITY MUST BE ENTERED".
037600     PERFORM ACCEPT-VENDOR-CITY.
037700
037800 ENTER-VENDOR-STATE.
037900     PERFORM ACCEPT-VENDOR-STATE.
038000     PERFORM RE-ACCEPT-VENDOR-STATE
038100          UNTIL VENDOR-STATE NOT = SPACES AND
038200              STATE-RECORD-FOUND = "Y".
038300
038400 ACCEPT-VENDOR-STATE.
038500     DISPLAY "ENTER VENDOR STATE".
038600     ACCEPT VENDOR-STATE.
038700     PERFORM EDIT-CHECK-VENDOR-STATE.
038800
038900 RE-ACCEPT-VENDOR-STATE.
039000     DISPLAY ERROR-MESSAGE.
039100     PERFORM ACCEPT-VENDOR-STATE.
039200
039300 EDIT-CHECK-VENDOR-STATE.
039400     PERFORM EDIT-VENDOR-STATE.
039500     PERFORM CHECK-VENDOR-STATE.
039600
039700 EDIT-VENDOR-STATE.
039800     INSPECT VENDOR-STATE
039900          CONVERTING LOWER-ALPHA
040000          TO              UPPER-ALPHA.
040100
040200 CHECK-VENDOR-STATE.
040300     PERFORM VENDOR-STATE-REQUIRED.
040400     IF VENDOR-STATE NOT = SPACES
040500          PERFORM VENDOR-STATE-ON-FILE.
040600
040700 VENDOR-STATE-REQUIRED.
040800     IF VENDOR-STATE = SPACE
040900          MOVE "VENDOR STATE MUST BE ENTERED"
041000              TO ERROR-MESSAGE.
041100
041200 VENDOR-STATE-ON-FILE.
041300     MOVE VENDOR-STATE TO STATE-CODE.
041400     PERFORM READ-STATE-RECORD.
041500     IF STATE-RECORD-FOUND = "N"
041600          MOVE "STATE CODE NOT FOUND IN CODES FILE"
041700              TO ERROR-MESSAGE.
041800
041900 ENTER-VENDOR-ZIP.
042000     PERFORM ACCEPT-VENDOR-ZIP.
042100     PERFORM RE-ACCEPT-VENDOR-ZIP
```

```
042200           UNTIL VENDOR-ZIP NOT = SPACE.
042300
042400 ACCEPT-VENDOR-ZIP.
042500     DISPLAY "ENTER VENDOR ZIP".
042600     ACCEPT VENDOR-ZIP.
042700     INSPECT VENDOR-ZIP
042800         CONVERTING LOWER-ALPHA
042900         TO          UPPER-ALPHA.
043000
043100 RE-ACCEPT-VENDOR-ZIP.
043200     DISPLAY "VENDOR ZIP MUST BE ENTERED".
043300     PERFORM ACCEPT-VENDOR-ZIP.
043400
043500 ENTER-VENDOR-CONTACT.
043600     DISPLAY "ENTER VENDOR CONTACT".
043700     ACCEPT VENDOR-CONTACT.
043800     INSPECT VENDOR-CONTACT
043900         CONVERTING LOWER-ALPHA
044000         TO          UPPER-ALPHA.
044100
044200 ENTER-VENDOR-PHONE.
044300     PERFORM ACCEPT-VENDOR-PHONE.
044400     PERFORM RE-ACCEPT-VENDOR-PHONE
044500         UNTIL VENDOR-PHONE NOT = SPACE.
044600
044700 ACCEPT-VENDOR-PHONE.
044800     DISPLAY "ENTER VENDOR PHONE".
044900     ACCEPT VENDOR-PHONE.
045000     INSPECT VENDOR-PHONE
045100         CONVERTING LOWER-ALPHA
045200         TO          UPPER-ALPHA.
045300
045400 RE-ACCEPT-VENDOR-PHONE.
045500     DISPLAY "VENDOR PHONE MUST BE ENTERED".
045600     PERFORM ACCEPT-VENDOR-PHONE.
045700
045800*--------------------------------
045900* Routines shared by Change,
046000* Inquire and Delete
046100*--------------------------------
046200 GET-EXISTING-RECORD.
046300     PERFORM ACCEPT-EXISTING-KEY.
046400     PERFORM RE-ACCEPT-EXISTING-KEY
046500         UNTIL VENDOR-RECORD-FOUND = "Y" OR
046600               VENDOR-NUMBER = ZEROES.
046700
046800 ACCEPT-EXISTING-KEY.
046900     PERFORM INIT-VENDOR-RECORD.
047000     PERFORM ENTER-VENDOR-NUMBER.
047100     IF VENDOR-NUMBER NOT = ZEROES
047200         PERFORM READ-VENDOR-RECORD.
047300
047400 RE-ACCEPT-EXISTING-KEY.
047500     DISPLAY "RECORD NOT FOUND"
047600     PERFORM ACCEPT-EXISTING-KEY.
047700
```

18

continues

Listing 18.11. continued

```
047800 DISPLAY-ALL-FIELDS.
047900     DISPLAY " ".
048000     PERFORM DISPLAY-VENDOR-NUMBER.
048100     PERFORM DISPLAY-VENDOR-NAME.
048200     PERFORM DISPLAY-VENDOR-ADDRESS-1.
048300     PERFORM DISPLAY-VENDOR-ADDRESS-2.
048400     PERFORM DISPLAY-VENDOR-CITY.
048500     PERFORM DISPLAY-VENDOR-STATE.
048600     PERFORM DISPLAY-VENDOR-ZIP.
048700     PERFORM DISPLAY-VENDOR-CONTACT.
048800     PERFORM DISPLAY-VENDOR-PHONE.
048900     DISPLAY " ".
049000
049100 DISPLAY-VENDOR-NUMBER.
049200     DISPLAY "   VENDOR NUMBER: " VENDOR-NUMBER.
049300
049400 DISPLAY-VENDOR-NAME.
049500     DISPLAY "1. VENDOR NAME: " VENDOR-NAME.
049600
049700 DISPLAY-VENDOR-ADDRESS-1.
049800     DISPLAY "2. VENDOR ADDRESS-1: " VENDOR-ADDRESS-1.
049900
050000 DISPLAY-VENDOR-ADDRESS-2.
050100     DISPLAY "3. VENDOR ADDRESS-2: " VENDOR-ADDRESS-2.
050200
050300 DISPLAY-VENDOR-CITY.
050400     DISPLAY "4. VENDOR CITY: " VENDOR-CITY.
050500
050600 DISPLAY-VENDOR-STATE.
050700     PERFORM VENDOR-STATE-ON-FILE.
050800     IF STATE-RECORD-FOUND = "N"
050900         MOVE "**Not found**" TO STATE-NAME.
051000     DISPLAY "5. VENDOR STATE: "
051100             VENDOR-STATE " "
051200             STATE-NAME.
051300
051400 DISPLAY-VENDOR-ZIP.
051500     DISPLAY "6. VENDOR ZIP: " VENDOR-ZIP.
051600
051700 DISPLAY-VENDOR-CONTACT.
051800     DISPLAY "7. VENDOR CONTACT: " VENDOR-CONTACT.
051900
052000 DISPLAY-VENDOR-PHONE.
052100     DISPLAY "8. VENDOR PHONE: " VENDOR-PHONE.
052200
052300*--------------------------------
052400* File I-O Routines
052500*--------------------------------
052600 READ-VENDOR-RECORD.
052700     MOVE "Y" TO VENDOR-RECORD-FOUND.
052800     READ VENDOR-FILE RECORD
052900         INVALID KEY
053000             MOVE "N" TO VENDOR-RECORD-FOUND.
053100
```

18

```
053200*or  READ VENDOR-FILE RECORD WITH LOCK
053300*       INVALID KEY
053400*          MOVE "N" TO VENDOR-RECORD-FOUND.
053500
053600*or  READ VENDOR-FILE RECORD WITH HOLD
053700*       INVALID KEY
053800*          MOVE "N" TO VENDOR-RECORD-FOUND.
053900
054000 WRITE-VENDOR-RECORD.
054100    WRITE VENDOR-RECORD
054200       INVALID KEY
054300       DISPLAY "RECORD ALREADY ON FILE".
054400
054500 REWRITE-VENDOR-RECORD.
054600    REWRITE VENDOR-RECORD
054700       INVALID KEY
054800       DISPLAY "ERROR REWRITING VENDOR RECORD".
054900
055000 DELETE-VENDOR-RECORD.
055100    DELETE VENDOR-FILE RECORD
055200       INVALID KEY
055300       DISPLAY "ERROR DELETING VENDOR RECORD".
055400
055500 READ-STATE-RECORD.
055600    MOVE "Y" TO STATE-RECORD-FOUND.
055700    READ STATE-FILE RECORD
055800       INVALID KEY
055900       MOVE "N" TO STATE-RECORD-FOUND.
056000
```

The output of vndmnt04.cbl includes a full menu with several options:

```
PLEASE SELECT:

        1.   ADD RECORDS
        2.   CHANGE A RECORD
        3.   LOOK UP A RECORD
        4.   DELETE A RECORD
        5.   LOOK UP BY NAME
        6.   PRINT RECORDS
        7.   PRINT IN NAME ORDER

        0.   EXIT




YOUR CHOICE (0-7)?
```

18

ANALYSIS The calling routines are at lines 029400 through 031800, and they each use the method of closing the open files by performing CLOSING-PROCEDURE before calling their respective programs, and then calling OPENING-PROCEDURE on return. This is a handy way of closing all open files and reopening them on the way back.

Code and compile (and link if necessary) vndmnt04.cbl, and you will have a complete menu of the vendor file options.

Menu Programs

Menu programs that call other programs are even easier to write. Because a menu program probably has no files open, there is no closing of files involved.

Listing 18.12 is bilmnu01.cbl. This will become the main menu for the bills processing system.

TYPE Listing 18.12. Main menu for the bills processing system.

```
000100 IDENTIFICATION DIVISION.
000200 PROGRAM-ID. BILMNU01.
000300*--------------------------------
000400* Menu for the bill payment system.
000500*--------------------------------
000600 ENVIRONMENT DIVISION.
000700 INPUT-OUTPUT SECTION.
000800 FILE-CONTROL.
000900
001000 DATA DIVISION.
001100 FILE SECTION.
001200
001300 WORKING-STORAGE SECTION.
001400
001500 77  MENU-PICK                 PIC 9.
001600     88  MENU-PICK-IS-VALID     VALUES 0 THRU 2.
001700
001800 PROCEDURE DIVISION.
001900 PROGRAM-BEGIN.
002000     PERFORM OPENING-PROCEDURE.
002100     PERFORM MAIN-PROCESS.
002200     PERFORM CLOSING-PROCEDURE.
002300
002400 PROGRAM-EXIT.
002500     EXIT PROGRAM.
002600
002700 PROGRAM-DONE.
002800     STOP RUN.
002900
003000 OPENING-PROCEDURE.
003100
```

```
003200 CLOSING-PROCEDURE.
003300
003400 MAIN-PROCESS.
003500     PERFORM GET-MENU-PICK.
003600     PERFORM DO-THE-PICK
003700         UNTIL MENU-PICK = 0.
003800
003900*--------------------------------
004000* MENU
004100*--------------------------------
004200 GET-MENU-PICK.
004300     PERFORM DISPLAY-THE-MENU.
004400     PERFORM ACCEPT-MENU-PICK.
004500     PERFORM RE-ACCEPT-MENU-PICK
004600         UNTIL MENU-PICK-IS-VALID.
004700
004800 DISPLAY-THE-MENU.
004900     PERFORM CLEAR-SCREEN.
005000     DISPLAY "    PLEASE SELECT:".
005100     DISPLAY " ".
005200     DISPLAY "          1.   STATE CODE MAINTENANCE".
005300     DISPLAY "          2.   VENDOR MAINTENANCE".
005400     DISPLAY " ".
005500     DISPLAY "          0.   EXIT".
005600     PERFORM SCROLL-LINE 8 TIMES.
005700
005800 ACCEPT-MENU-PICK.
005900     DISPLAY "YOUR CHOICE (0-2)?".
006000     ACCEPT MENU-PICK.
006100
006200 RE-ACCEPT-MENU-PICK.
006300     DISPLAY "INVALID SELECTION - PLEASE RE-TRY.".
006400     PERFORM ACCEPT-MENU-PICK.
006500
006600 CLEAR-SCREEN.
006700     PERFORM SCROLL-LINE 25 TIMES.
006800
006900 SCROLL-LINE.
007000     DISPLAY " ".
007100
007200 DO-THE-PICK.
007300     IF MENU-PICK = 1
007400         PERFORM STATE-MAINTENANCE
007500     ELSE
007600     IF MENU-PICK = 2
007700         PERFORM VENDOR-MAINTENANCE.
007800
007900     PERFORM GET-MENU-PICK.
008000
008100*--------------------------------
008200* STATE
008300*--------------------------------
008400 STATE-MAINTENANCE.
```

continues

18

Listing 18.12. continued

```
008500      CALL "STCMNT04".
008600
008700*-------------------------------
008800* VENDOR
008900*-------------------------------
009000 VENDOR-MAINTENANCE.
009100      CALL "VNDMNT04".
009200
```

The output of `bilmnu01.cbl` and the programs that it calls shows the user selecting menu options and descending into lower programs, and then exiting back to the top level:

```
PLEASE SELECT:

        1.    STATE CODE MAINTENANCE
        2.    VENDOR MAINTENANCE

        0.    EXIT




YOUR CHOICE (0-2)?
2
    PLEASE SELECT:

        1.    ADD RECORDS
        2.    CHANGE A RECORD
        3.    LOOK UP A RECORD
        4.    DELETE A RECORD
        5.    LOOK UP BY NAME
        6.    PRINT RECORDS
        7.    PRINT IN NAME ORDER
        0.    EXIT




YOUR CHOICE (0-7)?
5
ENTER VENDOR NAME
abc
VENDOR NUMBER: 00002
1. VENDOR NAME: ABC PRINTING
2. VENDOR ADDRESS-1: 1624 FOOTHILL BLVD
```

```
3. VENDOR ADDRESS-2: SUITE 34
4. VENDOR CITY: LOS ANGELES
5. VENDOR STATE: CA CALIFORNIA
6. VENDOR ZIP: 91042
7. VENDOR CONTACT: CHARLES JOHANSSEN
8. VENDOR PHONE: (818) 555-4321
DISPLAY NEXT RECORD (Y/N)?
n
ENTER VENDOR NAME
```

(The user presses Enter here.)

```
    PLEASE SELECT:

        1.  ADD RECORDS
        2.  CHANGE A RECORD
        3.  LOOK UP A RECORD
        4.  DELETE A RECORD
        5.  LOOK UP BY NAME
        6.  PRINT RECORDS
        7.  PRINT IN NAME ORDER
        0.  EXIT
```

```
YOUR CHOICE (0-7)?
0
    PLEASE SELECT:
        1.  STATE CODE MAINTENANCE
        2.  VENDOR MAINTENANCE
        0.  EXIT
```

```
YOUR CHOICE (0-2)?
0
C>
```

ANALYSIS You should recognize quickly that `bilmnu01.cbl` displays a menu and then calls an appropriate program based on the pick. Code and compile (and link if necessary) `bilmnu01.cbl`. Run the program and you should be able to select a menu option, descend to a lower-level menu such as vendor maintenance, execute an option from that menu, and return up the menu tree to this top menu.

One point worth noting is the difference in the manner of exiting from menus and maintenance programs. The menus all use zeroes to exit the current menu and return to the previous menu or exit the entire program. Vendor Maintenance exits when the user enters 0, but State Code Maintenance exits when the user enters ZZ. In practice, it is much better to keep a common style to all the programs in a system so that a common exit method is used. In Listing 18.6, stcmnt04.cbl, changing the exit message and the code that causes an exit to 0 would improve the overall interface so that the user could become familiar with the idea that 0 always means exit. The sample changes are as follows:

```
025600 ACCEPT-STATE-CODE.
025700     DISPLAY " ".
025800     DISPLAY "ENTER STATE CODE OF THE STATE" .
025900     DISPLAY "TO " THE-MODE
026000              "(2 UPPER CASE CHARACTERS)".
026100     DISPLAY "or ENTER 0 TO STOP ENTRY".
026200     ACCEPT STATE-CODE.
026300

.  .  .  .
.  .  .  .
027200 GET-STATE-RECORD.
027300     PERFORM INIT-STATE-RECORD.
027400     PERFORM ENTER-STATE-CODE.
027500     MOVE "N" TO RECORD-FOUND.
027600     PERFORM FIND-STATE-RECORD
027700        UNTIL RECORD-FOUND = "Y" OR
027800              STATE-CODE = "0".
027900
```

Summary

In practice, a system is built of many programs that work in concert. In order to get these programs to work together for the user, you need to provide a menu with all the programs available as choices. Today, you learned the following basics:

- [ ] CALL can be used to execute one COBOL program from within another.
- [ ] CALL works as if it were a PERFORM that performs a whole program.
- [ ] STOP RUN stops all COBOL programs that you currently are running even if it is executed in a called program.
- [ ] Use EXIT PROGRAM combined with STOP RUN at the end of all programs and you will have a general-purpose end-of-program logic that works whether the program is a called or calling program.

18

Q&A

Q Can any program be executed by using a CALL?

A This is limited by the amount of memory that you have available. There may be other limitations on this based on your COBOL version. For example, the program being called must be a COBOL program, or it must have been compiled with the same COBOL compiler.

Q Can a called program make a CALL to the calling program? In other words, if PROGRAMA calls PROGRAMB, can PROGRAMB call PROGRAMA?

A No. A called program cannot call the parent program that called it, nor any other program above it. If PROGRAMA calls PROGRAMB, and PROGRAMB in turn calls PROGRAMC, PROGRAMC may not call either PROGRAMA or PROGRAMB. The compiler will allow you to do this, but the programs will not run correctly, and you will start to get unpredictable results.

Q Can a called program use variables defined in a calling program or vice versa?

A The short answer is no. The variables in the called and calling program are completely isolated from one another, and may even use identical data names without causing a naming conflict. There is a way for some variables in a calling program to be available to a called program. This is covered in Bonus Day 2, "Miscellaneous COBOL Syntax."

18

Workshop

Quiz

1. When one program calls another program, which of the following happens to the calling program?

   a. It continues executing.

   b. It remains in memory, but waits for the calling program to complete.

   c. It drops out of memory and disappears.

2. In a called program, which of the following commands causes the called program to finish execution and return control to the calling program?

   a. EXIT PROGRAM

   b. STOP RUN

   c. END PERFORM

Exercises

1. Locate vnddsp02.cbl, which you created as an exercise for Day 13, "Deleting Records and Other Indexed File Operations." Copy it to vnddsp03.cbl, modify it to use the new SELECT and FD for the vendor file, and add program exit logic to it. Don't forget to change the PROGRAM-ID. Compile the program so that it is ready to run.

2. Copy vndmnt04.cbl to vndmnt05.cbl. Add a menu pick to display all records, and have that pick call the new vnddsp03.cbl. Compile the new vndmnt05.cbl and, if necessary, link it.

3. Run vndmnt05 and select the new menu pick. You probably will find a bug in the way it displays. The last screen of the vendor list is displayed and then disappears to be replaced by the menu as in the following sample output. There should be a pause where noted in the display, but instead, the last page scrolls off the screen and the menu is immediately displayed:

```
PLEASE SELECT:

       1.   ADD RECORDS
       2.   CHANGE A RECORD
       3.   LOOK UP A RECORD
       4.   DELETE A RECORD
       5.   LOOK UP BY NAME
       6.   PRINT RECORDS
       7.   PRINT IN NAME ORDER
       8.   DISPLAY ALL RECORDS

       0.   EXIT
```

```
YOUR CHOICE (0-8)?
8
VENDOR LIST                PAGE:      1
NO    NAME-ADDRESS                     CONTACT-PHONE-ZIP
00001 AERIAL SIGNS                     HENRIETTA MARKSON
BURBANK AIRPORT                 (818) 555-6066
HANGAR 305
BURBANK            CA           90016
00002 ABC PRINTING                     CHARLES JOHANSSEN
1624 FOOTHILL BLVD              (818) 555-4321
SUITE 34
LOS ANGELES        CA           91042
00003 CHARLES SMITH AND SONS           MARTHA HARRISON
1435 SOUTH STREET               (213) 555-4432
LOS ANGELES        CA           90064
```

```
PRESS ENTER TO CONTINUE. . .
VENDOR LIST              PAGE:      2
NO     NAME-ADDRESS                    CONTACT-PHONE-ZIP
00005 ALIAS SMITH AND JONES           ROBIN COUSINS
1216 MAIN STREET               415 555-9203
PALO ALTO          CA          90061
00014 RANIER GRAPHICS                 JULIA SIMPSON
4433 WASHINGTON ST             (213) 555-6789
LOS ANGELES        CA          90032
00022 ARTFUL DODGER
123 UNDERWOOD LANE             202 555-1234
MARKHAM            WA          40466
PRESS ENTER TO CONTINUE. . .
VENDOR LIST              PAGE:      3
NO     NAME-ADDRESS                    CONTACT-PHONE-ZIP
00067 ABC PRINTING                    HARRIET NELSON
1606 SOUTH 7TH                 (815) 555-2020
POMONA             CA          90404
01176 ABERCROMBIE AND OTHERS
1234 45TH ST.                  (213) 555-6543
SUITE 17
LOS ANGELES        CA          92345
01440 ZINZINDORFF INC.
1604 7TH ST                    (213) 555-7234
LOS ANGELES        CA          90404
```

(The display should pause at this point and wait for the user to press Enter.)

```
    PLEASE SELECT:

        1.   ADD RECORDS
        2.   CHANGE A RECORD
        3.   LOOK UP A RECORD
        4.   DELETE A RECORD
        5.   LOOK UP BY NAME
        6.   PRINT RECORDS
        7.   PRINT IN NAME ORDER
        8.   DISPLAY ALL RECORDS

        0.   EXIT
```

18

```
YOUR CHOICE (0-8)?
```

The assignment in this exercise is to add a Press ENTER message to vndmnt05.cbl
that is executed immediately after the return from vnddsp03.cbl.

4. Copy bilmnu01.cbl to bilmnu02.cbl, and modify it to call vndmnt05 instead of
   vndmnt04. Be sure to change the PROGRAM-ID.

Day 19

Complex Data Entry Problems

Data entry frequently is more complicated than the maintenance program examples that you have explored so far. Validations might be more complicated, data fields such as dates frequently cause problems, and some maintenance modules don't use all of the modes (add, change, inquire, and delete). Today, you explore the following topics:

- ☐ What is a control file?
- ☐ Creating a control file.
- ☐ Maintaining a control file.
- ☐ Multiple maintenance programs.
- ☐ Designing the bills payment system.
- ☐ Creating the voucher file.
- ☐ Handling date display.
- ☐ Handling date entry.

☐ What is a redefined variable?

☐ Handling date validation.

☐ Flexible date handling.

What Is a Control File?

In any large system, there are basic values that have to be tracked in various programs within the system:

☐ A payroll system has an employee file, allows time and work entries, and prints payroll checks. A program to add employees to the system might have to keep track of the last employee number used. When an employee is added to the system, the add mode might extract the last employee number and automatically assign the next number to the new employee.

☐ There has to be some value that the data entry program uses as the number of hours an employee can work before his pay goes into overtime rates.

☐ During check-printing, a program has to keep track of the last check number used, and it might have to look up the account number to be used for payroll checks. Whenever checks are printed, the last check number should be extracted and checks start printing from the next check number. The payroll checking account number also should be extracted and printed on each check. At the end of the print run, the last check number used should be updated with the number used at the end of the print run.

This type of information usually is stored in a file called a control file. A control file frequently contains a single record. This single record contains fields that hold all the information required for the system. Listing 19.1 is an example of an FD for a payroll system control file containing some of the fields described in the preceding paragraph.

TYPE **Listing 19.1. A payroll control file FD.**

```
001000 FD  PAYROLL-CONTROL-FILE
001100     LABEL RECORDS ARE STANDARD.
001200 01  PAYROLL-CONTROL-RECORD.
001300     05  PAYROLL-CONTROL-KEY              PIC 9.
001400     05  PAYROLL-CONTROL-LAST-EMPLOYEE    PIC 9(5).
001500     05  PAYROLL-CONTROL-OVERTIME-HOURS   PIC 99V99.
001600     05  PAYROLL-CONTROL-LAST-CHECK       PIC 9(6).
001700     05  PAYROLL-CONTROL-CHECK-ACCOUNT    PIC X(15).
```

ANALYSIS The payroll control file is an indexed file containing only one record. The key to the record always is 1. Any program that needs information from the control file would open the file, move 1 to the key, and read the record. The record could be updated by rewriting it.

It might seem odd to use an indexed file to store a single record, but there are reasons that an indexed file is used. Indexed files are easier to REWRITE. Because control files frequently contain information that is updated, such as last check number, they are updated in one or more programs. Indexed files also are easier to share. In a large system, one user might be adding an employee, two others entering data for hours worked, and yet another printing checks. All these programs need to share the control file, even though each is using only one part of it.

The control file that is used in the bill payment system also is an indexed file. It contains a key that always is 1 and a single field, CONTROL-LAST-VOUCHER.

 In a bills paying system, each new invoice that is received for payment is assigned a tracking number. This tracking number is the key to the voucher file, or bills file, and the number usually is called a *voucher number*.

This control file is used to assign voucher numbers automatically whenever a new invoice is added to the system. Listings 19.2 is the COPY file slcontrl.cbl and contains the SELECT for this control file.

TYPE | **Listing 19.2. The SELECT statement for a control file.**

```
000100*--------------------------------
000200* SLCONTRL.CBL
000300*--------------------------------
000400     SELECT CONTROL-FILE
000500         ASSIGN TO "CONTROL"
000600         ORGANIZATION IS INDEXED
000700         RECORD KEY IS CONTROL-KEY
000800         ACCESS MODE IS DYNAMIC.
000900
```

Listing 19.3 is the COPY file fdcontrl.cbl and contains the FD for this control file.

TYPE | **Listing 19.3. The FD for a control file.**

```
000100*--------------------------------
000200* FDCONTRL.CBL
000300* Primary Key - CONTROL-KEY
000400* LAST-VOUCHER is used
000500* to track the last
000600* used voucher number.
000700* This is a single record file
```

continues

19

Listing 19.3. continued

```
000800* CONTROL-KEY always = 1.
000900*--------------------------------
001000 FD  CONTROL-FILE
001100     LABEL RECORDS ARE STANDARD.
001200 01  CONTROL-RECORD.
001300     05  CONTROL-KEY              PIC 9.
001400     05  CONTROL-LAST-VOUCHER     PIC 9(5).
001500
```

Creating a Control File

Creating a new control file for a system is slightly different from creating another file in the system. A control file of the type that is used for the bills payment system is always expected to have that single record in it.

Listing 19.4 is similar to other build programs, but at lines 002400 through 002600, it loads and writes a single record to the file. This record contains a last voucher number of zeroes.

TYPE **Listing 19.4. Creating a control file with an initial record.**

```
000100 IDENTIFICATION DIVISION.
000200 PROGRAM-ID. CTLBLD01.
000300*--------------------------------
000400* Create a Control file for the
000500* bills payment system and write
000600* the initial record.
000700*--------------------------------
000800 ENVIRONMENT DIVISION.
000900 INPUT-OUTPUT SECTION.
001000 FILE-CONTROL.
001100
001200     COPY "SLCONTRL.CBL".
001300
001400 DATA DIVISION.
001500 FILE SECTION.
001600
001700     COPY "FDCONTRL.CBL".
001800
001900 WORKING-STORAGE SECTION.
002000
002100 PROCEDURE DIVISION.
002200 PROGRAM-BEGIN.
002300     OPEN OUTPUT CONTROL-FILE.
002400     MOVE 1 TO CONTROL-KEY.
002500     MOVE ZEROES TO CONTROL-LAST-VOUCHER.
002600     WRITE CONTROL-RECORD.
002700     CLOSE CONTROL-FILE.
```

```
002800
002900 PROGRAM-EXIT.
003000     EXIT PROGRAM.
003100
003200 PROGRAM-DONE.
003300     STOP RUN.
003400
```

Code Listing 19.2 and Listing 19.3 to create the SELECT and FD for the control file. Then code, compile, and run ctlbld01.cbl to create the new control file with its single record.

Maintaining a Control File

Basically, maintaining a control file requires only the change and inquire modes from a standard maintenance module. You never want to add records, and you certainly never want to delete the record, so only the change and inquire options are left.

Do	Don't

DO allow a user, or more likely a system administrator, to look up information in the control file, and make it possible to change the information.

DON'T allow anyone to delete the control record from the control file. Don't provide delete mode in the maintenance program.

Listing 19.5 is a maintenance program for the control file. It uses only change and inquire mode, which gives a user the ability of looking up the control information or changing the control information. The control record cannot be deleted, nor can a new record be added.

Listing 19.5. Maintaining a control file using change and inquire mode only.

TYPE

```
000100 IDENTIFICATION DIVISION.
000200 PROGRAM-ID. CTLMNT01.
000300*-----------------------------
000400* Change and Inquire only
000500* for the bills system control
000600* file.
000700*-----------------------------
000800 ENVIRONMENT DIVISION.
000900 INPUT-OUTPUT SECTION.
001000 FILE-CONTROL.
```

continues

Listing 19.5. continued

```
001100
001200      COPY "SLCONTRL.CBL".
001300
001400 DATA DIVISION.
001500 FILE SECTION.
001600
001700      COPY "FDCONTRL.CBL".
001800
001900 WORKING-STORAGE SECTION.
002000
002100 77  MENU-PICK                PIC 9.
002200      88  MENU-PICK-IS-VALID   VALUES 0 THRU 2.
002300
002400 77  THE-MODE                 PIC X(7).
002500 77  RECORD-FOUND             PIC X.
002600 77  WHICH-FIELD              PIC 9.
002700 77  A-DUMMY                  PIC X.
002800
002900 PROCEDURE DIVISION.
003000 PROGRAM-BEGIN.
003100      PERFORM OPENING-PROCEDURE.
003200      PERFORM MAIN-PROCESS.
003300      PERFORM CLOSING-PROCEDURE.
003400
003500 PROGRAM-EXIT.
003600      EXIT PROGRAM.
003700
003800 PROGRAM-DONE.
003900      STOP RUN.
004000
004100 OPENING-PROCEDURE.
004200      OPEN I-O CONTROL-FILE.
004300
004400 CLOSING-PROCEDURE.
004500      CLOSE CONTROL-FILE.
004600
004700
004800 MAIN-PROCESS.
004900      PERFORM GET-MENU-PICK.
005000      PERFORM MAINTAIN-THE-FILE
005100          UNTIL MENU-PICK = 0.
005200
005300*------------------------------
005400* MENU
005500*------------------------------
005600 GET-MENU-PICK.
005700      PERFORM DISPLAY-THE-MENU.
005800      PERFORM ACCEPT-MENU-PICK.
005900      PERFORM RE-ACCEPT-MENU-PICK
006000          UNTIL MENU-PICK-IS-VALID.
006100
006200 DISPLAY-THE-MENU.
006300      PERFORM CLEAR-SCREEN.
006400      DISPLAY "    PLEASE SELECT:".
```

```
006500      DISPLAY " ".
006600      DISPLAY "          1.   CHANGE   CONTROL INFORMATION".
006700      DISPLAY "          2.   DISPLAY CONTROL INFORMATION".
006800      DISPLAY " ".
006900      DISPLAY "          0.   EXIT".
007000      PERFORM SCROLL-LINE 8 TIMES.
007100
007200 ACCEPT-MENU-PICK.
007300      DISPLAY "YOUR CHOICE (0-2)?".
007400      ACCEPT MENU-PICK.
007500
007600 RE-ACCEPT-MENU-PICK.
007700      DISPLAY "INVALID SELECTION - PLEASE RE-TRY.".
007800      PERFORM ACCEPT-MENU-PICK.
007900
008000 CLEAR-SCREEN.
008100      PERFORM SCROLL-LINE 25 TIMES.
008200
008300 SCROLL-LINE.
008400      DISPLAY " ".
008500
008600 MAINTAIN-THE-FILE.
008700      PERFORM DO-THE-PICK.
008800      PERFORM GET-MENU-PICK.
008900
009000 DO-THE-PICK.
009100      IF MENU-PICK = 1
009200          PERFORM CHANGE-MODE
009300      ELSE
009400      IF MENU-PICK = 2
009500          PERFORM INQUIRE-MODE.
009600
009700*-------------------------------
009800* CHANGE
009900*-------------------------------
010000 CHANGE-MODE.
010100      MOVE "CHANGE" TO THE-MODE.
010200      PERFORM GET-CONTROL-RECORD.
010300      IF RECORD-FOUND = "Y"
010400          PERFORM CHANGE-RECORDS.
010500
010600 CHANGE-RECORDS.
010700      PERFORM GET-FIELD-TO-CHANGE.
010800      PERFORM CHANGE-ONE-FIELD.
010900
011000      PERFORM GET-CONTROL-RECORD.
011100
011200 GET-FIELD-TO-CHANGE.
011300      PERFORM DISPLAY-ALL-FIELDS.
011400      PERFORM ASK-WHICH-FIELD.
011500
011600 ASK-WHICH-FIELD.
011700      MOVE 1 TO WHICH-FIELD.
011800
011900 CHANGE-ONE-FIELD.
```

continues

Listing 19.5. continued

```
012000      PERFORM CHANGE-THIS-FIELD.
012100
012200 CHANGE-THIS-FIELD.
012300      IF WHICH-FIELD = 1
012400           PERFORM ENTER-CONTROL-LAST-VOUCHER.
012500
012600      PERFORM REWRITE-CONTROL-RECORD.
012700
012800*-------------------------------
012900* INQUIRE
013000*-------------------------------
013100 INQUIRE-MODE.
013200      MOVE "DISPLAY" TO THE-MODE.
013300      PERFORM GET-CONTROL-RECORD.
013400      IF RECORD-FOUND = "Y"
013500           PERFORM INQUIRE-RECORDS.
013600
013700 INQUIRE-RECORDS.
013800      PERFORM DISPLAY-ALL-FIELDS.
013900      PERFORM PRESS-ENTER.
014000
014100 PRESS-ENTER.
014200      DISPLAY " ".
014300      DISPLAY "PRESS ENTER TO CONTINUE".
014400      ACCEPT A-DUMMY.
014500
014600*-------------------------------
014700* Routines for Change
014800*-------------------------------
014900 ENTER-CONTROL-LAST-VOUCHER.
015000      PERFORM ACCEPT-CONTROL-LAST-VOUCHER.
015100
015200 ACCEPT-CONTROL-LAST-VOUCHER.
015300      DISPLAY "ENTER LAST VOUCHER NUMBER".
015400      ACCEPT CONTROL-LAST-VOUCHER.
015500
015600*-------------------------------
015700* Routines shared by Change and Inquire
015800*-------------------------------
015900 INIT-CONTROL-RECORD.
016000      MOVE ZEROES TO CONTROL-RECORD.
016100
016200 ENTER-CONTROL-KEY.
016300      MOVE 1 TO CONTROL-KEY.
016400
016500 GET-CONTROL-RECORD.
016600      PERFORM INIT-CONTROL-RECORD.
016700      PERFORM ENTER-CONTROL-KEY.
016800      MOVE "N" TO RECORD-FOUND.
016900      PERFORM FIND-CONTROL-RECORD.
017000
017100 FIND-CONTROL-RECORD.
017200      PERFORM READ-CONTROL-RECORD.
```

```
017300     IF RECORD-FOUND = "N"
017400         DISPLAY "RECORD NOT FOUND"
017500         DISPLAY "YOU MUST RUN CTLBLD01"
017600         DISPLAY "TO CREATE THIS FILE".
017700
017800 DISPLAY-ALL-FIELDS.
017900     DISPLAY " ".
018000     PERFORM DISPLAY-CONTROL-LAST-VOUCHER.
018100     DISPLAY " ".
018200
018300 DISPLAY-CONTROL-LAST-VOUCHER.
018400     DISPLAY "1. LAST VOUCHER NUMBER: "
018500               CONTROL-LAST-VOUCHER.
018600
018700*--------------------------------
018800* File I-O Routines
018900*--------------------------------
019000 READ-CONTROL-RECORD.
019100     MOVE "Y" TO RECORD-FOUND.
019200     READ CONTROL-FILE RECORD
019300       INVALID KEY
019400         MOVE "N" TO RECORD-FOUND.
019500
019600*or  READ CONTROL-FILE RECORD WITH LOCK
019700*      INVALID KEY
019800*        MOVE "N" TO RECORD-FOUND.
019900
020000*or  READ CONTROL-FILE RECORD WITH HOLD
020100*      INVALID KEY
020200*        MOVE "N" TO RECORD-FOUND.
020300
020400 REWRITE-CONTROL-RECORD.
020500     REWRITE CONTROL-RECORD
020600         INVALID KEY
020700         DISPLAY "ERROR REWRITING CONTROL RECORD".
020800
```

ANALYSIS   There are two other features in the control maintenance program, the use of a permanent key value of 1, and the absence of the key value on the display. The key to the record always is a value of 1. Rather than asking the user to enter a value, at line 016200, the ENTER-CONTROL-KEY routine moves 1 to CONTROL-KEY.

If 1 is not a valid key for the record, something has gone wrong and the control record has been deleted somehow. The FIND-CONTROL-RECORD routine at line 017100 expands on the standard "RECORD NOT FOUND" message by adding some additional messages at lines 017500 and 017600.

The control key itself is not a number that the user ever needs to enter or even see, so the DISPLAY-ALL-FIELDS routine at line 017800 is reduced to displaying the single field in the control file, CONTROL-LAST-VOUCHER.

19

In other maintenance modules, the user is put into a loop to change or look up a record, the record is displayed and modified, and then the user is asked for the key of another record to display or change. With this control file, that loop would be pointless because there is only one record in the file, which causes a problem in inquire mode. The fields (in this case, a single field) are displayed and the user is not asked for another key, but is returned immediately to the menu. In inquire mode, the information flashes briefly on the screen and then the menu is displayed.

To slow down the display so that the user has a chance to read the information, INQUIRE-RECORDS at line 013700 includes a request to perform a PRESS-ENTER routine at line 013900. This enables the user to see the record and then press Enter before being returned to the menu.

There is an exercise at the end of today's lesson to compare a simple maintenance module such as stcmnt04.cbl with ctlmnt01.cbl. You might want to try this exercise right away.

Code, compile, and run ctlmnt01.cbl and ensure that you can change and display the last voucher number. Use ctlmnt01.cbl to reset this number to zeroes.

Multiple Maintenance Programs

The bills payment system will use more than one program to maintain the voucher file, which is shown in Listing 19.6 and which is a COPY file for the voucher FD.

TYPE   **Listing 19.6. The FD for the voucher file.**

```
000100*---------------------------------
000200* FDVOUCH.CBL
000300* Primary Key - VOUCHER-NUMBER
000400*Dates are in CCYYMMDD format
000500 FD   VOUCHER-FILE
000600      LABEL RECORDS ARE STANDARD.
000700 01   VOUCHER-RECORD.
000800      05   VOUCHER-NUMBER          PIC 9(5).
000900      05   VOUCHER-VENDOR          PIC 9(5).
001000      05   VOUCHER-INVOICE         PIC X(15).
001100      05   VOUCHER-FOR             PIC X(30).
001200      05   VOUCHER-AMOUNT          PIC S9(6)V99.
001300      05   VOUCHER-DATE            PIC 9(8).
001400      05   VOUCHER-DUE             PIC 9(8).
001500      05   VOUCHER-DEDUCTIBLE      PIC X.
001600      05   VOUCHER-SELECTED        PIC X.
001700      05   VOUCHER-PAID-AMOUNT     PIC S9(6)V99.
001800      05   VOUCHER-PAID-DATE       PIC 9(8).
001900      05   VOUCHER-CHECK-NO        PIC 9(6).
002000
```

ANALYSIS Whenever a new bill comes in, the user will use a standard maintenance module to add the information to the file. The voucher number will be assigned automatically in add mode. The user will be required to enter the vendor, vendor's invoice number, a comment on what the invoice is for, the amount of the invoice, the invoice date and due date, and a yes/no flag as to whether this is tax deductible. Basically, this encompasses all the fields from line 000900 through line 001500.

The remaining fields, from line 001600 through 001800, are filled in by the computer in add mode. VOUCHER-SELECTED is set to "N"; VOUCHER-PAID-AMOUNT, VOUCHER-PAID-DATE, and VOUCHER-CHECK-NO are set to zero.

All the date fields in the voucher file use an eight digit date in the form CCYYMMDD. CCYY represents a full four digit year, such as 1997. Until recently it has been a tradition, based on the original very expensive costs of memory and disk space, to store dates as YYMMDD. This practice is causing a major problem in the computer industry as the year 2000 approaches. This issue is covered extensively in Bonus Day 6, "Dates and the Year 2000."

A separate program enables the user to select which vouchers should be paid, and yet another program enables the user to enter the paid amount, paid date, and check number. Here is an example of more than one program maintaining a single file.

The voucher file has a single key—the voucher number—and Listing 19.7 is the COPY file slvouch.cbl containing the SELECT statement for the file.

TYPE **Listing 19.7. The SELECT statement for the voucher file.**

```
000100*- - - - - - - - - - - - - - - - - - - - - - - - - - - -
000200* SLVOUCH.CBL
000300*- - - - - - - - - - - - - - - - - - - - - - - - - - - -
000400    SELECT VOUCHER-FILE
000500        ASSIGN TO "VOUCHER"
000600        ORGANIZATION IS INDEXED
000700        RECORD KEY IS VOUCHER-NUMBER
000800        ACCESS MODE IS DYNAMIC.
000900
```

Designing the Bills Payment System

First, look at the basic design of the bills paying system, and then start putting together the programs you need to implement the system.

NEW TERM A *flowchart* is a graphic representation of how a program or activity moves through various processes or program routines. It uses symbols to represent the activities and arrows to represent the direction of activity through the processes.

You can use flowcharts to define the behavior of a single program or a system (a combination of programs).

Figure 19.1 shows a flowchart representing how the bills system operates. At step 1 in the diagram, the arrival of a new bill is represented by a shape used to stand for a document.

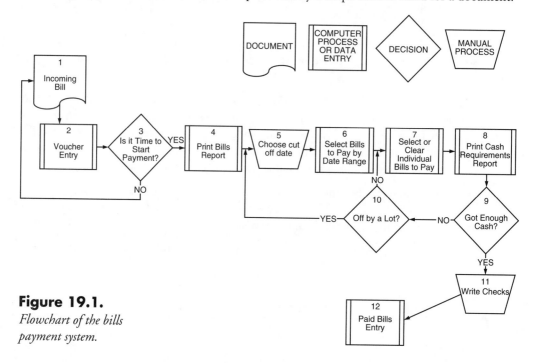

Figure 19.1.

Flowchart of the bills payment system.

At step 2, the bill is keyed into the computer as a voucher. Step 2 is a voucher entry program very much like a standard maintenance module, as described in the analysis of Listing 19.6.

At step 3, a decision is made whether to start bills payment. This decision is made by a person and usually is based on a regular bills payment schedule, which could be weekly or biweekly. If it is not time to start paying the bills, the flow of the system loops back up to await the arrival of any more bills. Steps 1, 2, and 3 are repeated while bills continue to come in.

When the decision is made to start the bill payment cycle, the bills report is printed at step 4. Step 4 is a program that prints all the outstanding vouchers (bills) in the voucher file.

This system is designed to pay by dateline, so step 5 defines a manual process of deciding through which date to pay bills. The decision involves someone sitting down with the bills report and making a decision about what cutoff date to use.

Step 6 is a program that enables the user to enter the selected cutoff date, and it flags all bills due within the cutoff date as ready to be paid by writing a "Y" to the VOUCHER-SELECTED flag.

Step 7 is a program that allows for the VOUCHER-SELECTED flag to be adjusted. This program can be used to set the flag to "Y" or "N" for any voucher (bill) that is as yet unpaid. This program enables the user to fine-tune the selections made in step 6 by including or excluding vouchers to pay.

Step 8 is a program that prints the cash requirements report. This report provides a total of all the cash needed to pay the bills selected in steps 6 and 7.

Step 9 is another human decision. Someone sits down with the cash requirements report and the bank balance and decides whether there is enough cash to fulfill the cash requirements.

If there is not enough cash, the user proceeds to step 10 where another decision is made: How bad is the shortfall? If the cash requirements grossly exceeds the available cash, the process returns to the beginning of the loop at step 5 where the user once again selects a cutoff date that will encompass fewer bills. If the shortfall is not large, the user returns to step 6 and uses the VOUCHER-SELECTED adjustment program to trim off some bills that won't be paid.

This process is continued until the answer to step 9 is yes and there is enough cash. Then the process continues to step 11, where the user manually writes the checks for each voucher in the final version of the cash requirements report.

At step 12, a data entry program enables the user to pull up the selected vouchers and mark them as paid. The system also includes some programs that enable you to report on paid bills.

Creating the Voucher File

Listing 19.8 is a familiar program used to create a new voucher file.

TYPE **Listing 19.8. Creating a voucher file.**

```
000100 IDENTIFICATION DIVISION.
000200 PROGRAM-ID. VCHBLD01.
000300*------------------------------
000400* Create a Voucher file for the
000500* bills payment system
000600*------------------------------
000700 ENVIRONMENT DIVISION.
000800 INPUT-OUTPUT SECTION.
000900 FILE-CONTROL.
001000
001100     COPY "SLVOUCH.CBL".
```

continues

Listing 19.8. continued

```
001200
001300 DATA DIVISION.
001400 FILE SECTION.
001500
001600     COPY "FDVOUCH.CBL".
001700
001800 WORKING-STORAGE SECTION.
001900
002000 PROCEDURE DIVISION.
002100 PROGRAM-BEGIN.
002200     OPEN OUTPUT VOUCHER-FILE.
002300     CLOSE VOUCHER-FILE.
002400
002500 PROGRAM-EXIT.
002600     EXIT PROGRAM.
002700
002800 PROGRAM-DONE.
002900     STOP RUN.
003000
```

Edit, compile, and run this program to create the new voucher file.

Handling Date Storage

Before launching into the actual maintenance module, you need to take a look at date handling.

The first problem with dates is storing them. Dates traditionally have been stored as a six-digit number in COBOL data files, either in YYMMDD format or MMDDYY format (in Europe, this is DDMMYY). January 7th, 1994 is stored as 940107 (YYMMDD), 010794 (MMDDYY), or 070194 (DDMMYY).

Storing a date in either MMDDYY or DDMMYY format presents some problems. In Table 19.1, several dates are listed in MMDDYY format and YYMMDD format. Each list contains the same dates. The first list, in MMDDYY format, is sorted correctly in numeric order, but is an incorrect sort for date order. The second list, in YYMMDD format, is sorted correctly as numbers and also is a correct sort for dates.

19

Table 19.1. Incorrect and correct sorts for date formats.

Sorted Dates in MMDDYY Format	Sorted Dates in YYMMDD Format
011592	870814
011593	870919
021291	880711
031492	890523
041893	900630
052389	910212
063090	911011
071188	920115
081487	920314
091987	921128
101191	930115
112892	930418
121693	931216

When the date format is changed to an eight-digit equivalent, MMDDCCYY, the sorting problem remains. Therefore, for the exercises in this book, you should store all dates in CCYYMMDD format so that date order and numeric order are the same.

The second problem is just an extension of the first problem. The approach of the year 2000 has caused a lot of consternation in COBOL circles. There are millions of lines of code currently in use that still use a six-digit date. The continued use of a six-digit date will cause big sorting problems even if the date is stored in YYMMDD format. When the user is looking for records dated between December 1, 1999, and February 28, 2000, the program will be looking at values that are stored as 991201 and 000228, because trying to store a four-digit year of 2000 in a two digit field only allows room for last two digits, 00.

One immediate solution is to start storing dates as eight digits by extending the year to the left and using a CCYYMMDD format where CCYY is a full four-digit year with CC representing the hundreds portion of the year. The voucher file provides for an eight-digit date. This isn't going to handle the millions of lines of code that aren't using four-digit years, but at least it won't compound the problem.

19

NOTE

When discussing dates in CCYYMMDD or similar formats with anyone, be sure that you understand the date format that he or she is discussing. Some people use CC or C to designate a "century indicator" that might not be an actual two-digit 19 or 20. In one system a zero represents 18, a 1 represents 19, a 2 represents 20, and so on. There are already a confusing number of date standards being propounded by various people. I use CC to indicate the two digits that represent the hundreds of years—18, 19, 20, and so on. Thus, CCYY format is the same as YYYY format.

The date problem for existing programs is covered in Bonus Day 6.

Handling Date Display

The third problem is formatting dates for display. If the date is stored in CCYYMMDD format, it has to be converted to MM/DD/CCYY format for displaying and printing. The CCYYMMDD format works well for the programmer who can use this format for correct sorting of dates, but users are accustomed to seeing dates as MM/DD/CCYY or MM-DD-CCYY.

You already have used editing characters to modify the way a number displays. Some of the editing characters, such as the comma (,), are inserted into a numeric field to change the way the field appears when it is displayed. Moving a value such as 09456.01 to a PIC ZZ,ZZZ.ZZ results in a display of 9,456.01. The leading zero is suppressed and the comma is inserted.

There is an editing character that was designed specifically for date handling. It is the slant or slash (/). A slash placed in a numeric field causes the field to become an edited field, and the slashes are inserted into any number moved into the field. Listing 19.9 is a code fragment showing the use of an edited numeric field used to display slashes within a date. The display at line 032100 would be 05/15/1997.

TYPE **Listing 19.9. Formatting a date field with slashes.**

```
011200 77  FORMATTED-DATE          PIC 99/99/9999.

032000     MOVE 05151997 TO FORMATTED-DATE.
032100     DISPLAY FORMATTED-DATE.
```

Zero suppression can be used in an edited date field, as shown in Listing 19.10. The output of this example would be 5/15/1997, with the leading zero suppressed.

TYPE **Listing 19.10. Zero suppression in a formatted date.**

```
011200 77  FORMATTED-DATE          PIC Z9/99/9999.

032000     MOVE 05151997 TO FORMATTED-DATE.
032100     DISPLAY FORMATTED-DATE.
```

The use of a simple edited field will add in the slashes, but both of the dates used in Listings 19.9 and 19.10 are in MMDDCCYY format. Listing 19.11 converts a date in CCYYMMDD format to MMDDCCYY, and then moves it to an edited field.

TYPE **Listing 19.11. Converting CCYYMMDD to MMDDCCYY.**

```
011200 77  FORMATTED-DATE          PIC Z9/99/9999.
011300 77  DATE-CCYYMMDD           PIC 9(8).
011400 77  DATE-MMDDCCYY           PIC 9(8).

031900     MOVE 19970515 TO DATE-CCYYMMDD.
032000     COMPUTE DATE-MMDDCCYY =
032100          DATE-CCYYMMDD * 10000.0001
032200     MOVE DATE-MMDDCCYY TO FORMATTED-DATE.
032300     DISPLAY FORMATTED-DATE.
```

ANALYSIS The formatted (edited) date field is defined at line 011200. Two separate PIC 9(8) variables are defined to hold the date in CCYYMMDD and MMDDCCYY at lines 011300 and 011400, respectively.

The code fragment at line 031900 starts by moving May 15, 1997, in CCYYMMDD format, to the appropriate variable.

The COMPUTE command is used to multiply DATE-CCYYMMDD by 10000.0001 and store the result in DATE-MMDDCCYY. This trick is used to convert the date.

The date starts out as 19970515. Multiplying it by 10000.0001 results in 199705151997, a 12-digit number. The COMPUTE command stores the result in DATE-MMDDCCYY, which is only eight digits long. Numeric variables are truncated on the left, so the initial 1997 is lost, leaving 05151997, which is the correct value for an MMDDCCYY format.

Handling Date Entry

The fourth problem with dates concerns the data entry format versus the storage format, which is partly the reverse of the date display. Users still are accustomed to entering dates as MM/DD/YY, and as the new century approaches, they may have to get used to entering values as MM/DD/CCYY. This format includes characters that are not stored in the file (the slashes), and the parts of the date are not arranged correctly for CCYYMMDD storage. An entry of MM/DD/CCYY has to be converted to CCYYMMDD to be stored correctly.

The easiest solution is to use a formatted date field as the data entry field, an example of which appears in Listing 19.12.

TYPE   **Listing 19.12. Accepting formatted dates.**

```
000100 IDENTIFICATION DIVISION.
000200 PROGRAM-ID. DATE01.
000300*-------------------------------
000400* Demo of Date Entry
000500*-------------------------------
000600 ENVIRONMENT DIVISION.
000700 INPUT-OUTPUT SECTION.
000800 FILE-CONTROL.
000900
001000 DATA DIVISION.
001100 FILE SECTION.
001200
001300 WORKING-STORAGE SECTION.
001400
001500 77   DATE-ENTRY-FIELD    PIC Z9/99/9999.
001600 77   DATE-MMDDCCYY       PIC 9(8).
001700 77   DATE-CCYYMMDD       PIC 9(8).
001800
001900 PROCEDURE DIVISION.
002000 PROGRAM-BEGIN.
002100     PERFORM OPENING-PROCEDURE.
002200     PERFORM MAIN-PROCESS.
002300     PERFORM CLOSING-PROCEDURE.
002400
002500 PROGRAM-EXIT.
002600     EXIT PROGRAM.
002700
002800 PROGRAM-DONE.
002900     STOP RUN.
003000
003100 OPENING-PROCEDURE.
003200
003300 CLOSING-PROCEDURE.
003400
003500 MAIN-PROCESS.
003600     PERFORM GET-A-DATE.
003700     PERFORM DISPLAY-AND-GET-DATE
003800         UNTIL DATE-MMDDCCYY = ZEROES.
003900
004000 GET-A-DATE.
004100     DISPLAY "ENTER A DATE (MM/DD/CCYY)".
004200     ACCEPT DATE-ENTRY-FIELD.
004300     MOVE DATE-ENTRY-FIELD TO DATE-MMDDCCYY.
004400     COMPUTE DATE-CCYYMMDD =
004500             DATE-MMDDCCYY * 10000.0001.
```

```
004600
004700 DISPLAY-AND-GET-DATE.
004800     PERFORM DISPLAY-A-DATE.
004900     PERFORM GET-A-DATE.
005000
005100 DISPLAY-A-DATE.
005200     MOVE DATE-MMDDCCYY TO DATE-ENTRY-FIELD.
000300     DISPLAY "FORMATTED DATE IS " DATE-ENTRY-FIELD.
005400     DISPLAY "DATE-MMDDCCYY IS " DATE-MMDDCCYY.
005500     DISPLAY "DATE-CCYYMMDD IS " DATE-CCYYMMDD.
005600
```

 Using the formatted date field defined at line 001500 for data entry allows the user to enter any eight digits, including optional slashes at line 004200 in the ACCEPT command.

The user can enter 01/22/1996 or 01221996, and either version is stored in DATE-MMDDCCYY as 01221996. That takes care of enabling the user to enter a date including slashes.

Some COBOL compilers will require that line 004300 read: MOVE WITH CONVERSION DATA-ENTRY-FIELD TO DATE-MMDDCCYY.

At lines 004400 and 004500, the same conversion trick is used to convert DATE-MMDDCCYY to DATE-CCYYMMDD. Try it out with a pencil and paper, and you will see that multiplying an eight-digit number by 10,000.0001, and then truncating the twelve-digit answer from the left to eight digits has the effect of swapping the left and right four digits of the eight-digit number.

At line 005100, the DISPLAY-A-DATE routine displays the various date formats.

Code, compile, and run date01.cbl and enter various valid eight-digit dates, with and without slashes. You will see the effect of using an edited field for the data entry.

What Is a Redefined Variable?

Run date01.cbl and enter some invalid dates, such as 12345 (not eight digits), or 31/64/2219 (month and day are both invalid). The date01.cbl program accepts these without question, because as far as date01.cbl is concerned it is accepting numbers that happen to have slashes in them. In order to ensure that the date is valid, you are going to have to do some work in the program.

In order to validate a date, you need to be able to take the date (either DATE-CCYYMMDD or DATE-MMDDCCYY) and break it into month, day, and year, and then validate each part of the date.

It seems at first glance that Listing 19.13 does the job, but there is a problem with this method of defining a date field. In Listing 19.13, DATE-CC represents the hundreds of years.

19

TYPE   **Listing 19.13. Trying to break up the date.**

```
001100 01   DATE-CCYYMMDD.
001200      05   DATE-CC          PIC 99.
001300      05   DATE-YY          PIC 99.
001400      05   DATE-MM          PIC 99.
001500      05   DATE-DD          PIC 99.
```

In order to understand this problem, it is necessary to take another look at structure variables. Recall that when variables are going to be used as a group, they can be combined into a single variable called a structure or a record. A structure or record is a variable containing one or more COBOL variables. In Listing 19.14, the variable named ALL-THE-VARIABLES contains the three variables 1ST-NUMBER, 2ND-NUMBER, and 3RD-NUMBER. ALL-THE-VARIABLES is a structure.

TYPE   **Listing 19.14. A structure variable.**

```
000900 01   ALL-THE-VARIABLES.
001000      05   1ST-NUMBER       PIC 99.
001100      05   2ND-NUMBER       PIC 99.
001200      05   3RD-NUMBER       PIC 99.
```

ANALYSIS   Listing 19.14 actually defines six bytes of memory that contain four variables: 1ST-NUMBER, 2ND-NUMBER, 3RD-NUMBER, and ALL-THE-VARIABLES.

1ST-NUMBER is two bytes long and is designed to hold a PIC 99. 2ND-NUMBER and 3RD-NUMBER also are designed to hold two-byte numbers. This is a total of six bytes.

The structure variable itself, ALL-THE-VARIABLES, is six bytes long and occupies the same six bytes as 1ST-NUMBER, 2ND-NUMBER, and 3RD-NUMBER.

When a structure variable is created, it doesn't matter what the pictures of the subordinate variables are. COBOL forces the structure variable to have an alphanumeric data type.

Because of the way COBOL treats structure variables, ALL-THE-VARIABLES has an implied alphanumeric data type, so its picture becomes PIC X(6).

In effect, line 000900 defines a six-byte variable with a PICTURE of X(6), and lines 001000 through 001200 redefine those six bytes as three variables each with a PICTURE of 99.

In COBOL, this redefinition occurs in any structure variable. The structure variable has an implied picture of PIC X(some number), and the subordinate variables can have numeric pictures.

19

At this point you might want to review Day 8, "Structured Data," which presents the organization of a structure variable in some detail.

In Listing 19.15, which is a repeat of the problem posed in Listing 19.13 (a date broken into separate elements), DATE-CCYYMMDD is an alphanumeric variable with a picture of PIC X(8), even though the individual parts are all PIC 99 fields. You need each of the individual parts of DATE-CCYYMMDD to have a PIC 99, but you also need DATE-CCYYMMDD to be numeric with a picture of PIC 9(8).

TYPE **Listing 19.15.** DATE-CCYYMMDD **is a** PIC X(8)**.**

```
001100 01   DATE-CCYYMMDD.
001200      05   DATE-CC         PIC 99.
001300      05   DATE-YY         PIC 99.
001400      05   DATE-MM         PIC 99.
001500      05   DATE-DD         PIC 99.
```

In COBOL, it is possible to create a variable that specifically redefines another variable. Listing 19.16 is an example of how this is done.

TYPE **Listing 19.16. A redefinition.**

```
001100 01   AN-X-FIELD              PIC X(6).
001200 01   A-9-FIELD REDEFINES
001300      AN-X-FIELD              PIC 9(6).
```

ANALYSIS In Listing 19.16, the variable defined at lines 001200 and 001300 is a redefinition of the variable defined at line 001100. The variable at line 001100 defines a six-byte variable that is used for alphanumeric data. The variable at lines 001200 and 001300 redefines the same six bytes as a variable to be used for numeric data.

In Listing 19.15, you end up with DATE-CCYYMMDD as a PIC X(8), but you really want it to be a PIC 9(8). You can use a REDEFINES to create that situation. A REDEFINES can be used to redefine any variable, even a structure variable, as shown in Listing 19.17.

TYPE **Listing 19.17. Using** REDEFINES **to define a new variable.**

```
001100 01   A-DATE.
001200      05   DATE-CC              PIC 99.
001300      05   DATE-YY              PIC 99.
001400      05   DATE-MM              PIC 99.
001500      05   DATE-DD              PIC 99.
001600 01   DATE-CCYYMMDD REDEFINES
001700      A-DATE                    PIC 9(8).
```

19

Lines 001100 through 001500 define a structure variable named A-DATE containing four variables that are each a PIC 99. A-DATE will become a PIC X(8). A-DATE is of little use, so the name used for the variable is unimportant.

At lines 001600 and 001700, the eight-byte variable A-DATE is redefined as a PIC 9(8) variable with the name DATE-CCYYMMDD. This redefinition creates the effect that you want. DATE-CCYYMMDD is a numeric variable with a picture of PIC 9(8). Each of the parts of the date is also numeric, having pictures of PIC 99.

If you move the value 19970315 to DATE-CCYYMMDD, the eight bytes of memory will contain the values for the number 19970315.

A-DATE will contain those eight bytes as "19970315", which are the same bytes but interpreted as characters. DATE-CC will contain two bytes: the number 19. DATE-YY will contain two bytes: the number 97. DATE-MM will contain two bytes: the number 03. DATE-DD will contain two bytes: the number 15.

In the preceding example, a structure variable A-DATE is redefined as an elementary (nonstructured) variable called DATE-CCYYMMDD. A-DATE is the redefined variable and DATE-CCYYMMDD is the redefining variable.

In a redefinition, either or both of the redefined and redefining variables can be structure variables.

In Listing 19.18, the positions of the two variables are reversed. DATE-CCYYMMDD becomes the redefined variable, and it is redefined with the structure variable, A-DATE. A-DATE is then broken into its elementary variables.

TYPE **Listing 19.18. Redefining a variable with a structure.**

```
001600 01   DATE-CCYYMMDD          PIC 9(8).
001700 01   A-DATE REDEFINES   DATE-CCYYMMDD.
001800      05   DATE-CC            PIC 99.
001900      05   DATE-YY            PIC 99.
002000      05   DATE-MM            PIC 99.
002100      05   DATE-DD            PIC 99.
```

A variable can be redefined by using the COBOL REDEFINES command. The redefined variable and the redefining variable must have the same level number.

The redefining variable must not have a length longer than the redefined variable. The compiler would complain about the example in Listing 19.19 because DATE-CCYYMMDD on line 001600 is only six bytes long, but A-DATE is 8 bytes long.

19

TYPE **Listing 19.19. An illegal** REDEFINES.

```
001600 01   DATE-CCYYMMDD          PIC 9(6).
001700 01   A-DATE REDEFINES   DATE-CCYYMMDD.
001800      05   DATE-CC           PIC 99.
001900      05   DATE-YY           PIC 99.
002000      05   DATE-MM           PIC 99.
002100      05   DATE-DD           PIC 99.
```

There is one more step you need to take to complete the redefinition of the date fields. A-DATE will never be used. All you want is the numeric versions of DATE-CCYYMMDD, DATE-CC, DATE-YY, and so on. Therefore, A-DATE can be converted to a FILLER as in Listing 19.20.

TYPE **Listing 19.20. The final date** REDEFINES.

```
001600 01   DATE-CCYYMMDD          PIC 9(8).
001700 01   FILLER REDEFINES   DATE-CCYYMMDD.
001800      05   DATE-CC           PIC 99.
001900      05   DATE-YY           PIC 99.
002000      05   DATE-MM           PIC 99.
002100      05   DATE-DD           PIC 99.
```

Handling Date Validation

Date validation is the process of taking a date apart and checking that the parts are valid. Listing 19.21, date02.cbl, includes a date validation routine.

TYPE **Listing 19.21. A demonstration of date validation.**

```
000100 IDENTIFICATION DIVISION.
000200 PROGRAM-ID. DATE02.
000300*---------------------------------
000400* Demo of Date Entry and validation
000500*---------------------------------
000600 ENVIRONMENT DIVISION.
000700 INPUT-OUTPUT SECTION.
000800 FILE-CONTROL.
000900
001000 DATA DIVISION.
001100 FILE SECTION.
001200
001300 WORKING-STORAGE SECTION.
001400
001500 77   DATE-ENTRY-FIELD   PIC Z9/99/9999.
```

continues

19

Listing 19.21. continued

```
001600 77   DATE-MMDDCCYY      PIC 9(8).
001700 77   DATE-QUOTIENT      PIC 9999.
001800 77   DATE-REMAINDER     PIC 9999.
001900
002000 77   VALID-DATE-FLAG    PIC X.
002100      88   DATE-IS-INVALID   VALUE "N".
002200      88   DATE-IS-ZERO      VALUE "0".
002300      88   DATE-IS-VALID     VALUE "Y".
002400      88   DATE-IS-OK        VALUES "Y" "0".
002500
002600 01   DATE-CCYYMMDD      PIC 9(8).
002700 01   FILLER REDEFINES DATE-CCYYMMDD.
002800      05   DATE-CCYY    PIC 9999.
002900      05   DATE-MM      PIC 99.
003000      05   DATE-DD      PIC 99.
003100
003200
003300 PROCEDURE DIVISION.
003400 PROGRAM-BEGIN.
003500      PERFORM OPENING-PROCEDURE.
003600      PERFORM MAIN-PROCESS.
003700      PERFORM CLOSING-PROCEDURE.
003800
003900 PROGRAM-EXIT.
004000      EXIT PROGRAM.
004100
004200 PROGRAM-DONE.
004300      STOP RUN.
004400
004500 OPENING-PROCEDURE.
004600
004700 CLOSING-PROCEDURE.
004800
004900 MAIN-PROCESS.
005000      PERFORM GET-A-DATE.
005100      PERFORM DISPLAY-AND-GET-DATE
005200          UNTIL DATE-MMDDCCYY = ZEROES.
005300
005400 GET-A-DATE.
005500      PERFORM ACCEPT-A-DATE.
005600      PERFORM RE-ACCEPT-A-DATE
005700          UNTIL DATE-IS-OK.
005800
005900 ACCEPT-A-DATE.
006000      DISPLAY "ENTER A DATE (MM/DD/CCYY)".
006100      ACCEPT DATE-ENTRY-FIELD.
006200
006300      PERFORM EDIT-CHECK-DATE.
006400
006500 RE-ACCEPT-A-DATE.
006600      DISPLAY "INVALID DATE".
006700      PERFORM ACCEPT-A-DATE.
006800
006900 EDIT-CHECK-DATE.
```

19

```
007000      PERFORM EDIT-DATE.
007100      PERFORM CHECK-DATE.
007200
007300 EDIT-DATE.
007400      MOVE DATE-ENTRY-FIELD TO DATE-MMDDCCYY.
007500      COMPUTE DATE-CCYYMMDD =
007600              DATE-MMDDCCYY * 10000.0001.
007700
007800*--------------------------------
007900* Assume that the date is good, then
008000* test the date in the following
008100* steps. The routine stops if any
008200* of these conditions is true,
008300* and sets the valid date flag.
008400* Condition 1 returns the valid date
008500* flag set to "0".
008600* If any other condition is true,
008700* the valid date flag is set to "N".
008800* 1.  Is the date zeroes
008900* 2.  Month > 12 or < 1
009000* 3.  Day < 1 or  > 31
009100* 4.  Day > 30 and
009200*     Month = 2 (February)  or
009300*              4 (April)    or
009400*              6 (June)     or
009500*              9 (September) or
009600*             11 (November)
009700*     Day > 29 and
009800*     Month = 2 (February)
009900* 5.  Day = 29 and Month = 2 and
010000*     Not a leap year
010100* ( A leap year is any year evenly
010200*   divisible by 4, but does not
010300*   end in 00 and that is
010400*   not evenly divisible by 400).
010500*--------------------------------
010600 CHECK-DATE.
010700      MOVE "Y" TO VALID-DATE-FLAG.
010800      PERFORM CHECK-IF-DATE-ZEROES.
010900      IF DATE-IS-VALID
011000         PERFORM CHECK-MM.
011100      IF DATE-IS-VALID
011200         PERFORM CHECK-DD.
011300      IF DATE-IS-VALID
011400         PERFORM CHECK-MMDD.
011500      IF DATE-IS-VALID
011600         PERFORM CHECK-LEAP-YEAR.
011700
011800 CHECK-IF-DATE-ZEROES.
011900      IF DATE-CCYYMMDD = ZEROES
012000         MOVE "0" TO VALID-DATE-FLAG.
012100
012200 CHECK-MM.
012300      IF DATE-MM < 1 OR DATE-MM > 12
012400         MOVE "N" TO VALID-DATE-FLAG.
```

continues

Listing 19.21. continued

```
012500
012600 CHECK-DD.
012700     IF DATE-DD < 1 OR DATE-DD > 31
012800         MOVE "N" TO VALID-DATE-FLAG.
012900
013000 CHECK-MMDD.
013100     IF (DATE-DD > 30) AND
013200         (DATE-MM = 2 OR 4 OR 6 OR 9 OR 11)
013300         MOVE "N" TO VALID-DATE-FLAG
013400     ELSE
013500     IF DATE-DD > 29 AND DATE-MM = 2
013600         MOVE "N" TO VALID-DATE-FLAG.
013700
013800 CHECK-LEAP-YEAR.
013900     IF DATE-DD = 29 AND DATE-MM = 2
014000         DIVIDE DATE-CCYY BY 400 GIVING DATE-QUOTIENT
014100                 REMAINDER DATE-REMAINDER
014200         IF DATE-REMAINDER = 0
014300             MOVE "Y" TO VALID-DATE-FLAG
014400         ELSE
014500             DIVIDE DATE-CCYY BY 100 GIVING DATE-QUOTIENT
014600                     REMAINDER DATE-REMAINDER
014700             IF DATE-REMAINDER = 0
014800                 MOVE "N" TO VALID-DATE-FLAG
014900             ELSE
015000                 DIVIDE DATE-CCYY BY 4 GIVING DATE-QUOTIENT
015100                         REMAINDER DATE-REMAINDER
015200                 IF DATE-REMAINDER = 0
015300                     MOVE "Y" TO VALID-DATE-FLAG
015400                 ELSE
015500                     MOVE "N" TO VALID-DATE-FLAG.
015600
015700 DISPLAY-AND-GET-DATE.
015800     PERFORM DISPLAY-A-DATE.
015900     PERFORM GET-A-DATE.
016000
016100 DISPLAY-A-DATE.
016200     MOVE DATE-MMDDCCYY TO DATE-ENTRY-FIELD.
016300     DISPLAY "FORMATTED DATE IS " DATE-ENTRY-FIELD.
016400     DISPLAY "DATE-MMDDCCYY IS " DATE-MMDDCCYY.
016500     DISPLAY "DATE-CCYYMMDD IS " DATE-CCYYMMDD.
016600
```

ANALYSIS The date-validation routine in Listing 19.21 has been created to be reasonably flexible. In working storage at lines 001700 and 001800, DATE-QUOTIENT and DATE-REMAINDER have been defined. These will be used in the date validation as part of the logic to check for a leap year.

At line 002000, the VALID-DATE-FLAG is defined. This flag is used to hold the result of the validation. It has three possible result values, which are defined with level 88 entries at lines

002100 through 002300. If the date is in error, the flag is set to "N". If the date is valid, the flag is set to "Y". If the date is zero, the flag is set to "0", which allows for a general-purpose date validation that will allow a zero date entry. In some fields, it might be okay to enter a date with a value of zero, so the two entries that are possibly okay, "0" and "Y", are defined with a level 88 at line 002400.

At line 002600, the DATE-CCYYMMDD variable is defined as a PIC 9(8). These eight bytes are redefined at lines 002700 through 003100 into four two-byte numeric fields.

The GET-A-DATE routine begins at line 005400 and is a standard field-entry routine that performs ACCEPT-A-DATE and then performs RE-ACCEPT-A-DATE until DATE-IS-OK.

ACCEPT-A-DATE at line 005900 displays a prompt, accepts the entry field, and then performs the edit check EDIT-CHECK-DATE. The editing logic at line 007300, EDIT-DATE, moves the entered field to DATE-MMDDCCYY and then converts this to DATE-CCYYMMDD.

It is the date validation logic that is extensive. It begins at line 007800 with a long comment explaining how the routine works.

The routine CHECK-DATE starts at line 010600. The routine assumes that DATE-CCYYMMDD has been filled in with the date to test (this was taken care of at lines 007500 and 007600) and that the date is valid. The routine moves "Y" to the VALID-DATE-FLAG.

The routine is a series of tests on the date. If any tested condition is true, there is something wrong with the date. The VALID-DATE-FLAG flag is set accordingly and the PERFORM commands in the rest of the paragraph are skipped.

There are three possible conditions for the date: valid, invalid, or zero. Zero is checked first at line 011900, and if the date is zero, the VALID-DATE-FLAG is set to "0" and the remainder of the paragraph is ignored.

If the date passes the zero test, a series of possible invalid conditions are tested.

At line 012200, CHECK-MM checks for an invalid month. At line 012600, CHECK-DD checks for an invalid day.

At line 013000, CHECK-MMDD begins checking for an invalid month and day combination, which is a day greater than 30 with a month that does not contain 31 days, or a day greater than 29 for the month of February.

The CHECK-LEAP-YEAR routine at line 013800 tests for a leap year when the date is February 29. A leap year is any year that is evenly divisible by 4, but not evenly divisible by 100, unless it is divisible by 400. The divisibility tests begin at lines 014000 and 014100, which perform the tests in what seems an upside down manner. The routine tests for a leap year by performing a series of divisions, and saving the results in DATE-QUOTIENT, and the remainder in DATE-REMAINDER. You don't care about the value in DATE-REMAINDER. First the routine tests if the year

19

is evenly divisible by 400. If it is, then it is definitely a leap year. If the year is not evenly divisible by 400, then it is tested to see if it is evenly divisible by 100. If it is, then the year is definitely not a leap year. The final check tests by dividing the year by 4. Trying to come up with different ways to test for a leap year is a good exercise that you should try.

As long as DATE-CCYYMMDD passes each test, the VALID-DATE-FLAG remains "Y"; any other condition changes the flag.

As is the case with any programming problem, there usually is more than one way to skin a cat. Listing 19.22 is extracted from date02.cbl, and some changes are made to the CHECK-DATE logic.

TYPE   **Listing 19.22. Another date validation.**

```
005100*---------------------------
005200* PLDATE.CBL
005300*---------------------------
005400 GET-A-DATE.
005500     PERFORM ACCEPT-A-DATE.
005600     PERFORM RE-ACCEPT-A-DATE
005700          UNTIL DATE-IS-OK.
005800
005900 ACCEPT-A-DATE.
006000     DISPLAY "ENTER A DATE (MM/DD/CCYY)".
006100     ACCEPT DATE-ENTRY-FIELD.
006200
006300     PERFORM EDIT-CHECK-DATE.
006400
006500 RE-ACCEPT-A-DATE.
006600     DISPLAY "INVALID DATE".
006700     PERFORM ACCEPT-A-DATE.
006800
006900 EDIT-CHECK-DATE.
007000     PERFORM EDIT-DATE.
007100     PERFORM CHECK-DATE.
007200
007300 EDIT-DATE.
007400     MOVE DATE-ENTRY-FIELD TO DATE-MMDDCCYY.
007500     COMPUTE DATE-CCYYMMDD =
007600          DATE-MMDDCCYY * 10000.0001.
007700
007800*--------------------------------
007900* Assume that the date is good, then
008000* test the date in the following
008100* steps. The routine stops if any
008200* of these conditions is true,
008300* and sets the valid date flag.
008400* Condition 1 returns the valid date
008500* flag set to "0".
```

```
008600* If any other condition is true,
008700* the valid date flag is set to "N".
008800* 1.  Is the date zeroes
008900* 2.  Month > 12 or < 1
009000* 3.  Day < 1 or  > 31
009100* 4.  Day > 30 and
009200*     Month = 2 (February)  or
009300*             4 (April)    or
009400*             6 (June)     or
009500*             9 (September) or
009600*            11 (November)
009700*     Day > 29 and
009800*     Month = 2 (February)
009900* 5.  Day = 29 and
010000*     Month = 2 and
010100*     Not a leap year
010200* ( A leap year is any year evenly
010300*   divisible by 400 or by 4
010400*   but not by 100 ).
010500*--------------------------------
010600 CHECK-DATE.
010700     MOVE "Y" TO VALID-DATE-FLAG.
010800     IF DATE-CCYYMMDD = ZEROES
010900         MOVE "0" TO VALID-DATE-FLAG
011000     ELSE
011100     IF DATE-MM < 1 OR DATE-MM > 12
011200         MOVE "N" TO VALID-DATE-FLAG
011300     ELSE
011400     IF DATE-DD < 1 OR DATE-DD > 31
011500         MOVE "N" TO VALID-DATE-FLAG
011600     ELSE
011700     IF (DATE-DD > 30) AND
011800         (DATE-MM = 2 OR 4 OR 6 OR 9 OR 11)
011900         MOVE "N" TO VALID-DATE-FLAG
012000     ELSE
012100     IF DATE-DD > 29 AND DATE-MM = 2
012200         MOVE "N" TO VALID-DATE-FLAG
012300     ELSE
012400     IF DATE-DD = 29 AND DATE-MM = 2
012500         DIVIDE DATE-CCYY BY 400 GIVING DATE-QUOTIENT
012600             REMAINDER DATE-REMAINDER
012700         IF DATE-REMAINDER = 0
012800            MOVE "Y" TO VALID-DATE-FLAG
012900         ELSE
013000            DIVIDE DATE-CCYY BY 100 GIVING DATE-QUOTIENT
013100                REMAINDER DATE-REMAINDER
013200            IF DATE-REMAINDER = 0
013300               MOVE "N" TO VALID-DATE-FLAG
013400            ELSE
013500               DIVIDE DATE-CCYY BY 4 GIVING DATE-QUOTIENT
013600                   REMAINDER DATE-REMAINDER
013700               IF DATE-REMAINDER = 0
013800                  MOVE "Y" TO VALID-DATE-FLAG
013900               ELSE
014000                  MOVE "N" TO VALID-DATE-FLAG.
014100
```

19

ANALYSIS The logic that appears at lines 010600 through 015600 in date02.cbl has been reduced to a single paragraph in Listing 19.22. The routine is a long series of IF ELSE tests. If any tested condition is true, there is something wrong with the date. The VALID-DATE-FLAG flag is set accordingly and the rest of the paragraph is skipped.

Flexible Date Handling

Date validation involves a great deal of code. It would be a lot of work to have to rewrite all of this code every time a date popped up in a program, so it seems that date handling could or should be put into a COPY file.

So far you have put values for a file definition or WORKING-STORAGE only into a COPY file, but it also is possible to put PROCEDURE DIVISION paragraphs and logic into COPY files.

The whole of Listing 19.22 can be copied into a file called pldate.cbl (the pl stands for program logic), and this creates the program logic needed to validate dates. Then copy lines 001500 through 003100 of Listing 19.21, date02.cbl, into a file called wsdate.cbl. This creates the needed WORKING-STORAGE. Listing 19.23, date04.cbl, is now all you need to create the same date-entry and validation programs date01.cbl. This gives you a routine that can be used for entering a date in any program.

TYPE **Listing 19.23. Using canned date handling.**

```
000100 IDENTIFICATION DIVISION.
000200 PROGRAM-ID. DATE04.
000300*--------------------------------
000400* Demo of Date Entry and validation
000500*--------------------------------
000600 ENVIRONMENT DIVISION.
000700 INPUT-OUTPUT SECTION.
000800 FILE-CONTROL.
000900
001000 DATA DIVISION.
001100 FILE SECTION.
001200
001300 WORKING-STORAGE SECTION.
001400
001500     COPY "WSDATE.CBL".
001600
001700 PROCEDURE DIVISION.
001800 PROGRAM-BEGIN.
001900     PERFORM OPENING-PROCEDURE.
002000     PERFORM MAIN-PROCESS.
002100     PERFORM CLOSING-PROCEDURE.
002200
```

```
002300 PROGRAM-EXIT.
002400     EXIT PROGRAM.
002500
002600 PROGRAM-DONE.
002700     STOP RUN.
002800
002900 OPENING-PROCEDURE.
003000
003100 CLOSING-PROCEDURE.
003200
003300 MAIN-PROCESS.
003400     PERFORM GET-A-DATE.
003500     PERFORM DISPLAY-AND-GET-DATE
003600         UNTIL DATE-MMDDCCYY = ZEROES.
003700
003800     COPY "PLDATE.CBL".
003900
004000 DISPLAY-AND-GET-DATE.
004100     PERFORM DISPLAY-A-DATE.
004200     PERFORM GET-A-DATE.
004300
004400 DISPLAY-A-DATE.
004500     MOVE DATE-MMDDCCYY TO DATE-ENTRY-FIELD.
004600     DISPLAY "FORMATTED DATE IS " DATE-ENTRY-FIELD.
004700     DISPLAY "DATE-MMDDCCYY IS " DATE-MMDDCCYY.
004800     DISPLAY "DATE-CCYYMMDD IS " DATE-CCYYMMDD.
004900
```

This code is almost, but not quite, adequate. The GET-A-DATE routine, which would end up being included within pldate.cbl, has a problem that makes it unsuitable as a general-purpose, date-entry routine: It isn't flexible enough. At line 006000 in Listing 19.22, the prompt for a date is forced to be "ENTER A DATE (MM/DD/CCYY)". You might want the user to see a different prompt, such as "ENTER THE INVOICE DATE (MM/DD/CCYY)".

At line 005700, the reaccept logic is performed until DATE-IS-OK. This allows an entry of zeroes, but you might have date fields that are required entries and cannot allow the user to enter zeroes.

Both of these "inflexible" situations are fine for date04.cbl, but this will not be the case for all date entry.

The way to handle these problems is to build the flexibility into the WORKING-STORAGE and program logic for date handling, and then create the COPY files containing the routines.

Listing 19.24, date05.cbl, has isolated a date-entry routine as well as other different types of date handling routines. The date05.cbl is written as a test program only to test these date routines. After they are tested, the WORKING-STORAGE and program logic can be extracted into COPY files.

19

TYPE Listing 19.24. Date handling routines.

```
000100 IDENTIFICATION DIVISION.
000200 PROGRAM-ID. DATE05.
000300*----------------------------------
000400* Testing Date Entry and handling
000500*----------------------------------
000600 ENVIRONMENT DIVISION.
000700 INPUT-OUTPUT SECTION.
000800 FILE-CONTROL.
000900
001000 DATA DIVISION.
001100 FILE SECTION.
001200
001300 WORKING-STORAGE SECTION.
001400
001500 77  ANY-DATE          PIC 9(8) VALUE ZEROES.
001600 77  REQUIRED-DATE      PIC 9(8) VALUE ZEROES.
001700
001800*----------------------------------
001900* Fields for date routines.
002000*----------------------------------
002100 77  FORMATTED-DATE     PIC Z9/99/9999.
002200 77  DATE-MMDDCCYY       PIC 9(8).
002300 77  DATE-QUOTIENT      PIC 9999.
002400 77  DATE-REMAINDER     PIC 9999.
002500
002600 77  VALID-DATE-FLAG    PIC X.
002700     88  DATE-IS-INVALID  VALUE "N".
002800     88  DATE-IS-ZERO     VALUE "0".
002900     88  DATE-IS-VALID    VALUE "Y".
003000     88  DATE-IS-OK       VALUES "Y" "0".
003100
003200 01  DATE-CCYYMMDD      PIC 9(8).
003300 01  FILLER REDEFINES DATE-CCYYMMDD.
003400     05  DATE-CCYY        PIC 9999.
003500
003600     05  DATE-MM          PIC 99.
003700     05  DATE-DD          PIC 99.
003800
003900*----------------------------------
004000* User can set these values before
004100* performing GET-A-DATE.
004200*----------------------------------
004300 77  DATE-PROMPT        PIC X(50) VALUE SPACE.
004400 77  DATE-ERROR-MESSAGE PIC X(50) VALUE SPACE.
004500*----------------------------------
004600* User can set this value before
004700* performing GET-A-DATE or CHECK-DATE.
004800*----------------------------------
004900 77  ZERO-DATE-IS-OK    PIC X VALUE "N".
005000
005100 PROCEDURE DIVISION.
005200 PROGRAM-BEGIN.
005300     PERFORM OPENING-PROCEDURE.
005400     PERFORM MAIN-PROCESS.
```

19

```
005500      PERFORM CLOSING-PROCEDURE.
005600
005700 PROGRAM-EXIT.
005800      EXIT PROGRAM.
005900
006000 PROGRAM-DONE.
006100      STOP RUN.
006200
006300 OPENING-PROCEDURE.
006400
006500 CLOSING-PROCEDURE.
006600
006700 MAIN-PROCESS.
006800      PERFORM GET-TWO-DATES.
006900      PERFORM DISPLAY-AND-GET-DATES
007000          UNTIL REQUIRED-DATE = 00010101.
007100
007200 GET-TWO-DATES.
007300      PERFORM GET-ANY-DATE.
007400      PERFORM GET-REQUIRED-DATE.
007500
007600 GET-ANY-DATE.
007700      MOVE "Y" TO ZERO-DATE-IS-OK.
007800      MOVE "ENTER AN OPTIONAL MM/DD/CCYY?" TO DATE-PROMPT.
007900      MOVE "MUST BE ANY VALID DATE" TO DATE-ERROR-MESSAGE.
008000      PERFORM GET-A-DATE.
008100      MOVE DATE-CCYYMMDD TO ANY-DATE.
008200
008300 GET-REQUIRED-DATE.
008400      MOVE "N" TO ZERO-DATE-IS-OK.
008500      MOVE SPACE TO DATE-PROMPT.
008600      MOVE "MUST ENTER A VALID DATE" TO DATE-ERROR-MESSAGE.
008700      PERFORM GET-A-DATE.
008800      MOVE DATE-CCYYMMDD TO REQUIRED-DATE.
008900
009000 DISPLAY-AND-GET-DATES.
009100      PERFORM DISPLAY-THE-DATES.
009200      PERFORM GET-TWO-DATES.
009300
009400 DISPLAY-THE-DATES.
009500      MOVE ANY-DATE TO DATE-CCYYMMDD.
009600      PERFORM FORMAT-THE-DATE.
009700      DISPLAY "ANY DATE IS " FORMATTED-DATE.
009800      MOVE REQUIRED-DATE TO DATE-CCYYMMDD.
009900      PERFORM FORMAT-THE-DATE.
010000      DISPLAY "REQUIRED DATE IS " FORMATTED-DATE.
010100
010200*--------------------------------
010300* USAGE:
010400*   MOVE "Y" (OR "N") TO ZERO-DATE-IS-OK.  (optional)
010500*   MOVE prompt TO DATE-PROMPT.            (optional)
010600*   MOVE message TO DATE-ERROR-MESSAGE     (optional)
010700*   PERFORM GET-A-DATE
010800* RETURNS:
010900*   DATE-IS-OK (ZERO OR VALID)
```

19

continues

Listing 19.24. continued

```
011000*    DATE-IS-VALID (VALID)
011100*    DATE-IS-INVALID (BAD DATE )
011200*
011300*    IF DATE IS VALID IT IS IN
011400*        DATE-CCYYMMDD AND
011500*        DATE-MMDDCCYY AND
011600*        FORMATTED-DATE (formatted)
011700*--------------------------------
011800 GET-A-DATE.
011900     PERFORM ACCEPT-A-DATE.
012000     PERFORM RE-ACCEPT-A-DATE
012100         UNTIL DATE-IS-OK.
012200
012300 ACCEPT-A-DATE.
012400     IF DATE-PROMPT = SPACE
012500         DISPLAY "ENTER A DATE (MM/DD/CCYY)"
012600     ELSE
012700         DISPLAY DATE-PROMPT.
012800
012900     ACCEPT FORMATTED-DATE.
013000
013100     PERFORM EDIT-CHECK-DATE.
013200
013300 RE-ACCEPT-A-DATE.
013400     IF DATE-ERROR-MESSAGE = SPACE
013500         DISPLAY "INVALID DATE"
013600     ELSE
013700         DISPLAY DATE-ERROR-MESSAGE.
013800
013900     PERFORM ACCEPT-A-DATE.
014000
014100 EDIT-CHECK-DATE.
014200     PERFORM EDIT-DATE.
014300     PERFORM CHECK-DATE.
014400     MOVE DATE-MMDDCCYY TO FORMATTED-DATE.
014500
014600 EDIT-DATE.
014700     MOVE FORMATTED-DATE TO DATE-MMDDCCYY.
014800     PERFORM CONVERT-TO-CCYYMMDD.
014900
015000*--------------------------------
015100* USAGE:
015200*  MOVE date(CCYYMMDD) TO DATE-CCYYMMDD.
015300*  PERFORM CONVERT-TO-MMDDCCYY.
015400*
015500* RETURNS:
015600*  DATE-MMDDCCYY.
015700*--------------------------------
015800 CONVERT-TO-MMDDCCYY.
015900     COMPUTE DATE-MMDDCCYY =
016000             DATE-CCYYMMDD * 10000.0001.
016100
016200*--------------------------------
016300* USAGE:
```

19

```
016400*   MOVE date(MMDDCCYY) TO DATE-MMDDCCYY.
016500*   PERFORM CONVERT-TO-CCYYMMDD.
016600*
016700* RETURNS:
016800*   DATE-CCYYMMDD.
016900*--------------------------------
017000 CONVERT-TO-CCYYMMDD.
017100     COMPUTE DATE-CCYYMMDD =
017200             DATE-MMDDCCYY * 10000.0001.
017300
017400*--------------------------------
017500* USAGE:
017600*   MOVE date(CCYYMMDD) TO DATE-CCYYMMDD.
017700*   MOVE "Y" (OR "N") TO ZERO-DATE-IS-OK.
017800*   PERFORM CHECK-DATE.
017900*
018000* RETURNS:
018100*   DATE-IS-OK      (ZERO OR VALID)
018200*   DATE-IS-VALID   (VALID)
018300*   DATE-IS-INVALID (BAD DATE )
018400*
018500* Assume that the date is good, then
018600* test the date in the following
018700* steps. The routine stops if any
018800* of these conditions is true,
018900* and sets the valid date flag.
019000* Condition 1 returns the valid date
019100* flag set to "0" if ZERO-DATE-IS-OK
019200* is "Y", otherwise it sets the
019300* valid date flag to "N".
019400* If any other condition is true,
019500* the valid date flag is set to "N".
019600* 1.  Is the date zeroes
019700* 2.  Month > 12 or < 1
019800* 3.  Day < 1 or  > 31
019900* 4.  Day > 30 and
020000*     Month = 2 (February)  or
020100*             4 (April)     or
020200*             6 (June)      or
020300*             9 (September) or
020400*            11 (November)
020500*     Day > 29 and
020600*     Month = 2 (February)
020700* 5.  Day = 29 and
020800*     Month = 2 and
020900*     Not a leap year
021000* ( A leap year is any year evenly
021100*   divisible by 400 or by 4
021200*   but not by 100 ).
021300*--------------------------------
021400 CHECK-DATE.
021500     MOVE "Y" TO VALID-DATE-FLAG.
021600     IF DATE-CCYYMMDD = ZEROES
021700         IF ZERO-DATE-IS-OK = "Y"
021800             MOVE "0" TO VALID-DATE-FLAG
```

continues

19

Listing 19.24. continued

```
021900          ELSE
022000             MOVE "N" TO VALID-DATE-FLAG
022100       ELSE
022200       IF DATE-MM < 1 OR DATE-MM > 12
022300          MOVE "N" TO VALID-DATE-FLAG
022400       ELSE
022500       IF DATE-DD < 1 OR DATE-DD > 31
022600          MOVE "N" TO VALID-DATE-FLAG
022700       ELSE
022800       IF (DATE-DD > 30) AND
022900          (DATE-MM = 2 OR 4 OR 6 OR 9 OR 11)
023000          MOVE "N" TO VALID-DATE-FLAG
023100       ELSE
023200       IF DATE-DD > 29 AND DATE-MM = 2
023300          MOVE "N" TO VALID-DATE-FLAG
023400       ELSE
023500       IF DATE-DD = 29 AND DATE-MM = 2
023600          DIVIDE DATE-CCYY BY 400 GIVING DATE-QUOTIENT
023700                REMAINDER DATE-REMAINDER
023800          IF DATE-REMAINDER = 0
023900             MOVE "Y" TO VALID-DATE-FLAG
024000          ELSE
024100             DIVIDE DATE-CCYY BY 100 GIVING DATE-QUOTIENT
024200                   REMAINDER DATE-REMAINDER
024300          IF DATE-REMAINDER = 0
024400             MOVE "N" TO VALID-DATE-FLAG
024500          ELSE
024600             DIVIDE DATE-CCYY BY 4 GIVING DATE-QUOTIENT
024700                   REMAINDER DATE-REMAINDER
024800          IF DATE-REMAINDER = 0
024900             MOVE "Y" TO VALID-DATE-FLAG
025000          ELSE
025100             MOVE "N" TO VALID-DATE-FLAG.
025200*- - - - - - - - - - - - - - - - - - - - - - - - - - - - - -
025300* USAGE:
025400*  MOVE date(CCYYMMDD) TO DATE-CCYYMMDD.
025500*  PERFORM FORMAT-THE-DATE.
025600*
025700* RETURNS:
025800*  FORMATTED-DATE
025900*  DATE-MMDDCCYY.
026000*- - - - - - - - - - - - - - - - - - - - - - - - - - - - - -
026100 FORMAT-THE-DATE.
026200     PERFORM CONVERT-TO-MMDDCCYY.
026300     MOVE DATE-MMDDCCYY TO FORMATTED-DATE.
026400
```

The output of date05.cbl displays errors when dates are incorrect depending on whether zero entry is allowed. The prompt and error messages for the fields change. The following is an example of the output for date05.cbl:

19

OUTPUT

```
ENTER AN OPTIONAL DATE(MM/DD/CCYY)?

ENTER A DATE (MM/DD/CCYY)

MUST ENTER A VALID DATE
ENTER A DATE (MM/DD/CCYY)
12171993
ANY DATE IS  0/00/0000
REQUIRED DATE IS 12/17/1993
ENTER AN OPTIONAL DATE(MM/DD/CCYY)?
454519922
MUST BE ANY VALID DATE
ENTER AN OPTIONAL DATE(MM/DD/CCYY)?
02291968
ENTER A DATE (MM/DD/CCYY)
03041997
ANY DATE IS  2/29/1968
REQUIRED DATE IS  3/04/1997
ENTER AN OPTIONAL DATE(MM/DD/CCYY)?

ENTER A DATE (MM/DD/CCYY)
01/01/0001

c>
```

ANALYSIS   The program accepts and displays two date fields. One can be entered as zeroes or a valid date (ANY-DATE); the other will accept only a valid date (REQUIRED-DATE). The program is set up to test whether the validation for these two types of entry is handled correctly.

Working storage for two dates is defined at lines 001500 and 001600. These are used for the testing program and will not be a part of the date logic directly.

The WORKING-STORAGE for the date routines is defined at lines 001800 through 004900. The DATE-ENTRY-FIELD is renamed FORMATTED-DATE at line 002100, but aside from this change, the fields will be familiar down through line 003700.

Starting at line 003900, three new fields are defined that are designed to make the date routines more flexible. DATE-PROMPT at line 004300 can be filled in by the user to provide a prompt for the date entry. DATE-ERROR-MESSAGE at line 004400 can be filled in to provide a specific error message if the date is invalid. ZERO-DATE-IS-OK at line 004900 is a flag that can be set to yes or no and controls the way the DATE-CHECK logic behaves. If ZERO-DATE-IS-OK is set to "N", a date entry of zero is invalid and the user will be forced to enter a valid date. If ZERO-DATE-IS-OK is set to "Y", the routine will accept zero as a valid entry.

Date handling routines begin at line 010200, and five separate routines have been created. At line 011800, GET-A-DATE can be used to perform date entry. At lines 015800 and 017000, the routines CONVERT-TO-MMDDCCYY and CONVERT-TO-CCYYMMDD have been created to convert back and forth between DATE-MMDDCCYY and DATE-CCYYMMDD.

19

At line 021400, CHECK-DATE can be used to validate a date that has been moved to DATE-CCYYMMDD.

Finally, at line 026100, the routine FORMAT-THE-DATE can be used to create a display or print a version of a date by moving it to DATE-CCYYMMDD and then performing FORMAT-THE-DATE.

The DATE-PROMPT variable is used in ACCEPT-A-DATE at line 012300. If DATE-PROMPT has been filled in, it is used; otherwise, a general-purpose prompt, "ENTER A DATE (MM/DD/CCYY)", is displayed.

The DATE-ERROR-MESSAGE field is used in a similar manner to DATE-PROMT—in RE-ACCEPT-A-DATE at line 013300. If DATE-ERROR-MESSAGE has been filled in, then DATE-ERROR-MESSAGE is displayed in the event of an error. If DATE-ERROR-MESSAGE is spaces, a general-purpose error message, "INVALID DATE", is displayed.

The ZERO-DATE-IS-OK flag is used in the routine that begins at line 021400. The result of the original test for a zero date has been changed slightly. If the date is a zero and if ZERO-DATE-IS-OK = "Y", "0" is moved to VALID-DATE-FLAG; otherwise, a zero date is considered to be an error and "N" is moved to VALID-DATE-FLAG.

The remaining date routines are fairly easy to follow.

The main logic of the program is to loop and repetitively accept two date fields. GET-ANY-DATE at 007600 allows zeroes to be entered, and DATE-PROMPT and DATE-ERROR-MESSAGE are modified before the data entry is done.

GET-REQUIRED-DATE at line 008300 does not allow zeroes, and clears the DATE-PROMPT so that the default prompt will be used, but does load a special error message into DATE-ERROR-MESSAGE.

The GET-ANY-DATE routine returns the entered date in DATE-CCYYMMDD, so at line 008100, immediately after performing GET-A-DATE, DATE-CCYYMMDD is moved to ANY-DATE. The same is done for REQUIRED-DATE at line 008800.

The date05.cbl program ends when the user enters a date of 01/01/0001 for the required date field.

Code, compile, and run date05.cbl. Test various date entries until you are satisfied that the routines are working correctly. Copy date05.cbl to wsdate01.cbl and delete everything except lines 001800 through 004900. This creates the WORKING-STORAGE for date handling. Copy date05.cbl to pldate01.cbl and delete everything except lines 010200 through 026400. This creates the program logic for date handling.

Finally, code and compile Listing 19.25, date06.cbl. Run it, testing that it behaves the same as date05.cbl. You now have a general-purpose date-entry and validation routine and date-handling routines.

19

TYPE   **Listing 19.25. Using the COPY files for date handling.**

```
000100 IDENTIFICATION DIVISION.
000200 PROGRAM-ID. DATE06.
000300*-------------------------------
000400* Testing Date Entry and handling
000500*-------------------------------
000600 ENVIRONMENT DIVISION.
000700 INPUT-OUTPUT SECTION.
000800 FILE-CONTROL.
000900
001000 DATA DIVISION.
001100 FILE SECTION.
001200
001300 WORKING-STORAGE SECTION.
001400
001500 77  ANY-DATE          PIC 9(8) VALUE ZEROES.
001600 77  REQUIRED-DATE      PIC 9(8) VALUE ZEROES.
001700
001800     COPY "WSDATE01.CBL".
001900
002000 PROCEDURE DIVISION.
002100 PROGRAM-BEGIN.
002200     PERFORM OPENING-PROCEDURE.
002300     PERFORM MAIN-PROCESS.
002400     PERFORM CLOSING-PROCEDURE.
002500
002600 PROGRAM-EXIT.
002700     EXIT PROGRAM.
002800
002900 PROGRAM-DONE.
003000     STOP RUN.
003100
003200 OPENING-PROCEDURE.
003300
003400 CLOSING-PROCEDURE.
003500
003600 MAIN-PROCESS.
003700     PERFORM GET-TWO-DATES.
003800     PERFORM DISPLAY-AND-GET-DATES
003900         UNTIL REQUIRED-DATE = 00010101.
004000
004100 GET-TWO-DATES.
004200     PERFORM GET-ANY-DATE.
004300     PERFORM GET-REQUIRED-DATE.
004400
004500 GET-ANY-DATE.
004600     MOVE "Y" TO ZERO-DATE-IS-OK.
004700     MOVE "ENTER AN OPTIONAL MM/DD/CCYY?" TO DATE-PROMPT.
004800     MOVE "MUST BE ANY VALID DATE" TO DATE-ERROR-MESSAGE.
004900     PERFORM GET-A-DATE.
005000     MOVE DATE-CCYYMMDD TO ANY-DATE.
005100
```

continues

Listing 19.25. continued

```
005200 GET-REQUIRED-DATE.
005300     MOVE "N" TO ZERO-DATE-IS-OK.
005400     MOVE SPACE TO DATE-PROMPT.
005500     MOVE "MUST ENTER A VALID DATE" TO DATE-ERROR-MESSAGE.
005600     PERFORM GET-A-DATE.
005700     MOVE DATE-CCYYMMDD TO REQUIRED-DATE.
005800
005900 DISPLAY-AND-GET-DATES.
006000     PERFORM DISPLAY-THE-DATES.
006100     PERFORM GET-TWO-DATES.
006200
006300 DISPLAY-THE-DATES.
006400     MOVE ANY-DATE TO DATE-CCYYMMDD.
006500     PERFORM FORMAT-THE-DATE.
006600     DISPLAY "ANY DATE IS " FORMATTED-DATE.
006700     MOVE REQUIRED-DATE TO DATE-CCYYMMDD.
006800     PERFORM FORMAT-THE-DATE.
006900     DISPLAY "REQUIRED DATE IS " FORMATTED-DATE.
007000
007100     COPY "PLDATE01.CBL".
007200
```

With the logic for date entry under control, you are ready to start work on entering data into the voucher file.

Summary

Data entry can be complicated. Validations and dates frequently cause problems and some maintenance modules don't use all the modes (add, change, inquire, and delete). Today, you learned the following basics:

☐ A control file is used to store basic values used in one or more parts of a COBOL system of programs.

☐ A control file usually is a single indexed record containing the key values.

☐ The maintenance program for a control file usually contains only change and inquire modes. It is different than a standard maintenance module because the user usually does not need to see or change the key to the file.

☐ Formatted dates can be displayed by using a field with the / edit character, for example, PIC 99/99/9999. This type of formatted field also can be used for entering dates.

☐ You can convert a date from MMDDCCYY format to CCYYMMDD format, and vice versa, by multiplying the date by 10000.0001.

☐ Use a REDEFINES command to define different types of variables that use the same space in memory.

☐ A leap year occurs on years that are evenly divisible by 400, or on years that are evenly divisible by 4 but not by 100.

☐ Date validation involves separating a date into its components—year, month, and day—and checking each of the parts.

Q&A

Q Does a date validation routine have to allow any year?

A No. You can specify that no date fall outside a certain range by adding an additional test to the date validation routine. The following listing prevents years prior to 1900 being entered. The lines that have been added have no line numbers so that they will stand out:

```
021500      MOVE "Y" TO VALID-DATE-FLAG.
021600      IF DATE-CCYYMMDD = ZEROES
021700          IF ZERO-DATE-IS-OK = "Y"
021800              MOVE "0" TO VALID-DATE-FLAG
021900          ELSE
022000              MOVE "N" TO VALID-DATE-FLAG
022100      ELSE
            IF DATE-CC < 19
                MOVE "N" TO VALID-DATE-FLAG
            ELSE
022200      IF DATE-MM < 1 OR DATE-MM > 12
022300          MOVE "N" TO VALID-DATE-FLAG
022400      ELSE
022500      IF DATE-DD < 1 OR DATE-DD > 31
022600          MOVE "N" TO VALID-DATE-FLAG
022700      ELSE
022800      IF (DATE-DD > 30) AND
022900         (DATE-MM = 2 OR 4 OR 6 OR 9 OR 11)
023000          MOVE "N" TO VALID-DATE-FLAG
023100      ELSE
023200      IF DATE-DD > 29 AND DATE-MM = 2
023300          MOVE "N" TO VALID-DATE-FLAG
023400      ELSE
023500      IF DATE-DD = 29 AND DATE-MM = 2
023600          DIVIDE DATE-CCYY BY 400 GIVING DATE-QUOTIENT
023700              REMAINDER DATE-REMAINDER
023800          IF DATE-REMAINDER = 0
023900              MOVE "Y" TO VALID-DATE-FLAG
024000          ELSE
024100              DIVIDE DATE-CCYY BY 100 GIVING DATE-QUOTIENT
024200                  REMAINDER DATE-REMAINDER
024300              IF DATE-REMAINDER = 0
024400                  MOVE "N" TO VALID-DATE-FLAG
024500              ELSE
```

19

```
024600                      DIVIDE DATE-CCYY BY 4 GIVING DATE-QUOTIENT
024700                          REMAINDER DATE-REMAINDER
024800                      IF DATE-REMAINDER = 0
024900                          MOVE "Y" TO VALID-DATE-FLAG
025000                      ELSE
025100                          MOVE "N" TO VALID-DATE-FLAG.
025200
```

Q Can REDEFINES appear within REDEFINES?

A Yes. In fact, if you need to test the full four-digit year, you might use a variable
definition that looks something like the next listing. This defines eight bytes that
contain six variables. DATE-CCYYMMDD is a numeric eight-byte field. DATE-CCYY is a
numeric four-byte field in the first four bytes. DATE-CC is a numeric two-byte field
in the first two bytes. DATE-YY is a numeric two-byte field in positions 3 and 4.
DATE-MM is a numeric two-byte field in positions 5 and 6, and DATE-DD is a numeric
two-byte field in positions 7 and 8.

```
003200 01  DATE-CCYYMMDD        PIC 9(8).
003300 01  FILLER REDEFINES DATE-CCYYMMDD.
003400     05  DATE-CCYY        PIC 9999.
003500     05  FILLER REDEFINES DATE-CCYY.
003600         10  DATE-CC      PIC 99.
003700         10  DATE-YY      PIC 99.
003800     05  DATE-MM          PIC 99.
003900     05  DATE-DD          PIC 99.
```

Workshop

Quiz

1. The variable defined in the following listing is used to store the time in hour,
   minute, second format (using a 24-hour clock) and includes a redefinition. How
   many bytes of memory are used by the definition?

```
000100  01  TIME-HHMMSS         PIC 9(6).
000200  01  FILLER REDEFINES TIME-HHMMSS.
000300      05  TIME-HH         PIC 99.
000400      05  TIME-MM         PIC 99.
000500      05  TIME-SS         PIC 99.
```

2. How long is TIME-HHMMSS and what type of data will it hold?

3. How long is TIME-HH and what type of data will it hold?

4. How long is TIME-MM and what type of data will it hold?

5. How long is TIME-SS and what type of data will it hold?

19

Exercises

1. Print out copies of `stcmnt04.cbl` from Day 18, "Calling Other Programs," and `ctlmnt01.cbl`, which is Listing 19.5 from today's lesson. Compare the change and inquire logic of `ctlmnt01.cbl` with the change and inquire logic of `stcmnt04.cbl`. Try to get a feel for the changes that were made to the logic flow for `ctlmnt01.cbl` to adjust for the fact that there is only one record, and for the fact that the user doesn't have to enter or even see the key field.

2. Using data defined in the listing in the Q&A section, question 2, modify the listing in the Q&A section, question 1, to exclude dates earlier than 1920, and later than the year 2150.

3. Print out `wsdate01.cbl` and `pldate01.cbl` and, using them as guides, create `WORKING-STORAGE` and a routine analogous to `CHECK-DATE`; however, this routine will be called `CHECK-TIME`, and will be used to validate time entries of hours, minutes, and seconds, with the following conditions: the hour can be in the range zero to 23, and minutes and seconds can be in the range 0 to 59.

   Hint: There is no data entry in this logic, so the logic will include only `WORKING-STORAGE`, as in the listing in the Q&A section, question 2, and a `VALID-TIME-FLAG`. `TIME-HHMMSS = 0` is a valid condition, so there will be no need for a `TIME-IS-ZERO` level 88.

   Don't feel bad if you have to peek at the answers. The answer to this exercise includes a program that can be used to test your logic.

19

Day **20**

More Complex Data Entry

You now have mastered some of the complex data entry problems that a program might have to tackle. It is time to put this new knowledge to use. Today and in Day 21, "Selecting, Sorting, and Reporting," you will complete all the pieces needed for the bills payment system described in Day 19, "Complex Data Entry Problems."

Today, you learn about the following parts of the bills payment system:

- ☐ Maintaining the voucher file
- ☐ Selecting individual vouchers
- ☐ Completing the payment cycle on a voucher

Maintaining the Voucher File

Figure 20.1 highlights the parts of the bills payment system that will be covered today—steps 2, 7, and 12. This section of the chapter deals with step 2 of the process.

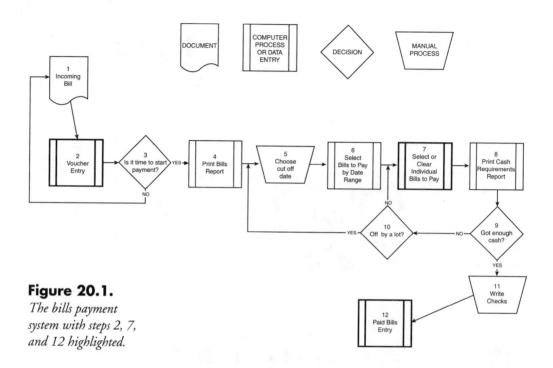

Figure 20.1.

The bills payment
system with steps 2, 7,
and 12 highlighted.

A voucher is created every time a bill arrives. The voucher record contains important information needed for selecting the bill for payment and for tracking the bill, such as due date, vendor, amount, and invoice number.

Voucher Entry, highlighted as step 2 of Figure 20.1, really is a maintenance program with a few extra features. Listing 20.1 is vchmnt01.cbl. When an invoice is received, the voucher entry cycle begins, starting with adding a voucher for the invoice to the system. Although the primary use of vchmnt01.cbl is to add new vouchers to the voucher file, it is possible at any time in the life of a voucher that it might have to be changed or deleted. vchmnt01.cbl is a complete maintenance module that primarily is used in add mode.

TYPE   **Listing 20.1. Voucher entry.**

```
000100 IDENTIFICATION DIVISION.
000200 PROGRAM-ID. VCHMNT01.
000300*--------------------------------
000400* Add, Change, Inquire and Delete
000500* for the Voucher File.
000600* All fields are displayed, but
000700* SELECTED, PAID-AMOUNT, PAID-DATE and
000800* CHECK-NO are not modifiable
000900*--------------------------------
```

```
001000 ENVIRONMENT DIVISION.
001100 INPUT-OUTPUT SECTION.
001200 FILE-CONTROL.
001300
001400     COPY "SLVND02.CBL".
001500
001600     COPY "SLVOUCH.CBL".
001700
001800     COPY "SLCONTRL.CBL".
001900
002000 DATA DIVISION.
002100 FILE SECTION.
002200
002300     COPY "FDVND04.CBL".
002400
002500     COPY "FDVOUCH.CBL".
002600
002700     COPY "FDCONTRL.CBL".
002800
002900 WORKING-STORAGE SECTION.
003000
003100 77  MENU-PICK                    PIC 9.
003200     88  MENU-PICK-IS-VALID        VALUES 0 THRU 4.
003300
003400 77  THE-MODE                     PIC X(7).
003500 77  WHICH-FIELD                  PIC 9.
003600 77  OK-TO-DELETE                 PIC X.
003700 77  VOUCHER-RECORD-FOUND         PIC X.
003800 77  CONTROL-RECORD-FOUND         PIC X.
003900 77  VENDOR-RECORD-FOUND          PIC X.
004000 77  A-DUMMY                      PIC X.
004100 77  ADD-ANOTHER                  PIC X.
004200
004300 77  VOUCHER-NUMBER-FIELD         PIC Z(5).
004400 77  VOUCHER-AMOUNT-FIELD         PIC ZZZ,ZZ9.99-.
004500 77  VOUCHER-PAID-AMOUNT-FIELD    PIC ZZZ,ZZ9.99-.
004600
004700 77  ERROR-MESSAGE                PIC X(79) VALUE SPACE.
004800
004900     COPY "WSCASE01.CBL".
005000
005100     COPY "WSDATE01.CBL".
005200
005300 PROCEDURE DIVISION.
005400 PROGRAM-BEGIN.
005500     PERFORM OPENING-PROCEDURE.
005600     PERFORM MAIN-PROCESS.
005700     PERFORM CLOSING-PROCEDURE.
005800
005900 PROGRAM-EXIT.
006000     EXIT PROGRAM.
006100
006200 PROGRAM-DONE.
006300     STOP RUN.
006400
```

20

continues

Listing 20.1. continued

```
006500 OPENING-PROCEDURE.
006600      OPEN I-O VOUCHER-FILE.
006700      OPEN I-O VENDOR-FILE.
006800      OPEN I-O CONTROL-FILE.
006900
007000 CLOSING-PROCEDURE.
007100      CLOSE VOUCHER-FILE.
007200      CLOSE VENDOR-FILE.
007300      CLOSE CONTROL-FILE.
007400
007500 MAIN-PROCESS.
007600      PERFORM GET-MENU-PICK.
007700      PERFORM MAINTAIN-THE-FILE
007800          UNTIL MENU-PICK = 0.
007900
008000*-------------------------------
008100* MENU
008200*-------------------------------
008300 GET-MENU-PICK.
008400      PERFORM DISPLAY-THE-MENU.
008500      PERFORM ACCEPT-MENU-PICK.
008600      PERFORM RE-ACCEPT-MENU-PICK
008700          UNTIL MENU-PICK-IS-VALID.
008800
008900 DISPLAY-THE-MENU.
009000      PERFORM CLEAR-SCREEN.
009100      DISPLAY "    PLEASE SELECT:".
009200      DISPLAY " ".
009300      DISPLAY "          1.  ADD RECORDS".
009400      DISPLAY "          2.  CHANGE A RECORD".
009500      DISPLAY "          3.  LOOK UP A RECORD".
009600      DISPLAY "          4.  DELETE A RECORD".
009700      DISPLAY " ".
009800      DISPLAY "          0.  EXIT".
009900      PERFORM SCROLL-LINE 8 TIMES.
010000
010100 ACCEPT-MENU-PICK.
010200      DISPLAY "YOUR CHOICE (0-4)?".
010300      ACCEPT MENU-PICK.
010400
010500 RE-ACCEPT-MENU-PICK.
010600      DISPLAY "INVALID SELECTION - PLEASE RE-TRY.".
010700      PERFORM ACCEPT-MENU-PICK.
010800
010900 CLEAR-SCREEN.
011000      PERFORM SCROLL-LINE 25 TIMES.
011100
011200 SCROLL-LINE.
011300      DISPLAY " ".
011400
011500 MAINTAIN-THE-FILE.
011600      PERFORM DO-THE-PICK.
011700      PERFORM GET-MENU-PICK.
011800
```

20

```
011900 DO-THE-PICK.
012000     IF MENU-PICK = 1
012100         PERFORM ADD-MODE
012200     ELSE
012300     IF MENU-PICK = 2
012400         PERFORM CHANGE-MODE
012500     ELSE
012600     IF MENU-PICK = 3
012700         PERFORM INQUIRE-MODE
012800     ELSE
012900     IF MENU-PICK = 4
013000         PERFORM DELETE-MODE.
013100
013200*-------------------------------
013300* ADD
013400*-------------------------------
013500 ADD-MODE.
013600     MOVE "ADD" TO THE-MODE.
013700     MOVE "Y" TO ADD-ANOTHER.
013800     PERFORM GET-NEW-RECORD-KEY.
013900     PERFORM ADD-RECORDS
014000         UNTIL ADD-ANOTHER = "N".
014100
014200 GET-NEW-RECORD-KEY.
014300     PERFORM ACCEPT-NEW-RECORD-KEY.
014400     PERFORM RE-ACCEPT-NEW-RECORD-KEY
014500         UNTIL VOUCHER-RECORD-FOUND = "N".
014600
014700     PERFORM DISPLAY-VOUCHER-NUMBER.
014800
014900 ACCEPT-NEW-RECORD-KEY.
015000     PERFORM INIT-VOUCHER-RECORD.
015100     PERFORM RETRIEVE-NEXT-VOUCHER-NUMBER.
015200
015300     PERFORM READ-VOUCHER-RECORD.
015400
015500 RE-ACCEPT-NEW-RECORD-KEY.
015600     PERFORM ACCEPT-NEW-RECORD-KEY.
015700
015800 RETRIEVE-NEXT-VOUCHER-NUMBER.
015900     PERFORM READ-CONTROL-RECORD.
016000     ADD 1 TO CONTROL-LAST-VOUCHER.
016100     MOVE CONTROL-LAST-VOUCHER TO VOUCHER-NUMBER.
016200     PERFORM REWRITE-CONTROL-RECORD.
016300
016400 ADD-RECORDS.
016500     PERFORM ENTER-REMAINING-FIELDS.
016600     PERFORM WRITE-VOUCHER-RECORD.
016700     PERFORM GET-ADD-ANOTHER.
016800
016900 GET-ADD-ANOTHER.
017000     PERFORM ACCEPT-ADD-ANOTHER.
017100     PERFORM RE-ACCEPT-ADD-ANOTHER
017200         UNTIL ADD-ANOTHER = "Y" OR "N".
017300
```

20

continues

Listing 20.1. continued

```
017400 ACCEPT-ADD-ANOTHER.
017500     DISPLAY "ADD ANOTHER VOUCHER(Y/N)?".
017600     ACCEPT ADD-ANOTHER.
017700
017800     INSPECT ADD-ANOTHER
017900         CONVERTING LOWER-ALPHA
018000         TO          UPPER-ALPHA.
018100
018200     IF ADD-ANOTHER = "Y"
018300         PERFORM GET-NEW-RECORD-KEY.
018400
018500 RE-ACCEPT-ADD-ANOTHER.
018600     DISPLAY "YOU MUST ENTER YES OR NO".
018700     PERFORM ACCEPT-ADD-ANOTHER.
018800
018900 ENTER-REMAINING-FIELDS.
019000     PERFORM ENTER-VOUCHER-VENDOR.
019100     PERFORM ENTER-VOUCHER-INVOICE.
019200     PERFORM ENTER-VOUCHER-FOR.
019300     PERFORM ENTER-VOUCHER-AMOUNT.
019400     PERFORM ENTER-VOUCHER-DATE.
019500     PERFORM ENTER-VOUCHER-DUE.
019600     PERFORM ENTER-VOUCHER-DEDUCTIBLE.
019700     PERFORM ENTER-VOUCHER-SELECTED.
019800
019900*-------------------------------
020000* CHANGE
020100*-------------------------------
020200 CHANGE-MODE.
020300     MOVE "CHANGE" TO THE-MODE.
020400     PERFORM GET-EXISTING-RECORD.
020500     PERFORM CHANGE-RECORDS
020600         UNTIL VOUCHER-NUMBER = ZEROES.
020700
020800 CHANGE-RECORDS.
020900     PERFORM GET-FIELD-TO-CHANGE.
021000     PERFORM CHANGE-ONE-FIELD
021100         UNTIL WHICH-FIELD = ZERO.
021200     PERFORM GET-EXISTING-RECORD.
021300
021400 GET-FIELD-TO-CHANGE.
021500     PERFORM DISPLAY-ALL-FIELDS.
021600     PERFORM ASK-WHICH-FIELD.
021700
021800 ASK-WHICH-FIELD.
021900     PERFORM ACCEPT-WHICH-FIELD.
022000     PERFORM RE-ACCEPT-WHICH-FIELD
022100         UNTIL WHICH-FIELD < 8.
022200
022300 ACCEPT-WHICH-FIELD.
022400     DISPLAY "ENTER THE NUMBER OF THE FIELD".
022500     DISPLAY "TO CHANGE (1-7) OR 0 TO EXIT".
022600     ACCEPT WHICH-FIELD.
022700
```

```
022800 RE-ACCEPT-WHICH-FIELD.
022900     DISPLAY "INVALID ENTRY".
023000     PERFORM ACCEPT-WHICH-FIELD.
023100
023200 CHANGE-ONE-FIELD.
023300     PERFORM CHANGE-THIS-FIELD.
023400     PERFORM GET-FIELD-TO-CHANGE.
023500
023600 CHANGE-THIS-FIELD.
023700     IF WHICH-FIELD = 1
023800         PERFORM ENTER-VOUCHER-VENDOR.
023900     IF WHICH-FIELD = 2
024000         PERFORM ENTER-VOUCHER-INVOICE.
024100     IF WHICH-FIELD = 3
024200         PERFORM ENTER-VOUCHER-FOR.
024300     IF WHICH-FIELD = 4
024400         PERFORM ENTER-VOUCHER-AMOUNT.
024500     IF WHICH-FIELD = 5
024600         PERFORM ENTER-VOUCHER-DATE.
024700     IF WHICH-FIELD = 6
024800         PERFORM ENTER-VOUCHER-DUE.
024900     IF WHICH-FIELD = 7
025000         PERFORM ENTER-VOUCHER-DEDUCTIBLE.
025100
025200     PERFORM REWRITE-VOUCHER-RECORD.
025300
025400*-------------------------------
025500* INQUIRE
025600*-------------------------------
025700 INQUIRE-MODE.
025800     MOVE "DISPLAY" TO THE-MODE.
025900     PERFORM GET-EXISTING-RECORD.
026000     PERFORM INQUIRE-RECORDS
026100         UNTIL VOUCHER-NUMBER = ZEROES.
026200
026300 INQUIRE-RECORDS.
026400     PERFORM DISPLAY-ALL-FIELDS.
026500     PERFORM GET-EXISTING-RECORD.
026600
026700*-------------------------------
026800* DELETE
026900*-------------------------------
027000 DELETE-MODE.
027100     MOVE "DELETE" TO THE-MODE.
027200     PERFORM GET-EXISTING-RECORD.
027300     PERFORM DELETE-RECORDS
027400         UNTIL VOUCHER-NUMBER = ZEROES.
027500
027600 DELETE-RECORDS.
027700     PERFORM DISPLAY-ALL-FIELDS.
027800
027900     PERFORM ASK-OK-TO-DELETE.
028000
028100     IF OK-TO-DELETE = "Y"
028200         PERFORM DELETE-VOUCHER-RECORD.
```

continues

Listing 20.1. continued

```
028300
028400      PERFORM GET-EXISTING-RECORD.
028500
028600 ASK-OK-TO-DELETE.
028700      PERFORM ACCEPT-OK-TO-DELETE.
028800
028900      PERFORM RE-ACCEPT-OK-TO-DELETE
029000          UNTIL OK-TO-DELETE = "Y" OR "N".
029100
029200 ACCEPT-OK-TO-DELETE.
029300      DISPLAY "DELETE THIS RECORD (Y/N)?".
029400      ACCEPT OK-TO-DELETE.
029500      INSPECT OK-TO-DELETE
029600       CONVERTING LOWER-ALPHA TO UPPER-ALPHA.
029700
029800 RE-ACCEPT-OK-TO-DELETE.
029900      DISPLAY "YOU MUST ENTER YES OR NO".
030000      PERFORM ACCEPT-OK-TO-DELETE.
030100
030200*-------------------------------
030300* Routines shared by all modes
030400*-------------------------------
030500 INIT-VOUCHER-RECORD.
030600      MOVE SPACE TO VOUCHER-INVOICE
030700                    VOUCHER-FOR
030800                    VOUCHER-DEDUCTIBLE
030900                    VOUCHER-SELECTED.
031000      MOVE ZEROES TO VOUCHER-NUMBER
031100                    VOUCHER-VENDOR
031200                    VOUCHER-AMOUNT
031300                    VOUCHER-DATE
031400                    VOUCHER-DUE
031500                    VOUCHER-PAID-AMOUNT
031600                    VOUCHER-PAID-DATE
031700                    VOUCHER-CHECK-NO.
031800
031900*-------------------------------
032000* Routines shared Add and Change
032100*-------------------------------
032200 ENTER-VOUCHER-VENDOR.
032300      PERFORM ACCEPT-VOUCHER-VENDOR.
032400      PERFORM RE-ACCEPT-VOUCHER-VENDOR
032500          UNTIL VOUCHER-VENDOR NOT = ZEROES AND
032600                VENDOR-RECORD-FOUND = "Y".
032700
032800 ACCEPT-VOUCHER-VENDOR.
032900      DISPLAY "ENTER VENDOR".
033000      ACCEPT VOUCHER-VENDOR.
033100      PERFORM EDIT-CHECK-VOUCHER-VENDOR.
033200      PERFORM DISPLAY-VOUCHER-VENDOR.
033300
033400 RE-ACCEPT-VOUCHER-VENDOR.
033500      DISPLAY ERROR-MESSAGE.
033600      PERFORM ACCEPT-VOUCHER-VENDOR.
```

```
033700
033800 EDIT-CHECK-VOUCHER-VENDOR.
033900     PERFORM EDIT-VOUCHER-VENDOR.
034000     PERFORM CHECK-VOUCHER-VENDOR.
034100
034200 EDIT-VOUCHER-VENDOR.
034300
034400 CHECK-VOUCHER-VENDOR.
034500     PERFORM VOUCHER-VENDOR-REQUIRED.
034600     IF VOUCHER-VENDOR NOT = ZEROES
034700         PERFORM VOUCHER-VENDOR-ON-FILE.
034800
034900 VOUCHER-VENDOR-REQUIRED.
035000     IF VOUCHER-VENDOR = ZEROES
035100         MOVE "VENDOR MUST BE ENTERED"
035200             TO ERROR-MESSAGE.
035300
035400 VOUCHER-VENDOR-ON-FILE.
035500     MOVE VOUCHER-VENDOR TO VENDOR-NUMBER.
035600     PERFORM READ-VENDOR-RECORD.
035700     IF VENDOR-RECORD-FOUND = "N"
035800         MOVE "VENDOR NOT ON FILE"
035900             TO ERROR-MESSAGE.
036000
036100 ENTER-VOUCHER-INVOICE.
036200     PERFORM ACCEPT-VOUCHER-INVOICE.
036300     PERFORM RE-ACCEPT-VOUCHER-INVOICE
036400         UNTIL VOUCHER-INVOICE NOT = SPACE.
036500
036600 ACCEPT-VOUCHER-INVOICE.
036700     DISPLAY "ENTER INVOICE NUMBER".
036800     ACCEPT VOUCHER-INVOICE.
036900     INSPECT VOUCHER-INVOICE
037000         CONVERTING LOWER-ALPHA
037100         TO         UPPER-ALPHA.
037200
037300 RE-ACCEPT-VOUCHER-INVOICE.
037400     DISPLAY "INVOICE MUST BE ENTERED".
037500     PERFORM ACCEPT-VOUCHER-INVOICE.
037600
037700 ENTER-VOUCHER-FOR.
037800     PERFORM ACCEPT-VOUCHER-FOR.
037900     PERFORM RE-ACCEPT-VOUCHER-FOR
038000         UNTIL VOUCHER-FOR NOT = SPACE.
038100
038200 ACCEPT-VOUCHER-FOR.
038300     DISPLAY "WHAT FOR?".
038400     ACCEPT VOUCHER-FOR.
038500     INSPECT VOUCHER-FOR
038600         CONVERTING LOWER-ALPHA
038700         TO         UPPER-ALPHA.
038800
038900 RE-ACCEPT-VOUCHER-FOR.
039000     DISPLAY "A DESCRIPTION MUST BE ENTERED".
039100     PERFORM ACCEPT-VOUCHER-FOR.
```

20

continues

Listing 20.1. continued

```
039200
039300 ENTER-VOUCHER-AMOUNT.
039400     PERFORM ACCEPT-VOUCHER-AMOUNT.
039500     PERFORM RE-ACCEPT-VOUCHER-AMOUNT
039600          UNTIL VOUCHER-AMOUNT NOT = ZEROES.
039700
039800 ACCEPT-VOUCHER-AMOUNT.
039900     DISPLAY "ENTER INVOICE AMOUNT".
040000     ACCEPT VOUCHER-AMOUNT-FIELD.
040100     MOVE VOUCHER-AMOUNT-FIELD TO VOUCHER-AMOUNT.
040200
040300 RE-ACCEPT-VOUCHER-AMOUNT.
040400     DISPLAY "AMOUNT MUST NOT BE ZERO".
040500     PERFORM ACCEPT-VOUCHER-AMOUNT.
040600
040700 ENTER-VOUCHER-DATE.
040800     MOVE "N" TO ZERO-DATE-IS-OK.
040900     MOVE "ENTER INVOICE DATE(MM/DD/CCYY)?"
041000          TO DATE-PROMPT.
041100     MOVE "AN INVOICE DATE IS REQUIRED"
041200          TO DATE-ERROR-MESSAGE.
041300     PERFORM GET-A-DATE.
041400     MOVE DATE-CCYYMMDD TO VOUCHER-DATE.
041500
041600 ENTER-VOUCHER-DUE.
041700     MOVE "N" TO ZERO-DATE-IS-OK.
041800     MOVE "ENTER DUE DATE(MM/DD/CCYY)?"
041900          TO DATE-PROMPT.
042000     MOVE "A DUE DATE IS REQUIRED"
042100          TO DATE-ERROR-MESSAGE.
042200     PERFORM GET-A-DATE.
042300     MOVE DATE-CCYYMMDD TO VOUCHER-DUE.
042400
042500
042600 ENTER-VOUCHER-DEDUCTIBLE.
042700     PERFORM ACCEPT-VOUCHER-DEDUCTIBLE.
042800     PERFORM RE-ACCEPT-VOUCHER-DEDUCTIBLE
042900          UNTIL VOUCHER-DEDUCTIBLE = "Y" OR "N".
043000
043100 ACCEPT-VOUCHER-DEDUCTIBLE.
043200     DISPLAY "IS THIS TAX DEDUCTIBLE?".
043300     ACCEPT VOUCHER-DEDUCTIBLE.
043400     INSPECT VOUCHER-DEDUCTIBLE
043500          CONVERTING LOWER-ALPHA
043600          TO          UPPER-ALPHA.
043700
043800 RE-ACCEPT-VOUCHER-DEDUCTIBLE.
043900     DISPLAY "MUST BE YES OR NO".
044000     PERFORM ACCEPT-VOUCHER-DEDUCTIBLE.
044100
044200 ENTER-VOUCHER-SELECTED.
044300     MOVE "N" TO VOUCHER-SELECTED.
044400
044500*-------------------------------
```

```
044600* Routines shared by Change,
044700* Inquire and Delete
044800*--------------------------------
044900 GET-EXISTING-RECORD.
045000     PERFORM ACCEPT-EXISTING-KEY.
045100     PERFORM RE-ACCEPT-EXISTING-KEY
045200          UNTIL VOUCHER-RECORD-FOUND = "Y" OR
045300               VOUCHER-NUMBER = ZEROES.
045400
045500 ACCEPT-EXISTING-KEY.
045600     PERFORM INIT-VOUCHER-RECORD.
045700     PERFORM ENTER-VOUCHER-NUMBER.
045800     IF VOUCHER-NUMBER NOT = ZEROES
045900          PERFORM READ-VOUCHER-RECORD.
046000
046100 RE-ACCEPT-EXISTING-KEY.
046200     DISPLAY "RECORD NOT FOUND"
046300     PERFORM ACCEPT-EXISTING-KEY.
046400
046500 ENTER-VOUCHER-NUMBER.
046600     DISPLAY "ENTER VOUCHER NUMBER TO "
046700          THE-MODE.
046800     ACCEPT VOUCHER-NUMBER.
046900
047000 DISPLAY-ALL-FIELDS.
047100     DISPLAY " ".
047200     PERFORM DISPLAY-VOUCHER-NUMBER.
047300     PERFORM DISPLAY-VOUCHER-VENDOR.
047400     PERFORM DISPLAY-VOUCHER-INVOICE.
047500     PERFORM DISPLAY-VOUCHER-FOR.
047600     PERFORM DISPLAY-VOUCHER-AMOUNT.
047700     PERFORM DISPLAY-VOUCHER-DATE.
047800     PERFORM DISPLAY-VOUCHER-DUE.
047900     PERFORM DISPLAY-VOUCHER-DEDUCTIBLE.
048000     IF VOUCHER-PAID-DATE = ZEROES
048100          PERFORM DISPLAY-VOUCHER-SELECTED.
048200     IF VOUCHER-PAID-DATE NOT = ZEROES
048300          PERFORM DISPLAY-VOUCHER-PAID-AMOUNT
048400          PERFORM DISPLAY-VOUCHER-PAID-DATE
048500          PERFORM DISPLAY-VOUCHER-CHECK-NO.
048600     DISPLAY " ".
048700
048800 DISPLAY-VOUCHER-NUMBER.
048900     DISPLAY "   VOUCHER NUMBER: " VOUCHER-NUMBER.
049000
049100 DISPLAY-VOUCHER-VENDOR.
049200     PERFORM VOUCHER-VENDOR-ON-FILE.
049300     IF VENDOR-RECORD-FOUND = "N"
049400          MOVE "**Not found**" TO VENDOR-NAME.
049500     DISPLAY "1. VENDOR: "
049600          VOUCHER-VENDOR " "
049700          VENDOR-NAME.
049800
049900 DISPLAY-VOUCHER-INVOICE.
050000     DISPLAY "2. INVOICE: " VOUCHER-INVOICE.
```

continues

20

Listing 20.1. continued

```
050100
050200 DISPLAY-VOUCHER-FOR.
050300      DISPLAY "3. FOR: " VOUCHER-FOR.
050400
050500 DISPLAY-VOUCHER-AMOUNT.
050600      MOVE VOUCHER-AMOUNT TO VOUCHER-AMOUNT-FIELD.
050700      DISPLAY "4. AMOUNT: " VOUCHER-AMOUNT-FIELD.
050800
050900 DISPLAY-VOUCHER-DATE.
051000      MOVE VOUCHER-DATE TO DATE-CCYYMMDD.
051100      PERFORM FORMAT-THE-DATE.
051200      DISPLAY "5. INVOICE DATE: " FORMATTED-DATE.
051300
051400 DISPLAY-VOUCHER-DUE.
051500      MOVE VOUCHER-DUE TO DATE-CCYYMMDD.
051600      PERFORM FORMAT-THE-DATE.
051700      DISPLAY "6. DUE DATE: " FORMATTED-DATE.
051800
051900 DISPLAY-VOUCHER-DEDUCTIBLE.
052000      DISPLAY "7. DEDUCTIBLE: " VOUCHER-DEDUCTIBLE.
052100
052200 DISPLAY-VOUCHER-SELECTED.
052300      DISPLAY "   SELECTED FOR PAYMENT: " VOUCHER-SELECTED.
052400
052500 DISPLAY-VOUCHER-PAID-AMOUNT.
052600      MOVE VOUCHER-PAID-AMOUNT TO VOUCHER-PAID-AMOUNT-FIELD.
052700      DISPLAY "   PAID: " VOUCHER-PAID-AMOUNT-FIELD.
052800
052900 DISPLAY-VOUCHER-PAID-DATE.
053000      MOVE VOUCHER-PAID-DATE TO DATE-CCYYMMDD.
053100      PERFORM FORMAT-THE-DATE.
053200      DISPLAY "   PAID ON: " FORMATTED-DATE.
053300
053400 DISPLAY-VOUCHER-CHECK-NO.
053500      DISPLAY "   CHECK: " VOUCHER-CHECK-NO.
053600
053700*-------------------------------
053800* File I-O Routines
053900*-------------------------------
054000 READ-VOUCHER-RECORD.
054100      MOVE "Y" TO VOUCHER-RECORD-FOUND.
054200      READ VOUCHER-FILE RECORD
054300         INVALID KEY
054400            MOVE "N" TO VOUCHER-RECORD-FOUND.
054500
054600*or  READ VOUCHER-FILE RECORD WITH LOCK
054700*      INVALID KEY
054800*         MOVE "N" TO VOUCHER-RECORD-FOUND.
054900
055000*or  READ VOUCHER-FILE RECORD WITH HOLD
055100*      INVALID KEY
055200*         MOVE "N" TO VOUCHER-RECORD-FOUND.
055300
```

```
055400 WRITE-VOUCHER-RECORD.
055500     WRITE VOUCHER-RECORD
055600         INVALID KEY
055700         DISPLAY "RECORD ALREADY ON FILE".
055800
055900 REWRITE-VOUCHER-RECORD.
056000     REWRITE VOUCHER-RECORD
056100         INVALID KEY
056200         DISPLAY "ERROR REWRITING VENDOR RECORD".
056300
056400 DELETE-VOUCHER-RECORD.
056500     DELETE VOUCHER-FILE RECORD
056600         INVALID KEY
056700         DISPLAY "ERROR DELETING VENDOR RECORD".
056800
056900 READ-VENDOR-RECORD.
057000     MOVE "Y" TO VENDOR-RECORD-FOUND.
057100     READ VENDOR-FILE RECORD
057200       INVALID KEY
057300         MOVE "N" TO VENDOR-RECORD-FOUND.
057400
057500 READ-CONTROL-RECORD.
057600     MOVE 1 TO CONTROL-KEY.
057700     MOVE "Y" TO CONTROL-RECORD-FOUND.
057800     READ CONTROL-FILE RECORD
057900         INVALID KEY
058000         MOVE "N" TO CONTROL-RECORD-FOUND
058100         DISPLAY "CONTROL FILE IS INVALID".
058200
058300 REWRITE-CONTROL-RECORD.
058400     REWRITE CONTROL-RECORD
058500         INVALID KEY
058600         DISPLAY "ERROR REWRITING CONTROL RECORD".
058700
058800     COPY "PLDATE01.CBL".
058900
```

Here is the sample output of `vchmnt01.cbl` as new vouchers are added:

```
PLEASE SELECT:
1.  ADD RECORDS
2.  CHANGE A RECORD
3.  LOOK UP A RECORD
4.  DELETE A RECORD
0.  EXIT
YOUR CHOICE (0-4)?
1

VOUCHER NUMBER: 00004
ENTER VENDOR
2

1. VENDOR: 00002 ABC PRINTING
ENTER INVOICE NUMBER
cx-5055
```

```
WHAT FOR?
letter head
ENTER INVOICE AMOUNT
104.19
ENTER INVOICE DATE(MM/DD/CCYY)?
01/07/1997
ENTER DUE DATE(MM/DD/CCYY)?
02/07/1997
IS THIS TAX DEDUCTIBLE?
y
ADD ANOTHER VOUCHER(Y/N)?
n

PLEASE SELECT:
1.   ADD RECORDS
2.   CHANGE A RECORD
3.   LOOK UP A RECORD
4.   DELETE A RECORD
0.   EXIT
YOUR CHOICE (0-4)?
```

ANALYSIS   At lines 001200 through 002800, the file definitions for the control file, the voucher file, and the vendor file are included. OPENING-PROCEDURE and CLOSING-PROCEDURE, at lines 006500 and 007300, respectively, appropriately open and close these three files. The voucher file is the main file that is being modified. The vendor file is used to look up vendors when they are entered, and the control file is used to generate new voucher numbers in add mode.

The first big difference occurs in ACCEPT-NEW-RECORD-KEY at line 014900. Rather than ask the user to enter a new voucher number, one is generated automatically by performing RETRIEVE-NEXT-VOUCHER-NUMBER. The RETRIEVE-NEXT-VOUCHER-NUMBER routine at line 015800 reads the control file, adds 1 to the CONTROL-LAST-VOUCHER, and moves the new value to VOUCHER-NUMBER. The routine then rewrites the CONTROL-RECORD, causing the control file to be updated with the last used number. At line 015300, the voucher record is read. This loop, at lines 014900 through 015400, is performed at lines 014200 through 014500 until a voucher number is generated that is not on file. This logic is used in the event that the control file and voucher file get out of synch with each other. By repeating the logic until an unused voucher number is found, the two files become synchronized. This also is useful in multiuser systems where two or more people might be adding to a file at once.

After the new voucher number is generated successfully, it is displayed at line 014700. Usually, a data entry operator writes this voucher number at the top of the physical invoice received so that the invoice is associated with its voucher tracking number.

The data entry for the invoice date begins at line 040700. This routine uses GET-A-DATE in pldate01.cbl (which is included by a COPY statement at line 058800). At line 040800, a zero date is prevented; at lines 040900 through 041200, a special prompt and error message are set up, and then GET-A-DATE is performed. After returning from GET-A-DATE at line 041400, the entered date in DATE-CCYYMMDD is moved to VOUCHER-DATE.

The data entry for the invoice due date begins at line 041600 and uses the identical style of logic to get a valid date for VOUCHER-DUE.

ENTER-VOUCHER-VENDOR at line 032200 looks up the vendor that is entered in the vendor file. The vendor must be on file to be valid.

There is another difference from a standard maintenance module. Four of the fields are reserved to be entered by other programs. These are VOUCHER-SELECTED, VOUCHER-PAID-AMOUNT, VOUCHER-PAID-DATE, and VOUCHER-CHECK-NO.

VOUCHER-SELECTED is a flag that is set when a voucher is selected for payment. The remaining three fields are set when a voucher actually is paid. VOUCHER-SELECTED will be modified by steps 6 and 7 in Figure 20.1, and the other three fields will be modified by step 12 of Figure 20.1. However, there is no reason that the user should not be allowed to see these fields. When deleting records or changing values in the fields that can be modified, it might help if the user can see the selected and paid status of the voucher. In DISPLAY-ALL-FIELDS at line 047000, this program displays the four fields that cannot be modified by the program.

If a voucher is paid, the paid date will not be zeroes, and the VOUCHER-SELECTED field is irrelevant because the voucher obviously has been selected for payment as it has been paid. So, at line 048000, the VOUCHER-SELECTED field is displayed only if the VOUCHER-PAID-DATE is zeroes. Because the voucher has not been paid, the user might want to know whether it has been selected for payment.

If a voucher has been paid, the paid date, amount, and check number all have values. So, at lines 048200 through 048500, VOUCHER-PAID-AMOUNT, VOUCHER-PAID-DATE, and VOUCHER-CHECK-NO are displayed when the VOUCHER-PAID-DATE is not zero.

Code and compile vchmnt01.cbl. Print a list of vendors using the vendor report programs from earlier lessons, and then run vchmnt01.cbl and enter some vouchers as if real invoices had been received.

Selecting Individual Vouchers

The selection of individual vouchers to pay is performed by a maintenance program that runs in change mode only and allows only one field, VOUCHER-SELECTED, to be modified. Listing 20.2 is vchpic01.cbl and allows single vouchers to be selected and the VOUCHER-SELECTED flag to be entered to a *yes* or *no*. Step 7 of the flowchart shows where individual selection of bills fits into the flow of activities in the bills payment system. (Refer to Figure 20.1.)

20

TYPE **Listing 20.2. Selecting records to be paid.**

```
000100 IDENTIFICATION DIVISION.
000200 PROGRAM-ID. VCHPIC01.
000300*-------------------------------
000400* Change only.
000500* Allows the user to change
000600* the VOUCHER-SELECTED flag
000700* for unpaid vouchers
000800*-------------------------------
000900 ENVIRONMENT DIVISION.
001000 INPUT-OUTPUT SECTION.
001100 FILE-CONTROL.
001200
001300     COPY "SLVND02.CBL".
001400
001500     COPY "SLVOUCH.CBL".
001600
001700     COPY "SLCONTRL.CBL".
001800
001900 DATA DIVISION.
002000 FILE SECTION.
002100
002200     COPY "FDVND04.CBL".
002300
002400     COPY "FDVOUCH.CBL".
002500
002600     COPY "FDCONTRL.CBL".
002700
002800 WORKING-STORAGE SECTION.
002900
003000 77  MENU-PICK                 PIC 9.
003100     88  MENU-PICK-IS-VALID     VALUES 0 THRU 4.
003200
003300 77  WHICH-FIELD               PIC 9.
003400 77  VOUCHER-RECORD-FOUND      PIC X.
003500 77  VENDOR-RECORD-FOUND       PIC X.
003600
003700 77  VOUCHER-NUMBER-FIELD      PIC Z(5).
003800 77  VOUCHER-AMOUNT-FIELD      PIC ZZZ,ZZ9.99-.
003900 77  VOUCHER-PAID-AMOUNT-FIELD PIC ZZZ,ZZ9.99-.
004000
004100 77  ERROR-MESSAGE             PIC X(79) VALUE SPACE.
004200
004300     COPY "WSCASE01.CBL".
004400
004500     COPY "WSDATE01.CBL".
004600
004700 PROCEDURE DIVISION.
004800 PROGRAM-BEGIN.
004900     PERFORM OPENING-PROCEDURE.
005000     PERFORM MAIN-PROCESS.
005100     PERFORM CLOSING-PROCEDURE.
005200
005300 PROGRAM-EXIT.
005400     EXIT PROGRAM.
```

20

```
005500
005600 PROGRAM-DONE.
005700      STOP RUN.
005800
005900 OPENING-PROCEDURE.
006000      OPEN I-O VOUCHER-FILE.
006100      OPEN I-O VENDOR-FILE.
006200
006300 CLOSING-PROCEDURE.
006400      CLOSE VOUCHER-FILE.
006500      CLOSE VENDOR-FILE.
006600
006700 MAIN-PROCESS.
006800      PERFORM CHANGE-MODE.
006900
007000*--------------------------------
007100* CHANGE
007200*--------------------------------
007300 CHANGE-MODE.
007400      PERFORM GET-EXISTING-RECORD.
007500      PERFORM CHANGE-RECORDS
007600          UNTIL VOUCHER-NUMBER = ZEROES.
007700
007800 CHANGE-RECORDS.
007900      PERFORM GET-FIELD-TO-CHANGE.
008000      IF VOUCHER-PAID-DATE = ZEROES
008100          PERFORM CHANGE-ONE-FIELD.
008200      PERFORM GET-EXISTING-RECORD.
008300
008400 GET-FIELD-TO-CHANGE.
008500      PERFORM DISPLAY-ALL-FIELDS.
008600      PERFORM ASK-WHICH-FIELD.
008700
008800 ASK-WHICH-FIELD.
008900      MOVE 1 TO WHICH-FIELD.
009000
009100 CHANGE-ONE-FIELD.
009200      PERFORM CHANGE-THIS-FIELD.
009300
009400 CHANGE-THIS-FIELD.
009500      IF WHICH-FIELD = 1
009600          PERFORM ENTER-VOUCHER-SELECTED.
009700
009800      PERFORM REWRITE-VOUCHER-RECORD.
009900
010000*--------------------------------
010100* Routines shared by all modes
010200*--------------------------------
010300 INIT-VOUCHER-RECORD.
010400      MOVE SPACE TO VOUCHER-INVOICE
010500                      VOUCHER-FOR
010600                      VOUCHER-DEDUCTIBLE
010700                      VOUCHER-SELECTED.
010800      MOVE ZEROES TO VOUCHER-NUMBER
010900                      VOUCHER-VENDOR
```

continues

Listing 20.2. continued

```
011000                      VOUCHER-AMOUNT
011100                      VOUCHER-DATE
011200                      VOUCHER-DUE
011300                      VOUCHER-PAID-AMOUNT
011400                      VOUCHER-PAID-DATE
011500                      VOUCHER-CHECK-NO.
011600
011700*--------------------------------
011800* Routines shared Add and Change
011900*--------------------------------
012000 ENTER-VOUCHER-SELECTED.
012100     PERFORM ACCEPT-VOUCHER-SELECTED.
012200     PERFORM RE-ACCEPT-VOUCHER-SELECTED
012300         UNTIL VOUCHER-SELECTED = "Y" OR "N".
012400
012500 ACCEPT-VOUCHER-SELECTED.
012600     DISPLAY "SELECT THIS VOUCHER (Y/N)?".
012700     ACCEPT VOUCHER-SELECTED.
012800
012900     INSPECT VOUCHER-SELECTED
013000        CONVERTING LOWER-ALPHA
013100        TO UPPER-ALPHA.
013200
013300 RE-ACCEPT-VOUCHER-SELECTED.
013400     DISPLAY "YOU MUST ENTER YES OR NO".
013500     PERFORM ACCEPT-VOUCHER-SELECTED.
013600
013700*--------------------------------
013800* Routines shared by Change,
013900* Inquire and Delete
014000*--------------------------------
014100 GET-EXISTING-RECORD.
014200     PERFORM ACCEPT-EXISTING-KEY.
014300     PERFORM RE-ACCEPT-EXISTING-KEY
014400         UNTIL VOUCHER-RECORD-FOUND = "Y" OR
014500             VOUCHER-NUMBER = ZEROES.
014600
014700 ACCEPT-EXISTING-KEY.
014800     PERFORM INIT-VOUCHER-RECORD.
014900     PERFORM ENTER-VOUCHER-NUMBER.
015000     IF VOUCHER-NUMBER NOT = ZEROES
015100         PERFORM READ-VOUCHER-RECORD.
015200
015300 RE-ACCEPT-EXISTING-KEY.
015400     DISPLAY "RECORD NOT FOUND".
015500     PERFORM ACCEPT-EXISTING-KEY.
015600
015700 ENTER-VOUCHER-NUMBER.
015800     DISPLAY "ENTER VOUCHER NUMBER TO SELECT OR CLEAR ".
015900     ACCEPT VOUCHER-NUMBER.
016000
016100 DISPLAY-ALL-FIELDS.
016200     DISPLAY " ".
016300     IF VOUCHER-PAID-DATE NOT = ZEROES
```

```
016400          DISPLAY " !!! THIS VOUCHER IS ALREADY PAID !!!".
016500      PERFORM DISPLAY-VOUCHER-NUMBER.
016600      PERFORM DISPLAY-VOUCHER-VENDOR.
016700      PERFORM DISPLAY-VOUCHER-INVOICE.
016800      PERFORM DISPLAY-VOUCHER-FOR.
016900      PERFORM DISPLAY-VOUCHER-AMOUNT.
017000      PERFORM DISPLAY-VOUCHER-DATE.
017100      PERFORM DISPLAY-VOUCHER-DUE.
017200      PERFORM DISPLAY-VOUCHER-DEDUCTIBLE.
017300      IF VOUCHER-PAID-DATE = ZEROES
017400          PERFORM DISPLAY-VOUCHER-SELECTED.
017500      IF VOUCHER-PAID-DATE NOT = ZEROES
017600          PERFORM DISPLAY-VOUCHER-PAID-AMOUNT
017700          PERFORM DISPLAY-VOUCHER-PAID-DATE
017800          PERFORM DISPLAY-VOUCHER-CHECK-NO.
017900      DISPLAY " ".
018000
018100 DISPLAY-VOUCHER-NUMBER.
018200      DISPLAY "   VOUCHER NUMBER: " VOUCHER-NUMBER.
018300
018400 DISPLAY-VOUCHER-VENDOR.
018500      PERFORM VOUCHER-VENDOR-ON-FILE.
018600      IF VENDOR-RECORD-FOUND = "N"
018700          MOVE "**Not found**" TO VENDOR-NAME.
018800      DISPLAY "   VENDOR: "
018900             VOUCHER-VENDOR " "
019000             VENDOR-NAME.
019100
019200 VOUCHER-VENDOR-ON-FILE.
019300      MOVE VOUCHER-VENDOR TO VENDOR-NUMBER.
019400      PERFORM READ-VENDOR-RECORD.
019500      IF VENDOR-RECORD-FOUND = "N"
019600          MOVE "VENDOR NOT ON FILE"
019700             TO ERROR-MESSAGE.
019800
019900 DISPLAY-VOUCHER-INVOICE.
020000      DISPLAY "   INVOICE: " VOUCHER-INVOICE.
020100
020200 DISPLAY-VOUCHER-FOR.
020300      DISPLAY "   FOR: " VOUCHER-FOR.
020400
020500 DISPLAY-VOUCHER-AMOUNT.
020600      MOVE VOUCHER-AMOUNT TO VOUCHER-AMOUNT-FIELD.
020700      DISPLAY "   AMOUNT: " VOUCHER-AMOUNT-FIELD.
020800
020900 DISPLAY-VOUCHER-DATE.
021000      MOVE VOUCHER-DATE TO DATE-CCYYMMDD.
021100      PERFORM FORMAT-THE-DATE.
021200      DISPLAY "   INVOICE DATE: " FORMATTED-DATE.
021300
021400 DISPLAY-VOUCHER-DUE.
021500      MOVE VOUCHER-DUE TO DATE-CCYYMMDD.
021600      PERFORM FORMAT-THE-DATE.
021700      DISPLAY "   DUE DATE: " FORMATTED-DATE.
021800
```

20

continues

Listing 20.2. continued

```
021900 DISPLAY-VOUCHER-DEDUCTIBLE.
022000      DISPLAY "  DEDUCTIBLE: " VOUCHER-DEDUCTIBLE.
022100
022200 DISPLAY-VOUCHER-SELECTED.
022300      DISPLAY "1. SELECTED FOR PAYMENT: " VOUCHER-SELECTED.
022400
022500 DISPLAY-VOUCHER-PAID-AMOUNT.
022600      MOVE VOUCHER-PAID-AMOUNT TO VOUCHER-PAID-AMOUNT-FIELD.
022700      DISPLAY "   PAID: " VOUCHER-PAID-AMOUNT-FIELD.
022800
022900 DISPLAY-VOUCHER-PAID-DATE.
023000      MOVE VOUCHER-PAID-DATE TO DATE-CCYYMMDD.
023100      PERFORM FORMAT-THE-DATE.
023200      DISPLAY "   PAID ON: " FORMATTED-DATE.
023300
023400 DISPLAY-VOUCHER-CHECK-NO.
023500      DISPLAY "   CHECK: " VOUCHER-CHECK-NO.
023600
023700*-------------------------------
023800* File I-O Routines
023900*-------------------------------
024000 READ-VOUCHER-RECORD.
024100      MOVE "Y" TO VOUCHER-RECORD-FOUND.
024200      READ VOUCHER-FILE RECORD
024300        INVALID KEY
024400          MOVE "N" TO VOUCHER-RECORD-FOUND.
024500
024600*or  READ VOUCHER-FILE RECORD WITH LOCK
024700*        INVALID KEY
024800*          MOVE "N" TO VOUCHER-RECORD-FOUND.
024900
025000*or  READ VOUCHER-FILE RECORD WITH HOLD
025100*        INVALID KEY
025200*          MOVE "N" TO VOUCHER-RECORD-FOUND.
025300
025400 REWRITE-VOUCHER-RECORD.
025500      REWRITE VOUCHER-RECORD
025600          INVALID KEY
025700          DISPLAY "ERROR REWRITING VENDOR RECORD".
025800
025900 READ-VENDOR-RECORD.
026000      MOVE "Y" TO VENDOR-RECORD-FOUND.
026100      READ VENDOR-FILE RECORD
026200        INVALID KEY
026300          MOVE "N" TO VENDOR-RECORD-FOUND.
026400
026500      COPY "PLDATE01.CBL".
026600
```

The output of vchpic01.cbl for a paid and an unpaid voucher follows:

20

```
ENTER VOUCHER NUMBER TO SELECT OR CLEAR
2
!!! THIS VOUCHER IS ALREADY PAID !!!
VOUCHER NUMBER: 00002
VENDOR: 00002 ABC PRINTING
INVOICE: CX-1407
FOR: BUSINESS CARDS
AMOUNT:     98.97
INVOICE DATE:  1/22/1997
DUE DATE:  2/22/1997
DEDUCTIBLE: Y
PAID:    98.97
PAID ON:  1/28/1997
CHECK: 000466
ENTER VOUCHER NUMBER TO SELECT OR CLEAR
3
VOUCHER NUMBER: 00003
VENDOR: 00003 CHARLES SMITH AND SONS
INVOICE: 5057
FOR: OFFICE SUPPLIES
AMOUNT:     27.76
INVOICE DATE:  1/15/1997
DUE DATE:  1/31/1997
DEDUCTIBLE: Y
1. SELECTED FOR PAYMENT: N
SELECT THIS VOUCHER (Y/N)?
Y
```

ANALYSIS The `vchpic01.cbl` program is a cross between `vchmnt01.cbl` and a single-field maintenance program such as `stcmnt04.cbl`—with an extra feature. The user is asked to select a voucher to change. The voucher information is displayed, and the user is asked to enter *yes* or *no* for the VOUCHER-SELECTED field.

The extra feature ensures that if the voucher is paid, the record is displayed with a warning message that it has been paid, and the user is not asked to enter the VOUCHER-SELECTED field.

The warning message appears in DISPLAY-ALL-FIELDS at lines 016300 and 016400. The program tests whether VOUCHER-PAID-DATE NOT = ZEROES and displays the warning before displaying the rest of the record.

Data entry for the selected field is prevented at lines 008000 and 008100 in CHANGE-RECORDS. CHANGE-ONE-FIELD is performed only if VOUCHER-PAID-DATE = ZEROES.

A couple of minor changes exist, such as the prompt for the voucher number at line 015800.

Completing the Payment Cycle on a Voucher

It might seem odd to skip to step 12 of the bills payment flowchart at this point, but the programs needed for steps 2, 7, and 12 are closely related. Refer to Figure 20.1 and note the last step of the bills payment cycle. In this section, you look at vchpay01.cbl, the program that flags vouchers as paid.

You might have noticed that programs that allow changes to one or more fields in a file tend to be based on standard add, change, inquire, or delete maintenance modes. The vchpay01.cbl program in Listing 20.3 is no exception.

TYPE **Listing 20.3. Paying vouchers.**

```
000100 IDENTIFICATION DIVISION.
000200 PROGRAM-ID. VCHPAY01.
000300*-------------------------------
000400* Change only.
000500* User can request a voucher.
000600* If the voucher is already paid,
000700* the user is asked if they
000800* would like to clear the payment
000900* and reopen the voucher.
001000* If the voucher is not paid,
001100* the user is required to enter
001200* a payment date, amount and check
001300* number.
001400* Only maintains PAID-DATE
001500* CHECK-NO and PAID-AMOUNT.
001600*-------------------------------
001700 ENVIRONMENT DIVISION.
001800 INPUT-OUTPUT SECTION.
001900 FILE-CONTROL.
002000
002100     COPY "SLVND02.CBL".
002200
002300     COPY "SLVOUCH.CBL".
002400
002500     COPY "SLCONTRL.CBL".
002600
002700 DATA DIVISION.
002800 FILE SECTION.
002900
003000     COPY "FDVND04.CBL".
003100
003200     COPY "FDVOUCH.CBL".
003300
003400     COPY "FDCONTRL.CBL".
003500
003600 WORKING-STORAGE SECTION.
003700
003800 77  WHICH-FIELD              PIC 9.
003900 77  OK-TO-PROCESS            PIC X.
004000 77  FULL-PAYMENT             PIC X.
004100 77  NEW-VOUCHER              PIC X.
004200
004300 77  VOUCHER-RECORD-FOUND     PIC X.
004400 77  VENDOR-RECORD-FOUND      PIC X.
```

```
004500 77  CONTROL-RECORD-FOUND        PIC X.
004600 77  VOUCHER-NUMBER-FIELD        PIC Z(5).
004700 77  AN-AMOUNT-FIELD             PIC ZZZ,ZZ9.99-.
004800 77  CHECK-NO-FIELD              PIC Z(6).
004900
005000 77  PROCESS-MESSAGE             PIC X(79) VALUE SPACE.
005100
005200 77  SAVE-VOUCHER-RECORD         PIC X(103).
005300
005400     COPY "WSDATE01.CBL".
005500
005600     COPY "WSCASE01.CBL".
005700
005800 PROCEDURE DIVISION.
005900 PROGRAM-BEGIN.
006000     PERFORM OPENING-PROCEDURE.
006100     PERFORM MAIN-PROCESS.
006200     PERFORM CLOSING-PROCEDURE.
006300
006400 PROGRAM-EXIT.
006500     EXIT PROGRAM.
006600
006700 PROGRAM-DONE.
006800     STOP RUN.
006900
007000 OPENING-PROCEDURE.
007100     OPEN I-O VOUCHER-FILE.
007200     OPEN I-O VENDOR-FILE.
007300     OPEN I-O CONTROL-FILE.
007400
007500 CLOSING-PROCEDURE.
007600     CLOSE VOUCHER-FILE.
007700     CLOSE VENDOR-FILE.
007800     CLOSE CONTROL-FILE.
007900
008000 MAIN-PROCESS.
008100     PERFORM CHANGE-MODE.
008200
008300*--------------------------------
008400* CHANGE
008500*--------------------------------
008600 CHANGE-MODE.
008700     PERFORM GET-EXISTING-RECORD.
008800     PERFORM CHANGE-RECORDS
008900         UNTIL VOUCHER-NUMBER = ZEROES.
009000
009100 CHANGE-RECORDS.
009200     PERFORM DISPLAY-ALL-FIELDS.
009300     IF VOUCHER-PAID-DATE = ZEROES
009400         PERFORM CHANGE-TO-PAID
009500     ELSE
009600         PERFORM CHANGE-TO-UNPAID.
009700
009800     PERFORM GET-EXISTING-RECORD.
009900
```

continues

Listing 20.3. continued

```
010000*-------------------------------
010100* Ask if the user wants to pay this
010200* voucher and if so:
010300* Change the voucher to paid status
010400* by getting PAID-DATE, PAID-AMOUNT
010500* and CHECK-NO.
010600*-------------------------------
010700 CHANGE-TO-PAID.
010800     PERFORM ASK-OK-TO-PAY.
010900     IF OK-TO-PROCESS = "Y"
011000         PERFORM CHANGE-ALL-FIELDS.
011100
011200 ASK-OK-TO-PAY.
011300     MOVE "PROCESS THIS VOUCHER AS PAID (Y/N)?"
011400         TO PROCESS-MESSAGE.
011500     PERFORM ASK-OK-TO-PROCESS.
011600
011700 CHANGE-ALL-FIELDS.
011800     PERFORM CHANGE-THIS-FIELD
011900         VARYING WHICH-FIELD FROM 1 BY 1
012000             UNTIL WHICH-FIELD > 3.
012100
012200     PERFORM REWRITE-VOUCHER-RECORD.
012300
012400     IF NEW-VOUCHER = "Y"
012500         PERFORM GENERATE-NEW-VOUCHER.
012600
012700 CHANGE-THIS-FIELD.
012800     IF WHICH-FIELD = 1
012900         PERFORM ENTER-VOUCHER-PAID-DATE.
013000     IF WHICH-FIELD = 2
013100         PERFORM ENTER-VOUCHER-PAYMENT.
013200     IF WHICH-FIELD = 3
013300         PERFORM ENTER-VOUCHER-CHECK-NO.
013400
013500*-------------------------------
013600* Ask if the user wants to re-open
013700* this voucher and if so:
013800* Move zeroes to PAID-DATE,
013900* PAID-AMOUNT and CHECK-NO.
014000*-------------------------------
014100 CHANGE-TO-UNPAID.
014200     PERFORM ASK-OK-TO-OPEN.
014300     IF OK-TO-PROCESS = "Y"
014400         PERFORM CLEAR-PAID-AND-REWRITE
014500         DISPLAY "VOUCHER HAS BEEN RE OPENED".
014600
014700 CLEAR-PAID-AND-REWRITE.
014800     PERFORM CLEAR-PAID-FIELDS.
014900     PERFORM REWRITE-VOUCHER-RECORD.
015000
015100 CLEAR-PAID-FIELDS.
015200     MOVE ZEROES TO VOUCHER-PAID-DATE
015300                    VOUCHER-PAID-AMOUNT
```

```
015400              VOUCHER-CHECK-NO.
015500
015600 ASK-OK-TO-OPEN.
015700      MOVE "RE-OPEN THIS VOUCHER (Y/N)?" TO PROCESS-MESSAGE.
015800      PERFORM ASK-OK-TO-PROCESS.
015900
016000*--------------------------------
016100* This routine is used by both
016200* ASK-OK-TO-PAY which is part of
016300* the CHANGE-TO-PAID logic, and
016400* ASK-OK-TO-OPEN which is part
016500* of the CHANGE-TO-UNPAID LOGIC.
016600*--------------------------------
016700 ASK-OK-TO-PROCESS.
016800      PERFORM ACCEPT-OK-TO-PROCESS.
016900
017000      PERFORM RE-ACCEPT-OK-TO-PROCESS
017100          UNTIL OK-TO-PROCESS = "Y" OR "N".
017200
017300 ACCEPT-OK-TO-PROCESS.
017400      DISPLAY PROCESS-MESSAGE.
017500      ACCEPT OK-TO-PROCESS.
017600      INSPECT OK-TO-PROCESS
017700        CONVERTING LOWER-ALPHA TO UPPER-ALPHA.
017800
017900 RE-ACCEPT-OK-TO-PROCESS.
018000      DISPLAY "YOU MUST ENTER YES OR NO".
018100      PERFORM ACCEPT-OK-TO-PROCESS.
018200
018300*--------------------------------
018400* Field entry routines.
018500*--------------------------------
018600 ENTER-VOUCHER-PAID-DATE.
018700      MOVE "N" TO ZERO-DATE-IS-OK.
018800      MOVE "ENTER PAID DATE(MM/DD/CCYY)?"
018900          TO DATE-PROMPT.
019000      MOVE "A VALID PAID DATE IS REQUIRED"
019100          TO DATE-ERROR-MESSAGE.
019200      PERFORM GET-A-DATE.
019300      MOVE DATE-CCYYMMDD TO VOUCHER-PAID-DATE.
019400
019500*--------------------------------
019600* Voucher payment is entered by
019700* asking if the payment is for
019800* the exact amount of the voucher.
019900* If it is, VOUCHER-AMOUNT
020000* is moved in to VOUCHER-PAID-AMOUNT.
020100* If it is not, then the user is
020200* asked to enter the amount
020300* to be paid.
020400* If the paid amount is less than
020500* the voucher amount, the user
020600* is also asked if a new voucher
020700* should be generated for
020800* the balance. This allows
020900* for partial payments.
```

20

continues

Listing 20.3. continued

```
021000*------------------------------
021100 ENTER-VOUCHER-PAYMENT.
021200     MOVE "N" TO NEW-VOUCHER.
021300     PERFORM ASK-FULL-PAYMENT.
021400     IF FULL-PAYMENT = "Y"
021500         MOVE VOUCHER-AMOUNT TO VOUCHER-PAID-AMOUNT
021600     ELSE
021700         PERFORM ENTER-VOUCHER-PAID-AMOUNT
021800         IF VOUCHER-PAID-AMOUNT < VOUCHER-AMOUNT
021900             PERFORM ASK-NEW-VOUCHER.
022000
022100 ASK-FULL-PAYMENT.
022200     PERFORM ACCEPT-FULL-PAYMENT.
022300     PERFORM RE-ACCEPT-FULL-PAYMENT
022400         UNTIL FULL-PAYMENT = "Y" OR "N".
022500
022600 ACCEPT-FULL-PAYMENT.
022700     MOVE VOUCHER-AMOUNT TO AN-AMOUNT-FIELD.
022800     DISPLAY "PAY THE EXACT AMOUNT "
022900             AN-AMOUNT-FIELD
023000             " (Y/N)?".
023100     ACCEPT FULL-PAYMENT.
023200     INSPECT FULL-PAYMENT
023300      CONVERTING LOWER-ALPHA TO UPPER-ALPHA.
023400
023500 RE-ACCEPT-FULL-PAYMENT.
023600     DISPLAY "YOU MUST ENTER YES OR NO".
023700     PERFORM ACCEPT-FULL-PAYMENT.
023800
023900 ASK-NEW-VOUCHER.
024000     PERFORM ACCEPT-NEW-VOUCHER.
024100     PERFORM RE-ACCEPT-NEW-VOUCHER
024200         UNTIL NEW-VOUCHER = "Y" OR "N".
024300
024400 ACCEPT-NEW-VOUCHER.
024500     MOVE VOUCHER-AMOUNT TO AN-AMOUNT-FIELD.
024600     DISPLAY "GENERATE A NEW VOUCHER".
024700     DISPLAY " FOR THE BALANCE (Y/N)?".
024800     ACCEPT NEW-VOUCHER.
024900     INSPECT NEW-VOUCHER
025000      CONVERTING LOWER-ALPHA TO UPPER-ALPHA.
025100
025200 RE-ACCEPT-NEW-VOUCHER.
025300     DISPLAY "YOU MUST ENTER YES OR NO".
025400     PERFORM ACCEPT-NEW-VOUCHER.
025500
025600 ENTER-VOUCHER-PAID-AMOUNT.
025700     PERFORM ACCEPT-VOUCHER-PAID-AMOUNT.
025800     PERFORM RE-ACCEPT-VOUCHER-PAID-AMOUNT
025900         UNTIL VOUCHER-PAID-AMOUNT NOT = ZEROES
026000             AND VOUCHER-PAID-AMOUNT NOT > VOUCHER-AMOUNT.
026100
026200 ACCEPT-VOUCHER-PAID-AMOUNT.
026300     DISPLAY "ENTER AMOUNT PAID".
```

```
026400      ACCEPT AN-AMOUNT-FIELD.
026500      MOVE AN-AMOUNT-FIELD TO VOUCHER-PAID-AMOUNT.
026600
026700 RE-ACCEPT-VOUCHER-PAID-AMOUNT.
026800      MOVE VOUCHER-AMOUNT TO AN-AMOUNT-FIELD.
026900      DISPLAY "A PAYMENT MUST BE ENTERED THAT IS".
027000      DISPLAY "NOT GREATER THAN " AN-AMOUNT-FIELD.
027100      PERFORM ACCEPT-VOUCHER-PAID-AMOUNT.
027200
027300 ENTER-VOUCHER-CHECK-NO.
027400      PERFORM ACCEPT-VOUCHER-CHECK-NO.
027500
027600 ACCEPT-VOUCHER-CHECK-NO.
027700      DISPLAY "ENTER THE CHECK NUMBER".
027800      DISPLAY "ENTER 0 FOR CASH PAYMENT".
027900      ACCEPT CHECK-NO-FIELD.
028000      MOVE CHECK-NO-FIELD TO VOUCHER-CHECK-NO.
028100
028200*-------------------------------
028300* A new voucher is generated by
028400* 1. Saving the existing voucher
028500*    record.
028600* 2. Locating a new voucher number
028700*    that is not in use by using
028800*    the control file and attempting
028900*    to read a voucher with the
029000*    number offered by the control
029100*    file.
029200* 3. Restoring the saved voucher record
029300*    but using the new voucher number.
029400* 4. Setting the new voucher amount
029500*    to the original amount minus
029600*    the amount paid.
029700* 5. Resetting the paid date,
029800*    paid amount and check number.
029900* 6. Setting the selected flag to "N".
030000* 7. Writing this new record.
030100*-------------------------------
030200 GENERATE-NEW-VOUCHER.
030300      MOVE VOUCHER-RECORD TO SAVE-VOUCHER-RECORD.
030400      PERFORM GET-NEW-RECORD-KEY.
030500      PERFORM CREATE-NEW-VOUCHER-RECORD.
030600      PERFORM DISPLAY-NEW-VOUCHER.
030700
030800 CREATE-NEW-VOUCHER-RECORD.
030900      MOVE SAVE-VOUCHER-RECORD TO VOUCHER-RECORD.
031000      MOVE CONTROL-LAST-VOUCHER TO VOUCHER-NUMBER.
031100      SUBTRACT VOUCHER-PAID-AMOUNT FROM VOUCHER-AMOUNT.
031200      MOVE "N" TO VOUCHER-SELECTED.
031300      PERFORM CLEAR-PAID-FIELDS.
031400      PERFORM WRITE-VOUCHER-RECORD.
031500
031600 DISPLAY-NEW-VOUCHER.
031700      MOVE VOUCHER-NUMBER TO VOUCHER-NUMBER-FIELD.
031800      MOVE VOUCHER-AMOUNT TO AN-AMOUNT-FIELD.
```

20

continues

Listing 20.3. continued

```
031900        DISPLAY "VOUCHER " VOUCHER-NUMBER-FIELD
032000                " CREATED FOR " AN-AMOUNT-FIELD.
032100
032200*--------------------------------
032300* Standard change mode routines to
032400* get a voucher number, read the
032500* voucher record.
032600*--------------------------------
032700 GET-NEW-RECORD-KEY.
032800        PERFORM ACCEPT-NEW-RECORD-KEY.
032900        PERFORM RE-ACCEPT-NEW-RECORD-KEY
033000             UNTIL VOUCHER-RECORD-FOUND = "N".
033100
033200
033300
033400 ACCEPT-NEW-RECORD-KEY.
033500        PERFORM INIT-VOUCHER-RECORD.
033600        PERFORM RETRIEVE-NEXT-VOUCHER-NUMBER.
033700
033800        PERFORM READ-VOUCHER-RECORD.
033900
034000 RE-ACCEPT-NEW-RECORD-KEY.
034100        PERFORM ACCEPT-NEW-RECORD-KEY.
034200
034300 RETRIEVE-NEXT-VOUCHER-NUMBER.
034400        PERFORM READ-CONTROL-RECORD.
034500        ADD 1 TO CONTROL-LAST-VOUCHER.
034600        MOVE CONTROL-LAST-VOUCHER TO VOUCHER-NUMBER.
034700        PERFORM REWRITE-CONTROL-RECORD.
034800
034900 GET-EXISTING-RECORD.
035000        PERFORM ACCEPT-EXISTING-KEY.
035100        PERFORM RE-ACCEPT-EXISTING-KEY
035200             UNTIL VOUCHER-RECORD-FOUND = "Y" OR
035300                   VOUCHER-NUMBER = ZEROES.
035400
035500 ACCEPT-EXISTING-KEY.
035600        PERFORM INIT-VOUCHER-RECORD.
035700        PERFORM ENTER-VOUCHER-NUMBER.
035800        IF VOUCHER-NUMBER NOT = ZEROES
035900           PERFORM READ-VOUCHER-RECORD.
036000
036100 RE-ACCEPT-EXISTING-KEY.
036200        DISPLAY "RECORD NOT FOUND".
036300        PERFORM ACCEPT-EXISTING-KEY.
036400
036500 ENTER-VOUCHER-NUMBER.
036600        DISPLAY "ENTER VOUCHER NUMBER TO PROCESS".
036700        ACCEPT VOUCHER-NUMBER.
036800
036900*--------------------------------
037000* Standard routines to display
037100* voucher fields.
037200*--------------------------------
```

```
037300 DISPLAY-ALL-FIELDS.
037400     DISPLAY " ".
037500     PERFORM DISPLAY-VOUCHER-NUMBER.
037600     PERFORM DISPLAY-VOUCHER-VENDOR.
037700     PERFORM DISPLAY-VOUCHER-INVOICE.
037800     PERFORM DISPLAY-VOUCHER-FOR.
037900     PERFORM DISPLAY-VOUCHER-AMOUNT.
038000     PERFORM DISPLAY-VOUCHER-DATE.
038100     PERFORM DISPLAY-VOUCHER-DUE.
038200     PERFORM DISPLAY-VOUCHER-DEDUCTIBLE.
038300     PERFORM DISPLAY-VOUCHER-SELECTED.
038400     PERFORM DISPLAY-VOUCHER-PAID-DATE.
038500     PERFORM DISPLAY-VOUCHER-PAID-AMOUNT.
038600     PERFORM DISPLAY-VOUCHER-CHECK-NO.
038700     DISPLAY " ".
038800
038900 DISPLAY-VOUCHER-NUMBER.
039000     DISPLAY "    VOUCHER NUMBER: " VOUCHER-NUMBER.
039100
039200 DISPLAY-VOUCHER-VENDOR.
039300     PERFORM VOUCHER-VENDOR-ON-FILE.
039400     IF VENDOR-RECORD-FOUND = "N"
039500         MOVE "**Not found**" TO VENDOR-NAME.
039600     DISPLAY "    VENDOR: "
039700            VOUCHER-VENDOR " "
039800            VENDOR-NAME.
039900
040000 DISPLAY-VOUCHER-INVOICE.
040100     DISPLAY "    INVOICE: " VOUCHER-INVOICE.
040200
040300 DISPLAY-VOUCHER-FOR.
040400     DISPLAY "    FOR: " VOUCHER-FOR.
040500
040600 DISPLAY-VOUCHER-AMOUNT.
040700     MOVE VOUCHER-AMOUNT TO AN-AMOUNT-FIELD.
040800     DISPLAY "    AMOUNT: " AN-AMOUNT-FIELD.
040900
041000 DISPLAY-VOUCHER-DATE.
041100     MOVE VOUCHER-DATE TO DATE-CCYYMMDD.
041200     PERFORM FORMAT-THE-DATE.
041300     DISPLAY "    INVOICE DATE: " FORMATTED-DATE.
041400
041500 DISPLAY-VOUCHER-DUE.
041600     MOVE VOUCHER-DUE TO DATE-CCYYMMDD.
041700     PERFORM FORMAT-THE-DATE.
041800     DISPLAY "    DUE DATE: " FORMATTED-DATE.
041900
042000 DISPLAY-VOUCHER-DEDUCTIBLE.
042100     DISPLAY "    DEDUCTIBLE: " VOUCHER-DEDUCTIBLE.
042200
042300 DISPLAY-VOUCHER-SELECTED.
042400     DISPLAY "    SELECTED FOR PAYMENT: " VOUCHER-SELECTED.
042500
042600 DISPLAY-VOUCHER-PAID-DATE.
042700     MOVE VOUCHER-PAID-DATE TO DATE-CCYYMMDD.
```

20

continues

Listing 20.3. continued

```
042800        PERFORM FORMAT-THE-DATE.
042900        DISPLAY "1. PAID ON: " FORMATTED-DATE.
043000
043100 DISPLAY-VOUCHER-PAID-AMOUNT.
043200        MOVE VOUCHER-PAID-AMOUNT TO AN-AMOUNT-FIELD.
043300        DISPLAY "2. PAID: " AN-AMOUNT-FIELD.
043400
043500 DISPLAY-VOUCHER-CHECK-NO.
043600        DISPLAY "3. CHECK: " VOUCHER-CHECK-NO.
043700
043800*--------------------------------
043900* File activity Routines
044000*--------------------------------
044100 INIT-VOUCHER-RECORD.
044200        MOVE SPACE TO VOUCHER-INVOICE
044300                            VOUCHER-FOR
044400                            VOUCHER-DEDUCTIBLE
044500                            VOUCHER-SELECTED.
044600        MOVE ZEROES TO VOUCHER-NUMBER
044700                            VOUCHER-VENDOR
044800                    .       VOUCHER-AMOUNT
044900                            VOUCHER-DATE
045000                            VOUCHER-DUE
045100                            VOUCHER-PAID-AMOUNT
045200                            VOUCHER-PAID-DATE
045300                            VOUCHER-CHECK-NO.
045400
045500 READ-VOUCHER-RECORD.
045600        MOVE "Y" TO VOUCHER-RECORD-FOUND.
045700        READ VOUCHER-FILE RECORD
045800          INVALID KEY
045900              MOVE "N" TO VOUCHER-RECORD-FOUND.
046000
046100*or  READ VOUCHER-FILE RECORD WITH LOCK
046200*        INVALID KEY
046300*            MOVE "N" TO VOUCHER-RECORD-FOUND.
046400
046500*or  READ VOUCHER-FILE RECORD WITH HOLD
046600*        INVALID KEY
046700*            MOVE "N" TO VOUCHER-RECORD-FOUND.
046800
046900 WRITE-VOUCHER-RECORD.
047000        WRITE VOUCHER-RECORD
047100          INVALID KEY
047200            DISPLAY "RECORD ALREADY ON FILE".
047300
047400 REWRITE-VOUCHER-RECORD.
047500        REWRITE VOUCHER-RECORD
047600          INVALID KEY
047700            DISPLAY "ERROR REWRITING VENDOR RECORD".
047800
047900 VOUCHER-VENDOR-ON-FILE.
048000        MOVE VOUCHER-VENDOR TO VENDOR-NUMBER.
048100        PERFORM READ-VENDOR-RECORD.
```

```
048200
048300 READ-VENDOR-RECORD.
048400     MOVE "Y" TO VENDOR-RECORD-FOUND.
048500     READ VENDOR-FILE RECORD
048600        INVALID KEY
048700           MOVE "N" TO VENDOR-RECORD-FOUND.
048800
048900 READ-CONTROL-RECORD.
049000     MOVE 1 TO CONTROL-KEY.
049100     MOVE "Y" TO CONTROL-RECORD-FOUND.
049200     READ CONTROL-FILE RECORD
049300        INVALID KEY
049400         MOVE "N" TO CONTROL-RECORD-FOUND
049500         DISPLAY "CONTROL FILE IS INVALID".
049600
049700 REWRITE-CONTROL-RECORD.
049800     REWRITE CONTROL-RECORD
049900        INVALID KEY
050000         DISPLAY "ERROR REWRITING CONTROL RECORD".
050100
050200*-------------------------------
050300* General utility routines
050400*-------------------------------
050500     COPY "PLDATE01.CBL".
050600
```

The sample output for vchpay01.cbl shows voucher 2 being processed as a partial payment of $50.00 on an invoice that was for $98.97. The program indicates that voucher 10 was generated for the balance. Voucher 10 then is processed, and the display confirms that a voucher was created for the balance of the original invoice, $48.97. Voucher 10 is not processed. Finally, voucher 3 is reopened. Here is the output:

OUTPUT

```
ENTER VOUCHER NUMBER TO PROCESS
2
VOUCHER NUMBER: 00002
VENDOR: 00002 ABC PRINTING
INVOICE: CX-1407
FOR: BUSINESS CARDS
AMOUNT:      98.97
INVOICE DATE:  1/22/1997
DUE DATE:  2/22/1997
DEDUCTIBLE: Y
SELECTED FOR PAYMENT: N
1. PAID ON:  0/00/0000
2. PAID:        0.00
3. CHECK: 000000
PROCESS THIS VOUCHER AS PAID (Y/N)?
y
ENTER PAID DATE(MM/DD/CCYY)?
1/27/1997
PAY THE EXACT AMOUNT      98.97  (Y/N)?
n
ENTER AMOUNT PAID
```

20

```
50
GENERATE A NEW VOUCHER
FOR THE BALANCE (Y/N)?
y
ENTER THE CHECK NUMBER
ENTER 0 FOR CASH PAYMENT
107
VOUCHER     10 CREATED FOR        48.97
ENTER VOUCHER NUMBER TO PROCESS
10
VOUCHER NUMBER: 00010
VENDOR: 00002 ABC PRINTING
INVOICE: CX-1407
FOR: BUSINESS CARDS
AMOUNT:      48.97
INVOICE DATE:  1/22/1997
DUE DATE:  2/22/1997
DEDUCTIBLE: Y
SELECTED FOR PAYMENT: N
1. PAID ON:  0/00/0000
2. PAID:      0.00
3. CHECK: 000000
PROCESS THIS VOUCHER AS PAID (Y/N)?
n
ENTER VOUCHER NUMBER TO PROCESS
3
VOUCHER NUMBER: 00003
VENDOR: 00003 CHARLES SMITH AND SONS
INVOICE: 5057
FOR: OFFICE SUPPLIES
AMOUNT:      27.76
INVOICE DATE:  1/15/1997
DUE DATE:  1/31/1997
DEDUCTIBLE: Y
SELECTED FOR PAYMENT: N
1. PAID ON:  1/22/1997
2. PAID:      27.76
3. CHECK: 000106
RE-OPEN THIS VOUCHER (Y/N)?
y
VOUCHER HAS BEEN RE OPENED
ENTER VOUCHER NUMBER TO PROCESS
```

ANALYSIS Before you look in detail at the analysis of the program, you need to know about some differences between vchpay01.cbl and a standard maintenance module.

The program is in change mode only, but within change mode a user could be making two possible changes. The user could be intending to change a voucher from unpaid to paid, which would be the usual action of the program.

The user might also want to change the status from paid to unpaid for various reasons, such as, if a voucher were flagged as paid in error, or for some reason the actual payment was not valid (because the check bounced or all the cash was counterfeit).

The program also has a special feature that allows the user to enter a partial payment on a voucher. When a partial payment is entered, the voucher is flagged as paid, and a new voucher is written for the balance unpaid. This creates an add records action in the middle of change mode. This is described in more detail in the analysis of the program, and in the description that follows here.

Change mode actually is broken into two different types of changes to handle this: CHANGE-TO-PAID and CHANGE-TO-UNPAID. Either one affects three fields—VOUCHER-PAID-DATE, VOUCHER-PAID-AMOUNT, and VOUCHER-CHECK-NO—but in slightly different ways.

In changing a voucher from unpaid to paid, the user must enter values for all three of these fields. It would be incorrect to enter a paid date, but no paid amount or check number. The user must be forced to enter all three fields and cannot be given the usual choice in change mode of selecting which field to modify.

Reversing the process reopens a voucher by resetting the paid date, paid amount, and check number to zeroes. There is no point in asking the user to enter zeroes for each of these fields, so this is done automatically in the program if reopening of a voucher is selected.

The usual process of the program, changing a voucher from unpaid to paid, is more complicated than just accepting entry of the three fields. On any voucher, you might want to pay the exact amount, overpay the amount (because of late charges), or underpay the amount (as a partial payment).

Rather than directly asking for the amount to be paid, the program first asks the user whether the exact amount of the voucher is to be paid. If so, VOUCHER-AMOUNT is moved to VOUCHER-PAID-AMOUNT, and the user is not required to enter the amount. Otherwise, the user must enter the amount.

In a full accounts payable system (a bills payment system with accounting functions), overpayment probably would not be allowed. If late charges or additional charges were created for an invoice, either the original voucher would have to be modified, or a new voucher would have to be created with the additional charges. The original voucher and the late charges voucher could be paid by the same check. The vchpay01.cbl program also will not allow overpayment.

The last feature of vchpay01.cbl is designed to handle underpayment. The program assumes that underpayment is a partial payment and asks the user whether a new voucher should be generated automatically for the balance of the voucher that was just paid.

This new voucher will sit in the voucher file waiting for the next bills payment cycle. The automated generation saves the user having to hand-enter another copy of the same voucher with the new balance now owing on the invoice and, in the process, also reduces potential data error entries.

20

Now that you know what to expect in the way of differences, you can look at the program in some detail.

The first difference is apparent in CHANGE-RECORDS, which begins at line 009100. At this point, the voucher record has been read and is displayed at line 009200. If VOUCHER-PAID-DATE = ZEROES, the voucher is unpaid, and the logic performs CHANGE-TO-PAID. Otherwise, the voucher is paid, and presumably the user wants to CHANGE-TO-UNPAID, which is performed at line 009600.

The CHANGE-TO-UNPAID logic is the simpler of the two types of logic. The user has just seen the voucher displayed on-screen, and you cannot assume that it must be changed. The user could have typed the wrong voucher number accidentally, and to move straight into the logic to clear the fields would cause a voucher to be modified incorrectly.

CHANGE-TO-UNPAID and its related paragraphs extend from lines 014100 through 015900. The first action at line 014200 is to ask the user whether it is okay to reopen this voucher (ASK-OK-TO-OPEN). If the user says yes, zeroes are moved to VOUCHER-PAID-DATE, VOUCHER-PAID-AMOUNT, and VOUCHER-CHECK-NO. The voucher record is rewritten and the user is given a message saying "VOUCHER HAS BEEN RE OPENED".

CHANGE-TO-PAID and its related paragraphs extend from lines 010700 through 013400, and it is a bit more complicated. At line 010800, the user immediately is asked whether this is the voucher to pay. If so, CHANGE-ALL-FIELDS at line 011700 asks for an entry for each of the fields by performing CHANGE-THIS-FIELD while varying WHICH-FIELD from 1 through 3. CHANGE-THIS-FIELD at line 012700 performs the data entry routines for each field.

In CHANGE-ALL-FIELDS at line 012200, the record is rewritten. At lines 012400 and 012500, a test is done to see whether NEW-VOUCHER = "Y". If so, the GENERATE-NEW-VOUCHER routine is performed.

The field-entry routines start at line 018300 and extend to line 028100. ENTER-VOUCHER-PAID-DATE at line 018600 is a standard date-entry routine that does not allow a zero date to be entered.

At line 027300, ENTER-VOUCHER-CHECK-NO is another simple entry routine for the check number. The user is allowed to enter a zero check number to signal that payment is by cash (or at least not by check).

The meatiest data entry routine starts at line 021100, ENTER-VOUCHER-PAYMENT. The routine starts by setting the NEW-VOUCHER flag to "N" and performing ASK-FULL-PAYMENT. This routine at line 022100 asks the user whether the voucher payment is for the exact amount of the voucher. If the user answers yes, at line 021500, the VOUCHER-AMOUNT is moved to the VOUCHER-PAID-AMOUNT, and the user is not required to enter the amount to be paid. Otherwise, at line 021700, the user is asked to ENTER-VOUCHER-PAID-AMOUNT. This routine at line 025600 requires that the user enter an amount greater than zero, but not greater than VOUCHER-AMOUNT. Upon return to line 021800, IF VOUCHER-PAID-AMOUNT < VOUCHER-AMOUNT, the user is asked whether a new voucher should be created. ASK-NEW-VOUCHER at line 023900 is a simple yes/no entry routine that accepts a value into NEW-VOUCHER.

The last key part of the program begins at line 030200, the routine to GENERATE-NEW-VOUCHER. A new voucher is generated by creating a new voucher with all the same information as the original voucher, a new voucher number, and a voucher amount that is the original amount minus the amount just paid.

Most of the information that is needed to create the new voucher record is in the VOUCHER-RECORD, but you do need to locate a new voucher number that can be used. The GET-NEW-RECORD-KEY routine, taken from vchmnt01.cbl, locates a usable voucher number, but in the process might destroy the needed information in the VOUCHER-RECORD. To preserve the values in VOUCHER-RECORD, at line 030300, it is moved to a SAVE-VOUCHER-RECORD. This is defined in WORKING-STORAGE at line 005200 and is a space set aside for saving a copy of the voucher record. When the voucher record is preserved, it is possible to perform GET-NEW-RECORD-KEY, which returns a new voucher number in VOUCHER-NUMBER and in CONTROL-LAST-VOUCHER.

The next step is CREATE-NEW-VOUCHER-RECORD at line 030800. This routine moves the SAVE-VOUCHER-RECORD back to the VOUCHER-RECORD. This destroys the new voucher number that was set up in VOUCHER-NUMBER, but another copy of that number is available in CONTROL-LAST-VOUCHER. This is moved to VOUCHER-NUMBER.

At this point, the voucher record contains all the information that was placed in the record after the voucher was entered as paid but also contains the new voucher number. To set up the record so that the VOUCHER-AMOUNT is correct, it is necessary to subtract the VOUCHER-PAID-AMOUNT from the VOUCHER-AMOUNT. The voucher is flagged as not selected for payment at the VOUCHER-PAID-AMOUNT, and VOUCHER-PAID-DATE and VOUCHER-CHECK-NO are reset to zero. Finally, this new voucher record is written at line 031400.

Follow thoroughly what is happening in CREATE-NEW-VOUCHER-RECORD because it contains much that is new to you.

The last routine in this series, DISPLAY-NEW-VOUCHER at line 031600, informs the user that a new voucher has been created for the balance, and what the new voucher number is.

Code, compile, and run vchpay01.cbl against some trial vouchers created with vchmnt01.cbl. Pay some in full, and make some partial payments. Then try reopening some of those vouchers.

20

Summary

Today, you created a maintenance module that actually is used as a voucher-entry program. This used a control file to generate the new voucher number in add mode, thus avoiding the step of having the user look up the next voucher number each time a voucher needs to be added. You also explored the following:

☐ Another maintenance-based program to allow selection of individual vouchers to pay

☐ A third variation on a maintenance program, used as the basis for the program that allows vouchers to be flagged as paid

☐ Several features that can be added to a standard change mode maintenance module in order to assist the user while doing data entry, including recognition of whether a user wants to change a voucher status from paid to unpaid, or vice versa, and automatic generation of new vouchers for underpayment

Q&A

Q Why add all these features to a maintenance module?

A There are two answers to this. A computer is supposed to take the workload off the user. The more it can do so, the better the program is. The second part of the answer has to do with data accuracy. In vchpay01.cbl, a new voucher is generated automatically on an underpayment. The computer easily can calculate the difference between the amount paid and the amount owed and generate a voucher for the new amount. A user would have to do this subtraction by hand or with an adding machine, opening up the possibility of an error. When thinking about features for a program, always think in terms of whether it gets more work done and whether it achieves more accuracy.

Workshop

Quiz

1. The original routine to enter the paid amount in vchpay01.cbl (shown in Listing 20.3) allowed the entry of only a voucher amount less than or equal to the voucher amount. The program has been modified as shown in the following listing:

```
025600 ENTER-VOUCHER-PAID-AMOUNT.
025700     PERFORM ACCEPT-VOUCHER-PAID-AMOUNT.
025800     PERFORM RE-ACCEPT-VOUCHER-PAID-AMOUNT
025900         UNTIL VOUCHER-PAID-AMOUNT NOT = ZEROES.
026000
026100
026200 ACCEPT-VOUCHER-PAID-AMOUNT.
```

20

```
026300        DISPLAY "ENTER AMOUNT PAID".
026400        ACCEPT AN-AMOUNT-FIELD.
026500        MOVE AN-AMOUNT-FIELD TO VOUCHER-PAID-AMOUNT.
026600
026700 RE-ACCEPT-VOUCHER-PAID-AMOUNT.
026800        MOVE VOUCHER-AMOUNT TO AN-AMOUNT-FIELD.
026900        DISPLAY "A PAYMENT MUST BE ENTERED".
027000        DISPLAY "AGAINST " AN-AMOUNT-FIELD.
027100        PERFORM ACCEPT-VOUCHER-PAID-AMOUNT.
027200
```

Compare this to lines 025600 through 027100 in vchpay01.cbl (shown in Listing 20.3). What is the effect of this change?

Exercise

Copy vchpay01.cbl to vchpay02.cbl and using the listing in Quiz question 1, make the changes indicated. Compile and run the program and try some overpayments and underpayments. Make sure the program works correctly. The vchpay02.cbl program will be used in the next chapter, Day 21, "Selecting, Sorting, and Reporting," so be sure to complete this exercise.

20

Day 21

Selecting, Sorting, and Reporting

Reporting is the most visible part of any program. Hard-copy reports tend to circulate and be seen by many users. Reports tend to be the area where most modification requests come in. You need several tools to handle reports effectively.

Today, you learn about the following topics:

- ☐ Selecting records
- ☐ Sorting a file
- ☐ Printing totals
- ☐ Programming control breaks
- ☐ The cash requirements report

Continuing the Bills Payment System

Figure 21.1 shows the flowchart from Day 20. Steps 2, 7, and 12, shown in light gray, were completed on that day. In today's lesson, you complete steps 4, 6, and 8 shown in dark gray. This will complete all of the computer processes in the bills payment system.

You start with step 6, the selection of records by date range.

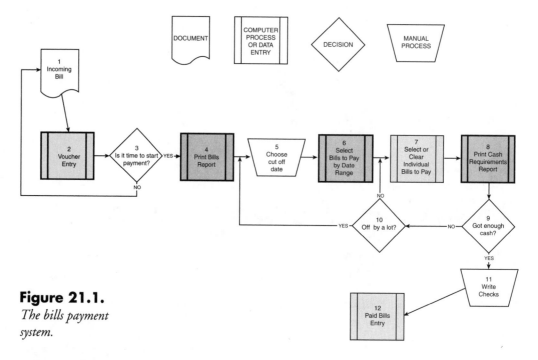

Figure 21.1.
The bills payment system.

Selecting Records

In many programs, it is necessary to read through a file, picking out records that require processing. Step 4 in Figure 21.1 is to report on all unpaid bills. That report has to select for printing all voucher records in which the VOUCHER-PAID-DATE is zeroes. In step 8, the cash-requirements report selects for printing all vouchers that are unpaid (VOUCHER-PAID-DATE = ZEROES) and that are selected for payment (VOUCHER-SELECTED = "Y").

There are several solutions to this selection problem, but one of the most efficient methods is to stick with the basic processing-loop design. Listing 21.1 shows the pseudocode for this style of processing.

21

TYPE Listing 21.1. Pseudocode for a selected records-processing loop.

```
process-records
    read-first-valid-record
    perform process-loop
        until file-at-end
process-loop
    process-this-record
    read-next-valid-record
```

ANALYSIS In some programs, such as those covered in Day 17, "Alternate Keys," it is necessary to use a START command to change the key path in the file before reading through the file. In such a program, the read-first-valid-record action is used to set up the file so that it can be read.

In other programs, you don't need to do any setting up. The OPEN positions the file so that the first READ NEXT will return the first record on the primary key path. In this type of program, there is no difference between a read-first-valid-record and a read-next-valid-record.

The read-next-valid-record logic reads a record and makes all the decisions necessary to determine that this record fits the selection criteria. The read-first-valid-record action sets up the file, reads a record, and then uses the same decisions used in read-next-valid-record. Listing 21.2 shows how this code might look on the voucher file.

TYPE Listing 21.2. Code for a selected records processing loop.

```
010100 PROCESS-VOUCHERS.
010200     PERFORM READ-FIRST-VALID-VOUCHER.
010300     PERFORM PROCESS-ALL-VOUCHERS
010400         UNTIL VOUCHER-FILE-AT-END = "Y".
010500
010600 PROCESS-ALL-VOUCHERS.
010700     PERFORM PROCESS-THIS-VOUCHER.
010800     PERFORM READ-NEXT-VALID-VOUCHER.
```

Step 6 in Figure 21.1, selecting vouchers by range, is really a two-step process. Selecting vouchers for payment the first time is simple, but if the user wants to change the selection, there must be some way to clear out existing selections in order to start over again. This process of clearing existing selections and selecting could be combined into one program, but for ease of illustration, it is broken down here into two separate programs.

The vchclr01.cbl program in Listing 21.3 clears all VOUCHER-SELECTED flags, and vchsel01.cbl (which you'll see soon) selects vouchers by range.

21

TYPE **Listing 21.3. Clearing existing selections.**

```
000100 IDENTIFICATION DIVISION.
000200 PROGRAM-ID. VCHCLR01.
000300*-------------------------------
000400* Asks the user if all selected
000500* vouchers should be cleared.
000600*
000700* 1. Searches the voucher file for
000800*    unpaid vouchers that are
000900*    selected and clears the
001000*    selected flag
001100*-------------------------------
001200 ENVIRONMENT DIVISION.
001300 INPUT-OUTPUT SECTION.
001400 FILE-CONTROL.
001500
001600     COPY "SLVOUCH.CBL".
001700
001800 DATA DIVISION.
001900 FILE SECTION.
002000
002100     COPY "FDVOUCH.CBL".
002200
002300 WORKING-STORAGE SECTION.
002400
002500 77  OK-TO-CLEAR            PIC X.
002600 77  VOUCHER-FILE-AT-END    PIC X.
002700
002800     COPY "WSCASE01.CBL".
002900
003000 PROCEDURE DIVISION.
003100 PROGRAM-BEGIN.
003200     PERFORM OPENING-PROCEDURE.
003300     PERFORM MAIN-PROCESS.
003400     PERFORM CLOSING-PROCEDURE.
003500
003600 PROGRAM-EXIT.
003700     EXIT PROGRAM.
003800
003900 PROGRAM-DONE.
004000     STOP RUN.
004100
004200 OPENING-PROCEDURE.
004300     OPEN I-O VOUCHER-FILE.
004400
004500 CLOSING-PROCEDURE.
004600     CLOSE VOUCHER-FILE.
004700
004800 MAIN-PROCESS.
004900     PERFORM GET-OK-TO-CLEAR.
005000     IF OK-TO-CLEAR = "Y"
005100         PERFORM PROCESS-VOUCHERS.
005200
005300 GET-OK-TO-CLEAR.
005400     PERFORM ACCEPT-OK-TO-CLEAR.
```

21

```
005500      PERFORM RE-ACCEPT-OK-TO-CLEAR
005600          UNTIL OK-TO-CLEAR = "Y" OR "N".
005700
005800 ACCEPT-OK-TO-CLEAR.
005900      DISPLAY "CLEAR ALL PREVIOUS SELECTIONS (Y/N)?".
006000      ACCEPT OK-TO-CLEAR.
006100      INSPECT OK-TO-CLEAR
006200        CONVERTING LOWER-ALPHA
006300        TO            UPPER-ALPHA.
006400
006500
006600 RE-ACCEPT-OK-TO-CLEAR.
006700      DISPLAY "YOU MUST ENTER YES OR NO".
006800      PERFORM ACCEPT-OK-TO-CLEAR.
006900
007000*--------------------------------
007100* Clear all previous selections.
007200*--------------------------------
007300 PROCESS-VOUCHERS.
007400      PERFORM READ-FIRST-VALID-VOUCHER.
007500      PERFORM PROCESS-ALL-VOUCHERS
007600          UNTIL VOUCHER-FILE-AT-END = "Y".
007700
007800 PROCESS-ALL-VOUCHERS.
007900      PERFORM PROCESS-THIS-VOUCHER.
008000      PERFORM READ-NEXT-VALID-VOUCHER.
008100
008200 PROCESS-THIS-VOUCHER.
008300      MOVE "N" TO VOUCHER-SELECTED
008400      PERFORM REWRITE-VOUCHER-RECORD.
008500
008600*--------------------------------
008700* Read first, read next routines
008800*--------------------------------
008900 READ-FIRST-VALID-VOUCHER.
009000      PERFORM READ-NEXT-VALID-VOUCHER.
009100
009200 READ-NEXT-VALID-VOUCHER.
009300      PERFORM READ-NEXT-VOUCHER-RECORD.
009400      PERFORM READ-NEXT-VOUCHER-RECORD
009500          UNTIL VOUCHER-FILE-AT-END = "Y"
009600             OR (   VOUCHER-PAID-DATE = ZEROES
009700                 AND VOUCHER-SELECTED = "Y").
009800
009900 READ-NEXT-VOUCHER-RECORD.
010000      MOVE  "N" TO VOUCHER-FILE-AT-END.
010100      READ VOUCHER-FILE NEXT RECORD
010200        AT END
010300          MOVE "Y" TO VOUCHER-FILE-AT-END.
010400
010500*--------------------------------
010600* Other File I-O routines.
010700*--------------------------------
010800 REWRITE-VOUCHER-RECORD.
010900      REWRITE VOUCHER-RECORD
011000          INVALID KEY
011100          DISPLAY "ERROR REWRITING VENDOR RECORD".
011200
```

21

ANALYSIS The MAIN-PROCESS of the program at line 004800 starts by asking the user whether to "CLEAR ALL PREVIOUS SELECTIONS (Y/N)?". This gives the user a chance to back out in case the program was run incorrectly. The routines to ask the user extend from line 005300 through line 006800. If the user answers yes, PROCESS-VOUCHERS at line 007300 is performed. This logic extends from line 007300 through line 008400 and follows the format of a selected records processing loop.

The actual processing of the voucher is at line 008200 in PROCESS-THIS-VOUCHER. This routine moves "N" to VOUCHER-SELECTED and rewrites the record. This takes care of what is to be done to the records, but the selection of which records it will be done to still needs attention.

READ-FIRST-VALID-VOUCHER and READ-NEXT-VALID-VOUCHER are at lines 008900 and 009200. No special setup is needed for the READ-FIRST-VALID-VOUCHER routine, so it simply performs READ-NEXT-VALID-VOUCHER.

The real action takes place in READ-NEXT-VALID-VOUCHER at line 009200. At first glance, the paragraph seems odd because it appears to read the next voucher record twice. Remember that the UNTIL in a PERFORM UNTIL is tested once before anything is performed. Lines 009200 through 009700 actually do the following:

1. Read the next voucher record.
2. Test whether the file is at end or paid date is zeroes and the selected flag is "Y".
3. If none of the conditions is true, read the next voucher record and go back to step 2.

It is easy to forget that the test in a PERFORM UNTIL occurs before the PERFORM because of the way the command is structured.

The overall effect is that READ-NEXT-VALID-VOUCHER continues reading through the file until either the file is exhausted (at end), or a record is found that matches the two conditions of VOUCHER-PAID-DATE = ZEROES and VOUCHER-SELECTED = "Y". The READ-NEXT-VOUCHER-RECORD routine at line 009900 is a standard read-next routine that sets an at-end flag.

The pseudocode for record selection now can be extended to incorporate the logic for reading the first and next selected records, as in Listing 21.4.

TYPE **Listing 21.4. An extended selected record-processing loop.**

```
process-records
    read-first-valid-record
    perform process-loop
        until file-at-end
process-loop
    process-this-record
    read-next-valid-record
```

21

```
read-first-valid-record
    start-the-file
    read-next-valid-record
read-next-valid-record
    read-next-record
    perform read-next-record
        until file is at end
        or (the selection condition is met)
```

The second half of the selection problem is solved with vchsel01.cbl, shown in Listing 21.5.
This program enables the user to select vouchers for payment by a cutoff date. The user enters
a cutoff date, and all unpaid vouchers due on or before that date are selected for payment.
The vchsel01.cbl program that you are about to create (vchclr01.cbl) and vchpic01.cbl
created in Day 20, "More Complex Data Entry," can be used repeatedly to select and reselect
vouchers. This will be done as long as the cash requirements report (step 8 of Figure 21.1)
produces a number that is too large to pay.

TYPE   **Listing 21.5. Selecting by cutoff date.**

```
000100 IDENTIFICATION DIVISION.
000200 PROGRAM-ID. VCHSEL01.
000300*--------------------------------
000400* Asks the user for a cutoff
000500* date
000600*
000700* 1. Searches the voucher file for
000800*    unpaid vouchers that are
000900*    within the cut off date
001000*    and reflags them as selected
001100*--------------------------------
001200 ENVIRONMENT DIVISION.
001300 INPUT-OUTPUT SECTION.
001400 FILE-CONTROL.
001500
001600     COPY "SLVOUCH.CBL".
001700
001800 DATA DIVISION.
001900 FILE SECTION.
002000
002100     COPY "FDVOUCH.CBL".
002200
002300 WORKING-STORAGE SECTION.
002400
002500 77  OK-TO-PROCESS          PIC X.
002600 77  VOUCHER-FILE-AT-END     PIC X.
002700
002800 77  CUT-OFF-DATE            PIC 9(8).
002900
003000     COPY "WSCASE01.CBL".
```

continues

Listing 21.5. continued

```
003100
003200      COPY "WSDATE01.CBL".
003300
003400 PROCEDURE DIVISION.
003500 PROGRAM-BEGIN.
003600      PERFORM OPENING-PROCEDURE.
003700      PERFORM MAIN-PROCESS.
003800      PERFORM CLOSING-PROCEDURE.
003900
004000 PROGRAM-EXIT.
004100      EXIT PROGRAM.
004200
004300 PROGRAM-DONE.
004400      STOP RUN.
004500
004600 OPENING-PROCEDURE.
004700      OPEN I-O VOUCHER-FILE.
004800
004900 CLOSING-PROCEDURE.
005000      CLOSE VOUCHER-FILE.
005100
005200 MAIN-PROCESS.
005300      PERFORM GET-OK-TO-PROCESS.
005400      IF OK-TO-PROCESS = "Y"
005500          PERFORM GET-CUT-OFF-DATE
005600          PERFORM PROCESS-VOUCHERS.
005700
005800 GET-OK-TO-PROCESS.
005900      PERFORM ACCEPT-OK-TO-PROCESS.
006000      PERFORM RE-ACCEPT-OK-TO-PROCESS
006100          UNTIL OK-TO-PROCESS = "Y" OR "N".
006200
006300 ACCEPT-OK-TO-PROCESS.
006400      DISPLAY "SELECT VOUCHER BY DATE RANGE (Y/N)?".
006500      ACCEPT OK-TO-PROCESS.
006600      INSPECT OK-TO-PROCESS
006700        CONVERTING LOWER-ALPHA
006800        TO          UPPER-ALPHA.
006900
007000
007100 RE-ACCEPT-OK-TO-PROCESS.
007200      DISPLAY "YOU MUST ENTER YES OR NO".
007300      PERFORM ACCEPT-OK-TO-PROCESS.
007400
007500 GET-CUT-OFF-DATE.
007600      MOVE "N" TO ZERO-DATE-IS-OK.
007700      MOVE "SELECT ON OR BEFORE (MM/DD/CCYY)?"
007800              TO DATE-PROMPT.
007900      PERFORM GET-A-DATE.
008000      MOVE DATE-CCYYMMDD TO CUT-OFF-DATE.
008100
008200*--------------------------------
008300* Clear all previous selections.
008400*--------------------------------
```

21

```
008500 PROCESS-VOUCHERS.
008600     PERFORM READ-FIRST-VALID-VOUCHER.
008700     PERFORM PROCESS-ALL-VOUCHERS
008800         UNTIL VOUCHER-FILE-AT-END = "Y".
008900
009000 PROCESS-ALL-VOUCHERS.
009100     PERFORM PROCESS-THIS-VOUCHER.
009200     PERFORM READ-NEXT-VALID-VOUCHER.
009300
009400 PROCESS-THIS-VOUCHER.
009500     MOVE "Y" TO VOUCHER-SELECTED
009600     PERFORM REWRITE-VOUCHER-RECORD.
009700
009800*------------------------------
009900* Read first, read next routines
010000*------------------------------
010100 READ-FIRST-VALID-VOUCHER.
010200     PERFORM READ-NEXT-VALID-VOUCHER.
010300
010400 READ-NEXT-VALID-VOUCHER.
010500     PERFORM READ-NEXT-VOUCHER-RECORD.
010600     PERFORM READ-NEXT-VOUCHER-RECORD
010700         UNTIL VOUCHER-FILE-AT-END = "Y"
010800         OR (   VOUCHER-PAID-DATE = ZEROES
010900             AND VOUCHER-DUE NOT > CUT-OFF-DATE).
011000
011100 READ-NEXT-VOUCHER-RECORD.
011200     MOVE  "N" TO VOUCHER-FILE-AT-END.
011300     READ VOUCHER-FILE NEXT RECORD
011400       AT END
011500         MOVE "Y" TO VOUCHER-FILE-AT-END.
011600
011700*------------------------------
011800* Other File I-O routines.
011900*------------------------------
012000 REWRITE-VOUCHER-RECORD.
012100     REWRITE VOUCHER-RECORD
012200         INVALID KEY
012300         DISPLAY "ERROR REWRITING VENDOR RECORD".
012400*------------------------------
012500* Utility routines.
012600*------------------------------
012700     COPY "PLDATE01.CBL".
012800
```

ANALYSIS This program is similar to vchclr01.cbl. The user is asked at line 005300 whether to continue. If the answer is yes, GET-CUT-OFF-DATE is performed to get a date range to use for the selection process. This is a simple routine at line 007500 that asks the user for a required date and stores it in CUT-OFF-DATE. It uses the GET-A-DATE routine that was created in pldate01.cbl. This is copied at the end of the program. After the cutoff date is entered, the flow of the program is identical to vchclr01.cbl.

21

The only real differences are at line 009500 in PROCESS-THIS-VOUCHER, which moves "Y" instead of "N" to VOUCHER-SELECTED, and in the record selection logic at lines 010700 through 010900. The selection is for records with VOUCHER-PAID-DATE = ZEROES and VOUCHER-DUE NOT > CUT-OFF-DATE.

Sorting a File

The bills report lists all the outstanding bills. It is step 4 of the flowchart in Figure 21.1. Figure 21.2 is a printer spacing chart for the bills report. The column headed S will be used to print the VOUCHER-SELECTED flag.

Figure 21.2.

The printer chart for bilrpt01.cbl.

Listing 21.6 is the simplest version of this report.

TYPE   **Listing 21.6. The bills report.**

```
000100 IDENTIFICATION DIVISION.
000200 PROGRAM-ID. BILRPT01.
000300*-------------------------------
000400* Bills report in Due Date order
000500*-------------------------------
000600 ENVIRONMENT DIVISION.
000700 INPUT-OUTPUT SECTION.
000800 FILE-CONTROL.
000900
001000     COPY "SLVOUCH.CBL".
001100
001200     COPY "SLVND02.CBL".
001300
001400     SELECT PRINTER-FILE
001500         ASSIGN TO PRINTER
001600         ORGANIZATION IS LINE SEQUENTIAL.
001700
001800 DATA DIVISION.
001900 FILE SECTION.
002000
002100     COPY "FDVOUCH.CBL".
002200
002300     COPY "FDVND04.CBL".
002400
002500 FD  PRINTER-FILE
002600     LABEL RECORDS ARE OMITTED.
```

```
002700 01  PRINTER-RECORD          PIC X(80).
002800
002900 WORKING-STORAGE SECTION.
003000
003100 77  OK-TO-PROCESS           PIC X.
003200
003300     COPY "WSCASE01.CBL".
003400
003500 01  DETAIL-LINE.
003600     05  PRINT-NUMBER         PIC ZZZZ9.
003700     05  FILLER               PIC X(3) VALUE SPACE.
003800     05  PRINT-NAME           PIC X(30).
003900     05  FILLER               PIC X(1) VALUE SPACE.
004000     05  PRINT-DUE-DATE        PIC Z9/99/9999.
004100     05  FILLER               PIC X(1) VALUE SPACE.
004200     05  PRINT-AMOUNT          PIC ZZZ,ZZ9.99.
004300     05  FILLER               PIC X(1) VALUE SPACE.
004400     05  PRINT-INVOICE         PIC X(15).
004500     05  FILLER               PIC X(1) VALUE SPACE.
004600     05  PRINT-SELECTED        PIC X(1) VALUE SPACE.
004700
004800 01  TOTAL-THRU.
004900     05  FILLER               PIC X(20) VALUE SPACE.
005000     05  FILLER               PIC X(10) VALUE "TOTAL THRU".
005100
005200 01  COLUMN-LINE.
005300     05  FILLER         PIC X(7)  VALUE "VOUCHER".
005400     05  FILLER         PIC X(1)  VALUE SPACE.
005500     05  FILLER         PIC X(10) VALUE "VENDOR/For".
005600     05  FILLER         PIC X(23) VALUE SPACE.
005700     05  FILLER         PIC X(8)  VALUE "DUE DATE".
005800     05  FILLER         PIC X(1)  VALUE SPACE.
005900     05  FILLER         PIC X(10) VALUE "AMOUNT DUE".
006000     05  FILLER         PIC X(1)  VALUE SPACE.
006100     05  FILLER         PIC X(7)  VALUE "INVOICE".
006200     05  FILLER         PIC X(9)  VALUE SPACE.
006300     05  FILLER         PIC X(1)  VALUE "S".
006400
006500 01  TITLE-LINE.
006600     05  FILLER               PIC X(30) VALUE SPACE.
006700     05  FILLER               PIC X(12)
006800         VALUE "BILLS REPORT".
006900     05  FILLER               PIC X(19) VALUE SPACE.
007000     05  FILLER               PIC X(5) VALUE "PAGE:".
007100     05  FILLER               PIC X(1) VALUE SPACE.
007200     05  PRINT-PAGE-NUMBER    PIC ZZZ9.
007300
007400 77  VOUCHER-FILE-AT-END      PIC X.
007500 77  VENDOR-RECORD-FOUND      PIC X.
007600
007700 77  LINE-COUNT               PIC 999 VALUE ZERO.
007800 77  PAGE-NUMBER              PIC 9999 VALUE ZERO.
007900 77  MAXIMUM-LINES            PIC 999 VALUE 55.
008000
008100 77  RECORD-COUNT             PIC 9999 VALUE ZEROES.
```

continues

21

Listing 21.6. continued

```
008200
008300     COPY "WSDATE01.CBL".
008400
008500 PROCEDURE DIVISION.
008600 PROGRAM-BEGIN.
008700
008800     PERFORM OPENING-PROCEDURE.
008900     PERFORM MAIN-PROCESS.
009000     PERFORM CLOSING-PROCEDURE.
009100
009200 PROGRAM-EXIT.
009300     EXIT PROGRAM.
009400
009500 PROGRAM-DONE.
009600     STOP RUN.
009700
009800 OPENING-PROCEDURE.
009900     OPEN I-O VENDOR-FILE.
010000
010100     OPEN OUTPUT PRINTER-FILE.
010200
010300 MAIN-PROCESS.
010400     PERFORM GET-OK-TO-PROCESS.
010500     IF OK-TO-PROCESS = "Y"
010600         PERFORM PRINT-THE-REPORT.
010700
010800 CLOSING-PROCEDURE.
010900     CLOSE VENDOR-FILE.
011000     PERFORM END-LAST-PAGE.
011100     CLOSE PRINTER-FILE.
011200
011300 GET-OK-TO-PROCESS.
011400     PERFORM ACCEPT-OK-TO-PROCESS.
011500     PERFORM RE-ACCEPT-OK-TO-PROCESS
011600         UNTIL OK-TO-PROCESS = "Y" OR "N".
011700
011800 ACCEPT-OK-TO-PROCESS.
011900     DISPLAY "PRINT BILLS REPORT (Y/N)?".
012000     ACCEPT OK-TO-PROCESS.
012100     INSPECT OK-TO-PROCESS
012200       CONVERTING LOWER-ALPHA
012300       TO          UPPER-ALPHA.
012400
012500 RE-ACCEPT-OK-TO-PROCESS.
012600     DISPLAY "YOU MUST ENTER YES OR NO".
012700     PERFORM ACCEPT-OK-TO-PROCESS.
012800
012900 PRINT-THE-REPORT.
013000     OPEN INPUT VOUCHER-FILE.
013100     PERFORM START-ONE-REPORT.
013200     PERFORM PROCESS-VOUCHERS.
013300     PERFORM END-ONE-REPORT.
013400     CLOSE VOUCHER-FILE.
013500
```

21

```
013600 START-ONE-REPORT.
013700     PERFORM INITIALIZE-REPORT.
013800     PERFORM START-NEW-PAGE.
013900
014000 INITIALIZE-REPORT.
014100     MOVE ZEROES TO LINE-COUNT PAGE-NUMBER.
014200
014300 END-ONE-REPORT.
014400     IF RECORD-COUNT = ZEROES
014500         MOVE "NO RECORDS FOUND" TO PRINTER-RECORD
014600         PERFORM WRITE-TO-PRINTER.
014700
014800 PROCESS-VOUCHERS.
014900     PERFORM READ-FIRST-VALID-VOUCHER.
015000     PERFORM PROCESS-ALL-VOUCHERS
015100         UNTIL VOUCHER-FILE-AT-END = "Y".
015200
015300 PROCESS-ALL-VOUCHERS.
015400     PERFORM PROCESS-THIS-VOUCHER.
015500     PERFORM READ-NEXT-VALID-VOUCHER.
015600
015700 PROCESS-THIS-VOUCHER.
015800     ADD 1 TO RECORD-COUNT.
015900     IF LINE-COUNT > MAXIMUM-LINES
016000         PERFORM START-NEXT-PAGE.
016100     PERFORM PRINT-THE-RECORD.
016200
016300 PRINT-THE-RECORD.
016400     PERFORM PRINT-LINE-1.
016500     PERFORM PRINT-LINE-2.
016600     PERFORM LINE-FEED.
016700
016800 PRINT-LINE-1.
016900     MOVE SPACE TO DETAIL-LINE.
017000     MOVE VOUCHER-NUMBER TO PRINT-NUMBER.
017100
017200     MOVE VOUCHER-VENDOR TO VENDOR-NUMBER.
017300     PERFORM READ-VENDOR-RECORD.
017400     IF VENDOR-RECORD-FOUND = "Y"
017500         MOVE VENDOR-NAME TO PRINT-NAME
017600     ELSE
017700         MOVE "*VENDOR NOT ON FILE*" TO PRINT-NAME.
017800
017900     MOVE VOUCHER-DUE TO DATE-CCYYMMDD.
018000     PERFORM CONVERT-TO-MMDDCCYY.
018100     MOVE DATE-MMDDCCYY TO PRINT-DUE-DATE.
018200
018300     MOVE VOUCHER-AMOUNT TO PRINT-AMOUNT.
018400     MOVE VOUCHER-INVOICE TO PRINT-INVOICE.
018500
018600     IF VOUCHER-SELECTED = "Y"
018700         MOVE VOUCHER-SELECTED TO PRINT-SELECTED
018800     ELSE
018900         MOVE SPACE TO PRINT-SELECTED.
019000
```

21

continues

Listing 21.6. continued

```
019100      MOVE DETAIL-LINE TO PRINTER-RECORD.
019200      PERFORM WRITE-TO-PRINTER.
019300
019400 PRINT-LINE-2.
019500      MOVE SPACE TO DETAIL-LINE.
019600      MOVE VOUCHER-FOR TO PRINT-NAME.
019700      MOVE DETAIL-LINE TO PRINTER-RECORD.
019800      PERFORM WRITE-TO-PRINTER.
019900
020000 WRITE-TO-PRINTER.
020100      WRITE PRINTER-RECORD BEFORE ADVANCING 1.
020200      ADD 1 TO LINE-COUNT.
020300
020400 LINE-FEED.
020500      MOVE SPACE TO PRINTER-RECORD.
020600      PERFORM WRITE-TO-PRINTER.
020700
020800 START-NEXT-PAGE.
020900      PERFORM END-LAST-PAGE.
021000      PERFORM START-NEW-PAGE.
021100
021200 START-NEW-PAGE.
021300      ADD 1 TO PAGE-NUMBER.
021400      MOVE PAGE-NUMBER TO PRINT-PAGE-NUMBER.
021500      MOVE TITLE-LINE TO PRINTER-RECORD.
021600      PERFORM WRITE-TO-PRINTER.
021700      PERFORM LINE-FEED.
021800      MOVE COLUMN-LINE TO PRINTER-RECORD.
021900      PERFORM WRITE-TO-PRINTER.
022000      PERFORM LINE-FEED.
022100
022200 END-LAST-PAGE.
022300      PERFORM FORM-FEED.
022400      MOVE ZERO TO LINE-COUNT.
022500
022600 FORM-FEED.
022700      MOVE SPACE TO PRINTER-RECORD.
022800      WRITE PRINTER-RECORD BEFORE ADVANCING PAGE.
022900
023000*-------------------------------
023100* Read first, read next routines
023200*-------------------------------
023300 READ-FIRST-VALID-VOUCHER.
023400      PERFORM READ-NEXT-VALID-VOUCHER.
023500
023600 READ-NEXT-VALID-VOUCHER.
023700      PERFORM READ-NEXT-VOUCHER-RECORD.
023800      PERFORM READ-NEXT-VOUCHER-RECORD
023900          UNTIL VOUCHER-FILE-AT-END = "Y"
024000              OR VOUCHER-PAID-DATE = ZEROES.
024100
024200 READ-NEXT-VOUCHER-RECORD.
024300      MOVE "N" TO VOUCHER-FILE-AT-END.
024400      READ VOUCHER-FILE NEXT RECORD
```

```
024500          AT END MOVE "Y" TO VOUCHER-FILE-AT-END.
024600
024700*-------------------------------
024800* Other File IO routines
024900*-------------------------------
025000 READ-VENDOR-RECORD.
025100     MOVE "Y" TO VENDOR-RECORD-FOUND.
025200     READ VENDOR-FILE RECORD
025300        INVALID KEY
025400           MOVE "N" TO VENDOR-RECORD-FOUND.
025500
025600*-------------------------------
025700* Utility Routines
025800*-------------------------------
025900     COPY "PLDATE01.CBL".
026000
```

The sample report output from `bilrpt01.cbl` lists vouchers in voucher number order that are not yet paid:

```
                              BILLS REPORT                    PAGE:   1
VOUCHER VENDOR/For                         DUE DATE AMOUNT DUE INVOICE     S
     3   CHARLES SMITH AND SONS            2/22/1997    27.76 5057
OFFICE SUPPLIES
     4   ABC PRINTING                      2/07/1997   104.19 CX-5055
LETTER HEAD
     7   ABC PRINTING                      2/22/1997    48.97 CX-1407
BUSINESS CARDS
     8   ABC PRINTING                      1/27/1997    48.97 CX-1566
BUSINESS CARDS
    13   MA BELL                           1/23/1997    94.96 50577
PHONE LINE 555-6067
    14   AERIAL SIGNS                      1/17/1997 1,046.97 FA1234
SIGN OVER ZUMA BEACH
    15   ABERCROMBIE AND OTHERS            1/31/1997   657.19 MONTHLY
RENT
    16   CHARLES SMITH AND SONS            1/16/1997    25.97 5098
1997 DAY RUNNER
    17   RANIER GRAPHICS                   2/25/1997 4,057.07 ZO-1515
2 PAGE AD LAYOUT WITH RACE CAR
    19   MA BELL                           1/23/1997    34.95 50577
PHONE LINE 555-9098
```

The logic to process selected records begins at line 014800 with PROCESS-VOUCHERS. The actual processing loop, PROCESS-THIS-VOUCHER at line 015700, is printing logic to print the record information.

The READ-NEXT-VALID-VOUCHER routine at line 023600 is simpler than the previous examples because all you want are records where VOUCHER-PAID-DATE = ZEROES.

One unusual thing in `bilrpt01.cbl` is the opening and closing of VOUCHER-FILE at lines 013000 and 013400, rather than in the OPENING-PROCEDURE and CLOSING-PROCEDURE. If this were the

21

final version of the program, the OPEN and CLOSE would have been placed correctly in OPENING-PROCEDURE and CLOSING-PROCEDURE. You are working up to another version of this program, so allow this discrepancy for the moment and it will be explained. This program still works correctly.

Code, compile, and run bilrpt01.cbl. Make sure that it works correctly, and make sure that you understand how it works. You are about to add several things to this program, and if you understand this one fairly well, the additions should not cause any confusion.

Although it is possible simply to write a report of the information in the voucher file, as in bilrpt01.cbl, the report would be more useful if it were organized in order of the dates on which the bills are due. Anyone reading the report would know that bills appearing earlier in the report are the more urgent ones because their due dates are closer.

This presents a problem. The voucher file does not have an alternate key for the due date. Should you go back, redefine the file, add a key, and go through a file conversion? You could, but there is another solution. Alternate keys carry an overhead in a file. They slow down the writing of a new record because the alternate key information has to be updated during the write. They also increase the size of the file on the disk. Whether to create an alternate key or to use a sort on a field (which you learn about in this section) is a part of database and file design, trading off different kinds of costs to produce an efficient compromise.

A file can be sorted on any field or fields in the record by using the COBOL SORT command. The SORT command creates a new file in the process. It is a sequential file that has the same FD as the original file, but it is not keyed. The SORT command requires three files to work correctly:

- ☐ The input-file is the file that is being sorted.
- ☐ The output-file is the new file containing the sorted records.
- ☐ The sort-file is a special file used as a temporary work file for the SORT command.

The SORT command has many options. Here is an example of a common syntax for the SORT command:

```
SORT sort-file
  ON ASCENDING KEY sort-field
  USING input-file
  GIVING output-file
```

The following is an example:

```
SORT SORT-FILE
  ON ASCENDING KEY SORT-DATE
  USING VOUCHER-FILE
  GIVING WORK-FILE.
```

The KEY in a SORT command is not an indexed key, but simply a way of indicating the field on which the file will be sorted. Because the SORT command uses two extra files, both files must be defined in the ENVIRONMENT DIVISION and the DATA DIVISION. The easiest way to understand this is to look at an example of a sort. Listing 21.7 is bilrpt02.cbl, a modified version of bilrpt01.cbl that includes a sort.

TYPE **Listing 21.7. The bills report sorted in due date order.**

```
000100 IDENTIFICATION DIVISION.
000200 PROGRAM-ID. BILRPT02.
000300*------------------------------
000400* Bills report in Due Date order
000500*------------------------------
000600 ENVIRONMENT DIVISION.
000700 INPUT-OUTPUT SECTION.
000800 FILE-CONTROL.
000900
001000     COPY "SLVOUCH.CBL".
001100
001200     COPY "SLVND02.CBL".
001300
001400     COPY "SLSTATE.CBL".
001500
001600     SELECT WORK-FILE
001700         ASSIGN TO "WORK"
001800         ORGANIZATION IS SEQUENTIAL.
001900
002000     SELECT SORT-FILE
002100         ASSIGN TO "SORT".
002200
002300     SELECT PRINTER-FILE
002400         ASSIGN TO PRINTER
002500         ORGANIZATION IS LINE SEQUENTIAL.
002600
002700 DATA DIVISION.
002800 FILE SECTION.
002900
003000     COPY "FDVOUCH.CBL".
003100
003200     COPY "FDVND04.CBL".
003300
003400     COPY "FDSTATE.CBL".
003500
003600 FD  WORK-FILE
003700     LABEL RECORDS ARE STANDARD.
003800 01  WORK-RECORD.
003900     05  WORK-NUMBER        PIC 9(5).
004000     05  WORK-VENDOR        PIC 9(5).
004100     05  WORK-INVOICE       PIC X(15).
004200     05  WORK-FOR           PIC X(30).
004300     05  WORK-AMOUNT        PIC S9(6)V99.
004400     05  WORK-DATE          PIC 9(8).
004500     05  WORK-DUE           PIC 9(8).
004600     05  WORK-DEDUCTIBLE    PIC X.
```

21

continues

Listing 21.7. continued

```
004700       05   WORK-SELECTED          PIC X.
004800       05   WORK-PAID-AMOUNT       PIC S9(6)V99.
004900       05   WORK-PAID-DATE         PIC 9(8).
005000       05   WORK-CHECK-NO          PIC 9(6).
005100
005200 SD  SORT-FILE.
005300
005400 01  SORT-RECORD.
005500       05   SORT-NUMBER            PIC 9(5).
005600       05   SORT-VENDOR            PIC 9(5).
005700       05   SORT-INVOICE           PIC X(15).
005800       05   SORT-FOR               PIC X(30).
005900       05   SORT-AMOUNT            PIC S9(6)V99.
006000       05   SORT-DATE              PIC 9(8).
006100       05   SORT-DUE               PIC 9(8).
006200       05   SORT-DEDUCTIBLE        PIC X.
006300       05   SORT-SELECTED          PIC X.
006400       05   SORT-PAID-AMOUNT       PIC S9(6)V99.
006500       05   SORT-PAID-DATE         PIC 9(8).
006600       05   SORT-CHECK-NO          PIC 9(6).
006700
006800 FD  PRINTER-FILE
006900      LABEL RECORDS ARE OMITTED.
007000 01  PRINTER-RECORD               PIC X(80).
007100
007200 WORKING-STORAGE SECTION.
007300
007400 77  OK-TO-PROCESS        PIC X.
007500
007600      COPY "WSCASE01.CBL".
007700
007800 01  DETAIL-LINE.
007900       05   PRINT-NUMBER      PIC ZZZZ9.
008000       05   FILLER           PIC X(3) VALUE SPACE.
008100       05   PRINT-NAME       PIC X(30).
008200       05   FILLER           PIC X(1) VALUE SPACE.
008300       05   PRINT-DUE-DATE   PIC Z9/99/9999.
008400       05   FILLER           PIC X(1) VALUE SPACE.
008500       05   PRINT-AMOUNT     PIC ZZZ,ZZ9.99.
008600       05   FILLER           PIC X(1) VALUE SPACE.
008700       05   PRINT-INVOICE    PIC X(15).
008800       05   FILLER           PIC X(1) VALUE SPACE.
008900       05   PRINT-SELECTED   PIC X(1) VALUE SPACE.
009000
009100 01  TOTAL-THRU.
009200       05   FILLER           PIC X(20) VALUE SPACE.
009300       05   FILLER           PIC X(10) VALUE "TOTAL THRU".
009400
009500 01  COLUMN-LINE.
009600       05   FILLER       PIC X(7)  VALUE "VOUCHER".
009700       05   FILLER       PIC X(1)  VALUE SPACE.
009800       05   FILLER       PIC X(10) VALUE "VENDOR/For".
009900       05   FILLER       PIC X(23) VALUE SPACE.
010000       05   FILLER       PIC X(8)  VALUE "DUE DATE".
```

21

```
010100     05  FILLER          PIC X(1)  VALUE SPACE.
010200     05  FILLER          PIC X(10) VALUE "AMOUNT DUE".
010300     05  FILLER          PIC X(1)  VALUE SPACE.
010400     05  FILLER          PIC X(7)  VALUE "INVOICE".
010500     05  FILLER          PIC X(9)  VALUE SPACE.
010600     05  FILLER          PIC X(1)  VALUE "S".
010700
010800 01  TITLE-LINE.
010900     05  FILLER              PIC X(30) VALUE SPACE.
011000     05  FILLER              PIC X(12)
011100         VALUE "BILLS REPORT".
011200     05  FILLER              PIC X(19) VALUE SPACE.
011300     05  FILLER              PIC X(5) VALUE "PAGE:".
011400     05  FILLER              PIC X(1) VALUE SPACE.
011500     05  PRINT-PAGE-NUMBER   PIC ZZZ9.
011600
011700 77  WORK-FILE-AT-END      PIC X.
011800 77  VENDOR-RECORD-FOUND    PIC X.
011900
012000 77  LINE-COUNT             PIC 999 VALUE ZERO.
012100 77  PAGE-NUMBER            PIC 9999 VALUE ZERO.
012200 77  MAXIMUM-LINES          PIC 999 VALUE 55.
012300
012400 77  RECORD-COUNT           PIC 9999 VALUE ZEROES.
012500
012600     COPY "WSDATE01.CBL".
012700
012800 PROCEDURE DIVISION.
012900 PROGRAM-BEGIN.
013000
013100     PERFORM OPENING-PROCEDURE.
013200     PERFORM MAIN-PROCESS.
013300     PERFORM CLOSING-PROCEDURE.
013400
013500 PROGRAM-EXIT.
013600     EXIT PROGRAM.
013700
013800 PROGRAM-DONE.
013900     STOP RUN.
014000
014100 OPENING-PROCEDURE.
014200     OPEN I-O VENDOR-FILE.
014300
014400     OPEN OUTPUT PRINTER-FILE.
014500
014600 MAIN-PROCESS.
014700     PERFORM GET-OK-TO-PROCESS.
014800     IF OK-TO-PROCESS = "Y"
014900         PERFORM SORT-DATA-FILE
015000         PERFORM PRINT-THE-REPORT.
015100
015200 CLOSING-PROCEDURE.
015300     CLOSE VENDOR-FILE.
015400     PERFORM END-LAST-PAGE.
015500     CLOSE PRINTER-FILE.
```

21

continues

Listing 21.7. continued

```
015600
015700 GET-OK-TO-PROCESS.
015800     PERFORM ACCEPT-OK-TO-PROCESS.
015900     PERFORM RE-ACCEPT-OK-TO-PROCESS
016000         UNTIL OK-TO-PROCESS = "Y" OR "N".
016100
016200 ACCEPT-OK-TO-PROCESS.
016300     DISPLAY "PRINT BILLS REPORT (Y/N)?".
016400     ACCEPT OK-TO-PROCESS.
016500     INSPECT OK-TO-PROCESS
016600       CONVERTING LOWER-ALPHA
016700       TO           UPPER-ALPHA.
016800
016900 RE-ACCEPT-OK-TO-PROCESS.
017000     DISPLAY "YOU MUST ENTER YES OR NO".
017100     PERFORM ACCEPT-OK-TO-PROCESS.
017200
017300*--------------------------------
017400* Sorting logic
017500*--------------------------------
017600 SORT-DATA-FILE.
017700     SORT SORT-FILE
017800         ON ASCENDING KEY SORT-DUE
017900           USING VOUCHER-FILE
018000           GIVING WORK-FILE.
018100
018200 PRINT-THE-REPORT.
018300     OPEN INPUT WORK-FILE.
018400     PERFORM START-ONE-REPORT.
018500     PERFORM PROCESS-VOUCHERS.
018600     PERFORM END-ONE-REPORT.
018700     CLOSE WORK-FILE.
018800
018900 START-ONE-REPORT.
019000     PERFORM INITIALIZE-REPORT.
019100     PERFORM START-NEW-PAGE.
019200
019300 INITIALIZE-REPORT.
019400     MOVE ZEROES TO LINE-COUNT PAGE-NUMBER.
019500
019600 END-ONE-REPORT.
019700     IF RECORD-COUNT = ZEROES
019800         MOVE "NO RECORDS FOUND" TO PRINTER-RECORD
019900         PERFORM WRITE-TO-PRINTER.
020000
020100 PROCESS-VOUCHERS.
020200     PERFORM READ-FIRST-VALID-WORK.
020300     PERFORM PROCESS-ALL-VOUCHERS
020400         UNTIL WORK-FILE-AT-END = "Y".
020500
020600 PROCESS-ALL-VOUCHERS.
020700     PERFORM PROCESS-THIS-VOUCHER.
020800     PERFORM READ-NEXT-VALID-WORK.
020900
```

```
021000 PROCESS-THIS-VOUCHER.
021100     ADD 1 TO RECORD-COUNT.
021200     IF LINE-COUNT > MAXIMUM-LINES
021300         PERFORM START-NEXT-PAGE.
021400     PERFORM PRINT-THE-RECORD.
021500
021600 PRINT-THE-RECORD.
021700     PERFORM PRINT-LINE-1.
021800     PERFORM PRINT-LINE-2.
021900     PERFORM LINE-FEED.
022000
022100 PRINT-LINE-1.
022200     MOVE SPACE TO DETAIL-LINE.
022300     MOVE WORK-NUMBER TO PRINT-NUMBER.
022400
022500     MOVE WORK-VENDOR TO VENDOR-NUMBER.
022600     PERFORM READ-VENDOR-RECORD.
022700     IF VENDOR-RECORD-FOUND = "Y"
022800         MOVE VENDOR-NAME TO PRINT-NAME
022900     ELSE
023000         MOVE "*VENDOR NOT ON FILE*" TO PRINT-NAME.
023100
023200     MOVE WORK-DUE TO DATE-CCYYMMDD.
023300     PERFORM CONVERT-TO-MMDDCCYY.
023400     MOVE DATE-MMDDCCYY TO PRINT-DUE-DATE.
023500
023600     MOVE WORK-AMOUNT TO PRINT-AMOUNT.
023700     MOVE WORK-INVOICE TO PRINT-INVOICE.
023800
023900     IF WORK-SELECTED = "Y"
024000         MOVE WORK-SELECTED TO PRINT-SELECTED
024100     ELSE
024200         MOVE SPACE TO PRINT-SELECTED.
024300
024400     MOVE DETAIL-LINE TO PRINTER-RECORD.
024500     PERFORM WRITE-TO-PRINTER.
024600
024700 PRINT-LINE-2.
024800     MOVE SPACE TO DETAIL-LINE.
024900     MOVE WORK-FOR TO PRINT-NAME.
025000     MOVE DETAIL-LINE TO PRINTER-RECORD.
025100     PERFORM WRITE-TO-PRINTER.
025200
025300 WRITE-TO-PRINTER.
025400     WRITE PRINTER-RECORD BEFORE ADVANCING 1.
025500     ADD 1 TO LINE-COUNT.
025600
025700 LINE-FEED.
025800     MOVE SPACE TO PRINTER-RECORD.
025900     PERFORM WRITE-TO-PRINTER.
026000
026100 START-NEXT-PAGE.
026200     PERFORM END-LAST-PAGE.
026300     PERFORM START-NEW-PAGE.
026400
```

21

continues

Listing 21.7. continued

```
026500 START-NEW-PAGE.
026600     ADD 1 TO PAGE-NUMBER.
026700     MOVE PAGE-NUMBER TO PRINT-PAGE-NUMBER.
026800     MOVE TITLE-LINE TO PRINTER-RECORD.
026900     PERFORM WRITE-TO-PRINTER.
027000     PERFORM LINE-FEED.
027100     MOVE COLUMN-LINE TO PRINTER-RECORD.
027200     PERFORM WRITE-TO-PRINTER.
027300     PERFORM LINE-FEED.
027400
027500 END-LAST-PAGE.
027600     PERFORM FORM-FEED.
027700     MOVE ZERO TO LINE-COUNT.
027800
027900 FORM-FEED.
028000     MOVE SPACE TO PRINTER-RECORD.
028100     WRITE PRINTER-RECORD BEFORE ADVANCING PAGE.
028200
028300*--------------------------------
028400* Read first, read next routines
028500*--------------------------------
028600 READ-FIRST-VALID-WORK.
028700     PERFORM READ-NEXT-VALID-WORK.
028800
028900 READ-NEXT-VALID-WORK.
029000     PERFORM READ-NEXT-WORK-RECORD.
029100     PERFORM READ-NEXT-WORK-RECORD
029200         UNTIL WORK-FILE-AT-END = "Y"
029300             OR WORK-PAID-DATE = ZEROES.
029400
029500 READ-NEXT-WORK-RECORD.
029600     MOVE "N" TO WORK-FILE-AT-END.
029700     READ WORK-FILE NEXT RECORD
029800         AT END MOVE "Y" TO WORK-FILE-AT-END.
029900
030000*--------------------------------
030100* Other File IO routines
030200*--------------------------------
030300 READ-VENDOR-RECORD.
030400     MOVE "Y" TO VENDOR-RECORD-FOUND.
030500     READ VENDOR-FILE RECORD
030600         INVALID KEY
030700         MOVE "N" TO VENDOR-RECORD-FOUND.
030800
030900*--------------------------------
031000* Utility Routines
031100*--------------------------------
031200     COPY "PLDATE01.CBL".
031300
```

The output of `bilrpt02.cbl` is sorted in due-date order, improving the usefulness of the report:

```
                                      BILLS REPORT                    PAGE: 1
          VOUCHER VENDOR/For                    DUE DATE AMOUNT DUE INVOICE   S
          16    CHARLES SMITH AND SONS          1/16/1997    25.97 5098
          1997 DAY RUNNER
          14    AERIAL SIGNS                    1/17/1997  1,046.97 FA1234
          SIGN OVER ZUMA BEACH
          13    MA BELL                         1/23/1997    94.96 50577
          PHONE LINE 555-6067
          19    MA BELL                         1/23/1997    34.95 50577
          PHONE LINE 555-9098
          8    ABC PRINTING                     1/27/1997    48.97 CX-1566     Y
          BUSINESS CARDS
          15    ABERCROMBIE AND OTHERS          1/31/1997   657.19 MONTHLY
          RENT
          4    ABC PRINTING                     2/07/1997   104.19 CX-5055     Y
          LETTER HEAD
          3    CHARLES SMITH AND SONS           2/22/1997    27.76 5057
          OFFICE SUPPLIES
          7    ABC PRINTING                     2/22/1997    48.97 CX-1407
          BUSINESS CARDS
          17    RANIER GRAPHICS                 2/25/1997  4,057.07 ZO-1515
          2 PAGE AD LAYOUT WITH RACE CAR
```

ANALYSIS   This program is identical to `bilrpt01.cbl` except that the voucher file is sorted into a work file, and the report is printed using the data in the work file rather than directly from the voucher file.

The FILE-CONTROL paragraph of the INPUT-OUTPUT SECTION in the ENVIRONMENT DIVISION contains SELECT clauses for two new files. WORK-FILE at line 001600 will be used as the output of the sort, and SORT-FILE at line 002000 will be used as a temporary file by the SORT command. Note that the organization of the WORK-FILE is SEQUENTIAL because it will have no key. No organization is specified for the SORT-FILE.

The organization of a sort file is omitted, because it is a special type of file used by the SORT command. The actual organization of the file probably is nothing like any of the standard COBOL file organizations. It is set up by your version of COBOL to produce the fastest possible sorting of another file.

In the FILE SECTION of the DATA DIVISION, the FD for the WORK-FILE is defined at lines 003600 through 005000. It is an exact duplicate of the VOUCHER-FILE, but it uses the prefix WORK- for all fields. This work version of the voucher file will have exactly the same record layout as the voucher file, but it will be a SEQUENTIAL file, not an INDEXED file.

The FD for the SORT-FILE begins at line 005200. Notice that it is not given a level number of FD but is called an SD (sort descriptor). This again highlights the special nature of a sort file. The SD serves to set the file apart from others as a special file that will be used only by the SORT command. It cannot be used as a standard file. Aside from the SD, the remainder of the sort file is identical to the VOUCHER-FILE, but all fields use the prefix SORT-.

21

The actual sort is done at lines 017600 through 018000 in the SORT-DATA-FILE paragraph. You can think of the SORT command as a series of steps:

1. Copy the voucher file to the sort file.
2. Sort the sort file on the SORT-DUE field.
3. Copy the resulting sorted file to the work file.

This version of the SORT command automatically opens the input file (VOUCHER-FILE) and the output file (WORK-FILE) before the sort and closes them when the sort is done. The SORT command fails if you have opened either of these files in your program already. If you do need to open a file that is used in a sort for any reason, it must be closed again before the SORT command is used. There is no OPEN or CLOSE of VOUCHER-FILE or WORK-FILE in OPENING-PROCEDURE or CLOSING-PROCEDURE.

The work file cannot be opened until after the sort is completed, but it must be opened for the report. The opening and closing of the WORK-FILE is performed at lines 018300 and 018700, respectively—which are the top and bottom of the PRINT-THE-REPORT paragraph—just as the VOUCHER-FILE is handled in bilrpt01.cbl.

To execute the sort, it is inserted into MAIN-PROCESS after the user has said yes to go ahead with the report, but before performing PRINT-THE-REPORT (at line 014900).

From PRINT-THE-REPORT at line 018200 to the end of the program, the processing is identical to bilrpt01.cbl except for one point. The bilrpt01.cbl program prints out the voucher file and bilrpt02.cbl is printing out the work file, so all fields have been changed to WORK-. Values now are moved from the work file to the print record.

Code, compile, and run bilrpt02.cbl; you should get a report with the same information, but sorted in due-date order.

Printing Totals

The bilrpt02.cbl program still leaves the user the task of totaling the dollars and working out the total due day by day, and it seems that the computer should be able to do the mathematics.

Figure 21.3 is a modified layout for the bills report program that provides a running total at the end of each day.

The problem is to print the same report but to keep a running total of the amount owed as each voucher is processed, with a running total printed at the end of each due date.

Figure 21.3.

A layout with totals.

NEW TERM The interruption of the usual printing of a report program to print a total or subtotal is called a *control break* or *level break*. In the following example, the report breaks at the end of each vendor, prints a subtotal for that vendor, and then breaks at the end of the report and prints a total for the report. These are control breaks:

```
Vendor          DUE DATE      AMOUNT
ABC Printing    1/23/1997      27.95
ABC Printing    1/31/1997      15.54
ABC Printing    2/16/1997      10.17
Total        53.66
GTE             1/17/1997      34.97
GTE             1/24/1997      17.54
Total        52.51
Grand Total     106.17
```

Programming Control Breaks

A control break in a program usually is programmed by setting up the program so that it prints until the value in one of the fields changes. In the previous example, the report prints until the vendor name changes and then prints a total. In the problem you are dealing with, the report prints until the due date changes. When the field changes, a subtotal or running total is printed.

In all control breaking, the data file is sorted on the field that will be used for controlling the break. In the case of `bilrpt03.cbl` in Listing 21.8, the control field will be WORK-DUE and the file already is sorted on this field.

Listing 21.8. Sorted bills report with totals.

```
000100 IDENTIFICATION DIVISION.
000200 PROGRAM-ID. BILRPT03.
000300*-------------------------------
000400* Bills Report with totals by day.
000500*-------------------------------
000600 ENVIRONMENT DIVISION.
000700 INPUT-OUTPUT SECTION.
000800 FILE-CONTROL.
000900
```

21

continues

Listing 21.8. continued

```
001000       COPY "SLVOUCH.CBL".
001100
001200       COPY "SLVND02.CBL".
001300
001400       COPY "SLSTATE.CBL".
001500
001600       SELECT WORK-FILE
001700           ASSIGN TO "WORK"
001800           ORGANIZATION IS SEQUENTIAL.
001900
002000       SELECT SORT-FILE
002100           ASSIGN TO "SORT".
002200
002300       SELECT PRINTER-FILE
002400           ASSIGN TO PRINTER
002500           ORGANIZATION IS LINE SEQUENTIAL.
002600
002700 DATA DIVISION.
002800 FILE SECTION.
002900
003000       COPY "FDVOUCH.CBL".
003100
003200       COPY "FDVND04.CBL".
003300
003400       COPY "FDSTATE.CBL".
003500
003600 FD  WORK-FILE
003700       LABEL RECORDS ARE STANDARD.
003800 01  WORK-RECORD.
003900       05   WORK-NUMBER          PIC 9(5).
004000       05   WORK-VENDOR          PIC 9(5).
004100       05   WORK-INVOICE         PIC X(15).
004200       05   WORK-FOR             PIC X(30).
004300       05   WORK-AMOUNT          PIC S9(6)V99.
004400       05   WORK-DATE            PIC 9(8).
004500       05   WORK-DUE             PIC 9(8).
004600       05   WORK-DEDUCTIBLE      PIC X.
004700       05   WORK-SELECTED        PIC X.
004800       05   WORK-PAID-AMOUNT     PIC S9(6)V99.
004900       05   WORK-PAID-DATE       PIC 9(8).
005000       05   WORK-CHECK-NO        PIC 9(6).
005100
005200 SD  SORT-FILE.
005300
005400 01  SORT-RECORD.
005500       05   SORT-NUMBER          PIC 9(5).
005600       05   SORT-VENDOR          PIC 9(5).
005700       05   SORT-INVOICE         PIC X(15).
005800       05   SORT-FOR             PIC X(30).
005900       05   SORT-AMOUNT          PIC S9(6)V99.
006000       05   SORT-DATE            PIC 9(8).
006100       05   SORT-DUE             PIC 9(8).
006200       05   SORT-DEDUCTIBLE      PIC X.
006300       05   SORT-SELECTED        PIC X.
```

21

```
006400        05   SORT-PAID-AMOUNT      PIC S9(6)V99.
006500        05   SORT-PAID-DATE        PIC 9(8).
006600        05   SORT-CHECK-NO         PIC 9(6).
006700
006800 FD   PRINTER-FILE
006900        LABEL RECORDS ARE OMITTED.
007000 01   PRINTER-RECORD               PIC X(80).
007100
007200 WORKING-STORAGE SECTION.
007300
007400 77   OK-TO-PROCESS         PIC X.
007500
007600        COPY "WSCASE01.CBL".
007700
007800 01   DETAIL-LINE.
007900        05   PRINT-NUMBER     PIC ZZZZ9.
008000        05   FILLER           PIC X(3) VALUE SPACE.
008100        05   PRINT-NAME       PIC X(30).
008200        05   FILLER           PIC X(1) VALUE SPACE.
008300        05   PRINT-DUE-DATE   PIC Z9/99/9999.
008400        05   FILLER           PIC X(1) VALUE SPACE.
008500        05   PRINT-AMOUNT     PIC ZZZ,ZZ9.99.
008600        05   FILLER           PIC X(1) VALUE SPACE.
008700        05   PRINT-INVOICE    PIC X(15).
008800        05   FILLER           PIC X(1) VALUE SPACE.
008900        05   PRINT-SELECTED   PIC X(1) VALUE SPACE.
009000
009100 01   TOTAL-THRU.
009200        05   FILLER           PIC X(20) VALUE SPACE.
009300        05   FILLER           PIC X(10) VALUE "TOTAL THRU".
009400
009500 01   COLUMN-LINE.
009600        05   FILLER       PIC X(7)  VALUE "VOUCHER".
009700        05   FILLER       PIC X(1)  VALUE SPACE.
009800        05   FILLER       PIC X(10) VALUE "VENDOR/For".
009900        05   FILLER       PIC X(23) VALUE SPACE.
010000        05   FILLER       PIC X(8)  VALUE "DUE DATE".
010100        05   FILLER       PIC X(1)  VALUE SPACE.
010200        05   FILLER       PIC X(10) VALUE "AMOUNT DUE".
010300        05   FILLER       PIC X(1)  VALUE SPACE.
010400        05   FILLER       PIC X(7)  VALUE "INVOICE".
010500        05   FILLER       PIC X(9)  VALUE SPACE.
010600        05   FILLER       PIC X(1)  VALUE "S".
010700
010800 01   TITLE-LINE.
010900        05   FILLER           PIC X(30) VALUE SPACE.
011000        05   FILLER           PIC X(12)
011100           VALUE "BILLS REPORT".
011200        05   FILLER           PIC X(19) VALUE SPACE.
011300        05   FILLER           PIC X(5) VALUE "PAGE:".
011400        05   FILLER           PIC X(1) VALUE SPACE.
011500        05   PRINT-PAGE-NUMBER  PIC ZZZ9.
011600
011700 77   WORK-FILE-AT-END     PIC X.
011800 77   VENDOR-RECORD-FOUND    PIC X.
```

continues

21

Listing 21.8. continued

```
011900
012000 77  LINE-COUNT              PIC 999 VALUE ZERO.
012100 77  PAGE-NUMBER             PIC 9999 VALUE ZERO.
012200 77  MAXIMUM-LINES           PIC 999 VALUE 55.
012300
012400 77  RECORD-COUNT            PIC 9999 VALUE ZEROES.
012500
012600 77  SAVE-DUE                PIC 9(8).
012700
012800 77  RUNNING-TOTAL           PIC S9(6)V99.
012900
013000     COPY "WSDATE01.CBL".
013100
013200 PROCEDURE DIVISION.
013300 PROGRAM-BEGIN.
013400
013500     PERFORM OPENING-PROCEDURE.
013600     PERFORM MAIN-PROCESS.
013700     PERFORM CLOSING-PROCEDURE.
013800
013900 PROGRAM-EXIT.
014000     EXIT PROGRAM.
014100
014200 PROGRAM-DONE.
014300     STOP RUN.
014400
014500 OPENING-PROCEDURE.
014600     OPEN I-O VENDOR-FILE.
014700
014800     OPEN OUTPUT PRINTER-FILE.
014900
015000 MAIN-PROCESS.
015100     PERFORM GET-OK-TO-PROCESS.
015200     IF OK-TO-PROCESS = "Y"
015300         PERFORM SORT-DATA-FILE
015400         PERFORM PRINT-THE-REPORT.
015500
015600 CLOSING-PROCEDURE.
015700     CLOSE VENDOR-FILE.
015800     PERFORM END-LAST-PAGE.
015900     CLOSE PRINTER-FILE.
016000
016100 GET-OK-TO-PROCESS.
016200     PERFORM ACCEPT-OK-TO-PROCESS.
016300     PERFORM RE-ACCEPT-OK-TO-PROCESS
016400         UNTIL OK-TO-PROCESS = "Y" OR "N".
016500
016600 ACCEPT-OK-TO-PROCESS.
016700     DISPLAY "PRINT BILLS REPORT (Y/N)?".
016800     ACCEPT OK-TO-PROCESS.
016900     INSPECT OK-TO-PROCESS
017000         CONVERTING LOWER-ALPHA
017100         TO          UPPER-ALPHA.
017200
```

```
017300 RE-ACCEPT-OK-TO-PROCESS.
017400     DISPLAY "YOU MUST ENTER YES OR NO".
017500     PERFORM ACCEPT-OK-TO-PROCESS.
017600
017700*-------------------------------
017800* Sorting logic
017900*-------------------------------
018000 SORT-DATA-FILE.
018100     SORT SORT-FILE
018200         ON ASCENDING KEY SORT-DUE
018300         USING VOUCHER-FILE
018400         GIVING WORK-FILE.
018500
018600 PRINT-THE-REPORT.
018700     OPEN INPUT WORK-FILE.
018800     PERFORM START-ONE-REPORT.
018900     PERFORM PROCESS-VOUCHERS.
019000     PERFORM END-ONE-REPORT.
019100     CLOSE WORK-FILE.
019200
019300 START-ONE-REPORT.
019400     PERFORM INITIALIZE-REPORT.
019500     PERFORM START-NEW-PAGE.
019600     MOVE ZEROES TO RUNNING-TOTAL.
019700
019800 INITIALIZE-REPORT.
019900     MOVE ZEROES TO LINE-COUNT PAGE-NUMBER.
020000
020100 END-ONE-REPORT.
020200     IF RECORD-COUNT = ZEROES
020300         MOVE "NO RECORDS FOUND" TO PRINTER-RECORD
020400         PERFORM WRITE-TO-PRINTER.
020500
020600 PROCESS-VOUCHERS.
020700     PERFORM READ-FIRST-VALID-WORK.
020800     PERFORM PROCESS-ALL-DATES
020900         UNTIL WORK-FILE-AT-END = "Y".
021000
021100 PROCESS-ALL-DATES.
021200     PERFORM START-ONE-DATE.
021300
021400     PERFORM PROCESS-ALL-VOUCHERS
021500         UNTIL WORK-FILE-AT-END = "Y"
021600             OR WORK-DUE NOT = SAVE-DUE.
021700
021800     PERFORM END-ONE-DATE.
021900
022000 START-ONE-DATE.
022100     MOVE WORK-DUE TO SAVE-DUE.
022200
022300 END-ONE-DATE.
022400     PERFORM PRINT-RUNNING-TOTAL.
022500
022600 PRINT-RUNNING-TOTAL.
022700     MOVE SPACE TO DETAIL-LINE.
```

21

continues

Listing 21.8. continued

```
022800          MOVE SAVE-DUE TO DATE-CCYYMMDD.
022900          PERFORM CONVERT-TO-MMDDCCYY.
023000          MOVE DATE-MMDDCCYY TO PRINT-DUE-DATE.
023100          MOVE RUNNING-TOTAL TO PRINT-AMOUNT.
023200          MOVE TOTAL-THRU TO PRINT-NAME.
023300          MOVE DETAIL-LINE TO PRINTER-RECORD.
023400          PERFORM WRITE-TO-PRINTER.
023500          PERFORM LINE-FEED 2 TIMES.
023600
023700 PROCESS-ALL-VOUCHERS.
023800          PERFORM PROCESS-THIS-VOUCHER.
023900          PERFORM READ-NEXT-VALID-WORK.
024000
024100 PROCESS-THIS-VOUCHER.
024200          ADD 1 TO RECORD-COUNT.
024300          IF LINE-COUNT > MAXIMUM-LINES
024400              PERFORM START-NEXT-PAGE.
024500          PERFORM PRINT-THE-RECORD.
024600          ADD WORK-AMOUNT TO RUNNING-TOTAL.
024700
024800 PRINT-THE-RECORD.
024900          PERFORM PRINT-LINE-1.
025000          PERFORM PRINT-LINE-2.
025100          PERFORM LINE-FEED.
025200
025300 PRINT-LINE-1.
025400          MOVE SPACE TO DETAIL-LINE.
025500          MOVE WORK-NUMBER TO PRINT-NUMBER.
025600
025700          MOVE WORK-VENDOR TO VENDOR-NUMBER.
025800          PERFORM READ-VENDOR-RECORD.
025900          IF VENDOR-RECORD-FOUND = "Y"
026000              MOVE VENDOR-NAME TO PRINT-NAME
026100          ELSE
026200              MOVE "*VENDOR NOT ON FILE*" TO PRINT-NAME.
026300
026400          MOVE WORK-DUE TO DATE-CCYYMMDD.
026500          PERFORM CONVERT-TO-MMDDCCYY.
026600          MOVE DATE-MMDDCCYY TO PRINT-DUE-DATE.
026700
026800          MOVE WORK-AMOUNT TO PRINT-AMOUNT.
026900          MOVE WORK-INVOICE TO PRINT-INVOICE.
027000
027100          IF WORK-SELECTED = "Y"
027200              MOVE WORK-SELECTED TO PRINT-SELECTED
027300          ELSE
027400              MOVE SPACE TO PRINT-SELECTED.
027500
027600          MOVE DETAIL-LINE TO PRINTER-RECORD.
027700          PERFORM WRITE-TO-PRINTER.
027800
027900 PRINT-LINE-2.
028000          MOVE SPACE TO DETAIL-LINE.
028100          MOVE WORK-FOR TO PRINT-NAME.
```

21

```
028200      MOVE DETAIL-LINE TO PRINTER-RECORD.
028300      PERFORM WRITE-TO-PRINTER.
028400
028500 WRITE-TO-PRINTER.
028600      WRITE PRINTER-RECORD BEFORE ADVANCING 1.
028700      ADD 1 TO LINE-COUNT.
028800
028900 LINE-FEED.
029000      MOVE SPACE TO PRINTER-RECORD.
029100      PERFORM WRITE-TO-PRINTER.
029200
029300 START-NEXT-PAGE.
029400      PERFORM END-LAST-PAGE.
029500      PERFORM START-NEW-PAGE.
029600
029700 START-NEW-PAGE.
029800      ADD 1 TO PAGE-NUMBER.
029900      MOVE PAGE-NUMBER TO PRINT-PAGE-NUMBER.
030000      MOVE TITLE-LINE TO PRINTER-RECORD.
030100      PERFORM WRITE-TO-PRINTER.
030200      PERFORM LINE-FEED.
030300      MOVE COLUMN-LINE TO PRINTER-RECORD.
030400      PERFORM WRITE-TO-PRINTER.
030500      PERFORM LINE-FEED.
030600
030700 END-LAST-PAGE.
030800      PERFORM FORM-FEED.
030900      MOVE ZERO TO LINE-COUNT.
031000
031100 FORM-FEED.
031200      MOVE SPACE TO PRINTER-RECORD.
031300      WRITE PRINTER-RECORD BEFORE ADVANCING PAGE.
031400
031500*-------------------------------
031600* Read first, read next routines
031700*-------------------------------
031800 READ-FIRST-VALID-WORK.
031900      PERFORM READ-NEXT-VALID-WORK.
032000
032100 READ-NEXT-VALID-WORK.
032200      PERFORM READ-NEXT-WORK-RECORD.
032300      PERFORM READ-NEXT-WORK-RECORD
032400          UNTIL WORK-FILE-AT-END = "Y"
032500              OR WORK-PAID-DATE = ZEROES.
032600
032700 READ-NEXT-WORK-RECORD.
032800      MOVE "N" TO WORK-FILE-AT-END.
032900      READ WORK-FILE NEXT RECORD
033000          AT END MOVE "Y" TO WORK-FILE-AT-END.
033100
033200*-------------------------------
033300* Other File IO routines
033400*-------------------------------
033500 READ-VENDOR-RECORD.
033600      MOVE "Y" TO VENDOR-RECORD-FOUND.
```

21

continues

Listing 21.8. continued

```
033700     READ VENDOR-FILE RECORD
033800         INVALID KEY
033900           MOVE "N" TO VENDOR-RECORD-FOUND.
034000
034100*-------------------------------
034200* Utility Routines
034300*-------------------------------
034400     COPY "PLDATE01.CBL".
034500
```

The output of `bilrpt03.cbl` includes running totals for each day:

```
                                  BILLS REPORT                      PAGE:    1
VOUCHER VENDOR/For                             DUE DATE AMOUNT DUE INVOICE    S
16    CHARLES SMITH AND SONS                1/16/1997      25.97 5098
1997 DAY RUNNER
TOTAL THRU   1/16/1997      25.97
14    AERIAL SIGNS                          1/17/1997   1,046.97 FA1234
SIGN OVER ZUMA BEACH
TOTAL THRU   1/17/1997    1,072.94
13    MA BELL                               1/23/1997      94.96 50577
PHONE LINE 555-6067
19    MA BELL                               1/23/1997      34.95 50577
PHONE LINE 555-9098
TOTAL THRU   1/23/1997    1,202.85
8    ABC PRINTING                           1/27/1997      48.97 CX-1566       Y
BUSINESS CARDS
TOTAL THRU   1/27/1997    1,251.82
15    ABERCROMBIE AND OTHERS                1/31/1997     657.19 MONTHLY
RENT
TOTAL THRU   1/31/1997    1,909.01
4    ABC PRINTING                           2/07/1997     104.19 CX-5055       Y
LETTER HEAD
TOTAL THRU   2/07/1997    2,013.20
3    CHARLES SMITH AND SONS                 2/22/1997      27.76 5057
OFFICE SUPPLIES
7    ABC PRINTING                           2/22/1997      48.97 CX-1407
BUSINESS CARDS
TOTAL THRU   2/22/1997    2,089.93
17    RANIER GRAPHICS                       2/25/1997   4,057.07 ZO-1515
2 PAGE AD LAYOUT WITH RACE CAR
TOTAL THRU   2/25/1997    6,147.00
```

ANALYSIS   In Listing 21.8, a totaling field has been added to keep a running total of the amount owed. RUNNING-TOTAL is defined at line 012800. This is kept up to date inside the PROCESS-THIS-VOUCHER processing loop at line 024600, where WORK-AMOUNT is added to RUNNING-TOTAL. At line 012600, SAVE-DUE is defined. This field will be used to save the values in the due-date field so that it is possible to tell whether it has changed from one record to the next.

21

The original PROCESS-ALL-VOUCHERS routine is a processing loop that processes all voucher records. You need a higher-level loop that processes the group of all records that have the same due date. The control break logic PROCESS-ALL-DATES is inserted as a level between PRINT-THE-REPORT and PROCESS-ALL-VOUCHERS at line 021100.

Rather than performing PROCESS-ALL-VOUCHERS, PRINT-THE-REPORT performs PROCESS-ALL-DATES. PROCESS-ALL-DATES in turn performs PROCESS-ALL-VOUCHERS.

PROCESS-ALL-DATES is the clue to the control break. It starts by performing START-ONE-DATE. This is a routine at line 022000 that saves WORK-DUE in SAVE-DUE. After this is saved, it is possible at line 021400 to perform PROCESS-ALL-VOUCHERS until WORK-FILE-AT-END = "Y" or WORK-DUE NOT = SAVE-DUE.

This PERFORM causes the primary logic of the program to print individual records from the voucher file until a read on the work file pulls up a voucher record with a different due date.

After this break happens at line 021800, END-ONE-DATE is performed. END-ONE-DATE at line 022300 in turn performs PRINT-RUNNING-TOTAL. This routine at line 022600 prints the running total so far for this date by printing the SAVE-DATE and the RUNNING-TOTAL, along with a total message.

At this point, PROCESS-ALL-DATES ends and the logic returns to lines 020800 and 020900. If WORK-FILE-AT-END = "Y" the whole loop ends, but if it is only a change of date, PROCESS-ALL-DATES is performed again. This continues until WORK-FILE-AT-END = "Y".

The remainder of the program is identical to bilrpt02.cbl.

Code, compile, and run bilrpt03.cbl to see a report like the one given in the sample output. This report helps a user determine what date line to use as the cutoff date for selecting records using vchsel01.cbl.

Several different methods can be used to organize a control breaking report. Listing 21.8, bilrpt02.cbl, illustrates one flexible method that I like.

The Cash Requirements Report

The cash requirements report is the final program that you need in order to complete the bills payment system shown in Figure 21.1. It is step 8 of the bills payment system.

The cash requirements report in Listing 21.9 is not much different from bilrpt03.cbl. It prints only vouchers that are selected, so the "S" column has been removed from the report.

21

TYPE   **Listing 21.9. The cash requirements report.**

```
000100 IDENTIFICATION DIVISION.
000200 PROGRAM-ID. CSHREQ01.
000300*--------------------------------
000400* Cash Requirements Report
000500*--------------------------------
000600 ENVIRONMENT DIVISION.
000700 INPUT-OUTPUT SECTION.
000800 FILE-CONTROL.
000900
001000     COPY "SLVOUCH.CBL".
001100
001200     COPY "SLVND02.CBL".
001300
001400     COPY "SLSTATE.CBL".
001500
001600     SELECT WORK-FILE
001700         ASSIGN TO "WORK"
001800         ORGANIZATION IS SEQUENTIAL.
001900
002000     SELECT SORT-FILE
002100         ASSIGN TO "SORT".
002200
002300     SELECT PRINTER-FILE
002400         ASSIGN TO PRINTER
002500         ORGANIZATION IS LINE SEQUENTIAL.
002600
002700 DATA DIVISION.
002800 FILE SECTION.
002900
003000     COPY "FDVOUCH.CBL".
003100
003200     COPY "FDVND04.CBL".
003300
003400     COPY "FDSTATE.CBL".
003500
003600 FD  WORK-FILE
003700     LABEL RECORDS ARE STANDARD.
003800 01  WORK-RECORD.
003900     05  WORK-NUMBER         PIC 9(5).
004000     05  WORK-VENDOR         PIC 9(5).
004100     05  WORK-INVOICE        PIC X(15).
004200     05  WORK-FOR            PIC X(30).
004300     05  WORK-AMOUNT         PIC S9(6)V99.
004400     05  WORK-DATE           PIC 9(8).
004500     05  WORK-DUE            PIC 9(8).
004600     05  WORK-DEDUCTIBLE     PIC X.
004700     05  WORK-SELECTED       PIC X.
004800     05  WORK-PAID-AMOUNT    PIC S9(6)V99.
004900     05  WORK-PAID-DATE      PIC 9(8).
005000     05  WORK-CHECK-NO       PIC 9(6).
005100
005200 SD  SORT-FILE.
005300
005400 01  SORT-RECORD.
```

21

```
005500      05  SORT-NUMBER          PIC 9(5).
005600      05  SORT-VENDOR          PIC 9(5).
005700      05  SORT-INVOICE         PIC X(15).
005800      05  SORT-FOR             PIC X(30).
005900      05  SORT-AMOUNT          PIC S9(6)V99.
006000      05  SORT-DATE            PIC 9(8).
006100      05  SORT-DUE             PIC 9(8).
006200      05  SORT-DEDUCTIBLE      PIC X.
006300      05  SORT-SELECTED        PIC X.
006400      05  SORT-PAID-AMOUNT     PIC S9(6)V99.
006500      05  SORT-PAID-DATE       PIC 9(8).
006600      05  SORT-CHECK-NO        PIC 9(6).
006700
006800 FD  PRINTER-FILE
006900      LABEL RECORDS ARE OMITTED.
007000 01  PRINTER-RECORD           PIC X(80).
007100
007200 WORKING-STORAGE SECTION.
007300
007400 77  OK-TO-PROCESS            PIC X.
007500
007600      COPY "WSCASE01.CBL".
007700
007800 01  DETAIL-LINE.
007900      05  PRINT-NUMBER         PIC ZZZZ9.
008000      05  FILLER               PIC X(3) VALUE SPACE.
008100      05  PRINT-NAME           PIC X(30).
008200      05  FILLER               PIC X(1) VALUE SPACE.
008300      05  PRINT-DUE-DATE       PIC Z9/99/9999.
008400      05  FILLER               PIC X(1) VALUE SPACE.
008500      05  PRINT-AMOUNT         PIC ZZZ,ZZ9.99.
008600      05  FILLER               PIC X(1) VALUE SPACE.
008700      05  PRINT-INVOICE        PIC X(15).
008800
008900 01  TOTAL-THRU.
009000      05  FILLER               PIC X(20) VALUE SPACE.
009100      05  FILLER               PIC X(10) VALUE "TOTAL THRU".
009200
009300 01  COLUMN-LINE.
009400      05  FILLER            PIC X(7)  VALUE "VOUCHER".
009500      05  FILLER            PIC X(1)  VALUE SPACE.
009600      05  FILLER            PIC X(10) VALUE "VENDOR/For".
009700      05  FILLER            PIC X(23) VALUE SPACE.
009800      05  FILLER            PIC X(8)  VALUE "DUE DATE".
009900      05  FILLER            PIC X(1)  VALUE SPACE.
010000      05  FILLER            PIC X(10) VALUE "AMOUNT DUE".
010100      05  FILLER            PIC X(1)  VALUE SPACE.
010200      05  FILLER            PIC X(7)  VALUE "INVOICE".
010300
010400 01  TITLE-LINE.
010500      05  FILLER               PIC X(28) VALUE SPACE.
010600      05  FILLER               PIC X(17)
010700           VALUE "CASH REQUIREMENTS".
010800      05  FILLER               PIC X(16) VALUE SPACE.
010900      05  FILLER               PIC X(5) VALUE "PAGE:".
```

continues

21

Listing 21.9. continued

```
011000      05  FILLER              PIC X(1) VALUE SPACE.
011100      05  PRINT-PAGE-NUMBER   PIC ZZZ9.
011200
011300 77  WORK-FILE-AT-END     PIC X.
011400 77  VENDOR-RECORD-FOUND  PIC X.
011500
011600 77  LINE-COUNT           PIC 999 VALUE ZERO.
011700 77  PAGE-NUMBER          PIC 9999 VALUE ZERO.
011800 77  MAXIMUM-LINES        PIC 999 VALUE 55.
011900
012000 77  RECORD-COUNT         PIC 9999 VALUE ZEROES.
012100
012200 77  SAVE-DUE             PIC 9(8).
012300
012400 77  RUNNING-TOTAL        PIC S9(6)V99.
012500
012600     COPY "WSDATE01.CBL".
012700
012800 PROCEDURE DIVISION.
012900 PROGRAM-BEGIN.
013000
013100     PERFORM OPENING-PROCEDURE.
013200     PERFORM MAIN-PROCESS.
013300     PERFORM CLOSING-PROCEDURE.
013400
013500 PROGRAM-EXIT.
013600     EXIT PROGRAM.
013700
013800 PROGRAM-DONE.
013900     STOP RUN.
014000
014100 OPENING-PROCEDURE.
014200     OPEN I-O VENDOR-FILE.
014300
014400     OPEN OUTPUT PRINTER-FILE.
014500
014600 MAIN-PROCESS.
014700     PERFORM GET-OK-TO-PROCESS.
014800     IF OK-TO-PROCESS = "Y"
014900         PERFORM SORT-DATA-FILE
015000         PERFORM PRINT-THE-REPORT.
015100
015200 CLOSING-PROCEDURE.
015300     CLOSE VENDOR-FILE.
015400     PERFORM END-LAST-PAGE.
015500     CLOSE PRINTER-FILE.
015600
015700 GET-OK-TO-PROCESS.
015800     PERFORM ACCEPT-OK-TO-PROCESS.
015900     PERFORM RE-ACCEPT-OK-TO-PROCESS
016000         UNTIL OK-TO-PROCESS = "Y" OR "N".
016100
016200 ACCEPT-OK-TO-PROCESS.
016300     DISPLAY "PRINT CASH REQUIREMENTS REPORT (Y/N)?".
```

21

```
016400     ACCEPT OK-TO-PROCESS.
016500     INSPECT OK-TO-PROCESS
016600        CONVERTING LOWER-ALPHA
016700        TO           UPPER-ALPHA.
016800
016900 RE-ACCEPT-OK-TO-PROCESS.
017000     DISPLAY "YOU MUST ENTER YES OR NO".
017100     PERFORM ACCEPT-OK-TO-PROCESS.
017200
017300*-------------------------------
017400* Sorting logic
017500*-------------------------------
017600 SORT-DATA-FILE.
017700     SORT SORT-FILE
017800        ON ASCENDING KEY SORT-DUE
017900           USING VOUCHER-FILE
018000           GIVING WORK-FILE.
018100
018200 PRINT-THE-REPORT.
018300     OPEN INPUT WORK-FILE.
018400     PERFORM START-ONE-REPORT.
018500     PERFORM PROCESS-VOUCHERS.
018600     PERFORM END-ONE-REPORT.
018700     CLOSE WORK-FILE.
018800
018900 START-ONE-REPORT.
019000     PERFORM INITIALIZE-REPORT.
019100     PERFORM START-NEW-PAGE.
019200     MOVE ZEROES TO RUNNING-TOTAL.
019300
019400 INITIALIZE-REPORT.
019500     MOVE ZEROES TO LINE-COUNT PAGE-NUMBER.
019600
019700 END-ONE-REPORT.
019800     IF RECORD-COUNT = ZEROES
019900        MOVE "NO RECORDS FOUND" TO PRINTER-RECORD
020000        PERFORM WRITE-TO-PRINTER.
020100
020200 PROCESS-VOUCHERS.
020300     PERFORM READ-FIRST-VALID-WORK.
020400     PERFORM PROCESS-ALL-DATES
020500        UNTIL WORK-FILE-AT-END = "Y".
020600
020700 PROCESS-ALL-DATES.
020800     PERFORM START-ONE-DATE.
020900
021000     PERFORM PROCESS-ALL-VOUCHERS
021100        UNTIL WORK-FILE-AT-END = "Y"
021200           OR WORK-DUE NOT = SAVE-DUE.
021300
021400     PERFORM END-ONE-DATE.
021500
021600 START-ONE-DATE.
021700     MOVE WORK-DUE TO SAVE-DUE.
021800
```

21

continues

Listing 21.9. continued

```
021900 END-ONE-DATE.
022000     PERFORM PRINT-RUNNING-TOTAL.
022100
022200 PRINT-RUNNING-TOTAL.
022300     MOVE SPACE TO DETAIL-LINE.
022400     MOVE SAVE-DUE TO DATE-CCYYMMDD.
022500     PERFORM CONVERT-TO-MMDDCCYY.
022600     MOVE DATE-MMDDCCYY TO PRINT-DUE-DATE.
022700     MOVE RUNNING-TOTAL TO PRINT-AMOUNT.
022800     MOVE TOTAL-THRU TO PRINT-NAME.
022900     MOVE DETAIL-LINE TO PRINTER-RECORD.
023000     PERFORM WRITE-TO-PRINTER.
023100     PERFORM LINE-FEED 2 TIMES.
023200
023300 PROCESS-ALL-VOUCHERS.
023400     PERFORM PROCESS-THIS-VOUCHER.
023500     PERFORM READ-NEXT-VALID-WORK.
023600
023700 PROCESS-THIS-VOUCHER.
023800     ADD 1 TO RECORD-COUNT.
023900     IF LINE-COUNT > MAXIMUM-LINES
024000         PERFORM START-NEXT-PAGE.
024100     PERFORM PRINT-THE-RECORD.
024200     ADD WORK-AMOUNT TO RUNNING-TOTAL.
024300
024400 PRINT-THE-RECORD.
024500     PERFORM PRINT-LINE-1.
024600     PERFORM PRINT-LINE-2.
024700     PERFORM LINE-FEED.
024800
024900 PRINT-LINE-1.
025000     MOVE SPACE TO DETAIL-LINE.
025100     MOVE WORK-NUMBER TO PRINT-NUMBER.
025200
025300     MOVE WORK-VENDOR TO VENDOR-NUMBER.
025400     PERFORM READ-VENDOR-RECORD.
025500     IF VENDOR-RECORD-FOUND = "Y"
025600         MOVE VENDOR-NAME TO PRINT-NAME
025700     ELSE
025800         MOVE "*VENDOR NOT ON FILE*" TO PRINT-NAME.
025900
026000     MOVE WORK-DUE TO DATE-CCYYMMDD.
026100     PERFORM CONVERT-TO-MMDDCCYY.
026200     MOVE DATE-MMDDCCYY TO PRINT-DUE-DATE.
026300
026400     MOVE WORK-AMOUNT TO PRINT-AMOUNT.
026500     MOVE WORK-INVOICE TO PRINT-INVOICE.
026600
026700     MOVE DETAIL-LINE TO PRINTER-RECORD.
026800     PERFORM WRITE-TO-PRINTER.
026900
027000 PRINT-LINE-2.
027100     MOVE SPACE TO DETAIL-LINE.
027200     MOVE WORK-FOR TO PRINT-NAME.
```

21

```
027300      MOVE DETAIL-LINE TO PRINTER-RECORD.
027400      PERFORM WRITE-TO-PRINTER.
027500
027600 WRITE-TO-PRINTER.
027700      WRITE PRINTER-RECORD BEFORE ADVANCING 1.
027800      ADD 1 TO LINE-COUNT.
027900
028000 LINE-FEED.
028100      MOVE SPACE TO PRINTER-RECORD.
028200      PERFORM WRITE-TO-PRINTER.
028300
028400 START-NEXT-PAGE.
028500      PERFORM END-LAST-PAGE.
028600      PERFORM START-NEW-PAGE.
028700
028800 START-NEW-PAGE.
028900      ADD 1 TO PAGE-NUMBER.
029000      MOVE PAGE-NUMBER TO PRINT-PAGE-NUMBER.
029100      MOVE TITLE-LINE TO PRINTER-RECORD.
029200      PERFORM WRITE-TO-PRINTER.
029300      PERFORM LINE-FEED.
029400      MOVE COLUMN-LINE TO PRINTER-RECORD.
029500      PERFORM WRITE-TO-PRINTER.
029600      PERFORM LINE-FEED.
029700
029800 END-LAST-PAGE.
029900      PERFORM FORM-FEED.
030000      MOVE ZERO TO LINE-COUNT.
030100
030200 FORM-FEED.
030300      MOVE SPACE TO PRINTER-RECORD.
030400      WRITE PRINTER-RECORD BEFORE ADVANCING PAGE.
030500
030600*--------------------------------
030700* Read first, read next routines
030800*--------------------------------
030900 READ-FIRST-VALID-WORK.
031000      PERFORM READ-NEXT-VALID-WORK.
031100
031200 READ-NEXT-VALID-WORK.
031300      PERFORM READ-NEXT-WORK-RECORD.
031400      PERFORM READ-NEXT-WORK-RECORD
031500          UNTIL WORK-FILE-AT-END = "Y"
031600             OR ( WORK-PAID-DATE = ZEROES AND
031700                 WORK-SELECTED = "Y").
031800
031900 READ-NEXT-WORK-RECORD.
032000      MOVE "N" TO WORK-FILE-AT-END.
032100      READ WORK-FILE NEXT RECORD
032200          AT END MOVE "Y" TO WORK-FILE-AT-END.
032300
032400*--------------------------------
032500* Other File IO routines
032600*--------------------------------
032700 READ-VENDOR-RECORD.
```

continues

Listing 21.9. continued

```
032800          MOVE "Y" TO VENDOR-RECORD-FOUND.
032900          READ VENDOR-FILE RECORD
033000              INVALID KEY
033100                  MOVE "N" TO VENDOR-RECORD-FOUND.
033200
033300*-------------------------------
033400* Utility Routines
033500*-------------------------------
033600          COPY "PLDATE01.CBL".
033700
```

In the sample output report from cshrq01.cbl, the user has selected all vouchers through 01/23/1997, using vchsel01.cbl, and has additionally selected vouchers numbered 3 and 4, using vchpic01.cbl:

```
                                  CASH REQUIREMENTS                    PAGE:    1
       VOUCHER VENDOR/For                       DUE DATE AMOUNT DUE INVOICE
       16    CHARLES SMITH AND SONS             1/16/1997       25.97 5098
       1997 DAY RUNNER
       TOTAL THRU  1/16/1997       25.97
       14    AERIAL SIGNS                       1/17/1997    1,046.97 FA1234
       SIGN OVER ZUMA BEACH
       TOTAL THRU  1/17/1997    1,072.94
       13    MA BELL                            1/23/1997       94.96 50577
       PHONE LINE 555-6067
       19    MA BELL                            1/23/1997       34.95 50577
       PHONE LINE 555-9098
       TOTAL THRU  1/23/1997    1,202.85
       4    ABC PRINTING                        2/07/1997      104.19 CX-5055
       LETTER HEAD
       TOTAL THRU  2/07/1997    1,307.04
       3    CHARLES SMITH AND SONS              2/22/1997       27.76 5057
       OFFICE SUPPLIES
       TOTAL THRU  2/22/1997    1,334.80
```

ANALYSIS The TITLE-LINE is changed at lines 010600 and 010700. The main change is in the record selection logic in READ-NEXT-VALID-WORK at line 031200. A test has been added at line 031700 so that records are selected only when WORK-PAID-DATE = ZEROES and WORK-SELECTED = "Y". This additional test eliminates unselected records.

Completing the System

The last steps needed to tie all the programs together are to get all the parts on menus by creating a new menu, and making some changes to an existing menu. Listing 21.10 is a menu of the voucher processes in the order they are used in the bills processing system. This menu program calls VCHPAY02, which you should have created in Exercise 1 of the previous chapter,

Day 20, "More Complex Data Entry." If you did not create it for that exercise, go back and do so now.

TYPE | **Listing 21.10. A menu for voucher handling.**

```
000100 IDENTIFICATION DIVISION.
000200 PROGRAM-ID. VCHMNU01.
000300*-----------------------------
000400* Menu for Voucher Processing
000500*-----------------------------
000600 ENVIRONMENT DIVISION.
000700 INPUT-OUTPUT SECTION.
000800 FILE-CONTROL.
000900
001000 DATA DIVISION.
001100 FILE SECTION.
001200
001300 WORKING-STORAGE SECTION.
001400
001500 77  MENU-PICK                 PIC 9.
001600     88  MENU-PICK-IS-VALID     VALUES 0 THRU 7.
001700
001800 PROCEDURE DIVISION.
001900 PROGRAM-BEGIN.
002000     PERFORM OPENING-PROCEDURE.
002100     PERFORM MAIN-PROCESS.
002200     PERFORM CLOSING-PROCEDURE.
002300
002400 PROGRAM-EXIT.
002500     EXIT PROGRAM.
002600
002700 PROGRAM-DONE.
002800     STOP RUN.
002900
003000 OPENING-PROCEDURE.
003100
003200 CLOSING-PROCEDURE.
003300
003400 MAIN-PROCESS.
003500     PERFORM GET-MENU-PICK.
003600     PERFORM DO-THE-PICK
003700         UNTIL MENU-PICK = 0.
003800
003900*-----------------------------
004000* MENU
004100*-----------------------------
004200 GET-MENU-PICK.
004300     PERFORM DISPLAY-THE-MENU.
004400     PERFORM ACCEPT-MENU-PICK.
004500     PERFORM RE-ACCEPT-MENU-PICK
004600         UNTIL MENU-PICK-IS-VALID.
004700
```

continues

21

Listing 21.10. continued

```
004800 DISPLAY-THE-MENU.
004900     PERFORM CLEAR-SCREEN.
005000     DISPLAY "    PLEASE SELECT:".
005100     DISPLAY " ".
005200     DISPLAY "         1.  VOUCHER ENTRY".
005300     DISPLAY "         2.  BILLS REPORT".
005400     DISPLAY "         3.  SELECT VOUCHERS BY DUE DATE RANGE".
005500     DISPLAY "         4.  SELECT INDIVIDUAL VOUCHERS".
005600     DISPLAY "         5.  CLEAR PREVIOUS SELECTIONS".
005700     DISPLAY "         6.  CASH REQUIREMENTS REPORT".
005800     DISPLAY "         7.  PAID BILLS ENTRY".
005900     DISPLAY " ".
006000     DISPLAY "         0.  EXIT".
006100     PERFORM SCROLL-LINE 8 TIMES.
006200
006300 ACCEPT-MENU-PICK.
006400     DISPLAY "YOUR CHOICE (0-7)?".
006500     ACCEPT MENU-PICK.
006600
006700 RE-ACCEPT-MENU-PICK.
006800     DISPLAY "INVALID SELECTION - PLEASE RE-TRY.".
006900     PERFORM ACCEPT-MENU-PICK.
007000
007100 CLEAR-SCREEN.
007200     PERFORM SCROLL-LINE 25 TIMES.
007300
007400 SCROLL-LINE.
007500     DISPLAY " ".
007600
007700 DO-THE-PICK.
007800     IF MENU-PICK = 1
007900         PERFORM VOUCHER-ENTRY
008000     ELSE
008100     IF MENU-PICK = 2
008200         PERFORM BILLS-REPORT
008300     ELSE
008400     IF MENU-PICK = 3
008500         PERFORM DATE-SELECTION
008600     ELSE
008700     IF MENU-PICK = 4
008800         PERFORM SINGLE-SELECTION
008900     ELSE
009000     IF MENU-PICK = 5
009100         PERFORM CLEAR-SELECTIONS
009200     ELSE
009300     IF MENU-PICK = 6
009400         PERFORM CASH-REQUIREMENTS
009500     ELSE
009600     IF MENU-PICK = 7
009700         PERFORM PAID-ENTRY.
009800
009900     PERFORM GET-MENU-PICK.
010000
010100 VOUCHER-ENTRY.
```

21

```
010200     CALL "VCHMNT01".
010300
010400 BILLS-REPORT.
010500     CALL "BILRPT03".
010600
010700 DATE-SELECTION.
010800     CALL "VCHSEL01".
010900
011000 SINGLE-SELECTION.
011100     CALL "VCHPIC01".
011200
011300 CLEAR-SELECTIONS.
011400     CALL "VCHCLR01".
011500
011600 CASH-REQUIREMENTS.
011700     CALL "CSHREQ01".
011800
011900 PAID-ENTRY.
012000     CALL "VCHPAY02".
012100
012200
```

The following is the output:

```
PLEASE SELECT:
1.   VOUCHER ENTRY
2.   BILLS REPORT
3.   SELECT VOUCHERS BY DUE DATE RANGE
4.   SELECT INDIVIDUAL VOUCHERS
5.   CLEAR PREVIOUS SELECTIONS
6.   CASH REQUIREMENTS REPORT
7.   PAID BILLS ENTRY
0.   EXIT
YOUR CHOICE (0-7)?
```

Finally, the bills payment system main menu must be modified to call the new voucher-processing menu. Listing 21.11, `bilmnu03.cbl`, adds a single pick to the main menu.

Listing 21.11. An extended main menu.

```
000100 IDENTIFICATION DIVISION.
000200 PROGRAM-ID. BILMNU03.
000300*--------------------------------
000400* Menu for the bill payment system.
000500* Including Vouchers
000600*--------------------------------
000700 ENVIRONMENT DIVISION.
000800 INPUT-OUTPUT SECTION.
000900 FILE-CONTROL.
001000
001100 DATA DIVISION.
```

continues

Listing 21.11. continued

```
001200 FILE SECTION.
001300
001400 WORKING-STORAGE SECTION.
001500
001600 77  MENU-PICK                  PIC 9.
001700     88  MENU-PICK-IS-VALID      VALUES 0 THRU 3.
001800
001900 PROCEDURE DIVISION.
002000 PROGRAM-BEGIN.
002100     PERFORM OPENING-PROCEDURE.
002200     PERFORM MAIN-PROCESS.
002300     PERFORM CLOSING-PROCEDURE.
002400
002500 PROGRAM-EXIT.
002600     EXIT PROGRAM.
002700
002800 PROGRAM-DONE.
002900     STOP RUN.
003000
003100 OPENING-PROCEDURE.
003200
003300 CLOSING-PROCEDURE.
003400
003500 MAIN-PROCESS.
003600     PERFORM GET-MENU-PICK.
003700     PERFORM DO-THE-PICK
003800         UNTIL MENU-PICK = 0.
003900
004000*-----------------------------
004100* MENU
004200*-----------------------------
004300 GET-MENU-PICK.
004400     PERFORM DISPLAY-THE-MENU.
004500     PERFORM ACCEPT-MENU-PICK.
004600     PERFORM RE-ACCEPT-MENU-PICK
004700         UNTIL MENU-PICK-IS-VALID.
004800
004900 DISPLAY-THE-MENU.
005000     PERFORM CLEAR-SCREEN.
005100     DISPLAY "    PLEASE SELECT:".
005200     DISPLAY " ".
005300     DISPLAY "         1.   STATE CODE MAINTENANCE".
005400     DISPLAY "         2.   VENDOR MAINTENANCE".
005500     DISPLAY "         3.   VOUCHER PROCESSING".
005600     DISPLAY " ".
005700     DISPLAY "         0.   EXIT".
005800     PERFORM SCROLL-LINE 8 TIMES.
005900
006000 ACCEPT-MENU-PICK.
006100     DISPLAY "YOUR CHOICE (0-3)?".
006200     ACCEPT MENU-PICK.
006300
006400 RE-ACCEPT-MENU-PICK.
006500     DISPLAY "INVALID SELECTION - PLEASE RE-TRY.".
```

```
006600      PERFORM ACCEPT-MENU-PICK.
006700
006800 CLEAR-SCREEN.
006900      PERFORM SCROLL-LINE 25 TIMES.
007000
007100 SCROLL-LINE.
007200      DISPLAY " ".
007300
007400 DO-THE-PICK.
007500      IF MENU-PICK = 1
007600          PERFORM STATE-MAINTENANCE
007700      ELSE
007800      IF MENU-PICK = 2
007900          PERFORM VENDOR-MAINTENANCE
008000      ELSE
008100      IF MENU-PICK = 3
008200          PERFORM VOUCHER-PROCESSING.
008300
008400      PERFORM GET-MENU-PICK.
008500
008600*-------------------------------
008700* STATE
008800*-------------------------------
008900 STATE-MAINTENANCE.
009000      CALL "STCMNT04".
009100
009200*-------------------------------
009300* VENDOR
009400*-------------------------------
009500 VENDOR-MAINTENANCE.
009600      CALL "VNDMNT05".
009700
009800*-------------------------------
009900* VOUCHERS
010000*-------------------------------
010100 VOUCHER-PROCESSING.
010200      CALL "VCHMNU01".
010300
```

Here is the output:

```
PLEASE SELECT:
1.   STATE CODE MAINTENANCE
2.   VENDOR MAINTENANCE
3.   VOUCHER PROCESSING
0.   EXIT
YOUR CHOICE (0-3)?
```

In Closing

This course has not covered all of COBOL syntax, nor has it covered all the commands and their versions. It has covered working COBOL not just at an individual level, but at a system level, trying to give you an idea of how programs work together to get a job done.

21

A piece of advice frequently given to writers is, "If you want to learn how to write, write." The same is true of programming. If you want to learn how to program, you should program.

Go back to earlier sections of the book. Pick up the phone book maintenance program that was started, and work out how to do it better. Create an indexed phone file. Program your own phone book program with fields for home, office, car, beeper, and fax numbers. Design a report that prints all this information. Add an alternate key to the name field so that a phone number can be looked up by user name.

Write a program to keep track of your to-do list in a file containing the project description, priority, and due date. Write reports that print the to-do list in priority order and in due-date order.

It really doesn't matter what the project is or how simple it is; in fact, the simpler the better. Just keep writing!

This completes your 21-day course, and you now have an excellent grounding in COBOL. With practice, you can become an expert.

COBOL is a comprehensive language, and you never really stop learning about it. I still study it whenever I have the chance. To enable you to continue your progress in COBOL, this book includes six Bonus Day lessons! These expand on topics already covered and open up some new areas.

The Bonus Day chapters also cover the issue that is filling the computer news these days: the year 2000, its effect on COBOL programs, and what needs to be done to fix the problem.

So pat yourself on the back. You've done a terrific job so far. Onward to a few more days of work.

Summary

Reporting is the most visible part of any program. Today, you learned these basics:

☐ A processing loop that requires record selection can be handled by using the logic flow demonstrated by the following pseudocode:

```
process-records
    read-first-valid-record
    perform process-loop
        until file-at-end
process-loop
    process-this-record.
    read-next-valid-record
read-first-valid-record
    start-the-file
    read-next-valid-record
```

21

```
read-next-valid-record
    read-next-record
    perform read-next-record
        until file is at end
        or (the selection condition is met)
```

☐ A SORT command can be used to sort a file on a field that is not a key in the file. You can think of the SORT command as a series of steps:

1. Copy the input file to the sort file.

2. Sort the sort file on one or more fields in the sort record.

3. Copy the resulting sorted file to the output file.

☐ The interruption of the normal printing of a report program to print a total or subtotal is called a control break or level break.

☐ You can create a control break for any field on which a file has been sorted.

☐ You can create menus to tie the whole report together.

Q&A

Q **Some of the fields in the VOUCHER-FILE are never used in reports such as the VOUCHER-DEDUCTIBLE. What happens to this field?**

A See the exercises in the Workshop section.

Workshop

Quiz

1. What is the SORT command used for?

2. Before the following command is used, in which state must the VOUCHER-FILE and WORK-FILE be?

```
SORT SORT-FILE
    ON ASCENDING KEY SORT-DATE
    USING VOUCHER-FILE
    GIVING WORK-FILE
```

   a. Open

   b. Closed

   c. Doesn't matter

21

Exercises

1. Copy `cshreq01.cbl` to `deduct01.cbl`, and modify the program to do the following:

   a. Change the `PROGRAM-ID` to `DEDUCT01`.

   b. Modify the comment to indicate that this will be the deductibles report.

   c. Modify `TITLE-LINE` to read `"DEDUCTIBLES"`.

   d. Modify the column headings in `COLUMN-LINE` to read `DATE` and `AMOUNT` instead of `DUE DATE` and `AMOUNT DUE`.

   e. Change the variable `SAVE-DUE` to `SAVE-PAID-DATE`.

   f. Modify `ACCEPT-OK-TO-PROCESS` to display `"PRINT DEDUCTIBLES REPORT (Y/N)?"`.

   g. Sort by `SORT-PAID-DATE`.

   h. Modify `PROCESS-ALL-DATES` and `START-ONE-DATE` to save `WORK-PAID-DATE` and process until `WORK-PAID-DATE NOT = SAVE-PAID-DATE`.

   i. Modify `PRINT-RUNNING-TOTAL` to print `SAVE-PAID-DATE` instead of `SAVE-DUE`.

   j. Modify `PROCESS-THIS-VOUCHER` to move `WORK-PAID-AMOUNT` to the print line instead of `WORK-AMOUNT`.

   k. Modify `PRINT-LINE-1` to print the `WORK-PAID-AMOUNT` and `WORK-PAID-DATE`.

2. Modify `READ-NEXT-VALID-WORK` to select records when (`WORK-PAID-DATE NOT = ZEROES AND WORK-DEDUCTIBLE = "Y"`).

3. Compile and run this program. It should give you a report on any paid vouchers that have the `VOUCHER-DEDUCTIBLE` flag set to `"Y"`.

21

In Review

Congratulations! You've accomplished your goal of learning COBOL in 21 days. Now that you're on a roll, you can move ahead to the bonus days that have been provided for those who are ambitious enough to take what they've learned in 21 days and add real-world experiences.

15

16

17

18

19

20

21

Let's take a moment to reflect on what you've learned this week. The concepts of data integrity were intentionally woven into each day because your users will need to know that they can depend on your program's reliability. This trust isn't placed lightly. An unreliable program serves no purpose. The first two days of this week focused on the concepts of data integrity and how to look up information in tables and arrays. These skills ensure that you treat data properly and provide the means for your users to look up information on demand. Who wants to remember everything when you have a computer on hand to look up data? Day 17 enhanced your understanding of index files and provided the means for alternate keys. Day 18 showed you how to call other programs from your program. This concept escapes many programmers, but it significantly increases the power you can give your users. Days 19 and 20 completed the concepts of data entry, one of the primary reasons users will come to count on your COBOL programming prowess. Finally, Day 21 tied together the processes of selecting, sorting, and reporting.

If you choose to tackle the bonus days, you'll find that they aren't necessarily more difficult than any of the previous days. These six days have been included to enhance your real-world understanding of COBOL programming and finish preparing you for situations you might encounter but that are difficult to include in a 21-day course.

Congratulations on a job well done!

Day 1

Control Breaks

Control breaks, covered briefly on Day 21, "Selecting, Sorting, and Reporting," are an important part of reports. On this first bonus day, you learn how to use them more effectively. You also learn about the following topics:

- ☐ Control breaks
- ☐ Control break variables
- ☐ The mechanics of a control break
- ☐ Control break levels
- ☐ Control break logic
- ☐ Using control breaks for totals
- ☐ Using control breaks for formatting
- ☐ Multilevel control breaks

Control breaks are important in reports and are used extensively for totaling and subtotaling. Recall that a control break is a break inserted into the normal processing of a program (usually a report program) to cause groups of records to be processed together as one unit. The interruption of the normal printing of a report program to print a total or subtotal is a control break or level break. In the example shown in Figure B1.1, the report breaks at the end of each vendor and prints a subtotal for that vendor, and then breaks at the end of the report and prints a total for the report.

Figure B1.1.

Control breaks for printing subtotals and a report total.

```
Vendor              DUE DATE    AMOUNT
ABC Printing        1/23/1994    27.95
ABC Printing        1/31/1994    15.54
ABC Printing        2/16/1994    10.17
                    Sub Total    53.66

Phone Co            1/17/1994    34.97
Phone Co            1/24/1994    17.54
Phone Co            1/31/1994    27.15
                    Sub Total    79.66

Moon Mountain Inc.  1/06/1994    39.95
Moon Mountain Inc.  1/16/1994    47.55
                    Sub Total    87.50
                    Grand Total 220.82
```

Using the definition of a control break, the subtotals for ABC Printing, Phone Co, and Moon Mountain Inc. are generated by treating all records with the same vendor as a unit. The report total is generated by treating all records in the file as a unit.

Control Break Variables

The actual records in the file might look something like the ones in Figure B1.2. The fields (name, date, and amount) have some space inserted between them so that you can see them more easily. The file has been sorted in vendor name order.

Figure B1.2.

The records used in Figure B1.1.

```
ABC Printing          19940123    00027.95
ABC Printing          19940131    00015.54
ABC Printing          19940216    00010.17
Phone Co              19940117    00034.97
Phone Co              19940124    00017.54
Phone Co              19940131    00027.15
Moon Mountain Inc.    19940106    00039.95
Moon Mountain Inc.    19940116    00047.55
```

If you compare Figure B1.1 to the records in Figure B1.2, you will see immediately that in addition to the values in the record, you need variables to hold the subtotals for each vendor and the grand total for the report. The obvious choice would be totals for all needed values, as shown in Listing B1.1.

TYPE **Listing B1.1. The total for control breaks.**

```
000500 77   ABC-TOTAL          PIC S9(6)V99.
000600 77   PHONE-TOTAL        PIC S9(6)V99.
000700 77   MOON-TOTAL         PIC S9(6)V99.
000800 77   GRAND-TOTAL        PIC S9(6)V99.
```

Unfortunately, when you're processing a file, you have no idea what values, which vendors, or how many vendors are in the file. You cannot create a separate variable to hold a subtotal for each vendor.

You need one variable that is filled and emptied over and over for each vendor, and one that fills just for the whole report, as shown in Listing B1.2.

TYPE **Listing B1.2. Just two variables for the control breaks.**

```
000700 77   VENDOR-TOTAL       PIC S9(6)V99.
000800 77   GRAND-TOTAL        PIC S9(6)V99.
```

ANALYSIS The VENDOR-TOTAL is set to zero at the start of each new vendor. As records are processed, the amount in the record is added to VENDOR-TOTAL. After the last record with that vendor name is processed, a line is formatted and the VENDOR-TOTAL is printed.

The Mechanics of a Control Break

Table B1.1 illustrates what is happening in a control break. The left column shows the record as it is read from the file. These are numbered in the figure for reference. The right column shows the steps being taken. The steps also are numbered for reference. The steps are only those connected with the control break, and they do not include the actions necessary to print each line of the report. Imagine the actions on the right being taken in response to each record read on the left.

Table B1.1. An idealized model of control breaking.

Record			Action
			1. MOVE ZERO TO GRAND-TOTAL
			2. MOVE ZERO TO VENDOR-TOTAL
1. ABC Printing	19940123	00027.95	3. ADD 27.95 TO VENDOR-TOTAL
2. ABC Printing	19940131	00015.54	4. ADD 15.54 TO VENDOR-TOTAL
3. ABC Printing	19940216	00010.17	5. ADD 10.17 TO VENDOR-TOTAL

continues

Table B1.1. continued

Record			Action
			6. PRINT VENDOR-TOTAL
			7. ADD VENDOR-TOTAL TO GRAND-TOTAL
			8. MOVE ZERO TO VENDOR-TOTAL
4. Phone Co	19940117	00034.97	9. ADD 34.97 TO VENDOR-TOTAL
5. Phone Co	19940124	00017.54	10. ADD 17.54 TO VENDOR-TOTAL
6. Phone Co	19940131	00027.15	11. ADD 27.15 TO VENDOR-TOTAL
			12. PRINT VENDOR-TOTAL
			13. ADD VENDOR-TOTAL TO GRAND-TOTAL
			14. MOVE ZERO TO VENDOR-TOTAL
7. Moon Mountain Inc.	19940106	00039.95	15. ADD 39.95 TO VENDOR-TOTAL
8. Moon Mountain Inc.	19940116	00047.55	16. ADD 47.55 TO VENDOR-TOTAL
			17. PRINT VENDOR-TOTAL
			18. ADD VENDOR-TOTAL TO GRAND-TOTAL
			19. PRINT GRAND-TOTAL

This is an idealized model of control breaking. If you look at steps 6, 7, and 8 in the right column, you see that after the last ABC Printing record is read, the total for ABC Printing is printed and then added to the grand total for the report. These steps are sensible enough for a human being. You can scan up and down through the records and quickly establish the breaking points; but how would the computer know that ABC Printing was finished and that a new vendor was about to begin, unless it had already read the next record in the file? This makes the programming of control breaks somewhat tricky. It is necessary to read the file past the point that you want, and then execute the control break logic.

Table B1.2 shows a truer picture of what happens in a programmed control break.

Table B1.2. A truer picture of a programmed control break.

Record			Action
1. ABC Printing	19940123	00027.95	1. MOVE ZERO TO GRAND-TOTAL
			2. MOVE ZERO TO VENDOR-TOTAL
			3. ADD 27.95 TO VENDOR-TOTAL

Record				Action
2. ABC Printing		19940131	00015.54	4. ADD 15.54 TO VENDOR-TOTAL
3. ABC Printing		19940216	00010.17	5. ADD 10.17 TO VENDOR-TOTAL
4. Phone Co		19940117	00034.97	6. PRINT VENDOR-TOTAL
				7. ADD VENDOR-TOTAL TO GRAND-TOTAL
				8. MOVE ZERO TO VENDOR-TOTAL
				9. ADD 34.97 TO VENDOR-TOTAL
5. Phone Co		19940124	00017.54	10. ADD 17.54 TO VENDOR-TOTAL
6. Phone Co		19940131	00027.15	11. ADD 27.15 TO VENDOR-TOTAL
7. Moon Mountain Inc.		19940106	00039.95	12. PRINT VENDOR-TOTAL
				13. ADD VENDOR-TOTAL TO GRAND-TOTAL
				14. MOVE ZERO TO VENDOR-TOTAL
				15. ADD 39.95 TO VENDOR-TOTAL
8. Moon Mountain Inc.		19940116	00047.55	16. ADD 47.55 TO VENDOR-TOTAL
9. END OF FILE				17. PRINT VENDOR-TOTAL
				18. ADD VENDOR-TOTAL TO GRAND-TOTAL
				19. PRINT GRAND-TOTAL

BD
1

 In the left column, the first record is read from the file. This triggers the start of a report, and step 1 moves zero to the GRAND-TOTAL. This first record also triggers the beginning of a vendor, and step 2 moves zeroes to the VENDOR-TOTAL.

Step 3 is the action taken based on the actual record. The value in the record is added to the VENDOR-TOTAL. Record 2 is read, causing step 4 to be taken. Record 3 is read, causing step 5 to be taken. When record 4 is read, the vendor name changes. The change of name signals the end of a vendor. Steps 6 and 7 print the VENDOR-TOTAL and add it to the GRAND-TOTAL. Record 4 also signals the beginning of a new vendor, and step 8 sets the VENDOR-TOTAL back to zero for the beginning of this new vendor.

Step 9 adds the value in the record to VENDOR-TOTAL, and the values read from records 5 and 6 also are added in steps 10 and 11. When record 7 is read, the vendor name changes again. This signals an end of a vendor, and steps 12 and 13 print the VENDOR-TOTAL and add it to the GRAND-TOTAL. Record 7 also signals a new vendor, and step 14 zeroes the VENDOR-TOTAL again. Steps 15 and 16 add the values for records 7 and 8.

The last read on the file (labeled record 9) does not retrieve a record but creates an end-of-file condition. This condition triggers the end of a vendor, and steps 17 and 18 print the VENDOR-TOTAL and add it to the GRAND-TOTAL. The end-of-file condition also triggers the end of the report and, finally, step 19 prints the GRAND-TOTAL.

Control Break Levels

Control breaks are usually thought of in terms of levels. In the example shown in Table B1.2, the senior, or highest, level is the level that includes all records in the file. The next level below that is the level that includes all records with the same vendor.

The senior level control break can be called the level-1 break. The vendor break would then be called the level-2 break. Any file processing can have more than two level breaks, but this example works with only two. There are several key parts to a control break.

NEW TERM   The *control break field* or *control field* is the field in the record that causes a control break to occur when it changes. In Table B1.2, the vendor name is a control break field.

The control break field is the field on which the file is sorted. One special type of control break field is used at level 1. Level 1 is usually at the level of the complete file, or all records. The break on level 1 is not a field, but an end-of-file condition. The control break field for a level-1 break can be thought of as the whole file, and the condition that determines the break is that of no more records to process (end of file).

NEW TERM   The *control break current value* or *control current value* is a field created in WORKING-STORAGE that holds a copy of the control break field. The control break current value is sometimes called the *control break holding area* or *control holding area*.

The control break current value is filled in at the beginning of a control break level with the value in the control break field. As the processing continues, the control break field is compared to the control break current value to determine whether a control break has occurred. In Table B1.2, a control break current value field was created in WORKING-STORAGE that is filled in with the vendor name from the record. When reading a record creates the condition that the control break field does not match the control break current value, the logic for that control break is executed.

NEW TERM   *Control break accumulators* or *control accumulators* are any variables used for summing or counting values within a control break. In Table B1.2, there are two accumulators: a grand total accumulator, and a vendor accumulator.

Control Break Logic

The mechanics of a control break make it seem difficult, but the logic of a control break is quite easy to express. Listing B1.3 is a general statement of the logic of a control break. The example is for a level-2 control break. I have shown the pseudocode for a level-2 break because the level-1 break (all records) behaves slightly differently.

TYPE | **Listing B1.3. Pseudocode for a control break.**

```
process-level-2-control-break
    perform start-level-2-control-break
    perform process-level-3-control-break
        until file at end
            or level-2-control-field not = level-2-current-value
    perform end-level-2
start-level-2
    move level-2-control-field to level-2-current-value.
    move zeroes to level-2 accumulators.
    any other starting actions
end-level-2
    perform process-level-2-accumulators
    perform add-level-2 accumulators to level-1 accumulators
    any other ending actions
```

ANALYSIS   A control break starts by saving the control break field in the control break current value and zeroing the accumulators for that control level.

The body of the break performs the next lower-level control break until the file is at the end or the control break field no longer matches the control break value field.

The control break ends by processing the level accumulators. For a report program, this involves printing the subtotals. Finally, it adds the accumulators for this level to the next higher level.

Listing B1.4 is the pseudocode for a level-1 (all records) control break.

TYPE | **Listing B1.4. A level-1 control break.**

```
process-level-1-control-break
    perform start-level-1
    perform process-level-2-control-break
        until file-at-end
    perform end-level-1
start-level-1
    read first valid record
    move zeroes to level-1-accumulators.
    any other starting actions
```

continues

Listing B1.4. continued

```
end-level-1
    perform process-level-1-accumulators
    any other ending actions
```

 A level-1 break varies from any other break because there is no true control break current value; the start-level-1 logic starts by executing a read first valid record.

The body of the level-1 break performs level 2 until the file is at end. The end of a level-1 break does not add accumulators to the next higher level because there is no next higher level.

Using Control Breaks for Totals

A good way to get a feel for control breaks is to see them in action. Figure B1.3 is a printer spacing chart for a Bills by Vendor report. This report produces a level-1 break for the complete file and a level-2 break for each vendor.

Figure B1.3.

A printer layout chart for blbyvn01.cbl.

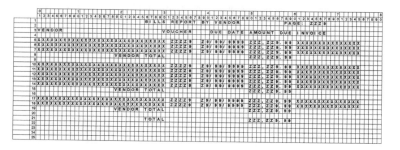

Listing B1.5 is blbyvn01.cbl, the report program. It sorts on the vendor number, prints subtotals for each vendor, and prints a grand total at the end of the report.

TYPE   Listing B1.5. More control breaks.

```
000100 IDENTIFICATION DIVISION.
000200 PROGRAM-ID. BLBYVN01.
000300*---------------------------------
000400* Bills Report by vendor
000500*---------------------------------
000600 ENVIRONMENT DIVISION.
000700 INPUT-OUTPUT SECTION.
000800 FILE-CONTROL.
000900
001000     COPY "SLVOUCH.CBL".
001100
001200     COPY "SLVND02.CBL".
```

```
001300
001400        COPY "SLSTATE.CBL".
001500
001600        SELECT WORK-FILE
001700            ASSIGN TO "WORK"
001800            ORGANIZATION IS SEQUENTIAL.
001900
002000        SELECT SORT-FILE
002100            ASSIGN TO "SORT".
002200
002300        SELECT PRINTER-FILE
002400            ASSIGN TO PRINTER
002500            ORGANIZATION IS LINE SEQUENTIAL.
002600
002700 DATA DIVISION.
002800 FILE SECTION.
002900
003000        COPY "FDVOUCH.CBL".
003100
003200        COPY "FDVND04.CBL".
003300
003400        COPY "FDSTATE.CBL".
003500
003600 FD   WORK-FILE
003700        LABEL RECORDS ARE STANDARD.
003800 01   WORK-RECORD.
003900        05   WORK-NUMBER          PIC 9(5).
004000        05   WORK-VENDOR          PIC 9(5).
004100        05   WORK-INVOICE         PIC X(15).
004200        05   WORK-FOR             PIC X(30).
004300        05   WORK-AMOUNT          PIC S9(6)V99.
004400        05   WORK-DATE            PIC 9(8).
004500        05   WORK-DUE             PIC 9(8).
004600        05   WORK-DEDUCTIBLE      PIC X.
004700        05   WORK-SELECTED        PIC X.
004800        05   WORK-PAID-AMOUNT     PIC S9(6)V99.
004900        05   WORK-PAID-DATE       PIC 9(8).
005000        05   WORK-CHECK-NO        PIC 9(6).
005100
005200 SD   SORT-FILE.
005300
005400 01   SORT-RECORD.
005500        05   SORT-NUMBER          PIC 9(5).
005600        05   SORT-VENDOR          PIC 9(5).
005700        05   SORT-INVOICE         PIC X(15).
005800        05   SORT-FOR             PIC X(30).
005900        05   SORT-AMOUNT          PIC S9(6)V99.
006000        05   SORT-DATE            PIC 9(8).
006100        05   SORT-DUE             PIC 9(8).
006200        05   SORT-DEDUCTIBLE      PIC X.
006300        05   SORT-SELECTED        PIC X.
006400        05   SORT-PAID-AMOUNT     PIC S9(6)V99.
006500        05   SORT-PAID-DATE       PIC 9(8).
006600        05   SORT-CHECK-NO        PIC 9(6).
006700
006800 FD   PRINTER-FILE
```

continues

Listing B1.5. continued

```
006900        LABEL RECORDS ARE OMITTED.
007000 01  PRINTER-RECORD              PIC X(80).
007100
007200 WORKING-STORAGE SECTION.
007300
007400 77  OK-TO-PROCESS              PIC X.
007500
007600        COPY "WSCASE01.CBL".
007700
007800 01  DETAIL-LINE.
007900        05  PRINT-NAME          PIC X(30).
008000        05  FILLER              PIC X(1) VALUE SPACE.
008100        05  PRINT-NUMBER        PIC ZZZZ9.
008200        05  FILLER              PIC X(3) VALUE SPACE.
008300        05  PRINT-DUE-DATE      PIC Z9/99/9999.
008400        05  FILLER              PIC X(1) VALUE SPACE.
008500        05  PRINT-AMOUNT        PIC ZZZ,ZZ9.99.
008600        05  FILLER              PIC X(1) VALUE SPACE.
008700        05  PRINT-INVOICE       PIC X(15).
008800
008900 01  VENDOR-TOTAL-LITERAL.
009000        05  FILLER              PIC X(18) VALUE SPACE.
009100        05  FILLER              PIC X(12) VALUE "VENDOR TOTAL".
009200
009300 01  GRAND-TOTAL-LITERAL.
009400        05  FILLER              PIC X(25) VALUE SPACE.
009500        05  FILLER              PIC X(5) VALUE "TOTAL".
009600
009700 01  COLUMN-LINE.
009800        05  FILLER          PIC X(6) VALUE "VENDOR".
009900        05  FILLER          PIC X(23) VALUE SPACE.
010000        05  FILLER          PIC X(7)  VALUE "VOUCHER".
010100        05  FILLER          PIC X(5)  VALUE SPACE.
010200        05  FILLER          PIC X(8)  VALUE "DUE DATE".
010300        05  FILLER          PIC X(1)  VALUE SPACE.
010400        05  FILLER          PIC X(10) VALUE "AMOUNT DUE".
010500        05  FILLER          PIC X(1)  VALUE SPACE.
010600        05  FILLER          PIC X(7)  VALUE "INVOICE".
010700
010800 01  TITLE-LINE.
010900        05  FILLER              PIC X(25) VALUE SPACE.
011000        05  FILLER              PIC X(22)
011100           VALUE "BILLS REPORT BY VENDOR".
011200        05  FILLER              PIC X(11) VALUE SPACE.
011300        05  FILLER              PIC X(5) VALUE "PAGE:".
011400        05  FILLER              PIC X(1) VALUE SPACE.
011500        05  PRINT-PAGE-NUMBER   PIC ZZZ9.
011600
011700 77  WORK-FILE-AT-END      PIC X.
011800 77  VENDOR-RECORD-FOUND   PIC X.
011900
012000 77  LINE-COUNT            PIC 999 VALUE ZERO.
012100 77  PAGE-NUMBER          PIC 9999 VALUE ZERO.
012200 77  MAXIMUM-LINES        PIC 999 VALUE 55.
```

```
012300
012400 77  RECORD-COUNT              PIC 9999 VALUE ZEROES.
012500
012600* Control break current value for vendor
012700 77  CURRENT-VENDOR           PIC 9(5).
012800
012900* Control break accumulators
013000* GRAND TOTAL is the level 1 accumulator for the whole file
013100* VENDOR TOTAL is the level 2 accumulator
013200 77  GRAND-TOTAL              PIC S9(6)V99.
013300 77  VENDOR-TOTAL             PIC S9(6)V99.
013400
013500     COPY "WSDATE01.CBL".
013600
013700 PROCEDURE DIVISION.
013800 PROGRAM-BEGIN.
013900
014000     PERFORM OPENING-PROCEDURE.
014100     PERFORM MAIN-PROCESS.
014200     PERFORM CLOSING-PROCEDURE.
014300
014400 PROGRAM-EXIT.
014500     EXIT PROGRAM.
014600
014700 PROGRAM-DONE.
014800     STOP RUN.
014900
015000 OPENING-PROCEDURE.
015100     OPEN I-O VENDOR-FILE.
015200
015300     OPEN OUTPUT PRINTER-FILE.
015400
015500 MAIN-PROCESS.
015600     PERFORM GET-OK-TO-PROCESS.
015700     PERFORM PROCESS-THE-FILE
015800         UNTIL OK-TO-PROCESS = "N".
015900
016000 CLOSING-PROCEDURE.
016100     CLOSE VENDOR-FILE.
016200     CLOSE PRINTER-FILE.
016300
016400 GET-OK-TO-PROCESS.
016500     PERFORM ACCEPT-OK-TO-PROCESS.
016600     PERFORM RE-ACCEPT-OK-TO-PROCESS
016700         UNTIL OK-TO-PROCESS = "Y" OR "N".
016800
016900 ACCEPT-OK-TO-PROCESS.
017000     DISPLAY "PRINT BILLS BY VENDOR (Y/N)?".
017100     ACCEPT OK-TO-PROCESS.
017200     INSPECT OK-TO-PROCESS
017300        CONVERTING LOWER-ALPHA
017400        TO           UPPER-ALPHA.
017500
017600 RE-ACCEPT-OK-TO-PROCESS.
017700     DISPLAY "YOU MUST ENTER YES OR NO".
017800     PERFORM ACCEPT-OK-TO-PROCESS.
```

continues

Listing B1.5. continued

```
017900
018000 PROCESS-THE-FILE.
018100     PERFORM START-THE-FILE.
018200     PERFORM PRINT-ONE-REPORT.
018300     PERFORM END-THE-FILE.
018400
018500*    PERFORM GET-OK-TO-PROCESS.
018600     MOVE "N" TO OK-TO-PROCESS.
018700
018800 START-THE-FILE.
018900     PERFORM SORT-DATA-FILE.
019000     OPEN INPUT WORK-FILE.
019100
019200 END-THE-FILE.
019300     CLOSE WORK-FILE.
019400
019500 SORT-DATA-FILE.
019600     SORT SORT-FILE
019700         ON ASCENDING KEY SORT-VENDOR
019800             USING VOUCHER-FILE
019900             GIVING WORK-FILE.
020000
020100* LEVEL 1 CONTROL BREAK
020200 PRINT-ONE-REPORT.
020300     PERFORM START-ONE-REPORT.
020400     PERFORM PROCESS-ALL-VENDORS
020500         UNTIL WORK-FILE-AT-END = "Y".
020600     PERFORM END-ONE-REPORT.
020700
020800 START-ONE-REPORT.
020900     PERFORM READ-FIRST-VALID-WORK.
021000     MOVE ZEROES TO GRAND-TOTAL.
021100
021200     PERFORM START-NEW-REPORT.
021300
021400 START-NEW-REPORT.
021500    MOVE SPACE TO DETAIL-LINE.
021600    MOVE ZEROES TO LINE-COUNT PAGE-NUMBER.
021700    PERFORM START-NEW-PAGE.
021800
021900 END-ONE-REPORT.
022000    IF RECORD-COUNT = ZEROES
022100        MOVE "NO RECORDS FOUND" TO PRINTER-RECORD
022200        PERFORM WRITE-TO-PRINTER
022300    ELSE
022400        PERFORM PRINT-GRAND-TOTAL.
022500
022600    PERFORM END-LAST-PAGE.
022700
022800 PRINT-GRAND-TOTAL.
022900    MOVE GRAND-TOTAL TO PRINT-AMOUNT.
023000    MOVE GRAND-TOTAL-LITERAL TO PRINT-NAME.
023100    MOVE DETAIL-LINE TO PRINTER-RECORD.
023200    PERFORM WRITE-TO-PRINTER.
023300    PERFORM LINE-FEED 2 TIMES.
```

```
023400      MOVE SPACE TO DETAIL-LINE.
023500
023600* LEVEL 2 CONTROL BREAK
023700 PROCESS-ALL-VENDORS.
023800      PERFORM START-ONE-VENDOR.
023900
024000      PERFORM PROCESS-ALL-VOUCHERS
024100          UNTIL WORK-FILE-AT-END = "Y"
024200              OR WORK-VENDOR NOT = CURRENT-VENDOR.
024300
024400      PERFORM END-ONE-VENDOR.
024500
024600 START-ONE-VENDOR.
024700      MOVE WORK-VENDOR TO CURRENT-VENDOR.
024800      MOVE ZEROES TO VENDOR-TOTAL.
024900
025000 END-ONE-VENDOR.
025100      PERFORM PRINT-VENDOR-TOTAL.
025200      ADD VENDOR-TOTAL TO GRAND-TOTAL.
025300
025400 PRINT-VENDOR-TOTAL.
025500      MOVE VENDOR-TOTAL TO PRINT-AMOUNT.
025600      MOVE VENDOR-TOTAL-LITERAL TO PRINT-NAME.
025700      MOVE DETAIL-LINE TO PRINTER-RECORD.
025800      PERFORM WRITE-TO-PRINTER.
025900      PERFORM LINE-FEED.
026000      MOVE SPACE TO DETAIL-LINE.
026100
026200* PROCESS ONE RECORD LEVEL
026300 PROCESS-ALL-VOUCHERS.
026400      PERFORM PROCESS-THIS-VOUCHER.
026500      ADD WORK-AMOUNT TO VENDOR-TOTAL.
026600      ADD 1 TO RECORD-COUNT.
026700      PERFORM READ-NEXT-VALID-WORK.
026800
026900 PROCESS-THIS-VOUCHER.
027000      IF LINE-COUNT > MAXIMUM-LINES
027100          PERFORM START-NEXT-PAGE.
027200      PERFORM PRINT-THE-RECORD.
027300
027400 PRINT-THE-RECORD.
027500      MOVE WORK-NUMBER TO PRINT-NUMBER.
027600
027700      PERFORM LOAD-VENDOR-NAME.
027800
027900      MOVE WORK-DUE TO DATE-CCYYMMDD.
028000      PERFORM CONVERT-TO-MMDDCCYY.
028100      MOVE DATE-MMDDCCYY TO PRINT-DUE-DATE.
028200
028300      MOVE WORK-AMOUNT TO PRINT-AMOUNT.
028400      MOVE WORK-INVOICE TO PRINT-INVOICE.
028500
028600      MOVE DETAIL-LINE TO PRINTER-RECORD.
028700      PERFORM WRITE-TO-PRINTER.
028800      MOVE SPACE TO DETAIL-LINE.
028900
```

continues

Listing B1.5. continued

```
029000 LOAD-VENDOR-NAME.
029100     MOVE WORK-VENDOR TO VENDOR-NUMBER.
029200     PERFORM READ-VENDOR-RECORD.
029300     IF VENDOR-RECORD-FOUND = "Y"
029400         MOVE VENDOR-NAME TO PRINT-NAME
029500     ELSE
029600         MOVE "*VENDOR NOT ON FILE*" TO PRINT-NAME.
029700
029800* PRINTING ROUTINES
029900 WRITE-TO-PRINTER.
030000     WRITE PRINTER-RECORD BEFORE ADVANCING 1.
030100     ADD 1 TO LINE-COUNT.
030200
030300 LINE-FEED.
030400     MOVE SPACE TO PRINTER-RECORD.
030500     PERFORM WRITE-TO-PRINTER.
030600
030700 START-NEXT-PAGE.
030800     PERFORM END-LAST-PAGE.
030900     PERFORM START-NEW-PAGE.
031000
031100 START-NEW-PAGE.
031200     ADD 1 TO PAGE-NUMBER.
031300     MOVE PAGE-NUMBER TO PRINT-PAGE-NUMBER.
031400     MOVE TITLE-LINE TO PRINTER-RECORD.
031500     PERFORM WRITE-TO-PRINTER.
031600     PERFORM LINE-FEED.
031700     MOVE COLUMN-LINE TO PRINTER-RECORD.
031800     PERFORM WRITE-TO-PRINTER.
031900     PERFORM LINE-FEED.
032000
032100 END-LAST-PAGE.
032200     PERFORM FORM-FEED.
032300     MOVE ZERO TO LINE-COUNT.
032400
032500 FORM-FEED.
032600     MOVE SPACE TO PRINTER-RECORD.
032700     WRITE PRINTER-RECORD BEFORE ADVANCING PAGE.
032800
032900*-------------------------------
033000* Read first, read next routines
033100*-------------------------------
033200 READ-FIRST-VALID-WORK.
033300     PERFORM READ-NEXT-VALID-WORK.
033400
033500 READ-NEXT-VALID-WORK.
033600     PERFORM READ-NEXT-WORK-RECORD.
033700     PERFORM READ-NEXT-WORK-RECORD
033800         UNTIL WORK-FILE-AT-END = "Y"
033900             OR WORK-PAID-DATE = ZEROES.
034000
034100 READ-NEXT-WORK-RECORD.
034200     MOVE "N" TO WORK-FILE-AT-END.
034300     READ WORK-FILE NEXT RECORD
```

```
034400          AT END MOVE "Y" TO WORK-FILE-AT-END.
034500
034600*--------------------------------
034700* Other File IO routines
034800*--------------------------------
034900 READ-VENDOR-RECORD.
035000     MOVE "Y" TO VENDOR-RECORD-FOUND.
035100     READ VENDOR-FILE RECORD
035200         INVALID KEY
035300             MOVE "N" TO VENDOR-RECORD-FOUND.
035400
035500*--------------------------------
035600* Utility Routines
035700*--------------------------------
035800     COPY "PLDATE01.CBL".
035900
```

The output of the Bills by Vendor report provides subtotals for each vendor and a grand total at the end of the report:

OUTPUT

```
                         BILLS REPORT BY VENDOR            PAGE:    1
VENDOR                   VOUCHER      DUE DATE AMOUNT DUE INVOICE
AERIAL SIGNS                  14     1/17/1994   1,046.97 FA1234
VENDOR TOTAL             1,046.97
ABC PRINTING                   4     2/07/1994     104.19 CX-5055
ABC PRINTING                   7     2/22/1994      48.97 CX-1407
ABC PRINTING                   8     1/27/1994      48.97 CX-1566
VENDOR TOTAL               202.13
CHARLES SMITH AND SONS         3     2/22/1994      27.76 5057
CHARLES SMITH AND SONS        16     1/16/1994      25.97 5098
VENDOR TOTAL                53.73
MA BELL                       13     1/23/1994      94.96 50577
MA BELL                       19     1/23/1994      34.95 50577
VENDOR TOTAL               129.91
RANIER GRAPHICS               20     2/25/1994   2,057.07 ZO-1515
VENDOR TOTAL             2,057.07
ABERCROMBIE AND OTHERS        15     1/31/1994     657.19 MONTHLY
VENDOR TOTAL               657.19
TOTAL               4,147.00
```

ANALYSIS The program has two control level breaks: level 1 at file level (all records) and level 2 at vendor-number level.

The control break field for level 1 is the entire WORK-RECORD. When there are no more work records, the level 1 break is completed. The control break current value for this level is really the WORK-FILE-AT-END flag defined at line 011700.

The control break field for level 2 is WORK-VENDOR, defined in the work file at line 004000. The control break current value for the vendor level is defined at line 012700, a CURRENT-VENDOR that will hold the value of the vendor that is currently undergoing processing.

The control break accumulators are GRAND-TOTAL and VENDOR-TOTAL, defined at lines 013200 and 013300, respectively. The RECORD-COUNT defined at line 012400 also is used as a control break accumulator because it counts all the records processed by the report portion of the program.

The program starts by asking the user whether to proceed with the report. This logic is handled in MAIN-PROCESS at line 015500 by performing GET-OK-TO-PROCESS. This routine at line 016400 requires that the user enter yes or no and place "Y" or "N" in OK-TO-PROCESS. MAIN-PROCESS then performs the main loop, PROCESS-THE-FILE, until OK-TO-PROCESS = "N".

When the user has agreed to print the report, PROCESS-THE-FILE at line 018000 starts by performing START-THE-FILE. This routine at line 018800 sorts the voucher file on the vendor number into a work file and opens the work file ready for processing. The actual sort routine is at line 019500. PROCESS-THE-FILE continues by printing the report and then performing END-THE-FILE, which closes the work file. The last action of PROCESS-THE-FILE is to decide whether to process again. The code includes two solutions at lines 018500 and 018600. One possibility at line 018500 is to ask the user whether to print the report again. This option is commented out. The second option at line 018600 moves "N" to OK-TO-PROCESS. Either one of these will resolve the main loop condition that will PROCESS-THE-FILE UNTIL OK-TO-PROCESS = "N". The first enables the user to decide, and the second forces no further processing.

The sort step is important because the file must be in vendor number order for a control break to work correctly on the vendor number.

The level-1 (all records) control break, PRINT-ONE-REPORT, and related routines are at lines 020100 through 023400. The logic follows a pattern similar to the pseudocode in Listing B1.4 for a level-1 control break. The additional start level actions in START-NEW-REPORT at line 021400 include setting up a report ready to be printed.

END-ONE-REPORT at line 021900 prints either a grand total or a "NO RECORDS FOUND" message and then ends the report by performing END-LAST-PAGE to issue a final form feed to the printer.

The level-2 control logic, PROCESS-ALL-VENDORS, and related routines are found at lines 023600 through 026100. This logic follows Listing B1.3, pseudocode for standard level break.

The level that processes single records, PROCESS-ALL-VOUCHERS at line 026300, performs a routine to PROCESS-THIS-VOUCHER. When this is done, the WORK-AMOUNT is added to the VENDOR-TOTAL, and the RECORD-COUNT is increased by 1. The last action of PROCESS-ALL-VOUCHERS is READ-NEXT-VALID-WORK.

The printing-level routine, PROCESS-THIS-VOUCHER, performs fairly routine actions to print a single record. One routine worth noting at line 029000 is LOAD-VENDOR-NAME, which is used to look up the WORK-VENDOR in the VENDOR-FILE and print the vendor name instead of the vendor number.

Using Control Breaks for Formatting

In blbyvn01.cbl, the control breaking logic was used to create additional lines to print with vendor subtotals and grand totals. Control breaking also is frequently used to eliminate the repetition of a control field on a report. Figure B1.4 is a printer-spacing chart for a modified version of blbyvn01.cbl.

Figure B1.4.

A printer layout chart for blbyvn02.cbl.

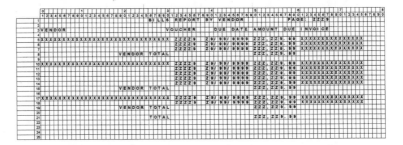

In this version, the vendor name is printed on only the first line of a group of records with the same vendor. This prevents the vendor name from repeating on each line.

Listing B1.6, blbyvn02.cbl, implements this change by removing the vendor name from the detail line printing and moving it up to become part of START-ONE-VENDOR.

TYPE **Listing B1.6. Another control break problem.**

```
000100 IDENTIFICATION DIVISION.
000200 PROGRAM-ID. BLBYVN02.
000300*-----------------------------
000400* Bills Report by vendor
000500*-----------------------------
000600 ENVIRONMENT DIVISION.
000700 INPUT-OUTPUT SECTION.
000800 FILE-CONTROL.
000900
001000     COPY "SLVOUCH.CBL".
001100
001200     COPY "SLVND02.CBL".
001300
001400     COPY "SLSTATE.CBL".
001500
001600     SELECT WORK-FILE
001700         ASSIGN TO "WORK"
001800         ORGANIZATION IS SEQUENTIAL.
001900
002000     SELECT SORT-FILE
002100         ASSIGN TO "SORT".
002200
002300     SELECT PRINTER-FILE
```

continues

Listing B1.6. continued

```
002400          ASSIGN TO PRINTER
002500          ORGANIZATION IS LINE SEQUENTIAL.
002600
002700 DATA DIVISION.
002800 FILE SECTION.
002900
003000     COPY "FDVOUCH.CBL".
003100
003200     COPY "FDVND04.CBL".
003300
003400     COPY "FDSTATE.CBL".
003500
003600 FD  WORK-FILE
003700     LABEL RECORDS ARE STANDARD.
003800 01  WORK-RECORD.
003900     05  WORK-NUMBER          PIC 9(5).
004000     05  WORK-VENDOR          PIC 9(5).
004100     05  WORK-INVOICE         PIC X(15).
004200     05  WORK-FOR             PIC X(30).
004300     05  WORK-AMOUNT          PIC S9(6)V99.
004400     05  WORK-DATE            PIC 9(8).
004500     05  WORK-DUE             PIC 9(8).
004600     05  WORK-DEDUCTIBLE      PIC X.
004700     05  WORK-SELECTED        PIC X.
004800     05  WORK-PAID-AMOUNT     PIC S9(6)V99.
004900     05  WORK-PAID-DATE       PIC 9(8).
005000     05  WORK-CHECK-NO        PIC 9(6).
005100
005200 SD  SORT-FILE.
005300
005400 01  SORT-RECORD.
005500     05  SORT-NUMBER          PIC 9(5).
005600     05  SORT-VENDOR          PIC 9(5).
005700     05  SORT-INVOICE         PIC X(15).
005800     05  SORT-FOR             PIC X(30).
005900     05  SORT-AMOUNT          PIC S9(6)V99.
006000     05  SORT-DATE            PIC 9(8).
006100     05  SORT-DUE             PIC 9(8).
006200     05  SORT-DEDUCTIBLE      PIC X.
006300     05  SORT-SELECTED        PIC X.
006400     05  SORT-PAID-AMOUNT     PIC S9(6)V99.
006500     05  SORT-PAID-DATE       PIC 9(8).
006600     05  SORT-CHECK-NO        PIC 9(6).
006700
006800 FD  PRINTER-FILE
006900     LABEL RECORDS ARE OMITTED.
007000 01  PRINTER-RECORD           PIC X(80).
007100
007200 WORKING-STORAGE SECTION.
007300
007400 77  OK-TO-PROCESS        PIC X.
007500
007600     COPY "WSCASE01.CBL".
007700
```

```
007800 01   DETAIL-LINE.
007900      05   PRINT-NAME         PIC X(30).
008000      05   FILLER            PIC X(1) VALUE SPACE.
008100      05   PRINT-NUMBER       PIC ZZZZ9.
008200      05   FILLER            PIC X(3) VALUE SPACE.
008300      05   PRINT-DUE-DATE     PIC Z9/99/9999.
008400      05   FILLER            PIC X(1) VALUE SPACE.
008500      05   PRINT-AMOUNT       PIC ZZZ,ZZ9.99.
008600      05   FILLER            PIC X(1) VALUE SPACE.
008700      05   PRINT-INVOICE      PIC X(15).
008800
008900 01   VENDOR-TOTAL-LITERAL.
009000      05   FILLER            PIC X(18) VALUE SPACE.
009100      05   FILLER            PIC X(12) VALUE "VENDOR TOTAL".
009200
009300 01   GRAND-TOTAL-LITERAL.
009400      05   FILLER            PIC X(25) VALUE SPACE.
009500      05   FILLER            PIC X(5) VALUE "TOTAL".
009600
009700 01   COLUMN-LINE.
009800      05   FILLER       PIC X(6) VALUE "VENDOR".
009900      05   FILLER       PIC X(23) VALUE SPACE.
010000      05   FILLER       PIC X(7)  VALUE "VOUCHER".
010100      05   FILLER       PIC X(5)  VALUE SPACE.
010200      05   FILLER       PIC X(8)  VALUE "DUE DATE".
010300      05   FILLER       PIC X(1)  VALUE SPACE.
010400      05   FILLER       PIC X(10) VALUE "AMOUNT DUE".
010500      05   FILLER       PIC X(1)  VALUE SPACE.
010600      05   FILLER       PIC X(7)  VALUE "INVOICE".
010700
010800 01   TITLE-LINE.
010900      05   FILLER             PIC X(25) VALUE SPACE.
011000      05   FILLER             PIC X(22)
011100         VALUE "BILLS REPORT BY VENDOR".
011200      05   FILLER             PIC X(11) VALUE SPACE.
011300      05   FILLER             PIC X(5) VALUE "PAGE:".
011400      05   FILLER             PIC X(1) VALUE SPACE.
011500      05   PRINT-PAGE-NUMBER   PIC ZZZ9.
011600
011700 77   WORK-FILE-AT-END      PIC X.
011800 77   VENDOR-RECORD-FOUND    PIC X.
011900
012000 77   LINE-COUNT            PIC 999 VALUE ZERO.
012100 77   PAGE-NUMBER           PIC 9999 VALUE ZERO.
012200 77   MAXIMUM-LINES         PIC 999 VALUE 55.
012300
012400 77   RECORD-COUNT          PIC 9999 VALUE ZEROES.
012500
012600* Control break current value for vendor
012700 77   CURRENT-VENDOR        PIC 9(5).
012800
012900* Control break accumulators
013000* GRAND TOTAL is the level 1 accumulator for the whole file
013100* VENDOR TOTAL is the level 2 accumulator
013200 77   GRAND-TOTAL          PIC S9(6)V99.
013300 77   VENDOR-TOTAL         PIC S9(6)V99.
```

continues

Listing B1.6. continued

```
013400
013500     COPY "WSDATE01.CBL".
013600
013700 PROCEDURE DIVISION.
013800 PROGRAM-BEGIN.
013900
014000     PERFORM OPENING-PROCEDURE.
014100     PERFORM MAIN-PROCESS.
014200     PERFORM CLOSING-PROCEDURE.
014300
014400 PROGRAM-EXIT.
014500     EXIT PROGRAM.
014600
014700 PROGRAM-DONE.
014800     STOP RUN.
014900
015000 OPENING-PROCEDURE.
015100     OPEN I-O VENDOR-FILE.
015200
015300     OPEN OUTPUT PRINTER-FILE.
015400
015500 MAIN-PROCESS.
015600     PERFORM GET-OK-TO-PROCESS.
015700     PERFORM PROCESS-THE-FILE
015800         UNTIL OK-TO-PROCESS = "N".
015900
016000 CLOSING-PROCEDURE.
016100     CLOSE VENDOR-FILE.
016200     CLOSE PRINTER-FILE.
016300
016400 GET-OK-TO-PROCESS.
016500     PERFORM ACCEPT-OK-TO-PROCESS.
016600     PERFORM RE-ACCEPT-OK-TO-PROCESS
016700         UNTIL OK-TO-PROCESS = "Y" OR "N".
016800
016900 ACCEPT-OK-TO-PROCESS.
017000     DISPLAY "PRINT BILLS BY VENDOR (Y/N)?".
017100     ACCEPT OK-TO-PROCESS.
017200     INSPECT OK-TO-PROCESS
017300       CONVERTING LOWER-ALPHA
017400       TO          UPPER-ALPHA.
017500
017600 RE-ACCEPT-OK-TO-PROCESS.
017700     DISPLAY "YOU MUST ENTER YES OR NO".
017800     PERFORM ACCEPT-OK-TO-PROCESS.
017900
018000 PROCESS-THE-FILE.
018100     PERFORM START-THE-FILE.
018200     PERFORM PRINT-ONE-REPORT.
018300     PERFORM END-THE-FILE.
018400
018500*    PERFORM GET-OK-TO-PROCESS.
018600     MOVE "N" TO OK-TO-PROCESS.
018700
```

```
018800 START-THE-FILE.
018900     PERFORM SORT-DATA-FILE.
019000     OPEN INPUT WORK-FILE.
019100
019200 END-THE-FILE.
019300     CLOSE WORK-FILE.
019400
019500 SORT-DATA-FILE.
019600     SORT SORT-FILE
019700         ON ASCENDING KEY SORT-VENDOR
019800             USING VOUCHER-FILE
019900             GIVING WORK-FILE.
020000
020100* LEVEL 1 CONTROL BREAK
020200 PRINT-ONE-REPORT.
020300     PERFORM START-ONE-REPORT.
020400     PERFORM PROCESS-ALL-VENDORS
020500         UNTIL WORK-FILE-AT-END = "Y".
020600     PERFORM END-ONE-REPORT.
020700
020800 START-ONE-REPORT.
020900     PERFORM READ-FIRST-VALID-WORK.
021000     MOVE ZEROES TO GRAND-TOTAL.
021100
021200     PERFORM START-NEW-REPORT.
021300
021400 START-NEW-REPORT.
021500     MOVE SPACE TO DETAIL-LINE.
021600     MOVE ZEROES TO LINE-COUNT PAGE-NUMBER.
021700     PERFORM START-NEW-PAGE.
021800
021900 END-ONE-REPORT.
022000     IF RECORD-COUNT = ZEROES
022100         MOVE "NO RECORDS FOUND" TO PRINTER-RECORD
022200         PERFORM WRITE-TO-PRINTER
022300     ELSE
022400         PERFORM PRINT-GRAND-TOTAL.
022500
022600     PERFORM END-LAST-PAGE.
022700
022800 PRINT-GRAND-TOTAL.
022900     MOVE GRAND-TOTAL TO PRINT-AMOUNT.
023000     MOVE GRAND-TOTAL-LITERAL TO PRINT-NAME.
023100     MOVE DETAIL-LINE TO PRINTER-RECORD.
023200     PERFORM WRITE-TO-PRINTER.
023300     PERFORM LINE-FEED 2 TIMES.
023400     MOVE SPACE TO DETAIL-LINE.
023500
023600* LEVEL 2 CONTROL BREAK
023700 PROCESS-ALL-VENDORS.
023800     PERFORM START-ONE-VENDOR.
023900
024000     PERFORM PROCESS-ALL-VOUCHERS
024100         UNTIL WORK-FILE-AT-END = "Y"
024200             OR WORK-VENDOR NOT = CURRENT-VENDOR.
024300
```

continues

Listing B1.6. continued

```
024400      PERFORM END-ONE-VENDOR.
024500
024600 START-ONE-VENDOR.
024700      MOVE WORK-VENDOR TO CURRENT-VENDOR.
024800      MOVE ZEROES TO VENDOR-TOTAL.
024900
025000      PERFORM LOAD-VENDOR-NAME.
025100
025200 LOAD-VENDOR-NAME.
025300      MOVE WORK-VENDOR TO VENDOR-NUMBER.
025400      PERFORM READ-VENDOR-RECORD.
025500      IF VENDOR-RECORD-FOUND = "Y"
025600          MOVE VENDOR-NAME TO PRINT-NAME
025700      ELSE
025800          MOVE "*VENDOR NOT ON FILE*" TO PRINT-NAME.
025900
026000 END-ONE-VENDOR.
026100      PERFORM PRINT-VENDOR-TOTAL.
026200      ADD VENDOR-TOTAL TO GRAND-TOTAL.
026300
026400 PRINT-VENDOR-TOTAL.
026500      MOVE VENDOR-TOTAL TO PRINT-AMOUNT.
026600      MOVE VENDOR-TOTAL-LITERAL TO PRINT-NAME.
026700      MOVE DETAIL-LINE TO PRINTER-RECORD.
026800      PERFORM WRITE-TO-PRINTER.
026900      PERFORM LINE-FEED.
027000      MOVE SPACE TO DETAIL-LINE.
027100
027200* PROCESS ONE RECORD LEVEL
027300 PROCESS-ALL-VOUCHERS.
027400      PERFORM PROCESS-THIS-VOUCHER.
027500      ADD WORK-AMOUNT TO VENDOR-TOTAL.
027600      ADD 1 TO RECORD-COUNT.
027700      PERFORM READ-NEXT-VALID-WORK.
027800
027900 PROCESS-THIS-VOUCHER.
028000      IF LINE-COUNT > MAXIMUM-LINES
028100          PERFORM START-NEXT-PAGE.
028200      PERFORM PRINT-THE-RECORD.
028300
028400 PRINT-THE-RECORD.
028500      MOVE WORK-NUMBER TO PRINT-NUMBER.
028600
028700 .    MOVE WORK-DUE TO DATE-CCYYMMDD.
028800      PERFORM CONVERT-TO-MMDDCCYY.
028900      MOVE DATE-MMDDCCYY TO PRINT-DUE-DATE.
029000
029100      MOVE WORK-AMOUNT TO PRINT-AMOUNT.
029200      MOVE WORK-INVOICE TO PRINT-INVOICE.
029300
029400      MOVE DETAIL-LINE TO PRINTER-RECORD.
029500      PERFORM WRITE-TO-PRINTER.
029600      MOVE SPACE TO DETAIL-LINE.
029700
```

```
029800* PRINTING ROUTINES
029900 WRITE-TO-PRINTER.
030000     WRITE PRINTER-RECORD BEFORE ADVANCING 1.
030100     ADD 1 TO LINE-COUNT.
030200
030300 LINE-FEED.
030400     MOVE SPACE TO PRINTER-RECORD.
030500     PERFORM WRITE-TO-PRINTER.
030600
030700 START-NEXT-PAGE.
030800     PERFORM END-LAST-PAGE.
030900     PERFORM START-NEW-PAGE.
031000
031100 START-NEW-PAGE.
031200     ADD 1 TO PAGE-NUMBER.
031300     MOVE PAGE-NUMBER TO PRINT-PAGE-NUMBER.
031400     MOVE TITLE-LINE TO PRINTER-RECORD.
031500     PERFORM WRITE-TO-PRINTER.
031600     PERFORM LINE-FEED.
031700     MOVE COLUMN-LINE TO PRINTER-RECORD.
031800     PERFORM WRITE-TO-PRINTER.
031900     PERFORM LINE-FEED.
032000
032100 END-LAST-PAGE.
032200     PERFORM FORM-FEED.
032300     MOVE ZERO TO LINE-COUNT.
032400
032500 FORM-FEED.
032600     MOVE SPACE TO PRINTER-RECORD.
032700     WRITE PRINTER-RECORD BEFORE ADVANCING PAGE.
032800
032900*-------------------------------
033000* Read first, read next routines
033100*-------------------------------
033200 READ-FIRST-VALID-WORK.
033300     PERFORM READ-NEXT-VALID-WORK.
033400
033500 READ-NEXT-VALID-WORK.
033600     PERFORM READ-NEXT-WORK-RECORD.
033700     PERFORM READ-NEXT-WORK-RECORD
033800         UNTIL WORK-FILE-AT-END = "Y"
033900           OR WORK-PAID-DATE = ZEROES.
034000
034100 READ-NEXT-WORK-RECORD.
034200     MOVE "N" TO WORK-FILE-AT-END.
034300     READ WORK-FILE NEXT RECORD
034400        AT END MOVE "Y" TO WORK-FILE-AT-END.
034500
034600*-------------------------------
034700* Other File IO routines
034800*-------------------------------
034900 READ-VENDOR-RECORD.
035000     MOVE "Y" TO VENDOR-RECORD-FOUND.
035100     READ VENDOR-FILE RECORD
035200         INVALID KEY
035300         MOVE "N" TO VENDOR-RECORD-FOUND.
```

continues

Listing B1.6. continued

```
035400
035500*- - - - - - - - - - - - - - - - - - - - - - - - - - - - - - -
035600* Utility Routines
035700*- - - - - - - - - - - - - - - - - - - - - - - - - - - - - - -
035800      COPY "PLDATE01.CBL".
035900
```

The output of `blbyvn02.cbl` prints the vendor name only once for each group of vouchers attached to the same vendor:

OUTPUT

```
                                 BILLS REPORT BY VENDOR              PAGE:    1
        VENDOR                         VOUCHER      DUE DATE AMOUNT DUE INVOICE
        AERIAL SIGNS                        14     1/17/1994  1,046.97 FA1234
        VENDOR TOTAL                  1,046.97
        ABC PRINTING                         4     2/07/1994    104.19 CX-5055
        7     2/22/1994       48.97 CX-1407
        8     1/27/1994       48.97 CX-1566
        VENDOR TOTAL                    202.13
        CHARLES SMITH AND SONS              3     2/22/1994     27.76 5057
        16    1/16/1994      25.97 5098
        VENDOR TOTAL                     53.73
        MA BELL                             13     1/23/1994     94.96 50577
        19    1/23/1994      34.95 50577
        VENDOR TOTAL                    129.91
        RANIER GRAPHICS                     20     2/25/1994  2,057.07 ZO-1515
        VENDOR TOTAL                  2,057.07
        ABERCROMBIE AND OTHERS              15     1/31/1994    657.19 MONTHLY
        VENDOR TOTAL                    657.19
        TOTAL                         4,147.00
```

ANALYSIS START-ONE-VENDOR at line 024600 is identical to the same paragraph in `blbyvn01.cbl` (shown in Listing B1.5), but it adds logic to perform LOAD-VENDOR-NAME. This routine originally was performed in PRINT-THE-RECORD, which begins at line 028400 in this version of the program. The vendor name is loaded into the detail line only once at the beginning of each new vendor.

Multilevel Control Breaks

The logic of a multilevel control breaking program is quite easy to express. Listing B1.7 is a general statement of control breaking in a file-processing program down to four levels. Level 1 is the all-records level and the `level-1-accumulators` will be the grand totals for the whole file.

TYPE **Listing B1.7. A general logic flow for control breaks.**

```
process-the-file
    perform start-the-file
    perform process-level-1-control-break
    perform end-the-file
start-the-file
    create-the-file
    open the file
create-the-file
    sort the file on
        level-2-control-field
        level-3-control-field
        level-4-control-field
end-the-file
    close the file
process-level-1-control-break
    perform start-level-1
    perform process-level-2-control-break
        until file-at-end
    perform end-level-1
start-level-1
    read first valid record
    move zeroes to level-1-accumulators
    any other starting actions
end-level-1
    perform process-level-1-accumulators
    any other ending actions
process-level-2-control-break
    perform start-level-2
    perform process-level-3-control-break
        until file-at-end
            or level-2-control-field not = level-2-current-value
    perform end-level-2
start-level-2
    move level-2-control-field to level-2-current-value
    move zeroes to level-2-accumulators
    any other starting actions
end-level-2
    perform process-level-2-accumulators
    perform add-level-2-accumulators to level-1-accumulators
    any other ending actions
process-level-3-control-break
    perform start-level-3
    perform process-level-4-control-break
        until file-at-end
            or level-2-control-field not = level-2-current-value
            or level-3-control-field not = level-3-current-value
    perform end-level-3
start-level-3
    move level-3-control-field to level-3-current-value
    move zeroes to level-3-accumulators
    any other starting actions
end-level-3
    perform process-level-3-accumulators
    perform add-level-3-accumulators to level-2-accumulators
```

continues

Listing B1.7. continued

```
       any other ending actions
process-level-4-control-break
    perform start-level-4
    perform process-one-record
        until file-at-end
            or level-2-control-field not = level-2-current-value
            or level-3-control-field not = level-3-current-value
            or level-4-control-field not = level-4-current-value
    perform end-level-4
start-level-4
    move level-4-control-field to level-4-current-value
    move zeroes to level-4-accumulators
    any other starting actions
end-level-4
    perform process-level-4-accumulators
    perform add-level-4-accumulators to level-3-accumulators
    any other ending actions
process-one-record
    perform process-this-record
    add record-values to level-4-accumulators
    read next valid record
```

This example carries the control breaking to four levels, and this can be repeated for as many levels as necessary as long as the file is sorted on each of the control break fields.

Remember that the level-1 break is controlled by the end of the file, and notice that the conditions that cause level breaks are cumulative as you descend to lower levels.

Using Multilevel Control Breaks

In order to illustrate a multilevel control breaking report, it is necessary to create a test file with multiple levels in it.

For this example, you create a chain of six retail stores that sell sporting goods. All of the goods are divided into 12 categories. The categories are allocated to departments, and the departments fall under three main divisions. Table B1.3 shows the breakdown of divisions, departments, and categories.

Table B1.3. Divisions, departments, and categories of a hypothetical sporting goods store.

Div. Name	Division Name	Dep.	Department Name	Cat.	Category
01	Athletics	01	Exercise	01	Weights
				02	Machines
		02	Miscellaneous	03	Sunglasses
				04	Vitamins

Div. Name	Division Name	Dep.	Department Name	Cat.	Category
02	Sporting Goods	03	Sport Clothes	05	Men's Clothes
				06	Women's Clothes
		04	Equipment	07	Tennis
				08	Soccer
03	Camping	05	Camp Equipment	09	Tents
				10	Sleeping Bags
		06	Camping Clothes	11	Clothing
				12	Hiking Boots

Each day, the six stores send in their sales figures by category. A program looks up the division and department and creates a temporary file of sales information that includes the store number, division number, department number, category number, and sales figures. Listings B1.8 and B1.9 are the SELECT and FD for this temporary file. The file is not indexed because it is used only for reporting.

TYPE   **Listing B1.8. The SELECT statement for the sales file.**

```
000100*------------------------------
000200* SLSALES.CBL
000300*------------------------------
000400     SELECT SALES-FILE
000500        ASSIGN TO "SALES"
000600        ORGANIZATION IS SEQUENTIAL.
000700
```

TYPE   **Listing B1.9. The FD for the sales file.**

```
000100*------------------------------
000200* FDSALES.CBL
000400* Temporary daily sales file.
000600*------------------------------
000700 FD  SALES-FILE
000800     LABEL RECORDS ARE STANDARD.
000900 01  SALES-RECORD.
001000     05  SALES-STORE         PIC 9(2).
001100     05  SALES-DIVISION      PIC 9(2).
001200     05  SALES-DEPARTMENT    PIC 9(2).
001300     05  SALES-CATEGORY      PIC 9(2).
001400     05  SALES-AMOUNT        PIC S9(6)V99.
001500
```

Because you do not actually have a retail chain at your disposal, you have to create a test file containing random sales figures. Listing B1.10, slsgen01.cbl, generates a collection of random sales records for all stores and all categories.

TYPE **Listing B1.10. Generating test sales data.**

```
000100 IDENTIFICATION DIVISION.
000200 PROGRAM-ID. SLSGEN01.
000300*-------------------------------
000400* Generate test sales data
000500*-------------------------------
000600 ENVIRONMENT DIVISION.
000700 INPUT-OUTPUT SECTION.
000800 FILE-CONTROL.
000900
001000*-------------------------------
001100* SLSALES.CBL
001200*-------------------------------
001300     SELECT SALES-FILE
001400         ASSIGN TO "SALES"
001500         ORGANIZATION IS SEQUENTIAL.
001600
001700 DATA DIVISION.
001800 FILE SECTION.
001900
002000*-------------------------------
002100* FDSALES.CBL
002200* Temporary daily sales file.
002300*-------------------------------
002400 FD  SALES-FILE
002500     LABEL RECORDS ARE STANDARD.
002600 01  SALES-RECORD.
002700     05  SALES-STORE          PIC 9(2).
002800     05  SALES-DIVISION       PIC 9(2).
002900     05  SALES-DEPARTMENT     PIC 9(2).
003000     05  SALES-CATEGORY       PIC 9(2).
003100     05  SALES-AMOUNT         PIC S9(6)V99.
003200
003300 WORKING-STORAGE SECTION.
003400
003500 77  THE-STORE                PIC 99.
003600 77  THE-DIVISION             PIC 99.
003700 77  THE-DEPARTMENT           PIC 99.
003800 77  THE-CATEGORY             PIC 99.
003900
004000 77  THE-AMOUNT               PIC S9(6)V99.
004100
004200 PROCEDURE DIVISION.
004300 PROGRAM-BEGIN.
004400     PERFORM OPENING-PROCEDURE.
004500     PERFORM MAIN-PROCESS.
004600     PERFORM CLOSING-PROCEDURE.
004700
```

```
004800 PROGRAM-EXIT.
004900     EXIT PROGRAM.
005000
005100 PROGRAM-DONE.
005200     STOP RUN.
005300
005400 OPENING-PROCEDURE.
005500     OPEN OUTPUT SALES-FILE.
005600
005700 CLOSING-PROCEDURE.
005800     CLOSE SALES-FILE.
005900
006000 MAIN-PROCESS.
006100     MOVE ZEROES TO THE-AMOUNT.
006200     PERFORM GENERATE-STORE-SALES
006300         VARYING THE-STORE FROM 1 BY 1
006400             UNTIL THE-STORE > 6.
006500
006600 GENERATE-STORE-SALES.
006700     PERFORM GENERATE-CATEGORY-SALES
006800         VARYING THE-CATEGORY FROM 1 BY 1
006900             UNTIL THE-CATEGORY > 12.
007000
007100 GENERATE-CATEGORY-SALES.
007200     ADD 237.57 TO THE-AMOUNT.
007300     IF THE-AMOUNT > 800
007400         SUBTRACT 900 FROM THE-AMOUNT.
007500
007600     MOVE THE-AMOUNT TO SALES-AMOUNT.
007700     MOVE THE-STORE TO SALES-STORE.
007800     MOVE THE-CATEGORY TO SALES-CATEGORY.
007900
008000     PERFORM GENERATE-THE-DEPARTMENT.
008100     PERFORM GENERATE-THE-DIVISION.
008200
008300     WRITE SALES-RECORD.
008400
008500 GENERATE-THE-DEPARTMENT.
008600     ADD 1 TO THE-CATEGORY.
008700     DIVIDE THE-CATEGORY BY 2
008800         GIVING THE-DEPARTMENT.
008900     MOVE THE-DEPARTMENT TO SALES-DEPARTMENT.
009000     SUBTRACT 1 FROM THE-CATEGORY.
009100
009200 GENERATE-THE-DIVISION.
009300     ADD 1 TO THE-DEPARTMENT
009400     DIVIDE THE-DEPARTMENT BY 2
009500         GIVING THE-DIVISION.
009600     MOVE THE-DIVISION TO SALES-DIVISION.
009700
```

ANALYSIS   The OPENING-PROCEDURE opens the file in output mode so that it is created.

The main process starts by moving zeroes to THE-AMOUNT at line 006100. This field will be used to create some random sales numbers. MAIN-PROCESS then performs GENERATE-STORE-SALES for each of the six stores at line 006200.

The GENERATE-STORE-SALES routine at line 006600 performs GENERATE-CATEGORY-SALES for each of the 12 categories of goods.

The GENERATE-CATEGORY-SALES starts at line 007100. It uses some tricks to generate amounts at lines 007200 through 007400. On each entry to GENERATE-CATEGORY-SALES, 237.57 is added to THE-AMOUNT. If THE-AMOUNT has exceeded 800, 900 is subtracted from THE-AMOUNT. This method was chosen as an arbitrary way of creating random sales figures for each category. Subtracting 900 when the number exceeds 800 allows some categories to be negative (because of refunds).

At lines 007600 through 007800, THE-AMOUNT, THE-STORE, and THE-CATEGORY are moved into the SALES-RECORD.

Another trick is used to determine the department number for each category. From Table B1.3, you see that department 1 includes categories 1 and 2, and department 2 includes categories 3 and 4. If you add 1 to the category and divide it by 2, the result (ignoring fractions) will be the department number. This is just a convenient trick that gets the department number quickly. This logic is taken care of in GENERATE-THE-DEPARTMENT, which starts at line 008500. After 1 is added to the category, it is divided by 2 and the result is placed directly in THE-DEPARTMENT. THE-DEPARTMENT has no decimal, so any decimal result of the division is truncated. Finally, THE-DEPARTMENT is moved to SALES-DEPARTMENT. Because THE-CATEGORY is being used as a loop-control variable (in lines 006700 through 006900), it is necessary to subtract 1 from it to return it to its original value.

A similar trick is used in GENERATE-THE-DIVISION, which starts at line 009200 to generate the division number from the department number.

After the department number and division number are filled in, all fields of the record are filled in, and at line 008300 the program writes the SALES-RECORD.

Code, compile, and run slsgen01.cbl. It should create 72 test records, one for each of 12 departments in six stores.

Now that you have the test data that you need, you can build a multilevel control breaking report that reports sales titles by store, division, department, and category.

Figure B1.5 is the printer spacing chart for slsrpt01.cbl. Line 7 is a detail line. Line 8 also is a detail line, but because the division and department have not changed, they are not printed again on this line. Line 9 is an example of a department subtotal. Line 15 is an example of a division subtotal. Lines 27 and 29 are store and grand totals. Each store will start on a new page. This report is an example of several of the types of problems encountered when working on control breaking reports.

Listing B1.11 is the report program that will generate the report using the test sales file that has been created.

Figure B1.5.

Printer layout chart for slsrpt01.cbl.

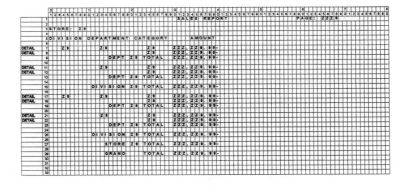

TYPE | **Listing B1.11. A report with multiple control breaks.**

```
000100 IDENTIFICATION DIVISION.
000200 PROGRAM-ID. SLSRPT01.
000300*--------------------------------
000400* Print test sales data
000500*--------------------------------
000600 ENVIRONMENT DIVISION.
000700 INPUT-OUTPUT SECTION.
000800 FILE-CONTROL.
000900
001000*--------------------------------
001100* SLSALES.CBL
001200*--------------------------------
001300     SELECT SALES-FILE
001400         ASSIGN TO "SALES"
001500         ORGANIZATION IS SEQUENTIAL.
001600
001700     SELECT WORK-FILE
001800         ASSIGN TO "WORK"
001900         ORGANIZATION IS SEQUENTIAL.
002000
002100     SELECT SORT-FILE
002200         ASSIGN TO "SORT".
002300
002400     SELECT PRINTER-FILE
002500         ASSIGN TO PRINTER
002600         ORGANIZATION IS LINE SEQUENTIAL.
002700
002800 DATA DIVISION.
002900 FILE SECTION.
003000
003100*--------------------------------
003200* FDSALES.CBL
003300* Temporary daily sales file.
```

continues

Listing B1.11. continued

```
003400*------------------------------------
003500 FD  SALES-FILE
003600     LABEL RECORDS ARE STANDARD.
003700 01  SALES-RECORD.
003800     05  SALES-STORE           PIC 9(2).
003900     05  SALES-DIVISION        PIC 9(2).
004000     05  SALES-DEPARTMENT      PIC 9(2).
004100     05  SALES-CATEGORY        PIC 9(2).
004200     05  SALES-AMOUNT          PIC S9(6)V99.
004300
004400 FD  WORK-FILE
004500     LABEL RECORDS ARE STANDARD.
004600 01  WORK-RECORD.
004700     05  WORK-STORE            PIC 9(2).
004800     05  WORK-DIVISION         PIC 9(2).
004900     05  WORK-DEPARTMENT       PIC 9(2).
005000     05  WORK-CATEGORY         PIC 9(2).
005100     05  WORK-AMOUNT           PIC S9(6)V99.
005200
005300 SD  SORT-FILE
005400     LABEL RECORDS ARE STANDARD.
005500 01  SORT-RECORD.
005600     05  SORT-STORE            PIC 9(2).
005700     05  SORT-DIVISION         PIC 9(2).
005800     05  SORT-DEPARTMENT       PIC 9(2).
005900     05  SORT-CATEGORY         PIC 9(2).
006000     05  SORT-AMOUNT           PIC S9(6)V99.
006100
006200 FD  PRINTER-FILE
006300     LABEL RECORDS ARE OMITTED.
006400 01  PRINTER-RECORD            PIC X(80).
006500
006600 WORKING-STORAGE SECTION.
006700
006800 77 OK-TO-PROCESS       PIC X.
006900
007000     COPY "WSCASE01.CBL".
007100
007200 01  LEGEND-LINE.
007300     05  FILLER            PIC X(6) VALUE "STORE:".
007400     05  FILLER            PIC X(1) VALUE SPACE.
007500     05  PRINT-STORE       PIC Z9.
007600
007700 01  DETAIL-LINE.
007800     05  FILLER            PIC X(3) VALUE SPACE.
007900     05  PRINT-DIVISION    PIC Z9.
008000     05  FILLER            PIC X(4) VALUE SPACE.
008100     05  FILLER            PIC X(3) VALUE SPACE.
008200     05  PRINT-DEPARTMENT  PIC Z9.
008300     05  FILLER            PIC X(6) VALUE SPACE.
008400     05  FILLER            PIC X(3) VALUE SPACE.
008500     05  PRINT-CATEGORY    PIC Z9.
008600     05  FILLER            PIC X(4) VALUE SPACE.
008700     05  PRINT-AMOUNT      PIC ZZZ,ZZ9.99-.
```

```
008800
008900 01  COLUMN-LINE.
009000     05  FILLER        PIC X(8)   VALUE "DIVISION".
009100     05  FILLER        PIC X(1)   VALUE SPACE.
009200     05  FILLER        PIC X(10)  VALUE "DEPARTMENT".
009300     05  FILLER        PIC X(1)   VALUE SPACE.
009400     05  FILLER        PIC X(8)   VALUE "CATEGORY".
009500     05  FILLER        PIC X(1)   VALUE SPACE.
009600     05  FILLER        PIC X(4)   VALUE SPACE.
009700     05  FILLER        PIC X(6)   VALUE "AMOUNT".
009800
009900 01  TITLE-LINE.
010000     05  FILLER            PIC X(30) VALUE SPACE.
010100     05  FILLER            PIC X(12)
010200         VALUE "SALES REPORT".
010300     05  FILLER            PIC X(16) VALUE SPACE.
010400     05  FILLER            PIC X(5) VALUE "PAGE:".
010500     05  FILLER            PIC X(1) VALUE SPACE.
010600     05  PRINT-PAGE-NUMBER PIC ZZZ9.
010700
010800 01  TOTAL-LINE.
010900     05  FILLER            PIC X(11) VALUE SPACE.
011000     05  TOTAL-TYPE        PIC X(8).
011100     05  FILLER            PIC X(1) VALUE SPACE.
011200     05  TOTAL-NUMBER      PIC Z9.
011300     05  FILLER            PIC X(1) VALUE SPACE.
011400     05  TOTAL-LITERAL     PIC X(5) VALUE "TOTAL".
011500     05  FILLER            PIC X(1) VALUE SPACE.
011600     05  PRINT-TOTAL       PIC ZZZ,ZZ9.99-.
011700
011800 77  GRAND-TOTAL-LITERAL      PIC X(8) VALUE "   GRAND".
011900 77  STORE-TOTAL-LITERAL      PIC X(8) VALUE "   STORE".
012000 77  DIVISION-TOTAL-LITERAL   PIC X(8) VALUE "DIVISION".
012100 77  DEPARTMENT-TOTAL-LITERAL PIC X(8) VALUE "    DEPT".
012200
012300 77  WORK-FILE-AT-END    PIC X.
012400
012500 77  LINE-COUNT          PIC 999 VALUE ZERO.
012600 77  PAGE-NUMBER         PIC 9999 VALUE ZERO.
012700 77  MAXIMUM-LINES       PIC 999 VALUE 55.
012800
012900 77  RECORD-COUNT        PIC 9999 VALUE ZEROES.
013000
013100* Control break current values for store, division
013200* department.
013300 77  CURRENT-STORE       PIC 99.
013400 77  CURRENT-DIVISION    PIC 99.
013500 77  CURRENT-DEPARTMENT  PIC 99.
013600
013700* Control break accumulators
013800* GRAND TOTAL is the level 1 accumulator for the whole file
013900* STORE TOTAL is the level 2 accumulator
014000* DIVISION TOTAL is the level 3 accumulator
014100* DEPARTMENT TOTAL is the level 4 accumulator.
014200 77  GRAND-TOTAL         PIC S9(6)V99.
014300 77  STORE-TOTAL         PIC S9(6)V99.
```

BD
1

continues

Listing B1.11. continued

```
014400 77  DIVISION-TOTAL         PIC S9(6)V99.
014500 77  DEPARTMENT-TOTAL       PIC S9(6)V99.
014600
014700 PROCEDURE DIVISION.
014800 PROGRAM-BEGIN.
014900
015000     PERFORM OPENING-PROCEDURE.
015100     PERFORM MAIN-PROCESS.
015200     PERFORM CLOSING-PROCEDURE.
015300
015400 PROGRAM-EXIT.
015500     EXIT PROGRAM.
015600
015700 PROGRAM-DONE.
015800     STOP RUN.
015900
016000 OPENING-PROCEDURE.
016100
016200     OPEN OUTPUT PRINTER-FILE.
016300
016400 MAIN-PROCESS.
016500     PERFORM GET-OK-TO-PROCESS.
016600     PERFORM PROCESS-THE-FILE
016700         UNTIL OK-TO-PROCESS = "N".
016800
016900 CLOSING-PROCEDURE.
017000     CLOSE PRINTER-FILE.
017100
017200 GET-OK-TO-PROCESS.
017300     PERFORM ACCEPT-OK-TO-PROCESS.
017400     PERFORM RE-ACCEPT-OK-TO-PROCESS
017500         UNTIL OK-TO-PROCESS = "Y" OR "N".
017600
017700 ACCEPT-OK-TO-PROCESS.
017800     DISPLAY "PRINT SALES REPORT (Y/N)?".
017900     ACCEPT OK-TO-PROCESS.
018000     INSPECT OK-TO-PROCESS
018100       CONVERTING LOWER-ALPHA
018200       TO        UPPER-ALPHA.
018300
018400 RE-ACCEPT-OK-TO-PROCESS.
018500     DISPLAY "YOU MUST ENTER YES OR NO".
018600     PERFORM ACCEPT-OK-TO-PROCESS.
018700
018800 PROCESS-THE-FILE.
018900     PERFORM START-THE-FILE.
019000     PERFORM PRINT-ONE-REPORT.
019100     PERFORM END-THE-FILE.
019200
019300*    PERFORM GET-OK-TO-PROCESS.
019400     MOVE "N" TO OK-TO-PROCESS.
019500
019600 START-THE-FILE.
019700     PERFORM SORT-DATA-FILE.
```

```
019800     OPEN INPUT WORK-FILE.
019900
020000 END-THE-FILE.
020100     CLOSE WORK-FILE.
020200
020300 SORT-DATA-FILE.
020400     SORT SORT-FILE
020500         ON ASCENDING KEY SORT-STORE
020600             ASCENDING KEY SORT-DIVISION
020700             ASCENDING KEY SORT-DEPARTMENT
020800             ASCENDING KEY SORT-CATEGORY
020900             USING SALES-FILE
021000             GIVING WORK-FILE.
021100
021200* LEVEL 1 CONTROL BREAK
021300 PRINT-ONE-REPORT.
021400     PERFORM START-ONE-REPORT.
021500     PERFORM PROCESS-ALL-STORES
021600         UNTIL WORK-FILE-AT-END = "Y".
021700     PERFORM END-ONE-REPORT.
021800
021900 START-ONE-REPORT.
022000     PERFORM READ-FIRST-VALID-WORK.
022100     MOVE ZEROES TO GRAND-TOTAL.
022200
022300     PERFORM START-NEW-REPORT.
022400
022500 START-NEW-REPORT.
022600     MOVE SPACE TO DETAIL-LINE.
022700     MOVE ZEROES TO LINE-COUNT PAGE-NUMBER.
022800
022900 END-ONE-REPORT.
023000     IF RECORD-COUNT = ZEROES
023100         MOVE "NO RECORDS FOUND" TO PRINTER-RECORD
023200         PERFORM WRITE-TO-PRINTER
023300     ELSE
023400         PERFORM PRINT-GRAND-TOTAL.
023500
023600     PERFORM END-LAST-PAGE.
023700
023800 PRINT-GRAND-TOTAL.
023900     MOVE SPACE TO TOTAL-LINE.
024000     MOVE GRAND-TOTAL TO PRINT-TOTAL.
024100     MOVE GRAND-TOTAL-LITERAL TO TOTAL-TYPE.
024200     MOVE "TOTAL" TO TOTAL-LITERAL.
024300     MOVE TOTAL-LINE TO PRINTER-RECORD.
024400     PERFORM WRITE-TO-PRINTER.
024500     PERFORM LINE-FEED 2 TIMES.
024600     MOVE SPACE TO DETAIL-LINE.
024700
024800* LEVEL 2 CONTROL BREAK
024900 PROCESS-ALL-STORES.
025000     PERFORM START-ONE-STORE.
025100
025200     PERFORM PROCESS-ALL-DIVISIONS
025300         UNTIL WORK-FILE-AT-END = "Y"
```

continues

Listing B1.11. continued

```
025400              OR WORK-STORE NOT = CURRENT-STORE.
025500
025600          PERFORM END-ONE-STORE.
025700
025800 START-ONE-STORE.
025900          MOVE WORK-STORE TO CURRENT-STORE.
026000          MOVE ZEROES TO STORE-TOTAL.
026100          MOVE WORK-STORE TO PRINT-STORE.
026200
026300          PERFORM START-NEXT-PAGE.
026400
026500 END-ONE-STORE.
026600          PERFORM PRINT-STORE-TOTAL.
026700          ADD STORE-TOTAL TO GRAND-TOTAL.
026800
026900 PRINT-STORE-TOTAL.
027000          MOVE SPACE TO TOTAL-LINE.
027100          MOVE STORE-TOTAL TO PRINT-TOTAL.
027200          MOVE CURRENT-STORE TO TOTAL-NUMBER.
027300          MOVE STORE-TOTAL-LITERAL TO TOTAL-TYPE.
027400          MOVE "TOTAL" TO TOTAL-LITERAL.
027500          MOVE TOTAL-LINE TO PRINTER-RECORD.
027600          PERFORM WRITE-TO-PRINTER.
027700          PERFORM LINE-FEED.
027800          MOVE SPACE TO DETAIL-LINE.
027900
028000* LEVEL 3 CONTROL BREAK
028100 PROCESS-ALL-DIVISIONS.
028200          PERFORM START-ONE-DIVISION.
028300
028400          PERFORM PROCESS-ALL-DEPARTMENTS
028500              UNTIL WORK-FILE-AT-END = "Y"
028600                  OR WORK-STORE NOT = CURRENT-STORE
028700                  OR WORK-DIVISION NOT = CURRENT-DIVISION.
028800
028900          PERFORM END-ONE-DIVISION.
029000
029100 START-ONE-DIVISION.
029200          MOVE WORK-DIVISION TO CURRENT-DIVISION.
029300          MOVE ZEROES TO DIVISION-TOTAL.
029400          MOVE WORK-DIVISION TO PRINT-DIVISION.
029500
029600 END-ONE-DIVISION.
029700          PERFORM PRINT-DIVISION-TOTAL.
029800          ADD DIVISION-TOTAL TO STORE-TOTAL.
029900
030000 PRINT-DIVISION-TOTAL.
030100          MOVE SPACE TO TOTAL-LINE.
030200          MOVE DIVISION-TOTAL TO PRINT-TOTAL.
030300          MOVE CURRENT-DIVISION TO TOTAL-NUMBER.
030400          MOVE DIVISION-TOTAL-LITERAL TO TOTAL-TYPE.
030500          MOVE "TOTAL" TO TOTAL-LITERAL.
030600          MOVE TOTAL-LINE TO PRINTER-RECORD.
030700          PERFORM WRITE-TO-PRINTER.
```

1

```
030800     PERFORM LINE-FEED.
030900     MOVE SPACE TO DETAIL-LINE.
031000
031100* LEVEL 4 CONTROL BREAK
031200 PROCESS-ALL-DEPARTMENTS.
031300     PERFORM START-ONE-DEPARTMENT.
031400
031500     PERFORM PROCESS-ALL-CATEGORIES
031600         UNTIL WORK-FILE-AT-END = "Y"
031700             OR WORK-STORE NOT = CURRENT-STORE
031800             OR WORK-DIVISION NOT = CURRENT-DIVISION
031900             OR WORK-DEPARTMENT NOT = CURRENT-DEPARTMENT.
032000
032100     PERFORM END-ONE-DEPARTMENT.
032200
032300 START-ONE-DEPARTMENT.
032400     MOVE WORK-DEPARTMENT TO CURRENT-DEPARTMENT.
032500     MOVE ZEROES TO DEPARTMENT-TOTAL.
032600     MOVE WORK-DEPARTMENT TO PRINT-DEPARTMENT.
032700
032800 END-ONE-DEPARTMENT.
032900     PERFORM PRINT-DEPARTMENT-TOTAL.
033000     ADD DEPARTMENT-TOTAL TO DIVISION-TOTAL.
033100
033200 PRINT-DEPARTMENT-TOTAL.
033300     MOVE SPACE TO TOTAL-LINE.
033400     MOVE DEPARTMENT-TOTAL TO PRINT-TOTAL.
033500     MOVE CURRENT-DEPARTMENT TO TOTAL-NUMBER.
033600     MOVE DEPARTMENT-TOTAL-LITERAL TO TOTAL-TYPE.
033700     MOVE "TOTAL" TO TOTAL-LITERAL.
033800     MOVE TOTAL-LINE TO PRINTER-RECORD.
033900     PERFORM WRITE-TO-PRINTER.
034000     PERFORM LINE-FEED.
034100     MOVE SPACE TO DETAIL-LINE.
034200
034300* PROCESS ONE RECORD LEVEL
034400 PROCESS-ALL-CATEGORIES.
034500     PERFORM PROCESS-THIS-CATEGORY.
034600     ADD WORK-AMOUNT TO DEPARTMENT-TOTAL.
034700     ADD 1 TO RECORD-COUNT.
034800     PERFORM READ-NEXT-VALID-WORK.
034900
035000 PROCESS-THIS-CATEGORY.
035100     IF LINE-COUNT > MAXIMUM-LINES
035200         PERFORM START-NEXT-PAGE.
035300     PERFORM PRINT-THE-RECORD.
035400
035500 PRINT-THE-RECORD.
035600     MOVE WORK-CATEGORY TO PRINT-CATEGORY.
035700
035800     MOVE WORK-AMOUNT TO PRINT-AMOUNT.
035900
036000     MOVE DETAIL-LINE TO PRINTER-RECORD.
036100     PERFORM WRITE-TO-PRINTER.
036200     MOVE SPACE TO DETAIL-LINE.
036300
```

continues

Listing B1.11. continued

```
036400* PRINTING ROUTINES
036500 WRITE-TO-PRINTER.
036600     WRITE PRINTER-RECORD BEFORE ADVANCING 1.
036700     ADD 1 TO LINE-COUNT.
036800
036900 LINE-FEED.
037000     MOVE SPACE TO PRINTER-RECORD.
037100     PERFORM WRITE-TO-PRINTER.
037200
037300 START-NEXT-PAGE.
037400     PERFORM END-LAST-PAGE.
037500     PERFORM START-NEW-PAGE.
037600
037700 START-NEW-PAGE.
037800     ADD 1 TO PAGE-NUMBER.
037900     MOVE PAGE-NUMBER TO PRINT-PAGE-NUMBER.
038000     MOVE TITLE-LINE TO PRINTER-RECORD.
038100     PERFORM WRITE-TO-PRINTER.
038200     PERFORM LINE-FEED.
038300     MOVE LEGEND-LINE TO PRINTER-RECORD.
038400     PERFORM WRITE-TO-PRINTER.
038500     PERFORM LINE-FEED.
038600     MOVE COLUMN-LINE TO PRINTER-RECORD.
038700     PERFORM WRITE-TO-PRINTER.
038800     PERFORM LINE-FEED.
038900
039000 END-LAST-PAGE.
039100     IF PAGE-NUMBER > 0
039200         PERFORM FORM-FEED.
039300     MOVE ZERO TO LINE-COUNT.
039400
039500 FORM-FEED.
039600     MOVE SPACE TO PRINTER-RECORD.
039700     WRITE PRINTER-RECORD BEFORE ADVANCING PAGE.
039800
039900*--------------------------------
040000* Read first, read next routines
040100*--------------------------------
040200 READ-FIRST-VALID-WORK.
040300     PERFORM READ-NEXT-VALID-WORK.
040400
040500 READ-NEXT-VALID-WORK.
040600     PERFORM READ-NEXT-WORK-RECORD.
040700
040800 READ-NEXT-WORK-RECORD.
040900     MOVE "N" TO WORK-FILE-AT-END.
041000     READ WORK-FILE NEXT RECORD
041100         AT END MOVE "Y" TO WORK-FILE-AT-END.
041200
```

The output of `slsrpt01` shows four levels of control breaks: all records, store, division, and department:

BD 1

OUTPUT

```
SALES REPORT                  PAGE:    1
STORE:  1
DIVISION DEPARTMENT CATEGORY     AMOUNT
1          1          1      237.57
2          475.14
DEPT  1 TOTAL     712.71
2          3          712.71
4          50.28
DEPT  2 TOTAL     762.99
DIVISION  1 TOTAL    1,475.70
2          3          5      287.85
6          525.42
DEPT  3 TOTAL     813.27
4          7          762.99
8          100.56
DEPT  4 TOTAL     863.55
DIVISION  2 TOTAL    1,676.82
3          5          9      338.13
10         575.70
DEPT  5 TOTAL     913.83
6          11          86.73-
12         150.84
DEPT  6 TOTAL      64.11
DIVISION  3 TOTAL     977.94
STORE   1 TOTAL    4,130.46

SALES REPORT                  PAGE:    2
STORE:  2
DIVISION DEPARTMENT CATEGORY     AMOUNT
1          1          1      388.41
2          625.98
DEPT  1 TOTAL    1,014.39
2          3           36.45-
4          201.12
DEPT  2 TOTAL     164.67
DIVISION  1 TOTAL    1,179.06
2          3          5      438.69
6          676.26
DEPT  3 TOTAL    1,114.95
4          7           13.83
8          251.40
DEPT  4 TOTAL     265.23
DIVISION  2 TOTAL    1,380.18
3          5          9      488.97
10         726.54
DEPT  5 TOTAL    1,215.51
6          11           64.11
12         301.68
DEPT  6 TOTAL     365.79
DIVISION  3 TOTAL    1,581.30
STORE   2 TOTAL    4,140.54

SALES REPORT                  PAGE:    3
```

```
STORE:  3
DIVISION DEPARTMENT CATEGORY      AMOUNT
1        1          1        539.25
2        776.82
DEPT  1 TOTAL   1,316.07
2          3         114.39
4        351.96
DEPT  2 TOTAL    466.35
DIVISION  1 TOTAL   1,782.42
2          3         5        589.53
6         72.90-
DEPT  3 TOTAL    516.63
4          7         164.67
8        402.24
DEPT  4 TOTAL    566.91
DIVISION  2 TOTAL   1,083.54
3          5         9        639.81
10         22.62-
DEPT  5 TOTAL    617.19
6          11        214.95
12        452.52
DEPT  6 TOTAL    667.47
DIVISION  3 TOTAL   1,284.66
STORE  3 TOTAL   4,150.62

SALES REPORT                PAGE:     4
STORE:  4
DIVISION DEPARTMENT CATEGORY      AMOUNT
1        1          1        690.09
2         27.66
DEPT  1 TOTAL    717.75
2          3         265.23
4        502.80
DEPT  2 TOTAL    768.03
DIVISION  1 TOTAL   1,485.78
2          3         5        740.37
6         77.94
DEPT  3 TOTAL    818.31
4          7         315.51
8        553.08
DEPT  4 TOTAL    868.59
DIVISION  2 TOTAL   1,686.90
3          5         9        790.65
10        128.22
DEPT  5 TOTAL    918.87
6          11        365.79
12        603.36
DEPT  6 TOTAL    969.15
DIVISION  3 TOTAL   1,888.02
STORE  4 TOTAL   5,060.70

SALES REPORT                PAGE:     5
STORE:  5
DIVISION DEPARTMENT CATEGORY      AMOUNT
1        1          1        59.07-
2        178.50
DEPT  1 TOTAL    119.43
```

```
2         3         416.07
4         653.64
DEPT  2 TOTAL    1,069.71
DIVISION  1 TOTAL    1,189.14
2         3         5          8.79-
6         228.78
DEPT  3 TOTAL    219.99
4         7         466.35
8         703.92
DEPT  4 TOTAL    1,170.27
DIVISION  2 TOTAL    1,390.26
3         5         9          41.49
10        279.06
DEPT  5 TOTAL    320.55
6         11        516.63
12        754.20
DEPT  6 TOTAL    1,270.83
DIVISION  3 TOTAL    1,591.38
STORE  5 TOTAL    4,170.78

SALES REPORT                PAGE:      6
STORE:  6
DIVISION DEPARTMENT CATEGORY     AMOUNT
1         1         1          91.77
2         329.34
DEPT  1 TOTAL    421.11
2         3         566.91
4         95.52-
DEPT  2 TOTAL    471.39
DIVISION  1 TOTAL    892.50
2         3         5          142.05
6         379.62
DEPT  3 TOTAL    521.67
4         7         617.19
8         45.24-
DEPT  4 TOTAL    571.95
DIVISION  2 TOTAL    1,093.62
3         5         9          192.33
10        429.90
DEPT  5 TOTAL    622.23
6         11        667.47
12        5.04
DEPT  6 TOTAL    672.51
DIVISION  3 TOTAL    1,294.74
STORE  6 TOTAL    3,280.86
GRAND    TOTAL    24,933.96
```

ANALYSIS The report contains four level breaks: all records, store, division, and department. The first thing you would expect of a report like this is that the input data file must be sorted. Lines 003500, 004400, and 005300 contain the definitions for the sales file, a work file, and a sort file, respectively.

The sort itself is at lines 020400 through 021000. Note the wording of the multiple sort. When a multiple key sort is done, the first key named is the first sort. Records then are sorted in order of the second key, within the first sort, and so on. The sort keys are given in the order SORT-STORE, SORT-DIVISION, SORT-DEPARTMENT, and then SORT-CATEGORY. When the sort is complete, the primary order of the file will be by store. Then within each store, the records are sorted by division. Within each division, the records are in department order, and within each department, the records are in category order. The file is sorted on four keys, but only three of them are used. Category is not a control break, but adding category to the sort will cause the records within a department break to print in category order.

The level-1 control break extends from lines 021200 through 024700. It is similar to level-1 logic in earlier programs, with one exception. The logic to START-NEXT-PAGE is not performed as part of START-ONE-REPORT. A new page will be started on each new store, so this logic has been moved down to level 2 where it is performed in START-ONE-STORE.

The level-2 control break, PROCESS-ALL-STORES, extends from lines 024900 to 027800. This has two special features. The logic to START-NEXT-PAGE is performed inside START-ONE-STORE, at line 026300. Usually, this routine is performed as part of START-ONE-REPORT. The store information is printed on a special line, which is defined in WORKING-STORAGE at line 007200. This is named LEGEND-LINE, a name frequently used for an extra line such as this one that appears between the title of a report and the column lines of a report.

The printing of the LEGEND-LINE has been added to the START-NEW-PAGE routine at lines 038300 through 038500.

The END-ONE-STORE logic at line 026500 handles the printing of the store total. This begins at line 026900. A special totaling line is defined in WORKING-STORAGE at lines 010800 through 011600. This line can be filled in with the total type, and the store, division, or department number. The PRINT-STORE-TOTAL logic at line 026900 fills this in with the STORE-TOTAL and appropriate other values, and then it is printed.

The PRINT-STORE-TOTAL logic for the store control break is imitated at line 030000, PRINT-DIVISION-TOTAL, for printing the division total, and at line 033200, PRINT-DEPARTMENT-TOTAL, for printing the department total.

Code, compile, and run slsrpt01.cbl, and look at the sample output. You will see that control breaks are just a repetitive series of steps for each level.

1

Summary

Control breaks are an important part of reports, and you should know how to use them more effectively. Today, you learned these basics:

☐ Control breaks are important to report and file processing. A control break is a break inserted into the normal processing of a program (usually a report program) to cause groups of records to be processed together as one unit. The interruption of the normal printing of a report program to print a total or subtotal is a control break or level break.

☐ The control break field or control field is the field in the record that causes a control break to occur when the field changes.

☐ The control break current value or control current value is a field created in WORKING-STORAGE that holds a copy of the control break field. The control break current value is filled in at the beginning of a control break level with the value in the control break field. As the processing continues, the control break field is compared to the control break current value to determine whether a control break has occurred.

☐ Control break accumulators or control accumulators are variables used for summing or counting values within a control break.

☐ The pseudocode for a level-2 or lower control break is the following:

```
process-level-2-control-break
    perform start-level-2-control-break
    perform process-level-3-control-break
        until file at end
            or level-2-control-field not = level-2-current-value
    perform end-level-2
start-level-2
    move level-2-control-field to level-2-current-value.
    move zeroes to level-2 accumulators.
    any other starting actions
end-level-2
    perform process-level-2-accumulators
    perform add-level-2 accumulators to level-1 accumulators
    any other ending actions
```

A control break starts by saving the control break field in the control break current value and zeroing the accumulators for that control level.

The body of the break performs the next lower level control break until the file is at end or the control break field no longer matches the control break value field.

The control break ends by processing the level accumulators. For a report program, this involves printing the subtotals. Finally, it adds the accumulators for this level to the next higher level.

☐ A level-1 break varies from any other break because there is no true control break current value, so the start-level-1 logic begins by executing a read first valid record.

☐ The body of the level-1 break performs level-2 breaks until the file is at end. The end of a level-1 break does not add accumulators to the next higher level because there is no higher level.

☐ The pseudocode for a level 1 control break is the following:

```
process-level-1-control-break
    perform start-level-1
    perform process-level-2-control-break
        until file-at-end
    perform end-level-1
start-level-1
    read first valid record
    move zeroes to level-1-accumulators.
    any other starting actions
end-level-1
    perform process-level-1-accumulators
    any other ending actions
```

☐ Control breaking can be repeated for as many levels as necessary, as long as the file is sorted on each of the control break fields.

Q&A

Q **Is a control break the same as a level break?**

A Because control breaks usually are organized in levels, control break and level break sometimes are used interchangeably as terms for a control break.

Workshop

Quiz

1. What is a control break?
2. What is the function of a control break field?
3. What is the function of a control break current value field?
4. What is the function of a control break accumulator?
5. Why is a level-1 control break different from other levels?

Exercises

1. Copy slsrpt01.cbl to slsrpt02.cbl. Modify it so that the division number and department number are printed on each detail line.

   Hint: Code in START-ONE-DIVISION and START-ONE-DEPARTMENT needs to be moved to PRINT-THE-RECORD.

2. Copy slsrpt01.cbl to slssum01.cbl. Modify the new program so that no detail lines are printed at all. This will become a sales summary report that prints only the totals for the control breaks.

   Hint: The key to this problem is to prevent the printing of the detail line somewhere between lines 035000 and 036300.

BD
1

Day **2**

Miscellaneous COBOL Syntax

Although the 21-day course covered the meat of COBOL, many areas of the language and the use of COBOL in programming have not been touched. This chapter rounds out some of those areas, touching on different topics that are not necessarily related. They are common issues that will come up when you work with COBOL.

Today, you learn about the following topics:

- ☐ Internal tables
- ☐ STRING
- ☐ UNSTRING
- ☐ INSPECT
- ☐ CALL USING
- ☐ ACCEPT FROM DATE or TIME
- ☐ Computational fields

☐ Numbering paragraphs
☐ Qualified data names
☐ MOVE CORRESPONDING
☐ Continuation characters

Internal Tables

You learned to use tables on Day 16, "Using Look Up and Arrays." In that lesson you created a table for state codes and loaded the table from the state codes file. The table then was used in the program to look up state codes while printing a report on the vendor file.

It also is possible to create tables or arrays in memory that already are filled in with values, rather than loading them from a file.

Today, you improve the appearance of the sales reports created on Bonus Day 1, "Control Breaks," by printing the division, department, and category names on the report. First, a quick review of tables. A table or an array is an area of memory that has been set aside and organized in such a way that it can hold multiple occurrences of the same type of information.

On Day 16, you created a table that looked like Listing B2.1.

TYPE   **Listing B2.1. A state code table.**

```
007000 01  TABLE-STATE-RECORD OCCURS 50 TIMES
007100       INDEXED BY STATE-INDEX.
007200     05  TABLE-STATE-CODE       PIC XX.
007300     05  TABLE-STATE-NAME       PIC X(20).
```

For the sales report, you need a table of division names, a table of department names, and a table of category names. Table B2.1 shows the list of names for these subdivisions.

Table B2.1. Names for the sales report.

Div	Division Name	Dep	Department Name	Cat	Category Name
01	Athletics	01	Exercise	01	Weights
				02	Machines
		02	Miscellaneous	03	Sunglasses
				04	Vitamins
02	Sporting Goods	03	Sport Clothes	05	Men's Clothes
				06	Women's Clothes

Div	Division Name	Dep	Department Name	Cat	Category Name
		04	Equipment	07	Tennis
				08	Soccer
03	Camping	05	Camp Equipment	09	Tents
				10	Sleeping Bags
		06	Camping Clothes	11	Clothing
				12	Hiking Boots

Listing B2.2 is a table that is good enough for the divisions.

TYPE   **Listing B2.2.** WORKING-STORAGE **for a division table.**

```
007000 01   DIVISION-TABLE OCCURS 3 TIMES
007100          INDEXED BY DIVISION-INDEX.
007200      05  DIVISION-NUMBER          PIC 99.
007300      05  DIVISION-NAME            PIC X(15).
```

This table could be loaded in the program with a series of commands, as shown in Listing B2.3.

TYPE   **Listing B2.3. Loading a table in the program.**

```
010700          MOVE 1 TO DIVISION-NUMBER(1).
010800          MOVE "ATHLETICS" TO DIVISION-NAME(1).
010900          MOVE 2 TO DIVISION-NUMBER(2).
011000          MOVE "SPORTING GOODS" TO DIVISION-NAME(2).
011100          MOVE 3 TO DIVISION-NUMBER(3).
011200          MOVE "CAMPING" TO DIVISION-NAME(3).
```

However, the usual method for loading a table is to initialize it directly in working storage when it is defined. This is done by first creating a variable that has all the needed values and space, as shown in Listing B2.4.

TYPE   **Listing B2.4. Creating the needed values in** WORKING-STORAGE.

```
007000 01   THE-DIVISIONS.
007100      05  FILLER          PIC 99 VALUE 01.
007200      05  FILLER          PIC X(15) VALUE "ATHLETICS".
```

continues

Listing B2.4. continued

```
007100     05  FILLER       PIC 99 VALUE 02.
007200     05  FILLER       PIC X(15) VALUE "SPORTING GOODS".
007100     05  FILLER       PIC 99 VALUE 01.
007200     05  FILLER       PIC X(15) VALUE "CAMPING".
```

This variable is then redefined as a table, as shown in Listing B2.5.

TYPE **Listing B2.5. Redefining the variable.**

```
007000 01  THE-DIVISIONS.
007100     05  FILLER       PIC 99 VALUE 01.
007200     05  FILLER       PIC X(15) VALUE "ATHLETICS".
007100     05  FILLER       PIC 99 VALUE 02.
007200     05  FILLER       PIC X(15) VALUE "SPORTING GOODS".
007100     05  FILLER       PIC 99 VALUE 03.
007200     05  FILLER       PIC X(15) VALUE "CAMPING".
007300 01  FILLER REDEFINES THE-DIVISIONS.
007400     05  DIVISION-TABLE OCCURS 3 TIMES
007500         INDEXED BY DIVISION-INDEX.
007600         10  DIVISION-NUMBER      PIC 99.
007700         10  DIVISION-NAME        PIC X(15).
```

Using Internal Tables

Figure B2.1 is a printer spacing chart for a version of the sales report that includes the name of each division, department, or category. Listing B2.6 is slsrpt03.cbl. It is based on slsrpt01.cbl, but the layout has been modified to accommodate an extra 15-character name for division, department, and category.

Figure B2.1.

Printer layout chart
for slsrpt03.cbl.

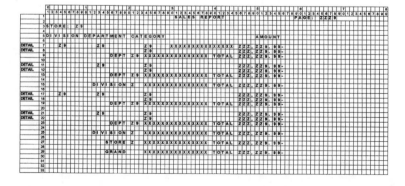

TYPE **Listing B2.6. Printing the subdivision names.**

```
000100 IDENTIFICATION DIVISION.
000200 PROGRAM-ID. SLSRPT03.
000300*--------------------------------
000400* Print test sales data
000500*--------------------------------
000600 ENVIRONMENT DIVISION.
000700 INPUT-OUTPUT SECTION.
000800 FILE-CONTROL.
000900
001000*--------------------------------
001100* SLSALES.CBL
001200*--------------------------------
001300     SELECT SALES-FILE
001400         ASSIGN TO "SALES"
001500         ORGANIZATION IS SEQUENTIAL.
001600
001700     SELECT WORK-FILE
001800         ASSIGN TO "WORK"
001900         ORGANIZATION IS SEQUENTIAL.
002000
002100     SELECT SORT-FILE
002200         ASSIGN TO "SORT".
002300
002400     SELECT PRINTER-FILE
002500         ASSIGN TO PRINTER
002600         ORGANIZATION IS LINE SEQUENTIAL.
002700
002800 DATA DIVISION.
002900 FILE SECTION.
003000
003100*--------------------------------
003200* FDSALES.CBL
003300* Temporary daily sales file.
003400*--------------------------------
003500 FD   SALES-FILE
003600      LABEL RECORDS ARE STANDARD.
003700 01   SALES-RECORD.
003800      05   SALES-STORE          PIC 9(2).
003900      05   SALES-DIVISION       PIC 9(2).
004000      05   SALES-DEPARTMENT     PIC 9(2).
004100      05   SALES-CATEGORY       PIC 9(2).
004200      05   SALES-AMOUNT         PIC S9(6)V99.
004300
004400 FD   WORK-FILE
004500      LABEL RECORDS ARE STANDARD.
004600 01   WORK-RECORD.
004700      05   WORK-STORE           PIC 9(2).
004800      05   WORK-DIVISION        PIC 9(2).
004900      05   WORK-DEPARTMENT      PIC 9(2).
```

continues

Listing B2.6. continued

```
005000      05  WORK-CATEGORY           PIC 9(2).
005100      05  WORK-AMOUNT             PIC S9(6)V99.
005200
005300 SD  SORT-FILE
005400      LABEL RECORDS ARE STANDARD.
005500 01  SORT-RECORD.
005600      05  SORT-STORE              PIC 9(2).
005700      05  SORT-DIVISION           PIC 9(2).
005800      05  SORT-DEPARTMENT         PIC 9(2).
005900      05  SORT-CATEGORY           PIC 9(2).
006000      05  SORT-AMOUNT             PIC S9(6)V99.
006100
006200 FD  PRINTER-FILE
006300      LABEL RECORDS ARE OMITTED.
006400 01  PRINTER-RECORD              PIC X(80).
006500
006600 WORKING-STORAGE SECTION.
006700
006800 01  THE-DIVISIONS.
006900      05  FILLER     PIC 99 VALUE 01.
007000      05  FILLER     PIC X(15) VALUE "ATHLETICS".
007100      05  FILLER     PIC 99 VALUE 02.
007200      05  FILLER     PIC X(15) VALUE "SPORTING GOODS".
007300      05  FILLER     PIC 99 VALUE 03.
007400      05  FILLER     PIC X(15) VALUE "CAMPING".
007500 01  FILLER REDEFINES THE-DIVISIONS.
007600      05  DIVISION-TABLE OCCURS 3 TIMES
007700          INDEXED BY DIVISION-INDEX.
007800          10  DIVISION-NUMBER      PIC 99.
007900          10  DIVISION-NAME        PIC X(15).
008000
008100 01  THE-DEPARTMENTS.
008200      05  FILLER     PIC 99 VALUE 01.
008300      05  FILLER     PIC X(15) VALUE "EXERCISE".
008400      05  FILLER     PIC 99 VALUE 02.
008500      05  FILLER     PIC X(15) VALUE "MISCELLANEOUS".
008600      05  FILLER     PIC 99 VALUE 03.
008700      05  FILLER     PIC X(15) VALUE "SPORT CLOTHES".
008800      05  FILLER     PIC 99 VALUE 04.
008900      05  FILLER     PIC X(15) VALUE "EQUIPMENT".
009000      05  FILLER     PIC 99 VALUE 05.
009100      05  FILLER     PIC X(15) VALUE "CAMP EQUIPMENT".
009200      05  FILLER     PIC 99 VALUE 06.
009300      05  FILLER     PIC X(15) VALUE "CAMPING CLOTHES".
009400 01  FILLER REDEFINES THE-DEPARTMENTS.
009500      05  DEPARTMENT-TABLE OCCURS 6 TIMES
009600          INDEXED BY DEPARTMENT-INDEX.
009700          10  DEPARTMENT-NUMBER      PIC 99.
009800          10  DEPARTMENT-NAME        PIC X(15).
009900
010000 01  THE-CATEGORIES.
010100      05  FILLER     PIC 99 VALUE 01.
010200      05  FILLER     PIC X(15) VALUE "WEIGHTS".
010300      05  FILLER     PIC 99 VALUE 02.
```

```
010400      05  FILLER           PIC X(15) VALUE "MACHINES".
010500      05  FILLER           PIC 99 VALUE 03.
010600      05  FILLER           PIC X(15) VALUE "SUN GLASSES".
010700      05  FILLER           PIC 99 VALUE 04.
010800      05  FILLER           PIC X(15) VALUE "VITAMINS".
010900      05  FILLER           PIC 99 VALUE 05.
011000      05  FILLER           PIC X(15) VALUE "MEN'S CLOTHES".
011100      05  FILLER           PIC 99 VALUE 06.
011200      05  FILLER           PIC X(15) VALUE "WOMEN'S CLOTHES".
011300      05  FILLER           PIC 99 VALUE 07.
011400      05  FILLER           PIC X(15) VALUE "TENNIS".
011500      05  FILLER           PIC 99 VALUE 08.
011600      05  FILLER           PIC X(15) VALUE "SOCCER".
011700      05  FILLER           PIC 99 VALUE 09.
011800      05  FILLER           PIC X(15) VALUE "TENTS".
011900      05  FILLER           PIC 99 VALUE 10.
012000      05  FILLER           PIC X(15) VALUE "SLEEPING BAGS".
012100      05  FILLER           PIC 99 VALUE 11.
012200      05  FILLER           PIC X(15) VALUE "CLOTHING".
012300      05  FILLER           PIC 99 VALUE 12.
012400      05  FILLER           PIC X(15) VALUE "HIKING BOOTS".
012500 01  FILLER REDEFINES THE-CATEGORIES.
012600      05  CATEGORY-TABLE OCCURS 12 TIMES
012700          INDEXED BY CATEGORY-INDEX.
012800          10  CATEGORY-NUMBER       PIC 99.
012900          10  CATEGORY-NAME         PIC X(15).
013000
013100 77  OK-TO-PROCESS          PIC X.
013200
013300     COPY "WSCASE01.CBL".
013400
013500 01  LEGEND-LINE.
013600      05  FILLER           PIC X(6) VALUE "STORE:".
013700      05  FILLER           PIC X(1) VALUE SPACE.
013800      05  PRINT-STORE      PIC Z9.
013900
014000 01  DETAIL-LINE.
014100      05  FILLER             PIC X(3) VALUE SPACE.
014200      05  PRINT-DIVISION     PIC Z9.
014300      05  FILLER             PIC X(4) VALUE SPACE.
014400      05  FILLER             PIC X(3) VALUE SPACE.
014500      05  PRINT-DEPARTMENT   PIC Z9.
014600      05  FILLER             PIC X(6) VALUE SPACE.
014700      05  FILLER             PIC X(3) VALUE SPACE.
014800      05  PRINT-CATEGORY     PIC Z9.
014900      05  FILLER             PIC X(4) VALUE SPACE.
015000      05  PRINT-CATEGORY-NAME PIC X(15).
015100      05  FILLER             PIC X(1) VALUE SPACE.
015200      05  PRINT-AMOUNT       PIC ZZZ,ZZ9.99-.
015300
015400 01  COLUMN-LINE.
015500      05  FILLER           PIC X(8)  VALUE "DIVISION".
015600      05  FILLER           PIC X(1)  VALUE SPACE.
015700      05  FILLER           PIC X(10) VALUE "DEPARTMENT".
015800      05  FILLER           PIC X(1)  VALUE SPACE.
```

continues

Listing B2.6. continued

```
015900     05  FILLER       PIC X(8)   VALUE "CATEGORY".
016000     05  FILLER       PIC X(1)   VALUE SPACE.
016100     05  FILLER       PIC X(15)  VALUE SPACE.
016200     05  FILLER       PIC X(5)   VALUE SPACE.
016300     05  FILLER       PIC X(6)   VALUE "AMOUNT".
016400
016500 01  TITLE-LINE.
016600     05  FILLER              PIC X(30) VALUE SPACE.
016700     05  FILLER              PIC X(12)
016800         VALUE "SALES REPORT".
016900     05  FILLER              PIC X(16) VALUE SPACE.
017000     05  FILLER              PIC X(5) VALUE "PAGE:".
017100     05  FILLER              PIC X(1) VALUE SPACE.
017200     05  PRINT-PAGE-NUMBER   PIC ZZZ9.
017300
017400 01  TOTAL-LINE.
017500     05  FILLER              PIC X(11) VALUE SPACE.
017600     05  TOTAL-TYPE          PIC X(8).
017700     05  FILLER              PIC X(1) VALUE SPACE.
017800     05  TOTAL-NUMBER        PIC Z9.
017900     05  FILLER              PIC X(1) VALUE SPACE.
018000     05  TOTAL-NAME          PIC X(15) VALUE SPACE.
018100     05  FILLER              PIC X(1) VALUE SPACE.
018200     05  TOTAL-LITERAL       PIC X(5) VALUE "TOTAL".
018300     05  FILLER              PIC X(1) VALUE SPACE.
018400     05  PRINT-TOTAL         PIC ZZZ,ZZ9.99-.
018500
018600 77  GRAND-TOTAL-LITERAL      PIC X(8) VALUE "   GRAND".
018700 77  STORE-TOTAL-LITERAL      PIC X(8) VALUE "   STORE".
018800 77  DIVISION-TOTAL-LITERAL   PIC X(8) VALUE "DIVISION".
018900 77  DEPARTMENT-TOTAL-LITERAL PIC X(8) VALUE "    DEPT".
019000
019100 77  WORK-FILE-AT-END        PIC X.
019200
019300 77  LINE-COUNT              PIC 999 VALUE ZERO.
019400 77  PAGE-NUMBER             PIC 9999 VALUE ZERO.
019500 77  MAXIMUM-LINES           PIC 999 VALUE 55.
019600
019700 77  RECORD-COUNT            PIC 9999 VALUE ZEROES.
019800
019900* Control break current values for store, division
020000* department.
020100 77  CURRENT-STORE           PIC 99.
020200 77  CURRENT-DIVISION        PIC 99.
020300 77  CURRENT-DEPARTMENT      PIC 99.
020400
020500* Control break accumulators
020600* GRAND TOTAL is the level 1 accumulator for the whole file
020700* STORE TOTAL is the level 2 accumulator
020800* DIVISION TOTAL is the level 3 accumulator
020900* DEPARTMENT TOTAL is the level 4 accumulator.
021000 77  GRAND-TOTAL             PIC S9(6)V99.
021100 77  STORE-TOTAL             PIC S9(6)V99.
021200 77  DIVISION-TOTAL          PIC S9(6)V99.
```

2

```
021300 77  DEPARTMENT-TOTAL        PIC S9(6)V99.
021400
021500 PROCEDURE DIVISION.
021600 PROGRAM-BEGIN.
021700
021800     PERFORM OPENING-PROCEDURE.
021900     PERFORM MAIN-PROCESS.
022000     PERFORM CLOSING-PROCEDURE.
022100
022200 PROGRAM-EXIT.
022300     EXIT PROGRAM.
022400
022500 PROGRAM-DONE.
022600     STOP RUN.
022700
022800 OPENING-PROCEDURE.
022900
023000     OPEN OUTPUT PRINTER-FILE.
023100
023200 MAIN-PROCESS.
023300     PERFORM GET-OK-TO-PROCESS.
023400     PERFORM PROCESS-THE-FILE
023500         UNTIL OK-TO-PROCESS = "N".
023600
023700 CLOSING-PROCEDURE.
023800     CLOSE PRINTER-FILE.
023900
024000 GET-OK-TO-PROCESS.
024100     PERFORM ACCEPT-OK-TO-PROCESS.
024200     PERFORM RE-ACCEPT-OK-TO-PROCESS
024300         UNTIL OK-TO-PROCESS = "Y" OR "N".
024400
024500 ACCEPT-OK-TO-PROCESS.
024600     DISPLAY "PRINT SALES REPORT (Y/N)?".
024700     ACCEPT OK-TO-PROCESS.
024800     INSPECT OK-TO-PROCESS
024900       CONVERTING LOWER-ALPHA
025000       TO            UPPER-ALPHA.
025100
025200 RE-ACCEPT-OK-TO-PROCESS.
025300     DISPLAY "YOU MUST ENTER YES OR NO".
025400     PERFORM ACCEPT-OK-TO-PROCESS.
025500
025600 PROCESS-THE-FILE.
025700     PERFORM START-THE-FILE.
025800     PERFORM PRINT-ONE-REPORT.
025900     PERFORM END-THE-FILE.
026000
026100*    PERFORM GET-OK-TO-PROCESS.
026200     MOVE "N" TO OK-TO-PROCESS.
026300
026400 START-THE-FILE.
026500     PERFORM SORT-DATA-FILE.
026600     OPEN INPUT WORK-FILE.
```

BD
2

continues

Listing B2.6. continued

```
026700
026800 END-THE-FILE.
026900     CLOSE WORK-FILE.
027000
027100 SORT-DATA-FILE.
027200     SORT SORT-FILE
027300         ON ASCENDING KEY SORT-STORE
027400             ASCENDING KEY SORT-DIVISION
027500             ASCENDING KEY SORT-DEPARTMENT
027600             ASCENDING KEY SORT-CATEGORY
027700         USING SALES-FILE
027800         GIVING WORK-FILE.
027900
028000* LEVEL 1 CONTROL BREAK
028100 PRINT-ONE-REPORT.
028200     PERFORM START-ONE-REPORT.
028300     PERFORM PROCESS-ALL-STORES
028400         UNTIL WORK-FILE-AT-END = "Y".
028500     PERFORM END-ONE-REPORT.
028600
028700 START-ONE-REPORT.
028800     PERFORM READ-FIRST-VALID-WORK.
028900     MOVE ZEROES TO GRAND-TOTAL.
029000
029100     PERFORM START-NEW-REPORT.
029200
029300 START-NEW-REPORT.
029400     MOVE SPACE TO DETAIL-LINE.
029500     MOVE ZEROES TO LINE-COUNT PAGE-NUMBER.
029600
029700 END-ONE-REPORT.
029800     IF RECORD-COUNT = ZEROES
029900         MOVE "NO RECORDS FOUND" TO PRINTER-RECORD
030000         PERFORM WRITE-TO-PRINTER
030100     ELSE
030200         PERFORM PRINT-GRAND-TOTAL.
030300
030400     PERFORM END-LAST-PAGE.
030500
030600 PRINT-GRAND-TOTAL.
030700     MOVE SPACE TO TOTAL-LINE.
030800     MOVE GRAND-TOTAL TO PRINT-TOTAL.
030900     MOVE GRAND-TOTAL-LITERAL TO TOTAL-TYPE.
031000     MOVE "TOTAL" TO TOTAL-LITERAL.
031100     MOVE TOTAL-LINE TO PRINTER-RECORD.
031200     PERFORM WRITE-TO-PRINTER.
031300     PERFORM LINE-FEED 2 TIMES.
031400     MOVE SPACE TO DETAIL-LINE.
031500
031600* LEVEL 2 CONTROL BREAK
031700 PROCESS-ALL-STORES.
031800     PERFORM START-ONE-STORE.
031900
032000     PERFORM PROCESS-ALL-DIVISIONS
```

```
032100          UNTIL WORK-FILE-AT-END = "Y"
032200               OR WORK-STORE NOT = CURRENT-STORE.
032300
032400      PERFORM END-ONE-STORE.
032500
032600 START-ONE-STORE.
032700      MOVE WORK-STORE TO CURRENT-STORE.
032800      MOVE ZEROES TO STORE-TOTAL.
032900      MOVE WORK-STORE TO PRINT-STORE.
033000
033100      PERFORM START-NEXT-PAGE.
033200
033300 END-ONE-STORE.
033400      PERFORM PRINT-STORE-TOTAL.
033500      ADD STORE-TOTAL TO GRAND-TOTAL.
033600
033700 PRINT-STORE-TOTAL.
033800      MOVE SPACE TO TOTAL-LINE.
033900      MOVE STORE-TOTAL TO PRINT-TOTAL.
034000      MOVE CURRENT-STORE TO TOTAL-NUMBER.
034100      MOVE STORE-TOTAL-LITERAL TO TOTAL-TYPE.
034200      MOVE "TOTAL" TO TOTAL-LITERAL.
034300      MOVE TOTAL-LINE TO PRINTER-RECORD.
034400      PERFORM WRITE-TO-PRINTER.
034500      PERFORM LINE-FEED.
034600      MOVE SPACE TO DETAIL-LINE.
034700
034800* LEVEL 3 CONTROL BREAK
034900 PROCESS-ALL-DIVISIONS.
035000      PERFORM START-ONE-DIVISION.
035100
035200      PERFORM PROCESS-ALL-DEPARTMENTS
035300          UNTIL WORK-FILE-AT-END = "Y"
035400               OR WORK-STORE NOT = CURRENT-STORE
035500               OR WORK-DIVISION NOT = CURRENT-DIVISION.
035600
035700      PERFORM END-ONE-DIVISION.
035800
035900 START-ONE-DIVISION.
036000      MOVE WORK-DIVISION TO CURRENT-DIVISION.
036100      MOVE ZEROES TO DIVISION-TOTAL.
036200      MOVE WORK-DIVISION TO PRINT-DIVISION.
036300
036400 END-ONE-DIVISION.
036500      PERFORM PRINT-DIVISION-TOTAL.
036600      ADD DIVISION-TOTAL TO STORE-TOTAL.
036700
036800 PRINT-DIVISION-TOTAL.
036900      MOVE SPACE TO TOTAL-LINE.
037000      MOVE DIVISION-TOTAL TO PRINT-TOTAL.
037100      MOVE CURRENT-DIVISION TO TOTAL-NUMBER.
037200      MOVE DIVISION-TOTAL-LITERAL TO TOTAL-TYPE.
037300      MOVE "TOTAL" TO TOTAL-LITERAL.
037400      PERFORM LOAD-DIVISION-NAME.
```

BD
2

continues

Listing B2.6. continued

```
037500      MOVE TOTAL-LINE TO PRINTER-RECORD.
037600      PERFORM WRITE-TO-PRINTER.
037700      PERFORM LINE-FEED.
037800      MOVE SPACE TO DETAIL-LINE.
037900
038000 LOAD-DIVISION-NAME.
038100      SET DIVISION-INDEX TO 1.
038200      SEARCH DIVISION-TABLE
038300          AT END
038400              MOVE "NOT FOUND" TO TOTAL-NAME
038500          WHEN
038600              DIVISION-NUMBER(DIVISION-INDEX) =
038700                  CURRENT-DIVISION
038800                  MOVE DIVISION-NAME(DIVISION-INDEX) TO
038900                      TOTAL-NAME.
039000
039100* LEVEL 4 CONTROL BREAK
039200 PROCESS-ALL-DEPARTMENTS.
039300      PERFORM START-ONE-DEPARTMENT.
039400
039500      PERFORM PROCESS-ALL-CATEGORIES
039600          UNTIL WORK-FILE-AT-END = "Y"
039700              OR WORK-STORE NOT = CURRENT-STORE
039800              OR WORK-DIVISION NOT = CURRENT-DIVISION
039900              OR WORK-DEPARTMENT NOT = CURRENT-DEPARTMENT.
040000
040100      PERFORM END-ONE-DEPARTMENT.
040200
040300 START-ONE-DEPARTMENT.
040400      MOVE WORK-DEPARTMENT TO CURRENT-DEPARTMENT.
040500      MOVE ZEROES TO DEPARTMENT-TOTAL.
040600      MOVE WORK-DEPARTMENT TO PRINT-DEPARTMENT.
040700
040800 END-ONE-DEPARTMENT.
040900      PERFORM PRINT-DEPARTMENT-TOTAL.
041000      ADD DEPARTMENT-TOTAL TO DIVISION-TOTAL.
041100
041200 PRINT-DEPARTMENT-TOTAL.
041300      MOVE SPACE TO TOTAL-LINE.
041400      MOVE DEPARTMENT-TOTAL TO PRINT-TOTAL.
041500      MOVE CURRENT-DEPARTMENT TO TOTAL-NUMBER.
041600      MOVE DEPARTMENT-TOTAL-LITERAL TO TOTAL-TYPE.
041700      MOVE "TOTAL" TO TOTAL-LITERAL.
041800      PERFORM LOAD-DEPARTMENT-NAME.
041900      MOVE TOTAL-LINE TO PRINTER-RECORD.
042000      PERFORM WRITE-TO-PRINTER.
042100      PERFORM LINE-FEED.
042200      MOVE SPACE TO DETAIL-LINE.
042300
042400 LOAD-DEPARTMENT-NAME.
042500      SET DEPARTMENT-INDEX TO 1.
042600      SEARCH DEPARTMENT-TABLE
042700          AT END
042800              MOVE "NOT FOUND" TO TOTAL-NAME
```

2

```
042900          WHEN
043000            DEPARTMENT-NUMBER(DEPARTMENT-INDEX) =
043100                CURRENT-DEPARTMENT
043200                MOVE DEPARTMENT-NAME(DEPARTMENT-INDEX) TO
043300                    TOTAL-NAME.
043400
043500* PROCESS ONE RECORD LEVEL
043600 PROCESS-ALL-CATEGORIES.
043700      PERFORM PROCESS-THIS-CATEGORY.
043800      ADD WORK-AMOUNT TO DEPARTMENT-TOTAL.
043900      ADD 1 TO RECORD-COUNT.
044000      PERFORM READ-NEXT-VALID-WORK.
044100
044200 PROCESS-THIS-CATEGORY.
044300      IF LINE-COUNT > MAXIMUM-LINES
044400          PERFORM START-NEXT-PAGE.
044500      PERFORM PRINT-THE-RECORD.
044600
044700 PRINT-THE-RECORD.
044800      MOVE WORK-CATEGORY TO PRINT-CATEGORY.
044900
045000      PERFORM LOAD-CATEGORY-NAME.
045100
045200      MOVE WORK-AMOUNT TO PRINT-AMOUNT.
045300
045400      MOVE DETAIL-LINE TO PRINTER-RECORD.
045500      PERFORM WRITE-TO-PRINTER.
045600      MOVE SPACE TO DETAIL-LINE.
045700
045800 LOAD-CATEGORY-NAME.
045900      SET CATEGORY-INDEX TO 1.
046000      SEARCH CATEGORY-TABLE
046100          AT END
046200            MOVE "NOT FOUND" TO TOTAL-NAME
046300          WHEN
046400            CATEGORY-NUMBER(CATEGORY-INDEX) =
046500                WORK-CATEGORY
046600                MOVE CATEGORY-NAME(CATEGORY-INDEX) TO
046700                    PRINT-CATEGORY-NAME.
046800
046900* PRINTING ROUTINES
047000 WRITE-TO-PRINTER.
047100      WRITE PRINTER-RECORD BEFORE ADVANCING 1.
047200      ADD 1 TO LINE-COUNT.
047300
047400 LINE-FEED.
047500      MOVE SPACE TO PRINTER-RECORD.
047600      PERFORM WRITE-TO-PRINTER.
047700
047800 START-NEXT-PAGE.
047900      PERFORM END-LAST-PAGE.
048000      PERFORM START-NEW-PAGE.
048100
048200 START-NEW-PAGE.
```

BD
2

continues

Listing B2.6. continued

```
048300        ADD 1 TO PAGE-NUMBER.
048400        MOVE PAGE-NUMBER TO PRINT-PAGE-NUMBER.
048500        MOVE TITLE-LINE TO PRINTER-RECORD.
048600        PERFORM WRITE-TO-PRINTER.
048700        PERFORM LINE-FEED.
048800        MOVE LEGEND-LINE TO PRINTER-RECORD.
048900        PERFORM WRITE-TO-PRINTER.
049000        PERFORM LINE-FEED.
049100        MOVE COLUMN-LINE TO PRINTER-RECORD.
049200        PERFORM WRITE-TO-PRINTER.
049300        PERFORM LINE-FEED.
049400
049500 END-LAST-PAGE.
049600     IF PAGE-NUMBER > 0
049700          PERFORM FORM-FEED.
049800     MOVE ZERO TO LINE-COUNT.
049900
050000 FORM-FEED.
050100     MOVE SPACE TO PRINTER-RECORD.
050200     WRITE PRINTER-RECORD BEFORE ADVANCING PAGE.
050300
050400*--------------------------------
050500* Read first, read next routines
050600*--------------------------------
050700 READ-FIRST-VALID-WORK.
050800     PERFORM READ-NEXT-VALID-WORK.
050900
051000 READ-NEXT-VALID-WORK.
051100     PERFORM READ-NEXT-WORK-RECORD.
051200
051300 READ-NEXT-WORK-RECORD.
051400     MOVE "N" TO WORK-FILE-AT-END.
051500     READ WORK-FILE NEXT RECORD
051600          AT END MOVE "Y" TO WORK-FILE-AT-END.
051700
```

```
                                   SALES REPORT              PAGE:    1
 STORE:   1

 DIVISION DEPARTMENT CATEGORY                     AMOUNT

        1          1          1     WEIGHTS       237.57
                               2     MACHINES      475.14
                     DEPT  1 EXERCISE     TOTAL    712.71

                   2          3     SUN GLASSES   712.71
                               4     VITAMINS       50.28
```

```
            DEPT  2 MISCELLANEOUS   TOTAL    762.99

         DIVISION  1 ATHLETICS        TOTAL   1,475.70

   2        3          5     MEN'S CLOTHES      287.85
                       6     WOMEN'S CLOTHES    525.42
            DEPT  3 SPORT CLOTHES   TOTAL    813.27

            4          7     TENNIS             762.99
                       8     SOCCER             100.56
            DEPT  4 EQUIPMENT       TOTAL    863.55

         DIVISION  2 SPORTING GOODS  TOTAL   1,676.82

   3        5          9     TENTS              338.13
                      10     SLEEPING BAGS      575.70
            DEPT  5 CAMP EQUIPMENT  TOTAL    913.83

            6         11     CLOTHING            86.73-
                      12     HIKING BOOTS       150.84
            DEPT  6 CAMPING CLOTHES TOTAL     64.11

         DIVISION  3 CAMPING         TOTAL    977.94


            STORE  1               TOTAL   4,130.46
                              SALES REPORT              PAGE:    2
```

STORE: 2

```
DIVISION DEPARTMENT CATEGORY            AMOUNT

   1        1          1     WEIGHTS            388.41
                       2     MACHINES           625.98
            DEPT  1 EXERCISE        TOTAL   1,014.39

            2          3     SUN GLASSES         36.45-
                       4     VITAMINS           201.12
            DEPT  2 MISCELLANEOUS   TOTAL    164.67

         DIVISION  1 ATHLETICS        TOTAL   1,179.06

   2        3          5     MEN'S CLOTHES      438.69
                       6     WOMEN'S CLOTHES    676.26
            DEPT  3 SPORT CLOTHES   TOTAL   1,114.95

            4          7     TENNIS              13.83
                       8     SOCCER             251.40
            DEPT  4 EQUIPMENT       TOTAL    265.23

         DIVISION  2 SPORTING GOODS  TOTAL   1,380.18

   3        5          9     TENTS              488.97
                      10     SLEEPING BAGS      726.54
            DEPT  5 CAMP EQUIPMENT  TOTAL   1,215.51
```

BD
2

```
            6          11    CLOTHING              64.11
                       12    HIKING BOOTS         301.68
                  DEPT 6 CAMPING CLOTHES TOTAL    365.79

            DIVISION 3 CAMPING          TOTAL   1,581.30


                  STORE 2                 TOTAL   4,140.54
```

                                SALES REPORT   PAGE: 3

STORE: 3

DIVISION DEPARTMENT CATEGORY   AMOUNT

```
      1          1          1    WEIGHTS              539.25
                            2    MACHINES             776.82
                  DEPT 1 EXERCISE        TOTAL   1,316.07

                 2          3    SUN GLASSES          114.39
                            4    VITAMINS             351.96
                  DEPT 2 MISCELLANEOUS   TOTAL     466.35

            DIVISION 1 ATHLETICS         TOTAL   1,782.42

      2          3          5    MEN'S CLOTHES        589.53
                            6    WOMEN'S CLOTHES       72.90-
                  DEPT 3 SPORT CLOTHES   TOTAL     516.63

                 4          7    TENNIS               164.67
                            8    SOCCER               402.24
                  DEPT 4 EQUIPMENT       TOTAL     566.91

            DIVISION 2 SPORTING GOODS  TOTAL   1,083.54

      3          5          9    TENTS                639.81
                           10    SLEEPING BAGS         22.62-
                  DEPT 5 CAMP EQUIPMENT  TOTAL     617.19

                 6         11    CLOTHING             214.95
                           12    HIKING BOOTS         452.52
                  DEPT 6 CAMPING CLOTHES TOTAL     667.47

            DIVISION 3 CAMPING          TOTAL   1,284.66


                  STORE 3                 TOTAL   4,150.62
```

                                SALES REPORT   PAGE: 4

STORE: 4

DIVISION DEPARTMENT CATEGORY   AMOUNT

```
      1          1          1    WEIGHTS              690.09
                            2    MACHINES              27.66
                  DEPT 1 EXERCISE        TOTAL     717.75
```

```
          2            3      SUN GLASSES      265.23
                       4      VITAMINS         502.80
              DEPT  2 MISCELLANEOUS   TOTAL    768.03

          DIVISION  1 ATHLETICS       TOTAL  1,485.78

   2       3            5      MEN'S CLOTHES    740.37
                        6      WOMEN'S CLOTHES   77.94
              DEPT  3 SPORT CLOTHES   TOTAL     818.31

           4            7      TENNIS           315.51
                        8      SOCCER           553.08
              DEPT  4 EQUIPMENT       TOTAL     868.59

          DIVISION  2 SPORTING GOODS  TOTAL  1,686.90

   3       5            9      TENTS            790.65
                       10      SLEEPING BAGS    128.22
              DEPT  5 CAMP EQUIPMENT   TOTAL    918.87

           6           11      CLOTHING         365.79
                       12      HIKING BOOTS     603.36
              DEPT  6 CAMPING CLOTHES TOTAL     969.15

          DIVISION  3 CAMPING         TOTAL  1,888.02

              STORE  4               TOTAL  5,060.70
                                SALES REPORT          PAGE:   5

STORE:  5

DIVISION DEPARTMENT CATEGORY                   AMOUNT

   1       1            1      WEIGHTS           59.07-
                        2      MACHINES         178.50
              DEPT  1 EXERCISE        TOTAL     119.43

           2            3      SUN GLASSES      416.07
                        4      VITAMINS         653.64
              DEPT  2 MISCELLANEOUS   TOTAL   1,069.71

          DIVISION  1 ATHLETICS       TOTAL  1,189.14

   2       3            5      MEN'S CLOTHES      8.79-
                        6      WOMEN'S CLOTHES  228.78
              DEPT  3 SPORT CLOTHES   TOTAL     219.99

           4            7      TENNIS           466.35
                        8      SOCCER           703.92
              DEPT  4 EQUIPMENT       TOTAL   1,170.27

          DIVISION  2 SPORTING GOODS  TOTAL  1,390.26

   3       5            9      TENTS             41.49
```

```
                    10    SLEEPING BAGS      279.06
          DEPT  5 CAMP EQUIPMENT   TOTAL    320.55

             6      11    CLOTHING           516.63
                    12    HIKING BOOTS       754.20
          DEPT  6 CAMPING CLOTHES TOTAL   1,270.83

      DIVISION  3 CAMPING          TOTAL   1,591.38

          STORE  5                  TOTAL   4,170.78
```

```
                              SALES REPORT                    PAGE:    6

          STORE:   6

          DIVISION DEPARTMENT CATEGORY              AMOUNT

             1        1        1    WEIGHTS           91.77
                               2    MACHINES         329.34
                      DEPT  1 EXERCISE      TOTAL    421.11

                      2        3    SUN GLASSES      566.91
                               4    VITAMINS          95.52-
                      DEPT  2 MISCELLANEOUS  TOTAL    471.39

                 DIVISION  1 ATHLETICS      TOTAL    892.50

             2        3        5    MEN'S CLOTHES    142.05
                               6    WOMEN'S CLOTHES  379.62
                      DEPT  3 SPORT CLOTHES  TOTAL    521.67

                      4        7    TENNIS           617.19
                               8    SOCCER            45.24-
                      DEPT  4 EQUIPMENT      TOTAL    571.95

                 DIVISION  2 SPORTING GOODS  TOTAL  1,093.62

             3        5        9    TENTS            192.33
                              10    SLEEPING BAGS    429.90
                      DEPT  5 CAMP EQUIPMENT  TOTAL   622.23

                      6       11    CLOTHING         667.47
                              12    HIKING BOOTS       5.04
                      DEPT  6 CAMPING CLOTHES TOTAL   672.51

                 DIVISION  3 CAMPING        TOTAL  1,294.74

                 STORE  6                   TOTAL  3,280.86

                 GRAND                      TOTAL 24,933.96
```

 ANALYSIS The tables for THE-DIVISIONS, THE-DEPARTMENTS, and THE-CATEGORIES are defined at lines 006800, 008100, and 010000, respectively.

2

The division name is loaded in the END-ONE-DIVISION as part of PRINT-DIVISION-TOTAL at line 036800. This paragraph performs LOAD-DIVISION-NAME at line 037400. LOAD-DIVISION-NAME at line 038000 uses the SEARCH verb to locate the division name using the CURRENT-DIVISION.

The department name is loaded using similar logic in the END-ONE-DEPARTMENT as part of PRINT-DEPARTMENT-TOTAL at line 041200. This paragraph performs LOAD-DEPARTMENT-NAME at line 042400. LOAD-DEPARTMENT-NAME at line 042400 uses the SEARCH verb to locate the department name using the CURRENT-DEPARTMENT.

The category name is loaded in the detail printing as part of PRINT-THE-RECORD at line 044700. This paragraph performs LOAD-CATEGORY-NAME at line 045000. LOAD-CATEGORY-NAME at line 045800 uses the SEARCH verb to locate the category name using the CURRENT-CATEGORY.

Code, compile, and run slsrpt03.cbl to see these internal tables being used to fill in the names.

STRING

The STRING verb can be used to combine several fields into one by appending the input fields end to end.

 The action of appending fields one behind the other into a single field is called *concatenation*.

In Figure B2.2, 30 bytes have been used to define three variables, each containing a ten-character portion of a name.

The data definition for the fields described in Figure B2.2 is illustrated in Listing B2.7.

Figure B2.2.

Three separate name fields.

Field Name	LAST-NAME										FIRST-NAME										MIDDLE-NAME									
Character	J	O	N	E	S						J	O	H	N							P	A	U	L						
Position	1	2	3	4	5	6	7	8	9	10	11	12	13	14	15	16	17	18	19	20	21	22	23	24	25	26	27	28	29	30

TYPE **Listing B2.7. The data definition of three names.**

```
000900 01  THE-NAME
001000     05  LAST-NAME        PIC X(10).
001100     05  FIRST-NAME       PIC X(10).
001200     05  MIDDLE-NAME      PIC X(10).
```

If these fields were printed by moving them to print fields, as shown in Listing B2.8, the resulting printed name would contain all the extra spaces at the end of each name.

TYPE Listing B2.8. Printing the names.

```
001300 01  DETAIL-LINE.
001400     05  PRINT-FIRST        PIC X(10).
001500     05  FILLER             PIC X(1).
001600     05  PRINT-MIDDLE       PIC X(10).
001700     05  FILLER             PIC X(1).
001800     05  PRINT-LAST         PIC X(10).
.......
010300         MOVE SPACE TO DETAIL-LINE.
010400         MOVE FIRST-NAME TO PRINT-FIRST.
010500         MOVE MIDDLE-NAME TO PRINT-MIDDLE.
010600         MOVE LAST-NAME TO PRINT-MIDDLE.
010700         PERFORM PRINT-DETAIL-LINE.
```

OUTPUT

```
JOHN        PAUL        JONES
```

A better approach is to use the STRING verb. This can be used to concatenate all three fields, ignoring the spaces in each field. A STRING verb will combine two or more fields into a destination field. The input fields may be truncated by a value used to specify that the STRING action is to stop at a specific character. The input field may also be included by its full length. This is the STRING syntax:

```
STRING
  value
    DELIMITED BY delimiter
  value
    DELIMITED BY delimiter
  INTO variable.
```

The following is an example:

```
STRING
  FIRST-NAME
    DELIMITED BY SPACE
  LAST-NAME
    DELIMITED BY SPACE
  INTO FULL-NAME.
```

The output of the code fragment in Listing B2.9 is better, but now we have eliminated all spaces.

TYPE Listing B2.9. Using STRING to put fields together.

```
001300 01  DETAIL-LINE.
001400     05  PRINT-WHOLE-NAME     PIC X(30).
.......
010300         MOVE SPACE TO DETAIL-LINE.
010400         STRING
```

```
010500        FIRST-NAME DELIMITED BY SPACE
010600        MIDDLE-NAME DELIMITED BY SPACE
010700        LAST-NAME DELIMITED BY SPACE
010800          INTO PRINT-WHOLE-NAME.
010900        PERFORM PRINT-DETAIL-LINE.
```

OUTPUT   JOHNPAULJONES

ANALYSIS   The STRING must add spaces to break the fields apart. PRINT-WHOLE-NAME is increased to accommodate a name that fills all 30 spaces and also needs the two extra spaces to separate the names. In Listing B2.10 at lines 010600 and 010800, a space is inserted between each field.

TYPE   ## Listing B2.10. Adding extra spaces.

```
001300 01  DETAIL-LINE.
001400     05  PRINT-WHOLE-NAME      PIC X(32).
.......
010300        MOVE SPACE TO DETAIL-LINE.
010400        STRING
010500         FIRST-NAME DELIMITED BY SPACE
010600         " " DELIMITED BY SIZE
010700         MIDDLE-NAME DELIMITED BY SPACE
010800         " " DELIMITED BY SIZE
010900         LAST-NAME DELIMITED BY SPACE
011000           INTO PRINT-WHOLE-NAME.
011100         PERFORM PRINT-DETAIL-LINE.
```

OUTPUT   JOHN PAUL JONES

The STRING verb frequently is used to format names to print envelopes and for other mailing list activities.

UNSTRING

As indicated by the name, the UNSTRING verb does the opposite of the STRING verb, enabling you to break a single field on a specific character into several separate fields. It is used less often than the STRING verb. The following is the UNSTRING syntax:

```
UNSTRING variable
  DELIMITED BY [ALL] delimiter
         [ OR [ALL] delimiter ]
  INTO variable . . .
```

Here is an example:

```
UNSTRING INPUT-DATA
   DELIMITED BY SPACE
   INTO FIRST-NAME
        LAST-NAME
```

UNSTRING can be used to make data entry seem more natural and then break the results into separate fields. Listing B2.11 is an example of using UNSTRING.

TYPE **Listing B2.11. Unstringing input.**

```
001100 01   INPUT-DATA              PIC X(50).
001200
001300 01   FORMATTED-NAME.
001400      05  FIRST-NAME          PIC X(25).
001500      05  LAST-NAME           PIC X(25).
......
010700      DISPLAY "ENTER FIRST AND LAST NAMES".
010800      DISPLAY "WITH A SPACE BETWEEN THE NAMES".
010900      ACCEPT INPUT-DATA.
011000      MOVE SPACE TO FORMATTED-NAME.
011100      UNSTRING INPUT-DATA
011200         DELIMITED BY ALL SPACE
011300         INTO FIRST-NAME
011400               LAST-NAME.
011500
```

INSPECT

The INSPECT verb, which you used to convert lowercase to uppercase, has two other formats.

INSPECT can be used to count characters in a field. In the following example, SLASH-COUNTER (if it starts with a zero value) will contain the number of / characters that appear in DATE-FIELD. Here is the syntax:

```
INSPECT variable
   TALLYING counter
      FOR [ALL] character
```

and the example:

```
INSPECT DATE-FIELD
   TALLYING SLASH-COUNTER
      FOR ALL "/"
```

The second version of INSPECT is more useful. INSPECT can be used to convert a single character in much the same way it is used to convert multiple characters. Multiple characters are converted by using INSPECT CONVERTING; a single character is converted by using INSPECT REPLACING. This is the syntax:

```
INSPECT variable
  REPLACING [ALL]
    character BY character.
```

and the example:

```
INSPECT FORMATTED-DATE
  REPLACING ALL
    "/" BY "-"
```

This version can be used to change formatting characters after a value has been moved into an edited field. In Listing B2.12, the date is changed to display with dashes instead of slashes.

TYPE **Listing B2.12. Using INSPECT.**

```
000900 01  FORMATTED-DATE      PIC Z9/99/9999.
001000 01  DATE-MMDDCCYY        PIC 9(8).
......
010100     MOVE 02141995 TO DATE-MMDDCCYY.
010200     MOVE DATE-MMDDCCYY TO FORMATTED-DATE.
010300     DISPLAY FORMATTED-DATE.
010400     INSPECT FORMATTED-DATE
010500       REPLACING ALL "\" BY "-".
010600     DISPLAY FORMATTED-DATE.
```

OUTPUT The output of Listing B2.12 illustrates the date format, before and after the INSPECT is used to change the formatting characters:

```
2/14/1995
2-14-1995
```

CALL USING

The CALL verb is used to execute one COBOL program from within another. In Day 18, "Calling Other Programs," you used the CALL verb to build a menu that executed different programs. In those and subsequent examples, there was no way for the called and calling program to share information. The DATA DIVISION of both the called and calling program were separate from each other, and neither program could access variables in the other program.

It is possible to CALL a program and pass it a variable from the calling program with this syntax:

```
CALL "TIMEDIT"
  USING variable
        [variable . . ]
```

The following is an example:

```
CALL "TIMEDIT"
    USING TIME-HHMMSS
          FORMATTED-TIME
          ZERO-TIME-IS-OK
```

The calling program, the program that passes the value to another program, contains the definition of the data to be passed in WORKING-STORAGE just like any other data item. The variable can be shared by the calling and called program, but the variable really exists only in the DATA DIVISION of the calling program. The USING phrase in CALL USING is really a signal to the compiler that a value must be passed to let the called program know where the variables exist in the calling program.

The called program must receive the value. The definition of the data item in a called program is a bit more complicated. Variables that exist in a calling program but are used in a called program are defined in a special section of the DATA DIVISION in the called program. This is the LINKAGE SECTION, and an example is shown starting at line 002100 in Listing B2.13.

TYPE **Listing B2.13. The LINKAGE SECTION.**

```
001000 DATA DIVISION.
001100 FILE SECTION.
001200
001300 WORKING-STORAGE SECTION.
001400
001500 77  VALID-TIME-FLAG     PIC X.
001600     88  TIME-IS-INVALID  VALUE "N".
001700     88  TIME-IS-ZERO     VALUE "0".
001800     88  TIME-IS-VALID    VALUE "Y".
001900     88  TIME-IS-OK       VALUES "Y" "0".
002000
002100 LINKAGE SECTION.
002200*--------------------------------
002300* Fields passed for TIME routines.
002400*--------------------------------
002500 77  FORMATTED-TIME      PIC Z9/99/99.
002600
002700 01  TIME-HHMMSS     PIC 9(6).
002800 01  FILLER REDEFINES TIME-HHMMSS.
002900     05  TIME-HH      PIC 99.
003000     05  TIME-MM      PIC 99.
003100     05  TIME-SS      PIC 99.
003200
003300 77  ZERO-TIME-IS-OK    PIC X VALUE "N".
003400
```

ANALYSIS The LINKAGE SECTION starts at line 002100. It contains a description of the data that is expected to be passed by the calling program. The LINKAGE SECTION is used by the called program as a description of the variables that are passed by the calling program. However, variables defined in the LINKAGE SECTION do not exist in the called program; they exist in the calling program.

For example, at line 002700, TIME-HHMMSS is defined as a PIC 9(6). This indicates that 6 bytes of data that are passed by the calling program are to be treated as a PIC 9(6) in the called program. The called program will use the name TIME-HHMMSS as the name of these 6 bytes. These 6 bytes could be passed to a called program that used the value to format a formatted time for display, or to be printed at the top of a report along with the date to indicate the date and time that report was run.

One other thing that a called program must do is name the variables that are passed from the calling program in the order in which they are passed. This is taken care of by adding USING to the PROCEDURE DIVISION of a called program, as shown in Listing B2.14.

TYPE **Listing B2.14. PROCEDURE DIVISION USING.**

```
003500 PROCEDURE DIVISION
003600     USING TIME-HHMMSS FORMATTED-TIME
003700          ZERO-TIME-IS-OK.
003800
```

 At lines 003500–003700, the PROCEDURE DIVISION is extended by adding a USING list. The USING list in the called program must match, in sequence, the variables passed in the CALL USING list of the calling program.

Listing B2.15 is a program to enter time values and display them. Instead of doing the data entry and validation in the program, it calls another program to do this.

TYPE **Listing B2.15. A calling program.**

```
000100 IDENTIFICATION DIVISION.
000200 PROGRAM-ID. TIME02.
000300*-------------------------------
000400* Testing Time Entry and handling
000500*-------------------------------
000600 ENVIRONMENT DIVISION.
000700 INPUT-OUTPUT SECTION.
000800 FILE-CONTROL.
000900
001000 DATA DIVISION.
001100 FILE SECTION.
001200
001300 WORKING-STORAGE SECTION.
001400
001500 77  ANY-TIME          PIC 9(6) VALUE ZEROES.
001600
001700 77  ANY-FORMATTED     PIC X(8).
001800
001900 77  FORMATTED-TIME    PIC Z9/99/99.
002000
002100 77  THE-TIME          PIC 9(6).
```

continues

Listing B2.15. continued

```
002200
002300 77  ZERO-IS-OK     PIC X VALUE "N".
002400
002500 PROCEDURE DIVISION.
002600 PROGRAM-BEGIN.
002700     PERFORM OPENING-PROCEDURE.
002800     PERFORM MAIN-PROCESS.
002900     PERFORM CLOSING-PROCEDURE.
003000
003100 PROGRAM-EXIT.
003200     EXIT PROGRAM.
003300
003400 PROGRAM-DONE.
003500     STOP RUN.
003600
003700 OPENING-PROCEDURE.
003800
003900 CLOSING-PROCEDURE.
004000
004100 MAIN-PROCESS.
004200     PERFORM GET-ANY-TIME.
004300     PERFORM DISPLAY-AND-GET-ANY-TIME
004400         UNTIL ANY-TIME = 000001.
004500
004600 GET-ANY-TIME.
004700     MOVE "Y" TO ZERO-IS-OK.
004800     PERFORM GET-THE-TIME.
004900     MOVE THE-TIME TO ANY-TIME.
005000     MOVE FORMATTED-TIME TO ANY-FORMATTED.
005100
005200 GET-THE-TIME.
005300     CALL "TIMEDIT" USING
005400         THE-TIME FORMATTED-TIME
005500         ZERO-IS-OK.
005600
005700 DISPLAY-AND-GET-ANY-TIME.
005800     PERFORM DISPLAY-THE-TIME.
005900     PERFORM GET-ANY-TIME.
006000
006100 DISPLAY-THE-TIME.
006200     DISPLAY "ANY TIME IS " ANY-FORMATTED.
006300
```

ANALYSIS The time02.cbl program calls timedit.cbl to do the data entry and testing of the field. The two programs must pass three values back and forth between the called and calling program.

The first is a field that will hold the time as a six-digit number when the data entry is completed. This field is filled in by timedit.cbl during the data entry process. The second field is a formatted version of the time. This field also is filled in by timedit.cbl and returned to `time02.cbl`. The third field is filled by `time02.cbl` and is a flag indicating whether `timedit.cbl` should accept a time entry of zeroes.

These variables are all defined in the WORKING-STORAGE section of `time02.cbl` at lines 001900, 002100, and 002300. The values are passed to `timedit.cbl` at lines 005300–005500.

Listing B2.16 is the called program. It has a LINKAGE SECTION in the DATA DIVISION.

TYPE **Listing B2.16. The called program.**

```
000100 IDENTIFICATION DIVISION.
000200 PROGRAM-ID. TIMEDIT.
000300*--------------------------------
000400* TIME ENTRY AND VALIDATION SUB PROGRAM
000500*--------------------------------
000600 ENVIRONMENT DIVISION.
000700 INPUT-OUTPUT SECTION.
000800 FILE-CONTROL.
000900
001000 DATA DIVISION.
001100 FILE SECTION.
001200
001300 WORKING-STORAGE SECTION.
001400
001500 77  VALID-TIME-FLAG      PIC X.
001600     88  TIME-IS-INVALID   VALUE "N".
001700     88  TIME-IS-ZERO      VALUE "0".
001800     88  TIME-IS-VALID     VALUE "Y".
001900     88  TIME-IS-OK        VALUES "Y" "0".
002000
002100 LINKAGE SECTION.
002200*--------------------------------
002300* Fields passed for TIME routines.
002400*--------------------------------
002500 77  FORMATTED-TIME       PIC Z9/99/99.
002600
002700 01  TIME-HHMMSS          PIC 9(6).
002800 01  FILLER REDEFINES TIME-HHMMSS.
002900     05  TIME-HH          PIC 99.
003000     05  TIME-MM          PIC 99.
003100     05  TIME-SS          PIC 99.
003200
003300 77  ZERO-TIME-IS-OK      PIC X VALUE "N".
003400
003500 PROCEDURE DIVISION
003600     USING TIME-HHMMSS FORMATTED-TIME
003700          ZERO-TIME-IS-OK.
003800
003900 PROGRAM-BEGIN.
004000     PERFORM OPENING-PROCEDURE.
004100     PERFORM MAIN-PROCESS.
```

continues

Listing B2.16. continued

```
004200      PERFORM CLOSING-PROCEDURE.
004300
004400 PROGRAM-EXIT.
004500      EXIT PROGRAM.
004600
004700 PROGRAM-DONE.
004800      STOP RUN.
004900
005000 OPENING-PROCEDURE.
005100
005200 CLOSING-PROCEDURE.
005300
005400 MAIN-PROCESS.
005500      PERFORM GET-A-TIME.
005600
005700 GET-A-TIME.
005800      PERFORM ACCEPT-A-TIME.
005900      PERFORM RE-ACCEPT-A-TIME
006000          UNTIL TIME-IS-OK.
006100
006200 ACCEPT-A-TIME.
006300      DISPLAY "ENTER A TIME (HH:MM:SS)".
006400
006500      ACCEPT FORMATTED-TIME.
006600
006700      PERFORM EDIT-CHECK-TIME.
006800
006900 RE-ACCEPT-A-TIME.
007000      DISPLAY "INVALID TIME".
007100
007200      PERFORM ACCEPT-A-TIME.
007300
007400 EDIT-CHECK-TIME.
007500      PERFORM EDIT-TIME.
007600      PERFORM CHECK-TIME.
007700      PERFORM FORMAT-THE-TIME.
007800
007900 EDIT-TIME.
008000      MOVE FORMATTED-TIME TO TIME-HHMMSS.
008100
008200 CHECK-TIME.
008300      MOVE "Y" TO VALID-TIME-FLAG.
008400      IF TIME-HHMMSS = ZEROES
008500          IF ZERO-TIME-IS-OK = "Y"
008600              MOVE "0" TO VALID-TIME-FLAG
008700          ELSE
008800              MOVE "N" TO VALID-TIME-FLAG
008900      ELSE
009000      IF TIME-HH > 24
009100          MOVE "N" TO VALID-TIME-FLAG
009200      ELSE
009300      IF TIME-MM > 59
009400          MOVE "N" TO VALID-TIME-FLAG
009500      ELSE
009600      IF TIME-SS > 59
```

```
009700          MOVE "N" TO VALID-TIME-FLAG
009800       ELSE
009900       IF TIME-HHMMSS > 240000
010000          MOVE "N" TO VALID-TIME-FLAG.
010100
010200 FORMAT-THE-TIME.
010300    MOVE TIME-HHMMSS TO FORMATTED-TIME.
010400    INSPECT FORMATTED-TIME
010500      REPLACING ALL "/" BY ":".
010600
```

OUTPUT The output of the combined time02.cbl and timedit.cbl shows the two programs working together. Each line of output is marked to indicate which program is doing the work:

```
ENTER A TIME (HH:MM:SS)————————————————— timedit.cbl
111495 ————————————————————————————————— user entry still in timedit.cbl
INVALID TIME—————————————————————————————error message from timedit.cbl
ENTER A TIME (HH:MM:SS) ——————————————————still in timedit.cbl
111435 ——————————————————————————————————user tries again in timedit.cbl
ANY TIME IS 11:14:35—————————————————————displayed in time02.cbl
ENTER A TIME (HH:MM:SS)——————————————————back in timedit.cbl
```

ANALYSIS The entries in the LINKAGE SECTION at lines 002500, 002700, and 003300 describe three variables that are expected to be passed from the calling program. The variables don't have to have the same names, but they must be the same size (same number of bytes).

After the "shape" of the variables is described in the LINKAGE SECTION, the PROCEDURE DIVISION at lines 003500–003700 lists the values that are passed from the calling program.

If you compare this list with lines 005300–005500 in time02.cbl, Listing B2.15, you will find that the variables match in length.

The first variable is a 6-byte field called THE-TIME in time02.cbl and TIME-HHMMSS in timedit.cbl. The second variable is an 8-byte edited field called FORMATTED-TIME in both programs. The third field is a single byte called ZERO-IS-OK in time02.cbl and ZERO-TIME-IS-OK in timedit.cbl.

The timedit.cbl program is a fairly straightforward program that accepts data entry of a time field and checks whether it is valid. If the passed flag indicates that a zero entry is OK, the program allows the user to enter zeroes; otherwise, it forces an entry of a valid time in the range of 000001–240000.

One notable piece of code appears at lines 010300–010500 and uses the INSPECT REPLACING verb to convert the slashes (/) in the formatted field to colons (:), which are more appropriate for time formatting (for example, 11:14:29).

Code and compile time02.cbl and timedit.cbl and link them if necessary. Run time02.cbl and see that the called program timedit.cbl is correctly entering and validating the time fields. Enter a value of 1 for the time to stop the program.

ACCEPT FROM DATE or TIME

Usually, the ACCEPT verb is used to receive input keyboard information into a field. The ACCEPT verb has an implied KEYBOARD as the device from which information is being accepted:

```
ACCEPT INPUT-DATA [FROM KEYBOARD].
```

You also may accept data from the computer's internal system clock. This clock provides at least two pieces of information that you might want in a program: today's date and the current time. To extract the date, you must ACCEPT FROM DATE. To extract the time, ACCEPT FROM TIME. Use this syntax:

```
ACCEPT variable
    FROM DATE

ACCEPT variable
    FROM TIME
```

The following is an example:

```
ACCEPT TODAYS-DATE
    FROM DATE

ACCEPT THE-TIME
    FROM TIME.
```

The variable used for today's date must be defined as a PIC 9(6), and the date is returned in YYMMDD format. Another mechanism has been developed for 8-digit dates as the year 2000 approaches. The variable for the time must be a PIC 9(8), and the value returned is hours, minutes, seconds, and hundredths of seconds. The time used is a 24-hour clock, so 3:56 PM would be returned as 15560000.

System date and time can be used to identify the run date and time of a report, as shown in Listing B2.17, a code fragment that could be used in a report program.

TYPE **Listing B2.17. Using the system date and time.**

```
000100 IDENTIFICATION DIVISION.
000200 PROGRAM-ID. SLSRPT04.
000300*-------------------------------
000400* Print test sales data
000500*-------------------------------
000600 ENVIRONMENT DIVISION.
000700 INPUT-OUTPUT SECTION.
000800 FILE-CONTROL.
000900
001000*-------------------------------
001100* SLSALES.CBL
001200*-------------------------------
001300     SELECT SALES-FILE
001400         ASSIGN TO "SALES"
001500         ORGANIZATION IS SEQUENTIAL.
001600
```

```
001700     SELECT WORK-FILE
001800         ASSIGN TO "WORK"
001900         ORGANIZATION IS SEQUENTIAL.
002000
002100     SELECT SORT-FILE
002200         ASSIGN TO "SORT".
002300
002400     SELECT PRINTER-FILE
002500         ASSIGN TO PRINTER
002600         ORGANIZATION IS LINE SEQUENTIAL.
002700
002800 DATA DIVISION.
002900 FILE SECTION.
003000
003100*--------------------------------
003200* FDSALES.CBL
003300* Temporary daily sales file.
003400*--------------------------------
003500 FD  SALES-FILE
003600     LABEL RECORDS ARE STANDARD.
003700 01  SALES-RECORD.
003800     05  SALES-STORE          PIC 9(2).
003900     05  SALES-DIVISION       PIC 9(2).
004000     05  SALES-DEPARTMENT     PIC 9(2).
004100     05  SALES-CATEGORY       PIC 9(2).
004200     05  SALES-AMOUNT         PIC S9(6)V99.
004300
004400 FD  WORK-FILE
004500     LABEL RECORDS ARE STANDARD.
004600 01  WORK-RECORD.
004700     05  WORK-STORE           PIC 9(2).
004800     05  WORK-DIVISION        PIC 9(2).
004900     05  WORK-DEPARTMENT      PIC 9(2).
005000     05  WORK-CATEGORY        PIC 9(2).
005100     05  WORK-AMOUNT          PIC S9(6)V99.
005200
005300 SD  SORT-FILE
005400     LABEL RECORDS ARE STANDARD.
005500 01  SORT-RECORD.
005600     05  SORT-STORE           PIC 9(2).
005700     05  SORT-DIVISION        PIC 9(2).
005800     05  SORT-DEPARTMENT      PIC 9(2).
005900     05  SORT-CATEGORY        PIC 9(2).
006000     05  SORT-AMOUNT          PIC S9(6)V99.
006100
006200 FD  PRINTER-FILE
006300     LABEL RECORDS ARE OMITTED.
006400 01  PRINTER-RECORD           PIC X(80).
006500
006600 WORKING-STORAGE SECTION.
006700
006800 01  THE-DIVISIONS.
006900     05  FILLER      PIC 99 VALUE 01.
007000     05  FILLER      PIC X(15) VALUE "ATHLETICS".
007100     05  FILLER      PIC 99 VALUE 02.
```

continues

Listing B2.17. continued

```
007200       05  FILLER       PIC X(15) VALUE "SPORTING GOODS".
007300       05  FILLER       PIC 99 VALUE 03.
007400       05  FILLER       PIC X(15) VALUE "CAMPING".
007500 01  FILLER REDEFINES THE-DIVISIONS.
007600       05  DIVISION-TABLE OCCURS 3 TIMES
007700            INDEXED BY DIVISION-INDEX.
007800            10  DIVISION-NUMBER         PIC 99.
007900            10  DIVISION-NAME           PIC X(15).
008000
008100 01  THE-DEPARTMENTS.
008200       05  FILLER       PIC 99 VALUE 01.
008300       05  FILLER       PIC X(15) VALUE "EXERCISE".
008400       05  FILLER       PIC 99 VALUE 02.
008500       05  FILLER       PIC X(15) VALUE "MISCELLANEOUS".
008600       05  FILLER       PIC 99 VALUE 03.
008700       05  FILLER       PIC X(15) VALUE "SPORT CLOTHES".
008800       05  FILLER       PIC 99 VALUE 04.
008900       05  FILLER       PIC X(15) VALUE "EQUIPMENT".
009000       05  FILLER       PIC 99 VALUE 05.
009100       05  FILLER       PIC X(15) VALUE "CAMP EQUIPMENT".
009200       05  FILLER       PIC 99 VALUE 06.
009300       05  FILLER       PIC X(15) VALUE "CAMPING CLOTHES".
009400 01  FILLER REDEFINES THE-DEPARTMENTS.
009500       05  DEPARTMENT-TABLE OCCURS 6 TIMES
009600            INDEXED BY DEPARTMENT-INDEX.
009700            10  DEPARTMENT-NUMBER       PIC 99.
009800            10  DEPARTMENT-NAME         PIC X(15).
009900
010000 01  THE-CATEGORIES.
010100       05  FILLER       PIC 99 VALUE 01.
010200       05  FILLER       PIC X(15) VALUE "WEIGHTS".
010300       05  FILLER       PIC 99 VALUE 02.
010400       05  FILLER       PIC X(15) VALUE "MACHINES".
010500       05  FILLER       PIC 99 VALUE 03.
010600       05  FILLER       PIC X(15) VALUE "SUN GLASSES".
010700       05  FILLER       PIC 99 VALUE 04.
010800       05  FILLER       PIC X(15) VALUE "VITAMINS".
010900       05  FILLER       PIC 99 VALUE 05.
011000       05  FILLER       PIC X(15) VALUE "MEN'S CLOTHES".
011100       05  FILLER       PIC 99 VALUE 06.
011200       05  FILLER       PIC X(15) VALUE "WOMEN'S CLOTHES".
011300       05  FILLER       PIC 99 VALUE 07.
011400       05  FILLER       PIC X(15) VALUE "TENNIS".
011500       05  FILLER       PIC 99 VALUE 08.
011600       05  FILLER       PIC X(15) VALUE "SOCCER".
011700       05  FILLER       PIC 99 VALUE 09.
011800       05  FILLER       PIC X(15) VALUE "TENTS".
011900       05  FILLER       PIC 99 VALUE 10.
012000       05  FILLER       PIC X(15) VALUE "SLEEPING BAGS".
012100       05  FILLER       PIC 99 VALUE 11.
012200       05  FILLER       PIC X(15) VALUE "CLOTHING".
012300       05  FILLER       PIC 99 VALUE 12.
012400       05  FILLER       PIC X(15) VALUE "HIKING BOOTS".
012500 01  FILLER REDEFINES THE-CATEGORIES.
```

```
012600     05  CATEGORY-TABLE OCCURS 12 TIMES
012700         INDEXED BY CATEGORY-INDEX.
012800       10  CATEGORY-NUMBER          PIC 99.
012900       10  CATEGORY-NAME            PIC X(15).
013000
013100 77 OK-TO-PROCESS          PIC X.
013200
013300     COPY "WSCASE01.CBL".
013400
013500 01  LEGEND-LINE.
013600     05  FILLER              PIC X(6) VALUE "STORE:".
013700     05  FILLER              PIC X(1) VALUE SPACE.
013800     05  PRINT-STORE         PIC Z9.
013900
014000 01  DETAIL-LINE.
014100     05  FILLER                 PIC X(3) VALUE SPACE.
014200     05  PRINT-DIVISION         PIC Z9.
014300     05  FILLER                 PIC X(4) VALUE SPACE.
014400     05  FILLER                 PIC X(3) VALUE SPACE.
014500     05  PRINT-DEPARTMENT       PIC Z9.
014600     05  FILLER                 PIC X(6) VALUE SPACE.
014700     05  FILLER                 PIC X(3) VALUE SPACE.
014800     05  PRINT-CATEGORY         PIC Z9.
014900     05  FILLER                 PIC X(4) VALUE SPACE.
015000     05  PRINT-CATEGORY-NAME    PIC X(15).
015100     05  FILLER                 PIC X(1) VALUE SPACE.
015200     05  PRINT-AMOUNT           PIC ZZZ,ZZ9.99-.
015300
015400 01  COLUMN-LINE.
015500     05  FILLER        PIC X(8)  VALUE "DIVISION".
015600     05  FILLER        PIC X(1)  VALUE SPACE.
015700     05  FILLER        PIC X(10) VALUE "DEPARTMENT".
015800     05  FILLER        PIC X(1)  VALUE SPACE.
015900     05  FILLER        PIC X(8)  VALUE "CATEGORY".
016000     05  FILLER        PIC X(1)  VALUE SPACE.
016100     05  FILLER        PIC X(15) VALUE SPACE.
016200     05  FILLER        PIC X(5)  VALUE SPACE.
016300     05  FILLER        PIC X(6)  VALUE "AMOUNT".
016400
016500 01  TITLE-LINE.
016600     05  FILLER              PIC X(4) VALUE "RUN:".
016700     05  FORMATTED-RUN-DATE  PIC X(10).
016800     05  FILLER              PIC X(4) VALUE " AT ".
016900     05  FORMATTED-RUN-TIME  PIC X(8).
017000     05  FILLER              PIC X(10) VALUE SPACE.
017100     05  FILLER              PIC X(12)
017200         VALUE "SALES REPORT".
017300     05  FILLER              PIC X(10) VALUE SPACE.
017400     05  FILLER              PIC X(5) VALUE "PAGE:".
017500     05  FILLER              PIC X(1) VALUE SPACE.
017600     05  PRINT-PAGE-NUMBER   PIC ZZZ9.
017700
017800 01  TOTAL-LINE.
017900     05  FILLER              PIC X(11) VALUE SPACE.
```

continues

Listing B2.17. continued

```
018000      05   TOTAL-TYPE           PIC X(8).
018100      05   FILLER               PIC X(1) VALUE SPACE.
018200      05   TOTAL-NUMBER         PIC Z9.
018300      05   FILLER               PIC X(1) VALUE SPACE.
018400      05   TOTAL-NAME           PIC X(15) VALUE SPACE.
018500      05   FILLER               PIC X(1) VALUE SPACE.
018600      05   TOTAL-LITERAL        PIC X(5) VALUE "TOTAL".
018700      05   FILLER               PIC X(1) VALUE SPACE.
018800      05   PRINT-TOTAL          PIC ZZZ,ZZ9.99-.
018900
019000 77   GRAND-TOTAL-LITERAL       PIC X(8) VALUE "   GRAND".
019100 77   STORE-TOTAL-LITERAL       PIC X(8) VALUE "   STORE".
019200 77   DIVISION-TOTAL-LITERAL    PIC X(8) VALUE "DIVISION".
019300 77   DEPARTMENT-TOTAL-LITERAL  PIC X(8) VALUE "    DEPT".
019400
019500 77   WORK-FILE-AT-END          PIC X.
019600
019700 77   LINE-COUNT                PIC 999 VALUE ZERO.
019800 77   PAGE-NUMBER               PIC 9999 VALUE ZERO.
019900 77   MAXIMUM-LINES             PIC 999 VALUE 55.
020000
020100 77   RECORD-COUNT              PIC 9999 VALUE ZEROES.
020200
020300* Control break current values for store, division
020400* department.
020500 77   CURRENT-STORE             PIC 99.
020600 77   CURRENT-DIVISION          PIC 99.
020700 77   CURRENT-DEPARTMENT        PIC 99.
020800
020900* Control break accumulators
021000* GRAND TOTAL is the level 1 accumulator for the whole file
021100* STORE TOTAL is the level 2 accumulator
021200* DIVISION TOTAL is the level 3 accumulator
021300* DEPARTMENT TOTAL is the level 4 accumulator.
021400 77   GRAND-TOTAL               PIC S9(6)V99.
021500 77   STORE-TOTAL               PIC S9(6)V99.
021600 77   DIVISION-TOTAL            PIC S9(6)V99.
021700 77   DEPARTMENT-TOTAL          PIC S9(6)V99.
021800
021900* System date and time
022000 77   RUN-DATE            PIC 9(6).
022100 77   RUN-TIME            PIC 9(8).
022200
022300*-------------------------------------
022400* Fields for date routines.
022500*-------------------------------------
022600 77   FORMATTED-DATE      PIC Z9/99/9999.
022700 77   DATE-MMDDCCYY       PIC 9(8).
022800 01   DATE-CCYYMMDD       PIC 9(8).
022900 01   FILLER REDEFINES DATE-CCYYMMDD.
023000      05   DATE-CC        PIC 99.
023100      05   DATE-YY        PIC 99.
023200      05   DATE-MM        PIC 99.
023300      05   DATE-DD        PIC 99.
```

```
023400
023500*--------------------------------
023600* Fields for TIME routines.
023700*--------------------------------
023800 77  FORMATTED-TIME    PIC Z9/99/99.
023900
024000 01  TIME-HHMMSS       PIC 9(6).
024100 01  FILLER REDEFINES TIME-HHMMSS.
024200     05  TIME-HH       PIC 99.
024300     05  TIME-MM       PIC 99.
024400     05  TIME-SS       PIC 99.
024500
024600 PROCEDURE DIVISION.
024700 PROGRAM-BEGIN.
024800
024900     PERFORM OPENING-PROCEDURE.
025000     PERFORM MAIN-PROCESS.
025100     PERFORM CLOSING-PROCEDURE.
025200
025300 PROGRAM-EXIT.
025400     EXIT PROGRAM.
025500
025600 PROGRAM-DONE.
025700     STOP RUN.
025800
025900 OPENING-PROCEDURE.
026000
026100     OPEN OUTPUT PRINTER-FILE.
026200
026300 MAIN-PROCESS.
026400     PERFORM GET-OK-TO-PROCESS.
026500     PERFORM PROCESS-THE-FILE
026600         UNTIL OK-TO-PROCESS = "N".
026700
026800 CLOSING-PROCEDURE.
026900     CLOSE PRINTER-FILE.
027000
027100 GET-OK-TO-PROCESS.
027200     PERFORM ACCEPT-OK-TO-PROCESS.
027300     PERFORM RE-ACCEPT-OK-TO-PROCESS
027400         UNTIL OK-TO-PROCESS = "Y" OR "N".
027500
027600 ACCEPT-OK-TO-PROCESS.
027700     DISPLAY "PRINT SALES REPORT (Y/N)?".
027800     ACCEPT OK-TO-PROCESS.
027900     INSPECT OK-TO-PROCESS
028000        CONVERTING LOWER-ALPHA
028100        TO         UPPER-ALPHA.
028200
028300 RE-ACCEPT-OK-TO-PROCESS.
028400     DISPLAY "YOU MUST ENTER YES OR NO".
028500     PERFORM ACCEPT-OK-TO-PROCESS.
028600
028700 PROCESS-THE-FILE.
028800     PERFORM START-THE-FILE.
```

continues

Listing B2.17. continued

```
028900        PERFORM PRINT-ONE-REPORT.
029000        PERFORM END-THE-FILE.
029100
029200*       PERFORM GET-OK-TO-PROCESS.
029300        MOVE "N" TO OK-TO-PROCESS.
029400
029500 START-THE-FILE.
029600        PERFORM SORT-DATA-FILE.
029700        OPEN INPUT WORK-FILE.
029800
029900 END-THE-FILE.
030000        CLOSE WORK-FILE.
030100
030200 SORT-DATA-FILE.
030300        SORT SORT-FILE
030400            ON ASCENDING KEY SORT-STORE
030500               ASCENDING KEY SORT-DIVISION
030600               ASCENDING KEY SORT-DEPARTMENT
030700               ASCENDING KEY SORT-CATEGORY
030800            USING SALES-FILE
030900            GIVING WORK-FILE.
031000
031100* LEVEL 1 CONTROL BREAK
031200 PRINT-ONE-REPORT.
031300        PERFORM START-ONE-REPORT.
031400        PERFORM PROCESS-ALL-STORES
031500            UNTIL WORK-FILE-AT-END = "Y".
031600        PERFORM END-ONE-REPORT.
031700
031800 START-ONE-REPORT.
031900        PERFORM READ-FIRST-VALID-WORK.
032000        MOVE ZEROES TO GRAND-TOTAL.
032100
032200        PERFORM START-NEW-REPORT.
032300
032400 START-NEW-REPORT.
032500        MOVE SPACE TO DETAIL-LINE.
032600        MOVE ZEROES TO LINE-COUNT PAGE-NUMBER.
032700
032800        ACCEPT RUN-DATE FROM DATE.
032900        MOVE RUN-DATE TO DATE-CCYYMMDD.
033000        IF DATE-YY > 90
033100            MOVE 19 TO DATE-CC
033200        ELSE
033300            MOVE 20 TO DATE-CC.
033400
033500        PERFORM FORMAT-THE-DATE.
033600        MOVE FORMATTED-DATE TO FORMATTED-RUN-DATE.
033700
033800        ACCEPT RUN-TIME FROM TIME.
033900        COMPUTE TIME-HHMMSS = RUN-TIME / 100.
034000        PERFORM FORMAT-THE-TIME.
034100        MOVE FORMATTED-TIME TO FORMATTED-RUN-TIME.
034200
034300
```

2

```
034400 END-ONE-REPORT.
034500     IF RECORD-COUNT = ZEROES
034600         MOVE "NO RECORDS FOUND" TO PRINTER-RECORD
034700         PERFORM WRITE-TO-PRINTER
034800     ELSE
034900         PERFORM PRINT-GRAND-TOTAL.
035000
035100     PERFORM END-LAST-PAGE.
035200
035300 PRINT-GRAND-TOTAL.
035400     MOVE SPACE TO TOTAL-LINE.
035500     MOVE GRAND-TOTAL TO PRINT-TOTAL.
035600     MOVE GRAND-TOTAL-LITERAL TO TOTAL-TYPE.
035700     MOVE "TOTAL" TO TOTAL-LITERAL.
035800     MOVE TOTAL-LINE TO PRINTER-RECORD.
035900     PERFORM WRITE-TO-PRINTER.
036000     PERFORM LINE-FEED 2 TIMES.
036100     MOVE SPACE TO DETAIL-LINE.
036200
036300* LEVEL 2 CONTROL BREAK
036400 PROCESS-ALL-STORES.
036500     PERFORM START-ONE-STORE.
036600
036700     PERFORM PROCESS-ALL-DIVISIONS
036800         UNTIL WORK-FILE-AT-END = "Y"
036900             OR WORK-STORE NOT = CURRENT-STORE.
037000
037100     PERFORM END-ONE-STORE.
037200
037300 START-ONE-STORE.
037400     MOVE WORK-STORE TO CURRENT-STORE.
037500     MOVE ZEROES TO STORE-TOTAL.
037600     MOVE WORK-STORE TO PRINT-STORE.
037700
037800     PERFORM START-NEXT-PAGE.
037900
038000 END-ONE-STORE.
038100     PERFORM PRINT-STORE-TOTAL.
038200     ADD STORE-TOTAL TO GRAND-TOTAL.
038300
038400 PRINT-STORE-TOTAL.
038500     MOVE SPACE TO TOTAL-LINE.
038600     MOVE STORE-TOTAL TO PRINT-TOTAL.
038700     MOVE CURRENT-STORE TO TOTAL-NUMBER.
038800     MOVE STORE-TOTAL-LITERAL TO TOTAL-TYPE.
038900     MOVE "TOTAL" TO TOTAL-LITERAL.
039000     MOVE TOTAL-LINE TO PRINTER-RECORD.
039100     PERFORM WRITE-TO-PRINTER.
039200     PERFORM LINE-FEED.
039300     MOVE SPACE TO DETAIL-LINE.
039400
039500* LEVEL 3 CONTROL BREAK
039600 PROCESS-ALL-DIVISIONS.
039700     PERFORM START-ONE-DIVISION.
039800
```

BD
2

continues

Listing B2.17. continued

```
039900      PERFORM PROCESS-ALL-DEPARTMENTS
040000          UNTIL WORK-FILE-AT-END = "Y"
040100             OR WORK-STORE NOT = CURRENT-STORE
040200             OR WORK-DIVISION NOT = CURRENT-DIVISION.
040300
040400      PERFORM END-ONE-DIVISION.
040500
040600 START-ONE-DIVISION.
040700      MOVE WORK-DIVISION TO CURRENT-DIVISION.
040800      MOVE ZEROES TO DIVISION-TOTAL.
040900      MOVE WORK-DIVISION TO PRINT-DIVISION.
041000
041100 END-ONE-DIVISION.
041200      PERFORM PRINT-DIVISION-TOTAL.
041300      ADD DIVISION-TOTAL TO STORE-TOTAL.
041400
041500 PRINT-DIVISION-TOTAL.
041600      MOVE SPACE TO TOTAL-LINE.
041700      MOVE DIVISION-TOTAL TO PRINT-TOTAL.
041800      MOVE CURRENT-DIVISION TO TOTAL-NUMBER.
041900      MOVE DIVISION-TOTAL-LITERAL TO TOTAL-TYPE.
042000      MOVE "TOTAL" TO TOTAL-LITERAL.
042100      PERFORM LOAD-DIVISION-NAME.
042200      MOVE TOTAL-LINE TO PRINTER-RECORD.
042300      PERFORM WRITE-TO-PRINTER.
042400      PERFORM LINE-FEED.
042500      MOVE SPACE TO DETAIL-LINE.
042600
042700 LOAD-DIVISION-NAME.
042800      SET DIVISION-INDEX TO 1.
042900      SEARCH DIVISION-TABLE
043000          AT END
043100             MOVE "NOT FOUND" TO TOTAL-NAME
043200          WHEN
043300             DIVISION-NUMBER(DIVISION-INDEX) =
043400                 CURRENT-DIVISION
043500                 MOVE DIVISION-NAME(DIVISION-INDEX) TO
043600                     TOTAL-NAME.
043700
043800* LEVEL 4 CONTROL BREAK
043900 PROCESS-ALL-DEPARTMENTS.
044000      PERFORM START-ONE-DEPARTMENT.
044100
044200      PERFORM PROCESS-ALL-CATEGORIES
044300          UNTIL WORK-FILE-AT-END = "Y"
044400             OR WORK-STORE NOT = CURRENT-STORE
044500             OR WORK-DIVISION NOT = CURRENT-DIVISION
044600             OR WORK-DEPARTMENT NOT = CURRENT-DEPARTMENT.
044700
044800      PERFORM END-ONE-DEPARTMENT.
044900
045000 START-ONE-DEPARTMENT.
045100      MOVE WORK-DEPARTMENT TO CURRENT-DEPARTMENT.
045200      MOVE ZEROES TO DEPARTMENT-TOTAL.
045300      MOVE WORK-DEPARTMENT TO PRINT-DEPARTMENT.
```

2

```
045400
045500 END-ONE-DEPARTMENT.
045600     PERFORM PRINT-DEPARTMENT-TOTAL.
045700     ADD DEPARTMENT-TOTAL TO DIVISION-TOTAL.
045800
045900 PRINT-DEPARTMENT-TOTAL.
046000     MOVE SPACE TO TOTAL-LINE.
046100     MOVE DEPARTMENT-TOTAL TO PRINT-TOTAL.
046200     MOVE CURRENT-DEPARTMENT TO TOTAL-NUMBER.
046300     MOVE DEPARTMENT-TOTAL-LITERAL TO TOTAL-TYPE.
046400     MOVE "TOTAL" TO TOTAL-LITERAL.
046500     PERFORM LOAD-DEPARTMENT-NAME.
046600     MOVE TOTAL-LINE TO PRINTER-RECORD.
046700     PERFORM WRITE-TO-PRINTER.
046800     PERFORM LINE-FEED.
046900     MOVE SPACE TO DETAIL-LINE.
047000
047100 LOAD-DEPARTMENT-NAME.
047200     SET DEPARTMENT-INDEX TO 1.
047300     SEARCH DEPARTMENT-TABLE
047400         AT END
047500           MOVE "NOT FOUND" TO TOTAL-NAME
047600         WHEN
047700           DEPARTMENT-NUMBER(DEPARTMENT-INDEX) =
047800               CURRENT-DEPARTMENT
047900               MOVE DEPARTMENT-NAME(DEPARTMENT-INDEX) TO
048000                   TOTAL-NAME.
048100
048200* PROCESS ONE RECORD LEVEL
048300 PROCESS-ALL-CATEGORIES.
048400     PERFORM PROCESS-THIS-CATEGORY.
048500     ADD WORK-AMOUNT TO DEPARTMENT-TOTAL.
048600     ADD 1 TO RECORD-COUNT.
048700     PERFORM READ-NEXT-VALID-WORK.
048800
048900 PROCESS-THIS-CATEGORY.
049000     IF LINE-COUNT > MAXIMUM-LINES
049100         PERFORM START-NEXT-PAGE.
049200     PERFORM PRINT-THE-RECORD.
049300
049400 PRINT-THE-RECORD.
049500     MOVE WORK-CATEGORY TO PRINT-CATEGORY.
049600
049700     PERFORM LOAD-CATEGORY-NAME.
049800
049900     MOVE WORK-AMOUNT TO PRINT-AMOUNT.
050000
050100     MOVE DETAIL-LINE TO PRINTER-RECORD.
050200     PERFORM WRITE-TO-PRINTER.
050300     MOVE SPACE TO DETAIL-LINE.
050400
050500 LOAD-CATEGORY-NAME.
050600     SET CATEGORY-INDEX TO 1.
050700     SEARCH CATEGORY-TABLE
050800         AT END
```

continues

Listing B2.17. continued

```
050900            MOVE "NOT FOUND" TO TOTAL-NAME
051000          WHEN
051100            CATEGORY-NUMBER(CATEGORY-INDEX) =
051200              WORK-CATEGORY
051300              MOVE CATEGORY-NAME(CATEGORY-INDEX) TO
051400                  PRINT-CATEGORY-NAME.
051500
051600* PRINTING ROUTINES
051700 WRITE-TO-PRINTER.
051800    WRITE PRINTER-RECORD BEFORE ADVANCING 1.
051900    ADD 1 TO LINE-COUNT.
052000
052100 LINE-FEED.
052200    MOVE SPACE TO PRINTER-RECORD.
052300    PERFORM WRITE-TO-PRINTER.
052400
052500 START-NEXT-PAGE.
052600    PERFORM END-LAST-PAGE.
052700    PERFORM START-NEW-PAGE.
052800
052900 START-NEW-PAGE.
053000    ADD 1 TO PAGE-NUMBER.
053100    MOVE PAGE-NUMBER TO PRINT-PAGE-NUMBER.
053200    MOVE TITLE-LINE TO PRINTER-RECORD.
053300    PERFORM WRITE-TO-PRINTER.
053400    PERFORM LINE-FEED.
053500    MOVE LEGEND-LINE TO PRINTER-RECORD.
053600    PERFORM WRITE-TO-PRINTER.
053700    PERFORM LINE-FEED.
053800    MOVE COLUMN-LINE TO PRINTER-RECORD.
053900    PERFORM WRITE-TO-PRINTER.
054000    PERFORM LINE-FEED.
054100
054200 END-LAST-PAGE.
054300    IF PAGE-NUMBER > 0
054400        PERFORM FORM-FEED.
054500    MOVE ZERO TO LINE-COUNT.
054600
054700 FORM-FEED.
054800    MOVE SPACE TO PRINTER-RECORD.
054900    WRITE PRINTER-RECORD BEFORE ADVANCING PAGE.
055000
055100*--------------------------------
055200* Read first, read next routines
055300*--------------------------------
055400 READ-FIRST-VALID-WORK.
055500    PERFORM READ-NEXT-VALID-WORK.
055600
055700 READ-NEXT-VALID-WORK.
055800    PERFORM READ-NEXT-WORK-RECORD.
055900
056000 READ-NEXT-WORK-RECORD.
056100    MOVE "N" TO WORK-FILE-AT-END.
056200    READ WORK-FILE NEXT RECORD
056300        AT END MOVE "Y" TO WORK-FILE-AT-END.
056400
```

```
056500* Date and time routines
056600 FORMAT-THE-DATE.
056700     PERFORM CONVERT-TO-MMDDCCYY.
056800     MOVE DATE-MMDDCCYY TO FORMATTED-DATE.
056900
057000 CONVERT-TO-MMDDCCYY.
057100     COMPUTE DATE-MMDDCCYY =
057200          DATE-CCYYMMDD * 10000.0001.
057300
057400 FORMAT-THE-TIME.
057500     MOVE TIME-HHMMSS TO FORMATTED-TIME.
057600     INSPECT FORMATTED-TIME
057700       REPLACING ALL "/" BY ":".
057800
```

 The output of slsrpt04.cbl shows a run date and time printed at the top of the report with each title line:

```
RUN: 2/19/1997 AT 17:14:59        SALES REPORT              PAGE:    1

STORE:  1

DIVISION DEPARTMENT CATEGORY                    AMOUNT

        1         1          1     WEIGHTS       237.57
                             2     MACHINES      475.14
                  DEPT  1 EXERCISE       TOTAL   712.71

                  2          3     SUN GLASSES   712.71
                             4     VITAMINS       50.28
                  DEPT  2 MISCELLANEOUS   TOTAL  762.99

        DIVISION  1 ATHLETICS        TOTAL     1,475.70

        2         3          5     MEN'S CLOTHES   287.85
                             6     WOMEN'S CLOTHES 525.42
                  DEPT  3 SPORT CLOTHES  TOTAL     813.27

                  4          7     TENNIS        762.99
                             8     SOCCER        100.56
                  DEPT  4 EQUIPMENT      TOTAL     863.55

        DIVISION  2 SPORTING GOODS  TOTAL      1,676.82

        3         5          9     TENTS         338.13
                             10    SLEEPING BAGS 575.70
                  DEPT  5 CAMP EQUIPMENT  TOTAL    913.83

                  6          11    CLOTHING       86.73-
                             12    HIKING BOOTS  150.84
                  DEPT  6 CAMPING CLOTHES TOTAL    64.11

        DIVISION  3 CAMPING         TOTAL        977.94

             STORE  1              TOTAL      4,130.46
```

```
RUN: 2/19/1997 AT 17:14:59          SALES REPORT              PAGE:    2

STORE:  2

DIVISION DEPARTMENT CATEGORY                        AMOUNT

     1           1          1    WEIGHTS            388.41
                            2    MACHINES           625.98
                 DEPT  1 EXERCISE      TOTAL      1,014.39

                 2          3    SUN GLASSES         36.45-
                            4    VITAMINS           201.12
                 DEPT  2 MISCELLANEOUS  TOTAL       164.67

          DIVISION  1 ATHLETICS        TOTAL      1,179.06

     2           3          5    MEN'S CLOTHES      438.69
                            6    WOMEN'S CLOTHES    676.26
                 DEPT  3 SPORT CLOTHES  TOTAL     1,114.95

                 4          7    TENNIS              13.83
                            8    SOCCER             251.40
                 DEPT  4 EQUIPMENT      TOTAL       265.23

          DIVISION  2 SPORTING GOODS  TOTAL      1,380.18

     3           5          9    TENTS              488.97
                           10    SLEEPING BAGS      726.54
                 DEPT  5 CAMP EQUIPMENT  TOTAL    1,215.51

                 6         11    CLOTHING            64.11
                           12    HIKING BOOTS       301.68
                 DEPT  6 CAMPING CLOTHES TOTAL      365.79

          DIVISION  3 CAMPING          TOTAL      1,581.30

             STORE  2                   TOTAL      4,140.54

RUN: 2/19/1997 AT 17:14:59          SALES REPORT              PAGE:    3

STORE:  3

DIVISION DEPARTMENT CATEGORY                        AMOUNT

     1           1          1    WEIGHTS            539.25
                            2    MACHINES           776.82
                 DEPT  1 EXERCISE      TOTAL      1,316.07

                 2          3    SUN GLASSES        114.39
                            4    VITAMINS           351.96
                 DEPT  2 MISCELLANEOUS  TOTAL       466.35

          DIVISION  1 ATHLETICS        TOTAL      1,782.42

     2           3          5    MEN'S CLOTHES      589.53
                            6    WOMEN'S CLOTHES     72.90-
```

```
           DEPT  3 SPORT CLOTHES   TOTAL     516.63

      4           7    TENNIS               164.67
                  8    SOCCER               402.24
           DEPT  4 EQUIPMENT       TOTAL     566.91

      DIVISION  2 SPORTING GOODS   TOTAL   1,083.54

3     5           9    TENTS                639.81
                 10    SLEEPING BAGS         22.62-
           DEPT  5 CAMP EQUIPMENT  TOTAL     617.19

      6          11    CLOTHING             214.95
                 12    HIKING BOOTS         452.52
           DEPT  6 CAMPING CLOTHES TOTAL     667.47

      DIVISION  3 CAMPING          TOTAL   1,284.66

           STORE  3                TOTAL   4,150.62
RUN: 2/19/1997 AT 17:14:59          SALES REPORT                    PAGE:    4

STORE:   4

DIVISION DEPARTMENT CATEGORY                AMOUNT

      1     1           1    WEIGHTS              690.09
                        2    MACHINES              27.66
                 DEPT  1 EXERCISE        TOTAL     717.75

            2           3    SUN GLASSES          265.23
                        4    VITAMINS             502.80
                 DEPT  2 MISCELLANEOUS   TOTAL     768.03

            DIVISION  1 ATHLETICS        TOTAL   1,485.78

      2     3           5    MEN'S CLOTHES        740.37
                        6    WOMEN'S CLOTHES       77.94
                 DEPT  3 SPORT CLOTHES   TOTAL     818.31

            4           7    TENNIS               315.51
                        8    SOCCER               553.08
                 DEPT  4 EQUIPMENT       TOTAL     868.59

            DIVISION  2 SPORTING GOODS   TOTAL   1,686.90

      3     5           9    TENTS                790.65
                       10    SLEEPING BAGS        128.22
                 DEPT  5 CAMP EQUIPMENT  TOTAL     918.87

            6          11    CLOTHING             365.79
                       12    HIKING BOOTS         603.36
                 DEPT  6 CAMPING CLOTHES TOTAL     969.15

            DIVISION  3 CAMPING          TOTAL   1,888.02

                 STORE  4                TOTAL   5,060.70
```

```
RUN: 2/19/1997 AT 17:14:59        SALES REPORT                PAGE:    5

STORE:  5

DIVISION DEPARTMENT CATEGORY                      AMOUNT

      1         1          1     WEIGHTS            59.07-
                           2     MACHINES          178.50
                DEPT  1 EXERCISE        TOTAL       119.43

                2          3     SUN GLASSES        416.07
                           4     VITAMINS           653.64
                DEPT  2 MISCELLANEOUS   TOTAL     1,069.71

           DIVISION  1 ATHLETICS        TOTAL     1,189.14

      2         3          5     MEN'S CLOTHES       8.79-
                           6     WOMEN'S CLOTHES   228.78
                DEPT  3 SPORT CLOTHES   TOTAL       219.99

                4          7     TENNIS            466.35
                           8     SOCCER            703.92
                DEPT  4 EQUIPMENT       TOTAL     1,170.27

           DIVISION  2 SPORTING GOODS   TOTAL     1,390.26

      3         5          9     TENTS              41.49
                          10     SLEEPING BAGS     279.06
                DEPT  5 CAMP EQUIPMENT  TOTAL       320.55

                6         11     CLOTHING          516.63
                          12     HIKING BOOTS      754.20
                DEPT  6 CAMPING CLOTHES TOTAL     1,270.83

           DIVISION  3 CAMPING          TOTAL     1,591.38

                STORE  5               TOTAL     4,170.78

RUN: 2/19/1997 AT 17:14:59        SALES REPORT                PAGE:    6

STORE:  6

DIVISION DEPARTMENT CATEGORY                      AMOUNT

      1         1          1     WEIGHTS            91.77
                           2     MACHINES          329.34
                DEPT  1 EXERCISE        TOTAL       421.11

                2          3     SUN GLASSES        566.91
                           4     VITAMINS           95.52-
                DEPT  2 MISCELLANEOUS   TOTAL       471.39

           DIVISION  1 ATHLETICS        TOTAL       892.50
```

2

```
    2         3          5     MEN'S CLOTHES         142.05
                         6     WOMEN'S CLOTHES       379.62
                  DEPT   3 SPORT CLOTHES    TOTAL    521.67

              4          7     TENNIS               617.19
                         8     SOCCER                45.24-
                  DEPT   4 EQUIPMENT        TOTAL    571.95

          DIVISION   2 SPORTING GOODS       TOTAL  1,093.62

    3         5          9     TENTS                192.33
                        10     SLEEPING BAGS        429.90
                  DEPT   5 CAMP EQUIPMENT   TOTAL    622.23

              6         11     CLOTHING             667.47
                        12     HIKING BOOTS           5.04
                  DEPT   6 CAMPING CLOTHES TOTAL     672.51

          DIVISION   3 CAMPING             TOTAL  1,294.74

              STORE  6                      TOTAL  3,280.86

              GRAND                         TOTAL 24,933.96
```

ANALYSIS   At lines 016500–017600, TITLE-LINE has been modified to allow room for a run date and time.

Variables for extracting the date and time and formatting them are defined at lines 021900–024400. The extraction and formatting of the date and time are done in START-NEW-REPORT, which begins at line 032400.

At lines 032800 and 032900, RUN-DATE is accepted from DATE and moved to DATE-CCYYMMDD.

Because you accept the current date, the year portion of the date will come back as 94. When the year turns over, it will return as 95, and so on up to 1999. In the year 2000, the year portion of the date will come back as 00, then 01, and so on. The effect of this is that we have to assume that any year from 94 through 99 is 1994 through 1999. Sometime when the century turns, the years will start coming back as 00, 01, and so on. If the year is greater than 90, then the first two digits must be 19; otherwise, they are set to 20. This logic appears at lines 033000–033300. The date is formatted at line 033500 and then moved into the title line at line 033600. Of course, in about 110 years this program won't work correctly.

At line 033800, RUN-TIME is accepted from TIME. This time had hundredths that are not needed, so it is computed into TIME-HHMMSS by dividing it by 100. At lines 034000 and 034100, the time is formatted and moved into the title line.

Lines 056500–057700 contain the routines for formatting the date and time.

Computational Fields

Numbers are stored in COBOL in several different ways. The methods used were chosen as compromises between speed of calculation and saving space in memory.

In all the programs you have worked on so far, you have used a type of storage called zoned. This is the default storage for a number in COBOL:

```
01   A-NUMBER              PIC S9(5)V99.
```

This definition creates zoned numeric storage. Each digit in the number uses one byte of storage; the sign and decimal point do not use any space.

The decimal point is saved in the PIC, and the sign is saved by combining it with the first or last digit of the number. The first or last digit in a zoned field actually is a code that represents both the digit value and the sign. The field is 7 bytes long.

The other main type of storage used in COBOL is called computational. The most common form of computational storage is COMPUTATIONAL-3 or COMP-3. This is so common that it frequently is just called "comp" by programmers, even though different COBOL versions require that it be called COMP-3. In some versions of COBOL, it is the only version of computational storage that is supported.

Computational storage comes in many different types, and is used to squeeze more than one digit into a byte. Just as the sign and a digit of a zoned field are encoded into a single byte, computational takes this encoding even further.

A COMP-3 field is created by adding COMP-3 after the picture:

```
01   A-NUMBER              PIC S9(5)V99 COMP-3.
```

In versions of COBOL that support only COMPUTATIONAL-3, you might be required only to add COMP after the picture:

```
01   A-NUMBER              PIC S9(5)V99 COMP.
```

ACUCOBOL, Micro Focus Personal COBOL, LPI COBOL, and VAX COBOL all require that the field be named COMP-3.

A computational field can be treated like any other numeric field in all respects. The only difference in a computational field is the number of bytes used for the storage of a number.

You should know how to determine the size of a COMP-3 field for counting record lengths and table sizes. The digits and sign of a COMP-3 field are stored two to a byte. If the picture does not contain a sign, a sign is still created for the storage.

The steps for calculating the size of a COMP-3 field are simple:

1. Count the number of digits in the number.
2. Add 1 for the sign (even if the number does not have a sign in the PICTURE).
3. If the result is an odd number, add 1 to make it even.
4. Divide this result by 2.

Step 3 is used because a byte cannot be split. If the total number of digits and sign equals 7, the number would be stored in 3 1/2 bytes, except that a byte cannot be split. Rounding up to an even number always makes the result divisible by 2. Table B2.2 shows the steps for calculating the size of a PIC 9(8) COMP-3 definition.

Table B2.2. Calculating the size of PIC 9 (8) COMP-3 field.

Step	Function	Result
Beginning total number of digits		8
Add 1 for the sign (even though not in PIC)	+	1
Calculate the result	=	9
Round up to the next even number	+	1
Calculate the new result	=	10
Divide by 2	/	2
The number of bytes used by ANOTHER-NUMBER	=	5

Computational storage is frequently used to reduce the size of a file. The size of accounting files that contain many numeric fields can be drastically reduced by converting zone numeric fields to computational fields.

Numbering Paragraphs

Paragraph numbering is not required by the COBOL language, but it is a style that is used so commonly that you should see an example of it to be familiar with it.

The basic idea of paragraph numbering is that the program is a series of layers. The top layer performs one or more routines in the next lower layer, the second layer performs one or more routines in the next lower layer, and so on. The paragraphs in each layer are given related paragraph numbers and are kept together in the source code file to make reading and analyzing easier. The numbers help to keep the paragraphs together physically on the page, and help to indicate the relationships between various routines quickly.

Listing B2.18 is an example of a numbered paragraph listing. It was created by using slsprt04.cbl as the base and renaming it slsrpt05.cbl. Note that the general-purpose routines starting at line 051600 are not numbered. They could be left unnumbered or given general-purpose numbers to indicate that they are utility routines, such as G000-WRITE-TO-PRINTER (G for general routine) or P000-WRITE-TO-PRINTER (P for print routine).

TYPE **Listing B2.18. Numbered paragraphs.**

```
000100 IDENTIFICATION DIVISION.
000200 PROGRAM-ID. SLSRPT05.
000300*-------------------------------
000400* Print test sales data
000500*-------------------------------
000600 ENVIRONMENT DIVISION.
000700 INPUT-OUTPUT SECTION.
000800 FILE-CONTROL.
000900
001000*-------------------------------
001100* SLSALES.CBL
001200*-------------------------------
001300     SELECT SALES-FILE
001400         ASSIGN TO "SALES"
001500         ORGANIZATION IS SEQUENTIAL.
001600 .
001700     SELECT WORK-FILE
001800         ASSIGN TO "WORK"
001900         ORGANIZATION IS SEQUENTIAL.
002000
002100     SELECT SORT-FILE
002200         ASSIGN TO "SORT".
002300
002400     SELECT PRINTER-FILE
002500         ASSIGN TO PRINTER
002600         ORGANIZATION IS LINE SEQUENTIAL.
002700
002800 DATA DIVISION.
002900 FILE SECTION.
003000
003100*-------------------------------
003200* FDSALES.CBL
003300* Temporary daily sales file.
003400*-------------------------------
003500 FD  SALES-FILE
003600     LABEL RECORDS ARE STANDARD.
003700 01  SALES-RECORD.
003800     05  SALES-STORE          PIC 9(2).
003900     05  SALES-DIVISION       PIC 9(2).
004000     05  SALES-DEPARTMENT     PIC 9(2).
004100     05  SALES-CATEGORY       PIC 9(2).
004200     05  SALES-AMOUNT         PIC S9(6)V99.
004300
004400 FD  WORK-FILE
004500     LABEL RECORDS ARE STANDARD.
```

```
004600 01   WORK-RECORD.
004700      05   WORK-STORE           PIC 9(2).
004800      05   WORK-DIVISION        PIC 9(2).
004900      05   WORK-DEPARTMENT      PIC 9(2).
005000      05   WORK-CATEGORY        PIC 9(2).
005100      05   WORK-AMOUNT          PIC S9(6)V99.
005200
005300 SD   SORT-FILE
005400      LABEL RECORDS ARE STANDARD.
005500 01   SORT-RECORD.
005600      05   SORT-STORE           PIC 9(2).
005700      05   SORT-DIVISION        PIC 9(2).
005800      05   SORT-DEPARTMENT      PIC 9(2).
005900      05   SORT-CATEGORY        PIC 9(2).
006000      05   SORT-AMOUNT          PIC S9(6)V99.
006100
006200 FD   PRINTER-FILE
006300      LABEL RECORDS ARE OMITTED.
006400 01   PRINTER-RECORD           PIC X(80).
006500
006600 WORKING-STORAGE SECTION.
006700
006800 01   THE-DIVISIONS.
006900      05   FILLER        PIC 99 VALUE 01.
007000      05   FILLER        PIC X(15) VALUE "ATHLETICS".
007100      05   FILLER        PIC 99 VALUE 02.
007200      05   FILLER        PIC X(15) VALUE "SPORTING GOODS".
007300      05   FILLER        PIC 99 VALUE 03.
007400      05   FILLER        PIC X(15) VALUE "CAMPING".
007500 01   FILLER REDEFINES THE-DIVISIONS.
007600      05   DIVISION-TABLE OCCURS 3 TIMES
007700           INDEXED BY DIVISION-INDEX.
007800          10   DIVISION-NUMBER       PIC 99.
007900          10   DIVISION-NAME         PIC X(15).
008000
008100 01   THE-DEPARTMENTS.
008200      05   FILLER        PIC 99 VALUE 01.
008300      05   FILLER        PIC X(15) VALUE "EXERCISE".
008400      05   FILLER        PIC 99 VALUE 02.
008500      05   FILLER        PIC X(15) VALUE "MISCELLANEOUS".
008600      05   FILLER        PIC 99 VALUE 03.
008700      05   FILLER        PIC X(15) VALUE "SPORT CLOTHES".
008800      05   FILLER        PIC 99 VALUE 04.
008900      05   FILLER        PIC X(15) VALUE "EQUIPMENT".
009000      05   FILLER        PIC 99 VALUE 05.
009100      05   FILLER        PIC X(15) VALUE "CAMP EQUIPMENT".
009200      05   FILLER        PIC 99 VALUE 06.
009300      05   FILLER        PIC X(15) VALUE "CAMPING CLOTHES".
009400 01   FILLER REDEFINES THE-DEPARTMENTS.
009500      05   DEPARTMENT-TABLE OCCURS 6 TIMES
009600           INDEXED BY DEPARTMENT-INDEX.
009700          10   DEPARTMENT-NUMBER     PIC 99.
009800          10   DEPARTMENT-NAME       PIC X(15).
009900
010000 01   THE-CATEGORIES.
```

continues

Listing B2.18. continued

```
010100      05   FILLER       PIC 99 VALUE 01.
010200      05   FILLER       PIC X(15) VALUE "WEIGHTS".
010300      05   FILLER       PIC 99 VALUE 02.
010400      05   FILLER       PIC X(15) VALUE "MACHINES".
010500      05   FILLER       PIC 99 VALUE 03.
010600      05   FILLER       PIC X(15) VALUE "SUN GLASSES".
010700      05   FILLER       PIC 99 VALUE 04.
010800      05   FILLER       PIC X(15) VALUE "VITAMINS".
010900      05   FILLER       PIC 99 VALUE 05.
011000      05   FILLER       PIC X(15) VALUE "MEN'S CLOTHES".
011100      05   FILLER       PIC 99 VALUE 06.
011200      05   FILLER       PIC X(15) VALUE "WOMEN'S CLOTHES".
011300      05   FILLER       PIC 99 VALUE 07.
011400      05   FILLER       PIC X(15) VALUE "TENNIS".
011500      05   FILLER       PIC 99 VALUE 08.
011600      05   FILLER       PIC X(15) VALUE "SOCCER".
011700      05   FILLER       PIC 99 VALUE 09.
011800      05   FILLER       PIC X(15) VALUE "TENTS".
011900      05   FILLER       PIC 99 VALUE 10.
012000      05   FILLER       PIC X(15) VALUE "SLEEPING BAGS".
012100      05   FILLER       PIC 99 VALUE 11.
012200      05   FILLER       PIC X(15) VALUE "CLOTHING".
012300      05   FILLER       PIC 99 VALUE 12.
012400      05   FILLER       PIC X(15) VALUE "HIKING BOOTS".
012500 01   FILLER REDEFINES THE-CATEGORIES.
012600      05   CATEGORY-TABLE OCCURS 12 TIMES
012700           INDEXED BY CATEGORY-INDEX.
012800         10   CATEGORY-NUMBER      PIC 99.
012900         10   CATEGORY-NAME        PIC X(15).
013000
013100 77 OK-TO-PROCESS        PIC X.
013200
013300      COPY "WSCASE01.CBL".
013400
013500 01  LEGEND-LINE.
013600      05   FILLER        PIC X(6) VALUE "STORE:".
013700      05   FILLER        PIC X(1) VALUE SPACE.
013800      05   PRINT-STORE   PIC Z9.
013900
014000 01  DETAIL-LINE.
014100      05   FILLER            PIC X(3) VALUE SPACE.
014200      05   PRINT-DIVISION    PIC Z9.
014300      05   FILLER            PIC X(4) VALUE SPACE.
014400      05   FILLER            PIC X(3) VALUE SPACE.
014500      05   PRINT-DEPARTMENT  PIC Z9.
014600      05   FILLER            PIC X(6) VALUE SPACE.
014700      05   FILLER            PIC X(3) VALUE SPACE.
014800      05   PRINT-CATEGORY    PIC Z9.
014900      05   FILLER            PIC X(4) VALUE SPACE.
015000      05   PRINT-CATEGORY-NAME  PIC X(15).
015100      05   FILLER            PIC X(1) VALUE SPACE.
015200      05   PRINT-AMOUNT      PIC ZZZ,ZZ9.99-.
015300
015400 01  COLUMN-LINE.
015500      05   FILLER        PIC X(8)  VALUE "DIVISION".
```

```
015600      05  FILLER          PIC X(1)  VALUE SPACE.
015700      05  FILLER          PIC X(10) VALUE "DEPARTMENT".
015800      05  FILLER          PIC X(1)  VALUE SPACE.
015900      05  FILLER          PIC X(8)  VALUE "CATEGORY".
016000      05  FILLER          PIC X(1)  VALUE SPACE.
016100      05  FILLER          PIC X(15)  VALUE SPACE.
016200      05  FILLER          PIC X(5)  VALUE SPACE.
016300      05  FILLER          PIC X(6)  VALUE "AMOUNT".
016400
016500 01  TITLE-LINE.
016600      05  FILLER              PIC X(4) VALUE "RUN:".
016700      05  FORMATTED-RUN-DATE  PIC X(10).
016800      05  FILLER              PIC X(4) VALUE " AT ".
016900      05  FORMATTED-RUN-TIME  PIC X(8).
017000      05  FILLER              PIC X(10) VALUE SPACE.
017100      05  FILLER              PIC X(12)
017200          VALUE "SALES REPORT".
017300      05  FILLER              PIC X(10) VALUE SPACE.
017400      05  FILLER              PIC X(5) VALUE "PAGE:".
017500      05  FILLER              PIC X(1) VALUE SPACE.
017600      05  PRINT-PAGE-NUMBER   PIC ZZZ9.
017700
017800 01  TOTAL-LINE.
017900      05  FILLER          PIC X(11) VALUE SPACE.
018000      05  TOTAL-TYPE      PIC X(8).
018100      05  FILLER          PIC X(1) VALUE SPACE.
018200      05  TOTAL-NUMBER    PIC Z9.
018300      05  FILLER          PIC X(1) VALUE SPACE.
018400      05  TOTAL-NAME      PIC X(15) VALUE SPACE.
018500      05  FILLER          PIC X(1) VALUE SPACE.
018600      05  TOTAL-LITERAL   PIC X(5) VALUE "TOTAL".
018700      05  FILLER          PIC X(1) VALUE SPACE.
018800      05  PRINT-TOTAL     PIC ZZZ,ZZ9.99-.
018900
019000 77  GRAND-TOTAL-LITERAL      PIC X(8) VALUE "   GRAND".
019100 77  STORE-TOTAL-LITERAL      PIC X(8) VALUE "   STORE".
019200 77  DIVISION-TOTAL-LITERAL   PIC X(8) VALUE "DIVISION".
019300 77  DEPARTMENT-TOTAL-LITERAL PIC X(8) VALUE "    DEPT".
019400
019500 77  WORK-FILE-AT-END     PIC X.
019600
019700 77  LINE-COUNT          PIC 999 VALUE ZERO.
019800 77  PAGE-NUMBER         PIC 9999 VALUE ZERO.
019900 77  MAXIMUM-LINES       PIC 999 VALUE 55.
020000
020100 77  RECORD-COUNT        PIC 9999 VALUE ZEROES.
020200
020300* Control break current values for store, division
020400* department.
020500 77  CURRENT-STORE       PIC 99.
020600 77  CURRENT-DIVISION    PIC 99.
020700 77  CURRENT-DEPARTMENT  PIC 99.
020800
020900* Control break accumulators
021000* GRAND TOTAL is the level 1 accumulator for the whole file
```

continues

Listing B2.18. continued

```
021100* STORE TOTAL is the level 2 accumulator
021200* DIVISION TOTAL is the level 3 accumulator
021300* DEPARTMENT TOTAL is the level 4 accumulator.
021400 77   GRAND-TOTAL          PIC S9(6)V99.
021500 77   STORE-TOTAL          PIC S9(6)V99.
021600 77   DIVISION-TOTAL       PIC S9(6)V99.
021700 77   DEPARTMENT-TOTAL     PIC S9(6)V99.
021800
021900* System date and time
022000 77   RUN-DATE         PIC 9(6).
022100 77   RUN-TIME         PIC 9(8).
022200
022300*-------------------------------
022400* Fields for date routines.
022500*-------------------------------
022600 77   FORMATTED-DATE      PIC Z9/99/9999.
022700 77   DATE-MMDDCCYY       PIC 9(8).
022800 01   DATE-CCYYMMDD       PIC 9(8).
022900 01   FILLER REDEFINES DATE-CCYYMMDD.
023000      05   DATE-CC        PIC 99.
023100      05   DATE-YY        PIC 99.
023200      05   DATE-MM        PIC 99.
023300      05   DATE-DD        PIC 99.
023400
023500*-------------------------------
023600* Fields for TIME routines.
023700*-------------------------------
023800 77   FORMATTED-TIME      PIC Z9/99/99.
023900
024000 01   TIME-HHMMSS      PIC 9(6).
024100 01   FILLER REDEFINES TIME-HHMMSS.
024200      05   TIME-HH       PIC 99.
024300      05   TIME-MM       PIC 99.
024400      05   TIME-SS       PIC 99.
024500
024600 PROCEDURE DIVISION.
024700 1000-PROGRAM-BEGIN.
024800
024900      PERFORM 1300-OPENING-PROCEDURE.
025000      PERFORM 2000-MAIN-PROCESS.
025100      PERFORM 1400-CLOSING-PROCEDURE.
025200
025300 1100-PROGRAM-EXIT.
025400      EXIT PROGRAM.
025500
025600 1200-PROGRAM-DONE.
025700      STOP RUN.
025800
025900 1300-OPENING-PROCEDURE.
026000
026100      OPEN OUTPUT PRINTER-FILE.
026200
026300 1400-CLOSING-PROCEDURE.
026400      CLOSE PRINTER-FILE.
026500
```

```
026600 2000-MAIN-PROCESS.
026700     PERFORM 2100-GET-OK-TO-PROCESS.
026800     PERFORM 3000-PROCESS-THE-FILE
026900         UNTIL OK-TO-PROCESS = "N".
027000
027100 2100-GET-OK-TO-PROCESS.
027200     PERFORM 2110-ACCEPT-OK-TO-PROCESS.
027300     PERFORM 2120-RE-ACCEPT-OK-TO-PROCESS
027400         UNTIL OK-TO-PROCESS = "Y" OR "N".
027500
027600 2110-ACCEPT-OK-TO-PROCESS.
027700     DISPLAY "PRINT SALES REPORT (Y/N)?".
027800     ACCEPT OK-TO-PROCESS.
027900     INSPECT OK-TO-PROCESS
028000        CONVERTING LOWER-ALPHA
028100        TO          UPPER-ALPHA.
028200
028300 2120-RE-ACCEPT-OK-TO-PROCESS.
028400     DISPLAY "YOU MUST ENTER YES OR NO".
028500     PERFORM 2110-ACCEPT-OK-TO-PROCESS.
028600
028700 3000-PROCESS-THE-FILE.
028800     PERFORM 3100-START-THE-FILE.
028900     PERFORM 4000-PRINT-ONE-REPORT.
029000     PERFORM 3200-END-THE-FILE.
029100
029200     MOVE "N" TO OK-TO-PROCESS.
029300
029400 3100-START-THE-FILE.
029500     PERFORM 3110-SORT-DATA-FILE.
029600     OPEN INPUT WORK-FILE.
029700
029800 3110-SORT-DATA-FILE.
029900     SORT SORT-FILE
030000         ON ASCENDING KEY SORT-STORE
030100            ASCENDING KEY SORT-DIVISION
030200            ASCENDING KEY SORT-DEPARTMENT
030300            ASCENDING KEY SORT-CATEGORY
030400         USING SALES-FILE
030500         GIVING WORK-FILE.
030600
030700 3200-END-THE-FILE.
030800     CLOSE WORK-FILE.
030900
031000* LEVEL 1 CONTROL BREAK
031100 4000-PRINT-ONE-REPORT.
031200     PERFORM 4100-START-ONE-REPORT.
031300     PERFORM 5000-PROCESS-ALL-STORES
031400         UNTIL WORK-FILE-AT-END = "Y".
031500     PERFORM 4200-END-ONE-REPORT.
031600
031700 4100-START-ONE-REPORT.
031800     PERFORM READ-FIRST-VALID-WORK.
031900     MOVE ZEROES TO GRAND-TOTAL.
032000
```

BD
2

continues

Listing B2.18. continued

```
032100       PERFORM 4110-START-NEW-REPORT.
032200
032300 4110-START-NEW-REPORT.
032400       MOVE SPACE TO DETAIL-LINE.
032500       MOVE ZEROES TO LINE-COUNT PAGE-NUMBER.
032600
032700       ACCEPT RUN-DATE FROM DATE.
032800       MOVE RUN-DATE TO DATE-CCYYMMDD.
032900       IF DATE-YY > 90
033000           MOVE 19 TO DATE-CC
033100       ELSE
033200           MOVE 20 TO DATE-CC.
033300
033400       PERFORM FORMAT-THE-DATE.
033500       MOVE FORMATTED-DATE TO FORMATTED-RUN-DATE.
033600
033700       ACCEPT RUN-TIME FROM TIME.
033800       COMPUTE TIME-HHMMSS = RUN-TIME / 100.
033900       PERFORM FORMAT-THE-TIME.
034000       MOVE FORMATTED-TIME TO FORMATTED-RUN-TIME.
034100
034200
034300 4200-END-ONE-REPORT.
034400       IF RECORD-COUNT = ZEROES
034500           MOVE "NO RECORDS FOUND" TO PRINTER-RECORD
034600           PERFORM WRITE-TO-PRINTER
034700       ELSE
034800           PERFORM 4210-PRINT-GRAND-TOTAL.
034900
035000       PERFORM END-LAST-PAGE.
035100
035200 4210-PRINT-GRAND-TOTAL.
035300       MOVE SPACE TO TOTAL-LINE.
035400       MOVE GRAND-TOTAL TO PRINT-TOTAL.
035500       MOVE GRAND-TOTAL-LITERAL TO TOTAL-TYPE.
035600       MOVE "TOTAL" TO TOTAL-LITERAL.
035700       MOVE TOTAL-LINE TO PRINTER-RECORD.
035800       PERFORM WRITE-TO-PRINTER.
035900       PERFORM LINE-FEED 2 TIMES.
036000       MOVE SPACE TO DETAIL-LINE.
036100
036200* LEVEL 2 CONTROL BREAK
036300 5000-PROCESS-ALL-STORES.
036400       PERFORM 5100-START-ONE-STORE.
036500
036600       PERFORM 6000-PROCESS-ALL-DIVISIONS
036700           UNTIL WORK-FILE-AT-END = "Y"
036800               OR WORK-STORE NOT = CURRENT-STORE.
036900
037000       PERFORM 5200-END-ONE-STORE.
037100
037200 5100-START-ONE-STORE.
037300       MOVE WORK-STORE TO CURRENT-STORE.
037400       MOVE ZEROES TO STORE-TOTAL.
```

```
037500     MOVE WORK-STORE TO PRINT-STORE.
037600
037700     PERFORM START-NEXT-PAGE.
037800
037900 5200-END-ONE-STORE.
038000     PERFORM 5210-PRINT-STORE-TOTAL.
038100     ADD STORE-TOTAL TO GRAND-TOTAL.
038200
038300 5210-PRINT-STORE-TOTAL.
038400     MOVE SPACE TO TOTAL-LINE.
038500     MOVE STORE-TOTAL TO PRINT-TOTAL.
038600     MOVE CURRENT-STORE TO TOTAL-NUMBER.
038700     MOVE STORE-TOTAL-LITERAL TO TOTAL-TYPE.
038800     MOVE "TOTAL" TO TOTAL-LITERAL.
038900     MOVE TOTAL-LINE TO PRINTER-RECORD.
039000     PERFORM WRITE-TO-PRINTER.
039100     PERFORM LINE-FEED.
039200     MOVE SPACE TO DETAIL-LINE.
039300
039400* LEVEL 3 CONTROL BREAK
039500 6000-PROCESS-ALL-DIVISIONS.
039600     PERFORM 6100-START-ONE-DIVISION.
039700
039800     PERFORM 7000-PROCESS-ALL-DEPARTMENTS
039900         UNTIL WORK-FILE-AT-END = "Y"
040000             OR WORK-STORE NOT = CURRENT-STORE
040100             OR WORK-DIVISION NOT = CURRENT-DIVISION.
040200
040300     PERFORM 6200-END-ONE-DIVISION.
040400
040500 6100-START-ONE-DIVISION.
040600     MOVE WORK-DIVISION TO CURRENT-DIVISION.
040700     MOVE ZEROES TO DIVISION-TOTAL.
040800     MOVE WORK-DIVISION TO PRINT-DIVISION.
040900
041000 6200-END-ONE-DIVISION.
041100     PERFORM 6210-PRINT-DIVISION-TOTAL.
041200     ADD DIVISION-TOTAL TO STORE-TOTAL.
041300
041400 6210-PRINT-DIVISION-TOTAL.
041500     MOVE SPACE TO TOTAL-LINE.
041600     MOVE DIVISION-TOTAL TO PRINT-TOTAL.
041700     MOVE CURRENT-DIVISION TO TOTAL-NUMBER.
041800     MOVE DIVISION-TOTAL-LITERAL TO TOTAL-TYPE.
041900     MOVE "TOTAL" TO TOTAL-LITERAL.
042000     PERFORM 6220-LOAD-DIVISION-NAME.
042100     MOVE TOTAL-LINE TO PRINTER-RECORD.
042200     PERFORM WRITE-TO-PRINTER.
042300     PERFORM LINE-FEED.
042400     MOVE SPACE TO DETAIL-LINE.
042500
042600 6220-LOAD-DIVISION-NAME.
042700     SET DIVISION-INDEX TO 1.
042800     SEARCH DIVISION-TABLE
042900         AT END
```

continues

Listing B2.18. continued

```
043000            MOVE "NOT FOUND" TO TOTAL-NAME
043100          WHEN
043200            DIVISION-NUMBER(DIVISION-INDEX) =
043300              CURRENT-DIVISION
043400            MOVE DIVISION-NAME(DIVISION-INDEX) TO
043500              TOTAL-NAME.
043600
043700* LEVEL 4 CONTROL BREAK
043800 7000-PROCESS-ALL-DEPARTMENTS.
043900     PERFORM 7100-START-ONE-DEPARTMENT.
044000
044100     PERFORM 8000-PROCESS-ALL-CATEGORIES
044200         UNTIL WORK-FILE-AT-END = "Y"
044300            OR WORK-STORE NOT = CURRENT-STORE
044400            OR WORK-DIVISION NOT = CURRENT-DIVISION
044500            OR WORK-DEPARTMENT NOT = CURRENT-DEPARTMENT.
044600
044700     PERFORM 7200-END-ONE-DEPARTMENT.
044800
044900 7100-START-ONE-DEPARTMENT.
045000     MOVE WORK-DEPARTMENT TO CURRENT-DEPARTMENT.
045100     MOVE ZEROES TO DEPARTMENT-TOTAL.
045200     MOVE WORK-DEPARTMENT TO PRINT-DEPARTMENT.
045300
045400 7200-END-ONE-DEPARTMENT.
045500     PERFORM 7210-PRINT-DEPARTMENT-TOTAL.
045600     ADD DEPARTMENT-TOTAL TO DIVISION-TOTAL.
045700
045800 7210-PRINT-DEPARTMENT-TOTAL.
045900     MOVE SPACE TO TOTAL-LINE.
046000     MOVE DEPARTMENT-TOTAL TO PRINT-TOTAL.
046100     MOVE CURRENT-DEPARTMENT TO TOTAL-NUMBER.
046200     MOVE DEPARTMENT-TOTAL-LITERAL TO TOTAL-TYPE.
046300     MOVE "TOTAL" TO TOTAL-LITERAL.
046400     PERFORM LOAD-DEPARTMENT-NAME.
046500     MOVE TOTAL-LINE TO PRINTER-RECORD.
046600     PERFORM WRITE-TO-PRINTER.
046700     PERFORM LINE-FEED.
046800     MOVE SPACE TO DETAIL-LINE.
046900
047000 LOAD-DEPARTMENT-NAME.
047100     SET DEPARTMENT-INDEX TO 1.
047200     SEARCH DEPARTMENT-TABLE
047300        AT END
047400          MOVE "NOT FOUND" TO TOTAL-NAME
047500        WHEN
047600          DEPARTMENT-NUMBER(DEPARTMENT-INDEX) =
047700            CURRENT-DEPARTMENT
047800            MOVE DEPARTMENT-NAME(DEPARTMENT-INDEX) TO
047900              TOTAL-NAME.
048000
048100* PROCESS ONE RECORD LEVEL
048200 8000-PROCESS-ALL-CATEGORIES.
048300     PERFORM 8100-PROCESS-THIS-CATEGORY.
```

```
048400        ADD WORK-AMOUNT TO DEPARTMENT-TOTAL.
048500        ADD 1 TO RECORD-COUNT.
048600        PERFORM READ-NEXT-VALID-WORK.
048700
048800 8100-PROCESS-THIS-CATEGORY.
048900        IF LINE-COUNT > MAXIMUM-LINES
049000            PERFORM START-NEXT-PAGE.
049100        PERFORM 8110-PRINT-THE-RECORD.
049200
049300 8110-PRINT-THE-RECORD.
049400        MOVE WORK-CATEGORY TO PRINT-CATEGORY.
049500
049600        PERFORM 8120-LOAD-CATEGORY-NAME.
049700
049800        MOVE WORK-AMOUNT TO PRINT-AMOUNT.
049900
050000        MOVE DETAIL-LINE TO PRINTER-RECORD.
050100        PERFORM WRITE-TO-PRINTER.
050200        MOVE SPACE TO DETAIL-LINE.
050300
050400 8120-LOAD-CATEGORY-NAME.
050500        SET CATEGORY-INDEX TO 1.
050600        SEARCH CATEGORY-TABLE
050700            AT END
050800              MOVE "NOT FOUND" TO TOTAL-NAME
050900            WHEN
051000              CATEGORY-NUMBER(CATEGORY-INDEX) =
051100                  WORK-CATEGORY
051200                  MOVE CATEGORY-NAME(CATEGORY-INDEX) TO
051300                      PRINT-CATEGORY-NAME.
051400
051500* PRINTING ROUTINES
051600 WRITE-TO-PRINTER.
051700        WRITE PRINTER-RECORD BEFORE ADVANCING 1.
051800        ADD 1 TO LINE-COUNT.
051900
052000 LINE-FEED.
052100        MOVE SPACE TO PRINTER-RECORD.
052200        PERFORM WRITE-TO-PRINTER.
052300
052400 START-NEXT-PAGE.
052500        PERFORM END-LAST-PAGE.
052600        PERFORM START-NEW-PAGE.
052700
052800 START-NEW-PAGE.
052900        ADD 1 TO PAGE-NUMBER.
053000        MOVE PAGE-NUMBER TO PRINT-PAGE-NUMBER.
053100        MOVE TITLE-LINE TO PRINTER-RECORD.
053200        PERFORM WRITE-TO-PRINTER.
053300        PERFORM LINE-FEED.
053400        MOVE LEGEND-LINE TO PRINTER-RECORD.
053500        PERFORM WRITE-TO-PRINTER.
053600        PERFORM LINE-FEED.
053700        MOVE COLUMN-LINE TO PRINTER-RECORD.
053800        PERFORM WRITE-TO-PRINTER.
```

BD
2

continues

Listing B2.18. continued

```
053900      PERFORM LINE-FEED.
054000
054100 END-LAST-PAGE.
054200      IF PAGE-NUMBER > 0
054300          PERFORM FORM-FEED.
054400      MOVE ZERO TO LINE-COUNT.
054500
054600 FORM-FEED.
054700      MOVE SPACE TO PRINTER-RECORD.
054800      WRITE PRINTER-RECORD BEFORE ADVANCING PAGE.
054900
055000*-------------------------------
055100* Read first, read next routines
055200*-------------------------------
055300 READ-FIRST-VALID-WORK.
055400      PERFORM READ-NEXT-VALID-WORK.
055500
055600 READ-NEXT-VALID-WORK.
055700      PERFORM READ-NEXT-WORK-RECORD.
055800
055900 READ-NEXT-WORK-RECORD.
056000      MOVE "N" TO WORK-FILE-AT-END.
056100      READ WORK-FILE NEXT RECORD
056200          AT END MOVE "Y" TO WORK-FILE-AT-END.
056300
056400* Date and time routines
056500 FORMAT-THE-DATE.
056600      PERFORM CONVERT-TO-MMDDCCYY.
056700      MOVE DATE-MMDDCCYY TO FORMATTED-DATE.
056800
056900 CONVERT-TO-MMDDCCYY.
057000      COMPUTE DATE-MMDDCCYY =
057100          DATE-CCYYMMDD * 10000.0001.
057200
057300 FORMAT-THE-TIME.
057400      MOVE TIME-HHMMSS TO FORMATTED-TIME.
057500      INSPECT FORMATTED-TIME
057600        REPLACING ALL "/" BY ":".
057700
```

Qualified Data Names

Although data names should be unique within a program, there is a way around this—using a qualified data name that became available in the COBOL-74 standard. Data names do not need to be unique, as long as the name exists within a hierarchy of names in such a way that the name can be made unique by reference to one or more of the higher-level names. Use this syntax:

```
QUALIFIED NAMES
01  a-structure-name
    05  variable-1   picture
```

```
        05  variable-2   picture

01  another-structure
        05  variable-1   picture
        05  variable-2   picture

statement variable-1
        of another-structure
```

The following is an example:

```
01  STORE-TOTALS
        05 SALES-AMT   PIC S9(5)V99
        05 TAX-AMT     PIC S9(3)V99.

01  GRAND-TOTALS
        05 SALES-AMT   PIC S9(5)V99
        05 TAX-AMT     PIC S9(3)V99.

ADD SALES-AMT OF STORE-TOTALS
        TO SALES-AMT OF GRAND-TOTALS
ADD TAX-AMT OF STORE-TOTALS
        TO TAX-AMT OF GRAND-TOTALS.
```

Listing B2.19 shows `slsprt06.cbl`, based on `slsrpt04.cbl`.

TYPE **Listing B2.19. Qualified data names.**

```
000100 IDENTIFICATION DIVISION.
000200 PROGRAM-ID. SLSRPT06.
000300*-------------------------------
000400* Print test sales data
000500* Uses qualified data names.
000600*-------------------------------
000700 ENVIRONMENT DIVISION.
000800 INPUT-OUTPUT SECTION.
000900 FILE-CONTROL.
001000
001100*-------------------------------
001200* SLSALES.CBL
001300*-------------------------------
001400     SELECT SALES-FILE
001500         ASSIGN TO "SALES"
001600         ORGANIZATION IS SEQUENTIAL.
001700
001800     SELECT WORK-FILE
001900         ASSIGN TO "WORK"
002000         ORGANIZATION IS SEQUENTIAL.
002100
002200     SELECT SORT-FILE
002300         ASSIGN TO "SORT".
002400
002500     SELECT PRINTER-FILE
002600         ASSIGN TO PRINTER
002700         ORGANIZATION IS LINE SEQUENTIAL.
```

continues

Listing B2.19. continued

```
002800
002900 DATA DIVISION.
003000 FILE SECTION.
003100
003200*-------------------------------
003300* FDSALES.CBL
003400* Temporary daily sales file.
003500*-------------------------------
003600 FD  SALES-FILE
003700     LABEL RECORDS ARE STANDARD.
003800 01  SALES-RECORD.
003900     05  SALES-STORE          PIC 9(2).
004000     05  SALES-DIVISION       PIC 9(2).
004100     05  SALES-DEPARTMENT     PIC 9(2).
004200     05  SALES-CATEGORY       PIC 9(2).
004300     05  SALES-AMOUNT         PIC S9(6)V99.
004400
004500 FD  WORK-FILE
004600     LABEL RECORDS ARE STANDARD.
004700 01  WORK-RECORD.
004800     05  SALES-STORE          PIC 9(2).
004900     05  SALES-DIVISION       PIC 9(2).
005000     05  SALES-DEPARTMENT     PIC 9(2).
005100     05  SALES-CATEGORY       PIC 9(2).
005200     05  SALES-AMOUNT         PIC S9(6)V99.
005300
005400 SD  SORT-FILE
005500     LABEL RECORDS ARE STANDARD.
005600 01  SORT-RECORD.
005700     05  SALES-STORE          PIC 9(2).
005800     05  SALES-DIVISION       PIC 9(2).
005900     05  SALES-DEPARTMENT     PIC 9(2).
006000     05  SALES-CATEGORY       PIC 9(2).
006100     05  SALES-AMOUNT         PIC S9(6)V99.
006200
006300 FD  PRINTER-FILE
006400     LABEL RECORDS ARE OMITTED.
006500 01  PRINTER-RECORD           PIC X(80).
006600
006700 WORKING-STORAGE SECTION.
006800
006900 01  THE-DIVISIONS.
007000     05  FILLER      PIC 99 VALUE 01.
007100     05  FILLER      PIC X(15) VALUE "ATHLETICS".
007200     05  FILLER      PIC 99 VALUE 02.
007300     05  FILLER      PIC X(15) VALUE "SPORTING GOODS".
007400     05  FILLER      PIC 99 VALUE 03.
007500     05  FILLER      PIC X(15) VALUE "CAMPING".
007600 01  FILLER REDEFINES THE-DIVISIONS.
007700     05  DIVISION-TABLE OCCURS 3 TIMES
007800         INDEXED BY DIVISION-INDEX.
007900     10  DIVISION-NUMBER      PIC 99.
008000     10  DIVISION-NAME        PIC X(15).
008100
```

```
008200 01   THE-DEPARTMENTS.
008300      05  FILLER        PIC 99 VALUE 01.
008400      05  FILLER        PIC X(15) VALUE "EXERCISE".
008500      05  FILLER        PIC 99 VALUE 02.
008600      05  FILLER        PIC X(15) VALUE "MISCELLANEOUS".
008700      05  FILLER        PIC 99 VALUE 03.
008800      05  FILLER        PIC X(15) VALUE "SPORT CLOTHES".
008900      05  FILLER        PIC 99 VALUE 04.
009000      05  FILLER        PIC X(15) VALUE "EQUIPMENT".
009100      05  FILLER        PIC 99 VALUE 05.
009200      05  FILLER        PIC X(15) VALUE "CAMP EQUIPMENT".
009300      05  FILLER        PIC 99 VALUE 06.
009400      05  FILLER        PIC X(15) VALUE "CAMPING CLOTHES".
009500 01   FILLER REDEFINES THE-DEPARTMENTS.
009600      05  DEPARTMENT-TABLE OCCURS 6 TIMES
009700          INDEXED BY DEPARTMENT-INDEX.
009800          10  DEPARTMENT-NUMBER        PIC 99.
009900          10  DEPARTMENT-NAME          PIC X(15).
010000
010100 01   THE-CATEGORIES.
010200      05  FILLER        PIC 99 VALUE 01.
010300      05  FILLER        PIC X(15) VALUE "WEIGHTS".
010400      05  FILLER        PIC 99 VALUE 02.
010500      05  FILLER        PIC X(15) VALUE "MACHINES".
010600      05  FILLER        PIC 99 VALUE 03.
010700      05  FILLER        PIC X(15) VALUE "SUN GLASSES".
010800      05  FILLER        PIC 99 VALUE 04.
010900      05  FILLER        PIC X(15) VALUE "VITAMINS".
011000      05  FILLER        PIC 99 VALUE 05.
011100      05  FILLER        PIC X(15) VALUE "MEN'S CLOTHES".
011200      05  FILLER        PIC 99 VALUE 06.
011300      05  FILLER        PIC X(15) VALUE "WOMEN'S CLOTHES".
011400      05  FILLER        PIC 99 VALUE 07.
011500      05  FILLER        PIC X(15) VALUE "TENNIS".
011600      05  FILLER        PIC 99 VALUE 08.
011700      05  FILLER        PIC X(15) VALUE "SOCCER".
011800      05  FILLER        PIC 99 VALUE 09.
011900      05  FILLER        PIC X(15) VALUE "TENTS".
012000      05  FILLER        PIC 99 VALUE 10.
012100      05  FILLER        PIC X(15) VALUE "SLEEPING BAGS".
012200      05  FILLER        PIC 99 VALUE 11.
012300      05  FILLER        PIC X(15) VALUE "CLOTHING".
012400      05  FILLER        PIC 99 VALUE 12.
012500      05  FILLER        PIC X(15) VALUE "HIKING BOOTS".
012600 01   FILLER REDEFINES THE-CATEGORIES.
012700      05  CATEGORY-TABLE OCCURS 12 TIMES
012800          INDEXED BY CATEGORY-INDEX.
012900          10  CATEGORY-NUMBER          PIC 99.
013000          10  CATEGORY-NAME            PIC X(15).
013100
013200 77   OK-TO-PROCESS        PIC X.
013300
013400      COPY "WSCASE01.CBL".
013500
013600 01   LEGEND-LINE.
```

continues

Listing B2.19. continued

```
013700      05  FILLER          PIC X(6) VALUE "STORE:".
013800      05  FILLER          PIC X(1) VALUE SPACE.
013900      05  PRINT-STORE     PIC Z9.
014000
014100 01  DETAIL-LINE.
014200      05  FILLER               PIC X(3) VALUE SPACE.
014300      05  PRINT-DIVISION       PIC Z9.
014400      05  FILLER               PIC X(4) VALUE SPACE.
014500      05  FILLER               PIC X(3) VALUE SPACE.
014600      05  PRINT-DEPARTMENT     PIC Z9.
014700      05  FILLER               PIC X(6) VALUE SPACE.
014800      05  FILLER               PIC X(3) VALUE SPACE.
014900      05  PRINT-CATEGORY       PIC Z9.
015000      05  FILLER               PIC X(4) VALUE SPACE.
015100      05  PRINT-CATEGORY-NAME  PIC X(15).
015200      05  FILLER               PIC X(1) VALUE SPACE.
015300      05  PRINT-AMOUNT         PIC ZZZ,ZZ9.99-.
015400
015500 01  COLUMN-LINE.
015600      05  FILLER          PIC X(8)  VALUE "DIVISION".
015700      05  FILLER          PIC X(1)  VALUE SPACE.
015800      05  FILLER          PIC X(10) VALUE "DEPARTMENT".
015900      05  FILLER          PIC X(1)  VALUE SPACE.
016000      05  FILLER          PIC X(8)  VALUE "CATEGORY".
016100      05  FILLER          PIC X(1)  VALUE SPACE.
016200      05  FILLER          PIC X(15) VALUE SPACE.
016300      05  FILLER          PIC X(5)  VALUE SPACE.
016400      05  FILLER          PIC X(6)  VALUE "AMOUNT".
016500
016600 01  TITLE-LINE.
016700      05  FILLER               PIC X(4) VALUE "RUN:".
016800      05  FORMATTED-RUN-DATE   PIC X(10).
016900      05  FILLER               PIC X(4) VALUE " AT ".
017000      05  FORMATTED-RUN-TIME   PIC X(8).
017100      05  FILLER               PIC X(10) VALUE SPACE.
017200      05  FILLER               PIC X(12)
017300          VALUE "SALES REPORT".
017400      05  FILLER               PIC X(10) VALUE SPACE.
017500      05  FILLER               PIC X(5) VALUE "PAGE:".
017600      05  FILLER               PIC X(1) VALUE SPACE.
017700      05  PRINT-PAGE-NUMBER    PIC ZZZ9.
017800
017900 01  TOTAL-LINE.
018000      05  FILLER          PIC X(11) VALUE SPACE.
018100      05  TOTAL-TYPE      PIC X(8).
018200      05  FILLER          PIC X(1) VALUE SPACE.
018300      05  TOTAL-NUMBER    PIC Z9.
018400      05  FILLER          PIC X(1) VALUE SPACE.
018500      05  TOTAL-NAME      PIC X(15) VALUE SPACE.
018600      05  FILLER          PIC X(1) VALUE SPACE.
018700      05  TOTAL-LITERAL   PIC X(5) VALUE "TOTAL".
018800      05  FILLER          PIC X(1) VALUE SPACE.
018900      05  PRINT-TOTAL     PIC ZZZ,ZZ9.99-.
019000
```

```
019100 77  GRAND-TOTAL-LITERAL      PIC X(8) VALUE "   GRAND".
019200 77  STORE-TOTAL-LITERAL      PIC X(8) VALUE "   STORE".
019300 77  DIVISION-TOTAL-LITERAL   PIC X(8) VALUE "DIVISION".
019400 77  DEPARTMENT-TOTAL-LITERAL PIC X(8) VALUE "    DEPT".
019500
019600 77  WORK-FILE-AT-END         PIC X.
019700
019800 77  LINE-COUNT               PIC 999 VALUE ZERO.
019900 77  PAGE-NUMBER              PIC 9999 VALUE ZERO.
020000 77  MAXIMUM-LINES            PIC 999 VALUE 55.
020100
020200 77  RECORD-COUNT             PIC 9999 VALUE ZEROES.
020300
020400* Control break current values for store, division
020500* department.
020600 77  CURRENT-STORE            PIC 99.
020700 77  CURRENT-DIVISION         PIC 99.
020800 77  CURRENT-DEPARTMENT       PIC 99.
020900
021000* Control break accumulators
021100* GRAND TOTAL is the level 1 accumulator for the whole file
021200* STORE TOTAL is the level 2 accumulator
021300* DIVISION TOTAL is the level 3 accumulator
021400* DEPARTMENT TOTAL is the level 4 accumulator.
021500 77  GRAND-TOTAL              PIC S9(6)V99.
021600 77  STORE-TOTAL              PIC S9(6)V99.
021700 77  DIVISION-TOTAL           PIC S9(6)V99.
021800 77  DEPARTMENT-TOTAL         PIC S9(6)V99.
021900
022000* System date and time
022100 77  RUN-DATE          PIC 9(6).
022200 77  RUN-TIME          PIC 9(8).
022300
022400*------------------------------
022500* Fields for date routines.
022600*------------------------------
022700 77  FORMATTED-DATE    PIC Z9/99/9999.
022800 77  DATE-MMDDCCYY      PIC 9(8).
022900 01  DATE-CCYYMMDD      PIC 9(8).
023000 01  FILLER REDEFINES DATE-CCYYMMDD.
023100     05  DATE-CC        PIC 99.
023200     05  DATE-YY        PIC 99.
023300     05  DATE-MM        PIC 99.
023400     05  DATE-DD        PIC 99.
023500
023600*------------------------------
023700* Fields for TIME routines.
023800*------------------------------
023900 77  FORMATTED-TIME    PIC Z9/99/99.
024000
024100 01  TIME-HHMMSS     PIC 9(6).
024200 01  FILLER REDEFINES TIME-HHMMSS.
024300     05  TIME-HH        PIC 99.
024400     05  TIME-MM        PIC 99.
024500     05  TIME-SS        PIC 99.
```

continues

Listing B2.19. continued

```
024600
024700 PROCEDURE DIVISION.
024800 PROGRAM-BEGIN.
024900
025000     PERFORM OPENING-PROCEDURE.
025100     PERFORM MAIN-PROCESS.
025200     PERFORM CLOSING-PROCEDURE.
025300
025400 PROGRAM-EXIT.
025500     EXIT PROGRAM.
025600
025700 PROGRAM-DONE.
025800     STOP RUN.
025900
026000 OPENING-PROCEDURE.
026100
026200     OPEN OUTPUT PRINTER-FILE.
026300
026400 MAIN-PROCESS.
026500     PERFORM GET-OK-TO-PROCESS.
026600     PERFORM PROCESS-THE-FILE
026700         UNTIL OK-TO-PROCESS = "N".
026800
026900 CLOSING-PROCEDURE.
027000     CLOSE PRINTER-FILE.
027100
027200 GET-OK-TO-PROCESS.
027300     PERFORM ACCEPT-OK-TO-PROCESS.
027400     PERFORM RE-ACCEPT-OK-TO-PROCESS
027500         UNTIL OK-TO-PROCESS = "Y" OR "N".
027600
027700 ACCEPT-OK-TO-PROCESS.
027800     DISPLAY "PRINT SALES REPORT (Y/N)?".
027900     ACCEPT OK-TO-PROCESS.
028000     INSPECT OK-TO-PROCESS
028100       CONVERTING LOWER-ALPHA
028200       TO          UPPER-ALPHA.
028300
028400 RE-ACCEPT-OK-TO-PROCESS.
028500     DISPLAY "YOU MUST ENTER YES OR NO".
028600     PERFORM ACCEPT-OK-TO-PROCESS.
028700
028800 PROCESS-THE-FILE.
028900     PERFORM START-THE-FILE.
029000     PERFORM PRINT-ONE-REPORT.
029100     PERFORM END-THE-FILE.
029200
029300*    PERFORM GET-OK-TO-PROCESS.
029400     MOVE "N" TO OK-TO-PROCESS.
029500
029600 START-THE-FILE.
029700     PERFORM SORT-DATA-FILE.
029800     OPEN INPUT WORK-FILE.
029900
```

```
030000 END-THE-FILE.
030100     CLOSE WORK-FILE.
030200
030300 SORT-DATA-FILE.
030400     SORT SORT-FILE
030500         ON ASCENDING KEY SALES-STORE OF SORT-RECORD
030600             ASCENDING KEY SALES-DIVISION OF SORT-RECORD
030700             ASCENDING KEY SALES-DEPARTMENT OF SORT-RECORD
030800             ASCENDING KEY SALES-CATEGORY OF SORT-RECORD
030900         USING SALES-FILE
031000         GIVING WORK-FILE.
031100
031200* LEVEL 1 CONTROL BREAK
031300 PRINT-ONE-REPORT.
031400     PERFORM START-ONE-REPORT.
031500     PERFORM PROCESS-ALL-STORES
031600         UNTIL WORK-FILE-AT-END = "Y".
031700     PERFORM END-ONE-REPORT.
031800
031900 START-ONE-REPORT.
032000     PERFORM READ-FIRST-VALID-WORK.
032100     MOVE ZEROES TO GRAND-TOTAL.
032200
032300     PERFORM START-NEW-REPORT.
032400
032500 START-NEW-REPORT.
032600     MOVE SPACE TO DETAIL-LINE.
032700     MOVE ZEROES TO LINE-COUNT PAGE-NUMBER.
032800
032900     ACCEPT RUN-DATE FROM DATE.
033000     MOVE RUN-DATE TO DATE-CCYYMMDD.
033100     IF DATE-YY > 90
033200         MOVE 19 TO DATE-CC
033300     ELSE
033400         MOVE 20 TO DATE-CC.
033500
033600     PERFORM FORMAT-THE-DATE.
033700     MOVE FORMATTED-DATE TO FORMATTED-RUN-DATE.
033800
033900     ACCEPT RUN-TIME FROM TIME.
034000     COMPUTE TIME-HHMMSS = RUN-TIME / 100.
034100     PERFORM FORMAT-THE-TIME.
034200     MOVE FORMATTED-TIME TO FORMATTED-RUN-TIME.
034300
034400
034500 END-ONE-REPORT.
034600     IF RECORD-COUNT = ZEROES
034700         MOVE "NO RECORDS FOUND" TO PRINTER-RECORD
034800         PERFORM WRITE-TO-PRINTER
034900     ELSE
035000         PERFORM PRINT-GRAND-TOTAL.
035100
035200     PERFORM END-LAST-PAGE.
035300
035400 PRINT-GRAND-TOTAL.
```

continues

Listing B2.19. continued

```
035500        MOVE SPACE TO TOTAL-LINE.
035600        MOVE GRAND-TOTAL TO PRINT-TOTAL.
035700        MOVE GRAND-TOTAL-LITERAL TO TOTAL-TYPE.
035800        MOVE "TOTAL" TO TOTAL-LITERAL.
035900        MOVE TOTAL-LINE TO PRINTER-RECORD.
036000        PERFORM WRITE-TO-PRINTER.
036100        PERFORM LINE-FEED 2 TIMES.
036200        MOVE SPACE TO DETAIL-LINE.
036300
036400* LEVEL 2 CONTROL BREAK
036500 PROCESS-ALL-STORES.
036600        PERFORM START-ONE-STORE.
036700
036800        PERFORM PROCESS-ALL-DIVISIONS
036900            UNTIL WORK-FILE-AT-END = "Y"
037000              OR SALES-STORE OF WORK-RECORD
037100                  NOT = CURRENT-STORE.
037200
037300        PERFORM END-ONE-STORE.
037400
037500 START-ONE-STORE.
037600        MOVE SALES-STORE OF WORK-RECORD TO CURRENT-STORE.
037700        MOVE ZEROES TO STORE-TOTAL.
037800        MOVE SALES-STORE OF WORK-RECORD TO PRINT-STORE.
037900
038000        PERFORM START-NEXT-PAGE.
038100
038200 END-ONE-STORE.
038300        PERFORM PRINT-STORE-TOTAL.
038400        ADD STORE-TOTAL TO GRAND-TOTAL.
038500
038600 PRINT-STORE-TOTAL.
038700        MOVE SPACE TO TOTAL-LINE.
038800        MOVE STORE-TOTAL TO PRINT-TOTAL.
038900        MOVE CURRENT-STORE TO TOTAL-NUMBER.
039000        MOVE STORE-TOTAL-LITERAL TO TOTAL-TYPE.
039100        MOVE "TOTAL" TO TOTAL-LITERAL.
039200        MOVE TOTAL-LINE TO PRINTER-RECORD.
039300        PERFORM WRITE-TO-PRINTER.
039400        PERFORM LINE-FEED.
039500        MOVE SPACE TO DETAIL-LINE.
039600
039700* LEVEL 3 CONTROL BREAK
039800 PROCESS-ALL-DIVISIONS.
039900        PERFORM START-ONE-DIVISION.
040000
040100        PERFORM PROCESS-ALL-DEPARTMENTS
040200            UNTIL WORK-FILE-AT-END = "Y"
040300              OR SALES-STORE OF WORK-RECORD
040400                  NOT = CURRENT-STORE
040500              OR SALES-DIVISION OF WORK-RECORD
040600                  NOT = CURRENT-DIVISION.
040700
040800        PERFORM END-ONE-DIVISION.
```

```
040900
041000 START-ONE-DIVISION.
041100     MOVE SALES-DIVISION OF WORK-RECORD TO CURRENT-DIVISION.
041200     MOVE ZEROES TO DIVISION-TOTAL.
041300     MOVE SALES-DIVISION OF WORK-RECORD TO PRINT-DIVISION.
041400
041500 END-ONE-DIVISION.
041600     PERFORM PRINT-DIVISION-TOTAL.
041700     ADD DIVISION-TOTAL TO STORE-TOTAL.
041800
041900 PRINT-DIVISION-TOTAL.
042000     MOVE SPACE TO TOTAL-LINE.
042100     MOVE DIVISION-TOTAL TO PRINT-TOTAL.
042200     MOVE CURRENT-DIVISION TO TOTAL-NUMBER.
042300     MOVE DIVISION-TOTAL-LITERAL TO TOTAL-TYPE.
042400     MOVE "TOTAL" TO TOTAL-LITERAL.
042500     PERFORM LOAD-DIVISION-NAME.
042600     MOVE TOTAL-LINE TO PRINTER-RECORD.
042700     PERFORM WRITE-TO-PRINTER.
042800     PERFORM LINE-FEED.
042900     MOVE SPACE TO DETAIL-LINE.
043000
043100 LOAD-DIVISION-NAME.
043200     SET DIVISION-INDEX TO 1.
043300     SEARCH DIVISION-TABLE
043400         AT END
043500             MOVE "NOT FOUND" TO TOTAL-NAME
043600         WHEN
043700             DIVISION-NUMBER(DIVISION-INDEX) =
043800                 CURRENT-DIVISION
043900                 MOVE DIVISION-NAME(DIVISION-INDEX) TO
044000                     TOTAL-NAME.
044100
044200* LEVEL 4 CONTROL BREAK
044300 PROCESS-ALL-DEPARTMENTS.
044400     PERFORM START-ONE-DEPARTMENT.
044500
044600     PERFORM PROCESS-ALL-CATEGORIES
044700         UNTIL WORK-FILE-AT-END = "Y"
044800             OR SALES-STORE OF WORK-RECORD
044900             NOT = CURRENT-STORE
045000             OR SALES-DIVISION OF WORK-RECORD
045100             NOT = CURRENT-DIVISION
045200             OR SALES-DEPARTMENT OF WORK-RECORD
045300             NOT = CURRENT-DEPARTMENT.
045400
045500     PERFORM END-ONE-DEPARTMENT.
045600
045700 START-ONE-DEPARTMENT.
045800     MOVE SALES-DEPARTMENT OF WORK-RECORD
045900         TO CURRENT-DEPARTMENT.
046000     MOVE ZEROES TO DEPARTMENT-TOTAL.
046100     MOVE SALES-DEPARTMENT OF WORK-RECORD
046200         TO PRINT-DEPARTMENT.
046300
```

continues

Listing B2.19. continued

```
046400 END-ONE-DEPARTMENT.
046500     PERFORM PRINT-DEPARTMENT-TOTAL.
046600     ADD DEPARTMENT-TOTAL TO DIVISION-TOTAL.
046700
046800 PRINT-DEPARTMENT-TOTAL.
046900     MOVE SPACE TO TOTAL-LINE.
047000     MOVE DEPARTMENT-TOTAL TO PRINT-TOTAL.
047100     MOVE CURRENT-DEPARTMENT TO TOTAL-NUMBER.
047200     MOVE DEPARTMENT-TOTAL-LITERAL TO TOTAL-TYPE.
047300     MOVE "TOTAL" TO TOTAL-LITERAL.
047400     PERFORM LOAD-DEPARTMENT-NAME.
047500     MOVE TOTAL-LINE TO PRINTER-RECORD.
047600     PERFORM WRITE-TO-PRINTER.
047700     PERFORM LINE-FEED.
047800     MOVE SPACE TO DETAIL-LINE.
047900
048000 LOAD-DEPARTMENT-NAME.
048100     SET DEPARTMENT-INDEX TO 1.
048200     SEARCH DEPARTMENT-TABLE
048300         AT END
048400           MOVE "NOT FOUND" TO TOTAL-NAME
048500         WHEN
048600           DEPARTMENT-NUMBER(DEPARTMENT-INDEX) =
048700               CURRENT-DEPARTMENT
048800               MOVE DEPARTMENT-NAME(DEPARTMENT-INDEX) TO
048900                   TOTAL-NAME.
049000
049100* PROCESS ONE RECORD LEVEL
049200 PROCESS-ALL-CATEGORIES.
049300     PERFORM PROCESS-THIS-CATEGORY.
049400     ADD SALES-AMOUNT OF WORK-RECORD
049500      TO DEPARTMENT-TOTAL.
049600     ADD 1 TO RECORD-COUNT.
049700     PERFORM READ-NEXT-VALID-WORK.
049800
049900 PROCESS-THIS-CATEGORY.
050000     IF LINE-COUNT > MAXIMUM-LINES
050100         PERFORM START-NEXT-PAGE.
050200     PERFORM PRINT-THE-RECORD.
050300
050400 PRINT-THE-RECORD.
050500     MOVE SALES-CATEGORY OF WORK-RECORD
050600      TO PRINT-CATEGORY.
050700
050800     PERFORM LOAD-CATEGORY-NAME.
050900
051000     MOVE SALES-AMOUNT OF WORK-RECORD
051100      TO PRINT-AMOUNT.
051200
051300     MOVE DETAIL-LINE TO PRINTER-RECORD.
051400     PERFORM WRITE-TO-PRINTER.
051500     MOVE SPACE TO DETAIL-LINE.
051600
051700 LOAD-CATEGORY-NAME.
051800     SET CATEGORY-INDEX TO 1.
```

```
051900     SEARCH CATEGORY-TABLE
052000         AT END
052100            MOVE "NOT FOUND" TO TOTAL-NAME
052200         WHEN
052300            CATEGORY-NUMBER(CATEGORY-INDEX) =
052400               SALES-CATEGORY OF WORK-RECORD
052500               MOVE CATEGORY-NAME(CATEGORY-INDEX) TO
052600                  PRINT-CATEGORY-NAME.
052700
052800* PRINTING ROUTINES
052900 WRITE-TO-PRINTER.
053000     WRITE PRINTER-RECORD BEFORE ADVANCING 1.
053100     ADD 1 TO LINE-COUNT.
053200
053300 LINE-FEED.
053400     MOVE SPACE TO PRINTER-RECORD.
053500     PERFORM WRITE-TO-PRINTER.
053600
053700 START-NEXT-PAGE.
053800     PERFORM END-LAST-PAGE.
053900     PERFORM START-NEW-PAGE.
054000
054100 START-NEW-PAGE.
054200     ADD 1 TO PAGE-NUMBER.
054300     MOVE PAGE-NUMBER TO PRINT-PAGE-NUMBER.
054400     MOVE TITLE-LINE TO PRINTER-RECORD.
054500     PERFORM WRITE-TO-PRINTER.
054600     PERFORM LINE-FEED.
054700     MOVE LEGEND-LINE TO PRINTER-RECORD.
054800     PERFORM WRITE-TO-PRINTER.
054900     PERFORM LINE-FEED.
055000     MOVE COLUMN-LINE TO PRINTER-RECORD.
055100     PERFORM WRITE-TO-PRINTER.
055200     PERFORM LINE-FEED.
055300
055400 END-LAST-PAGE.
055500     IF PAGE-NUMBER > 0
055600         PERFORM FORM-FEED.
055700     MOVE ZERO TO LINE-COUNT.
055800
055900 FORM-FEED.
056000     MOVE SPACE TO PRINTER-RECORD.
056100     WRITE PRINTER-RECORD BEFORE ADVANCING PAGE.
056200
056300*-------------------------------
056400* Read first, read next routines
056500*-------------------------------
056600 READ-FIRST-VALID-WORK.
056700     PERFORM READ-NEXT-VALID-WORK.
056800
056900 READ-NEXT-VALID-WORK.
057000     PERFORM READ-NEXT-WORK-RECORD.
057100
057200 READ-NEXT-WORK-RECORD.
057300     MOVE "N" TO WORK-FILE-AT-END.
```

continues

Listing B2.19. continued

```
057400      READ WORK-FILE NEXT RECORD
057500          AT END MOVE "Y" TO WORK-FILE-AT-END.
057600
057700* Date and time routines
057800 FORMAT-THE-DATE.
057900      PERFORM CONVERT-TO-MMDDCCYY.
058000      MOVE DATE-MMDDCCYY TO FORMATTED-DATE.
058100
058200 CONVERT-TO-MMDDCCYY.
058300      COMPUTE DATE-MMDDCCYY =
058400          DATE-CCYYMMDD * 10000.0001.
058500
058600 FORMAT-THE-TIME.
058700      MOVE TIME-HHMMSS TO FORMATTED-TIME.
058800      INSPECT FORMATTED-TIME
058900        REPLACING ALL "/" BY ":".
059000
```

ANALYSIS Rather than using different names for each of the fields in the three records used by the program, all the fields are given the same names (see lines `003900–004300`, `004800–005200`, and `005700–006100`). This apparent naming conflict can be resolved by referring to the field with a qualifier `OF RECORD-NAME`. Throughout the program, qualifiers are added to the names of the fields to clarify which field is meant.

At lines `030500–030800`, all the sort fields are qualified by adding `OF SORT-RECORD` after the field name. All the fields in the `WORK-RECORD` are qualified by adding `OF WORK-RECORD`. Some examples of this are at lines `037600`, `037800`, `040300–0406000`, `044800–045300`, and `052400`. There are many other examples in the program.

Code, compile, and run slsrpt06.cbl, and satisfy yourself that it runs with the same result as slsrpt04.cbl. Then edit the file and remove one of the `OF WORK-RECORD` phrases from any variable. Attempt to compile the program and you should receive an error such as `"Qualifier needed"` or `"Ambiguous reference to variable."` Micro Focus Personal COBOL produces the error `"User-name not unique."`

MOVE CORRESPONDING

The use of qualified variables makes it possible to use `MOVE` to move more than one field at a time. In Listing B2.20, the `DETAIL-LINE` has been defined using the same data names as some of the fields in the `SALES-RECORD`.

TYPE **Listing B2.20. Using** MOVE CORRESPONDING.

```
003600 FD  SALES-FILE
003700     LABEL RECORDS ARE STANDARD.
003800 01  SALES-RECORD.
003900     05  SALES-STORE           PIC 9(2).
004000     05  SALES-DIVISION        PIC 9(2).
004100     05  SALES-DEPARTMENT      PIC 9(2).
004200     05  SALES-CATEGORY        PIC 9(2).
004300     05  SALES-AMOUNT          PIC S9(6)V99.
......
014100 01  DETAIL-LINE.
014200     05  FILLER                PIC X(3) VALUE SPACE.
014300     05  SALES-DIVISION        PIC Z9.
014400     05  FILLER                PIC X(4) VALUE SPACE.
014500     05  FILLER                PIC X(3) VALUE SPACE.
014600     05  SALES-DEPARTMENT      PIC Z9.
014700     05  FILLER                PIC X(6) VALUE SPACE.
014800     05  FILLER                PIC X(3) VALUE SPACE.
014900     05  SALES-CATEGORY        PIC Z9.
015000     05  FILLER                PIC X(4) VALUE SPACE.
015300     05  SALES-AMOUNT          PIC ZZZ,ZZ9.99-.
......
020100     MOVE CORRESPONDING SALES-RECORD TO DETAIL-LINE.
```

ANALYSIS At line 020100, the MOVE CORRESPONDING will cause fields in the SALES-RECORD that have the same name as fields in the DETAIL-LINE to be moved one by one to corresponding fields in the detail line. These moves happen as if each field were moved individually.

SALES-DIVISION, SALES-DEPARTMENT, SALES-CATEGORY, and SALES-AMOUNT will be moved. SALES-STORE will not be moved because there is no corresponding field in the DETAIL-LINE.

Continuation Characters

When an alphanumeric value is too long to fit on a single line, it may be continued on the next line by using a continuation character. In Listing B2.21, the columns have been included. The message must be continued to the end of Area B (column 72) and ends without a closing quote. The next line begins with a hyphen (-) in column 7 to indicate that the previous quoted string is being continued. The rest of the message starts with a quote and continues as long as is necessary to complete the message. Lines can be continued over more than one line if necessary.

TYPE **Listing B2.21. The continuation character.**

```
000500 01  LONG-MESSAGE    PIC X(80) VALUE "This is an incredibly long
000600-         "message that will take more than one line to define".
```

Summary

Today, you learned about some common issues that will come up when you work with COBOL, including these basics:

☐ A table may be initialized in WORKING-STORAGE by first defining a variable containing the needed values, and then redefining this variable as a table.

☐ The STRING verb can be used to concatenate several fields into one by appending the input fields end to end.

☐ An UNSTRING verb can be used to break a longer field into smaller pieces.

☐ A calling program may pass a variable to a called program. If the variable is changed by either the called or calling program, that change affects the variable in both programs.

☐ Computational numeric storage can be used to save space in memory or in a file.

☐ The steps for calculating the size of a COMP-3 field are

    1. Count the number of digits in the number.

    2. Add 1 for the sign (even if the number does not have a sign in the PICTURE).

    3. If the result is an odd number, add 1 to make it even.

    4. Divide this result by two.

☐ One style of COBOL coding uses paragraph numbers to break the paragraphs of a program into sections of code that can be easily located on a printed listing, and helps to indicate the relationships between various routines.

☐ Data names do not have to be unique, as long as the name exists within a hierarchy of names in such a way that the name can be made unique by reference to one or more of the higher-level names. A data name can be made unique by qualifying it.

☐ MOVE CORRESPONDING can be used to move individual fields with the same names from one record to another.

☐ A continuation character can be used to continue a literal on one or more subsequent lines.

Q&A

Q Do I need to number paragraphs?

A No. It is not part of the COBOL language, but you might end up working for a company that requires it as part of its coding style.

2

Q What would a continuation look like for a literal that extended over more than two lines?

A The following code presents a much longer continuation:

```
000500 01  LONG-MESSAGE     PIC X(200) VALUE   "This is an incredibly lon
000600-    "g message that will take more than one line to define. In fa
000700-    "ct this now extends over several lines."
```

Q What happens on the display if an alphanumeric value longer than 80 characters is displayed? Does it wrap to the next line, or is it truncated?

A Usually, values that are longer than 80 characters wrap to the next line. However, some versions of COBOL display only the first 80 characters on a single line and truncate the remaining characters.

Workshop

Quiz

1. What is the output of the STRING operation described in the following code, using JONES and JOHN as the values in LAST-NAME and FIRST-NAME, and PAUL as the value in MIDDLE-NAME?

```
001300 01  DETAIL-LINE.
001400     05  PRINT-WHOLE-NAME       PIC X(32).
.......
010300     MOVE SPACE TO DETAIL-LINE.
010400     STRING
010500      LAST-NAME DELIMITED BY SPACE
010600      "," DELIMITED BY SIZE
010700      " " DELIMITED BY SIZE
010800      FIRST-NAME DELIMITED BY SPACE
010900      " " DELIMITED BY SIZE
011000      MIDDLE-NAME DELIMITED BY SPACE
011100       INTO PRINT-WHOLE-NAME.
011200     PERFORM PRINT-DETAIL-LINE.
```

2. After executing the following code, what will be the values in FIRST-NAME and LAST-NAME if the user enters JANE JOHANSEN?

```
001100 01  INPUT-DATA         PIC X(50).
001200
001300 01  FORMATTED-NAME.
001400     05  FIRST-NAME      PIC X(25).
001500     05  LAST-NAME       PIC X(25).
......
010700     DISPLAY "ENTER FIRST AND LAST NAMES".
010800     DISPLAY "WITH A SPACE BETWEEN THE NAMES".
010900     ACCEPT INPUT-DATA.
011000     MOVE SPACE TO FORMATTED-NAME.
011100     UNSTRING INPUT-DATA
```

```
011200          DELIMITED BY ALL SPACE
011300          INTO FIRST-NAME
011400               LAST-NAME.
011500
```

Exercise

Write a program named yesorno.cbl that can be called, and that will ask the user to answer yes or no.

Hint: This program should only have to be passed one field, a single PIC X that is filled in by the program. You should be able to pattern this on timedit.cbl. Appendix A, "Answers," includes a short program that can be used to test your program.

Day **3**

Full-Screen I/O

So far you have worked with COBOL programs that display and accept all data by scrolling up from the bottom of the screen. All activity you have encountered so far occurs one line at a time.

Several modern versions of COBOL enable a more polished method of handling user input by enabling the program to display and accept a full screen of information at a time. Full-screen I/O is not a standard part of the COBOL language, but it is so common in modern COBOL that you should have some understanding of how this works. Because full-screen I/O is not a standard part of the language, there are variations on how each version of COBOL handles this problem. There are enough similarities, however, that a general understanding of how some versions of COBOL handle full-screen I/O will be usable with almost any version of COBOL.

Today, you learn about the following topics:

- [ ] What is full-screen I/O?
- [ ] The keyboard
- [ ] Formatting full screens

☐ Defining a screen to maintain a file

☐ A maintenance module for the file

☐ Boilerplate

What Is Full-Screen I/O?

Full-screen I/O enables you to define a complete screen (24 rows by 80 columns) containing prompts and fields to be entered. This screen can be displayed to the user, which enables the user to enter data in the fields, move the cursor around the screen to different fields, modify the fields in any order, and then complete the entry by pressing a key to indicate that all fields are complete.

Figure B3.1 is an example of what a full screen might look like. The screen is a series of prompts followed by one or more fields into which information can be typed.

Most versions of COBOL make this feature available by providing an enhanced version of the ACCEPT and DISPLAY verbs. These enhanced features usually allow for the following:

☐ Fields to be positioned by row and column

☐ Fields to be given special attributes, such as blinking, highlighting, or underlining

☐ The cursor to be positioned by row and column

☐ Keys on the keyboard to be defined with special functions

Figure B3.1.

An example of full-screen I/O.

```
         VENDOR NUMBER:           2

         VENDOR NAME:         ABC PRINTING_____

         VENDOR ADDRESS:      1624 FOOTHILL BLVD
                              SUITE 34
         VENDOR CITY:         LOS ANGELES

         VENDOR STATE:        CA   CALIFORNIA

         VENDOR ZIP:          91042

         VENDOR CONTACT:      CHARLES JOHANSSEN

         VENDOR PHONE:        (818) 555-4321


CHANGE FIELDS
CONTINUE WITH CHANGES (Y/N)?        Y
```

The Keyboard

The keyboard usually behaves differently during full-screen I/O, and you will have to experiment with it once you have your first program up and running. Usually, the Tab key and arrow keys move you around the screen from field to field, and the Enter key causes the screen input to terminate and sends the data you have entered back to the program. This might cause confusion for some PC users who are used to using the Enter key to move the cursor to the next field.

Formatting Full Screens

The simplest screen to format for data entry usually is a menu screen. It has several values that are displayed onscreen, and usually only one data entry field, which is the selection by the user.

First look at the following proposed output for a full-screen menu:

```
                            PLEASE SELECT:

                                1.  STATE CODE MAINTENANCE
                                2.  VENDOR MAINTENANCE
                                3.  VOUCHER PROCESSING

                                0.  EXIT




            YOUR SELECTION 5
            INVALID SELECTION - PLEASE RE-TRY.
```

Now look at the code to create this screen. Listing B3.1 is `bilmnu04.cbl`, and is a full-screen version of the billing system menu for Micro Focus Personal or Professional COBOL, ACUCOBOL, and with slight revisions LPI COBOL.

TYPE **Listing B3.1. A full-screen menu.**

```
000100 IDENTIFICATION DIVISION.
000200 PROGRAM-ID. BILMNU04.
000300*--------------------------------
000400* Menu for the bill payment system.
000500* Including Vouchers
000600* Using full screen IO.
000700*--------------------------------
000800 ENVIRONMENT DIVISION.
000900 INPUT-OUTPUT SECTION.
001000 FILE-CONTROL.
001100
001200 DATA DIVISION.
001300 FILE SECTION.
```

continues

Listing B3.1. continued

```
001400
001500 WORKING-STORAGE SECTION.
001600
001700 77  MENU-PICK                 PIC 9 VALUE 0.
001800     88  MENU-PICK-IS-VALID     VALUES 0 THRU 3.
001900
002000 77  ERROR-MESSAGE     PIC X(79).
002100
002200 SCREEN SECTION.
002300 01  MENU-SCREEN.
002400     05  BLANK SCREEN.
002500     05  LINE  6 COL 20 VALUE "PLEASE SELECT:".
002600     05  LINE  8 COL 25 VALUE "1. STATE CODE MAINTENANCE".
002700     05  LINE  9 COL 25 VALUE "2. VENDOR MAINTENANCE".
002800     05  LINE 10 COL 25 VALUE "3. VOUCHER PROCESSING".
002900     05  LINE 12 COL 25 VALUE "0. EXIT".
003000     05  LINE 20 COL  1 VALUE "YOUR SELECTION".
003100     05  LINE 20 COL 16 PIC Z USING MENU-PICK.
003200     05  LINE 24 COL  1 PIC X(79) FROM ERROR-MESSAGE.
003300
003400 PROCEDURE DIVISION.
003500 PROGRAM-BEGIN.
003600     PERFORM OPENING-PROCEDURE.
003700     PERFORM MAIN-PROCESS.
003800     PERFORM CLOSING-PROCEDURE.
003900
004000 PROGRAM-EXIT.
004100     EXIT PROGRAM.
004200
004300 PROGRAM-DONE.
004400     STOP RUN.
004500
004600 OPENING-PROCEDURE.
004700
004800 CLOSING-PROCEDURE.
004900
005000 MAIN-PROCESS.
005100     PERFORM GET-MENU-PICK.
005200     PERFORM DO-THE-PICK
005300         UNTIL MENU-PICK = 0.
005400
005500*--------------------------------
005600* MENU
005700*--------------------------------
005800 GET-MENU-PICK.
005900     PERFORM DISPLAY-MENU-SCREEN.
006000     PERFORM ACCEPT-MENU-SCREEN.
006100     PERFORM RE-ACCEPT-MENU-SCREEN
006200         UNTIL MENU-PICK-IS-VALID.
006300
006400 DISPLAY-MENU-SCREEN.
006500
006600     DISPLAY MENU-SCREEN.
006700
```

```
006800 ACCEPT-MENU-SCREEN.
006900     ACCEPT MENU-SCREEN.
007000     MOVE SPACE TO ERROR-MESSAGE.
007100
007200 RE-ACCEPT-MENU-SCREEN.
007300     MOVE "INVALID SELECTION - PLEASE RE-TRY."
007400         TO ERROR-MESSAGE.
007500     PERFORM DISPLAY-MENU-SCREEN.
007600     PERFORM ACCEPT-MENU-SCREEN.
007700
007800 DO-THE-PICK.
007900     IF MENU-PICK = 1
008000         PERFORM STATE-MAINTENANCE
008100     ELSE
008200     IF MENU-PICK = 2
008300         PERFORM VENDOR-MAINTENANCE
008400     ELSE
008500     IF MENU-PICK = 3
008600         PERFORM VOUCHER-PROCESSING.
008700
008800     PERFORM GET-MENU-PICK.
008900
009000*------------------------------
009100* STATE
009200*------------------------------
009300 STATE-MAINTENANCE.
009400     CALL "STCMNT04".
009500
009600*------------------------------
009700* VENDOR
009800*------------------------------
009900 VENDOR-MAINTENANCE.
010000     CALL "VNDMNT05".
010100
010200*------------------------------
010300* VOUCHERS
010400*------------------------------
010500 VOUCHER-PROCESSING.
010600     CALL "VCHMNU01".
010700
```

ANALYSIS The SCREEN SECTION begins at line 002200. The screen definition for MENU-SCREEN begins at line 002200.

The first variable within MENU-SCREEN is BLANK SCREEN at line 002400. This is not really a value, but an instruction to blank the screen when DISPLAY MENU-SCREEN is executed.

Lines 002500 through 002900 define values that will be displayed onscreen. Each field is defined with a LINE (row), COL (column), and a VALUE definition of the literal.

Line 003100 defines a data entry field. This definition includes a line and column (LINE 20 COL 16), a picture (PIC Z), and a USING clause (USING MENU-PICK) that names the field to be used for receiving the entered data. When the MENU-SCREEN is processed, this definition causes various things to happen.

During DISPLAY MENU-SCREEN, the cursor is positioned at row 20 and column 16. The value in MENU-PICK is moved to the screen and displayed using zero suppression (PIC Z).

During ACCEPT MENU-PICK, the cursor is positioned at row 20 and column 16. The value entered by the user is saved. When the user presses Enter, the saved value is moved to MENU-PICK.

It is important to note that MENU-PICK is defined in WORKING-STORAGE at line 001700, and not in the SCREEN SECTION. The field that is displayed or entered is always processed by moving it to a temporary area and then displaying it, or accepting it into a temporary area and moving it back to the field. This moving back and forth is performed automatically by displaying or accepting a full screen. The field itself is not part of the screen definition, but is used by the screen definition.

The last field in MENU-SCREEN is defined at line 003200. This has a row and column position (LINE 24 COL 1), a picture (PIC X(79)), and a FROM clause (FROM ERROR-MESSAGE).

A FROM clause affects only the way DISPLAY behaves. During DISPLAY MENU-SCREEN the cursor is positioned at row 24 and column 1. The value in ERROR-MESSAGE is moved to the screen and displayed as a PIC X(79) field.

The logic of bilmnu04.cbl is similar to bilmnu03.cbl, but uses full screens instead of individual fields.

GET-MENU-PICK at line 005800 displays the menu, then accepts the user entry, and, if necessary, reaccepts entry until a valid value is entered.

The DISPLAY-MENU-SCREEN routine at line 006400 displays the whole MENU-SCREEN.

The ACCEPT-MENU-SCREEN routine at line 006800 accepts the entire MENU-SCREEN. Only one field is defined in MENU-SCREEN at line 003100; the field that will accept data into MENU-PICK. The ACCEPT of MENU-SCREEN actually causes data entry to take place only for that single field.

The routine to RE-ACCEPT-MENU-SCREEN, at line 007200, moves an error message to ERROR-MESSAGE, displays the entire MENU-SCREEN, and then accepts the MENU-SCREEN again.

One short point worth noting is that MENU-PICK must be initialized when it is defined. If it is not, the first DISPLAY MENU-SCREEN will cause an error, because MENU-PICK will contain an invalid numeric value.

TIP

Some versions of COBOL will not accept COL as an abbreviation for COLUMN in a screen definition. LPI COBOL is one that does not. If your compiler complains about the use of COL, change all of them to COLUMN and try to compile again.

Code, compile, and run `bilmnu04.cbl` to see the effect of full-screen I/O. It will compile and run correctly for Micro Focus Personal COBOL, ACUCOBOL, LPI COBOL by changing `COL` to `COLUMN`, and probably others. It will not work for VAX COBOL, which does not support full-screen I/O.

Try entering some valid and invalid menu choices to see how the field at the bottom of the screen is either filled with error messages or cleared, depending on the validity of the choice.

Defining a Screen to Maintain a File

In the next example, you create a full-screen version of vendor maintenance. First, you need to define the screens. A screen can be designed on printer spacing paper by using 80 columns and 24 lines of the chart. Figure B3.2 is a layout chart for the menu portion of the program.

Figure B3.2.

Screen layout for the menu.

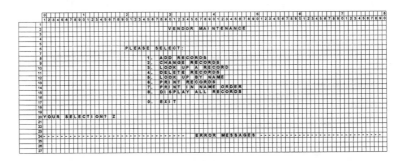

Listing B3.2 shows the menu screen to be used in vendor maintenance. It has only one modifiable field, `MENU-PICK`, which must be defined in `WORKING-STORAGE`.

TYPE **Listing B3.2. The menu screen.**

```
004800 01  MENU-SCREEN.
004900     05  BLANK SCREEN.
005000     05  LINE  2 COLUMN 30 VALUE "VENDOR MAINTENANCE".
005100     05  LINE  6 COLUMN 20 VALUE "PLEASE SELECT:".
005200     05  LINE  8 COLUMN 25 VALUE "1. ADD RECORDS".
005300     05  LINE  9 COLUMN 25 VALUE "2. CHANGE A RECORD".
005400     05  LINE 10 COLUMN 25 VALUE "3. LOOK UP A RECORD".
005500     05  LINE 11 COLUMN 25 VALUE "4. DELETE A RECORD".
005600     05  LINE 12 COLUMN 25 VALUE "5. LOOK UP BY NAME".
005700     05  LINE 13 COLUMN 25 VALUE "6. PRINT RECORDS".
005800     05  LINE 14 COLUMN 25 VALUE "7. PRINT IN NAME ORDER".
005900     05  LINE 15 COLUMN 25 VALUE "8. DISPLAY ALL RECORDS".
006000     05  LINE 17 COLUMN 25 VALUE "0. EXIT".
006100     05  LINE 20 COLUMN  1 VALUE "YOUR SELECTION? ".
006200     05  LINE 20 COLUMN 17 PIC Z USING MENU-PICK.
006300     05  LINE 24 COLUMN  1 PIC X(79) FROM ERROR-MESSAGE.
```

Figure B3.3 is a screen layout chart for the new vendor maintenance program. The layout includes prompts and entry fields for each of the fields in the vendor file. The extra field on line 12 is a 20-character field to hold the state name retrieved from the state codes file. This field cannot be modified; it is for display only.

Figure B3.3.

Screen layout chart for vendor maintenance.

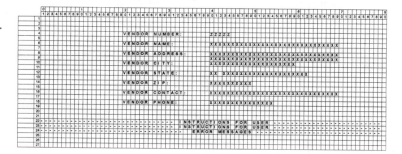

The DATA DIVISION definition of the basic screen for vendor maintenance is shown in Listing B3.3. It includes modifiable entry fields for all of the fields in the vendor file.

TYPE   Listing B3.3. Basic vendor maintenance screen.

```
007200 01   VENDOR-SCREEN.
007300      05   BLANK SCREEN.
007400      05   LINE   4 COLUMN 20 VALUE "VENDOR NUMBER:".
007500      05   LINE   4 COLUMN 40 PIC Z(5) USING VENDOR-NUMBER.
007600      05   LINE   6 COLUMN 20 VALUE "VENDOR NAME: ".
007700      05   LINE   6 COLUMN 40 PIC X(30) USING VENDOR-NAME.
007800      05   LINE   8 COLUMN 20 VALUE "VENDOR ADDRESS:".
007900      05   LINE   8 COLUMN 40 PIC X(30) USING VENDOR-ADDRESS-1.
008000      05   LINE   9 COLUMN 40 PIC X(30) USING VENDOR-ADDRESS-2.
008100      05   LINE  10 COLUMN 20 VALUE "VENDOR CITY:".
008200      05   LINE  10 COLUMN 40 PIC X(20) USING VENDOR-CITY.
008300      05   LINE  12 COLUMN 20 VALUE "VENDOR STATE:".
008400      05   LINE  12 COLUMN 40 PIC XX USING VENDOR-STATE.
008500      05   LINE  12 COLUMN 45 PIC X(20) FROM STATE-NAME.
008600      05   LINE  14 COLUMN 20 VALUE "VENDOR ZIP:".
008700      05   LINE  14 COLUMN 40 PIC X(10) USING VENDOR-ZIP.
008800      05   LINE  16 COLUMN 20 VALUE "VENDOR CONTACT:".
008900      05   LINE  16 COLUMN 40 PIC X(30) USING VENDOR-CONTACT.
009000      05   LINE  18 COLUMN 20 VALUE "VENDOR PHONE:".
009100      05   LINE  18 COLUMN 40 PIC X(15) USING VENDOR-PHONE.
009200      05   LINE  22 COLUMN   1 PIC X(79) FROM FOOTER-FIELD.
009300      05   LINE  22 COLUMN   1 PIC X(79) FROM 2ND-FOOTER-FIELD.
009400      05   LINE  24 COLUMN   1 PIC X(79) FROM ERROR-MESSAGE.
009500
```

A maintenance program that uses full-screen I/O faces one problem. When a field is defined in a screen, it can be defined as a USING field, such as line 007500 in Listing B3.3. This definition will allow data entry. A field also can be defined with a FROM clause, as in line 008500 of Listing B3.3. A FROM field cannot be modified. There are times during maintenance when you want a field to be modifiable, and there are other times when you do not. How can you define a field to be both modifiable and nonmodifiable?

Some versions of COBOL allow you to change whether a field can be modified while the program is running, but some do not. The solution should take as many versions of COBOL into account as possible. One solution that works on many different versions of COBOL is to define several different screens.

You will need three screens. The first screen allows the user to enter only the values that make up the primary key to the file; in this case, the VENDOR-NUMBER. The second screen allows the user to enter all fields except the primary key fields. The third screen displays all fields, but allows none of them to be entered.

The key screen is used by all modes (add, change, inquire, and delete) to get the user entry of the vendor number to process. The change screen is used by add and change modes to enable the user to enter or update the fields in the file. The display-only screen is used by inquire and delete modes to enable the user to view or review a record before deciding to delete it.

Ignoring the user instructions and error messages, Listing B3.4 is a listing of the three screens that will be used in the program. A few more fields will be added for the actual program, but these are the basic screen definitions.

TYPE

Listing B3.4. Example of screen definitions for vendor maintenance.

```
006500 01  KEY-SCREEN.
006600     05  BLANK SCREEN.
006700     05  LINE  4 COLUMN 20 VALUE "VENDOR NUMBER:".
006800     05  LINE  4 COLUMN 40 PIC Z(5) USING VENDOR-NUMBER.
......
007100
007200 01  ENTRY-SCREEN.
007300     05  BLANK SCREEN.
007400     05  LINE  4 COLUMN 20 VALUE "VENDOR NUMBER:".
007500     05  LINE  4 COLUMN 40 PIC Z(5) FROM VENDOR-NUMBER.
007600     05  LINE  6 COLUMN 20 VALUE "VENDOR NAME: ".
007700     05  LINE  6 COLUMN 40 PIC X(30) USING VENDOR-NAME.
007800     05  LINE  8 COLUMN 20 VALUE "VENDOR ADDRESS:".
007900     05  LINE  8 COLUMN 40 PIC X(30) USING VENDOR-ADDRESS-1.
008000     05  LINE  9 COLUMN 40 PIC X(30) USING VENDOR-ADDRESS-2.
008100     05  LINE 10 COLUMN 20 VALUE "VENDOR CITY:".
008200     05  LINE 10 COLUMN 40 PIC X(20) USING VENDOR-CITY.
008300     05  LINE 12 COLUMN 20 VALUE "VENDOR STATE:".
008400     05  LINE 12 COLUMN 40 PIC XX USING VENDOR-STATE.
008500     05  LINE 12 COLUMN 45 PIC X(20) FROM STATE-NAME.
```

continues

BD
3

Listing B3.4. continued

```
008600      05   LINE 14 COLUMN 20 VALUE "VENDOR ZIP:".
008700      05   LINE 14 COLUMN 40 PIC X(10) USING VENDOR-ZIP.
008800      05   LINE 16 COLUMN 20 VALUE "VENDOR CONTACT:".
008900      05   LINE 16 COLUMN 40 PIC X(30) USING VENDOR-CONTACT.
009000      05   LINE 18 COLUMN 20 VALUE "VENDOR PHONE:".
009100      05   LINE 18 COLUMN 40 PIC X(15) USING VENDOR-PHONE.
......
009600
009700 01   DISPLAY-SCREEN.
009800      05   BLANK SCREEN.
009900      05   LINE  4 COLUMN 20 VALUE "VENDOR NUMBER:".
010000      05   LINE  4 COLUMN 40 PIC Z(5) FROM VENDOR-NUMBER.
010100      05   LINE  6 COLUMN 20 VALUE "VENDOR NAME: ".
010200      05   LINE  6 COLUMN 40 PIC X(30) FROM VENDOR-NAME.
010300      05   LINE  8 COLUMN 20 VALUE "VENDOR ADDRESS:".
010400      05   LINE  8 COLUMN 40 PIC X(30) FROM VENDOR-ADDRESS-1.
010500      05   LINE  9 COLUMN 40 PIC X(30) FROM VENDOR-ADDRESS-2.
010600      05   LINE 10 COLUMN 20 VALUE "VENDOR CITY:".
010700      05   LINE 10 COLUMN 40 PIC X(20) FROM VENDOR-CITY.
010800      05   LINE 12 COLUMN 20 VALUE "VENDOR STATE:".
010900      05   LINE 12 COLUMN 40 PIC XX FROM VENDOR-STATE.
011000      05   LINE 12 COLUMN 45 PIC X(20) FROM STATE-NAME.
011100      05   LINE 14 COLUMN 20 VALUE "VENDOR ZIP:".
011200      05   LINE 14 COLUMN 40 PIC X(10) FROM VENDOR-ZIP.
011300      05   LINE 16 COLUMN 20 VALUE "VENDOR CONTACT:".
011400      05   LINE 16 COLUMN 40 PIC X(30) FROM VENDOR-CONTACT.
011500      05   LINE 18 COLUMN 20 VALUE "VENDOR PHONE:".
011600      05   LINE 18 COLUMN 40 PIC X(15) FROM VENDOR-PHONE.
```

ANALYSIS The KEY-SCREEN at line 006500 contains only a prompt for the vendor number and a field for entry of the vendor number.

The ENTRY-SCREEN at line 007200 is similar to the VENDOR-SCREEN in Listing B3.3, but at line 007500, the VENDOR-NUMBER is not modifiable because it is defined with a FROM clause.

The DISPLAY-SCREEN at line 009700 is the same as ENTRY-SCREEN, except that all fields are defined with USING clauses, which makes all fields nonmodifiable.

A Maintenance Module for the File

With the screens worked out, it is possible to complete the maintenance module. Listing B3.5 contains add, change, inquire, and delete modes.

TYPE Listing B3.5. Maintenance using full-screen I/O.

```
000100 IDENTIFICATION DIVISION.
000200 PROGRAM-ID. VNDMNT06.
000300*-------------------------------
000400* Add, Change, Inquire and Delete
```

```
000500* for the Vendor File.
000600* This includes Inquire by name
000700* The vendor report, and the vendor
000800* report in name order.
000900* Added Display all records.
001000* Uses full screen IO
001100*-------------------------------
001200 ENVIRONMENT DIVISION.
001300 INPUT-OUTPUT SECTION.
001400 FILE-CONTROL.
001500
001600     COPY "SLVND02.CBL".
001700
001800     COPY "SLSTATE.CBL".
001900
002000 DATA DIVISION.
002100 FILE SECTION.
002200
002300     COPY "FDVND04.CBL".
002400
002500     COPY "FDSTATE.CBL".
002600
002700 WORKING-STORAGE SECTION.
002800
002900 77  MENU-PICK                    PIC 9 VALUE ZERO.
003000     88  MENU-PICK-IS-VALID       VALUES 0 THRU 8.
003100
003200 77  VENDOR-RECORD-FOUND          PIC X.
003300 77  STATE-RECORD-FOUND           PIC X.
003400
003500 77  SCREEN-ERROR                 PIC X.
003600 77  ERROR-MESSAGE                PIC X(79) VALUE SPACE.
003700
003800 77  CONTINUE-MESSAGE             PIC X(40) VALUE SPACE.
003900 77  OK-TO-CONTINUE               PIC X.
004000
004100 01  FOOTER-FIELD.
004200     05  FOOTER-1-FIELD           PIC X(40) VALUE SPACE.
004300     05  FOOTER-2-FIELD           PIC X(39) VALUE SPACE.
004400
004500     COPY "WSCASE01.CBL".
004600
004700 SCREEN SECTION.
004800 01  MENU-SCREEN.
004900     05  BLANK SCREEN.
005000     05  LINE  2 COLUMN 30 VALUE "VENDOR MAINTENANCE".
005100     05  LINE  6 COLUMN 20 VALUE "PLEASE SELECT:".
005200     05  LINE  8 COLUMN 25 VALUE "1. ADD RECORDS".
005300     05  LINE  9 COLUMN 25 VALUE "2. CHANGE A RECORD".
005400     05  LINE 10 COLUMN 25 VALUE "3. LOOK UP A RECORD".
005500     05  LINE 11 COLUMN 25 VALUE "4. DELETE A RECORD".
005600     05  LINE 12 COLUMN 25 VALUE "5. LOOK UP BY NAME".
005700     05  LINE 13 COLUMN 25 VALUE "6. PRINT RECORDS".
005800     05  LINE 14 COLUMN 25 VALUE "7. PRINT IN NAME ORDER".
005900     05  LINE 15 COLUMN 25 VALUE "8. DISPLAY ALL RECORDS".
006000     05  LINE 17 COLUMN 25 VALUE "0. EXIT".
```

continues

Listing B3.5. continued

```
006100      05   LINE 20 COLUMN  1 VALUE "YOUR SELECTION? ".
006200      05   LINE 20 COLUMN 17 PIC Z USING MENU-PICK.
006300      05   LINE 24 COLUMN  1 PIC X(79) FROM ERROR-MESSAGE.
006400
006500 01  KEY-SCREEN.
006600      05   BLANK SCREEN.
006700      05   LINE  4 COLUMN 20 VALUE "VENDOR NUMBER:".
006800      05   LINE  4 COLUMN 40 PIC Z(5) USING VENDOR-NUMBER.
006900      05   LINE 22 COLUMN  1 PIC X(79) FROM FOOTER-FIELD.
007000      05   LINE 24 COLUMN  1 PIC X(79) FROM ERROR-MESSAGE.
007100
007200 01  ENTRY-SCREEN.
007300      05   BLANK SCREEN.
007400      05   LINE  4 COLUMN 20 VALUE "VENDOR NUMBER:".
007500      05   LINE  4 COLUMN 40 PIC Z(5) FROM VENDOR-NUMBER.
007600      05   LINE  6 COLUMN 20 VALUE "VENDOR NAME: ".
007700      05   LINE  6 COLUMN 40 PIC X(30) USING VENDOR-NAME.
007800      05   LINE  8 COLUMN 20 VALUE "VENDOR ADDRESS:".
007900      05   LINE  8 COLUMN 40 PIC X(30) USING VENDOR-ADDRESS-1.
008000      05   LINE  9 COLUMN 40 PIC X(30) USING VENDOR-ADDRESS-2.
008100      05   LINE 10 COLUMN 20 VALUE "VENDOR CITY:".
008200      05   LINE 10 COLUMN 40 PIC X(20) USING VENDOR-CITY.
008300      05   LINE 12 COLUMN 20 VALUE "VENDOR STATE:".
008400      05   LINE 12 COLUMN 40 PIC XX USING VENDOR-STATE.
008500      05   LINE 12 COLUMN 45 PIC X(20) FROM STATE-NAME.
008600      05   LINE 14 COLUMN 20 VALUE "VENDOR ZIP:".
008700      05   LINE 14 COLUMN 40 PIC X(10) USING VENDOR-ZIP.
008800      05   LINE 16 COLUMN 20 VALUE "VENDOR CONTACT:".
008900      05   LINE 16 COLUMN 40 PIC X(30) USING VENDOR-CONTACT.
009000      05   LINE 18 COLUMN 20 VALUE "VENDOR PHONE:".
009100      05   LINE 18 COLUMN 40 PIC X(15) USING VENDOR-PHONE.
009200      05   LINE 22 COLUMN  1 PIC X(79) FROM FOOTER-FIELD.
009300      05   LINE 23 COLUMN  1 PIC X(40) FROM CONTINUE-MESSAGE.
009400      05   LINE 23 COLUMN 41 PIC X USING OK-TO-CONTINUE.
009500      05   LINE 24 COLUMN  1 PIC X(79) FROM ERROR-MESSAGE.
009600
009700 01  DISPLAY-SCREEN.
009800      05   BLANK SCREEN.
009900      05   LINE  4 COLUMN 20 VALUE "VENDOR NUMBER:".
010000      05   LINE  4 COLUMN 40 PIC Z(5) FROM VENDOR-NUMBER.
010100      05   LINE  6 COLUMN 20 VALUE "VENDOR NAME: ".
010200      05   LINE  6 COLUMN 40 PIC X(30) FROM VENDOR-NAME.
010300      05   LINE  8 COLUMN 20 VALUE "VENDOR ADDRESS:".
010400      05   LINE  8 COLUMN 40 PIC X(30) FROM VENDOR-ADDRESS-1.
010500      05   LINE  9 COLUMN 40 PIC X(30) FROM VENDOR-ADDRESS-2.
010600      05   LINE 10 COLUMN 20 VALUE "VENDOR CITY:".
010700      05   LINE 10 COLUMN 40 PIC X(20) FROM VENDOR-CITY.
010800      05   LINE 12 COLUMN 20 VALUE "VENDOR STATE:".
010900      05   LINE 12 COLUMN 40 PIC XX FROM VENDOR-STATE.
011000      05   LINE 12 COLUMN 45 PIC X(20) FROM STATE-NAME.
011100      05   LINE 14 COLUMN 20 VALUE "VENDOR ZIP:".
011200      05   LINE 14 COLUMN 40 PIC X(10) FROM VENDOR-ZIP.
011300      05   LINE 16 COLUMN 20 VALUE "VENDOR CONTACT:".
011400      05   LINE 16 COLUMN 40 PIC X(30) FROM VENDOR-CONTACT.
011500      05   LINE 18 COLUMN 20 VALUE "VENDOR PHONE:".
```

```
011600      05  LINE 18 COLUMN 40 PIC X(15) FROM VENDOR-PHONE.
011700      05  LINE 23 COLUMN  1 PIC X(40) FROM CONTINUE-MESSAGE.
011800      05  LINE 23 COLUMN 41 PIC X USING OK-TO-CONTINUE.
011900      05  LINE 24 COLUMN  1 PIC X(79) FROM ERROR-MESSAGE.
012000
012100 PROCEDURE DIVISION.
012200 PROGRAM-BEGIN.
012300      PERFORM OPENING-PROCEDURE.
012400      PERFORM MAIN-PROCESS.
012500      PERFORM CLOSING-PROCEDURE.
012600
012700 PROGRAM-EXIT.
012800      EXIT PROGRAM.
012900
013000 PROGRAM-DONE.
013100      STOP RUN.
013200
013300 OPENING-PROCEDURE.
013400      OPEN I-O VENDOR-FILE.
013500      OPEN I-O STATE-FILE.
013600
013700 CLOSING-PROCEDURE.
013800      CLOSE VENDOR-FILE.
013900      CLOSE STATE-FILE.
014000
014100 MAIN-PROCESS.
014200      PERFORM GET-MENU-PICK.
014300      PERFORM MAINTAIN-THE-FILE
014400          UNTIL MENU-PICK = 0.
014500
014600*-------------------------------
014700* MENU
014800*-------------------------------
014900 GET-MENU-PICK.
015000      PERFORM INITIALIZE-MENU-PICK.
015100      PERFORM DISPLAY-ACCEPT-MENU.
015200      PERFORM RE-DISPLAY-ACCEPT-MENU
015300          UNTIL MENU-PICK-IS-VALID.
015400
015500 INITIALIZE-MENU-PICK.
015600      MOVE 0 TO MENU-PICK.
015700
015800 DISPLAY-ACCEPT-MENU.
015900      DISPLAY MENU-SCREEN.
016000      ACCEPT MENU-SCREEN.
016100      MOVE SPACE TO ERROR-MESSAGE.
016200
016300 RE-DISPLAY-ACCEPT-MENU.
016400      MOVE "INVALID SELECTION - PLEASE RE-TRY."
016500          TO ERROR-MESSAGE.
016600      PERFORM DISPLAY-ACCEPT-MENU.
016700
016800 MAINTAIN-THE-FILE.
016900      PERFORM DO-THE-PICK.
017000      PERFORM GET-MENU-PICK.
```

continues

Listing B3.5. continued

```
017100
017200 DO-THE-PICK.
017300     IF MENU-PICK = 1
017400         PERFORM ADD-MODE
017500     ELSE
017600     IF MENU-PICK = 2
017700         PERFORM CHANGE-MODE
017800     ELSE
017900     IF MENU-PICK = 3
018000         PERFORM INQUIRE-MODE
018100     ELSE
018200     IF MENU-PICK = 4
018300         PERFORM DELETE-MODE
018400     ELSE
018500     IF MENU-PICK = 5
018600         PERFORM INQUIRE-BY-NAME
018700     ELSE
018800     IF MENU-PICK = 6
018900         PERFORM PRINT-VENDOR-REPORT
019000     ELSE
019100     IF MENU-PICK = 7
019200         PERFORM PRINT-BY-NAME
019300     ELSE
019400     IF MENU-PICK = 8
019500         PERFORM DISPLAY-ALL.
019600
019700*-------------------------------
019800* ADD
019900*-------------------------------
020000 ADD-MODE.
020100     PERFORM INITIALIZE-ADD-MODE.
020200     PERFORM GET-NEW-RECORD-KEY.
020300     PERFORM ADD-RECORDS
020400         UNTIL VENDOR-NUMBER = ZEROES.
020500
020600 INITIALIZE-ADD-MODE.
020700     MOVE "ENTER THE VENDOR NUMBER TO ADD"
020800         TO FOOTER-1-FIELD.
020900
021000 GET-NEW-RECORD-KEY.
021100     PERFORM ACCEPT-NEW-RECORD-KEY.
021200     PERFORM RE-ACCEPT-NEW-RECORD-KEY
021300         UNTIL VENDOR-NUMBER = ZEROES
021400             OR VENDOR-RECORD-FOUND = "N".
021500
021600 ACCEPT-NEW-RECORD-KEY.
021700     PERFORM INITIALIZE-VENDOR-FIELDS.
021800     PERFORM ENTER-VENDOR-NUMBER.
021900     IF VENDOR-NUMBER NOT = ZEROES
022000         PERFORM READ-VENDOR-RECORD.
022100
022200 RE-ACCEPT-NEW-RECORD-KEY.
022300     MOVE "RECORD ALREADY ON FILE" TO ERROR-MESSAGE.
022400     PERFORM ACCEPT-NEW-RECORD-KEY.
022500
```

```
022600 ADD-RECORDS.
022700     PERFORM INITIALIZE-TO-ADD-FIELDS.
022800     PERFORM ENTER-REMAINING-FIELDS.
022900     IF OK-TO-CONTINUE = "Y"
023000         PERFORM WRITE-VENDOR-RECORD.
023100     PERFORM GET-NEW-RECORD-KEY.
023200
023300 INITIALIZE-TO-ADD-FIELDS.
023400     MOVE "ADD NEW FIELDS" TO FOOTER-FIELD.
023500     MOVE "CONTINUE WITH ADDITIONS (Y/N)?"
023600         TO CONTINUE-MESSAGE.
023700     MOVE "Y" TO OK-TO-CONTINUE.
023800
023900*-------------------------------
024000* CHANGE
024100*-------------------------------
024200 CHANGE-MODE.
024300     PERFORM INITIALIZE-CHANGE-MODE.
024400     PERFORM GET-EXISTING-RECORD.
024500     PERFORM CHANGE-RECORDS
024600         UNTIL VENDOR-NUMBER = ZEROES.
024700
024800 INITIALIZE-CHANGE-MODE.
024900     MOVE "ENTER THE VENDOR NUMBER TO CHANGE"
025000         TO FOOTER-1-FIELD.
025100
025200 CHANGE-RECORDS.
025300     PERFORM INITIALIZE-TO-CHANGE-FIELDS.
025400     PERFORM ENTER-REMAINING-FIELDS.
025500     IF OK-TO-CONTINUE = "Y"
025600         PERFORM REWRITE-VENDOR-RECORD.
025700     PERFORM GET-EXISTING-RECORD.
025800
025900 INITIALIZE-TO-CHANGE-FIELDS.
026000     MOVE "CHANGE FIELDS" TO FOOTER-FIELD.
026100     MOVE "CONTINUE WITH CHANGES (Y/N)?"
026200         TO CONTINUE-MESSAGE.
026300     MOVE "Y" TO OK-TO-CONTINUE.
026400
026500*-------------------------------
026600* INQUIRE
026700*-------------------------------
026800 INQUIRE-MODE.
026900     PERFORM INITIALIZE-INQUIRE-MODE.
027000     PERFORM GET-EXISTING-RECORD.
027100     PERFORM INQUIRE-RECORDS
027200         UNTIL VENDOR-NUMBER = ZEROES.
027300
027400 INITIALIZE-INQUIRE-MODE.
027500     MOVE "ENTER THE VENDOR NUMBER TO DISPLAY"
027600         TO FOOTER-1-FIELD.
027700
027800 INQUIRE-RECORDS.
027900     PERFORM INITIALIZE-TO-INQUIRE.
028000     PERFORM DISPLAY-ACCEPT-ALL-FIELDS.
```

continues

Listing B3.5. continued

```
028100        PERFORM GET-EXISTING-RECORD.
028200
028300 INITIALIZE-TO-INQUIRE.
028400        MOVE "PRESS ENTER TO CONTINUE" TO CONTINUE-MESSAGE.
028500        MOVE SPACE TO OK-TO-CONTINUE.
028600
028700*--------------------------------
028800* DELETE
028900*--------------------------------
029000 DELETE-MODE.
029100        PERFORM INITIALIZE-DELETE-MODE.
029200        PERFORM GET-EXISTING-RECORD.
029300        PERFORM DELETE-RECORDS
029400            UNTIL VENDOR-NUMBER = ZEROES.
029500
029600 INITIALIZE-DELETE-MODE.
029700        MOVE "ENTER THE VENDOR NUMBER TO DELETE"
029800            TO FOOTER-1-FIELD.
029900
030000 DELETE-RECORDS.
030100        PERFORM INITIALIZE-TO-DELETE-RECORD.
030200        PERFORM ASK-OK-TO-DELETE.
030300        IF OK-TO-CONTINUE = "Y"
030400            PERFORM DELETE-VENDOR-RECORD.
030500        PERFORM GET-EXISTING-RECORD.
030600
030700 INITIALIZE-TO-DELETE-RECORD.
030800        MOVE "OK TO DELETE(Y/N)?" TO CONTINUE-MESSAGE.
030900        MOVE "N" TO OK-TO-CONTINUE.
031000
031100 ASK-OK-TO-DELETE.
031200        PERFORM DISPLAY-ACCEPT-ALL-FIELDS.
031300        PERFORM RE-DISPLAY-ACCEPT-ALL-FIELDS
031400            UNTIL OK-TO-CONTINUE = "Y" OR "N".
031500
031600 RE-DISPLAY-ACCEPT-ALL-FIELDS.
031700        MOVE "YOU MUST ENTER YES OR NO"
031800            TO ERROR-MESSAGE.
031900        PERFORM DISPLAY-ACCEPT-ALL-FIELDS.
032000
032100*--------------------------------
032200* Routines shared by all modes
032300*--------------------------------
032400 INITIALIZE-VENDOR-FIELDS.
032500        MOVE SPACE TO VENDOR-RECORD.
032600        MOVE ZEROES TO VENDOR-NUMBER.
032700        MOVE SPACE TO STATE-NAME.
032800
032900 ENTER-VENDOR-NUMBER.
033000        MOVE "ENTER 0 TO QUIT" TO FOOTER-2-FIELD.
033100        DISPLAY KEY-SCREEN.
033200        ACCEPT KEY-SCREEN.
033300        MOVE SPACE TO ERROR-MESSAGE.
033400
033500*--------------------------------
```

```
033600* Routines shared Add and Change
033700*-------------------------------
033800 ENTER-REMAINING-FIELDS.
033900     PERFORM DISPLAY-ACCEPT-ENTRY-SCREEN.
034000     PERFORM DISPLAY-ACCEPT-ENTRY-SCREEN
034100         UNTIL SCREEN-ERROR = "N"
034200            OR OK-TO-CONTINUE = "N".
034300
034400 DISPLAY-ACCEPT-ENTRY-SCREEN.
034500     DISPLAY ENTRY-SCREEN.
034600     ACCEPT ENTRY-SCREEN.
034700     MOVE SPACE TO ERROR-MESSAGE.
034800
034900     INSPECT OK-TO-CONTINUE
035000      CONVERTING LOWER-ALPHA TO UPPER-ALPHA.
035100
035200     IF OK-TO-CONTINUE = "Y"
035300         PERFORM EDIT-CHECK-FIELDS.
035400
035500 EDIT-CHECK-FIELDS.
035600     MOVE "N" TO SCREEN-ERROR.
035700     PERFORM EDIT-CHECK-VENDOR-NAME.
035800     IF SCREEN-ERROR NOT = "Y"
035900         PERFORM EDIT-CHECK-VENDOR-ADDRESS-1.
036000     IF SCREEN-ERROR NOT = "Y"
036100         PERFORM EDIT-CHECK-VENDOR-ADDRESS-2.
036200     IF SCREEN-ERROR NOT = "Y"
036300         PERFORM EDIT-CHECK-VENDOR-CITY.
036400     IF SCREEN-ERROR NOT = "Y"
036500         PERFORM EDIT-CHECK-VENDOR-STATE.
036600     IF SCREEN-ERROR NOT = "Y"
036700         PERFORM EDIT-CHECK-VENDOR-ZIP.
036800     IF SCREEN-ERROR NOT = "Y"
036900         PERFORM EDIT-CHECK-VENDOR-CONTACT.
037000     IF SCREEN-ERROR NOT = "Y"
037100         PERFORM EDIT-CHECK-VENDOR-PHONE.
037200
037300 EDIT-CHECK-VENDOR-NAME.
037400     INSPECT VENDOR-NAME
037500         CONVERTING LOWER-ALPHA
037600         TO          UPPER-ALPHA.
037700
037800     IF VENDOR-NAME = SPACES
037900         MOVE "Y" TO SCREEN-ERROR
038000         MOVE "VENDOR NAME MUST BE ENTERED"
038100             TO ERROR-MESSAGE.
038200 EDIT-CHECK-VENDOR-ADDRESS-1.
038300     INSPECT VENDOR-ADDRESS-1
038400         CONVERTING LOWER-ALPHA
038500         TO          UPPER-ALPHA.
038600     IF VENDOR-ADDRESS-1 = SPACE
038700         MOVE "Y" TO SCREEN-ERROR
038800         MOVE "VENDOR ADDRESS-1 MUST BE ENTERED"
038900             TO ERROR-MESSAGE.
039000
```

continues

Listing B3.5. continued

```
039100 EDIT-CHECK-VENDOR-ADDRESS-2.
039200     INSPECT VENDOR-ADDRESS-2
039300         CONVERTING LOWER-ALPHA
039400         TO          UPPER-ALPHA.
039500
039600 EDIT-CHECK-VENDOR-CITY.
039700     INSPECT VENDOR-CITY
039800         CONVERTING LOWER-ALPHA
039900         TO          UPPER-ALPHA.
040000
040100     IF VENDOR-CITY = SPACE
040200         MOVE "Y" TO SCREEN-ERROR
040300         MOVE   "VENDOR CITY MUST BE ENTERED"
040400             TO ERROR-MESSAGE.
040500
040600 EDIT-CHECK-VENDOR-STATE.
040700     PERFORM EDIT-VENDOR-STATE.
040800     PERFORM CHECK-VENDOR-STATE.
040900
041000 EDIT-VENDOR-STATE.
041100     INSPECT VENDOR-STATE
041200         CONVERTING LOWER-ALPHA
041300         TO          UPPER-ALPHA.
041400
041500 CHECK-VENDOR-STATE.
041600     PERFORM VENDOR-STATE-REQUIRED.
041700     IF VENDOR-STATE NOT = SPACES
041800         PERFORM VENDOR-STATE-ON-FILE.
041900
042000 VENDOR-STATE-REQUIRED.
042100     IF VENDOR-STATE = SPACE
042200         MOVE "Y" TO SCREEN-ERROR
042300         MOVE "VENDOR STATE MUST BE ENTERED"
042400             TO ERROR-MESSAGE.
042500
042600 VENDOR-STATE-ON-FILE.
042700     MOVE VENDOR-STATE TO STATE-CODE.
042800     PERFORM READ-STATE-RECORD.
042900     IF STATE-RECORD-FOUND = "N"
043000         MOVE "Y" TO SCREEN-ERROR
043100         MOVE "STATE CODE NOT FOUND IN CODES FILE"
043200             TO ERROR-MESSAGE.
043300
043400 EDIT-CHECK-VENDOR-ZIP.
043500     INSPECT VENDOR-ZIP
043600         CONVERTING LOWER-ALPHA
043700         TO          UPPER-ALPHA.
043800     IF VENDOR-ZIP = SPACE
043900         MOVE "Y" TO SCREEN-ERROR
044000         MOVE "VENDOR ZIP MUST BE ENTERED"
044100             TO ERROR-MESSAGE.
044200
044300 EDIT-CHECK-VENDOR-CONTACT.
044400     INSPECT VENDOR-CONTACT
044500         CONVERTING LOWER-ALPHA
044600         TO          UPPER-ALPHA.
```

3

```
044700
044800 EDIT-CHECK-VENDOR-PHONE.
044900     INSPECT VENDOR-PHONE
045000          CONVERTING LOWER-ALPHA
045100          TO           UPPER-ALPHA.
045200     IF VENDOR-PHONE = SPACE
045300          MOVE "Y" TO SCREEN-ERROR
045400          MOVE "ENTER VENDOR PHONE"
045500               TO ERROR-MESSAGE.
045600
045700*------------------------------
045800* Routines shared by Change,
045900* Inquire and Delete
046000*------------------------------
046100 GET-EXISTING-RECORD.
046200     PERFORM INITIALIZE-VENDOR-FIELDS.
046300     PERFORM ACCEPT-EXISTING-KEY.
046400     PERFORM RE-ACCEPT-EXISTING-KEY
046500          UNTIL VENDOR-RECORD-FOUND = "Y" OR
046600               VENDOR-NUMBER = ZEROES.
046700
046800 ACCEPT-EXISTING-KEY.
046900     PERFORM ENTER-VENDOR-NUMBER.
047000     IF VENDOR-NUMBER NOT = ZEROES
047100          PERFORM READ-VENDOR-AND-STATE.
047200
047300 RE-ACCEPT-EXISTING-KEY.
047400     MOVE "RECORD NOT FOUND" TO ERROR-MESSAGE.
047500     PERFORM ACCEPT-EXISTING-KEY.
047600
047700*------------------------------
047800* Routines shared by delete and inquire
047900*------------------------------
048000 DISPLAY-ACCEPT-ALL-FIELDS.
048100     DISPLAY DISPLAY-SCREEN.
048200     ACCEPT DISPLAY-SCREEN.
048300     MOVE SPACE TO ERROR-MESSAGE.
048400     INSPECT OK-TO-CONTINUE
048500      CONVERTING LOWER-ALPHA TO UPPER-ALPHA.
048600
048700*------------------------------
048800* File I-O Routines
048900*------------------------------
049000 READ-VENDOR-AND-STATE.
049100     PERFORM READ-VENDOR-RECORD.
049200     IF VENDOR-RECORD-FOUND = "Y"
049300          MOVE VENDOR-STATE TO STATE-CODE
049400          PERFORM READ-STATE-RECORD
049500          IF STATE-RECORD-FOUND = "N"
049600               MOVE "*** NOT FOUND ***" TO STATE-NAME.
049700
049800 READ-VENDOR-RECORD.
049900     MOVE "Y" TO VENDOR-RECORD-FOUND.
050000     READ VENDOR-FILE RECORD
050100       INVALID KEY
050200          MOVE "N" TO VENDOR-RECORD-FOUND.
050300
```

BD
3

continues

Listing B3.5. continued

```
050400 WRITE-VENDOR-RECORD.
050500     WRITE VENDOR-RECORD
050600         INVALID KEY
050700             DISPLAY "RECORD ALREADY ON FILE".
050800
050900 REWRITE-VENDOR-RECORD.
051000     REWRITE VENDOR-RECORD
051100         INVALID KEY
051200             DISPLAY "ERROR REWRITING VENDOR RECORD".
051300
051400 DELETE-VENDOR-RECORD.
051500     DELETE VENDOR-FILE RECORD
051600         INVALID KEY
051700             DISPLAY "ERROR DELETING VENDOR RECORD".
051800
051900 READ-STATE-RECORD.
052000     MOVE "Y" TO STATE-RECORD-FOUND.
052100     READ STATE-FILE RECORD
052200       INVALID KEY
052300           MOVE "N" TO STATE-RECORD-FOUND.
052400
052500*-------------------------------
052600* CALLS TO OTHER PROGRAMS
052700*-------------------------------
052800
052900*-------------------------------
053000* INQUIRE BY NAME
053100*-------------------------------
053200 INQUIRE-BY-NAME.
053300     PERFORM CLOSING-PROCEDURE.
053400     CALL "VNINNM03".
053500     PERFORM OPENING-PROCEDURE.
053600
053700*-------------------------------
053800* PRINT
053900*-------------------------------
054000 PRINT-VENDOR-REPORT.
054100     PERFORM CLOSING-PROCEDURE.
054200     DISPLAY "VENDOR REPORT IN PROGRESS".
054300     CALL "VNDRPT04".
054400     PERFORM OPENING-PROCEDURE.
054500
054600*-------------------------------
054700* PRINT BY NAME
054800*-------------------------------
054900 PRINT-BY-NAME.
055000     PERFORM CLOSING-PROCEDURE.
055100     DISPLAY " REPORT BY NAME IN PROGRESS".
055200     CALL "VNBYNM02".
055300     PERFORM OPENING-PROCEDURE.
055400
055500*-------------------------------
055600* DISPLAY ALL
055700*-------------------------------
055800 DISPLAY-ALL.
055900     PERFORM CLOSING-PROCEDURE.
```

3

```
056000      CALL "VNDDSP03".
056100      DISPLAY "DISPLAY COMPLETE".
056200      DISPLAY "PRESS ENTER TO CONTINUE".
056300      ACCEPT OK-TO-CONTINUE.
056400      PERFORM OPENING-PROCEDURE.
056500
```

 The following output of vndmnt06.cbl illustrates some of the full screens that are created by the program:

```
                        VENDOR MAINTENANCE
                PLEASE SELECT:
                        1. ADD RECORDS
                        2. CHANGE A RECORD
                        3. LOOK UP A RECORD
                        4. DELETE A RECORD
                        5. LOOK UP BY NAME
                        6. PRINT RECORDS
                        7. PRINT IN NAME ORDER
                        8. DISPLAY ALL RECORDS
                        0. EXIT
     YOUR SELECTION?
- - - - - - - - - - - - - - - - - - - - - - - - - - - - - - - - - - - - - - - - -
                  VENDOR NUMBER:        _____
     ENTER THE VENDOR NUMBER TO CHANGE  ENTER 0 TO QUIT
- - - - - - - - - - - - - - - - - - - - - - - - - - - - - - - - - - - - - - - - -
                  VENDOR NUMBER:        __606
     ENTER THE VENDOR NUMBER TO CHANGE  ENTER 0 TO QUIT
     RECORD NOT FOUND
- - - - - - - - - - - - - - - - - - - - - - - - - - - - - - - - - - - - - - - - -
                  VENDOR NUMBER:             2
                  VENDOR NAME:          ABC PRINTING_____
                  VENDOR ADDRESS:       1624 FOOTHILL BLVD
                                        SUITE 34
                  VENDOR CITY:          LOS ANGELES
                  VENDOR STATE:         CA   CALIFORNIA
                  VENDOR ZIP:           91042
                  VENDOR CONTACT:       CHARLES JOHANSSEN
                  VENDOR PHONE:         (818) 555-4321
     CHANGE FIELDS
     CONTINUE WITH CHANGES (Y/N)?       Y
- - - - - - - - - - - - - - - - - - - - - - - - - - - - - - - - - - - - - - - - -
                  VENDOR NUMBER:             2
                  VENDOR NAME:          ABC PRINTING
                  VENDOR ADDRESS:       1624 FOOTHILL BLVD
                                        SUITE 34
                  VENDOR CITY:          LOS ANGELES
                  VENDOR STATE:         CA   CALIFORNIA
                  VENDOR ZIP:           91042
                  VENDOR CONTACT:       CHARLES JOHANSSEN
                  VENDOR PHONE:         (818) 555-4321
     OK TO DELETE(Y/N)?                 N
- - - - - - - - - - - - - - - - - - - - - - - - - - - - - - - - - - - - - - - - -
```

ANALYSIS   The screens are defined at lines 004800, 006500, 007200, and 009700 in the SCREEN
SECTION. All of the fields used in the screen definitions are defined either in the
WORKING-STORAGE SECTION or in the FILE SECTION.

At lines 003500 and 003600, fields are defined to handle error logic, a SCREEN-ERROR flag, and
an ERROR-MESSAGE that will be displayed on the screens.

The user instructions fields on rows 23 and 24 are defined at lines 0003800 through 004300,
which consist of a CONTINUE-MESSAGE flag, an OK-TO-CONTINUE flag, and a FOOTER-FIELD that
is broken into two smaller fields, FOOTER-1-FIELD and FOOTER-2-FIELD.

When through the menu, all modes start by using the ENTER-VENDOR-NUMBER routine at line
032900. This routine is used to display and accept entry of the KEY-SCREEN.

ADD-MODE begins at line 020000. It uses INITIALIZE-ADD-MODE to set up a message in FOOTER-
1-FIELD, and then performs GET-NEW-RECORD-KEY at line 021000.

The task of GET-NEW-RECORD-KEY is to get the user to enter a vendor number that is not on file
or enter 0 to indicate that the user wants to exit. The GET-NEW-RECORD-KEY paragraph uses
ENTER-VENDOR-NUMBER and the KEY-SCREEN to do this. After the user has entered a valid vendor
number (a new number or a zero), ADD-RECORDS at line 020300 is performed until VENDOR-
NUMBER = ZEROES.

ADD-RECORDS at line 022600 initializes for adding fields, and then performs ENTER-REMAINING-
FIELDS. If on the return from ENTER-REMAINING-FIELDS the test for OK-TO-CONTINUE = "Y" is
true, the new vendor record is written. Another new record key is asked of the user and ADD-
RECORDS continues until the user enters 0.

ENTER-REMAINING-FIELDS at line 033800 is probably the largest routine in the file. Its job is to
display and accept the ENTRY-SCREEN, and to edit and validate all of the entered fields. It starts
by performing DISPLAY-ACCEPT-ENTRY-SCREEN and then repeating DISPLAY-ACCEPT-ENTRY-
SCREEN UNTIL SCREEN-ERROR = "N" OR OK-TO-CONTINUE = "N". The OK-TO-CONTINUE flag gives
the user a chance to bail out if the data entry cycle began in error.

This bail-out takes place in DISPLAY-ACCEPT-ENTRY-SCREEN, which begins at line 034400. After
displaying and accepting the screens at line 034900, the OK-TO-CONTINUE flag is converted to
uppercase, and if OK-TO-CONTINUE = "Y" is true, the edit-check is performed.

The edit-checks are performed on the basis that all editing and checking stops on the first field
that contains an error. EDIT-CHECK-FIELDS at line 035500 performs each edit-check, field by
field, as long as SCREEN-ERROR NOT = "Y" is true.

The actual checks are at lines 037300 through 045500. Each edit-check must set up two
conditions if an error occurs in a field. It must MOVE "Y" TO SCREEN-ERROR and it must move
an error message to ERROR-MESSAGE.

3

Change mode, which is similar to add mode, first locates the key of a record that does exist, and then uses ENTER-REMAINING-FIELDS to enable the user to change values. Inquire mode and delete mode are simple; they are left for you to analyze.

Code and compile vndmnt06.cbl. Print out a copy of the program and as you run it, follow where you are at each point in the maintenance program.

Boilerplate

The cobsh104.cbl program is a boilerplate, though a very simple one. The vndmnt06.cbl program can be used as a boilerplate for full-screen maintenance programs. Replace the data and statements that are specific to the vendor file with those from another file.

> **NEW TERM** A *boilerplate* is a program that can be used as the basic starting block for other programs.

As your coding improves, you gradually will develop something that you are happy with as the basic way a file should be maintained and that will become your boilerplate. For now, you can use vndmnt06.cbl as a boilerplate and for the exercises of today's lesson.

Summary

Several modern versions of COBOL enable a more polished method of handling user input by allowing the program to display and accept a full screen of information at a time. Today, you learned these basics:

- [ ] Full-screen I/O allows a screen of 24 rows and 80 columns to be defined and then displayed and accepted as a single unit.
- [ ] Full-screen I/O is an extension to several versions of COBOL. Because it is not defined as a standard component of the language, there are slight variations from version to version.
- [ ] Full-screen I/O creates a more professional look and feel to the program.

Q&A

Q Do I have to use full-screen I/O?

A No, but you probably will. After you become more familiar with COBOL, you will want to try these "slicker" screens. If you land a job working in COBOL, you will almost certainly have to code in full-screen mode.

Q Can I use a mouse with COBOL programs?

A A mouse is not supported as a standard part of the COBOL language, but several modern COBOL compilers include programs or routines that can be called upon that will return mouse positions and mouse clicks. Micro Focus Personal COBOL supports mouse commands, but this is beyond the scope of this book.

Workshop

Quiz

1. The following code is a fragment of a screen definition. Which lines create fields on the screen that cannot be modified?

```
008300        05  LINE 12 COLUMN 20 VALUE "VENDOR STATE:".
008400        05  LINE 12 COLUMN 40 PIC XX USING VENDOR-STATE.
008500        05  LINE 12 COLUMN 45 PIC X(20) FROM STATE-NAME.
```

2. Which line or lines of the code in question 1 create fields on the screen that can be modified?

Exercise

Using vndmnt06.cbl as a pattern, create stcmnt05.cbl as a full-screen maintenance module for the state codes file.

3

Day 4

Using a Symbolic Debugger

Today you'll learn about symbolic debugging. You should be familiar with using a debugger, because it's an indispensable tool. Today's lesson shows you the main activities for which a symbolic debugger may be used.

Today you will learn

- [ ] What a symbolic debugger is
- [ ] How to prepare a program for symbolic debugging
- [ ] How to start and run a symbolic debugger

The Symbolic Debugger

The symbolic debugger is probably the single most powerful tool that you will ever use to understand a program. Unfortunately, there is no such thing as a standard debugger. However, certain common features of a debugger can be discussed.

NEW TERM   A *symbolic debugger* lets you execute a program in small increments (usually a line at a time) and watch the code as it's being executed. A symbolic debugger also lets you display the values of variables using the variable name. It is called a *symbolic debugger* because it lets you display the variables using the symbolic name that the variable was given in the original source-code program.

Learning to use a debugger requires a complete course in itself, but knowing even the fundamentals makes your programming life easier.

It's not easy to create a lesson on this subject, because debuggers vary, but an example using the Micro Focus Personal COBOL debugger will give you an idea of how powerful debuggers are. You must read your debugger's manual and practice with it to learn how to use it. The steps shown here are fairly common to all debuggers. Examples for different machines are given. If you're using Micro Focus Personal COBOL, follow along with these steps.

Preparing for Debugging

The first step in debugging is often to compile the program for debugging. In these examples, you will compile and run wrdsrt01.cbl from Day 4, "Decision Making." This simple program illustrates the debugger's power. Adding debugging information to a compiled program usually increases the size of the program and slows down the compiler. It also slows down the program itself when it runs. Most versions of COBOL require that the program be compiled in a special way to allow for debugging:

☐ Micro Focus Personal COBOL has no special requirements. The Micro Focus Personal COBOL compiler is set up to automatically compile with debugging.

Press F2 until Check is displayed, and then press Enter. The program will be compiled with debugging information included. Unless you have deleted the earlier compiled version of wrdsrt01.cbl, you don't need to follow this step, but it doesn't hurt to do it anyway.

☐ For ACUCOBOL, add -Zd to the command line:

```
ccbl -Zd -owrdsrt01 wrdsrt01.cbl
```

☐ For VAX COBOL, add /DEBUG=ALL to the compile command line and /DEBUG to the link command line:

```
COBOL/DEBUG=ALL WRDSRT01.COB

LINK/DEBUG/EXE=WRDSRT01 WRDSRT01.OBJ
```

Starting the Debugger

Some versions of COBOL require that a program be run in a special way in order to be debugged:

☐ For Micro Focus Personal COBOL, you must run the program through the debugger, called the Animator. If you have just loaded and compiled, you have already loaded the program into the editor. Otherwise, start by loading it into the editor:

```
PCOBOL WRDSRT01
```

Press F2 until Animate is displayed, and then press Enter.

☐ For ACUCOBOL, add -d to the command line:

```
runcbl -d wrdsrt01
```

☐ For VAX COBOL, a program compiled and linked with debug information will start automatically in debug mode:

```
RUN WRDSRT01.EXE
```

Running the Debugger

You already have seen considerable differences between compiling for debugging and starting the debugger. Once the debugger is running, the differences in the behavior of debuggers are too complex to cover here. The following steps show a series of common debugging actions using the Animator debugger in Micro Focus Personal COBOL.

When the debugger first comes up, the screen displays a portion of the code on rows 1 through 21. Rows 22, 23, and 24 contain a menu of various commands you can give to the debugger. The next line of code to be executed is highlighted on the display, as shown in Figure B4.1.

Figure B4.1.

The first screen from the debugger.

```
15 PROGRAM-BEGIN.
16
17     PERFORM INITIALIZE-PROGRAM.
18     PERFORM ENTER-THE-WORDS.
19     PERFORM DISPLAY-THE-WORDS.
20
21 PROGRAM-DONE.
22     STOP RUN.
23
24* Level 2 Routines
25
26 INITIALIZE-PROGRAM.
27     MOVE " " TO WORD-1.
28     MOVE " " TO WORD-2.
29
30 ENTER-THE-WORDS.
31     DISPLAY "This program will accept 2 words,".
32     DISPLAY "and then display them".
33     DISPLAY "in ASCII order.".
34
35     DISPLAY "Please enter the first word.".
Animate-WRDSRT01────────────────Level=01-Speed=5-Ins-Caps-Num-Scroll
F1=help F2=view F3=align F4=exchange F5=where F6=look-up  F9/F10=word-</> Escape
Step Go Zoom next-If Perform Reset Break Env Query Find Locate Text Do 0-9=speed
```

Pressing S causes a single step of the program (the next line) to be executed. The line to be executed is PERFORM INITIALIZE-PROGRAM.

After this line is executed, the highlight moves to line 27, the first line of INITIALIZE-PROGRAM. The highlight indicates that the next line of code to be executed is MOVE " " TO WORD-1.

Press S again to step to the next line of code. Line 27 is executed, and the highlight is now ready to execute line 28.

Pressing S again steps through line 28, completing the INITIALIZE-PROGRAM paragraph. The highlight is now set to line 18.

Press S four more times, and you step one line at a time until the highlight is set to line 35. The 21 rows at the top of the screen might shift around while you're doing this to display different sets of lines.

Pressing S one more time moves the highlight to line 36 and displays a new group of 21 lines, including line 36. Line 36 is ready to be executed.

Pressing S at this point causes the display to shift to the screen as the user would see it. The debugger is executing an ACCEPT verb and needs input from the keyboard. Type the word beta and press Enter. The screen should look like this:

```
* Accepted - CONFIRM
This program will accept 2 words,
and then display them
in ASCII order.
Please enter the first word.
beta
```

The debugger returns to the debug screen, ready to execute line 38.

Press S once more to advance the highlight to line 39, ready to accept WORD-2.

Pressing S one more time displays a user screen again into which you should type the word alpha. The screen should look like this:

```
* Accepted - CONFIRM
This program will accept 2 words,
and then display them
in ASCII order.
Please enter the first word.
beta
Please enter the second word.
alpha
```

The debug screen returns, having completed the ENTER-THE-WORDS paragraph, ready to execute line 19.

Using the Debugger to View Variables

Now you should examine the values in WORD-1 and WORD-2. Press Q to start a query. Row 24 changes to allow various new options.

Press E to enter a name. Row 24 again changes, and a blinking cursor appears in row 25. You can now type the variable name. Type word-1 and press Enter.

As shown in Figure B4.2, row 25 now displays the value beta, the value that you entered for word-1.

Figure B4.2.

Displaying the value of a variable.

```
 17     PERFORM INITIALIZE-PROGRAM.
 18     PERFORM ENTER-THE-WORDS.
 19     PERFORM DISPLAY-THE-WORDS.
 20
 21  PROGRAM-DONE.
 22     STOP RUN.
 23
 24* Level 2 Routines
 25
 26  INITIALIZE-PROGRAM.
 27     MOVE " " TO WORD-1.
 28     MOVE " " TO WORD-2.
 29
 30  ENTER-THE-WORDS.
 31     DISPLAY "This program will accept 2 words,".
 32     DISPLAY "and then display them".
 33     DISPLAY "in ASCII order.".
 34
 35     DISPLAY "Please enter the first word.".
 36     ACCEPT WORD-1.
 37
Query:    WORD-1──────────────────Level=01-Speed=5-Ins-Caps-Num-Scroll
F1=help F2=clear F3=hex  F4=monitor                 ↑ ↓ =up/down data
F7=containing F8=contained F9=same level            ←┘    Alt  Ctrl  Escape
beta                                         ]
```

The ability to enter a variable name and display the contents of the value is what gives a symbolic debugger its power. Prior to the advent of symbolic debuggers, the programmer had to know where each of the program's variables were in memory. Then a request was made to display the values at the memory address. This made debugging very tedious and error-prone.

Press Esc, Q, E to enter a new variable, and then change word-1 to word-2 and press Enter. The value in word-2, alpha, is displayed on row 25.

While this has been going on, the highlight bar has been waiting patiently at line 19, ready for the next step command. Press Esc, and then press S to continue stepping through the program. This lets you examine how the IF logic in lines 45 through 51 is processed. Continue to press S until the highlight is on STOP RUN. Press S one more time, and a final message is displayed on row 25, concluding the program. Leave the program sitting at this point in the debugger because you will continue working with this program in the next section.

BD
4

You can see that the debugger makes it possible to examine in detail what's going on in a program. You can step through the action one line at a time and examine the values in variables at any point. This is a very useful tool to find out what a program is doing, and especially to find out why a program is doing something wrong.

Stopping the Program at a Specific Line

Before leaving the debugger, you should examine one more feature, called a *breakpoint*.

In a large program, it would be tedious to step through all the lines of code one by one to get to the area of code where you know your program is having trouble.

This example illustrates how to use a breakpoint to get to a section of a program quickly. Restart the program by pressing R, S to reset and start the program. This sets the highlight back to line 17.

Press the down arrow twice. This moves the cursor (not the highlight) down two lines to line 19. Press B to set a breakpoint and S to set it at the current cursor position. Figure B4.3 shows the debugger screen after B is pressed.

Figure B4.3.

The debugger is ready to set a breakpoint.

```
16
17      PERFORM INITIALIZE-PROGRAM.
18      PERFORM ENTER-THE-WORDS.
19      PERFORM DISPLAY-THE-WORDS.
20
21  PROGRAM-DONE.
22      STOP RUN.
23
24* Level 2 Routines
25
26  INITIALIZE-PROGRAM.
27      MOVE " " TO WORD-1.
28      MOVE " " TO WORD-2.
29
30  ENTER-THE-WORDS.
31      DISPLAY "This program will accept 2 words,".
32      DISPLAY "and then display them".
33      DISPLAY "in ASCII order.".
34
35      DISPLAY "Please enter the first word.".
36      ACCEPT WORD-1.
Break-points─On-count=unset─────────Level=01─Speed=5─Ins─Caps─Num─Scroll
F1=help F2=view F3=align F4=exchange F5=where F6=look-up  F9/F10=word-</> Escape
Set Unset Cancel-all Examine If Do On-count
```

When the breakpoint is set, press Z to zoom. This starts the program running as if it were not in the debugger. The debugger screen clears, and you're asked for the two words, just as you would be in the usual running:

OUTPUT
```
This program will accept 2 words,
and then display them
in ASCII order.
Please enter the first word.
dog
Please enter the second word.
cat
```

4

Enter any value for both fields, and the program will continue running as usual.

This usual running continues until the line with the breakpoint is encountered—line 19. The program reverts to debugging mode, and the debug screen is displayed with line 19 highlighted as the next line to be executed. Row 25 displays the message `Breakpoint encountered`.

From this point you may examine variables, single-step through the program, or set another breakpoint further on in the program and zoom to it.

Summary

Symbolic debuggers improve debugging capability. There is no such thing as a "standard" symbolic debugger, because debuggers vary from one software vendor to another, but they all have common commands that can be used to examine a program. Today you learned these basics:

- [ ] Programs usually must be compiled in a special way to so that they can be executed by a symbolic debugger.
- [ ] A symbolic debugger loads a program and then waits for the user to press a key to start the program.
- [ ] When a program is running, it can usually be stopped.
- [ ] A symbolic debugger lets you inspect the value of a variable in the program.
- [ ] A symbolic debugger lets you set a breakpoint at a line of code. The program will run normally until that line of code is about to be executed, and then the program will stop in the debugger window and wait for commands from the user.

BD
4

Q&A

Q If a breakpoint is set on a line, does the debugger stop the program before or after the line is executed?

A Every debugger I have ever worked with (about 40 different ones) stops the program before the line is executed. I would be very surprised to have it break after, but I suppose this is possible.

Q How can I learn a different symbolic debugger?

A Ask for the manual. Although COBOL is a fairly standard language, the tools used to develop and test COBOL programs are not. It's not uncommon to have to read the manuals to learn a linker, an editor, and a debugger.

Workshop

Quiz

1. The following code is a fragment of a program being run in the debugger. Assuming the normal breakpoint behavior of breaking before, what value would be displayed in A-NUMBER if the program broke at line 018500? At line 018600?

```
008300 01  A-NUMBER             PIC 999.
 . . . . . .
018400      COMPUTE A-NUMBER = 110 / 11.
018500      COMPUTE A-NUMBER =  110 / 10.
018600      DISPLAY A-NUMBER.
```

Exercises

1. Find a program that you don't understand perfectly and compile it for debugging. Load it into the debugger and step through it using the debugger until you understand what the program does.

2. If you're working on a different computer system, locate the manual for your debugger and find out how to prepare a program for debugging, start the debugger, examine the contents of a variable, and set a breakpoint. Practice with the debugger if you can get permission.

4

Day 5

Intrinsic Functions and the Year 2000

Part of the reason for this chapter is to prepare you for the manpower shortage that is already resulting from the year 2000 problem. (This subject is covered in greater detail in Bonus Day 6, "Dates and the Year 2000.") Recent versions of COBOL include several tools designed to help you handle year 2000 problems and date issues. These tools are called *intrinsic functions*. Intrinsic functions aren't limited to handling date problems, but many intrinsic functions are targeted at dates.

NEW TERM   *intrinsic*—Belonging to the essential nature or constitution of something.

NEW TERM   *function*—A computer subroutine—specifically, one that performs an action using zero, one, or more variables from a program and supplies the program with a single result.

Today you will learn about the following topics:

☐ What intrinsic functions are

☐ How to use arguments with intrinsic functions

☐ Numeric intrinsic functions

Understanding Intrinsic Functions

Intrinsic functions were added to the COBOL 85 standard. You've already seen something that looks and acts somewhat like an intrinsic function:

```
ACCEPT SYSTEM-DATE FROM DATE
```

The ACCEPT...FROM DATE syntax was covered in Bonus Day 2, "Miscellaneous COBOL Syntax." In the preceding example, DATE isn't a data item—it is a request for the system date from the operating system. DATE doesn't really exist as something on the system. It is actually a routine that looks up, builds, and returns a six-digit date. It does this dynamically while the program is running. If you run the program on two separate days, DATE will return two separate dates from the operating system, even though you haven't changed the program.

The CURRENT-DATE Intrinsic Function

Intrinsic functions are similar to DATE, but their syntax is different. They are easier to understand with an example. The first intrinsic function we will look at is CURRENT-DATE. The CURRENT-DATE function returns the current date as a PIC X(21) that is broken down into a date and time and a number of hours difference from Greenwich Mean Time (GMT). The date fills the first eight positions with digits in the form of CCYYMMDD (where CC represents the hundredths of years of the four-digit year). The next eight positions are the time down to hundredths of a second in the form HHMMSSDD (where DD represents hundredths). The next five positions give you the difference in hours and minutes of local time from GMT.

The five-character GMT is broken down into a sign and four digits. The sign is – if local time is earlier than GMT. The sign is + if local time is the same as or later than GMT. The sign is set to 0 if the difference from GMT is not available on this system. Using Micro Focus Personal COBOL on an MS-DOS-based machine, this character will always be 0, because MS-DOS doesn't store information about your local time zone. The remaining four character positions are the hour and minute difference from GMT if the sign is not 0. Many operating systems store the difference from GMT, and you will see these five-character positions filled in when you use CURRENT-DATE on larger computers.

Listing B5.1, CURDAT.CBL, uses the CURRENT-DATE intrinsic function to extract the current date information.

TYPE **Listing B5.1.** CURDAT.CBL **uses** CURRENT-DATE.

```
000100 IDENTIFICATION DIVISION.
000200 PROGRAM-ID. CURDAT.
000300 AUTHOR. MO BUDLONG.
000400 INSTALLATION.
000500 DATE-WRITTEN. 09/07/96.
000600 DATE-COMPILED.
000700 SECURITY. NONE
000800 ENVIRONMENT DIVISION.
000900 INPUT-OUTPUT SECTION.
001000 FILE-CONTROL.
001100 DATA DIVISION.
001200 FILE SECTION.
001300 WORKING-STORAGE SECTION.
001400
001500 01  CD-DATE                    PIC X(21).
001600 01  FILLER REDEFINES CD-DATE.
001700     05  CD-CYMD                PIC 9(8).
001800     05  CD-HMSD                PIC 9(8).
001900     05  CD-GMT-OFF             PIC S9(4) SIGN LEADING SEPARATE.
002000     05  FILLER REDEFINES CD-GMT-OFF.
002100         10  CD-GMT-OFF-SIGN  PIC X.
002200         10  CD-GMT-OFF-HM    PIC 9(4).
002300
002400 01  CD-MDCY                    PIC 9(8).
002500 01  CD-FORMATTED-MDCY          PIC Z9/99/9999.
002600 01  CD-FORMATTED-HMSD          PIC Z9/99/99/99.
002700 01  CD-FORMATTED-GMT-OFF       PIC 99/99.
002800
002900 01  DUMMY     PIC X.
003000
003100 PROCEDURE DIVISION.
003200 MAIN-LOGIC SECTION.
003300 PROGRAM-BEGIN.
003400
003500     PERFORM OPENING-PROCEDURE.
003600     PERFORM MAIN-PROCESS.
003700     PERFORM CLOSING-PROCEDURE.
003800
003900 EXIT-PROGRAM.
004000     EXIT PROGRAM.
004100 STOP-RUN.
004200     STOP RUN.
004300
004400
004500 THE-OTHER SECTION.
004600
004700 OPENING-PROCEDURE.
004800 CLOSING-PROCEDURE.
004900 MAIN-PROCESS.
005000
005100     MOVE FUNCTION CURRENT-DATE TO CD-DATE.
005200
005300     DISPLAY CD-DATE.
005400     COMPUTE CD-MDCY = CD-CYMD * 10000.0001.
```

continues

Listing B5.1. continued

```
005500        MOVE CD-MDCY TO CD-FORMATTED-MDCY.
005600        MOVE CD-HMSD TO CD-FORMATTED-HMSD.
005700        INSPECT CD-FORMATTED-HMSD REPLACING ALL '/' BY ':'.
005800        MOVE CD-GMT-OFF-HM TO CD-FORMATTED-GMT-OFF.
005900        INSPECT CD-FORMATTED-GMT-OFF REPLACING ALL '/' BY ':'.
006000        DISPLAY "DATE       = " CD-FORMATTED-MDCY.
006100        DISPLAY "TIME       = " CD-FORMATTED-HMSD.
006200        DISPLAY "GMT OFFSET = " CD-GMT-OFF-SIGN CD-FORMATTED-GMT-OFF.
006300        ACCEPT DUMMY.
006400
```

The following output was created by running CURDAT.CBL three times in a row. You will see
the time portion of the displayed data change each time you run the program, because the
system time has moved forward each time.

```
Personal COBOL version 2.0 from Micro Focus
PCOBRUN V2.0.02  Copyright(C)  1983-1993 Micro Focus Ltd.
199701052258001100000
DATE        =  1/05/1997
TIME        = 22:58:00:11
GMT OFFSET = 000:00
C:\pcobol\DATE8\intrnsic>pcobrun curdat
Personal COBOL version 2.0 from Micro Focus
PCOBRUN V2.0.02  Copyright (C) 1983-1993 Micro Focus Ltd.
199701052258210400000
DATE        =  1/05/1997
TIME        = 22:58:21:04
GMT OFFSET = 000:00
C:\pcobol\DATE8\intrnsic>pcobrun curdat
Personal COBOL version 2.0 from Micro Focus
PCOBRUN V2.0.02  Copyright (C) 1983-1993 Micro Focus Ltd.
199701052258572300000
DATE        =  1/05/1997
TIME        = 22:58:57:23
GMT OFFSET = 000:00
```

The key syntax for using CURRENT-DATE is on line 005100:

```
005100     MOVE FUNCTION CURRENT-DATE TO CD-DATE.
```

As I mentioned earlier, an intrinsic function behaves as if it were a data item. It doesn't have
to be defined in WORKING-STORAGE—it is there already. In order for the compiler to recognize
that it is dealing with a function as a pseudo-data item rather than a real data item, the
keyword FUNCTION appears before the function name.

The destination of the MOVE, CD-DATE, is a real data item and is defined in WORKING-STORAGE
on lines 001500 through 002200. The execution of the statement on line 005100 causes the
program to create a temporary variable of a PIC X(21) size. This variable is filled with eight
digits of current date, eight digits of current time, and a sign plus four digits of GMT offset

information. The resulting 21 bytes are moved to CD-DATE, just as if CURRENT-DATE had already existed in WORKING-STORAGE and had been filled in somewhere else in the program.

The remainder of the program displays CD-DATE as it was received from CURRENT-DATE and then formats and displays the parts of CD-DATE.

Passing Arguments to an Intrinsic Function

Some intrinsic functions act on data that is passed to the function. Data passed to a function is similar to arguments passed in linkage to called programs (as covered in Bonus Day 2).

Listing B5.2, UPPER.CBL, illustrates the use of the UPPER-CASE intrinsic function. This function requires an alphabetic or alphanumeric argument, and it will convert the argument to uppercase. You coded an uppercase conversion program, UPPER01.CBL, on Day 15, "Data Integrity," but you will see that the intrinsic function makes the case conversion problem easier to solve.

TYPE **Listing B5.2.** UPPER.CBL **converts an argument to uppercase.**

```
000100 IDENTIFICATION DIVISION.
000200 PROGRAM-ID. UPPER.
000300 AUTHOR. MO BUDLONG.
000400 INSTALLATION.
000500 DATE-WRITTEN. 09/07/96.
000600 DATE-COMPILED.
000700 SECURITY. NONE
000800 ENVIRONMENT DIVISION.
000900 INPUT-OUTPUT SECTION.
001000 FILE-CONTROL.
001100 DATA DIVISION.
001200 FILE SECTION.
001300 WORKING-STORAGE SECTION.
001400
001500 01   ALPHA-FIELD              PIC X(20).
001600
001700 01   DUMMY     PIC X.
001800
001900 PROCEDURE DIVISION.
002000 MAIN-LOGIC SECTION.
002100 PROGRAM-BEGIN.
002200
002300     PERFORM OPENING-PROCEDURE.
002400     PERFORM MAIN-PROCESS.
002500     PERFORM CLOSING-PROCEDURE.
002600
002700 EXIT-PROGRAM.
002800     EXIT PROGRAM.
002900 STOP-RUN.
```

BD 5

continues

Listing B5.2. continued

```
003000      STOP RUN.
003100
003200
003300 THE-OTHER SECTION.
003400
003500 OPENING-PROCEDURE.
003600 CLOSING-PROCEDURE.
003700 MAIN-PROCESS.
003800
003900      MOVE FUNCTION UPPER-CASE("goodbye") TO ALPHA-FIELD.
004000
004100      DISPLAY ALPHA-FIELD.
004200
004300      MOVE "hello" TO ALPHA-FIELD.
004400
004500      DISPLAY FUNCTION UPPER-CASE(ALPHA-FIELD).
004600
004700      ACCEPT DUMMY.
004800
```

```
C:\pcobol\DATE8\intrnsic>pcobrun upper
Personal COBOL version 2.0 from Micro Focus
PCOBRUN V2.0.02  Copyright (C) 1983-1993 Micro Focus Ltd.
GOODBYE
HELLO
```

UPPER.CBL provides two separate examples of using the UPPER-CASE function. In the first, UPPER-CASE("goodbye") is used as the source of a MOVE statement, and the result is moved to ALPHA-FIELD and then displayed on lines 003900 through 004100.

In this example, the running program creates a temporary variable, calls the subroutine UPPER-CASE, and passes it "goodbye". The result of converting it to uppercase is moved to the temporary variable. The temporary variable is then moved to ALPHA-FIELD.

UPPER-CASE(*constant or data-item*) acts like a data item, so it should be possible to directly display the result of an UPPER-CASE function call. Lines 004300 through 004500 illustrate this by moving a value to ALPHA-FIELD and then using DISPLAY UPPER-CASE(ALPHA-FIELD) to place the information onscreen.

In this use of UPPER-CASE, a temporary variable is created, and then the uppercase subroutine is called and passed the contents of ALPHA-FIELD. The result is moved to the temporary variable. The temporary variable is then displayed as if it had always existed in WORKING-STORAGE.

FUNCTION UPPER-CASE("goodbye") acts as if it were a single PIC X item containing the uppercase version of "goodbye", just as FUNCTION UPPER-CASE(ALPHA-FIELD) acts as if it were a single PIC X item containing the uppercase version of whatever is in ALPHA-FIELD. In either case, you can move from it or display it.

Limitations of Intrinsic Functions

Because an intrinsic function is actually a call to a subroutine that acts like a data item, you can't use an intrinsic function as the destination of a MOVE or in any command that attempts to use it as a destination type data item. An intrinsic function acts like a constant or a read-only value.

The following statements are illegal because the intrinsic function is being used as the destination of a MOVE or STRING:

```
MOVE "1997010112361748000000" TO FUNCTION CURRENT-DATE.
STRING
    "1997010112361748000000" DELIMITED BY SIZE
    INTO FUNCTION CURRENT-DATE.
```

An intrinsic function doesn't actually modify the data item arguments that it operates on. Instead, it creates a temporary variable and acts on that. In the following example, after the two statements are executed, ALPHA-FIELD still contains the lowercase "hello", while OTHER-FIELD now contains "HELLO". The call to FUNCTION UPPER-CASE(ALPHA-FIELD) doesn't modify the contents of ALPHA-FIELD:

```
MOVE "hello" TO ALPHA-FIELD.
MOVE FUNCTION UPPER-CASE(ALPHA-FIELD) TO OTHER-FIELD.
```

Intrinsic String Functions

The complementary intrinsic function FUNCTION LOWER-CASE (*argument*) creates a lowercase version of its argument. There is also an intrinsic function, REVERSE, that reverses its argument:

```
MOVE FUNCTION REVERSE("hello") TO BACK-WARDS.
```

In this example, REVERSE will produce the value olleh in BACK-WARDS.

Listing B5.3, STRNG.CBL, illustrates the three string-handling functions: FUNCTION UPPER-CASE(*argument*), FUNCTION LOWER-CASE (*argument*), and FUNCTION REVERSE(*argument*). It also highlights some additional actions you can take with an intrinsic, such as using an intrinsic as the source of a STRING command.

BD
5

TYPE   **Listing B5.3.** STRNG.CBL **shows some string functions.**

```
000100 IDENTIFICATION DIVISION.
000200 PROGRAM-ID. STRNG.
000300 AUTHOR. MO BUDLONG.
000400 INSTALLATION.
000500 DATE-WRITTEN. 09/07/96.
```

continues

Listing B5.3. continued

```
000600 DATE-COMPILED.
000700 SECURITY. NONE
000800 ENVIRONMENT DIVISION.
000900 INPUT-OUTPUT SECTION.
001000 FILE-CONTROL.
001100 DATA DIVISION.
001200 FILE SECTION.
001300 WORKING-STORAGE SECTION.
001400
001500 01  ALPHA-FIELD            PIC X(26).
001600 01  SECOND-FIELD           PIC X(26).
001700
001800 01  DUMMY     PIC X.
001900
002000 PROCEDURE DIVISION.
002100 MAIN-LOGIC SECTION.
002200 PROGRAM-BEGIN.
002300
002400     PERFORM OPENING-PROCEDURE.
002500     PERFORM MAIN-PROCESS.
002600     PERFORM CLOSING-PROCEDURE.
002700
002800 EXIT-PROGRAM.
002900     EXIT PROGRAM.
003000 STOP-RUN.
003100     STOP RUN.
003200
003300
003400 THE-OTHER SECTION.
003500
003600 OPENING-PROCEDURE.
003700 CLOSING-PROCEDURE.
003800 MAIN-PROCESS.
003900
004000     MOVE FUNCTION UPPER-CASE("goodbye") TO ALPHA-FIELD.
004100
004200     DISPLAY ALPHA-FIELD.
004300
004400     MOVE FUNCTION LOWER-CASE(ALPHA-FIELD) TO SECOND-FIELD.
004500
004600     DISPLAY "ALPHA  = " ALPHA-FIELD.
004700     DISPLAY "SECOND = " SECOND-FIELD.
004800
004900     MOVE "abcdefghijklmnopqrstuvwxyz" TO ALPHA-FIELD.
005000
005100     STRING
005200      FUNCTION UPPER-CASE( "hello") DELIMITED BY SIZE
005300      INTO ALPHA-FIELD.
005400
005500     DISPLAY FUNCTION REVERSE(ALPHA-FIELD).
005600
005700     ACCEPT DUMMY.
005800
```

OUTPUT

```
C:\pcobol\DATE8\intrnsic>pcobrun strng
Personal COBOL version 2.0 from Micro Focus
PCOBRUN V2.0.02  Copyright (C) 1983-1993 Micro Focus Ltd.
GOODBYE
ALPHA  = GOODBYE
SECOND = goodbye
zyxwvutsrqponmlkjihgfOLLEH
```

ANALYSIS   On lines 004000 and 004200, goodbye is converted to uppercase, stored in ALPHA-FIELD, and then displayed. On line 004400, ALPHA-FIELD is converted to lowercase and stored in SECOND-FIELD, and then, on lines 004600 and 004700, ALPHA-FIELD and SECOND-FIELD are displayed.

On line 004900, a new value is moved to ALPHA-FIELD that contains the letters of the alphabet. On lines 005100 through 005300, the STRING verb moves an uppercase version of hello into the same field.

Remember that the STRING verb won't clear out the rest of ALPHA-FIELD, which would have happened if a MOVE verb had been used. Instead, the uppercase letters HELLO are moved over the first five positions of the contents of ALPHA-FIELD.

Finally, on line 005500, a reversed version of ALPHA-FIELD is displayed.

Numeric Intrinsic Functions

An intrinsic function acts like a data item. Data items can be numeric or alphanumeric, so there must be some intrinsic functions that can act like numbers. There are several, including intrinsic functions that act on dates. For the moment, we will look at a simple intrinsic function that doesn't involve dates so that you can get a feel for them.

Listing B5.4, REMEX.CBL, illustrates the REM function. REM returns the remainder of a division between two numbers. The REM function behaves as a numeric data item, but in the Micro Focus personal COBOL compiler, a numeric function can't be used as the source of a MOVE. Other compilers also have this limitation. The best way to use a numeric function is in a COMPUTE statement, as shown in Listing B5.4.

TYPE   **Listing B5.4.** REMEX.CBL **uses the** REM **intrinsic function.**

```
000100 IDENTIFICATION DIVISION.
000200 PROGRAM-ID. REMEX.
000300 AUTHOR. MO BUDLONG.
000400 INSTALLATION.
000500 DATE-WRITTEN. 09/07/96.
000600 DATE-COMPILED.
000700 SECURITY. NONE
000800 ENVIRONMENT DIVISION.
```

continues

BD
5

Listing B5.4. continued

```
000900 INPUT-OUTPUT SECTION.
001000 FILE-CONTROL.
001100 DATA DIVISION.
001200 FILE SECTION.
001300 WORKING-STORAGE SECTION.
001400
001500 01  NUMERIC-1              PIC 9(9).
001600 01  NUMERIC-2              PIC 9(9).
001700 01  NUMERIC-3              PIC 9(9).
001800
001900 01  DUMMY      PIC X.
002000
002100 PROCEDURE DIVISION.
002200 MAIN-LOGIC SECTION.
002300 PROGRAM-BEGIN.
002400
002500     PERFORM OPENING-PROCEDURE.
002600     PERFORM MAIN-PROCESS.
002700     PERFORM CLOSING-PROCEDURE.
002800
002900 EXIT-PROGRAM.
003000     EXIT PROGRAM.
003100 STOP-RUN.
003200     STOP RUN.
003300
003400
003500 THE-OTHER SECTION.
003600
003700 OPENING-PROCEDURE.
003800 CLOSING-PROCEDURE.
003900 MAIN-PROCESS.
004000     MOVE 1 TO NUMERIC-1, NUMERIC-2.
004100     PERFORM ENTER-PARAMETERS.
004200     PERFORM TEST-REM UNTIL
004300         NUMERIC-1 = 0
004400       OR NUMERIC-2 = 0.
004500
004600 ENTER-PARAMETERS.
004700     DISPLAY "ENTER LARGER NUMBER (0 TO QUIT)".
004800     ACCEPT NUMERIC-1.
004900
005000     IF NUMERIC-1 NOT = 0
005100         DISPLAY "ENTER SMALLER NUMBER (0 TO QUIT)"
005200         ACCEPT NUMERIC-2.
005300
005400 TEST-REM.
005500     COMPUTE NUMERIC-3 =
005600         FUNCTION REM (NUMERIC-1, NUMERIC-2).
005700
005800     DISPLAY "REMAINDER OF " NUMERIC-1 "/" NUMERIC-2 " IS ".
005900     DISPLAY NUMERIC-3.
006000     DISPLAY "PRESS ENTER TO CONTINUE . . . "
006100     ACCEPT DUMMY.
006200
006300     PERFORM ENTER-PARAMETERS.
006400
```

5

The output illustrates several remainder calculations.

```
C:\pcobol\DATE8\intrnsic>pcobrun remex
Personal COBOL version 2.0 from Micro Focus
PCOBRUN V2.0.02  Copyright (C) 1983-1993 Micro Focus Ltd.
ENTER LARGER NUMBER (0 TO QUIT)
23
ENTER SMALLER NUMBER (0 TO QUIT)
7
REMAINDER OF 000000023/000000007 IS
000000002
PRESS ENTER TO CONTINUE . . .
ENTER LARGER NUMBER (0 TO QUIT)
4266
ENTER SMALLER NUMER (0 TO QUIT)
11
REMAINDER OF 000004266/000000011 IS
000000009
PRESS ENTER TO CONTINUE . . .
ENTER LARGER NUMBER (0 TO QUIT)
0
C:\pcobol\DATE8\intrnsic>
```

On lines 004600 through 005300, a larger number and a smaller number are accepted as input. TEST-REM, on lines 005400 through 006400, displays the remainder of dividing the larger number by the smaller. MAIN-PROCESS, on lines 003900 through 004500, creates a loop that repeats until the user enters 0.

Summary

Today you learned about intrinsic functions, why they were introduced in the COBOL 85 standard, and how to use several of them in your programs. You explored the following:

☐ The CURRENT-DATE function, which extracts an eight-digit date, time, and other information.

☐ How to pass arguments to functions and how to use the values created and returned by functions.

☐ String-handling functions such as UPPER-CASE, LOWER-CASE, and REVERSE.

☐ How to use the numeric function REM.

BD
5

Q&A

Q Are there other intrinsic functions?

A Yes. You will learn about several other intrinsic functions on Bonus Day 6, "Dates and the Year 2000."

Workshop

Quiz

What does the following call to REM return as a value that is stored in RESULT?

```
COMPUTE RESULT = REM(15, 4).
```

Exercise

Review the date routines in Day 19, "Complex Data Entry Problems," and work out a way to use the REM function to check for leap years.

5

Day 6

Dates and the Year 2000

The approach of the year 2000 (just around the corner now) has produced a great deal of activity regarding dates. The biggest issue is solving the problem of millions of lines of code that use only two digits to represent years. There are also issues involving the rules for leap years and new standards for storing and retrieving date information

Today, you learn about the following parts of the bills-payment system:

- ☐ A short history of the modern calendar used in computer dating
- ☐ The correct rules for determining a leap year
- ☐ Date formats and calendars used in computer dating, including the Julian calendar, Julian period dating, Julian format dates, the Gregorian calendar, Gregorian format dates, Lilian dates, and ANSI/ISO dates

☐ Using computer dating to calculate the day of the week and to add days to a date to calculate a new date

☐ The year 2000 problem

☐ Using intrinsic functions to help solve year 2000 problems

☐ Solutions currently being used in the industry for the year 2000 problem

More Than You Ever Wanted to Know About Dates

This section covers dating systems and calendars so that you'll understand how computers calculate dates (or miscalculate dates) and the dating techniques used by computers.

I won't make this a history lesson, but suffice it to say that calendars were a source of great consternation in the past (not that we're doing much better these days). They were based on either the lunar month (about 29$\frac{1}{2}$ days), the solar year (about 365$\frac{1}{4}$ days—note the use of "about" here; it will come back to haunt us), or a combination of both.

There are as many versions of history as there are historians. I would like to say that the following information on the Greco-Roman origins of the calendar is etched-in-bronze irrefutable fact, but the truth is that no one really knows, and calendar historians love to argue about it. For the purposes of this early history, the following should be called the story of the calendar, or perhaps even the legend of the calendar, rather than its history.

The modern Western calendar as we know it has its roots in a Roman calendar that was borrowed from the Greeks. It had 10 months of varying lengths that made up a year of 304 days. The remaining 61 (or 62) days were just left over, lying around for whatever you wanted to do with them. The 10 months were Martius, Aprilis, Maius, Junius, Quintilis, Sextilis, Septembris, Octobris, Novembris, and Decembris. Greedy rulers (gee, Rome had those too?), notably Numa Pompilius, realized that they could collect more taxes if there were more months in a year, so they scooped up the spare days, placed them at the end of the year, and divided them into two more months, Januarius and Februarius. The year started on Martius 1 and ended on the last day of Februarius. In this arrangement, you can see the beginnings of a proto-modern calendar.

The First Julian Calendar

There were still some loose days lying around, and seasons drifted around, appearing in different months in some years. In 46 B.C.E. (Before the Common Era), Julius Caesar grabbed the astronomer Sosigenes and told him to sort things out. Sosigenes devised a year with 12 months of 30 or 31 days each, except for Februarius, which had 29. Every four years, one extra day was added to Februarius to keep the calendar year synchronized with the solar year. In order to align the year with the seasons, Julius declared that the current year should have begun on Januarius 1, and that henceforth each year would begin on that date. The population was also informed that Januarius 1 hadn't occurred when they thought it had, but that it had actually happened more than 20 days earlier. Therefore, the year 46 B.C.E. had many extra days to compensate for all this date-shifting. Romans called it the year of confusion.

In order to honor the calendar reform, and presumably with a fair bit of pressure from Julius himself, the Roman Senate renamed the month Quintilis to Julius (which, of course, is now July).

Does all this sound familiar? You have a 12-month year starting in Januarius; each month has 30 or 31 days, except Februarius, which has 29; and Februarius gains an extra day every four years.

Interestingly, Sosigenes, who actually devised this scheme and was *almost* right, was never honored in the calendar. Otherwise, Americans might be celebrating the 4th of Sosigeny as Independence Day.

The Calendar According to Augustus

Julius Caesar's successor, Emperor Augustus, who felt that he was every bit as cool as his predecessor, had the month Sextilis renamed Augustus. Officially, the Senate proclaimed this renaming, but it isn't difficult to guess who was lobbying for it.

Unfortunately, the month Julius had 31 days, and the renamed Augustus had only 30. Augustus, upset that his month wasn't as big as Julius's, took a day from Februarius and stuck it onto the end of Augustus, so February ended up having only 28 days most of the time.

The change caused by Augustus was not a very big one, so the calendar was still called the Julian calendar for another 1,500 years.

A final warning. Some serious calendar scholars claim that the whole story so far is learned claptrap and a medieval fabrication by calendar reformers who wanted to create some "history" for their own scheme to regularize the calendar.

BD
6

Leap Year Drift

Earlier I said that the solar year was about $365\frac{1}{4}$ days long. It's actually 11 minutes and 14 seconds shorter than that. You might think that this isn't much to worry about. In the course of a 70-year lifetime, the calendar would drift by only about 13 hours. However, over 1,500 years, the drift was beginning to show. In 1582, the spring equinox, one of those inescapably observable astronomical phenomena, had drifted back to March 11, 10 days earlier than its traditional March 21 date. Something had to be done, and quickly. After all, in another 140 years, the spring equinox would slip to March 10.

The Gregorian Calendar

Pope Gregory XIII turned this problem over to the scholar Aloysius Lilius. He and his brother came up with a solution that involved further fiddling with poor old Februarius. Having an extra day every four years was almost right, but the system could be further tuned with two additional rules.

Here was the original rule:

☐ Years that are evenly divisible by 4 are leap years.

Here were the additional new rules:

☐ Years that are divisible by 100 (that is, years that end in 00) are not leap years, even though they are evenly divisible by 4.

☐ Years that end in 00 and that are evenly divisible by 400 are leap years.

So, for example, 1700, 1800, and 1900 are not leap years, but 2000 is, and 1600 was.

These are the leap year rules that are used in the current calendar.

With all the attention to the year 2000, considerable significance has been attached to the fact that the year 2000 is a leap year. This was caused by a notable series of goofs by more than one software company that applied only the old rule and the first new rule to the year 2000 and determined that 2000 was not a leap year.

So much attention is attached to this issue that you might be asked about it in a job interview. Is the year 2000 a leap year, and why or why not?

Adjusting the Drift

The new rules worked well, but something had to be done about the 10-day drift. The Pope handled this by proclaiming that the day that should have been October 5, 1582 would be October 15, 1582. So the days October 5 through October 14, 1582 don't actually exist in the Gregorian calendar.

Of course, the new calendar didn't roll out overnight. The average man-in-the-street (in those days known as the average peasant-in-ye-muddy-rutted-path) didn't have the benefit of the 9 o'clock news to warn him of the changes. There was also political resistance to the change. It took Great Britain 200 years to get with the program. They went Gregorian in 1752, calling it the New Style calendar, and declared that the day following September 2, 1752 would be

September 14, 1752. They also ordered all colonies to adopt the new date conventions. Note that because Great Britain waited 200 years before adopting the Gregorian calendar, it had to drop 11 days, September 3 through 13, one day more than Gregory had to drop in 1582 (October 5 through 14).

Turkey didn't adopt the new calendar until 1927. Since each country adopted the calendar at a different time, calendar adjustments happened at different times in various parts of the world. There are missing days in different periods for each location, depending on when the country in question adopted the calendar and which days were disposed of to adjust for the adoption.

The Gregorian calendar is very accurate in keeping pace with the solar year. It is still about 26 seconds too long, so in a few thousand years, that pesky spring equinox will have drifted off by a day. I guess we will cross that bridge when we come to it.

The Gregorian calendar is not the only calendar. The Islamic calendar is based on a lunar calendar with leap year adjustments and is quite accurate, although the year drifts through a complete cycle every 30 years. On the Hebrew calendar, the current year (1997) is 5757, and their year begins in autumn. There are many more. Because the Gregorian calendar is used for most business computing, it is the calendar that this chapter deals with.

The Other Julian System

In 1582, Joseph Scaliger devised another dating system called the Julian period. He numbered days starting from noon on January 1, 4713 B.C.E. Noon on December 31, 1994 was the beginning of Julian Day 2,449,718.

The starting date for the Julian period was chosen because it was the convergence in recent history of three earlier chronological cycles that were used for determining dates: the 28-year solar cycle, the 19-year lunar cycle, and the 15-year Roman Tax cycle, also called the indiction cycle. Julian period dating is used today in astronomy as a convenient method of dating astronomical events. This has advantages on an international scale because the Gregorian calendar was adopted at different times in different places. June 3, 1602 is not the same day to an Italian astronomer whose country was on the Gregorian calendar and an English astronomer whose country was not. Scaliger named the system after his father, Julius, not after the Julian calendar. This Julian period dating system is frequently called the Julian calendar or Julian Day, which causes some confusion with the Julius Caesar version.

BD
6

Julian Dates

Just to throw another Julian into the pot, the computer industry has developed a date format containing five or seven digits, composed of a two- or four-digit year and a three-digit day of the year. This format does not have a month in it but simply counts the days from the beginning of the year with January 1 being day 1. Thus, January 1, 1997 is 97001 or 1997001, and February 2, 1998 becomes 1998033 or 98033. This date format is used in a lot of military software. This format should be called Ordinal Day of the Year or Ordinal Year Day Format, but somewhere along the line the name Julian was applied, and it stuck.

Gregorian Versus Julian Formats

In the computer business, two naming conventions have arisen for two date formats: Julian format, as already described, and Gregorian format. Gregorian dates are those stored with a year (2 or 4 digit), a month, and a day (without regard to the order of these numbers) as 970213 or 02131997.

Both Julian and Gregorian formats use the underlying Gregorian calendar, but the term *Julian date* has been in use long enough now that it will persist. Even IBM uses the terms Julian date and Julian format to refer to the ordinal day of the year format of a two- or four-digit year followed by a three-digit day of the year.

A Final Note on the Julians

With so much attention on the year 2000, a new breed of programmer has appeared—the arcane date trivia buff. These folks are characterized by a tendency to correct you vehemently whenever you refer to a date as a Julian date when it is in Julian format. They will trot out either the Julian calendar (Caesar's) or the Julian period dating system (Scaliger's) and proceed to beat you over the head with it to illustrate what a dolt you are for not knowing that the year-year-day-day-day format is actually in the Gregorian calendar but uses the ordinal day and year format.

These folks usually also know all about Scaliger's Julian period or Julian Day dates and incorrectly call it the Julian calendar and then criticize you for defining the Julian calendar as the calendar developed at Julius Caesar's order in 46 B.C.E., or vice versa.

A third piece of information that these date buffs love thrusting down your throat is the fact that the year 2000 is *not* the beginning of the 21st century; it is the last year of the 19th century. Because there is no year 0, the 1st century was years 1 through 100, the 2nd century was years 101 through 200, and so on up to the 20th century, which is the years 1901 through 2000. 2001 is the first year of the 21st century. This has nothing to do with computer date problems, but when some people get going, they just can't stop. It does mean that we will have two great New Year's celebrations back to back: the first to incorrectly celebrate the end of the 20th century on December 31, 1999, and the other to correctly celebrate it on December 31, 2000.

Don't be too hard on these people just because you now know the correct answers. Just smile and refer them to a good encyclopedia.

Lilian Dates

The Lilian dating system was named for Aloysius Lilius, one of the two brothers who were instrumental in developing the Gregorian calendar. The Lilian dating system is based on counting the number of days since October 14, 1582. The Gregorian calendar was deployed by papal decree on October 15, 1582, or Lilian day 1.

This system of creating dates by counting days from a specified date in the past has been used in various calendars and dating systems, including the Julian period system devised by Joseph Scaliger. The American National Standards Institute (ANSI) adopted a system of counting days starting from December 31, 1600 as Day 0. Thus, January 1, 1601 is ANSI Day 1. This format is referred to as the ANSI or ISO (International Standards Organization) date format.

The Lilian and ANSI date formats are two examples of a style of dating usually called *integer-day* dating systems or *day-as-integer* dates.

The Lilian and ANSI day dating systems use large numbers to store the number of days since a particular start date. For example, January 1, 1998 will be ANSI day 145,002.

Dating Systems Used on Computers

What does all this have to do with computers? You will commonly find the following seven date types on computers:

- [ ] Gregorian calendar dates: Most business computers use the Gregorian calendar. Regardless of how dates are displayed to the user—1/1/98 or 1998001 or 1-JAN-1998—these are all methods of expressing dates in the Gregorian calendar.

- [ ] Gregorian format dates: A Gregorian calendar date stored as a two- or four-digit year, a two-digit month, and a two-digit day. Usually 19980101.

- [ ] Julian format dates: A Gregorian calendar date stored as a two- or four-digit year and a three-digit day of the year. Usually 1998001.

- [ ] Lilian dates: A date stored as a number of days from October 14, 1582 as Day 0.

- [ ] ANSI (or ISO) dates: A date stored as a number of days from December 31, 1600 as Day 0.

- [ ] Integer day dates: A date stored as a number of days from a fixed date. Some mainframes and minicomputers have an option during the initial setting up of the computer that allows the installer to choose a start date. Thereafter, dates are tracked as days from the user-entered date in a manner similar to Lilian or ANSI dates.

BD
6

☐ Integer interval dates: A date and time stored as a number of seconds, hundredths of seconds, computer clock ticks, or similar measurements from a fixed date in the past. Because this method of storing dates produces very large numbers, the starting date for these systems is almost always something recent, such as January 1, 1990.

If you work on computers that store astronomical data, you might run into Julian period dates, in which a date is stored as a number of days from noon on January 1, 4713 B.C.E. Julian period dates are beyond the scope of this chapter.

Even less likely and also beyond the scope of this chapter might be software that tracks archaeological finds or historical documents on the Julian (Caesar's) calendar, the Mayan calendar, or any other possible dating system based on the culture associated with the artifact.

Intrinsic Functions for Dates

Several intrinsic functions are designed to handle dates. Table B6.1 lists each function, its arguments, and its return values.

Bonus Day 5, "Intrinsic Functions and the Year 2000," covered the CURRENT-DATE function, so let's look at some of the others.

Day of the Week

One of the reasons that the ANSI committee chose January 1, 1601 to be Day 1 of the ANSI date-recording technique is that January 1, 1601 also happens to be a Monday. This makes it possible to combine the REM function with the INTEGER-OF-DATE function to calculate the day of the week for dates equal to or greater than January 1, 1601, which is day 1 of the ANSI dating system.

Table B6.2 shows you how the day of the week is calculated using the ANSI date in days, dividing it by 7, and using the remainder to determine the actual day of the week for that date. It lists a date starting from January 1, 1601, the ANSI day, which is the remainder of dividing the ANSI day by 7 and the day of the week for the date. The pattern shows a remainder of 1 for Mondays, 2 for Tuesdays, and so on through to Sunday, which returns a remainder of zero. This pattern repeats for successive dates all the way to the present. A remainder of 0 represents a Sunday, 1 is a Monday, and so on through Friday, which is 6. Hark back to your early elementary school long division classes when looking at the table, and you will remember that 1 divided by 7 produces a result of 0 and a remainder of 1, 2 divided by 7 also produces a result of 0 but a remainder of 2, and so on.

6

Table B6.1. Date functions.

Function Name	Content of Arguments	Data Type of Arguments	Content of Returned Value	Data Type of Returned Value
CURRENT-DATE	None	None	Current date, time, and GMT difference[1]	Alphanumeric
DATE-OF-INTEGER	ANSI date[2]	Integer	Gregorian date[3]	Integer
DAY-OF-INTEGER	ANSI date[2]	Integer	Julian date[4]	Integer
INTEGER-OF-DATE	Gregorian date[3]	Integer	ANSI date[2]	Integer
INTEGER-OF-DAY	Julian date[4]	Integer	ANSI date[2]	Integer

An integer is a whole number.

[1] Current date, time, and Greenwich Mean Time (GMT) difference. A date and time in the format CCYYMMDDHHMMSSDD followed by a sign and four digits of difference from GMT in HHMM format. In the format CC = hundreds of years, YY = years, MM = month 1-12, DD = day 1-31, HH = hour 0-23, MM = minutes 0-59, SS = seconds 0-59 and DD = hundredths of a second 0-99. When it is 7:55 pm in Greenwich, it is also 7:55 pm in Dublin, Ireland, and the GMT difference will appear as +0000. In Moscow it will be 10:55 pm, and the GMT difference will be +0300. Los Angeles, California is eight hours earlier than GMT. The time there will be 11:55 am, and the GMT difference will be -0800. All of these numbers ignore any shifts that occur for Daylight savings time.

[2] The number of days since December 31, 1600.

[3] A date in the format YYYYMMDD.

[4] A date in the format YYYYDDD.

BD
6

To determine the day of the week for any date from January 1, 1601, you need to convert the date to ANSI days using the INTEGER-OF-DATE function and find the remainder of dividing that number by 7 using the REM function. The INTEGER-OF-DATE function will not work correctly for dates prior to January 1, 1601.

Table B6.2. Day-of-the-week calculations.

Date	ANSI Date	REM (Remainder of ANSI Date Divided by 7)	Day of the Week
Jan 1, 1601	1	1	Monday
Jan 2, 1601	2	2	Tuesday
Jan 3, 1601	3	3	Wednesday
Jan 4, 1601	4	4	Thursday
Jan 5, 1601	5	5	Friday
Jan 6, 1601	6	6	Saturday
Jan 7, 1601	7	0	Sunday
Jan 8, 1601	8	1	Monday
Jan 9, 1601	9	2	Tuesday
Jan 10, 1601	10	3	Wednesday
Jan 11, 1601	11	4	Thursday
Jan 12, 1601	12	5	Friday
Jan 13, 1601	13	6	Saturday
Jan 14, 1601	14	0	Sunday
Jan 15, 1601	15	1	Monday

Listing B6.1, DOW.CBL, uses the REM and the INTEGER-OF-DATE functions to calculate the day of the week of the current system date and a date entered by the user. It does this using two different styles.

TYPE   **Listing B6.1.** DOW.CBL.

```
000100 IDENTIFICATION DIVISION.
000200 PROGRAM-ID. DOW.
000300 AUTHOR. MO BUDLONG.
000400 INSTALLATION.
000500 DATE-WRITTEN. 09/07/96.
000600 DATE-COMPILED.
000700 SECURITY. NONE
```

```
000800 ENVIRONMENT DIVISION.
000900 INPUT-OUTPUT SECTION.
001000 FILE-CONTROL.
001100 DATA DIVISION.
001200 FILE SECTION.
001300 WORKING-STORAGE SECTION.
001400
001500 01   CD-DATE.
001600      05   CD-YYYYMMDD         PIC 9(8).
001700      05   FILLER              PIC X(13).
001800 01   THE-DATE                 PIC 9(8).
001900 01   ANSI-DATE                PIC 9(6).
002000 01   THE-DOW                  PIC 9.
002100
002200 01   DAYS-OF-WEEK.
002300      05   FILLER              PIC X(9) VALUE "SUNDAY".
002400      05   FILLER              PIC X(9) VALUE "MONDAY".
002500      05   FILLER              PIC X(9) VALUE "TUESDAY".
002600      05   FILLER              PIC X(9) VALUE "WEDNESDAY".
002700      05   FILLER              PIC X(9) VALUE "THURSDAY".
002800      05   FILLER              PIC X(9) VALUE "FRIDAY".
002900      05   FILLER              PIC X(9) VALUE "SATURDAY".
003000 01   FILLER REDEFINES DAYS-OF-WEEK.
003100      05   THE-DAY             PIC X(9) OCCURS 7 TIMES.
003200
003300 01   DOW-SUB                  PIC 9.
003400
003500 01   DUMMY     PIC X.
003600
003700 PROCEDURE DIVISION.
003800 MAIN-LOGIC SECTION.
003900 PROGRAM-BEGIN.
004000
004100      PERFORM OPENING-PROCEDURE.
004200      PERFORM MAIN-PROCESS.
004300      PERFORM CLOSING-PROCEDURE.
004400
004500 EXIT-PROGRAM.
004600      EXIT PROGRAM.
004700 STOP-RUN.
004800      STOP RUN.
004900
005000
005100 THE-OTHER SECTION.
005200
005300 OPENING-PROCEDURE.
005400 CLOSING-PROCEDURE.
005500 MAIN-PROCESS.
005600      MOVE 1 TO THE-DATE.
005700      PERFORM ENTER-PARAMETERS.
005800      PERFORM TEST-DOW UNTIL
005900          THE-DATE = 0.
006000
006100 ENTER-PARAMETERS.
006200      DISPLAY "ENTER A DATE IN YYYYMMDD FORMAT (0 TO QUIT)".
```

continues

BD
6

Listing B6.1. continued

```
006300        ACCEPT THE-DATE.
006400
006500 TEST-DOW.
006600        MOVE FUNCTION CURRENT-DATE TO CD-DATE.
006700
006800        COMPUTE ANSI-DATE = FUNCTION INTEGER-OF-DATE(CD-YYYYMMDD).
006900        COMPUTE THE-DOW = FUNCTION REM(ANSI-DATE,7).
007000        COMPUTE DOW-SUB = THE-DOW + 1.
007100
007200        DISPLAY "TODAY IS " CD-YYYYMMDD " A "
007300            THE-DAY(DOW-SUB).
007400
007500        COMPUTE DOW-SUB = FUNCTION REM(
007600            FUNCTION INTEGER-OF-DATE(THE-DATE), 7) + 1.
007700
007800        DISPLAY THE-DATE " IS A "
007900            THE-DAY(DOW-SUB).
008000
008100        DISPLAY "PRESS ENTER TO CONTINUE . . . "
008200        ACCEPT DUMMY.
008300
008400        PERFORM ENTER-PARAMETERS.
008500
```

OUTPUT

```
C:\pcobol\DATE8\intrnsic>PCOBRUN DOW
Personal COBOL version 2.0 from Micro Focus
PCOBRUN V2.0.02  Copyright (C) 1983-1993 Micro Focus Ltd.
ENTER A DATE IN YYYYMMDD FORMAT (0 TO QUIT)
16010101
TODAY IS 19970112 A SUNDAY
16010101 IS A MONDAY
PRESS ENTER TO CONTINUE . . .
ENTER A DATE IN YYYYMMDD FORMAT (0 TO QUIT)
19970113
TODAY IS 19970112 A SUNDAY
19970113 IS A MONDAY
PRESS ENTER TO CONTINUE . . .
ENTER A DATE IN YYYYMMDD FORMAT (0 TO QUIT)
19480304
TODAY IS 19970112 A SUNDAY
19480304 IS A THURSDAY
PRESS ENTER TO CONTINUE . . .
ENTER A DATE IN YYYYMMDD FORMAT (0 TO QUIT)
```

ANALYSIS   In lines 006600 through 007400, the CURRENT-DATE is extracted and then converted to an ANSI date. The remainder division is performed on the ANSI date, and the result is placed in DOW. DOW is used to create a subscript DOW-SUB into the DAYS-OF-WEEK table, and the result is displayed.

The second version starting on line 007500 uses a feature of intrinsic functions. The result of an intrinsic function can be used directly as an argument to another intrinsic function. The second version computes the value of DOW-SUB in one statement on lines 007500 and 007600. Let's analyze this statement and see how it works while the computer executes the statement. First, it helps to scrunch everything onto one line:

```
COMPUTE DOW-SUB = FUNCTION REM( FUNCTION INTEGER-OF-DATE(THE-DATE), 7) + 1.
```

For this example, I will assume that the entered date is 16010108 (January 8, 1601), a Monday. Functions, just like arithmetic statements, are evaluated from the inside out. The first thing the computer does is replace the THE-DATE for the INTEGER-OF-DATE function with the actual value that was entered, 16010108:

```
COMPUTE DOW-SUB = FUNCTION REM( FUNCTION INTEGER-OF-DATE(16010108), 7) + 1.
```

The inner function, FUNCTION INTEGER-OF-DATE(16010108), is resolved to ANSI Day 8, and the statement becomes

```
COMPUTE DOW-SUB = FUNCTION REM(8, 7) + 1.
```

Now the REM(8, 7) function is performed and resolves to 1:

```
COMPUTE DOW-SUB = 1 + 1.
```

Finally, the value 2 is assigned to DOW-SUB, which points to the value "MONDAY" in the DAYS-OF-WEEK table, which is what we were after.

Adding Days to a Date

It's possible to use INTEGER-OF-DATE and the inverse function DATE-OF-INTEGER to calculate a new date when a number of days are added to an existing date. Listing B6.2, DADD.CBL, illustrates one method of doing this by adding a positive or negative number to the current date.

TYPE   **Listing B6.2. DADD.CBL: Adds days to a date.**

```
000100 IDENTIFICATION DIVISION.
000200 PROGRAM-ID. DADD.
000300 AUTHOR. MO BUDLONG.
000400 INSTALLATION.
000500 DATE-WRITTEN. 09/07/96.
000600 DATE-COMPILED.
000700 SECURITY. NONE
000800 ENVIRONMENT DIVISION.
000900 INPUT-OUTPUT SECTION.
001000 FILE-CONTROL.
001100 DATA DIVISION.
001200 FILE SECTION.
```

BD
6

continues

Listing B6.2. continued

```
001300 WORKING-STORAGE SECTION.
001400
001500 01   CD-DATE.
001600      05   CD-YYYYMMDD          PIC 9(8).
001700      05   FILLER               PIC X(13).
001800 01   NEW-DATE                  PIC 9(8).
001900 01   DAYS-TO-ADD               PIC S9(5).
002000 01   FORMAT-DAYS-TO-ADD        PIC ZZZZ9-.
002100
002200 01   DUMMY      PIC X.
002300
002400 PROCEDURE DIVISION.
002500 MAIN-LOGIC SECTION.
002600 PROGRAM-BEGIN.
002700
002800      PERFORM OPENING-PROCEDURE.
002900      PERFORM MAIN-PROCESS.
003000      PERFORM CLOSING-PROCEDURE.
003100
003200 EXIT-PROGRAM.
003300      EXIT PROGRAM.
003400 STOP-RUN.
003500      STOP RUN.
003600
003700
003800 THE-OTHER SECTION.
003900
004000 OPENING-PROCEDURE.
004100 CLOSING-PROCEDURE.
004200 MAIN-PROCESS.
004300      MOVE 1 TO DAYS-TO-ADD.
004400      PERFORM ENTER-PARAMETERS.
004500      PERFORM TEST-DADD UNTIL
004600          DAYS-TO-ADD = 0.
004700
004800 ENTER-PARAMETERS.
004900      DISPLAY "ENTER NUMBER-OF-DAYS TO ADD (0 TO QUIT)".
005000      ACCEPT DAYS-TO-ADD.
005100      MOVE DAYS-TO-ADD TO FORMAT-DAYS-TO-ADD.
005200
005300 TEST-DADD.
005400      MOVE FUNCTION CURRENT-DATE TO CD-DATE.
005500
005600      COMPUTE NEW-DATE =
005700          FUNCTION DATE-OF-INTEGER(
005800             FUNCTION INTEGER-OF-DATE(CD-YYYYMMDD)
005900          + DAYS-TO-ADD).
006000
006100      DISPLAY "CURRENT DATE " CD-YYYYMMDD
006200             " + " FORMAT-DAYS-TO-ADD
006300             " WILL BE " NEW-DATE.
006400
006500      PERFORM ENTER-PARAMETERS.
006600
```

```
Accepted - CONFIRM
ENTER NUMBER-OF-DAYS TO ADD (0 TO QUIT)
15
CURRENT DATE 19970112 +     15  WILL BE 19970127
ENTER NUMBER-OF-DAYS TO ADD (0 TO QUIT)
-1
CURRENT DATE 19970112 +      1- WILL BE 19970111
ENTER NUMBER-OF-DAYS TO ADD (0 TO QUIT)
-30
CURRENT DATE 19970112 +     30- WILL BE 19961213
ENTER NUMBER-OF-DAYS TO ADD (0 TO QUIT)
-500
CURRENT DATE 19970112 +    500- WILL BE 19950831
ENTER NUMBER-OF-DAYS TO ADD (0 TO QUIT)
-365
CURRENT DATE 19970112 +    365- WILL BE 19960113
ENTER NUMBER-OF-DAYS TO ADD (0 TO QUIT)
-366
CURRENT DATE 19970112 +    366- WILL BE 19960112
ENTER NUMBER-OF-DAYS TO ADD (0 TO QUIT)
+365
CURRENT DATE 19970112 +    365  WILL BE 19980112
ENTER NUMBER-OF-DAYS TO ADD (0 TO QUIT)
```

ANALYSIS The technique of using the return value of a function as an argument to another function is used in lines 005600 through 005900. In the following example, the line is too wide for this book's margins, so it is broken into two lines. The statement starts out as follows:

```
COMPUTE NEW-DATE = FUNCTION DATE-OF-INTEGER (
➥FUNCTION INTEGER-OF-DATE(CD-YYYYMMDD) + DAYS-TO-ADD).
```

Assuming that the current date is 19970112 and that the user entered -30 as the days offset, the function resolves in stages. Again, the following line is split across two lines. First, the value of the current date is plugged into the INTEGER-OF-DATE function:

```
COMPUTE NEW-DATE = FUNCTION DATE-OF-INTEGER (
➥FUNCTION INTEGER-OF-DATE(19970112) + DAYS-TO-ADD).
```

The ANSI days are calculated by calling INTEGER-OF-DATE and replacing the function call:

```
COMPUTE NEW-DATE = FUNCTION DATE-OF-INTEGER(144,648 + DAYS-TO-ADD).
```

DAYS-TO-ADD is plugged into the formula, and the arithmetic is done:

```
COMPUTE NEW-DATE = FUNCTION DATE-OF-INTEGER(144,648 + (-30)).
COMPUTE NEW-DATE = FUNCTION DATE-OF-INTEGER(144,618).
```

Finally, the DATE-OF-INTEGER function is called with this value and returns 19961231, which is assigned to NEW-DATE:

```
COMPUTE NEW-DATE = 19961231.
```

BD
6

What Is the Year 2000 Problem?

Now that you have seen what can be done with intrinsic functions operating on dates, it's time to look at the year 2000 problem. COBOL programs, as well as other software, including even the software that displays the date and time on your IBM-compatible PC, use a six-digit date. The date, in YYMMDD or MMDDYY format, and the accompanying code assume 19 for the first part of the year and store, for example, November 12, 1997 as 971112 or 111297. January 1, 2000 would become 000101. This will mess up a lot of sorting logic and other parts of the program.

For many, the problem is upon them already. Financial institutions are currently dealing with the maturation date of five-year CDs, for example. My insurance company has calculated my life insurance premium based on an actuarial table that estimates my death in a four-digit year that begins with a 20, not an assumed 19. At least I hope so!

For other companies, the problem will have to be solved by the beginning of 1999. This will allow purchase orders, due dates, delivery dates, and other future-based transactions to be processed correctly.

Some people erroneously believe that the problem has already been solved. I recently attended a demonstration of a payroll package that displayed dates with a four-digit year. After I used the package and tried a few options, something struck me as odd about the dates. I ran a few quick tests. I wasn't allowed to see the source code, but I hypothesized that the logic read something like this:

```
IF YY > 20
    PERFORM FORMAT-AS-1900
ELSE
    PERFORM FORMAT-AS-2000
```

The date hadn't been converted to YYYY format. Instead, a simple hack had been put in to display years ending in 21 and greater as 1921, 1922, and so on, and years ending in 00 to 20 as 2000, 2001, and so on.

The logic didn't hold up under a few simple sorts. Reports showed the year 2001 as occurring prior to the year 1921. The package cost almost $60,000, and the sales representative was devastated when I pointed out the nature of the internal coding error. I wrote it up in detail so that their technical people could see the problem. Many months of coding will be required to correct the mistake and all the other date problems that presumably exist in the system. By then I will have chosen another package in which the problem has truly been solved, and the sale will have been lost. This is one example of the problem.

In systems that use six-digit YYMMDD formatted dates or five-digit YYDDD Julian Dates, routines already exist to handle standard business calculations such as calculating the day of the week using a five- or six-digit date or adding days to an existing date and coming up with the new date. To move these routines to the larger date format needed to accommodate the year 2000, all of these routines would have to be rewritten to accommodate the four-digit year format. Additionally, the DATE used in ACCEPT statements such as ACCEPT SYSTEM-DATE FROM DATE is a six-digit date, and extracting the system date in an eight-digit format would require complex coding and calling techniques. Fortunately, intrinsic functions make this task much easier.

Other difficult date problems are sitting on systems based on coding practices that have developed. At one time, it was common to use a date of 990909 to indicate some special condition for a date. It was frequently used to mean "forever." An archive file or tape might be given an expiration date of 990909 to indicate that it was a permanent archive, never to be deleted. Of course, in a couple of years, "forever" will actually arrive, and unless the date is fixed, archives could be inadvertently deleted. Other popular "forever" dates are 990101 and 991231.

Solutions for Year 2000 Problems

The year 2000 problem goes far beyond business date routines. Intrinsic functions take care of many of the existing business routines, but they don't address the real core of the problem. Dates that are stored with a two-digit year are time bombs waiting to explode the first time someone tries to enter or process transactions with a date of January 1, 2000 or greater. This problem could easily surface on a large scale in early 1999 when users try to enter future receiving dates for inventory on order.

Incorrect date handling is already a problem in some credit card machines. Cards with an expiration date in the year 2000 or beyond are being refused. Credit card companies that have completed their year 2000 programming are finding their cards are rejected by credit card machines because the machine itself extracts only the last two digits of the year—00, 01, 02, or whatever—and assumes that the card is expired. The machine doesn't even try to connect to the central clearinghouse to clear the transaction.

As we get closer to 2000, the problem will become more and more severe. All data that is stored with a two-digit date must be modified to allow for these upcoming dates—either by modifying the dates in the file and the programs that read the file, or by modifying the way programs interpret the data in the file. Either way, millions of lines of code will need to be modified to handle this situation over the next three years.

There are two basic methods for solving the year 2000 problem:

☐ Change the data in all files to reflect a new date format that includes two extra digits for the year portion of the date. Then change all the programs to read or write this new full date to and from files. Programs that sort or format this new date will also have to be changed.

BD
6

☐ Change the data in all files to reflect a new way of storing dates, but use the same amount of space currently used for dates. Then change all the programs to read, sort, or format this new date. This method breaks down into four main sub-methods:

Fixed-window dating uses the two digits of the year and provides a break or rollover point in the programs. For example, all years stored as 51 to 99 represent 1951 to 1999, and all years stored as 00 to 50 represent 2000 to 2050. Even if your computer processes a maximum of 100 years worth of data, this method will eventually need revision sometime before 2049.

Sliding-window dating is similar to fixed-window dating, but instead of a fixed rollover, the rollover point slides in time. The rollover point is defined as the current system date, and limits are set for the bottom and top of the 100-year limit. As an example, an inventory system might have to deal with dates received on goods as much as five years ago and dates of expected shipment on new goods that are as much as two years in the future. The sliding window could be set so that the system could store 40 years into the past and 60 years into the future. During 1997, years 37 through 99 represent 1937 through 1999, and years 00 through 36 represent 2000 through 2036. When the system date moves to 1999, years 39 through 99 represent 1939 through 1999, and years 00 through 38 represent 2000 through 2038. This assumes that material is retired from the system so that the sliding window doesn't slide up over old dates and that the system doesn't process more than a 100-year range of dates.

Encoding dates involves modifying dates in the files to use a new coding scheme that lets the date be stored as other than just digits. A wide variety of methods has been suggested. Alphabetical characters and hexadecimal digits are two suggestions that show up frequently, but at the moment, no coding scheme stands out as a favorite. This involves modifying all date-handling logic to convert to and from this encoded scheme.

Use the six digits currently used to store year month and day to store the ANSI days date (or the Lilian days date on many IBM systems). Again, all programs must be modified to convert between YYYYMMDD format and ANSI days format when reading from and writing to a file. The six digits of days would allow for about 2,739 years worth of dates, or January 1, 1601 to some date in the year 4339.

Additional Information

The year 2000 situation is rapidly changing, and it is impossible to keep up-to-date on everything. The intent of this chapter isn't to help you sweep into a company to fix all its date problems, but to help you become an employable resource who can be used as part of a date-handling team. For further information on the year 2000 problem, I recommend reading the following:

☐ *The Year 2000 and 2-Digit Dates: A Guide for Planning and Implementation,* published by IBM (914-432-9405).

☐ *Dates and the Year 2000,* published by King Computer Services, Inc. (818-951-5240).

Summary

The year 2000 problem will demand huge programming resources. This will include extremely skilled analysts who can sort out the problem and determine how to approach it, as well as many people who can code and test the solutions that the analyst comes up with. In this lesson, you learned the following:

☐ How to use intrinsic functions to handle date problems

☐ The importance of correcting dates

☐ Some of the methods used to correct dates

☐ What the year 2000 problem is

☐ Some methods in use to handle the year 2000 problem

Q&A

Q Where are Lilian Dates used?

A IBM has adopted Lilian dates in many instances as an alternative to ANSI dates. Some of their machines and systems provide routines that perform the same functions as INTEGER-FROM-DATE and DATE-FROM-INTEGER but use the Lilian date as the base date. The main difference in using Lilian dates is that Lilian Day 1—October 15, 1582—was a Friday, while ANSI Day 1—January 1, 1601—was a Monday. This changes the behavior of any day-of-the-week logic:

Date	Lilian Date	REM (Lilian Date Divided by 7)	Day of the Week
Oct 15, 1582	1	1	Friday
Oct 16, 1582	2	2	Saturday
Oct 17, 1582	3	3	Sunday
Oct 18, 1582	4	4	Monday

continues

BD
6

Date	Lilian Date	REM (Lilian Date Divided by 7)	Day of the Week
Oct 19, 1582	5	5	Tuesday
Oct 20, 1582	6	6	Wednesday
Oct 21, 1582	7	0	Thursday
Oct 22, 1582	1	1	Friday
Oct 23, 1582	2	2	Saturday
Oct 24, 1582	3	3	Sunday
Oct 25, 1582	4	4	Monday
Oct 26, 1582	5	5	Tuesday
Oct 27, 1582	6	6	Wednesday
Oct 28, 1582	7	0	Thursday

Q Is there a fix or simple software solution for year 2000 problems?

A So far there isn't, and it seems very unlikely that there will be. Several expensive software packages on the market analyze the problem by searching through source code for DATE, YMD, YYMMDD, and other similar words. These packages perform a variety of source-code analysis tricks to point you toward the problem, but so far, the work of fixing and testing is a manual task. An automated solution is unlikely.

One example from a school is a file containing a data item:

```
05  THE-SEMESTER              PICTURE 9(3).
```

This is actually a two-digit year and a one-digit month (3, 6, or 9) for the beginning month of the semester, a YYM format. No analysis program would ever pick this up as a date problem, because nothing in the data item THE-SEMESTER or PICTURE 9(3) would cause an automated computer program to think this might be a date.

Q Can ANSI days be used to calculate days and dates prior to January 1, 1601?

A Some systems might allow it, but Microfocus Personal COBOL does not. The ANSI days date format is defined as "days since December 31, 1600," which implies only going forward in time from that date.

Workshop

Quiz

1. How are the Lilian days date format and the ANSI days date format similar?
2. What does the following call to REM return as a value that is stored in RESULT?

```
COMPUTE RESULT = REM(15, 4).
```

3. What are the rules for determining if a year is a leap year?
4. Which of the following are leap years?

    1600
    1700
    1901
    1955
    1996
    2000

Exercise

Develop a program that will let you enter two dates and will then tell you the number-of-days difference between the two.

Hint: If you convert the two dates to ANSI dates using INTEGER-OF-DATE, the two numbers can be subtracted from one another.

BD
6

APPENDIX

A

Answers

Answers to Day 1, "Your First COBOL Program"

Quiz

1. The output of the sample program BYEBYE is the following:

   ```
   Bye bye birdie
   ```

2. The byebye.cbl program contains four divisions: the IDENTIFICATION DIVISION, the ENVIRONMENT DIVISION, the DATA DIVISION, and the PROCEDURE DIVISION.

3. The program contains three paragraphs: PROGRAM-ID in the IDENTIFICATION DIVISION, PROGRAM-BEGIN in the PROCEDURE DIVISION, and PROGRAM-STOP in the PROCEDURE DIVISION.

4. The program contains two sentences: DISPLAY "Bye bye birdie" and STOP RUN. It also is possible to consider BYEBYE (the PROGRAM-ID) a sentence.

5. The bad01.cbl program contains no DATA DIVISION and, therefore, is missing one of the four standard divisions. ANSI-85 COBOL allows the ENVIRONMENT DIVISION and the DATA DIVISION to be omitted if there is nothing to put in them. Do not get into a habit of leaving these out, as your code might have to run on a version of COBOL that does not allow this option.

6. The bad02.cbl program contains a sentence, DISPLAY "I'm bad!", that begins in Area A.

7. The bad03.cbl program contains a comment, but there is no asterisk in column 7. The compiler will attempt to compile the comment "This program displays a message." and will fail because it is not in COBOL syntax.

Exercises

1. One method of solving the problem is shown in Listing A.1, iam.cbl.

TYPE **Listing A.1. Another simple display.**

```
000100 IDENTIFICATION DIVISION.
000200 PROGRAM-ID. IAM.
000300 ENVIRONMENT DIVISION.
000400 DATA DIVISION.
000500 PROCEDURE DIVISION.
000600
000700 PROGRAM-BEGIN.
000800     DISPLAY "I am a COBOL programmer".
000900 PROGRAM-DONE.
001000     STOP RUN.
```

2. Make a note of the errors.

3. Add a DATA DIVISION under the ENVIRONMENT DIVISION:

```
000100 IDENTIFICATION DIVISION.
000200 PROGRAM-ID. BAD01FIX.
000300 ENVIRONMENT DIVISION.
000400 DATA DIVISION.
000500 PROCEDURE DIVISION.
000600
000700 PROGRAM-BEGIN.
000800     DISPLAY "I'm bad!".
000900 PROGRAM-DONE.
001000     STOP RUN.
```

4. Move the DISPLAY statement to the right so that it begins in column 12 or higher:

```
000100 IDENTIFICATION DIVISION.
000200 PROGRAM-ID. BAD01FIX.
000300 ENVIRONMENT DIVISION.
000400 DATA DIVISION.
```

```
000500 PROCEDURE DIVISION.
000600
000700 PROGRAM-BEGIN.
000800     DISPLAY "I'm bad!".
000900 PROGRAM-DONE.
001000     STOP RUN.
```

5. Place an asterisk in column 7 of a line containing a comment:

```
000100 IDENTIFICATION DIVISION.
000200 PROGRAM-ID. BAD03FIX.
000300 ENVIRONMENT DIVISION.
000400 DATA DIVISION.
000500 PROCEDURE DIVISION.
000600*    This program displays a message.
000700 PROGRAM-BEGIN.
000800     DISPLAY "I'm really bad!".
000900 PROGRAM-DONE.
001100     STOP RUN.
```

Answers to Day 2, "Using Variables and Constants"

Quiz

1. 30 bytes.

2. Alphanumeric data.

3. The remaining character positions are filled with spaces by the MOVE verb.

4. The largest value is 9,999.

5. The smallest value is 0, which would be stored as 0000.

6. The four places are filled with 0012.

Exercises

1. Adding a one-line DISPLAY informs the user of what's happening (as shown in Listing A.2).

TYPE | **Listing A.2. Keeping the user informed.**

```
000100 IDENTIFICATION DIVISION.
000200 PROGRAM-ID. ADD03.
000300 ENVIRONMENT DIVISION.
000400 DATA DIVISION.
000500
000600 WORKING-STORAGE SECTION.
000700
000800 01  FIRST-NUMBER      PICTURE IS 99.
```

continues

Listing A.2. continued

```
000900 01  SECOND-NUMBER      PICTURE IS 99.
001000 01  THE-RESULT         PICTURE IS 999.
001100
001200 PROCEDURE DIVISION.
001300
001400 PROGRAM-BEGIN.
001500     DISPLAY "This program will add 2 numbers.".
001600     DISPLAY "Enter the first number.".
001700
001800     ACCEPT FIRST-NUMBER.
001900
002000     DISPLAY "Enter the second number.".
002100
002200     ACCEPT SECOND-NUMBER.
002300
002400     COMPUTE THE-RESULT = FIRST-NUMBER + SECOND-NUMBER.
002500
002600     DISPLAY "The result is " THE-RESULT.
002700
002800
002900 PROGRAM-DONE.
003000     STOP RUN.
003100
```

The following is sample output for Listing A.2:

OUTPUT

```
C>pcobrun add03

This program will add 2 numbers.
Enter the first number.
16
Enter the second number.
44
The result is 060

C>
```

2. For my selection of a verse, I have chosen the sad tale of the Lady of Eiger, which is recounted with numbered lines in Listing A.3. Of course, your program will contain a verse of your own choosing.

TYPE ## Listing A.3. Numbering a longer phrase.

```
000100 IDENTIFICATION DIVISION.
000200 PROGRAM-ID. EIGER01.
000300 ENVIRONMENT DIVISION.
000400 DATA DIVISION.
000500
000600 WORKING-STORAGE SECTION.
000700
000800 01  THE-MESSAGE      PIC X(50).
```

```
000900 01  THE-NUMBER        PIC 9(2).
001000 01  A-SPACE           PIC X.
001100
001200 PROCEDURE DIVISION.
001300 PROGRAM-BEGIN.
001400
001500* Initialize the space variable
001600      MOVE " " TO A-SPACE.
001700
001800* Set up and display line 1
001900      MOVE 1 TO THE-NUMBER.
002000      MOVE "There once was a lady from Eiger,"
002100          TO THE-MESSAGE.
002200      DISPLAY
002300          THE-NUMBER
002400          A-SPACE
002500          THE-MESSAGE.
002600
002700* Set up and Display line 2
002800      ADD 1 TO THE-NUMBER.
002900      MOVE "Who smiled and rode forth on a tiger."
003000          TO THE-MESSAGE.
003100      DISPLAY
003200          THE-NUMBER
003300          A-SPACE
003400          THE-MESSAGE.
003500
003600* Set up and display line 3
003700      ADD 1 TO THE-NUMBER.
003800      MOVE "They returned from the ride" TO THE-MESSAGE.
003900      DISPLAY
004000          THE-NUMBER
004100          A-SPACE
004200          THE-MESSAGE.
004300
004400* Set up and display line 4
004500      ADD 1 TO THE-NUMBER.
004600      MOVE "With the lady inside," TO THE-MESSAGE.
004700      DISPLAY
004800          THE-NUMBER
004900          A-SPACE
005000          THE-MESSAGE.
005100
005200* Set up and display line 5
005300      ADD 1 TO THE-NUMBER.
005400      MOVE "And the smile on the face of the tiger."
005500          TO THE-MESSAGE.
005600      DISPLAY
005700          THE-NUMBER
005800          A-SPACE
005900          THE-MESSAGE.
006000
006100
006200 PROGRAM-DONE.
006300      STOP RUN.
006400
```

The following is sample output for Listing A.3:

```
01 There once was a lady from Eiger,
02 Who smiled and rode forth on a tiger.
03 They returned from the ride
04 With the lady inside,
05 And the smile on the face of the tiger.


C>
C>
```

3. Listing A.4 reprises the sad tale with line numbers in increments of 5.

Listing A.4. Incrementing by 5.

```
000100 IDENTIFICATION DIVISION.
000200 PROGRAM-ID. EIGER02.
000300 ENVIRONMENT DIVISION.
000400 DATA DIVISION.
000500
000600 WORKING-STORAGE SECTION.
000700
000800 01  THE-MESSAGE       PIC X(50).
000900 01  THE-NUMBER        PIC 9(2).
001000 01  A-SPACE           PIC X.
001100
001200 PROCEDURE DIVISION.
001300 PROGRAM-BEGIN.
001400
001500* Initialize the space variable
001600     MOVE " " TO A-SPACE.
001700
001800* Set up and display line 1
001900     MOVE 5 TO THE-NUMBER.
002000     MOVE "There once was a lady from Eiger,"
002100          TO THE-MESSAGE.
002200     DISPLAY
002300          THE-NUMBER
002400          A-SPACE
002500          THE-MESSAGE.
002600
002700* Set up and Display line 2
002800     ADD 5 TO THE-NUMBER.
002900     MOVE "Who smiled and rode forth on a tiger."
003000          TO THE-MESSAGE.
003100     DISPLAY
003200          THE-NUMBER
003300          A-SPACE
003400          THE-MESSAGE.
003500
003600* Set up and display line 3
003700     ADD 5 TO THE-NUMBER.
003800     MOVE "They returned from the ride" TO THE-MESSAGE.
003900     DISPLAY
```

```
004000          THE-NUMBER
004100          A-SPACE
004200          THE-MESSAGE.
004300
004400* Set up and display line 4
004500     ADD 5 TO THE-NUMBER.
004600     MOVE "With the lady inside," TO THE-MESSAGE.
004700     DISPLAY
004800          THE-NUMBER
004900          A-SPACE
005000          THE-MESSAGE.
005100
005200* Set up and display line 5
005300     ADD 5 TO THE-NUMBER.
005400     MOVE "And the smile on the face of the tiger."
005500          TO THE-MESSAGE.
005600     DISPLAY
005700          THE-NUMBER
005800          A-SPACE
005900          THE-MESSAGE.
006000
006100
006200 PROGRAM-DONE.
006300     STOP RUN.
006400
```

The following is sample output for Listing A.4:

```
05 There once was a lady from Eiger,
10 Who smiled and rode forth on a tiger.
15 They returned from the ride
20 With the lady inside,
25 And the smile on the face of the tiger.


C>
C>
```

Answers to Day 3, "A First Look at Structured COBOL"

Quiz

1. c. LOCATE-OVERDUE-CUSTOMERS best describes the function of the paragraph.

2. There are two ways to number the program. In the first example, the paragraph names as well as the sentences being executed are numbered:

```
000100 IDENTIFICATION DIVISION.
000200 PROGRAM-ID. MSG01.
000300
000400 ENVIRONMENT DIVISION.
```

```
000500 DATA DIVISION.
000600
000700 WORKING-STORAGE SECTION.
000800
000900 PROCEDURE DIVISION.
001000
001100 PROGRAM-BEGIN. ————————————————————————————— 1
001200
001300     PERFORM MAIN-LOGIC. ——————————————————— 2
001400
001500 PROGRAM-DONE. —————————————————————————————10
001600     STOP RUN. —————————————————————————————11
001700
001800 MAIN-LOGIC. ——————————————————————————————— 3
001900     PERFORM DISPLAY-MSG-1. ————————————————— 4
002000     PERFORM DISPLAY-MSG-2. ————————————————— 7
002100
002200 DISPLAY-MSG-1. ———————————————————————————— 5
002300     DISPLAY "This is message 1.". ——————————— 6
002400
002500 DISPLAY-MSG-2. ———————————————————————————— 8
002600     DISPLAY "This is message 2.". ——————————— 9
002700
```

In this example, only the sentences are numbered:

```
000100 IDENTIFICATION DIVISION.
000200 PROGRAM-ID. MSG01.
000300
000400 ENVIRONMENT DIVISION.
000500 DATA DIVISION.
000600
000700 WORKING-STORAGE SECTION.
000800
000900 PROCEDURE DIVISION.
001000
001100 PROGRAM-BEGIN.
001200
001300     PERFORM MAIN-LOGIC. ——————————————————— 1
001400
001500 PROGRAM-DONE.
001600     STOP RUN. ————————————————————————————— 6
001700
001800 MAIN-LOGIC.
001900     PERFORM DISPLAY-MSG-1. ————————————————— 2
002000     PERFORM DISPLAY-MSG-2. ————————————————— 4
002100
002200 DISPLAY-MSG-1.
002300     DISPLAY "This is message 1.". ——————————— 3
002400
002500 DISPLAY-MSG-2.
002600     DISPLAY "This is message 2.". ——————————— 5
002700
```

Exercises

1. In Listing A.5, PROGRAM-DONE and STOP RUN have been removed.

 Listing A.5. Missing a STOP RUN.

```
000100 IDENTIFICATION DIVISION.
000200 PROGRAM-ID. HELLO06.
000300
000400* This program illustrates the use of a PERFORM
000500
000600 ENVIRONMENT DIVISION.
000700 DATA DIVISION.
000800 PROCEDURE DIVISION.
000900
001000 PROGRAM-BEGIN.
001100     DISPLAY "Today's message is:".
001200     PERFORM SAY-HELLO.
001300
001400 SAY-HELLO.
001500     DISPLAY "Hello world".
001600
```

The following output from hello06.cbl is similar to the output of hello05.cbl in Day 3:

OUTPUT
```
Today's message is:
Hello world
Hello world


C>
C>
```

You must have a STOP RUN in your program that appears before any paragraphs that are PERFORMed.

2. The flow of hello06.cbl is the following:

Line 001000. Internally note that the PROGRAM-BEGIN paragraph has started.

Line 001100. Display "Today's message is:" on-screen.

Line 001200. Jump to line 001400, the beginning of SAY-HELLO.

Line 001400. Internally note that the SAY-HELLO paragraph has started.

Line 001500. Display "Hello world" on-screen.

End of file. Recognize that the SAY-HELLO paragraph has ended. Because this is in the middle of a PERFORM requested on line 001200, return to the end of line 001200, where no further actions are requested.

Line 001200. No other actions on this line.

Line 001400. Internally note that the SAY-HELLO paragraph has started.

Line 001500. Display "Hello world" on-screen.

End of file. Recognize that the SAY-HELLO paragraph has ended. There is no active PERFORM requested, so the program ends here. The end of the program might cause an error in your version of COBOL after this display.

3. Insert a STOP RUN at line 001300 to prevent this problem.

4. Listing A.6, add08.cbl, adds three numbers together and displays the result.

TYPE **Listing A.6. Adding three numbers.**

```
000100 IDENTIFICATION DIVISION.
000200 PROGRAM-ID. ADD08.
000300 ENVIRONMENT DIVISION.
000400 DATA DIVISION.
000500
000600 WORKING-STORAGE SECTION.
000700
000800 01   FIRST-NUMBER       PICTURE IS 99.
000900 01   SECOND-NUMBER      PICTURE IS 99.
001000 01   THIRD-NUMBER       PICTURE IS 99.
001100 01   THE-RESULT         PICTURE IS 999.
001200
001300 PROCEDURE DIVISION.
001400
001500 PROGRAM-BEGIN.
001600
001700     PERFORM ADVISE-THE-USER.
001800     PERFORM GET-FIRST-NUMBER.
001900     PERFORM GET-SECOND-NUMBER.
002000     PERFORM GET-THIRD-NUMBER.
002100     PERFORM COMPUTE-AND-DISPLAY.
002200
002300 PROGRAM-DONE.
002400     STOP RUN.
002500
002600 ADVISE-THE-USER.
002700     DISPLAY "This program will add 3 numbers.".
002800
002900 GET-FIRST-NUMBER.
003000
003100     DISPLAY "Enter the first number.".
003200     ACCEPT FIRST-NUMBER.
003300
003400 GET-SECOND-NUMBER.
003500
003600     DISPLAY "Enter the second number.".
003700     ACCEPT SECOND-NUMBER.
003800
003900 GET-THIRD-NUMBER.
004000
004100     DISPLAY "Enter the third number.".
```

```
004200     ACCEPT THIRD-NUMBER.
004300
004400 COMPUTE-AND-DISPLAY.
004500
004600     COMPUTE THE-RESULT = FIRST-NUMBER +
004700                          SECOND-NUMBER +
004800                          THIRD-NUMBER.
004900     DISPLAY "The result is " THE-RESULT.
005000
```

The following is sample output for Listing A.6:

OUTPUT

```
This program will add 3 numbers.
Enter the first number.
12
Enter the second number.
64
Enter the third number.
99
The result is 175


C>
C>
```

5. Listing A.7, `add09.cbl`, provides a sample method of breaking `add02.cbl` into performed paragraphs.

TYPE **Listing A.7. Adding two numbers using PERFORM.**

```
000100 IDENTIFICATION DIVISION.
000200 PROGRAM-ID. ADD09.
000300 ENVIRONMENT DIVISION.
000400 DATA DIVISION.
000500
000600 WORKING-STORAGE SECTION.
000700
000800 01  FIRST-NUMBER      PICTURE IS 99.
000900 01  SECOND-NUMBER     PICTURE IS 99.
001000 01  THE-RESULT        PICTURE IS 999.
001100
001200 PROCEDURE DIVISION.
001300
001400 PROGRAM-BEGIN.
001500
001600     PERFORM ENTER-THE-FIRST-NUMBER.
001700     PERFORM ENTER-THE-SECOND-NUMBER.
001800     PERFORM COMPUTE-AND-DISPLAY.
001900
002000 PROGRAM-DONE.
002100     STOP RUN.
002200
```

continues

Listing A.7. continued

```
002300 ENTER-THE-FIRST-NUMBER.
002400
002500     DISPLAY "Enter the first number.".
002600
002700     ACCEPT FIRST-NUMBER.
002800
002900 ENTER-THE-SECOND-NUMBER.
003000
003100     DISPLAY "Enter the second number.".
003200
003300     ACCEPT SECOND-NUMBER.
003400
003500 COMPUTE-AND-DISPLAY.
003600
003700     COMPUTE THE-RESULT = FIRST-NUMBER + SECOND-NUMBER.
003800
003900     DISPLAY "The result is " THE-RESULT.
004000
```

Answers to Day 4, "Decision Making"

Quiz

1. Lines 005500 and 005600.

2. Line 005800.

3. Lines 005500 and 005600.

4. Line 005800.

Exercises

1. Listing A.8 shows one method of providing for three possible answers.

TYPE **Listing A.8. Allowing for three valid answers.**

```
000100 IDENTIFICATION DIVISION.
000200 PROGRAM-ID. MAYBE01.
000300*-----------------------------------------------------
000400* This program asks for a Y or N answer, and then
000500* displays whether the user chose yes or no.
000600* The edit logic allows for entry of Y, y, N, or n.
000700*-----------------------------------------------------
000800 ENVIRONMENT DIVISION.
000900 DATA DIVISION.
001000 WORKING-STORAGE SECTION.
001100
001200 01  YES-OR-NO      PIC X.
001300
```

```
001400 PROCEDURE DIVISION.
001500 PROGRAM-BEGIN.
001600
001700     PERFORM GET-THE-ANSWER.
001800
001900     PERFORM EDIT-THE-ANSWER.
002000
002100     PERFORM DISPLAY-THE-ANSWER.
002200
002300 PROGRAM-DONE.
002400     STOP RUN.
002500
002600 GET-THE-ANSWER.
002700
002800     DISPLAY "Is the answer Yes, No or Maybe? (Y/N/M)".
002900     ACCEPT YES-OR-NO.
003000
003100 EDIT-THE-ANSWER.
003200
003300     IF YES-OR-NO = "y"
003400         MOVE "Y" TO YES-OR-NO.
003500
003600     IF YES-OR-NO = "n"
003700         MOVE "N" TO YES-OR-NO.
003800
003900     IF YES-OR-NO = "m"
004000         MOVE "M" TO YES-OR-NO.
004100
004200 DISPLAY-THE-ANSWER.
004300     IF YES-OR-NO = "Y"
004400         DISPLAY "You answered Yes.".
004500
004600     IF YES-OR-NO = "N"
004700         DISPLAY "You answered No.".
004800
004900     IF YES-OR-NO = "M"
005000         DISPLAY "You answered Maybe.".
```

2. Listing A.9 shows one way of adding Maybe as an option. You can test three conditions as well as two, as in this example.

TYPE   **Listing A.9. Using OR to test three conditions.**

```
000100 IDENTIFICATION DIVISION.
000200 PROGRAM-ID. MAYBE02.
000300*------------------------------------------------
000400* This program asks for a Y, N, or M answer, and
000500* displays the user's choice.
000600* The edit allows for Y, y, N, n, M, or m.
000700*------------------------------------------------
000800 ENVIRONMENT DIVISION.
000900 DATA DIVISION.
001000 WORKING-STORAGE SECTION.
```

A

continues

Listing A.9. continued

```
001100
001200 01  YES-OR-NO        PIC X.
001300
001400 PROCEDURE DIVISION.
001500 PROGRAM-BEGIN.
001600
001700     PERFORM GET-THE-ANSWER.
001800
001900     PERFORM EDIT-THE-ANSWER.
002000
002100     PERFORM DISPLAY-THE-ANSWER.
002200
002300 PROGRAM-DONE.
002400     STOP RUN.
002500
002600 GET-THE-ANSWER.
002700
002800     DISPLAY "Is the answer Yes, No or Maybe? (Y/N/M)".
002900     ACCEPT YES-OR-NO.
003000
003100 EDIT-THE-ANSWER.
003200
003300     IF YES-OR-NO = "y"
003400         MOVE "Y" TO YES-OR-NO.
003500
003600     IF YES-OR-NO = "n"
003700         MOVE "N" TO YES-OR-NO.
003800
003900     IF YES-OR-NO = "m"
004000         MOVE "M" TO YES-OR-NO.
004100
004200 DISPLAY-THE-ANSWER.
004300
004400     IF YES-OR-NO = "Y" OR
004500         YES-OR-NO = "N" OR
004600         YES-OR-NO = "M"
004700         PERFORM DISPLAY-YES-NO-OR-MAYBE
004800     ELSE
004900         DISPLAY "Your answer was invalid.".
005000
005100 DISPLAY-YES-NO-OR-MAYBE.
005200     IF YES-OR-NO = "Y"
005300         DISPLAY "You answered Yes.".
005400
005500     IF YES-OR-NO = "N"
005600         DISPLAY "You answered No.".
005700
005800     IF YES-OR-NO = "M"
005900         DISPLAY "You answered Maybe.".
006000
```

Answers to Day 5, "Using PERFORM, GO TO, and IF to Control Programs"

Quiz

1. Assuming that the program contains the correct structure, with a STOP RUN located in the correct place in the code, 10 times.

2. 5 times.

3. In the listing for question 1, the loop control is at line 003600 and the processing loop is at lines 003800 through 003900:

```
003600      PERFORM DISPLAY-HELLO 10 TIMES.
003700
003800 DISPLAY-HELLO.
003900      DISPLAY "hello".
004000
```

In the listing for question 2, the loop control is at lines 003600 through 003800. The processing loop is at lines 004000 through 004100:

```
003600      PERFORM DISPLAY-HELLO
003700          VARYING THE-COUNT FROM 1 BY 1
003800          UNTIL THE-COUNT > 5.
003900
004000 DISPLAY-HELLO.
004100      DISPLAY "hello".
004200
```

Exercise

There are several ways to do this. The following are four possible examples.

The following uses the TIMES option of the PERFORM verb.

```
003900      PERFORM A-PARAGRAPH 8 TIMES.
```

The following example uses THE-COUNT as a variable that is controlled by a VARYING option of the PERFORM verb.

```
003900      PERFORM A-PARAGRAPH
004000          VARYING THE-COUNT FROM 1 BY 1
004100              UNTIL THE-COUNT > 8.
```

The following example uses THE-COUNT as a variable that is tested with the UNTIL option of the PERFORM verb. The value of the variable is changed in the paragraph that is being PERFORMed.

```
003800      MOVE 1 TO THE-COUNT.
003900      PERFORM A-PARAGRAPH
004000              UNTIL THE-COUNT > 8.
......
......
```

A

```
005600 A-PARAGRAPH.
005700* Some processing code goes here
......
......
006500       ADD 1 TO THE-COUNT.
```

This example uses a GO TO and will be frowned on by some:

```
003800       MOVE 1 TO THE-COUNT.
003900       PERFORM A-PARAGRAPH.
......
......
005600 A-PARAGRAPH.
005700* Some processing code goes here
......
......
006500       ADD 1 TO THE-COUNT.
006600       IF THE-COUNT NOT > 8
006700           GO TO A-PARAGRAPH.
006800
```

Answers to Day 6, "Using Data and COBOL Operators"

Quiz

1. 04976.

2. 76.

3. The integer portion of the value, 1000, is too large to fit in a PIC 999, so the 1 is truncated, resulting in a value of 000. The decimal portion .001 is truncated on the right when it is moved to the V99 portion of the picture. The overall result is that the far left 1 and the far right 1 are both truncated in the move, leaving a 000.00 in the variable.

Exercises

1. Note any errors or warnings and look them up.

2. Note the errors and look them up.

Answers to Day 7, "Basics of Design"

Quiz

1. The step to be performed to continue the design is to break the job description into smaller tasks.

2. The first six steps of design are as follows:

1. Create a job description for the program.

2. Break the job description into tasks until the tasks approximate what the computer will do.

3. Identify the processing loops.

4. Identify the main processing loop if it has not become apparent during step 3.

5. Write the program in pseudocode.

6. Convert the pseudocode into actual code.

Exercises

1. The design steps for a sales tax calculator are as follows:

a. Job: Ask the user for sales amounts and sales tax rates, and use these values to calculate the sales tax on the amount.

b. Tasks: Ask the user for a sales amount, ask the user for a sales tax percentage, and calculate the sales tax (over and over).

c. Processing loops: There is only one processing loop in the task list, *calculate the sales tax (over and over)*.

d. Main loop: The main loop is the loop for calculating the sales tax.

e. Pseudocode:

```
THE-PROGRAM
    MOVE "Y" TO YES-NO.
    PERFORM CALCULATE-SALES-TAX
        UNTIL YES-NO = "N".

CALCULATE-SALES-TAX.
    PERFORM GET-SALES-AMOUNT.
    PERFORM GET-TAX-PERCENT.
    PERFORM CALCULATE-TAX-AMOUNT.
    PERFORM DISPLAY-TAX-AMOUNT.
    PERFORM GO-AGAIN.

GET-SALES-AMOUNT.
    (between 0.01 and 9999.99)

GET-TAX-PERCENT.
    (between 0.1% and 20.0%)

CALCULATE-TAX-AMOUNT.
    COMPUTE SALES-TAX ROUNDED =
        SALES-AMOUNT * TAX-AS-DECIMAL.
```

A

```
DISPLAY-TAX-AMOUNT.
    (sales tax = SALES-TAX)

GO-AGAIN.
    (yes or no)
```

f. Code. Listing A.10 is an example of the code that could result from this design. Remember to adjust the ACCEPT WITH CONVERSION statements at lines 004700 and 005800. Listing A.10 is coded for versions of COBOL that require ACCEPT WITH CONVERSION. If you are using Micro Focus Personal COBOL, just use ACCEPT.

TYPE   **Listing A.10. A sales tax calculator.**

```
000100 IDENTIFICATION DIVISION.
000200 PROGRAM-ID. SLSTAX01.
000300*-----------------------------------------------
000400* Calculates sales tax based on entered sales
000500* amounts and tax rates.
000600*-----------------------------------------------
000700 ENVIRONMENT DIVISION.
000800 DATA DIVISION.
000900 WORKING-STORAGE SECTION.
001000
001100 01  YES-NO          PIC X.
001200 01  ENTRY-OK        PIC X.
001300 01  TAX-PERCENT     PIC 99V99.
001400 01  TAX-AS-DECIMAL  PIC V9999.
001500
001600 01  SALES-AMOUNT    PIC 9(4)V99.
001700 01  SALES-TAX       PIC 9(4)V99.
001800
001900 01  ENTRY-FIELD     PIC Z(4).ZZ.
002000 01  DISPLAY-SALES-TAX PIC Z,ZZ9.99.
002100
002200
002300 PROCEDURE DIVISION.
002400 PROGRAM-BEGIN.
002500
002600     MOVE "Y" TO YES-NO.
002700     PERFORM CALCULATE-SALES-TAX
002800        UNTIL YES-NO = "N".
002900
003000 PROGRAM-DONE.
003100     STOP RUN.
003200
003300 CALCULATE-SALES-TAX.
003400     PERFORM GET-SALES-AMOUNT.
003500     PERFORM GET-TAX-PERCENT.
003600     PERFORM CALCULATE-TAX-AMOUNT.
003700     PERFORM DISPLAY-TAX-AMOUNT.
003800     PERFORM GO-AGAIN.
003900
004000 GET-SALES-AMOUNT.
```

```
004100       MOVE "N" TO ENTRY-OK.
004200       PERFORM ENTER-SALES-AMOUNT
004300           UNTIL ENTRY-OK = "Y".
004400
004500 ENTER-SALES-AMOUNT.
004600       DISPLAY "SALES AMOUNT (0.01 TO 9999.99)?".
004700       ACCEPT ENTRY-FIELD WITH CONVERSION.
004800       MOVE ENTRY-FIELD TO SALES-AMOUNT.
004900       IF SALES-AMOUNT < .01 OR
005000           SALES-AMOUNT > 9999.99
005100             DISPLAY "INVALID ENTRY"
005200       ELSE
005300           MOVE "Y" TO ENTRY-OK.
005400
005500 GET-TAX-PERCENT.
005600       DISPLAY "SALES TAX PERCENT (.01% TO 20.00%)?".
005700       ACCEPT ENTRY-FIELD WITH CONVERSION.
005800       MOVE ENTRY-FIELD TO TAX-PERCENT.
005900       IF TAX-PERCENT < .01 OR
006000           TAX-PERCENT > 20.0
006100             DISPLAY "INVALID ENTRY"
006200       ELSE
006300           MOVE "Y" TO ENTRY-OK
006400           COMPUTE TAX-AS-DECIMAL = TAX-PERCENT / 100.
006500
006600 CALCULATE-TAX-AMOUNT.
006700       COMPUTE SALES-TAX ROUNDED =
006800           SALES-AMOUNT * TAX-AS-DECIMAL.
006900
007000 DISPLAY-TAX-AMOUNT.
007100       MOVE SALES-TAX TO DISPLAY-SALES-TAX.
007200       DISPLAY "SALES TAX = " DISPLAY-SALES-TAX.
007300
007400 GO-AGAIN.
007500       DISPLAY "GO AGAIN?".
007600       ACCEPT YES-NO.
007700       IF YES-NO = "y"
007800           MOVE "Y" TO YES-NO.
007900       IF YES-NO NOT = "Y"
008000           MOVE "N" TO YES-NO.
008100
```

The sample output for slstax01.cbl is as follows:

OUTPUT

```
SALES AMOUNT (0.01 TO 9999.99)?
22.95
SALES TAX PERCENT (.01% TO 20.00%)?
8.25
SALES TAX =      1.89
GO AGAIN?
y
SALES AMOUNT (0.01 TO 9999.99)?
432.17
SALES TAX PERCENT (.01% TO 20.00%)?
6.5
SALES TAX =     28.09
GO AGAIN?
```

2. Get the program working correctly before proceeding to the next exercise. Refer to the previous example for tips on how to do this.

3. Listing A.11 is an example of one way to change the program to ask for the sales tax rate only once. Study the difference between slstax01.cbl and slstax02.cbl—in particular, the fact that the sales tax percentage is asked for outside of the main loop. Remember the rule for a processing loop: You set up any values needed for the first entry into the loop. This applies even if setting up the initial value requires a DISPLAY and ACCEPT statement or even more complicated logic. Remember to change the ACCEPT WITH CONVERSION statements to ACCEPT statements as necessary.

TYPE **Listing A.11. Asking for the tax rate once.**

```
000100 IDENTIFICATION DIVISION.
000200 PROGRAM-ID. SLSTAX02.
000300*-------------------------------------------------
000400* Accepts tax rate from the user and then
000500* calculates sales tax over and over based on
000600* entered sales amounts.
000700*-------------------------------------------------
000800 ENVIRONMENT DIVISION.
000900 DATA DIVISION.
001000 WORKING-STORAGE SECTION.
001100
001200 01   YES-NO          PIC X.
001300 01   ENTRY-OK        PIC X.
001400 01   TAX-PERCENT     PIC 99V99.
001500 01   TAX-AS-DECIMAL  PIC V9999.
001600
001700 01   SALES-AMOUNT    PIC 9(4)V99.
001800 01   SALES-TAX       PIC 9(4)V99.
001900
002000 01   ENTRY-FIELD       PIC Z(4).ZZ.
002100 01   DISPLAY-SALES-TAX PIC Z,ZZ9.99.
002200
002300 PROCEDURE DIVISION.
002400 PROGRAM-BEGIN.
002500
002600     PERFORM GET-TAX-PERCENT.
002700     MOVE "Y" TO YES-NO.
002800     PERFORM CALCULATE-SALES-TAX
002900         UNTIL YES-NO = "N".
003000
003100 PROGRAM-DONE.
003200     STOP RUN.
003300
003400 CALCULATE-SALES-TAX.
003500     PERFORM GET-SALES-AMOUNT.
003600     PERFORM CALCULATE-TAX-AMOUNT.
003700     PERFORM DISPLAY-TAX-AMOUNT.
003800     PERFORM GO-AGAIN.
003900
```

```
004000 GET-SALES-AMOUNT.
004100     MOVE "N" TO ENTRY-OK.
004200     PERFORM ENTER-SALES-AMOUNT
004300         UNTIL ENTRY-OK = "Y".
004400
004500 ENTER-SALES-AMOUNT.
004600     DISPLAY "SALES AMOUNT (0.01 TO 9999.99)?".
004700     ACCEPT ENTRY-FIELD WITH CONVERSION.
004800     MOVE ENTRY-FIELD TO SALES-AMOUNT.
004900     IF SALES-AMOUNT < .01 OR
005000         SALES-AMOUNT > 9999.99
005100         DISPLAY "INVALID ENTRY"
005200     ELSE
005300         MOVE "Y" TO ENTRY-OK.
005400
005500 GET-TAX-PERCENT.
005600     DISPLAY "SALES TAX PERCENT (.01% TO 20.00%)?".
005700     ACCEPT ENTRY-FIELD WITH CONVERSION.
005800     MOVE ENTRY-FIELD TO TAX-PERCENT.
005900     IF TAX-PERCENT < .01 OR
006000         TAX-PERCENT > 20.0
006100         DISPLAY "INVALID ENTRY"
006200     ELSE
006300         MOVE "Y" TO ENTRY-OK
006400         COMPUTE TAX-AS-DECIMAL = TAX-PERCENT / 100.
006500
006600 CALCULATE-TAX-AMOUNT.
006700     COMPUTE SALES-TAX ROUNDED =
006800         SALES-AMOUNT * TAX-AS-DECIMAL.
006900
007000 DISPLAY-TAX-AMOUNT.
007100     MOVE SALES-TAX TO DISPLAY-SALES-TAX.
007200     DISPLAY "SALES TAX = " DISPLAY-SALES-TAX.
007300
007400 GO-AGAIN.
007500     DISPLAY "GO AGAIN?".
007600     ACCEPT YES-NO.
007700     IF YES-NO = "y"
007800         MOVE "Y" TO YES-NO.
007900     IF YES-NO NOT = "Y"
008000         MOVE "N" TO YES-NO.
008100
```

Here is the output:

OUTPUT

```
SALES TAX PERCENT (.01% TO 20.00%)?
8.75
SALES AMOUNT (0.01 TO 9999.99)?
312.95
SALES TAX =     27.38
GO AGAIN?
y
SALES AMOUNT (0.01 TO 9999.99)?
419.15
SALES TAX =     36.68
GO AGAIN?
```

Answers to Day 8, "Structured Data"

Quiz

1. THE-WHOLE-MESSAGE is 53 bytes long.

2. The implied PICTURE for THE-WHOLE-MESSAGE is PIC X(53).

3. A data structure is a method of combining several variables into one larger variable, frequently for display purposes.

4. The values are destroyed and replaced by whatever was moved into the structure.

5. ```
004600   IF ANSWER-IS-YES
```

6. ```
004600    IF ANSWER-IS-VALID
```

7. ```
001800 01 YES-NO   PIC X.
001900   88 ANSWER-IS-VALID   VALUES "Y", "y", "N", "n".

004600   IF ANSWER-IS-VALID
004700   PERFORM DO-SOMETHING.
```

## Exercises

1. Listing A.12 is one possible way of setting up a structure to display the results.

### Listing A.12. Displaying multiplication tables with a structure.

**TYPE**

```
000100 IDENTIFICATION DIVISION.
000200 PROGRAM-ID. MULT09.
000300*---
000400* This program asks the user for a number for a
000500* multiplication table, and a table size
000600* and then displays a table for that number
000700* times the values 1 through HOW-MANY.
000800*
000900* The display is paused after each 15 lines.
001000*---
001100 ENVIRONMENT DIVISION.
001200 DATA DIVISION.
001300 WORKING-STORAGE SECTION.
001400
001500 01 THE-TABLE   PIC 99.
001600 01 THE-ENTRY   PIC 999.
001700 01 THE-PRODUCT   PIC 9999.
001800 01 HOW-MANY-ENTRIES   PIC 99.
001900 01 SCREEN-LINES   PIC 99.
002000
002100 01 A-DUMMY   PIC X.
002200
```
```

```
002300 01  YES-NO                PIC X VALUE "Y".
002400
002500 01 THE-TABLE-LINE.
002600     05  DISPLAY-THE-TABLE   PIC ZZ9.
002700     05  FILLER              PIC XXX VALUE " * ".
002800     05  DISPLAY-THE-ENTRY   PIC ZZ9.
002900     05  FILLER              PIC XXX VALUE " = ".
003000     05  DISPLAY-THE-PRODUCT PIC ZZZ9.
003100
003200
003300 PROCEDURE DIVISION.
003400
003500 PROGRAM-BEGIN.
003600     MOVE "Y" TO YES-NO.
003700     PERFORM DISPLAY-ONE-TABLE
003800         UNTIL YES-NO = "N".
003900
004000 PROGRAM-DONE.
004100     STOP RUN.
004200
004300 DISPLAY-ONE-TABLE.
004400     PERFORM GET-WHICH-TABLE.
004500     PERFORM DISPLAY-TABLE.
004600     PERFORM GO-AGAIN.
004700
004800 GET-WHICH-TABLE.
004900     DISPLAY
005000      "Which multiplication table(01-99)?".
005100     ACCEPT THE-TABLE.
005200
005300 DISPLAY-TABLE.
005400     PERFORM GET-HOW-MANY-ENTRIES.
005500
005600     MOVE 0 TO SCREEN-LINES.
005700
005800     PERFORM DISPLAY-ONE-ENTRY
005900         VARYING THE-ENTRY
006000           FROM 1 BY 1
006100           UNTIL THE-ENTRY > HOW-MANY-ENTRIES.
006200
006300 GO-AGAIN.
006400     DISPLAY "Go Again (Y/N)?".
006500     ACCEPT YES-NO.
006600     IF YES-NO = "y"
006700         MOVE "Y" TO YES-NO.
006800     IF YES-NO NOT = "Y"
006900         MOVE "N" TO YES-NO.
007000
007100 GET-HOW-MANY-ENTRIES.
007200     DISPLAY
007300      "How many entries would you like (01-99)?".
007400     ACCEPT HOW-MANY-ENTRIES.
007500
007600 DISPLAY-ONE-ENTRY.
007700
```

continues

Listing A.12. continued

```
007800        IF SCREEN-LINES = 15
007900            PERFORM PRESS-ENTER.
008000        COMPUTE THE-PRODUCT = THE-TABLE * THE-ENTRY.
008100        MOVE THE-TABLE TO DISPLAY-THE-TABLE.
008200        MOVE THE-ENTRY TO DISPLAY-THE-ENTRY.
008300        MOVE THE-PRODUCT TO DISPLAY-THE-PRODUCT.
008400        DISPLAY THE-TABLE-LINE.
008500
008600        ADD 1 TO SCREEN-LINES.
008700
008800 PRESS-ENTER.
008900        DISPLAY "Press ENTER to continue . . .".
009000        ACCEPT A-DUMMY.
009100        MOVE 0 TO SCREEN-LINES.
009200
```

The following is the first screen of output of mult09.cbl:

```
Which multiplication table(01-99)?
15
How many entries would you like (01-99)?
33
15 *   1 =    15
15 *   2 =    30
15 *   3 =    45
15 *   4 =    60
15 *   5 =    75
15 *   6 =    90
15 *   7 =   105
15 *   8 =   120
15 *   9 =   135
15 *  10 =   150
15 *  11 =   165
15 *  12 =   180
15 *  13 =   195
15 *  14 =   210
15 *  15 =   225
Press ENTER to continue . . .
```

2.
```
001100 01  CUST-DATA.
001200     05  CUST-NUMBER      PIC 9(5).
001300     05  CUST-NAME        PIC X(30).
001400     05  CUST-ADDRESS     PIC X(50).
001500     05  CUST-ZIP         PIC 9(5).
```

3.
```
001100 01  CUST-DATA.
001200     05  CUST-NUMBER      PIC 9(5)  VALUE ZEROES.
001300     05  CUST-NAME        PIC X(30) VALUE SPACES.
001400     05  CUST-ADDRESS     PIC X(50) VALUE SPACES.
001500     05  CUST-ZIP         PIC 9(5)  VALUE ZEROES.
```

Answers to Day 9, "File I/O"

Quiz

No, the file must be opened with the same logical and physical definition that was used to create the file. In this case, the file definition is longer than the actual physical records in the file.

Exercises

1. Listing A.13 adds the extra field, and it prompts for the extension.

TYPE | **Listing A.13. Adding a phone extension.**

```
000100 IDENTIFICATION DIVISION.
000200 PROGRAM-ID. PHNADD02.
000300*------------------------------------------------
000400* This program creates a new data file if necessary
000500* and adds records to the file from user entered
000600* data.
000700*------------------------------------------------
000800 ENVIRONMENT DIVISION.
000900 INPUT-OUTPUT SECTION.
001000 FILE-CONTROL.
001100     SELECT OPTIONAL PHONE-FILE
001200*or  SELECT PHONE-FILE
001300         ASSIGN TO "phone.dat"
001400*or       ASSIGN TO "phone"
001500         ORGANIZATION IS SEQUENTIAL.
001600
001700 DATA DIVISION.
001800 FILE SECTION.
001900 FD  PHONE-FILE
002000     LABEL RECORDS ARE STANDARD.
002100 01  PHONE-RECORD.
002200     05  PHONE-LAST-NAME      PIC X(20).
002300     05  PHONE-FIRST-NAME     PIC X(20).
002400     05  PHONE-NUMBER         PIC X(15).
002500     05  PHONE-EXTENSION      PIC X(5).
002600
002700 WORKING-STORAGE SECTION.
002800
002900* Variables for SCREEN ENTRY
003000 01  PROMPT-1              PIC X(9) VALUE "Last Name".
003100 01  PROMPT-2              PIC X(10) VALUE "First Name".
003200 01  PROMPT-3              PIC X(6) VALUE "Number".
003300 01  PROMPT-4              PIC X(9) VALUE "Extension".
003400
003500 01  YES-NO                PIC X.
003600 01  ENTRY-OK              PIC X.
003700
```

continues

Listing A.13. continued

```
003800 PROCEDURE DIVISION.
003900 MAIN-LOGIC SECTION.
004000 PROGRAM-BEGIN.
004100
004200     PERFORM OPENING-PROCEDURE.
004300     MOVE "Y" TO YES-NO.
004400     PERFORM ADD-RECORDS
004500         UNTIL YES-NO = "N".
004600     PERFORM CLOSING-PROCEDURE.
004700
004800 PROGRAM-DONE.
004900     STOP RUN.
005000
005100* OPENING AND CLOSING
005200
005300 OPENING-PROCEDURE.
005400     OPEN EXTEND PHONE-FILE.
005500
005600 CLOSING-PROCEDURE.
005700     CLOSE PHONE-FILE.
005800
005900 ADD-RECORDS.
006000     MOVE "N" TO ENTRY-OK.
006100     PERFORM GET-FIELDS
006200         UNTIL ENTRY-OK = "Y".
006300     PERFORM ADD-THIS-RECORD.
006400     PERFORM GO-AGAIN.
006500
006600 GET-FIELDS.
006700     MOVE SPACE TO PHONE-RECORD.
006800     DISPLAY PROMPT-1 " ? ".
006900     ACCEPT PHONE-LAST-NAME.
007000     DISPLAY PROMPT-2 " ? ".
007100     ACCEPT PHONE-FIRST-NAME.
007200     DISPLAY PROMPT-3 " ? ".
007300     ACCEPT PHONE-NUMBER.
007400     DISPLAY PROMPT-4 " ? ".
007500     ACCEPT PHONE-EXTENSION.
007600     PERFORM VALIDATE-FIELDS.
007700
007800 VALIDATE-FIELDS.
007900     MOVE "Y" TO ENTRY-OK.
008000     IF PHONE-LAST-NAME = SPACE
008100         DISPLAY "LAST NAME MUST BE ENTERED"
008200         MOVE "N" TO ENTRY-OK.
008300
008400 ADD-THIS-RECORD.
008500     WRITE PHONE-RECORD.
008600
008700 GO-AGAIN.
008800     DISPLAY "GO AGAIN?".
008900     ACCEPT YES-NO.
009000     IF YES-NO = "y"
009100         MOVE "Y" TO YES-NO.
```

```
009200     IF YES-NO NOT = "Y"
009300         MOVE "N" TO YES-NO.
009400
```

Here is the output of phnadd02.cbl:

OUTPUT
```
Last Name  ?
KARENINA
First Name ?
ANA
Number     ?
 (818) 555-4567
Extension ?
123
GO AGAIN?
Y
Last Name  ?
SMITH
First Name ?
MICHAEL VALENTINE
Number     ?
 (415) 555-1234
Extension ?
6065
GO AGAIN?
```

2. Listing A.14 displays the extra field. Note that the prompts at lines 003000, 003200, 003400, and 003600 had to be shortened to enable the record to fit on an 80-column screen.

TYPE ## Listing A.14. Displaying the extension.

```
000100 IDENTIFICATION DIVISION.
000200 PROGRAM-ID. PHNLST02.
000300*-------------------------------------------------
000400* This program displays the contents of the
000500* phone file.
000600*-------------------------------------------------
000700 ENVIRONMENT DIVISION.
000800 INPUT-OUTPUT SECTION.
000900 FILE-CONTROL.
001000     SELECT OPTIONAL PHONE-FILE
001100*or   SELECT PHONE-FILE
001200         ASSIGN TO "phone.dat"
001300*or      ASSIGN TO "phone"
001400         ORGANIZATION IS SEQUENTIAL.
001500
001600 DATA DIVISION.
001700 FILE SECTION.
001800 FD  PHONE-FILE
001900     LABEL RECORDS ARE STANDARD.
002000 01  PHONE-RECORD.
```

continues

Listing A.14. continued

```
002100     05   PHONE-LAST-NAME      PIC X(20).
002200     05   PHONE-FIRST-NAME     PIC X(20).
002300     05   PHONE-NUMBER         PIC X(15).
002400     05   PHONE-EXTENSION      PIC X(5).
002500
002600 WORKING-STORAGE SECTION.
002700
002800* Structure for SCREEN DISPLAY
002900 01  FIELDS-TO-DISPLAY.
003000     05   PROMPT-1             PIC X(4) VALUE "Lst:".
003100     05   DISPLAY-LAST-NAME    PIC X(20).
003200     05   PROMPT-2             PIC X(4) VALUE "1st:".
003300     05   DISPLAY-FIRST-NAME   PIC X(20).
003400     05   PROMPT-3             PIC X(3) VALUE "NO:".
003500     05   DISPLAY-NUMBER       PIC X(15).
003600     05   PROMPT-4             PIC X(4) VALUE "Xtn:".
003700     05   DISPLAY-EXTENSION    PIC X(5).
003800
003900 01  END-OF-FILE              PIC X.
004000
004100 01  SCREEN-LINES            PIC 99.
004200 01  A-DUMMY                 PIC X.
004300
004400 PROCEDURE DIVISION.
004500 MAIN-LOGIC SECTION.
004600 PROGRAM-BEGIN.
004700
004800     PERFORM OPENING-PROCEDURE.
004900     MOVE ZEROES TO SCREEN-LINES.
005000     MOVE "N" TO END-OF-FILE.
005100     PERFORM READ-NEXT-RECORD.
005200     PERFORM DISPLAY-RECORDS
005300         UNTIL END-OF-FILE = "Y".
005400     PERFORM CLOSING-PROCEDURE.
005500
005600 PROGRAM-DONE.
005700     STOP RUN.
005800
005900 OPENING-PROCEDURE.
006000     OPEN INPUT PHONE-FILE.
006100
006200 CLOSING-PROCEDURE.
006300     CLOSE PHONE-FILE.
006400
006500 DISPLAY-RECORDS.
006600     PERFORM DISPLAY-FIELDS.
006700     PERFORM READ-NEXT-RECORD.
006800
006900 DISPLAY-FIELDS.
007000     IF SCREEN-LINES = 15
007100         PERFORM PRESS-ENTER.
007200     MOVE PHONE-LAST-NAME TO DISPLAY-LAST-NAME.
007300     MOVE PHONE-FIRST-NAME TO DISPLAY-FIRST-NAME.
007400     MOVE PHONE-NUMBER TO DISPLAY-NUMBER.
```

```
007500      MOVE PHONE-EXTENSION TO DISPLAY-EXTENSION.
007600      DISPLAY FIELDS-TO-DISPLAY.
007700
007800      ADD 1 TO SCREEN-LINES.
007900
008000 READ-NEXT-RECORD.
008100     READ PHONE-FILE NEXT RECORD
008200        AT END
008300          MOVE "Y" TO END-OF-FILE.
008400
008500 PRESS-ENTER.
008600     DISPLAY "Press ENTER to continue . . ".
008700     ACCEPT A-DUMMY.
008800     MOVE ZEROES TO SCREEN-LINES.
008900
```

The output of `phnlst02.cbl` follows:

```
C>pcobrun phnlst01
Personal COBOL version 2.0 from Micro Focus
PCOBRUN V2.0.02  Copyright (C) 1983-1993 Micro Focus Ltd.
Lst:KARENINA        1st:ANA           NO:555-4567         Xtn:
Lst:ARBUTHNOT       1st:ARTHUR        NO:(515) 555-1234   Xtn:
Lst:BUDLONG         1st:MO            NO:(818) 555-4444   Xtn:
Lst:WRIGHT          1st:ORVILLE       NO:606-555-7777     Xtn:23
Lst:ZERILDA         1st:MARSHA        NO:555-4567         Xtn:
Lst:WAYNE           1st:BOB           NO:555-4332         Xtn:
Lst:ADALE           1st:ALAN          NO:415-555 6666     Xtn:4466
Lst:NOTTINGHAM      1st:SHERIFF       NO:415-555-6789     Xtn:
Lst:TUCK            1st:FRIAR         NO:213-5552345      Xtn:
Lst:SCARLET         1st:WILL          NO:202-5556789      Xtn:
Lst:PLUM            1st:PROFESSOR     NO:202-555-5678     Xtn:802
Lst:RED             1st:ERIC THE      NO:424-555-3456     Xtn:
Lst:SCOTT           1st:W.R.          NO:616-555-2345     Xtn:297
Lst:BACH            1st:J.S.          NO:555-6789         Xtn:
Lst:RUTH            1st:BABE          NO:555-9876         Xtn:12
Press ENTER to continue . .
```

Answers to Day 10, "Printing"

Quiz

Using NEXT-PAGE at the start of the report usually causes a blank page to be fed out of the printer before the first page of the report is printed. Some modern printers, particularly laser and inkjet/bubble-jet types, might not eject the initial blank page.

Exercises

1. All the changes are in COLUMN-HEADINGS and DETAIL-LINE, and involve increasing the FILLER between the headings and the detail fields by 1 (as shown in Listing A.15).

   The printer spacing sheet for the modified report is shown in Figure A.1.

Figure A.1.

*A printer spacing sheet
for the modified
report.*

TYPE   **Listing A.15. Two spaces between fields.**

```
000100 IDENTIFICATION DIVISION.
000200 PROGRAM-ID. PHNPRT03.
000300*----------------------------------------------------
000400* This program prints the contents of the
000500* phone file.
000600*----------------------------------------------------
000700 ENVIRONMENT DIVISION.
000800 INPUT-OUTPUT SECTION.
000900 FILE-CONTROL.
001000     SELECT OPTIONAL PHONE-FILE
001100*or  SELECT PHONE-FILE
001200         ASSIGN TO "phone.dat"
001300*or      ASSIGN TO "phone"
001400         ORGANIZATION IS SEQUENTIAL.
001500
001600     SELECT PRINTER-FILE
001700         ASSIGN TO PRINTER
001800         ORGANIZATION IS LINE SEQUENTIAL.
001900
002000 DATA DIVISION.
002100 FILE SECTION.
002200 FD  PHONE-FILE
002300     LABEL RECORDS ARE STANDARD.
002400 01  PHONE-RECORD.
002500     05   PHONE-LAST-NAME      PIC X(20).
002600     05   PHONE-FIRST-NAME     PIC X(20).
002700     05   PHONE-NUMBER         PIC X(15).
002800     05   PHONE-EXTENSION      PIC X(5).
002900
003000 FD  PRINTER-FILE
003100     LABEL RECORDS ARE OMITTED.
003200 01  PRINTER-RECORD            PIC X(80).
003300
003400 WORKING-STORAGE SECTION.
003500
003600* Structure for printing a title line
003700 01  TITLE-LINE.
003800     05   FILLER               PIC X(21) VALUE SPACE.
003900     05   FILLER               PIC X(17) VALUE
004000     "PHONE BOOK REPORT".
004100     05   FILLER               PIC X(15) VALUE SPACE.
004200     05   FILLER               PIC X(5) VALUE "Page:".
004300     05   PRINT-PAGE-NUMBER    PIC ZZZZ9.
004400
```

```
004500* Structure for printing a column heading
004600 01  COLUMN-HEADINGS.
004700     05  FILLER              PIC X(9)  VALUE "Last Name".
004800     05  FILLER              PIC X(13) VALUE SPACE.
004900     05  FILLER              PIC X(10) VALUE "First Name".
005000     05  FILLER              PIC X(12) VALUE SPACE.
005100     05  FILLER              PIC X(6)  VALUE "Number".
005200     05  FILLER              PIC X(11) VALUE SPACE.
005300     05  FILLER              PIC X(4)  VALUE "Ext.".
005400
005500 01 DETAIL-LINE.
005600     05  PRINT-LAST-NAME     PIC X(20).
005700     05  FILLER              PIC X(2) VALUE SPACE.
005800     05  PRINT-FIRST-NAME    PIC X(20).
005900     05  FILLER              PIC X(2) VALUE SPACE.
006000     05  PRINT-NUMBER        PIC X(15).
006100     05  FILLER              PIC X(2) VALUE SPACE.
006200     05  PRINT-EXTENSION     PIC X(5).
006300
006400 01  END-OF-FILE            PIC X.
006500
006600 01  PRINT-LINES           PIC 99.
006700 01  PAGE-NUMBER           PIC 9(5).
006800
006900 PROCEDURE DIVISION.
007000 MAIN-LOGIC SECTION.
007100 PROGRAM-BEGIN.
007200
007300     PERFORM OPENING-PROCEDURE.
007400     MOVE ZEROES TO PRINT-LINES
007500                    PAGE-NUMBER.
007600     PERFORM START-NEW-PAGE.
007700     MOVE "N" TO END-OF-FILE.
007800     PERFORM READ-NEXT-RECORD.
007900     IF END-OF-FILE = "Y"
008000         MOVE "No records found" TO PRINTER-RECORD
008100         WRITE PRINTER-RECORD BEFORE ADVANCING 1.
008200     PERFORM PRINT-RECORDS
008300         UNTIL END-OF-FILE = "Y".
008400     PERFORM CLOSING-PROCEDURE.
008500
008600 PROGRAM-DONE.
008700     STOP RUN.
008800
008900 OPENING-PROCEDURE.
009000     OPEN INPUT PHONE-FILE.
009100     OPEN OUTPUT PRINTER-FILE.
009200
009300 CLOSING-PROCEDURE.
009400     CLOSE PHONE-FILE.
009500     PERFORM END-LAST-PAGE.
009600     CLOSE PRINTER-FILE.
009700
009800 PRINT-RECORDS.
009900     PERFORM PRINT-FIELDS.
```

continues

Listing A.15. continued

```
010000      PERFORM READ-NEXT-RECORD.
010100
010200 PRINT-FIELDS.
010300      IF PRINT-LINES NOT < 55
010400          PERFORM NEXT-PAGE.
010500      MOVE PHONE-LAST-NAME TO PRINT-LAST-NAME.
010600      MOVE PHONE-FIRST-NAME TO PRINT-FIRST-NAME.
010700      MOVE PHONE-NUMBER TO PRINT-NUMBER.
010800      MOVE PHONE-EXTENSION TO PRINT-EXTENSION.
010900      MOVE DETAIL-LINE TO PRINTER-RECORD.
011000      WRITE PRINTER-RECORD BEFORE ADVANCING 1.
011100
011200      ADD 1 TO PRINT-LINES.
011300
011400 READ-NEXT-RECORD.
011500      READ PHONE-FILE NEXT RECORD
011600          AT END
011700          MOVE "Y" TO END-OF-FILE.
011800
011900 NEXT-PAGE.
012000      PERFORM END-LAST-PAGE.
012100      PERFORM START-NEW-PAGE.
012200
012300 START-NEW-PAGE.
012400      ADD 1 TO PAGE-NUMBER.
012500      MOVE PAGE-NUMBER TO PRINT-PAGE-NUMBER.
012600      MOVE TITLE-LINE TO PRINTER-RECORD.
012700      WRITE PRINTER-RECORD BEFORE ADVANCING 2.
012800      MOVE COLUMN-HEADINGS TO PRINTER-RECORD.
012900      WRITE PRINTER-RECORD BEFORE ADVANCING 2.
013000      MOVE 4 TO PRINT-LINES.
013100
013200 END-LAST-PAGE.
013300      MOVE SPACE TO PRINTER-RECORD.
013400      WRITE PRINTER-RECORD BEFORE ADVANCING PAGE.
013500      MOVE ZEROES TO PRINT-LINES.
013600
```

2. Figure A.2 is one example of a possible layout for the customer report.

Figure A.2.

A possible customer report layout.

Answers to Day 11, "Indexed File I/O"

Quiz

1. CONTACT-BIRTH-DATE will not be unique. Even with as few as 200 records, the chance of a duplicate birth date is very high. Once you start putting hundreds of records in a file, birth dates won't stay unique.

2. The CONTACT-PHONE-NUMBER has a better chance of being unique, but there is still a possibility of having two contacts at the same phone number. The best solution is to create an additional numeric field in the record called CONTACT-NUMBER. Each contact added to the file is assigned a new number.

Exercises

1. Listings A.16 and A.17 present a better way of defining the record, and CONTACT-NUMBER will be assigned during data entry to ensure that it is unique.

TYPE **Listing A.16. The FD for a contact file.**

```
000900 FD  CONTACT-FILE
001000     LABEL RECORDS ARE STANDARD.
001100 01  CONTACT-RECORD.
001200     05  CONTACT-NUMBER        PIC 9(5).
001300     05  CONTACT-BIRTH-DATE    PIC 9(6).
001400     05  CONTACT-NAME          PIC X(20).
001500     05  CONTACT-ADDRESS-1     PIC X(20).
001600     05  CONTACT-ADDRESS-2     PIC X(20).
001700     05  CONTACT-ZIP           PIC 9(5).
001800     05  CONTACT-PHONE.
001900         10  CONTACT-AREA-CODE  PIC 9(3).
002000         10  CONTACT-PREFIX     PIC 9(3).
002200         10  CONTACT-PHONE-NO   PIC 9(4).
```

TYPE **Listing A.17. The SELECT statement for a contact file.**

```
000300     SELECT CONTACT-FILE
000400         ASSIGN TO "contact"
000500         ORGANIZATION IS INDEXED
000600         RECORD KEY IS CONTACT-NUMBER
000700         ACCESS MODE IS DYNAMIC.
```

A

2. DISPLAY-NAME is 30 bytes long with an implied picture of X and is therefore a PIC X(30). Everywhere it is used in the program, it is unaffected by the fact that subordinate variables are within DISPLAY-NAME. DISPLAY-CITY and DISPLAY-STATE are now within DISPLAY-NAME, and consequently within DETAIL-LINE, so the move that used to exist at line 014400 is no longer needed.

3. Listings A.18 and A.19 compare PHNPRT02 and VNDDSP01. I have inserted comments without line numbers so that they will stand out in the listings. The comments provide the comparisons between the two programs.

TYPE **Listing A.18. PHNPRT02 compared to VNDDSP01.**

```
       * PHNPRT02 prints records to paper
000100 IDENTIFICATION DIVISION.
000200 PROGRAM-ID. PHNPRT02.
000300*--------------------------------------------
000400* This program prints the contents of the
000500* phone file.
000600*--------------------------------------------
000700 ENVIRONMENT DIVISION.
000800 INPUT-OUTPUT SECTION.
000900 FILE-CONTROL.
001000      SELECT OPTIONAL PHONE-FILE
001100*or   SELECT PHONE-FILE
001200         ASSIGN TO "phone.dat"
001300*or      ASSIGN TO "phone"
001400         ORGANIZATION IS SEQUENTIAL.
001500
001600      SELECT PRINTER-FILE
001700         ASSIGN TO PRINTER
001800         ORGANIZATION IS LINE SEQUENTIAL.
001900
002000 DATA DIVISION.
002100 FILE SECTION.
002200 FD  PHONE-FILE
002300     LABEL RECORDS ARE STANDARD.
002400 01  PHONE-RECORD.
002500     05  PHONE-LAST-NAME    PIC X(20).
002600     05  PHONE-FIRST-NAME   PIC X(20).
002700     05  PHONE-NUMBER       PIC X(15).
002800     05  PHONE-EXTENSION    PIC X(5).
002900
003000 FD  PRINTER-FILE
003100     LABEL RECORDS ARE OMITTED.
003200 01  PRINTER-RECORD         PIC X(80).
003300
003400 WORKING-STORAGE SECTION.
003500
003600* Structure for printing a title line
003700 01  TITLE-LINE.
003800     05  FILLER             PIC X(21) VALUE SPACE.
003900     05  FILLER             PIC X(17) VALUE
004000     "PHONE BOOK REPORT".
004100     05  FILLER             PIC X(15) VALUE SPACE.
004200     05  FILLER             PIC X(5) VALUE "Page:".
004300     05  PRINT-PAGE-NUMBER  PIC ZZZZ9.
004400
004500* Structure for printing a column heading
004600 01  COLUMN-HEADINGS.
004700     05  FILLER             PIC X(9)  VALUE "Last Name".
```

```
004800      05   FILLER              PIC X(12) VALUE SPACE.
004900      05   FILLER              PIC X(10) VALUE "First Name".
005000      05   FILLER              PIC X(11) VALUE SPACE.
005100      05   FILLER              PIC X(6)  VALUE "Number".
005200      05   FILLER              PIC X(10) VALUE SPACE.
005300      05   FILLER              PIC X(4)  VALUE "Ext.".
005400
005500 01 DETAIL-LINE.
005600      05   PRINT-LAST-NAME     PIC X(20).
005700      05   FILLER              PIC X(1) VALUE SPACE.
005800      05   PRINT-FIRST-NAME    PIC X(20).
005900      05   FILLER              PIC X(1) VALUE SPACE.
006000      05   PRINT-NUMBER        PIC X(15).
006100      05   FILLER              PIC X(1) VALUE SPACE.
006200      05   PRINT-EXTENSION     PIC X(5).
006300
006400 01   END-OF-FILE             PIC X.
006500
006600 01   PRINT-LINES            PIC 99.
006700 01   PAGE-NUMBER            PIC 9(5).
006800
006900 PROCEDURE DIVISION.
007000 MAIN-LOGIC SECTION.

     * The main logic at lines 007100 through 007800 is almost
     * identical to the same logic at lines 007600 through
     * 008500 of VNDDSP01.
007100 PROGRAM-BEGIN.
007200
007300      PERFORM OPENING-PROCEDURE.
007400      MOVE ZEROES TO PRINT-LINES
007500                     PAGE-NUMBER.
007600      PERFORM START-NEW-PAGE.
007700      MOVE "N" TO END-OF-FILE.
007800      PERFORM READ-NEXT-RECORD.

     * The logic at lines 007900 through 008300 prints a message
     * if no records are found in the file. This is similar to
     * lines 008600 through 009100 in VNDDSP01 which display a
     * message if no records are found.
007900      IF END-OF-FILE = "Y"
008000         MOVE "No records found" TO PRINTER-RECORD
008100         WRITE PRINTER-RECORD BEFORE ADVANCING 1.
008200      PERFORM PRINT-RECORDS
008300         UNTIL END-OF-FILE = "Y".
008400      PERFORM CLOSING-PROCEDURE.
008500
008600 PROGRAM-DONE.
008700      STOP RUN.
008800
008900 OPENING-PROCEDURE.
009000      OPEN INPUT PHONE-FILE.
009100      OPEN OUTPUT PRINTER-FILE.
009200
009300 CLOSING-PROCEDURE.
```

continues

Listing A.18. continued

```
009400        CLOSE PHONE-FILE.
009500        PERFORM END-LAST-PAGE.
009600        CLOSE PRINTER-FILE.
009700

          * Lines 009800 through 011200 start a new page when needed,
          * print records one at a time and read the next record.
          * VNDDSP01 does the same functions at lines 010500 through
          * 015200. The big difference in VNDDSP01 is that vendor
          * information is displayed on multiple lines.
009800 PRINT-RECORDS.
009900        PERFORM PRINT-FIELDS.
010000        PERFORM READ-NEXT-RECORD.
010100
010200 PRINT-FIELDS.
010300        IF PRINT-LINES NOT < 55
010400            PERFORM NEXT-PAGE.
010500        MOVE PHONE-LAST-NAME TO PRINT-LAST-NAME.
010600        MOVE PHONE-FIRST-NAME TO PRINT-FIRST-NAME.
010700        MOVE PHONE-NUMBER TO PRINT-NUMBER.
010800        MOVE PHONE-EXTENSION TO PRINT-EXTENSION.
010900        MOVE DETAIL-LINE TO PRINTER-RECORD.
011000        WRITE PRINTER-RECORD BEFORE ADVANCING 1.
011100
011200        ADD 1 TO PRINT-LINES.
011300
011400 READ-NEXT-RECORD.
011500        READ PHONE-FILE NEXT RECORD
011600            AT END
011700            MOVE "Y" TO END-OF-FILE.
011800

          * The logic at lines 011900 through 013500 controls what to
          * do when a new page is needed and special processing to
          * handle the last page. VNDDSP01 does the same sort of
          * processing but for the display at lines 016100
          * through 018200.
011900 NEXT-PAGE.
012000        PERFORM END-LAST-PAGE.
012100        PERFORM START-NEW-PAGE.
012200
012300 START-NEW-PAGE.
012400        ADD 1 TO PAGE-NUMBER.
012500        MOVE PAGE-NUMBER TO PRINT-PAGE-NUMBER.
012600        MOVE TITLE-LINE TO PRINTER-RECORD.
012700        WRITE PRINTER-RECORD BEFORE ADVANCING 2.
012800        MOVE COLUMN-HEADINGS TO PRINTER-RECORD.
012900        WRITE PRINTER-RECORD BEFORE ADVANCING 2.
013000        MOVE 4 TO PRINT-LINES.
013100
013200 END-LAST-PAGE.
013300        MOVE SPACE TO PRINTER-RECORD.
013400        WRITE PRINTER-RECORD BEFORE ADVANCING PAGE.
013500        MOVE ZEROES TO PRINT-LINES.
013600
```

Listing A.19. VNDDSP01 **compared to** PHNPRT02.

```
         * VNDDSP01 displays records on a screen.
000100 IDENTIFICATION DIVISION.
000200 PROGRAM-ID. VNDDSP01.
000300*----------------------------------------
000400* Display records in the Vendor File.
000500*----------------------------------------
000600 ENVIRONMENT DIVISION.
000700 INPUT-OUTPUT SECTION.
000800 FILE-CONTROL.
000900
001000     SELECT VENDOR-FILE
001100         ASSIGN TO "vendor"
001200         ORGANIZATION IS INDEXED
001300         RECORD KEY IS VENDOR-NUMBER
001400         ACCESS MODE IS DYNAMIC.
001500
001600 DATA DIVISION.
001700 FILE SECTION.
001800
001900 FD  VENDOR-FILE
002000     LABEL RECORDS ARE STANDARD.
002100 01  VENDOR-RECORD.
002200     05  VENDOR-NUMBER                PIC 9(5).
002300     05  VENDOR-NAME                  PIC X(30).
002400     05  VENDOR-ADDRESS-1             PIC X(30).
002500     05  VENDOR-ADDRESS-2             PIC X(30).
002600     05  VENDOR-CITY                  PIC X(20).
002700     05  VENDOR-STATE                 PIC X(2).
002800     05  VENDOR-ZIP                   PIC X(10).
002900     05  VENDOR-CONTACT               PIC X(30).
003000     05  VENDOR-PHONE                 PIC X(15).
003100
003200
003300
003400
003500 WORKING-STORAGE SECTION.
003600
003700
003800
003900 01  DETAIL-LINE.
004000     05  DISPLAY-NUMBER    PIC 9(5).
004100     05  FILLER            PIC X      VALUE SPACE.
004200     05  DISPLAY-NAME      PIC X(30).
004300     05  FILLER            PIC X      VALUE SPACE.
004400     05  DISPLAY-CONTACT   PIC X(30).
004500
004600 01  CITY-STATE-DETAIL.
004700     05  DISPLAY-CITY      PIC X(20).
004800     05  FILLER            PIC X VALUE SPACE.
004900     05  DISPLAY-STATE     PIC X(2).
005000
005100 01  COLUMN-LINE.
```

continues

Listing A.19. continued

```
005200      05  FILLER          PIC X(2)  VALUE "NO".
005300      05  FILLER          PIC X(4) VALUE SPACE.
005400      05  FILLER          PIC X(12) VALUE "NAME-ADDRESS".
005500      05  FILLER          PIC X(19) VALUE SPACE.
005600      05  FILLER          PIC X(17) VALUE "CONTACT-PHONE-ZIP".
005700
005800 01  TITLE-LINE.
005900      05  FILLER               PIC X(15) VALUE SPACE.
006000      05  FILLER               PIC X(11)
006100          VALUE "VENDOR LIST".
006200      05  FILLER               PIC X(15) VALUE SPACE.
006300      05  FILLER               PIC X(5) VALUE "PAGE:".
006400      05  FILLER               PIC X(1) VALUE SPACE.
006500      05  DISPLAY-PAGE-NUMBER PIC ZZZZ9.
006600
006700 77  FILE-AT-END          PIC X.
006800 77  A-DUMMY              PIC X.
006900 77  LINE-COUNT           PIC 999 VALUE ZERO.
007000 77  PAGE-NUMBER          PIC 99999 VALUE ZERO.
007100 77  MAXIMUM-LINES        PIC 999 VALUE 15.
007200
007300 77  DISPLAY-RECORD       PIC X(79).
007400
007500 PROCEDURE DIVISION.

       * The main logic at lines 007600 through 008500 is almost
       * identical to the same logic at lines 007100 through
       * 007800 of PHNPRT02.
007600 PROGRAM-BEGIN.
007700
007800      PERFORM OPENING-PROCEDURE.
007900      MOVE ZEROES TO LINE-COUNT
008000                     PAGE-NUMBER.
008100
008200      PERFORM START-NEW-PAGE.
008300
008400      MOVE "N" TO FILE-AT-END.
008500      PERFORM READ-NEXT-RECORD.

1234567890123456789012345678901234567890123456789012345
       * The logic at lines 008600 through 009100 displays a message
       * if no records are found in the file. This is similar to
       * lines 007900 through 008300 in PHNPRT02 which prints a
       * message if no records are found.
008600      IF FILE-AT-END = "Y"
008700         MOVE "NO RECORDS FOUND" TO DISPLAY-RECORD
008800         PERFORM WRITE-DISPLAY-RECORD
008900      ELSE
009000         PERFORM DISPLAY-VENDOR-FIELDS
009100            UNTIL FILE-AT-END = "Y".
009200
009300      PERFORM CLOSING-PROCEDURE.
009400
009500
```

```
009600 PROGRAM-DONE.
009700      STOP RUN.
009800
009900 OPENING-PROCEDURE.
010000      OPEN I-O VENDOR-FILE.
010100
010200 CLOSING-PROCEDURE.
010300      CLOSE VENDOR-FILE.
010400

          * Lines 010500 through 015200 start a new screen's worth
          * of display information when needed,
          * display records one at a time and read the next record.
          * PHNPRT02 does the same functions at lines 009800 through
          * 011200. The big difference in PHNPRT02 is that phone
          * information is printed on a sinlge line.
010500 DISPLAY-VENDOR-FIELDS.
010600      IF LINE-COUNT > MAXIMUM-LINES
010700          PERFORM START-NEXT-PAGE.
010800      PERFORM DISPLAY-THE-RECORD.
010900      PERFORM READ-NEXT-RECORD.
011000
011100 DISPLAY-THE-RECORD.
011200      PERFORM DISPLAY-LINE-1.
011300      PERFORM DISPLAY-LINE-2.
011400      PERFORM DISPLAY-LINE-3.
011500      PERFORM DISPLAY-LINE-4.
011600      PERFORM LINE-FEED.
011700
011800 DISPLAY-LINE-1.
011900      MOVE SPACE TO DETAIL-LINE.
012000      MOVE VENDOR-NUMBER TO DISPLAY-NUMBER.
012100      MOVE VENDOR-NAME TO DISPLAY-NAME.
012200      MOVE VENDOR-CONTACT TO DISPLAY-CONTACT.
012300      MOVE DETAIL-LINE TO DISPLAY-RECORD.
012400      PERFORM WRITE-DISPLAY-RECORD.
012500
012600 DISPLAY-LINE-2.
012700      MOVE SPACE TO DETAIL-LINE.
012800      MOVE VENDOR-ADDRESS-1 TO DISPLAY-NAME.
012900      MOVE VENDOR-PHONE TO DISPLAY-CONTACT.
013000      MOVE DETAIL-LINE TO DISPLAY-RECORD.
013100      PERFORM WRITE-DISPLAY-RECORD.
013200
013300 DISPLAY-LINE-3.
013400      MOVE SPACE TO DETAIL-LINE.
013500      MOVE VENDOR-ADDRESS-2 TO DISPLAY-NAME.
013600      IF VENDOR-ADDRESS-2 NOT = SPACE
013700          MOVE DETAIL-LINE TO DISPLAY-RECORD
013800          PERFORM WRITE-DISPLAY-RECORD.
013900
014000 DISPLAY-LINE-4.
014100      MOVE SPACE TO DETAIL-LINE.
014200      MOVE VENDOR-CITY TO DISPLAY-CITY.
014300      MOVE VENDOR-STATE TO DISPLAY-STATE.
```

continues

Listing A.19. continued

```
014400        MOVE CITY-STATE-DETAIL TO DISPLAY-NAME.
014500        MOVE VENDOR-ZIP TO DISPLAY-CONTACT.
014600        MOVE DETAIL-LINE TO DISPLAY-RECORD.
014700        PERFORM WRITE-DISPLAY-RECORD.
014800
014900 READ-NEXT-RECORD.
015000        READ VENDOR-FILE NEXT RECORD
015100            AT END MOVE "Y" TO FILE-AT-END.
015200
015300 WRITE-DISPLAY-RECORD.
015400        DISPLAY DISPLAY-RECORD.
015500        ADD 1 TO LINE-COUNT.
015600
015700 LINE-FEED.
015800        MOVE SPACE TO DISPLAY-RECORD.
015900        PERFORM WRITE-DISPLAY-RECORD.
016000

          * The logic at lines 016100 through 018200 controls what to
          * do when a new screen is needed and special processing to
          * handle the last screen. PHNPRT02 does the same sort of
          * processing but for printed pages at lines 011900
          * through 013500.
016100 START-NEXT-PAGE.
016200
016300        PERFORM END-LAST-PAGE.
016400        PERFORM START-NEW-PAGE.
016500
016600 START-NEW-PAGE.
016700        ADD 1 TO PAGE-NUMBER.
016800        MOVE PAGE-NUMBER TO DISPLAY-PAGE-NUMBER.
016900        MOVE TITLE-LINE TO DISPLAY-RECORD.
017000        PERFORM WRITE-DISPLAY-RECORD.
017100        PERFORM LINE-FEED.
017200        MOVE COLUMN-LINE TO DISPLAY-RECORD.
017300        PERFORM WRITE-DISPLAY-RECORD.
017400        PERFORM LINE-FEED.
017500
017600 END-LAST-PAGE.
017700        PERFORM PRESS-ENTER.
017800        MOVE ZERO TO LINE-COUNT.
017900
018000 PRESS-ENTER.
018100        DISPLAY "PRESS ENTER TO CONTINUE. . .".
018200        ACCEPT A-DUMMY.
018300
```

Answers to Day 12, "More on Indexed Files"

Quiz

The example reproduced in Listing A.20 has a bug at line 003800. The logic is set up so that if a record is not found, an attempt is made to change the record; and, if the record is found, an attempt is made to add the record. This is the reverse of what was intended. Line 003800 should read as follows:

```
003800      IF RECORD-FOUND-FLAG = "Y"
```

TYPE **Listing A.20. Reading a record in a file.**

```
003200 ADD-OR-UPDATE.
003300      MOVE "Y" TO RECORD-FOUND-FLAG.
003400      MOVE NEW-NUMBER TO VENDOR-NUMBER.
003500      READ VENDOR-RECORD
003600          INVALID KEY
003700          MOVE "N" TO RECORD-FOUND-FLAG.
003800      IF RECORD-FOUND-FLAG = "N"
003900          PERFORM CHANGE-THIS-RECORD
004000      ELSE
004100          PERFORM ADD-THIS-RECORD.
004200
004300 CHANGE-THIS-RECORD.
004400      PERFORM LOAD-RECORD-VALUES.
004500      REWRITE VENDOR-RECORD
004600          INVALID KEY
004700          DISPLAY "ERROR CHANGING THE RECORD".
004800
004900 ADD-THIS-RECORD.
005000      PERFORM LOAD-RECORD-VALUES.
005100      WRITE VENDOR-RECORD
005200          INVALID KEY
005300          DISPLAY "ERROR ADDING THE RECORD".
005400
005500 LOAD-RECORD-VALUES.
005600      MOVE NEW-NAME TO VENDOR-NAME.
005700      MOVE NEW-ADDRESS-1 TO VENDOR-ADDRESS-1.
005800      MOVE NEW-ADDRESS-2 TO VENDOR-ADDRESS-2.
005900      MOVE NEW-CITY TO VENDOR-CITY.
006000      MOVE NEW-STATE TO VENDOR-STATE.
006100      MOVE NEW-ZIP TO VENDOR-ZIP.
006200      MOVE NEW-CONTACT TO VENDOR-CONTACT.
006300      MOVE NEW-PHONE TO VENDOR-PHONE.
006400
```

A

Exercises

1. The IF test is wrong, causing the program to attempt to change a record when it doesn't exist and add a record when it does exist.

2. The correction is shown in Listing A.21.

TYPE **Listing A.21. Correcting the bug.**

```
003200 ADD-OR-UPDATE.
003300     MOVE "Y" TO RECORD-FOUND-FLAG.
003400     MOVE NEW-NUMBER TO VENDOR-NUMBER.
003500     READ VENDOR-RECORD
003600         INVALID KEY
003700         MOVE "N" TO RECORD-FOUND-FLAG.
003800     IF RECORD-FOUND-FLAG = "Y"
003900         PERFORM CHANGE-THIS-RECORD
004000     ELSE
004100         PERFORM ADD-THIS-RECORD.
004200
004300 CHANGE-THIS-RECORD.
004400     PERFORM LOAD-RECORD-VALUES.
004500     REWRITE VENDOR-RECORD
004600         INVALID KEY
004700         DISPLAY "ERROR CHANGING THE RECORD".
004800
004900 ADD-THIS-RECORD.
005000     PERFORM LOAD-RECORD-VALUES.
005100     WRITE VENDOR-RECORD
005200         INVALID KEY
005300         DISPLAY "ERROR ADDING THE RECORD".
005400
005500 LOAD-RECORD-VALUES.
005600     MOVE NEW-NAME TO VENDOR-NAME.
005700     MOVE NEW-ADDRESS-1 TO VENDOR-ADDRESS-1.
005800     MOVE NEW-ADDRESS-2 TO VENDOR-ADDRESS-2.
005900     MOVE NEW-CITY TO VENDOR-CITY.
006000     MOVE NEW-STATE TO VENDOR-STATE.
006100     MOVE NEW-ZIP TO VENDOR-ZIP.
006200     MOVE NEW-CONTACT TO VENDOR-CONTACT.
006300     MOVE NEW-PHONE TO VENDOR-PHONE.
006400
```

Answers to Day 13, "Deleting Records and Other Indexed File Operations"

Quiz

1. c. Change, inquire, and delete modes frequently are similar.

2. Change, inquire, and delete modes all require the user to enter a key value of a
   record that is looked up in the file. This record must be found before the remainder
   of the change, inquire, or delete action is undertaken.

Exercise

Listing A.22 uses COPY directives.

TYPE   **Listing A.22. Using COPY directives.**

```
000100 IDENTIFICATION DIVISION.
000200 PROGRAM-ID. VNDDSP02.
000300*-----------------------------------------------
000400* Display records in the Vendor File.
000500*-----------------------------------------------
000600 ENVIRONMENT DIVISION.
000700 INPUT-OUTPUT SECTION.
000800 FILE-CONTROL.
000900
001000     COPY "SLVND01.CBL".
001100
001200 DATA DIVISION.
001300 FILE SECTION.
001400
001500     COPY "FDVND02.CBL".
001600
001700 WORKING-STORAGE SECTION.
001800
001900 01  DETAIL-LINE.
002000     05  DISPLAY-NUMBER      PIC 9(5).
002100     05  FILLER             PIC X       VALUE SPACE.
002200     05  DISPLAY-NAME       PIC X(30).
002300     05  FILLER             PIC X       VALUE SPACE.
002400     05  DISPLAY-CONTACT    PIC X(30).
002500
002600 01  CITY-STATE-DETAIL.
002700     05  DISPLAY-CITY       PIC X(20).
002800     05  FILLER             PIC X VALUE SPACE.
002900     05  DISPLAY-STATE      PIC X(2).
003000
003100 01  COLUMN-LINE.
003200     05  FILLER         PIC X(2)  VALUE "NO".
003300     05  FILLER         PIC X(4) VALUE SPACE.
003400     05  FILLER         PIC X(12) VALUE "NAME-ADDRESS".
003500     05  FILLER         PIC X(19) VALUE SPACE.
003600     05  FILLER         PIC X(17) VALUE "CONTACT-PHONE-ZIP".
003700
003800 01  TITLE-LINE.
003900     05  FILLER             PIC X(15) VALUE SPACE.
004000     05  FILLER             PIC X(11)
004100         VALUE "VENDOR LIST".
004200     05  FILLER             PIC X(15) VALUE SPACE.
```

continues

Listing A.22. continued

```
004300     05   FILLER              PIC X(5) VALUE "PAGE:".
004400     05   FILLER              PIC X(1) VALUE SPACE.
004500     05   DISPLAY-PAGE-NUMBER PIC ZZZZ9.
004600
004700 77 FILE-AT-END              PIC X.
004800 77 A-DUMMY                  PIC X.
004900 77 LINE-COUNT               PIC 999 VALUE ZERO.
005000 77 PAGE-NUMBER              PIC 99999 VALUE ZERO.
005100 77 MAXIMUM-LINES            PIC 999 VALUE 15.
005200
005300 77 DISPLAY-RECORD           PIC X(79).
005400
005500 PROCEDURE DIVISION.
005600 PROGRAM-BEGIN.
005700
005800     PERFORM OPENING-PROCEDURE.
005900     MOVE ZEROES TO LINE-COUNT
006000                    PAGE-NUMBER.
006100
006200     PERFORM START-NEW-PAGE.
006300
006400     MOVE "N" TO FILE-AT-END.
006500     PERFORM READ-NEXT-RECORD.
006600     IF FILE-AT-END = "Y"
006700         MOVE "NO RECORDS FOUND" TO DISPLAY-RECORD
006800         PERFORM WRITE-DISPLAY-RECORD
006900     ELSE
007000         PERFORM DISPLAY-VENDOR-FIELDS
007100             UNTIL FILE-AT-END = "Y".
007200
007300     PERFORM CLOSING-PROCEDURE.
007400
007500
007600 PROGRAM-DONE.
007700     STOP RUN.
007800
007900 OPENING-PROCEDURE.
008000     OPEN I-O VENDOR-FILE.
008100
008200 CLOSING-PROCEDURE.
008300     CLOSE VENDOR-FILE.
008400
008500 DISPLAY-VENDOR-FIELDS.
008600     IF LINE-COUNT > MAXIMUM-LINES
008700         PERFORM START-NEXT-PAGE.
008800     PERFORM DISPLAY-THE-RECORD.
008900     PERFORM READ-NEXT-RECORD.
009000
009100 DISPLAY-THE-RECORD.
009200     PERFORM DISPLAY-LINE-1.
009300     PERFORM DISPLAY-LINE-2.
009400     PERFORM DISPLAY-LINE-3.
009500     PERFORM DISPLAY-LINE-4.
009600     PERFORM LINE-FEED.
```

```
009700
009800 DISPLAY-LINE-1.
009900      MOVE SPACE TO DETAIL-LINE.
010000      MOVE VENDOR-NUMBER TO DISPLAY-NUMBER.
010100      MOVE VENDOR-NAME TO DISPLAY-NAME.
010200      MOVE VENDOR-CONTACT TO DISPLAY-CONTACT.
010300      MOVE DETAIL-LINE TO DISPLAY-RECORD.
010400      PERFORM WRITE-DISPLAY-RECORD.
010500
010600 DISPLAY-LINE-2.
010700      MOVE SPACE TO DETAIL-LINE.
010800      MOVE VENDOR-ADDRESS-1 TO DISPLAY-NAME.
010900      MOVE VENDOR-PHONE TO DISPLAY-CONTACT.
011000      MOVE DETAIL-LINE TO DISPLAY-RECORD.
011100      PERFORM WRITE-DISPLAY-RECORD.
011200
011300 DISPLAY-LINE-3.
011400      MOVE SPACE TO DETAIL-LINE.
011500      MOVE VENDOR-ADDRESS-2 TO DISPLAY-NAME.
011600      IF VENDOR-ADDRESS-2 NOT = SPACE
011700          MOVE DETAIL-LINE TO DISPLAY-RECORD
011800          PERFORM WRITE-DISPLAY-RECORD.
011900
012000 DISPLAY-LINE-4.
012100      MOVE SPACE TO DETAIL-LINE.
012200      MOVE VENDOR-CITY TO DISPLAY-CITY.
012300      MOVE VENDOR-STATE TO DISPLAY-STATE.
012400      MOVE CITY-STATE-DETAIL TO DISPLAY-NAME.
012500      MOVE VENDOR-ZIP TO DISPLAY-CONTACT.
012600      MOVE DETAIL-LINE TO DISPLAY-RECORD.
012700      PERFORM WRITE-DISPLAY-RECORD.
012800
012900 READ-NEXT-RECORD.
013000      READ VENDOR-FILE NEXT RECORD
013100          AT END MOVE "Y" TO FILE-AT-END.
013200
013300 WRITE-DISPLAY-RECORD.
013400      DISPLAY DISPLAY-RECORD.
013500      ADD 1 TO LINE-COUNT.
013600
013700 LINE-FEED.
013800      MOVE SPACE TO DISPLAY-RECORD.
013900      PERFORM WRITE-DISPLAY-RECORD.
014000
014100 START-NEXT-PAGE.
014200
014300      PERFORM END-LAST-PAGE.
014400      PERFORM START-NEW-PAGE.
014500
014600 START-NEW-PAGE.
014700      ADD 1 TO PAGE-NUMBER.
014800      MOVE PAGE-NUMBER TO DISPLAY-PAGE-NUMBER.
014900      MOVE TITLE-LINE TO DISPLAY-RECORD.
015000      PERFORM WRITE-DISPLAY-RECORD.
015100      PERFORM LINE-FEED.
```

continues

Listing A.22. continued

```
015200      MOVE COLUMN-LINE TO DISPLAY-RECORD.
015300      PERFORM WRITE-DISPLAY-RECORD.
015400      PERFORM LINE-FEED.
015500
015600 END-LAST-PAGE.
015700      PERFORM PRESS-ENTER.
015800      MOVE ZERO TO LINE-COUNT.
015900
016000 PRESS-ENTER.
016100      DISPLAY "PRESS ENTER TO CONTINUE. . .".
016200      ACCEPT A-DUMMY.
016300
```

Answers to Day 14, "A Review of Indexed Files"

Quiz

1. Remember: Write or rewrite a record; do everything else to a file. The correct command for reading a record in the file is b:

```
READ CUSTOMER-FILE RECORD
    INVALID KEY MOVE "N" TO RECORD-FOUND.
```

2. Remember: Write or rewrite a record; do everything else to a file. The correct command for writing a new record to the file is a:

```
WRITE CUSTOMER-RECORD
    INVALID KEY
      DISPLAY "RECORD ALREADY ON FILE".
```

Exercises

1. Listings A.23, A.24, A.25, and A.26 are each highlighted in bold type for add, change, inquire, and delete mode, respectively.

TYPE   Listing A.23. Add mode.

```
000100 IDENTIFICATION DIVISION.
000200 PROGRAM-ID. VNDMNT01.
000300*-------------------------------
000400* Add, Change, Inquire and Delete
000500* for the Vendor File.
000600*-------------------------------
000700 ENVIRONMENT DIVISION.
000800 INPUT-OUTPUT SECTION.
000900 FILE-CONTROL.
```

```
001000
001100     COPY "SLVND01.CBL".
001200
001300 DATA DIVISION.
001400 FILE SECTION.
001500
001600     COPY "FDVND02.CBL".
001700
001800 WORKING-STORAGE SECTION.
001900
002000 77  MENU-PICK                    PIC 9.
002100     88  MENU-PICK-IS-VALID        VALUES 0 THRU 4.
002200
002300 77  THE-MODE                     PIC X(7).
002400 77  WHICH-FIELD                  PIC 9.
002500 77  OK-TO-DELETE                 PIC X.
002600 77  RECORD-FOUND                 PIC X.
002700 77  VENDOR-NUMBER-FIELD          PIC Z(5).
002800
002900 PROCEDURE DIVISION.
003000 PROGRAM-BEGIN.
003100     PERFORM OPENING-PROCEDURE.
003200     PERFORM MAIN-PROCESS.
003300     PERFORM CLOSING-PROCEDURE.
003400
003500 PROGRAM-DONE.
003600     STOP RUN.
003700
003800 OPENING-PROCEDURE.
003900     OPEN I-O VENDOR-FILE.
004000
004100 CLOSING-PROCEDURE.
004200     CLOSE VENDOR-FILE.
004300
004400
004500 MAIN-PROCESS.
004600     PERFORM GET-MENU-PICK.
004700     PERFORM MAINTAIN-THE-FILE
004800         UNTIL MENU-PICK = 0.
004900
005000*- - - - - - - - - - - - - - - - - - - - - - - - - - - -
005100* MENU
005200*- - - - - - - - - - - - - - - - - - - - - - - - - - - -
005300 GET-MENU-PICK.
005400     PERFORM DISPLAY-THE-MENU.
005500     PERFORM GET-THE-PICK.
005600     PERFORM MENU-RETRY
005700         UNTIL MENU-PICK-IS-VALID.
005800
005900 DISPLAY-THE-MENU.
006000     PERFORM CLEAR-SCREEN.
006100     DISPLAY "    PLEASE SELECT:".
006200     DISPLAY " ".
006300     DISPLAY "         1.  ADD RECORDS".
006400     DISPLAY "         2.  CHANGE A RECORD".
```

continues

Listing A.23. continued

```
006500        DISPLAY "       3.   LOOK UP A RECORD".
006600        DISPLAY "       4.   DELETE A RECORD".
006700        DISPLAY " ".
006800        DISPLAY "       0.   EXIT".
006900        PERFORM SCROLL-LINE 8 TIMES.
007000
007100 GET-THE-PICK.
007200        DISPLAY "YOUR CHOICE (0-4)?".
007300        ACCEPT MENU-PICK.
007400 MENU-RETRY.
007500        DISPLAY "INVALID SELECTION - PLEASE RE-TRY.".
007600        PERFORM GET-THE-PICK.
007700 CLEAR-SCREEN.
007800        PERFORM SCROLL-LINE 25 TIMES.
007900
008000 SCROLL-LINE.
008100        DISPLAY " ".
008200
008300 MAINTAIN-THE-FILE.
008400        PERFORM DO-THE-PICK.
008500        PERFORM GET-MENU-PICK.
008600
008700 DO-THE-PICK.
008800        IF MENU-PICK = 1
008900            PERFORM ADD-MODE
009000        ELSE
009100        IF MENU-PICK = 2
009200            PERFORM CHANGE-MODE
009300        ELSE
009400        IF MENU-PICK = 3
009500            PERFORM INQUIRE-MODE
009600        ELSE
009700        IF MENU-PICK = 4
009800            PERFORM DELETE-MODE.
009900
010000*-------------------------------
010100* ADD
010200*-------------------------------
010300 ADD-MODE.
010400        MOVE "ADD" TO THE-MODE.
010500        PERFORM GET-NEW-VENDOR-NUMBER.
010600        PERFORM ADD-RECORDS
010700            UNTIL VENDOR-NUMBER = ZEROES.
010800
010900 GET-NEW-VENDOR-NUMBER.
011000        PERFORM INIT-VENDOR-RECORD.
011100        PERFORM ENTER-VENDOR-NUMBER.
011200        MOVE "Y" TO RECORD-FOUND.
011300        PERFORM FIND-NEW-VENDOR-RECORD
011400            UNTIL RECORD-FOUND = "N" OR
011500                  VENDOR-NUMBER = ZEROES.
011600
011700 FIND-NEW-VENDOR-RECORD.
011800        PERFORM READ-VENDOR-RECORD.
```

```
011900     IF RECORD-FOUND = "Y"
012000         DISPLAY "RECORD ALREADY ON FILE"
012100         PERFORM ENTER-VENDOR-NUMBER.
012200
012300 ADD-RECORDS.
012400     PERFORM ENTER-REMAINING-FIELDS.
012500     PERFORM WRITE-VENDOR-RECORD.
012600     PERFORM GET-NEW-VENDOR-NUMBER.
012700
012800 ENTER-REMAINING-FIELDS.
012900     PERFORM ENTER-VENDOR-NAME.
013000     PERFORM ENTER-VENDOR-ADDRESS-1.
013100     PERFORM ENTER-VENDOR-ADDRESS-2.
013200     PERFORM ENTER-VENDOR-CITY.
013300     PERFORM ENTER-VENDOR-STATE.
013400     PERFORM ENTER-VENDOR-ZIP.
013500     PERFORM ENTER-VENDOR-CONTACT.
013600     PERFORM ENTER-VENDOR-PHONE.
013700
013800*------------------------------
013900* CHANGE
014000*------------------------------
014100 CHANGE-MODE.
014200     MOVE "CHANGE" TO THE-MODE.
014300     PERFORM GET-VENDOR-RECORD.
014400     PERFORM CHANGE-RECORDS
014500         UNTIL VENDOR-NUMBER = ZEROES.
014600
014700 CHANGE-RECORDS.
014800     PERFORM GET-FIELD-TO-CHANGE.
014900     PERFORM CHANGE-ONE-FIELD
015000         UNTIL WHICH-FIELD = ZERO.
015100     PERFORM GET-VENDOR-RECORD.
015200
015300 GET-FIELD-TO-CHANGE.
015400     PERFORM DISPLAY-ALL-FIELDS.
015500     PERFORM ASK-WHICH-FIELD.
015600
015700 ASK-WHICH-FIELD.
015800     DISPLAY "ENTER THE NUMBER OF THE FIELD".
015900     DISPLAY "TO CHANGE (1-8) OR 0 TO EXIT".
016000     ACCEPT WHICH-FIELD.
016100     IF WHICH-FIELD > 8
016200         DISPLAY "INVALID ENTRY".
016300
016400 CHANGE-ONE-FIELD.
016500     PERFORM CHANGE-THIS-FIELD.
016600     PERFORM GET-FIELD-TO-CHANGE.
016700
016800 CHANGE-THIS-FIELD.
016900     IF WHICH-FIELD = 1
017000         PERFORM ENTER-VENDOR-NAME.
017100     IF WHICH-FIELD = 2
017200         PERFORM ENTER-VENDOR-ADDRESS-1.
017300     IF WHICH-FIELD = 3
```

continues

Listing A.23. continued

```
017400          PERFORM ENTER-VENDOR-ADDRESS-2.
017500     IF WHICH-FIELD = 4
017600          PERFORM ENTER-VENDOR-CITY.
017700     IF WHICH-FIELD = 5
017800          PERFORM ENTER-VENDOR-STATE.
017900     IF WHICH-FIELD = 6
018000          PERFORM ENTER-VENDOR-ZIP.
018100     IF WHICH-FIELD = 7
018200          PERFORM ENTER-VENDOR-CONTACT.
018300     IF WHICH-FIELD = 8
018400          PERFORM ENTER-VENDOR-PHONE.
018500
018600     PERFORM REWRITE-VENDOR-RECORD.
018700
018800*------------------------------
018900* INQUIRE
019000*------------------------------
019100 INQUIRE-MODE.
019200     MOVE "DISPLAY" TO THE-MODE.
019300     PERFORM GET-VENDOR-RECORD.
019400     PERFORM INQUIRE-RECORDS
019500          UNTIL VENDOR-NUMBER = ZEROES.
019600
019700 INQUIRE-RECORDS.
019800     PERFORM DISPLAY-ALL-FIELDS.
019900     PERFORM GET-VENDOR-RECORD.
020000
020100*------------------------------
020200* DELETE
020300*------------------------------
020400 DELETE-MODE.
020500     MOVE "DELETE" TO THE-MODE.
020600     PERFORM GET-VENDOR-RECORD.
020700     PERFORM DELETE-RECORDS
020800          UNTIL VENDOR-NUMBER = ZEROES.
020900
021000 DELETE-RECORDS.
021100     PERFORM DISPLAY-ALL-FIELDS.
021200     MOVE "X" TO OK-TO-DELETE.
021300
021400     PERFORM ASK-TO-DELETE
021500          UNTIL OK-TO-DELETE = "Y" OR "N".
021600
021700     IF OK-TO-DELETE = "Y"
021800          PERFORM DELETE-VENDOR-RECORD.
021900
022000     PERFORM GET-VENDOR-RECORD.
022100
022200 ASK-TO-DELETE.
022300     DISPLAY "DELETE THIS RECORD (Y/N)?".
022400     ACCEPT OK-TO-DELETE.
022500     IF OK-TO-DELETE = "y"
022600          MOVE "Y" TO OK-TO-DELETE.
022700     IF OK-TO-DELETE = "n"
```

```
022800          MOVE "N" TO OK-TO-DELETE.
022900      IF OK-TO-DELETE NOT = "Y" AND
023000          OK-TO-DELETE NOT = "N"
023100          DISPLAY "YOU MUST ENTER YES OR NO".
023200
023300*-------------------------------
023400* Routines shared by all modes
023500*-------------------------------
023600 INIT-VENDOR-RECORD.
023700      MOVE SPACE TO VENDOR-RECORD.
023800      MOVE ZEROES TO VENDOR-NUMBER.
023900
024000 ENTER-VENDOR-NUMBER.
024100      DISPLAY " ".
024200      DISPLAY "ENTER VENDOR NUMBER OF THE VENDOR" .
024300      DISPLAY "TO " THE-MODE " (1-99999)".
024400      DISPLAY "ENTER 0 TO STOP ENTRY".
024500      ACCEPT VENDOR-NUMBER-FIELD.
024600*OR   ACCEPT VENDOR-NUMBER-FIELD WITH CONVERSION.
024700
024800      MOVE VENDOR-NUMBER-FIELD TO VENDOR-NUMBER.
024900
025000 GET-VENDOR-RECORD.
025100      PERFORM INIT-VENDOR-RECORD.
025200      PERFORM ENTER-VENDOR-NUMBER.
025300      MOVE "N" TO RECORD-FOUND.
025400      PERFORM FIND-VENDOR-RECORD
025500          UNTIL RECORD-FOUND = "Y" OR
025600              VENDOR-NUMBER = ZEROES.
025700
025800*-------------------------------
025900* Routines shared Add and Change
026000*-------------------------------
026100 FIND-VENDOR-RECORD.
026200      PERFORM READ-VENDOR-RECORD.
026300      IF RECORD-FOUND = "N"
026400          DISPLAY "RECORD NOT FOUND"
026500        * PERFORM ENTER-VENDOR-NUMBER.
026600
026700 ENTER-VENDOR-NAME.
026800      DISPLAY "ENTER VENDOR NAME".
026900      ACCEPT VENDOR-NAME.
027000
027100 ENTER-VENDOR-ADDRESS-1.
027200      DISPLAY "ENTER VENDOR ADDRESS-1".
027300      ACCEPT VENDOR-ADDRESS-1.
027400
027500 ENTER-VENDOR-ADDRESS-2.
027600      DISPLAY "ENTER VENDOR ADDRESS-2".
027700      ACCEPT VENDOR-ADDRESS-2.
027800
027900 ENTER-VENDOR-CITY.
028000      DISPLAY "ENTER VENDOR CITY".
028100      ACCEPT VENDOR-CITY.
028200
```

continues

Listing A.23. continued

```
028300 ENTER-VENDOR-STATE.
028400      DISPLAY "ENTER VENDOR STATE".
028500      ACCEPT VENDOR-STATE.
028600
028700 ENTER-VENDOR-ZIP.
028800      DISPLAY "ENTER VENDOR ZIP".
028900      ACCEPT VENDOR-ZIP.
029000
029100 ENTER-VENDOR-CONTACT.
029200      DISPLAY "ENTER VENDOR CONTACT".
029300      ACCEPT VENDOR-CONTACT.
029400
029500 ENTER-VENDOR-PHONE.
029600      DISPLAY "ENTER VENDOR PHONE".
029700      ACCEPT VENDOR-PHONE.
029800
029900*--------------------------------
030000* Routines shared by Change,
030100* Inquire and Delete
030200*--------------------------------
030300 DISPLAY-ALL-FIELDS.
030400      DISPLAY " ".
030500      PERFORM DISPLAY-VENDOR-NUMBER.
030600      PERFORM DISPLAY-VENDOR-NAME.
030700      PERFORM DISPLAY-VENDOR-ADDRESS-1.
030800      PERFORM DISPLAY-VENDOR-ADDRESS-2.
030900      PERFORM DISPLAY-VENDOR-CITY.
031000      PERFORM DISPLAY-VENDOR-STATE.
031100      PERFORM DISPLAY-VENDOR-ZIP.
031200      PERFORM DISPLAY-VENDOR-CONTACT.
031300      PERFORM DISPLAY-VENDOR-PHONE.
031400      DISPLAY " ".
031500
031600 DISPLAY-VENDOR-NUMBER.
031700      DISPLAY "   VENDOR NUMBER: " VENDOR-NUMBER.
031800
031900 DISPLAY-VENDOR-NAME.
032000      DISPLAY "1. VENDOR NAME: " VENDOR-NAME.
032100
032200 DISPLAY-VENDOR-ADDRESS-1.
032300      DISPLAY "2. VENDOR ADDRESS-1: " VENDOR-ADDRESS-1.
032400
032500 DISPLAY-VENDOR-ADDRESS-2.
032600      DISPLAY "3. VENDOR ADDRESS-2: " VENDOR-ADDRESS-2.
032700
032800 DISPLAY-VENDOR-CITY.
032900      DISPLAY "4. VENDOR CITY: " VENDOR-CITY.
033000
033100 DISPLAY-VENDOR-STATE.
033200      DISPLAY "5. VENDOR STATE: " VENDOR-STATE.
033300
033400 DISPLAY-VENDOR-ZIP.
033500      DISPLAY "6. VENDOR ZIP: " VENDOR-ZIP.
033600
```

```
033700 DISPLAY-VENDOR-CONTACT.
033800     DISPLAY "7. VENDOR CONTACT: " VENDOR-CONTACT.
033900
034000 DISPLAY-VENDOR-PHONE.
034100     DISPLAY "8. VENDOR PHONE: " VENDOR-PHONE.
034200
034300*-------------------------------
034400* File I-O Routines
034500*-------------------------------
034600 READ-VENDOR-RECORD.
034700     MOVE "Y" TO RECORD-FOUND.
034800     READ VENDOR-FILE RECORD
034900        INVALID KEY
035000           MOVE "N" TO RECORD-FOUND.
035100
035200*or  READ VENDOR-FILE RECORD WITH LOCK
035300*       INVALID KEY
035400*          MOVE "N" TO RECORD-FOUND.
035500
035600*or  READ VENDOR-FILE RECORD WITH HOLD
035700*       INVALID KEY
035800*          MOVE "N" TO RECORD-FOUND.
035900
036000 WRITE-VENDOR-RECORD.
036100     WRITE VENDOR-RECORD
036200        INVALID KEY
036300        DISPLAY "RECORD ALREADY ON FILE".
036400
036500 REWRITE-VENDOR-RECORD.
036600     REWRITE VENDOR-RECORD
036700        INVALID KEY
036800        DISPLAY "ERROR REWRITING VENDOR RECORD".
036900
037000 DELETE-VENDOR-RECORD.
037100     DELETE VENDOR-FILE RECORD
037200        INVALID KEY
037300        DISPLAY "ERROR DELETING VENDOR RECORD".
037400
```

TYPE | **Listing A.24. Change mode.**

```
000100 IDENTIFICATION DIVISION.
000200 PROGRAM-ID. VNDMNT01.
000300*-------------------------------
000400* Add, Change, Inquire and Delete
000500* for the Vendor File.
000600*-------------------------------
000700 ENVIRONMENT DIVISION.
000800 INPUT-OUTPUT SECTION.
000900 FILE-CONTROL.
001000
001100     COPY "SLVND01.CBL".
```

continues

Listing A.24. continued

```
001200
001300 DATA DIVISION.
001400 FILE SECTION.
001500
001600     COPY "FDVND02.CBL".
001700
001800 WORKING-STORAGE SECTION.
001900
002000 77  MENU-PICK                 PIC 9.
002100     88  MENU-PICK-IS-VALID     VALUES 0 THRU 4.
002200
002300 77  THE-MODE                  PIC X(7).
002400 77  WHICH-FIELD               PIC 9.
002500 77  OK-TO-DELETE              PIC X.
002600 77  RECORD-FOUND              PIC X.
002700 77  VENDOR-NUMBER-FIELD       PIC Z(5).
002800
002900 PROCEDURE DIVISION.
003000 PROGRAM-BEGIN.
003100     PERFORM OPENING-PROCEDURE.
003200     PERFORM MAIN-PROCESS.
003300     PERFORM CLOSING-PROCEDURE.
003400
003500 PROGRAM-DONE.
003600     STOP RUN.
003700
003800 OPENING-PROCEDURE.
003900     OPEN I-O VENDOR-FILE.
004000
004100 CLOSING-PROCEDURE.
004200     CLOSE VENDOR-FILE.
004300
004400
004500 MAIN-PROCESS.
004600     PERFORM GET-MENU-PICK.
004700     PERFORM MAINTAIN-THE-FILE
004800         UNTIL MENU-PICK = 0.
004900
005000*-------------------------------
005100* MENU
005200*-------------------------------
005300 GET-MENU-PICK.
005400     PERFORM DISPLAY-THE-MENU.
005500     PERFORM GET-THE-PICK.
005600     PERFORM MENU-RETRY
005700         UNTIL MENU-PICK-IS-VALID.
005800
005900 DISPLAY-THE-MENU.
006000     PERFORM CLEAR-SCREEN.
006100     DISPLAY "    PLEASE SELECT:".
006200     DISPLAY " ".
006300     DISPLAY "       1.  ADD RECORDS".
006400     DISPLAY "       2.  CHANGE A RECORD".
006500     DISPLAY "       3.  LOOK UP A RECORD".
```

```
006600      DISPLAY "           4.   DELETE A RECORD".
006700      DISPLAY " ".
006800      DISPLAY "           0.   EXIT".
006900      PERFORM SCROLL-LINE 8 TIMES.
007000
007100 GET-THE-PICK.
007200      DISPLAY "YOUR CHOICE (0-4)?".
007300      ACCEPT MENU-PICK.
007400 MENU-RETRY.
007500      DISPLAY "INVALID SELECTION - PLEASE RE-TRY.".
007600      PERFORM GET-THE-PICK.
007700 CLEAR-SCREEN.
007800      PERFORM SCROLL-LINE 25 TIMES.
007900
008000 SCROLL-LINE.
008100      DISPLAY " ".
008200
008300 MAINTAIN-THE-FILE.
008400      PERFORM DO-THE-PICK.
008500      PERFORM GET-MENU-PICK.
008600
008700 DO-THE-PICK.
008800      IF MENU-PICK = 1
008900          PERFORM ADD-MODE
009000      ELSE
009100      IF MENU-PICK = 2
009200          PERFORM CHANGE-MODE
009300      ELSE
009400      IF MENU-PICK = 3
009500          PERFORM INQUIRE-MODE
009600      ELSE
009700      IF MENU-PICK = 4
009800          PERFORM DELETE-MODE.
009900
010000*-------------------------------
010100* ADD
010200*-------------------------------
010300 ADD-MODE.
010400      MOVE "ADD" TO THE-MODE.
010500      PERFORM GET-NEW-VENDOR-NUMBER.
010600      PERFORM ADD-RECORDS
010700          UNTIL VENDOR-NUMBER = ZEROES.
010800
010900 GET-NEW-VENDOR-NUMBER.
011000      PERFORM INIT-VENDOR-RECORD.
011100      PERFORM ENTER-VENDOR-NUMBER.
011200      MOVE "Y" TO RECORD-FOUND.
011300      PERFORM FIND-NEW-VENDOR-RECORD
011400          UNTIL RECORD-FOUND = "N" OR
011500                VENDOR-NUMBER = ZEROES.
011600
011700 FIND-NEW-VENDOR-RECORD.
011800      PERFORM READ-VENDOR-RECORD.
011900      IF RECORD-FOUND = "Y"
012000          DISPLAY "RECORD ALREADY ON FILE"
```

continues

Listing A.24. continued

```
012100          PERFORM ENTER-VENDOR-NUMBER.
012200
012300 ADD-RECORDS.
012400          PERFORM ENTER-REMAINING-FIELDS.
012500          PERFORM WRITE-VENDOR-RECORD.
012600          PERFORM GET-NEW-VENDOR-NUMBER.
012700
012800 ENTER-REMAINING-FIELDS.
012900          PERFORM ENTER-VENDOR-NAME.
013000          PERFORM ENTER-VENDOR-ADDRESS-1.
013100          PERFORM ENTER-VENDOR-ADDRESS-2.
013200          PERFORM ENTER-VENDOR-CITY.
013300          PERFORM ENTER-VENDOR-STATE.
013400          PERFORM ENTER-VENDOR-ZIP.
013500          PERFORM ENTER-VENDOR-CONTACT.
013600          PERFORM ENTER-VENDOR-PHONE.
013700
013800*------------------------------
013900* CHANGE
014000*------------------------------
014100 CHANGE-MODE.
014200          MOVE "CHANGE" TO THE-MODE.
014300          PERFORM GET-VENDOR-RECORD.
014400          PERFORM CHANGE-RECORDS
014500              UNTIL VENDOR-NUMBER = ZEROES.
014600
014700 CHANGE-RECORDS.
014800          PERFORM GET-FIELD-TO-CHANGE.
014900          PERFORM CHANGE-ONE-FIELD
015000              UNTIL WHICH-FIELD = ZERO.
015100          PERFORM GET-VENDOR-RECORD.
015200
015300 GET-FIELD-TO-CHANGE.
015400          PERFORM DISPLAY-ALL-FIELDS.
015500          PERFORM ASK-WHICH-FIELD.
015600
015700 ASK-WHICH-FIELD.
015800          DISPLAY "ENTER THE NUMBER OF THE FIELD".
015900          DISPLAY "TO CHANGE (1-8) OR 0 TO EXIT".
016000          ACCEPT WHICH-FIELD.
016100          IF WHICH-FIELD > 8
016200              DISPLAY "INVALID ENTRY".
016300
016400 CHANGE-ONE-FIELD.
016500          PERFORM CHANGE-THIS-FIELD.
016600          PERFORM GET-FIELD-TO-CHANGE.
016700
016800 CHANGE-THIS-FIELD.
016900          IF WHICH-FIELD = 1
017000              PERFORM ENTER-VENDOR-NAME.
017100          IF WHICH-FIELD = 2
017200              PERFORM ENTER-VENDOR-ADDRESS-1.
017300          IF WHICH-FIELD = 3
017400              PERFORM ENTER-VENDOR-ADDRESS-2.
```

```
017500     IF WHICH-FIELD = 4
017600         PERFORM ENTER-VENDOR-CITY.
017700     IF WHICH-FIELD = 5
017800         PERFORM ENTER-VENDOR-STATE.
017900     IF WHICH-FIELD = 6
018000         PERFORM ENTER-VENDOR-ZIP.
018100     IF WHICH-FIELD = 7
018200         PERFORM ENTER-VENDOR-CONTACT.
018300     IF WHICH-FIELD = 8
018400         PERFORM ENTER-VENDOR-PHONE.
018500
018600     PERFORM REWRITE-VENDOR-RECORD.
018700
018800*------------------------------
018900* INQUIRE
019000*------------------------------
019100 INQUIRE-MODE.
019200     MOVE "DISPLAY" TO THE-MODE.
019300     PERFORM GET-VENDOR-RECORD.
019400     PERFORM INQUIRE-RECORDS
019500         UNTIL VENDOR-NUMBER = ZEROES.
019600
019700 INQUIRE-RECORDS.
019800     PERFORM DISPLAY-ALL-FIELDS.
019900     PERFORM GET-VENDOR-RECORD.
020000
020100*------------------------------
020200* DELETE
020300*------------------------------
020400 DELETE-MODE.
020500     MOVE "DELETE" TO THE-MODE.
020600     PERFORM GET-VENDOR-RECORD.
020700     PERFORM DELETE-RECORDS
020800         UNTIL VENDOR-NUMBER = ZEROES.
020900
021000 DELETE-RECORDS.
021100     PERFORM DISPLAY-ALL-FIELDS.
021200     MOVE "X" TO OK-TO-DELETE.
021300
021400     PERFORM ASK-TO-DELETE
021500         UNTIL OK-TO-DELETE = "Y" OR "N".
021600
021700     IF OK-TO-DELETE = "Y"
021800         PERFORM DELETE-VENDOR-RECORD.
021900
022000     PERFORM GET-VENDOR-RECORD.
022100
022200 ASK-TO-DELETE.
022300     DISPLAY "DELETE THIS RECORD (Y/N)?".
022400     ACCEPT OK-TO-DELETE.
022500     IF OK-TO-DELETE = "y"
022600         MOVE "Y" TO OK-TO-DELETE.
022700     IF OK-TO-DELETE = "n"
022800         MOVE "N" TO OK-TO-DELETE.
022900     IF OK-TO-DELETE NOT = "Y" AND
```

continues

Listing A.24. continued

```
023000          OK-TO-DELETE NOT = "N"
023100            DISPLAY "YOU MUST ENTER YES OR NO".
023200
023300*--------------------------------
023400* Routines shared by all modes
023500*--------------------------------
023600 INIT-VENDOR-RECORD.
023700      MOVE SPACE TO VENDOR-RECORD.
023800      MOVE ZEROES TO VENDOR-NUMBER.
023900
024000 ENTER-VENDOR-NUMBER.
024100      DISPLAY " ".
024200      DISPLAY "ENTER VENDOR NUMBER OF THE VENDOR" .
024300      DISPLAY "TO " THE-MODE " (1-99999)".
024400      DISPLAY "ENTER 0 TO STOP ENTRY".
024500      ACCEPT VENDOR-NUMBER-FIELD.
024600*OR  ACCEPT VENDOR-NUMBER-FIELD WITH CONVERSION.
024700
024800      MOVE VENDOR-NUMBER-FIELD TO VENDOR-NUMBER.
024900
025000 GET-VENDOR-RECORD.
025100      PERFORM INIT-VENDOR-RECORD.
025200      PERFORM ENTER-VENDOR-NUMBER.
025300      MOVE "N" TO RECORD-FOUND.
025400      PERFORM FIND-VENDOR-RECORD
025500          UNTIL RECORD-FOUND = "Y" OR
025600              VENDOR-NUMBER = ZEROES.
025700
025800*--------------------------------
025900* Routines shared by Add and Change
026000*--------------------------------
026100 FIND-VENDOR-RECORD.
026200      PERFORM READ-VENDOR-RECORD.
026300      IF RECORD-FOUND = "N"
026400          DISPLAY "RECORD NOT FOUND"
026500          PERFORM ENTER-VENDOR-NUMBER.
026600
026700 ENTER-VENDOR-NAME.
026800      DISPLAY "ENTER VENDOR NAME".
026900      ACCEPT VENDOR-NAME.
027000
027100 ENTER-VENDOR-ADDRESS-1.
027200      DISPLAY "ENTER VENDOR ADDRESS-1".
027300      ACCEPT VENDOR-ADDRESS-1.
027400
027500 ENTER-VENDOR-ADDRESS-2.
027600      DISPLAY "ENTER VENDOR ADDRESS-2".
027700      ACCEPT VENDOR-ADDRESS-2.
027800
027900 ENTER-VENDOR-CITY.
028000      DISPLAY "ENTER VENDOR CITY".
028100      ACCEPT VENDOR-CITY.
028200
028300 ENTER-VENDOR-STATE.
```

```
028400      DISPLAY "ENTER VENDOR STATE".
028500      ACCEPT VENDOR-STATE.
028600
028700 ENTER-VENDOR-ZIP.
028800      DISPLAY "ENTER VENDOR ZIP".
028900      ACCEPT VENDOR-ZIP.
029000
029100 ENTER-VENDOR-CONTACT.
029200      DISPLAY "ENTER VENDOR CONTACT".
029300      ACCEPT VENDOR-CONTACT.
029400
029500 ENTER-VENDOR-PHONE.
029600      DISPLAY "ENTER VENDOR PHONE".
029700      ACCEPT VENDOR-PHONE.
029800
029900*-------------------------------
030000* Routines shared by Change,
030100* Inquire and Delete
030200*-------------------------------
030300 DISPLAY-ALL-FIELDS.
030400      DISPLAY " ".
030500      PERFORM DISPLAY-VENDOR-NUMBER.
030600      PERFORM DISPLAY-VENDOR-NAME.
030700      PERFORM DISPLAY-VENDOR-ADDRESS-1.
030800      PERFORM DISPLAY-VENDOR-ADDRESS-2.
030900      PERFORM DISPLAY-VENDOR-CITY.
031000      PERFORM DISPLAY-VENDOR-STATE.
031100      PERFORM DISPLAY-VENDOR-ZIP.
031200      PERFORM DISPLAY-VENDOR-CONTACT.
031300      PERFORM DISPLAY-VENDOR-PHONE.
031400      DISPLAY " ".
031500
031600 DISPLAY-VENDOR-NUMBER.
031700      DISPLAY "   VENDOR NUMBER: " VENDOR-NUMBER.
031800
031900 DISPLAY-VENDOR-NAME.
032000      DISPLAY "1. VENDOR NAME: " VENDOR-NAME.
032100
032200 DISPLAY-VENDOR-ADDRESS-1.
032300      DISPLAY "2. VENDOR ADDRESS-1: " VENDOR-ADDRESS-1.
032400
032500 DISPLAY-VENDOR-ADDRESS-2.
032600      DISPLAY "3. VENDOR ADDRESS-2: " VENDOR-ADDRESS-2.
032700
032800 DISPLAY-VENDOR-CITY.
032900      DISPLAY "4. VENDOR CITY: " VENDOR-CITY.
033000
033100 DISPLAY-VENDOR-STATE.
033200      DISPLAY "5. VENDOR STATE: " VENDOR-STATE.
033300
033400 DISPLAY-VENDOR-ZIP.
033500      DISPLAY "6. VENDOR ZIP: " VENDOR-ZIP.
033600
033700 DISPLAY-VENDOR-CONTACT.
033800      DISPLAY "7. VENDOR CONTACT: " VENDOR-CONTACT.
```

continues

Listing A.24. continued

```
033900
034000 DISPLAY-VENDOR-PHONE.
034100     DISPLAY "8. VENDOR PHONE: " VENDOR-PHONE.
034200
034300*-------------------------------
034400* File I-O Routines
034500*-------------------------------
034600 READ-VENDOR-RECORD.
034700     MOVE "Y" TO RECORD-FOUND.
034800     READ VENDOR-FILE RECORD
034900        INVALID KEY
035000           MOVE "N" TO RECORD-FOUND.
035100
035200*or  READ VENDOR-FILE RECORD WITH LOCK
035300*       INVALID KEY
035400*          MOVE "N" TO RECORD-FOUND.
035500
035600*or  READ VENDOR-FILE RECORD WITH HOLD
035700*       INVALID KEY
035800*          MOVE "N" TO RECORD-FOUND.
035900
036000 WRITE-VENDOR-RECORD.
036100     WRITE VENDOR-RECORD
036200        INVALID KEY
036300        DISPLAY "RECORD ALREADY ON FILE".
036400
036500 REWRITE-VENDOR-RECORD.
036600     REWRITE VENDOR-RECORD
036700        INVALID KEY
036800        DISPLAY "ERROR REWRITING VENDOR RECORD".
036900
037000 DELETE-VENDOR-RECORD.
037100     DELETE VENDOR-FILE RECORD
037200        INVALID KEY
037300        DISPLAY "ERROR DELETING VENDOR RECORD".
037400
```

TYPE **Listing A.25. Inquire mode.**

```
000100 IDENTIFICATION DIVISION.
000200 PROGRAM-ID. VNDMNT01.
000300*-------------------------------
000400* Add, Change, Inquire and Delete
000500* for the Vendor File.
000600*-------------------------------
000700 ENVIRONMENT DIVISION.
000800 INPUT-OUTPUT SECTION.
000900 FILE-CONTROL.
001000
001100     COPY "SLVND01.CBL".
001200
```

```
001300 DATA DIVISION.
001400 FILE SECTION.
001500
001600      COPY "FDVND02.CBL".
001700
001800 WORKING-STORAGE SECTION.
001900
002000 77  MENU-PICK                    PIC 9.
002100      88  MENU-PICK-IS-VALID       VALUES 0 THRU 4.
002200
002300 77  THE-MODE                     PIC X(7).
002400 77  WHICH-FIELD                  PIC 9.
002500 77  OK-TO-DELETE                 PIC X.
002600 77  RECORD-FOUND                 PIC X.
002700 77  VENDOR-NUMBER-FIELD          PIC Z(5).
002800
002900 PROCEDURE DIVISION.
003000 PROGRAM-BEGIN.
003100      PERFORM OPENING-PROCEDURE.
003200      PERFORM MAIN-PROCESS.
003300      PERFORM CLOSING-PROCEDURE.
003400
003500 PROGRAM-DONE.
003600      STOP RUN.
003700
003800 OPENING-PROCEDURE.
003900      OPEN I-O VENDOR-FILE.
004000
004100 CLOSING-PROCEDURE.
004200      CLOSE VENDOR-FILE.
004300
004400
004500 MAIN-PROCESS.
004600      PERFORM GET-MENU-PICK.
004700      PERFORM MAINTAIN-THE-FILE
004800          UNTIL MENU-PICK = 0.
004900
005000*-------------------------------
005100* MENU
005200*-------------------------------
005300 GET-MENU-PICK.
005400      PERFORM DISPLAY-THE-MENU.
005500      PERFORM GET-THE-PICK.
005600      PERFORM MENU-RETRY
005700          UNTIL MENU-PICK-IS-VALID.
005800
005900 DISPLAY-THE-MENU.
006000      PERFORM CLEAR-SCREEN.
006100      DISPLAY "    PLEASE SELECT:".
006200      DISPLAY " ".
006300      DISPLAY "        1.  ADD RECORDS".
006400      DISPLAY "        2.  CHANGE A RECORD".
006500      DISPLAY "        3.  LOOK UP A RECORD".
006600      DISPLAY "        4.  DELETE A RECORD".
006700      DISPLAY " ".
```

continues

Listing A.25. continued

```
006800      DISPLAY "           0.   EXIT".
006900      PERFORM SCROLL-LINE 8 TIMES.
007000
007100 GET-THE-PICK.
007200      DISPLAY "YOUR CHOICE (0-4)?".
007300      ACCEPT MENU-PICK.
007400 MENU-RETRY.
007500      DISPLAY "INVALID SELECTION - PLEASE RE-TRY.".
007600      PERFORM GET-THE-PICK.
007700 CLEAR-SCREEN.
007800      PERFORM SCROLL-LINE 25 TIMES.
007900
008000 SCROLL-LINE.
008100      DISPLAY " ".
008200
008300 MAINTAIN-THE-FILE.
008400      PERFORM DO-THE-PICK.
008500      PERFORM GET-MENU-PICK.
008600
008700 DO-THE-PICK.
008800      IF MENU-PICK = 1
008900          PERFORM ADD-MODE
009000      ELSE
009100      IF MENU-PICK = 2
009200          PERFORM CHANGE-MODE
009300      ELSE
009400      IF MENU-PICK = 3
009500          PERFORM INQUIRE-MODE
009600      ELSE
009700      IF MENU-PICK = 4
009800          PERFORM DELETE-MODE.
009900
010000*------------------------------
010100* ADD
010200*------------------------------
010300 ADD-MODE.
010400      MOVE "ADD" TO THE-MODE.
010500      PERFORM GET-NEW-VENDOR-NUMBER.
010600      PERFORM ADD-RECORDS
010700          UNTIL VENDOR-NUMBER = ZEROES.
010800
010900 GET-NEW-VENDOR-NUMBER.
011000      PERFORM INIT-VENDOR-RECORD.
011100      PERFORM ENTER-VENDOR-NUMBER.
011200      MOVE "Y" TO RECORD-FOUND.
011300      PERFORM FIND-NEW-VENDOR-RECORD
011400          UNTIL RECORD-FOUND = "N" OR
011500              VENDOR-NUMBER = ZEROES.
011600
011700 FIND-NEW-VENDOR-RECORD.
011800      PERFORM READ-VENDOR-RECORD.
011900      IF RECORD-FOUND = "Y"
012000          DISPLAY "RECORD ALREADY ON FILE"
012100          PERFORM ENTER-VENDOR-NUMBER.
```

```
012200
012300 ADD-RECORDS.
012400      PERFORM ENTER-REMAINING-FIELDS.
012500      PERFORM WRITE-VENDOR-RECORD.
012600      PERFORM GET-NEW-VENDOR-NUMBER.
012700
012800 ENTER-REMAINING-FIELDS.
012900      PERFORM ENTER-VENDOR-NAME.
013000      PERFORM ENTER-VENDOR-ADDRESS-1.
013100      PERFORM ENTER-VENDOR-ADDRESS-2.
013200      PERFORM ENTER-VENDOR-CITY.
013300      PERFORM ENTER-VENDOR-STATE.
013400      PERFORM ENTER-VENDOR-ZIP.
013500      PERFORM ENTER-VENDOR-CONTACT.
013600      PERFORM ENTER-VENDOR-PHONE.
013700
013800*------------------------------
013900* CHANGE
014000*------------------------------
014100 CHANGE-MODE.
014200      MOVE "CHANGE" TO THE-MODE.
014300      PERFORM GET-VENDOR-RECORD.
014400      PERFORM CHANGE-RECORDS
014500          UNTIL VENDOR-NUMBER = ZEROES.
014600
014700 CHANGE-RECORDS.
014800      PERFORM GET-FIELD-TO-CHANGE.
014900      PERFORM CHANGE-ONE-FIELD
015000          UNTIL WHICH-FIELD = ZERO.
015100      PERFORM GET-VENDOR-RECORD.
015200
015300 GET-FIELD-TO-CHANGE.
015400      PERFORM DISPLAY-ALL-FIELDS.
015500      PERFORM ASK-WHICH-FIELD.
015600
015700 ASK-WHICH-FIELD.
015800      DISPLAY "ENTER THE NUMBER OF THE FIELD".
015900      DISPLAY "TO CHANGE (1-8) OR 0 TO EXIT".
016000      ACCEPT WHICH-FIELD.
016100      IF WHICH-FIELD > 8
016200          DISPLAY "INVALID ENTRY".
016300
016400 CHANGE-ONE-FIELD.
016500      PERFORM CHANGE-THIS-FIELD.
016600      PERFORM GET-FIELD-TO-CHANGE.
016700
016800 CHANGE-THIS-FIELD.
016900      IF WHICH-FIELD = 1
017000          PERFORM ENTER-VENDOR-NAME.
017100      IF WHICH-FIELD = 2
017200          PERFORM ENTER-VENDOR-ADDRESS-1.
017300      IF WHICH-FIELD = 3
017400          PERFORM ENTER-VENDOR-ADDRESS-2.
017500      IF WHICH-FIELD = 4
017600          PERFORM ENTER-VENDOR-CITY.
```

continues

Listing A.25. continued

```
017700      IF WHICH-FIELD = 5
017800          PERFORM ENTER-VENDOR-STATE.
017900      IF WHICH-FIELD = 6
018000          PERFORM ENTER-VENDOR-ZIP.
018100      IF WHICH-FIELD = 7
018200          PERFORM ENTER-VENDOR-CONTACT.
018300      IF WHICH-FIELD = 8
018400          PERFORM ENTER-VENDOR-PHONE.
018500
018600      PERFORM REWRITE-VENDOR-RECORD.
018700
018800*-------------------------------
018900* INQUIRE
019000*-------------------------------
019100 INQUIRE-MODE.
019200      MOVE "DISPLAY" TO THE-MODE.
019300      PERFORM GET-VENDOR-RECORD.
019400      PERFORM INQUIRE-RECORDS
019500          UNTIL VENDOR-NUMBER = ZEROES.
019600
019700 INQUIRE-RECORDS.
019800      PERFORM DISPLAY-ALL-FIELDS.
019900      PERFORM GET-VENDOR-RECORD.
020000
020100*-------------------------------
020200* DELETE
020300*-------------------------------
020400 DELETE-MODE.
020500      MOVE "DELETE" TO THE-MODE.
020600      PERFORM GET-VENDOR-RECORD.
020700      PERFORM DELETE-RECORDS
020800          UNTIL VENDOR-NUMBER = ZEROES.
020900
021000 DELETE-RECORDS.
021100      PERFORM DISPLAY-ALL-FIELDS.
021200      MOVE "X" TO OK-TO-DELETE.
021300
021400      PERFORM ASK-TO-DELETE
021500          UNTIL OK-TO-DELETE = "Y" OR "N".
021600
021700      IF OK-TO-DELETE = "Y"
021800          PERFORM DELETE-VENDOR-RECORD.
021900
022000      PERFORM GET-VENDOR-RECORD.
022100
022200 ASK-TO-DELETE.
022300      DISPLAY "DELETE THIS RECORD (Y/N)?".
022400      ACCEPT OK-TO-DELETE.
022500      IF OK-TO-DELETE = "y"
022600          MOVE "Y" TO OK-TO-DELETE.
022700      IF OK-TO-DELETE = "n"
022800          MOVE "N" TO OK-TO-DELETE.
022900      IF OK-TO-DELETE NOT = "Y" AND
023000          OK-TO-DELETE NOT = "N"
```

```
023100          DISPLAY "YOU MUST ENTER YES OR NO".
023200
023300*---------------------------------
023400* Routines shared by all modes
023500*---------------------------------
023600 INIT-VENDOR-RECORD.
023700     MOVE SPACE TO VENDOR-RECORD.
023800     MOVE ZEROES TO VENDOR-NUMBER.
023900
024000 ENTER-VENDOR-NUMBER.
024100     DISPLAY " ".
024200     DISPLAY "ENTER VENDOR NUMBER OF THE VENDOR" .
024300     DISPLAY "TO " THE-MODE " (1-99999)".
024400     DISPLAY "ENTER 0 TO STOP ENTRY".
024500     ACCEPT VENDOR-NUMBER-FIELD.
024600*OR  ACCEPT VENDOR-NUMBER-FIELD WITH CONVERSION.
024700
024800     MOVE VENDOR-NUMBER-FIELD TO VENDOR-NUMBER.
024900
025000 GET-VENDOR-RECORD.
025100     PERFORM INIT-VENDOR-RECORD.
025200     PERFORM ENTER-VENDOR-NUMBER.
025300     MOVE "N" TO RECORD-FOUND.
025400     PERFORM FIND-VENDOR-RECORD
025500         UNTIL RECORD-FOUND = "Y" OR
025600             VENDOR-NUMBER = ZEROES.
025700
025800*---------------------------------
025900* Routines shared Add and Change
026000*---------------------------------
026100 FIND-VENDOR-RECORD.
026200     PERFORM READ-VENDOR-RECORD.
026300     IF RECORD-FOUND = "N"
026400         DISPLAY "RECORD NOT FOUND"
026500         PERFORM ENTER-VENDOR-NUMBER.
026600
026700 ENTER-VENDOR-NAME.
026800     DISPLAY "ENTER VENDOR NAME".
026900     ACCEPT VENDOR-NAME.
027000
027100 ENTER-VENDOR-ADDRESS-1.
027200     DISPLAY "ENTER VENDOR ADDRESS-1".
027300     ACCEPT VENDOR-ADDRESS-1.
027400
027500 ENTER-VENDOR-ADDRESS-2.
027600     DISPLAY "ENTER VENDOR ADDRESS-2".
027700     ACCEPT VENDOR-ADDRESS-2.
027800
027900 ENTER-VENDOR-CITY.
028000     DISPLAY "ENTER VENDOR CITY".
028100     ACCEPT VENDOR-CITY.
028200
028300 ENTER-VENDOR-STATE.
028400     DISPLAY "ENTER VENDOR STATE".
028500     ACCEPT VENDOR-STATE.
```

continues

Listing A.25. continued

```
028600
028700 ENTER-VENDOR-ZIP.
028800     DISPLAY "ENTER VENDOR ZIP".
028900     ACCEPT VENDOR-ZIP.
029000
029100 ENTER-VENDOR-CONTACT.
029200     DISPLAY "ENTER VENDOR CONTACT".
029300     ACCEPT VENDOR-CONTACT.
029400
029500 ENTER-VENDOR-PHONE.
029600     DISPLAY "ENTER VENDOR PHONE".
029700     ACCEPT VENDOR-PHONE.
029800
029900*-------------------------------
030000* Routines shared by Change,
030100* Inquire and Delete
030200*-------------------------------
030300 DISPLAY-ALL-FIELDS.
030400     DISPLAY " ".
030500     PERFORM DISPLAY-VENDOR-NUMBER.
030600     PERFORM DISPLAY-VENDOR-NAME.
030700     PERFORM DISPLAY-VENDOR-ADDRESS-1.
030800     PERFORM DISPLAY-VENDOR-ADDRESS-2.
030900     PERFORM DISPLAY-VENDOR-CITY.
031000     PERFORM DISPLAY-VENDOR-STATE.
031100     PERFORM DISPLAY-VENDOR-ZIP.
031200     PERFORM DISPLAY-VENDOR-CONTACT.
031300     PERFORM DISPLAY-VENDOR-PHONE.
031400     DISPLAY " ".
031500
031600 DISPLAY-VENDOR-NUMBER.
031700     DISPLAY "   VENDOR NUMBER: " VENDOR-NUMBER.
031800
031900 DISPLAY-VENDOR-NAME.
032000     DISPLAY "1. VENDOR NAME: " VENDOR-NAME.
032100
032200 DISPLAY-VENDOR-ADDRESS-1.
032300     DISPLAY "2. VENDOR ADDRESS-1: " VENDOR-ADDRESS-1.
032400
032500 DISPLAY-VENDOR-ADDRESS-2.
032600     DISPLAY "3. VENDOR ADDRESS-2: " VENDOR-ADDRESS-2.
032700
032800 DISPLAY-VENDOR-CITY.
032900     DISPLAY "4. VENDOR CITY: " VENDOR-CITY.
033000
033100 DISPLAY-VENDOR-STATE.
033200     DISPLAY "5. VENDOR STATE: " VENDOR-STATE.
033300
033400 DISPLAY-VENDOR-ZIP.
033500     DISPLAY "6. VENDOR ZIP: " VENDOR-ZIP.
033600
033700 DISPLAY-VENDOR-CONTACT.
033800     DISPLAY "7. VENDOR CONTACT: " VENDOR-CONTACT.
033900
```

```
034000 DISPLAY-VENDOR-PHONE.
034100     DISPLAY "8. VENDOR PHONE: " VENDOR-PHONE.
034200
034300*-------------------------------
034400* File I-O Routines
034500*-------------------------------
034600 READ-VENDOR-RECORD.
034700     MOVE "Y" TO RECORD-FOUND.
034800     READ VENDOR-FILE RECORD
034900        INVALID KEY
035000           MOVE "N" TO RECORD-FOUND.
035100
035200*or   READ VENDOR-FILE RECORD WITH LOCK
035300*        INVALID KEY
035400*           MOVE "N" TO RECORD-FOUND.
035500
035600*or   READ VENDOR-FILE RECORD WITH HOLD
035700*        INVALID KEY
035800*           MOVE "N" TO RECORD-FOUND.
035900
036000 WRITE-VENDOR-RECORD.
036100     WRITE VENDOR-RECORD
036200        INVALID KEY
036300           DISPLAY "RECORD ALREADY ON FILE".
036400
036500 REWRITE-VENDOR-RECORD.
036600     REWRITE VENDOR-RECORD
036700        INVALID KEY
036800           DISPLAY "ERROR REWRITING VENDOR RECORD".
036900
037000 DELETE-VENDOR-RECORD.
037100     DELETE VENDOR-FILE RECORD
037200        INVALID KEY
037300           DISPLAY "ERROR DELETING VENDOR RECORD".
037400
```

TYPE ## Listing A.26. Delete mode.

```
000100 IDENTIFICATION DIVISION.
000200 PROGRAM-ID. VNDMNT01.
000300*-------------------------------
000400* Add, Change, Inquire and Delete
000500* for the Vendor File.
000600*-------------------------------
000700 ENVIRONMENT DIVISION.
000800 INPUT-OUTPUT SECTION.
000900 FILE-CONTROL.
001000
001100     COPY "SLVND01.CBL".
001200
001300 DATA DIVISION.
001400 FILE SECTION.
```

continues

Listing A.26. continued

```
001500
001600     COPY "FDVND02.CBL".
001700
001800 WORKING-STORAGE SECTION.
001900
002000 77  MENU-PICK                  PIC 9.
002100     88  MENU-PICK-IS-VALID      VALUES 0 THRU 4.
002200
002300 77  THE-MODE                   PIC X(7).
002400 77  WHICH-FIELD                PIC 9.
002500 77  OK-TO-DELETE               PIC X.
002600 77  RECORD-FOUND               PIC X.
002700 77  VENDOR-NUMBER-FIELD        PIC Z(5).
002800
002900 PROCEDURE DIVISION.
003000 PROGRAM-BEGIN.
003100     PERFORM OPENING-PROCEDURE.
003200     PERFORM MAIN-PROCESS.
003300     PERFORM CLOSING-PROCEDURE.
003400
003500 PROGRAM-DONE.
003600     STOP RUN.
003700
003800 OPENING-PROCEDURE.
003900     OPEN I-O VENDOR-FILE.
004000
004100 CLOSING-PROCEDURE.
004200     CLOSE VENDOR-FILE.
004300
004400
004500 MAIN-PROCESS.
004600     PERFORM GET-MENU-PICK.
004700     PERFORM MAINTAIN-THE-FILE
004800         UNTIL MENU-PICK = 0.
004900
005000*-------------------------------
005100* MENU
005200*-------------------------------
005300 GET-MENU-PICK.
005400     PERFORM DISPLAY-THE-MENU.
005500     PERFORM GET-THE-PICK.
005600     PERFORM MENU-RETRY
005700         UNTIL MENU-PICK-IS-VALID.
005800
005900 DISPLAY-THE-MENU.
006000     PERFORM CLEAR-SCREEN.
006100     DISPLAY "    PLEASE SELECT:".
006200     DISPLAY " ".
006300     DISPLAY "        1.   ADD RECORDS".
006400     DISPLAY "        2.   CHANGE A RECORD".
006500     DISPLAY "        3.   LOOK UP A RECORD".
006600     DISPLAY "        4.   DELETE A RECORD".
006700     DISPLAY " ".
006800     DISPLAY "        0.   EXIT".
```

```
006900      PERFORM SCROLL-LINE 8 TIMES.
007000
007100 GET-THE-PICK.
007200      DISPLAY "YOUR CHOICE (0-4)?".
007300      ACCEPT MENU-PICK.
007400 MENU-RETRY.
007500      DISPLAY "INVALID SELECTION - PLEASE RE-TRY.".
007600      PERFORM GET-THE-PICK.
007700 CLEAR-SCREEN.
007800      PERFORM SCROLL-LINE 25 TIMES.
007900
008000 SCROLL-LINE.
008100      DISPLAY " ".
008200
008300 MAINTAIN-THE-FILE.
008400      PERFORM DO-THE-PICK.
008500      PERFORM GET-MENU-PICK.
008600
008700 DO-THE-PICK.
008800      IF MENU-PICK = 1
008900          PERFORM ADD-MODE
009000      ELSE
009100      IF MENU-PICK = 2
009200          PERFORM CHANGE-MODE
009300      ELSE
009400      IF MENU-PICK = 3
009500          PERFORM INQUIRE-MODE
009600      ELSE
009700      IF MENU-PICK = 4
009800          PERFORM DELETE-MODE.
009900
010000*-------------------------------
010100* ADD
010200*-------------------------------
010300 ADD-MODE.
010400      MOVE "ADD" TO THE-MODE.
010500      PERFORM GET-NEW-VENDOR-NUMBER.
010600      PERFORM ADD-RECORDS
010700          UNTIL VENDOR-NUMBER = ZEROES.
010800
010900 GET-NEW-VENDOR-NUMBER.
011000      PERFORM INIT-VENDOR-RECORD.
011100      PERFORM ENTER-VENDOR-NUMBER.
011200      MOVE "Y" TO RECORD-FOUND.
011300      PERFORM FIND-NEW-VENDOR-RECORD
011400          UNTIL RECORD-FOUND = "N" OR
011500                VENDOR-NUMBER = ZEROES.
011600
011700 FIND-NEW-VENDOR-RECORD.
011800      PERFORM READ-VENDOR-RECORD.
011900      IF RECORD-FOUND = "Y"
012000          DISPLAY "RECORD ALREADY ON FILE"
012100          PERFORM ENTER-VENDOR-NUMBER.
012200
012300 ADD-RECORDS.
```

continues

Listing A.26. continued

```
012400      PERFORM ENTER-REMAINING-FIELDS.
012500      PERFORM WRITE-VENDOR-RECORD.
012600      PERFORM GET-NEW-VENDOR-NUMBER.
012700
012800 ENTER-REMAINING-FIELDS.
012900      PERFORM ENTER-VENDOR-NAME.
013000      PERFORM ENTER-VENDOR-ADDRESS-1.
013100      PERFORM ENTER-VENDOR-ADDRESS-2.
013200      PERFORM ENTER-VENDOR-CITY.
013300      PERFORM ENTER-VENDOR-STATE.
013400      PERFORM ENTER-VENDOR-ZIP.
013500      PERFORM ENTER-VENDOR-CONTACT.
013600      PERFORM ENTER-VENDOR-PHONE.
013700
013800*-------------------------------
013900* CHANGE
014000*-------------------------------
014100 CHANGE-MODE.
014200      MOVE "CHANGE" TO THE-MODE.
014300      PERFORM GET-VENDOR-RECORD.
014400      PERFORM CHANGE-RECORDS
014500          UNTIL VENDOR-NUMBER = ZEROES.
014600
014700 CHANGE-RECORDS.
014800      PERFORM GET-FIELD-TO-CHANGE.
014900      PERFORM CHANGE-ONE-FIELD
015000          UNTIL WHICH-FIELD = ZERO.
015100      PERFORM GET-VENDOR-RECORD.
015200
015300 GET-FIELD-TO-CHANGE.
015400      PERFORM DISPLAY-ALL-FIELDS.
015500      PERFORM ASK-WHICH-FIELD.
015600
015700 ASK-WHICH-FIELD.
015800      DISPLAY "ENTER THE NUMBER OF THE FIELD".
015900      DISPLAY "TO CHANGE (1-8) OR 0 TO EXIT".
016000      ACCEPT WHICH-FIELD.
016100      IF WHICH-FIELD > 8
016200          DISPLAY "INVALID ENTRY".
016300
016400 CHANGE-ONE-FIELD.
016500      PERFORM CHANGE-THIS-FIELD.
016600      PERFORM GET-FIELD-TO-CHANGE.
016700
016800 CHANGE-THIS-FIELD.
016900      IF WHICH-FIELD = 1
017000          PERFORM ENTER-VENDOR-NAME.
017100      IF WHICH-FIELD = 2
017200          PERFORM ENTER-VENDOR-ADDRESS-1.
017300      IF WHICH-FIELD = 3
017400          PERFORM ENTER-VENDOR-ADDRESS-2.
017500      IF WHICH-FIELD = 4
017600          PERFORM ENTER-VENDOR-CITY.
017700      IF WHICH-FIELD = 5
```

```
017800          PERFORM ENTER-VENDOR-STATE.
017900     IF WHICH-FIELD = 6
018000          PERFORM ENTER-VENDOR-ZIP.
018100     IF WHICH-FIELD = 7
018200          PERFORM ENTER-VENDOR-CONTACT.
018300     IF WHICH-FIELD = 8
018400          PERFORM ENTER-VENDOR-PHONE.
018500
018600     PERFORM REWRITE-VENDOR-RECORD.
018700
018800*------------------------------
018900* INQUIRE
019000*------------------------------
019100 INQUIRE-MODE.
019200     MOVE "DISPLAY" TO THE-MODE.
019300     PERFORM GET-VENDOR-RECORD.
019400     PERFORM INQUIRE-RECORDS
019500          UNTIL VENDOR-NUMBER = ZEROES.
019600
019700 INQUIRE-RECORDS.
019800     PERFORM DISPLAY-ALL-FIELDS.
019900     PERFORM GET-VENDOR-RECORD.
020000
020100*------------------------------
020200* DELETE
020300*------------------------------
020400 DELETE-MODE.
020500     MOVE "DELETE" TO THE-MODE.
020600     PERFORM GET-VENDOR-RECORD.
020700     PERFORM DELETE-RECORDS
020800          UNTIL VENDOR-NUMBER = ZEROES.
020900
021000 DELETE-RECORDS.
021100     PERFORM DISPLAY-ALL-FIELDS.
021200     MOVE "X" TO OK-TO-DELETE.
021300
021400     PERFORM ASK-TO-DELETE
021500          UNTIL OK-TO-DELETE = "Y" OR "N".
021600
021700     IF OK-TO-DELETE = "Y"
021800          PERFORM DELETE-VENDOR-RECORD.
021900
022000     PERFORM GET-VENDOR-RECORD.
022100
022200 ASK-TO-DELETE.
022300     DISPLAY "DELETE THIS RECORD (Y/N)?".
022400     ACCEPT OK-TO-DELETE.
022500     IF OK-TO-DELETE = "y"
022600          MOVE "Y" TO OK-TO-DELETE.
022700     IF OK-TO-DELETE = "n"
022800          MOVE "N" TO OK-TO-DELETE.
022900     IF OK-TO-DELETE NOT = "Y" AND
023000          OK-TO-DELETE NOT = "N"
023100          DISPLAY "YOU MUST ENTER YES OR NO".
023200
```

A

continues

Listing A.26. continued

```
023300*-------------------------------
023400* Routines shared by all modes
023500*-------------------------------
023600 INIT-VENDOR-RECORD.
023700      MOVE SPACE TO VENDOR-RECORD.
023800      MOVE ZEROES TO VENDOR-NUMBER.
023900
024000 ENTER-VENDOR-NUMBER.
024100      DISPLAY " ".
024200      DISPLAY "ENTER VENDOR NUMBER OF THE VENDOR" .
024300      DISPLAY "TO " THE-MODE " (1-99999)".
024400      DISPLAY "ENTER 0 TO STOP ENTRY".
024500      ACCEPT VENDOR-NUMBER-FIELD.
024600*OR  ACCEPT VENDOR-NUMBER-FIELD WITH CONVERSION.
024700
024800      MOVE VENDOR-NUMBER-FIELD TO VENDOR-NUMBER.
024900
025000 GET-VENDOR-RECORD.
025100      PERFORM INIT-VENDOR-RECORD.
025200      PERFORM ENTER-VENDOR-NUMBER.
025300      MOVE "N" TO RECORD-FOUND.
025400      PERFORM FIND-VENDOR-RECORD
025500          UNTIL RECORD-FOUND = "Y" OR
025600              VENDOR-NUMBER = ZEROES.
025700
025800*-------------------------------
025900* Routines shared Add and Change
026000*-------------------------------
026100 FIND-VENDOR-RECORD.
026200      PERFORM READ-VENDOR-RECORD.
026300      IF RECORD-FOUND = "N"
026400          DISPLAY "RECORD NOT FOUND"
026500          PERFORM ENTER-VENDOR-NUMBER.
026600
026700 ENTER-VENDOR-NAME.
026800      DISPLAY "ENTER VENDOR NAME".
026900      ACCEPT VENDOR-NAME.
027000
027100 ENTER-VENDOR-ADDRESS-1.
027200      DISPLAY "ENTER VENDOR ADDRESS-1".
027300      ACCEPT VENDOR-ADDRESS-1.
027400
027500 ENTER-VENDOR-ADDRESS-2.
027600      DISPLAY "ENTER VENDOR ADDRESS-2".
027700      ACCEPT VENDOR-ADDRESS-2.
027800
027900 ENTER-VENDOR-CITY.
028000      DISPLAY "ENTER VENDOR CITY".
028100      ACCEPT VENDOR-CITY.
028200
028300 ENTER-VENDOR-STATE.
028400      DISPLAY "ENTER VENDOR STATE".
028500      ACCEPT VENDOR-STATE.
028600
```

```
028700 ENTER-VENDOR-ZIP.
028800      DISPLAY "ENTER VENDOR ZIP".
028900      ACCEPT VENDOR-ZIP.
029000
029100 ENTER-VENDOR-CONTACT.
029200      DISPLAY "ENTER VENDOR CONTACT".
029300      ACCEPT VENDOR-CONTACT.
029400
029500 ENTER-VENDOR-PHONE.
029600      DISPLAY "ENTER VENDOR PHONE".
029700      ACCEPT VENDOR-PHONE.
029800
029900*--------------------------------
030000* Routines shared by Change,
030100* Inquire and Delete
030200*--------------------------------
030300 DISPLAY-ALL-FIELDS.
030400      DISPLAY " ".
030500      PERFORM DISPLAY-VENDOR-NUMBER.
030600      PERFORM DISPLAY-VENDOR-NAME.
030700      PERFORM DISPLAY-VENDOR-ADDRESS-1.
030800      PERFORM DISPLAY-VENDOR-ADDRESS-2.
030900      PERFORM DISPLAY-VENDOR-CITY.
031000      PERFORM DISPLAY-VENDOR-STATE.
031100      PERFORM DISPLAY-VENDOR-ZIP.
031200      PERFORM DISPLAY-VENDOR-CONTACT.
031300      PERFORM DISPLAY-VENDOR-PHONE.
031400      DISPLAY " ".
031500
031600 DISPLAY-VENDOR-NUMBER.
031700      DISPLAY "   VENDOR NUMBER: " VENDOR-NUMBER.
031800
031900 DISPLAY-VENDOR-NAME.
032000      DISPLAY "1. VENDOR NAME: " VENDOR-NAME.
032100
032200 DISPLAY-VENDOR-ADDRESS-1.
032300      DISPLAY "2. VENDOR ADDRESS-1: " VENDOR-ADDRESS-1.
032400
032500 DISPLAY-VENDOR-ADDRESS-2.
032600      DISPLAY "3. VENDOR ADDRESS-2: " VENDOR-ADDRESS-2.
032700
032800 DISPLAY-VENDOR-CITY.
032900      DISPLAY "4. VENDOR CITY: " VENDOR-CITY.
033000
033100 DISPLAY-VENDOR-STATE.
033200      DISPLAY "5. VENDOR STATE: " VENDOR-STATE.
033300
033400 DISPLAY-VENDOR-ZIP.
033500      DISPLAY "6. VENDOR ZIP: " VENDOR-ZIP.
033600
033700 DISPLAY-VENDOR-CONTACT.
033800      DISPLAY "7. VENDOR CONTACT: " VENDOR-CONTACT.
033900
034000 DISPLAY-VENDOR-PHONE.
034100      DISPLAY "8. VENDOR PHONE: " VENDOR-PHONE.
```

A

continues

Listing A.26. continued

```
034200
034300*------------------------------
034400* File I-O Routines
034500*------------------------------
034600 READ-VENDOR-RECORD.
034700     MOVE "Y" TO RECORD-FOUND.
034800     READ VENDOR-FILE RECORD
034900         INVALID KEY
035000             MOVE "N" TO RECORD-FOUND.
035100
035200*or  READ VENDOR-FILE RECORD WITH LOCK
035300*         INVALID KEY
035400*             MOVE "N" TO RECORD-FOUND.
035500
035600*or  READ VENDOR-FILE RECORD WITH HOLD
035700*         INVALID KEY
035800*             MOVE "N" TO RECORD-FOUND.
035900
036000 WRITE-VENDOR-RECORD.
036100     WRITE VENDOR-RECORD
036200         INVALID KEY
036300         DISPLAY "RECORD ALREADY ON FILE".
036400
036500 REWRITE-VENDOR-RECORD.
036600     REWRITE VENDOR-RECORD
036700         INVALID KEY
036800         DISPLAY "ERROR REWRITING VENDOR RECORD".
036900
037000 DELETE-VENDOR-RECORD.
037100     DELETE VENDOR-FILE RECORD
037200         INVALID KEY
037300         DISPLAY "ERROR DELETING VENDOR RECORD".
037400
```

    a. The routine that is incorrectly placed is GET-VENDOR-RECORD at line 025000 and FIND-VENDOR-RECORD at line 026100. GET-VENDOR-RECORD is placed in a section that is commented as a routine used in all modes, but it is not used in add mode. FIND-VENDOR-RECORD is placed in a section that is commented as a routine used in add and change mode, but it is not used in add mode.

    b. These routines should be below line 030200 in the section for routines used in change, inquire, and delete modes because they are used in all of those modes.

    c. All modes use READ-VENDOR-RECORD.

    d. Add mode.

    e. Change mode.

    f. Delete mode.

2. Listing A.27 highlights in bold type the menu actions in vndmnt01.cbl.

TYPE Listing A.27. Menu actions.

```
000100 IDENTIFICATION DIVISION.
000200 PROGRAM-ID. VNDMNT01.
000300*--------------------------------
000400* Add, Change, Inquire and Delete
000500* for the Vendor File.
000600*--------------------------------
000700 ENVIRONMENT DIVISION.
000800 INPUT-OUTPUT SECTION.
000900 FILE-CONTROL.
001000
001100      COPY "SLVND01.CBL".
001200
001300 DATA DIVISION.
001400 FILE SECTION.
001500
001600      COPY "FDVND02.CBL".
001700
001800 WORKING-STORAGE SECTION.
001900
002000 77  MENU-PICK                  PIC 9.
002100     88  MENU-PICK-IS-VALID     VALUES 0 THRU 4.
002200
002300 77  THE-MODE                   PIC X(7).
002400 77  WHICH-FIELD                PIC 9.
002500 77  OK-TO-DELETE               PIC X.
002600 77  RECORD-FOUND               PIC X.
002700 77  VENDOR-NUMBER-FIELD        PIC Z(5).
002800
002900 PROCEDURE DIVISION.
003000 PROGRAM-BEGIN.
003100      PERFORM OPENING-PROCEDURE.
003200      PERFORM MAIN-PROCESS.
003300      PERFORM CLOSING-PROCEDURE.
003400
003500 PROGRAM-DONE.
003600      STOP RUN.
003700
003800 OPENING-PROCEDURE.
003900      OPEN I-O VENDOR-FILE.
004000
004100 CLOSING-PROCEDURE.
004200      CLOSE VENDOR-FILE.
004300
004400
004500 MAIN-PROCESS.
004600      PERFORM GET-MENU-PICK.
004700      PERFORM MAINTAIN-THE-FILE
004800          UNTIL MENU-PICK = 0.
004900
005000*--------------------------------
005100* MENU
005200*--------------------------------
005300 GET-MENU-PICK.
```

continues

Listing A.27. continued

```
005400      PERFORM DISPLAY-THE-MENU.
005500      PERFORM GET-THE-PICK.
005600      PERFORM MENU-RETRY
005700          UNTIL MENU-PICK-IS-VALID.
005800
005900 DISPLAY-THE-MENU.
006000      PERFORM CLEAR-SCREEN.
006100      DISPLAY "    PLEASE SELECT:".
006200      DISPLAY " ".
006300      DISPLAY "          1.  ADD RECORDS".
006400      DISPLAY "          2.  CHANGE A RECORD".
006500      DISPLAY "          3.  LOOK UP A RECORD".
006600      DISPLAY "          4.  DELETE A RECORD".
006700      DISPLAY " ".
006800      DISPLAY "          0.  EXIT".
006900      PERFORM SCROLL-LINE 8 TIMES.
007000
007100 GET-THE-PICK.
007200      DISPLAY "YOUR CHOICE (0-4)?".
007300      ACCEPT MENU-PICK.
007400 MENU-RETRY.
007500      DISPLAY "INVALID SELECTION - PLEASE RE-TRY.".
007600      PERFORM GET-THE-PICK.
007700 CLEAR-SCREEN.
007800      PERFORM SCROLL-LINE 25 TIMES.
007900
008000 SCROLL-LINE.
008100      DISPLAY " ".
008200
008300 MAINTAIN-THE-FILE.
008400      PERFORM DO-THE-PICK.
008500      PERFORM GET-MENU-PICK.
008600
008700 DO-THE-PICK.
008800      IF MENU-PICK = 1
008900          PERFORM ADD-MODE
009000      ELSE
009100      IF MENU-PICK = 2
009200          PERFORM CHANGE-MODE
009300      ELSE
009400      IF MENU-PICK = 3
009500          PERFORM INQUIRE-MODE
009600      ELSE
009700      IF MENU-PICK = 4
009800          PERFORM DELETE-MODE.
009900
010000*-------------------------------
010100* ADD
010200*-------------------------------
010300 ADD-MODE.
010400      MOVE "ADD" TO THE-MODE.
010500      PERFORM GET-NEW-VENDOR-NUMBER.
010600      PERFORM ADD-RECORDS
010700          UNTIL VENDOR-NUMBER = ZEROES.
```

```
010800
010900 GET-NEW-VENDOR-NUMBER.
011000      PERFORM INIT-VENDOR-RECORD.
011100      PERFORM ENTER-VENDOR-NUMBER.
011200      MOVE "Y" TO RECORD-FOUND.
011300      PERFORM FIND-NEW-VENDOR-RECORD
011400          UNTIL RECORD-FOUND = "N" OR
011500              VENDOR-NUMBER = ZEROES.
011600
011700 FIND-NEW-VENDOR-RECORD.
011800      PERFORM READ-VENDOR-RECORD.
011900      IF RECORD-FOUND = "Y"
012000          DISPLAY "RECORD ALREADY ON FILE"
012100          PERFORM ENTER-VENDOR-NUMBER.
012200
012300 ADD-RECORDS.
012400      PERFORM ENTER-REMAINING-FIELDS.
012500      PERFORM WRITE-VENDOR-RECORD.
012600      PERFORM GET-NEW-VENDOR-NUMBER.
012700
012800 ENTER-REMAINING-FIELDS.
012900      PERFORM ENTER-VENDOR-NAME.
013000      PERFORM ENTER-VENDOR-ADDRESS-1.
013100      PERFORM ENTER-VENDOR-ADDRESS-2.
013200      PERFORM ENTER-VENDOR-CITY.
013300      PERFORM ENTER-VENDOR-STATE.
013400      PERFORM ENTER-VENDOR-ZIP.
013500      PERFORM ENTER-VENDOR-CONTACT.
013600      PERFORM ENTER-VENDOR-PHONE.
013700
013800*-------------------------------
013900* CHANGE
014000*-------------------------------
014100 CHANGE-MODE.
014200      MOVE "CHANGE" TO THE-MODE.
014300      PERFORM GET-VENDOR-RECORD.
014400      PERFORM CHANGE-RECORDS
014500          UNTIL VENDOR-NUMBER = ZEROES.
014600
014700 CHANGE-RECORDS.
014800      PERFORM GET-FIELD-TO-CHANGE.
014900      PERFORM CHANGE-ONE-FIELD
015000          UNTIL WHICH-FIELD = ZERO.
015100      PERFORM GET-VENDOR-RECORD.
015200
015300 GET-FIELD-TO-CHANGE.
015400      PERFORM DISPLAY-ALL-FIELDS.
015500      PERFORM ASK-WHICH-FIELD.
015600
015700 ASK-WHICH-FIELD.
015800      DISPLAY "ENTER THE NUMBER OF THE FIELD".
015900      DISPLAY "TO CHANGE (1-8) OR 0 TO EXIT".
016000      ACCEPT WHICH-FIELD.
016100      IF WHICH-FIELD > 8
016200          DISPLAY "INVALID ENTRY".
```

continues

Listing A.27. continued

```
016300
016400 CHANGE-ONE-FIELD.
016500     PERFORM CHANGE-THIS-FIELD.
016600     PERFORM GET-FIELD-TO-CHANGE.
016700
016800 CHANGE-THIS-FIELD.
016900     IF WHICH-FIELD = 1
017000         PERFORM ENTER-VENDOR-NAME.
017100     IF WHICH-FIELD = 2
017200         PERFORM ENTER-VENDOR-ADDRESS-1.
017300     IF WHICH-FIELD = 3
017400         PERFORM ENTER-VENDOR-ADDRESS-2.
017500     IF WHICH-FIELD = 4
017600         PERFORM ENTER-VENDOR-CITY.
017700     IF WHICH-FIELD = 5
017800         PERFORM ENTER-VENDOR-STATE.
017900     IF WHICH-FIELD = 6
018000         PERFORM ENTER-VENDOR-ZIP.
018100     IF WHICH-FIELD = 7
018200         PERFORM ENTER-VENDOR-CONTACT.
018300     IF WHICH-FIELD = 8
018400         PERFORM ENTER-VENDOR-PHONE.
018500
018600     PERFORM REWRITE-VENDOR-RECORD.
018700
018800*--------------------------------
018900* INQUIRE
019000*--------------------------------
019100 INQUIRE-MODE.
019200     MOVE "DISPLAY" TO THE-MODE.
019300     PERFORM GET-VENDOR-RECORD.
019400     PERFORM INQUIRE-RECORDS
019500         UNTIL VENDOR-NUMBER = ZEROES.
019600
019700 INQUIRE-RECORDS.
019800     PERFORM DISPLAY-ALL-FIELDS.
019900     PERFORM GET-VENDOR-RECORD.
020000
020100*--------------------------------
020200* DELETE
020300*--------------------------------
020400 DELETE-MODE.
020500     MOVE "DELETE" TO THE-MODE.
020600     PERFORM GET-VENDOR-RECORD.
020700     PERFORM DELETE-RECORDS
020800         UNTIL VENDOR-NUMBER = ZEROES.
020900
021000 DELETE-RECORDS.
021100     PERFORM DISPLAY-ALL-FIELDS.
021200     MOVE "X" TO OK-TO-DELETE.
021300
021400     PERFORM ASK-TO-DELETE
021500         UNTIL OK-TO-DELETE = "Y" OR "N".
021600
```

```
021700      IF OK-TO-DELETE = "Y"
021800          PERFORM DELETE-VENDOR-RECORD.
021900
022000      PERFORM GET-VENDOR-RECORD.
022100
022200 ASK-TO-DELETE.
022300      DISPLAY "DELETE THIS RECORD (Y/N)?".
022400      ACCEPT OK-TO-DELETE.
022500      IF OK-TO-DELETE = "y"
022600          MOVE "Y" TO OK-TO-DELETE.
022700      IF OK-TO-DELETE = "n"
022800          MOVE "N" TO OK-TO-DELETE.
022900      IF OK-TO-DELETE NOT = "Y" AND
023000          OK-TO-DELETE NOT = "N"
023100          DISPLAY "YOU MUST ENTER YES OR NO".
023200
023300*-------------------------------
023400* Routines shared by all modes
023500*-------------------------------
023600 INIT-VENDOR-RECORD.
023700      MOVE SPACE TO VENDOR-RECORD.
023800      MOVE ZEROES TO VENDOR-NUMBER.
023900
024000 ENTER-VENDOR-NUMBER.
024100      DISPLAY " ".
024200      DISPLAY "ENTER VENDOR NUMBER OF THE VENDOR" .
024300      DISPLAY "TO " THE-MODE " (1-99999)".
024400      DISPLAY "ENTER 0 TO STOP ENTRY".
024500      ACCEPT VENDOR-NUMBER-FIELD.
024600*OR   ACCEPT VENDOR-NUMBER-FIELD WITH CONVERSION.
024700
024800      MOVE VENDOR-NUMBER-FIELD TO VENDOR-NUMBER.
024900
025000 GET-VENDOR-RECORD.
025100      PERFORM INIT-VENDOR-RECORD.
025200      PERFORM ENTER-VENDOR-NUMBER.
025300      MOVE "N" TO RECORD-FOUND.
025400      PERFORM FIND-VENDOR-RECORD
025500          UNTIL RECORD-FOUND = "Y" OR
025600                VENDOR-NUMBER = ZEROES.
025700
025800*-------------------------------
025900* Routines shared Add and Change
026000*-------------------------------
026100 FIND-VENDOR-RECORD.
026200      PERFORM READ-VENDOR-RECORD.
026300      IF RECORD-FOUND = "N"
026400          DISPLAY "RECORD NOT FOUND"
026500          PERFORM ENTER-VENDOR-NUMBER.
026600
026700 ENTER-VENDOR-NAME.
026800      DISPLAY "ENTER VENDOR NAME".
026900      ACCEPT VENDOR-NAME.
027000
027100 ENTER-VENDOR-ADDRESS-1.
```

continues

Listing A.27. continued

```
027200      DISPLAY "ENTER VENDOR ADDRESS-1".
027300      ACCEPT VENDOR-ADDRESS-1.
027400
027500 ENTER-VENDOR-ADDRESS-2.
027600      DISPLAY "ENTER VENDOR ADDRESS-2".
027700      ACCEPT VENDOR-ADDRESS-2.
027800
027900 ENTER-VENDOR-CITY.
028000      DISPLAY "ENTER VENDOR CITY".
028100      ACCEPT VENDOR-CITY.
028200
028300 ENTER-VENDOR-STATE.
028400      DISPLAY "ENTER VENDOR STATE".
028500      ACCEPT VENDOR-STATE.
028600
028700 ENTER-VENDOR-ZIP.
028800      DISPLAY "ENTER VENDOR ZIP".
028900      ACCEPT VENDOR-ZIP.
029000
029100 ENTER-VENDOR-CONTACT.
029200      DISPLAY "ENTER VENDOR CONTACT".
029300      ACCEPT VENDOR-CONTACT.
029400
029500 ENTER-VENDOR-PHONE.
029600      DISPLAY "ENTER VENDOR PHONE".
029700      ACCEPT VENDOR-PHONE.
029800
029900*-------------------------------
030000* Routines shared by Change,
030100* Inquire and Delete
030200*-------------------------------
030300 DISPLAY-ALL-FIELDS.
030400      DISPLAY " ".
030500      PERFORM DISPLAY-VENDOR-NUMBER.
030600      PERFORM DISPLAY-VENDOR-NAME.
030700      PERFORM DISPLAY-VENDOR-ADDRESS-1.
030800      PERFORM DISPLAY-VENDOR-ADDRESS-2.
030900      PERFORM DISPLAY-VENDOR-CITY.
031000      PERFORM DISPLAY-VENDOR-STATE.
031100      PERFORM DISPLAY-VENDOR-ZIP.
031200      PERFORM DISPLAY-VENDOR-CONTACT.
031300      PERFORM DISPLAY-VENDOR-PHONE.
031400      DISPLAY " ".
031500
031600 DISPLAY-VENDOR-NUMBER.
031700      DISPLAY "   VENDOR NUMBER: " VENDOR-NUMBER.
031800
031900 DISPLAY-VENDOR-NAME.
032000      DISPLAY "1. VENDOR NAME: " VENDOR-NAME.
032100
```

```
032200 DISPLAY-VENDOR-ADDRESS-1.
032300     DISPLAY "2. VENDOR ADDRESS-1: " VENDOR-ADDRESS-1.
032400
032500 DISPLAY-VENDOR-ADDRESS-2.
032600     DISPLAY "3. VENDOR ADDRESS-2: " VENDOR-ADDRESS-2.
032700
032800 DISPLAY-VENDOR-CITY.
032900     DISPLAY "4. VENDOR CITY: " VENDOR-CITY.
033000
033100 DISPLAY-VENDOR-STATE.
033200     DISPLAY "5. VENDOR STATE: " VENDOR-STATE.
033300
033400 DISPLAY-VENDOR-ZIP.
033500     DISPLAY "6. VENDOR ZIP: " VENDOR-ZIP.
033600
033700 DISPLAY-VENDOR-CONTACT.
033800     DISPLAY "7. VENDOR CONTACT: " VENDOR-CONTACT.
033900
034000 DISPLAY-VENDOR-PHONE.
034100     DISPLAY "8. VENDOR PHONE: " VENDOR-PHONE.
034200
034300*-------------------------------
034400* File I-O Routines
034500*-------------------------------
034600 READ-VENDOR-RECORD.
034700     MOVE "Y" TO RECORD-FOUND.
034800     READ VENDOR-FILE RECORD
034900       INVALID KEY
035000         MOVE "N" TO RECORD-FOUND.
035100
035200*or  READ VENDOR-FILE RECORD WITH LOCK
035300*      INVALID KEY
035400*        MOVE "N" TO RECORD-FOUND.
035500
035600*or  READ VENDOR-FILE RECORD WITH HOLD
035700*      INVALID KEY
035800*        MOVE "N" TO RECORD-FOUND.
035900
036000 WRITE-VENDOR-RECORD.
036100     WRITE VENDOR-RECORD
036200         INVALID KEY
036300         DISPLAY "RECORD ALREADY ON FILE".
036400
036500 REWRITE-VENDOR-RECORD.
036600     REWRITE VENDOR-RECORD
036700         INVALID KEY
036800         DISPLAY "ERROR REWRITING VENDOR RECORD".
036900
037000 DELETE-VENDOR-RECORD.
037100     DELETE VENDOR-FILE RECORD
037200         INVALID KEY
037300         DISPLAY "ERROR DELETING VENDOR RECORD".
037400
```

A

Answers to Day 15, "Data Integrity"

Quiz

1. a. Data always should be validated before it is put in a data file.

2. INSPECT CONVERTING can be used to convert a field to uppercase.

3. A field could be converted to lowercase by reversing the compare field and the replace field.

   If Listing A.28 converts DATA-FIELD to uppercase, Listing A.29 will convert DATA-FIELD to lowercase.

TYPE **Listing A.28. Converting to uppercase.**

```
010300       INSPECT DATA FIELD
010400          CONVERTING LOWER-ALPHA
010500          TO         UPPER-ALPHA.
```

TYPE **Listing A.29. Converting to lowercase.**

```
010300       INSPECT DATA FIELD
010400          CONVERTING UPPER-ALPHA
010500          TO         LOWER-ALPHA.
```

Exercises

1. The routine in Listing A.30 is one way of entering and converting the vendor name.

TYPE **Listing A.30. Entering, validating, and converting a VENDOR-NAME.**

```
ENTER-VENDOR-NAME.
    PERFORM ACCEPT-VENDOR-NAME.
    PERFORM RE-ACCEPT-VENDOR-NAME
       UNTIL VENDOR-NAME NOT = SPACES.

ACCEPT-VENDOR-NAME.
    DISPLAY "ENTER VENDOR NAME".
    ACCEPT VENDOR-NAME.

INSPECT VENDOR-NAME
    CONVERTING LOWER-ALPHA
    TO         UPPER-ALPHA.
```

```
RE-ACCEPT-VENDOR-NAME.
    DISPLAY "VENDOR NAME MUST BE ENTERED".
    PERFORM ACCEPT-VENDOR-NAME.
```

2. Figure A.3 compares ENTER-VENDOR-NAME to a standard field-entry routine.

Figure A.3.

ENTER-VENDOR-NAME *as a standard field-entry routine.*

```
ENTER-VENDOR-NAME.                          enter-the-data
    PERFORM ACCEPT-VENDOR-NAME.                  PERFORM accept-the-data.
    PERFORM RE-ACCEPT-VENDOR-NAME               PERFORM re-accept-the-data
        UNTIL VENDOR-NAME NOT = SPACES.             UNTIL the-data is valid.

ACCEPT-VENDOR-NAME.                          accept-the-data.
    DISPLAY "ENTER VENDOR NAME".                 DISPLAY a-prompt.
    ACCEPT VENDOR-NAME.                          ACCEPT the-data.

    INSPECT VENDOR-NAME                         edit check the data.
        CONVERTING LOWER-ALPHA
        TO         UPPER-ALPHA.

RE-ACCEPT-VENDOR-NAME.                       re-accept-the-data.
    DISPLAY "VENDOR NAME MUST BE ENTERED".      DISPLAY error-message.
    PERFORM ACCEPT-VENDOR-NAME.                 PERFORM accept-the-data.
```

Answers to Day 16, "Using Look Up and Arrays"

Quiz

1. SET VENDOR-INDEX UP BY 1.

2. STATE-INDEX will contain 14.

3. TABLE-STATE-CODE(STATE-INDEX) will contain "XX".

Exercises

1. Listing A.31 would be a suitable table for 100 vendor records.

TYPE **Listing A.31. 100 vendors.**

```
002000 01  TABLE-VENDOR-RECORD OCCURS 100 TIMES
002000     INDEXED BY VENDOR-INDEX.
002100     05  TABLE-VENDOR-NUMBER        PIC 9(5).
002200     05  TABLE-VENDOR-NAME          PIC X(30).
002300     05  TABLE-VENDOR-ADDRESS-1     PIC X(30).
002400     05  TABLE-VENDOR-ADDRESS-2     PIC X(30).
002500     05  TABLE-VENDOR-CITY          PIC X(20).
002600     05  TABLE-VENDOR-STATE         PIC X(2).
002700     05  TABLE-VENDOR-ZIP           PIC X(10).
002800     05  TABLE-VENDOR-CONTACT       PIC X(30).
002900     05  TABLE-VENDOR-PHONE         PIC X(15).
```

2. The size of the vendor table in exercise 1 would be 100 times the length of a single record. The record is 172 bytes long, so the whole table is 17,200 bytes.

Answers to Day 17, "Alternate Keys"

Quiz

1. OMEGA MANUFACTURING. The value "LINCOLN" in the VENDOR-NAME would not be matched by any vendor name on the file. The next key that is equal to or greater than "LINCOLN" is OMEGA MANUFACTURING.

2. The keys to the PART-FILE are the following:

   PART-NUMBER
   PART-VENDOR
   PART-DEPARTMENT
   PART-VENDOR-NUMBER

   PART-NUMBER is the primary key.

3. Duplicate keys are allowed in the following:

   PART-VENDOR
   PART-DEPARTMENT

   Duplicate keys are not allowed in the following:

   PART-NUMBER
   PART-VENDOR-NUMBER

Exercise

Listing A.32 defines the necessary keys.

TYPE | **Listing A.32. Multiple keys for the customer file.**

```
000400      SELECT CUSTOMER-FILE
000500          ASSIGN TO "CUST"
000600          ORGANIZATION IS INDEXED
000700          RECORD KEY IS CUSTOMER-NUMBER
000800          ALTERNATE KEY IS CUSTOMER-NAME WITH DUPLICATES
000900          ALTERNATE KEY IS CUSTOMER-ZIP WITH DUPLICATES
001000          ACCESS MODE IS DYNAMIC.
001100
```

Answers to Day 18, "Calling Other Programs"

Quiz

1. b. It remains in memory, but waits for the calling program to complete.

2. a. EXIT PROGRAM.

Exercises

1. Listing A.33 is a code fragment that includes all the changes you need to create vnddsp03.cbl.

TYPE **Listing A.33. Changes to** `vnddsp03.cbl`**.**

```
000100 IDENTIFICATION DIVISION.
000200 PROGRAM-ID. VNDDSP03.
000300*-------------------------------------------------
000400* Display records in the Vendor File.
000500*-------------------------------------------------
000600 ENVIRONMENT DIVISION.
000700 INPUT-OUTPUT SECTION.
000800 FILE-CONTROL.
000900
001000     COPY "SLVND02.CBL".
001100
001200 DATA DIVISION.
001300 FILE SECTION.
001400
001500     COPY "FDVND04.CBL".
001600
001700 WORKING-STORAGE SECTION.
001800
001900 01   DETAIL-LINE.
002000     05   DISPLAY-NUMBER      PIC 9(5).
002100     05   FILLER              PIC X      VALUE SPACE.
002200     05   DISPLAY-NAME        PIC X(30).
002300     05   FILLER              PIC X      VALUE SPACE.
002400     05   DISPLAY-CONTACT     PIC X(30).
002500
002600 01   CITY-STATE-DETAIL.
002700     05   DISPLAY-CITY        PIC X(20).
002800     05   FILLER              PIC X VALUE SPACE.
002900     05   DISPLAY-STATE       PIC X(2).
003000
003100 01   COLUMN-LINE.
003200     05   FILLER          PIC X(2)  VALUE "NO".
003300     05   FILLER          PIC X(4)  VALUE SPACE.
003400     05   FILLER          PIC X(12) VALUE "NAME-ADDRESS".
003500     05   FILLER          PIC X(19) VALUE SPACE.
```

continues

A

Listing A.33. continued

```
003600      05  FILLER           PIC X(17) VALUE "CONTACT-PHONE-ZIP".
003700
003800 01  TITLE-LINE.
003900      05  FILLER               PIC X(15) VALUE SPACE.
004000      05  FILLER               PIC X(11)
004100          VALUE "VENDOR LIST".
004200      05  FILLER               PIC X(15) VALUE SPACE.
004300      05  FILLER               PIC X(5) VALUE "PAGE:".
004400      05  FILLER               PIC X(1) VALUE SPACE.
004500      05  DISPLAY-PAGE-NUMBER PIC ZZZZ9.
004600
004700 77  FILE-AT-END          PIC X.
004800 77  A-DUMMY              PIC X.
004900 77  LINE-COUNT           PIC 999 VALUE ZERO.
005000 77  PAGE-NUMBER          PIC 99999 VALUE ZERO.
005100 77  MAXIMUM-LINES        PIC 999 VALUE 15.
005200
005300 77  DISPLAY-RECORD       PIC X(79).
005400
005500 PROCEDURE DIVISION.
005600 PROGRAM-BEGIN.
005700
005800      PERFORM OPENING-PROCEDURE.
005900      MOVE ZEROES TO LINE-COUNT
006000                      PAGE-NUMBER.
006100
006200      PERFORM START-NEW-PAGE.
006300
006400      MOVE "N" TO FILE-AT-END.
006500      PERFORM READ-NEXT-RECORD.
006600      IF FILE-AT-END = "Y"
006700          MOVE "NO RECORDS FOUND" TO DISPLAY-RECORD
006800          PERFORM WRITE-DISPLAY-RECORD
006900      ELSE
007000          PERFORM DISPLAY-VENDOR-FIELDS
007100              UNTIL FILE-AT-END = "Y".
007200
007300      PERFORM CLOSING-PROCEDURE.
007400
007500 PROGRAM-EXIT.
007600      EXIT PROGRAM.
007700
007800 PROGRAM-DONE.
007900      STOP RUN.
008000
```

2. Listing A.34 includes the changes for this exercise and the next.

3. Listing A.34 includes the changes for this exercise and the preceding one.

TYPE   **Listing A.34. Changes for** `vndmnt05.cbl.`

```
000100 IDENTIFICATION DIVISION.
000200 PROGRAM-ID. VNDMNT05.
000300*------------------------------
000400* Add, Change, Inquire and Delete
000500* for the Vendor File.
000600* This includes Inquire by name
000700* The vendor report, and the vendor
000800* report in name order.
000900* Added Display all records.
001000*------------------------------
001100 ENVIRONMENT DIVISION.
001200 INPUT-OUTPUT SECTION.
001300 FILE-CONTROL.
001400
001500     COPY "SLVND02.CBL".
001600
001700     COPY "SLSTATE.CBL".
001800
001900 DATA DIVISION.
002000 FILE SECTION.
002100
002200     COPY "FDVND04.CBL".
002300
002400     COPY "FDSTATE.CBL".
002500
002600 WORKING-STORAGE SECTION.
002700
002800 77  MENU-PICK                 PIC 9.
002900     88  MENU-PICK-IS-VALID     VALUES 0 THRU 8.
003000
003100 77  THE-MODE                  PIC X(7).
003200 77  WHICH-FIELD               PIC 9.
003300 77  OK-TO-DELETE              PIC X.
003400 77  VENDOR-RECORD-FOUND       PIC X.
003500 77  STATE-RECORD-FOUND        PIC X.
003600 77  A-DUMMY                   PIC X.
003700
003800 77  VENDOR-NUMBER-FIELD       PIC Z(5).
003900
004000 77  ERROR-MESSAGE             PIC X(79) VALUE SPACE.
004100
004200     COPY "WSCASE01.CBL".
004300
004400 PROCEDURE DIVISION.
004500 PROGRAM-BEGIN.
004600     PERFORM OPENING-PROCEDURE.
004700     PERFORM MAIN-PROCESS.
004800     PERFORM CLOSING-PROCEDURE.
004900
005000 PROGRAM-EXIT.
005100     EXIT PROGRAM.
005200
005300 PROGRAM-DONE.
```

continues

Listing A.34. continued

```
005400      STOP RUN.
005500
005600 OPENING-PROCEDURE.
005700      OPEN I-O VENDOR-FILE.
005800      OPEN I-O STATE-FILE.
005900
006000 CLOSING-PROCEDURE.
006100      CLOSE VENDOR-FILE.
006200      CLOSE STATE-FILE.
006300
006400 MAIN-PROCESS.
006500      PERFORM GET-MENU-PICK.
006600      PERFORM MAINTAIN-THE-FILE
006700          UNTIL MENU-PICK = 0.
006800
006900*--------------------------------
007000* MENU
007100*--------------------------------
007200 GET-MENU-PICK.
007300      PERFORM DISPLAY-THE-MENU.
007400      PERFORM ACCEPT-MENU-PICK.
007500      PERFORM RE-ACCEPT-MENU-PICK
007600          UNTIL MENU-PICK-IS-VALID.
007700
007800 DISPLAY-THE-MENU.
007900      PERFORM CLEAR-SCREEN.
008000      DISPLAY "    PLEASE SELECT:".
008100      DISPLAY " ".
008200      DISPLAY "         1.  ADD RECORDS".
008300      DISPLAY "         2.  CHANGE A RECORD".
008400      DISPLAY "         3.  LOOK UP A RECORD".
008500      DISPLAY "         4.  DELETE A RECORD".
008600      DISPLAY "         5.  LOOK UP BY NAME".
008700      DISPLAY "         6.  PRINT RECORDS".
008800      DISPLAY "         7.  PRINT IN NAME ORDER".
008900      DISPLAY "         8.  DISPLAY ALL RECORDS".
009000      DISPLAY " ".
009100      DISPLAY "         0.  EXIT".
009200      PERFORM SCROLL-LINE 8 TIMES.
009300
009400 ACCEPT-MENU-PICK.
009500      DISPLAY "YOUR CHOICE (0-8)?".
009600      ACCEPT MENU-PICK.
009700
009800 RE-ACCEPT-MENU-PICK.
009900      DISPLAY "INVALID SELECTION - PLEASE RE-TRY.".
010000      PERFORM ACCEPT-MENU-PICK.
010100
010200 CLEAR-SCREEN.
010300      PERFORM SCROLL-LINE 25 TIMES.
010400
010500 SCROLL-LINE.
010600      DISPLAY " ".
010700
```

```
010800 MAINTAIN-THE-FILE.
010900     PERFORM DO-THE-PICK.
011000     PERFORM GET-MENU-PICK.
011100
011200 DO-THE-PICK.
011300     IF MENU-PICK = 1
011400         PERFORM ADD-MODE
011500     ELSE
011600     IF MENU-PICK = 2
011700         PERFORM CHANGE-MODE
011800     ELSE
011900     IF MENU-PICK = 3
012000         PERFORM INQUIRE-MODE
012100     ELSE
012200     IF MENU-PICK = 4
012300         PERFORM DELETE-MODE
012400     ELSE
012500     IF MENU-PICK = 5
012600         PERFORM INQUIRE-BY-NAME
012700     ELSE
012800     IF MENU-PICK = 6
012900         PERFORM PRINT-VENDOR-REPORT
013000     ELSE
013100     IF MENU-PICK = 7
013200         PERFORM PRINT-BY-NAME
013300     ELSE
013400     IF MENU-PICK = 8
013500         PERFORM DISPLAY-ALL.
013600
013700*-------------------------------
013800* ADD
013900*-------------------------------
014000 ADD-MODE.
014100     MOVE "ADD" TO THE-MODE.
014200     PERFORM GET-NEW-RECORD-KEY.
014300     PERFORM ADD-RECORDS
014400         UNTIL VENDOR-NUMBER = ZEROES.
014500
014600 GET-NEW-RECORD-KEY.
014700     PERFORM ACCEPT-NEW-RECORD-KEY.
014800     PERFORM RE-ACCEPT-NEW-RECORD-KEY
014900         UNTIL VENDOR-RECORD-FOUND = "N" OR
015000               VENDOR-NUMBER = ZEROES.
015100
015200 ACCEPT-NEW-RECORD-KEY.
015300     PERFORM INIT-VENDOR-RECORD.
015400     PERFORM ENTER-VENDOR-NUMBER.
015500     IF VENDOR-NUMBER NOT = ZEROES
015600         PERFORM READ-VENDOR-RECORD.
015700
015800 RE-ACCEPT-NEW-RECORD-KEY.
015900     DISPLAY "RECORD ALREADY ON FILE"
016000     PERFORM ACCEPT-NEW-RECORD-KEY.
016100
016200 ADD-RECORDS.
```

continues

Listing A.34. continued

```
016300      PERFORM ENTER-REMAINING-FIELDS.
016400      PERFORM WRITE-VENDOR-RECORD.
016500      PERFORM GET-NEW-RECORD-KEY.
016600
016700 ENTER-REMAINING-FIELDS.
016800      PERFORM ENTER-VENDOR-NAME.
016900      PERFORM ENTER-VENDOR-ADDRESS-1.
017000      PERFORM ENTER-VENDOR-ADDRESS-2.
017100      PERFORM ENTER-VENDOR-CITY.
017200      PERFORM ENTER-VENDOR-STATE.
017300      PERFORM ENTER-VENDOR-ZIP.
017400      PERFORM ENTER-VENDOR-CONTACT.
017500      PERFORM ENTER-VENDOR-PHONE.
017600
017700*--------------------------------
017800* CHANGE
017900*--------------------------------
018000 CHANGE-MODE.
018100      MOVE "CHANGE" TO THE-MODE.
018200      PERFORM GET-EXISTING-RECORD.
018300      PERFORM CHANGE-RECORDS
018400          UNTIL VENDOR-NUMBER = ZEROES.
018500
018600 CHANGE-RECORDS.
018700      PERFORM GET-FIELD-TO-CHANGE.
018800      PERFORM CHANGE-ONE-FIELD
018900          UNTIL WHICH-FIELD = ZERO.
019000      PERFORM GET-EXISTING-RECORD.
019100
019200 GET-FIELD-TO-CHANGE.
019300      PERFORM DISPLAY-ALL-FIELDS.
019400      PERFORM ASK-WHICH-FIELD.
019500
019600 ASK-WHICH-FIELD.
019700      PERFORM ACCEPT-WHICH-FIELD.
019800      PERFORM RE-ACCEPT-WHICH-FIELD
019900          UNTIL WHICH-FIELD < 9.
020000
020100 ACCEPT-WHICH-FIELD.
020200      DISPLAY "ENTER THE NUMBER OF THE FIELD".
020300      DISPLAY "TO CHANGE (1-8) OR 0 TO EXIT".
020400      ACCEPT WHICH-FIELD.
020500
020600 RE-ACCEPT-WHICH-FIELD.
020700      DISPLAY "INVALID ENTRY".
020800      PERFORM ACCEPT-WHICH-FIELD.
020900
021000 CHANGE-ONE-FIELD.
021100      PERFORM CHANGE-THIS-FIELD.
021200      PERFORM GET-FIELD-TO-CHANGE.
021300
021400 CHANGE-THIS-FIELD.
021500      IF WHICH-FIELD = 1
021600          PERFORM ENTER-VENDOR-NAME.
```

```
021700        IF WHICH-FIELD = 2
021800            PERFORM ENTER-VENDOR-ADDRESS-1.
021900        IF WHICH-FIELD = 3
022000            PERFORM ENTER-VENDOR-ADDRESS-2.
022100        IF WHICH-FIELD = 4
022200            PERFORM ENTER-VENDOR-CITY.
022300        IF WHICH-FIELD = 5
022400            PERFORM ENTER-VENDOR-STATE.
022500        IF WHICH-FIELD = 6
022600            PERFORM ENTER-VENDOR-ZIP.
022700        IF WHICH-FIELD = 7
022800            PERFORM ENTER-VENDOR-CONTACT.
022900        IF WHICH-FIELD = 8
023000            PERFORM ENTER-VENDOR-PHONE.
023100
023200        PERFORM REWRITE-VENDOR-RECORD.
023300
023400*-------------------------------
023500* INQUIRE
023600*-------------------------------
023700 INQUIRE-MODE.
023800        MOVE "DISPLAY" TO THE-MODE.
023900        PERFORM GET-EXISTING-RECORD.
024000        PERFORM INQUIRE-RECORDS
024100            UNTIL VENDOR-NUMBER = ZEROES.
024200
024300 INQUIRE-RECORDS.
024400        PERFORM DISPLAY-ALL-FIELDS.
024500        PERFORM GET-EXISTING-RECORD.
024600
024700*-------------------------------
024800* DELETE
024900*-------------------------------
025000 DELETE-MODE.
025100        MOVE "DELETE" TO THE-MODE.
025200        PERFORM GET-EXISTING-RECORD.
025300        PERFORM DELETE-RECORDS
025400            UNTIL VENDOR-NUMBER = ZEROES.
025500
025600 DELETE-RECORDS.
025700        PERFORM DISPLAY-ALL-FIELDS.
025800
025900        PERFORM ASK-OK-TO-DELETE.
026000
026100        IF OK-TO-DELETE = "Y"
026200            PERFORM DELETE-VENDOR-RECORD.
026300
026400        PERFORM GET-EXISTING-RECORD.
026500
026600 ASK-OK-TO-DELETE.
026700        PERFORM ACCEPT-OK-TO-DELETE.
026800
026900        PERFORM RE-ACCEPT-OK-TO-DELETE
027000            UNTIL OK-TO-DELETE = "Y" OR "N".
027100
```

continues

Listing A.34. continued

```
027200 ACCEPT-OK-TO-DELETE.
027300     DISPLAY "DELETE THIS RECORD (Y/N)?".
027400     ACCEPT OK-TO-DELETE.
027500     INSPECT OK-TO-DELETE
027600      CONVERTING LOWER-ALPHA TO UPPER-ALPHA.
027700
027800 RE-ACCEPT-OK-TO-DELETE.
027900     DISPLAY "YOU MUST ENTER YES OR NO".
028000     PERFORM ACCEPT-OK-TO-DELETE.
028100
028200*------------------------------
028300* Routines shared by all modes
028400*------------------------------
028500 INIT-VENDOR-RECORD.
028600     MOVE SPACE TO VENDOR-RECORD.
028700     MOVE ZEROES TO VENDOR-NUMBER.
028800
028900 ENTER-VENDOR-NUMBER.
029000     DISPLAY " ".
029100     DISPLAY "ENTER VENDOR NUMBER OF THE VENDOR" .
029200     DISPLAY "TO " THE-MODE " (1-99999)".
029300     DISPLAY "ENTER 0 TO STOP ENTRY".
029400     ACCEPT VENDOR-NUMBER-FIELD.
029500*OR  ACCEPT VENDOR-NUMBER-FIELD WITH CONVERSION.
029600
029700     MOVE VENDOR-NUMBER-FIELD TO VENDOR-NUMBER.
029800
029900*------------------------------
030000* INQUIRE BY NAME
030100*------------------------------
030200 INQUIRE-BY-NAME.
030300     PERFORM CLOSING-PROCEDURE.
030400     CALL "VNINNM03".
030500     PERFORM OPENING-PROCEDURE.
030600
030700*------------------------------
030800* PRINT
030900*------------------------------
031000 PRINT-VENDOR-REPORT.
031100     PERFORM CLOSING-PROCEDURE.
031200     DISPLAY "VENDOR REPORT IN PROGRESS".
031300     CALL "VNDRPT04".
031400     PERFORM OPENING-PROCEDURE.
031500
031600*------------------------------
031700* PRINT BY NAME
031800*------------------------------
031900 PRINT-BY-NAME.
032000     PERFORM CLOSING-PROCEDURE.
032100     DISPLAY " REPORT BY NAME IN PROGRESS".
032200     CALL "VNBYNM02".
032300     PERFORM OPENING-PROCEDURE.
032400
032500*------------------------------
```

```
032600* DISPLAY ALL
032700*------------------------------
032800 DISPLAY-ALL.
032900     PERFORM CLOSING-PROCEDURE.
033000     CALL "VNDDSP03".
033100     DISPLAY "DISPLAY COMPLETE".
033200     DISPLAY "PRESS ENTER TO CONTINUE".
033300     ACCEPT A-DUMMY.
033400     PERFORM OPENING-PROCEDURE.
033500
033600*------------------------------
033700* Routines shared Add and Change
033800*------------------------------
033900 ENTER-VENDOR-NAME.
034000     PERFORM ACCEPT-VENDOR-NAME.
034100     PERFORM RE-ACCEPT-VENDOR-NAME
034200         UNTIL VENDOR-NAME NOT = SPACE.
034300
034400 ACCEPT-VENDOR-NAME.
034500     DISPLAY "ENTER VENDOR NAME".
034600     ACCEPT VENDOR-NAME.
034700     INSPECT VENDOR-NAME
034800         CONVERTING LOWER-ALPHA
034900         TO          UPPER-ALPHA.
035000
035100 RE-ACCEPT-VENDOR-NAME.
035200     DISPLAY "VENDOR NAME MUST BE ENTERED".
035300     PERFORM ACCEPT-VENDOR-NAME.
035400
035500 ENTER-VENDOR-ADDRESS-1.
035600     PERFORM ACCEPT-VENDOR-ADDRESS-1.
035700     PERFORM RE-ACCEPT-VENDOR-ADDRESS-1
035800         UNTIL VENDOR-ADDRESS-1 NOT = SPACE.
035900
036000 ACCEPT-VENDOR-ADDRESS-1.
036100     DISPLAY "ENTER VENDOR ADDRESS-1".
036200     ACCEPT VENDOR-ADDRESS-1.
036300     INSPECT VENDOR-ADDRESS-1
036400         CONVERTING LOWER-ALPHA
036500         TO          UPPER-ALPHA.
036600
036700 RE-ACCEPT-VENDOR-ADDRESS-1.
036800     DISPLAY "VENDOR ADDRESS-1 MUST BE ENTERED".
036900     PERFORM ACCEPT-VENDOR-ADDRESS-1.
037000
037100 ENTER-VENDOR-ADDRESS-2.
037200     DISPLAY "ENTER VENDOR ADDRESS-2".
037300     ACCEPT VENDOR-ADDRESS-2.
037400     INSPECT VENDOR-ADDRESS-2
037500         CONVERTING LOWER-ALPHA
037600         TO          UPPER-ALPHA.
037700
037800 ENTER-VENDOR-CITY.
037900     PERFORM ACCEPT-VENDOR-CITY.
038000     PERFORM RE-ACCEPT-VENDOR-CITY
```

continues

Listing A.34. continued

```
038100          UNTIL VENDOR-CITY NOT = SPACE.
038200
038300 ACCEPT-VENDOR-CITY.
038400     DISPLAY "ENTER VENDOR CITY".
038500     ACCEPT VENDOR-CITY.
038600     INSPECT VENDOR-CITY
038700          CONVERTING LOWER-ALPHA
038800          TO          UPPER-ALPHA.
038900
039000 RE-ACCEPT-VENDOR-CITY.
039100     DISPLAY "VENDOR CITY MUST BE ENTERED".
039200     PERFORM ACCEPT-VENDOR-CITY.
039300
039400 ENTER-VENDOR-STATE.
039500     PERFORM ACCEPT-VENDOR-STATE.
039600     PERFORM RE-ACCEPT-VENDOR-STATE
039700          UNTIL VENDOR-STATE NOT = SPACES AND
039800               STATE-RECORD-FOUND = "Y".
039900
040000 ACCEPT-VENDOR-STATE.
040100     DISPLAY "ENTER VENDOR STATE".
040200     ACCEPT VENDOR-STATE.
040300     PERFORM EDIT-CHECK-VENDOR-STATE.
040400
040500 RE-ACCEPT-VENDOR-STATE.
040600     DISPLAY ERROR-MESSAGE.
040700     PERFORM ACCEPT-VENDOR-STATE.
040800
040900 EDIT-CHECK-VENDOR-STATE.
041000     PERFORM EDIT-VENDOR-STATE.
041100     PERFORM CHECK-VENDOR-STATE.
041200
041300 EDIT-VENDOR-STATE.
041400     INSPECT VENDOR-STATE
041500          CONVERTING LOWER-ALPHA
041600          TO          UPPER-ALPHA.
041700
041800 CHECK-VENDOR-STATE.
041900     PERFORM VENDOR-STATE-REQUIRED.
042000     IF VENDOR-STATE NOT = SPACES
042100          PERFORM VENDOR-STATE-ON-FILE.
042200
042300 VENDOR-STATE-REQUIRED.
042400     IF VENDOR-STATE = SPACE
042500          MOVE "VENDOR STATE MUST BE ENTERED"
042600               TO ERROR-MESSAGE.
042700
042800 VENDOR-STATE-ON-FILE.
042900     MOVE VENDOR-STATE TO STATE-CODE.
043000     PERFORM READ-STATE-RECORD.
043100     IF STATE-RECORD-FOUND = "N"
043200          MOVE "STATE CODE NOT FOUND IN CODES FILE"
043300               TO ERROR-MESSAGE.
043400
```

```
043500 ENTER-VENDOR-ZIP.
043600     PERFORM ACCEPT-VENDOR-ZIP.
043700     PERFORM RE-ACCEPT-VENDOR-ZIP
043800         UNTIL VENDOR-ZIP NOT = SPACE.
043900
044000 ACCEPT-VENDOR-ZIP.
044100     DISPLAY "ENTER VENDOR ZIP".
044200     ACCEPT VENDOR-ZIP.
044300     INSPECT VENDOR-ZIP
044400         CONVERTING LOWER-ALPHA
044500         TO         UPPER-ALPHA.
044600
044700 RE-ACCEPT-VENDOR-ZIP.
044800     DISPLAY "VENDOR ZIP MUST BE ENTERED".
044900     PERFORM ACCEPT-VENDOR-ZIP.
045000
045100 ENTER-VENDOR-CONTACT.
045200     DISPLAY "ENTER VENDOR CONTACT".
045300     ACCEPT VENDOR-CONTACT.
045400     INSPECT VENDOR-CONTACT
045500         CONVERTING LOWER-ALPHA
045600         TO         UPPER-ALPHA.
045700
045800 ENTER-VENDOR-PHONE.
045900     PERFORM ACCEPT-VENDOR-PHONE.
046000     PERFORM RE-ACCEPT-VENDOR-PHONE
046100         UNTIL VENDOR-PHONE NOT = SPACE.
046200
046300 ACCEPT-VENDOR-PHONE.
046400     DISPLAY "ENTER VENDOR PHONE".
046500     ACCEPT VENDOR-PHONE.
046600     INSPECT VENDOR-PHONE
046700         CONVERTING LOWER-ALPHA
046800         TO         UPPER-ALPHA.
046900
047000 RE-ACCEPT-VENDOR-PHONE.
047100     DISPLAY "VENDOR PHONE MUST BE ENTERED".
047200     PERFORM ACCEPT-VENDOR-PHONE.
047300
047400*--------------------------------
047500* Routines shared by Change,
047600* Inquire and Delete
047700*--------------------------------
047800 GET-EXISTING-RECORD.
047900     PERFORM ACCEPT-EXISTING-KEY.
048000     PERFORM RE-ACCEPT-EXISTING-KEY
048100         UNTIL VENDOR-RECORD-FOUND = "Y" OR
048200             VENDOR-NUMBER = ZEROES.
048300
048400 ACCEPT-EXISTING-KEY.
048500     PERFORM INIT-VENDOR-RECORD.
048600     PERFORM ENTER-VENDOR-NUMBER.
048700     IF VENDOR-NUMBER NOT = ZEROES
048800         PERFORM READ-VENDOR-RECORD.
048900
```

continues

Listing A.34. continued

```
049000 RE-ACCEPT-EXISTING-KEY.
049100     DISPLAY "RECORD NOT FOUND"
049200     PERFORM ACCEPT-EXISTING-KEY.
049300
049400 DISPLAY-ALL-FIELDS.
049500     DISPLAY " ".
049600     PERFORM DISPLAY-VENDOR-NUMBER.
049700     PERFORM DISPLAY-VENDOR-NAME.
049800     PERFORM DISPLAY-VENDOR-ADDRESS-1.
049900     PERFORM DISPLAY-VENDOR-ADDRESS-2.
050000     PERFORM DISPLAY-VENDOR-CITY.
050100     PERFORM DISPLAY-VENDOR-STATE.
050200     PERFORM DISPLAY-VENDOR-ZIP.
050300     PERFORM DISPLAY-VENDOR-CONTACT.
050400     PERFORM DISPLAY-VENDOR-PHONE.
050500     DISPLAY " ".
050600
050700 DISPLAY-VENDOR-NUMBER.
050800     DISPLAY "   VENDOR NUMBER: " VENDOR-NUMBER.
050900
051000 DISPLAY-VENDOR-NAME.
051100     DISPLAY "1. VENDOR NAME: " VENDOR-NAME.
051200
051300 DISPLAY-VENDOR-ADDRESS-1.
051400     DISPLAY "2. VENDOR ADDRESS-1: " VENDOR-ADDRESS-1.
051500
051600 DISPLAY-VENDOR-ADDRESS-2.
051700     DISPLAY "3. VENDOR ADDRESS-2: " VENDOR-ADDRESS-2.
051800
051900 DISPLAY-VENDOR-CITY.
052000     DISPLAY "4. VENDOR CITY: " VENDOR-CITY.
052100
052200 DISPLAY-VENDOR-STATE.
052300     PERFORM VENDOR-STATE-ON-FILE.
052400     IF STATE-RECORD-FOUND = "N"
052500         MOVE "**Not found**" TO STATE-NAME.
052600     DISPLAY "5. VENDOR STATE: "
052700             VENDOR-STATE " "
052800             STATE-NAME.
052900
053000 DISPLAY-VENDOR-ZIP.
053100     DISPLAY "6. VENDOR ZIP: " VENDOR-ZIP.
053200
053300 DISPLAY-VENDOR-CONTACT.
053400     DISPLAY "7. VENDOR CONTACT: " VENDOR-CONTACT.
053500
053600 DISPLAY-VENDOR-PHONE.
053700     DISPLAY "8. VENDOR PHONE: " VENDOR-PHONE.
053800
053900*------------------------------
054000* File I-O Routines
054100*------------------------------
054200 READ-VENDOR-RECORD.
054300     MOVE "Y" TO VENDOR-RECORD-FOUND.
```

```
054400     READ VENDOR-FILE RECORD
054500        INVALID KEY
054600           MOVE "N" TO VENDOR-RECORD-FOUND.
054700
054800*or  READ VENDOR-FILE RECORD WITH LOCK
054900*       INVALID KEY
055000*          MOVE "N" TO VENDOR-RECORD-FOUND.
055100
055200*or  READ VENDOR-FILE RECORD WITH HOLD
055300*       INVALID KEY
055400*          MOVE "N" TO VENDOR-RECORD-FOUND.
055500
055600 WRITE-VENDOR-RECORD.
055700     WRITE VENDOR-RECORD
055800        INVALID KEY
055900        DISPLAY "RECORD ALREADY ON FILE".
056000
056100 REWRITE-VENDOR-RECORD.
056200     REWRITE VENDOR-RECORD
056300        INVALID KEY
056400        DISPLAY "ERROR REWRITING VENDOR RECORD".
056500
056600 DELETE-VENDOR-RECORD.
056700     DELETE VENDOR-FILE RECORD
056800        INVALID KEY
056900        DISPLAY "ERROR DELETING VENDOR RECORD".
057000
057100 READ-STATE-RECORD.
057200     MOVE "Y" TO STATE-RECORD-FOUND.
057300     READ STATE-FILE RECORD
057400        INVALID KEY
057500           MOVE "N" TO STATE-RECORD-FOUND.
```

4. Listing A.35 includes the changes needed to create `bilmnu02.cbl`.

TYPE **Listing A.35. The changes for** `bilmnu02.cbl`.

```
000100 IDENTIFICATION DIVISION.
000200 PROGRAM-ID. BILMNU02.
000300*-------------------------------
000400* Menu for the bill payment system.
000500*-------------------------------
000600 ENVIRONMENT DIVISION.
000700 INPUT-OUTPUT SECTION.
000800 FILE-CONTROL.
000900
001000 DATA DIVISION.
001100 FILE SECTION.
001200
001300 WORKING-STORAGE SECTION.
001400
001500 77  MENU-PICK                PIC 9.
```

continues

Listing A.35. continued

```
001600      88  MENU-PICK-IS-VALID        VALUES 0 THRU 2.
001700
001800 PROCEDURE DIVISION.
001900 PROGRAM-BEGIN.
002000      PERFORM OPENING-PROCEDURE.
002100      PERFORM MAIN-PROCESS.
002200      PERFORM CLOSING-PROCEDURE.
002300
002400 PROGRAM-EXIT.
002500      EXIT PROGRAM.
002600
002700 PROGRAM-DONE.
002800      STOP RUN.
002900
003000 OPENING-PROCEDURE.
003100
003200 CLOSING-PROCEDURE.
003300
003400 MAIN-PROCESS.
003500      PERFORM GET-MENU-PICK.
003600      PERFORM DO-THE-PICK
003700          UNTIL MENU-PICK = 0.
003800
003900*------------------------------
004000* MENU
004100*------------------------------
004200 GET-MENU-PICK.
004300      PERFORM DISPLAY-THE-MENU.
004400      PERFORM ACCEPT-MENU-PICK.
004500      PERFORM RE-ACCEPT-MENU-PICK
004600          UNTIL MENU-PICK-IS-VALID.
004700
004800 DISPLAY-THE-MENU.
004900      PERFORM CLEAR-SCREEN.
005000      DISPLAY "     PLEASE SELECT:".
005100      DISPLAY " ".
005200      DISPLAY "          1.  STATE CODE MAINTENANCE".
005300      DISPLAY "          2.  VENDOR MAINTENANCE".
005400      DISPLAY " ".
005500      DISPLAY "          0.  EXIT".
005600      PERFORM SCROLL-LINE 8 TIMES.
005700
005800 ACCEPT-MENU-PICK.
005900      DISPLAY "YOUR CHOICE (0-2)?".
006000      ACCEPT MENU-PICK.
006100
006200 RE-ACCEPT-MENU-PICK.
006300      DISPLAY "INVALID SELECTION - PLEASE RE-TRY.".
006400      PERFORM ACCEPT-MENU-PICK.
006500
006600 CLEAR-SCREEN.
006700      PERFORM SCROLL-LINE 25 TIMES.
006800
006900 SCROLL-LINE.
```

```
007000     DISPLAY " ".
007100
007200 DO-THE-PICK.
007300     IF MENU-PICK = 1
007400         PERFORM STATE-MAINTENANCE
007500     ELSE
007600     IF MENU-PICK = 2
007700         PERFORM VENDOR-MAINTENANCE.
007800
007900     PERFORM GET-MENU-PICK.
008000
008100*-------------------------------
008200* STATE
008300*-------------------------------
008400 STATE-MAINTENANCE.
008500     CALL "STCMNT04".
008600
008700*-------------------------------
008800* VENDOR
008900*-------------------------------
009000 VENDOR-MAINTENANCE.
009100     CALL "VNDMNT05".
009200
```

Answers to Day 19, "Complex Data Entry Problems"

Quiz

1. The variable represents six bytes of memory.

2. TIME-HHMMSS is six bytes long and will hold numeric data.

3. TIME-HH is two bytes long and will hold numeric data.

4. TIME-MM is two bytes long and will hold numeric data.

5. TIME-SS is two bytes long and will hold numeric data.

Exercises

1. Figure A.4 highlights the differences between a simple maintenance module such as stcmnt04.cbl and a control-file maintenance module such as ctlmnt01.cbl. Both of these listings had to be rewritten here to allow them to fit side by side within the 80-column limit of this book's layout. The new programs, stcmntxx.cbl and ctlmntxx.cbl, function in the same way as the originals, but the lines and line breaks have been extensively shifted to squeeze everything into the side-by-side format. You will recognize all the parts of the original programs as you review these two programs.

A

Figure A.4.

Comparing
stcmntxx.cbl *and*
ctlmntxx.cbl.

```
stcmntxx.cbl
000100 IDENTIFICATION DIVISION.
000200 PROGRAM-ID. STCMNTXX.
000300*--------------------------------
000400* Add, Change, Inquire and
000500* Delete for the State Code.
000600* Calls the State Codes Report.
000700*--------------------------------
000800 ENVIRONMENT DIVISION.
000900 INPUT-OUTPUT SECTION.
001000 FILE-CONTROL.
001100
001200     COPY "SLSTATE.CBL".
001300
001400 DATA DIVISION.
001500 FILE SECTION.
001600
001700     COPY "FDSTATE.CBL".
001800
001900 WORKING-STORAGE SECTION.
002000
002100 77  MENU-PICK          PIC 9.
002200     88  PICK-IS-VALID
002300             VALUES 0 THRU 5.
002400
002500 77  THE-MODE          PIC X(7).
002600 77  OK-TO-DELETE      PIC X.
002700 77  RECORD-FOUND      PIC X.
002800 77  WHICH-FIELD       PIC 9.
002900
003000     COPY "WSCASE01.CBL".
003100
003200 PROCEDURE DIVISION.
003300 PROGRAM-BEGIN.
003400     PERFORM OPENING-PROCEDURE.
003500     PERFORM MAIN-PROCESS.
003600     PERFORM CLOSING-PROCEDURE.
003700
003800 PROGRAM-EXIT.
003900     EXIT PROGRAM.
004000
004100 PROGRAM-DONE.
004200     STOP RUN.
004300
004400 OPENING-PROCEDURE.
004500     OPEN I-O STATE-FILE.
004600
004700 CLOSING-PROCEDURE.
004800     CLOSE STATE-FILE.
004900
005000
005100 MAIN-PROCESS.
005200     PERFORM GET-MENU-PICK.
005300     PERFORM MAINTAIN-THE-FILE
005400         UNTIL MENU-PICK = 0.
005500
005600*--------------------------------
005700* MENU
005800*--------------------------------
005900 GET-MENU-PICK.
006000     PERFORM DISPLAY-THE-MENU.
006100     PERFORM ACCEPT-MENU-PICK.
006200     PERFORM RE-ACCEPT-MENU-PICK
006300         UNTIL PICK-IS-VALID.
006400
006500 DISPLAY-THE-MENU.
006600     PERFORM CLEAR-SCREEN.
006700     DISPLAY
006800        "   PLEASE SELECT:".
```

```
ctlmntxx.cbl
000100 IDENTIFICATION DIVISION.
000200 PROGRAM-ID. CTLMNTXX.
000300*--------------------------------
000400* Change and Inquire only
000500* for the bills system control
000600* file.
000700*--------------------------------
000800 ENVIRONMENT DIVISION.
000900 INPUT-OUTPUT SECTION.
001000 FILE-CONTROL.
001100
001200     COPY "SLCONTRL.CBL".
001300
001400 DATA DIVISION.
001500 FILE SECTION.
001600
001700     COPY "FDCONTRL.CBL".
001800
001900 WORKING-STORAGE SECTION.
002000
002100 77  MENU-PICK          PIC 9.
002200     88  PICK-IS-VALID
002300             VALUES 0 THRU 2.
002400
002500 77  THE-MODE          PIC X(7).
002600 77  RECORD-FOUND      PIC X.
002700 77  WHICH-FIELD       PIC 9.
002800 77  A-DUMMY           PIC X.
002900

003000 PROCEDURE DIVISION.
003100 PROGRAM-BEGIN.
003200     PERFORM OPENING-PROCEDURE.
003300     PERFORM MAIN-PROCESS.
003400     PERFORM CLOSING-PROCEDURE.
003500
003600 PROGRAM-EXIT.
003700     EXIT PROGRAM.
003800
003900 PROGRAM-DONE.
004000     STOP RUN.
004100
004200 OPENING-PROCEDURE.
004300     OPEN I-O CONTROL-FILE.
004400
004500 CLOSING-PROCEDURE.
004600     CLOSE CONTROL-FILE.
004700

004800 MAIN-PROCESS.
004900     PERFORM GET-MENU-PICK.
005000     PERFORM MAINTAIN-THE-FILE
005100         UNTIL MENU-PICK = 0.
005200
005300*--------------------------------
005400* MENU
005500*--------------------------------
005600 GET-MENU-PICK.
005700     PERFORM DISPLAY-THE-MENU.
005800     PERFORM ACCEPT-MENU-PICK.
005900     PERFORM RE-ACCEPT-MENU-PICK
006000         UNTIL PICK-IS-VALID.
006100
006200 DISPLAY-THE-MENU.
006300     PERFORM CLEAR-SCREEN.
006400     DISPLAY
006500        "   PLEASE SELECT:".
```

```
006900      DISPLAY " ".                    006600  DISPLAY " ".
007000      DISPLAY "            "           006700  DISPLAY "            "
007100         "1.  ADD RECORDS".           006800     "1.  CHANGE CONTROL "
007200      DISPLAY "            "           006900     "INFORMATION".
007300         "2.  CHANGE A "              007000  DISPLAY "            "
007400         "RECORD".                    007100     "2. DISPLAY "
007500      DISPLAY "            "           007200     "CONTROL INFORMATION".
007600         "3.  LOOK UP A "             007300  DISPLAY " ".
007700         "RECORD".                    007400  DISPLAY "        0.  EXIT".
007800      DISPLAY "            "           007500  PERFORM SCROLL-LINE 8 TIMES.
007900         "4.  DELETE A "              007600
008000         "RECORD".
008100      DISPLAY "            "
008200         "5.  PRINT RECORDS".
008300      DISPLAY " ".
008400      DISPLAY "            "
008500         "0.  EXIT".
008600      PERFORM SCROLL-LINE 8 TIMES.
008700
008800 ACCEPT-MENU-PICK.                    007700 ACCEPT-MENU-PICK.
008900      DISPLAY                          007800      DISPLAY "YOUR CHOICE "
009000      "YOUR CHOICE (0-5)?".           007900          "(0-2)?".
009100      ACCEPT MENU-PICK.               008000      ACCEPT MENU-PICK.
009200                                       008100
009300 RE-ACCEPT-MENU-PICK.                  008200 RE-ACCEPT-MENU-PICK.
009400      DISPLAY                          008300      DISPLAY "INVALID SELECTION "
009500      "INVALID SELECTION - "          008400          "- PLEASE RE-TRY.".
009600      "PLEASE RE-TRY.".               008500      PERFORM ACCEPT-MENU-PICK.
009700      PERFORM ACCEPT-MENU-PICK.       008600
009800
009900 CLEAR-SCREEN.                        008700 CLEAR-SCREEN.
010000      PERFORM SCROLL-LINE             008800      PERFORM SCROLL-LINE
010100         25 TIMES.                    008900         25 TIMES.
010200                                       009000
010300 SCROLL-LINE.                         009100 SCROLL-LINE.
010400      DISPLAY " ".                     009200      DISPLAY " ".
010500                                       009300
010600 MAINTAIN-THE-FILE.                   009400 MAINTAIN-THE-FILE.
010700      PERFORM DO-THE-PICK.            009500      PERFORM DO-THE-PICK.
010800      PERFORM GET-MENU-PICK.          009600      PERFORM GET-MENU-PICK.
010900                                       009700
011000 DO-THE-PICK.                         009800 DO-THE-PICK.
011100      IF MENU-PICK = 1                009900      IF MENU-PICK = 1
011200        PERFORM ADD-MODE              010000        PERFORM CHANGE-MODE
011300      ELSE                            010100      ELSE
011400      IF MENU-PICK = 2                010200      IF MENU-PICK = 2
011500        PERFORM CHANGE-MODE           010300        PERFORM INQUIRE-MODE.
011600      ELSE                            010400
011700      IF MENU-PICK = 3
011800        PERFORM INQUIRE-MODE
011900      ELSE
012000      IF MENU-PICK = 4
012100        PERFORM DELETE-MODE
012200      ELSE
012300      IF MENU-PICK = 5
012400        PERFORM PRINT-THE-RECORDS.
012500
012600*----------------------------
012700* ADD
012800*----------------------------
012900 ADD-MODE.
013000      MOVE "ADD" TO THE-MODE.
013100      PERFORM GET-NEW-STATE-CODE.
013200      PERFORM ADD-RECORDS
013300         UNTIL STATE-CODE = "ZZ".
013400
013500 GET-NEW-STATE-CODE.
```

continues

Figure A.4.

continued

```
013600        PERFORM INIT-STATE-RECORD.
013700        PERFORM ENTER-STATE-CODE.
013800        MOVE "Y" TO RECORD-FOUND.
013900        PERFORM
014000          FIND-NEW-STATE-RECORD
014100            UNTIL
014200              RECORD-FOUND = "N" OR
014300              STATE-CODE = "ZZ".
014400
014500 FIND-NEW-STATE-RECORD.
014600        PERFORM READ-STATE-RECORD.
014700        IF RECORD-FOUND = "Y"
014800          DISPLAY "RECORD ALREADY "
014900                  "ON FILE"
015000          PERFORM ENTER-STATE-CODE.
015100
015200 ADD-RECORDS.
015300        PERFORM
015400            ENTER-REMAINING-FIELDS.
015500        PERFORM WRITE-STATE-RECORD.
015600        PERFORM GET-NEW-STATE-CODE.
015700
015800 ENTER-REMAINING-FIELDS.
015900        PERFORM ENTER-STATE-NAME.
016000
016100*------------------------------    010500*----------------------------
016200* CHANGE                            010600* CHANGE
016300*------------------------------    010700*----------------------------
016400 CHANGE-MODE.                       010800 CHANGE-MODE.
016500        MOVE "CHANGE" TO THE-MODE.  010900        MOVE "CHANGE" TO THE-MODE.
016600        PERFORM GET-STATE-RECORD.   011000        PERFORM GET-CONTROL-RECORD.
016700        PERFORM CHANGE-RECORDS      011100        IF RECORD-FOUND = "Y"
016800            UNTIL STATE-CODE = "ZZ". 011200          PERFORM CHANGE-RECORDS.
016900                                     011300
017000 CHANGE-RECORDS.                    011400 CHANGE-RECORDS.
017100        PERFORM GET-FIELD-TO-CHANGE. 011500        PERFORM GET-FIELD-TO-CHANGE.
017200*       PERFORM CHANGE-ONE-FIELD     011600        PERFORM CHANGE-ONE-FIELD.
017300*         UNTIL WHICH-FIELD = ZERO.  011700
017400        PERFORM CHANGE-ONE-FIELD.    011800        PERFORM GET-CONTROL-RECORD.
017500                                     011900
017600        PERFORM GET-STATE-RECORD.
017700
017800 GET-FIELD-TO-CHANGE.               012000 GET-FIELD-TO-CHANGE.
017900        PERFORM DISPLAY-ALL-FIELDS.  012100        PERFORM DISPLAY-ALL-FIELDS.
018000        PERFORM ASK-WHICH-FIELD.     012200        PERFORM ASK-WHICH-FIELD.
018100                                     012300
018200 ASK-WHICH-FIELD.                   012400 ASK-WHICH-FIELD.
018300*       PERFORM ACCEPT-WHICH-FIELD.  012500        MOVE 1 TO WHICH-FIELD.
018400*       PERFORM                      012600
018500*         RE-ACCEPT-WHICH-FIELD
018600*         UNTIL WHICH-FIELD NOT > 1.
018700        MOVE 1 TO WHICH-FIELD.
018800
018900*ACCEPT-WHICH-FIELD.
019000*       DISPLAY "ENTER THE "
019100*               "NUMBER OF THE FIELD".
019200*       DISPLAY "TO CHANGE (1) "
019300*               "OR 0 TO EXIT".
019400*       ACCEPT WHICH-FIELD.
019500*
019600*RE-ACCEPT-WHICH-FIELD.
019700*       DISPLAY "INVALID ENTRY".
019800*       PERFORM ACCEPT-WHICH-FIELD.
019900
020000 CHANGE-ONE-FIELD.                  012700 CHANGE-ONE-FIELD.
020100        PERFORM CHANGE-THIS-FIELD.   012800        PERFORM CHANGE-THIS-FIELD.
020200*       PERFORM GET-FIELD-TO-CHANGE. 012900
020300                                     013000 CHANGE-THIS-FIELD.
020400 CHANGE-THIS-FIELD.                  013100        IF WHICH-FIELD = 1
```

```
020500      IF WHICH-FIELD = 1          013200      PERFORM
020600          PERFORM ENTER-STATE-NAME.  013300      ENTER-CONTROL-LAST-VOUCHER.
020700                                   013400
020800      PERFORM                      013500      PERFORM
020900          REWRITE-STATE-RECORD.    013600      REWRITE-CONTROL-RECORD.
021000                                   013700
021100*--------------------------       013800*--------------------------
021200* INQUIRE                          013900* INQUIRE
021300*--------------------------       014000*--------------------------
021400 INQUIRE-MODE.                     014100 INQUIRE-MODE.
021500      MOVE "DISPLAY" TO THE-MODE.  014200      MOVE "DISPLAY" TO THE-MODE.
021600      PERFORM GET-STATE-RECORD.    014300      PERFORM GET-CONTROL-RECORD.
021700      PERFORM INQUIRE-RECORDS      014400      IF RECORD-FOUND = "Y"
021800          UNTIL STATE-CODE = "ZZ". 014500          PERFORM INQUIRE-RECORDS.
021900                                   014600
022000 INQUIRE-RECORDS.                  014700 INQUIRE-RECORDS.
022100      PERFORM DISPLAY-ALL-FIELDS.  014800      PERFORM DISPLAY-ALL-FIELDS.
022200      PERFORM GET-STATE-RECORD.    014900      PERFORM PRESS-ENTER.
022300                                   015000
                                         015100 PRESS-ENTER.
                                         015200      DISPLAY " ".
                                         015300      DISPLAY "PRESS ENTER "
                                         015400          "TO CONTINUE".
                                         015500      ACCEPT A-DUMMY.
                                         015600

022400*--------------------------
022500* DELETE
022600*--------------------------
022700 DELETE-MODE.
022800      MOVE "DELETE" TO THE-MODE.
022900      PERFORM GET-STATE-RECORD.
023000      PERFORM DELETE-RECORDS
023100          UNTIL STATE-CODE = "ZZ".
023200
023300 DELETE-RECORDS.
023400      PERFORM DISPLAY-ALL-FIELDS.
023500
023600      PERFORM ASK-OK-TO-DELETE
023700      IF OK-TO-DELETE = "Y"
023800       PERFORM
023900        DELETE-STATE-RECORD.
024000
024100      PERFORM GET-STATE-RECORD.
024200
024300 ASK-OK-TO-DELETE.
024400      PERFORM ACCEPT-OK-TO-DELETE.
024500      PERFORM
024600       RE-ACCEPT-OK-TO-DELETE
024700          UNTIL OK-TO-DELETE = "Y"
024800                      OR "N".
024900
025000 ACCEPT-OK-TO-DELETE.
025100      DISPLAY "DELETE THIS "
025200          "RECORD (Y/N)?".
025300      ACCEPT OK-TO-DELETE.
025400
025500      INSPECT OK-TO-DELETE
025600       CONVERTING LOWER-ALPHA
025700       TO         UPPER-ALPHA.
025800
025900 RE-ACCEPT-OK-TO-DELETE.
026000      DISPLAY "YOU MUST ENTER "
026100          "YES OR NO".
026200      PERFORM ACCEPT-OK-TO-DELETE.
026300
026400*--------------------------
026500* PRINT
026600*--------------------------
```

continues

Figure A.4.

continued

```
026700 PRINT-THE-RECORDS.
026800     CLOSE STATE-FILE.
026900     DISPLAY "REPORT IN "
027000         "PROGRESS".
027100     CALL "STCRPT02".
027200     OPEN I-O STATE-FILE.
027300
027400*-----------------------------     015700*--------------------------
027500* Routines shared by all modes     015800* Routines shared by
027600*-----------------------------     015900* Change and Inquire
027700 INIT-STATE-RECORD.                016000*--------------------------
027800     MOVE SPACE TO STATE-RECORD.   016100 INIT-CONTROL-RECORD.
027900                                   016200     MOVE ZEROES
028000 ENTER-STATE-CODE.                 016300         TO CONTROL-RECORD.
028100     PERFORM ACCEPT-STATE-CODE.    016400
028200     PERFORM RE-ACCEPT-STATE-CODE  016500 ENTER-CONTROL-KEY.
028300         UNTIL STATE-CODE          016600     MOVE 1 TO CONTROL-KEY.
028400             NOT = SPACE.          016700
028500
028600 ACCEPT-STATE-CODE.
028700     DISPLAY " ".
028800     DISPLAY "ENTER STATE CODE "
028900         "OF THE STATE" .
029000     DISPLAY "TO " THE-MODE
029100     "(2 UPPER CASE CHARACTERS)".
029200     DISPLAY "ENTER ZZ TO "
029300         "STOP ENTRY".
029400     ACCEPT STATE-CODE.
029500
029600     INSPECT STATE-CODE
029700       CONVERTING LOWER-ALPHA
029800       TO        UPPER-ALPHA.
029900
030000 RE-ACCEPT-STATE-CODE.
030100     DISPLAY "STATE CODE MUST "
030200         "BE ENTERED".
030300     PERFORM ACCEPT-STATE-CODE.
030400
030500 GET-STATE-RECORD.                 016800 GET-CONTROL-RECORD.
030600     PERFORM INIT-STATE-RECORD.    016900     PERFORM INIT-CONTROL-RECORD.
030700     PERFORM ENTER-STATE-CODE.     017000     PERFORM ENTER-CONTROL-KEY.
030800     MOVE "N" TO RECORD-FOUND.     017100     MOVE "N" TO RECORD-FOUND.
030900     PERFORM FIND-STATE-RECORD     017200     PERFORM FIND-CONTROL-RECORD.
031000       UNTIL RECORD-FOUND = "Y" OR 017300
031100           STATE-CODE = "ZZ".
031200
031300*-----------------------------
031400* Routines for Add and Change
031500*-----------------------------
031600 FIND-STATE-RECORD.                017400 FIND-CONTROL-RECORD.
031700     PERFORM READ-STATE-RECORD.    017500     PERFORM READ-CONTROL-RECORD.
031800     IF RECORD-FOUND = "N"         017600     IF RECORD-FOUND = "N"
031900       DISPLAY "RECORD NOT FOUND"  017700       DISPLAY "RECORD NOT FOUND"
032000       PERFORM ENTER-STATE-CODE.   017800           "FOUND"
032100                                   017900       DISPLAY "YOU MUST RUN "
                                         018000           "CTLBLD01"
                                         018100       DISPLAY "TO CREATE "
                                         018200           "THIS FILE".
                                         018300
                                         018400*--------------------------
                                         018500* Routines for Change
                                         018600*--------------------------
032200 ENTER-STATE-NAME.                 018700 ENTER-CONTROL-LAST-VOUCHER.
032300     PERFORM ACCEPT-STATE-NAME.    018800     PERFORM
032400     PERFORM RE-ACCEPT-STATE-NAME  018900     ACCEPT-CONTROL-LAST-VOUCHER.
032500       UNTIL                       019000
032600         STATE-NAME NOT = SPACES.  019100 ACCEPT-CONTROL-LAST-VOUCHER.
032700                                   019200     DISPLAY "ENTER LAST "
032800 ACCEPT-STATE-NAME.                019300         "VOUCHER NUMBER".
```

```
032900     DISPLAY "ENTER STATE NAME".     019400     ACCEPT CONTROL-LAST-VOUCHER.
033000     ACCEPT STATE-NAME.              019500
033100
033200     INSPECT STATE-NAME
033300       CONVERTING LOWER-ALPHA
033400       TO          UPPER-ALPHA.
033500
033600 RE-ACCEPT-STATE-NAME.
033700     DISPLAY "STATE NAME "
033800             "MUST BE ENTERED".
033900     PERFORM ACCEPT-STATE-NAME.
034000
034100*---------------------------
034200* Routines shared by Change,
034300* Inquire and Delete
034400*---------------------------
034500 DISPLAY-ALL-FIELDS.                 019600 DISPLAY-ALL-FIELDS.
034600     DISPLAY " ".                    019700     DISPLAY " ".
034700     PERFORM DISPLAY-STATE-CODE.     019800     PERFORM
034800     PERFORM DISPLAY-STATE-NAME.     019900     DISPLAY-CTRL-LAST-VOUCHER
034900     DISPLAY " ".                    020000
035000                                     020100     DISPLAY " ".
035100 DISPLAY-STATE-CODE.                 020200
035200     DISPLAY                         020300 DISPLAY-CTRL-LAST-VOUCHER.
035300        "  STATE CODE: "             020400     DISPLAY
035400        STATE-CODE.                  020500       "1. LAST VOUCHER NUMBER: "
035500                                     020600        CONTROL-LAST-VOUCHER.
035600 DISPLAY-STATE-NAME.                 020700
035700     DISPLAY
035800       "1. STATE NAME: "
035900          STATE-NAME.
036000
036100*---------------------------         020800*---------------------------
036200* File I-O Routines                  020900* File I-O Routines
036300*---------------------------         021000*---------------------------
036400 READ-STATE-RECORD.                  021100 READ-CONTROL-RECORD.
036500     MOVE "Y" TO RECORD-FOUND.       021200     MOVE "Y" TO RECORD-FOUND.
036600     READ STATE-FILE RECORD          021300     READ CONTROL-FILE RECORD
036700       INVALID KEY                   021400       INVALID KEY
036800       MOVE "N" TO RECORD-FOUND.     021500       MOVE "N" TO RECORD-FOUND.
036900                                     021600
037000*or  READ STATE-FILE RECORD          021700*or  READ CONTROL-FILE RECORD
037100*          WITH LOCK                 021800*          WITH LOCK
037200*      INVALID KEY                   021900*      INVALID KEY
037300*      MOVE "N" TO RECORD-FOUND.     022000*      MOVE "N" TO RECORD-FOUND.
037400                                     022100
037500*or  READ STATE-FILE RECORD          022200*or  READ CONTROL-FILE RECORD
037600*          WITH HOLD                 022300*          WITH HOLD
037700*      INVALID KEY                   022400*      INVALID KEY
037800*      MOVE "N" TO RECORD-FOUND.     022500*      MOVE "N" TO RECORD-FOUND.
037900                                     022600
038000 WRITE-STATE-RECORD.
038100     WRITE STATE-RECORD
038200       INVALID KEY
038300       DISPLAY "RECORD ALREADY "
038400               "ON FILE".
038500
038600 REWRITE-STATE-RECORD.               022700 REWRITE-CONTROL-RECORD.
038700     REWRITE STATE-RECORD            022800     REWRITE CONTROL-RECORD
038800       INVALID KEY                   022900       INVALID KEY
038900       DISPLAY "ERROR REWRITING "    023000       DISPLAY "ERROR REWRITING "
039000               "STATE RECORD".       023100               "CONTROL RECORD".
039100
039200 DELETE-STATE-RECORD.
039300     DELETE STATE-FILE RECORD
039400       INVALID KEY
039500       DISPLAY "ERROR DELETING "
039600               "STATE RECORD".
```

A

2. Listing A.36 makes it possible to directly test DATE-CCYY for a value, as shown in Listing A.37.

TYPE **Listing A.36.** REDEFINES **within a** REDEFINES.

```
003200 01  DATE-CCYYMMDD       PIC 9(8).
003300 01  FILLER REDEFINES DATE-CCYYMMDD.
003400     05  DATE-CCYY       PIC 9999.
003500     05  FILLER REDEFINES DATE-CCYY.
003600         10  DATE-CC     PIC 99.
003700         10  DATE-YY     PIC 99.
003800     05  DATE-MM         PIC 99.
003900     05  DATE-DD         PIC 99.
```

TYPE **Listing A.37. Testing the whole year.**

```
021500     MOVE "Y" TO VALID-DATE-FLAG.
021600     IF DATE-CCYYMMDD = ZEROES
021700         IF ZERO-DATE-IS-OK = "Y"
021800             MOVE "0" TO VALID-DATE-FLAG
021900         ELSE
022000             MOVE "N" TO VALID-DATE-FLAG
022100     ELSE
           IF DATE-CCYY < 1920 OR DATE-CCYY > 2150
               MOVE "N" TO VALID-DATE-FLAG
           ELSE
022200     IF DATE-MM < 1 OR DATE-MM > 12
022300         MOVE "N" TO VALID-DATE-FLAG
022400     ELSE
022500     IF DATE-DD < 1 OR DATE-DD > 31
022600         MOVE "N" TO VALID-DATE-FLAG
022700     ELSE
022800     IF (DATE-DD > 30) AND
022900        (DATE-MM = 2 OR 4 OR 6 OR 9 OR 11)
023000         MOVE "N" TO VALID-DATE-FLAG
023100     ELSE
023200     IF DATE-DD > 29 AND DATE-MM = 2
023300         MOVE "N" TO VALID-DATE-FLAG
023400     ELSE
023500     IF DATE-DD = 29 AND DATE-MM = 2
. . . . .
. . . . .
024100
```

3. One answer is shown in the following two listings, A.38 and A.39. A CHECK-TIME routine would use WORKING-STORAGE as in Listing A.38. Create this file and name it WSTIME01.CBL. The logic for checking the time is in Listing A.39, which you should create and call PLTIME01.CBL.

TYPE **Listing A.38.** WORKING-STORAGE **for** CHECK-TIME.

```
000100*-------------------------------
000200* Fields for CHECK-TIME
000300*-------------------------------
000400 77  VALID-TIME-FLAG      PIC X.
000500     88  TIME-IS-INVALID  VALUE "N".
000600     88  TIME-IS-VALID    VALUE "Y".
000700
000800 01  TIME-HHMMSS          PIC 9(6).
000900 01  FILLER REDEFINES TIME-HHMMSS.
001000     05  TIME-HH          PIC 99.
001100     05  TIME-MM          PIC 99.
001200     05  TIME-SS          PIC 99.
001300
```

TYPE **Listing A.39. The** CHECK-TIME **routine.**

```
000100*-------------------------------
000200* USAGE:
000300*    MOVE TIME(hhmmss) TO TIME-HHMMSS.
000400*    PERFORM CHECK-TIME.
000500*
000600* RETURNS:
000700*    TIME-IS-VALID   (VALID)
000800*    TIME-IS-INVALID (BAD TIME )
000900*
001000* Assume that the time is good, then
001100* test the time in the following
001200* steps. The routine stops if any
001300* of these conditions is true,
001400* and sets the valid time flag to "N".
001500* 1.  Hours > 23
001600* 2.  Minutes > 59
001700* 3.  Seconds > 59
001800*-------------------------------
001900 CHECK-TIME.
002000     MOVE "Y" TO VALID-TIME-FLAG.
002100     IF TIME-HH > 23
002200         MOVE "N" TO VALID-TIME-FLAG
002300     ELSE
002400     IF TIME-MM > 59
002500         MOVE "N" TO VALID-TIME-FLAG
002600     ELSE
002700     IF TIME-SS > 59
002800         MOVE "N" TO VALID-TIME-FLAG.
002900
```

You can use Listing A.40 to check your logic.

TYPE   **Listing A.40.** TIME01 **testing time logic.**

```
000100 IDENTIFICATION DIVISION.
000200 PROGRAM-ID. TIME01.
000300*-------------------------------
000400* Testing CHECK-TIME
000500*-------------------------------
000600 ENVIRONMENT DIVISION.
000700 INPUT-OUTPUT SECTION.
000800 FILE-CONTROL.
000900
001000 DATA DIVISION.
001100 FILE SECTION.
001200
001300 WORKING-STORAGE SECTION.
001400
001500 77  ANY-TIME           PIC 9(6) VALUE ZEROES.
001600
001700 77  TIME-FIELD         PIC Z(6).
001800
001900     COPY "WSTIME01.CBL".
002000
002100 PROCEDURE DIVISION.
002200 PROGRAM-BEGIN.
002300     PERFORM OPENING-PROCEDURE.
002400     PERFORM MAIN-PROCESS.
002500     PERFORM CLOSING-PROCEDURE.
002600
002700 PROGRAM-EXIT.
002800     EXIT PROGRAM.
002900
003000 PROGRAM-DONE.
003100     STOP RUN.
003200
003300 OPENING-PROCEDURE.
003400
003500 CLOSING-PROCEDURE.
003600
003700 MAIN-PROCESS.
003800     PERFORM GET-A-TIME.
003900     PERFORM DISPLAY-AND-GET-TIME
004000         UNTIL ANY-TIME = 000001.
004100
004200 GET-A-TIME.
004300     PERFORM ACCEPT-A-TIME.
004400     PERFORM RE-ACCEPT-A-TIME
004500         UNTIL TIME-IS-VALID.
004600     MOVE TIME-HHMMSS TO ANY-TIME.
004700
004800 ACCEPT-A-TIME.
004900     DISPLAY "ENTER A TIME (HHMMSS)"
005000     ACCEPT TIME-FIELD.
005100     PERFORM EDIT-CHECK-TIME.
005200
005300 RE-ACCEPT-A-TIME.
005400     DISPLAY "INVALID TIME"
```

```
005500     PERFORM ACCEPT-A-TIME.
005600
005700 EDIT-CHECK-TIME.
005800     PERFORM EDIT-TIME.
005900     PERFORM CHECK-TIME.
006000
006100 EDIT-TIME.
006200     MOVE TIME-FIELD TO TIME-HHMMSS.
006300
006400 DISPLAY-AND-GET-TIME.
006500     PERFORM DISPLAY-THE-TIME.
006600     PERFORM GET-A-TIME.
006700
006800 DISPLAY-THE-TIME.
006900     DISPLAY "ANY TIME IS " ANY-TIME.
007000
007100     COPY "PLTIME01.CBL".
007200
```

Answers to Day 20, "More Complex Data Entry"

Quiz

The original routine prevented the entry of values greater than VOUCHER-AMOUNT by using this logic:

```
025600 ENTER-VOUCHER-PAID-AMOUNT.
025700     PERFORM ACCEPT-VOUCHER-PAID-AMOUNT.
025800     PERFORM RE-ACCEPT-VOUCHER-PAID-AMOUNT
025900         UNTIL VOUCHER-PAID-AMOUNT NOT = ZEROES
026000             AND VOUCHER-PAID-AMOUNT NOT > VOUCHER-AMOUNT.
```

The new logic prevents only a zero amount from being entered:

```
025600 ENTER-VOUCHER-PAID-AMOUNT.
025700     PERFORM ACCEPT-VOUCHER-PAID-AMOUNT.
025800     PERFORM RE-ACCEPT-VOUCHER-PAID-AMOUNT
025900         UNTIL VOUCHER-PAID-AMOUNT NOT = ZEROES.
026000
```

The user can enter any amount other than zero for the voucher paid amount.

Exercise

Listing A.41 implements the changes from the quiz question.

A

TYPE   **Listing A.41. Allowing overpayment.**

```
000100 IDENTIFICATION DIVISION.
000200 PROGRAM-ID. VCHPAY02.
000300*-------------------------------
000400* Change only.
000500* User can request a voucher.
000600* If the voucher is already paid,
000700* the user is asked whether
000800* to clear the payment
000900* and reopen the voucher.
001000* If the voucher is not paid,
001100* the user is required to enter
001200* a payment date, amount and check
001300* number.
001400* Only maintains PAID-DATE
001500* CHECK-NO and PAID-AMOUNT.
001600*-------------------------------
001700 ENVIRONMENT DIVISION.
001800 INPUT-OUTPUT SECTION.
001900 FILE-CONTROL.
002000
002100     COPY "SLVND02.CBL".
002200
002300     COPY "SLVOUCH.CBL".
002400
002500     COPY "SLCONTRL.CBL".
002600
002700 DATA DIVISION.
002800 FILE SECTION.
002900
003000     COPY "FDVND04.CBL".
003100
003200     COPY "FDVOUCH.CBL".
003300
003400     COPY "FDCONTRL.CBL".
003500
003600 WORKING-STORAGE SECTION.
003700
003800 77  WHICH-FIELD                PIC 9.
003900 77  OK-TO-PROCESS              PIC X.
004000 77  FULL-PAYMENT               PIC X.
004100 77  NEW-VOUCHER                PIC X.
004200
004300 77  VOUCHER-RECORD-FOUND       PIC X.
004400 77  VENDOR-RECORD-FOUND        PIC X.
004500 77  CONTROL-RECORD-FOUND       PIC X.
004600 77  VOUCHER-NUMBER-FIELD       PIC Z(5).
004700 77  AN-AMOUNT-FIELD            PIC ZZZ,ZZ9.99-.
004800 77  CHECK-NO-FIELD             PIC Z(6).
004900
005000 77  PROCESS-MESSAGE            PIC X(79) VALUE SPACE.
005100
005200 77  SAVE-VOUCHER-RECORD        PIC X(103).
005300
005400     COPY "WSDATE01.CBL".
```

```
005500
005600     COPY "WSCASE01.CBL".
005700
005800 PROCEDURE DIVISION.
005900 PROGRAM-BEGIN.
006000     PERFORM OPENING-PROCEDURE.
006100     PERFORM MAIN-PROCESS.
006200     PERFORM CLOSING-PROCEDURE.
006300
006400 PROGRAM-EXIT.
006500     EXIT PROGRAM.
006600
006700 PROGRAM-DONE.
006800     STOP RUN.
006900
007000 OPENING-PROCEDURE.
007100     OPEN I-O VOUCHER-FILE.
007200     OPEN I-O VENDOR-FILE.
007300     OPEN I-O CONTROL-FILE.
007400
007500 CLOSING-PROCEDURE.
007600     CLOSE VOUCHER-FILE.
007700     CLOSE VENDOR-FILE.
007800     CLOSE CONTROL-FILE.
007900
008000 MAIN-PROCESS.
008100     PERFORM CHANGE-MODE.
008200
008300*-------------------------------
008400* CHANGE
008500*-------------------------------
008600 CHANGE-MODE.
008700     PERFORM GET-EXISTING-RECORD.
008800     PERFORM CHANGE-RECORDS
008900         UNTIL VOUCHER-NUMBER = ZEROES.
009000
009100 CHANGE-RECORDS.
009200     PERFORM DISPLAY-ALL-FIELDS.
009300     IF VOUCHER-PAID-DATE = ZEROES
009400         PERFORM CHANGE-TO-PAID
009500     ELSE
009600         PERFORM CHANGE-TO-UNPAID.
009700
009800     PERFORM GET-EXISTING-RECORD.
009900
010000*-------------------------------
010100* Ask if the user wants to pay this
010200* voucher and if so:
010300* Change the voucher to paid status
010400* by getting PAID-DATE, PAID-AMOUNT
010500* and CHECK-NO.
010600*-------------------------------
010700 CHANGE-TO-PAID.
010800     PERFORM ASK-OK-TO-PAY.
010900     IF OK-TO-PROCESS = "Y"
```

continues

Listing A.41. continued

```
011000          PERFORM CHANGE-ALL-FIELDS.
011100
011200 ASK-OK-TO-PAY.
011300     MOVE "PROCESS THIS VOUCHER AS PAID (Y/N)?"
011400         TO PROCESS-MESSAGE.
011500     PERFORM ASK-OK-TO-PROCESS.
011600
011700 CHANGE-ALL-FIELDS.
011800     PERFORM CHANGE-THIS-FIELD
011900         VARYING WHICH-FIELD FROM 1 BY 1
012000           UNTIL WHICH-FIELD > 3.
012100
012200     PERFORM REWRITE-VOUCHER-RECORD.
012300
012400     IF NEW-VOUCHER = "Y"
012500         PERFORM GENERATE-NEW-VOUCHER.
012600
012700 CHANGE-THIS-FIELD.
012800     IF WHICH-FIELD = 1
012900         PERFORM ENTER-VOUCHER-PAID-DATE.
013000     IF WHICH-FIELD = 2
013100         PERFORM ENTER-VOUCHER-PAYMENT.
013200     IF WHICH-FIELD = 3
013300         PERFORM ENTER-VOUCHER-CHECK-NO.
013400
013500*--------------------------------
013600* Ask if the user wants to re-open
013700* this voucher and if so:
013800* Move zeroes to PAID-DATE,
013900* PAID-AMOUNT and CHECK-NO.
014000*--------------------------------
014100 CHANGE-TO-UNPAID.
014200     PERFORM ASK-OK-TO-OPEN.
014300     IF OK-TO-PROCESS = "Y"
014400         PERFORM CLEAR-PAID-AND-REWRITE
014500         DISPLAY "VOUCHER HAS BEEN REOPENED".
014600
014700 CLEAR-PAID-AND-REWRITE.
014800     PERFORM CLEAR-PAID-FIELDS.
014900     PERFORM REWRITE-VOUCHER-RECORD.
015000
015100 CLEAR-PAID-FIELDS.
015200     MOVE ZEROES TO VOUCHER-PAID-DATE
015300                    VOUCHER-PAID-AMOUNT
015400                    VOUCHER-CHECK-NO.
015500
015600 ASK-OK-TO-OPEN.
015700     MOVE "RE-OPEN THIS VOUCHER (Y/N)?" TO PROCESS-MESSAGE.
015800     PERFORM ASK-OK-TO-PROCESS.
015900
016000*--------------------------------
016100* This routine is used by both
016200* ASK-OK-TO-PAY which is part of
016300* the CHANGE-TO-PAID logic, and
```

```
016400* ASK-OK-TO-OPEN which is part
016500* of the CHANGE-TO-UNPAID LOGIC.
016600*-------------------------------
016700 ASK-OK-TO-PROCESS.
016800     PERFORM ACCEPT-OK-TO-PROCESS.
016900
017000     PERFORM RE-ACCEPT-OK-TO-PROCESS
017100        UNTIL OK-TO-PROCESS = "Y" OR "N".
017200
017300 ACCEPT-OK-TO-PROCESS.
017400     DISPLAY PROCESS-MESSAGE.
017500     ACCEPT OK-TO-PROCESS.
017600     INSPECT OK-TO-PROCESS
017700      CONVERTING LOWER-ALPHA TO UPPER-ALPHA.
017800
017900 RE-ACCEPT-OK-TO-PROCESS.
018000     DISPLAY "YOU MUST ENTER YES OR NO".
018100     PERFORM ACCEPT-OK-TO-PROCESS.
018200
018300*-------------------------------
018400* Field entry routines.
018500*-------------------------------
018600 ENTER-VOUCHER-PAID-DATE.
018700     MOVE "N" TO ZERO-DATE-IS-OK.
018800     MOVE "ENTER PAID DATE(MM/DD/YYYY)?"
018900        TO DATE-PROMPT.
019000     MOVE "A VALID PAID DATE IS REQUIRED"
019100        TO DATE-ERROR-MESSAGE.
019200     PERFORM GET-A-DATE.
019300     MOVE DATE-CCYYMMDD TO VOUCHER-PAID-DATE.
019400
019500*-------------------------------
019600* Voucher payment is entered by
019700* asking if the payment is for the
019800* the exact amount of the voucher.
019900* If it is, VOUCHER-AMOUNT is
020000* moved in to VOUCHER-PAID-AMOUNT.
020100* If it is not, then the user is
020200* asked to enter the amount
020300* to be paid.
020400* If the paid amount is less than
020500* the voucher amount, the user
020600* is also asked if a new voucher
020700* should be generated for the
020800* the balance. This allows
020900* for partial payments.
021000*-------------------------------
021100 ENTER-VOUCHER-PAYMENT.
021200     MOVE "N" TO NEW-VOUCHER.
021300     PERFORM ASK-FULL-PAYMENT.
021400     IF FULL-PAYMENT = "Y"
021500        MOVE VOUCHER-AMOUNT TO VOUCHER-PAID-AMOUNT
021600     ELSE
021700        PERFORM ENTER-VOUCHER-PAID-AMOUNT
021800        IF VOUCHER-PAID-AMOUNT < VOUCHER-AMOUNT
```

continues

Listing A.41. continued

```
021900              PERFORM ASK-NEW-VOUCHER.
022000
022100 ASK-FULL-PAYMENT.
022200     PERFORM ACCEPT-FULL-PAYMENT.
022300     PERFORM RE-ACCEPT-FULL-PAYMENT
022400         UNTIL FULL-PAYMENT = "Y" OR "N".
022500
022600 ACCEPT-FULL-PAYMENT.
022700     MOVE VOUCHER-AMOUNT TO AN-AMOUNT-FIELD.
022800     DISPLAY "PAY THE EXACT AMOUNT "
022900             AN-AMOUNT-FIELD
023000             " (Y/N)?".
023100     ACCEPT FULL-PAYMENT.
023200     INSPECT FULL-PAYMENT
023300      CONVERTING LOWER-ALPHA TO UPPER-ALPHA.
023400
023500 RE-ACCEPT-FULL-PAYMENT.
023600     DISPLAY "YOU MUST ENTER YES OR NO".
023700     PERFORM ACCEPT-FULL-PAYMENT.
023800
023900 ASK-NEW-VOUCHER.
024000     PERFORM ACCEPT-NEW-VOUCHER.
024100     PERFORM RE-ACCEPT-NEW-VOUCHER
024200         UNTIL NEW-VOUCHER = "Y" OR "N".
024300
024400 ACCEPT-NEW-VOUCHER.
024500     MOVE VOUCHER-AMOUNT TO AN-AMOUNT-FIELD.
024600     DISPLAY "GENERATE A NEW VOUCHER".
024700     DISPLAY " FOR THE BALANCE (Y/N)?".
024800     ACCEPT NEW-VOUCHER.
024900     INSPECT NEW-VOUCHER
025000      CONVERTING LOWER-ALPHA TO UPPER-ALPHA.
025100
025200 RE-ACCEPT-NEW-VOUCHER.
025300     DISPLAY "YOU MUST ENTER YES OR NO".
025400     PERFORM ACCEPT-NEW-VOUCHER.
025500
025600 ENTER-VOUCHER-PAID-AMOUNT.
025700     PERFORM ACCEPT-VOUCHER-PAID-AMOUNT.
025800     PERFORM RE-ACCEPT-VOUCHER-PAID-AMOUNT
025900         UNTIL VOUCHER-PAID-AMOUNT NOT = ZEROES.
026000
026100
026200 ACCEPT-VOUCHER-PAID-AMOUNT.
026300     DISPLAY "ENTER AMOUNT PAID".
026400     ACCEPT AN-AMOUNT-FIELD.
026500     MOVE AN-AMOUNT-FIELD TO VOUCHER-PAID-AMOUNT.
026600
026700 RE-ACCEPT-VOUCHER-PAID-AMOUNT.
026800     MOVE VOUCHER-AMOUNT TO AN-AMOUNT-FIELD.
026900     DISPLAY "A PAYMENT MUST BE ENTERED".
027000     DISPLAY "AGAINST " AN-AMOUNT-FIELD.
027100     PERFORM ACCEPT-VOUCHER-PAID-AMOUNT.
027200
```

```
027300 ENTER-VOUCHER-CHECK-NO.
027400     PERFORM ACCEPT-VOUCHER-CHECK-NO.
027500
027600 ACCEPT-VOUCHER-CHECK-NO.
027700     DISPLAY "ENTER THE CHECK NUMBER".
027800     DISPLAY "ENTER 0 FOR CASH PAYMENT".
027900     ACCEPT CHECK-NO-FIELD.
028000     MOVE CHECK-NO-FIELD TO VOUCHER-CHECK-NO.
028100
028200*-------------------------------
028300* A new voucher is generated by
028400* 1. Saving the existing voucher
028500*    record.
028600* 2. Locating a new voucher number
028700*    that is not in use by using
028800*    the control file and attempting
028900*    to read a voucher with the
029000*    number offered by the control
029100*    file.
029200* 3. Restoring the saved voucher record
029300*    but using the new voucher number.
029400* 4. Setting the new voucher amount
029500*    to the original amount minus
029600*    the amount paid.
029700* 5. Resetting the paid date,
029800*    paid amount and check number
029900* 6. Setting the selected flag to "N".
030000* 7. Writing this new record.
030100*-------------------------------
030200 GENERATE-NEW-VOUCHER.
030300     MOVE VOUCHER-RECORD TO SAVE-VOUCHER-RECORD.
030400     PERFORM GET-NEW-RECORD-KEY.
030500     PERFORM CREATE-NEW-VOUCHER-RECORD.
030600     PERFORM DISPLAY-NEW-VOUCHER.
030700
030800 CREATE-NEW-VOUCHER-RECORD.
030900     MOVE SAVE-VOUCHER-RECORD TO VOUCHER-RECORD.
031000     MOVE CONTROL-LAST-VOUCHER TO VOUCHER-NUMBER.
031100     SUBTRACT VOUCHER-PAID-AMOUNT FROM VOUCHER-AMOUNT.
031200     MOVE "N" TO VOUCHER-SELECTED.
031300     PERFORM CLEAR-PAID-FIELDS.
031400     PERFORM WRITE-VOUCHER-RECORD.
031500
031600 DISPLAY-NEW-VOUCHER.
031700     MOVE VOUCHER-NUMBER TO VOUCHER-NUMBER-FIELD.
031800     MOVE VOUCHER-AMOUNT TO AN-AMOUNT-FIELD.
031900     DISPLAY "VOUCHER " VOUCHER-NUMBER-FIELD
032000             " CREATED FOR " AN-AMOUNT-FIELD.
032100
032200*-------------------------------
032300* Standard change mode routines to
032400* get a voucher number, read the
032500* voucher record.
032600*-------------------------------
032700 GET-NEW-RECORD-KEY.
```

continues

Listing A.41. continued

```
032800      PERFORM ACCEPT-NEW-RECORD-KEY.
032900      PERFORM RE-ACCEPT-NEW-RECORD-KEY
033000          UNTIL VOUCHER-RECORD-FOUND = "N".
033100
033200
033300
033400 ACCEPT-NEW-RECORD-KEY.
033500      PERFORM INIT-VOUCHER-RECORD.
033600      PERFORM RETRIEVE-NEXT-VOUCHER-NUMBER.
033700
033800      PERFORM READ-VOUCHER-RECORD.
033900
034000 RE-ACCEPT-NEW-RECORD-KEY.
034100      PERFORM ACCEPT-NEW-RECORD-KEY.
034200
034300 RETRIEVE-NEXT-VOUCHER-NUMBER.
034400      PERFORM READ-CONTROL-RECORD.
034500      ADD 1 TO CONTROL-LAST-VOUCHER.
034600      MOVE CONTROL-LAST-VOUCHER TO VOUCHER-NUMBER.
034700      PERFORM REWRITE-CONTROL-RECORD.
034800
034900 GET-EXISTING-RECORD.
035000      PERFORM ACCEPT-EXISTING-KEY.
035100      PERFORM RE-ACCEPT-EXISTING-KEY
035200          UNTIL VOUCHER-RECORD-FOUND = "Y" OR
035300              VOUCHER-NUMBER = ZEROES.
035400
035500 ACCEPT-EXISTING-KEY.
035600      PERFORM INIT-VOUCHER-RECORD.
035700      PERFORM ENTER-VOUCHER-NUMBER.
035800      IF VOUCHER-NUMBER NOT = ZEROES
035900          PERFORM READ-VOUCHER-RECORD.
036000
036100 RE-ACCEPT-EXISTING-KEY.
036200      DISPLAY "RECORD NOT FOUND".
036300      PERFORM ACCEPT-EXISTING-KEY.
036400
036500 ENTER-VOUCHER-NUMBER.
036600      DISPLAY "ENTER VOUCHER NUMBER TO PROCESS".
036700      ACCEPT VOUCHER-NUMBER.
036800
036900*--------------------------------
037000* Standard routines to display
037100* voucher fields.
037200*--------------------------------
037300 DISPLAY-ALL-FIELDS.
037400      DISPLAY " ".
037500      PERFORM DISPLAY-VOUCHER-NUMBER.
037600      PERFORM DISPLAY-VOUCHER-VENDOR.
037700      PERFORM DISPLAY-VOUCHER-INVOICE.
037800      PERFORM DISPLAY-VOUCHER-FOR.
037900      PERFORM DISPLAY-VOUCHER-AMOUNT.
038000      PERFORM DISPLAY-VOUCHER-DATE.
038100      PERFORM DISPLAY-VOUCHER-DUE.
```

```
038200          PERFORM DISPLAY-VOUCHER-DEDUCTIBLE.
038300          PERFORM DISPLAY-VOUCHER-SELECTED.
038400          PERFORM DISPLAY-VOUCHER-PAID-DATE.
038500          PERFORM DISPLAY-VOUCHER-PAID-AMOUNT.
038600          PERFORM DISPLAY-VOUCHER-CHECK-NO.
038700          DISPLAY " ".
038800
038900 DISPLAY-VOUCHER-NUMBER.
039000          DISPLAY "   VOUCHER NUMBER: " VOUCHER-NUMBER.
039100
039200 DISPLAY-VOUCHER-VENDOR.
039300          PERFORM VOUCHER-VENDOR-ON-FILE.
039400          IF VENDOR-RECORD-FOUND = "N"
039500              MOVE "**Not found**" TO VENDOR-NAME.
039600          DISPLAY "   VENDOR: "
039700                  VOUCHER-VENDOR " "
039800                  VENDOR-NAME.
039900
040000 DISPLAY-VOUCHER-INVOICE.
040100          DISPLAY "   INVOICE: " VOUCHER-INVOICE.
040200
040300 DISPLAY-VOUCHER-FOR.
040400          DISPLAY "   FOR: " VOUCHER-FOR.
040500
040600 DISPLAY-VOUCHER-AMOUNT.
040700          MOVE VOUCHER-AMOUNT TO AN-AMOUNT-FIELD.
040800          DISPLAY "   AMOUNT: " AN-AMOUNT-FIELD.
040900
041000 DISPLAY-VOUCHER-DATE.
041100          MOVE VOUCHER-DATE TO DATE-CCYYMMDD.
041200          PERFORM FORMAT-THE-DATE.
041300          DISPLAY "   INVOICE DATE: " FORMATTED-DATE.
041400
041500 DISPLAY-VOUCHER-DUE.
041600          MOVE VOUCHER-DUE TO DATE-CCYYMMDD.
041700          PERFORM FORMAT-THE-DATE.
041800          DISPLAY "   DUE DATE: " FORMATTED-DATE.
041900
042000 DISPLAY-VOUCHER-DEDUCTIBLE.
042100          DISPLAY "   DEDUCTIBLE: " VOUCHER-DEDUCTIBLE.
042200
042300 DISPLAY-VOUCHER-SELECTED.
042400          DISPLAY "   SELECTED FOR PAYMENT: " VOUCHER-SELECTED.
042500
042600 DISPLAY-VOUCHER-PAID-DATE.
042700          MOVE VOUCHER-PAID-DATE TO DATE-CCYYMMDD.
042800          PERFORM FORMAT-THE-DATE.
042900          DISPLAY "1. PAID ON: " FORMATTED-DATE.
043000
043100 DISPLAY-VOUCHER-PAID-AMOUNT.
043200          MOVE VOUCHER-PAID-AMOUNT TO AN-AMOUNT-FIELD.
043300          DISPLAY "2. PAID: " AN-AMOUNT-FIELD.
043400
043500 DISPLAY-VOUCHER-CHECK-NO.
043600          DISPLAY "3. CHECK: " VOUCHER-CHECK-NO.
```

continues

Listing A.41. continued

```
043700
043800*-------------------------------
043900* File activity Routines
044000*-------------------------------
044100 INIT-VOUCHER-RECORD.
044200     MOVE SPACE TO VOUCHER-INVOICE
044300                    VOUCHER-FOR
044400                    VOUCHER-DEDUCTIBLE
044500                    VOUCHER-SELECTED.
044600     MOVE ZEROES TO VOUCHER-NUMBER
044700                    VOUCHER-VENDOR
044800                    VOUCHER-AMOUNT
044900                    VOUCHER-DATE
045000                    VOUCHER-DUE
045100                    VOUCHER-PAID-AMOUNT
045200                    VOUCHER-PAID-DATE
045300                    VOUCHER-CHECK-NO.
045400
045500 READ-VOUCHER-RECORD.
045600     MOVE "Y" TO VOUCHER-RECORD-FOUND.
045700     READ VOUCHER-FILE RECORD
045800       INVALID KEY
045900         MOVE "N" TO VOUCHER-RECORD-FOUND.
046000
046100*or  READ VOUCHER-FILE RECORD WITH LOCK
046200*      INVALID KEY
046300*        MOVE "N" TO VOUCHER-RECORD-FOUND.
046400
046500*or  READ VOUCHER-FILE RECORD WITH HOLD
046600*      INVALID KEY
046700*        MOVE "N" TO VOUCHER-RECORD-FOUND.
046800
046900 WRITE-VOUCHER-RECORD.
047000     WRITE VOUCHER-RECORD
047100         INVALID KEY
047200         DISPLAY "RECORD ALREADY ON FILE".
047300
047400 REWRITE-VOUCHER-RECORD.
047500     REWRITE VOUCHER-RECORD
047600         INVALID KEY
047700         DISPLAY "ERROR REWRITING VENDOR RECORD".
047800
047900 VOUCHER-VENDOR-ON-FILE.
048000     MOVE VOUCHER-VENDOR TO VENDOR-NUMBER.
048100     PERFORM READ-VENDOR-RECORD.
048200
048300 READ-VENDOR-RECORD.
048400     MOVE "Y" TO VENDOR-RECORD-FOUND.
048500     READ VENDOR-FILE RECORD
048600       INVALID KEY
048700         MOVE "N" TO VENDOR-RECORD-FOUND.
048800
048900 READ-CONTROL-RECORD.
049000     MOVE 1 TO CONTROL-KEY.
```

```
049100     MOVE "Y" TO CONTROL-RECORD-FOUND.
049200     READ CONTROL-FILE RECORD
049300         INVALID KEY
049400           MOVE "N" TO CONTROL-RECORD-FOUND
049500           DISPLAY "CONTROL FILE IS INVALID".
049600
049700 REWRITE-CONTROL-RECORD.
049800     REWRITE CONTROL-RECORD
049900         INVALID KEY
050000           DISPLAY "ERROR REWRITING CONTROL RECORD".
050100
050200*--------------------------------
050300* General utility routines
050400*--------------------------------
050500     COPY "PLDATE01.CBL".
050600
```

The output of vchpay02.cbl allows overpayment:

OUTPUT
```
ENTER VOUCHER NUMBER TO PROCESS
2

VOUCHER NUMBER: 00002
VENDOR: 00002 ABC PRINTING
INVOICE: CX-1407
FOR: BUSINESS CARDS
AMOUNT:      98.97
INVOICE DATE:  1/22/1994
DUE DATE:  2/22/1994
DEDUCTIBLE: Y
SELECTED FOR PAYMENT: N
1. PAID ON:  0/00/0000
2. PAID:        0.00
3. CHECK: 000000

PROCESS THIS VOUCHER AS PAID (Y/N)?
y
ENTER PAID DATE(MM/DD/YYYY)?
01/27/1994
PAY THE EXACT AMOUNT      98.97   (Y/N)?
n
ENTER AMOUNT PAID
105
ENTER THE CHECK NUMBER
ENTER 0 FOR CASH PAYMENT
207
ENTER VOUCHER NUMBER TO PROCESS
2

VOUCHER NUMBER: 00002
VENDOR: 00002 ABC PRINTING
INVOICE: CX-1407
FOR: BUSINESS CARDS
AMOUNT:      98.97
INVOICE DATE:  1/22/1994
```

```
DUE DATE:  2/22/1994
DEDUCTIBLE: Y
SELECTED FOR PAYMENT: N
1. PAID ON:  1/27/1994
2. PAID:      105.00
3. CHECK: 000207

RE-OPEN THIS VOUCHER (Y/N)?
```

Answers to Day 21, "Selecting, Sorting, and Reporting"

Quiz

1. The SORT command is used to sort a file on a field that is not a key to the file.

2. b. Closed.

Exercises

1. Listing A.42 is deduct01.cbl, a report on paid bills that are tax-deductible.

TYPE   **Listing A.42. Deductibles report.**

```
000100 IDENTIFICATION DIVISION.
000200 PROGRAM-ID. DEDUCT01.
000300*-------------------------------
000400* Deductibles Report
000500*-------------------------------
000600 ENVIRONMENT DIVISION.
000700 INPUT-OUTPUT SECTION.
000800 FILE-CONTROL.
000900
001000     COPY "SLVOUCH.CBL".
001100
001200     COPY "SLVND02.CBL".
001300
001400     COPY "SLSTATE.CBL".
001500
001600     SELECT WORK-FILE
001700         ASSIGN TO "WORK"
001800         ORGANIZATION IS SEQUENTIAL.
001900
002000     SELECT SORT-FILE
002100         ASSIGN TO "SORT".
002200
002300     SELECT PRINTER-FILE
002400         ASSIGN TO PRINTER
002500         ORGANIZATION IS LINE SEQUENTIAL.
002600
002700 DATA DIVISION.
002800 FILE SECTION.
```

```
002900
003000      COPY "FDVOUCH.CBL".
003100
003200      COPY "FDVND04.CBL".
003300
003400      COPY "FDSTATE.CBL".
003500
003600 FD  WORK-FILE
003700      LABEL RECORDS ARE STANDARD.
003800 01  WORK-RECORD.
003900      05  WORK-NUMBER            PIC 9(5).
004000      05  WORK-VENDOR            PIC 9(5).
004100      05  WORK-INVOICE           PIC X(15).
004200      05  WORK-FOR               PIC X(30).
004300      05  WORK-AMOUNT            PIC S9(6)V99.
004400      05  WORK-DATE              PIC 9(8).
004500      05  WORK-DUE               PIC 9(8).
004600      05  WORK-DEDUCTIBLE        PIC X.
004700      05  WORK-SELECTED          PIC X.
004800      05  WORK-PAID-AMOUNT       PIC S9(6)V99.
004900      05  WORK-PAID-DATE         PIC 9(8).
005000      05  WORK-CHECK-NO          PIC 9(6).
005100
005200 SD  SORT-FILE.
005300
005400 01  SORT-RECORD.
005500      05  SORT-NUMBER            PIC 9(5).
005600      05  SORT-VENDOR            PIC 9(5).
005700      05  SORT-INVOICE           PIC X(15).
005800      05  SORT-FOR               PIC X(30).
005900      05  SORT-AMOUNT            PIC S9(6)V99.
006000      05  SORT-DATE              PIC 9(8).
006100      05  SORT-DUE               PIC 9(8).
006200      05  SORT-DEDUCTIBLE        PIC X.
006300      05  SORT-SELECTED          PIC X.
006400      05  SORT-PAID-AMOUNT       PIC S9(6)V99.
006500      05  SORT-PAID-DATE         PIC 9(8).
006600      05  SORT-CHECK-NO          PIC 9(6).
006700
006800 FD  PRINTER-FILE
006900      LABEL RECORDS ARE OMITTED.
007000 01  PRINTER-RECORD              PIC X(80).
007100
007200 WORKING-STORAGE SECTION.
007300
007400 77  OK-TO-PROCESS      PIC X.
007500
007600      COPY "WSCASE01.CBL".
007700
007800 01  DETAIL-LINE.
007900      05  PRINT-NUMBER      PIC ZZZZ9.
008000      05  FILLER            PIC X(3) VALUE SPACE.
008100      05  PRINT-NAME        PIC X(30).
008200      05  FILLER            PIC X(1) VALUE SPACE.
008300      05  PRINT-DUE-DATE    PIC Z9/99/9999.
```

continues

Listing A.42. continued

```
008400      05  FILLER          PIC X(1) VALUE SPACE.
008500      05  PRINT-AMOUNT    PIC ZZZ,ZZ9.99.
008600      05  FILLER          PIC X(1) VALUE SPACE.
008700      05  PRINT-INVOICE   PIC X(15).
008800
008900 01  TOTAL-THRU.
009000      05  FILLER              PIC X(20) VALUE SPACE.
009100      05  FILLER              PIC X(10) VALUE "TOTAL THRU".
009200
009300 01  COLUMN-LINE.
009400      05  FILLER      PIC X(7)  VALUE "VOUCHER".
009500      05  FILLER      PIC X(1)  VALUE SPACE.
009600      05  FILLER      PIC X(10) VALUE "VENDOR/For".
009700      05  FILLER      PIC X(23) VALUE SPACE.
009800      05  FILLER      PIC X(8)  VALUE "DATE".
009900      05  FILLER      PIC X(1)  VALUE SPACE.
010000      05  FILLER      PIC X(10) VALUE "    AMOUNT".
010100      05  FILLER      PIC X(1)  VALUE SPACE.
010200      05  FILLER      PIC X(7)  VALUE "INVOICE".
010300
010400 01  TITLE-LINE.
010500      05  FILLER              PIC X(31) VALUE SPACE.
010600      05  FILLER              PIC X(11)
010700          VALUE "DEDUCTIBLES".
010800      05  FILLER              PIC X(19) VALUE SPACE.
010900      05  FILLER              PIC X(5) VALUE "PAGE:".
011000      05  FILLER              PIC X(1) VALUE SPACE.
011100      05  PRINT-PAGE-NUMBER   PIC ZZZ9.
011200
011300 77  WORK-FILE-AT-END      PIC X.
011400 77  VENDOR-RECORD-FOUND   PIC X.
011500
011600 77  LINE-COUNT           PIC 999 VALUE ZERO.
011700 77  PAGE-NUMBER          PIC 9999 VALUE ZERO.
011800 77  MAXIMUM-LINES        PIC 999 VALUE 55.
011900
012000 77  RECORD-COUNT         PIC 9999 VALUE ZEROES.
012100
012200 77  SAVE-PAID-DATE       PIC 9(8).
012300
012400 77  RUNNING-TOTAL        PIC S9(6)V99.
012500
012600     COPY "WSDATE01.CBL".
012700
012800 PROCEDURE DIVISION.
012900 PROGRAM-BEGIN.
013000
013100     PERFORM OPENING-PROCEDURE.
013200     PERFORM MAIN-PROCESS.
013300     PERFORM CLOSING-PROCEDURE.
013400
013500 PROGRAM-EXIT.
013600     EXIT PROGRAM.
013700
```

```
013800 PROGRAM-DONE.
013900     STOP RUN.
014000
014100 OPENING-PROCEDURE.
014200     OPEN I-O VENDOR-FILE.
014300
014400     OPEN OUTPUT PRINTER-FILE.
014500
014600 MAIN-PROCESS.
014700     PERFORM GET-OK-TO-PROCESS.
014800     IF OK-TO-PROCESS = "Y"
014900         PERFORM SORT-DATA-FILE
015000         PERFORM PRINT-THE-REPORT.
015100
015200 CLOSING-PROCEDURE.
015300     CLOSE VENDOR-FILE.
015400     PERFORM END-LAST-PAGE.
015500     CLOSE PRINTER-FILE.
015600
015700 GET-OK-TO-PROCESS.
015800     PERFORM ACCEPT-OK-TO-PROCESS.
015900     PERFORM RE-ACCEPT-OK-TO-PROCESS
016000         UNTIL OK-TO-PROCESS = "Y" OR "N".
016100
016200 ACCEPT-OK-TO-PROCESS.
016300     DISPLAY "PRINT DEDUCTIBLES REPORT (Y/N)?".
016400     ACCEPT OK-TO-PROCESS.
016500     INSPECT OK-TO-PROCESS
016600       CONVERTING LOWER-ALPHA
016700       TO          UPPER-ALPHA.
016800
016900 RE-ACCEPT-OK-TO-PROCESS.
017000     DISPLAY "YOU MUST ENTER YES OR NO".
017100     PERFORM ACCEPT-OK-TO-PROCESS.
017200
017300*-------------------------------
017400* Sorting logic
017500*-------------------------------
017600 SORT-DATA-FILE.
017700     SORT SORT-FILE
017800         ON ASCENDING KEY SORT-PAID-DATE
017900           USING VOUCHER-FILE
018000           GIVING WORK-FILE.
018100
018200 PRINT-THE-REPORT.
018300     OPEN INPUT WORK-FILE.
018400     PERFORM START-ONE-REPORT.
018500     PERFORM PROCESS-VOUCHERS.
018600     PERFORM END-ONE-REPORT.
018700     CLOSE WORK-FILE.
018800
018900 START-ONE-REPORT.
019000     PERFORM INITIALIZE-REPORT.
019100     PERFORM START-NEW-PAGE.
019200     MOVE ZEROES TO RUNNING-TOTAL.
```

continues

Listing A.42. continued

```
019300
019400 INITIALIZE-REPORT.
019500     MOVE ZEROES TO LINE-COUNT PAGE-NUMBER.
019600
019700 END-ONE-REPORT.
019800     IF RECORD-COUNT = ZEROES
019900         MOVE "NO RECORDS FOUND" TO PRINTER-RECORD
020000         PERFORM WRITE-TO-PRINTER.
020100
020200 PROCESS-VOUCHERS.
020300     PERFORM READ-FIRST-VALID-WORK.
020400     PERFORM PROCESS-ALL-DATES
020500         UNTIL WORK-FILE-AT-END = "Y".
020600
020700 PROCESS-ALL-DATES.
020800     PERFORM START-ONE-DATE.
020900
021000     PERFORM PROCESS-ALL-VOUCHERS
021100         UNTIL WORK-FILE-AT-END = "Y"
021200             OR WORK-PAID-DATE NOT = SAVE-PAID-DATE.
021300
021400     PERFORM END-ONE-DATE.
021500
021600 START-ONE-DATE.
021700     MOVE WORK-PAID-DATE TO SAVE-PAID-DATE.
021800
021900 END-ONE-DATE.
022000     PERFORM PRINT-RUNNING-TOTAL.
022100
022200 PRINT-RUNNING-TOTAL.
022300     MOVE SPACE TO DETAIL-LINE.
022400     MOVE SAVE-PAID-DATE TO DATE-CCYYMMDD.
022500     PERFORM CONVERT-TO-MMDDCCYY.
022600     MOVE DATE-MMDDCCYY TO PRINT-DUE-DATE.
022700     MOVE RUNNING-TOTAL TO PRINT-AMOUNT.
022800     MOVE TOTAL-THRU TO PRINT-NAME.
022900     MOVE DETAIL-LINE TO PRINTER-RECORD.
023000     PERFORM WRITE-TO-PRINTER.
023100     PERFORM LINE-FEED 2 TIMES.
023200
023300 PROCESS-ALL-VOUCHERS.
023400     PERFORM PROCESS-THIS-VOUCHER.
023500     PERFORM READ-NEXT-VALID-WORK.
023600
023700 PROCESS-THIS-VOUCHER.
023800     ADD 1 TO RECORD-COUNT.
023900     IF LINE-COUNT > MAXIMUM-LINES
024000         PERFORM START-NEXT-PAGE.
024100     PERFORM PRINT-THE-RECORD.
024200     ADD WORK-PAID-AMOUNT TO RUNNING-TOTAL.
024300
024400 PRINT-THE-RECORD.
024500     PERFORM PRINT-LINE-1.
024600     PERFORM PRINT-LINE-2.
```

```
024700     PERFORM LINE-FEED.
024800
024900 PRINT-LINE-1.
025000     MOVE SPACE TO DETAIL-LINE.
025100     MOVE WORK-NUMBER TO PRINT-NUMBER.
025200
025300     MOVE WORK-VENDOR TO VENDOR-NUMBER.
025400     PERFORM READ-VENDOR-RECORD.
025500     IF VENDOR-RECORD-FOUND = "Y"
025600         MOVE VENDOR-NAME TO PRINT-NAME
025700     ELSE
025800         MOVE "*VENDOR NOT ON FILE*" TO PRINT-NAME.
025900
026000     MOVE WORK-PAID-DATE TO DATE-CCYYMMDD.
026100     PERFORM CONVERT-TO-MMDDCCYY.
026200     MOVE DATE-MMDDCCYY TO PRINT-DUE-DATE.
026300
026400     MOVE WORK-PAID-AMOUNT TO PRINT-AMOUNT.
026500     MOVE WORK-INVOICE TO PRINT-INVOICE.
026600
026700     MOVE DETAIL-LINE TO PRINTER-RECORD.
026800     PERFORM WRITE-TO-PRINTER.
026900
027000 PRINT-LINE-2.
027100     MOVE SPACE TO DETAIL-LINE.
027200     MOVE WORK-FOR TO PRINT-NAME.
027300     MOVE DETAIL-LINE TO PRINTER-RECORD.
027400     PERFORM WRITE-TO-PRINTER.
027500
027600 WRITE-TO-PRINTER.
027700     WRITE PRINTER-RECORD BEFORE ADVANCING 1.
027800     ADD 1 TO LINE-COUNT.
027900
028000 LINE-FEED.
028100     MOVE SPACE TO PRINTER-RECORD.
028200     PERFORM WRITE-TO-PRINTER.
028300
028400 START-NEXT-PAGE.
028500     PERFORM END-LAST-PAGE.
028600     PERFORM START-NEW-PAGE.
028700
028800 START-NEW-PAGE.
028900     ADD 1 TO PAGE-NUMBER.
029000     MOVE PAGE-NUMBER TO PRINT-PAGE-NUMBER.
029100     MOVE TITLE-LINE TO PRINTER-RECORD.
029200     PERFORM WRITE-TO-PRINTER.
029300     PERFORM LINE-FEED.
029400     MOVE COLUMN-LINE TO PRINTER-RECORD.
029500     PERFORM WRITE-TO-PRINTER.
029600     PERFORM LINE-FEED.
029700
029800 END-LAST-PAGE.
029900     PERFORM FORM-FEED.
030000     MOVE ZERO TO LINE-COUNT.
030100
```

continues

Listing A.42. continued

```
030200 FORM-FEED.
030300     MOVE SPACE TO PRINTER-RECORD.
030400     WRITE PRINTER-RECORD BEFORE ADVANCING PAGE.
030500
030600*--------------------------------
030700* Read first, read next routines
030800*--------------------------------
030900 READ-FIRST-VALID-WORK.
031000     PERFORM READ-NEXT-VALID-WORK.
031100
031200 READ-NEXT-VALID-WORK.
031300     PERFORM READ-NEXT-WORK-RECORD.
031400     PERFORM READ-NEXT-WORK-RECORD
031500         UNTIL WORK-FILE-AT-END = "Y"
031600             OR ( WORK-PAID-DATE NOT =  ZEROES AND
031700                 WORK-DEDUCTIBLE = "Y").
031800
031900 READ-NEXT-WORK-RECORD.
032000     MOVE "N" TO WORK-FILE-AT-END.
032100     READ WORK-FILE NEXT RECORD
032200         AT END MOVE "Y" TO WORK-FILE-AT-END.
032300
032400*--------------------------------
032500* Other File IO routines
032600*--------------------------------
032700 READ-VENDOR-RECORD.
032800     MOVE "Y" TO VENDOR-RECORD-FOUND.
032900     READ VENDOR-FILE RECORD
033000         INVALID KEY
033100         MOVE "N" TO VENDOR-RECORD-FOUND.
033200
033300*--------------------------------
033400* Utility Routines
033500*--------------------------------
033600     COPY "PLDATE01.CBL".
033700
```

2. The sample output of deduct01.cbl lists paid bills that were flagged as tax-deductible:

```
OUTPUT   DEDUCTIBLES                     PAGE:    1

         VOUCHER VENDOR/For                     DATE       AMOUNT INVOICE

         2    ABC PRINTING              1/27/1994     105.00 CX-1407
         BUSINESS CARDS

         11   ABC PRINTING              1/27/1994      51.03 CX-1407
         BUSINESS CARDS

         12   ABC PRINTING              1/27/1994       6.03 CX-1407
         BUSINESS CARDS

         TOTAL THRU  1/27/1994      162.06
```

3. Study the report from DEDUCT01. Frequently, an entry screen will be used to allow the user to print the same basic information in a variety of ways. For example, when the user runs a report program, the user could be asked SHOW ONLY UNPAID ITEMS (Y/N)? followed by SHOW ONLY DEDUCTIBLE ITEMS (Y/N)? After criteria such as these are added in to the report, the READ-NEXT-VALID logic can become complicated. In the following example, the next record is read and if no select criteria has been requested, the logic returns with the record just read. Otherwise, it tries to match one or the other of the selected criteria.

```
031200 READ-NEXT-VALID-WORK.
031300     PERFORM READ-NEXT-WORK-RECORD.
031400     IF SHOW-ONLY-UNPAID-ITEMS = "Y" OR
031500         SHOW-ONLY-DEDUCTIBLE-ITEMS = "Y"
031600         PERFORM READ-NEXT-WORK-RECORD
031700             UNTIL WORK-FILE-AT-END = "Y"
031800             OR ( WORK-PAID-DATE NOT =  ZEROES AND
031700                 SHOW-ONLY-UNPAID-ITEMS = "Y").
031900             OR ( WORK-DEDUCTIBLE = "Y" AND
032000                 SHOW-ONLY-DEDUCTIBLE = "Y").
032100
```

Answers to Bonus Day 1, "Control Breaks"

Quiz

1. A control break is a break inserted into the normal processing of a program (usually a report program) to cause groups of records to be processed together as one unit. The interruption of the normal printing of a report program to print a total or subtotal would be a control break or level break.

2. The control break field or control field is the field in the record that causes a control break to occur when the record changes.

3. The control break current value or control current value is a field created in WORKING-STORAGE that holds a copy of the control break field. The control break current value is filled in at the beginning of a control break level with the value in the control break field. As the processing continues, the control break field is compared to the control break current value to determine whether a control break has occurred.

4. Control break accumulators or control accumulators are variables used for summing or counting values within a control break.

5. A level 1 break varies from any other break because there is no true control break current value. The level 1 break starts at the beginning of the file and completes at

the end of the file. The logic to start level 1 begins by executing a read-first valid record.

The end of a level 1 break does not add accumulators to the next higher level because there is no next higher level.

Exercises

1. Listing A.43 is slsrpt02.cbl, modified from slsrpt01.cbl. The lines that were moved have been commented out, and the changes are highlighted in the listing.

TYPE | **Listing A.43. The changes needed to create slsrpt02.cbl.**

```
000100 IDENTIFICATION DIVISION.
000200 PROGRAM-ID. SLSRPT02.
000300*--------------------------------
000400* Generate test sales data
000500*--------------------------------
000600 ENVIRONMENT DIVISION.
000700 INPUT-OUTPUT SECTION.
000800 FILE-CONTROL.
000900
001000*--------------------------------
001100* SLSALES.CBL
001200*--------------------------------
001300     SELECT SALES-FILE
001400         ASSIGN TO "SALES"
001500         ORGANIZATION IS SEQUENTIAL.
001600
001700     SELECT WORK-FILE
001800         ASSIGN TO "WORK"
001900         ORGANIZATION IS SEQUENTIAL.
002000
002100     SELECT SORT-FILE
002200         ASSIGN TO "SORT".
002300
002400     SELECT PRINTER-FILE
002500         ASSIGN TO PRINTER
002600         ORGANIZATION IS LINE SEQUENTIAL.
002700
002800 DATA DIVISION.
002900 FILE SECTION.
003000
003100*--------------------------------
003200* FDSALES.CBL
003300* Temporary daily sales file.
003400*--------------------------------
003500 FD  SALES-FILE
003600     LABEL RECORDS ARE STANDARD.
003700 01  SALES-RECORD.
003800     05  SALES-STORE          PIC 9(2).
003900     05  SALES-DIVISION       PIC 9(2).
```

```
004000     05  SALES-DEPARTMENT        PIC 9(2).
004100     05  SALES-CATEGORY          PIC 9(2).
004200     05  SALES-AMOUNT            PIC S9(6)V99.
004300
004400 FD  WORK-FILE
004500     LABEL RECORDS ARE STANDARD.
004600 01  WORK-RECORD.
004700     05  WORK-STORE              PIC 9(2).
004800     05  WORK-DIVISION           PIC 9(2).
004900     05  WORK-DEPARTMENT         PIC 9(2).
005000     05  WORK-CATEGORY           PIC 9(2).
005100     05  WORK-AMOUNT             PIC S9(6)V99.
005200
005300 SD  SORT-FILE
005400     LABEL RECORDS ARE STANDARD.
005500 01  SORT-RECORD.
005600     05  SORT-STORE              PIC 9(2).
005700     05  SORT-DIVISION           PIC 9(2).
005800     05  SORT-DEPARTMENT         PIC 9(2).
005900     05  SORT-CATEGORY           PIC 9(2).
006000     05  SORT-AMOUNT             PIC S9(6)V99.
006100
006200 FD  PRINTER-FILE
006300     LABEL RECORDS ARE OMITTED.
006400 01  PRINTER-RECORD              PIC X(80).
006500
006600 WORKING-STORAGE SECTION.
006700
006800 77  OK-TO-PROCESS              PIC X.
006900
007000     COPY "WSCASE01.CBL".
007100
007200 01  LEGEND-LINE.
007300     05  FILLER                 PIC X(6) VALUE "STORE:".
007400     05  FILLER                 PIC X(1) VALUE SPACE.
007500     05  PRINT-STORE            PIC Z9.
007600
007700 01  DETAIL-LINE.
007800     05  FILLER                 PIC X(3) VALUE SPACE.
007900     05  PRINT-DIVISION         PIC Z9.
008000     05  FILLER                 PIC X(4) VALUE SPACE.
008100     05  FILLER                 PIC X(3) VALUE SPACE.
008200     05  PRINT-DEPARTMENT       PIC Z9.
008300     05  FILLER                 PIC X(6) VALUE SPACE.
008400     05  FILLER                 PIC X(3) VALUE SPACE.
008500     05  PRINT-CATEGORY         PIC Z9.
008600     05  FILLER                 PIC X(4) VALUE SPACE.
008700     05  PRINT-AMOUNT           PIC ZZZ,ZZ9.99-.
008800
008900 01  COLUMN-LINE.
009000     05  FILLER           PIC X(8)  VALUE "DIVISION".
009100     05  FILLER           PIC X(1)  VALUE SPACE.
009200     05  FILLER           PIC X(10) VALUE "DEPARTMENT".
009300     05  FILLER           PIC X(1)  VALUE SPACE.
009400     05  FILLER           PIC X(8)  VALUE "CATEGORY".
```

continues

Listing A.43. continued

```
009500       05  FILLER        PIC X(1)  VALUE SPACE.
009600       05  FILLER        PIC X(4)  VALUE SPACE.
009700       05  FILLER        PIC X(6)  VALUE "AMOUNT".
009800
009900 01  TITLE-LINE.
010000       05  FILLER                  PIC X(30) VALUE SPACE.
010100       05  FILLER                  PIC X(12)
010200            VALUE "SALES REPORT".
010300       05  FILLER                  PIC X(16) VALUE SPACE.
010400       05  FILLER                  PIC X(5) VALUE "PAGE:".
010500       05  FILLER                  PIC X(1) VALUE SPACE.
010600       05  PRINT-PAGE-NUMBER       PIC ZZZ9.
010700
010800 01  TOTAL-LINE.
010900       05  FILLER                  PIC X(11) VALUE SPACE.
011000       05  TOTAL-TYPE              PIC X(8).
011100       05  FILLER                  PIC X(1) VALUE SPACE.
011200       05  TOTAL-NUMBER            PIC Z9.
011300       05  FILLER                  PIC X(1) VALUE SPACE.
011400       05  TOTAL-LITERAL           PIC X(5) VALUE "TOTAL".
011500       05  FILLER                  PIC X(1) VALUE SPACE.
011600       05  PRINT-TOTAL             PIC ZZZ,ZZ9.99-.
011700
011800 77  GRAND-TOTAL-LITERAL      PIC X(8) VALUE "   GRAND".
011900 77  STORE-TOTAL-LITERAL      PIC X(8) VALUE "   STORE".
012000 77  DIVISION-TOTAL-LITERAL   PIC X(8) VALUE "DIVISION".
012100 77  DEPARTMENT-TOTAL-LITERAL PIC X(8) VALUE "    DEPT".
012200
012300 77  WORK-FILE-AT-END         PIC X.
012400
012500 77  LINE-COUNT               PIC 999 VALUE ZERO.
012600 77  PAGE-NUMBER              PIC 9999 VALUE ZERO.
012700 77  MAXIMUM-LINES            PIC 999 VALUE 55.
012800
012900 77  RECORD-COUNT             PIC 9999 VALUE ZEROES.
013000
013100* Control break current values for store, division
013200* department.
013300 77  CURRENT-STORE            PIC 99.
013400 77  CURRENT-DIVISION         PIC 99.
013500 77  CURRENT-DEPARTMENT       PIC 99.
013600
013700* Control break accumulators
013800* GRAND TOTAL is the level 1 accumulator for the whole file
013900* STORE TOTAL is the level 2 accumulator
014000* DIVISION TOTAL is the level 3 accumulator
014100* DEPARTMENT TOTAL is the level 4 accumulator.
014200 77  GRAND-TOTAL              PIC S9(6)V99.
014300 77  STORE-TOTAL              PIC S9(6)V99.
014400 77  DIVISION-TOTAL           PIC S9(6)V99.
014500 77  DEPARTMENT-TOTAL         PIC S9(6)V99.
014600
014700 PROCEDURE DIVISION.
```

```
014800 PROGRAM-BEGIN.
014900
015000     PERFORM OPENING-PROCEDURE.
015100     PERFORM MAIN-PROCESS.
015200     PERFORM CLOSING-PROCEDURE.
015300
015400 PROGRAM-EXIT.
015500     EXIT PROGRAM.
015600
015700 PROGRAM-DONE.
015800     STOP RUN.
015900
016000 OPENING-PROCEDURE.
016100
016200     OPEN OUTPUT PRINTER-FILE.
016300
016400 MAIN-PROCESS.
016500     PERFORM GET-OK-TO-PROCESS.
016600     PERFORM PROCESS-THE-FILE
016700         UNTIL OK-TO-PROCESS = "N".
016800
016900 CLOSING-PROCEDURE.
017000     CLOSE PRINTER-FILE.
017100
017200 GET-OK-TO-PROCESS.
017300     PERFORM ACCEPT-OK-TO-PROCESS.
017400     PERFORM RE-ACCEPT-OK-TO-PROCESS
017500         UNTIL OK-TO-PROCESS = "Y" OR "N".
017600
017700 ACCEPT-OK-TO-PROCESS.
017800     DISPLAY "PRINT SALES REPORT (Y/N)?".
017900     ACCEPT OK-TO-PROCESS.
018000     INSPECT OK-TO-PROCESS
018100       CONVERTING LOWER-ALPHA
018200       TO          UPPER-ALPHA.
018300
018400 RE-ACCEPT-OK-TO-PROCESS.
018500     DISPLAY "YOU MUST ENTER YES OR NO".
018600     PERFORM ACCEPT-OK-TO-PROCESS.
018700
018800 PROCESS-THE-FILE.
018900     PERFORM START-THE-FILE.
019000     PERFORM PRINT-ONE-REPORT.
019100     PERFORM END-THE-FILE.
019200
019300*    PERFORM GET-OK-TO-PROCESS.
019400     MOVE "N" TO OK-TO-PROCESS.
019500
019600 START-THE-FILE.
019700     PERFORM SORT-DATA-FILE.
019800     OPEN INPUT WORK-FILE.
019900
020000 END-THE-FILE.
020100     CLOSE WORK-FILE.
020200
```

continues

Listing A.43. continued

```
020300 SORT-DATA-FILE.
020400     SORT SORT-FILE
020500        ON ASCENDING KEY SORT-STORE
020600            ASCENDING KEY SORT-DIVISION
020700            ASCENDING KEY SORT-DEPARTMENT
020800            ASCENDING KEY SORT-CATEGORY
020900          USING SALES-FILE
021000          GIVING WORK-FILE.
021100
021200* LEVEL 1 CONTROL BREAK
021300 PRINT-ONE-REPORT.
021400     PERFORM START-ONE-REPORT.
021500     PERFORM PROCESS-ALL-STORES
021600        UNTIL WORK-FILE-AT-END = "Y".
021700     PERFORM END-ONE-REPORT.
021800
021900 START-ONE-REPORT.
022000     PERFORM READ-FIRST-VALID-WORK.
022100     MOVE ZEROES TO GRAND-TOTAL.
022200
022300     PERFORM START-NEW-REPORT.
022400
022500 START-NEW-REPORT.
022600     MOVE SPACE TO DETAIL-LINE.
022700     MOVE ZEROES TO LINE-COUNT PAGE-NUMBER.
022800
022900 END-ONE-REPORT.
023000     IF RECORD-COUNT = ZEROES
023100        MOVE "NO RECORDS FOUND" TO PRINTER-RECORD
023200            PERFORM WRITE-TO-PRINTER
023300     ELSE
023400            PERFORM PRINT-GRAND-TOTAL.
023500
023600     PERFORM END-LAST-PAGE.
023700
023800 PRINT-GRAND-TOTAL.
023900     MOVE SPACE TO TOTAL-LINE.
024000     MOVE GRAND-TOTAL TO PRINT-TOTAL.
024100     MOVE GRAND-TOTAL-LITERAL TO TOTAL-TYPE.
024200     MOVE "TOTAL" TO TOTAL-LITERAL.
024300     MOVE TOTAL-LINE TO PRINTER-RECORD.
024400     PERFORM WRITE-TO-PRINTER.
024500     PERFORM LINE-FEED 2 TIMES.
024600     MOVE SPACE TO DETAIL-LINE.
024700
024800* LEVEL 2 CONTROL BREAK
024900 PROCESS-ALL-STORES.
025000     PERFORM START-ONE-STORE.
025100
025200     PERFORM PROCESS-ALL-DIVISIONS
025300        UNTIL WORK-FILE-AT-END = "Y"
025400            OR WORK-STORE NOT = CURRENT-STORE.
025500
```

```
025600      PERFORM END-ONE-STORE.
025700
025800 START-ONE-STORE.
025900      MOVE WORK-STORE TO CURRENT-STORE.
026000      MOVE ZEROES TO STORE-TOTAL.
026100      MOVE WORK-STORE TO PRINT-STORE.
026200
026300      PERFORM START-NEXT-PAGE.
026400
026500 END-ONE-STORE.
026600      PERFORM PRINT-STORE-TOTAL.
026700      ADD STORE-TOTAL TO GRAND-TOTAL.
026800
026900 PRINT-STORE-TOTAL.
027000      MOVE SPACE TO TOTAL-LINE.
027100      MOVE STORE-TOTAL TO PRINT-TOTAL.
027200      MOVE CURRENT-STORE TO TOTAL-NUMBER.
027300      MOVE STORE-TOTAL-LITERAL TO TOTAL-TYPE.
027400      MOVE "TOTAL" TO TOTAL-LITERAL.
027500      MOVE TOTAL-LINE TO PRINTER-RECORD.
027600      PERFORM WRITE-TO-PRINTER.
027700      PERFORM LINE-FEED.
027800      MOVE SPACE TO DETAIL-LINE.
027900
028000* LEVEL 3 CONTROL BREAK
028100 PROCESS-ALL-DIVISIONS.
028200      PERFORM START-ONE-DIVISION.
028300
028400      PERFORM PROCESS-ALL-DEPARTMENTS
028500          UNTIL WORK-FILE-AT-END = "Y"
028600              OR WORK-STORE NOT = CURRENT-STORE
028700              OR WORK-DIVISION NOT = CURRENT-DIVISION.
028800
028900      PERFORM END-ONE-DIVISION.
029000
029100 START-ONE-DIVISION.
029200      MOVE WORK-DIVISION TO CURRENT-DIVISION.
029300      MOVE ZEROES TO DIVISION-TOTAL.
029400*     MOVE WORK-DIVISION TO PRINT-DIVISION.
029500
029600 END-ONE-DIVISION.
029700      PERFORM PRINT-DIVISION-TOTAL.
029800      ADD DIVISION-TOTAL TO STORE-TOTAL.
029900
030000 PRINT-DIVISION-TOTAL.
030100      MOVE SPACE TO TOTAL-LINE.
030200      MOVE DIVISION-TOTAL TO PRINT-TOTAL.
030300      MOVE CURRENT-DIVISION TO TOTAL-NUMBER.
030400      MOVE DIVISION-TOTAL-LITERAL TO TOTAL-TYPE.
030500      MOVE "TOTAL" TO TOTAL-LITERAL.
030600      MOVE TOTAL-LINE TO PRINTER-RECORD.
030700      PERFORM WRITE-TO-PRINTER.
030800      PERFORM LINE-FEED.
030900      MOVE SPACE TO DETAIL-LINE.
031000
```

continues

Listing A.43. continued

```
031100* LEVEL 4 CONTROL BREAK
031200 PROCESS-ALL-DEPARTMENTS.
031300     PERFORM START-ONE-DEPARTMENT.
031400
031500     PERFORM PROCESS-ALL-CATEGORIES
031600         UNTIL WORK-FILE-AT-END = "Y"
031700             OR WORK-STORE NOT = CURRENT-STORE
031800             OR WORK-DIVISION NOT = CURRENT-DIVISION
031900             OR WORK-DEPARTMENT NOT = CURRENT-DEPARTMENT.
032000
032100     PERFORM END-ONE-DEPARTMENT.
032200
032300 START-ONE-DEPARTMENT.
032400     MOVE WORK-DEPARTMENT TO CURRENT-DEPARTMENT.
032500     MOVE ZEROES TO DEPARTMENT-TOTAL.
032600*    MOVE WORK-DEPARTMENT TO PRINT-DEPARTMENT.
032700
032800 END-ONE-DEPARTMENT.
032900     PERFORM PRINT-DEPARTMENT-TOTAL.
033000     ADD DEPARTMENT-TOTAL TO DIVISION-TOTAL.
033100
033200 PRINT-DEPARTMENT-TOTAL.
033300     MOVE SPACE TO TOTAL-LINE.
033400     MOVE DEPARTMENT-TOTAL TO PRINT-TOTAL.
033500     MOVE CURRENT-DEPARTMENT TO TOTAL-NUMBER.
033600     MOVE DEPARTMENT-TOTAL-LITERAL TO TOTAL-TYPE.
033700     MOVE "TOTAL" TO TOTAL-LITERAL.
033800     MOVE TOTAL-LINE TO PRINTER-RECORD.
033900     PERFORM WRITE-TO-PRINTER.
034000     PERFORM LINE-FEED.
034100     MOVE SPACE TO DETAIL-LINE.
034200
034300* PROCESS ONE RECORD LEVEL
034400 PROCESS-ALL-CATEGORIES.
034500     PERFORM PROCESS-THIS-CATEGORY.
034600     ADD WORK-AMOUNT TO DEPARTMENT-TOTAL.
034700     ADD 1 TO RECORD-COUNT.
034800     PERFORM READ-NEXT-VALID-WORK.
034900
035000 PROCESS-THIS-CATEGORY.
035100     IF LINE-COUNT > MAXIMUM-LINES
035200         PERFORM START-NEXT-PAGE.
035300     PERFORM PRINT-THE-RECORD.
035400
035500 PRINT-THE-RECORD.
035600     MOVE WORK-DIVISION TO PRINT-DIVISION.
035700     MOVE WORK-DEPARTMENT TO PRINT-DEPARTMENT.
035800     MOVE WORK-CATEGORY TO PRINT-CATEGORY.
035900
036000     MOVE WORK-AMOUNT TO PRINT-AMOUNT.
036100
036200     MOVE DETAIL-LINE TO PRINTER-RECORD.
036300     PERFORM WRITE-TO-PRINTER.
```

```
036400      MOVE SPACE TO DETAIL-LINE.
036500
036600* PRINTING ROUTINES
036700 WRITE-TO-PRINTER.
036800      WRITE PRINTER-RECORD BEFORE ADVANCING 1.
036900      ADD 1 TO LINE-COUNT.
037000
037100 LINE-FEED.
037200      MOVE SPACE TO PRINTER-RECORD.
037300      PERFORM WRITE-TO-PRINTER.
037400
037500 START-NEXT-PAGE.
037600      PERFORM END-LAST-PAGE.
037700      PERFORM START-NEW-PAGE.
037800
037900 START-NEW-PAGE.
038000      ADD 1 TO PAGE-NUMBER.
038100      MOVE PAGE-NUMBER TO PRINT-PAGE-NUMBER.
038200      MOVE TITLE-LINE TO PRINTER-RECORD.
038300      PERFORM WRITE-TO-PRINTER.
038400      PERFORM LINE-FEED.
038500      MOVE LEGEND-LINE TO PRINTER-RECORD.
038600      PERFORM WRITE-TO-PRINTER.
038700      PERFORM LINE-FEED.
038800      MOVE COLUMN-LINE TO PRINTER-RECORD.
038900      PERFORM WRITE-TO-PRINTER.
039000      PERFORM LINE-FEED.
039100
039200 END-LAST-PAGE.
039300      IF PAGE-NUMBER > 0
039400          PERFORM FORM-FEED.
039500      MOVE ZERO TO LINE-COUNT.
039600
039700 FORM-FEED.
039800      MOVE SPACE TO PRINTER-RECORD.
039900      WRITE PRINTER-RECORD BEFORE ADVANCING PAGE.
040000
040100*--------------------------------
040200* Read first, read next routines
040300*--------------------------------
040400 READ-FIRST-VALID-WORK.
040500      PERFORM READ-NEXT-VALID-WORK.
040600
040700 READ-NEXT-VALID-WORK.
040800      PERFORM READ-NEXT-WORK-RECORD.
040900
041000 READ-NEXT-WORK-RECORD.
041100      MOVE "N" TO WORK-FILE-AT-END.
041200      READ WORK-FILE NEXT RECORD
041300          AT END MOVE "Y" TO WORK-FILE-AT-END.
041400
```

A

The output of slsrpt02.cbl shows full detail on each line:

```
Ⓞ UTPUT                                  SALES REPORT                    PAGE:    1

         STORE:  1

         DIVISION DEPARTMENT CATEGORY       AMOUNT

         1         1          1         237.57
         1         1          2         475.14
         DEPT  1 TOTAL       712.71

         1         2          3         712.71
         1         2          4          50.28
         DEPT  2 TOTAL       762.99

         DIVISION  1 TOTAL     1,475.70

         2         3          5         287.85
         2         3          6         525.42
         DEPT  3 TOTAL       813.27

         2         4          7         762.99
         2         4          8         100.56
         DEPT  4 TOTAL       863.55

         DIVISION  2 TOTAL     1,676.82

         3         5          9         338.13
         3         5         10         575.70
         DEPT  5 TOTAL       913.83

         3         6         11          86.73-
         3         6         12         150.84
         DEPT  6 TOTAL        64.11

         DIVISION  3 TOTAL      977.94

         STORE  1 TOTAL    4,130.46

         ---------------------<page break>----------------------------


                                          SALES REPORT                    PAGE:    2

         STORE:  2

         DIVISION DEPARTMENT CATEGORY       AMOUNT

         1         1          1         388.41
         1         1          2         625.98
         DEPT  1 TOTAL     1,014.39

         1         2          3          36.45-
         1         2          4         201.12
         DEPT  2 TOTAL       164.67
```

```
DIVISION  1 TOTAL    1,179.06

2        3         5        438.69
2        3         6        676.26
DEPT  3 TOTAL    1,114.95

2        4         7         13.83
2        4         8        251.40
DEPT  4 TOTAL     265.23

DIVISION  2 TOTAL    1,380.18

3        5         9        488.97
3        5        10        726.54
DEPT  5 TOTAL    1,215.51

3        6        11         64.11
3        6        12        301.68
DEPT  6 TOTAL     365.79

DIVISION  3 TOTAL    1,581.30

STORE  2 TOTAL    4,140.54

--------------------<page break>-----------------------------


                              SALES REPORT            PAGE:    3

STORE:  3

DIVISION DEPARTMENT CATEGORY     AMOUNT

1        1         1        539.25
1        1         2        776.82
DEPT  1 TOTAL    1,316.07

1        2         3        114.39
1        2         4        351.96
DEPT  2 TOTAL     466.35

DIVISION  1 TOTAL    1,782.42

2        3         5        589.53
2        3         6         72.90-
DEPT  3 TOTAL     516.63

2        4         7        164.67
2        4         8        402.24
DEPT  4 TOTAL     566.91

DIVISION  2 TOTAL    1,083.54

3        5         9        639.81
3        5        10         22.62-
DEPT  5 TOTAL     617.19
```

```
3        6        11        214.95
3        6        12        452.52
DEPT  6 TOTAL    667.47

DIVISION  3 TOTAL   1,284.66

STORE  3 TOTAL   4,150.62
```

----------------------<page break>--------------------------------

```
                              SALES REPORT              PAGE:    4

STORE:   4

DIVISION DEPARTMENT CATEGORY     AMOUNT

1        1        1         690.09
1        1        2          27.66
DEPT  1 TOTAL    717.75

1        2        3         265.23
1        2        4         502.80
DEPT  2 TOTAL    768.03

DIVISION  1 TOTAL   1,485.78

2        3        5         740.37
2        3        6          77.94
DEPT  3 TOTAL    818.31

2        4        7         315.51
2        4        8         553.08
DEPT  4 TOTAL    868.59

DIVISION  2 TOTAL   1,686.90

3        5        9         790.65
3        5        10        128.22
DEPT  5 TOTAL    918.87

3        6        11        365.79
3        6        12        603.36
DEPT  6 TOTAL    969.15

DIVISION  3 TOTAL   1,888.02

STORE  4 TOTAL   5,060.70
```

----------------------<page break>--------------------------------

```
                              SALES REPORT              PAGE:    5

STORE:   5
```

```
DIVISION DEPARTMENT CATEGORY      AMOUNT

1         1          1          59.07-
1         1          2         178.50
DEPT  1 TOTAL      119.43

1         2          3         416.07
1         2          4         653.64
DEPT  2 TOTAL    1,069.71

DIVISION  1 TOTAL    1,189.14

2         3          5           8.79-
2         3          6         228.78
DEPT  3 TOTAL      219.99

2         4          7         466.35
2         4          8         703.92
DEPT  4 TOTAL    1,170.27

DIVISION  2 TOTAL    1,390.26

3         5          9          41.49
3         5         10         279.06
DEPT  5 TOTAL      320.55

3         6         11         516.63
3         6         12         754.20
DEPT  6 TOTAL    1,270.83

DIVISION  3 TOTAL    1,591.38

STORE  5 TOTAL    4,170.78

- - - - - - - - - - - - - - - - - - <page break> - - - - - - - - - - - - - - - - - - - - - - - - - - - - - -


                                    SALES REPORT          PAGE:    6

STORE:  6

DIVISION DEPARTMENT CATEGORY      AMOUNT

1         1          1          91.77
1         1          2         329.34
DEPT  1 TOTAL      421.11

1         2          3         566.91
1         2          4          95.52-
DEPT  2 TOTAL      471.39

DIVISION  1 TOTAL      892.50

2         3          5         142.05
2         3          6         379.62
DEPT  3 TOTAL      521.67
```

```
2          4          7          617.19
2          4          8           45.24-
DEPT   4  TOTAL    571.95

DIVISION   2  TOTAL    1,093.62

3          5          9          192.33
3          5          10         429.90
DEPT   5  TOTAL    622.23

3          6          11         667.47
3          6          12           5.04
DEPT   6  TOTAL    672.51

DIVISION   3  TOTAL    1,294.74

STORE   6  TOTAL    3,280.86

GRAND     TOTAL   24,933.96
```

2. Listing A.44 removes all detail printing and prints only the control breaks. All changes are highlighted, but only the change of removing (by commenting out) lines 035300 through 036200 was necessary to remove the printing of the detail lines.

The key cosmetic change is the removal of lines 038600 through 038800, which print the column line. All other highlighted changes are the removal of things not needed for a summary version of the report, or small cosmetic changes such as the title of the report.

TYPE **Listing A.44. Printing control breaks only.**

```
000100 IDENTIFICATION DIVISION.
000200 PROGRAM-ID. SLSSUM01.
000300*--------------------------------
000400* Generate test sales data
000500*--------------------------------
000600 ENVIRONMENT DIVISION.
000700 INPUT-OUTPUT SECTION.
000800 FILE-CONTROL.
000900
001000*--------------------------------
001100* SLSALES.CBL
001200*--------------------------------
001300     SELECT SALES-FILE
001400         ASSIGN TO "SALES"
001500         ORGANIZATION IS SEQUENTIAL.
001600
001700     SELECT WORK-FILE
001800         ASSIGN TO "WORK"
001900         ORGANIZATION IS SEQUENTIAL.
002000
002100     SELECT SORT-FILE
```

```
002200         ASSIGN TO "SORT".
002300
002400     SELECT PRINTER-FILE
002500         ASSIGN TO PRINTER
002600         ORGANIZATION IS LINE SEQUENTIAL.
002700
002800 DATA DIVISION.
002900 FILE SECTION.
003000
003100*------------------------------
003200* FDSALES.CBL
003300* Temporary daily sales file.
003400*------------------------------
003500 FD  SALES-FILE
003600     LABEL RECORDS ARE STANDARD.
003700 01  SALES-RECORD.
003800     05  SALES-STORE           PIC 9(2).
003900     05  SALES-DIVISION        PIC 9(2).
004000     05  SALES-DEPARTMENT      PIC 9(2).
004100     05  SALES-CATEGORY        PIC 9(2).
004200     05  SALES-AMOUNT          PIC S9(6)V99.
004300
004400 FD  WORK-FILE
004500     LABEL RECORDS ARE STANDARD.
004600 01  WORK-RECORD.
004700     05  WORK-STORE            PIC 9(2).
004800     05  WORK-DIVISION         PIC 9(2).
004900     05  WORK-DEPARTMENT       PIC 9(2).
005000     05  WORK-CATEGORY         PIC 9(2).
005100     05  WORK-AMOUNT           PIC S9(6)V99.
005200
005300 SD  SORT-FILE
005400     LABEL RECORDS ARE STANDARD.
005500 01  SORT-RECORD.
005600     05  SORT-STORE            PIC 9(2).
005700     05  SORT-DIVISION         PIC 9(2).
005800     05  SORT-DEPARTMENT       PIC 9(2).
005900     05  SORT-CATEGORY         PIC 9(2).
006000     05  SORT-AMOUNT           PIC S9(6)V99.
006100
006200 FD  PRINTER-FILE
006300     LABEL RECORDS ARE OMITTED.
006400 01  PRINTER-RECORD            PIC X(80).
006500
006600 WORKING-STORAGE SECTION.
006700
006800 77  OK-TO-PROCESS            PIC X.
006900
007000     COPY "WSCASE01.CBL".
007100
007200 01  LEGEND-LINE.
007300     05  FILLER                PIC X(6) VALUE "STORE:".
007400     05  FILLER                PIC X(1) VALUE SPACE.
007500     05  PRINT-STORE           PIC Z9.
007600
```

continues

Listing A.44. continued

```
007700*01  DETAIL-LINE.
007800*    05  FILLER           PIC X(3) VALUE SPACE.
007900*    05  PRINT-DIVISION   PIC Z9.
008000*    05  FILLER           PIC X(4) VALUE SPACE.
008100*    05  FILLER           PIC X(3) VALUE SPACE.
008200*    05  PRINT-DEPARTMENT PIC Z9.
008300*    05  FILLER           PIC X(6) VALUE SPACE.
008400*    05  FILLER           PIC X(3) VALUE SPACE.
008500*    05  PRINT-CATEGORY   PIC Z9.
008600*    05  FILLER           PIC X(4) VALUE SPACE.
008700*    05  PRINT-AMOUNT     PIC ZZZ,ZZ9.99-.
008800
008900*01  COLUMN-LINE.
009000*    05  FILLER       PIC X(8)  VALUE "DIVISION".
009100*    05  FILLER       PIC X(1)  VALUE SPACE.
009200*    05  FILLER       PIC X(10) VALUE "DEPARTMENT".
009300*    05  FILLER       PIC X(1)  VALUE SPACE.
009400*    05  FILLER       PIC X(8)  VALUE "CATEGORY".
009500*    05  FILLER       PIC X(1)  VALUE SPACE.
009600*    05  FILLER       PIC X(4)  VALUE SPACE.
009700*    05  FILLER       PIC X(6)  VALUE "AMOUNT".
009800
009900 01  TITLE-LINE.
010000     05  FILLER           PIC X(30) VALUE SPACE.
010100     05  FILLER           PIC X(13)
010200         VALUE "SALES SUMMARY".
010300     05  FILLER           PIC X(15) VALUE SPACE.
010400     05  FILLER           PIC X(5) VALUE "PAGE:".
010500     05  FILLER           PIC X(1) VALUE SPACE.
010600     05  PRINT-PAGE-NUMBER PIC ZZZ9.
010700
010800 01  TOTAL-LINE.
010900     05  FILLER           PIC X(11) VALUE SPACE.
011000     05  TOTAL-TYPE       PIC X(8).
011100     05  FILLER           PIC X(1) VALUE SPACE.
011200     05  TOTAL-NUMBER     PIC Z9.
011300     05  FILLER           PIC X(1) VALUE SPACE.
011400     05  TOTAL-LITERAL    PIC X(5) VALUE "TOTAL".
011500     05  FILLER           PIC X(1) VALUE SPACE.
011600     05  PRINT-TOTAL      PIC ZZZ,ZZ9.99-.
011700
011800 77  GRAND-TOTAL-LITERAL      PIC X(8) VALUE "   GRAND".
011900 77  STORE-TOTAL-LITERAL      PIC X(8) VALUE "   STORE".
012000 77  DIVISION-TOTAL-LITERAL   PIC X(8) VALUE "DIVISION".
012100 77  DEPARTMENT-TOTAL-LITERAL PIC X(8) VALUE "    DEPT".
012200
012300 77  WORK-FILE-AT-END     PIC X.
012400
012500 77  LINE-COUNT           PIC 999 VALUE ZERO.
012600 77  PAGE-NUMBER          PIC 9999 VALUE ZERO.
012700 77  MAXIMUM-LINES        PIC 999 VALUE 55.
012800
012900 77  RECORD-COUNT         PIC 9999 VALUE ZEROES.
013000
```

```
013100* Control break current values for store, division
013200* department.
013300 77  CURRENT-STORE            PIC 99.
013400 77  CURRENT-DIVISION         PIC 99.
013500 77  CURRENT-DEPARTMENT       PIC 99.
013600
013700* Control break accumulators
013800* GRAND TOTAL is the level 1 accumulator for the whole file
013900* STORE TOTAL is the level 2 accumulator
014000* DIVISION TOTAL is the level 3 accumulator
014100* DEPARTMENT TOTAL is the level 4 accumulator.
014200 77  GRAND-TOTAL              PIC S9(6)V99.
014300 77  STORE-TOTAL              PIC S9(6)V99.
014400 77  DIVISION-TOTAL           PIC S9(6)V99.
014500 77  DEPARTMENT-TOTAL         PIC S9(6)V99.
014600
014700 PROCEDURE DIVISION.
014800 PROGRAM-BEGIN.
014900
015000     PERFORM OPENING-PROCEDURE.
015100     PERFORM MAIN-PROCESS.
015200     PERFORM CLOSING-PROCEDURE.
015300
015400 PROGRAM-EXIT.
015500     EXIT PROGRAM.
015600
015700 PROGRAM-DONE.
015800     STOP RUN.
015900
016000 OPENING-PROCEDURE.
016100
016200     OPEN OUTPUT PRINTER-FILE.
016300
016400 MAIN-PROCESS.
016500     PERFORM GET-OK-TO-PROCESS.
016600     PERFORM PROCESS-THE-FILE
016700         UNTIL OK-TO-PROCESS = "N".
016800
016900 CLOSING-PROCEDURE.
017000     CLOSE PRINTER-FILE.
017100
017200 GET-OK-TO-PROCESS.
017300     PERFORM ACCEPT-OK-TO-PROCESS.
017400     PERFORM RE-ACCEPT-OK-TO-PROCESS
017500         UNTIL OK-TO-PROCESS = "Y" OR "N".
017600
017700 ACCEPT-OK-TO-PROCESS.
017800     DISPLAY "PRINT SALES SUMMARY (Y/N)?".
017900     ACCEPT OK-TO-PROCESS.
018000     INSPECT OK-TO-PROCESS
018100       CONVERTING LOWER-ALPHA
018200       TO          UPPER-ALPHA.
018300
018400 RE-ACCEPT-OK-TO-PROCESS.
018500     DISPLAY "YOU MUST ENTER YES OR NO".
```

continues

Listing A.44. continued

```
018600      PERFORM ACCEPT-OK-TO-PROCESS.
018700
018800 PROCESS-THE-FILE.
018900      PERFORM START-THE-FILE.
019000      PERFORM PRINT-ONE-REPORT.
019100      PERFORM END-THE-FILE.
019200
019300*     PERFORM GET-OK-TO-PROCESS.
019400      MOVE "N" TO OK-TO-PROCESS.
019500
019600 START-THE-FILE.
019700      PERFORM SORT-DATA-FILE.
019800      OPEN INPUT WORK-FILE.
019900
020000 END-THE-FILE.
020100      CLOSE WORK-FILE.
020200
020300 SORT-DATA-FILE.
020400      SORT SORT-FILE
020500          ON ASCENDING KEY SORT-STORE
020600              ASCENDING KEY SORT-DIVISION
020700              ASCENDING KEY SORT-DEPARTMENT
020800              ASCENDING KEY SORT-CATEGORY
020900          USING SALES-FILE
021000          GIVING WORK-FILE.
021100
021200* LEVEL 1 CONTROL BREAK
021300 PRINT-ONE-REPORT.
021400      PERFORM START-ONE-REPORT.
021500      PERFORM PROCESS-ALL-STORES
021600          UNTIL WORK-FILE-AT-END = "Y".
021700      PERFORM END-ONE-REPORT.
021800
021900 START-ONE-REPORT.
022000      PERFORM READ-FIRST-VALID-WORK.
022100      MOVE ZEROES TO GRAND-TOTAL.
022200
022300      PERFORM START-NEW-REPORT.
022400
022500 START-NEW-REPORT.
022600*     MOVE SPACE TO DETAIL-LINE.
022700      MOVE ZEROES TO LINE-COUNT PAGE-NUMBER.
022800
022900 END-ONE-REPORT.
023000      IF RECORD-COUNT = ZEROES
023100          MOVE "NO RECORDS FOUND" TO PRINTER-RECORD
023200          PERFORM WRITE-TO-PRINTER
023300      ELSE
023400          PERFORM PRINT-GRAND-TOTAL.
023500
023600      PERFORM END-LAST-PAGE.
023700
023800 PRINT-GRAND-TOTAL.
023900      MOVE SPACE TO TOTAL-LINE.
```

```
024000      MOVE GRAND-TOTAL TO PRINT-TOTAL.
024100      MOVE GRAND-TOTAL-LITERAL TO TOTAL-TYPE.
024200      MOVE "TOTAL" TO TOTAL-LITERAL.
024300      MOVE TOTAL-LINE TO PRINTER-RECORD.
024400      PERFORM WRITE-TO-PRINTER.
024500      PERFORM LINE-FEED 2 TIMES.
024600*     MOVE SPACE TO DETAIL-LINE.
024700
024800* LEVEL 2 CONTROL BREAK
024900 PROCESS-ALL-STORES.
025000      PERFORM START-ONE-STORE.
025100
025200      PERFORM PROCESS-ALL-DIVISIONS
025300          UNTIL WORK-FILE-AT-END = "Y"
025400              OR WORK-STORE NOT = CURRENT-STORE.
025500
025600      PERFORM END-ONE-STORE.
025700
025800 START-ONE-STORE.
025900      MOVE WORK-STORE TO CURRENT-STORE.
026000      MOVE ZEROES TO STORE-TOTAL.
026100      MOVE WORK-STORE TO PRINT-STORE.
026200
026300      PERFORM START-NEXT-PAGE.
026400
026500 END-ONE-STORE.
026600      PERFORM PRINT-STORE-TOTAL.
026700      ADD STORE-TOTAL TO GRAND-TOTAL.
026800
026900 PRINT-STORE-TOTAL.
027000      MOVE SPACE TO TOTAL-LINE.
027100      MOVE STORE-TOTAL TO PRINT-TOTAL.
027200      MOVE CURRENT-STORE TO TOTAL-NUMBER.
027300      MOVE STORE-TOTAL-LITERAL TO TOTAL-TYPE.
027400      MOVE "TOTAL" TO TOTAL-LITERAL.
027500      MOVE TOTAL-LINE TO PRINTER-RECORD.
027600      PERFORM WRITE-TO-PRINTER.
027700      PERFORM LINE-FEED.
027800*     MOVE SPACE TO DETAIL-LINE.
027900
028000* LEVEL 3 CONTROL BREAK
028100 PROCESS-ALL-DIVISIONS.
028200      PERFORM START-ONE-DIVISION.
028300
028400      PERFORM PROCESS-ALL-DEPARTMENTS
028500          UNTIL WORK-FILE-AT-END = "Y"
028600              OR WORK-STORE NOT = CURRENT-STORE
028700              OR WORK-DIVISION NOT = CURRENT-DIVISION.
028800
028900      PERFORM END-ONE-DIVISION.
029000
029100 START-ONE-DIVISION.
029200      MOVE WORK-DIVISION TO CURRENT-DIVISION.
029300      MOVE ZEROES TO DIVISION-TOTAL.
029400*     MOVE WORK-DIVISION TO PRINT-DIVISION.
```

A

continues

Listing A.44. continued

```
029500
029600 END-ONE-DIVISION.
029700      PERFORM PRINT-DIVISION-TOTAL.
029800      ADD DIVISION-TOTAL TO STORE-TOTAL.
029900
030000 PRINT-DIVISION-TOTAL.
030100      MOVE SPACE TO TOTAL-LINE.
030200      MOVE DIVISION-TOTAL TO PRINT-TOTAL.
030300      MOVE CURRENT-DIVISION TO TOTAL-NUMBER.
030400      MOVE DIVISION-TOTAL-LITERAL TO TOTAL-TYPE.
030500      MOVE "TOTAL" TO TOTAL-LITERAL.
030600      MOVE TOTAL-LINE TO PRINTER-RECORD.
030700      PERFORM WRITE-TO-PRINTER.
030800      PERFORM LINE-FEED.
030900*     MOVE SPACE TO DETAIL-LINE.
031000
031100* LEVEL 4 CONTROL BREAK
031200 PROCESS-ALL-DEPARTMENTS.
031300      PERFORM START-ONE-DEPARTMENT.
031400
031500      PERFORM PROCESS-ALL-CATEGORIES
031600          UNTIL WORK-FILE-AT-END = "Y"
031700              OR WORK-STORE NOT = CURRENT-STORE
031800              OR WORK-DIVISION NOT = CURRENT-DIVISION
031900              OR WORK-DEPARTMENT NOT = CURRENT-DEPARTMENT.
032000
032100      PERFORM END-ONE-DEPARTMENT.
032200
032300 START-ONE-DEPARTMENT.
032400      MOVE WORK-DEPARTMENT TO CURRENT-DEPARTMENT.
032500      MOVE ZEROES TO DEPARTMENT-TOTAL.
032600*     MOVE WORK-DEPARTMENT TO PRINT-DEPARTMENT.
032700
032800 END-ONE-DEPARTMENT.
032900      PERFORM PRINT-DEPARTMENT-TOTAL.
033000      ADD DEPARTMENT-TOTAL TO DIVISION-TOTAL.
033100
033200 PRINT-DEPARTMENT-TOTAL.
033300      MOVE SPACE TO TOTAL-LINE.
033400      MOVE DEPARTMENT-TOTAL TO PRINT-TOTAL.
033500      MOVE CURRENT-DEPARTMENT TO TOTAL-NUMBER.
033600      MOVE DEPARTMENT-TOTAL-LITERAL TO TOTAL-TYPE.
033700      MOVE "TOTAL" TO TOTAL-LITERAL.
033800      MOVE TOTAL-LINE TO PRINTER-RECORD.
033900      PERFORM WRITE-TO-PRINTER.
034000      PERFORM LINE-FEED.
034100*     MOVE SPACE TO DETAIL-LINE.
034200
034300* PROCESS ONE RECORD LEVEL
034400 PROCESS-ALL-CATEGORIES.
034500      PERFORM PROCESS-THIS-CATEGORY.
034600      ADD WORK-AMOUNT TO DEPARTMENT-TOTAL.
034700      ADD 1 TO RECORD-COUNT.
034800      PERFORM READ-NEXT-VALID-WORK.
```

```
034900
035000 PROCESS-THIS-CATEGORY.
035100     IF LINE-COUNT > MAXIMUM-LINES
035200          PERFORM START-NEXT-PAGE.
035300*    PERFORM PRINT-THE-RECORD.
035400
035500*PRINT-THE-RECORD.
035600*    MOVE WORK-CATEGORY TO PRINT-CATEGORY.
035700*
035800*    MOVE WORK-AMOUNT TO PRINT-AMOUNT.
035900*
036000*    MOVE DETAIL-LINE TO PRINTER-RECORD.
036100*    PERFORM WRITE-TO-PRINTER.
036200*    MOVE SPACE TO DETAIL-LINE.
036300
036400* PRINTING ROUTINES
036500 WRITE-TO-PRINTER.
036600     WRITE PRINTER-RECORD BEFORE ADVANCING 1.
036700     ADD 1 TO LINE-COUNT.
036800
036900 LINE-FEED.
037000     MOVE SPACE TO PRINTER-RECORD.
037100     PERFORM WRITE-TO-PRINTER.
037200
037300 START-NEXT-PAGE.
037400     PERFORM END-LAST-PAGE.
037500     PERFORM START-NEW-PAGE.
037600
037700 START-NEW-PAGE.
037800     ADD 1 TO PAGE-NUMBER.
037900     MOVE PAGE-NUMBER TO PRINT-PAGE-NUMBER.
038000     MOVE TITLE-LINE TO PRINTER-RECORD.
038100     PERFORM WRITE-TO-PRINTER.
038200     PERFORM LINE-FEED.
038300     MOVE LEGEND-LINE TO PRINTER-RECORD.
038400     PERFORM WRITE-TO-PRINTER.
038500     PERFORM LINE-FEED.
038600*    MOVE COLUMN-LINE TO PRINTER-RECORD.
038700*    PERFORM WRITE-TO-PRINTER.
038800*    PERFORM LINE-FEED.
038900
039000 END-LAST-PAGE.
039100     IF PAGE-NUMBER > 0
039200          PERFORM FORM-FEED.
039300     MOVE ZERO TO LINE-COUNT.
039400
039500 FORM-FEED.
039600     MOVE SPACE TO PRINTER-RECORD.
039700     WRITE PRINTER-RECORD BEFORE ADVANCING PAGE.
039800
039900*-------------------------------
040000* Read first, read next routines
040100*-------------------------------
040200 READ-FIRST-VALID-WORK.
040300     PERFORM READ-NEXT-VALID-WORK.
```

continues

Listing A.44. continued

```
040400
040500 READ-NEXT-VALID-WORK.
040600     PERFORM READ-NEXT-WORK-RECORD.
040700
040800 READ-NEXT-WORK-RECORD.
040900     MOVE "N" TO WORK-FILE-AT-END.
041000     READ WORK-FILE NEXT RECORD
041100         AT END MOVE "Y" TO WORK-FILE-AT-END.
041200
```

The output of s1ssum01.cbl prints only the control breaks and no detail lines:

OUTPUT

```
                            SALES SUMMARY              PAGE:    1

   STORE:  1

   DEPT  1 TOTAL     712.71

   DEPT  2 TOTAL     762.99

   DIVISION  1 TOTAL   1,475.70

   DEPT  3 TOTAL     813.27

   DEPT  4 TOTAL     863.55

   DIVISION  2 TOTAL   1,676.82

   DEPT  5 TOTAL     913.83

   DEPT  6 TOTAL      64.11

   DIVISION  3 TOTAL    977.94

   STORE  1 TOTAL   4,130.46

   --------------------<page break>-------------------------------


                            SALES SUMMARY              PAGE:    2

   STORE:  2

   DEPT  1 TOTAL   1,014.39

   DEPT  2 TOTAL     164.67

   DIVISION  1 TOTAL   1,179.06

   DEPT  3 TOTAL   1,114.95

   DEPT  4 TOTAL     265.23
```

```
DIVISION  2 TOTAL   1,380.18

DEPT  5 TOTAL   1,215.51

DEPT  6 TOTAL    365.79

DIVISION  3 TOTAL   1,581.30

STORE  2 TOTAL   4,140.54

--------------------<page break>-----------------------------


                          SALES SUMMARY          PAGE:    3

STORE:  3

DEPT  1 TOTAL   1,316.07

DEPT  2 TOTAL    466.35

DIVISION  1 TOTAL   1,782.42

DEPT  3 TOTAL    516.63

DEPT  4 TOTAL    566.91

DIVISION  2 TOTAL   1,083.54

DEPT  5 TOTAL    617.19

DEPT  6 TOTAL    667.47

DIVISION  3 TOTAL   1,284.66

STORE  3 TOTAL   4,150.62

--------------------<page break>-----------------------------


                          SALES SUMMARY          PAGE:    4

STORE:  4

DEPT  1 TOTAL    717.75

DEPT  2 TOTAL    768.03

DIVISION  1 TOTAL   1,485.78

DEPT  3 TOTAL    818.31

DEPT  4 TOTAL    868.59

DIVISION  2 TOTAL   1,686.90
```

A

```
DEPT  5 TOTAL     918.87

DEPT  6 TOTAL     969.15

DIVISION  3 TOTAL   1,888.02

STORE  4 TOTAL   5,060.70
---------------------<page break>-------------------------------

                                SALES SUMMARY           PAGE:    5

STORE:  5

DEPT  1 TOTAL     119.43

DEPT  2 TOTAL   1,069.71

DIVISION  1 TOTAL   1,189.14

DEPT  3 TOTAL     219.99

DEPT  4 TOTAL   1,170.27

DIVISION  2 TOTAL   1,390.26

DEPT  5 TOTAL     320.55

DEPT  6 TOTAL   1,270.83

DIVISION  3 TOTAL   1,591.38

STORE  5 TOTAL   4,170.78

---------------------<page break>-------------------------------

                                SALES SUMMARY           PAGE:    6

STORE:  6

DEPT  1 TOTAL     421.11

DEPT  2 TOTAL     471.39

DIVISION  1 TOTAL    892.50

DEPT  3 TOTAL     521.67

DEPT  4 TOTAL     571.95

DIVISION  2 TOTAL   1,093.62

DEPT  5 TOTAL     622.23
```

```
DEPT  6 TOTAL      672.51

DIVISION  3 TOTAL   1,294.74

STORE  6 TOTAL    3,280.86

GRAND     TOTAL  24,933.96
```

Answers to Bonus Day 2, "Miscellaneous COBOL Syntax"

Quiz

1. The output will be the last name, a comma, a space, the first name, a space, and the middle name:

   JONES, JOHN PAUL

2. FIRST-NAME will contain JANE with spaces to the end of the field. LAST-NAME will contain JOHANSEN with spaces to the end of the field.

Exercise

Listing A.45 is an example of how such a program might work.

TYPE **Listing A.45. A subroutine to get YES or NO.**

```
000100 IDENTIFICATION DIVISION.
000200 PROGRAM-ID. YESORNO.
000300*------------------------------
000400* Force user to enter yes or no
000500*------------------------------
000600 ENVIRONMENT DIVISION.
000700 INPUT-OUTPUT SECTION.
000800 FILE-CONTROL.
000900
001000 DATA DIVISION.
001100 FILE SECTION.
001200
001300 WORKING-STORAGE SECTION.
001400
001500 LINKAGE SECTION.
001600*------------------------------
001700* Field is filled in and returned
001800* to the calling program
001900*------------------------------
002000 77  YES-OR-NO          PIC X.
002100
002200 PROCEDURE DIVISION
002300     USING YES-OR-NO.
```

continues

Listing A.45. continued

```
002400
002500 PROGRAM-BEGIN.
002600     PERFORM OPENING-PROCEDURE.
002700     PERFORM MAIN-PROCESS.
002800     PERFORM CLOSING-PROCEDURE.
002900
003000 PROGRAM-EXIT.
003100     EXIT PROGRAM.
003200
003300 PROGRAM-DONE.
003400     STOP RUN.
003500
003600 OPENING-PROCEDURE.
003700
003800 CLOSING-PROCEDURE.
003900
004000 MAIN-PROCESS.
004100     PERFORM GET-YES-OR-NO.
004200
004300 GET-YES-OR-NO.
004400     PERFORM ACCEPT-YES-OR-NO.
004500     PERFORM RE-ACCEPT-YES-OR-NO
004600         UNTIL YES-OR-NO = "Y" OR "N".
004700
004800 ACCEPT-YES-OR-NO.
004900     DISPLAY "ENTER YES OR NO (Y/N)?".
005000
005100     ACCEPT YES-OR-NO.
005200
005300     PERFORM EDIT-CHECK-YES-OR-NO.
005400
005500 RE-ACCEPT-YES-OR-NO.
005600     DISPLAY "YOU MUST ENTER 'Y' OR 'N'".
005700
005800     PERFORM ACCEPT-YES-OR-NO.
005900
006000 EDIT-CHECK-YES-OR-NO.
006100     PERFORM EDIT-YES-OR-NO.
006200     PERFORM CHECK-YES-OR-NO.
006300     PERFORM FORMAT-YES-OR-NO.
006400
006500 EDIT-YES-OR-NO.
006600     IF YES-OR-NO = "y"
006700         MOVE "Y" TO YES-OR-NO.
006800
006900     IF YES-OR-NO = "n"
007000         MOVE "N" TO YES-OR-NO.
007100
007200 CHECK-YES-OR-NO.
007300* NO CHECKING NEEDED
007400
007500 FORMAT-YES-OR-NO.
007600* NO FORMATTING NEEDED.
007700
```

You can use listing A.46 to test yesorno.cbl. Code, compile, and link, if necessary, both programs. Then run yntest01.cbl.

TYPE **Listing A.46. Testing** yesorno.cbl.

```
000100 IDENTIFICATION DIVISION.
000200 PROGRAM-ID. YNTEST01.
000300*--------------------------------
000400* Testing YESORNO Entry
000500*--------------------------------
000600 ENVIRONMENT DIVISION.
000700 INPUT-OUTPUT SECTION.
000800 FILE-CONTROL.
000900
001000 DATA DIVISION.
001100 FILE SECTION.
001200
001300 WORKING-STORAGE SECTION.
001400
001500 77  YES-NO          PIC X.
001600
001700 PROCEDURE DIVISION.
001800 PROGRAM-BEGIN.
001900     PERFORM OPENING-PROCEDURE.
002000     PERFORM MAIN-PROCESS.
002100     PERFORM CLOSING-PROCEDURE.
002200
002300 PROGRAM-EXIT.
002400     EXIT PROGRAM.
002500
002600 PROGRAM-DONE.
002700     STOP RUN.
002800
002900 OPENING-PROCEDURE.
003000
003100 CLOSING-PROCEDURE.
003200
003300 MAIN-PROCESS.
003400     PERFORM DO-WE-CONTINUE.
003500
003600     IF YES-NO = "Y"
003700        DISPLAY "YOU DO WANT TO CONTINUE"
003800     ELSE
003900        DISPLAY "YOU DON'T WANT TO CONTINUE".
004000
004100 DO-WE-CONTINUE.
004200     DISPLAY "SHALL I CONTINUE?".
004300     CALL "YESORNO" USING YES-NO.
004400
```

The output of yntest01.cbl and yesorno.cbl is marked to indicate which program is producing which part of the display:

```
OUTPUT   SHALL I CONTINUE?                    <- yntest01.cbl
         ENTER YES OR NO (Y/N)?               <- yesorno.cbl
         X                                    <- user entry in yesorno.cbl
         YOU MUST ENTER 'Y' OR 'N'            <- yesorno.cbl
         ENTER YES OR NO (Y/N)?               <- yesorno.cbl
         Y                                    <- user entry in yesorno.cbl
         YOU DO WANT TO CONTINUE              <- yntest01.cbl
```

Answers to Bonus Day 3, "Full-Screen I/O"

Quiz

1. Lines 008300 and 008500 will create display fields that are not modifiable.

2. Line 008400 will create a display field that is modifiable.

Exercise

Listing A.47 will maintain the state code file using full screens.

TYPE   **Listing A.47. State code maintenance.**

```
000100 IDENTIFICATION DIVISION.
000200 PROGRAM-ID. STCMNT05.
000300*-------------------------------
000400* Add, Change, Inquire and Delete
000500* for the State Codes File.
000600* Calls the state codes report
000700* Uses full screen IO
000800*-------------------------------
000900 ENVIRONMENT DIVISION.
001000 INPUT-OUTPUT SECTION.
001100 FILE-CONTROL.
001200
001300     COPY "SLSTATE.CBL".
001400
001500 DATA DIVISION.
001600 FILE SECTION.
001700
001800     COPY "FDSTATE.CBL".
001900
002000 WORKING-STORAGE SECTION.
002100
002200 77  MENU-PICK                 PIC 9 VALUE ZERO.
002300     88  MENU-PICK-IS-VALID     VALUES 0 THRU 5.
002400
002500 77  STATE-RECORD-FOUND        PIC X.
002600
002700 77  SCREEN-ERROR              PIC X.
002800 77  ERROR-MESSAGE             PIC X(79) VALUE SPACE.
002900
```

```
003000 77  CONTINUE-MESSAGE           PIC X(40) VALUE SPACE.
003100 77  OK-TO-CONTINUE             PIC X.
003200
003300 01  FOOTER-FIELD.
003400     05  FOOTER-1-FIELD         PIC X(40) VALUE SPACE.
003500     05  FOOTER-2-FIELD         PIC X(39) VALUE SPACE.
003600
003700     COPY "WSCASE01.CBL".
003800
003900 SCREEN SECTION.
004000 01  MENU-SCREEN.
004100     05  BLANK SCREEN.
004200     05  LINE  2 COLUMN 30 VALUE "STATE CODE MAINTENANCE".
004300     05  LINE  6 COLUMN 20 VALUE "PLEASE SELECT:".
004400     05  LINE  8 COLUMN 25 VALUE "1. ADD RECORDS".
004500     05  LINE  9 COLUMN 25 VALUE "2. CHANGE A RECORD".
004600     05  LINE 10 COLUMN 25 VALUE "3. LOOK UP A RECORD".
004700     05  LINE 11 COLUMN 25 VALUE "4. DELETE A RECORD".
004800     05  LINE 12 COLUMN 25 VALUE "5. PRINT RECORDS".
004900     05  LINE 14 COLUMN 25 VALUE "0. EXIT".
005000     05  LINE 20 COLUMN  1 VALUE "YOUR SELECTION? ".
005100     05  LINE 20 COLUMN 17 PIC Z USING MENU-PICK.
005200     05  LINE 24 COLUMN  1 PIC X(79) FROM ERROR-MESSAGE.
005300
005400 01  KEY-SCREEN.
005500     05  BLANK SCREEN.
005600     05  LINE  8 COLUMN 20 VALUE "STATE CODE:".
005700     05  LINE  8 COLUMN 40 PIC XX USING STATE-CODE.
005800     05  LINE 22 COLUMN  1 PIC X(79) FROM FOOTER-FIELD.
005900     05  LINE 24 COLUMN  1 PIC X(79) FROM ERROR-MESSAGE.
006000
006100 01  ENTRY-SCREEN.
006200     05  BLANK SCREEN.
006300     05  LINE  8 COLUMN 20 VALUE "STATE CODE:".
006400     05  LINE  8 COLUMN 40 PIC XX FROM STATE-CODE.
006500     05  LINE 10 COLUMN 20 VALUE "STATE NAME: ".
006600     05  LINE 10 COLUMN 40 PIC X(20) USING STATE-NAME.
006700     05  LINE 22 COLUMN  1 PIC X(79) FROM FOOTER-FIELD.
006800     05  LINE 23 COLUMN  1 PIC X(40) FROM CONTINUE-MESSAGE.
006900     05  LINE 23 COLUMN 41 PIC X USING OK-TO-CONTINUE.
007000     05  LINE 24 COLUMN  1 PIC X(79) FROM ERROR-MESSAGE.
007100
007200 01  DISPLAY-SCREEN.
007300     05  BLANK SCREEN.
007400     05  LINE  8 COLUMN 20 VALUE "STATE CODE:".
007500     05  LINE  8 COLUMN 40 PIC XX FROM STATE-CODE.
007600     05  LINE 10 COLUMN 20 VALUE "STATE NAME: ".
007700     05  LINE 10 COLUMN 40 PIC X(20) FROM STATE-NAME.
007800     05  LINE 23 COLUMN  1 PIC X(40) FROM CONTINUE-MESSAGE.
007900     05  LINE 23 COLUMN 41 PIC X USING OK-TO-CONTINUE.
008000     05  LINE 24 COLUMN  1 PIC X(79) FROM ERROR-MESSAGE.
008100
008200 PROCEDURE DIVISION.
008300 PROGRAM-BEGIN.
008400     PERFORM OPENING-PROCEDURE.
```

continues

Listing A.47. continued

```
008500      PERFORM MAIN-PROCESS.
008600      PERFORM CLOSING-PROCEDURE.
008700
008800 PROGRAM-EXIT.
008900      EXIT PROGRAM.
009000
009100 PROGRAM-DONE.
009200      STOP RUN.
009300
009400 OPENING-PROCEDURE.
009500      OPEN I-O STATE-FILE.
009600
009700 CLOSING-PROCEDURE.
009800      CLOSE STATE-FILE.
009900
010000 MAIN-PROCESS.
010100      PERFORM GET-MENU-PICK.
010200      PERFORM MAINTAIN-THE-FILE
010300          UNTIL MENU-PICK = 0.
010400
010500*-------------------------------
010600* MENU
010700*-------------------------------
010800 GET-MENU-PICK.
010900      PERFORM INITIALIZE-MENU-PICK.
011000      PERFORM DISPLAY-ACCEPT-MENU.
011100      PERFORM RE-DISPLAY-ACCEPT-MENU
011200          UNTIL MENU-PICK-IS-VALID.
011300
011400 INITIALIZE-MENU-PICK.
011500      MOVE 0 TO MENU-PICK.
011600
011700 DISPLAY-ACCEPT-MENU.
011800      DISPLAY MENU-SCREEN.
011900      ACCEPT MENU-SCREEN.
012000      MOVE SPACE TO ERROR-MESSAGE.
012100
012200 RE-DISPLAY-ACCEPT-MENU.
012300      MOVE "INVALID SELECTION - PLEASE RE-TRY."
012400          TO ERROR-MESSAGE.
012500      PERFORM DISPLAY-ACCEPT-MENU.
012600
012700 MAINTAIN-THE-FILE.
012800      PERFORM DO-THE-PICK.
012900      PERFORM GET-MENU-PICK.
013000
013100 DO-THE-PICK.
013200      IF MENU-PICK = 1
013300          PERFORM ADD-MODE
013400      ELSE
013500      IF MENU-PICK = 2
013600          PERFORM CHANGE-MODE
013700      ELSE
013800      IF MENU-PICK = 3
013900          PERFORM INQUIRE-MODE
```

```
014000     ELSE
014100     IF MENU-PICK = 4
014200         PERFORM DELETE-MODE
014300     ELSE
014400     IF MENU-PICK = 5
014500         PERFORM PRINT-STATE-REPORT.
014600
014700*-------------------------------
014800* ADD
014900*-------------------------------
015000 ADD-MODE.
015100     PERFORM INITIALIZE-ADD-MODE.
015200     PERFORM GET-NEW-RECORD-KEY.
015300     PERFORM ADD-RECORDS
015400         UNTIL STATE-CODE = "ZZ".
015500
015600 INITIALIZE-ADD-MODE.
015700     MOVE "ENTER THE STATE CODE TO ADD"
015800         TO FOOTER-1-FIELD.
015900
016000 GET-NEW-RECORD-KEY.
016100     PERFORM ACCEPT-NEW-RECORD-KEY.
016200     PERFORM RE-ACCEPT-NEW-RECORD-KEY
016300         UNTIL STATE-CODE = "ZZ"
016400             OR STATE-RECORD-FOUND = "N".
016500
016600 ACCEPT-NEW-RECORD-KEY.
016700     PERFORM INITIALIZE-STATE-FIELDS.
016800     PERFORM ENTER-STATE-CODE.
016900     PERFORM ENTER-STATE-CODE
017000         UNTIL STATE-CODE NOT = SPACE.
017100     IF STATE-CODE NOT = "ZZ"
017200         PERFORM READ-STATE-RECORD.
017300
017400 RE-ACCEPT-NEW-RECORD-KEY.
017500     MOVE "RECORD ALREADY ON FILE" TO ERROR-MESSAGE.
017600     PERFORM ACCEPT-NEW-RECORD-KEY.
017700
017800 ADD-RECORDS.
017900     PERFORM INITIALIZE-TO-ADD-FIELDS.
018000     PERFORM ENTER-REMAINING-FIELDS.
018100     IF OK-TO-CONTINUE = "Y"
018200         PERFORM WRITE-STATE-RECORD.
018300     PERFORM GET-NEW-RECORD-KEY.
018400
018500 INITIALIZE-TO-ADD-FIELDS.
018600     MOVE "ADD NEW FIELDS" TO FOOTER-FIELD.
018700     MOVE "CONTINUE WITH ADDITIONS (Y/N)?"
018800         TO CONTINUE-MESSAGE.
018900     MOVE "Y" TO OK-TO-CONTINUE.
019000
019100*-------------------------------
019200* CHANGE
019300*-------------------------------
019400 CHANGE-MODE.
```

continues

Listing A.47. continued

```
019500      PERFORM INITIALIZE-CHANGE-MODE.
019600      PERFORM GET-EXISTING-RECORD.
019700      PERFORM CHANGE-RECORDS
019800          UNTIL STATE-CODE = "ZZ".
019900
020000 INITIALIZE-CHANGE-MODE.
020100      MOVE "ENTER THE STATE CODE TO CHANGE"
020200          TO FOOTER-1-FIELD.
020300
020400 CHANGE-RECORDS.
020500      PERFORM INITIALIZE-TO-CHANGE-FIELDS.
020600      PERFORM ENTER-REMAINING-FIELDS.
020700      IF OK-TO-CONTINUE = "Y"
020800          PERFORM REWRITE-STATE-RECORD.
020900      PERFORM GET-EXISTING-RECORD.
021000
021100 INITIALIZE-TO-CHANGE-FIELDS.
021200      MOVE "CHANGE FIELDS" TO FOOTER-FIELD.
021300      MOVE "CONTINUE WITH CHANGES (Y/N)?"
021400          TO CONTINUE-MESSAGE.
021500      MOVE "Y" TO OK-TO-CONTINUE.
021600
021700*------------------------------
021800* INQUIRE
021900*------------------------------
022000 INQUIRE-MODE.
022100      PERFORM INITIALIZE-INQUIRE-MODE.
022200      PERFORM GET-EXISTING-RECORD.
022300      PERFORM INQUIRE-RECORDS
022400          UNTIL STATE-CODE = "ZZ".
022500
022600 INITIALIZE-INQUIRE-MODE.
022700      MOVE "ENTER THE STATE CODE TO DISPLAY"
022800          TO FOOTER-1-FIELD.
022900
023000 INQUIRE-RECORDS.
023100      PERFORM INITIALIZE-TO-INQUIRE.
023200      PERFORM DISPLAY-ACCEPT-ALL-FIELDS.
023300      PERFORM GET-EXISTING-RECORD.
023400
023500 INITIALIZE-TO-INQUIRE.
023600      MOVE "PRESS ENTER TO CONTINUE" TO CONTINUE-MESSAGE.
023700      MOVE SPACE TO OK-TO-CONTINUE.
023800
023900*------------------------------
024000* DELETE
024100*------------------------------
024200 DELETE-MODE.
024300      PERFORM INITIALIZE-DELETE-MODE.
024400      PERFORM GET-EXISTING-RECORD.
024500      PERFORM DELETE-RECORDS
024600          UNTIL STATE-CODE = "ZZ".
024700
024800 INITIALIZE-DELETE-MODE.
024900      MOVE "ENTER THE STATE CODE TO DELETE"
```

```
025000        TO FOOTER-1-FIELD.
025100
025200 DELETE-RECORDS.
025300     PERFORM INITIALIZE-TO-DELETE-RECORD.
025400     PERFORM ASK-OK-TO-DELETE.
025500     IF OK-TO-CONTINUE = "Y"
025600         PERFORM DELETE-STATE-RECORD.
025700     PERFORM GET-EXISTING-RECORD.
025800
025900 INITIALIZE-TO-DELETE-RECORD.
026000     MOVE "OK TO DELETE(Y/N)?" TO CONTINUE-MESSAGE.
026100     MOVE "N" TO OK-TO-CONTINUE.
026200
026300 ASK-OK-TO-DELETE.
026400     PERFORM DISPLAY-ACCEPT-ALL-FIELDS.
026500     PERFORM RE-DISPLAY-ACCEPT-ALL-FIELDS
026600         UNTIL OK-TO-CONTINUE = "Y" OR "N".
026700
026800 RE-DISPLAY-ACCEPT-ALL-FIELDS.
026900     MOVE "YOU MUST ENTER YES OR NO"
027000         TO ERROR-MESSAGE.
027100     PERFORM DISPLAY-ACCEPT-ALL-FIELDS.
027200
027300*------------------------------
027400* Routines shared by all modes
027500*------------------------------
027600 INITIALIZE-STATE-FIELDS.
027700     MOVE SPACE TO STATE-RECORD.
027800
027900 ENTER-STATE-CODE.
028000     MOVE "ENTER 'ZZ' TO QUIT" TO FOOTER-2-FIELD.
028100     DISPLAY KEY-SCREEN.
028200     ACCEPT KEY-SCREEN.
028300     MOVE SPACE TO ERROR-MESSAGE.
028400
028500     INSPECT STATE-CODE
028600         CONVERTING LOWER-ALPHA
028700         TO          UPPER-ALPHA.
028800
028900     IF STATE-CODE = SPACE
029000         MOVE "YOU MUST ENTER STATE CODE"
029100           TO ERROR-MESSAGE.
029200
029300*------------------------------
029400* Routines shared Add and Change
029500*------------------------------
029600 ENTER-REMAINING-FIELDS.
029700     PERFORM DISPLAY-ACCEPT-ENTRY-SCREEN.
029800     PERFORM DISPLAY-ACCEPT-ENTRY-SCREEN
029900         UNTIL SCREEN-ERROR = "N"
030000           OR OK-TO-CONTINUE = "N".
030100
030200 DISPLAY-ACCEPT-ENTRY-SCREEN.
030300     DISPLAY ENTRY-SCREEN.
030400     ACCEPT ENTRY-SCREEN.
```

continues

Listing A.47. continued

```
030500      MOVE SPACE TO ERROR-MESSAGE.
030600
030700      INSPECT OK-TO-CONTINUE
030800        CONVERTING LOWER-ALPHA TO UPPER-ALPHA.
030900
031000      IF OK-TO-CONTINUE = "Y"
031100          PERFORM EDIT-CHECK-FIELDS.
031200
031300 EDIT-CHECK-FIELDS.
031400      MOVE "N" TO SCREEN-ERROR.
031500      PERFORM EDIT-CHECK-STATE-NAME.
031600
031700 EDIT-CHECK-STATE-NAME.
031800      INSPECT STATE-NAME
031900          CONVERTING LOWER-ALPHA
032000          TO          UPPER-ALPHA.
032100
032200      IF STATE-NAME = SPACES
032300          MOVE "Y" TO SCREEN-ERROR
032400          MOVE "STATE NAME MUST BE ENTERED"
032500              TO ERROR-MESSAGE.
032600
032700*-------------------------------
032800* Routines shared by Change,
032900* Inquire and Delete
033000*-------------------------------
033100 GET-EXISTING-RECORD.
033200      PERFORM INITIALIZE-STATE-FIELDS.
033300      PERFORM ACCEPT-EXISTING-KEY.
033400      PERFORM RE-ACCEPT-EXISTING-KEY
033500          UNTIL STATE-RECORD-FOUND = "Y" OR
033600              STATE-CODE = "ZZ".
033700
033800 ACCEPT-EXISTING-KEY.
033900      PERFORM ENTER-STATE-CODE.
034000      PERFORM ENTER-STATE-CODE
034100          UNTIL STATE-CODE NOT = SPACE.
034200      IF STATE-CODE NOT = "ZZ"
034300          PERFORM READ-STATE-RECORD.
034400
034500 RE-ACCEPT-EXISTING-KEY.
034600      MOVE "RECORD NOT FOUND" TO ERROR-MESSAGE.
034700      PERFORM ACCEPT-EXISTING-KEY.
034800
034900*-------------------------------
035000* Routines shared by delete and inquire
035100*-------------------------------
035200 DISPLAY-ACCEPT-ALL-FIELDS.
035300      DISPLAY DISPLAY-SCREEN.
035400      ACCEPT DISPLAY-SCREEN.
035500      MOVE SPACE TO ERROR-MESSAGE.
035600      INSPECT OK-TO-CONTINUE
035700        CONVERTING LOWER-ALPHA TO UPPER-ALPHA.
035800
035900*-------------------------------
```

```
036000* File I-O Routines
036100*--------------------------------
036200 WRITE-STATE-RECORD.
036300     WRITE STATE-RECORD
036400         INVALID KEY
036500         DISPLAY "RECORD ALREADY ON FILE".
036600
036700 REWRITE-STATE-RECORD.
036800     REWRITE STATE-RECORD
036900         INVALID KEY
037000         DISPLAY "ERROR REWRITING STATE RECORD".
037100
037200 DELETE-STATE-RECORD.
037300     DELETE STATE-FILE RECORD
037400         INVALID KEY
037500         DISPLAY "ERROR DELETING STATE RECORD".
037600
037700 READ-STATE-RECORD.
037800     MOVE "Y" TO STATE-RECORD-FOUND.
037900     READ STATE-FILE RECORD
038000       INVALID KEY
038100         MOVE "N" TO STATE-RECORD-FOUND.
038200
038300*--------------------------------
038400* CALLS TO OTHER PROGRAMS
038500*--------------------------------
038600
038700*--------------------------------
038800* PRINT
038900*--------------------------------
039000 PRINT-STATE-REPORT.
039100     PERFORM CLOSING-PROCEDURE.
039200     DISPLAY "REPORT IN PROGRESS".
039300     CALL "STCRPT02".
039400     PERFORM OPENING-PROCEDURE.
039500
```

Sample output from stcmnt05.cbl illustrates some of the screens created by the program:

```
                    STATE CODE MAINTENANCE




          PLEASE SELECT:

                  1. ADD RECORDS
                  2. CHANGE A RECORD
                  3. LOOK UP A RECORD
                  4. DELETE A RECORD
                  5. PRINT RECORDS

                  0. EXIT
```

YOUR SELECTION?

-----------------------------<next screen>-----------------------

                         STATE CODE: __

ENTER THE STATE CODE TO CHANGE   ENTER 'ZZ' TO QUIT

-----------------------------<next screen>-----------------------

                         STATE CODE: wx

ENTER THE STATE CODE TO CHANGE   ENTER 'ZZ' TO QUIT
RECORD NOT FOUND

Answers to Bonus Day 4, "Using a Symbolic Debugger"

Quiz

The value in A-NUMBER before Line 018500 will be 10. The value before line 018600 will be 11.

Exercises

1. No answer, just practice with the debugger.
2. No answer, just practice with the debugger.

Answers to Bonus Day 5, "Intrinsic Functions and the Year 2000"

Quiz

The value in RESULT will be the remainder of 15 divided by 4, which is 3.

Exercise

Listing A.48 is the original DATE-CHECK routine from PLDATE01.CBL. Listing A.49 is an alternative routine using the REM function. Listing A.50 provides another solution. In Listing A.50 the REM function is used directly to return a numeric value, and the DATE-REMAINDER field is not needed in WORKING-STORAGE.

TYPE **Listing A.48. The original CHECK-DATE routine.**

```
021400 CHECK-DATE.
021500     MOVE "Y" TO VALID-DATE-FLAG.
021600     IF DATE-CCYYMMDD = ZEROES
021700         IF ZERO-DATE-IS-OK = "Y"
021800             MOVE "0" TO VALID-DATE-FLAG
021900         ELSE
022000             MOVE "N" TO VALID-DATE-FLAG
022100     ELSE
022200     IF DATE-MM < 1 OR DATE-MM > 12
022300         MOVE "N" TO VALID-DATE-FLAG
022400     ELSE
022500     IF DATE-DD < 1 OR DATE-DD > 31
022600         MOVE "N" TO VALID-DATE-FLAG
022700     ELSE
022800     IF (DATE-DD > 30) AND
```

continues

Listing A.48. continued

```
022900              (DATE-MM = 2 OR 4 OR 6 OR 9 OR 11)
023000                  MOVE "N" TO VALID-DATE-FLAG
023100          ELSE
023200          IF DATE-DD > 29 AND DATE-MM = 2
023300              MOVE "N" TO VALID-DATE-FLAG
023400          ELSE
023500          IF DATE-DD = 29 AND DATE-MM = 2
023600              DIVIDE DATE-CCYY BY 400 GIVING DATE-QUOTIENT
023700                  REMAINDER DATE-REMAINDER
023800              IF DATE-REMAINDER = 0
023900                 MOVE "Y" TO VALID-DATE-FLAG
024000              ELSE
024100                 DIVIDE DATE-CCYY BY 100 GIVING DATE-QUOTIENT
024200                     REMAINDER DATE-REMAINDER
024300                 IF DATE-REMAINDER = 0
024400                     MOVE "N" TO VALID-DATE-FLAG
024500                 ELSE
024600                     DIVIDE DATE-CCYY BY 4 GIVING DATE-QUOTIENT
024700                         REMAINDER DATE-REMAINDER
024800                     IF DATE-REMAINDER = 0
024900                         MOVE "Y" TO VALID-DATE-FLAG
025000                     ELSE
025100                         MOVE "N" TO VALID-DATE-FLAG.
```

TYPE Listing A.49. CHECK-DATE **using the** REM **Function.**

```
021400 CHECK-DATE.
021500     MOVE "Y" TO VALID-DATE-FLAG.
021600     IF DATE-CCYYMMDD = ZEROES
021700         IF ZERO-DATE-IS-OK = "Y"
021800             MOVE "0" TO VALID-DATE-FLAG
021900         ELSE
022000             MOVE "N" TO VALID-DATE-FLAG
022100     ELSE
022200     IF DATE-MM < 1 OR DATE-MM > 12
022300         MOVE "N" TO VALID-DATE-FLAG
022400     ELSE
022500     IF DATE-DD < 1 OR DATE-DD > 31
022600         MOVE "N" TO VALID-DATE-FLAG
022700     ELSE
022800     IF (DATE-DD > 30) AND
022900        (DATE-MM = 2 OR 4 OR 6 OR 9 OR 11)
023000         MOVE "N" TO VALID-DATE-FLAG
023100     ELSE
023200     IF DATE-DD > 29 AND DATE-MM = 2
023300         MOVE "N" TO VALID-DATE-FLAG
023400     ELSE
023500     IF DATE-DD = 29 AND DATE-MM = 2
023600         COMPUTE DATE-REMAINDER = FUNCTION REM(DATE-CCYY, 400)
023700
023800             IF DATE-REMAINDER = 0
```

```
023900                    MOVE "Y" TO VALID-DATE-FLAG
024000                ELSE
024100                    COMPUTE DATE-REMAINDER = FUNCTION REM(DATE-CCYY,100)
024200
024300                    IF DATE-REMAINDER = 0
024400                        MOVE "N" TO VALID-DATE-FLAG
024500                    ELSE
024600                        COMPUTE DATE-REMAINDER =
024700                                FUNCTION REM(DATE-CCYY,100)
024800                        IF DATE-REMAINDER = 0
024900                            MOVE "Y" TO VALID-DATE-FLAG
025000                        ELSE
025100                            MOVE "N" TO VALID-DATE-FLAG.
```

TYPE | **Listing A.50. Another version of CHECK-DATE.**

```
021400 CHECK-DATE.
021500      MOVE "Y" TO VALID-DATE-FLAG.
021600      IF DATE-CCYYMMDD = ZEROES
021700          IF ZERO-DATE-IS-OK = "Y"
021800              MOVE "0" TO VALID-DATE-FLAG
021900          ELSE
022000              MOVE "N" TO VALID-DATE-FLAG
022100      ELSE
022200      IF DATE-MM < 1 OR DATE-MM > 12
022300          MOVE "N" TO VALID-DATE-FLAG
022400      ELSE
022500      IF DATE-DD < 1 OR DATE-DD > 31
022600          MOVE "N" TO VALID-DATE-FLAG
022700      ELSE
022800      IF (DATE-DD > 30) AND
022900         (DATE-MM = 2 OR 4 OR 6 OR 9 OR 11)
023000          MOVE "N" TO VALID-DATE-FLAG
023100      ELSE
023200      IF DATE-DD > 29 AND DATE-MM = 2
023300          MOVE "N" TO VALID-DATE-FLAG
023400      ELSE
023500      IF DATE-DD = 29 AND DATE-MM = 2
023600          IF FUNCTION REM(DATE-CCYY, 400) = 0
023700              MOVE "Y" TO VALID-DATE-FLAG
023800          ELSE
023900              IF FUNCTION REM(DATE-CCYY,100) = 0
024000                  MOVE "N" TO VALID-DATE-FLAG
024100              ELSE
024200                  IF FUNCTION REM(DATE-CCYY,100) = 0
024300                      MOVE "Y" TO VALID-DATE-FLAG
024400                  ELSE
024500                      MOVE "N" TO VALID-DATE-FLAG.
```

A

Answers to Bonus Day 6, "Dates and the Year 2000"

Quiz

1. Lilian and ANSI days dating both use a base date and calculate dates as a number of days from the base date. Lilian uses Friday, October 15, 1582 as day 1; ANSI uses Monday, January 1, 1601 as day 1.

2. The remainder of 15 divided by 4 is 3, the value that will be stored in RESULT.

3. A year is a leap year if it is

   ☐ Evenly divisible by 4

   ☐ But not if it is evenly divisible by 100

   ☐ Unless it is also evenly divisible by 400.

4. 1996, 2000, and 1600 are all leap years. 1700, 1901, and 1955 are not.

Exercise

Listing A.51 shows DDIF.CBL is one possible solution to the day difference problem.

TYPE **Listing A.51. DDIF.CBL calculating the number of days between two dates.**

```
000100 IDENTIFICATION DIVISION.
000200 PROGRAM-ID. DDIF.
000300 AUTHOR. MO BUDLONG.
000400 INSTALLATION.
000500 DATE-WRITTEN. 09/07/96.
000600 DATE-COMPILED.
000700 SECURITY. NONE
000800 ENVIRONMENT DIVISION.
000900 INPUT-OUTPUT SECTION.
001000 FILE-CONTROL.
001100 DATA DIVISION.
001200 FILE SECTION.
001300 WORKING-STORAGE SECTION.
001400
001500 01  LARGER-DATE            PIC 9(8).
001600 01  SMALLER-DATE           PIC 9(8).
001700 01  LARGER-ANSI            PIC 9(8).
001800 01  SMALLER-ANSI           PIC 9(8).
001900 01  DAYS-DIFF              PIC S9(5).
002000 01  FORMAT-DAYS-DIFF       PIC ZZZZ9-.
002100
002200 01  DUMMY      PIC X.
```

```
002300
002400 PROCEDURE DIVISION.
002500 MAIN-LOGIC SECTION.
002600 PROGRAM-BEGIN.
002700
002800      PERFORM OPENING-PROCEDURE.
002900      PERFORM MAIN-PROCESS.
003000      PERFORM CLOSING-PROCEDURE.
003100
003200 EXIT-PROGRAM.
003300      EXIT PROGRAM.
003400 STOP-RUN.
003500      STOP RUN.
003600
003700
003800 THE-OTHER SECTION.
003900
004000 OPENING-PROCEDURE.
004100 CLOSING-PROCEDURE.
004200 MAIN-PROCESS.
004300      MOVE 1 TO LARGER-DATE, SMALLER-DATE.
004400      PERFORM ENTER-PARAMETERS.
004500      PERFORM TEST-DDIF UNTIL
004600           LARGER-DATE = 0
004700        OR SMALLER-DATE = 0.
004800
004900 ENTER-PARAMETERS.
005000      DISPLAY "ENTER LARGER DATE AS YYYYMMDD(0 TO QUIT)".
005100      ACCEPT LARGER-DATE.
005200      IF LARGER-DATE NOT = 0
005300         DISPLAY "ENTER SMALLER DATE AS YYYYMMDD (0 TO QUIT)"
005400         ACCEPT SMALLER-DATE.
005500
005600 TEST-DDIF.
005700      COMPUTE LARGER-ANSI =
005800       FUNCTION INTEGER-OF-DATE(LARGER-DATE).
005900      COMPUTE SMALLER-ANSI =
006000       FUNCTION INTEGER-OF-DATE(SMALLER-DATE).
006100
006200      COMPUTE DAYS-DIFF = LARGER-ANSI - SMALLER-ANSI.
006300      MOVE DAYS-DIFF TO FORMAT-DAYS-DIFF.
006400      DISPLAY
006500        "DIFFERENCE BETWEEN " LARGER-DATE
006600        " AND " SMALLER-DATE
006700        " IS " FORMAT-DAYS-DIFF.
006800
006900      PERFORM ENTER-PARAMETERS.
007000
```

The following is a sample output screen from the program, showing that the answer is still correct even if the user enters the information incorrectly.

A

OUTPUT

```
* Accepted - CONFIRM
ENTER LARGER DATE AS YYYYMMDD(0 TO QUIT)
19970112
ENTER SMALLER DATE AS YYYYMMDD (0 TO QUIT)
19970110
DIFFERENCE BETWEEN 19970112 AND 19970110 IS     2
ENTER LARGER DATE AS YYYYMMDD(0 TO QUIT)
19970112
ENTER SMALLER DATE AS YYYYMMDD (0 TO QUIT)
19970114
DIFFERENCE BETWEEN 19970112 AND 19970114 IS     2-
ENTER LARGER DATE AS YYYYMMDD(0 TO QUIT)
```

APPENDIX B

ASCII

ASCII (American Standard Code for Information Interchange) uses 128 numbers to represent the characters of the alphabet, the digits, punctuation characters, and some special characters that are used to control printers, terminals, and other computer devices. The 128 values are numbered beginning with zero, so the numbers used are 0 through 127.

The ASCII character set includes all the digits, the upper- and lowercase letters of the alphabet, and punctuation characters. All the printable characters (letters, digits, and punctuation) have values between 32 and 126. The values 0 through 31 and 127 are used for control characters.

Table B.1 is a brief ASCII chart with the decimal value of each entry, and its ASCII name or character. Several of the ASCII codes represent nonprintable characters, and these are represented by their names. You might be familiar with some of these.

Table B.1. ASCII chart with decimal values.

0	NUL	32	SP	64	@	96	'
1	SOH	33	!	65	A	97	a
2	STX	34	"	66	B	98	b
3	ETX	35	#	67	C	99	c
4	EOT	36	$	68	D	100	d
5	ENQ	37	%	69	E	101	e
6	ACK	38	&	70	F	102	f
7	BEL	39	'	71	G	103	g
8	BS	40	(	72	H	104	h
9	HT	41	)	73	I	105	i
10	LF	42	*	74	J	106	j
11	VT	43	+	75	K	107	k
12	FF	44	,	76	L	108	l
13	CR	45	-	77	M	109	m
14	SO	46	.	78	N	110	n
15	SI	47	/	79	O	111	o
16	DLE	48	0	80	P	112	p
17	DC1	49	1	81	Q	113	q
18	DC2	50	2	82	R	114	r
19	DC3	51	3	83	S	115	s
20	DC4	52	4	84	T	116	t

21	NAK	53	5	85	U	117	u
22	SYN	54	6	86	V	118	v
23	ETB	55	7	87	W	119	w
24	CAN	56	8	88	X	120	x
25	EM	57	9	89	Y	121	y
26	SUB	58	:	90	Z	122	z
27	ESC	59	;	91	[	123	{
28	FS	60	<	92	\	124	|
29	GS	61	=	93	]	125	}
30	RS	62	>	94	^	126	~
31	US	63	?	95	_	127	DEL

A control character is a single character that can be sent to a computer device, such as a printer or monitor, that controls the behavior of the device (rather than printing an actual character). For example, the value 13 (CR) is a carriage return. This value sent to a printer causes the print head to return to column 1. A CR also is the code usually sent by the Return or Enter key on the keyboard. Value 7 (BEL), when sent by the computer to the terminal, usually causes a beep or rings an alarm.

The following are some of the other control characters:

HT (Horizontal Tab) value 9. This character, sent to a printer or a screen, causes the cursor or print head to advance to the next column.

SO (Shift Out) and SI (Shift In), values 14 and 15. Many printers are set up with two built-in fonts. Sending an SI causes the printer to shift to the second font. Sending an SO causes the printer to shift back to the first font.

The values from 32 through 126 are printable characters. Value 32 (SP) is a space. Whether a space is actually a "printable" character is a debatable issue. A space does not usually put ink on the paper; instead, it places a character containing no image. Some printers create this by simply advancing the print head one position.

The characters in the range below 32 are used extensively in telecommunications. For example, 02 and 03 (STX and ETX) are often used at the start and end of a block of transmitted information. 06 and 21 (ACK and NAK) are often used by a receiving computer to signal acknowledgement (ACK for well-received) or a negative acknowledgement (NAK for not well-received, please retransmit).

For a detailed and excellent description of ASCII, read *The C Programmer's Guide to Serial Communications, Second Edition*, by Joe Campbell (Sams Publishing). Chapter 1 on ASCII alone makes the book worth the cover price.

APPENDIX

C

Editing, Compiling, and Linking

To use this book effectively, you need to set up an area on your computer's disks where you can do your work and become familiar with your tools.

Setting up includes installing the COBOL compiler and creating a directory where you can do the lessons and experiment with ideas you might have while studying. The tools you need to become familiar with are an editor, the COBOL compiler, and perhaps a linker. You also need to learn how to run the completed program.

You'll perform this edit-compile-run sequence many times before you complete this book. Get comfortable with these steps. Without them, you will be unable to see your programs running, and your study will become an exercise in theory without practice.

This appendix explains the steps you need to take to set up a development area for various different COBOL compilers and computer systems, and how to use the tools to edit, compile, and link your program. If you use Micro Focus Personal COBOL or Acucobol, refer to the installation instructions distributed with your package. If the system you are using is not included, you have to consult the COBOL manual, editor manual, and system administrator or course instructor to work out this process.

Installation

First, install the COBOL compiler and associated software. If you will be working on a system that already has a COBOL compiler installed, you can skip installation.

Workspace

On almost any system, the workspace is a directory.

Windows

Under Windows, most of the compilers that you use will run within an MS-DOS Window. For Windows 3.x, double-click the group named Main, and double-click the MS-DOS icon. For Windows 95, click the Start button and select Programs. Within the programs listed, you will find one for MS-DOS Prompt. Click this selection.

When you are running MS-DOS under Windows, the MS-DOS window might appear as a smaller window on the main screen, or it might fill the entire screen, replacing the Windows desktop with a blank MS-DOS screen. After you have an MS-DOS screen or window open, you may type commands in that window or screen as if you were in MS-DOS. Follow the directions in the section "MS-DOS." When you are finished with your MS-DOS or COBOL programming session, type **exit** at the prompt to close the MS-DOS window or screen and return to the Windows desktop.

MS-DOS

On an MS-DOS system, change to the root directory by entering the following:

```
cd \
```

Then create a working directory by entering the following:

```
mkdir cobol21
```

This creates a directory in which you can do all your development. Whenever you are ready to work on a lesson, start by changing to that directory by entering the following:

```
cd \cobol21
```

UNIX

If you work on a UNIX-based operating system, change to your home directory by entering the following:

```
cd
```

Then create a directory in which you can do all your development by entering the following:

```
mkdir cobol21
```

Whenever you are ready to work on a lesson, change to that directory by entering the following:

```
cd $HOME
cd cobol21
```

or

```
cd $HOME/cobol21
```

VAX VMS

Log on to the system so that you are in your home directory. Create a directory in which you can do all your development by entering the following:

```
CREATE /DIR [.COBOL21]
```

Whenever you plan to work on a lesson, change to that directory by entering the following:

```
SET DEFAULT [.COBOL21]
```

Editing

The editor is your most important tool when you are programming. It is important to become familiar with it and to be able to use it easily.

- ☐ If you are working with ACUCOBOL COBOL under MS-DOS, I recommend that you use the editor that is now being distributed with MS-DOS called EDIT.

- ☐ If you are working on a UNIX system, I recommend that you learn how to use vi. It is a cranky editor, but it is available on all UNIX systems and therefore gives you access to editing on all systems.

- ☐ VAX VMS comes with a number of editors: EDIT, EDT, TPU, and others. Pick one that you like and stick with it. EMACS is another popular editor that is freely available for many computer systems.

For any editor, make sure that you can create a new file, add text to it, and save it. Practice the following steps, using the correct name of your editor:

1. Change to your working directory.

2. Start the editor on a new text file. For example, for MS-DOS, type the following:

```
EDIT new.txt
```

3. After the screen comes up, type a couple of lines and then save the results.

Open an existing file (such as new.txt) that you already have created, make changes, and save it.

These are editor basics. As you work through the lessons, if you are not familiar with your editor, have the editor manual or a crib sheet handy so that you gradually can learn how to work with it (cutting and pasting, searching for text, and so on). The more you know about your editor, the easier the job of programming is; programmers spend 90% of their programming time working with a source code file (a text file) in the editor.

Filenames

Some versions of COBOL require that your COBOL source code files have a particular extension. Under VAX VMS, all COBOL source code files must be created with the extension .COB. The source code for a program called MATH is created with the following command:

```
EDIT MATH.COB
```

ACUCOBOL does not care what extension you use, but it is common to use .cob or .cbl for COBOL source code files to make them easier to identify. The ACUCOBOL examples in this book use the extension .cbl. The math program source code is edited with a command such as the following:

```
EDIT math.cbl
```

Compiling

After you create or edit a program, you must compile it. Unless you have a programming environment that enables you to compile from within the editor, you have to exit the editor and start the compiler as a separate action by doing the following:

☐ For ACUCOBOL, enter the following:

```
ccbl -o progname progname.cbl
```

This compiles progname.cbl and creates a file called progname, where progname is the name of your program. The -o in the command name is called a switch or command-line option. ACUCOBOL comes with several options.

☐ For VAX VMS, enter the following:

```
COBOL PROGNAME.COB
```

This compiles and creates a file named PROGNAME.OBJ.

Linking

No linking is required for ACUCOBOL. Under VAX VMS, type the following:

```
LINK /EXE=PROGNAME PROGNAME.OBJ
```

This creates a program named PROGNAME.EXE.

Running

ACUCOBOL uses a runtime program, runcbl, that must be named on the command line. To execute the program, enter the following:

```
runcbl progname
```

On VAX VMS, enter the following:

```
RUN PROGNAME
```

APPENDIX

D

Handling Compiler Errors

One of the difficulties of COBOL is dealing with compiler error messages. COBOL is very fussy about the syntax of the program. Some simple errors can produce problems that are difficult to find.

Rules for Locating Errors

The following are two rules to remember at all times:

☐ Check for spelling errors. Check that you haven't misspelled IDENTIFICATION DIVISION or any of the other divisions. Check that you haven't omitted or added a period. Check that you haven't typed a zero when you meant to type the letter O.

☐ If the error that the compiler gives you doesn't seem to make sense after checking the line that contains the error, look earlier in the code for an error.

General Problem Areas

The following are general procedural and typing errors to watch for and avoid:

☐ Misspelling the name of a DIVISION. In Micro Focus Personal COBOL, misspelling IDENTIFICATION DIVISION produces an error of PROCEDURE DIVISION MISSING. This is a devil to locate because everything around PROCEDURE DIVISION might look good. You have to go all the way back to the top of the program to locate the error.

☐ Misspelling the name of a required SECTION.

☐ Misspelling the name of any required PARAGRAPH.

☐ Starting a DIVISION, SECTION, or PARAGRAPH outside of Area A. Area A is columns 8–11.

☐ Leaving a period off the end of a DIVISION, SECTION, or PARAGRAPH.

☐ Adding an unnecessary hyphen to a DIVISION or SECTION name. For example, IDENTIFICATION-DIVISION or WORKING-STORAGE-SECTION is wrong.

Specific Errors for Different Compilers

The following is a list of some errors that are hard to catch:

☐ Any type of error with a whole DIVISION. For example, the compiler might print a message such as the following:

```
MISSING PROCEDURE DIVISION
```

or

```
Expected DATA DIVISION but found something else.
```

If the DIVISION is in the program and seems to be okay, the error is in an earlier DIVISION. Check the spelling and punctuation.

☐ An unexpected end-of-file error message. This error can happen with some compilers when you omit the period from the last statement in the program.

☐ The compiler error indicates that a paragraph name or data name is invalid, but when you inspect the name there doesn't seem to be anything wrong with it.

This error can be caused by using the same name for a paragraph and a variable. For example, this type of error can occur if you have a variable with a name such as

```
01  SAVE-THE-TOTAL              PIC 9999.
```

and in the program you have a paragraph named the following:

```
SAVE-THE-TOTAL.
    PERFORM DO-SOMETHING.
```

When this occurs, compilers do not always provide a clear description of the error. Paragraph and data names should be unique.

☐ The compiler produces an error indicating that a variable name is ambiguous, such as the following:

```
MOVE 12 TO ANOTHER-NUMBER
```

```
Error: Destination is ambiguous
```

This error is caused by having two different variables with the same name. There is another way to get around this problem, but it is much simpler if every variable has a unique name. Bonus Day 2, "Miscellaneous COBOL Syntax," covers the use of qualified data names and explains how you can use variables with the same name when it is necessary.

☐ One common error in COBOL is accidentally typing a 0 (zero) when you intended an O (uppercase letter O). For example, the following might cause the compiler to generate strange errors:

```
MOVE 10 T0 THE-NUMBER
```

The error might look like the following:

```
OPERAND not declared.
```

Upon inspection, THE-NUMBER is found to be declared, so what's the problem? On closer inspection, the T0 is spelled with a zero, so the compiler error message just confuses the issue.

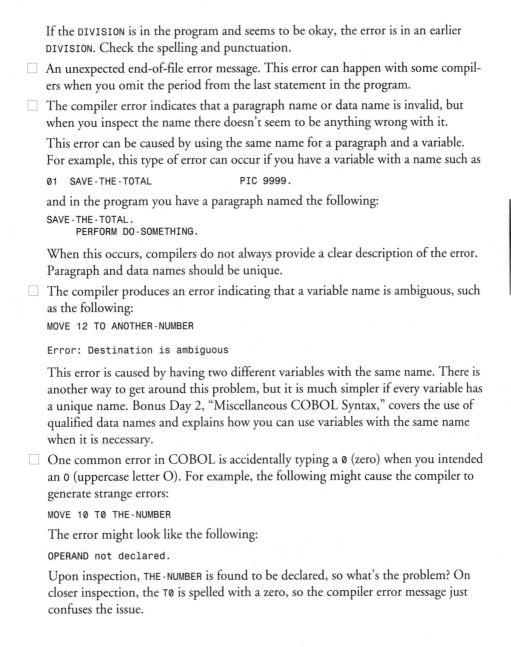

D

☐ The program seems to keep running when it should have stopped.

This problem is produced by a combination of errors. First, the compiler usually is one that does not care about sentences and paragraphs starting in the correct positions. Second, the command to stop the program, STOP RUN, has been typed incorrectly as STOP-RUN, with a hyphen.

When the compiler sees something like the following, it does not see this as a paragraph containing the sentence STOP RUN:

```
005500 PROGRAM-DONE.
005600     STOP-RUN.\
```

Instead, it sees it as a paragraph named PROGRAM-DONE containing no sentences and a paragraph named STOP-RUN containing no sentences.

☐ An unusual problem that produces oddball compiler errors is surprising reserved words. I ran into one while writing this book. In one program, I had created variables named DISPLAY-1, DISPLAY-2, DISPLAY-3, and DISPLAY-4. This program compiled and ran fine under ACUCOBOL, but produced a very strange error when compiled under Micro Focus Personal COBOL. It turned out that DISPLAY-1 is a reserved word in Micro Focus Personal COBOL, and its use as a variable name made the compiler a bit nuts.

APPENDIX

E

Summary of COBOL Syntax

This appendix presents a working summary of the syntax for various commands covered in this book. This summary is neither the whole syntax for a command nor is it all the commands supported by COBOL; however, it is enough to work with the command. For a full description of the syntax, consult the manual for your COBOL compiler.

Defining General Terms in Syntax Listings

Syntax Term	Description
... (ellipsis)	Indicates that the preceding item might be repeated a number of times.
[ ] (brackets)	An optional clause in the syntax.
¦ (vertical bar)	Two or more words separated by a vertical bar indicates that one of the values can be used.
alphanumeric variable	An alphanumeric variable defined in WORKING-STORAGE
arithmetic expression	An expression representing one or more addition, subtraction, multiplication, or division operations involving numeric values.
condition	An expression representing one or more comparisons between values optionally joined by AND or OR.
constant	For alphanumeric values, a set of characters enclosed in quotes, such as "ABC". For numeric values, an expression representing a number, such as 1296.54.
do something	Any COBOL command.
file-field-name	A COBOL variable that is a field in a record of a file described in an FD or SD (sort descriptor).
file-name	The name of a file described in an FD.
file-record	A COBOL variable that is the record of a file described in an FD.
index	A variable defined in WORKING-STORAGE used as an index for a table or array.
mode	One of the four open modes for a file: OUTPUT, EXTEND, I-O, or INPUT.
numeric value	A numeric constant or a numeric variable.
numeric variable	A numeric variable defined in WORKING-STORAGE.

Syntax Term	Description
paragraph	A paragraph name in the COBOL program.
procedure	A paragraph or section.
program-name	A COBOL program name.
sort-file	The name of a file described in an SD.
value	A constant or a variable.
variable	A variable defined in WORKING-STORAGE.

Command Syntax

The following syntax might not exactly match your chosen compiler. You should consult the COBOL reference manual distributed with your compiler.

ACCEPT

Syntax:

```
ACCEPT variable
    [WITH CONVERSION]

ACCEPT variable
    [CONVERT]
```

Some versions of COBOL do not use the WITH CONVERSION or CONVERT option.

Examples:

```
ACCEPT NUMERIC-ENTRY-FIELD
    WITH CONVERSION

ACCEPT ENTRY-FIELD
```

ADD

Syntax:

```
ADD numeric value TO
    numeric value
    GIVING variable [ROUNDED]
    [ ON SIZE ERROR
      do something ]

ADD numeric value TO
    numeric variable [ROUNDED]
    [ ON SIZE ERROR
    do something ]
```

Examples:

```
ADD 17.5 TO THE-VALUE
    GIVING THE-SUM ROUNDED
    ON SIZE ERROR
    DISPLAY "Add - overflow"

ADD 1.17 TO THE-VALUE ROUNDED
    ON SIZE ERROR
    DISPLAY "Add - overflow"
```

BEGIN TRANSACTION

Syntax:

```
BEGIN TRANSACTION
REWRITE file-record
    [ INVALID KEY
       do something ]
[ REWRITE file-record
    [ INVALID KEY
       do something ] ]
COMMIT¦ROLLBACK TRANSACTION
```

Examples:

```
BEGIN TRANSACTION
REWRITE VENDOR-RECORD
    INVALID KEY
       MOVE "E" TO TRANSACTION-FLAG

WRITE VENDOR-LOG-RECORD
    INVALID KEY
       MOVE "E" TO TRANSACTION-FLAG

IF TRANSACTION-FLAG = "E"
    ROLLBACK TRANSACTION

ELSE
    COMMIT TRANSACTION
```

CALL

Syntax:

```
CALL "program-name"

CALL "program-name"
    USING variable . . .
```

Examples:

```
CALL "VNDRPT03"

CALL "MYPROG"
    USING NUMERIC-DATA, DATE-FIELD.
```

CLOSE

Syntax:

```
CLOSE file-name
```

Examples:

```
CLOSE PHONE-FILE
```

COMPUTE

Syntax:

```
COMPUTE numeric variable
    [ROUNDED] =
    arithmetic expression
    [ ON SIZE ERROR
      do something else ]
```

Examples:

```
COMPUTE THE-RESULT ROUNDED =
  (BASE-VALUE * 10) +
  (A-VALUE / 50)
  ON SIZE ERROR
  DISPLAY "Warning Size error."
```

COPY

Syntax:

```
COPY "filename.ext".
```

Examples:

```
COPY "FDVENDOR.CBL".
```

DELETE

Syntax:

```
DELETE file-name RECORD
    [ INVALID KEY
      so something ]
```

Examples:

```
DELETE VOUCHER-FILE RECORD
  INVALID KEY
   DISPLAY "ERROR DELETING"
```

DISPLAY

Syntax:

```
DISPLAY value
```

Examples:

```
DISPLAY "HELLO WORLD".

DISPLAY ERROR-MESSAGE.
```

DIVIDE

Syntax:

```
DIVIDE value
    INTO variable [ROUNDED]
    [ ON SIZE ERROR
      do something ]

DIVIDE value BY value
    GIVING variable [ROUNDED]
    [ ON SIZE ERROR
      do something ]

DIVIDE value BY value
    GIVING variable [ROUNDED]
    REMAINDER variable
    [ ON SIZE ERROR
      do something ]

DIVIDE value INTO value
    GIVING variable [ROUNDED]
    [ ON SIZE ERROR
      do something ]

DIVIDE value INTO value
    GIVING variable [ROUNDED]
    REMAINDER variable
    [ ON SIZE ERROR
      do something ]
```

Examples:

```
DIVIDE 56.2
  INTO THE-VALUE ROUNDED
  ON SIZE ERROR
  DISPLAY "Divide-error"

DIVIDE 56.2 BY THE-VALUE
  GIVING THE-QUOTIENT ROUNDED
  ON SIZE ERROR
  DISPLAY "Divide-error"
```

```
DIVIDE 15 BY 7
   GIVING THE-QUOTIENT ROUNDED
   REMAINDER THE-REMAINDER
   ON SIZE ERROR
   DISPLAY "Divide-error"

DIVIDE 56.2 INTO THE-VALUE
   GIVING THE-QUOTIENT ROUNDED
   ON SIZE ERROR
   DISPLAY "Divide-error"

DIVIDE 15 INTO THE-VALUE
   GIVING THE-QUOTIENT ROUNDED
   REMAINDER THE-REMAINDER
   ON SIZE ERROR
   DISPLAY "Divide-error"
```

EXIT

Syntax:

```
EXIT PROGRAM
```

Examples:

```
PROGRAM-EXIT.
    EXIT PROGRAM.
```

GO TO

Syntax:

```
GO TO paragraph
```

Examples:

```
GO TO PROGRAM-EXIT.
```

IF ELSE

Syntax:

```
IF condition
    do something
    do something
ELSE
    do something
```

Examples:

```
IF RECORD-FOUND = "N"
    DISPLAY "RECORD NOT FOUND"
    MOVE "ERROR" TO ERROR-CODE
ELSE
    PERFORM DISPLAY-RECORD
```

INSPECT

Syntax:

```
INSPECT variable
   CONVERTING compare list
   TO          replace list
```

Examples:

```
INSPECT ENTRY-FIELD
   CONVERTING LOWER-ALPHA
   TO          UPPER-ALPHA
```

MOVE

Syntax:

```
MOVE value TO variable
                [variable . . .]
```

Examples:

```
MOVE 19 TO THE-VALUE
            ANOTHER-VALUE
            YET-ANOTHER-VALUE
```

MULTIPLY

Syntax:

```
MULTIPLY value
     BY variable [ROUNDED]
     [ ON SIZE ERROR
     do something ]

MULTIPLY value BY value
     GIVING variable [ROUNDED]
     [ ON SIZE ERROR
       do something ]
```

Examples:

```
MULTIPLY 1.17
   BY THE-VALUE ROUNDED
   ON SIZE ERROR
   DISPLAY "Multiply-overflow"

MULTIPLY 17.5 BY THE-VALUE
   GIVING THE-PRODUCT ROUNDED
   ON SIZE ERROR
   DISPLAY "Multiply-overflow"
```

OPEN

Syntax:

```
OPEN mode file-name
```

Examples:

```
OPEN OUTPUT PHONE-FILE

OPEN EXTEND PHONE-FILE

OPEN INPUT PHONE-FILE

OPEN I-O PHONE-FILE
```

PERFORM

Syntax:

```
PERFORM paragraph
    VARYING variable
    FROM value
    BY    value
    UNTIL condition
PERFORM paragraph

PERFORM paragraph
    value TIMES

PERFORM paragraph
    UNTIL condition
```

Examples:

```
PERFORM CALCULATE-AND-DISPLAY
    VARYING THE-MULTIPLIER
    FROM INITIAL-VALUE
    BY    1
    UNTIL THE-MULTIPLIER > 12.

PERFORM CALCULATE-AND-DISPLAY

PERFORM CALCULATE-AND-DISPLAY
    12 TIMES

PERFORM CALCULATE-AND-DISPLAY
    THE-COUNT TIMES

PERFORM CALCULATE-AND-DISPLAY
    UNTIL THE-MULTIPLIER > 12
```

READ

Syntax:

```
READ file-name [NEXT] RECORD
    AT END
      do something
```

For a SEQUENTIAL file, READ and READ NEXT RECORD are identical:

```
READ file-name RECORD
    INVALID KEY
      do something
```

Examples:

```
READ PHONE-FILE NEXT RECORD
    AT END
        MOVE "Y" TO END-OF-FILE

READ VENDOR-FILE RECORD
    INVALID KEY
        MOVE "N" TO RECORD-FOUND.
```

REWRITE

Syntax:

```
REWRITE file-record
    [ INVALID KEY
        do something ]
```

Examples:

```
REWRITE VENDOR-RECORD
    INVALID KEY
        DISPLAY "REWRITE ERROR"
```

SEARCH

Syntax:

```
SEARCH table name
  [AT END
    do something ]
  WHEN condition
    do something
```

Examples:

```
SET STATE-INDEX TO 1.
SEARCH TABLE-STATE-RECORD
 AT END
  PERFORM SEARCH-FAILED
WHEN
  VENDOR-STATE =
  TABLE-STATE-CODE(STATE-INDEX)
   PERFORM SEARCH-SUCCEEDED
```

SET

Syntax:

```
SET index
  UP¦DOWN BY value

SET index variable TO value
```

Examples:

```
SET STATE-INDEX UP BY 1.

SET STATE-INDEX
  DOWN BY LAST-VALUE.

SET STATE-INDEX TO 1

SET STATE-INDEX TO LAST-VALUE.
```

SORT

Syntax:

```
SORT sort-file
  ON ASCENDING KEY sort-field
  USING input-file
  GIVING output-file
```

Examples:

```
SORT SORT-FILE
  ON ASCENDING KEY SORT-DATE
  USING VOUCHER-FILE
  GIVING WORK-FILE.
```

START

Syntax:

```
START file name
 KEY NOT < key name
  [ INVALID KEY
     do something ]

START file name
 KEY > key name
  [ INVALID KEY
     do something ]

START file name
 KEY EQUALS¦NOT <¦GREATER THAN
  key name
  [ INVALID KEY
     do something ]
```

Examples:

```
MOVE SPACE TO VENDOR-NAME.
START VENDOR-FILE
  KEY NOT < VENDOR-NAME
   INVALID KEY
    MOVE "Y" TO FILE-AT-END.
```

```
MOVE "AZZZZZZZZZZZZZZZZZZZ"
    TO VENDOR-NAME.
START VENDOR-FILE
  KEY > VENDOR-NAME
    INVALID KEY
     MOVE "Y" TO FILE-AT-END.

MOVE "JONES AND SONS"
    TO VENDOR-NAME.
START VENDOR-FILE
  KEY EQUALS VENDOR-NAME
    INVALID KEY
     MOVE "N" TO RECORD-FOUND.

MOVE SPACE
    TO VENDOR-NAME.
START VENDOR-FILE
  KEY NOT < VENDOR-NAME
    INVALID KEY
     MOVE "N" TO RECORD-FOUND.
```

SUBTRACT

Syntax:

```
SUBTRACT value
    FROM variable [ROUNDED]
    [ ON SIZE ERROR
    do something ]

SUBTRACT value FROM value
    GIVING variable [ROUNDED]
    [ ON SIZE ERROR
      do something ]
```

Examples:

```
SUBTRACT  1.17
  FROM THE-VALUE ROUNDED
  ON SIZE ERROR
  DISPLAY "Subtract - overflow"

SUBTRACT 17.5 FROM THE-VALUE
  GIVING THE-SUM ROUNDED
  ON SIZE ERROR
  DISPLAY "Subtract-overflow"
```

WRITE

Syntax:

```
WRITE file-record
    [FROM variable]
    [ INVALID KEY
      do something]
```

```
WRITE file-record
    AFTER¦BEFORE
    ADVANCING
    PAGE¦value LINES
```

Examples:

```
WRITE PHONE-RECORD
```

```
WRITE PHONE-RECORD
    FROM WORK-DATA
```

```
WRITE VENDOR-RECORD
    INVALID KEY
        MOVE "Y" TO DUPLICATE-FLAG
```

```
WRITE PRINTER-RECORD
    BEFORE ADVANCING 1 LINE
```

```
WRITE PRINTER-RECORD
    AFTER ADVANCING PAGE
```

APPENDIX

F

Transaction Processing

Transaction processing is an additional area of COBOL that you should know something about.

The Basics of Transaction Processing

Transactions are used to force a group of two or more writes, rewrites, or deletes to one or more files to be treated as a single group in which all of the file updates must occur successfully.

In general terms, a transaction consists of the input data, the existing data in the file that is being changed, the transfer of the data from the input computer to the computer where it will be stored, locking the records to be changed, changing the records and recording the changes, releasing locks on records, and logging the changes.

The Steps of a Transaction

The steps of a transaction are generally as follows:

1. Inputting the data frequently involves keying in the information at a terminal. Sometimes it involves inputting information from another source, such as a floppy disk containing payroll information to be processed.

2. Temporarily saving the existing data is a significant step if the input data is making changes to already existing information. Existing data must be preserved in such a way that a partial update does not occur. A transaction is an all-or-nothing proposition, and the simple rule is either all of the requested new data is written or rewritten to the file, or none of it is.

3. Transferring the data from source to destination can be a complex step in a distributed environment. You can key in information at a PC or other terminal, and then send it as a packet of information to a remote computer. Some transaction systems are responsible for ensuring that the information travels from source to destination without data corruption.

4. Locking or holding the records to be changed prevents multiuser corruption. For example, if two users are both updating purchase order number 12345, whose information is actually written to the disk? A transaction processing system allows one user in and locks the other user out.

5. Changing the records is the core of a transaction processing system. The whole point of a transaction is to make some change to the information in a file or files. Recording the information to be written to the disk is the task of making the changes permanent and involves ensuring that all changes are recorded or none is

recorded. In this step, either the new information is recorded, or the existing information saved in a previous step might be restored because of a failure to record the new data.

6. Releasing locks on records is done so that other users can now have access to and can update the same information.

7. Logging the changes is done by all transaction processing systems. In some systems, the logged information can be accessed by special programs that can be used by a system programmer or system administrator who is trying to trace a problem, or by a security administrator who is trying to track down a security breach. More commonly, the transaction system logs the information internally and uses it in the processing of the previous steps.

The Need for Transactions

At least two very good reasons exist for using transactions in processing data. Multiple users might be trying to update the same information at the same time, and a transaction might involve more than one file.

When multiple users are trying to update the same information, there is no guarantee that they are entering the same data. Two users entering information for the same employee, but entering different addresses, could cause a data disaster, unless there were some mechanism to ensure that only one user at a time can update the information.

When multiple files are involved, there is the risk of a system problem as information is being updated. Take the case of an invoice file that is actually made up of two separate files. One file might contain the name and address of the customer, the invoice number, and the total amount of the invoice. The second file might contain several records, including one line for each of the items being purchased on the invoice and the amount for each item. If the invoice is changed, it is essential that the invoice and invoice lines all be updated simultaneously, or the total amount will no longer correctly reflect the sum of all the invoice lines. A mechanism is needed here to ensure that updates occur for both files or for neither file.

The mechanism that ensures this process is transaction processing.

COBOL Transactions

COBOL transaction processing is implemented in different ways by different versions of COBOL, but the following is a fairly common set of steps used in COBOL transaction processing:

1. Signal the beginning of a transaction. This usually uses the following syntax:

```
BEGIN TRANSACTION
```

2. Issue one or more writes or rewrites to a file. This usually involves standard COBOL file I-O syntax, such as

```
REWRITE CUSTOMER-RECORD
    INVALID KEY
        MOVE "E" TO TRANSACTION-FLAG.

WRITE PO-RECORD
    INVALID KEY
        MOVE "E" TO TRANSACTION-FLAG.
```

3. Complete the transaction or abort the transaction. These usually use the keyword COMMIT to signal that the transaction is completed successfully, or the keyword ROLLBACK to indicate that the transaction is to be aborted. The following is the syntax:

```
IF TRANSACTION-FLAG = "E"
    ROLLBACK TRANSACTION
ELSE
    COMMIT TRANSACTION.
```

All file writes or rewrites are saved up from the point that a BEGIN TRANSACTION is executed until a COMMIT or a ROLLBACK is executed. At that point, all writes and rewrites are either executed or abandoned, causing an all-or-nothing update to the disk drives.

Designing with Transactions

Designing a system with transaction processing involves careful planning of what constitutes a complete transaction.

Beginners frequently bundle large numbers of file writes and rewrites together and call these a transaction, which causes performance problems and prevents other users from being able to update the same files.

A more disastrous error is that of starting a transaction but never finishing it. This can happen when a COMMIT or ROLLBACK is not executed because of an error in the flow of the program that somehow skips the statements. A GO TO that skips over a crucial piece of code or placing the COMMIT or ROLLBACK in a separate paragraph and then neglecting to perform it are examples of possible errors.

Be sure that each transaction is as small as it can be while ensuring the integrity of the information in the files.

APPENDIX G

Glossary

accounts-payable system: A system that tracks your bills, their due dates, and what has been paid. It sometimes gives you information on future cash requirements needed to pay bills as they come due.

address: A numeric value representing a location in a computer's memory.

aggregate: A COBOL data type composed of one or more basic COBOL data types. Arrays and structures are both aggregates. *Aggregate* is the opposite of *atomic* when applied to COBOL data types. In the following code fragment, SOME-VALUES is an aggregate, and VALUE-1 and VALUE-2 are atomic:

```
01   SOME-VALUES.
     05   VALUE-1    PIC 9(4).
     05   VALUE-2    PIC 9(3).
```

alphanumeric: Any of the printable characters, A to Z, a to z, 0 to 9, and punctuation marks such as spaces, quotes, exclamation marks, and so on. An alphanumeric variable of four characters could hold any of the values "ABCD", "12XY", "1234", or "(**)" because these are all printable characters.

alternate index: An alternate index is an additional index in an indexed file that defines an alternative path along which records can be retrieved.

alternate key: See *alternate index*.

area: One of the five areas in a COBOL program in ANSI format. The areas of a COBOL program are arranged in columns.

The *sequence area* includes columns 1 through 6 and can be used for line numbering.

The *indicator area* is column 7. Single characters in this column cause different behavior.

The * character causes the remainder of the line to be ignored, effectively creating a comment.

The / character is similar to *, but additionally causes the printer to form feed when the listing of the program is being printed.

The D character indicates that the line is compiled only when compiling for debugging.

The - character indicates a continuation for a literal that was too long to fit on the preceding line.

Area A is columns 8 through 11. Various parts of the COBOL program must begin in Area A, including division names, section names, paragraph names, and data items having a level number of 01, 77, SD, and FD.

Area B is columns 12 through 72. Sentences and data items having levels other than 01, 77, SD, and FD are expected to begin and end in Area B.

The modification area includes columns 73 through 80. The area is used for modification codes by tradition, although the area is not officially designated for this use.

Area A: See *area*.

Area B: See *area*.

array: 1. An area of memory that has been set aside and organized in such a way that it can hold multiple occurrences of the same type of information. 2. A variable that contains a repeated occurrence of the same type of data. The following fragment defines an array of 6 numeric variables:

```
01  A-VALUE  PIC 9(5)  OCCURS 6 TIMES.
```

ASCII: American Standard Code for Information Interchange. A code used by computers to represent the letters of the alphabet, spaces, tabs, and other control information for terminals and printers. See Appendix B, "ASCII."

ASCII collating sequence: The sequence in which the characters are defined in the ASCII chart. (See Appendix B.)

atomic: This term generally refers to something that cannot be broken into smaller parts. In COBOL, atomic variables are given pictures. They cannot be reduced to smaller parts. Arrays and structures are not atomic because they are composed of smaller data types. *Atomic* is the opposite of *aggregate* when applied to data types. In the following code fragment, SOME-VALUES is an aggregate, and VALUE-1 and VALUE-2 are atomic:

```
01  SOME-VALUES.
    05  VALUE-1   PIC 9(4).
    05  VALUE-2   PIC 9(3).
```

bar code reader: An input device that reads a bar code and transmits the information to the computer. Bar codes are extensively used to encode part numbers on goods in retail stores.

binary: A numbering system using only 0 and 1 as digits in base 2.

block mode screen: Most computers operate a terminal on a character-by-character basis, sending each character to the screen one at a time and accepting one character at a time from the keyboard. Block mode screens such as the IBM 3270 send and receive complete screens (usually 1920 characters) at a time. This usually affects the way a series of DISPLAY verbs are displayed.

called program: A program that has been called to be executed by another program.

calling program: A program that calls another program and executes it.

G

carriage control: Any commands sent to a printer that control the positioning of the print head, such as a carriage return or line feed command.

carriage return: 1. See *CR.* 2. A command sent to a printer that causes the print head to return to the leftmost margin of the paper. Starting a new line on a printer usually involves sending a carriage return command followed by a line feed command. See *line feed.*

CD-ROM: Compact disc-read-only memory. A read-only storage device that uses optical disks to store data.

central processing unit: The heart of the computer, which performs addition, subtraction, multiplication, and division. It also moves data from one location to another. This is abbreviated *CPU.*

COBOL: Common Business Oriented Language, a computer programming language designed and used primarily for business applications.

comparison operator: The symbols used between two values when the values are being compared. The short and long versions of COBOL comparison operators are as follows:

Short	*Long*
=	IS EQUAL
NOT =	IS NOT EQUAL
>	IS GREATER THAN
NOT >	IS NOT GREATER THAN
<	IS LESS THAN
NOT <	IS NOT LESS THAN

compiler: A program that takes a source code file, processes it, and generates a translated version of the source code that the computer can understand. This translation is called an *object* and is usually saved in an *object file.*

compiler directive: A command to the compiler, telling it to do something while it is compiling the source code file, or telling the compiler to change the way it would normally behave. The COPY command is not a programming command. It is a command to the compiler to tell it to pull the pieces of different files together into one file, and then compile the resulting file. The COPY command is sometimes called the COPY directive, and it looks like this:

```
001100     COPY "FDVENDOR.CBL".
```

computer: A machine that can add, subtract, multiply, divide, move, and perform other mathematical and logical functions on numbers.

control break: A break inserted into the normal processing of a program (usually a report program) to cause groups of records to be processed together as one unit. The interruption of the normal printing of a report program to print a total or subtotal would be a *control break* or *level break*. In the following example, the report breaks at the end of each vendor and prints a subtotal for that vendor. Then it breaks at the end of the report and prints a total for the report.

```
Vendor           DUE DATE     AMOUNT
ABC Printing     1/23/1994     27.95
ABC Printing     1/31/1994     15.54
ABC Printing     2/16/1994     10.17
                 Total         53.66

GTE              1/17/1994     34.97
GTE              1/24/1994     17.54
                 Total         52.51

                 Grand Total  106.17
```

CPU: See *central processing unit.*

CR: ASCII name for a carriage return character. This has a value of 13 (hex 0D) and causes terminals and printers to move the cursor or print head to the leftmost column of the display or page.

CR-LF: A carriage return and line feed pair. These characters are used to end a line of text in a text file on an MS-DOS computer. They also are the standard behavior of a cursor or print head at the end of a line. See *CR* and *LF.*

DATA DIVISION: The DATA DIVISION describes the data used by the program. The DATA DIVISION and the PROCEDURE DIVISION are the most important divisions in a COBOL program and do 95 percent of the work. See *DIVISION.*

data name: The variable name assigned to each field, record, and file in a COBOL program.

data validation: Any technique used to decrease the errors in data entered into the computer.

debug: To test a program to eliminate errors.

default: A condition, value, or action that is executed or set up without having to be requested.

desk checking: Checking source code created with an editor before compiling it to check for typographical and other errors.

DIVISION: One of the four divisions in a COBOL program—IDENTIFICATION DIVISION, ENVIRONMENT DIVISION, DATA DIVISION, and PROCEDURE DIVISION.

G

edited numeric variable: A numeric variable that contains an editing character. Edited numeric variables should be used only to display values and cannot be used in calculations. There are other editing characters, but these are the main ones. The following is an example:

```
01  DISPLAY-VALUE    PIC ZZZ,ZZ9.99-.
```

editing characters: The characters minus (-), decimal point (.), comma (,) and Z are called editing characters when used in a PICTURE. See *edited numeric variable*.

element: An individual variable in an array of the same type of variables, or an individual variable in a structure that might contain dissimilar variables.

end of file: A condition that exists when the last record has been read from a file.

ENVIRONMENT DIVISION: The ENVIRONMENT DIVISION describes the physical environment in which the program is running. The main use of the ENVIRONMENT DIVISION is to describe the physical structure of files that will be used in the program. The following is an example:

```
000300 ENVIRONMENT DIVISION.
```

executable: A file containing an executable program that has been created by linking one or more objects.

explicit: A way of stating something in a computer language so that a value or action is apparent by content. In the following example, EMP-NUMBER has an explicit picture of PIC 9999, and EMP-HOURLY has an explicit picture of PIC Z9.99. Compare this with the definition of implicit.

```
000900 01  EMPLOYEE-DATA.
001000     05  FILLER       PIC X(4)
001100         VALUE "Emp ".
001200     05  EMP-NUMBER   PIC 9999.
001300     05  FILLER       PIC X(7)
001400         VALUE " earns ".
001500     05  EMP-HOURLY    PIC Z9.99.
```

FD: See *file description*.

field: A *field* or *data field* is one piece of data contained in a record. In the customer file, the customer name is one field, and the customer phone number is one field. COBOL data files are organized as one or more records containing the same fields in each record. For example, a record for a personal phone book might contain fields for a last name, a first name, and a phone number. See also *file* and *record*.

file: In a COBOL program, a file is a collection of related units of data within a category of data. For example, a file might contain all the data (related units of data) about customers (category of data) for a company. This customer file would contain information on each customer and is usually called a *data file* or a *logical file*. In order for it to exist at all, a physical file must be on the disk, but when this file is logically arranged so that a COBOL program can access the information, it becomes a data file to a COBOL program. See also *field* and *record.*

file at end: See *end of file.*

file description: Entries used to describe a file, its records, and its fields.

file descriptor: See *file description.*

FILE SECTION: A reserved name for the section of the DATA DIVISION that is used to define files used in a program.

FILE-CONTROL: A reserved name for a paragraph in the INPUT-OUTPUT section of the ENVIRON-MENT DIVISION that is used to define physical files used in a program.

FILLER: A COBOL reserved word that reserves space in memory for a field that will not be accessed in the program.

flag: A variable in working in storage that is used to indicate the presence or absence of some condition in the program. For example, a FILE-AT-END might be used as a flag to indicate that the last record of the data file has been read.

flowchart: A graphic representation of the logic or steps in a program or system. A flowchart represents how a program or activity moves through various processes or program routines. It uses symbols to represent the activities, and it uses arrows to represent the direction of activity through the processes. Flowcharts can be used to define the behavior of a single program or a system (a combination of programs).

form feed: A command sent to a printer that causes the printer to eject the last sheet of paper and ready itself to start printing at the top of a new sheet.

hexadecimal: A numbering system using 16 digits—0 through 9 and A, B, C, D, E, and F in base 16.

hierarchy of operators: See *precedence.*

I-O-CONTROL: A reserved name for a paragraph in the INPUT-OUTPUT section of the ENVIRONMENT DIVISION that is used to define what areas of memory will be used by the files while they are being processed. This paragraph is used to cut down on memory usage when memory is at a premium.

IDENTIFICATION DIVISION: The IDENTIFICATION DIVISION marks the beginning of a COBOL program and serves to name and comment the program.

implicit: Implied by context, or the rules of a computer language, but not stated. In the following example, EMPLOYEE-DATA has an implicit (implied but not stated) picture of PIC X(20). See also *explicit*.

```
000900 01   EMPLOYEE-DATA.
001000      05  FILLER       PIC X(4)
001100          VALUE "Emp ".
001200      05  EMP-NUMBER   PIC 9999.
001300      05  FILLER       PIC X(7)
001400          VALUE " earns ".
001500      05  EMP-HOURLY   PIC Z9.99.
```

implied decimal: A decimal point that does not explicitly appear in a number, but the existence of the decimal and its position are recorded elsewhere. In the following example, EMP-HOURLY contains an explicit decimal and EMP-WAGE contains an implicit decimal:

```
001300      05  EMP-WAGE     PIC 9999V99.
001400
001500      05  EMP-HOURLY   PIC Z9.99.
```

index variable: When you define a table (array), you also can define a variable that is specifically intended to be used as the index for that table. It is called an index variable. In the following example, STATE-INDEX is an index variable for the TABLE-STATE-RECORD array:

```
01   TABLE-STATE-RECORD OCCURS 50 TIMES
        INDEXED BY STATE-INDEX.
     05   TABLE-STATE-CODE       PIC XX.
     05   TABLE-STATE-NAME       PIC X(20).
```

indexed file: A file containing one or more indexes that allow records to be retrieved by a specific value or in a particular sort order.

indicator area: Character position 7 is called the *indicator area*. This seventh position is usually blank. If an asterisk is placed in this column, everything else on that line is ignored by the compiler. This is used as a method to include comments in a source code file. Other single characters in this column cause different behavior:

The / character is similar to *, but it additionally causes the printer to form feed when the listing of the program is being printed.

The D character indicates that the line is compiled only when compiling for debugging.

The - character indicates a continuation for a literal that was too long to fit on the preceding line.

infinite loop: An error condition in a program that causes a processing loop to be performed forever. Caused by incorrectly setting or testing loop-control variables.

initialize: Set a variable to a starting value.

input device: A device that allows input of information to a computer. The most common input device is a keyboard. Other devices for input include bar code readers, optical character readers, scanners, and telecommunications input devices such as modems. Modems are used to input data from other computers.

INPUT-OUTPUT SECTION: A reserved name for the section of the ENVIRONMENT DIVISION that is used to define physical files used in a program and what areas of memory will be used by the files while they are being processed.

ISAM: Indexed Sequential Access Method. Originally a method of creating and accessing indexed files that allowed record storage and retrieval by a key value in the record. The term tends to be used loosely to refer to any method of storing and retrieving indexed records.

K: An abbreviation for kilobytes.

key path: The natural sorted order of records as they are returned from the file using a particular key.

kilobyte: 1,024 bytes.

level break: See *control break*.

level number: A number from 01 to 49 indicating the hierarchy of data in a structure variable. Levels above 49 are reserved for special uses in COBOL.

LF: The ASCII name for a line feed character. This has a value of 10 (hex 0A) and causes terminals and printers to move the cursor or print head to the next line on the display or page.

line feed: See *LF*. A command sent to a printer that causes the print head to move down one line. Starting a new line on a printer usually involves sending a carriage return command followed by a line feed command. See *carriage return*.

listing file: A report produced by the compiler on the program that it has just compiled. This can be sent directly to the printer, or it can be created as a separate file that can be displayed or sent to the printer. Sometimes called a *listing*.

loop: A series of one or more commands executed a number of times or until a certain condition is met in the program.

M: An abbreviation for *megabyte*.

main memory: This is a storage area inside the computer that is used as a giant scratch pad for programs to load and use data. Main memory is usually built from random access memory (RAM) chips.

maintenance program: A program that allows a user to add, change, delete, or look up records in a file.

G

megabyte: 1,048,576 bytes.

menu: A program that offers the user a number of choices, each of which executes a different program or different part or screen of the current program.

mod code: See *modification code.*

modem: Computers transmit data using high and low voltages in a kind of Morse code used to represent computer bytes. A modem is used to translate high and low voltages from a computer into tones (sounds) that can be transmitted on a telephone line.

modification area: COBOL was designed as an 80-column language, but there is no formal definition of character positions 73 through 80. This area is left to the designer of the COBOL editor to use as needed. COBOL editors on large computers usually allow you to define an eight-character modification code. If you edit a line of an existing program, or insert lines, these are added to the source code file with the modification code placed in positions 73 through 80. This is a handy way of tagging all the changes made to a program for a specific purpose. This method of modification code marking usually depends on a specific editor being set up for COBOL and having the capability to insert these modification codes automatically. You probably won't see modification codes using COBOL on a PC. The modification area includes columns 73 through 80. The area is used for modification codes by tradition, although the area is not officially designated for this use.

modification code: COBOL editors on large computers usually allow you to define an eight-character modification code. If you edit a line of an existing program, or insert lines, these are added to the source code file with the modification code placed in positions 73 through 80. This is a handy way of tagging all the changes made to a program for a specific purpose. This method of modification code marking usually depends on a specific editor being set up for COBOL and having the capability to insert these modification codes automatically.

MS-DOS: Microsoft-Disk Operating System. An operating system developed by the Microsoft Corporation for IBM-compatible computers. See also *operating system.*

NUL: The ASCII name for the character that has a value of zero.

object file: A file containing codes that can be understood by a computer, and created by compiling a source code file. See also *compiler* and *source code.*

online processing: See *transaction processing.*

operating system: A master program that controls a computer's basic functions and allows other programs to access the computer's resources such as disk drive, printer, keyboard, and screen.

optical character reader: A device similar to a scanner (see *scanner*) that reads a document, but either transmits the information to the computer as readable text, or sends the graphic image to the computer to be interpreted back to the original text by a program.

order of operators: See *precedence.*

output device: Devices that allow output of information from a computer. The most common output devices are monitors and printers. Other output devices include telecommunications devices such as modems, which are used to output data to another computer.

paragraph: A subdivision of a COBOL program containing sentences.

pass by address: A method of passing a variable to a function by passing the address of the variable in memory. If the called program modifies the variable by using the address to locate the variable and changing the value, then the value is changed in both the called program and the calling program. Sometimes called *pass by reference.*

pass by copy: See *pass by value.*

pass by reference: See *pass by address.*

pass by value: A method of passing a variable to a program by making a copy of the variable and giving it to the called program. If the called program changes the variable, it does not affect the value of the variable in the calling program. Sometimes called *pass by copy.*

precedence: The order in which operators are applied to an expression or a statement. Usually called precedence of operators. Also called *order of operators* or *hierarchy of operators.* In the expression

```
COMPUTE VALUE-X = 1 + 3 * 4.
```

the * operator has a higher precedence than the + operator. The * operator, multiplication operator, is applied first. The expression is evaluated as

```
COMPUTE VALUE-X = 1 + (3 * 4).
```

rather than

```
COMPUTE VALUE-X = (1 + 3) * 4.
```

which sets VALUE-X to 13 and not 16.

primary key: In a COBOL indexed file, one field must be designed so that it will contain a unique value for each record. This field is then set up as the primary index for the file. This primary index is called the *primary key* or simply the *key.* See also *alternate key.*

primary memory: See *main memory.*

primary storage: See *main memory.*

print queue manager: See *spooler.*

printer layout chart: See *printer spacing chart.*

G

printer spacing chart: A layout tool similar to graph paper used to work out the spacing of values on a printed report.

PROCEDURE DIVISION: The PROCEDURE DIVISION contains the COBOL statements that the program executes. The PROCEDURE DIVISION is the real workhorse of a COBOL program. It includes all the commands that actually do something.

processing loop: One or more paragraphs or sections of a program that are executed over and over.

program: A series of steps to be executed by a computer.

programming language: A computer tool that allows a programmer to write commands in a format that is more easily understood or remembered by a person, and in such a way that they can be translated into codes that the computer can understand and execute.

prompt: Something indicating to the user that the computer is waiting for user input. Some sample prompts are the blinking cursor, a question mark, or a question or request displayed on the screen.

RAM: See *random access memory*.

random access memory: The primary working memory of a computer that can be used for rapid storage and retrieval characters or bytes of information. See also *main memory*.

real-time processing: 1. A computer system that functions in such a way that information entered at a terminal must be responded to by the computer within a short period of time. An airline reservation system that must respond with available seats on a flight, or a point of sale system that must quickly look up stock availability and prices; these are two examples of real-time systems. 2. By extension of this concept, real-time in modern usage has come to be used to describe a very fast response computer system such as one that might be used to control factory processes. A real-time system might have a sensor that reads the temperature of a vat of chemicals, and a method of sending signals to the heater for the vat. As the temperature rises or falls slightly, the computer switches the heater on and off to keep a consistent temperature in the vat.

record: See *structure, file,* and *field*.

record selection: Any process that reads through records in a file, accepting or rejecting records for processing based on testing conditions for each record.

relational operator: An operator that is used to compare two expressions usually used in an `if` statement. The following are some COBOL relational operators:

```
IF VALUE-X IS NOT EQUAL VALUE-Y
IF VALUE-X IS EQUAL VALUE-Y
IF VALUE-X IS LESS THAN VALUE-Y
```

COBOL usually includes one or two variations of the same relational operator so that comparisons can be written with words or with symbols:

```
IF VALUE-X NOT = VALUE-Y
IF VALUE-X = VALUE-Y
IF VALUE-X < VALUE-Y    is less than
```

reserved word: In any programming language, certain words have special meanings in the language. In COBOL, `DISPLAY "Hello"` causes the word `Hello` to be displayed on the screen. `DISPLAY` has a special meaning in COBOL. It tells the computer to put the next thing on the screen. Also in COBOL, the words `DATA` and `DIVISION` appearing together mean that the section of the program where data is defined is beginning. The words `DATA DIVISION` and `DISPLAY` are called reserved words because they are reserved in the language to have a special meaning, and the programmer cannot use these words for some other purpose. For example, it is incorrect to name a program `DISPLAY`, like this:

```
PROGRAM-ID. DISPLAY.
```

If you attempt this, the compiler probably will complain of an invalid program name, because `DISPLAY` is reserved for a special meaning in COBOL.

routine: Any set of instructions designed to perform a specific task. In COBOL programs, a routine consists of one or more paragraphs.

scanner: A device that can input data to a computer by scanning a graphic image and sending signals representing the graphic image to the computer. A scanner works somewhat like a photocopying machine, but instead of sending the pulses of lightness and darkness of the input document to be copied to another page of paper, the pulses are transmitted to the computer.

SD: See *sort description*.

secondary storage: Secondary storage is permanent after power is gone. Common secondary storage devices are diskettes, hard drives, and tapes. CD-ROM is becoming popular as a very large secondary storage device. There are many newer forms of secondary storage becoming available, such as memory cards that contain 10 year batteries.

sentence: One or more COBOL commands ending with a period.

G

sequence area: Columns 1 through 6 of a COBOL program are the sequence area and can be used for line numbering.

sort description: Entries used to describe a sort file, its records, and its sort keys. Also called a *sort descriptor*.

source code: A text file containing statements in a programming language. Also called *source*, *source file*, and *source program*.

spooler: A program, usually on a multiuser system, that queues print files for one or more printers and sends them to the printer one at a time. Sometimes called a *print queue manager*.

statement: A single instruction or command.

string: A sequence of characters, usually printable. In COBOL, strings are set off by double quotes, like this:

```
"Hello World," and "123-Z55" are strings.
```

structure: When variables will be used as a group, they can be combined into a single variable called a *structure* or a *record*. A structure or record is a variable containing one or more COBOL variables. In the following example, the variable named THE-WHOLE-MESSAGE contains the three variables THE-NUMBER, A-SPACE, and THE-MESSAGE. THE-WHOLE-MESSAGE is a structure.

```
01   THE-WHOLE-MESSAGE.
     05   THE-NUMBER          PIC 9(2).
     05   A-SPACE             PIC X(1).
     05   THE-MESSAGE         PIC X(50).
```

subscript: A number in parentheses that identifies one element of an array:

```
01   A-VALUE  PIC 99 OCCURS 4 TIMES.
     MOVE 16 TO A-VALUE(2)
```

The 2 is a subscript identifying a single element of the data array.

suppressing zeroes: See *zero suppression*.

symbolic debugger: A debugger enables a programmer to execute a program in small increments (usually one line at a time) and watch the program as it is being executed. A symbolic debugger also enables a programmer to display the lines of the original source code file, and the values of variables by referencing the variable name. It is called a symbolic debugger because variables and paragraphs are accessed by using the names given to them in the source code file.

syntax: The rules that specify how a command or instruction should be given to a computer so that the computer can understand how to execute the instruction.

syntax error: A programming error caused by a violation of the rules that specify how a command or instruction should be given to a computer.

table: See *array*.

transaction processing: The process of adding, changing, deleting, or looking up a record in a data file by entering the data at a terminal. Most transaction processing systems also include a method of ensuring that all the information entered as a transaction is simultaneously saved to disk.

variable: A named area of memory in a computer program that can contain data that changes as the program runs.

vendor: Someone who sells you goods or services and to whom you end up paying money for those goods or services. The vendor file is one of the main files in an accounts payable system.

voucher number: In a bills paying system, each new invoice that is received for payment is assigned a tracking number. This tracking number is the key to the voucher file or bills file, and the number is usually called a voucher number.

white space: Spaces between words in a program. Some languages allow tabs as white space; traditional COBOL allows only the space character.

WORKING-STORAGE SECTION: A reserved name for the section of the DATA DIVISION that is used to define data used in a program.

x: The X in a picture indicates that it can be used for alphanumeric values. The picture XXXX indicates that four characters can be stored in this variable. A variable with a picture of XXXX could hold any of the values "ABCD", "12XY", "1234", or "(**)" because they are all printable characters. The variable also holds the values "A", "12X", and "aa" because they are also alphanumeric and small enough to fit in a four-character space.

zero suppression: Editing of a numeric field so that leading zeroes are replaced with spaces in displaying or printing the field.

G

INDEX

TOOLS TO HELP YOU WITH YOUR COBOL TRAINING

COMPANION SOURCE CODE DISKETTE
for Teach Yourself COBOL in 21 Days

The companion source code disk contains the code for all of the complete programs and many of the code samples in this book.

It is particularly useful for cross-checking your own practice code from the exercises to locate any errors. Typographical errors can enter into printed text, but code on the disk has been tested. Students are encouraged to hand code their programs and exercises, but if you are just brushing up, copying the code will save you much typing.

The Source Code Diskette costs $15.00. Shipping (USA $2.00) (Non USA $5.00)

MICRO FOCUS PERSONAL COBOL COMPILER

The perfect compiler for learning COBOL and developing business applications on personal computers. It provides an integrated editor-compiler-debugger package that will get you started quickly and provide the tools you need to learn and develop personal and small business applications.

Micro Focus Personal COBOL costs $99.00. Shipping (USA $8.00) (Non USA $15.00)

EZ-COMPARE
File Comparison Utility

A useful programming tool to help locate those hard-to-find errors in your code.

An additional tool that beginners and experienced programmers alike will find useful is a file comparison utility, EZ-COMPARE. The EZ-COMPARE utility is useful for any course that has accompanying code on a disk, and it enables the student to compare the code he has written to the code on the diskette. EZ-COMPARE is especially useful for teaching new students who are unfamiliar with code because it displays the two files to be compared on the screen. When lines do not match, they are highlighted. It displays files that are wider than 80 columns, which makes it popular with programmers for comparing source code or text files to find changes.

EZ-COMPARE costs $49.95. ($39.95 for book purchasers.) Shipping (USA $5.00) (Non USA $10.00)

(This offer is made by Mo Budlong, King Computer Services, Inc., not by Sams Publishing.)

The COBOL COOK BOOK

This book contains general-purpose information addressing common COBOL programming problems, with tips and tricks on how to solve them. Examples are illustrated with listings and code, as well as canned general-purpose routines that you can include in your own programs.

If you are coding in COBOL on any machine, this book will provide a wealth of useful tips, including *bubble sorts, string manipulation, case conversion, debugging, reverse date keys, printing tricks, black boxes, sorting arrays, read previous, logical files, and more.*

The COBOL Cook Book costs $49.95. Shipping (USA $8.00) (Non USA $15.00)

GEN-CODE
STANDARD STRUCTURED COBOL CODE GENERATOR

Get the most out of COBOL with this easy-to-use programming tool.

GEN-CODE quickly produces Add, Change, Inquire, and Delete programs to your specifications. You provide the File description and screen format, fill in information about each field, and put GEN-CODE to work. In a matter of minutes, you will have fully functional source code that you can compile, run, and easily modify and maintain.

BY TEST ON A COMPLEX CARGO TRACKING SYSTEM USED IN THE PORT OF LOS ANGELES, THIS TOOL REDUCED DEVELOPMENT TIME BY 40% TO 60%.

GEN-CODE costs $299.00. Shipping (USA $8.00) (Non USA $15.00)

(This offer is made by Mo Budlong, King Computer Services, Inc., not by Sams Publishing.)

COBOL, Dates and the Year 2000—Technical Report with Source Code

If you have COBOL programs on your system, you **must** read this book. You need to prepare and execute a sensible plan *now* that will take your company into the year 2000. Don't leave it to the last minute when time and resources will be at a premium. This invaluable book addresses the problems that you must deal with to prepare for the year 2000. Solutions range from simple to complex, depending upon the nature of your system and the approach you choose to fix the problems. Its comprehensive technical tour takes you through the various methods of implementing solutions.

Topics covered include the following: *basic approaches to handling date problems, dates in files and on screens, Gregorian and Julian dates, routines for date entry, validation, conversions and system date, fiscal date handling routines, common date pitfalls, common date handling routines for day differences, adding days to dates, days of the week, and comparing dates. The book also includes source code for routines to help you locate dates and do conversions.*

COBOL, Dates and the Year 2000 costs $99.00. Source code on diskette costs $99.00.

COBOL, JUST IN TIME! COBOL CRASH COURSE

Featured on the front page of COMPUTER WORLD, and in Accounting Professional, ITAA, Unisphere, and other magazines.

This course is designed to help create resources to handle Year 2000 problems. Tailored for individual study at home, at school, or in the workplace, the course needs no instructor, only access to a PC.

The course package contains all the materials and tools a student will need to quickly gain entry-level proficiency in COBOL. It includes a comprehensive study guide, the *Teach Yourself COBOL in 21 Days* book, a complete compiler, the EZ-COMPARE Utility, a Computer Dictionary, and a book on computer basics. The course extends into intermediate-level programming with four additional lessons, a booklet on dates in the year 2000, and a "Cook Book" of professional tips and tricks for COBOL programmers that take the student into more advanced programming. The detailed study guide includes a complete sequential list of everything the student needs to do and learn, shown on an easy gradient so that the student can master one skill before starting on the next—from installing the compiler and using the editor through programming, compiling, and debugging.

In a *ComputerWorld* article on COBOL training, Sheldon Glasser, a 35 year COBOL veteran and president of the consulting firm R. Dunn Associates, recommends that graduates of the course be used on maintenance work to free up experienced programmers to work on more complex year 2000 problems. "The smart thing to do," he says "is to hire a bunch of younger or older programmers, teach them COBOL, and have them do some of the simpler work."

In an *Inside Technology Training* article, Rick Prouser, Director of IS at Oregon Mutual Insurance, says he bought three packages for his training class and is planning to buy more. "The students are able to be technically proficient for our Year 2000 projects in a short amount of time. That's definitely worth a couple of hundred dollars."

COBOL, Just-in-Time costs $350.00. Shipping (USA $15.00) (Non USA $30.00)

(This offer is made by Mo Budlong, King Computer Services, Inc., not by Sams Publishing.)

ORDER FORM

To order: Fill in the form and mail with your payment or Purchase Order to:

King Computer Services, Inc.

10350 Samoa Avenue, Tujunga, CA 91042

Or for faster service, call 818-951-5240 or Fax 818-353-1278

Credit card orders accepted.

Billing and Shipping Information:

Name _____ Title _____

Address _____ City _____

State _____ Zip _____ Phone # _____

Signature (required) _____ Date _____

Please send me the following:

Qty	ITEM	COST	TOTAL
	Teach Yourself COBOL in 21 Days	35.00	
	Companion 3.5" disk of source code	15.00	
	MICRO FOCUS COBOL COMPILER	99.00	
	The COBOL Cook Book Vol. I	49.95	
	EZ-COMPARE	39.95	
	GEN-CODE (Micro Focus)	299.00	
	GEN-CODE (ACUCOBOL)	299.00	
	COBOL, Dates and the Year 2000 Technical Report	99.00	
	COBOL, Dates and the Year 2000 diskette	99.00	
	COBOL, Just-in-Time! course	350.00	
	SUBTOTAL		
	CA Sales tax @ 8.25%		
	*Shipping		
	TOTAL		

* SHIPPING: The product description page has the general shipping costs for each item. If you have special shipping needs (rush, overnight, COD), or if you are ordering a number of products or making a non US order, call for shipping costs for the items you are ordering.

ORDERING INFORMATION: Government and Company Purchase orders, Visa, MasterCard, and American Express accepted. Otherwise, please send payment with order. (COD extra)

FOREIGN ORDERS: Prices are US dollars. Make payment by International Money Order in US dollars. Please print your mailing address in the format required by your post office.

(This offer is made by Mo Budlong, King Computer Services, Inc., not by Sams Publishing.)

Teach Yourself C in 21 Days, Fourth Edition

—*Brad Jones & Peter Aitken*

With its ever-expanding installed base, C continues to be one of the most popular programming languages on the market. This fact, along with the *Teach Yourself* series' reputation as the most popular way to learn programming languages, guarantees that *Teach Yourself C in 21 Days, Fourth Edition* is clearly headed for the best-seller lists. This book covers ANSI C—a standard for all compilers, including Visual C++, Borland C++, Turbo C++ for Windows, UNIX C, Mac C, and more. The book also includes a bonus week covering advanced topics such as coding styles and portability issues, and it teaches the basics of C, including variables, constants, conditional statements, loops, pointers, data structures, input/output, and functions.

$29.99 USA/$42.95 CAN   *User level: New–Casual*
ISBN: 0-672-31069-4

Teach Yourself C++ in 21 Days, Second Edition

—*Jesse Liberty*

The proven, best-selling elements of the *Teach Yourself* series and the immense popularity of the C++ programming language make *Teach Yourself C++ in 21 Days, Second Edition* the most efficient way to learn programming with C++. And because it doesn't focus on one particular compiler, it allows readers to jump from one compiler to another. This book teaches the basics of object-oriented programming with C++. It is completely revised to ANSI standards and can be used with any of the C++ compilers on the market.

$29.99 USA/$42.95 CAN   *User level: Beginning–Intermediate*
ISBN: 0-672-31070-8

Teach Yourself Perl 5 for Windows NT in 21 Days

—*David Till & Tony Zhang*

Perl, a powerful programming language in the UNIX arena, can be used for manipulating text, generating reports, and performing system tasks. Assuming no prior programming knowledge, this easy-to-use guide shows readers how to use this language to quickly develop dynamic user interfaces into Windows NT databases. Extensive coverage of scripting model architecture, lists and array variables, subroutines, mathematical functions, scalar conversion functions, debugging, and more are included. The book's CD-ROM is packed with author source code, sample scripts, and various third-party utilities.

$39.99 USA/$56.95 CAN   *User level: New–Casual*
ISBN: 0-672-31047-3   *Internet Programming*

Teach Yourself C++ in 24 Hours

—*Jesse Liberty*

Teach Yourself C++ in 24 Hours follows the step-by-step approach of the *Teach Yourself* series to show readers C++ basics in a quick, easy-to-learn method. Because it doesn't focus on any one compiler, readers learn to program in C++ using the compiler of their choice. This book teaches the basics of C++ in an easy, task-oriented format, and it covers ANSI C++, which is one of the core languages being taught in schools. The book's CD-ROM includes a C++ compiler, third-party programming tools, and all sample source code from the text.

$24.99 USA/$35.95 CAN   *User level: Beginning–Intermediate*
ISBN: 0-672-31067-8

Add to Your Sams Library Today with the Best Books for Programming, Operating Systems, and New Technologies

The easiest way to order is to pick up the phone and call

1-800-428-5331

between 9:00 a.m. and 5:00 p.m. EST.

For fastest service please have your credit card available.

ISBN	Quantity	Description of Item	Unit Cost	Total Cost
0-672-31069-4		Teach Yourself C in 21 Days, 4E	$29.99	
0-672-31070-8		Teach Yourself C++ in 21 Days, 2E	$29.99	
0-672-31047-3		Teach Yourself Perl 5 for Windows NT in 21 Days	$39.99	
0-672-31067-8		Teach Yourself C++ in 24 Hours	$24.99	
		Shipping and handling: See information below.		
		TOTAL		

Shipping and handling: $4.00 for the first book and $1.75 for each additional book. If you need to have it immediately, we can ship your order to you in 24 hours for an additional charge of approximately $18.00, and you will receive your order overnight or in two days. Overseas shipping and handling costs an additional $2.00 per book. Prices subject to change. Call between 9:00 a.m. and 5:00 p.m. EST for availability and pricing information on latest editions.

201 W. 103rd Street, Indianapolis, Indiana 46290

1-800-428-5331 — Orders   1-800-835-3202 — FAX   1-800-858-7674 — Customer Service

Book ISBN 0-672-31137-2

MACMILLAN COMPUTER PUBLISHING USA

A VIACOM COMPANY

Technical ---- **Support:**

If you need assistance with the information in this book or with a CD/Disk accompanying the book, please access the Knowledge Base on our Web site at **http://www.superlibrary.com/general/support**. Our most Frequently Asked Questions are answered there. If you do not find the answer to your questions on our Web site, you may contact Macmillan Technical Support **(317) 581-3833** or e-mail us at **support@mcp.com**.